HANDBOOK OF LATIN AMERICAN STUDIES: No. 52

A Selective and Annotated Guide to Recent Publications in Art, History, Language, Literature, Music, and Philosophy

VOLUME 53 WILL BE DEVOTED TO THE SOCIAL SCIENCES: ANTHROPOLOGY, ECONOMICS, GEOGRAPHY, GOVERNMENT AND POLITICS, INTERNATIONAL RELATIONS, AND SOCIOLOGY

EDITORIAL NOTE: Comments concerning the *Handbook of Latin American Studies* should be sent directly to the Editor, *Handbook of Latin American Studies*, Hispanic Division, Library of Congress, Washington, D.C. 20540.

HANDBOOK OF LATIN AMERICAN STUDIES: NO. 52

HUMANITIES

Prepared by a Number of Scholars
for the Hispanic Division of The Library of Congress

Edited by DOLORES MOYANO MARTIN

1993

UNIVERSITY OF TEXAS PRESS   *Austin*

International Standard Book Number 0-292-75156-7
International Standard Serial Number 0072-9833
Library of Congress Catalog Card Number 36-32633
Copyright © 1993 by the University of Texas Press
All rights reserved
Printed in the United States of America

Requests for permission to reproduce material
from this work should be sent to
Permissions, University of Texas Press
Box 7819, Austin, Texas 78713-7819.

First Edition, 1993

The paper used in this publication meets
the minimum requirements of American National
Standard for Information Sciences—Permanence
of Paper for Printed Library Materials,
ANSI Z39.48-1984 ⊗

CONTRIBUTING EDITORS

HUMANITIES

Barbara von Barghahn, *George Washington University*, ART
María Luisa Bastos, *Lehman College, CUNY*, LITERATURE
Judith Ishmael Bissett, *Miami University, Ohio*, LITERATURE
Alvaro Félix Bolaños, *Tulane University*, LITERATURE
Sara Castro-Klarén, *The Johns Hopkins University*, LITERATURE
Flora S. Clancy, *University of New Mexico*, ART
S.L. Cline, *University of California, Santa Barbara*, HISTORY
Don M. Coerver, *Texas Christian University*, HISTORY
Noble David Cook, *Florida International University*, HISTORY
Edith B. Couturier, *National Endowment for the Humanities*, HISTORY
Edward Cox, *Rice University*, HISTORY
Joseph T. Criscenti, *Boston College*, HISTORY
Ethel O. Davie, *West Virginia State College*, LITERATURE
Ralph E. Dimmick, *Organization of American States*, LITERATURE
Marshall Eakin, *Vanderbilt University*, HISTORY
Luis Eyzaguirre, *University of Connecticut*, LITERATURE
Fernando García Núñez, *University of Texas at El Paso*, LITERATURE
Magdalena García Pinto, *University of Missouri, Columbia*, LITERATURE
Naomi M. Garrett, *West Virginia State College*, LITERATURE
Jaime Giordano, *The Ohio State University*, LITERATURE
Rubén González, *State University of New York at Old Westbury*, LITERATURE
María Cristina Guiñazú, *Lehman College-CUNY*, LITERATURE
Linda B. Hall, *University of New Mexico*, HISTORY
Michael T. Hamerly, *University of Guam*, HISTORY
Carl A. Hanson, *Trinity University*, HISTORY
José M. Hernández, *Georgetown University*, HISTORY
Rosemarijn Hoefte, *Royal Institute of Linguistics and Anthropology*, HISTORY
Carlos R. Hortas, *Hunter College-CUNY*, LITERATURE
Regina Igel, *University of Maryland*, LITERATURE
Nils P. Jacobsen, *University of Illinois*, HISTORY
William H. Katra, *University of Wisconsin-Eau Claire*, LITERATURE
Norma Klahn, *University of California, Santa Cruz*, LITERATURE
Pedro Lastra, *State University of New York at Stony Brook*, LITERATURE
Asunción Lavrin, *Howard University*, HISTORY
Maria Angélica Guimarães Lopes, *University of South Carolina*, LITERATURE
Lionel V. Loroña, *The New York Public Library*, BIBLIOGRAPHY AND GENERAL
    WORKS
Carol Maier, *Kent State University*, TRANSLATIONS
Wilson Martins, *New York University*, LITERATURE

Alida C. Metcalf, *Trinity University*, HISTORY
José M. Neistein, *Brazilian-American Cultural Institute, Washington*, ART
José Miguel Oviedo, *University of Pennsylvania*, LITERATURE
Daphne Patai, *University of Massachusetts at Amherst*, LITERATURE
Anne Pérotin-Dumon, *University of Virginia*, HISTORY
Michael D. Powers, *Ebon Research Systems*, LANGUAGE
Richard A. Preto-Rodas, *University of South Florida*, LITERATURE
René Prieto, *Southern Methodist University*, LITERATURE
José Promis, *University of Arizona*, LITERATURE
Jane M. Rausch, *University of Massachusetts-Amherst*, HISTORY
James D. Riley, *The Catholic University of America*, HISTORY
Oscar Rivera-Rodas, *University of Tennessee, Knoxville*, LITERATURE
Bélgica Rodríguez, *Organization of American States*, ART
Humberto Rodríguez-Camilloni, *Virginia Polytechnic Institute and State University*, ART
Armando Romero, *University of Cincinnati*, LITERATURE
Enrique Sacerio-Garí, *Bryn Mawr College*, LITERATURE
William F. Sater, *California State University, Long Beach*, HISTORY
Francisco Scarano, *University of Wisconsin-Madison*, HISTORY
Susan M. Socolow, *Emory University*, HISTORY
Saúl Sosnowski, *University of Maryland*, LITERATURE
Robert Stevenson, *University of California, Los Angeles*, MUSIC
Barbara A. Tenenbaum, *Encyclopedia of Latin-American History*, HISTORY
Juan Carlos Torchia Estrada, *Organization of American States*, PHILOSOPHY
Kathy Waldron, *Citibank, N.A., New York*, HISTORY
Stephen Webre, *Louisiana Tech University*, HISTORY
Raymond Williams, *University of Colorado*, LITERATURE
Ralph Lee Woodward, Jr., *Tulane University*, HISTORY
George Woodyard, *University of Kansas*, LITERATURE
Winthrop R. Wright, *University of Maryland*, HISTORY
George Yudice, *Hunter College-CUNY*, LITERATURE

SOCIAL SCIENCES

Juan del Aguila, *Emory University*, GOVERNMENT AND POLITICS
Amalia Alberti, *US Agency for International Development*, SOCIOLOGY
G. Pope Atkins, *United States Naval Academy*, INTERNATIONAL RELATIONS
Melissa H. Birch, *University of Virginia*, ECONOMICS
Roderic A. Camp, *Tulane University*, GOVERNMENT AND POLITICS
William L. Canak, *Loyola University, New Orleans*, SOCIOLOGY
César Caviedes, *University of Florida*, GEOGRAPHY
Lambros Comitas, *Columbia University*, ANTHROPOLOGY
David W. Dent, *Towson State University*, GOVERNMENT AND POLITICS
Clinton R. Edwards, *University of Wisconsin-Milwaukee*, GEOGRAPHY
Gary S. Elbow, *Texas Tech University*, GEOGRAPHY
Malva Espinosa, *Instituto Latinoamericano de Estudios Transnacionales*, SOCIOLOGY
Damián Fernández, *Florida International University*, INTERNATIONAL RELATIONS
Michael Fleet, *Marquette University*, GOVERNMENT AND POLITICS

Magnus Mörner, *Göteborgs Universitet, Sweden,* SCANDINAVIAN LANGUAGES
Małgorzata Nalewajko, *Academia de Ciencias de Polonia, Warszawa, Poland,* POL-
ISH LANGUAGE
László Scholz, *Eötvös Loránd University, Budapest, Hungary,* HUNGARIAN
LANGUAGE

Special Contributing Editors

Barbara Dash, *Library of Congress,* RUSSIAN LANGUAGE
Georgette M. Dorn, *Library of Congress,* GERMAN AND HUNGARIAN LANGUAGES
George J. Kovtun, *Library of Congress,* CZECH LANGUAGE
Vincent C. Peloso, *Howard University,* ITALIAN LANGUAGE
Juan Manuel Pérez, *Library of Congress,* GALICIAN LANGUAGE
Maria Luisa Wagner, *Georgetown University,* GERMAN LANGUAGE
Iêda Siqueira Wiarda, *Library of Congress,* SPECIAL MATERIAL IN PORTUGUESE
LANGUAGE
Hasso von Winning *Southwest Museum, Los Angeles,* GERMAN MATERIAL ON ME-
SOAMERICAN ARCHAEOLOGY

CONTENTS

HISTORY

LITERATURE

EDITOR'S NOTE

I. GENERAL AND REGIONAL TRENDS

The number of publications that commemorate the quincentennial of Columbus' voyage constitutes the leading trend in this volume. Many important Spanish figures and events are also being celebrated in 1992. Among the more notable individuals are Bartolomé de las Casas, that exemplary friar, defender, and protector of the New World's Indians, and King Charles III, his reign, and reforms. These commemorations have generated important research on Spanish exploration, Iberian mentalities, the impact of Europe on the New World, the nature of late-Bourbon policies, and the essential nature and unique evolution of Latin American art (p. 26 and p. 104–105). The most ambitious and controversial art exhibit and publication devoted to the quincentennial was the massive show and catalog entitled *Mexico: splendors of thirty centuries* (item **127**). This exhibit and book/catalog encompassed an extraordinary array of Mexican art ranging from the ancient Olmecs to 20th-century muralists. Implicit in the show is the assumption of a deep continuity or affinity in art that runs from the remote past through the present, a notion subject to scholarly scrutiny in items **140** and **146** (p. 22). In contrast to the rest of Spanish America, little has been written on colonial Central America, with the exception of a biography of conquistador Pedro de Alvarado (item **1386,** and p. 184).

As in the case of Spanish figures in the Americas, this biennium also produced a number of exceptional works on the indigenous populations of the New World. The *Handbook's* Mesoamerican ethnohistorian emphasizes that "the last eight years have seen an explosion in the writing of indigenous history" (p. 78). It is worthwhile to pause and contemplate the extraordinary development of indigenous history or ethnohistory, a field of study pioneered by the Hispanic Division of the Library of Congress and especially by the *Handbook of Latin American Studies.* As noted by the ethnohistorian cited above, "in the early 1960s, there were only a few stalwart ethnohistorians," and all of them served as contributors to the *Handbook* (p. 78). These pioneers were the Chief of the Hispanic Division, Howard Cline, in addition to Charles Gibson, H.B. Nicholson, and Donald Robertson, all of them Mesoamericanists; and John Murra, the founding father of South American ethnohistory, who was the only one in the 1960s studying the history of Andean populations. Now, in this volume of the *Handbook,* some of the best and most prolific recent research is devoted to the Central Andes, an area in which Peruvian scholars dominate despite their country's ominous slide into political and economic anarchy. An interesting consensus among these scholars is that Peru's indigenous history "profoundly activates the nation's present," and that her true past is that of her native Americans (p. 87). And indeed, that formidable native American historian of the Andes, Guamán Poma de Ayala, continues to attract intense interest as exemplified by Mercedes López-Baralt's monumental analysis of his writings (item **3327,** p. 466). Equally rigorous and revealing are recent ethnohistorical studies that examine the Spanish confessional as a tool of Christianization in Mesoamerica, analyses which are yielding an "increasingly sophisticated understanding of the Nahua worldview and its colonial transformation" (items **518** and **530,** p. 77).

From its inception in the 1960s, ethnohistory has exemplified the direction and praxis of Latin American studies today. Those who wanted to study the past record of indigenous populations soon realized that attainment of such knowledge was impossible without acquiring additional expertise in unfamiliar and, what were then, arcane fields. Today, observes one contributor, such cross disciplinary incursions are taken for granted with "historians venturing into the realm of the pictorial; art historians examining the alphabetic texts in colonial codices; and anthropologists and archaeologists studying the colonial period" (p. 78). Indeed, observes a historian of the Dutch Caribbean, "it is remarkable that anthropologists have written most of the historical works" on slavery and Maroon societies in Suriname, Curaçao, Aruba, and other formerly Dutch territories (p. 208).

As in the above case of Latin America's indigenous past, the histories of other Latin American populations continue to command much interest in this *Handbook.* For example, in Mexico the long-standing interest in studies of the hacienda and landownership have "ceded their former preeminence to studies of interethnic relations at the social and economic levels" (p. 132). In Puerto Rico, Fernando Picó's "suggestive history of a free black community in the periphery of San Juan has advanced our understanding of the politics of resistance and evasion among the island's poor" (item **1582** and p. 210). Winthrop Wright has written the first history of anti-black bias in Venezuela by examining the evolution of images of Africans since colonial times in an original and revealing study (item **2337**). Important symposia on the history of the African populations of Colombia and Ecuador attest to the growing interest in black studies in South America (items **2416** and **2386**). And in Brazil, according to one contributor, there has been "a virtual flood of works" on slavery and the history of Afro-Brazilians, many of them issued in celebration of the centennial of abolition in Brazil in 1889 (p. 402). Among the more notable contributions is a book by Africanist Joseph Miller (item **2938**), of particular value to Brazilianists because of the author's "superb knowledge of the African side of the slave trade" (p. 402). And in literature, Afro-Brazilian writers have become so numerous, active, and well recognized that a journal devoted to their efforts, *Cadernos Negros*, has published at least 11 issues (item **4819,** and p. 658). Moreover, Brazilian literary critics in this *Handbook* remark on the quality of historical novels about Afro-Brazilians (items **4560** and **4559,** and p. 634) and the fact that the most notable theme of the Brazilian short story today is black liberation (e.g., items **4581, 4588, 4589, 4602,** and **4619,** and p. 642). The formation in Brazil of the "Quilombhoje Group" (i.e.,"Heroic Slave Liberation Today") attests to the emergence of a black consciousness movement there, but a uniquely Brazilian one that differs from both the American Black Power Movement and Caribbean *Négritude* (p. 642).

On the other hand, it is worth noting that while works on women are not as numerous as in previous *Handbooks,* the study of women is now a well entrenched field in all disciplines. Thus, what in the 1960s–70s was a controversial, contentious, and marginal topic has become in the 1990s a matter-of-fact, mainstream subject of study. The fortunate result of such recognition has been more light and less heat, or a notable rise in scholarship and a decline in polemics. Examples of such rigorous research are the following historical studies of Latin American women: Kathy Waldron's stunning piece on sexuality and society in colonial Venezuela (item **2051**); and on colonial Mexico, Asunción Lavrin's excellent study of sexuality and the Church (item **970**) as well as Edith Couturier's revealing examination of female philanthropy (item **962**); Richard Boyer's incisive analysis of women's perception of their rights in marriage (item **767**); Donna Guy's excellent study of prostitution in Argentina in the first decades of this century (item **2701**); and the following notable studies of Brazilian women–Sandra L. Graham's examination of domestic servants in the late 19th century (item **3028**), Maria da Silva Dias' and Rachel Soihet's respective works on poor women in the 19th century (items **3001** and **3105**), and Daphne Patai's fascinating account of the lives of contemporary women (item **2982**).

The high quality in works of history stated above is also evident in literary studies and biographies of Latin American women annotated in this *Handbook* (p. 466). That extraordinary 17th-century Mexican nun, Sor Juana Inés de la Cruz, continues to attract much attention. Among the best studies of the nun is Antonio Alatorre's splendid analysis of her famous letter to the priest who opposed her intellectual pursuits (item **3295**). Excellent studies of Brazilian female authors are devoted to Clarice Lispector (item **4809** and **4816**), Patricia Galvão (item **4801**) and Lygia Fagundes Telles (item **4814**). The world-wide success of Chilean novelist Isabel Allende may be partly responsible for both the first novel by Chile's leading female playwright, Isidora Aguirre (item **3765**), and for the emergence of several new women writers (p. 537, and item **3767**). In Puerto Rico, observes a literary critic, "Rosario Ferré (item **3611**) has become a literary elder stateswoman" who "continues to lead the way" for other female writers (p. 513). A collection of Puerto Rico's best women writers has been edited by Diana Vélez (item **4930**) and in Central America, Costa Rican women lead the way in terms of the quantity and quality of fiction published (p. 507).

The vigorous trend in regional history that we noted in *HLAS 50* (p. xxv) continues unabated in *HLAS 52*. The endeavors of regional historians are supported by the growing accessibility of regional archival sources. This is especially true in Mexico where the activities of local historical centers such as the Colegios of Michoacán and Guadalajara encourage the pursuit of regional studies (p. 132). In 19th-century Mexican history, regional works comprised over one third of the total contributions annotated in this *Handbook*, with almost 60 percent of these works written by Mexican historians (p. 155). Regional history also dominates studies of the Mexican Revolution and contemporary Mexico (p. 156). In Venezuela, regional works "continue to enlarge our understanding of the complexities" of the colonial period (p. 266).

In Colombia, scholars continue to focus on the history of the undeclared civil war of the 1940s–60s known as "La Violencia," as well as on the culture of violence that permeates the country's past and present (p. 320). Among the many new studies on the subject are Quintero Ospina's examination of the Gaitán assassination (item **2382**); two biographies of guerrilla fighters (items **2340** and **2388**); and testimonies of protagonists of the civil strife that dragged on between 1948 and 1985 (item **2341**). It is clear that Ilse Cohnen's bibliography on "La Violencia" (item **2343**) will soon have to be updated. Indeed, there is so much research underway on this subject in Colombia at present that the country now produces a type of expert commonly known as a *violentólogo*, or "violence specialist."

As we remarked in *HLAS 48* (p. xvii–xviii), studies of the Catholic Church, somewhat neglected in the 1970s–80s, are growing in number. In fact, according to one historian, "ecclesiastical history elicited considerable interest" in this biennium "perhaps as a result of a more intensive use of ecclesiastical records for social or mentalité studies, and their greater accessibility to researchers in recent years" (p. 133). Another historian welcomes as a positive development "the appearance of scholarly works on the Catholic Church in both Cuba and the Dominican Republic," a subject "which to date has received only spotty attention from historians" (p. 211). Examples of this scholarship are Solange Alberro's excellent study of the Mexican Inquisition (item **953**); Thomas E. Quigley's balanced examination of Church-State relations in present-day Cuba (item **1961**); José Sáez's two-volume history of the Jesuits in the Dominican Republic (item **1969**); Fernán González's examination of Church-State relations in 19th-century Colombia (item **2350**); Jeffrey Klaiber's judicious and comprehensive history of the Church in Peru (item **2489**); and Fernando Aliaga's analysis of the impact of the Church on Chilean society (item **2558**).

The publication of research is increasing in some regions and declining in others. Great increases are apparent in the historiography of Colombia and Chile (p. 271, and p. 318), and Ecuador, a country that generated little in the past, is now enjoying a notable boom in the quality and quantity of its historiography, especially "an unprecedented increase in the quantity of work being done on the Presidency of Quito" (p. 268). Also, the scholar Arturo A. Roig has shed much light in a few years on the history of ideas in Ecuador (item **5382**, and p. 754). Mexican literature is also undergoing a remarkable upsurge which can be attributed to three factors: a) the numerous writing workshops (*talleres literarios*) sponsored and established by the Instituto Nacional de Bellas Artes throughout the national territory; b) frequent writers conferences that are now held not only in the capital but in cities throughout Mexico; and, finally, c) the succesful promotion of new writing conducted by Mexican newspapers, magazines, and publishings houses, all of which encourage and support the works of new and young writers (p. 483, and p. 492–493). On the other hand, there has been a publishing decline in Brazil, particularly noticeable in previously prolific fields such as the history of ideas (p. 754), and in the number of Central American novels, a genre which has been virtually displaced by the short story (p. 506).

Finally, to conclude, we should mention four outstanding contributions singled out by contributors to this *Handbook.* They are: 1) Jorge Bernales Ballesteros' *Historia del arte hispanoamericano: siglos XVI a XVIII* (item **159**), a "copiously illustrated and thoroughly documented" work that reveals an "extraordinary breadth of knowledge about viceregal art and patronage" (p. 27); 2) Germán Franco Salamanca's *Templo de Santa Clara, Bogotá* (item **258**), "a masterful synthesis of the history of a single monument," and a "type of publication [that] will become critical for future studies of historic monuments undergoing restoration" (p. 41); 3) Iván Jaksic's *Academic rebels in Chile: the role of philosophy in higher education and politics* (item **5399**), an outstanding contribution in terms of the depth and breadth of its analysis; and 4) Enrique Krauze's study of José Vasconcelos (item **5335**), a work which confirms the fact that Krauze has become one of Latin America's finest essayists and interpreters (p. 753–754).

II. OBITUARIES

D. LINCOLN CANFIELD (1903–1991)

Lincoln Canfield, an internationally known linguist and a US pioneer in the study of the Spanish language of the Americas, died suddenly of an aneurysm on November 12, 1991, at Carbondale, Ill. He was 87 and, according to his wife, "still writing, traveling, lecturing, and riding his bicycle." From 1966 through 1986,

Lincoln Canfield served as contributing editor for the Spanish language chapter of the *Handbook*. He earned his doctorate at Columbia University in 1934, and devoted his life to the study and teaching of Spanish in a career that spanned more than 60 years. His principal scholarship was in Romance linguistics and the pronunciation of Spanish in Latin America. He also compiled the much acclaimed and used *University of Chicago dictionary of the Spanish language*. He was one of the few non-native Spanish speakers granted membership in the prestigious Real Academia Española or Royal Spanish Academy. We shall remember Lincoln Canfield both as a scholar and friend of the Hispanic Division.

FRAY LINO GOMEZ CANEDO (1908–1990)

Father Lino, as the indefatigable Franciscan historian was known to the *Handbook* staff, died of a heart attack in Mexico City on Christmas Eve 1990. From 1963 through 1970, Father Lino served as contributing editor for the *Handbook* chapter on South American colonial history. A Galician by birth and a Mexican by adoption, Father Lino was a graduate of the Gregorian University in Rome. His interest in Spanish American history began with the compilation of an early guide to Hispanic-American archives as well as through his early contacts with the Academy of American Franciscan History. Father Lino's notable contributions to colonial historiography are too numerous to list here. Above all, he excelled in the identification of sources, the erudite and painstaking reedition of classic works of Latin American colonial history, and in tracing the impact of the Franciscan Order in the region. His enthusiasm for and devotion to Hispanic America as well as his kindness and generosity towards all of us will be greatly missed.

III. CLOSING DATE FOR VOLUME 52

The closing date for most works annotated in this volume was early 1991. Most publications received and cataloged at the Library of Congress after that date will be annotated in the next humanities volume, *HLAS 54*.

IV . CHANGES IN VOLUME 52

Changes in Coverage

As we forewarned in our "Editor's Note" in *HLAS 48*, the history subsection devoted to the "Independence Period" of Spanish South America, prepared since 1957 by David Bushnell of the University of Florida, has been suspended. In his last two contributions, Bushnell remarked on "the continuing decline in scholarly attention to independence as compared to other topics," and attributed this downturn to the fact that "conceptual and methodological innovators are passing the independence period by, in the Río de la Plata as elsewhere" (see *HLAS 48*, p. 256; and *HLAS 50*, p. 284–285). As of this volume, *HLAS 52*, important works on the independence period of Spanish South America will be annotated by the various historians of the national period according to country (i.e., Colombia, Venezuela, Ecuador, Peru, Bolivia, Chile, Argentina, Uruguay, and Paraguay). Worthwhile studies that discuss the independence period from a continental or general viewpoint will appear in the HISTORY: SPANISH SOUTH AMERICA: GENERAL subsection.

Since its inception, the *HLAS* has taken the lead in supporting research in emerging fields in Latin American studies that are not among the traditional disciplines covered by the *Handbook*. Past examples are "Latin American Law," "Latin American Statistics," and "Latin American Labor and Social Welfare." Once these areas of study became well established in the United States, generating their own bibliographies, monographs, and serials, *HLAS* discontinued their bibliographic coverage. Two emerging fields whose development *HLAS* encouraged in the 1960s–70s, were "Latin American Folklore," and "Latin American Film." At the time there was very little published on these subjects. In 1968, *HLAS 30* featured a bibliography on folklore, compiled by renowned scholar Américo Paredes. By 1972 and in *HLAS 34*, we took the lead in promoting this new field and began annotating on a regular basis the rigorous research on folklore that began replacing the impressionistic works of the 1940s–50s. In 1974, the *HLAS* Advisory Board recommended that we also encourage the development of another emerging area of study in the region, one as important as folklore for the understanding of Latin American history and culture: film. Since lack of space did not allow us to cover both folklore and film in the humanities volume, in 1976 (*HLAS 38*), we began providing alternate coverage to these fields, a bibliography devoted to each appearing every four years.

Twenty years later, by the 1990s, both fields have come into their own in both academia and the popular press—in no small measure thanks to the early encouragement and support provided by the *Handbook* in the 1970s–80s. There are now numerous monographic studies of Latin American folklore and film—several authored by former contributors to *HLAS*—that include excellent bibliographies. Finally, there are a number of ongoing paper and machine-readable bibliographies and serial publications that also cover these fields (e.g., *Journal of Latin American Lore, The Hispanic American Periodical Index* or *HAPI*, the *MLA international bibliography of books and articles on the modern languages and literatures, The Cinéaste, Cinema Journal,* etc.). Therefore, as of *HLAS 52*, publications on Latin American folklore will be annotated by the ethnologist, sociologist, literary critic, historian, or musicologist according to the methodology used. Likewise, if a study of Latin American film is written from a strongly anthropological, sociological, literary, or historical perspective, it will be annotated by the appropriate contributor.

Art

Barbara von Barghahn of the George Washington University covered the literature on the colonial art of Middle America and the Caribbean. Bélgica Rodríguez, Director of the Museum of Latin American Art, Organization of American States, Washington D.C., annotated publications on the modern art of Latin America, except Brazil.

History

Noble David Cook, Florida International University, prepared the chapter on the ethnohistory of South America. Edward Cox, Rice University, covered publications on the history of the English-speaking Caribbean and Guyana. Rosemarijn Hoefte of The Netherlands' Royal Institute of Linguistics and Anthropology annotated the literature on the Dutch Caribbean islands and Suriname. Marshall C. Eakin of Vanderbilt University collaborated with Alida C. Metcalf and Carl A. Hanson of Trinity University, San Antonio, Texas, in the preparation of the chapter on the history of Brazil.

Literature

Alvaro Félix Bolaños, Tulane University, prepared the chapter on the colonial literature of Spanish America. Enrique Sacerio-Garí, Bryn Mawr College, covered the contemporary fiction and criticism of Cuba and the Dominican Republic. Raymond Williams, University of Colorado, annotated the contemporary fiction of

Colombia, Venezuela, Ecuador, Peru, and Bolivia. Rubén González, State University of New York at Westbury, covered the poetry and criticism of the Hispanic Caribbean. Daphne Patai, University of Massachusetts, Amherst, examined translations from the Portuguese into English.

Foreign Contributing Editors

Małgorzata Nalewajko, a scholar associated with the Institute of History, Polish Academy of Sciences, Warsaw, will be covering important publications in Polish.

Special Contributing Editors

Iêda Siqueira Wiarda, Luso-Brazilian Specialist for the Library of Congress' Hispanic Division, has been providing an invaluable service by selecting Brazilian and Uruguayan books and serials for review by the *Handbook's* contributors and by annotating special publications in the Portuguese language. Barbara Dash, a Librarian in the Rare Book and Special Collections Division of the Library of Congress and a specialist in Russian literature, has agreed to annotate important Russian titles in the humanities and social sciences.

Subject Index

The *Handbook* uses Library of Congress Subject Headings when they are consistent with usage among Latin Americanists. Differences in practice, however, make adaptation of LCSH headings necessary: 1) the *Handbook* index uses only two levels, while LC headings usually contain more; and 2) *Handbook* practice is to prefer a "subject-place" pattern, while LC practice generally uses a "place-subject" pattern. Automation of the *Handbook* has required that the subject index be compiled with two audiences in mind: users of the print edition of the *Handbook* and users of the online *Handbook* database. It has also demanded that index terms, once established, remain as stable as possible. Work has begun towards a complete thesaurus of *Handbook* subject index terms. In the meantime, cross references are included from subject terms used in *HLAS 48-HLAS 51* to terms used in this volume. Finally, since the *Handbook* is arranged by subject, users are encouraged to consult the table of contents for broad subject coverage.

Other Changes

Changes in the editorial staff of the *Handbook*, the administrative officers of the Library of Congress, and membership in the Advisory Board are reflected in the title pages of the present volume.

Dolores Moyano Martin

HANDBOOK OF
LATIN AMERICAN STUDIES:
No. 52

BIBLIOGRAPHY AND GENERAL WORKS

LIONEL V. LOROÑA, *The New York Public Library*

AN UNUSUALLY LARGE SELECTION of subject bibliographies, a varied and distinctive group of useful reference works and a trio of collective bio-bibliographical works are highlights this year. Beyond the highlights, however, there is still a considerable number of items deserving attention. This year has produced a profusion of good works; this introductory essay can only point out a few outstanding examples.

The opening subsection on "General Bibliographies" reaffirms European interest in Latin America in an extensive work, *El americanismo en Sevilla, 1900–1980* (item **1**), citing studies covering the greater part of this century. Albert Camarillo's *Latinos in the United States: a historical bibliography* (item **4**) deals with a narrower topic, but gives a fuller view, with over 1,300 citations backed by abstracts.

The subsection on "State, National, and Regional Bibliographies" is exceptionally rich this year. A model within this category is Josep Barnadas' *Introducción a los estudios bolivianos 1960–1984* (item **7**), which not only lists over 6,000 items, but illuminates each subject area with a review essay noting significant works and research trends. Ann Hartness' *Brazil in reference books, 1965–1988* (item **13**) provides excellent, annotated coverage of 1,669 items. Though unannotated, three state bibliographies (a genre far more prevalent than usual this year) are impressive for their size and seeming comprehensiveness: Germán Cardoza Galúe's *Bibliografía zuliana: ensayo, 1702–1975* (item **10**); Ramón Querales' *Contribución a la bibliografía y hemerografía del Estado Lara, 1557–1983* (item **18**), and the four-volume *Estado do Pará: pesquisa histórico* by Denise Farias de Souza *et al.* (item **20**). Lastly, it is interesting to note the current abundance of ISBN listings, best exemplified by the five-year Argentine cumulation, *Libros argentinos, ISBN: producción editorial registrada entre 1982 y 1986* (item **14**).

It is difficult to choose from among so many commendable works in the subject bibliography category although three titles in the fields of language and literature should be noted: Bobby J. Chamberlain's *Portuguese language and Luso-Brazilian literature: an annotated guide to selected reference works* (item **32**) provides an informed choice of over 500 works with descriptive and critical annotations; Flora Piñeiro de Rivera's *Un siglo de literatura infantil puertorriqueña* (item **46**) covers the field with an authoritative bibliographic essay and an array of comprehensive indexes; and finally, Walter Rela's *A bibliographical guide to Spanish American literature: twentieth century sources* (item **27**) surveys a wide field of well-annotated sources.

In matters relating to library science and services, one should note the prototypical set of conference proceedings concerned with current issues, *Bibliotecas populares: identidad y proceso* (item **67**), which records the attempts to evaluate the present and future state of libraries in Peru. In a related issue, José Arias Ordóñez and Moisés Pedrazo Robayo examine the current state of library and information science in Colombia in their article *Nuevas tendencias de la bibliotecología y necesidades del postgrado en Colombia* (item **68**).

Among the collective and personal bibliographies, one Latin American and one Caribbean writer receive superior treatment in fully annotated works: *Pablo Neruda: an annotated bibliography of critical studies* by Hensley C. Woodbridge and David S. Zubatsky (item **66**) and *V.S. Naipaul: a selective bibliography with annotations, 1957–1987* by Kelvin Jarvis (item **57**). Though not annotated, two extensive works on important literary figures are also worth mentioning: E.D. Carter's *Bibliografía de y sobre Julio Cortázar* (item **55**) and Ramiro Villaseñor y Villaseñor's *Biobibliografía Juan Rulfo* (item **64**). Three collective bio-bibliographical works are also particularly noteworthy: *Diccionario de la literatura venezolana* (2a ed., item **92**); *Women writers of Spanish America: an annotated bio-bibliographical guide* by Diane E. Marting (item **65**); and *Mexican autobiography: an annotated bibliography* by Richard D. Woods (item **60**).

Three catalogs which describe the contents of collections of interest to researchers in varying fields stand out in the "Acquisitions, Collections, and Catalogs" subsection: *Catálogo de la Colección Fondo Reservado de la Biblioteca Manuel Orozco y Berra* (item **79**), rich in Mexican history holdings; *Peronism and the three Peróns: a checklist of material . . . in the Hoover Institution Library and Archives . . .* by Laszlo Horvath (item **77**); and *Indians of North and South America: a bibliography based on the collection at the Willard E. Yager Library Museum . . .* by Carolyn E. Wolf and Nancy S. Chiang (item **82**). One also notes the Mexican Archivo General de la Nación's continuing program to inventory all municipal archives in the publication *Los archivos municipales del estado de México* (item **70**).

Heading the "Reference Works and Research" subsection is a discerning three-volume survey, *Latin American writers*, by Carlos A. Solé and María Isabel Abreu (item **93**), with critical essays and selective bibliographies for each subject. Two information-packed resource guides are welcome additions: *Libraries and special collections on Latin America and the Caribbean: a directory of European resources* by Roger Macdonald and Carole Travis (item **94**) and the *Tinker guide to Latin American and Caribbean policy and scholarly resources in Metropolitan New York* by Ronald G. Hellman and Beth Kempler Pfannl (item **100**). An unusual proliferation of biographical directories and encyclopedias is also very much in evidence. The two volume *Gran diccionario de Chile: biográfico-cultural* by Mario Céspedes and Lelia Garreaud (item **86**) is a good ready-reference source for information on historic people and historic/cultural events. Humberto Musacchio's four-volume *Diccionario enciclopédico de México* (item **96**) covers similar territory for Mexico. Germinal Nogues' *Diccionario biográfico de políticos argentinos* (item **97**) restricts itself to biography in a narrower field, while the two-volume *Diccionario enciclopédico dominicano* by Alejandro Paulino et al. (item **87**) attempts to cover everything to do with the Dominican Republic.

Finally, in the "General Works" subsection, we should point out that Aurelio Tanodi's detailed survey, *La situación de los archivos iberoamericanos*, (item **111**) is rich in information on specific archives, research guides, and legislation affecting accessibility.

GENERAL BIBLIOGRAPHIES

1   Calderón Quijano, José Antonio. El americanismo en Sevilla, 1900–1980. Prólogo de Antonio Muro Orejón. Sevilla: Escuela de Estudios Hispano-Americanos de Sevilla, Consejo Superior de Investigaciones Científicas, 1987. 507 p.: bibl. (Publicaciones de la Escuela de Estudios Hispano-Americanos de Sevilla; 326)

Ample bibliography of works published under the auspices of institutions in Seville, arranged by subject under each sponsoring institution. Bibliographies are preceded by short bibliographic essays which serve reasonably well as indexes to the works listed.

2   Inter-American Foundation. A guide to NGO directories: how to find over 11,000 nongovernmental organizations in Latin America and the Caribbean. Rosslyn, Virginia: Inter-American Foundation, 1990. 18 p.

Very useful compilation of 32 directories to 11,000 nongovernmental organizations in Latin America and the Caribbean. These NGO's are "each working to create a better life for its members and their communities" and are "proof of the hope and spirit of the poor throughout the region." The guide is available in English, Spanish and Portuguese from the Inter-American Foundation, 1515 Wilson Blvd., Rosslyn, Virginia 22209, USA. [Ed.]

3   International bibliography of biography. v. 1–12. London: Saur, 1988. 12 v.

List of biographical works published throughout the world contains both biographical and autobiographical titles. Covers historical as well as contemporary figures. Vols. 1–5 arranged by subject; vols. 6–12 arranged by author/title.

4   Latinos in the United States: a historical bibliography. Edited by Albert Camarillo. Santa Barbara, Calif.: ABC-Clio, 1986. 332 p.: indexes. (ABC-Clio research guides)

Contains 1,325 citations selected from *America: History and Life* taken primarily from the humanities and social sciences. Historical overview precedes chapters focusing on national origin groups. Each item has an abstract ranging from a sentence to a lengthy paragraph. Includes author and subject indexes.

5   Loroña, Lionel V. Bibliography of Latin American and Caribbean bibliographies, 1987–1988. Madison: Seminar on the Acquisition of Latin American Library Materials (SALALM), Memorial Library, Univ. of Wisconsin-Madison, 1988. 69 p. (SALALM Bibliography and Reference Series; 23)

Annual compilation of bibliographies in the social sciences and humanities appearing as monographs or periodical articles. Includes 477 unannotated items arranged by broad subject areas, with author and detailed subject indexes.

6   Loroña, Lionel V. Bibliography of Latin American and Caribbean Bibliographies, 1988–1989. Madison: Seminar on the Acquisition of Latin American Library Materials (SALALM), Memorial Library, Univ. of Wisconsin-Madison, 1989. 66 p. (SALALM Bibliography and Reference Series; 25)

Annual compilation of 457 unannotated items arranged by broad subject area. Includes author and detailed subject indexes.

STATE, NATIONAL, AND REGIONAL BIBLIOGRAPHIES

Acevedo Latorre, Eduardo. Colaboradores de Santander en la organización de la república. See item **2395.**

Barité, Mario and María Gladys Ceretta. Guía de revistas culturales uruguayas, 1885–1985. See item **3973.**

7   Barnadas, Josep M. Introducción a los estudios bolivianos contemporáneos, 1960–1984: manual de bibliografía. Revisado y corregido por Carlota Rosasco de Chacón. Cusco, Peru: Centro de Estudios Rurales Andinos Bartolomé de las Casas, 1987. 514 p.: indexes. (Archivos de historia andina; 6)

Excellent survey cites over 6,000 monographs and articles primarily in the humanities and social sciences. Eleven chapters deal with broad subject areas, each preceded by a review essay noting research trends as well as giving particulars on many items listed. Includes author and subject indexes.

8 Biblioteca CIES. Bibliografía colección Chiapas. San Cristóbal de Las Casas, México: Centro de Investigaciones Ecológicas del Sureste, 1986. 261 p.: indexes.

Lists materials in all subjects relating to Chiapas, arranged by subject. Most materials are in Spanish, but items in English, French, and German also appear. Contains name and title indexes.

9 Blakemore, Harold. Chile. Oxford, England; Santa Barbara, Calif.: Clio Press, 1988. 197 p., 2 p. of plates: indexes, maps. (World bibliographical series; 97)

Some 642 annotated items make up another in this series of selective bibliographies seeking to give a well-delineated profile of individual countries and their peoples. Aimed at the non-specialist English-speaking reader, it lists primarily contemporary works. Twenty-nine subject divisions cover a broad spectrum. Includes author, title, and subject indexes.

Boletín Bibliográfico. 1985–. See item **112.**

10 Cardozo Galué, Germán. Bibliografía zuliana: ensayo, 1702–1975. Maracaibo, Venezuela: Univ. del Zulia, Consejo de Desarrollo Científico y Humanístico, 1987. 483 p.: indexes.

Over 4,700 unannotated citations figure in this work covering all items published in, or written about, the state of Zulia. Includes books and pamphlets covering all subjects. Includes personal name and subject/institutional indexes.

11 Chambers, Frances. Guyana. Oxford, England; Santa Barbara, Calif.: Clio Press, 1989. 206 p.: indexes, map. (World bibliographical series; 96)

Made up of over 600 entries divided into broad subject areas, this work provides a good survey of the country and people of Guyana. Lists mostly current monographs and articles, and includes an overall index.

Cohnen, Ilse Valerie. *La Violencia* in Kolumbien. See item **2343.**

Dabydeen, David and **Nana Wilson-Tagoe.** Selected themes in West Indian literature: an annoted bibliography. See item **4905.**

Derkx, Jo and **Irene Rolfes.** Suriname: a bibliography, 1980–1989. See item **1544.**

12 Durón, Jorge Fidel. Bibliografía hondureña en 1985. (*Bol. Acad. Hondur. Leng.,* 28:29, dic. 1986, p. 109–124.)

Annual survey of Honduran imprints done in the form of a bibliographic essay. Considerable amount of data is presented in both monographs and serials, though complete bibliographic information is lacking.

13 Hartness, Ann. Brazil in reference books, 1965–1989: an annotated bibliography. Metuchen, N.J.: Scarecrow Press, 1991. 351 p.: indexes.

Excellent annotated bibliography lists 1,669 entries. Arrangement is by 29 broad subject areas, with further subdivisions by format, geographic unit, or narrower subjects; author and subject indexes enhance usefulness. What impresses most is the author's thoroughness and the fact that virtually all the publications were examined by her. Of greatest use to those interested in the humanities, fine arts, and social sciences. Other areas, such as education, natural history, and agriculture, are included, but with restricted coverage. Coverage is generally limited to books, pamphlets, and serials, such as yearbooks or regularly issued bibliographies. A special effort was made to identify publications by government agencies. Brazilianists, librarians, scholars, and policymakers are indebted to Hartness for a superb and extremely accessible bibliography. [Iêda Siqueira Wiarda]

Hoefte, Rosemarijn. Suriname. See item **1559.**

Información Bibliográfica. Año 3, no. 1, julio 1984–. See item **113.**

14 Libros argentinos. ISBN: producción editorial registrada entre 1982 y 1986. Buenos Aires: Cámara Argentina del Libro, 1987. 721 p.: indexes.

Cumulative listing of Argentine imprints, arranged alphabetically by title under broad subjects. Includes author and title indexes, as well as listings of commercial publishers and author publishers.

15 México en 500 libros. Coordinación de Enrique Florescano. México: Oceano, 1987. 187 p.: bibl., index. (Serie Historia)

Revises and updates 1980 edition (México: Editorial Nueva Imagen, 1980). Citations on all subjects relating to Mexico are accompanied by critical and descriptive annotations. Includes name index.

16   Myers, Robert A. Dominica. Oxford, England; Santa Barbara, Calif.: Clio Press, 1987. 190 p., 1 leaf of plates: index, map. (World bibliographical series; 82)
Deals with a wide variety of subjects covering all aspects of Dominica. Contemporary works make up the majority of nearly 500 well-annotated items. Aimed at the non-specialist English-speaking reader. Includes overall index.

17   Nickson, R. Andrew. Paraguay. Oxford, England; Santa Barbara, Calif.: Clio Press, 1987. 212 p., 1 leaf of plates: index, map. (World bibliographical series; 84)
Well-balanced bibliographic survey of Paraguay and its people includes 600 annotated items, primarily contemporary works, covering a variety of subjects. As with other volumes in this series, this work is intended for the non-specialist English-speaking reader. Includes overall index.

Pacheco Ladrón de Guevara, Lourdes C. Fuentes para el estudio de Nayarit. See item **941.**

18   Querales, Ramón. Contribución a la bibliografía y hemerografía del Estado Lara, 1557–1983. Barquisimeto, Venezuela: Gobernación del Estado Lara; Caracas: Instituto Autónomo Biblioteca Nacional y de Servicios de Bibliotecas, 1986. 2 v.: indexes.
This extensive bibliography is divided into: 1) reference works; 2) official publications published in, or about, Lara; 3) all other Lara imprints; and 4) journals and newspapers. Alphabetically arranged by author (by title if newspaper or journal). Includes personal name and subject indexes, and chronological and name indexes for the journals and newspapers.

Resistance and rebellion in Suriname: old and new. See item **1590.**

19   Romero de Solís, José Miguel. Bibliografía de Colima. v. 1. Zamora, Mexico: Colegio de Michoacán; Colima, Mexico: Univ. de Colima, 1986– . 1 v. (294 p.): indexes. (Sobre Colima y su rumbo; 1)
First of a two-part bibliography containing works by local authors as well as works published about Colima. Each citation gives source and location and often a descrip-

tive annotation. Name and subject indexes are appended.

Sarabia Viejo, María Justina. Bibliografía de México en la época colonial. See item **979.**

20   Souza, Denise Helena Farias de; Maria de Nazareth Moreira Martins de Barros; and Luiza Castro das Chegas. Estado do Pará: pesquisa histórico-bibliográfica. Belém, Brazil: Governo do Estado do Pará; Univ. Federal do Pará, 1986. 4 v.: bibl., indexes.
Over 1,200 annotated entries on the history of Pará from 1616 to date. Materials, all in Portuguese (although translations are included), are housed in local public and private libraries. Arranged by format (e.g., books, articles), work includes author and title indexes and location codes. Bibliography is preceded by historical narrative.

21   Woodward, Ralph Lee. El Salvador. Oxford, England; Santa Barbara, Calif.: Clio Press, 1988. 213 p.: index, map. (World bibliographical series; 98)
Contains 659 entries divided into broad subject areas profiling El Salvador and its people. Like others in this series, it is aimed at the non-specialist English-speaking reader but does contain some items in Spanish. Sources are mostly current. Includes overall index.

22   Yeager, Gertrude Matyoka. Bolivia. Oxford, England; Santa Barbara, Calif.: Clio Press, 1988. 228 p.: bibl., index, map. (World bibliographical series; 89)
Over 800 annotated works grouped in 33 broad subject areas provide a well-rounded picture of Bolivia. Aimed at the non-specialist English-speaking reader, annotations are primarily descriptive but informative. Includes overall index.

SUBJECT BIBLIOGRAPHIES

23   Arbeitsgemeinschaft Deutsche Lateinamerika-Forschung. Mitglieder- und Kompetenzregister (MuK) der Arbeitsgemeinschaft Deutsche Lateinamerikaforschung (ADLAF). herausgegeben von der Forschungsgruppe Lateinamerika der Westfälischen Wilhelms-Universität Münster. Münster, Germany: s.n., 1988. 98 p. (Münsteraner Beiträge zur Lateinamerikaforschung; Anuario 5)

Directory lists the members of the Latin American studies association (ADLAF) of the German Federal Republic, their fields of research and competence, and addresses. This annual publication is a most useful and welcome contribution. [G.M. Dorn]

24 Bansart, Andrés. El negro en la literatura hispanoamericana: bibliografía y hemerografía. Caracas: Equinoccio; Editorial de la Univ. Simón Bolívar, 1986. 113 p.: index. (Col. de bolsillo; 2)

Some 661 unannotated citations dating from the 19th century to the present are listed. Divided into two subject areas: 1) relation to Latin American literature; and 2) historic, linguistic, and anthropological aspects. Lists books, articles, and conference proceedings. Includes geographic index.

25 Bibliografía del Instituto Lingüístico de Verano de Centroamérica, 1952–1987. Recopilación de Rachel Engel. Guatemala: ILV, 1987. 144 p.

Publications listed are divided into three groups: 1) general interest; 2) items concerning linguistics of Mayan languages; and 3) items concerning linguistics of Central American languages other than Mayan. Within each language, items are further divided into: 1) ethnolinguistic studies; and 2) works written in the language itself. Numerous descriptive annotations.

Bibliografía sarmientina. See item **2644.**

26 Bibliografía sobre historia de Bogotá.
Recopilación de Fabiola Bohórquez de Briceño y Rubby Angel Giraldo. Bogotá: Cámara de Comercio de Bogotá, Vicepresidencia de Planeación y Desarrollo, Centro de Información Económica y Social de Bogotá, Red Distrital de Información Económica y Social, 1988. 103 p.: indexes.

Includes books, pamphlets, articles, and dissertations in 251 unannotated citations covering all aspects of Bogotá's history from 16th century to present. Alphabetically arranged by author with title and subject indexes.

27 A bibliographical guide to Spanish American literature: twentieth-century sources. Compiled by Walter Rela. Foreword by David William Foster. New York: Greenwood Press, 1988. 381 p.: indexes. (Bibliographies and indexes in world literature, 0742–6801; 13)

Close to 1,900 entries cover bibliographies, dictionaries, history and criticism, and anthologies. Each section is divided into general works, then by country. Most items have descriptive annotations; a good many have extensive notes. Includes author index.

28 Bibliography on Latin American psychology. [*in* Latin American psychology: a guide to research and training. Edited by Gerardo Marin, Steven Kennedy, and Barry Campbell Boyce. Washington: American Psychological Association, 1987, p. 174–217)

Lists books and articles appearing since 1970. General section is followed by sections on each Latin American country. Small percentage of citations have descriptive and, to a lesser extent, critical annotations.

29 Biblioteca Amadeu Amaral. Bibliografia afro-brasileira. Coordenação de Marisa Colnago Coelho e Raul Lody. Rio de Janeiro: FUNARTE, Instituto Nacional do Folclore, 1988. 105 p.: index. (Série Referência; 2)

Close to 1,000 unannotated titles, mostly contemporary, are included. Does not pretend to be exhaustive but hopes to list significant works. Arranged alphabetically by author, with fairly detailed subject index.

Bio-bibliografía de la filosofía en Chile desde 1980 hasta 1984. See item **5397.**

Bradley, Peter T. *Crónicas de Indias:* some recent editions. See item **768.**

Burgess, Ronald D. Building a basic Spanish-American theatre bibliography. See item **4432.**

30 Burt, Eugene C. Ethnoart: Africa, Oceania, and the Americas: a bibliography of theses and dissertations. New York: Garland Pub., 1988. 191 p.: indexes. (Garland reference library of the humanities; 840)

Includes 318 unannotated citations on Latin America, covering Aztecs, Mayas, and other Mexican and Andean ethnic groups, as well as some from Brazil and Colombia. Arranged geographically, by subject within each area, and then chronologically by date of thesis. Includes four indexes: author, subject, institution, and date of thesis completion.

Carone, Edgard. O marxismo no Brasil: das origens a 1964. See item **5407.**

31 Catálogo das dissertações e teses dos cursos de pós-graduação em História, 1973–1985. Organização de Carlos Humberto Corrêa. Florianópolis, Brazil: Editora da UFSC, 1987. 400 p.: indexes.

Theses in history from 14 Brazilian universities, arranged by academic institution. Includes author, subject, and faculty adviser indexes.

32 **Chamberlain, Bobby J.** Portuguese language and Luso-Brazilian literature: an annotated guide to selected reference works. New York: Modern Language Association of America, 1989. 95 p.: index. (Selected bibliographies in language and literature; 6)

Classified, annotated, and selective guide to over 500 reference works, including bibliographies, indexes, catalogs, guides, and directories, some broken down geographically or chronologically. Excellent descriptive and sometimes critical annotations. Includes index of authors, editors, and compilers.

33 **Cordasco, Francesco.** The new American immigration: evolving patterns of legal and illegal emigration: a bibliography of selected references. New York: Garland Pub., 1987. 418 p.: index. (Garland reference library of social science; 376)

Divided into four broad areas. Though this work lacks specific subject indexes, it contains rich research material within the numerous studies (many well-annotated) which examine the situation of Latin American and Caribbean immigrants, past and present. Cites monographs, documents, articles, and conference papers.

34 **Creative literature of Trinidad and Tobago: a bibliography.** Compiled by Beverly D. Wharton-Lake. Foreward by Val T. McComie. Washington: Columbus Memorial Library, Organization of American States, 1988. 102 p.: index. (Hipólito Unanue bibliographic series; 4)

Contains 842 unannotated citations in alphabetical sequence by author, followed by complete title index. "Does not pretend to be exhaustive but will hopefully identify some of the writers who range from the pioneers to the comtemporaries." No critical material is included.

35 **Criens, S.R.** Bibliografie Nederlandse Antillen en Aruba [Bibliography of Netherlands Antilles and Aruba]. Amsterdam: Univ. van de Nederlandse Antillen, Stichting voor Culturele Samenwerking, Bibliotheek der Rijksuniv. Utrecht, 1989. Microfiche

Bibliography of the Netherlands Antilles and Aruba published on microfiche contains 23,625 bibliographic descriptions of items in the collection of the Univ. of Utrecht, The Netherlands. The records refer to publications dealing entirely or partly with the Netherlands Antilles and Aruba, without restriction to subject, language, time, or place of publication. [R. Hoefte]

36 **Dabydeen, David** and **Nana Wilson-Tagoe.** Selected theses in West Indian literature: an annotated bibliography. (*Third World Q.*, 9, July 1987, p. 921–960)

Begins with a historical overview of West Indian literature followed by bibliographic essays. Essays are further illuminated by short annotated bibliographies citing major texts covering themes such as anti-imperialism, nationalism, migration, Rastafarians, Calypso, carnival, and post-independence critiques.

Donato, Hernâni. Dicionário das batalhas brasileiras. See item **2884.**

Epelbaum de Weinstein, Ana. Bibliografía sobre judaísmo argentino. v. 4, El movimiento obrero judío en la Argentina. See item **2673.**

Frank, Erwin H. Bibliografía anotada de fuentes con interés para la etnología y etnohistoria de los Uni. See item **609.**

García-Carranza, Araceli and **Josefina García Carranza.** Bibliografía cubana del comandante Ernesto Che Guevara. See item **1908.**

37 **García Luna Ortega, Margarita.** La prensa del Estado de México en el siglo diecinueve. México: Gobierno del Estado de México, Univ. Autónoma del Estado de México, 1986. 141 p.

Fully annotated listing of official and non-official newspapers and periodicals published in the state of Mexico, 1848–1910. All basic information is provided, plus editorial policy and descriptions of the political, social, economic, or educational aspects. Gives locations within Mexican resource centers.

38 **Gardosky, Angel R.** El gobierno de María Estela Martínez de Perón, 29 junio

1974—23 marzo 1976: bibliografía comentada. v. 1. Buenos Aires: Alberto Kleiner, 1988. 1 v.

This bibliography attempts to provide insights into the historical/political background of the period through the indexing of Argentine newspapers and periodicals of the political right and left. Brief abstracts are provided. Arranged alphabetically by subject.

39 Gardosky, Angel R. El período de transición Lanusse-Campora: bibliografía comentada sobre movimientos subversivos, guerrilla y fuerzas armadas. v. 1. Buenos Aires: Alberto Kleiner, 1988. 1 v.

Bibliography comprised of citations to newspaper and periodical articles of the period seeking to draw a picture of the historical and political situation at that time. Brief abstracts describe contents of articles. Arranged alphabetically by subject.

40 González, Nelly and **Scott Van Jacob.** Agrarian reform in Central America: a bibliography of bibliographies. (*in* Seminar on the Acquisition of Latin American Library Materials, *32nd, Miami, Fla., 1987.* Caribbean collections: recession management strategies for libraries. Madison: Univ. of Wisconsin, 1988, p. 266–281)

Compilation of bibliographies lists 52 citations, alphabetically arranged by author, with full descriptive and evaluative annotations.

41 López Cervantes, Gonzalo and **Rosa María García García.** Ensayo bibliográfico del período colonial de México. México: Instituto Nacional de Antropología e Historia, 1989. 235 p.: index. (Col. Fuentes)

Basic bibliography about colonial period in Mexico is organized by subject into 16 sections and concludes with an onomastic index. Very useful source for research in Mexican history. [B. von Barghahn]

42 McQuade, Frank. Exile and dictatorship in Latin America since 1945: an annotated bibliography. (*Third World Q.,* 9:1, Jan. 1987, p. 254–270)

Good descriptive annotations accompany over 100 citations covering not only historical and political aspects of exile and dictatorship, but also their depiction in Latin American literature.

43 Meléndez, Guillermo. Iglesia, cristianismo y religión en América Central: resumen bibliográfico, 1960–1988. San José: Editorial DEI, 1988. 96 p.: indexes. (Col. Cuadernos; 10)

Contains 917 unannotated citations to books, pamphlets, and articles. Begins with section on Central America, then lists material on individual countries. Includes name and subject indexes.

Miranda Francisco, Olivia. La bibliografía sobre Félix Valera. See item **1789.**

44 Nocte, Sofía E. Bibliografía comentada sobre derechos humanos en Argentina. v. 5–10, 12–13, 21–25. Buenos Aires: Ediciones S.J.L., 1986. 13 v.: ill., indexes.

Bibliography of (mainly) Argentine and Uruguayan articles, pamphlets, and documents on human rights. Each volume is arranged alphabetically by subject, including many covering individuals. Each volume has a separate name/subject index. A cumulative index is projected for vol. 26.

45 O'Brien, Mac Gregor. Bibliografía de las revistas literarias peruanas. (*Hispania/Teachers,* 71:1, March 1988, p. 61–74)

Over 300 mostly unannotated periodical titles are listed in alphabetical order. Information on each varies considerably but may include beginning dates, frequency, editor, publisher, and contributors.

Pérez Herrero, Pedro and **Pedro A. Vives.** Perfil bibliográfico de la América de Carlos III. See item **830.**

46 Piñeiro de Rivera, Flor. Un siglo de literatura infantil puertorriqueña = A century of Puerto Rican children's literature. Río Piedras, P.R.: Editorial de la Univ. de Puerto Rico, 1987. 139 p.: appendices, bibl., ill.

Body of this impressive bilingual work is a bibliographical essay covering all aspects of Puerto Rican children's and juvenile literature. Appendices include a catalog of the creative works themselves arranged by author, title, subject, and illustrator; a chronology; and an overall index. Includes illustrations and portraits.

47 Ramos, J.L. *et al.* El indio en la prensa nacional mexicana del siglo XIX: catálogo de noticias. v. 1–3. Coordinación de Teresa Rojas Rabiela. México: SEP, 1987. 3 v.: indexes. (Cuadernos de la Casa Chata; 137–139)

Ten 19th-century newspapers and periodicals are indexed in this catalog of citations. Gives name, date, and place of publication of source, along with its subject (ethnic group) and an abstract of its contents. Includes indexes by place-name and ethnic group.

48 **Romero Arteta, Oswaldo.** La literatura ecuatoriana en las tesis doctorales de las universidades norteamericanas desde 1943 a 1985. (*Rev. Iberoam.*, 54 : 144/145, julio/dic. 1988, p. 1011–1018)

Chronologically arranged listing of US dissertations on Ecuadorian literature. Most items from the last two decades have (sometimes extensive) descriptive annotations.

49 **Rouse-Jones, Margaret D.** Recent research in the history of Trinidad and Tobago: a review of the journal and conference literature, 1975–1985. (*in* Seminar on the Acquisition of Latin American Library Materials, *32nd, Miami, Fla., 1987.* Caribbean collections: recession management strategies for libraries. Madison: Univ. of Wisconsin, 1988, p. 169–194, appendices)

Fairly extensive bibliographic essay. Appendices contain sources of journal and conference literature discussed, and a brief guide to topics covered. Concludes with 78 full bibliographic citations to items discussed in essay.

Samara, Eni de Mesquita. A história da família no Brasil. See item **2900**.

50 **Selakoff, Judith.** Women in the non-Hispanic Caribbean: a selective bibliography. (*in* Seminar on the Acquisition of Latin American Library Materials, *32nd, Miami, Fla., 1987.* Caribbean collections: recession management strategies for libraries. Madison: Univ. of Wisconsin, 1988, p. 244–266)

Bibliography of 235 unannotated citations, mostly of recent vintage, from books, pamphlets, articles, and dissertations. The emphasis is on social sciences. Alphabetically arranged by author. No index.

51 **Select bibliography of education in the Commonwealth Caribbean, 1976–1985: a supplement to** *Select bibliography of education in the Commonwealth Caribbean, 1940–1975.* Compiled by Amy Robertson. Mona, Jamaica: Documentation Centre,

Faculty of Education, Univ. of West Indies, 1987. 174 p.: index.

Begins with general materials on the region, followed by materials on individual countries. This, in turn, is followed by a coverage of broad subject areas. Over 1,000 unannotated citations. Name index included.

Simposio sobre Bibliografía del Negro en Colombia, *1st, Bogotá, 1983.* El negro en la historia de Colombia: fuentes escritas y orales. See item **2386**.

Suárez, Santiago Gerardo. Las reales audiencias indianas: fuentes y bibliografía. See item **855**.

Tesauro de datos históricos: índice compendioso de la literatura histórica de Puerto Rico, incluyendo algunos datos inéditos, periodísticos y cartográficos. See item **1599**.

52 **Viajeros y cronistas en la Amazonia colombiana: catálogo colectivo.** Recopilación de Beatriz Alzate Angel. Bogotá: Corporación Araracuara; Misión Técnica Holandesa, 1987. 366 p.: indexes.

Close to 3,000 unannotated citations relating to travelers from 16th to mid-20th centuries. Includes monographs and articles, as well as manuscripts from local and foreign archives. Contains following indexes: author, geographic, subject, tribal groups, and missions established by religious groups.

53 **Witker Velásquez, Alejandro.** Bibliografía latinoamericana de política y partidos políticos. San José: CAPEL, 1988. 310 p. (Serie Elecciones y democracia)

Arranged by broad subject areas: 1) general materials; 2) politics on a continental basis; and 3) comprising the majority of the work, the politics of individual countries. For the most part, materials are current and unannotated. Includes no overall index, but a detailed table of contents is a fairly good finding aid.

54 **Women in the Third World: a historical bibliography.** Edited by Pamela R. Byrne and Suzanne R. Ontiveros. Santa Barbara, Calif.: ABC-Clio Information Services, 1986. 152 p.: indexes. (ABC-Clio research guides; 15)

Largest portion of this bibliography lists close to 300 citations, from current journal literature, on Latin American and Caribbean women. Mostly in English, but some foreign language material. Includes full abstracts of each item, and a detailed subject index.

COLLECTIVE AND PERSONAL BIBLIOGRAPHIES

55   Carter, E. Dale. Bibliografía de y sobre Julio Cortázar. (*Explic. Textos Lit.*, 17 : 1/2, 1988/1989, p. 251–327)

Extensive unannotated current bibliography which includes books, articles, and unpublished interviews, as well as critical works including books, articles, and reviews. Alphabetically arranged by author. For literary critic's comment see item **3923**.

En el quinto centenario de Bartolomé de las Casas. See item **786**.

56   García-Carranza, Araceli. Aproximación biobibliográfica al doctor Elías Entralgo Vallina: en el 850 aniversario de su nacimiento. (*Rev. Bibl. Nac. José Martí*, 30 : 1, enero/abril 1988, p. 129–171, index)

Chronologically arranged biographic sketch followed by bibliographies listing over 200 books, pamphlets, articles, conference proceedings, and book reviews of single and collaborative authorship. Includes some descriptive annotations; concludes with overall index.

García-Carranza, Araceli and **Josefina García-Carranza.** Biobibliografía de Carlos Rafael Rodríguez. See item **1909**.

García-Carranza, Araceli. Biobibliografía de Emilio Roig de Leuchsenring. See item **1910**.

57   Jarvis, Kelvin. V.S. Naipaul: a selective bibliography with annotations, 1957–1987. Metuchen, N.J.: Scarecrow Press, 1989. 205 p.: indexes. (Scarecrow author bibliographies; 83)

Solid piece of work, lists books, articles, bibliographies, critical studies, interviews, dissertations, and selected book reviews. Good descriptive and often critical annotations of most items. Overall arrangement is chronological. Emphasis is on American, British, Canadian, and Caribbean sources. Includes name and subject indexes.

58   José Emilio Pacheco ante la crítica. Selección y presentación de Hugo J. Ve-

rani. México: Dirección de Difusión Cultural, Univ. Autónoma Metropolitana, Depto. Editorial, 1987. 310 p.: bibl. (Col. de Cultura universitaria; 36)

Book of critical essays on this Mexican literary figure. Two bibliographies are appended: 1) works by Pacheco; and 2) works about him.

59   Luis Leal: a bibliography with interpretive and critical essays. Edited by Salvador Güereña. Berkeley, Calif.: Chicano Studies Library Publications Unit, Univ. of California at Berkeley, 1988. 119 p.: bibl., ill., index. (Chicano Studies Library publications series; 14)

Work is prefaced by an overview of Leal's contributions to the field of Hispanic literature, but the bulk is made up of an unannotated bibliography of 729 items by and about him. Includes books, articles, reviews, interviews, criticism, a professional chronology, and an overall index.

60   Mexican autobiography: an annotated bibliography = La autobiografía mexicana: una bibliografía razonada. Compiled by Richard Donovon Woods. Translated by Josefina Cruz-Meléndez. New York: Greenwood Press, 1988. 228 p.: indexes. (Bibliographies and indexes in world history, 0742–6852; 13)

This impressive and informative reference work includes 332 entries alphabetically arranged by author. Information includes basic bio-bibliographic data and an annotation with both descriptive and prescriptive comments. Indexes cover author, title, subject, profession, genre, and chronology.

61   Peña Fuenzalida, Carmen. Bibliografía [de Domingo Santa Cruz]. (*An. Univ. Chile*, 5 : 11, agosto 1986, p. 47–54, bibl.)

Bibliography of works by Domingo Santa Cruz lists 102 unannotated publications in the field of music. With one exception, they have been selected from his contributions to five noted Chilean music periodicals. For music specialist's comment see *HLAS 50 : 4464*.

Ruiz, Ernesto. Máximo Gómez: selección bibliográfica y documental. See item **1825**.

62   Sable, Martin Howard. Guide to the writings of pioneer Latinamericanists of the United States. (*Behav. Soc. Sci. Libr.*, 7 : 1/2, 1988, p. 1–159, index)

Arranged alphabetically by broad discipline and/or field of activity. Under each discipline, names are listed alphabetically. Lists two works by each of 567 individuals, providing information on research done in the field. Contains personal names index.

63 **Urbina, Nicasio.** Bibliografía crítica completa de Ernesto Sábato, con un índice temático. (*Rev. Crít. Lit. Latinoam.*, 14:27, 1988, p. 177–222)

Extensive unannotated list of works about Sábato, including books, articles, chapters, and dissertations, arranged alphabetically by author. Subject index begins with an overall index followed by citations relating to individual works.

64 **Villaseñor y Villaseñor, Ramiro.** Biobibliografía Juan Rulfo. Guadalajara, México: Gobierno de Jalisco, Secretaría General, Unidad Editorial, 1986. 80 p.: ill. (Col. Temática jalisciense; 13)

Work begins with a biographical sketch and continues with bibliographies of works by and about Juan Rulfo which include books, articles, and dissertations from Europe, Latin America, and the US published 1953–1986. No annotations.

65 **Women writers of Spanish America: an annotated bio-bibliographical guide.** Edited by Diane E. Marting. New York: Greenwood Press, 1987. 448 p.: appendices. (Bibliographies and indexes in women's studies, 0742–6941; 5)

Substantial guide to authors of creative literature, arranged alphabetically by author. Biographical sketches and analytical, informative annotations are often, but not always, provided. Appendices include lists of anthologies, authors born before 1900, dramatists, translations, bilingual editions, and a classified listing of authors by country.

66 **Woodbridge, Hensley Charles** and **David S. Zubatsky.** Pablo Neruda: an annotated bibliography of biographical and critical studies. New York: Garland Pub., 1988. 629 p.: indexes. (Garland reference library of the humanities; 593)

Substantial compilation of over 2,300 annotated items including bibliographies, biographical studies, general studies, special topics, and studies on individual works. An-notations, primarily in English and the romance languages, are descriptive rather than critical, but are full and informative. Includes author and title indexes.

LIBRARY SCIENCE AND SERVICES

67 **Bibliotecas populares: identidad y proceso.** Lima: CIDAP; TAREA, 1987. 255 p.: ill.

Volume is result of a 1987 conference held to evaluate the present and future state of libraries in Peru. Succeeding chapters discuss problems, plans, roles, and specific projects for both urban and rural libraries.

68 **Ordóñez, José Arias** and **Moisés Pedraza Robayo.** Nuevas tendencias de la bibliotecología y necesidades del postgrado en Colombia. (*Rev. Interam. Bibl.*, 10:2, julio/dic. 1987, p. 31–43, bibl., graphs, ill.)

Study examines current state of library and information sciences in Colombia. It posits the need not only for restructuring pre and post-graduate courses in the field, but for introducing new ones. These changes should result in the broadening and upgrading of professional productivity in these areas.

ACQUISITIONS, COLLECTIONS, AND CATALOGS

Andrés, Gregorio de. La biblioteca manuscrita del americanista Andrés González de Barcia, 1743, del Consejo y Cámara de Castilla. See item **755.**

Archivo General de Indias. Catálogo de las consultas del Consejo de Indias. v. 5, 1626–1636. See item **757.**

Archivo General de Indias. Catálogo de las consultas del Consejo de Indias. v. 8, 1644–1650. See item **758.**

69 **Archivo Histórico Diplomático Mexicano Genaro Estrada.** Archivo de la Embajada de México en Honduras, 1908–1976: guía documental. Coordinación de Edgar Andrade Jasso. México: Secretaría de Relaciones Exteriores, 1988. 207 p.: indexes. (Archivo histórico diplomático mexicano.

Cuarta época. Guía para la historia diplomática de México; 5)

Inventory of 806 archival files (with descriptions of papers included) listed in chronological order, dated 1920–83. Includes name, subject and geographic indexes. Valuable for information on Mexican-Central American relations during this period.

70 Los archivos municipales del Estado de México. México: Sistema Nacional de Archivos; Gobierno del Estado de México; Archivo General de la Nación, 1987. 263 p., 1 folded leaf of plates: bibl., ill., tables. (Archivos estatales y municipales de México; 5)

Inventory of 121 municipal archives, dating from the Conquest to present, is alphabetically arranged by city. Each listing gives information basic to accessibility followed by a breakdown by department, giving number of files and range of dates covered.

71 Baer, James. Archivo Histórico de la Ciudad de Buenos Aires. (*LARR*, 21:3, 1986, p. 137–143, bibl.)

Clear and concise description of documents recently made available by the *Archivo Histórico de la Ciudad de Buenos Aires*, focusing on the period 1856–1909. Existing bibliographic tools are cited, subjects encompassed are described, and specific examples are depicted which suggest usefulness of the archival holdings. Small bibliography appended.

Catalogue du fonds local, 1883–1985. See item **1529.**

72 Centro de Documentação do Pensamento Brasileiro. Catálogo do acervo. 2a. ed. Salvador, Brazil: Centro de Documentação do Pensamento Brasileiro, 1985. 443 p.: index.

Catalog of close to 3,000 20th-century unannotated titles is divided into collections on philosophy (by far the largest), political science, sociology, and anthropology. Includes books, articles, documents, and proceedings, primarily in Portuguese. Author index is appended with specific titles listed under each author's name.

73 Cortés Alonso, Vicenta. La documentación del Consejo de Indias en el Archivo Histórico Nacional, Madrid. (*Rev. Indias*, 47:179, enero/abril 1987, p. 13–37, bibl., tables)

Detailed, historical account of Consejo de Indias collections housed in the Archivo Histórico. Describes existing guides, catalogs, and inventories, and surveys past, present, and future work of archivists attempting to achieve bibliographic control over this material. For historian's comment see *HLAS 50:875.*

Ezquerra Abadía, Ramón. Las principales colecciones documentales colombinas. See item **787.**

74 Fisher de Figueroa, Marie-Claire. Al rescate del Caribe francés: descripción de las colecciones de dos bibliotecas de la Ciudad de México. (*in* Seminar on the Acquisition of Latin American Library Materials, *32nd, Miami, Fla., 1987.* Caribbean collections: recession management strategies for libraries. Madison: Univ. of Wisconsin, 1988, p. 195–211)

Historic overview precedes a bibliography of 66 sources with descriptive and evaluative annotations, and another related bibliography with 76 unannotated citations.

75 Hampe Martínez, Teodoro. La biblioteca del arzobispo Hernando Arias de Ugarte: bagaje intelectual de un prelado criollo, 1614. (*Thesaurus*, 42:2, mayo/agosto, 1987, p. 337–361.)

Catalog of private library of 17th-century archbishop is examined with an eye to relating its contents to intellectual history of that period. Catalog is divided into four areas: religious works, canon law, civil law, and history and other subjects.

76 Instituto Nacional de Estadística y Censos (Argentina). Catálogo de publicaciones seriadas argentinas. Buenos Aires: Instituto Nacional de Estadística y Censos, 1988. 170 p.: indexes. (Serie Biblioteca INDEC, 0327–0912; 1)

Arranged in two sections: 1) by name of publication, giving subject contents and types of statistical data; and 2) indexes, by institutional publisher, subject, statistical data, and acronyms.

77 Peronism and the three Perons: a checklist of material on peronism and on Juan Domingo, Eva, and Isabel Peron, and their writings, in the Hoover Institution Library and Archives and in the Stanford University Libraries. Compiled by Laszlo Horvath. Stanford, Calif.: Hoover Institution, Stanford Univ., 1988: 170 p. (Hoover Press bibliography; 71)

Exhaustive checklist of books, pamphlets, and archival materials held, for the most part, in the Hoover Institution. Divided into four parts: 1) Juan Perón and Peronism; 2) Eva Perón; 3) Isabel Perón; and 4) writings by all three. Provides location codes. No index or annotations.

78   Ramírez Ayala, Oliverio; Francisco Rodas de Coss; and Salvador Victoria.
Archivo de la Embajada de México en los Estados Unidos de América, 1822–1978: correspondencia encuadernada, 1822–1914. México: Secretaría de Relaciones Exteriores, 1987. 306 p.: index. (Archivo histórico diplomático mexicano. Cuarta época. Guías para la historia diplomática de México; 4)

Each of four sections contains records of correspondence between the embassy and various Mexican governmental departments. Lists close to 500 files dated 1822–1914, with descriptions of papers included. Includes good overall index.

79   Rivas Mata, Emma; María Esther Jasso Sáenz; and Gabriela Sánchez Vences.
Catálogo de la Colección Fondo reservado de la Biblioteca Manuel Orozco y Berra. México: Instituto Nacional de Antropología e Historia, 1985. 270 p.: facsims., indexes. (Col. Fuentes)

Catalog lists over 2,000 unannotated citations of a collection specializing in 19th-century Mexican history but containing other subjects as well. Arranged by Dewey Decimal Classification; includes author and subject indexes.

80   Torres Lanzas, Pedro. Catálogo de mapas y planos: Guatemala (Guatemala, San Salvador, Honduras, Nicaragua y Costa Rica). Madrid?: Ministerio de Cultura, Dirección General de Bellas Artes y Archivos, 1985. 214 p.: indexes.

One in a series of facsimile editions of early 20th-century catalogs of 16th to 19th-century Latin American maps and plans held in the Archivo General de Indias.

81   Vos, Jan de. Catálogo de los documentos históricos que se conservan en el fondo llamado "Provincia de Chiapas" del Archivo General de Centroamérica, Guatemala. v. 1–2. San Cristóbal de Las Casas,

Mexico: Centro de Estudios Indígenas, UNACH; Centro de Investigaciones Ecológicas del Sureste, 1985. 2 v. in 3: indexes, maps.

Catalog of documents in the Archivo General de Centro América pertaining to colonial history of Chiapas. Catalog is arranged by subject and contains geographic and name indexes. Succeeding volumes will deal with Chiapas-related colonial documents found in other locations.

82   Wolf, Carolyn E. and Nancy S. Chiang.
Indians of North and South America: a bibliography based on the collection at the Willard E. Yager Library-Museum, Hartwick College, Oneonta, N.Y.: Supplement. Metuchen, N.J.: Scarecrow Press, 1988. 654 p.: indexes.

Substantial supplement to original edition published in 1977. Contains 3,542 unannotated items arranged alphabetically by main entries. Collection includes books, articles, essays, documents, and dissertations, with title and subject indexes. Within an appended list of tribes cited in the subject index, over 50 are from Latin America.

REFERENCE WORKS AND RESEARCH

83   *The Americas*, Vol. 48, No. 1, July 1991– . Washington: Academy of American Franciscan History.

This cumulative index provides full author, title, and subject indexing for 629 articles and signed archival items published July 1964–April 1991. Book reviews are indexed by author and title only and the "Notes" sections are omitted, though these can still be accessed through the annual indices. Of particular interest are the numerous listings on archives and archival resources in Latin America.

84   Anuario parlamentar brasileiro, 1987.
Brasília: Semprel; São Paulo: Editora Tres Ltda., 1987. 1 v.: index.

Annual directory which, beginning with this edition (ano 2, 1988), includes biographical sketches of current members of the Assembléia Nacional Constituinte, Senado, and Câmara dos Deputados. Some personal biographical information is provided, but emphasis is on political accomplishments. Arranged geographically; includes personal name index.

Appleby, David P. Heitor Villa-Lobos: a bio-bibliography. See item **5120**.

85   **Baremboim, Javier E.** Periódicos y re-vistas políticas en Argentina: biblio-grafía comentada de publicaciones de parti-dos de izquierda, 1986. v. 1–7. Buenos Aires: Ediciones S.J.L., 1987. 7 v.

Index to Argentine periodicals of the left beginning with 1986. Articles in each volume are arranged first by subject and then in chronological order. Citations include short descriptive annotations. First seven volumes examined deal with one periodical title (838 citations).

Bizzarro, Salvatore. Historical dictionary of Chile. See item **2561**.

Boletín. No. 1, enero/feb. 1988–; No. 2, marzo/abril 1988–; No. 3, mayo/junio 1988– ; No. 4, julio/agosto 1988– ; No. 8, nov. 1988– ; No. 9, dic. 1988– . Bibliografía sobre Música Tradicional. See item **5114**.

86   **Céspedes, Mario** and **Lelia Garreaud.** Gran diccionario de Chile: biográfico-cultural. v. 1–2. 2a ed. Santiago: Importadora Alfa, 1988. 2 v.: appendices, bibl., ill., ports. (Col. Alfa divulgación. Serie Historia de Chile)

Intended as a ready reference source, this work includes concise but substantial information on noted personages as well as historical or cultural events of importance from the Conquest to the present. Appendi-ces include lists of heads of state, historic battles, and a bibliography.

87   **Diccionario enciclopédico domini-cano.** Redacción de Alejandro Paulino Ramos *et al.* Santo Dominigo: Sociedad Edi-torial Dominicana, 1988. 2 v.: appendices, bibl., ill., index, maps, ports.

Two-volume alphabetically-arranged encyclopedic work that attempts to cover all things Dominican. Entries are mostly brief but vary in size with the importance of the topic. Well illustrated with black and white photographs, including portraits. Appendices contain historical chronology, bibliography, and overall index.

88   **Dictionary of Brazilian literature.** Ed-ited by Irwin Stern. New York: Green-wood Press, 1988. 402 p.: bibl., index.

Good basic reference source contains approximately 300 entries covering not only significant writers but also literary schools and related cultural movements. Emphasis is on 20th century. Entries vary in length de-pending on importance of writer, with short bibliographies following most entries. Over-all index appended.

Duckles, Vincent Harris and **Michael A. Kel-ler.** Music reference and research materials: an annotated bibliography. See item **5071**.

89   **Estremadoyro Robles, Camila.** Dic-cionario histórico biográfico: peruanos ilustres: quinientas biografías, setenticinco pensamientos y frases célebres. Lima: Li-brería-Bazar Eureka, 1987. 506 p., 1 folded leaf of plates: bibl., ports.

Alphabetically-arranged reference work offers biographical information on 500 noted Peruvians, in all fields, from precolum-bian times to the present. Information ranges from a single paragraph to several pages.

90   **Guia brasileiro de fontes para a histó-ria da Africa, da escravidão negra e do negro na sociedade atual: fontes arquivísti-cas.** v. 1, Alagoas-Rio Grande do Sul. v. 2, Rio de Janeiro-Sergipe. Rio de Janeiro: Minis-tério da Justiça, Arquivo Nacional: Departa-mento de Impr. Nacional, 1988. 2 v.: indexes. (Guia de fontes para a história das nações. B, Africa. 11, Brasil.)

Extensive listing of Brazilian archival sources arranged alphabetically by state and within state by city. Descriptions of archives contain addresses, hours, curators, and sub-ject and size of collections. Actual details on materials available vary in length and speci-ficity. Includes indexes by city and subject.

Hartness, Ann. Brazil in reference books, 1965–1989: an annotated bibliography. See item **13**.

91   **Ibero-American publishers directory.** Compiled by Florencio Oscar García and Yolanda Olivas. Albuquerque, N.M.: FOG Publications, 1989. 100 p.: index.

Listing, alphabetically arranged by com-pany name, of 287 publishers and 91 printers in Latin America. Provides full names, ad-dresses, and (sometimes) telephone numbers. Publishers and printers are listed separately both in main body of entries as well as in an index by country.

92 Instituto de Investigaciones Literarias Gonzalo Picón Febres. Diccionario general de la literatura venezolana. v. 1–2. Ed. no. 2. Mérida, Venezuela: Editorial Venezolana; Consejo de Fomento; Consejo de Publicaciones, Univ. de los Andes, 1987. 2 v. (Libros de la Universidad de los Andes; 2419. Col. Ciencias sociales. Serie Letras)

Update of 1974 edition provides bio-bibliographic information on Venezuelan authors from 16th century to 1982. Also includes a few foreign authors who have written in, or about, Venezuela. Lists works by and about each subject.

Kuss, Malena. Toward a comprehensive approach to Latin American music bibliography: theoretical foundations for reference sources and research materials. See item **5077.**

Langevin, André. Música andina: breve introducción bibliográfica. See item **5078.**

93 Latin American writers. v. 1–3. Edited by Carlos A. Solé and Maria Isabel Abreu. New York: Scribner, 1989. 3 v.: bibl., indexes.

Interesting and informative work surveys over 175 authors, dating from conquest to present. Each writer is subject of critical essay followed by selective bibliography. Includes general and geographic indexes.

94 Macdonald, Roger and Carole Travis. Libraries and special collections on Latin America and the Caribbean: a directory of European resources. 2nd ed. London; Atlantic Highlands, N.J.: Published for the Institute of Latin American Studies, University of London [by] the Athlone Press, 1988. 339 p.: index. (Institute of Latin American Studies; 14)

Expanded revised edition which updates an excellent reference work published in 1975: *Directory of libraries and special collections on Latin America and the Caribbean.* Arranged geographically, each entry describes the collections and their accessibility, as well as services available. Includes overall index.

95 Mota Murillo, Rafael. Archivo Ibero-Americano, Indices: 1, Indice de autores y artículos. (*Arch. Ibero-Am.*, 49:193/194, enero/junio 1989, p. 195–297)

First part of a long-projected series of

indexes for this periodical consists of an author and title index of 1,207 citations covering the period 1914–88. Alphabetical list of authors notes articles by each.

96 Musacchio, Humberto. Diccionario enciclopédico de México. v. 1–4. México: A. Léon, Editor, 1989. 4 v.: ill.

Encyclopedic work comprised mainly of brief biographical sketches of Mexicans in all fields past and present. However, also includes articles on any place, personage, or subject relevant to historic/cultural background of Mexico. Contains many illustrations, including portraits; some are in color.

97 Nogués, Germinal. Diccionario biográfico de políticos argentinos. Buenos Aires: Grupo Editorial Planeta, 1989. 245 p.: bibl., ill.

Useful biographical directory of over 300 mostly contemporary Argentines actively involved in Argentine politics. Information is primarily concerned with political affiliations (which appear to span a fairly wide spectrum) and posts held within those political groups.

98 Rodríguez Rea, Miguel Angel. Indice de los primeros diez volúmenes de *Histórica*, 1977–1986. (*Histórica/Lima*, 11:2, dic. 1987, p. 207–238, bibl.)

Contains alphabetically-arranged author and subject indexes. Author index includes full bibliographic information on each article cited.

99 Sovetskaīa latinoamerikanistika, 1961–1986 [Soviet Latin American Studies, 1961–1986]. Edited by Viktor Vatslavovich Vol'skiĭ. Moskva: Akademiīa nauk SSSR, Institut Latinskoĭ Ameriki, 1986. 290 p.: bibl.

Informative collection of articles on Soviet scholarship on Latin America were published to mark the 25th anniversary of the Institute of Latin American Studies. Subjects include prominent Soviet scholars and publications in the field, ideological aims of the Insitute, influence of world events on Soviet scholarship, the Institute's international ties, and the methodology of Soviet studies on Latin America. Separate articles address geography, ethnography, history, and foreign relations. Many footnotes. [B. Dash]

100 Tinker guide to Latin American and Caribbean policy and scholarly re-

sources in metropolitan New York. Edited by Ronald G. Hellman and Beth Kempler Pfannl. New York: Bildner Center for Western Hemisphere Studies, Graduate School and University Center, City Univ. of New York, 1988. 217 p.: indexes.

Useful compilation listing institutions, organizations, and collections in the New York area that constitute sources of information and assistance to those interested in scholarly and policy-related issues; emphasizes social sciences. Appends lists of bookstores, publishing houses, publications, and media. Also has name and subject indexes.

101 Woods, Richard Donovon. Latin American reference books: an underappreciated genre. (*LARR*, 24:2, 1989, p. 231–245, bibl.)

Thoughtful survey of Latin American reference books in the last decade, noting trends and new disciplines in the field. Nine titles are carefully analyzed for their ability to support and provide further guidance in research.

102 The writings of Lewis Hanke. (*Rev. Interam. Bibliogr.*, 36:4, 1986, p. 427–451)

Books, articles, theses, interviews, and texts of speeches all form a part of this substantial bibliography in which 231 unannotated works, both published and unpublished, are listed in chronological order. Curriculum vitae is appended.

GENERAL WORKS

103 Dorn, Georgette M. Hispanic books in the Library of Congress, 1815–1965. (*in* Philosophy and literature in Latin America: a critical assessment of the current situation. Edited by Jorge J. E. Gracia and Mireya Camurati. Albany, N.Y.: State Univ. of New York Press, 1989, p. 173–181)

Article treads a clear path through the historic development of the Library of Congress' Hispanic collection from its Jeffersonian origins through the many vicissitudes which shaped it through the centuries. Benefactors, consultants, and directors all play leading parts in this narrative describing what led to the present-day collection.

104 Elkin, Judith Laikin. Building bibliography: the case of Latin American Jew-

ish studies. (*Rev. Interam. Bibliogr.*, 37:4, 1987, p. 473–479, bibl.)

Survey of past and present research in the field of Latin American Jewish studies describes both need and future plans for bibliographic control in the field by listing existing and projected bibliographic tools.

105 Ezquerra Abadía, Ramón. Las principales colecciones documentales colombinas. (*Rev. Indias*, 48:184, sept./dic. 1988, p. 661–691)

Extensive description of principal collections of Columbian documents collected from the beginning (by Columbus himself) to mid-20th century. Good historical accounts are augmented by precise details of contents and are supplemented by footnotes.

106 Peloso, Vincent. Hispanic books in the Library of Congress, 1815–1965: a comment. (*in* Philosophy and literature in Latin America: a critical assessment of the current situation. Edited by Jorge J. E. Gracia and Mireya Camurati. Albany, N.Y.: State Univ. of New York Press, 1989, p. 182–186)

Concise but informative article on the Hispanic Division. Focuses on the Reference Section and the *Handbook of Latin American Studies*, detailing strengths and weakness of both, as well as pointing out collections and items of interest.

107 Reunión Técnica Regional sobre Informática Aplicada a la Administración del Trabajo, La Habana, 1987. Informe final. v. 1–2. Lima: Centro Interamericano de Administración del Trabajo; Servicio Central de Biblioteca y Documentación (International Labour Organization); Havana: Comité Estatal de Trabajo y Seguridad Social, 1987. 2 v.: bibl., ill.

Ten Latin American countries, Spain, the International Labor Organization, and the Centro Interamericano de Administración del Trabajo participated in this conference promoted to exchange information on individual plans and programs for implementing computer systems used in extracting and dispensing information within their respective countries. The proceedings include program descriptions as well as resulting recommendations.

108 Rodríguez, Celso. The growing professionalism of Latin American journals. (*in* Philosophy and literature in Latin America: a critical assessment of the current situation. Edited by Jorge J. E. Gracia and Mireya Camurati. Albany, N.Y.: State Univ. of New York Press, 1989, p. 187–193)

Thoughtful survey of current Latin American journals in social sciences and humanities describes growth in number of important journals. Also relates their publishers' attempts to keep pace with growing professional demands and the problems many of them face in improving quality and expanding distribution.

109 Sarramía, Tomás. La revista *Las Antillas*, 1866–1867: un propósito hispanoamericanista. (*Rev. Interam. Bibliogr.*, 38:1, 1988, p. 61–68, index)

Historic sketch of this 19th-century periodical is followed by overall index in which titles of all articles that appeared are listed under their respective authors.

110 Siebenmann, Gustav. Os estudos latino-americanos nos países de idioma alemão. (*Let. Hoje*, 24:1, março 1989, p. 51–64)

Author traces growing scholarly interest in Latin American language and literature, from the 1960s onward, within cultural/educational institutions in German-speaking countries. Pinpoints the development of resources within particular institutions as well as resultant publications.

Smorkaloff, Pamela María. Literatura y edición de libros: la cultura literaria y el proceso social en Cuba. See item **3691.**

111 Tanodi, Aurelio. La situación de los archivos iberoamericanos. (*Jahrb. Gesch.*, 24, 1987, p. 41–109)

Lengthy and scholarly examination of present state of Iberoamerican archives. Covers historical descriptions of organizational patterns, a breakdown of official archival sources, problems of conservation, and maintenance and accessibility. Of particular interest are descriptions of specific archives, research guides, and legislation defining parameters of accessibility.

NEW SERIAL TITLES

112 *Boletín Bibliográfico.* 1985– . México: Agencia Mexicana del ISBN, Dirección General del Derecho del Autor.

Quarterly bibliography of current

Mexican ISBN listings issued as a supplement within the periodical *Libros de México*. Books are arranged by author, title, and subject. Full bibliographic information appears under author entry.

Boletín del Archivo Histórico Arquidiocesano Francisco de Paula García Paláez. Vol. 1, No. 1, julio 1988– . See item **1349.**

113 *Información Bibliográfica.* Año 3, no. 1, julio 1984– . Buenos Aires: Cámara Argentina del Libro.

Since the July 1984 issue, this special section of *Libros de edición argentina* carries Argentine ISBN listings corresponding to those registered the previous month. Listings are by author and subject, with full bibliographic information given in the subject listing.

Revista de la Academia Guatemalteca de Estudios Genealógicos, Heráldicos, e Históricos. Vol. 9, 1987– . See item **1366.**

JOURNAL ABBREVIATIONS

Americas/Francisc.   The Americas. Academy of American Franciscan History. Washington.

An. Univ. Chile.   Anales de la Universidad de Chile. Santiago.

Arch. Ibero-Am.   Archivo Ibero-Americano. Revista de Estudios Históricos. Los Padres Franciscanos. Madrid.

Behav. Soc. Sci. Libr.   Behavioral and Social Sciences Librarian. The Haworth Press, New York.

Bol. Acad. Hondur. Leng.   Boletín de la Academia Hondureña de la Lengua. Tegucigalpa.

Bol. Bibliogr./México.   Boletín Bibliográfico. Agencia Mexicana del ISBN, Dirección General del Derecho del Autor. Mexico.

Explic. Textos Lit.   Explicación de Textos Literarios. Dept. of Spanish and Portuguese, California State Univ. Sacramento.

Hispania/Teachers.   Hispania. American Assn. of Teachers of Spanish and Portuguese; Univ. of Southern California. Los Angeles.

Histórica/Lima.   Histórica. Pontificia Univ. Católica del Perú, Depto. de Humanidades. Lima.

Inf. Bibliogr. Información Bibliográfica. Libros de Edición Argentina; Cámara Argentina del Libro. Buenos Aires.

Jahrb. Gesch. Jahrbuch für Geschichte von Staat, Wirtschaft und Gesellschaft Lateinamerikas. Köln, Germany.

LARR. Latin American Research Review. Latin American Research Review Board. Univ. of New Mexico, Albuquerque, N.M.

Let. Hoje. Letras de Hoje. Pontifícia Univ. Católica do Rio Grande do Sul. Pôrto Alegre, Brazil.

Rev. Bibl. Nac. José Martí. Revista de la Biblioteca Nacional José Martí. La Habana.

Rev. Crít. Lit. Latinoam. Revista de Crítica Literaria Latinoamericana. Latinoamericana Editores. Lima.

Rev. Iberoam. Revista Iberoamericana. Instituto Internacional de Literatura Iberoamericana; Univ. de Pittsburgh. Pittsburgh, Penn.

Rev. Indias. Revista de Indias. Consejo Superior de Investigaciones Científicas, Instituto Gonzalo Fernández de Oviedo. Madrid.

Rev. Interam. Bibl. Revista Interamericana de Bibliotecología. Univ. de Antioquía, Escuela Interamericana de Bibliotecología. Medellin, Colombia.

Rev. Interam. Bibliogr. Revista Interamericana de Bibliografía. Organization of American States. Washington.

Thesaurus. Thesaurus. Instituto Caro y Cuervo. Bogotá.

Third World Q. Third World Quarterly. Third World Foundation; New Zealand House. London.

ART

SPANISH AMERICA
Precolumbian Art, Folk Art, and Popular Art

FLORA S. CLANCY, *Associate Professor of Art History,*
University of New Mexico, Albuquerque

IN THE LAST FEW YEARS I have observed intriguing shifts in the focus and in the intention of publications on Spanish American art, changes which may be the subtle result of the contemplation of meanings and histories engendered by the Quincentennial. In Spanish America, especially in the publications on folk and popular art, there is a shifting from the structural concerns with production and marketing towards a more historical (post-historical?) view that looks to the craft objects themselves as sources of information (item **140**). This does not mean that the descriptive, the nostalgic, and the lyrical tracts are disappearing. They are not (items **145, 151, 150,** and **128**). Still, greater methodological and even political risks are being taken in what is being published (items **139, 149, 148,** and **133**), not the least of which are the few attempts to achieve a descriptive overview of certain histories by combining archaeological information with art objects (items **117, 119,** and **121**).

There is also a shift to be observed in English-language publications, especially in the area of attempted overviews. Here the effort is to attempt a narrative history (items **144, 116,** and **135**) rather than a descriptive one, and seems brought about by greater confidence in abilities to render meaningful what was once thought to remain forever obscure, such as reading original texts, especially in the Maya area (item **135**), and eliciting "deep structures" from ethnographic sources (items **146** and **138**). The narrative history allows for an experimentation with point of view and subjective interpretation and that, I think, ultimately leads to more explicit statements of position on the part of the author(s).

The descriptive history (items **122, 134, 128, 121,** and **125**) usually relies on and illustrates more works of art than narrative history, but then it is more bound to the obvious and the material aspects of art as artifact. Narrative history can explore those things not manifest or obvious, the essence or "marrow" that Ortega y Gasset considered the substance of history.

One of the most common forms of publication is the edited volume that ranges from a tightly organized point of view or theme (items **138** and **126**) to a loose, disjointed compendium of various authors (items **142, 137,** and **115**). Many publishing houses are no longer as interested in this form of publication, and it is likely these will become fewer in number in the future. Still, such a format serves to make available information (item **137, 115,** and **125**) and differing points of view (items **142** and **149**) in a timely fashion. Although I think carefully envisioned overviews are badly needed, such efforts take long periods of time to research, think through, and write.

Catalogs of exhibitions and of collections have been numerous in the last few years, and although they sometimes, but not always, inspire essays of importance (items **117, 133,** and **136**), they do serve to make available works of art not often published (items **129, 130, 121,** and **125**). In this they offset the descriptive and the narrative histories discussed above, whose authors for some reason rely heavily on well-known and often-published works of art.

Oddly enough, few publications clearly take as a focus the many and various issues of the forthcoming Quincentennial. There certainly have been catalogs of exhibitions mounted with the Quincentennial in mind, but not as issue (items **129** and **125**). The most ambitious and controversial, perhaps, being the exhibition *Mexico: splendors of thirty centuries* (item **127**) that brought together in one show, and catalog, exemplary works of art from the early Mexican high culture of the Olmecs to the muralists of the 20th century. Implicit in the organization of the show is the idea that some kind of continuity or affinity runs uninterrupted from the deep past into the present, a topic that, hopefully, will continue to receive much needed scholarly attention (items **140** and **146**).

It is hoped as well that through the impetus of the Quincentennial, scholarly attention will be focused on the ways (beyond foodstuffs) that Amerindian cultures influenced 16th-century Europe, its economies, its philosophies, and even its folkways.

PRECOLUMBIAN

Agurto Calvo, Santiago. Estudios acerca de la construcción, arquitectura y planeamiento incas. See *HLAS 51:582.*

114   Bassie-Sweet, Karen. From the mouth of the dark cave: commemorative sculpture of the late classic Maya. Norman: Univ. of Oklahoma Press, 1991. 287 p.: bibl., ill., index, map.
Concerned with the ever provocative tablets from the Cross Group of the ancient Maya site of Palenque, author develops two lines of analysis: integration of text and image, and iconography of caves.

115   Classic Maya political history: hieroglyphic and archaeological evidence.
Edited by T. Patrick Culbert. Cambridge; New York: Cambridge Univ. Press, 1991. 396 p.: bibl., ill., index, maps. (School of American Research advanced seminar series)
Welcome volume tries to bring order to—or at least to bring together—the many new and different interpretations of late classic Maya history. Politics covered range from ancient times to present scholarly debates.

116   Clendinnen, Inga. Aztecs: an interpretation. Cambridge; New York: Cambridge Univ. Press, 1991. 398 p.: bibl., ill. (some col.), index, maps.
Remarkable and, at times, overwrought, effort to extract a human history and "daily life" from extant chronicles and histories of the Aztec-Mexica. Search is for the individual's sense of place and self within the (better known) social and cultural definitions of the Mexica world.

117   Culturas precolombinas: chimú. Lima: Banco de Crédito del Perú, 1988. 288 p.: bibl., ill. (some col.) (Col. Arte y tesoros del Perú)
Good piece of work combines basic, up-to-date knowledge of legends, ecology, and archaeology with a good and interesting interpretation of the chronicles. Illustrations are nicely photographed and have clear explanatory captions. Worth reading.

118   Czitrom, Carolyn Baus Reed. Los perros de la antigua provincia de Colima: estudio y corpus de sus representaciones en arcilla en las colecciónes del Museo Nacional de Antropología. México: Instituto Nacional de Antropología e Historia, 1988. 97 p.: bibl., ill. (Col. Catálogos de museos)
Monograph traces role played by the dog in ancient Mesoamerican thought.

Draws on chronicles and archaeological and ethnographic sources. Includes many useful and beautiful illustrations of ancient Colima ceramic sculptures of dogs.

119 Historia del arte hispanoamericano. v. 1, Arte precolombino [de] José Alcina Franch. Madrid: Alhambra, 1987. 1 v.: bibl., ill. (some col.)

Vol. 1 of four is devoted to precolumbian art. Author provides major overview of Hispanic American art intended for the college classroom. A responsible display of known works and issues. (For vols. 2–3, see items 159 and 289.)

120 Kubler, George. Esthetic recognition of ancient Amerindian art. New Haven: Yale Univ. Press, 1991. 276 p.: bibl., ill., index. (Yale publications in the history of art)

Every word in the title of the book receives a stunning and illuminating analysis, including, although more implicitly, the connecting preposition.

121 Larralde de Sáenz, Jacqueline. Crónicas en barro y piedra: arte prehispánico de México en la Colección Sáenz; el período formativo. Fotografías de Dolores Dahlhaus. México: Univ. Nacional Autónoma de México, Instituto de Investigaciones Estéticas, 1986. 250 p., 20 leaves of plates: bibl., ill. (some col.), indexes.

Volume's value lies in the inclusiveness of its examples, its clear organization, and responsible text.

Lathrap, Donald W.; Angelika Gebhart-Sayer; and Ann M. Mester. The roots of the Shipibo art style: three waves on Imiríacocha or there were "Incas" before the Incas. See *HLAS 51:608.*

Litvak King, Jaime. El estudio del arte mesoamericano: un punto de vista disidente. See *HLAS 51:188.*

122 Mangino Tazzer, Alejandro. Arquitectura mesoamericana: relaciones espaciales. México: Editorial Trillas, 1990. 239 p.: bibl., ill., index.

Architectural space is defined as a function of the observer in this clearly articulated analysis of architectual form and space.

123 Massing, Jean Michel. Early European images of America: the ethnographic approach. (*in* Circa 1492: art in the age of exploration. Edited by Jay A. Levenson. Washington: National Gallery of Art; New Haven: Yale Univ. Press, 1991, p. 515–520, photo, facsim.)

Discusses European influence in the meticulous but often inaccurate depictions of garments and artifacts of American Indians by Dürer (Aztecs) and Burgkmair (Brazil). Weiditz introduced a new approach in *Trachtenbuch* (1529) by recording individual characteristics, thus paralleling the efforts of sympathetic chroniclers like Peter Martyr and Sahagún. [H. von Winning]

124 Masuda, Yoshio *et al.* Kodai Andes bijutsu [Arts of the ancient Andes]. Tokyo: Iwanami Shoten, 1991. 253 p.: bibl., ill., index, photos.

Collection of ten papers on ancient Andean arts by archaeologists and historians from seven countries, including Japan. Peter Kaulicke, Izumi Shimada, and Patricia Knoblock analyze the arts of Chavin, Moche, and Huari respectively by using iconological interpretations; Luis Lumbreras explains the peoples and cultures of the Andes; and Patricia Lyon shows the genre and means of expression of their arts. Also includes Masuda's work on arts of the Incas and their conquest region, Nobuko Kajitani's work on ancient Andean textiles, and three other articles on the ancient arts of Ecuador, Chile, and Argentina. [K. Horisaka]

125 Los Mayas, el esplendor de una civilización: Centro Cultural de la Villa de Madrid, mayo 1990; Museu Etnológic de Barcelona, junio 1990. Madrid: Turner, 1990? 247 p.: bibl., ill. (some col.) (Col. Encuentros: Serie Catálogos)

Catalog published to accompany an exhibition held in Madrid and Barcelona. Consists of essays by well-known scholars and illustrations of exceptional works of art that are not commonly published. Essays are good, but general.

126 Mesoamerica after the decline of Teotihuacan, A.D. 700–900. Edited by Richard A. Diehl and Janet Catherine Berlo. Washington: Dumbarton Oaks Research Library and Collection, 1989. 244 p.: bibl., ill., index.

Articles included in this volume are not definitive, but taken together they provide a comprehensible and general picture of a transitional period in ancient Mesoamerican history.

127 Mexico: splendors of thirty centuries. Introduction by Octavio Paz. Translations by Edith Grossman *et al.* New York: Metropolitan Museum of Art; Boston: Little, Brown, 1990. 712 p.: bibl., ill. (some col.), index, maps.

Large and ambitious catalog produced to accompany "block buster" traveling exhibition encompassing all Mexican art, from precolumbian to present. Although essays are informative, photographs of objects work more clearly to illustrate perception of continuity suggested by title.

128 Montás, Onorio. Arte taíno. Fotografías de Onorio Montás y Pedro J. Borrell B. Texto de Frank Moya Pons. 2a ed. Santo Domingo: Banco Central de la República Dominicana, 1985. 231 p.: bibl., chiefly ill.

Text of second ed. of this 1983 publication illustrates the cultural patrimony expressed by the art of the Taino, and tries to understand ancient methods of integrating culture and economy. Illustrated images are extraordinary and are deserving of greater general knowledge.

129 Musees royaux d'Art et d'Histoire (Bruxelles). Inca-Peru: 3000 ans d'histoire. Gent, Belgium: Imschoot, Uitgevers, 1990. 2 v.

Two beautifully illustrated volumes provide an overview of ancient Peruvian cultures and artifacts from an anthropological point of view. Even without an organizing table of contents, these two volumes would make useful textbooks (for those who read French).

130 Parsons, Lee Allen; John B. Carlson; and **Peter David Joralemon.** The face of ancient America: the Wally and Brenda Zollman collection of Precolumbian art. Foreword by Michael D. Coe. Photographs by Justin Kerr. Indianapolis, Ind.: Indianapolis Museum of Art; Indiana Univ. Press, 1988. 223 p.: bibl., ill. (some col.)

Welcome, beautifully illustrated presentation of many unpublished works of art from the ancient cultures of the Olmec, the Maya, and the Coastal lowlands. Accompanying texts are predictable and book ul-

timately serves to validate this recently acquired (1983–88) collection.

131 Peterson, Jeanette Favrot and **Judith Strupp Green.** Precolumbian flora and fauna: continuity of plant and animal themes in Mesoamerican art. Designed by Martha Longenecker. San Diego, Calif.: Mingei International Museum of World Folk Art, 1990. 148 p.: bibl., ill. (some col.)

Plants and animals are the connecting themes of this impressive, but disjointed, exhibition of ancient Mesoamerican works of art and modern folk art. Accompanying texts are more coherent than the images of the exhibition.

132 Ramos, Carolyn. The art of Mexico: a heritage of lost civilization. Dubuque, Iowa: Kendall/Hunt Pub. Co., 1988. 236 p.: bibl., ill., index.

This book has bad maps, poor ilustrations, impossible citations and bibliography, confused descriptions, and no new point of view or insights.

133 Reichel-Dolmatoff, Gerardo. Orfebrería y chamanismo: un estudio iconográfico del Museo del Oro. Fotografía de Jorge Mario Múnera. Medellín, Colombia: Editorial Colina, 1988. 174 p.: bibl., col. ill.

Intriguing structural study organizes familiar precolumbian gold shapes into unfamiliar but convincing categories depicting the shamanic world. Beautifully illustrated.

134 Robertson, Merle Greene. The sculpture of Palenque. v. 4, The Cross Group, the North Group, the Olvidado, and other pieces. Princeton, N.J.: Princeton Univ. Press, 1991. 1 v.: bibl., ill. (some col.), indexes, map.

Vol. 4 of *The sculpture of Palenque* deals mainly with the famous Cross Group. This work of dedication is profusely illustrated by author's photographs and drawings.

135 Schele, Linda and **David A. Freidel.** A forest of kings: the untold story of the ancient Maya. Color photographs by Justin Kerr. New York: Morrow, 1990. 542 p., 16 p. of plates: bibl., ill. (some col.), index.

Compelling and coherent vision/version of ancient Maya history. Fulsome use of footnotes is oddly disjunctive with the narrative representatation of the "story."

136 Taube, Karl. The Albers Collection of Precolumbian Art. Foreword by Michael D. Coe. Preface by Nicholas Fox Weber. Photographs by William K. Sacco. New York: Hudson Hill Press; Rizzoli International, 1988. 176 p.: bibl., ill. (some col.), index.

Essays and short texts accompanying images are for the most part succinct, descriptive, and helpful. Author also introduces some new and intriguing insights. B/w photographs lack quality; color ones are good.

137 Vision and revision in Maya studies. Edited by Flora S. Clancy and Peter D. Harrison. Albuquerque: Univ. of New Mexico Press, 1990. 224 p.: bibl., ill., index, maps.

Based on the reexamination of old data or the presentation of new information, various authors suggest new structures and interpretations of ancient Maya life.

138 Word and image in Maya culture: explorations in language, writing, and representation. Edited by William F. Hanks and Don Stephen Rice. Salt Lake City: Univ. of Utah Press, 1989. 385 p.: bibl., ill.

Organized and edited in an effort to explicate ancient Maya thought-structures. Most contributions focus on extracting meaning through structural analyses.

FOLK AND POPULAR

139 Al-Chalabi, Mahboub. Arte mural popular en Venezuela. Caracas: BP, 1987. 135 p.: chiefly col. ill.

Author attempts to record an ephemeral but ancient activity—the creation of unofficial murals and graffiti. Author has categorized the murals by subject matter, but this takes second place to the many wonderful illustrations that record the indomitable human need to make images.

140 Arte popular en Bolivia. La Paz: Instituto Boliviano de Cultura; Quito: Instituto Andino de Artes Populares, 1988. 48 p.: bibl., ill.

Small book with a large purpose attempts to find historical continuity by finding "cultural stratigraphy" embedded in such artifacts as masks, legends, myths, textiles, and modern epic comedy.

141 Los artesanos nos dijeron. Recopilación de Rodolfo Becerril y Adalberto Ríos Szalay. México: Fondo Nacional para Actividades Sociales; Fondo Nacional para el Fomento de las Artesanías, 1981. 80 p. col. ill. ;

Poetic evocation and illustration of the crafts and popular arts of Mexico. The voice of the artisans themselves comprises the bulk of the text.

142 Behind the mask in Mexico. Edited by Janet Brody Esser. Santa Fe, N.M.: Museum of International Folk Art, Museum of New Mexico Press, 1988. 351 p.: bibl., ill. (some col.), index, map.

Catalog consists of illustrated essays written to accompany an ambitious and impressive exhibition. While individual essays are important and scholarly, there is no overview to connect them except for the ambiguous and general theme of masking.

143 Berdan, Frances and **Russell J. Barber.** Spanish thread on Indian looms: Mexican folk costume. Translated by Rafael E. Correa. San Bernardino: Univ. Art Gallery, California State Univ., 1988. 106 p.: bibl., ill. (some col.)

Bilingual catalog includes informative, short text on clothing forms, iconography, and history of Mexican textiles. Published examples do not include the Maya of Mexico.

144 Everton, Macduff. The modern Maya: a culture in transition. Edited by Ulrich Keller and Charles Demangate. Albuquerque: Univ. of New Mexico Press, 1991. 259 p.: bibl., ill., maps.

Both Everton's photographs and diaristic text are powerful evocations of his 20-year friendships with several Mayan families as they, and author, contend with the potent human issues of change, resistance, assimilation, and transcendence.

145 Hombres del sur. Santiago: Museo Chileno de Arte Precolombino, 1987. 100 p.: bibl., ill. (some col.)

Bilingual book strives to document the cultural history of Patagonia and Tierra del Fuego; a history on the point of extinction. Although there are brief archaeological and ethnographic essays, the main "texts" are the beautiful and artful photographs used in the apparent hope of eliciting a modern aesthetic response and, thus, "authenticating" the cultural artifacts. (For archaeologist's comment, see *HLAS 51:518*.)

146 Markman, Peter T. and **Roberta H. Markman.** Masks of the spirit: image and metaphor in Mesoamerica. Introduction by Joseph Campbell. Berkeley: Univ. of California Press, 1989. 254 p.: bibl., ill.

Synthetic effort to proclaim and explain ancient and modern Mesoamerican masks as agents of transformation and as symbols of creation and generation. Book is responsibly researched, but it has the predictable aura of mysticism.

147   Martínez Gracida, Manuel. Los indios oaxaqueños y sus monumentos arqueológicos. Oaxaca, Mexico: Gobierno del Estado de Oaxaca, 1986. 56 p.: ill. (some col.)

Intriguing *memoria* for a work of love and labor completed in 1910. Of original eight volumes of text and illustrations (unpublished), this publication presents an explanation of the work's history, some of the illustrations, and a contemporary (1910) newspaper article.

148   Mayén de Castellanos, Guisela; Idalma Mejía de Rodas; and Linda Asturias de Barrios. Tzute y jerarquía en Sololá. Guatemala: Museo Ixchel del Traje Indígena de Guatemala, 1986. 140 p.: bibl., ill. (some col.) (Ediciones del Museo Ixchel; 4)

Careful presentation of the *traje* of Sololá, Guatemala, aims to explain its social and historical contexts.

149   El mestizaje americano: octubre-diciembre 1985. Madrid: Museo de América; Ministerio de Cultura, Dirección General de Bellas Artes, 1985? 189 p.: bibl., ill. (some col.)

Report on exhibition of painting and sculpture illustrating various racial mixes in the Americas. Accompanying essays take differing points of view (e.g., ecological, historical, political, and cultural) of mestizaje.

150   Museo Regional de la Araucanía, Chile. Plata de la Araucanía: Colección Raúl Morris von Bennewitz. Talagante, Chile: Municipalidad de Talagante; Museo Regional de la Araucanía, 1980–1988. 65 p.: ill. (some col.)

Catalog's text, written by the collector, is a treatise stressing the importance of connoisseurship and historical and ethnographic knowledge. It is also an effort to "authenticate" Mapuche silverwork as an important human expression.

Peterson, Jeanette Favrot and **Judith Strupp Green.** Precolumbian flora and fauna: continuity of plant and animal themes in Mesoamerican art. See item **131.**

151   Valero Silva, José. El libro de la charrería. México: Ediciones Gacela, 1987. 222 p.: ill. (some col.)

Informative account of the Mexican "cowboy" traces its origins (back to precolumbian times) and traditions, as signalled by costumes and customs. Colorful and beautiful illustrations surround the text with nostalgic vistas that poignantly underwrite author's concern for the continuance of this uniquely Mexican tradition.

Colonial
General, Middle America, and the Caribbean

BARBARA VON BARGHAHN, *Professor of Art History, George Washington University*

AS THE QUINCENTENNIAL OF THE SPANISH ENCOUNTER in the New World approaches, scholars have provided a plethora of exemplary books and articles, the majority of which break new ground with documentary information. Besides this substantial research on the encounter, there are also publications that delve into problematic issues of patronage and reconstruction of lost monuments. Reformulation of traditional points of view and provocative arguments offering sociological insights are indicative of new avenues now being explored. However, this compendium suggests a course for future study: interpretative analyses of stylistic and iconographical crosscurrents between viceregal centers.

While the majority of texts concentrate upon the architecture, sculpture, painting and decorative arts of New Spain, the mantle of documentary and archival research has extended to cover many previously ignored sites. Recent publications in architecture include general comprehensive books (items **169, 167, 41,** and **226**) and more specific studies of regional buildings (items **177, 182, 206, 185,** and **227**). Particularly useful sources concern the colonial monuments of Oaxaca (items **180, 193, 202, 208,** and **216**), Jalisco and Michoacán (items **175, 197, 211, 212,** and **214**), Puebla (items **173, 190, 200,** and **203**), Zacatecas (items **198** and **213**), and the Yucatán (items **172** and **209**). Viceregal Mexico City is the subject of numerous works (items **171, 178, 187, 201, 207,** and **218**), and noteworthy documentary research on urbanization and secular architecture has also been provided (items **295, 222, 192, 199, 204, 217, 219,** and **224**).

Knowledge about commercial centers of art has been expanded, with studies covering Campeche (item **195**), Honduras (items **239** and **244**), El Salvador (item **233**), Panama (items **242** and **243**), Dominican Republic (item **231**), Cuba (item **355**), and Puerto Rico (item **247**). A study of Philippine ivories and the "Manila Galleon" trade is a vital resource for historians (item **221**).

Texts pertaining to the decorative arts encompass subjects ranging from the production of works in mother-of-pearl (item **184**) to metal works (items **166, 179, 210, 157,** and **160**). An important sociological and artistic study on the ritualistic usage of masks in Guatemala (item **238**) merits additional praise because of its bilingual text. Studies of ephemeral art also investigate royal exequies in the Americas (items **232** and **156**).

This biennial includes much pertinent material about Mexican and Guatemalan collections of colonial paintings and sculpture (items **168, 186, 189, 196, 241,** and **170**). Singular methodological contributions to the field of art history are monographs on Luis Juárez (item **162**), Juan Correa (item **164**), and patronage in New Spain (item **165**). Although iconography still remains a relatively unexplored area of art historical research (items **230** and **156**), scholars have investigated the influence of religious orders in Mexico and Guatemala (items **174, 235,** and **223**). Attention also has been directed towards museology, cultural projects of national patrimony, and legal issues (items **176, 183, 161, 215,** and **220**).

Among the imposing number of texts, *Historia del arte hispanoamericano: siglos XVI a XVIII* (item **159**) by Jorge Bernales Ballesteros is worthy of special recognition. Copiously illustrated and thoroughly documented, this work reveals an extraordinary breadth of knowledge about viceregal art and patronage. The premature death of Ballesteros in Seville leaves a void that will be hard to fill.

There are only a few specialists who are examining stylistic and iconographical crosscurrents between Andalusia and the New World (items **154** and **188**). However, *Presencia del arte hispánico en el mundo colonial americano* (item **152**) offers a commendable example of an interdisciplinary effort to address cultural encounters in the wake of the Spanish encounter. Conferences provide an active forum for debate and presentation of revolutionary approaches to traditional subjects. Symposia commemorating the Columbus Quincentennial should mark a trend towards reexamination of artistic legacies in the viceregal Americas. More bilingual publications would augment interest in colonial art history and aid in the dissemination of knowledge at US universities.

This section includes more than twice as many items as it did in *HLAS 50,* even after the great majority of applicable journal articles were eliminated due to space limitations. Readers are urged to consult the *Anales del Instituto de Investigaciones Estéticas* (México: Univ. Nacional Autónoma de México, 1986–1988, vols. 55–59) for many additional scholarly articles.

In completing this review of recently published books and articles, the contributing editor gratefully acknowledges the assistance of Ms. Evelyn Figueroa of The Smithsonian Institution.

GENERAL

152 Banda y Vargas, Antonio de la; Emilio Gómez Piñol; and Salvador Andrés Ordax. Presencia del arte hispánico en el mundo colonial americano. Mérida, Spain: Editora Regional de Extremadura, 1987. 48 p.: bibl. (Extremadura en clave 92)

Presented at a major conference in Extremadura, Spain, these thoroughly documented papers analyze the aesthetic forms that were brought to the New World by Spanish conquerors and artists and the unique forms that emerged from the fusion of European and indigenous forms.

153 Bayón, Damián and Murillo Marx. Historia del arte colonial sudamericano: Sudamérica Hispana y el Brasil. Barcelona, Spain: Ediciones Polígrafa, 1989. 441 p.: bibl., ill. (some col.), indexes.

Monumental synthesis of colonial South American architecture, painting, and sculpture, from Panama to Chile. Textual organization is strictly chronological by modern country, not necessarily reflecting the reality of artistic geography during colonial period. Presents a good balance of factual information, analysis, and interpretation. Catalog of principal monuments is also provided, including additional historical data and individual bibliographical references. The 891 illustrations are of consistently high quality and permit an excellent appreciation of the works discussed. Invaluable source for future studies. [H. Rodríguez-Camilloni]

154 Berlin-Neubart, Heinrich. Ensayos sobre historia del arte en Guatemala y México. Guatemala: Academia de Geografía e Historia de Guatemala, 1988. 181 p.: bibl., ill. (Publicación especial; 32)

Anthology of eight essays written about diverse themes such as colonial painting with Mexican influence in Guatemala, an artistic and architectonic description of the churches in Morelia, the Convent of Santa Clara, and a rural church in Oaxaca. Also includes references to architects, painters, and artisans of Guatemala.

155 Bomchil, Sara and Virginia Carreño. El mueble colonial de las Américas y su circunstancia histórica. Buenos Aires: Editorial Sudamericana, 1987. 919 p., 24 p. of plates: bibl., ill.

Ambitious attempt at a comprehensive history of furniture from Canada to Tierra del Fuego circa 1500–1800 relies heavily on European stylistic labels which may not be very helpful in defining particular qualities of works discussed. Text divided by country is a bit disjointed, but the fine line drawings make a useful reference catalog. A serious drawback, however, is lack of any reference to scale, even though the original architectural context is sometimes mentioned. [H. Rodríguez-Camilloni]

156 Cayol, Rafael. El rito fundacional español: ensayo histórico-arqueológico. Buenos Aires: R. Cayol, 1988. 82 p.: bibl., ill.

Attempts to analyze some archaic elements (i.e., Old Testament, Egyptian, Assyrian) as they relate to ceremonies of the colonial period sponsored by the Spanish Crown. Difficult reading.

157 Fernández, Alejandro; Rafael Munoa; and Jorge Rabasco. Enciclopedia de la plata española y virreinal americana. Suplemento a la primera edición. Prólogo de José Manuel Cruz Valdovinos. Madrid: Asociación Española de Joyeros, Plateros y Relojeros, 1985. 46 p.: bibl., ill.

Supplement updates first edition of this encyclopedic review of the silversmiths and hallmarks of the viceregal period. Contains a pertinent essay about the colonial center for production of silver, the Villa Imperial de Potosí.

158 Hardoy, Jorge Enrique and Mario R. dos Santos. Impacto de la urbanización

en los centros históricos latinoamericanos.
(*Rev. Parag. Sociol.*, 21:59, enero-abril 1984,
p. 199–231)

Brief version of technical report commissioned by the Lima-based Programa Regional de Patrimonio Cultural y Desarrollo (s.l.: PNUD-UNESCO, 1983, 183 p.) proposes new definitions for historic villages, historic cities, and historic centers, according to population size and socioeconomic condition. Convincing plea is made recommending that future historic restoration and conservation plans should not overlook well-being of the people who reside in such places today. [H. Rodríguez-Camilloni]

159   Historia del arte hispanoamericano.
v. 2., Siglos XVI a XVIII [de] Jorge Bernales Ballesteros. Madrid: Alhambra, 1987–1988. 368 p.: bibl., ill. (some col.)

Overview of Hispanic art during colonial period, particularly in New Spain and the Audiencia of Lima. Emphasizes Mannerist and Baroque influences in sculpture and architecture, in addition to Indian and Christian influences in painting. Good photographs; excellent research source. For v. 1 and v. 3, see items **119** and **289.**

160   Instituto de Cooperación Iberoamericana (Madrid). Orfebrería hispanoamericana, siglos XVI-XIX: obras civiles y religiosas en templos, museos y colecciones españolas. Madrid: Museo de America, 1986. 123 p.: bibl., ill. (some col.)

Excellent contribution to the study of silverwork production in Latin America during the colonial period. This exhibition catalog focuses on period from mid-16th century until end of 19th century in New Spain and Peru. Cristina Esteras Martín's essay provides succinct account of the silverwork production, an analysis of styles, and a well-documented description of 68 works of art from temples, museums and Spanish collections. Primarily b/w photographs and 13 color plates.

Jornadas de Andalucía y América, 4th, Univ. de Santa María de la Rábida, Sevilla, Spain, 1984. Andalucía y América en el siglo XVIII: actas. See item **805.**

161   Madrid, Miguel A. Glosario de términos museológicos. México: Coordinación de Difusión Cultural, UNAM-CISM, 1986. 130 p.: bibl., ill.

Glossary of museological terminology, with commentaries and definitions of some of the terms. Good source for students specializing in museology.

162   Ruiz Gomar, Rogelio. El pintor Luis Juárez: su vida y su obra. México: Univ. Nacional Autónoma de México, 1987. 366 p., 38 leaves of plates: bibl., ill. (some col.), index. (Monografías de arte; 15)

Luis Juárez was the best artist to represent the Mannerist influence in painting of New Spain. Excellent book traces the life and work of Juárez during the first third of the 17th century, analyzing his works and discussing the iconography represented in his paintings. Includes a comprehensive *catalogue raisonné* and good b/w plates.

163   Sebastián, Santiago. El barroco iberoamericano: mensaje iconográfico. Madrid: Ediciones Encuentro; Sociedad Estatal Quinto Centenario, 1990. 374 p.: bibl., ill. (many in color), indexes.

Exceptional volume in the "Pueblos y Culturas" series which is part of the "Biblioteca Quinto Centenario." This is the only publication to date of continental scope (including Mexico, Peru, and Brazil) concerned with iconographic studies of colonial art and architecture. Significantly expands author's earlier book, *Contrarreforma y barroco* (Madrid, 1981), presenting a wealth of new information, supported by an impressive corpus of spectacular b/w and color plates. Discusses in detail several iconographic themes common to Europe and Spanish and Portuguese America, as well as others which appear to have originated specifically in the New World. Notes at the end of each chapter provide indispensable references not always included in the general bibliography. [H. Rodríguez-Camilloni]

164   Vargas Lugo, Elisa and **José Guadalupe Victoria.** Juan Correa: su vida y su obra. v. 2, pt. 1–2. México: Univ. Nacional Autónoma de México, 1985. 2 v.: bibl., ill. (some col.)

The result of a nine-year extensive investigation of Correa's *oeuvre*, this text is an excellent resource for art historians. Correa's artistic production is classified and discussed according to subject, and each chapter contains an introduction. The *catalogue raisonné* consists of numerous photographs,

documentation, and information about conservation and iconography.

165 Victoria, José Guadalupe. Pintura y sociedad en Nueva España: siglo XVI. México: Univ. Nacional Autónoma de México, 1986. 183 p., 51 p. of plates: bibl., ill. (1 col.) (Estudios y fuentes del arte en México; 56)

Based on author's doctoral thesis, "Les problemes de la peinture en Nouvelle-Espagne entre la Renaissance et la Baroque, 1555–1625" (Univ. of Paris, 1982), this book is divided into two parts. First concerns history and culture of New Spain during first century after the Conquest and the artistic patronage of the Church. Second part examines the gremial system and the relationship between art and society. The study focuses upon three major artists of the last three decades of the 16th century: Simón Pereyns, Andrés de Concha and Baltazar de Echave Orio. Good photographs and bibliography.

MEXICO

166 Alcocer, Alfonso. La Campana de Dolores. México: Depto. del Distrito Federal, 1985. 122 p.: bibl., ill., ports.

Describes the bell of the Church of Dolores Hidalgo, its origin and significance during the independence movement, as well as its transfer to the National Palace (Mexico City). After the bell was replaced, copies of the political icon were cast and dispersed throughout Mexico.

167 Amerlinck, María Concepción et al. Atlas cultural de México. v. 6, Monumentos históricos. México: Secretaría de Educación Pública, Instituto Nacional de Antropología e Historia; Grupo Editorial Planeta, 1987–1988. 1 v.: bibl., ill. (some col.), index.

Provides general overview of historical monuments in Mexico which comprise part of the national patrimony. Focuses on religious, military, and civil architecture during colonial period and first century after Independence, and describes in general the transformations that occurred during different stages of urban development. Includes excellent color photographs and maps.

168 Anaya Larios, José Rodolfo. Historia de la escultura queretana. Querétaro: Univ. Autónoma de Querétaro, 1987. 132 p.: bibl., ill. (Col. Encuentro; 4)

Detailed examination of historical development of Querétaro's sculpture production, specifically artists, works of art, and techniques. Provides an important account of works of art that still exist in churches, museums, and private collections. Significant contribution to the study of colonial sculpture in Mexico.

169 Artigas H., Juan B. Arquitectura del virreinato: análisis y gráficas. México: Museo Universitario de Ciencias y Arte, Centro de Investigación y Servicios Museológicos, Coordinación de Extensión Universitaria, Univ. Nacional Autónoma de México, 1984. 47 p.: bibl., ill.

Catalog of an exhibition on Mexican viceregal architecture organized by Juan Artigas. Text includes historical information and analysis of architectural features of distinguishing Hispanic American monuments.

170 Arvizu García, Carlos et al. Museo Regional de Querétaro: 50 años. Imágenes de José Manuel Rivero Torres. Sur Querétaro, Mexico: Dirección de Patrimonio Cultural, Secretaría de Cultura y Bienestar Social, Gobierno del Estado de Querétaro, 1986. 238 p.: bibl., col. ill.

Published in honor of museum's founder, Germán Patino, book traces history of building that houses it. Built in 16th century as the Convento de los Franciscanos, the structure suffered many transformations and modifications. Few traces remain of its original architecture. Provides diagrams of the building and examines some works of art from museum's collection. Includes color photographs of paintings with detailed descriptions.

171 Báez Macías, Eduardo. El edificio del Hospital de Jesús: historia y documentos sobre su construcción. México: Univ. Nacional Autónoma de México, 1982. 164 p., 42 p. of plates: bibl., ill., index. (Monográfias de arte, Instituto de Investigaciones Estéticas; 6)

Historical monograph about Hospital de Jesús (Mexico City) covers the origin, construction, and architectural changes from 17th century to present. Based upon documentation from National Archives, book is a detailed study of a national monument and its social function.

Baird, Ellen T. Sahagún's *Codex Florentino:* the enigmatic A. See item **493.**

172 Bretos, Miguel A. Arquitectura y arte sacro en Yucatán, 1545–1823. Mérida, Mexico: Producción Editorial Dante, 1987. 277 p.: bibl., ill. (Sueste)

Contains seven essays about art and architecture in colonial Yucatán, such as influence of Franciscan missions in the region. Studies concern the Convent of San Bernardino de Sisal, the Camarín de la Virgen and the Orden Mariana, the Church of San Cristóbal de Mérida, and churches in western Yucatán. Also presents a discussion about silver production, the artistic works of Benito Ferráez, and the sculpture of Pascual Estrella. Good bibliography.

173 Calderón, Juan Alonso. Memorial histórico jurídico político de la Santa Iglesia Catedral de la Puebla de los Angeles, en la Nueva España: sobre restituirla las armas reales de Castilla, León, Aragón y Navarra, que puso en la capilla mayor de su iglesia, de que ha sido despojada injustamente. Edición y estudio preliminar de Efraín Castro Morales. Puebla, Mexico: Gobierno del Estado de Puebla, Secretaría de Cultura, 1988. 178 p.: bibl., ill.

Paleographic transcripts of a group of 17th-century Mexican documents pertaining to the Cathedral of Puebla of the Angels.

174 Campos Rebollo, Mario Ramón. La casa de los franciscanos en la Ciudad de México: reseña de los cambios que sufrió el Convento de San Francisco de los siglos XVI al XIX. México: Depto. del Distrito Federal, Secretaría General de Desarrollo Social, Dirección General de Acción Social, Cívica, Cultural y Turística, 1986. 89 p.: bibl., ill. (Col. Distrito Federal; 11)

Convent of San Francisco was the base for Christianization in Mexico during 16th century. Book presents history of convent since its colonial origin and its evolution during 17th, 18th, and 19th centuries. Excellent historical review provides reader with a perception of splendor and importance of the convent. Good illustrations and bibliography.

175 Castro Morales, Efraín. Arte virreinal en el Occidente. Madrid: La Muralla, 1987. 54 p.: bibl. (Historia del arte mexicano; 9)

Text serves as guide to churches and convents of Western Mexico: Michoacán, Colima, Jalisco, and Sinaloa, all located on Pacific Coast. Includes description and historical background of religious buildings as well as good slides.

176 Catálogo nacional, monumentos históricos inmuebles: municipios. México: Secretaría de Educación Pública, Instituto Nacional de Antropología e Historia; Programa Cultural de las Fronteras, 1986. 38 v.: bibl., ill.

Multi-volume catalog of historical monuments located in various municipalities of the Distrito Federal (3 vol.) and the following states: Baja California (1 vol.), Baja California Sur (7 vol.), Chihuahua (5 vol.), Coahuila (9 vol.), and Tamaulipas (13 vol.), with generally one volume per municipality. For example, Distrito Federal's 3-volume set covers Azcapotzalco, Iztapalapa, and Xochimilco. Prepared for conservation and administrative purposes, volumes include inventories of geographical locations, descriptions, photographs, and floor plans.

177 Catálogo nacional, monumentos históricos inmuebles. México: Secretaría de Educación Pública, Instituto Nacional de Antropología e Historia; Programa Cultural de las Fronteras, 1986. 19 v.: bibl., ill.

Multi-volume catalog of colonial architectural monuments in states of Baja California (1 vol.), Baja California Sur (1 vol.), Chihuahua (2 vol.), Coahuila (4 vol.), Mexico (3 vol.), Querétero (4 vol.), Tabasco (1 vol.), and Tamaulipas (3 vol.) was prepared for purposes of conservation and administration.

178 La Ciudad de México, espacio y sociedad, 1759–1910. México: Museo Nacional de Historia, 1984. 48 p.: ill.

Catalog of exhibition of same title which illustrated evolution of Mexico City in last years of Spanish dominion through the period known as the "Porfiriato." Highlights traditions of diverse castes of Mexican society and includes interesting essays, historical engravings, and photographs.

179 Cortina Portilla, Manuel. Algo sobre la plata en México en el siglo XVIII. México: Grupo Consa, 1986. 48 p., 1 folded leaf of plates: col. port.

Limited annual edition pertaining to silver production in 18th-century Mexico with purpose of promoting economic history of New Spain is divided into three chapters. Most important section discusses an 18th-century painting created by Fagoaga Arozqueta family, whose artists were closely involved with silver production.

180   Cruz Santos, Bertha and **Carlos Ramírez Montes.** Oaxaca: arquitectura religiosa; los templos cristianos de la Cd. de Oaxaca. Levantamientos arquitectónicos de Jorge Cosmes Gijon *et al.* Fotografía de Félix Villanueva Porras. México: Impr. Copioffset, 1989. 204 p.: bibl., ill.

Thesis presented at the Escuela de Arquitectura de la Univ. Autónoma Benito Juárez (Oaxaca) includes floor plans and external descriptions of colonial churches in Oaxaca.

181   Curiel, Gustavo. Nuevas noticias sobre un taller de artistas de la nobleza indígena. (*An. Inst. Invest. Estét.*, 59, 1988, p. 129–150, photos)

Finely documented essay discusses work on indigenous artist Tomás Xuárez, who headed a sculpture workshop in 17th-century New Spain. Xuárez's atelier was responsible for decoration of some of the most important colonial churches of New Spain. Includes chronological table containing important information about this Mexican workshop, copies of original documents, and photographs of some works.

182   Díaz, Marco. Itinerarios barrocos en Tlaxcala. Tlaxcala, Mexico: Instituto Tlaxcalteca de la Cultura, 1986. 56 p.: bibl., ill.

Good guide to monuments in Tlaxcala that have Baroque characteristics, organized according to five routes: 1) the road to Malintzin and San Miguel; 2) the royal road to San Martín; 3) the road in the highlands; 4) the road by the herd zone; and 5) the *pulque* zone road.

183   Díaz-Berrio Fernández, Salvador. Conservación de monumentos y zonas. México: Instituto Nacional de Antropología e Historia, 1985. 177 p.: bibl., ill. (Col. Fuentes)

Reproduces documents and agreements for preservation of cultural patrimony: *Carta de Atenas* (1931), *Carta de Venecia* (1964), *Recomendación del Consejo de Europa* (Bath), the Hague Convention (1954), and the recommendations of the International Council of Monuments and Sites. Sec-

ond part of book is dedicated to the Mexican legislation for conservation of cultural property, which includes archaeological, artistic, and historical monuments of the cities. Also includes UNESCO's *Convention for the Protection of Cultural Property* of 1972.

184   Dujovne, Marta. Las pinturas con incrustaciones de nácar. México: Univ. Nacional Autónoma de México, Instituto de Investigaciones Estéticas, 1984. 271 p.: ill. (Monografías de arte; 8)

General study of techniques, style, and iconography of mother-of-pearl paintings made in Mexico during second half of 17th century and first half of 18th century. Complemented with photographs and bibliography.

185   La escuadra y el cincel: documentos sobre la construcción de la Catedral de Morelia. Recopilación de Guillermina Ramírez Montes. México: Instituto de Investigaciones Estéticas, Univ. Nacional Autónoma de México, 1987. 181 p., 14 p. of plates: bibl., ill., index. (Monografías de arte; 7)

Compilation of documents about the construction of the Cathedral of Morelia, originally known as the Cathedral of Guayangareo, the name of its geographical area. Most of the documents belong to the Archivo Nacional de Indias and the Archivo General de la Nación de México, and are organized in chronological order from 1618–1744, the dates corresponding to cathedral's construction.

186   La escultura en México: siglos XVI al XIX. México: Centro de Investigación y Servicios Museológicos; Instituto de Investigaciones Bibliográficas; Coordinación de Extensión Universitaria, Univ. Nacional Autónoma de México, 1984 53 p.: ill. (some col.)

Catalog of exhibition "La Escultura en México" held at Ex-Templo de San Agustín, Univ. Nacional Autónoma de México consists of a selection of Mexican and European sculpture from Franz Mayer's estate. Although provenances of the works are not provided, text contains b/w photographs and 14 color plates.

187   Fernández García, Martha. Arquitectura y gobierno virreinal: los maestros mayores de la ciudad de México, siglo XVII. México: Univ. Nacional Autónoma de México, Instituto de Investigaciones Estéticas, 1985. 418 p., 38 p. of plates: bibl., ill. (some col.), indexes. (Estudios y fuentes del arte en México; 45)

Examines architecture of New Spain during 17th century, with emphasis upon artists and architects. Referring to documentation from the archives of Mexico and Spain, Fernández traces artistic development of each "maestro mayor," his works, his relationship with religious and political institutions, and his own guild of architects. Containing an excellent bibliography, prints, and b/w illustrations, this text is a seminal work for study of Mexican Viceregal patronage.

188   Fernández García, Martha. Retrato hablado: Diego de la Sierra, un arquitecto barroco en la Nueva España. México: Univ. Nacional Autónoma de México, Instituto de Investigaciones Estéticas, 1986. 297 p., 34 p. of plates: bibl., ill., indexes. (Monografías de arte; 14)

Detailed study of life, work, personality, and professional development of Diego de la Sierra, an artist from Seville who worked in Mexico from end of 17th century to beginning of 18th century, erecting many structures in Puebla.

189   Franz Mayer: una colección. México: Bancreser, 1984. 323 p.: bibl., ill. (some col.)

Text magnifies art collection of German collector Franz Mayer: an ensemble of colonial paintings and decorative appointments. A description of the "Templo de San Juan de Dios" and its adaptation to a museum for the Mayer collection is also presented with floor plans and color photographs.

190   García Zambrano, Angel Julián. El baldaquino de la Catedral de Puebla. Mérida, Venezuela: Ediciones La Imprenta, 1984. 145 p.: bibl., ill.

Analytical study of work of sculptor Manuel Tolsá and his architectural design of the *baldaquino* over main altar of Cathedral of Puebla is a comprehensive discussion of formal neoclassical style that evolved in New Spain as a response to exuberant designs of the Baroque. Thought-provoking study of the iconography of the "Cipres" is particularly intriguing. Good illustrations.

191   González Galván, Manuel. Una glosa reconstructiva ideal: el antiguo ciprés barroco de la Catedral de Morelia. (*An. Inst. Invest. Estét.*, 59, 1988, p. 93–100, facsims.)

Interprets a document in which 18th-century architect Isidoro Vicente de Balbas described the primary altarpiece of Cathedral of Valladolid (Michoacán). Very interesting analysis includes drawings and photographs.

192   González-Leal, Mariano. Apaseo el Grande: pasado y presente de un pueblo del Bajío. Apaseo el Grande, Mexico: Ayuntamiento de Apaseo el Grande, Guanajuato, 1988. 101 p.: bibl., ill. (some col.)

Short monograph about municipality of Apaseo el Grande from prehispanic period to present describes historical role of Apaseo, for whom the city was named.

193   Hernández Díaz, Gilberto. El Convento de San José de Oaxaca. México: s.n., 1987? 43 p., 4 p. of plates: bibl., ill. (Serie Monumentos; 1)

Historical review of the Convento de San José (Oaxaca) during 18th and 19th centuries, with special emphasis on the Mexican reform and the transformation of the convent into the "Escuela de las Artes de Oaxaca."

194   Hernández Pons, Elsa. El coro bajo de Santa Teresa la Antigua. (*Estud. Hist. Novohisp.*, 9, 1987, p. 219–230, bibl., facsims., ill., photos)

Archaeological description of lower chorus of Church of Santa Teresa la Antigua and the graves found in archaeological excavations. Author also describes funerary rituals practiced by nuns belonging to order of Carmelitas Descalzas. Drawings, photographs, architectural plans, good bibliography.

195   Las iglesias coloniales del Puerto de Campeche. Campeche, Mexico: Univ. del Sudeste, 1986. 132 p.: bibl., ill.

Compilation of previous studies on colonial religious architecture of Campeche, a primary port of Mexico. History of churches in Campeche from 16th to 19th centuries is noteworthy due to commercial importance of the center. Includes b/w illustrations.

196   Imagen de México. Santillana del Mar, Spain: Fundación Santillana, 1984. 56 p.: ill. (some col.) ;

Catalog of exhibition associated with "Imagen de México" (Cantabria, Spain) covers precolumbian through contemporary Mexican art. Includes essays by Paz Cabello Carro and Teresa del Conde.

197   Leal Briseño, Martha Leticia. Santa Mónica de La Barca en la época virreinal. Guadalajara, Mexico: Gobierno de Jalisco, Secretaría General, Unidad Editorial, 1987. 125 p.: bibl., ill. (Temática jalisciense; 18)

Short monograph focuses on the city, its Spanish origin, the landscape, natural resources, social life, and culture.

Lombardo de Ruiz, Sonia *et al.* **Y** todo- por una nación: historia social de la producción plástica de la Ciudad de México, 1781–1910. See item **936**.

López Cervantes, Gonzalo and **Rosa María García García.** Ensayo bibliográfico del periodo colonial de México. See item **41**.

198 López de Lara, J. Jesús. La Catedral de Zacatecas. Zacatecas, Mexico: Instituto Superior de Cultura Religiosa, 1989. 69 p.: ill.

Presents a short history of the construction and architectural design of the Cathedral of Zacatecas. Includes detailed photographs.

199 López Morales, Francisco Javier. Arquitectura vernácula en México. México: Fondo Internacional para la Promoción de la Cultura, UNESCO; Editorial Trillas, 1987. 274 p.: bibl., ill. (some col.)

Extensive, well-researched study on the indigenous architecture of Mexico and the manner in which prehispanic traditions were preserved. This excellent contribution to the history of Mexican architecture reviews diverse styles from precolumbian to colonial periods. Includes a good bibliography, floor plans, and b/w illustrations.

200 Luyando Lares, Adalberto. La Catedral de Puebla = The Cathedral of Puebla. Textos de Antonio Juárez Burgos. Traducción de Gertrudis Payás Puigarnau y María Cristina Martínez Montenegro. Puebla, Mexico: Univ. Autónoma de Puebla, 1986. 125 p.: bibl., chiefly ill., index.

This cathedral is one of the most important architectural monuments of colonial Mexico. Text in Spanish, English, and French describes cathedral's origin, construction, architectonic development, style, interior chapels, altars, and religious treasures. Luyando Lares provides excellent b/w photographs of architectonic details of building.

201 Maldonado López, Celia. La Ciudad de México en el siglo XVII. México:

Depto. del Distrito Federal, Secretaría General de Desarrollo Social, Comité Interno de Ediciones Gubernamentales, 1988. 85 p., 8 folded leaves of plates: bibl., ill. (Col. Distrito Federal; 21)

Detailed account of architectural development of Mexico City, capital of New Spain in 17th century. Describes urban development and architectural characteristics of main public buildings, churches, parks, plazas, convents, colleges, hospitals, and market of the period. Good illustrations and bibliography.

202 Martínez Vargas, Luciano and **Esteban Arroyo.** La nación chuchona y la monumental iglesia de Coixtlahuaca, Oax. México: s.n., s.d. 59 p.: bibl., ill.

Tourist guide of Coixtlahuaca covers some of the colonial churches and convents of the Chuchona kingdom, such as Teposcola and San Juan Bautista.

203 Méndez, Eloy. La conformación de la ciudad de Puebla, 1966–1980: una visión histórica. México: Univ. Autónoma de Puebla, 1987. 205 p.: bibl., ill. (Col. Historia)

Historical overview of urban center of Puebla from its construction in 1524 under the Franciscan Order to its present reconstruction. Divided into four chapters: 1) discussion of space as a reflection of social functions of the city; 2) description of principal monuments illustrating aspects of colonial heritage; 3) analysis of industrial development and urbanization; and 4) plans that summarize the evolution of Puebla during different epochs.

204 Mendiola Quezada, Vicente. Arquitectura del Estado de México: en los siglos XVI, XVII, XVIII y XIX. Ed. facsimilar a la de 1982, aum. con 43 ilustraciones. Toluca, Mexico: Gobierno del Estado de México, 1985. 363 p., 43 p. of plates: ill. (Documentos del Estado de México)

Covers colonial architecture and monuments of Mexico, establishing a difference between buildings constructed for Indians and mestizos and edifices intended for religious, military and civil use. Provides detailed descriptions of some edifices. Good art historical reference for Mexican viceregal period.

Mexico: splendors of thirty centuries. See item **127**.

205 Moffitt, John F. Tepozotlán: ¿el islam latente en América?; observaciones en torno a la portada esculpida hispánica. (*An. Inst. Invest. Estét.*, 57, 1986, p. 101–112, facsims., photos)

Good historical and aesthetic analysis of 18th-century facade of Seminario de San Martín church in Tepozotlán, Mexico. Constructed 1760–62, church is an excellent example of the retable facade that was so popular in colonial Mexican architecture. Includes photographs and drawings.

206 Montejano y Aguiñaga, Rafael. Templos y capillas potosinos desaparecidos. San Luis Potosí, Mexico: Univ. Autónoma de San Luis Potosí, 1987. 66 p.: bibl.

Compilation of historical details and information about some colonial churches and convents that are no longer extant. Contains a short bibliography.

207 Montoya Rivero, María Cristina. La Iglesia de la Santísima Trinidad. México: Univ. Nacional Autónoma de México, Escuela Nacional de Estudios Profesionales Acatlán, 1984. 195 p.: bibl., ill. (Nuevos cuadernos de apoyo a la docencia; 3)

Detailed account of history of this Mexico City church includes concise account of colonial religious architecture. Originally a thesis, book is divided into two parts: 1) historical perspective of architecture; and 2) aesthetical analysis of monuments.

208 Oaxaca: monumentos del centro histórico, patrimonio cultural de la humanidad. México: Secretaría de Desarrollo Urbano y Ecología, 1987. 353 p.: bibl., ill.

Written in response to UNESCO's declaring the city of Oaxaca "Patrimonio de la Humanidad," this book is a study of the historical evolution of this Mexican city, primarily the different styles of religious architecture. Twenty-six structures are analyzed for style and architectural characteristics. Includes very good b/w photogrpahs and floor plans.

209 Perry, Richard D. and **Rosalind Perry.** Maya missions: exploring the Spanish colonial churches of Yucatan. Drawings by Richard Perry. Santa Barbara, Calif.: Espadaña Press, 1988. 249 p.: bibl., ill., index.

After the Spanish conquest, many missions and churches were built in regions of the Yucatán Peninsula. This travel guide covers colonial architecture created by descendants of the ancient Maya. Includes well-documented historical background, description of sites and churches, drawings, glossary, and maps.

210 Plateros, plata y alhajas en Zacatecas, 1568–1782. Recopilación de Eugenio del Hoyo. Zacatecas, Mexico: Gobierno del Estado de Zacatecas, Instituto de Cultura de Zacatecas, 1986. 221 p., 4 leaves of plates: col. ill., index.

Compilation of 57 unpublished documents about silver crafts is a good source for future investigations on subject.

211 Ramírez Montes, Guillermina. La catedral de Vasco de Quiroga. Zamora, Mexico: Colegio de Michoacán, 1986. 212 p.: bibl., ill.

This cathedral in Pátzcuaro, Michoacán was one of the most important churches of colonial Mexico. It was named for Bishop Vasco de Quiroga who began its construction in 1538. Historical overview includes comments about the bishop, artisans, and artists of 16th century.

212 Ramírez Romero, Esperanza. Catálogo de monumentos y sitios de Tlalpujahua. México: Gobierno del Estado de Michoacán; Univ. Michoacana de San Nicolás de Hidalgo, 1985. 171 p., 62 p. of plates: bibl., ill. (Col. Monumentos y sitios de Michoacán)

Catalog and inventory of colonial churches, chapels, historical houses, paintings, and sculptures in Michoacán is a good administrative reference source, especially for the preservation and protection of artistic patrimony.

213 Ramos Dávila, Roberto. Plazas, plazuelas y jardines de Zacatecas. Zacatecas, Mexico H. Ayuntamiento, 1985. 125 p.: ill.

General tour guide of city of Zacatecas, Mexico, presents good description of municipal plazas and gardens.

214 Razo Zaragoza, José Luis. Guadalajara. 2a ed. Guadalajara, Mexico: Gobierno de Jalisco, Secretaría General, Unidad Editorial, 1986. 332 p.: ill.

Tourist guide of city of Guadalajara includes detailed description of places of interest such as Plaza de la Constitución, Plaza de la Rotonda, Plaza de la Liberación, Avenida 16 de Septiembre, Avenida Juárez, etc., and different routes to points beyond.

215 Reunión para Definir una Política Nacional de Conservación de Monumentos, 1st, México?, 1983? Primera Reunión para Definir una Política Nacional de Conservación de Monumentos: las legislaciones sobre la conservación de los monumentos históricos. México: Dirección de Monumentos Históricos, Instituto Nacional de Antropología e Historia, 1985. 121 p.: bibl. (Cuaderno de trabajo; 1)

Includes six short essays about Mexican law for conservation of historical monuments: 1) historical background of 18th and 19th centuries, by Sonia Lombardo; 2) laws from 1914–16, by Jorge A. Manrique; 3) laws from 1930–34, by Luz E. Galván; 4) General Law of National Cultural Patrimony, by Luis Ortiz Macedo; 5) organization of Instituto Nacional de Antropología e Historia, by Carlos San Juan; and 6) summary of first meeting to define national policy for conservation of monuments, by Sonia Lombardo.

216 Robles García, Nelly M.; Marcelo Leonardo Magadán; and Alfredo Moreira Quirós. Reconstrucción colonial en Mitla, Oaxaca. México: Escuela Nacional de Conservación, Restauración y Museografía, Instituto Nacional de Antropología e Historia, 1987. 78 p.: bibl., ill. (Cuaderno de trabajo; 1)

Analytical study of village of Mitla (Oaxaca), especially of the construction of the "Grupo del Curato" after Spanish invasion. Author gives important recommendations for historical conservation of this important colonial Mixtec national monument. Contains documentation and floor plans of restoration project and archaeological excavations. Good photographs.

217 Rojas, Pedro. La Casa de los Mascarones. México: Univ. Nacional Autónoma de México, Instituto de Investigaciones Estéticas, 1985. 83 p., 18 p. of plates: bibl., ill.

Detailed and documented study of history, architectural style, and architectural evolution of House of Mascarones (constructed 1562), one of the national monuments of Mexico City associated with José Diego Hurtado de Mendoza from 1766–71. Good documentation and very good illustrations.

218 Romero, Héctor Manuel. Crónica histórica de Tlatelolco. México: Cámara Nacional de Comercio de la Ciudad de México, 1985. 78 p.: bibl., ill. (some col.)

Historical summary of ancient Aztec city of Tlatelolco (now Mexico City), from prehispanic period until 1985.

219 Romero Quiroz, Javier. La Hacienda de San Juan de la Cruz. Toluca, Mexico: Gobierno del Estado de México, 1986. 46 leaves: bibl., ill.

Discussion about haciendas in Mexico, primarily in Oaxaca, focuses upon origin and history of the Hacienda de San Juan de la Cruz in Toluca. Good bibliography.

220 San Juan Bautista, Cuauhtinchan: restauración 1987. México: Secretaría de Desarrollo Urbano y Ecología, 1987. 140 p.: bibl., ill. (some col.)

Good report on history of San Juan Bautista Convent in Cuauhtinchan includes interesting essays about convent's restoration under aegis of Sergio Saldívar Guerra and conservation of retables, murals, and sculpture.

221 Sánchez Navarro de Pintado, Beatriz. Marfiles cristianos del oriente en México. Fotografía de Michel Zabé e Ignacio Urquiza. Dibujos de Xavier Talamante. México: Fomento Cultural Banamex, 1986. 128 p., 92 p. of plates: bibl., ill. (some col.), maps.

Artistic and historical examination of ivory sculpture production in New Spain presents an outstanding collection of religious oriental ivories of Christian subjects which came to New Spain in the "Galeón de Manila" during period of commercial trade between Mexico and Phillipines (16th-18th centuries). Provides a coherent study of the origin, aesthetic quality, and religious meaning of these sculptures, classifying them into two categories: "Chino-Hispanic" and "Indo-Portuguese." Important contribution to study of ivory sculpture in New Spain, a little-known subject in art history of colonial period. Excellent color photograhs.

222 Santiago Cruz, Francisco. Epigrafía de San Cristóbal de las Casas. San Cristóbal de las Casas, Mexico: Patronato Fray Bartolomé de las Casas, 1986 64 p: bibl.

Compilation of 32 epigraphies author collected in city of San Cristóbal de las Casas. Author describes houses and inscriptions and provides complete inventory of domestic colonial architecture featuring epigraphies. Lacks illustrations.

223 Sleight, Eleanor Friend. The many faces of Cuilapan: a historical digest of a sixteenth-century Dominican monastery and church complex and village, Oaxaca, Mexico. Orlando, Fla.: Pueblo Press, 1988. 177 p., 16 p. of plates: bibl., ill. (some col.), index, maps.

Historical and geographical account of village of Cuilapan in Oaxaca, Mexico contains historical and architectural description of 16th-century Dominican monastery and village churches. Includes bibliography, glossary, and excellent quality photographs.

224 Torre Villalpando, Guadalupe de la and **Jacinto Barrera Bassols.** Monumentos históricos: Baja California. México: Instituto Nacional de Antropología e Historia; Mexicali: Gobierno del Estado de Baja California, 1988. 85 p.: bibl., ill., maps (some col.) (Col. Monumentos históricos; 1)

Presents a chronological survey of the cities of Baja California with descriptions of major monuments, beginning with architecture of colonial epoch, continuing with the "ranchos," and culminating with structures of the political regime known as the "porfiriato." Missions of Tijuana, Mexicali, and Ensenada are among the colonial centers described.

225 Vargas Lugo, Elisa. Noticias sobre la construcción de la Casa Borda de Taxco. (*An. Inst. Invest. Estét.,* 55, 1986, p. 37–48, facsims., photos)

Examines history and construction of the Casa Borda de Taxco, Mexico, built in 1759 by Don Juan Joseph de Alva, professor of architecture. House was constructed for one of the most important figures in 18th-century mining sector, Don Joseph de la Borda (Real Minas de Taxco).

226 Vargas Lugo, Elisa. Las portadas religiosas de México. 2a ed. México: Univ. Nacional Autónoma de México, Instituto de Investigaciones Estéticas, 1986. 367 p., 188 p. of plates: bibl., ill. (some col.) (Estudios y fuentes del arte en México; 27)

General study on colonial religious art in Mexico describes facades of Hispanic churches in 26 cities. From an historical perspective, author discusses Mannerist and Ba-

roque influences, the presence of Renaissance, Mudéjar and Gothic forms, plus Mestizo and native forms. She establishes that churches in the 16th and 17th centuries are characterized by two elements: the floor and structure, which are static; and the facade and towers, which are dynamic, always changing with reconstructions. Contains information about colonial society and upholds concept that the Catholic Church should be viewed as an agent which defined differences between rich and poor in Mexico. Excellent bibliography.

227 Villegas, Víctor Manuel. Churriguera y Felipe de Ureña en Toluca: la Sacristía del Convento Franciscano de la Asunción de Toluca, los churriguera hasta Pedro Ribera y sus obras, la Ermita de Santa María del Puerto de Madrid; la restauración de la sacristía. Textos inéditos de René Taylor y Fernando Chueca Goitia. Toluca, Mexico: Gobierno Constitucional del Estado de México: Univ. Autónoma del Estado de México, 1981. 128 p: bibl., ill. (some col.)

Excellent monograph on colonial Mexican architecture which discusses Spanish influences in America, the "Indianization" of Spanish elements, the influence of Mannerist architecture, the presence of Baroque design, and especially the late 18th-century style known as Churrigueresque. Establishes differences between metropolitan and provincial architecture. Most important essay is dedicated to art and Churrigueresque expression during colonial period.

CENTRAL AMERICA AND THE CARIBBEAN

228 Alvarez Arévalo, Miguel. Reseña histórica de las imágenes procesionales de la Ciudad de Guatemala. Guatemala: Patronato de Amigos del Museo Nacional de Historia, 1984. 32 p.: bibl., ill. (Col. Imágenes de Guatemala; 5)

Explores general history of some of the ceremonial religious images that were used in old Guatemala, including manner in which the images and culture evolved over centuries. Provides pertinent analysis of the diverse icons of Christ venerated in Holy Week municipal processions.

229 Angulo Iñiquez, Diego. La arquitectura del siglo XVIII en Nicaragua. (*Bol.*

Nicar. Bibliogr. Doc., 57, mayo/julio 1988, p. 21–35, ill.)

Deftly compares religious architecture of two important Nicaraguan cities, León and Granada. Provides historical account of the origin of some important 18th-century churches and describes their Baroque style.

230 Avalos Austria, Gustavo Alejandro. El retablo guatemalteco: forma y expresión. México: Tredex Editores, 1988. 181 p.: bibl., ill. (some col.)

Originally presented as thesis requirement for Univ. del Valle de Guatemala in 1987, this book examines Guatemalan altarpieces of the viceregal period. Considers their style in relationship to architecture, as well as their social and religious meaning. Contains useful bibliography, diagrams of retables, black and white photographs, and color plates.

231 Báez López-Penha, José Ramón and **Eugenio Pérez Montás.** Restauración de antiguos monumentos dominicanos: planos e imágenes. Santo Domingo: Univ. Nacional Pedro Henríquez Ureña, 1986. 286 p.: bibl., ill.

General overview of colonial monuments of Dominican Republic contains excellent photographs, drawings, and floor plans. Accentuates military architecture (such as the Fortaleza de Santo Domingo), hospitals, and buildings erected for sugar production, but also includes information about convents, churches, and the Cathedral of Santo Domingo.

Bégot, Danielle. Imitation et créolité: une problématique des beaux-arts en espace créole insulaire; le cas des Antilles francophones, Martinique, Guadeloupe, Haïti, XVIII-XXe siècles. See item **1520.**

Bégot, Danielle. La révolution de Saint-Domingue à travers les peintres haïtiens. See item **1633.**

232 Berlin-Neubart, Heinrich and **Jorge Luján Muñoz.** Los túmulos funerarios en Guatemala. 1a ed. rev. Guatemala: Academia de Geografía e Historia de Guatemala, 1983. 88 p.: bibl., ill. (Publicación especial; 25)

Special publication focuses upon architectural monuments erected to commemorate death of Bourbon sovereigns during colonial period in Guatemala. Authors consulted viceregal documents as part of their research for this comprehensive study of exequies, a facet of colonial art history that is relatively unexplored. Complemented with illustrations and copies of documents, this text contributes to knowledge about *arquitectrua efímera.*

233 El Salvador. Dirección de Patrimonio Cultural. Departamento de Historia. Chalchuapa. San Salvador: Ministerio de Educación, Dirección de Publicaciones, 1985. 103 p.: bibl., ill.

Report of a study project on Chalchuapa and the Church of Santiago, its architectural characteristics, and significance for religious rituals. Includes description of an 1885 military event: the death of a Salvadoran national hero.

234 Escoffery, Gloria. The dynamics of metamorphosis: the 1988 Annual National Exhibition. (*Jam. J.*, 22:1, Feb./April 1989, p. 29–36, photos)

Author was a critic for 1988 annual exhibition of Jamaican art at National Gallery of Jamaica.

235 Jickling, David L. and **Elaine Elliott.** Façades and festivals of Antigua: a guide to church fronts and celebrations. Antigua, Guatemala: Casa del Sol, 1989. 75 p.: bibl., ill.

Useful and descriptive guide to churches and sacred places in villages of Guatemala emphasizes church facades, iconography of popular saints, and a calendar for religious feast days.

236 Lamothe, Eva S. The Cathedral of Antigua Guatemala: a colonial painting, ca. 1718. (*An. Inst. Invest. Estét.*, 56, 1986, p. 91–105, appendix, bibl., facsims.)

Originally part of author's M.A. thesis in art history at Tulane Univ., this article examines a colonial painting depicting the unfinished Cathedral of Antigua. Based upon her historical analysis, author gives painting a new date of 1718. Includes photographs, floor plan of the Cathedral, and bibliography.

Loupès, Philippe. Le modèle urbain a Saint-Domingue au XVIIIe siècle: la maison et l'habitat au Cap Français et à Port-au-Prince. See item **1672.**

237 Luján Muñoz, Luis. La escultura colonial guatemalteca en México. (*An. Inst. Invest. Estét.*, 59, 1988, p. 175–204, facsims., photos)

Discusses influence upon New Spain of sculpture production in colonial Guatemala during Baroque period (1676–1795). Excellent examination of stylistic transformations and reverberations.

238 Luján Muñoz, Luis. Máscaras y morerías de Guatemala = Masks and morerías of Guatemala. Guatemala: Museo Popol Vuh, Univ. Francisco Marroquín, 1987. 135 p.: bibl., ill.

Extensive study of masks, one of Guatemala's most important cultural expressions. Focuses on ritual dances in which masks have been used from precolumbian times to present. Role of Morero and Morerías in Guatemalan traditional folklore is also accented. Includes bilingual text and good photographs. Excellent research source.

239 Martínez, Mario Felipe. Catedral de la Inmaculada Concepción de Valladolid de Comayagua. Edición de Ramiro Colindres. Tegucigalpa: Graficentro Editores, 1988. 24 p.: ill.

Descriptive guide to Cathedral of Honduras includes a brief note on historical background. Lacks bibliography.

240 Morales, María Caridad; María Elena Orozco; and Lidia Margarita Martínez Bofill. Vestigios de la temprana arquitectura colonial de Santiago de Cuba. (*Santiago*, 65, junio 1987, p. 63–77, bibl., photos)

Historical examination of early architectural constructions in Santiago de Cuba since 16th century, when construction of the first villages began. Author explores relationship between civil and military architecture and the emergence of a unique domestic style during 16th, 17th, and 18th centuries.

241 Museo de Arte Colonial (Antigua, Guatemala). Museo de Arte Colonial, Antigua Guatemala. Antigua, Guatemala: Instituto de Antropología e Historia; Organización de Estados Americanos, 1986. 24 p.: ill. (some col.) (Serie Guías culturales; 1)

Catalog of museum located in the old building of the Univ. de San Carlos in Antigua, Guatemala. Although lacking information and documentation, guide presents a photographic survey of the museum's collection of colonial paintings and sculptures. For this reason, the text is useful.

242 Núñez, Aminta and Julio César Molo. Portobelo: diagnóstico de las condiciones socio-económicas, demográficas y monumentales; alternativas de desarrollo. Panamá: Instituto Nacional de Cultura, Dirección Nacional de Patrimonio Histórico, Proyecto de Desarrollo Cultural: PNUD, UNESCO, 1987. 119 p.: bibl., ill., maps. (Col. El Hombre y su cultura; 4)

General study of city of Portobelo includes social, economic, and historical perspectives. Prepared by UNESCO, it contains important documents for projects concerning preservation of Panama's national patrimony.

243 Osorio Osorio, Alberto. Santiago de Veragua colonial. Panamá: Impresora Real, 1989. 83 p.: bibl., ill.

Many cities in colonial America were named in honor of a religious patron or saint: Santiago de Veragua, a city on the Isthmus of Panama, was dedicated to Apostle St. James the Elder. Text explores origin, development, and history of this important province of Central America during viceregal epoch.

244 Palacios, Sergio. Las iglesias coloniales de la ciudad de Comayagua: guía histórica-turística. Tegucigalpa: Instituto Hondureño de Antropología e Historia, 1987. 70 p.: bibl., ill.

Short tour guide with historical summary of colonial churches in the town of Comayagua, Honduras.

245 Pérez Cisneros, Guy. Características de la evolución de la pintura en Cuba. Prólogo y edición de Guillermo de Zendegui. Miami, Fla.: Editorial Cubana, 1988. 1 v.: bibl.

Reprint of one of the few critical studies of Cuban painting during the colonial period. For original edition, see *HLAS 23:1405.* [J.M. Hernández]

246 Venegas Fornias, Carlos and Natalia Raola Ramos. Datos históricos de la Parroquia Mayor de San Juan Bautista de los Remedios. (*Islas*, 84, mayo/agosto 1987, p. 87–96, bibl., photos)

Documentation concerning construction of 16th-century Parroquia de San Juan Bautista de los Remedios (Cuba). Declared a national monument in 1949, the reconstruction of the edifice occurred 1944–54.

247 Vidal, Teodoro. Tres retratos pintados por Campeche. San Juan: Ediciones Alba, 1988. 32 p.: ill.

Short descriptive text about 18th-century Puerto Rican artist José Campeche Jordán. Material concerns three paintings from private collections in US.

South America

HUMBERTO RODRIGUEZ-CAMILLONI, *Associate Professor and Director, Center for Theory and History of Architecture, College of Architecture and Urban Studies, Virginia Polytechnic Institute and State University*

THE LITERATURE REVIEWED FOR THIS VOLUME OF *HLAS* once again offers a wide range of methodological approaches to the subject, ranging from general surveys by continent, country, or region, to detailed monographs on a single monument. In general, a high standard of scholarship is evident, reflecting the formal training in art and architectural history by a new generation of scholars. An increasing number of fine quality publications with excellent color plates facilitates a better appreciation of the rich artistic and architectural heritage of the colonial period.

Leading the list of noteworthy books is Damián Bayón and Murillo Marx's *Historia del arte colonial sudamericano* (item **153**), which despite its more limited scope rivals Santiago Sebastián, José de Mesa Figueroa and Teresa Gisbert's *Arte iberoamericano desde la colonización a la independencia* (Madrid, 1986, see *HLAS 50:191*). Written in collaboration with Myriam Ribeiro de Oliveira, Aurea Pereira da Silva and Hugo Segawa, Bayón and Marx's book provides a comprehensive survey of colonial architecture, painting, and sculpture in South America. Wherever possible, factual information is combined with critical commentaries guiding the reader to specific sources in the bibliography. Another important survey is the new edition of the pioneer work by Alfredo Benavides Rodríguez, *La arquitectura en el Virreinato del Perú y en la Capitanía General de Chile* (item **248**). Totally revised and updated with a new bibliography and improved visual material, this book now provides reliable information on urban centers and lesser-known rural areas in Peru and Chile.

Santiago Sebastián's *El barroco iberoamericano* (item **163**) may be singled out as an exceptional work entirely devoted to studies in iconography and iconology of Spanish and Portuguese American art and architecture. With painstaking rigor, the author thematically discusses the sources and meanings underlying works of art. It will serve as a methodological model for future studies.

Regional studies such as Patrick Rouillard's *Boyacá* (item **260**), Ramón Gutiérrez's *Evolución urbana y arquitectónica de Corrientes* (item **250**), and Luis Enrique Tord's *Arequipa artística y monumental* (item **275**) fill important voids in the field with a wealth of written and visual documentation on the subjects discussed. An outstanding book on a single monument is Germán Franco Salamanca's *Templo de Santa Clara, Bogotá* (item **258**).

Even though the vast majority of titles deal with architecture and urbanism, monographs on painting and sculpture are well represented by Jorge Bernales Ballesteros *et al.*'s *Pintura en el Virreinato del Perú* (item **272**), Francisco Gil Tovar *et al.*'s *Los Figueroa: aproximación a su época y a su pintura* (item **259**), and Carlos F. Duarte's *Historia de la escultura en Venezuela: época colonial* (item **257**). On the other hand, Sara Bomchil and Virginia Carreño's *El mueble colonial de las Américas y su circunstancia histórica* (item **155**) is a major contribution to a topic woefully neglected in the literature of colonial Latin American art.

Special mention should be made of the extraordinary contributions made by the Spanish government (sometimes in collaboration with national institutions of Latin American countries) toward cultural events and publications celebrating the quincentennial of the discovery of the Americas. Several series pertaining to art and architecture of the colonial period have been included in the "Biblioteca Quinto Centenario." For instance, volumes 4, 5, and 7 of Baltasar Jaime Martínez Compañón's *Trujillo del Perú al fines del siglo XVII* were released between 1989–90, thus nearly completing the splendid facsimile publication initiated by Ediciones Cultura Hispánica in 1978 (see *HLAS 50:249*). The Instituto de Cooperación Iberoamericana has also sponsored the handsome "Colección Ciudades Iberoamericanas," featuring photographic albums and essays on individual cities. Volumes in this series published to date include *La Habana* (1986), *Lima* (1987, item **271**), *Sucre* (1989), *Quito* (1989), *San Juan de Puerto Rico* (1989), *Potosí* (1990), *Cartegena de Indias* (1990), and *Santo Domingo* (1990).

Historic preservation and restoration projects conducted under the auspices of international organizations (e.g., UNESCO, The Organization of American States) in collaboration with national institutions (e.g., Peru's Instituto Nacional de Cultura, Instituto Colombiano de Cultura, Instituto Boliviano de Cultura) have produced a number of technical reports containing valuable information on historic buildings and works of art (items **158, 258, 272,** and **270**). Germán Franco Salamanca's book, mentioned above (item **258**), is a masterful synthesis of the history of a single monument, which also describes the restoration works and the criteria that guided them. This type of publication will become critical for future studies of historic monuments undergoing restoration.

A final word of recognition should go to a few academic institutions and private individuals in South America who, with very limited resources and against all odds, continue to contribute to the vital dissemination of scholarly research in the field. Although usually modest in their format and unpretentious in their circulation size, in most cases they have to be acknowledged as the *only* publications of their type in their respective countries. Journals that fall within this category include *DANA (Documentos de Arquitectura Nacional y Americana* published in Resistencia, Argentina, by the Instituto Argentino de Investigaciones en Historia de la Arquitectura y el Urbanismo under the direction of Ramón Gutiérrez and Ricardo J. Alexander; and, of more recent creation, *DAU (Documentos de Arquitectura y Urbanismo* under the direction of Pedro Belaúnde, and *HUACA* (Revista de la Facultad de Arquitectura, Urbanismo, y Artes de la Universidad Nacional de Ingeniería), both published in Lima, Peru. Let us hope that these and other similar publications will enjoy a prolonged life for years to come.

CHILE, ARGENTINA, PARAGUAY, AND URUGUAY

248   **Benavides Rodríguez, Alfredo.** La arquitectura en el Virreinato del Perú y en la Capitanía General de Chile. Edición ampliada y actualizada por Juan Benavides Courtois. 3a ed. Santiago: Editorial Andrés Bello, 1988. 282 p.: bibl., ill.

Third revised edition of pioneer study originally published in 1941 has been updated and expanded with a new bibliography, more footnotes, and better photographs and architectural plans. About two-thirds of book is devoted to Capitanía General de Chile, including important urban colonial centers as well as a wide selection of rural Andean areas.

249   **El Cabildo de Montevideo: 1730; 250o aniversario de su instalación, 1980.** Se-

lección de textos y prólogo de Alfredo Raúl Castellanos. Montevideo: Intendencia Municipal de Montevideo, 1979. 48 p.: bibl., ill.

Short history of Montevideo Cabildo is mainly a collection of primary and secondary source documents, complemented by a few reconstruction drawings of this historical building.

250 Gutiérrez, Ramón and **Angela Sánchez Negrette.** Evolución urbana y arquitectónica de Corrientes. t. 1, 1588–1850. t. 2, 1850–1988. Resistencia, Argentina: Instituto Argentino de Investigaciones de Historia de la Arquitectura y del Urbanismo, 1988. 2 v.: bibl., ill.

Exhaustive study of urban and architectural history of Corrientes from its foundation in 1588 to present day. Research was undertaken by team of professionals under the direction of distinguished architect/ architectural historian Ramón Gutiérrez. Supplies detailed information on city's material fabric, supported by wealth of archival material, measured plans, and historic and contemporary photographs. Indispensable reference for any future studies on the subject.

251 Larraín Aguirre, Alvaro. Santiago, iglesias antiguas. Santiago?: Impr. Gómez, 1986. 79 p.: bibl., ill.

Popular guide to oldest extant churches in Santiago, mostly dating from late 18th or 19th centuries. Each monument is described in a separate chapter which gives brief history of its origins and later reconstructions. B/w photographs show only exterior views and are generally of poor quality.

252 McNaspy, Clement J. Las ciudades perdidas del Paraguay: arte y arquitectura de las reducciones jesuíticas, 1607–1767. Fotografía de J.M. Blanch. Traducción de T. Rodríguez Miranda. Bilbao, Spain: Univ. de Deusto: Ediciones Mensajero, 1988? 159 p.: bibl., ill.

Faithful Spanish translation of *Lost cities of Paraguay* (see *HLAS 50:228*) provides a good introduction to the extant architectural remains and religious sculpture from the 30 Jesuit mission towns founded during the 17th and 18th centuries to protect the Guarani Indians from Portuguese slave trade

and the depredations of Spanish colonists, and to teach them the arts of Christian town life. Text is fluid and informative. Despite a tendency toward travelogue style, book contains sensitive and perceptive observations. Excellent b/w photographs supply a comprehensive visual survey of monuments discussed.

253 Schávelzon, Daniel. El Cabildo de Buenos Aires: la remodelación de Pedro Benoit en 1879–1881. (*Todo es Hist.*, 263, mayo 1989, p. 28–39, bibl., facsims., photos)

Well-documented history of construction of Cabildo of Buenos Aires and its neoclassic remodeling after plans by architect Pedro Benoit. Photographic and archaeological evidence is brought to light showing that several original elements of the 18th-century building were demolished later, during reconstruction of 1939–42 under direction of architect Mario J. Buschiazzo.

254 Schávelzon, Daniel. Un fuerte español cercano a Buenos Aires, 1671–1672. (*Todo es Hist.*, 268, oct. 1989, p. 38–47, bibl., facsims., photos)

Detailed account of little-known example of military architecture in vicinity of Buenos Aries dating from 17th century. Author calls attention to need for systematic archaeological exploration and conservation of this historic site.

COLOMBIA AND VENEZUELA

255 Castrillón Arboleda, Diego. Muros de papel. Bogotá: Banco Central Hipotecario, 1986? 623 p.: bibl., ill. (some col.), indexes.

History of city of Popayán is told through a survey of its architecture, including major public and private buildings and people associated with them. Combines factual information with stories, anecdotes, and poems which provide sociopolitical background to periods discussed. Old and recent photographs permit visual comparisons across time and give an appreciation of changes since devastating earthquake of 1983.

256 Chiquinquirá: 400 años. Edición de Octavio Arizmendi Posada. Bogotá: Litografía Arco, 1986. 172 p.: bibl., ill. (some col.)

Handsome publication celebrates 400th anniversary of apparition of the Virgin of Chiquinquirá on Dec. 26, 1586. Text by various authors is mostly devoted to history and legend surrounding the miraculous event, with only one art historical essay by Francisco Gil Tovar (p. 81–96) on its iconography. Reproduces 14 colonial paintings depicting Virgin of Chiquinquirá in fine color plates.

257 Duarte, Carlos F. Historia de la escultura en Venezuela: época colonial. Caracas: J.J. Castro, 1979. 131 p.: bibl., ill. (some col.)

Carefully documented history of colonial sculpture in Venezuela, with an impressive corpus of fine color and b/w photographs. Even though measurements of sculptures are omitted, captions provide valuable information on their manufacture and present location. Text concludes with catalog of 36 biographical notes on artists whose work is brought to light.

258 Franco Salamanca, Germán. Templo de Santa Clara, Bogotá. Bogotá: Instituto Colombiano de Cultura, 1987. 209 p.: bibl., ill. (some col.)

Thoroughly documented history of art, architecture, and restoration of the church and convent of Santa Clara in Bogotá. Descriptive material, analysis, and interpretation, complemented with fine measured drawings and b/w and color photographs, make this a model study. Restoration interventions on the fabric of the building as well as on the sculptural works and paintings are also discussed in detail, including the methodology and criteria used. Outstanding contribution to literature on this subject.

259 Museo de Arte Moderno (Bogotá). Los Figueroa: aproximación a su época y a su pintura. Edición de Benjamín Villegas Jiménez y Fernando Restrepo Uribe. Bogotá: Villegas Editores, 1986. 221 p.: bibl., ill. (some col.), indexes.

Important contribution toward a better appreciation of pictorial work of three colonial painters active in Colombia: Baltasar de Figueroa (ca. 1560–1659), Gaspar de Figueroa (ca. 1594–1658), and Baltasar Vargas de Figueroa (1629–67), grandfather, father, and

son, respectively. Most complete book to date on subject, with critical essays by Francisco Gil Tovar and Fernando Restrepo Uribe. Fine color reproductions of paintings, often filling the entire page, are supplemented by *catalogue raisonné* of works of each artist.

260 Rouillard, Patrick. Boyacá. Prólogo de Carlos E. Vargas Rubiano. Fotografía de Eduardo Vargas Jiménez. Traducción de Charles L. Roll. Medellín, Colombia: Compañía Litográfica Nacional, 1987. 103 p.: chiefly col. ill.

Impressive photographic album documents landscape, towns, and people of Boyacá department. Full-page color photographs capture beauty of natural setting, street scenes of daily life, historic monuments, and artistic treasures contained within. Text is limited to general prologue aimed at general public.

261 Tobón Botero, Néstor. Arquitectura de la colonización antioqueña. t. 2, Caldas. Bogotá: Banco Central Hipotecario, 1986. 1 v.: bibl., col. ill.

Volume visually surveys architecture and urban spaces of nine towns within department of Caldas, including Aguadas, Anserma, Manizales, Neira, Pácora, Pensilvania, Riosucio, and Salamina. Each town's history is briefly discussed in a separate chapter, followed by a collection of stunning color photographs documenting streetscapes, secular and religious monuments, and their ornamental details. Town plans and representative plans of individual buildings are also provided, as well as a useful bibliography with suggestions for further reading.

PERU, ECUADOR, AND BOLIVIA

262 Adorno, Rolena. Guamán Poma: writing and resistance in colonial Peru. Austin: Univ. of Texas Press, 1986. 189 p.: bibl., ill., index. (Latin American monographs/Institute of Latin American Studies, the University of Texas at Austin; 68)

Because Guamán Poma's *Nueva corónica y buen govierno* (c.1600) presents both text and image, author properly assesses the subtleties of both as well as their structural interrelatedness. Discussions of Guamán Poma's illustrations are insightful and daring.

For ethnohistorian's comment, see *HLAS 50: 567*. [F. Clancy]

263 Arte colonial de Ecuador: siglos XVI-XVII. Dirección de José María Vargas. Quito: Salvat Editores Ecuatoriana, 1985. 239 p.: ill. (some col.)

General survey of colonial art, architecture, and urbanism in Ecuador, predominantly but not exclusively with reference to city of Quito. The text, a collaboration by various authors under direction of José María Vargas, is uneven in quality but beautifully illustrated with an impressive collection of excellent color plates previously published in *Historia del arte ecuatoriano*, t. 2. (Quito: Salvat Editores Ecuatoriana, 1976). Regrettably, as in the earlier publication, no footnotes or bibliography are provided.

264 Becerra Casanovas, Rogers. Retablos coloniales del Beni: obras de arte religioso. La Paz?: A. Amabile; P. Godoy, 1984. 86 p., 15 p. of plates: bibl., col. ill.

Strictly descriptive inventory of religious monuments in northern dept. of El Beni, Bolivia. Shows that Jesuit churches, mostly rebuilt since colonial times, still house important collections of decorative arts, as well as *retablos* suggested by title. The few color photographs are generally of poor quality.

265 Caballero, Geraldine Byrne de and **Rodolfo Mercado Mercado.** Monumentos coloniales: inventario de los monumentos coloniales, civiles y religiosos del Departamento de Cochabamba. Cochabamba, Bolivia: Instituto de Investigaciones Antropológicas, Univ. Mayor de San Simón, 1986. 70 p., 41 p. of plates: bibl., ill.

Useful inventory of religious and secular colonial architecture in dept. of Cochabamba discusses each monument in a separate chapter, providing historic summary and description of its present condition. Visual material at end of book includes b/w photographs of general views and details, plans, and elevation drawings of most buildings.

266 Fraser, Valerie. The architecture of conquest: building in the Viceroyalty of Peru, 1535–1635. Cambridge, England; New York: Cambridge Univ. Press, 1989. 1 v.: bibl., index. (Cambridge Iberian and Latin American studies)

Important study of practice and ideology of architecture during early decades of Spanish Viceroyalty, with particular emphasis on province of Chucuito near Lake Titicaca. Author proposes that the deliberate display of certain European architectural motifs—such as the classical orders and the round arch—served the ends of political, religious, and economic conquest as symbols of Western civilization and Christianity.

267 García Bryce, José. Observaciones sobre cuatro obras atribuídas al Virrey Amat. (*Doc. Arquit. Urban.*, 1:4, agosto 1988, p. 12–29)

Serious study of four major 18th-century Lima buildings whose design is traditionally attributed to the Viceroy Manuel de Amat y Junient (1707–1782): Quinta de Presa, the church of Las Nazarenas, the Virgin's *camarín* in the church of La Merced, and the tower of the church of Santo Domingo. Even though no new documentary evidence is presented, author's careful formal analysis of the works strongly suggests their creation by a single hand. Visual comparative analysis between the works and other possible European sources is enhanced by fine illustrations, including several previously unpublished measured drawings.

268 Gisbert, Teresa and **José de Mesa.** La tradición bíblica en el arte virreinal. La Paz: Editorial los Amigos del Libro, 1986. 40 p.: bibl., ill. (Col. Texto y documento)

Brief but useful iconographic study of selected biblical themes in colonial art and architecture in Bolivia and Peru. The Temple of Solomon in Jerusalem, the menorah, the Solomonic column, and military angels are discussed in relation to specific monuments. Examines some of the reasons for their popularity in the Andean region and proposes a number of visual and written sources of inspiration.

269 Gutiérrez, Ramón; Cristina Esteras Martín; and **Alejandro Málaga Medina.** La arquitectura religiosa de las tierras altas del sur peruano: Colca, Chumbivilcas, Espinar. (*Doc. Arquit. Urban.*, 1:1, dic. 1986, p. 23–29)

Analyzes planiform architecture of the Valley of Colca in Arequipa as a regional style which includes the southernmost provinces of Chumbivilcas and Espinar in dept. of Cusco. Places major emphasis on socioeconomic, political, and religious factors in relation to settlement patterns during colonial period.

270 Instituto Boliviano de Cultura. Conservación de los monumentos virreinales de Bolivia. La Paz: Instituto Boliviano de Cultura; Embajada de España en Bolivia, 1987. 32 p.: ill.

Progress report on restoration work undertaken between 1970–87 on 14 colonial monuments located in depts. of La Paz, Oruro, and Potosí. Text, supplemented with architectural plans and b/w photographs, includes a brief history of each monument, technical information about its condition, and criteria used in restoration and conservation projects.

271 Méndez Guerrero, Manuel. Lima. Textos de César Pacheco Vélez y Juan Manuel Ugarte Eléspuru. Madrid: Ediciones Cultura Hispánica; Instituto de Cooperación Iberoamericana, 1986. 201 p.: ill. (some col.) (Col. Ciudades iberoamericanas)

Second volume in handsome series devoted to Spanish American cities. Distinguished photographer's artistic camera takes reader through a visual survey covering: 1) precolumbian origins of the City of Kings and its surroundings; 2) colonial religious, domestic, and military monuments; and 3) selected examples of 19th and 20th-century architecture. Introductory texts provide historical summary and poetic evocation of social milieu of city that remained for three centuries the undisputed capital of Hispanic South America.

272 Pintura en el Virreinato del Perú: el libro de arte del centenario. Lima: Banco de Crédito del Perú, 1989. 421 p.: bibl., ill. (some col.) (Col. Arte y tesoros del Perú)

Deluxe commemorative publication celebrates 100th anniversary of the institution that initiated the handsome art book series "Artes y Tesoros del Perú" 18 years ago. Ten critical studies by leading scholars, including Jorge Bernales Ballesteros, Ricardo Estabridis Cárdenas, Luis Enrique Tord, Juan Manuel Ugarte Eléspuru, César Pacheco Vélez, Duncan Kinkead, and Fernando Silva Santisteban, cover various topics on work of European and American masters and their circles during the viceregal period. Excellent color reproductions are by themselves a *tour*

de force. Of special significance is the detailed documentation of five years of restoration and conservation work that has shed new light on paintings attributed to such artists as Zurbarán and Juan de Valdés Leal and has permitted the identification of other unknown paintings by Mateo Pérez de Alesio and Pedro Pablo Morón. Concludes with a *catalogue raisonné* of the 170 restored paintings studied in the principal text.

273 San Cristóbal Sebastián, Antonio. Arquitectura virreynal religiosa de Lima. Lima: Librería Studium, 1988. 400 p.: bibl., ill., indexes.

Anthology of short essays, most originally published in the Lima newspaper *El Comercio.* Author discusses problems of chronology and attribution of religious art and architecture in 17th-century Lima in light of new documentation discovered in notarial archives of the Archivo General de la Nación. Unfortunately, no specific references to sources in footnotes are given and the b/w photographs suffer from poor quality printing of book.

274 San Cristóbal Sebastián, Antonio. El barroco de Lampa, Ayaviri, Asillo. (*Doc. Arquit. Urban.*, 1:1, dic. 1986, p. 31–36)

Examines in some detail exterior façades and portals of parish churches of Lampa, Ayaviri, and Asillo in dept. of Puno in an attempt to show their originality. Author argues that their design stands halfway between 17th-century Cusco churches and 18th-century Altiplano churches, but his frequent misuse of European stylistic labels—particularly the term "baroque"—is problematic.

275 Tord, Luis Enrique. Arequipa artística y monumental. Lima: Banco del Sur del Perú, 1987. 205 p., 6 folded leaves of plates: bibl., ill. (some col.)

Splendid monumental work by leading historian on art and architecture of the "White City of the Andes" and its surroundings is an outstanding contribution to subject. Text and visual material present an impressive corpus of region's artistic colonial heritage. Spectacular color photograhs shot especially for this publication, together with full-color reproductions of archival documents, make this an indispensable source for future studies. Final chapter is devoted to churches in Colca Valley which were discovered and documented by author in his pioneer book, *Templos coloniales del Colca, Arequipa* (see *HLAS 48:382*). Exhaustive bibliography provides complete guide to primary and secondary sources.

276 Villacorta Santamato, Luis. Iglesias rurales en Lima. (*HUACA*, 2, abril 1988, p. 53–64)

Well-documented typological study of a group of little-known rural churches in Lima and surroundings is a summary of author's thesis submitted to the Facultad de Arquitectura, Urbanismo y Artes de la Univ. Nacional de Ingeniería. Fine analytical drawings and old and contemporary photographs help clarify many points.

277 Villasís Gallo, Gino. Patrimonio artístico religioso de la ciudad de Latacunga y de la provincia de Cotopaxi. Quito: Libri Mundi, 1986. 138 p.: bibl., ill. (some col.)

First attempt at comprehensive survey of religious art and architecture in city of Latacunga and province of Cotopaxi in Ecuador. Text draws primarily from secondary sources, transcribed at length. Visual material is very uneven, particularly inventory of monuments printed at end of book on poor quality paper.

19th and 20th Centuries

BELGICA RODRIGUEZ, *Art Critic and Art Historian Specializing in 20th Century Latin American Art; Associate Professor of Latin American Art, Universidad Central de Venezuela; Director, Art Museum of the Americas, Organization of American States*

IN THE 1990S THE ARTISTIC BIBLIOGRAPHY for Latin America can no longer be considered as minor in comparison with other regions, as is evident in the quality and quantity of literature reviewed for this biennium. As usual, this section includes many entries from Mexico, Colombia, Venezuela, Argentina, and Chile, but it also contains a few items from countries such as Bolivia, Uruguay, Ecuador, and so on. It is especially important to notice the interest the Central American and Caribbean countries now have in producing books, catalogs and many other publications about their artistic development.

Another change which has to be taken into account is the publication of theoretical reflections and aesthetical proposals on art within the cultural development of Latin America as a whole, (e.g., *Arte moderno en America Latina*, by Damián Bayón *et al.*, item **280;** *The Latin American spirit: art and artists in the United States*, item **287;** and *Ensayos y ponencias latinoamericanistas* by Juan Acha, item **278**).

From more than 200 items, I initially chose 170 to review carefully, including 158 of these in this section. I cannot, definitely, say that the unannotated books are entirely lacking in interest; serious scholars must consult them in order to know what has been written to date. As Leonard Folgarait noted in *HLAS 48* and *HLAS 50*, the literature on Mexican art is once again the most numerous with 35 works. Next is the Caribbean (Jamaica, Trinidad and Tobago, Cuba, Haiti, Martinique, Dominican Republic, and Puerto Rico), with 22, Venezuela with 20, Colombia with 11, Argentina and Chile with ten, Perú with eight, Uruguay with five, Bolivia and El Salvador with three, and Ecuador, Guatemala, and Nicaragua with two each. To a certain extent, Costa Rica's seven entries can be considered as the singular surprise, due to the great difficulties of getting research published in small countries. Nevertheless, the strength of Costa Rican artistic development deserves this recognition.

One of the important facts uncovered while reviewing publications for this volume of *HLAS* was the number of works devoted to the study of Latin America as a whole. These 17 contributions constitute a serious attempt to analyze differences and similarities within Latin American artistic production as a continental cultural phenomenon. It cannot be said that this research on Latin America art has been neglected. On the contrary, the development of a Latin American art theory is based on the important research conducted so far by numerous Latin American scholars, such as Juan Acha, Aracy Amaral, Frederico Morais, Damián Bayón, Adelaida de Juan, Jorge Alberto Manrique, Rafael Squirru, Germán Rubiano Caballero, Angel Kalenberg, Bélgica Rodríguez, and the late Jorge Romero Brest and Marta Traba. We as researchers, docents, critics, and historians know the richness of the bibliography in each country. It is necessary to admit that, unfortunately, this information remains largely unknown because of the complicated logistics of distributing it. However, we are pleased to note that the trend mentioned in *HLAS 50* (p. 46) of declining receipts of 19th and 20th-century Spanish American art historical materials at the Library of Congress has been reversed.

One notable publication is *Pintura boliviana del siglo XX* (item **380**), important not only because it covers a major gap in the field, but also because of the beauty of the book, and mainly because of the comprehensive visual and historical information included. Other works one should note are two publications on Mexican art: Orozco's *Cuadernos* (item **318**), and *Dr. Atl, 1875–1964: conciencia y paisaje* (item **311**). Both publications provide reassessments of the importance of these artists and an understanding of their work. Many other contributions from several countries could also be mentioned, if space allowed: most are compilations in which the organization of the reference material, the clear criteria, and the research methodology, make for useful reference tools.

To conclude, Latin American art bibliography is no longer (nor has it been for the last 15 years) merely an accumulation of documentation, dates, and facts, but is a theoretically-based methodology, with new conclusions being reached from a conceptual and formal point of view. The only regret is that Latin American art has been analyzed within Latin American cultural development, and not as a hemispheric phenomenon. I propose a shift toward research which deals in comparative terms with what has happened in the whole Western hemisphere, in order to understand ourselves both within our own culture as well as that of the Hemisphere.

GENERAL

278 Acha, Juan. Ensayos y ponencias latinoamericanistas. Caracas: Ediciones GAN, 1984. 307 p.: ill. (Col. Galería: Serie Estudios)

Extremely important little book on Latin American artistic development as a conceptual process. This prestigious theoretician's essays are models for a serious approach to study of Latin American artistic production.

279 Ades, Dawn *et al.* Art in Latin America: the modern era, 1820–1980. New Haven: Yale Univ. Press, 1989. 361 p.: bibl., ill. (some col.)

Fine catalog of exhibition at London's Hayward Gallery is very well illustrated. Art from Independence and its heroes to the 1960s is treated in an extensive manner, emphasizing social realism as subject matter. Exhibition explores development of Latin American art from an historical and thematic point of view, trying to tie it to notion of national and cultural identity. Includes important documentary material such as manifestos, biographies, etc.

280 Amaral, Aracy A. *et al.* Arte moderno en América Latina. Edición de Damián Bayón. Madrid: Taurus, 1985. 349 p.: bibl., ill. (some col.) (Ensayistas; 267. Serie Maior)

Compilation of essays on development of modern art in Latin America written by distinguished Latin American art critics such as Aracy Amaral (Brazil), Jorge Alberto Manrique (Mexico), Alfredo Boulton (Venezuela), Roberto Pontual (Brazil), the late Marta Traba (Colombia), and Jorge Romero Brest (Argentina). All of these essays are theoretical reflections on architecture and visual arts in Latin America. Color and b/w illustrations lack identifying information.

281 Arte y arquitectura latinoamericana. Recopilación de Ivonne Pini. Bogotá: Univ. Nacional de Colombia, 1985. 189 p.: bibl. (Col. popular; 3)

Compilation of reports given at two symposiums, "XX Century Latin American Art and Architecture" and "Art and Anthropology," convened at International Congress of Americanists (45th, Bogotá, 1985). Subjects are varied, interesting, and very well formulated.

282 Baddeley, Oriana and **Valerie Fraser.** Drawing the line: art and cultural identity in contemporary Latin America. London; New York: Verso, 1989. 164 p.: bibl., ill. (some col.), index. (Critical studies in Latin American culture)

Authors show their superficial knowledge of the development of contemporary Latin American art, which is seen from their limited foreign point of view. Analysis covers commonplace stereotypes established as visual and conceptual characteristics of Latin American art. Authors assert that book's small bibliography reflects the lack of literature on the subject, which is simply not true.

283 Barrios Peña, Jaime. Arte mestizo en América Latina: discurso y mutación cultural; quinientos años después, 1492–1992. Buenos Aires?: Fénix Editorial, 1989. 195 p.: bibl., ill.

Reflections on mestizo culture of Latin America analyze historical conditions in development of Latin American culture. Author proposes the "anthropokinetic" theory to explain Latin American artistic production as a mestizo aesthetic.

284 Bayón, Damián. La transición a la modernidad. Bogotá: Tercer Mundo Editores, 1989. 242 p.: ill. (Artes)

Analyzes architecture, painting, and sculpture from end of 19th century to middle of 20th century. Well-written, easily understood work includes important names, dates, and facts on artistic production in Latin America. Includes b/w illustrations.

285 Bienal Internacional de Pintura, *2nd, Cuenca, Ecuador, 1989.* II Bienal, Cuenca, 1989. Cuenca, Ecuador: II Bienal Internacional de Pintura, 1989. 187 p.: ill. (some col.)

Catalog from International Biennial of Painting held in Cuenca. Each author is represented by a short biography and a color illustration of a work shown in the exhibition. Also includes general information about exhibit.

286 Brett, Guy; Lu Menezes; and **Paulo Venancio Filho.** Transcontinental: an investigation of reality; nine Latin American artists. London; New York: Verso, 1990. 112 p. : ill. ;

Catalog/book of exhibit of same name, in which nine avant-garde Latin American artists participated. Brett's interesting essay analyzes romantic stereotype by which Europeans see and perceive Latin American art, pigeonholing it as magic and fantastic. Includes important texts by and about artists from Brazil, Chile, and Argentina, three countries with a European cultural background.

287 Cancel, Luis R. *et al.* The Latin American spirit: art and artists in the United States, 1920–1970; essays. New York: Bronx Museum of the Arts; Harry N. Abrams, 1988. 343 p.: bibl., ill. (some col.), index.

In seven essays, Jacinto Quirarte, Marimar Benítez, Nelly Perazzo, Lowery Sims, Eva Cockcroft, Félix Angel, and Carla Stellweg analyze special theoretical subjects relating to artists who spent time in the US. Exhibition was divided into six stylistic groups covering 1920–70. Very well illustrated.

288 Chaplik, Dorothy. Latin American art: an introduction to works of the 20th century. Foreword by Angel Hurtado. Jefferson, N.C.: McFarland & Co., 1989. 183 p.: bibl., ill. (some col.), index.

Author describes visual content of a group of paintings which she believes can be analyzed according to specific formal elements: line, shape, space (?), etc. Paintings were apparently selected with no attention to their meanings: book in general is superficial and without interest.

Estrada, Leonel. Arte actual: diccionario de términos y tendencias. See item **3165.**

289　Historia del arte hispanoamericano.
v. 3, Siglos XIX y XX [de] Damián Bayón. Madrid: Alhambra, 1987–1988. 1 v.: bibl., ill. (some col.)

Bayón follows historical development of 19th and 20th-century art and architecture. Using a very simply approach, he characterizes each country according to geographical situation, giving extensive information on the subject. Enriched by numerous b/w illustrations. For v. 1–2, see items **119** and **159.**

290　Kul'tura Latinskoĭ Ameriki: problema natsional'nogo i obshcheregional'nogo; sbornik stateĭ [Latin American culture: the problem of nationality and regionality; a collection of articles]. Edited by V.A. Kuz'mishchev. Moscow: Nauka, 1990. 174 p.: bibl.

Seven Soviet scholars address the question of what makes Latin American arts distinctive in both form and content. They employ Soviet, Latin American, and other sources to develop discussions of regional and transregional literature, painting, architecture, theater, film, and folk music. For scholarly and general audiences. [B. Dash]

291　López Rangel, Rafael and Roberto Segre. Tendencias arquitectónicas y caos urbano en América Latina. Con la colaboración de Gustavo Adolfo Brito e Isolda Maur. México: GG, 1986. 183 p.: bibl., ill. (Arquitectura latinoamericana)

Analyzes architecture of important cities like Mexico City, La Habana, San Juan de Puerto Rico, Santa Fé de Bogotá, Caracas, Quito, Santiago de Chile, Buenos Aires, São Paulo, Lima, La Paz, Puebla, and Córdoba in order to characterize process of urban development and transformation that makes these cities "unique." Theoretical introduction

shows historical synthesis of this development. Includes b/w reproductions.

Ostrower, Fayga. Acasos e criação artística. See item **440.**

292　Squirru, Rafael F. Las exigencias del arte. Buenos Aires: Zurbarán Ediciones, 1989. 283 p.: facsims., index.

Compilation of notes and articles published by author in *La Nación* of Buenos Aires (Sept. 1985-Oct. 1988) lacks unifying theme. Articles are on Latin American and European art, as well as some general reflections on art.

293　Suárez Suárez, Orlando. La jaula invisible: neocolonialismo y plástica latinoamericana. La Habana: Editorial de Ciencias Sociales, 1986. 210 p., 16 p. of plates: bibl., ill. (Sociología)

Quasi-marxist approach to neocolonial conditions of development of culture and art in Latin America. Includes analysis of art market as a result of penetration and manipulation by international consumers.

294　El Surrealismo entre Viejo y Nuevo Mundo: 6 marzo-22 abril 1990: Sala de Exposiciones de la Fundación Cultural Mapfre Vida. Madrid: Quinto Centenario, 1990. 346 p.: bibl., ill. (some col.) (Col. Encuentros: Serie Catálogos)

Very well documented catalog of exhibition in Fundación Mapfre Vida gallery describes, through texts and reproductions, the stay of Spanish artists in Mexico, the Caribbean, and New York and Latin American artists Matta and Lamb in Europe. It is centered on the 1940s, the years of the American exile of André Breton, Benjamin Péret, and Antonin Artaud. Includes a large and complete chronology from 1925–66, color and b/w reproductions, and personal and documentary photos.

MEXICO

295　Altamirano R., Hugo. Ornamentación en la fachada de la Casa Regiomontana, 1900–1940. Monterrey, Mexico: Talleres de Editorial e Impr. del R. Ayuntamiento, 1984. 140 p.: bibl., ill.

Concerns different decorative styles characterizing houses, façades, portals, fenestrations, porches, etc. in early 20th-century

Monterrey. Particular attention is paid to the house known as "Regiomontana." [B. von Barghahn]

296 Amor, Inés. Una mujer en el arte mexicano: memorias de Inés Amor. Edición de Jorge Alberto Manrique y Teresa del Conde. México: Univ. Nacional Autónoma de México, Instituto de Investigaciones Estéticas, 1987. 271 p. (Cuadernos de historia del arte; 32)

Appealing book centered on legendary figure of Inés Amor. Two scholars and Amor herself present very fresh, well-written texts on Amor's exciting life and her gallery which opened in 1935 in Mexico City. In a lucid and humorous manner, Amor reflects on art and artists in Mexico, thus shedding light on their work.

297 Belkin, Arnold. Contra la amnesia: textos, 1960–1985. México: Editorial Domés: Univ. Autónoma Metropolitana, 1986. 305 p.: ill.

In prologue, Raquel Tibol explains that the book is a "self-anthology" and analyzes some aspects of the personality of the artist. Text is by Belkin, and he justifies this by explaining that the real artist must not remain silent, painting or carving only to please the buyer (?). This boring and pretentious book does not warrant Tibol's statement that it is obligatory reading for artists, scholars, art students, etc.

298 Beloff, Angelina. Memorias. Introducción de Bertha Taracena. Epílogo de Raquel Tibol. México: Coordinación de Difusión Cultural, Dirección de Literatura, UNAM; SEP, 1986. 98 p., 32 p. of plates: ill. (Textos de humanidades)

In memoirs translated from French into Spanish, Beloff describes her story, from departure from Moscow to her arrival in Paris and acquaintance with Diego Rivera. She lived with him for 10 years, spent some years alone in Paris, and later arrived in Mexico. Very well narrated, although at times incoherent. Thing that seemed to interest her most was to live near Rivera. This moving short biography is a pleasure to read.

299 Blanco, Lázaro. Luces y tiempos. Presentación de Guillermo Samperio. Edición de Mariana Yampolsky y Pablo Monas-

terio. México: Fondo de Cultura Económica, 1987. 61 p.: chiefly ill. (Col. Río de luz)

Interesting publication reproduces artistic photographs of Lázaro Blanco and includes poetic text explaining each.

300 Cardoza y Aragón, Luis. Ojo/voz. México: Ediciones Era, 1988. 105 p.: bibl., ill. (Biblioteca Era)

Previously published texts on Gunter Gerzso, Ricardo Martínez, Luis García Guerrero, Vicente Rojo, and Francisco Toledo. In very poetic vein, author writes about these important Mexican artists, but pays more attention to the external rather than internal properties of their work. Nevertheless, this is a very interesting book.

301 Cardoza y Aragón, Luis. Toledo: pintura y cerámica. México: Ediciones Era, 1987. 98 p.: bibl., ill. (some col.)

Poetic essay on imaginary and fantastic world of Toledo analyzes various aspects of his work, offering multiple possibilities for its interpretation. Outstanding color reproductions of Toledo's work (1960–84) make an interesting visual anthology of his artistic production. Includes important chronology and extensive bibliography. Highly recommended.

Catálogo nacional, monumentos históricos inmuebles: municipios. See item **176.**

302 Cimet, Esther *et al.* El público como propuesta: cuatro estudios sociológicos en museos de arte. México: INBA, Centro Nacional de Investigación, Documentación e Información de Artes Plásticas, Dirección de Investigación y Documentación de las Artes, 1987. 248 p.: bibl., ill. (Serie Investigación y documentación de las artes: Col. Artes plásticas; 3)

Result of research carried out in conjunction with four exhibitions in Mexico City from 1982–83 contains social analysis of the museum as a center of cultural dissemination and spectator's response to it. Based on this premise, the works examine official cultural and artistic politics as well as cultural needs, drawing important conclusions.

303 50 años de artes plásticas: Palacio de Bellas Artes. México: Instituto Nacional de Bellas Artes, Secretaría de Educación Pública, 1988. 327 p.: ill. (some col.)

Illustrated catalog shows cultural and plastic arts activity in Mexico between 1934–84. Book is very well documented with official and personal photographs, biographies, and reproductions. Finishes with a helpful synopsis which synthesizes country's cultural development during those years.

304 Coloquio de Historia del Arte, 8th, Univ. Nacional Autónoma de México, 1982. Los estudios sobre el arte mexicano: examen y prospectiva. México: Univ. Nacional Autónoma de México, 1986. 320 p., 1 leaf of plates: bibl. ill. (Estudios de arte y estética; 20)

Compilation of long essays with commentaries about different Mexican artistic manifestations: music, visual art, cinema, theater, and others. Good documentation.

305 Cuevas, José Luis. Exposición de José Luis Cuevas, "el hijo predilecto:" nov. de 1980. Monterrey, Mexico: Museo de Monterrey, 1980? 1 v.: ill. (some col.)

Catalog of exhibition of Cuevas' collection includes drawings of Cuevas by his artist friends and a series of letters he wrote to Tesende. Essays on Cuevas' work and life are of mixed quality, written by Ulalume González de León, José Emilio Pacheco, José Gómez Sicre, and Octavio Paz.

306 Cuevas, José Luis. Historias del viajero. México: Premià, 1987. 78 p. (La Red de Jonás: Literatura mexicana; 42)

Compilation of previously published articles by Cuevas surveys his travels, lovers, and experiences, his prices, and his extremely narcissistic life.

307 Del carnaval a la academia: homenaje a Ida Rodríguez Prampolini. Recopilación de Rita Eder y Olga Sáenz. México: Editorial Domés, 1987. 206 p., 10 p. of plates: bibl., ill.

Heterogeneous tribute to distinguished art critic and art historian Ida Rodríguez Prampolini includes: 1) texts analyzing her critical work; 2) texts dedicated to her; and 3) short stories written in her honor. Although book is interesting, it is difficult to read and lacks a conceptual spine. "Carnaval" is a very appropriate title.

308 Diego Rivera hoy: simposio sobre el artista en el centenario de su natalicio,

Sala Manuel M. Ponce, Palacio de Bellas Artes, México, D.F., agosto de 1986. México: Instituto Nacional de Bellas Artes, SEP, 1986? 256 p.: bibl., ill.

Compilation of reports presented to a symposium organized for the centennial of Rivera's birth. This very useful and welcome book treats many different aspects of Rivera's work, life, and his relation to Mexican cultural, artistic, political, and social life.

309 Goitia, Francisco. Goitia. Edición y selección de Beatriz L. Fernández y Mariana Yampolsky. México: ISSSTE, 1988. 80 p.: ill. (some col.)

Based mainly on color reproductions of paintings by Goitia (1882–1960), a fundamental figure in Mexican art. Reproduces artist's handwritten documents which give brief biographical information in chronological order from 1904–60. Majority of paintings are located in Museo Francisco Goitia in Zacatecas.

310 González Quijano, José. Manuel Felguérez: obra en Monterrey, octubre de 1984. Monterrey, Mexico: R. Cantú J., 1984. 1 v. (unpaged): ill. (some col.)

Catalog of exhibition of Felguérez in Monterrey, beautifully illustrated with color and b/w photos of works done by artist (1959–80). Introduction, a formal analysis begun when author was a student of art criticism in Florence, notes various stages of Felguérez's work. Includes chronological biography to 1983.

311 Hernández Campos, Jorge et al. Dr. Atl, 1875–1964: conciencia y paisaje. 2a. ed. Monterrey, Mexico: Seguros Monterrey; Museo de Monterrey, 1986. 135 p., 16 p. of plates: bibl., ill. (some col.)

Extremely valuable catalog of exhibition in Museum of Monterrey. Different essays cover extensive and eclectic activity of Dr. Atl: Jorge Alberto Manrique covers Atl's activity as a painter; Tomás Zurian Ugarte as an inventor; Paco Ignacio Taibo II as a politician; Francoise Perus as a writer; Jorge Hernández Campos as an influence in Mexican culture; etc. Includes good color photos and detailed biographical chronology.

312 Instituto Nacional de Bellas Artes (Mexico) Angelina Beloff: ilustradora y grabadora. México: Museo Estudio Diego Rivera, 1988. 95 p.: bibl., ill. (1 col.)

Romantic biography of Angelina Beloff (1879–1969), first wife of Diego Rivera, who accompanied him during his early, difficult days in Paris. Author looks at Angelina's memoirs and analyzes some of her works, her relation with Rivera, and her experiences living in Paris. Illustrations make this book more attractive.

Lombardo de Ruiz, Sonia *et al.* Y todo- por una nación: historia social de la producción plástica de la Ciudad de México, 1781–1910. See item **936.**

313 La Lotería de la Academia Nacional de San Carlos, 1841–1863. México: INBA; Lotería Nacional para la Asistencia Pública, 1987. 191 p.: bibl., ill. (some col.)

Catalog of exhibition showing relationship which developed from 1840–50 between local lottery and National Academy of San Carlos (1841–1863) in order to promote Mexican fine art. Reproductions are important evidences of quality of Mexican art during first half of 19th century.

314 Martín Hernández, Vicente *et al.* Catálogo de la exposición La Arquitectura en México: porfiriato y movimiento moderno. Coordinación de Víctor Jiménez. México: Secretaría de Educación Pública, Instituto Nacional de Bellas Artes, 1983. 109 p.: ill. (Cuadernos de arquitectura y conservación del patrimonio artístico, 0185–3562; 28–29: Serie Historia de la arquitectura mexicana del siglo XX)

Valuable overview on subject is divided into two chapters: 1) "The Porfiriato;" and 2) "The Modern Movement." Comprehensive and complete panoramic view of development of Mexican architecture during first half of this century includes numerous illustrations and some unpublished architectural plans.

Mendiola Quezada, Vicente. Arquitectura del Estado de México: en los siglos XVI, XVII, XVIII y XIX. See item **204.**

315 Mérida, Carlos. Escritos de Carlos Mérida sobre arte: el muralismo. Investigación, selección de textos y cronología de Xavier Guzmán *et al.* México: INBA, Centro Nacional de Investigación, Documentación e Información de Artes Plásticas, 1987. 202 p.: bibl., ill. (Serie Investigación y documentación de las artes: Col. Artes plásticas; 1)

Consists of two sections: mural painting and artistic integration. Twenty seven texts plus an appendix make this book an invaluable reference on Mérida's appreciation of Mexican muralism, as well as his very deep-seated concept of the integration of the arts. Mérida analyzes Mexican muralism as a fundamental part of artistic development of Mexican art, one very important in his own career. Includes chronology.

Mexico: splendors of thirty centuries. See item **127.**

316 Miguel Covarrubias: homenaje. Coordinación, investigación y edición de Lucía García-Noriega y Nieto. México: Centro Cultural/Arte Contemporáneo, 1987. 261 p.: bibl., ill. (some col.)

Huge catalog of documental and historical exhibition organized as tribute to Covarrubias. Paintings, drawings, books, documents, art magazines, his private collection, and a sort of bric-a-brac are reproduced in this catalog, accompanied by 12 texts written by different personalities from the Mexican intellectual and artistic scene. Chronology, bibliography, and notes make this book the only exhaustive study of work and life of this multifaceted artist.

317 Morales, Leonor. Wolfgang Paalen: introductor de la pintura surrealista en México. México: Univ. Nacional Autónoma de México, 1984. 142 p., 38 p. of plates: bibl., ill. (some col.) (Monografías de arte; 10)

Translations of Paalen's writings, a biographical text, and a short description of some of his paintings from the valuable core of this book. Author's thesis is that Paalen was the first to introduce Surrealism to Mexico, and that this was Mexico's first international contact. Excellent color photographs and chronology.

318 Orozco, José Clemente. Cuadernos. Organización y prólogo de Raquel Tibol. México: Cultura, SEP, 1983. 336 p.: chiefly ill.

Orozco's notebooks are invaluable for understanding and reconsidering his work. Their publication in quasi-facsimile was a highly important task. Raquel Tibol's introductory essay is clear and lucid; her analysis helps give an approach to Orozco's notebooks produced from 1931–34. Tibol divides them in six sections: theory; structure; and diagonal, plastic mechanic, color, and pictorial techniques. Very enjoyable reading.

Parker, Robert L. Diego Rivera, Frida Kahlo y Carlos Chávez: colaboración, desilusión y retribución. See item **5235**.

319 Rico, Araceli. Frida Kahlo: fantasía de un cuerpo herido. México: Plaza y Valdés, 1987. 178 p.: bibl., ill. (La Ciudad)

Analysis of Kahlo's paintings in regards to images from her personal life. Exaggerated analysis overemphasizes narcissistic side of Kahlo's tormented life instead of her creative needs. Important for understanding Kahlo's relationship to traditional folk and popular Mexican culture.

320 Rivera, Diego. Diego Rivera: Museo de Monterrey, junio-agosto 1983. Monterrey, Mexico: Museo de Monterrey, 1983. 71 p.: chiefly ill. (some col.)

Exhibition of Rivera's works from Dolores Olmedo's collection. Introduction tells how she acquired this collection. Well illustrated with color photos which show development of artist's career.

321 Rochfort, Desmond. The murals of Diego Rivera. Political chronology by Julia Engelhardt. London: South Bank Board; Journeyman, 1987. 103 p.

Extremely useful study of political content of murals in relation to social and political situations in which they were realized. Contains a clear, formal and referential analysis that is well organized. Includes numerous good color and b/w illustrations.

322 Ruptura, 1952–1965: catálogo de la exposición, Museo de Arte Alvar y Carmen T. de Carrillo Gil, Museo Biblioteca Pape. México: INBA, SEP, 1988. 191 p.: bibl., ill. (some col.)

Catalog of an exhibition organized to show the Carrillo Gil collection, centered mainly on work of: José Clemente Orozco; David Alfaro Siqueiros; a group of painters made famous by the Mexican Revolution; and the new generation of artists. Very well illustrated with color and b/w reproductions. Important essays by critics such as Rita Eder, Jorge Alberto Manrique, Juan García Ponce, Luis Cardoza y Aragón, and Carlos Monsiváis attempt to place younger generation within modern Mexican artistic scene. Artists José Luis Cuevas and Manuel Felguérez speak about their rupture with Mexican muralism.

323 Sims, Lowery Stokes. Julio Galán. Monterrey, Mexico: Museo de Monterrey, 1987. 1 v.: ill. (some col.)

Catalog of Galán exhibit in Museo de Monterrey has English and Spanish text and good color reproductions. Introduction presents biographical text, mainly anecdotal, and a clearly non-analytical appreciation of this important young Mexican artist's painting. Sims relates Galán's work to that of Frida Kahlo, and finishes by commenting on Galán's work within the New York art scene.

324 Los surrealistas en México. México: INBA, Museo Nacional de Arte; SEP, 1986. 115 p.: ill. (some col.)

Catalog of show which emphasized presence of international surrealism in Mexico, along with the discovery of Mexican art of the fantastic as surrealist. Erudite texts by Octavio Paz and specialist Ida Rodríguez Prampolini explain characteristics of this tendency in Mexico. Texts, artists, and b/w reproductions make catalog a very useful and interesting document for understanding the fantastic in Mexican art.

325 Tamayo, Rufino. Rufino Tamayo, pinturas: Centro de Arte Reina Sofía, 29 de junio-3 de octubre, 1988. Madrid: Ministerio de Cultura, Dirección General de Bellas Artes y Archivos, Centro Nacional de Exposiciones, 1988. 222 p.: bibl., ill. (some col.)

Essays by Raquel Tibol, Octavio Paz, and Julián Gallegos are included in magnificent catalog which, in a retrospective sense, offers a good complete account of Tamayo's work and life. Biography, documentation, and bibliography are substantial and up to date. Welcome excellent reference includes color reproductions of his work from 1928–88.

326 Tamayo, Rufino. Tamayo: Museo de Monterrey, enero-marzo 1986; catálogo de exhibición. Monterrey, Mexico: Museo de Monterrey, 1986. 1 v.: bibl., ill. (some col.)

Very valuable catalog in English and Spanish includes a major introduction by Teresa del Conde analyzing artist's creative periods. Juan Acha's important essay on Tamayo's graphic work studies color as an important issue. Contains extensive biography and color and b/w photos, including some of sculptures.

327 Tamayo, Rufino. Textos de Rufino Tamayo. Recopilación, prólogo y selección de viñetas de Raquel Tibol. México: Coordinación de Difusión Cultural, Dirección de Literatura, UNAM, 1987. 146 p., 32 p. of plates: ill. (Textos de humanidades)

Compilation of 32 texts written between 1934–83 show development of Tamayo's intellectual maturity and his convictions as a man and an artist. One of the central issues is his opposition to the "political" content of art. Excellent introduction by Raquel Tibol analyzes first criticisms of his early work. Includes his famous polemic with Mexican muralists.

328 Toledo, Francisco. Lo que el viento a Juárez. México: Ediciones Era, 1986. 16 p., 44 p. of plates: col. ill.

Carlos Monsivais' important introduction in English and Spanish analyzes why Toledo dedicates a book of his work to Benito Juárez: Toledo desacralizes this hero and sees him as a symbol of Mexican history and popular culture.

329 Vargas, Ismael. Ismael Vargas: Museo de Monterrey, noviembre-marzo 88–89. Monterrey, Mexico: Museo de Monterrey, 1988? 75 p.: ill. (some col.)

Two texts, in Spanish and English, analyze this Mexican artist's painting. Gamboa writes about Vargas' *barroco* sense, as evidenced by artist's use of images from "miniatures" of Mexican popular art. Sullivan discusses Vargas' subject matter, his technique, and his relation to Mexican popular art.

CENTRAL AMERICA

330 Altezor Fuentes, Carlos. Arquitectura urbana en Costa Rica: exploración histórica 1900–1950. Cartago: Editorial Tecnológica de Costa Rica, 1986. 272 p.: bibl., ill.

History of 50 years of Costa Rican ar-chitecture explores beginnings of modern architecture, especially after 1930, in relation to political and social changes. Includes chapters on city of San José, and chapters on three important Costa Rican architects: José María Barrantes Monge, José Francisco Salazar Quesada, and Paul Ehrenberg Brinkman. Very well illustrated.

331 Amighetti, Francisco. Francisco Amighetti. Diseño y edición gráfica de Sonia Calvo. San José: Editorial de la Univ. de Costa Rica, 1989. 167 p.: bibl., ill. (some col.)

Semi-autobiographical texts, in English and Spanish, are statements and poems by artist published previously in other books and catalogs. Presentation by Joaquín Gutiérrez is very poetic. Important color and b/w reproductions (1951–88) show different subject matter treated by Amighetti.

332 Arellano, Jorge Eduardo. Historia de la pintura nicaragüense. Managua: s.n., 1990. 200 p.: bibl., ill.

Modest but interesting book begins with short introduction on antecedents of Nicaraguan painting, and continues by analyzing each decade since 1940. Includes articles "Notes on Ten Nicaraguan Painters" by Rodrigo Peñalaba and "Contemporary Painting of Nicaragua" by Marta Traba. Lacks illustrations.

333 Echeverría, Carlos Francisco. Historia crítica del arte costarricense. San José: Editorial Univ. Estatal a Distancia, 1986. 168 p., 2 folded p. of plates: bibl., ill. (some col.), index.

Short study of development of Costa Rican art provides good information about artistic process and changes that occurred in techniques and subject matter in Costa Rica. Author claims that a special type of Costa Rican art, with its own characteristics and essence, does exist. Illustrated with b/w reproductions.

334 Ferrero, Luis. Cinco artistas costarricenses: pintores y escultores. San José: Editorial Univ. Estatal a Distancia, 1985. 145 p., 1 folded leaf of plates: bibl., ill. (some col.)

From historical rather than artistic point of view, author studies following artists and their art as representatives of different styles and periods in Costa Rica: Enrique

Echandi, Juan Rafael Chacón, Luisa González de Sáenz, Hernán Pérez, and Aquiles Jiménez. Also contains information about Costa Rican art milieu at the beginning of the 20th century.

335   Ferrero, Luis. Sociedad y arte en la Costa Rica del siglo 19. San José: Editorial Univ. Estatal a Distancia, 1986. 214 p., 2 p. of plates: bibl., ill. (some col.)

Precise and fluent introduction to 19th-century cultural milieu of Costa Rica. Key sections analyze 19th century influences on Costa Rican cultural development: intellectual influences (Enlightenment, Catholicism, positivism, etc.) and the introduction of photography to Costa Rica.

336   Gutiérrez, Samuel A. La arquitectura en dos archipiélagos caribeños: estudio comparado de Bocas del Toro, Panamá, y San Andrés y Providencia, Colombia. Panamá: EUPAN, 1986. 153 p.: bibl., ill. (1 col.)

Comparative research of typical architecture which developed in Caribbean cultural region, a type described by author as vernacular. This complete historical study contains architectural descriptions, genealogical roots, human resources, typologies, and parallels, as well as a series of conclusions and recommendations. Very well illustrated.

337   Lentini, Luigi *et al.* Arte y crítica en el siglo XX. San José: Univ. Estatal a Distancia, Círculo de Críticos de las Artes de Costa Rica, 1986. 149 p.: bibl., ports.

Eight essays on art and criticism written by Costa Rican scholars. Essays are uneven in terms of intellectual quality, although the majority are profound and serious.

338   Luján Muñoz, Luis. Carlos Mérida, precursor del arte contemporáneo latinoamericano. Guatemala: Esso, 1985. 292 p.: bibl., ill. (some col.)

Long biographical essay emphasizes Guatemalan origins of this artist. Exhibition is a Guatemalan tribute to Mérida's work, from his first work until his departure for Mexico. Includes many personal photos and illustrations of his early works, as well as some of his articles and notes on art.

339   Montero, Carlos Guillermo. Amighetti: 60 años de labor artística. San

José: Museo de Arte Costarricense, 1987. 177 p.: bibl., ill. (some col.)

Catalog of retrospective exhibition of Amighetti's sixty years of artistic production includes an introduction on his life and work. Amighetti's personal statements are extremely important to understand his work. Numerous illustrations in color and b/w give a clear idea of artist's different periods.

340   Mujeres por el arte: exposición de arte contemporáneo; Museo Nacional de Arte Moderno, 3–31 mayo 1989, catálogo. Guatemala: Ministerio de Cultura y Deportes, Dirección General de Difusión Cultural y Deportiva, 1989. 84 p.: ill. (some col.)

Exhibition of 42 Guatemalan women painters provides very confusing description of their work, biographies, and an exercise called "pictorial analisis," which is actually a drawing, rather than a verbal description of each. This attempt to include as many women artists as possible results in a pastiche with no coherence. Good quality of some of these artists is lost among bad taste and poor quality of others.

341   Solís, Armando. Conferencias. San Salvador: Editorial Abril Uno, 1987. 95 p.: ill.

Extremely confusing text of three lectures: "El Arte Social," "Joven Pintura Salvadoreña," and "Escultura Contemporánea de El Salvador." Useful only as a source for names of Salvadoran artists.

342   Tribute to Benjamín Cañas of El Salvador, 1933–1987. Washington: Museum of Modern Art of Latin America, 1989. 1 v.: ill.

Catalog in English and Spanish of retrospective exhibition of Salvadoran artist at the museum of the Organization of American States in Washington. Bélgica Rodríguez's introduction briefly analyzes exhibit. Includes useful short critical and chronological notes as well as a curriculum vita and color reproductions.

343   Unión Nacional de Artistas Plásticos (Nicaragua). Pintura contemporánea de Nicaragua. Managua: Editorial Nueva Nicaragua; Ediciones Monimbó, 1986. 69 p.: ill. (some col.)

Simple catalog of curricula vitae, reproductions of works, and personal photos of a very important sector of Nicaraguan artists: Alejandro Aróstegui, June Beer, Pablo Beteda, Manuel García, Arnaldo Guillén, Genaro Lugo, Santos Medina, Carlos Montenegro, Armando Morales, David Ocón, Roger Pérez de la Rocha, Leoncio Sáenz, Orlando Sobalvarro, Luis Urbina, and Leonel Vanegas.

THE CARIBBEAN

344 Archer Straw, Petrine and **Kim Robinson.** Jamaican art: an overview: with a focus on fifty artists. Foreword by David Boxer. Kingston, Jamaica: Kingston Publishers Ltd., 1990. 167 p.: ill. (some col.)

Succinct account of development of 20th-century Jamaican art is essentially a pictorial survey of 50 artists' work with explanatory texts. Well illustrated in both color and b/w. Very important document on Jamaican art.

Bégot, Danielle. Peinture et identité: l'imaginaire du paysage dans la peinture cubaine du XIXe siècle et dans la peinture haïtienne indigéniste. See item **1521.**

345 Building up the future from the past: studies on the architecture and historic monuments in the Dutch Caribbean. Edited by Henry E. Coomans, Michael A. Newton, and Maritza Coomans-Eustatia. Zutphen, Netherlands: Walburg Pers; Curaçao: Univ. Nashonal di Antia, 1990. 268 p.: bibl., ill. (UNA publications; 34)

Richly illustrated volume contains 23 essays on Antillean architecture, interior decoration and furniture, architectural aspects in Papiamentu prose, and on filligree goldsmithery in Curaçao. The articles are organized thematically in three chapters: 1) urban architecture; 2) the history of architecture and historic monuments; and 3) interiors, furniture, and jewellery. [R. Hoefte]

346 Calventi, Rafael. Arquitectura contemporánea en República Dominicana = Contemporary architecture in the Dominican Republic. Santo Domingo: Banco Nacional de la Vivienda, 1986. 222 p.: bibl., ill. (Col. Banco Nacional de la Vivienda)

History of architecture in Dominican Republic from 1914–65, followed by analysis of burst of development that took place from 1965–86 as a result of governmental and pri-

vate sector initiatives to construct public housing, schools, apartments, hotels, banks, and shopping centers. This very important book is profusely illustated.

347 Castillo, Efraim. Oviedo 25 años: trascendencia visual de una historia. Prólogo de Arnulfo Soto. Entrevista de Luis Pérez Casanovas. Santo Domingo: Amigo del Hogar, 1988. 138 p.: ill. (some col.)

Book/catalog of retrospective exhibit of this important artist. Work is analyzed in light of cultural context of Dominican Republic, throwing light on its development during past 25 years. Includes color reproductions and English summary.

348 Conferencia Internacional sobre la Plástica del Caribe, La Habana, 1986. Plástica del Caribe: ponencias de la conferencia internacional, II Bienal de La Habana. La Habana: Editorial Letras Cubanas, 1989. 318 p.: bibl. (Giraldilla)

Seriousness of these papers by such prestigious theoreticians as Juan Acha and Adelaida de Juan renders them obligatory reading. Analyzes and presents theories regarding different aspects of Caribbean culture, almost all dealing with concept of Africanness.

349 Conferencia Internacional sobre Wifredo Lam, La Habana, 1984. Sobre Wifredo Lam: ponencias de la conferencia internacional, I Bienal de La Habana. La Habana: Editorial Letras Cubanas, 1986. 179 p.: bibl. (Giraldilla)

Existing bibliography on Wifredo Lam is enriched by these papers which present new views of his work, many of them polemic in nature. This well organized work is highly recommended.

350 Delgado Mercado, Osiris. Ramón Frade León, pintor puertorriqueño, 1875–1954: un virtuoso del intelecto. San Juan: Centro de Estudios Avanzados de Puerto Rico y el Caribe; Instituto de Cultura Puertorriqueña, Academia Puertorriqueña de la Historia, 1989. 277 p., 36 p. of plates: bibl., ill. (some col.), indexes.

Well illustrated monograph describes life of Puerto Rican artist in unnecessarily minute detail, without attempting to analyze his work or place it in creative context. Contains useful short chronology and catalog of works.

351 Escoffery, Gloria. The Jamaican grand national. (*Jam. J.*, 20:1, Feb./April 1987, p. 61–67, ill.)

Account of 1986 annual national exhibition, analyzing some of the paintings exhibited and problems created by competitions such as this.

352 Gerón, Cándido. Antología de la pintura dominicana = Anthology of Dominican painting. Traducción de Doña Guillermina Nadal. Santo Domingo: Editora Tele 3, 1990. 148 p.: ill. (some col.)

Somewhat incomplete dictionary of Dominican painting covers artists from 1920s-40s, plus a few pioneers born at turn of century. Includes photographs of the artists and a few color reproductions, as well as author's comments on artists' aims. Adds little to knowledge of subject.

353 Gerón, Cándido. Presencia de once pintores dominicanos. Santo Domingo: Editora Taller, 1986. 121 p.: col. ill.

Flamboyant style renders text difficult to read, and analysis of works is superficial and incoherent. Includes important reproductions of works by Ada Balcacer, Antonio Guadalupe, Cándido Bidó, Fernando Peña Delfillo, Elsa Núñez, Dionisio Blanco, Domingo Liz, Antonio Peña, Ivan Tovar, and Tete Marella.

Gjessing, Frederik C. and **William P. MacLean.** Historic buildings of St. Thomas and St. John. See item **1549.**

Gutiérrez, Samuel A. La arquitectura en dos archipiélagos caribeños: estudio comparado de Bocas del Toro, Panamá, y San Andrés y Providencia, Colombia. See item **336.**

Huisken, Jacobine; Friso Lammertse; and **H.J. Scheepmaker.** Curaçao, an island of monuments. See item **1561.**

354 Lerebours, Michel Philippe. Haïti et ses peintres: de 1804 à 1980; souffrances & espoirs d'un peuple. v. 1–2. Préface de Henri Micciolo. Port-au-Prince: Imprimeur II, 1989. 2 v.: bibl., ill.

Doctoral dissertation along traditional academic lines is first complete work on subject. Analyzes painting in relation to other cultural values in Haiti, pointing out achievements which contradict the cliché that all Haitian art is primitive or naive. Includes b/w illustrations. Vol. 2 consists almost entirely of appendices of valuable documents.

355 Llanes, Llilian. Apuntes para una historia sobre los constructores cubanos. La Habana: Editorial Letras Cubanas, 1985. 83 p., 103 p. of plates: bibl., ill. (Col. Arquitectura cubana)

Historical review of origin and development of architectural and engineering professions as related to construction of Republic of Cuba from 19th-century to present. [B. von Barghahn]

356 Marillac, Jules. Jules Marillac, un peintre à la Martinique. Edición de Louis Mézin. Fort-de-France, Martinique: Musées départementaux de la Martinique; La Trinité, Martinique: Gondwana Editions, 1990. 86 p.: bibl., ill. (some col.)

Catalog published to celebrate centennial of Marillac's birth in 1888 gives information on his life and work. Includes illustrations of works from 1920–41. Important in view of scanty information on art of Martinique.

357 Mosquera, Gerard. Primitivismo y contemporaneidad en artistas jóvenes de Cuba. (*Am. Lat./Moscú*, 3, 1987, p. 63–67, photos)

Good illustrated article on three Cuban artists, José Bedia, Flavio Garciandía, and Ricardo Rodríguez Brey. Main theme is artists' interest in "primitivism" as a conceptual base for their work.

358 Norton, Noel. Noel Norton's Trinidad & Tobago. Compiled by Geoffrey MacLean. Port of Spain, Trinidad: Aquarela Galleries, 1988? 156 p.: chiefly col. ill.

Extraordinary color photographs of urban and natural landscape give an all but paradisiacal vision of people, customs, and folk life. Homes of the wealthy are shown alongside those of the poor.

359 Outside Cuba = Fuera de Cuba: an exhibition of contemporary Cuban artists. Edición de Ileana Fuentes-Pérez, Graciella Cruz-Taura, and Ricardo Pau-Llosa. New Brunswick, N.J.: Office of Hispanic Arts, Mason Gross School of the Arts of Rutgers State Univ. of New Jersey, 1987. 366 p.: plates, photos.

History of Cuban painting written by Cuban exiles emphasizes artists who work outside island. Unfortunately, many artists have made an intellectual profession out of their exile. Facts are manipulated, since not everyone left Cuba for the same reasons. Nonetheless, this well printed and profusely illustrated work is necessary for understanding Cuban artistic reality.

360 Pérez-Lizano, Manuel. Arte contemporáneo de Puerto Rico, 1950–1983: cerámica, escultura, pintura. San Juan?: Univ. Central de Bayamón, Ediciones Cruz Ansata, 1985. 324 p.: bibl., ill. (some col.)

Although dedicated to 1955–83 period, book offers useful historical background as far back as turn of century. Divided into sections on ceramics, sculpture, and painting. Gives clear picture of tendencies, periods, and development of individual artists, including biographical information and artists' personal statements. Good reproductions.

361 Pogolotti, Graziella. Oficio de leer. La Habana: Editorial Letras Cubanas, 1983. 176 p. (Col. Crítica)

First chapter is devoted to Cuban artists Víctor Manuel, Carlos Enrique, Mariano, Eduardo Abela, Servando Cabrera Moreno, Antonio Eiriz, and Raúl Martínez. Brief articles analyze work of each. Important essays.

362 Pogolotti, Graziella and **Ramón Vázquez Díaz.** René Portocarrero. Berlin: Henschel; La Habana: Letras Cubanas, 1987. 1 v. (unpaged): bibl., ill. (some col.) (El Mundo del arte)

Complete biography and chronology of Portocarrero, with color and b/w illustrations of principal works. Intelligent thematic and plastic arts analysis is important for understanding Cuban cultural context in which this artist developed.

363 Presencia africana en el arte del Caribe: exhibición de arte organizada por el Instituto de Estudios del Caribe, Facultad de Ciencias Sociales, Universidad de Puerto Rico, del 6 al 30 de septiembre de 1989, Museo de Arte e Historia, San Juan de Puerto Rico. San Juan?: s.n., 1989? 124 p.: bibl., ill. (some col.);

Five good essays written by specialists in visual arts and music, with b/w and color illustrations of paintings, sculptures, and folk art by artists from Barbados, Brazil, Cuba, Haiti, Puerto Rico, Suriname, Trinidad, and the US. Excellent bibliography.

364 Seoane Gallo, José. Eduardo Abela, cerca del cerco. La Habana: Editorial Letras Cubanas, 1986. 580 p.: bibl., ill.

Book is written from three points of view: that of the author, the artist, and his friends. Abela tells his story in a very entertaining fashion and much is added by statements from his 83 friends, among them Wifredo Lam, René Portocarrero, and poet Nicolás Guillén. Includes b/w illustrations.

365 Tananáeva, Larisa. Tiempo de renovación artística: pintura cubana en los años 20 y 30 del siglo XX. (*Am. Lat./Moscú,* 8:104, agosto 1986, p. 77–84, ill.)

Historical survey of development of Cuban painting from 1920–30 analyzes artistic vanguard according to political and social changes of country in that period.

366 Tolentino, Marianne de et al. 100 años de la pintura dominicana. Fotografía de José Ramón Andujar. Coordinación de Freddy Ginebra. Santo Domingo: Brugal, 1989. 291 p.: ill. (some col.), index.

Well illustrated documentary catalog of exhibit at Casa de Bastidas includes artists' biographies. Texts provide serious reflections on development of Dominican art. Important for understanding 20th-century events.

367 La xilografía en Puerto Rico, 1950–1986: exposición. Río Piedras, P.R.: Museo de la Univ. de Puerto Rico, Recinto de Río Piedras; Galería Nacional de Arte Moderno, Santo Domingo, 1987? 90 p.: bibl., ill.

Catalog of exhibit held at National Gallery of Modern Art in Santo Domingo. Reproductions and texts by variety of authors give fairly complete information on evolution of wood-engraving, a technique of fundamental importance for Puerto Rican art.

SOUTH AMERICA
Argentina

368 Alva Negri, Tomás. Alicia Penalba: o de la cadencia musical en la escultura. Buenos Aires: Ediciones de Arte Gaglianone, 1986. 77 p.: ill. ;

Short account of different periods of development of this important Argentine sculptress who died in France. Author compares her work to poetry of Pablo Neruda and César Vallejo and music of Bach and Beethoven: "Her forms, launched into space, resemble the sound effects achieved by the most eminent composer of our day." Does not include plastic arts analysis of her work.

369 Carril, Bonifacio del. Gericault: las litografías argentinas. Buenos Aires?: Emecé Editores, 1989. 30 p.: bibl., ill. (some col.)

Analyzes four lithographs Géricault made of Argentine subjects San Martín, Belgrano, and of the battles of Chacabuco and Maipú, with an interesting account of circumstances in which they were produced.

370 Contrastes visuales: homenaje de la Fundación Bodega J. Edmundo Navarro Correas a doce maestros argentinos; Salas Nacionales de Exposición, del 20 de abril al 10 de mayo de 1987. Buenos Aires: Salas Nacionales de Exposición, 1987. 29 p.: ill. (some col.)

Catalog of exhibit honoring 12 artists selected by a jury as typical of the many schools, techniques, and viewpoints which characterize contemporary Argentine painting. Includes information on Luis Benedict, Marcelo Bonevardi, Juan del Prete, Raquel Forner, Ricardo Garabito, Alfredo Hlito, Rómulo Macció, Guillermo Roux, and Antonio Seguí, as well as specially invited artists Carlos Alonso, Líbero Badii, and Pérez Celis.

371 Diomede, Miguel. Miguel Diomede, 1902–1974: exposición retrospectiva, 3 al 28 de agosto de 1989. Buenos Aires: Secretaría de Cultura de la Nación, Dirección Nacional de Artes Visuales, Salas Nacionales de Exposición, 1989. 1 v.: ill. (some col.)

Although catalog is short, texts and reproductions give adequate idea of importance of this artist for Argentine art scene. Contributors include Jorge Romero Brest, Luis Soane, Elena Poggio, Vicente Caride, and Romualdo Brughetti. Excellent presentation by art critic Osiris Chiérico.

372 Encuentro Nacional de Directores de Museos, 3rd, Mar del Plata, Argentina, 1986. Conclusiones y recomendaciones. Buenos Aires: Ministerio de Educación y Justicia, Secretaría de Cultura de la Nación, Dirección Nacional de Museos; General Pueyrredón: Secretaría de Educación y Cultura

de la Municipalidad del Partido de General Pueyrredón, 1986? 208 p.: ill.

Analysis of museums' responsibilities as instruments of preservation of country's cultural identities. Includes technical reports from four committees which studied "Museums and Identity," "Documentation of Collections," "Patrimony Conservation," and "Regional Museums."

373 Gradowczyk, Mario H. Alejandro Xul Solar, 1887–1963. Buenos Aires: Ediciones Anzilotti, 1988. 71 p.: bibl., ill. (some col.)

Relevant illustrated catalog honors centennial of birth of an artist of fundamental importance in Argentine art history. Includes poems and texts by Jorge Luis Borges, Jorge Calvetti, Cristian Morgenstein, and Xul Solar himself, as well as declarations by some of his friends.

374 King, John. El Di Tella y el desarrollo cultural argentino en la década del sesenta. Traducción de Carlos Gardini. Buenos Aires: Ediciones de Arte Gaglianone, 1985. 309 p.: bibl., ill. (Col. Ensayo)

This historical monograph is obligatory reading for an understanding of artistic events in Argentina since 1960s. Thanks to activity of the Instituto Torcuato Di Tella under the leadership of Jorge Romero Brest, Argentina now has an artistic avant-garde which should carry over into the next two decades. Well documented piece of research on this period, with a few b/w reproductions.

375 Oliveira Cézar, Lucrecia de. Los Guerrico: coleccionistas argentinos. Buenos Aires: Instituto Bonaerense de Numismática y Antigüedades, 1988. 140 p., 45 p. of plates: ill. (some col.)

History of art collecting in Argentina, particulary that of Guerrico family beginning in 1830. Detailed information and inventory of works gives book documentary value.

376 Salón Nacional de Grabado y Dibujo, 24th, Buenos Aires, 1988. Catálogo ilustrado y documental. Buenos Aires: Ministerio de Educación y Justicia, Secretaría de Cultura, Dirección Nacional de Artes Visuales, Salas Nacionales de Exposición, 1988. 88 p.: ill.

Well illustated and documented catalog which gives an idea of contemporary graphic work in Argentina and provides a list of artists and prices of works. Argentine artist Liliana Porter is named special honoree.

377 Squirru, Rafael F. Kenneth Kemble: ensayo crítico biográfico. Buenos Aires: Arte Gaglianone, 1987. 161 p.: bibl., ill. (some col.) (Col. Eveready)

Valuable profile of the man, the artist, and the critic: good analysis of his work; excellent color reproductions and personal photos; and selection of critical writings about his work. Provides important information on Kemble.

378 Whitelow, Guillermo. Raquel Forner. Buenos Aires: Ediciones de Arte Gaglianone, 1980. 186 p.: bibl., ill. (some col.) (Col. Maestros de la pintura)

Excellent study in English and Spanish of Forner's work includes splendid reproductions. Analyzes each period of her artistic development by itself and in relation to local Argentine context.

Bolivia

379 Imaná, Gil. Gil Imaná: obra de 1948 a 1989; exposición antológica, Casa de la Cultura Franz Tamayo, H. Municipalidad de La Paz, octubre-noviembre 1989. La Paz: La Casa, 1989? 1 v.: col. ill.

Catalog is important for its abundant color illustrations showing different periods of Imaná's work from 1949–89. Accompanied by short texts on his work.

380 Romero Moreno, Fernando. Pintura boliviana del siglo XX. Edición, recopilación y fotografía de Pedro Querejazu. La Paz: Ediciones INBO; Banco Hipotecario Nacional, 1989. 317 p.: bibl., ill. (some col.)

Expansive history of 20th-century Bolivian painting is a serious exploration, both historically and artistically, of the different periods and most representative artists. Fully illustrated with color reproductions, monograph includes general information about artists and their contexts.

381 Salazar Mostajo, Carlos. La pintura contemporánea de Bolivia. La Paz: Librería Editorial Juventud, 1989. 269 p., 40 p. of plates: bibl., ill. (some col.)

History of development of contemporary Bolivian painting explains historical details, especially in reference to what author

calls the "Spanish feudalism." One chapter is dedicated to 19th-century painting. Comprehensive text on subject.

Chile

382 Antúnez, Nemesio. Carta aérea: reproducción período, 1944–1988. Edición de Hernán Garfias. Santiago: Editorial Los Andes, 1988. 65 p.: ill. (some col.)

Autobiographical letter written by Antúnez to his son Pablo on artist's 50th birthday analyzes his life and work according to his own vision, giving important statements related to Chilean cultural life. Retrospective exhibition of paintings from 1944–1988. Full color reproductions.

383 Bindis, Ricardo. Marta Colvin: medio siglo de pasión artística. (Atenea/Concepción, 458, 1988, p. 13–41, photos)

Well illustrated article on life of important Chilean sculptress is a short survey of Colvin's life and work. Gives clear idea of her importance in Chilean artistic milieu.

384 Bindis, Ricardo. Rugendas en Chile. Santiago: Editorial Los Andes, 1989. 111 p.: bibl., ill. (some col.)

Fundamental biographical study of this European artist and his painting in relation to Chilean artistic scene during first half of 19th century. Also includes information about Rugendas' visits to Mexico and Brazil. Contains color illustrations and series of b/w drawings.

385 Fotografía chilena contemporánea = Contemporary Chilean photography. Edición de José Luis Granese Philipps. Santiago?: Kodak Chilena, 1985. 127 p.: chiefly ill.

Through b/w reproductions and personal statements, book attempts to show a good number of works by more than 30 artists/photographers who have worked with different techniques using various subjects and images. Gives a good idea of contemporary Chilean photography.

386 Galaz, Gaspar and **Milan Ivelić.** Chile, arte actual. Valparaíso: Ediciones Universitarias de Valparaíso, Univ. Católica de Valparaíso, 1988. 498 p.: bibl., ill., index. (Col. El Rescate)

Extremely comprehensive history of

Chilean contemporary art is complete up-to-date study. Includes many items relevant to understanding development of Chilean art during this century. Fully illustrated book gives wide range of information from visual point of view.

387   Jurado, María Cristina. Zañartu: reproducción período, 1946–1988. Santiago: Editorial Los Andes, 1989. 64 p.: ill. (some col.) (Serie Maestros del siglo XX)

Short anecdotal biography of Chilean artist who was born and has been living in Paris for many years. Artist's personal statements are relevant, as is his extensive curriculum vita. Very well illustrated with works from 1946–88.

388   Matta Echaurren, Roberto Sebastián. Matta: conversaciones. Entrevista de Eduardo Carrasco. Santiago: CENECA; CESOC, 1987. 295 p., 8 leaves of plates: bibl., col. ill. (Ediciones Chile y América)

Using humor and wit, Matta surveys his life and analyzes his painting. This excellent small book testifies to an extremely rich life: artist reveals his experiences—personal, artistic, and intellectual—and his deep knowledge of art and the creative phenomenon.

389   Plástica chilena horizonte universal. Santiago: El Mercurio, 1985. 73 p.: ill. (some col.), ports.

Catalog analyzes work of 15 Chilean artists: Tatiana Alamos, Carmen Aldunate, Samy Benmayor, Claudio Bravo, Mario Carreño, Aura Castro, Marta Colvin, Juan Egenau, Lily Garafulic, Gilda Hernández, Benjamín Lira, Osvaldo Peña, Raúl Valdivieso y Enrique Zañartu. Color reproductions show characteristic work by each artist.

390   Scarpa, Roque Esteban. Madurez de la luz. Concepción, Chile: Editorial de la Univ. de Concepcion, 1986. 138 p.: col. ill.

Poems written by Scarpa based on his contemplation of various artists' paintings and their titles. Each poem is illustrated with reproduction of painting that inspired it. Artists' curricula vitae are provided.

391   Universidad de Concepción (Chile). Generación del 13: colección pinacoteca de la Universidad de Concepción. Santiago: Biblioteca Nacional; Concepción: Univ. de Concepción; Santiago: Banco Concepción, 1987. 35 p.: ill. (some col.)

Very important selection of paintings by 22 artists who belonged to famous "Generación del 13," formed in early 20th century. Includes short biography of each artist as well as reproductions of works. Introduction summarizes Chilean artistic development during first decades of century, emphasizing contributions group made to Chilean modern art.

Colombia

392   50 años, Salón Nacional de Artistas. Edición y selección de Camilo Calderón Schrader. Bogotá: Instituto Colombiano de Cultura, 1990. 363 p.: bibl., ill. (some col.)

Good complete historical survey of this important artistic event in Colombia reproduces documents related to each of 50 salons: rules, list of artists, national and international juries, prices, etc., as well as photos of artists, juries, and works. Informative summary of Colombian art scene during last 50 years.

393   Corradine Angulo, Alberto. Historia de la arquitectura colombiana. v. 1., Colonia, 1538–1850. Cundinamarca, Colombia: Biblioteca de Cundinamarca, 1989. 1 v.: bibl., ill., index.

Historical survey of Colombian architecture from colonial period to 19th century focuses on architecture as a social and artistic discipline, emphasizing symbiotic relationship between urbanism and society and changes this relationship has undergone over time. Extremely well documented and illustrated.

394   Diseño en Colombia. Dirección general de Harry Child Williamson. Diseño y dirección editorial de Gustavo Gómez-Casallas. Bogotá: Prodiseño Ltda., 1989. 129 p.: ill. (some col.)

Good survey of design in Colombia: graphic, environmental, fashion, visual, and textile. Includes broad information about artists and their work, with numerous illustrations.

395   Forma y color Colombia: directorio arte y artistas de Colombia. Bogotá: Editorial Artico, 1989. 350 p.: ill. (some col.), index.

Guide to Colombian art and artists is

dedicated to late Colombian artist Darío Morales (1944–88). Although not a rigorous treatment, book does provide information on galleries, museums, and artists (biographies, addresses, etc.), and is illustrated with color reproductions. Artists are grouped according to decade their work began to be important in the Colombian art scene.

396 Gómez Campuzano, Ricardo. Ricardo Gómez Campuzano. Textos de Guillermo Hernández de Alba y Alvaro Rengifo Pardo. Bogotá: Villegas Editores, 1987. 191 p.: ill. (some col.)

Authors use straightforward language to give complete vision of life and work of this important Colombian artist. Sumptuous book edited as a tribute to Master Gómez Campuzano (1891–1981) is very well illustrated with color photographs. Includes important descriptions and analysis of artist's different creative periods as well as cohesion of subject matter he dealt with: landscapes, portraits, and scenes of daily life.

Gutiérrez, Samuel A. La arquitectura en dos archipiélagos caribeños: estudio comparado de Bocas del Toro, Panamá, y San Andrés y Providencia, Colombia. See item **336.**

397 Mejía de Millán, Beatriz Amelia. El arte colombiano en el siglo XX. Pereira, Colombia: s.n., 1988. 155 p.: bibl., ill. (Col. Universidad Tecnológica de Pereira: Serie Humanística; 1)

Schematic treatment begins with references to 19th-century Colombian art scene. Author dedicates a few lines to each artist and to each movement. More space is dedicated to well known Colombian artistic figures such as Andrés Santamaría, Botero, Villamizar, Negret, Obregón, and Grau.

398 Mendoza, Plinio Apuleyo. Nuestros pintores en París. Fotografía de Ignacio Gómez Pulido y Olga Lucía Jordán. Bogotá?: Ediciones Gamma, 1989. 147 p.: ill. (some col.)

Commentary on and personal anecdotes of two generations of Colombian artists in Paris includes color reproductions of works as well as personal photos of artists. Section on first generation covers Fernando Botero, Emma Reyes, Darío Morales, Luis Caballero, Antonio Barreda, Gregorio Cuartas, Heriberto Cuadrado Cogollo, Saturnino Ramírez, Jairo Tellez, Francisco Rocca and

Gloria Uribe. Coverage of second generation includes Heriberto Sojo, Gustavo Vejarano, Mario Ossaba, Patricia Tavera, María Teresa Viecco, Constanza Aguirre, Víctor Laignclet, Beatríz Duque, Homero Aguilar, Ramiro Arango, Gabriel Silva, Luis Fernando Zapata, and Jaime Gómez.

399 Panesso, Fausto. Alejandro Obregón—¡la visconversa!: conversaciones junto al mar. Bogotá: Ediciones Gamma, 1989. 129 p., 1 leaf of plates: ill. (some col.)

Colombian artist Obregón talks about his life and work, with Panesso commenting. This testimonial book's structure is based on free and spontaneous conversations: some parts are humorous, others are confused. Excellent color reproductions.

400 Paz Jaramillo, María de la. Mujer hombre objeto: julio-septiembre 1984; catálogo de exhibición. Monterrey, Mexico: Museo de Monterrey, 1984? 1 v. (unpaged): ill. (some col.)

Catalog contains introductory text, biographical dates, description of artist's curriculum, and different artistic periods. Important color reproductions.

401 Rodríguez Acevedo, José. José Rodríguez Acevedo: poeta de la piel. Bogotá: Litografía Arco, 1989. 119 p.: ill. (some col.)

Book is of interest only for its color and b/w reproductions. Taken from journals and art reviews, text is an unimportant chronicle of artist's exhibitions which fails to explain his work.

402 Santa María, Rodolfo and **Sergio Palleroni.** Carlos Mijares: tiempo y otras construcciones. Bogotá: Escala, 1989. 203 p.: bibl., ill. (some col.) (Col. SomoSur; 4)

Extensive bilingual English-Spanish text analyzes Mijares' work according to its contribution to development of contemporary Colombian architecture. Explores his incorporation of materials and traditional Colombian designs into architectural language, as well as in naturalistic and landscape values. Very well illustrated with plans, maquettes, drawings, and photographs of buildings.

Ecuador

403 Guayasamín, Oswaldo. El tiempo que me ha tocado vivir. Madrid: Fundación

Guayasamín: Instituto de Cooperación Ibe-roamericana, Quinto Centenario, 1988? 1 v.: ill. (some col.)

Extremely luxurious book is fully illustrated with color and b/w reproductions which show artist's prolific work (1942–88). Texts are personal statements and poetic evocations on his work.

404 Montana, Guido and Lenín Oña. Estuardo Maldonado: del símbolo al dimensionalismo. Introducción de Hernán Rodríguez Castelo. Edición de Estuardo Maldonado. Quito?: Ediciones EM, 1989. 251 p.: ill. (some col.)

Text in English, Spanish, and Italian surveys Maldonado's important work. Also includes extensive curriculum vitae, short introduction, and essays analyzing artist's work. Full color reproductions show his different periods (1947–80s). This impressive, easy-to-read edition is an art book in itself.

Peru

405 Antonio Máro: gemälde zeichnungen Skulpturen "Graphische Reflexionen." Hamburg, Germany: B.Wehn, 1990. l v.: ill.

Valuable catalog includes essay by Bélgica Rodríguez, interview by Lou Blum, and statements by this Peruvian artist, as well as color and b/w photos of his paintings, sculptures, and drawings.

406 Avendaño, Angel. Pintura contemporánea en el Cusco. Lima: Antarki Editores, 1987. 194 p., 52 p. of plates: bibl., ill. (some col.)

Chronological guide to artists and events from "Generación Centenario" to "Terremoto" (1950) and "Los Transeuntes" ends with 1960s "Ileary Group" and 1970s generation, with background information extending back to colonial period. It is difficult to understand author's statement that contemporary painting in Cusco began in 1903.

407 Falcón, Jorge. Simplemente Sabogal: centenario de su nacimiento 1888–1988. Lima: Ediciones Hora del Hombre, 1988. 71 p., 84 p. of plates: bibl., ill. (some col.)

Prologue, an impassioned plea for greater recognition of Sabogal, laments the criticism made of him during his lifetime as an "Indianist" painter. Includes lengthy chronology of artist's life along with good illustrations, but descriptions are so minute as to be bewildering. Contains valuable material on controversy surrounding appearance of Indianist School in Peru.

408 Lika Mutal: Silent Stone. New York: Nohra Haime Gallery, 1989.

Catalog with excellent color reproductions of Mutal's work done 1988–89 exhibited at Nohra Haime Gallery in New York. Includes complete biography of artist.

409 Moll, Eduardo. Ricardo Grau, 1907–1970. Lima: Editorial Navarrete, 1989. 127 p.: ill. (some col.)

Presents Grau as initiator of Modernism in Peru, combating Indianist tendencies in favor of work of universal character. Well illustrated, with lucid texts and ample documentation. Provides important information on art in Peru in first decades of 20th century. Includes interesting introduction by Fernando de Szyzslo.

410 Moll, Eduardo. Víctor Humareda, 1920–1986. Lima: Fondo del Libro, Banco Industrial del Perú, 1987. 217 p.: bibl., ill. (some col.)

Well organized biography of this important Peruvian artist is written in a simple and pleasant style. Well illustrated in b/w and color; also includes some personal photographs. Reproductions cover plastic analysis of paintings.

411 Torres Bohl, José. Apuntes sobre José Sabogal: vida y obra. Lima: Banco Central de Reserva del Perú, Fondo Editorial, 1989. 154 p.: bibl., ill. (some col.)

Views artist's life and work in sociocultural context of Peru from 1920 on. One chapter is dedicated to 1930s and apogee of the Indianist movement led by Sabogal. Provides good background information and color illustrations.

412 Zevallos, Andrés. Boceto biográfico del pintor Mario Urteaga. 2a ed. Lima: Lluvia Editores, 1987. 86 p.: ill. (some col.)

Little more than a first draft, narrative sequence is confusing and includes excessive number of local terms. Makes no attempt to situate artist in historical context. Although mediocre, book is important because it provides information on this important unknown Peruvian artist.

Uruguay

413 Crespi, Ana María and Nelson P. Inda. Renovación urbana: la Calle Piedras. Montevideo: Habitplan Consultores, 1989. 88 p.: bibl., ill. (Col. Documentos de arquitectura; 8)

Synthesizes report presented to the Ibero American Congress on Urbanism (Barcelona, 1988). Presents models and techniques for physical and social recuperation of the old center of Montevideo. Very well illustrated with b/w reproductions.

414 Haber, Alicia and Roberto de Espada. Arte uruguayo contemporáneo: cinco propuestas; Gustavo Alamón, José Pedro Costigliolo, Mario Lorieto, Luis A. Solari, Alfredo Testoni. Prólogo de Jorge Abbondanza. Montevideo: Alianza Francesa; Ediciones de la Banda Oriental, 1984. 93 p.: bibl., ill. (some col.)

Five critical essays, biographical information, and bibliographical list for each of five artists who exhibited their work in the Gallery of the Alliance Française in Montevideo. Emphasizes differences among these five and their importance in contemporary Uruguayan art scene. Color and b/w reproductions.

415 Haber, Alicia. Vernacular culture in Uruguayan art: an analysis of the documentary function of the works of Pedro Figari, Carlos González, and Luis Solari. Edited by Mark D. Szuchman. Miami, Fla.: Latin American and Caribbean Center, Florida International Univ., 1982. 31 p.: bibl., ill. (Occasional papers series; 2)

Analyzes work of three artists and their relationships with local sources of inspiration and international artistic scene. Each artist developed a personal language which became an autonomous expressive system.

416 Pereda, Raquel. Sáez: vida y obra de Carlos Federico Sáez. Montevideo: Ediciones de Jorge de Arteaga y Galería Latina, 1986. 237 p.: bibl., ill. (some col.)

Serious in-depth analysis of this Uruguayan's artistic work also looks at its relationship to 19th-century local cultural context. Author's research provided her with important information on the life of Sáez.

Numerous color reproductions show quality of artist's work.

417 Seis maestros de la pintura uruguaya: Museo Nacional de Bellas Artes, Buenos Aires, Argentina, 15 de setiembre al 15 de octubre de 1987. Organización y coordinación de Embajada del Uruguay en la República Argentina. Presentación del Museo Nacional de Artes Visuales de Montevideo. Buenos Aires: Museo Nacional de Bellas Artes, 1987. 171 p.: bibl., ill. (some col.)

Catalog of an extraordinary exhibition which included: Juan Manuel Blanes, Carlos Federico Sáez, Pedro Figari, Joaquín Torres García, Rafael Barradas, and José Cúneo. Principal text by Angel Kalenberg is fundamental for understanding the paintings of these artists and their relationship to Uruguay's modern art scene. Good documentation, notes, and articles on artists and their works, as well as biographies, make this catalog a very important source of information.

Venezuela

418 Aranguren, Willy. Contribución a la bibliografía de las artes plásticas venezolanas. t. 1, La obra de Juan Calzadilla. Caracas: Fondo Editorial Tropykos, 1989. 1 v.

Complete bibliography of multitudinous writings of critic and historian Juan Calzadilla concerning visual arts in Venezuela includes succinct chronology of Calzadilla's life. Important guide for researchers, historians, and students of Venezuelan art.

419 Botero, Fernando. Botero: la corrida; oleos, acuarelas, dibujos; catálogo de exhibición. Caracas: Museo de Arte Contemporáneo de Caracas: Armitano Arte, 1989. 1 v.: bibl., ill. (some col.) (Catálogo; 90)

Deluxe bilingual catalog with b/w and color reproductions of oils, drawings, and watercolors in the "Corrida" series exhibited at the Museo de Arte Contemporáneo de Caracas contains good information on artist and lengthy biography. Most important text is "Botero habla de Botero."

420 Boulton, Alfredo. El arte en Guri. Milán, Italia: A. Cordani, 1988. 80 p.: chiefly col. ill.

According to author, book was intended to be looked at rather than read. Contains handsome photos of Venezuelan Guayana's natural and "technological" landscapes as well as works of Alejandro Otero ("Torre Solar") and Carlos Cruz Diez ("Ambientación Cromática") which draw on that landscape.

421 Boulton, Alfredo. Homenaje a Alfredo Boulton: una visión integral del arte venezolano. Caracas: Museo de Arte Contemporáneo de Caracas, 1987. 152 p.: bibl., ill. (Catálogo; 83)

Well-printed book issued as catalog of exhibition honoring Venezuelan art historian Boulton reproduces photographs taken by Boulton, a pioneer of artistic photography and art history in Venezuela. Published conversations reveal his profound knowledge of subject.

422 Boulton, Alfredo. Reverón en cien años de pintura en Venezuela = Reverón in one hundred years of painting in Venezuela. Caracas: Museo de Arte Contemporáneo de Caracas, 1989. 132 p.: ill. (some col.) (Catálogo; 91)

Well-illustrated bilingual catalog of exhibit curated by Boulton to commemorate centennial of Reverón's birth contains good selection of works by Reverón and 14 contemporary Venezuelans: Federico Brandt, Rafael Monasterios, Manuel Cabré, Bárbaro Rivas, Marcos Castillo, Francisco Narváez, Héctor Poleo, Alejandro Otero, Jesús Soto, Carlos Cruz Diez, Luisa Richter, Marisol Escobar, Jacobo Borges, and Francisco Salazar. Includes useful short biography of each.

423 Calzadilla, Juan. Armando Reverón: exposición iconográfica y documental en el centenario de su nacimiento. Caracas: Galería de Arte Nacional, 1989. 136 p., 1 p. of plates: bibl., ill. (some col.)

Well-printed, excellently illustrated catalog of exhibit commemorates birth of artist of fundamental importance in Venezuelan modern painting. Text by Juan Calzadilla analyzes Reverón's work, reviews other critics' studies of him, and stresses aspects of paintings which have been considered of "minor" value, claiming they are basic to development of Reverón's characteristic style.

424 Calzadilla, Juan and **María Elena Ramos.** Marietta Berman: cosmovisión. Caracas: Armitano, 1990. 138, 6 p.: bibl., ill. (some col.)

Two studies cover Berman's work from artistic beginnings until her death in 1990. Calzadilla's analysis is historical and concentrates on plastic values. Ramos takes visual images presented by compositions as point of departure for poetic and literary metaphor. Includes important reflections by artist on her life and work and the creative process. Characteristically fine printing and color reproductions from Armitano Editores.

425 Díaz, Mariano. Fabuladores del color. Caracas: Fundación Bigott, 1988. 342 p.: ill. (some col.)

Handsome volume on Venezuelan popular art, introduced by subject specialist Perán Erminy, gives chronological and plastic analysis of development in this area. Díaz is responsible for the excellent photos and poetic texts on the 75 painters and their works. Interesting personal testimony by artists.

426 Diehl, Gaston. Poleo. Traducción de Bélgica Rodríguez. Caracas: Ernesto Armitano, 1989. 131 p.: col. ill., index.

Free translation into Spanish of French critic's analysis of the work and stages of development of Poleo. Gives an important historical account of Venezuelan artistic scene which forms background for several of Poleo's more important stages. Both author and translator are well grounded in subject. Carefully printed; excellent color reproductions.

427 Duarte, Carlos F. Juan Lovera, el pintor de los próceres. Caracas: Fundación Pampero, 1985. 182 p.: bibl., ill. (some col.), index.

Exhaustive, precise study of life and work of this important Venezuelan artist active in first half of 19th century. Includes succinct biography of Lovera and formal, thematic and iconographic analysis of his paintings. This significant new contribution for understanding Lovera's role in Venezuelan art of period is well printed, with excellent color reproductions.

428 Esteva Grillet, Roldán. Rafael Monasterios, un artista de su tiempo. Caracas: Fondo Editorial Tropykos, 1988. 128 p.: bibl., ill.

Generally good study of life and work of Venezuelan painter Rafael Monasterios includes account of Venezuelan artistic development from 1900–1940. However, "oral" testimony is taken from people whose acquaintance with aspects of his life and work is third- or fourth-hand. Abuse of local terms ("pata caliente," "chacota,") makes reading difficult for non-Venezuelans.

429 Guevara, Roberto. Veinticinco años de premios nacionales y el desarrollo del arte contemporáneo en Venezuela, 1961–1986. Caracas: Museo de Arte Contemporáneo de Caracas, 1987. 116 p.: bibl., ill. (some col.)

Catalog with good reproductions of exhibition of works awarded prizes at official salons which have been significant in Venezuelan artistic life since 1938. Resolutions, regulations, and bases governing salons are well documented. Guevara's introduction is vague and shows lack of research: lacks important dates, and complete names of some artists are missing. Nonetheless, this is an important reference work.

430 Komendant, August E. *et al.* Proyecto nueva sede, Galería de Arte Nacional, Caracas = New National Gallery of Art project, Caracas. Caracas: Galería de Arte Nacional, 1986. 77 p.: ill. (some col.)

First book to be published in Venezuela on a specific architectural project has bilingual text and excellent reproductions. Published by Fundación Pampero with aim of obtaining support for construction of new headquarters for the Galería de Arte Nacional, at that time under the direction of Bélgica Rodríguez. Authors of architectural project were Oscar Tenreiro and Francisco Sesto.

431 Padilla Bravo, Iván. Caracas, sus esquinas: imágenes y anhelos. Fotografía de Nélida Mosquera. Caracas: Panapo, 1988. 225 p.: bibl., ill.

Romantically nostalgic description of colonial Caracas with its red-tiled roofs. Interesting book, well-documented with photographs, explains in simple terms the urban and architectural changes Caracas has undergone since colonial times.

432 Rodríguez, Bélgica. Ramón Vásquez Brito: el hombre, el artista. Fotografía de Mariano Aldaca. Caracas?: Armitano, 1986? 134 p.: bibl., ill. (some col.)

Monograph on this Venezuelan artist

contains plastic analysis of his paintings as well as an historical account of his life and stages of development. Carefully printed; excellent color reproductions.

433 Sola Ricardo, Ricardo de. La reurbanización "El Silencio:" crónica 1942–1945. Caracas: Armitano, 1988. 320 p.: ill.

Important compilation of photographs and documents relating to construction of "El Silencio" project in central Caracas, analyzed as redevelopment of a marginal district into housing for middle class.

434 Velásquez, Lucila. Mateo Manaure: arte y conciencia. Caracas: Armitano, 1989. 127 p.: ill. (some col.)

Monograph on important Venezuelan artist begins by stressing lack of attention given at home to Manaure's indubitable talents, even though this is counterfactual. Good detailed account, in poetic language, of artist's life and stages of development. Does not include plastic analysis of his work or reference to cultural context in which it appeared. Excellent color reproductions.

435 Zawisza, Leszek M. Arquitectura y obras públicas en Venezuela: siglo XIX. v. 1–3. Caracas: Ediciones de la Presidencia de la República, 1988–1989. 3 v.: bibl., ill.

Highly exact study with abundant information on history of 19th-century architecture in Venezuela clearly shows change from modest colonial buildings to eclectic constructions of the 1800s. Analyzes development of architecture in relation to historical events and political, social, and economic situation with emphasis on the influence of upper-class taste on changes in building styles. Includes precise analysis of different types of public buildings and squares, prisons, and constructions for domestic purposes. Profusely illustrated with plans, views of cities, and photographs of buildings.

436 Zawisza, Leszek M. León Achiel Jerome Hoet, un ingeniero de la vieja Maracaibo. Maracaibo, Venezuela: Ars Gráfica, 1989. 225 p.: bibl., ill., maps.

Historical study of development of architecture in Maracaibo as seen in work of Belgian engineer Hoet, who practically designed the city. Ample documentation of presence of Belgian citizens and products in Venezuelan life of the day.

BRAZIL

JOSE M. NEISTEIN, *Executive Director, Brazilian-American Cultural Institute, Washington*

FEW BUT MOSTLY FINE ENTRIES mark the Brazilian subsections this year, with the exceptions of the "20th Century" and "City Planning, Architecture, and Landscape Architecture" subsections, which are proportionally larger in number and significance.

Among reference and theoretical works, the overall view of the São Paulo Biennials from 1951 to 1987 (item **437**) should be mentioned both for its wealth of information, as well as for the intrinsic importance of the institution itself. The dictionary of Indian crafts (item **441**) is very useful as it includes Latin and English equivalents, the catalog of the Brazilian art collection of the São Paulo "Pinacoteca" is a welcome tool for reference and research (item **438**).

Although lacking scholarship, "O barroco carioca" (item **447**) calls our attention to a lesser known field of colonial art in Brazil, namely the Baroque movement in Rio de Janeiro. Colonial painting, less studied than the other arts of the period is examined in the Bahian context by Ott (item **449**). Studies of the Dutch presence in 17th-century Pernambuco are gradually increasing as well (item **446**).

As 19th-century Brazilian fashion is not often researched, the pioneering study by Gilda de Mello e Souza is most welcome (item **454**). The contribution of German romantic painting to the development of Brazilian national culture was remarkable; Peixoto's handsome book does it justice, enriched with much information (item **452**).

As in previous volumes of the *Handbook*, the 20th-century subsection is the richest, both in terms of the quantity and quality of entries. Sacramento's book on Martins de Porangaba (item **469**) introduces to an international audience one of Brazil's very creative and vital modern painters, now reaching his first major artistic peak. The catalog of the "Modernidade" show in Paris is a gathering of information about the most comprehensive show of its kind ever exhibited abroad, or in Brazil (item **465**). A broad overview of Brazilian muralism is offered for the first time (item **456**) and the fine monograph on Gomide was long overdue (item **470**). Rubens Guerchman, who pioneered contemporary urban painting in Brazil, is the subject of an insightful book (item **461**). Cocchiarde and Berger's research highlights the many facets of the important 1950s abstract art movement, (item **455**). Pontual provides a catalog of Gilberto Chateaubriand's collection of 20th-century Brazilian art, the most important collection of its kind in Brazil (item **467**).

Folk art, Indian traditions and Afro-Brazilian traditions, otherwise rich avenues for Brazilian creativity, have not received enough scholarly attention in recent years. Each of these topics is represented by only one albeit a very fine book (items **472, 484, and 485**).

On the other hand, city planning, architecture and landscape architecture received much scholarly attention. Worthy of note are Fabris' book on eclecticism in Brazil (item **476**), Xavier's extensive monograph on modern architecture in Porto Alegre (item **483**), and Silva's in-depth research on Luso-Brazilian architecture in Maranhão (item **480**).

Included under the "Miscellaneous" category is Luiz Goldino's thorough and welcome study of the prehistory of Brazilian art (item **489**).

REFERENCE AND THEORETICAL WORKS

437 **Amarante, Leonor.** As bienais de São Paulo, 1951 a 1987. São Paulo: BFB; Projeto, 1989. 407 p.: bibl., ill. (some col.), indexes, ports.

Book celebrates 38 years of São Paulo Biennial. Of seminal importance for both artists and public alike, this institution was a major forum for the exchange and discussion of aesthetic ideas in Brazil, and at times, in the world. Handsomely produced book brings together a wealth of texts, reproductions, and photographs.

438 **Brazil. Estado de São Paulo. Pinacoteca do Estado.** Pinacoteca do Estado: catálogo geral de obras. São Paulo: Impr. Oficial do Estado, 1988. 447 p.: bibl., ill. (some col.), index.

Public collection assembled by government of São Paulo state from the larger traditional local families and purchases dating back to 1911 is one of the most comprehensive in the country. The "Pinacoteca" current collection, with nearly 3,500 works of paintings, sculptures, drawings, prints, photographs, and decorative arts, contains mostly Brazilian artists reflecting the tastes of several generations. Comprehensive catalog gives account of most of them, making it a welcome tool for reference and research.

439 **Lucarelli, Francesco.** Ouro Preto e Olinda: centri storici del Brasile "memória" per l'umanità. Contributo di Elvira Macchiarolli Petroncelli. Napoli: Edizioni scientifiche italiane, 1985. 373 p., 50 p. of plates: bibl., ill. (some col.).

Gradual scientific approach to restoration and conservation is taking over from more empirical, intuitive traditional methods. Political and social complexities are not to be underestimated. This study was supported in part by UNESCO, as Ouro Preto and Olinda have been declared universal monuments. Phenomenological investigation of great interest.

440 **Ostrower, Fayga.** Acasos e criação artística. Rio de Janeiro: Editora Campus, 1990. 289 p.: bibl., ill. (some col.), indexes.

A fine artist herself, Ostrower examines art and artistic creativity from the point of view of chance and necessity, using examples from both universal and Brazilian art. Topics include perception, meaning, forms and expressiveness, space and growth, computers and artistic forms, creation and style. Original contribution to ever intriguing mystery of artistic creativity.

441 **Ribeiro, Berta G.** Dicionário do artesanato indígena. Ilustrações de Hamilton Botelho Malhano. Belo Horizonte: Editora Itatiaia; São Paulo: Editora da Univ. de São Paulo, 1988. 343 p., xx p. of plates : ill. (some col.) (Col. Reconquista do Brasil; 3a. sér. especial, vol. 4)

Scholarly dictionary covers virtually all craft media of vast majority of Indian tribes in Brazil. Explains many technicalities and gives Latin and English equivalents. Many drawings and photographs complement texts.

442 **Schenberg, Mário.** Pensando a arte. São Paulo: Nova Stella, 1988. 221 p.: ill. (some col.)

Original interpretive contribution to the understanding of modern Brazilian art. Recently deceased physicist and art critic Mário Schenberg wrote extensively on the creative process of many Brazilian artists. Book gathers some of his most insightful texts written 1944–84. Covers most major trends, and includes plentiful and excellent reproductions.

443 **Strunck.** Identidade visual: a direção do olhar. Rio de Janeiro: Edição Europa, 1989. 123 p.: bibl., ill. (some col.)

Conceptual thinking has been partially replaced by visual thinking in recent decades. This study focuses on Brazilian style of visual civilizaton. Author points out that visual absorption of information takes considerably longer than the verbal process. Uses many examples from Brazilian visual systems and graphics.

COLONIAL PERIOD

444 **Artistas e artífices do Brasil: séculos XVI, XVII e XVIII.** São Paulo: Museu de Arte de São Paulo Assis Chateaubriand, 1977. 104 p.: ill. (some col.)

Over 70 private collectors from São Paulo loaned 240 significant works to this exhibition. Virtually all areas of Brazilian colonial art were represented at the show, the vast majority of which are reproduced in b/w and color in this valuable publication. (Not previously annotated in *HLAS*.)

445 Franceschi, Humberto Moraes. O ofício da prata no Brasil: Rio de Janeiro. Rio de Janeiro: Studio HMF, 1988. 325 p.: bibl., ill.

During a good part of Portuguese colonization of Brazil, silver was the precious metal by which wealth was measured. Quality of silver used and the objects created had to meet the highest standards for both secular and religious uses. Lisbon exercised tight control over silversmiths, many of whom worked on both sides of the Atlantic. Eventually, Brazil's output became distinctive. This book, a landmark on the subject, gives full coverage of the field, focusing on production in Rio de Janeiro from 17th-18th centuries. Includes excellent silvertone reproductions.

446 Imagens do Brasil holandês, 1630–1654. Texto de Evaldo Cabral de Mello. Rio de Janeiro?: Ministério da Cultura, Fundação Nacional Pró-Memória, 1987. 133 p.: facsims., ill. (some col.), ports.

Dutch presence in 17th-century Pernambuco left uneven imprints and documentation in Brazil. Much remains to be researched both in public and private archives and collections. This monograph gives an overview of Brazil reflected in the arts, crafts, and books produced by Dutch in 17th century. Useful, but all too short, text introduces this rather brief account.

447 Machado, Júlio César. O Barroco carioca. Rio de Janeiro: Rio Arte; GRD, 1987. 158 p.: bibl., ill. (some col.)

Although considerably less well known than their counterparts in Bahia, Minas, and Pernambuco, Baroque and rococo in Rio de Janeiro are nonetheless relevant in the Brazilian context. Although not very scholarly, publication gives fairly good idea of the variety in architecture, sculpture, and painting yet to be studied in depth. Author's illustrious predecessor was Clarival do Prado Valladares, who published *Barroco carioca* in 1977.

448 O Museu de Arte Sacra da Universidade Federal da Bahia. Redação de Pedro Moacir Maia. São Paulo: Banco Safra, 1987. 296 p.: chiefly ill. (some col.)

This museum is one of the best of its kind in the world and this book does it justice. P.M. Maia's insightful introductory essay and notes convey the richness and variety of this collection of Brazilian sacred art, while also highlighting museum's architectural beauty and high quality of the installation. Superb color reproductions.

449 Ott, Carlos. A escola bahiana de pintura, 1764–1850. Redação de Emanoel Araújo. São Paulo?: MWM Diesel, 1982. 153 p.: bibl., ill. (some col.)

Colonial architecture and sculpture in Bahia have been studied in depth since the 1940s, but as painting has not, this comprehensive, encompassing study is most welcome. In fact, this book is the result of 35 years of research in libraries and archives, as well as direct observation in many churches. José Teófilo de Jesus, José Joaquim da Rocha, and José Rodrigues Nunes are the major painters studied.

19TH CENTURY

450 150 anos de pintura no Brasil: 1820–1970. Ilustrado pela coleção de Sergio Sahione Fadel. Rio de Janeiro: Colorama Editora Artes Gráficas, 1989. 490 p.: col. ill.

Several essays from different perspectives introduce book: Ferreira Gullar gives insightful overall view of Brazilian art from 1820–1970; Rogério Falia throws new light on Brazilian 19th century. Includes good, but not extensive, bio-bibliographical information. Great variety and excellent quality reproductions.

451 Levy, Carlos Roberto Maciel. Giovanni Battista Castagneto, 1851–1900: o pintor do mar. Rio de Janeiro: Edições Pinakotheke, 1982. 235 p.: bibl., ill. (some col.), index.

Son of modest Italian immigrants from Liguria, Castagneto grew up and studied in Rio, and later in Toulon, France. He eventually became Brazil's most illustrious and creative seascape painter. It took many decades for Brazilian critics and art historians to realize his brilliance and sense of freedom vis-à-vis academy. This study, rich in details and critical insights, does him justice.

Poor color reproductions unfortunately tarnish an otherwise welcome book.

452 Peixoto, Maria Elizabete Santos. Pintores alemães no Brasil durante o século XIX = Deutsche Maler in Brasilien in XIX Jahrhundert = German painters in Brazil during the XIX century. Rio de Janeiro: Edições Pinakotheke, 1989. 244 p.: bibl., ill. (chiefly col.), indexes.

In the 19th century Brazil established and differentiated her national culture, in part due to the assimilation of international influences. Presence of some fine German romantic and late romantic painters was certainly a major contribution to the arts. Friedrich Hagedorn, Eduard Hildebrandt, Johann Georg Grimm, D.W. von Thevemin, and J.M. Rugendas are only a few among many others. Luxurious book includes extraordinary reproductions and much information.

453 Pinto, Lourdes Noronha. Antigas fazendas do Rio Grande do Sul. Porto Alegre, Brazil: Fundação Moinho Santista, 1989. 213 p.: ill. (some col.)

Beginning in the 18th century, farms expanded down the Jacuí river towards the South, where cattle was raised. Society there soon became affluent and, thanks to the Portuguese from Alentejo, a new, local, idiomatic architecture developed. Handsome book brings that tradition back to life, enhanced by clear historical descriptions and stylistic discussions. Excellent color photographs.

454 Souza, Gilda de Mello e. O espírito das roupas: a moda no século dezenove. São Paulo: Companhia das Letras, 1987. 255 p.: bibl., ill.

With sharp insights and accuracy, author captures fashion and its changes in 19th-century mass urban society of savage capitalism: happy few versus new emergent classes; provincial farmers as opposed to rich cosmopolitan farmers. Of special interest is discussion of fashion in 19th-century Brazil as seen from the social and political context vis-à-vis European perspectives.

20TH CENTURY

455 Abstracionismo, geométrico e informal: a vanguarda brasileira nos anos cinqüenta. Compilação de Fernando Cocchiarale e Anna Bella Geiger. Rio de Janeiro: FUNARTE, Instituto Nacional de Artes Plásticas, 1987. 308 p.: bibl., ill. (some col.), index. (Temas e debates; 5)

Fine contribution to history of contemporary Brazilian art gathers basic information, texts, interviews, iconography, and chronology on informal and geometrical abstract art, the two main trends in Brazil in 1950s. Differentiation of both tendencies enriched those avant-garde years and stimulated a creative interchange with European and US trends. Extensive bibliography.

456 Artistas do muralismo brasileiro = Brazilian mural artists. São Paulo?: Volkswagen do Brasil, 1988. 216 p.: col. ill.

Muralism is a new tradition in Brazil which started in the late 1930s with Portinari, who was influenced by the Mexican muralists. In the past five decades, many murals have been produced all over Brazil, and they often reflect aesthetic trends predominant in the years of their production. Handsome book gives glimpse into this rich and relatively little-known field, one that has become distinctly Brazilian over the years.

457 Bienal Internacional de São Paulo, 19th, São Paulo, 1987. Em busca da essência: elementos de redução na-arte brasileira. São Paulo: Fundação Bienal de São Paulo, 1987. 69 p.: bibl., ill. (chiefly col.)

"In Search of Essence," treating the theme of elements of reduction, was one of the representative shows of Brazilian art at the 19th São Paulo Biennial. Formal emptiness and expressiveness, the example given by Malevitch to his Brazilian followers, were brought together at this highly conceptual and intense exhibition.

458 Bienal Internacional de São Paulo, 19th, São Paulo, 1987. Imaginários singulares. São Paulo: Fundação Bienal de São Paulo, 1987. 131 p.: bibl., ill. (some col.)

"Unique Image Creators" was an exhibition that displayed a selection of Brazilian "fantastic" art at the 19th São Paulo Biennial. Primitivism and utopia were the main themes. Catalog reproduces all works selected both in color and b/w. Each artist is introduced by a biographical text. Curator Sheila Leirner wrote the text on controversies of the field; includes additional texts by Paulo Venancio Filho, Sônia Salzstein-Golberg and Ivo Mesquita.

459   Bracher, Carlos. Bracher. Redação de Olívio Tavares de Araújo. São Paulo: Métron, 1989. 176 p.: ill. (some col.)

An expressionist who has been painting alongside and even against the main streams of Brazilian painting in recent decades, Carlos Bracher has created a language of his own, meriting critical attention of some of Brazil's most noted theoreticians. This book gathers some of their best essays. Excellent color reproductions.

460   Furrer, Bruno. Carybé. Apresentação de Antônio Celestino. Introdução de Jorge Amado. Textos de Carybé, Lídia Besouchet, e José Cláudio da Silva. Pesquisa e biografia de Gardênia Melo. Salvador, Brazil: Odebrecht, 1989. 452 p.: ill. (chiefly col.)

An Argentine of Italo-Argentine parents, Carybé chose an Afro-Brazilian name for himself, and early in life adopted Brazil as his country. Over the past four decades he has become one of the most expressive artists of the Bahia region and its traditions. Splendidly printed book celebrates his life in art.

461   Gerchman, Rubens. Gerchman. Texto de Wilson Coutinho. Rio de Janeiro: Salamandra, 1989. 208 p.: ill. (chiefly col.)

Gerchman pioneered contemporary urban painting in Brazil by capturing the masses, the changes, the political faces of Brazilian cities from 1960s to late 1980s, becoming the visual chronicler of Rio de Janeiro. Kitsch and glamour, grandeur and banality, eroticism and manipulation converged on his canvasses, and an anti-rhetorical interpretation of the suburbs was brought to bear. Insightful essays; many excellent color reproductions.

462   Klintowitz, Jacob. O ofício da arte: a pintura. São Paulo, Brasil: SESC, 1987. 265 p.: col. ill.

Main theme is that Brazilian contemporary art is a vital statement of Brazil, and its international legitimacy is one of the consequences. Relationship between creative artists and national culture permeates entire book, and non-historical expressionism is focused upon as one of Brazil's most legitimate models of expression. Painting is chosen as

the artistic medium *par excellence*, and very representative artists were selected to portray Brazil's creativity. Fine selection of illustrations, excellent reproductions.

463   Klintowitz, Jacob. O ofício da arte: a escultura. São Paulo: SESC, 1988. 271 p.: col. ill.

Representative collection of Brazilian 20th-century sculptures by artists of several generations and diverse aesthetic orientations. Text is speculative and reflexive, rather than scholarly. Wealth of photographs conveys some of richness and variety of modern Brazilian sculpture, including folk sculpture, urban avant-garde, neo-classic, and an essay on use of materials.

464   Loureiro, Rita. Boi tema. Apresentação de Gilda de Mello e Souza. Rio de Janeiro: Philobiblion; São Paulo: Editora da Univ. de São Paulo, 1987. 22 p., 23 p. of plates: bibl., col. ill. (Col. Arte, sempre; 1)

After a very promising start as illustrator of *Macunaíma*, Rita Loureiro has gone on to become one of the most inventive contemporary Brazilian painters. This series, reminiscent of Bosch, Goya, and the Quattrocento, recreates Amazonian legends and folk celebrations, melding high European traditional standards with deep regional roots. Includes excellent introduction by Souza. Acceptable color reproductions.

465   Modernidade: art brésilien du 20e siècle; Musée d'art moderne de la ville de Paris, 10 décembre 1987–14 février 1988. Paris: Ministère des affaires étrangères, Association française d'action artistique, 1987. 426 p.: bibl., ill. (some col.), ports.

Catalog of most comprehensive panorama of 20th century Brazilian art ever shown abroad. Exhibition focused on the 1922 Week of Modern Art and its descendants in the following decades. Paris was chosen as the site because of its being the very center of international "modernité," but also because Brazilian artists and intellectuals rediscovered Brazil from the Parisian vantage. Many insightful essays, rich photographic documentation and excellent color reproductions make this a unique, most useful publication.

466   Monteiro, Fernando. Brennand. Fotografia de Tadeu Lubambo. Rio de Janeiro: Spala Editora, 1987. 143 p.: ill. (chiefly col.)

Plush, lavishly illustrated book treats unique Brazilian potter and his splendid studio in Pernambuco. Text focuses on artist's life as intertwined with his output, and his monumental sense of posterity. Grotesqueries, sensuous forms, and tropical colors give Brennand a special space among contemporary ceramicists.

467 Pontual, Roberto. Entre dois séculos: arte brasileira do século XX na Coleção Gilberto Chateaubriand. Rio de Janeiro: Editora JB, 1987. 585 p., 4 p. of plates: bibl., ill. (some col.), index.

Chateaubriand has been collecting since the early 1950s, assembling nearly 3,000 works, mainly paintings and drawings, in what has become the most important and comprehensive collection of 20th-century Brazilian art. Literally all major artists and trends are represented in this collection, now housed in Rio's Museum of Modern Art. Excellent text by Pontual, plus a wealth of information and many high quality reproductions.

468 Portinari, Cândido. Arte sacra. Apresentação de Alceu Amoroso Lima. Comentários de Bruno Palma. Rio de Janeiro: Edições Alumbramento, 1982. 123 p.: ill. (some col.)

Portinari was not a religious man, but his religious art is no less genuine because of this. He brings together Earth and Heaven, the modern and the eternal, in something akin to the spirit of the Renaissance. Includes an inspiring introductory essay by Alceu Amoroso Lima. Very fine color reproductions.

469 Sacramento, Enock. Martins de Porangaba. São Paulo: Y. Sanematsu, 1988 or 1989. 117 p.: bibl., ill. (some col.)

Basically self-taught, in spite of having enjoyed some formal training, Martins de Porangaba gives a highly personal response to Matisse, Braque, and Picasso. His vivid colors and cubistic and expressionistic approaches reveal a very talented painter now reaching his first peak: this is what Sacramento's book celebrates. Biographical information and critical discussion are complemented by excellent color reproductions and b/w photographs.

470 Vernaschi, Elvira. Gomide. São Paulo: Indústria Freios KNORR; MWM Motores Diesel; Univ. de São Paulo, 1989. 247 p.: bibl., ill. (some col.)

It has been said many times that Gomide was Brazil's best representative at the School of Paris. From his Art Deco beginning to his nativistic peak in 1960, this well-documented and handsomely printed book unfolds the itinerary of one of Brazil's finest 20th century painters. Also discusses his ties to the Renaissance.

471 Vieira, Ivone Luzia. A Escola Guignard na cultura modernista de Minas, 1944–1962. Pedro Leopoldo, Brazil: Companhia Empreendimento Sabará, 1988. 164 p.: bibl., ill. (some col.)

Guignard embodied modernism in Minas Gerais in a most personal way: he was seminal in teaching and supporting a whole new generation of Brazilian artists in the school that bears his name today. Details on how he influenced students and the ensuing creativity of the best of them are assembled here. Extensive and intensive historical and critical texts are complemented by excellent color reproductions.

FOLK ART

472 Artistas da cerâmica brasileira. São Paulo: Volkswagen do Brasil, 1985. 200 p.: chiefly col. ill.

Folk ceramicists from Caruarú, Jequitinhonha, and Taubaté, along with urban ceramic artists from São Paulo, Porto Alegre, Rio de Janeiro, and many other places exemplify the variety of technique and aesthetic trends in this medium. Extraordinary photography.

PHOTOGRAPHY

473 Maranhão. Fotografia de Pedro Oswaldo Cruz. São Paulo: Alcoa; Rio de Janeiro: Spala Editora, 1981. 200 p.: bibl., chiefly ill. (some col.)

Gorgeous book of photographs, perhaps the most beautiful ever printed on Maranhão. Chapters on architecture and on glazed tiles highlight the best of São Luís and Alcântara, but also illustrate how neglected most of these masterpieces are: ravages of time will require much conservation work to restore.

474 Santos, Angelo Oswaldo de Araújo. Ouro Preto: tempo sobre tempo = time upon time. Fotografia de Rui Cézar dos Santos. Rio de Janeiro: Spala Editora, 1985. 179 p.: bibl., col. ill.

Stunning book of photography on Ouro Preto's topography, city planning, architecture, painting, sculpture, and uniqueness. Includes many extraordinary details.

CITY PLANNING, ARCHITECTURE, AND LANDSCAPE ARCHITECTURE

475 Atlas dos monumentos históricos e artísticos de Minas Gerais: circuito de Santa Bárbara. v. 2, Região de Santa Bárbara, pt. 1. Belo Horizonte, Brazil: Secretaria de Estado do Planejamento e Coordenação Geral, Fundação João Pinheiro, Assessoria Técnica da Presidência, 1981. 1 v.: bibl.

This book on historic and artistic monuments includes minute details on city planning, architecture, sculpture, and painting of Santa Bárbara region in Minas Gerais, from its peak to downturn of gold cycle. Underscores role of religious brotherhood.

476 Lemos, Carlos Alberto Cerqueira et al. Ecletismo na arquitetura brasileira. Organização de Annateresa Fabris. São Paulo: Nobel; Edusp, 1987. 296 p.: bibl., ill.

Eclecticism in Brazil used to be synonymous with modernity and modernization. Ironically this first and most encompassing study arrives at a moment when real estate speculation is rapidly devastating whatever remains of this kind of architecture in Brazil. Includes examples from Rio, São Paulo, Minas, Pará, Pernambuco, Ceará, and Rio Grande do Sul. Many b/w photographs.

477 Mello Júnior, Donato. Rio de Janeiro: planos, plantas e aparências. Rio de Janeiro: Galeria de Arte do Centro Empresarial Rio, 1988. 267 p.: bibl., ill., maps.

In-depth study of several city planning projects in Rio de Janeiro's history. Parallel approach covers both technical demands and historical needs and makes this book an excellent source.

478 Moreno, Carlos A.B. et al. A gráfica urbana. São Paulo: Prefeitura do Município de São Paulo, Secretaria Municipal de Cultura; Centro de Documentação e Informação sobre Arte Brasileira Contemporânea, 1982. 91 p.: bibl., ill. (Cadernos; 7)

Studies presence of graphic expression in São Paulo city. Realism and abstraction, architecture as backing, graphics and landscape are some of the main themes. This original contribution contains many photographic examples, along with descriptive and polemical texts.

479 Segawa, Hugo M.; Cecília Rodrigues do Santos; and Ruth Verde Zein. Arquiteturas no Brasil, anos 80. São Paulo: Projeto Editores Associados, 1988? 1 v.: bibl., col. ill.

Landmarks of Brazilian architecture from mid 1940s to late-1980s are discussed by geographical region, grouped according to private or public use. Includes excellent color photographs, but no plans. Discusses technical details and aesthetic approaches.

480 Silva F., Olavo Pereira da. Arquitetura luso-brasileira no Maranhão. Brazil: Efecê Editora, 1986. 177 p.: bibl., ill. (some col.)

Maranhão did not reach its peak until second half of 19th century. When the Portuguese regained São Luís from the French in 1616, they developed their own orthogonal grid-patterned city plan and covered the many two story houses they had built with glazed tiles. Characterized by rural aristocracy in the beginning followed by urban textile industrialists, Maranhão testifies to strong presence of Portuguese architecture in religious, military, and civil buildings for 300 years. Styles, techniques, and materials are described with many details and abundant illustrations.

481 Torres, Mário Henrique Glicério. Palácio das Laranjeiras. Apresentação de Zoé Noronha Chagas Freitas. Fotografia de Pedro Oswaldo Cruz. Rio de Janeiro: Governo do Estado do Rio de Janeiro, BANERJ: SOBREART, 1982. 207 p., 7 p. of plates: bibl., ill. (some col.)

Laranjeiras Palace, the residence of the governor of Rio de Janeiro, is one of the gems of turn-of-the-century Brazil. Inspired by

French Belle Époque architecture, this building ended up being one of the very symbols of Rio's Belle Époque. Now fully restored to its original splendor, including paintings, sculptures, and furniture, this former residence of the Guinles is topic of this luxurious book. Also focuses upon decorative arts, lavish architectural details, and harmony of several different styles.

482 Vital Brazil, Alvaro. 50 anos de arquitetura. São Paulo: Nobel, 1986. 158 p.: bibl., ill., plans.

Opening of "Esther Building" in downtown São Paulo fifty years ago was a true splash. Its architect, Vital Brazil, always understood that architecture is the expression of a culture and an epoch. Long neglected, Vital's output and contribution to modern Brazilian architecture are now finally receiving the attention they deserve. Fine monograph is complemented by many plans and photographs.

483 Xavier, Alberto and **Ivan Mizoguchi.** Arquitetura moderna em Porto Alegre. Porto Alegre: FAUFRGS; São Paulo: Pini, 1987. 403 p.: ill., maps (some col.), indexes.

Excellent guide assembles, discusses, and illustrates chronologically (1945–83) a great variety of projects including high-rises, commercial buildings, private homes, banks, hospitals, gymnasiums, public buildings, industrial parks, and campuses.

AFRO-BRAZILIAN AND INDIAN TRADITIONS

484 Art plomari del Brasil: Fundació Joan Miró, Parc de Montjuïc, Barcelona, 16 de juny-21 d'agost de 1988. Barcelona: Fundació Joan Miró-Centre d'Estudis d'Art Contemporani, 1988? 63 p.: bibl., ill. (some col.)

Amazonian Indian feather art is now known internationally. This Barcelona exhibit, representative of several cultures, encompasses other areas of Brazil as well. Includes map of tribal groups' locations, excellent color reproductions, and texts by Fragoso, Nicola, Dorta, and Rowell.

485 A mão afro-brasileira: significado da contribuição artística e histórica. Organização de Emanoel Araújo. São Paulo:

TENENGE, Técnica Nacional de Engenharia, 1988. 398 p.: bibl., ill. (chiefly col.)

Afro-Brazilians' contribution to arts in Brazil has always been enormous. This luxurious book illustrates their major presence in architecture, sculpture, painting, decorative arts, and performing arts, from 17th-century to present. Texts convey a wealth of insights and information.

MISCELLANEOUS

486 Bardi, Pietro Maria. O ouro no Brasil. São Paulo: Banco Sudameris Brasil, 1988. 102 p.: bibl., ill. (some col.) (Arte e cultura; 11)

Over the centuries gold played a major role in Brazilian economy, art, jewelry, and numismatics. Text and illustrations cover all these aspects. Of special interest for this section is the chapter "Arte e Cultura."

487 Batista, Marta Rossetti and **Yone Soares de Lima.** Coleção Mário de Andrade: artes plásticas. São Paulo: Instituto de Estudos Brasileiros, Univ. de São Paulo, 1984. 373 p.: ill. (some col.)

Mário de Andrade was a consistent art collector throughout his life. After his death, his family sold Andrade's remarkable collection to the Univ. of São Paulo, along with his library, many of his manuscripts, and papers. Of all the segments, the one devoted to 20th-century Brazilian art—which he influenced in such a seminal way—is the most representative. This catalog is the standard work on the subject, a model in its own right.

488 Carelli, Mario. Brasil-França, cinco séculos de sedução = Cinq siècles de séduction, France-Brésil. Fotografia de Ivan Lima. Rio de Janeiro: Espaço e Tempo, 1989. 126 p.: ill. (some col.)

Ever since Rabelais' *Vie inestimable du grand Gargantua, père de Pantagruel* (1534), the French concept of the "marvelous" New World has been sustained by the "uniqueness" of Brazil. Beginning in 1503, French expeditions to Brazil were frequent. Although the "France Antartique" colony in Rio lasted only 3 years, the cultural, intellectual, and artistic presence of France in Brazil has been continuous for five centuries, as has France's attraction to Brazil. Last chapter is devoted to Brazil's artistic presence in France.

489 Galdino, Luiz. Itacoatiaras: uma pré-história da arte no Brasil = Itacoatiaras: a prehistory of art in Brazil. Tradução de Alasdair G. Burman. São Paulo: Editora Rios, 1988. 255 p.: bibl., ill. (some col.)

Galdino traveled all over Brazil to study Brazilian prehistorical art and to establish comparisons to the European counterpart. Dating is similar: ca. 30,000 years. Among Brazilian Indian tribes, Itacoatiaras means painted stone, but it is also used to denote a stone bearing marks or writing. Naturalistic and geometric groups are roughly the most distinctive, patterns also reminiscent of Altamira and Lascaux, as well as of similar cultures in other countries. This original scholarly contribution researches indigenous landmarks in depth, but the mystery of their origins remains.

490 Louzada, Júlio. Artes plásticas Brasil '90: seu mercado, seus leilões. v. 4. São Paulo: INTER/ARTE/BRASIL, 1990. 1211 p.

Practical guide to virtually all kinds of paintings, sculpture, and graphic arts that come up for auction in Brazil. Provides basic information on artists and prices fetched.

491 Universidade de São Paulo. Museu de Arte Contemporânea. Perfil de um acervo. Organização editorial e ensaio de Aracy A. Amaral. São Paulo: Techint, 1988. 391 p.: bibl., ill. (some col.)

Univ. of São Paulo's modern art collection is one of the finest in Brazil in terms of both international and national scope. Of great interest to this section is the Brazilian collection from 1945–85, which covers virtually all major trends of the past decades. Includes scholarly texts, many b/w reproductions, and a wealth of excellent color ones.

JOURNAL ABBREVIATIONS

Am. Lat./Moscú. América Latina. Academia de Ciencias de la Unión de Repúblicas Soviéticas Socialistas. Moscú.

An. Inst. Invest. Estét. Anales del Instituto de Investigaciones Estéticas. Univ. Nacional Autónoma de México. México.

Atenea/Concepción. Atenea. Univ. de Concepción. Chile.

Bol. Nicar. Bibliogr. Doc. Boletín Nicaragüense de Bibliografía y Documentación. Biblioteca, Banco Central de Nicaragua. Managua.

Doc. Arquit. Urban. Documentos de Arquitectura y Urbanismo: DAU. Instituto de Investigación de Arquitectura y Urbanismo. Lima.

Estud. Hist. Novohisp. Estudios de Historia Novohispana. Univ. Nacional Autónoma de México, México.

HUACA. Historia, Urbanismo, Arquitectura, Construcción, Arte: HUACA. Facultad de Arquitectura, Urbanismo y Artes de la Univ. Nacional de Ingeniería. Lima.

Islas. Islas. Univ. Central de Las Villas. Santa Clara, Cuba.

Jam. J. Jamaica Journal. Institute of Jamaica. Kingston.

Rev. Parag. Sociol. Revista Paraguaya de Sociología. Centro Paraguayo de Estudios Sociológicos. Asunción.

Santiago. Santiago. Univ. de Oriente. Santiago, Cuba.

Todo es Hist. Todo es Historia. Buenos Aires.

HISTORY

ETHNOHISTORY
Mesoamerica

S.L. CLINE, *Professor of History, University of California, Santa Barbara*

IN THE LAST TWO YEARS a number of fine monographs have appeared, dealing mainly with the Nahua and Maya spheres. Of particular note is a work by Louise Burkhart about the dynamics of the spiritual conquest of the Nahuas, particularly as seen through the Nahuatl texts created by the Spanish religious (items **498, 497,** and **496**). In her book Burkhart has done much to elucidate the Christianity which the natives absorbed, filtered through their own belief system. On the same theme, outright Nahua resistance to Spanish efforts at Christianization is seen in four case studies of Nahua "man-gods" in Serge Gruzinki's monograph (item **519**). Two articles on the confessional as a tool in the Christianization process contribute to the increasingly sophisticated understanding of the Nahua worldview and its colonial transformation. (items **518** and **530**). The translation of Alfredo López Austin's work on prehispanic Nahua ideology and religious beliefs as they pertain to the human body is a welcome addition to the English-language literature on Nahua beliefs. This work is of particular interest given the shifts in worldview and notion of the person which the Spanish religious were attempting to impose in the early colonial period (item **538**).

Other notable works in the Nahua sphere include Jacqueline Durand-Forest's study of Chimalpahin, the great native annalist whose writings are so valuable for understanding Nahua sociopolitical organization (item **504**). Prehispanic Aztec warfare and politics have received some attention (items **523, 503,** and **524**), as has the topic of land tenure (items **506, 522,** and **561**). Also worthy of note is Susan Gillespie's new analytical work on the Aztec kings and the recasting of their histories (item **512**).

In the Maya sphere, two major works on the early colonial period have appeared. Both Grant Jones' (item **528**) and Inga Clendinnen's (item **501**) works deal with Maya resistance to Spanish conquest. Although concerned with slightly different areas, time periods, and emphases, both studies illuminate the encounter between Spaniards and Indians, with particular emphasis on the native viewpoint. In both works, the history of the conquest and its aftermath has advanced considerably from earlier views, which generally focused on the Spanish sphere.

The last two years of publication in Mesoamerican ethnohistory have seen a slowdown in the production of facsimile and critical editions of major texts in the field. This may be a temporary hiatus, as publishers plan on issuing certain texts to coincide with the Columbus Quincentennial. One exception to this general paucity of publication of prehispanic and colonial texts is the facsimile of Bernardino de Sahagún's chronicle of the conquest of Mexico (item **550**).

Since this is my final contribution to the Mesoamerican Ethnohistory section, I would like to take the opportunity to reflect on the the condition of field. The last eight years have seen an explosion in the writing of indigenous history. The native peoples are now much more often the subjects rather than the objects of historical narrative. Their active role in shaping conquest and colonization is now more clearly seen. Only a decade ago it was noteworthy when major monographs on the colonial period relied substantially or solely on native-language materials: this is no longer the case for the Nahua and Maya spheres. Standard divisions in the field are breaking down. From its inception, ethnohistory has been an interdisciplinary field, with active participation from historians, anthropologists, linguists and art historians. However there has been a common categorization that historians and linguists work on the colonial period, while anthropologists and art historians work on the prehispanic. This can no longer be said to hold: historians are venturing into the realm of the pictorial; art historians are examining the alphabetic texts in the colonial codices; and anthropologists and archaeologists now study the colonial period. All this is profoundly encouraging, and can only contribute to the progress of the field. The number of Mexicans doing high level scholarly work has grown; this speaks well of Mexico's continued interest in the field of ethnohistory as well as of level of training available there. In North America, when this section of the *Handbook* was created in the early 1960s, there were only a few stalwart ethnohistorians such as Charles Gibson, Donald Roberston, H.B. Nicholson, and my father, Howard Cline. They often felt they were voices crying in the wilderness. I think they would be pleased by the state of our field today.

492 Albores Z., Beatriz A. La economía lacustre del Valle de Toluca. (*in* Sociedad Mexicana de Antropología. Mesa Redonda, *17th, San Cristobal de Las Casas, México, 1981*. Investigaciones recientes en el área maya. México: Sociedad Mexicana de Antropología, 1984, v. 3, p. 537–544, bibl.)

Brief but detailed description of economic activities including hunting, fishing, and plant gathering. Also includes description of tools used to pursue these activities.

493 Baird, Ellen T. Sahagún's *Codex Florentino:* the enigmatic A. (*Ethnohistory*, 34:3, Summer 1987, p. 289–306, bibl., ill.)

Brief contribution to Sahaguntine studies, arguing that one of Sahagún's sources was a treatise on architecture, possibly of Italian origin. There are implications for the skill of the copyists which suggest the state of contact with the larger world.

494 Barlow, Robert H. Tlatelolco, rival de Tenochtitlan. Recopilación de Jesús Monjarás-Ruiz, Elena Limón y María de la Cruz Paillés H. México: Instituto Nacional de Antropología e Historia; Puebla, Mexico: Univ. de las Américas, 1987. 164 p.: bibl., ill., index. (Obras de Robert H. Barlow; 1)

Vol. 1 of proposed series bringing together Barlow's publications. Contains one previously unpublished article, "La Guerra Civil; Moquíhuix," which treats the conflicts between Tlatelolco and Tenochtitlan (1466–73). Useful republication of difficult-to-obtain materials.

495 Berthe, Jean-Pierre. L'évangile et l'outil: le changement technique dans une village indien du Méxique au XVIe. siècle. (*Tech. Cult.*, 11, jan./juin 1988, p. 65–82, bibl.)

Examination of change in a Tarascan community based on late 16th-century *Relación geográfica* of Tiripitio. Long passages from the *Relación* are found in French translation.

496 Burkhart, Louise M. Moral deviance in sixteenth-century Nahua and Christian thought: the rabbit and the deer. (*J. Lat. Am. Lore*, 12:2, Winter 1986, p. 107–139, bibl., facsims.)

Illuminating discussion of Nahua concepts of deviance and their metaphorical expression as "deer" and "rabbit." Subtle textual analysis shows how Spanish friars' efforts to teach Christian concepts were pursued and how they might go awry.

497 **Burkhart, Louise M.** The slippery earth: Nahua-Christian moral dialogue in sixteenth-century Mexico. Tucson: Univ. of Arizona Press, 1989. 242 p.: bibl., ill., index.

Splendid extended analysis of the process of Nahua Christianization, with a keen eye for the mutual misunderstandings of Spaniards and Nahuas. Fine grounding in both the European and Indian belief systems and a sophisticated reading of the Nahua texts make this an outstanding contribution.

498 **Burkhart, Louise M.** The solar Christ in Nahuatl doctrinal texts of early colonial Mexico. (*Ethnohistory*, 35 : 3, Summer 1988, p. 234–256, bibl., facsim.)

Fine analysis of a 16th-century Christian motif. Suggests that Nahua views identifying Christ with the sun came directly out of Old World symbolism and thus constitute a Spanish introduction from the friars rather than an indigenous identification.

499 **Cantos y crónicas del México antiguo.** Recopilación de Miguel León Portilla. Madrid: Historia 16, 1986. 241 p.: bibl. (Crónicas de América; 24)

Good collection of Nahua texts and explications; representative selections from the relevant genres of *huehuetlatolli*: songs, poetry, chronicles, and histories.

500 **Carrasco, Pedro *et al.*** La sociedad indígena en el centro y occidente de México. Zamora, Mexico: Colegio de Michoacán, 1986. 305 p.: bibl.

Collection of essays on the Tarascan area. Ethnohistorical contributions include an important general article by Pedro Carrasco on prehispanic political and economic organization and analysis of the State and society by Ulises Beltrán.

Castro Leal, Marcia. Tzintzuntzan: capital de los tarascos. See *HLAS 51:161.*

Chance, John K. Conquest of the Sierra: Spaniards and Indians in colonial Oaxaca. See item **1004.**

501 **Clendinnen, Inga.** Ambivalent conquests: Maya and Spaniard in Yucatan, 1517–1570. Cambridge, England; New York: Cambridge Univ. Press, 1987. 245 p.: bibl., ill., index. (Cambridge Latin American studies; 61)

Subtle and masterful examination of Spanish-Maya relations in the early conquest and missionization period. Includes particularly good discussion of the shift in the Franciscans' attitudes after contact with the Maya, and a sophisticated discussion of the "spiritual conquest" from the Indian point of view.

Los códices mayas. See *HLAS 51:1119.*

502 **Coloquio de Arqueología y Etnohistoria del Estado de Guerrero, 1st, Chilpancingo de los Bravos, Mexico, 1984.** Primer coloquio de arqueología y etnohistoria del estado de Guerrero. México: Instituto Nacional de Antropología e Historia; Chilpancingo, Mexico?: Gobierno del Estado de Guerrero, 1986. 592 p.: bibl., ill.

Useful volume on a little-studied area of Mesoamerica. Worthwhile contributions include two on Nahuatl historical linguistics by Una Canger and Karen Dakin, and one on *encomienda* by Rafael Rubí Alarcón.

503 **Davies, Nigel.** The Aztec empire: the Toltec resurgence. Norman: Univ. of Oklahoma Press, 1987. 341 p.: bibl., ill., index. (The Civilization of the American Indian series; 187)

Analysis of the rise of the Aztec empire. Author believes key factor was assertion by the Mexica that they were successor to Tula. Includes discussion of the Aztec concept of history, structure of the Mexica State, trade, and trade-related warfare. Capstone to author's volumes on the Aztecs.

504 **Durand-Forest, Jacqueline de.** L'histoire de la Vallée de Mexico selon Chimalpahin Quauhtlehuanitzin. v. 1. Paris: L'Harmattan, 1987. 1 v.: bibl, ill., index. (Documents Amérique latine)

Vol. 1 of in-depth study of important 17th-century Nahua annalist. Key portions of the analysis focus on discussion of Chimalpahin's sources, tracing the history of Chalco according to Chimalpahin, particularly the royal dynasties. Useful and long-awaited contribution to our knowledge of the Nahua political system but also to our knowledge of this individual Indian.

505 Dürr, Michael von. Strategien india-
nischer Herrschaftslegitimierung im
kolonialzeitlichen Mesoamerika: ein Ver-
gleich der Argumentation im *Popol Vuh* und
im *Título de Totonicapán.* (*Sociologus,* 39:2,
1989, p. 172–181, bibl.)
Comparison of two parallel episodes in
the *Popul Vuh* and the *Título de Totonicapán* which shows that their differences center on arguments for legitimating rulership.
The first text places rulers firmly in the prehispanic religious sphere, and the second
within Christian ideology.

506 Dyckerhoff, Ursula. Indian corporate
landholding during colonial times: a
glimpse from the Valley of Puebla. (*in* Congreso Internacional de Americanistas, *45th,
Bogotá, 1985.* Etnohistoria e historia de las
Américas. Bogotá: Ediciones Uniandes, 1988,
p. 17–32, bibl., table)
Useful summary of early colonial land
tenure with special attention to Spanish legal
practices, which differentially preserved or
undermined communities' rights to land
and development of private holdings. Important for details on a specific region with possible implications for Indian land tenure
elsewhere.

507 Edmonson, Munro S. The book of the
year: Middle American calendrical systems. Salt Lake City: Univ. of Utah Press,
1988. 313 p.: bibl., ill., index.
Major contribution to the literature on
Mesoamerican calendars. Treats the structure of calendars, interrelationships among
60 calendars, the genealogy of the calendar
and its relationship to solar astronomy,
among other topics.

508 Edmonson, Munro S. Clase social en la
conquista de Yucatán. (*in* Sociedad
Mexicana de Antropología. Mesa Redonda,
*17th, San Cristobal de Las Casas, México,
1981.* Investigaciones recientes en el área
maya. México: Sociedad Mexicana de Antropología, 1984, v. 1, p. 247–255, bibl.)
Elegant interpretation examines role
of ethnic division and class-based civil war in
the context of a weakening political structure. Based on analysis of the *Codex Pérez*
and the *Chilam Balam.*

Farriss, Nancy M. Recordando el futuro, anticipando el pasado: tiempo histórico y tiempo

cósmico entre los mayas de Yucatán. See
item **1017.**

509 García Martínez, Bernardo. Los pueblos de la Sierra: el poder y el espacio
entre los indios del norte de Puebla hasta
1700. México: El Colegio de México, Centro
de Estudios Históricos, 1987. 424 p.: bibl.,
ill., index.
Work of high caliber examines shifts
in Nahua communities north of Puebla. Includes discussions of land tenure, migration,
race mixture, Indian government, and the interaction with the colonial system.

510 Garza, Mercedes de la. Los "angeles"
mayas. (*Estud. Cult. Maya,* 16, 1985,
p. 167–181)
Short discussion of Maya "angels"
(*canhelob*), which are confused with Christian angels. The Maya concept seemingly
never lost its true significance of association
with fertility. Interesting examination of an
idea through ethnohistorical sources.

511 Gasco, Janine. Una visión de conjunto
de la historia demográfica y económica
del Soconusco colonial. (*Mesoamérica/Anti-
gua,* 10:18, dic. 1989, p. 371–399)
Insightful discussion of factors affecting the demography and economy of a little-
studied region. Points to factors which made
possible small-scale agricultural development and which made difficult a transition
to a larger scale.

512 Gillespie, Susan D. The Aztec kings:
the construction of rulership in Mexica history. Tucson: Univ. of Arizona Press,
1989. 272 p.: bibl., ill., index.
Provocative and fruitful examination
of Aztec kings and kingship from a herme-
neutical rather than strictly ethnohistorical
point of view. Focuses on "women of discord" and "recycled kings," suggesting
changes in narrative to suit ideological
needs.

513 Gómez Canedo, Lino. Huicot: antecedentes misionales. (*Estud. Hist. Novohisp.,* 9, 1987, p. 95–145, bibl.)
Discussion, mainly from the Spanish
religious point of view, of the 16th-century
missionization of the little-studied region
encompassed by central Nayarit and the surrounding area.

514 Granados y Gálvez, José Joaquín.
Tardes americanas: gobierno gentil y

católico; breve y particular noticia de toda la historia indiana: sucesos, casos notables, y cosas ignoradas, desde la entrada de la gran nación tolteca a esta tierra de Anáhuac, hasta los presentes tiempos. Trabajadas por un indio y un español; sácalas a luz, José Joaquín Granados y Gálvez. México: Coordinación de Humanidades: M.A. Porrúa, 1987. 564 p., 2 leaves of plates: ill., index. (Biblioteca mexicana de escritores políticos)

Facsimile edition of late 18th-century text by the Bishop of Sonora. Text is set as a dialogue between a Spaniard and a native, with the Spaniard attempting to respond to the detractors of Spain and New Spain, and the Indian issuing apologies for Indian culture. Interesting source for cultural and intellectual history.

515 Graulich, Michel. Double immolations in ancient Mexican sacrificial ritual. (*Hist. Relig.*, 27:4, May 1988, p. 397–404, ill.)

Intriguing discussion of human sacrifice, delineating to which deities ordinary prisoners of war were sacrificed and offering a hypothesis as to why the sacrifices always involved both beheading and extraction of the heart.

516 Graulich, Michel. Miccailhuitl: the Aztec festivals of the deceased. (*Numen*, 36:1, June 1989, p. 43–71, bibl., tables)

Analysis of rituals surrounding greater and lesser festivals of the dead, emphasizing the linkages in the ritual calendar.

517 Graulich, Michel. Quetzalcoatl y el espejismo de Tollan. Antwerpen, Belgium: Instituut voor Amerikanistiek, v.z.w., 1988. 298 p.: bibl., indexes, tables.

Summary of cosmological traditions of the central Mexican highlands. Separate chapters treat various myths: migration, Quetzalcoatl, kings and conquests, and the end of Tollan. Careful analysis of relevant sources.

518 Gruzinski, Serge. Individualization and acculturation: confession among the Nahuas of Mexico from the sixteenth to the eighteenth century. (*in* Sexuality and marriage in colonial Latin America. Edited by Asunción Lavrin. Lincoln, Neb.: Univ. of Nebraska Press, 1989, p. 96–117, facsims.)

Important provocative contribution to studies of the spiritual conquest and acculturation of the Nahua, focusing on the Christian confession of sin as a form of ideological control and subjugation.

519 Gruzinski, Serge. Man-gods in the Mexican highlands: Indian power and colonial society, 1520–1800. Translated from the French by Eileen Corrigan. Stanford, Calif.: Stanford Univ. Press, 1989. 223 p.: bibl., index, maps.

Case studies of four Indian men who ran afoul of the Inquisition. Analysis suggests that these men expressed the Nahua concept of power. Intriguing study of Indian mentalities.

Gruzinski, Serge. La memoria mutilada: construcción del pasado y mecanismos de la memoria en un grupo otomí de la mitad del siglo XVII. See item **1031.**

520 Gutiérrez Solana, Nelly. Avances en los estudios sobre los códices mixtecos. (*An. Inst. Invest. Estét.*, 58, 1987, p. 35–45, bibl.)

Useful historiographical discussion summarizes advances in interpretation of Mixtec codices, including localization of towns found in assorted codices, interpretation of the obverse side of the *Codex Vindobonensis*, determination of the style of painters of several codices, and a better understanding of socio-political organization.

521 Hanks, William F. Authenticity and ambivalence in the text: a colonial Maya case. (*Am. Ethnol.*, 13:4, Nov. 1986, p. 721–744, bibl., tables)

Exploration of the situation of the Maya nobility who were both symbols of the indigenous system and leaders of acculturation. Article uses "discourse analysis" of native-language documents. Although laden with the jargon of literary criticism, the discussion of native-language documentation is worthwhile.

522 Harvey, Herbert R. The Oztoticpac Lands Map: a re-examination. (*in* Congreso Internacional de Americanistas, *45th, Bogotá, 1985*. Arqueología de las Américas. Bogotá: Fondo de Promoción de la Cultura, 1988, p. 339–353, bibl., facsims., tables)

Further analysis of a 1540 Texcocan region cadastral. Pays special attention to measurements of the parcels of land and provides particularly illuminating discussion of the arithmetical system in operation.

523 **Hassig, Ross.** Aztec warfare: imperial expansion and political control. Norman: Univ. of Oklahoma Press, 1988. 404 p.: bibl., ill., index. (The Civilization of the American Indian series; 188)

Full-length discussion of the significance of Aztec warfare mainly from a political and economic perspective, rather than from a religious or ideological viewpoint. Examines factors determining the decision to go to war and the consequences. Examines goals of and constraints on warfare within the context of the Aztec empire. For anthropologist's comment see *HLAS 51:177*.

524 **Hicks, Frederic.** La administración política y tributaria del Imperio Azteca. (*in* Congreso Internacional de Americanistas, *45th, Bogotá, 1985*.. Etnohistoria e historia de las Américas. Bogotá: Ediciones Uniandes, 1988, p. 49–58, bibl.)

Emphasizes role of exchange of gifts and the relation of social classes at the imperial level. Notes that many nobles were dependent while remaining in power, and that commoners were in greater servitude than before. Very useful and specific information regarding the exchange of gifts.

525 **Hill, Robert M.** and **John Monaghan.** Continuities in highland Maya social organization: ethnohistory in Sacapulas, Guatemala. Foreword by Victoria R. Bricker. Philadelphia: Univ. of Pennsylvania Press, 1987. 176 p.: bibl., ill., index. (Ethnohistory series)

Based on colonial land dispute in Sacapulas. Authors reconstruct the landholding system, concluding that landholding was based on a territorial unit similar to the *calpulli.*

526 **Hill, Robert M.** Instances of Maya witchcraft in the 18th-century Totonicapan area. (*Estud. Cult. Maya,* 17, 1988, p. 269–293, bibl.)

Fascinating elucidation of two 18th-century cases of witchcraft based on Indians' statements collected by Spanish officials during criminal investigations. Points to more modern origin of current beliefs concerning the supernatural.

Hill, Robert M. Social organization by decree in colonial highland Guatemala. See item **1387.**

527 **Izquierdo, Ana Luisa.** Documentos de la división del Beneficio de Yaxcabá: el castigo de una idolatría. (*Estud. Cult. Maya,* 17, 1988, p. 159–193, appendix, bibl.)

Seventeenth-century set of documents showing divisions of a Yucatecan ecclesiastical jurisdiction, along with extensive explication of the documents and their significance. Gives insight into ecclesiastical procedure and the extent to which native idolatry was a major problem.

Jansen, Maarten. Dzavuindanda, Ita Andehui y Iukano: historia y leyenda mixteca. See *HLAS 51:1148.*

528 **Jones, Grant D.** Maya resistance to Spanish rule: time and history on a colonial frontier. . Albuquerque: Univ. of New Mexico Press, 1989. 365 p.: appendix, bibl., ill., index.

Well-documented and carefully constructed portrait of Maya resistance to Spanish conquest in southeastern Yucatan. Author's largely successful attempt focuses attention on the Maya as "independent actors with their own historical agenda."

529 **Kellogg, Susan.** Cognatic kinship and religion: women in Aztec society. (*in* Smoke and mist: Mesoamerican studies in memory of Thelma D. Sullivan. Oxford, England: B.A.R., 1988, p. 665–681, bibl.)

Sophisticated discussion of women and religion goes beyond stereotyped categories and rhetoric to point out the complexities of the place of women in the functioning of society and their parallel roles in religion with men.

Kellogg, Susan. Households in late prehispanic and early colonial Mexico City: their structure and its implications for the study of historical demography. See item **1038.**

530 **Klor de Alva, J. Jorge.** Contar vidas: la autobiografía y la reconstrucción del ser nahua. (*Arbor,* 515/516, 1988, p. 49–78, bibl.)

Argues that for Nahuas the Christian confession required a new perception of their being which placed it at the center of a permanent body-soul conflict. Concludes that a new form of conscience emerged which allowed for colonial domination.

531 **Klor de Alva, J. Jorge.** Language, politics, and translation: colonial dis-

course and classic Nahuatl in New Spain. (*in* The art of translation: voices from the field. Edited by Rosanna Warren. Boston: Northeastern Univ. Press, 1989, p. 143–162, bibl.)

Argues that the development of classical Nahuatl as a colonial lingua franca was a self-conscious effort by colonial officials to create a language of domination and acculturation.

532 Lameiras, José. Los déspotas armados: un espectro de la guerra prehispánica. Zamora, Mexico: Colegio de Michoacán, 1985. 229 p.: bibl., index.

Takes the position that the last 200 years of prehispanic warfare was a condition of existence for which one always had to be prepared. Discusses warfare within the larger societal context. Useful scholarly treatment with reference to the theoretical literature on warfare.

Lemercinier, Geneviève. Les Miskitos au Nicaragua: notes chronologiques sur la population et l'histoire économico-politique de la Côte Atlantique. See *HLAS 51:711.*

533 León Portilla, Miguel. México-Tenochtitlán: su espacio y tiempo sagrados. México: Plaza y Valdés Editores, 1987. 159 p.: bibl., ill. (La Ciudad)

Insightful monograph on the Tenochca capital with chapters outlining the Tenochtitlan of myth, the sacred sites, and the place of myth within the social context. Book's second section consists of ethnohistorical sources on the city.

534 León Portilla, Miguel. Time and reality in the thought of the Maya. Foreword by J. Eric S. Thompson. Appendices by Alfonso Villa Rojas and Miguel León-Portilla. Translated by Charles L. Boilès, Fernando Horcasitas, and the author. 2nd ed., enl. Norman: Univ. of Oklahoma Press, 1988. 229 p.: appendices, bibl., ill., index. (The Civilization of the American Indian series; 190)

Expanded edition of important work leaves original 1968 text unchanged. Appendix dealing with recent developments in the literature on Maya space-time research indicates ethnographic confirmation of ideas first discussed in the earlier edition.

535 Lima, Oswaldo Gonçalves de. El maguey y el pulque en los códices mexicanos. Figuras de Honorina Lima. 2a ed. México: Fondo de Cultura Económica, 1986. 278 p.: bibl., ill. (Sección de obras de antropología)

Meticulous extended study of the maguey cactus and pulque. Includes review of the scientific literature, but most interesting for its thorough analysis of representations in the relevant pictorials.

Lizana, Bernardo de. Historia de Yucatán. See item **1042.**

536 Lobato, Rodolfo. Terrazas prehispánicas en la región del Río Usumacinta y su importancia en la agricultura maya. (*Estud. Cult. Maya,* 17, 1988, p. 19–58, ill., photos)

Careful description of prehispanic terraces in Chiapas with comparison to similar structures in Campeche and Belize. Existence of such terraces will modify notions of the form of agriculture of the region, generally thought to be slash-and-burn. Posits control of environment with the potential for higher food production and population growth.

537 Lockhart, James. A language transition in eighteenth-century Mexico: the change from Nahuatl to Spanish recordkeeping. (*in* Smoke and mist: Mesoamerican studies in memory of Thelma D. Sullivan. Oxford, England: B.A.R., 1988, p. 571–584, bibl.)

Close reading of several Nahuatl texts reveals shifts in language of recordkeeping which seem to be caused by Indians' desire to communicate with the Spanish sector, rather than by decay of the indigenous system. Fine example of insight into the Indians' world through their records.

538 López Austin, Alfredo. The human body and ideology: concepts of the ancient Nahuas. Salt Lake City: Univ. of Utah Press, 1988. 2 v.: appendices, bibl., ill.

English translation of a key work on the Nahua conceptualization of the world, focusing on the human body. Brilliant work, illuminating Nahua religious, social, and political beliefs. Topics include ideology and world view, equilibrium and desequilibrium of the body, the body in the universe, and the body and social stratification. Vol. 2 consists of Nahua texts concerning the human body and various philological appendices.

Luján Muñoz, Jorge. El reino pokomam de Petapa, Guatemala, hacia 1524. See item **1391.**

539 MacLeod, Murdo J. Dominican explanations for revolts and their suppression in colonial Chiapas, 1545–1715. (*in* Indian-religious relations in colonial Spanish America. Edited by Susan E. Ramírez. Syracuse, N.Y.: Maxwell School of Citizenship and Public Affairs, Syracuse Univ., 1989, p. 39–53, map)

Focuses particularly on the 1712–13 Tzeltal rebellion and attempts by the Dominicans to explain its causes. Explanation settled on was a cosmic struggle between God and the devil, good and evil, from which both Indians and Spaniards could learn to change their ways.

540 Markman, Sidney David. Comunidades chiapanecas y sus transformaciones después de la conquista española. (*in* Sociedad Mexicana de Antropología. Mesa Redonda, *17th, San Cristobal de Las Casas, México, 1981.* Investigaciones recientes en el área maya. México: Sociedad Mexicana de Antropología, 1984, v. 3, p. 319–325, bibl.)

Argues that the new urban centers created by the Dominicans were not important loci of earthly, civilized life; rather, they were viewed by the religious as antechambers for the *civitas* of heaven to come. Interesting, but more of an investigation of European rather than Indian attitudes.

541 Mesoamérica y el centro de México: una antología. Recopilación de Jesús Monjarás-Ruiz, Rosa Brambila y Emma Pérez-Rocha. México: Instituto Nacional de Antropología e Historia, 1985. 522 p., 2 folded leaves of plates: bibl., ill., index. (Serie Antropología: Col. Biblioteca del INAH)

Valuable collection of important articles from the last 30 years of Mesoamerican ethnohistory emphasizes political organization and social integration. Although many of these articles have been published previously, some are not readily available. Collection includes studies by P. Kirchhoff and A. Caso on land tenure; J. Litvak King on commerce; V. Castillo and P. Carrasco on the general economy; and M. Léon Portilla and A. López Austin on the State; among others.

542 Mohar Betancourt, Luz María. El tributo méxica en el siglo XVI: análisis de dos fuentes pictográficas. México: SEP; Centro de Investigaciones y Estudios Superiores en Antropología Social, 1987. 388 p.: bibl., ill. (Cuadernos de la casa chata; 154)

In-depth analysis of the tribute data in the *Codex Mendoza* and the *Matrícula de Tributos,* with a detailed comparison of the two. Worthwhile compilation for prehispanic economic history.

543 Moreno de los Arcos, Roberto. Autos seguidos por el provisor de naturales del arzobispado de México contra el ídolo del Gran Nayar, 1722–1723. (*Tlalocan,* 10, 1985, p. 377–447)

Transcription and some analysis of an 18th-century Spanish document concerning religious practices of a Corachol Indian group. Illuminates Spanish procedures against idolatrous native practices, and is an ethnohistorical source for the practices themselves.

544 Pascual Soto, Arturo. Los antiguos señores mixtecos de Acatlán, Puebla, en los códices *Sánchez Solís* y *Tulane.* (*An. Inst. Invest. Estét.,* 58, 1987, p. 55–71, bibl., facsims.)

Analysis of kinship and marriage among certain Mixtec lords. Marital alliance is seen as a way of averting conflicts and knitting together a network of elites. Provides painstaking identifications of the kin relations among these Mixtec lords.

Pietschmann, Horst. Grundzüge der Entwicklung des Bildungssystems im kolonialen Hispanoamerika. See item **832.**

545 Rojas, José Luis de. México Tenochtitlan, economía y sociedad en el siglo XVI. México: Fondo de Cultura Económica; Zamora, Mexico: Colegio de Michoacán, 1986. 329 p.: bibl., ill., index, maps. (Crónica de la Ciudad de México)

Focuses on the complexity of the social structure of a city with a large non-agricultural population. Separate treatment of the physical structure, demography, and occupational structures. Seeks to demonstrate the capacity of a preindustrial city with relatively underdeveloped technology and a large population.

546 Rojas, José Luis de. Tendencias de la etnohistoria del México central. (*Rev. Indias,* 49:185, enero/abril 1989, p. 195–204, bibl.)

Outline of what author considers salient features of ethnohistory, and an evaluation of certain ethnohistorical works. Contributions of anthropologists on the prehispanic era are better than those of historians on the colonial period.

547 Rosquillas Quiles, Hortensia. Huatlatlauca prehispánica en el contexto de la historia regional chichimeca. México: Dirección de Restauración del Patrimonio Cultural, Instituto Nacional de Antropología e Historia, 1986. 54 p.: bibl. (Cuaderno de trabajo; 1)

Localization and geographical description of the town of Huatlatlauca, Puebla. Includes discussion of the name of the town and colonial antecedents. Contains transcription of a 1579 *corregidor's* description of the town, likely a *relación geográfica* although not identified as such.

548 Ruz, Mario Humberto. Copanaguastla en un espejo: un pueblo tzeltal en el Virreinato. San Cristóbal de Las Casas, Mexico: Centro de Estudios Indígenas, Univ. Autónoma de Chiapas, 1985. 310 p., 16 p. of plates: bibl., ill. (some col.). (Serie Monografías; 2)

Fine historical reconstruction of daily life in a Tzeltal Maya community, based on texts by the first religious in the area, a Dominican. Topics discussed include flora and fauna, the family, the human body, sexuality, illnesses, etc. Intelligent and intriguing use of colonial texts.

549 Ruz, Mario Humberto and **Dolores Aramoni Calderón.** La *enfermedad que muda de matices:* caracterización del Mal del Pinto en Chiapas, siglo XVIII. (*Estud. Cult. Maya,* 17, 1988, p. 355–396, appendix, bibl., maps, tables)

Exhaustive study of a tropical malady often affecting native populations. Discusses extent of its spread and attempts at cure. Provides useful insights into the institutional Church and its relations with the native population.

550 Sahagún, Bernardino de. Conquest of New Spain: 1585 revision. Reproductions of Boston Public Library Manuscript and Carlos María de Bustamante 1840 edition. Translated by Howard F. Cline. Edited with an introduction and notes by S.L. Cline.

Salt Lake City : Univ. of Utah Press, 1989. 672 p., 1 leaf of plates: bibl., ill.

Facsimile edition of 19th-century copy of Sahagún's revised conquest narrative with transcription and translation into English. Introduction proposes reason why Sahagún was prompted to shift the focus of his conquest chronicle from an exclusively Indian one to one including a justification of the Spanish conquest. Also includes a republication of the virtually unavailable defective Bustamante edition.

551 Schroeder, Susan. Chimalpahin's view of Spanish ecclesiastics in colonial Mexico. (*in* Indian-religious relations in colonial Spanish America. Edited by Susan E. Ramírez. Syracuse, N.Y.: Maxwell School of Citizenship and Public Affairs, Syracuse Univ., 1989, p. 21–38, map)

Examination of the Spanish religious presence and Christian practice in the writings of Chimalpahin. Particularly interesting to gauge the understanding of these phenomena from the native viewpoint.

552 Smoke and mist: Mesoamerican studies in memory of Thelma D. Sullivan. Edited by J. Kathryn Josserand and Karen Dakin. Oxford, England: B.A.R., 1988. 2 vols.: bibl., ill., maps, tables. (B.A.R. International Series; 402)

Collection of nearly 50 articles, generally of high quality, which treat topics of interest to the late Thelma Sullivan. Separate sections on Sahagún, iconography and religion, linguistic and literary sources, and ethnography of the Nahua-speaking zone. (See also items **537** and **529**.) For anthropologist's comment see *HLAS 51:210.*

553 Thiemer-Sachse, Ursula von. Salzgewinnung und Salzhandel bei den Zapoteca Südmexikos in vorspanischer Zeit. (*Ethnogr.-Archäol. Z.,* 28:4, 1987, p. 565–574, bibl.)

Study of salt production and trade in precolumbian Oaxaca based primarily on *relaciones.* Salt was produced from beds in villages and saltworks on Pacific coast after subjugation just prior to Spanish conquest. Zapotecs traded primarily the clean, white, finely-grained sea salt within Oaxaca since they had no contact with trade routes between salt works of Yucatán and central Mexico. Salt trade was a secure source of wealth because of assured sales. More descriptive than analytical. Includes summaries in German, Russian, English, and Spanish. [M.L. Wagner]

554 Thompson, Philip C. The structure of the civil hierarchy in Tekanto, Yucatan, 1785–1820. (*Estud. Cult. Maya*, 16, 1985, p. 183–205, bibl., tables)

Highly informative discussion of career patterns of Maya officials based on Yucatecan language records, which relates the movement up through the hierarchy by many elite men.

555 Tomicki, Ryszard. Augurios de la conquista española entre los aztecas: el problema de la credibilitad de las fuentes históricas. (*Ethnol. Pol.*, 12, 1986, p. 51–78, bibl.)

Contribution to the debate on the reliability of the information foretelling the arrival of the Spanish in Nahua areas. Concentrates on analyzing direct and indirect contacts of Spaniards with Maya.

556 Tomicki, Ryszard. Ludzie i bogowie: Indianie meksykańscy wobec Hiszpanów we wczesnej fazie konkwisty [Men and gods: Mexican Indians and Spaniards in the early phase of the conquest]. Wrocaw, Poland: Zakad Narodowy im. Ossolińskich, 1990. 402 p.: bibl. (Biblioteka etnografii polskiej; 0067–7655: 43)

Attempts to reconstruct the "Indian history" of the conquest perceived as a confrontation of cultures. Discussion of Indian-Spanish contacts in 1519–20 follows a comprehensive analysis (Chap. 1–3) of the cultural context of Indian society. Imaginative, excellent ethnohistorical work based on extensive documentation. [M. Nalewajko]

557 Vicente Castro, Florencio and **José-Luis Rodríguez Molinero.** Bernardino de Sahagún: primer antropólogo en Nueva España, siglo XVI. Salamanca, Spain: Ediciones Univ. de Salamanca; León, Spain: Institución Fray Bernardino de Sahagún, 1986. 295 p.: bibl., facsims. (Acta Salmanticensia, Filosofía y letras; 181)

Recent discussion of the life and work of Sahagún containing interesting facsimiles from the Sahaguntine corpus.

558 Voorhies, Barbara. Late prehispanic sociopolitical organization in the Soco-

nusco at the southernmost frontier of the Aztec empire. (*in* Congreso Internacional de Americanistas, *45th, Bogotá, 1985*. Etnohistoria y historia de las Américas. Bogotá: Ediciones Uniandes, 1985, p. 33–48, bibl., facsims., maps, tables)

Working model of the Soconusco at the point of its integration into the Aztec empire. Proposes that the town of Soconusco was elevated to primary province-wide status by the Aztecs, and that regional organization did not exist previously because the chiefdoms of the region were homologous to one another.

559 Voorhies, Barbara. Un modelo del sistema político pre-azteca del Soconusco. (*Mesoamérica/Antigua*, 10:18, dic. 1989, p. 129–369, maps)

Offers model of southern Chiapas society before its 15th-century incorporation into the Aztec empire. Provides baseline for judging the effect of the Aztecs' conquest, and posits shifting political divisions. Includes archaeological and ethnohistorical perspectives.

560 Watson, Rodney C. Death and taxes and "wild liberty:" a basic model of population change and spatial dispersal at colonial Tila, Chiapas, 1595–1794. (*in* Sociedad Mexicana de Antropología. Mesa Redonda, *17th, San Cristobal de Las Casas, México, 1981.* Investigaciones recientes en el área maya. México: Sociedad Mexicana de Antropología, 1984, v. 3, p. 327–334, tables)

Intriguing discussion of population fluctuations tied to undernourishment and disease; but also to a system of croplands far from town, the development of cash crops, and the migration of native populations outside the area of effective Spanish control.

Werner, Gerd. Landshaftsumgestalung als folge von besiedlung, vegetationsänderung und landnutzung durch die altindianische bevölkerung im Staat Tlaxcala, Mexiko. See *HLAS 51:2950.*

Whitehead, Neil L. Lord of the tiger spirit: a history of the Caribs in colonial Venezuela and Guyana, 1498–1920. See *HLAS 51:850.*

561 Williams, Barbara J. The lands and political organization of a rural *tlaxilacalli* in Tepetlaoztoc, ca. AD 1540. (*in* Congreso Internacional de Americanistas, *45th,*

Bogotá, 1985. Arqueología de las Américas. Bogotá: Fondo de Promoción de la Cultura, 1988, p. 355–365, bibl., facsims., photos, tables)

Analysis using sources particularly rich for the Texcoco region. Documentation provides the dimension of spatial orientation and posits the distribution of local-level populations. Important for its findings of unequal distribution of population and resources, and for suggestions of the extent of control by elites.

South America

NOBLE DAVID COOK, *Professor of History, Florida International University*

THE CENTRAL ANDES continues to be the spatial focus of much of the best recent ethnohistorical research. In spite of pervasive political, social, and economic upheaval at the core, Peruvian contributions dominate. Indeed, perhaps because of the intellectual ferment in that country, there has been an impressive series of attempts at a new synthesis of the Andean past, including those by Manuel Burga (item **586**), Waldemar Espinosa Soriano (item **605**), Luis Millones (item **650**), and María Rostworowski de Diez Canseco (item **682**). Although interpretative differences abound, particularly on the nature of Inca polity, it is surprising that all agree that the past profoundly activates the nation's present, and that the true past is that of her native Americans, not the historical experience of the coastal Creoles.

The dominant ethnohistorian, in terms of monographic output during the past two years, seems to be Luis Millones. In addition to a masterly historical synthesis, he returned to a subject that has interested him for several years and compiled a volume (item **677**) on the Taki Onqoy movement. With linguist Mary Louise Pratt (item **649**) he broke new ground in an analysis of images of love and courtship in the Andes. Further, in a joint effort with Francisco Huamantinco and Edgar Sulca (item **651**), Millones used anthropological perspectives to untangle the web of meaning of dramatic enactments of the death of Atahualpa.

Four specific monographs deserve note. In two the authors combine linguistic and anthropological methods: Rolena Adorno's study of Guamán Poma de Ayala (item **563**), the culmination of several years of work on the important native chronicler, probes the individual as well as the meaning of symbolism within his illustrations; and Regina Harrison's examination of the translation of cultural norms (item **621**) shifts from the early colonial period to the contemporary songs of Ecuadorian women in an insightful blend. Two other works probe the complex structure of Inca society: Gary Urton examines the myths of the origin of the Incas and links to the local elite of the community of Pacariqtambo (item **704**), myths fostered during the early colonial era to gain prestige and power; and R. Tom Zuidema's analysis of the *ceque* system of Cusco, moiety, and *ayllu* is finally available in the English language (item **711**).

Several works have appeared on the Bolivian Aymara; most important are the fine synthesis by Thérèse Bouysse-Cassagne (item **585**), and articles by Thierry Saignes (items **684** and **685**). Each attempts to map contact or early colonial ethnic entities in the region from Lake Titicaca to Lake Poopó. Chilean ethnohistory continues to be dominated by the Araucanian, and Araucanian-Spanish relations. Publication of the ethnohistorical sources for population units in greater

Amazonia proceeds, along with mission histories of uneven value. In Colombia, Kathleen Romoli's lifelong study of the Cuevas (item **681**) is valuable, while in Venezuela, Fernando Arellano has provided a massive compilation on native peoples (item **575**).

Much exciting work was stimulated within the various sessions held at the International Congress of Americanists meeting (Bogotá, 1985). Of many excellent articles that were presented at Bogotá, Patricia Netherly's study of Inca penetration and control of Chimor (item **659**) and Frank Salomon's application of onomatical analysis to information provided in a 1559 *visita* of an encomienda in the Quito basin (item **686**) stand out. Such symposia provide one of the best forums for research on regional ethnohistorical issues, and are particularly valuable when publication of results is assured.

562 Acevedo, Edberto Oscar. Protestas indígenas contra aranceles eclesiásticos. (*Historia/Santiago,* 21, 1986, p. 9–30, bibl.)

Scrutinizes relationship between excessive ecclesiastical fees and native American protest movements in Upper Peru in the late colonial era.

563 Adorno, Rolena. Cronista y príncipe: la obra de don Felipe Guamán Poma de Ayala. Lima: Pontificia Univ. Católica del Perú, 1989. 276 p.: bibl., facsims.

Signficant contribution to our understanding of this important native chronicler. Author attempts to enter Guamán Poma's world, and explores the influences on his writing, his role as interpreter and witness, his views on women and the Church, and his spatial imagery.

564 Alaperrine-Bouyer, Monique. Des femmes dans le manuscrit de Huarochirí. (*Bull. Inst. fr. étud. andin.,* 16:3/4, 1987, p. 97–101, bibl.)

Short but informative essay on female religious forces, particularly Chaupiñamca, found in the Huarochirí cycle.

565 Albizu Labbe, Francisco. Apport pour l'étude du problème indien au Chili: le cas Mapuche. (*Etud. ibér. ibéro-am.,* 1:23, 1982, p. 11–29, graph, map)

Overview of relations of Chilean colonial and national governments with the Mapuche, stressing the difficulties of cultural survival.

566 Alcina Franch, José. El modelo teórico de la "jefatura" y su aplicación al área andina septentrional norte. (*in* Congreso Internacional de Americanistas, *45th, Bogotá, 1985.* Etnohistoria e historia de las Américas. Bogotá: Ediciones Uniandes, 1988, p. 97–116, bibl., tables)

Author develops a theoretical model based on 24 characteristics for analysis of a chiefdom, then tests it on the Pastos, Carangues, Cayambes, and Atacames peoples. Believes the model is adequate to allow the four to be ranked in hierarchical order.

567 Alcocer, Francisco. Ecología e historia: probanzas de indios y españoles referentes a las catastróficas lluvias de 1578, en los corregimientos de Trujillo y Saña. Versión paleográfica y comentarios de Lorenzo Huertas Vallejos. Chiclayo, Perú: CES Solidaridad, 1987. 208 p.: bibl., ill., indexes.

Fascinating information on a severe local disaster (1578) that had a massive impact on the native peoples of several valley systems. This is the earliest detailed description of the *Niño* effect. Lorenzo Huertas Vallejos provides a historical chronology of floods along the coast in a useful introductory essay.

568 Aliaga, Francisco. Astronomía y calendario Inka. (*in* Congreso Peruano de Hombre y la Cultura Andina, *6th, Lima, 1985.* Actas y trabajos. Recopilación de Francisco E. Iriarte Brenner. Lima: Univ. Inca Garcilaso de la Vega, Facultad de Ciencias Sociales, 1985, v. 2, p. 9–26)

Brief introduction stresses seasonal differences between coast and highlands, based on published sources and oral history.

569 Aliaga, Francisco. Dioses o divinidades. (*in* Congreso Peruano de Hombre y la Cultura Andina, *6th, Lima, 1985.* Actas y trabajos. Recopilación de Francisco E. Iriarte Brenner. Lima: Univ. Inca Garcilaso de la Vega, Facultad de Ciencias Sociales, 1985, v. 2, p. 27–40)

Another attempt to understand the nature of the principal Andean religious forces.

570 Alvarez, Silvia G. Recuperación y defensa de territorio étnico: el caso de Chanduy en la costa de Ecuador. (*Bol. Antropol. Am.*, 15, julio 1987, p. 105–121, bibl., facsims.)

In a short survey, author attempts to reconstruct the basic features of ethnic communities of the Santa Elena peninsula from conquest to present.

571 Alvarez, Silvia G. Recuperación y defensa de territorio étnico en la costa ecuatoriana: el caso de la antigua comunidad indígena de Chanduy, en la Península de Santa Elena. (*Bol. Am.*, 30:38, 1988, p. 117–139, bibl., maps)

Examines ethnic persistence in this geographically important, but little-studied region. Based on colonial documentation, and for the 20th century, contemporary informants.

572 Alvarez Lobo, Ricardo. Formación del mercado capitalista en la Amazonia peruana del Alto Ucayali. (*in* Congreso Internacional de Americanistas, *45th, Bogotá, 1985*. Etnohistoria e historia de las Américas. Bogotá: Ediciones Uniandes, 1988, p. 139–160)

Quick survey of economic development of Upper Ucayali and Peruvian *selva* from colonial times to present. Uses a deterministic model to stress impact of capitalist penetration on native peoples in general.

573 Angles Vargas, Víctor. Historia del Cusco incaico. v. 1–3. Lima: Industrial Gráfica, 1988. 3 v.: bibl., ill. (some col.), maps.

Encyclopedic introduction to the principal archaeological sites of the Cusco district based on secondary sources, with many maps, diagrams, and photographs.

574 Ardila Díaz, Isaías. El pueblo de los guanes: raíz gloriosa de Santander. 2a ed. Bogotá: Instituto Colombiano de Cultura, 1986. 550 p.: ill. (Col. Autores Nacionales, tercera serie; 4)

Effort by parish priest to reconstruct local past using Church and municipal archives, archaeological evidence, oral history, and published sources. Emphasizes civil organization, economy, culture, and religion.

575 Arellano, Fernando. Una introducción a la Venezuela prehispánica: culturas de las naciones indígenas venezolanas. Caracas: Univ. Católica Andrés Bello, 1987. 881 p.: bibl., index.

Challenging synthesis of precolumbian Venezuela based on recent monographic surveys and archival investigation. After providing broad historical overview, author takes a tribal approach. Useful college text.

576 Assadourian, Carlos Sempat. La crisis demográfica del siglo XVI y la transición del Tawantinsuyu al sistema mercantil colonial. (*in* Población y mano de obra en América Latina. Compilación de Nicolás Sánchez-Albornoz. Madrid: Alianza Editorial, 1985, p. 69–93, tables)

Argues that primary cause of Indian depopulation was strife, first between Huascar and Atahualpa factions, and then civil wars of the conquerors. Most rapid decline occurred between 1530–50. Viceroy Toledo's policies—settlement into towns, introduction of the amalgamation process in silver production, the *mita* labor draft—resulted in the transition to a full mercantile economy.

577 Assadourian, Carlos Sempat. La renta de la encomienda en la década de 1550: piedad cristiana y desconstrucción. (*Rev. Indias*, 48:182/183, enero/agosto 1988, p. 109–146, tables)

Detailed examination of the tribute assessment of *La Gasca* in 1549 and of the *retasas* that followed in the early 1550s. Argues that the shift away from extensive labor requirements continued the process of destruction of traditional Andean forms of tribute organization and weakened the role of the *curacas.*

578 Assadourian, Carlos Sempat. Los señores étnicos y los corregidores de indios en la conformación del Estado colonial. (*Anu. Estud. Am.*, 44, 1987, p. 325–426, appendix, bibl.)

Thorough review of Crown policy (1549–67) regarding Indian governance in Peru, stressing the shift of support away from the encomendero following establishment of the *corregimiento* system. Excellent evaluation of arguments of jurists and theologians over the perpetuity of the encomienda.

579 Autos da devassa contra os índios Mura do Rio Madeira e nações do Rio Tocantins, 1738–1739: facsímiles e transcrições paleográficas. Introdução de Adélia Engrácia de Oliveira. Transcrições de Raimundo Martins de Lima. Manaus, Brazil: Univ. do Amazonas, 1986. 169 p.: facsims., indexes. (Série Memória Histórica da Amazônia; 2)

Publication of important documents preserved in the Arquivo Histórico Ultramarino in Lisbon regarding the question of "just war."

580 Barrera, Eduardo. Guerras hispano wayuu del siglo XVIII. (*Univ. Humaníst.*, 17:29, enero/junio 1988, p. 123–143, bibl., maps)

Good synopsis of Spanish-Indian relations in the Guajira peninsula, concentrating on the bloody uprising of 1769. Capuchine missionaries failed to provide a buffer, with the area coming under the influence of Dutch and English traders as well as Spanish smugglers. *Mestizaje* contributed to Guajiro military successes.

581 Bauer, Brian S. Sistemas andinos de organización rural antes del establecimiento de reducciones: el ejemplo de Pacariqtambo, Perú. (*Rev. Andin.*, 5:1, julio 1987, p. 197–209, bibl., maps)

Archaeological and ethnohistorical investigations of the moiety and *ayllu* structures.

582 Benavides, Mariá A. Apuntes históricos y etnográficos del Valle del Río Colca, Arequipa, Perú, 1575–1980. (*Bol. Lima*, 9:50, marzo 1987, p. 7–20, maps, photos)

Valuable overview of ethnohistorical and ethnological sources for the Colca Valley of southern Peru.

583 Benchimol, Samuel. Introdução aos Autos da Devassa dos índios Mura. (*in* Congreso Internacional de Americanistas, *45th, Bogotá, 1985.* Etnohistoria e historia de las Américas. Bogotá: Ediciones Uniandes, 1988, p. 243–271)

Examines 18th-century Portuguese attempts to subjugate the Mura of the Madeira Valley, and application of the notion of a "just war" to validate military action.

584 Bernand-Muñoz, Carmen. Estrategias matrimoniales, apellidos y nombres de pila: libros parroquiales y civiles en el sur del Ecuador. (*in* Primer Simposio Europeo sobre Antropología del Ecuador: Memorias. Recopilación de Segundo E. Moreno Yáñez. Bonn:

Instituto de Antropología Cultural de la Univ. de Bonn; Quito: Ediciones Abya-Yala, 1985, p. 201–222, ill.)

Study based on examination of 15,000 entries in parish and civil registers of Pindilig, dating from mid-18th century to 1973. Finds five principal marriage strategies designed to conserve wealth and extend economic contacts beyond the community.

585 Bouysse-Cassagne, Thérèse. La identidad aymara; aproximación histórica: siglo XV, siglo XVI. La Paz: HISBOL-IFEA, 1987. 443 p.: bibl., ill. (Biblioteca andina; 3. Serie histórica; 1. Travaux de l'Institut français d'études andines; 34)

Mature account of the Aymaras, based on several years of investigation. Author deals with conquest, geography, demography, sources, languages, mythology, dualism, space, time and the calendar, the agricultural cycle, alliances, and warfare.

Bravo, Concepción. Un proceso de regionalización precoz en el Virreinato del Perú: el caso de Loja, siglos XVI-XIX. See item **2087.**

Buechler, Judith-Maria. Trade and market in Bolivia before 1953: an ethnologist in the garden of ethnohistory. See *HLAS 51:985.*

586 Burga, Manuel. Nacimiento de una utopia: muerte y resurrección de los incas. Lima: Instituto de Apoyo Agrario, 1988. 428 p., 48 p. of plates: bibl., ill. (some col.).

Mature and important examination of themes in Andean ethnohistory. Begins with evaluation of native modern dramas depicting death of Inca Atahualpa; then traces reality of the conquest, the resistance of Manco Capac, the Taki Onkoy movement, second death of the Inca (Tupac Amaru I), and 17th-century victory of the Christian world view; and finally relates the revolution in mentalities.

587 Caballero Girón, Luis Fredy. La batalla final de Tupac Amaru. Cusco, Perú: Talleres Gráficos de Impresores del Sur AL-FIL, 1985. 171 p., 7 leaves of plates: bibl., ill.

Another study of this late 18th-century revolt. Author argues it was a true independence movement, and attempts to provide an international perspective.

588 Caillavet, Chantal. Los grupos étnicos prehispánicos del sur del Ecuador según las fuentes etnohistóricas. (*in* Primer Simposio Europeo sobre Antropología del Ecuador: Memorias. Recopilación de Segundo E. Moreno Yáñez. Bonn: Instituto de Antropología Cultural de la Univ. de Bonn; Quito: Ediciones Abya-Yala, 1985, p. 127–157, bibl., facsims., map)

Attempts to identify and map ethnic entities in the region of Cuenca to Ayabaca in the 16th century. Important work based on research in Ecuadorian and Spanish archives.

589 Campos Harriet, Fernando. El corregimiento, después partido de Itata: 1600-1786-1818. (*Historia/Santiago,* 21, 1986, p. 111–144, bibl., table)

Synthesis of the historical evolution of colonial *corregimiento* of Itata, lying within the ecclesiastical jurisdiction of Concepción.

590 Casanova Guarda, Holdenis. Las rebeliones araucanas del siglo XVIII: mito y realidad. Temuco, Chile: Ediciones Univ. de la Frontera, 1987. 111 p.: bibl. (Serie Quinto centenario; 1)

Careful study of Araucanian rebellions of 1723 and 1766 and their impact. Notes increasing interpenetration of communities during the 18th century and a decline in antagonisms, partly the consequence of commerce, missionary activity, and *mestizaje.*

591 Chaumeil, Jean-Pierre. Nihamwo: los yagua del nor-oriente peruano. Traducción de María Victoria Santolaria de Ruda. Lima: Centro Amazónico de Antropología y Aplicación Práctica, 1987. 183 p., 8 p. of plates: bibl., ill. (some col.).

Solid ethnographic account of Yagua by French anthropologist. For annotation of author's *Historia y migraciones yagua de finales del siglo XVII hasta nuestros días,* see *HLAS 46:1608.*

592 Choy, Emilio. Antropología e historia. Lima: UNMSM, 1988. 3 v.: bibl., ill.

Essays by influential intellectual, some dealing with rebellion of Tupac Amaru. Of limited ethnohistorical value.

593 Contreras, Carlos. Estado republicano y tributo indígena en la sierra central en la post-independencia. (*Rev. Indias,* 48:182/183, enero/agosto 1988, p. 517–550, bibl., tables)

Useful study of the *contribución de indígenas* in early republican Peru. Argues that the contribution was not colonial tribute in disguise since at that time the individual paid directly, not the *ayllu* or community. Also states that the *curaca's* role in tribute collection was eliminated, and that free movement ended the *forastero—originario* distinction.

594 Contribuciones a los estudios de los Andes centrales. Recopilación de Shozo Masuda. Tokio: Univ. de Tokio, 1984. 405 p.: ill.

Series of important articles. Shozo Masuda, "Nueva técnica de investigación etnográfica andina (p. 1–21), points out the need for systematic study of the chroniclers using the computer to determine who borrowed from whom. Also by Masuda, "Informaciones acerca de la coca referidas en las Crónicas" (p. 22–58) applies the technique to coca. Jorge A. Flores Ochoa and Percy Paz Florez, in "El cultivo en Qocha en la Puna Sur Andina," examine raised field cultivation in the region of Lake Titicaca. Bente Bittman's "El programa cobija: investigaciones antropológico-multidisciplinarias en la Costa Centro Sur Andina: notas etnohistóricas" (p. 101–148) looks at the border region between Peru and Chile. Franklin Pease and Pedro Guibovich, in "Indice del Primer Libro Notorial de Moqueguas" (p. 149–383), provide a detailed index for years 1587–88, 1590, and 1593–95. Very useful compilation that includes many transactions of *curacas* involving commercial activities from near Arequipa to the Lake Titicaca basin.

595 Costales, Piedad Peñaherrera de and **Alfredo Costales Samaniego.** Nos, la plebe. Quito: Ediciones ABYA-YALA, 1986. 204 p.: bibl.

Study of social conflict in colonial Ecuador with focus on commoners, *mestizos,* artisans, and small shopkeepers during periods of crisis, especially the rebellion against the *alcabala* and a series of revolts in the third quarter of the 18th century.

596 Crónica que narra la entrada del Padre Vital en las zonas habitadas por los Cunibos y Campas en 1687. (*Amazonía Peru.,* 6:12, nov. 1985, p. 157–164)

Transcription by Julián Heras of important late 17th-century missionary report on the Cunibos and Campas of the Peruvian

Amazon basin. At the time, Franciscans and Jesuits were active in the region.

597 Cunha, Manuela Carneiro da and **Eduardo Batalha Viveiros de Castro.** Vingança e temporalidade: os Tupinambás. (*Anu. Antropol.*, 85, 1985, p. 57–78, bibl.)

Study of importance of warfare and ritual cannibalism for the Tupinambá and of the efforts of early Jesuits and colonial officials to erradicate the practice.

598 Dean, Warren. Indigenous populations of the São Paulo-Rio de Janeiro coast: trade, *aldeamento*, slavery and extinction. (*Rev. Hist./São Paulo*, 117, julho/dez. 1984, p. 3–26)

Careful study of the likely size of each native community in the São Paulo-Rio de Janeiro area in the 16th century. Starting with a population estimate of 57–63,000 in 1555, author uses a variety of techniques to extrapolate backwards, estimating that there were 103,000 individuals at contact. By 1600 the Tupinamba were virtually extinct in the region.

599 Dickason, Olive Patricia. The Brazilian connection: a look at the origin of French techniques for trading with Amerindians. (*Rev. fr. hist. Outre-mer*, 71:264/265, 1984, p. 129–146)

Argues that the experience gained by the French engaged in Indian trade in 16th-century Brazil provided a model that would be applied in Canada during the next century.

600 Dillehay, Tom D. and **Américo Gordon.** La actividad prehispánica de los incas y su influencia en la Araucania. (*in* Congreso Internacional de Americanistas, *45th, Bogotá, 1985.* Arqueología de las Américas. Bogotá: Fondo de Promoción de la Cultura, 1988, p. 145–156, bibl., facsim., map)

Socioeconomic frontier of the Inca may have extended into Araucanian territories far beyond the political boundary. Although the historical record is inconclusive, recent archaeological evidence shows Inca influence in pottery and textile designs as well as in gold and silver production.

601 Dillehay, Tom D. Estrategias políticas y económicas de las etnias locales del Valle del Chillón durante el período prehis-

pánico. (*Rev. Andin.*, 5:2, dic. 1987, p. 407–456, bibl., maps)

Tests "verticality" model in Chillón Valley of central coastal Peru. Finds ethnic groups gained economic self-sufficiency and political autonomy in various ways: colonization, economic interchange, migratory work groups, even warfare. Prefers concept of "strategic complementarity" to describe the socioeconomic dynamics of the valley.

602 Dzieje Inków przez nich samych opisane = Incas' history described by themselves. Selection by J. Szemiński. Warsaw: Państwowy Instytut Wydawniczy, 1989. 400 p.: ill.

Selection of chronicles by indigenous authors from the 16th century and beginning of the 17th: Titu Cusi Yupanqui, Joan de Santa Cruz Pachacuti Yamqui Salcamaygua, Collapiña, Supno, and other *kipu kamayuq.* Also contains fragments of the Indians' dispositions drawn from the case of Francisco Pizarro's heirs against the Spanish kingdom. Introduction presents sources on the history of Tahuantin-suyu in general, and describes the translated chronicles and their historical background. [M. Nalewajko]

603 Encuentro de Etnohistoriadores, *Santiago, 1987.* Encuentro de Etnohistoriadores. Recopilación de Osvaldo Silva G., Eduardo Medina Cárdenas, y Eduardo Téllez Lúgaro. Santiago: Depto. de Ciencias Históricas, Facultad de Filosofía, Humanidades y Educación, Univ. de Chile, 1988. 213 p.: bibl. (Serie Nuevo Mundo; 1)

Well-edited volume on Chilean ethnohistory consists of wide-ranging articles: Daniel Quiroz and Juan Olivares Toledo, "Nómades Canoeros de la Patagonia Occidental Insular Septentrional" (p. 10–33); Horacio Zapater, "Cuyo en 1658: Amenaza de Asalto de Tribus Indígenas Aliadas" (p. 34–52); José Luis Martínez, "Dispersión y Movilidad en Atacama Colonial" (p. 53–69); Jorge Pinto, "Misioneros y Mapuches: el Proyecto de Padre Luis de Valdivia y el Indigenismo de los Jesuitas en Chile" (p. 70–92); Leyla Marcha, "Fortificaciones Tempranas en el Valle del Toltem" (p. 93–101); Waldo Ricos Bordones, "Percepción de los Mecanismos de Solidaridad y Participación en los Andes: el Ritual del Corte de Pelo" (p. 102–110); Luis Alberto Galdames, "Principios de Percepción Espacial en los Andes a través de los Mitos de Petrificación" (p. 111–123); María Cristina Scatamacchia, "Etnohistoria y Arqueología: Algunas Consideraciones sobre la Historia Indígena" (p. 129–137); Sonia Pinto V., "Los Testamentos del Archivo de Escribanos de Santiago como Fuente Etnohistórica" (p. 138–152); Alberto Medina Rojas and Eduardo Téllez Lúgaro, "Francisco Martínez de Vergara y la Cacica de Chacabuco: un capítulo del Mestizaje 'Aristocrático' en el Chile Colonial" (p. 153–201); and Alberto Medina and María Teresa Prado, "Proposiciones acerca del Concepto de Medicina Tradicional" (p. 202–213).

604 Espinoza Soriano, Waldemar. Etnohistoria Carengue y Cayambe: lo investigado y lo que falta investigar. (*Bol. Lima,* 9:49, enero 1987, p. 89–95, bibl.)

Review of recent ethnohistorical research on peoples of the Quito district. Notes that important work remains to be done.

605 Espinoza Soriano, Waldemar. Los incas: economía, sociedad y Estado en la era del Tahuantinsuyo. La Victoria, Peru: Amaru Editores, 1987. 499 p.: bibl., ill.

Useful survey, and excellent introductory text, covering all aspects of life and society. Stresses impact of the environment, origin of the Incas, and State formation.

Estupiñán-Freile, Tamara. Testamento de Don Francisco Atagualpa. See item **2092.**

606 Fioravanti, Antoinette Molinié. El regreso de Viracocha. (*Bull. Inst. fr. étud. andin.,* 16:3/4, 1987, p. 71–83, bibl.)

Balanced inquiry into the reasons why Andeans referred to the European invaders as "Viracocha."

607 Fishman, Laura. Claude d'Abbeville and the Tupinamba: problems and goals of French missionary work in early seventeenth-century Brazil. (*Church Hist.,* 58:1, March 1989, p. 20–35)

Study of the three-year abortive French experience at Maranhão, particularly the missionary intent of d'Abbeville. The missionaries' legacy lies in the Capuchin's ethnographic account of the Tupinamba.

608 Flores Galindo, Alberto. Europa y el país de los incas: la utopía andina. Lima: Instituto de Apoyo Agrario, 1986. 89 p.: bibl., maps.

In brilliant tour-de-force, author argues that the idea of an Andean utopia is a European creation dating from the 16th century. Traces evolution of the concept of utopia, messianism, the Inkari myth, and the belief in cataclysmic ends ushering in new ages.

609 Frank, Erwin H. Bibliografía anotada de fuentes con interés para la etnología y etnohistoria de los Uni. (*Amazonía Peru.,* 14, 1987, p. 151–160)

Useful annotated bibliography on the Cashibo (i.e., Uni) of Peru's Amazonian lowlands.

610 Galdós Rodríguez, Guillermo. Comunidades prehispánicas de Arequipa. Arequipa, Peru: Fundación M.J. Bustamante de la Fuente, 1987. 391 p.: bibl., index, maps.

Author, director of the Archivo Provincial de Arequipa, has long been interested in the ethnic origins of the peoples of the district. Work provides documentation for a series of settlements surrounding the city: the Yarabayas, Copoatas, Socabaya, Porongoche, Yumina, Characato, and Chiguata.

611 Gambini, Roberto. O espelho índio: os jesuítas e a destruição da alma indígena. Rio de Janeiro: Espaço e Tempo, 1988. 222 p.: bibl., ill. (Col. Pensando o Brasil; 6)

Provocative attempt to apply Jungian analysis to the era of the conquest of Brazil. Author looks at the conflict of *mentalités* of Jesuits and 16th-century Brazilians, primarily on the basis of the Jesuits' annual letters.

612 Ganson, Barbara J. The Evueví of Paraguay: adaptive strategies and responses to colonialism, 1528–1811. (*Americas/Francisc.,* 45:4, April 1989, p. 461–488)

Excellent study of the non-sedentary and fiercely independent Guaycuruans, who dominated a section of the Paraguay/Paraná Rivers. Examines their adaptations to counter Spanish pressures, which allowed cultural survival under pressures of war, slaving operations, and missions.

613 García, Lorenzo. Historia de las misiones en la Amazonia Ecuatoriana. Quito: Ediciones Abya-Yala, 1985. 432 p., 7 leaves of plates (1 folded): bibl., ill., index, maps.

Uneven narrative history by Carmelite of missionary efforts in Ecuadorian Amazon basin.

614 Gareis, Iris. Religiöse Spezialisten des zentralen Andengebietes zur Zeit der Inka und während der spanischen Kolonialherrschaft. Hohenschäftlarn, Germany: Klaus Renner Verlag, 1987. 517 p.: bibl. (Münchner Beiträge zur Amerikanistik; 19k)

Careful systematic review of Inca State religion based on published sources. Looks at State cults, specialists, the *mamacuna* and *aqlla*, the priesthood and conquest, divination, and local religion. Useful bibliography.

615 Glave Testino, Luis Miguel. La producción de los trajines: coca y mercado interno colonial. (*in* Congreso Internacional de Americanistas, *45th, Bogotá, 1985.* Etnohistoria y historia de las Américas. Bogotá: Ediciones Uniandes, 1988, p. 119–138, bibl.)

Excellent study of the colonial transportation system, especially for Potosí. Notarial and other documents shed new light on shipment of coca, wine, and livestock by *encomienda* Indians in spite of royal decrees forbidding their employment in such transport.

616 Glave Testino, Luis Miguel. Tambos y caminos andinos en la formación del mercado interno colonial. (*Anu. Estud. Am.,* 45, 1988, p. 83–138, map)

Well-articulated study of transportation/communication system of the Viceroyalty of Peru and the shift in its control from the Inca to the Spanish. In spite of privatization of the *tambos* (way stations), native groups continued to play an important role in road and bridge maintenance, operation of the *tambos*, and transportation well into the 17th century.

617 Gómez L., Augusto. Llanos orientales: colonización y conflictos interétnicos, 1870–1970. (*Univ. Humaníst.,* 17:29, enero/junio 1988, p. 45–89, bibl., tables)

Examines impact of 19th-century Liberalism on native communities in the Llanos Orientales of Colombia, particularly the Guahibo, Arawak, Saliva, Chibcha, and Camigua-Tinigua. Finds despoliation of communal lands and finally genocide.

618 Grenand, Françoise and **Pierre Grenand.** La côte d'Amapa, de la bouche de l'Amazone à la baie d'Oyapock, atravers la tradition orale Palikur. (*Bol. Mus. Para.*

Goeldi, 3:1, dez. 1987, p. 1–77, appendices, bibl., maps, photos, tables)

Important ethnohistorical survey of the Amapá coast, north of the mouth of the Amazon River, based on documents, archaeology, and oral history. The region was culturally diverse, with linguistic elements of Arawak, Carib, and Tupi.

Grenand, Françoise. Dictionnaire wayãpi-français: lexique français-wayãpi, Guyane française. See *HLAS 51:1203.*

619 Guerrero, Andrés. Curagas y tenientes políticos: la ley de la costumbre y la ley del Estado, Otavalo, 1830–1875. (*Rev. Andin.,* 7:2, dic. 1989, p. 321–366, bibl.)

Independence of Ecuador did not end the colonial tribute regime. In the guise of a "personal contribution," ethnic entities continued to provide a primary source of government revenues. Examines new republican role of the ethnic leaders in the Otavalo district.

620 Guillén Guillén, Edmundo. Los mitos de origen inka y sus fuentes históricas. (*Bol. Lima,* 9:51, mayo 1987, p. 27–35)

Synopsis of principal variants of the Inca origin myths found in the major 16th and 17th-century chronicles.

621 Harrison, Regina. Signs, songs, and memory in the Andes: translating Quechua language and culture. Austin: Univ. of Texas Press, 1989. 233 p.: bibl., ill., index.

Series of stimulating essays that combine the methodologies of linguistics, literary criticism, and anthropology, written following several years of fieldwork in Ecuador. Themes center on the problems of cultural translation, the 16th-century confessionals, Felipillo and Martín as translators, the semiotics of Santacruz Pachacuti Yamqui, and the intricacies of the male-female relationship in the Andean world as depicted in song.

622 Hartmann, Roswith. Necrología y lista de publicaciones de Udo Oberem, 1923–1986. (*Jahrb. Gesch.,* 24, 1987, p. 21–30)

Synopsis of the work of a leading figure in Ecuadorian ethnohistory.

623 Hartmann, Roswith. Un predicador quechua del siglo XVI. (*in* Primer Simposio Europeo sobre Antropología del Ecuador. Memorias. Recopilación de Segundo E.

Moreno Yáñez. Bonn: Instituto de Antropología Cultural de la Univ. de Bonn; Quito: Ediciones Abya-Yala, 1985, p. 291–301, bibl.)

Biographical study of Diego Lobato de Sosa, mestizo offspring of a Spanish captain and one of the wives of the Inca, Atahualpa. Born about 1541, he was one of the few mestizos to be ordained. He achieved fame as a preacher in Quechua and as an examiner in the language.

624 Henley, Paul. Reconstructing Chaima and Cumanagoto kinship categories: an exercise in "tracking down ethnohistorical connections." (*Antropológica*, 63–64, 1985, p. 151–195, bibl., ill., tables)

Careful study of two late 17th-century dictionaries finds that the Chaima and Cumanagoto, two extinct Carib groups of eastern Venezuela, had "Dravidian" kinship structures and practiced cross-cousin and sister's-daughter marriage.

625 Hornborg, Alf. Stratification and exchange in the pre-columbian Andes. (*Ethnos*, 3/4, 1989, p. 217–228, bibl., map)

Widespread exchange of certain items, especially *spondylus* shell ornaments, is a persistent feature of the precolumbian Andean economy. Although specific goods and the mechanisms of exchange varied in time and place, the flow of articles continued in times of both independent regional polities and larger states.

626 The Huarochirí manuscript: a testament of ancient and Colonial Andean religion. Translation from Quechua by Frank Salomon and George L. Urioste; annotations and introductory essay by Frank Salomon. Austin: Univ. of Texas Press, 1991. p. cm.

Magnificent and well-edited version of native American narratives of the Huarochirí region of central Peru, collected during idolatry investigations of the late 16th to early 17th centuries. The book is of interest for both the specialist and the general reader, providing excellent insight into Andean religious concepts at the provincial level during a period in which Christianization efforts were still provisional.

627 Iglesias, Angel María. Los cañaris: aspectos históricos y culturales. Cañar, Ecuador: Impr. América, 1987. 156 p.: ill.

Uncritical survey of Cañari ethnic group, from pre-history to present.

628 Jaźwińska, Hanna. Análisis de un proceso de idolatria de la región de Checras del siglo XVII. (*Estud. Latinoam.*, 12, 1989, p. 139–172, ill., tables)

Interesting case of 1647 idolatry trial involving *kuraka* Tomás de Acosta of Checras, based on documents in the Archivo Arzobispal de Lima. The charges, based on a conspiracy by his illegitimate younger brother to remove him from office, were probably false.

629 Julien, Catherine J. How Inca decimal administration worked. (*Ethnohistory*, 35:3, Summer 1988, p. 257–279, bibl., map, tables)

Examines chronicler's accounts of Inca decimal system; then relates three case studies of utilization of Inca-period *quipos* in the 16th century (Chupacho, Chucuito, and Chachapoyas). Inca system of decimal organization led to modifications in the territorial structure of the provinces, bringing disparate parts into a coherent whole.

630 Kato, Takahiro. Estudios andinos en Japón en los años 80: balance y perspectivas. (*Rev. Andin.*, 9:2, dic. 1991, p. 487–511)

Surveys recent studies by Japanese scholars in Andean archaeology, ethnohistory, social anthropology, and linguistics. Presents extensive bibliography on these subjects in the 1980s. [K. Horisaka]

631 Kroemer, Gunter. Cuxiuara: o Purus dos indígenas: ensaio etno-histórico e etnográfico sobre os índios do médio Purus. São Paulo: Edições Loyola, 1985. 171 p.: bibl., ill. (Col. Missão aberta; 10)

View of the peoples of the Rio Purus area of Brazil from the standpoint of Jesuit missionaries, with historical survey of early contacts. Provides ethnographic account of Apurina, Jamamadi, Paumari, and Zuruaha.

632 Langer, Erick Detlef and **Robert H. Jackson.** Colonial and republican missions compared: the cases of Alta California and southeastern Bolivia. (*Comp. Stud. Soc. Hist.*, 30:2, April 1988, p. 286–311, graphs)

Comparison of Franciscan mission systems in Alta California (18th-19th centuries) and southeastern Bolivia (late 19th-early 20th centuries), stressing five factors: type of Indian society, nature of frontier, demography, acculturation, and resistance to change.

633 **Leiva, Arturo.** El primer avance a la Araucanía: Angol 1862. Temuco, Chile: Univ. de la Frontera, 1984. 220 p.: bibl.

Well-developed presentation of Chilean occupation of Angol and its environs in the mid-19th century, based on extensive archival research. Includes diary by one of the military commanders detailing the occupation.

634 **Lenz-Volland, Birgit** and **Martin Volland.** Algunas noticias acerca de los caciques de Daule durante el siglo XVII: estudio preliminar. (*in* Primer Simposio Europeo sobre Antropología del Ecuador. Memorias. Recopilación de Segundo E. Moreno Yáñez. Bonn: Instituto de Antropología Cultural de la Univ. de Bonn; Quito: Ediciones Abya-Yala, 1985, p. 189–200, bibl.)

Study of the Cayche *cacique* family of the Guayaquil district. Much of the foundation of the family's power was established by María Cayche during the administration of Daule (1590s-1644).

635 **León Solís, Leonardo.** Malocas araucanas en las fronteras de Chile, Cuyo y Buenos Aires: 1700–1800. (*Anu. Estud. Am.*, 44, 1987, p. 281–324, bibl.)

Thorough study of Araucanian raids in Argentina especially during the 18th century. The attacks on Spanish ranches, largely successful, were regular events after 1750 and peaked about 1780.

López-Baralt, Mercedes. Icono y conquista: Guamán Poma de Ayala. See item **3327.**

López-Baralt, Mercedes. La metáfora como *traslatio:* del código verbal al visual en la crónica ilustrada de Guamán Poma. See item **3328.**

636 **Lorandi, Ana María** and **Ricardo E. Rodríguez Molas.** Historia y antropología: hacia una nueva dimensión de la ciencia. (*Etnía*, 32, julio/dic. 1984, p. 53–80, bibl.)

Review of the state of the art of ethnohistory, especially its Andean variety, and of its potential contribution to a better understanding of Argentina's experience with its native peoples.

637 **Luna, Hugo Alberto.** Misión de Zenta: apuntes, actas y documentos para su historia. Salta, Argentina: Convento San Francisco, 1981. 126 p.: bibl., ill. (Conozca-

mos lo nuestro; 3) (Cuadernos franciscanos; 58. Itinerario; 22)

In-house mission history, of some ethnohistorical value, based on published documents from the Archivo del Convento de San Francisco de Tarija. Covers missions to Mataguayos and Vejoces, from about 1779–1820.

638 **Mallmann, Alfeu Nilson.** Retrato sem retoque das missões guaranis. Porto Alegre, Brazil: Martins Livreiro-Editor, 1986. 364 p.: bibl., ill.

Broad survey of the Jesuit missionary experience in Paraguay, based primarily on secondary sources.

639 **Manarelli, María Emma.** Inquisición y mujeres: las hechiceras en el Perú durante el siglo XVII. Lima: Centro de Documentación sobre la Mujer, 1987. 24 p.: bibl. (Cuadernos culturales. Serie I, La mujer en la historia)

Informative work that breaks new ground on an important topic.

640 **Mandrini, Raúl.** La agricultura indígena en la región pampeana y sus adyacencias, siglos XVIII y XIX. (*Anu. IEHS*, 1, 1986, p. 11–43, map)

Points out the clear evolution of agriculture among the native peoples of the Argentine pampas in the 18th and 19th centuries.

641 **Marriner, Harry Andrew.** El Rosal. S.l.: H.A. Marriner, 1988. 206 p.

Local history of El Rosal, based on archival investigation and oral history. Provides material on the Musca and their integration into the *encomienda* system, and on El Rosal from 1638–1870. Also includes a series of *hacienda* histories.

642 **Martínez C., José Luis.** Kurakas, rituales e insignias: una proposición. (*Histórica/Lima*, 12:1, julio 1988, p. 61–74, bibl.)

Systematic survey of symbols of power manipulated by *curacas:* trumpets, litters, fine *cumbi* cloth, feathers, and the *duho* seat. Also recounts the *curaca's* relation to local religious forces.

643 **Martínez de Salinas Alonso, María Luisa.** Los intentos de pacificación de los indios pijao, Nuevo Reino de Granada, a fines del siglo XVI. (*Rev. Indias*, 49:186, mayo/agosto 1989, p. 355–377, maps)

Traces Spanish attempts to subdue the Pijao, unsuccessful in spite of nearby gold deposits. The group earned the reputation as one of the most bellicose in the northeastern Andes.

644 Marzal, Manuel M. La religión andina persistente en Andagua a fines del Virreinato. (*Histórica/Lima*, 12:2, dic. 1988, p. 161–181, bibl.)

On the basis of two documents (1750 and 1813) in the Archivo Arzobispal de Lima, author attempts to reconstruct Andean religious beliefs. Notes that introduction of Christianity brought about profound changes; nevertheless native practices, especially relating to agriculture and the cure of illness, were retained.

645 Mehringer, Jakob. Pajonal-Asheninka, Campa-Indianer: ihre kulturelle Stellung im Rahmen der ostperuanischen Proto-Aruak Stämme. Hohenschäftlarn, Germany: Klaus Renner Verlag, 1986. 257 p., 52 p. of plates: bibl., ill., photos. (Münchner Beiträge zur Amerikanistik; 18)

Primarily modern ethnography of the montaña region of Peru, with some ethnohistorical background. Includes an excellent series of photographs of the subject area (1971–84).

Meliá, Bartomeu. El guaraní: conquistado y reducido; See *HLAS 51:946*.

646 Méndez Beltrán, Luz María. Trabajo indígena en la frontera araucana de Chile. (*Jahrb. Gesch.*, 24, 1987, p. 213–249)

Detailed investigation of evolution of native American labor systems on Araucanian frontier. Under royal protection, the group did not fall into the hands of private *encomenderos*. Yet labor was extracted with regulated salaries in a manner similar to the *mita* of Peru.

647 Michieli, Catalina Teresa. Los comechingones según *La crónica de Gerónimo de Bibar* y su confrontación con otras fuentes. San Juan, Argentina: Univ. Nacional de San Juan, Facultad de Filosofía, Humanidades y Artes, Instituto de Investigaciones Arqueológicas y Museo, 1985. 80 p. (Publicaciones; 13)

Bibar's chronicle, completed in 1558, included substantial mention of the *comechingones*, located just north of present-day

Córdoba. Author examines warfare, the economy, housing and settlement patterns, demography, religion, and social customs.

Michieli, Catalina Teresa. La región de Cuyo y sus naturales a través de la crónica de Gerónimo de Bibar y su confrontación con otras fuentes. Los indígenas de la Punta de los Venados a la llegada de los españoles. See item **2278.**

648 Michom, Martin. La economía subterránea y el mercado urbano: pulperos, "indias gateras," y "recatonas" del Quito colonial, siglos XVI-XVII. (*in* Primer Simposio Europeo sobre Antropología del Ecuador: Memorias. Recopilación de Segundo E. Moreno Yáñez. Bonn: Instituto de Antropología Cultural de la Univ. de Bonn; Quito: Ediciones Abya-Yala, 1985, p. 175–187, bibl.)

Early colonial Quito was supplied largely by an informal market (*tiánguez*) system dominated by Indian women. This system, based on barter, evolved in spite of Crown and *cabildo* legislation enacted to control the local economy.

649 Millones, Luis and **Mary Louise Pratt.** Amor brujo: images and culture of love in the Andes. Syracuse, N.Y.: Maxwell School of Citizenship and Public Affairs, Syracuse Univ., 1990. 79 p.: bibl., facsims., maps. (Foreign and comparative studies/ Latin American series; 10)

Unique interdisciplinary effort combines talents of an anthropologist (Millones) and a linguist (Pratt). Work uses interviews, local archives, drawings of Guamán Poma de Ayala, and the contemporary plank paintings of Sarhua (Ayacucho) to examine concepts of courtship, marriage, and Andean space and time.

650 Millones, Luis. Historia y poder en los Andes centrales: desde los orígenes al siglo XVII. Madrid: Alianza, 1987. 208 p.: bibl. (Alianza América; 14)

Important interpretive work by prominent anthropologist focuses on evolution of State and empire, examining Huari expansion, the Kingdom of Chimor and the Lupaca, and finally the Incas. Myth and religion play a role in rationalizing expansion and control of subjects. The Inca were in turn overthrown by European conquest and repression, provoking native resistance.

651 Millones, Luis; Francisco Huaman-tinco; and Edgar Sulca. Los incas en el recuerdo poético andino. (*Nuevo Texto Crít.,* 1:1, 1988, p. 7–33)

Drama of the death of the Inca Ata-hualpa, based on the poetic vision of Hermi-nio Ricaldi and his nephew Pío Campos from Junín Province. In this case there is an at-tempt to integrate native Andean oral tradi-tions with the modern nation-state.

652 Millones, Luis. Shamanismo y política en el Perú colonial: los curacas de Ayacucho. (*Bol. Antropol. Am.,* 15, julio 1987, p. 93–103, bibl., facsims., map)

Case study of a *kuraka* in the Aya-cucho district in the early 18th century. Demonstrates ways by which political au-thority could be maintained by shamanism. Here, colonial demands for the Huancavelica mines strained traditional leadership, creat-ing cleavages and factional battles. Spanish clerics and bureaucrats became enmeshed in these struggles.

653 Morales-Méndez, Filadelfo; María-elena Caprilles de Prada; and Horacio Biord Castillo. Historia Karíña de los siglos XVI y XVII. (*Bol. Acad. Nac. Hist./Caracas,* 70:277, enero/marzo 1987, p. 79–99, bibl.)

Brief sociocultural reconstruction of one largely Venezuelan Carib group at the time of the European conquest, based on pri-mary published sources.

Moreira Neto, Carlos de Araújo. Indios da Amazônia, de maioria a minoria, 1750–1850. See *HLAS 51:3280.*

654 Moreno Yáñez, Segundo. Alzamientos indígenas en la Audiencia de Quito, 1534–1803 Runacunapaj macanacuicuna. Versión quichua de Abel Inga Tenesaca y Carlos Moreno Maldonado. Quito: Ediciones Abya-Yala, 1987. 72 p.: bibl., ill.

Brief bilingual (Spanish-Quechua) ver-sion of a study of native resistance during the colonial era.

655 Moreno Yáñez, Segundo. Las "compo-siciones de tierras" y el despojo de la propiedad indígena en la región Latacunga-Ambato, siglo XVII. (*Cultura/Quito,* 8:24b, enero/abril 1986, p. 627–638, bibl.)

Case study of the impact of the *com-posiciones de tierras* first conducted in the Quito district in 1647–52. Similar to land title searches, *composiciones* involved pay-ment to the royal treasury to validate claims. Indian communities often suffered, but in this case, although fraud was uncovered, offi-cials were brought to trial.

656 Moreno Yáñez, Segundo. Don Leandro Sepla y Oro: un cacique andino de fi-nales de la colonia: estudio biográfico. (*in* Primer Simposio Europeo sobre Antropología del Ecuador: Memorias. Recopilación de Segundo E. Moreno Yáñez. Bonn: Instituto de Antropología Cultural de la Univ. de Bonn; Quito: Ediciones Abya-Yala, 1985, p. 223–244, bibl.)

Biographical study of *cacique* (1738–1810) of the Chimborazo province of Ecuador who collaborated closely with officials, help-ing to quell uprisings in 1764, 1778, and 1803. Shows the extent to which some *ca-ciques* could identify with the colonial re-gime, yet maintain their base.

657 Mott, Luiz Roberto de Barros. Aco-tundá: raízes setecentistas do sincre-tismo religioso afro-brasileiro. (*Rev. Mus. Paul.,* 31, 1986, p. 124–147, bibl., table)

Study of religious syncretism as exem-plified by the Acotundá dance of Nigerian origin which became widespread in Minas Gerais. The dance was suppressed by Brazil-ian authorities in 1747.

658 Nari, Marcela M. Alejandra. Deses-tructuración del mundo indígena. (*Rev. Hist. Am.,* 104, julio/dic. 1987, p. 7–18, bibl., ill., tables)

Author develops a case for a total breakdown of Andean society in the years immediately following European contact. Warfare, mine labor, *repartimientos*, and epi-demics were primary factors.

659 Netherly, Patricia. Las fronteras incas con el reino de Chimor. (*in* Congreso Internacional de Americanistas, 45th, Bo-gotá, 1985. Arqueología de las Américas. Bo-gotá: Fondo de Promoción de la Cultura, 1988, p. 103–118, bibl.)

Important systematic analysis of evo-lution of Inca control over coastal Chimor state. Local leaders were preoccupied with growing Inca hegemony and unsuccessfully attempted to block conquest of neighboring Huamachuco and Cajamarca. With victory, the Incas achieved domination by redefining frontiers and taking direct control of middle valleys; yet they allowed indirect rule in the Chimor core.

660 Niemeyer F., Hans and **Virgilio Schiappacasse F.** Patrones de asentamiento incaicos en el Norte Grande de Chile. (*in* Congreso Internacional de Americanistas, *45th, Bogotá, 1985.* Arqueología de las Américas. Bogotá: Fondo de Promoción de la Cultura, 1988, p. 119–144, bibl., facsims., maps)

Study of two principal zones of Inca control in Northern Chile: the Camarones Valley with resources of fish, shellfish, and guano; and the Cuenca del Salar de Atacama with minerals. Inca-style *tambos* were found in both valleys.

661 Ortiz, Juan Aurelio. Tinkunaco riojano. La Rioja, Argentina: Ediciones Tiempo Latinoamericano, 1987. 104 p., 14 leaves of plates: bibl., ill.

Touches on missionary efforts among the Diaguitas and on the activities of San Francisco Solano.

662 Ortiz de la Tabla Ducasse, Javier. La población ecuatoriana en el siglo XVI: fuentes y cálculos. (*in* Primer Simposio Europeo sobre Antropología del Ecuador: Memorias. Recopilación de Segundo E. Moreno Yáñez. Bonn: Instituto de Antropología Cultural de la Univ. de Bonn; Quito: Ediciones Abya-Yala, 1985, p. 159–173)

Evaluates state of knowledge of Ecuador's colonial population. Points out that while sources abound (general reports, geographical descriptions, Church documents, royal account records, *visitas*, and *encomienda* documents), no solid study has yet been done.

Palermo, Miguel Angel. La innovacion agropecuaria entre los indígenas pampeanopatagónicos: genesis y procesos. See item **2290.**

663 Palop Martínez, Josefina. Los cayapas en el siglo XVI. (*in* Congreso Internacional de Americanistas, *45th, Bogotá, 1985.* Etnohistoria e historia de las Américas. Bogotá: Ediciones Uniandes, 1988, p. 61–76, bibl., tables)

Ethnohistorical description of an indigenous group (ca. 1600) of the Esmeraldas province of Ecuador, based on documents from the Archivo General de Indias in Seville.

664 Paraiso, Maria Hilda Baqueiro. Os capuchinos e os índios no sul da Bahia: uma análise preliminar da sua atuação. (*Rev. Mus. Paul.*, 31, 1986, p. 148–196, bibl., tables)

The Capuchins were second only to the Jesuits in number of missionaries in Brazil; however, their attempts to convert the Indians have received little scholarly attention. Here is an overview of their work south of Bahia, primarily in the 19th century.

Patte, Marie France. De los Añun. See *HLAS 51:1220.*

665 Pease, Franklin. Las crónicas y los Andes. (*Rev. Crít. Lit. Latinoam.*, 14:28, 1988, p. 117–158, bibl.)

Balanced historiographical examination of the primary colonial chroniclers. Useful for both the specialist and beginner.

666 Pease, Franklin. Curacas coloniales: riqueza y actitudes. (*Rev. Indias*, 48:183/183, enero/agosto 1988, p. 87–107)

In the colonial era in the Andes many *curacas* amassed fortunes that led them to be ranked in strictly economic terms near the top of the socioeconomic scale. Such was true of the five individuals examined here.

667 Pease, Franklin. Nota sobre una nueva edición de la *Suma y narración de los incas.* (*Histórica/Lima*, 12:2, dic. 1988, p. 183–192, bibl.)

Historiographical evaluation of the work of Juan de Betanzos and of the significance of the newly discovered version of his *Suma y narración de los Incas*, published in 1987 by the Fundación Bartolomé March in Palma de Mallorca.

668 Pergola, Federico. Brujos y cuasi médicos en los inicios argentinos. Buenos Aires: EDIMED, 1986. 119 p.: bibl., ill. (Biblioteca de temas médicos)

Concise survey of folk curing for the general public by a professor of internal medicine and past president of the Argentine Society for the History of Medicine.

Peruvian prehistory: an overview of pre-Inca and Inca society. See *HLAS 51:624.*

669 Pineda Camacho, Roberto. Historia oral y proceso esclavista en el Caquetá. Bogotá: Fundación de Investigaciones Arqueológicas Nacionales, Banco de la República, 1985. 138 p.: bibl., ill. (some col.).

Examination of the lower Caquetá-Putumayo of Colombia, with chapters on Caguán culture and society, commerce and violence, and *brujos* and illnesses. Based on archival research and investigations in the field. Slaving expeditions had a substantial impact on the development of this region.

670 Platt, Tristan. Le calendrier économique des indiens de Lipez en Bolivie au XIXe siècle. (*Ann. écon. soc. civilis.*, 42:3, mai/juin 1987, p. 549–576, bibl., tables)

Important contribution to our understanding of the seasonal economy in one part of the Bolivian *altiplano*. Provides good example of the type of research needed on 19th-century topics.

671 Purizaga Vega, Medardo. El Inti Raymi como instrumento de dominación entre los Incas. (*in* Congreso Peruano de Hombre y la Cultura Andina, *6th, Lima, 1985*. Actas y trabajos. Recopilación de Francisco E. Iriarte Brenner. Lima: Univ. Inca Garcilaso de la Vega, Facultad de Ciencias Sociales, 1985, v. 2, p. 41–56)

Discusses significance of the placement of regional deities in Coricancha during the festival of Inti Raymi. Valuable for the study of the use of religion in Inca control over subjects.

672 Ramírez, Susan E. El "Dueño de Indios:" reflexiones sobre las consecuencias de cambios en las bases de poder del "curaca de los viejos antiguos" bajo los españoles en el Peru del siglo XVI. (*HISLA*, 10, 1987, p. 39–66, bibl., tables)

Important examination of the rapid change in the role and status of northern Peruvian *curacas* in the half century following conquest. Once commanding political authority and prestige, and control of water and resources, the *curacas*, under pressures of demographic collapse, war, forced migrations, the encomienda, and *reducciones*, soon lost the respect of subordinates.

673 Ramón Valarezo, Galo. Del cacicazgo andino a la hacienda: la transformación del espacio productivo en Cayambe. (*Cultura/Quito*, 8:24b, enero/abril 1986, p. 639–654, bibl., map)

Reducciones of 1576–79 broke the old spatial control over land and products exercised by *curacas* and led to the evolution of the Ecuadorian highland hacienda.

674 Randall, Robert. Del tiempo y del río: el ciclo de la historia y la energía en la cosmología incaica. (*Bol. Lima*, 9:54, nov. 1987, p. 69–95, bibl.)

Detailed and useful study of the concepts of the circulation of water and energy in Inca cosmology. Based on ethnohistorical sources, chronicles, and especially on dictionaries which the author argues are the "most pure sources" for reaching an understanding of the Andean mind.

675 Ravines, Rogger. El cuarto del rescate de Atahualpa, 1532–1987. (*Bol. Lima*, 9:50, marzo 1987, p. 51–60, bibl.)

Describes the archaeological restoration of the supposed building where the ransom of Inca ruler Atahualpa was collected. Useful from the standpoint of Inca regional-style architecture.

Reeve, Mary-Elizabeth. Cauchu Uras: lowland Quichua histories of the Amazon rubber boom. See *HLAS 51:932.*

676 Renard-Casevitz, France Marie; Thierry Saignes; and **Anne Christine Taylor.** L'Inca, l'Espagnol et les sauvages: rapports entre les sociétés amazoniennes et andines du XVe au XVIIe siècle. Paris: Editions Recherche sur les Civilisations, 1986. 411 p.: bibl., ill., indexes. (Synthèse, 0291–1663; 21)

Provides series of competent regional slices of Andean life shortly after European contact. Focuses on the highlands from Tarma to Guamanga, and on the eastern montaña from Carabaya to Cochabamba.

Requena, Francisco. Diario del viaje al Japurá. See item **2123.**

677 El Retorno de las Huacas: estudios y documentos sobre el Taki Onqoy. Recopilación de Luis Millones. Lima: Instituto de Estudios Peruanos; Sociedad Peruana de Psicoanálisis, 1990. 450 p.: bibl. (Biblioteca Peruana de Psicoanálisis; 2. Fuentes e Investigaciones para la Historia del Perú; 8)

Excellent series of articles on important native resistance movement of the 1560s. Probably the best work to date on the subject.

678 Ritos y tradiciones de Huarochirí: manuscrito quechua de comienzos del siglo XVII. Versión paleográfica, interpretación fonológica y traducción al castellano de Gérald Taylor. Estudio biográfico sobre Francisco de Avila de Antonio Acosta Rodríguez. Lima: Instituto de Estudios Peruanos; Instituto Francés de Estudios Andinos, 1987. 616 p.: bibl., ill., indexes. (Travaux de l'IFEA; 35. Historia andina; 12)

New basic edition of the Quechua text of the Huarochirí myths, with a Spanish translation. Important contribution, for the original Quechua provides the original meaning and nuances, both of which are sometimes lost in translation. Includes informative biographical study of Francisco de Avila by Antonio Acosta Rodríguez.

679   Rodríguez Achung, Martha. Poblamiento de la Amazonía desde el siglo XIX hasta 1940. (*Shupihui*, 11 : 39, enero/marzo 1986, p. 7–28, tables)

Outlines primarily Peruvian migration into the Amazonian region during the 19th century, and growth of Iquitos, Moyobamba, Tarapoto, Lamas, and Yurimaguas.

Rodríguez Molas, Ricardo E. Esclavitud africana, religión y origen étnico. See item **2292.**

680   Rodríguez Molas, Ricardo E. Los sometidos de la conquista: Argentina, Bolivia, Paraguay. Buenos Aires: Centro Editor de América Latina, 1985. 284 p. (Bibliotecas universitarias. Historia)

Series of contemporary documents relating to treatment of native Americans from 16th-17th centuries, with solid introductory essay.

681   Romoli, Kathleen. Los de la lengua de cueva: los grupos indígenas del istmo oriental en la época de la conquista española. Bogotá: Instituto Colombiano de Antropología; Instituto Colombiano de Cultura, 1987. 222 p.: bibl., ill.

Basic and important study of this Colombian group, based on archival research in Europe and America. The Cuevas disappeared early; the Cuna of the lower Atrato and Panama are different ethnic entities. Author, who spent some four decades researching the Cuevas, systematically examined all aspects of their culture.

682   Rostworowski de Diez Canseco, María. Historia del Tahuantinsuyu. Lima: Instituto de Estudios Peruanos; Ministerio de la Presidencia, Consejo Nacional de Ciencia y Tecnología, 1988. 332 p.: bibl., ill. (Historia andina; 13)

Analytical reevaluation of the Inca period by prominent specialist. Author begins with an examination of ethnohistorical sources and treats a variety of subjects including the nature of Cusco, the reasons for its expansion and development, and the social and economic nature of the regime.

683   Ruiz Lara, Guillermo. Castellví, el sabio y el hombre: la obra antecedente de la Iglesia y de los misioneros capuchinos. Medellín, Colombia: Editorial Zuluaga, 1986. 186 p., 1 leaf of plates: bibl. (Col. Academia Colombiana de Historia Eclesiástica; 7)

Laudatory biography of 20th-century Spanish Capuchine missionary and linguist who worked in Colombia.

684   Saignes, Thierry. Capoche, Potosí y la coca: el consumo popular de estimulantes en el siglo XVII. (*Rev. Indias*, 48 : 182/183, enero/agosto 1988, p. 207–235, appendix, bibl.)

Presents new documentary evidence on coca use in the 17th-century Andes. Stresses the ritual importance of consumption. During the course of the century, chicha, then wine, came to be substituted for coca, modifying traditional social relationships.

685   Saignes, Thierry. En busca del poblamiento étnico de los Andes bolivianos: siglos XV y XVI. La Paz: Museo Nacional de Etnografía y Folklore, 1986. 46 p.: map. (Avances de investigación; 3)

Important attempt to map spatial distribution of ethnic units, based on *encomienda* grants and the Toledo assessments of the 1570s. Author hoped to establish ethnic boundaries of the early colonial era and the period preceding Inca expansion. Here, oral traditions, modern toponymic identifications, and musical, linguistic, and juridical documents are mustered as evidence.

Salomon, Frank. Crisis y transformación de la sociedad aborigen invadida, 1528–1573. See item **2124.**

686   Salomon, Frank. Frontera aborigen y dualismo inca en el Ecuador prehispánico: pistas onomásticas. (*in* Congreso Internacional de Americanistas, *45th, Bogotá, 1985.* Arqueología de las Américas. Bogotá: Fondo de Promoción de la Cultura, 1988, p. 87–102, bibl., ill., map, tables)

Important interpretive application of onomastical analysis to the 1559 *visita* of an *encomienda* in the Quito basin. Finds that expansion of Inca frontier had two components: 1) military conquest; and 2) long-range cultural integration. Duality was an important facet of Inca domination here, as in the south.

687 Salomon, Frank. *YUMBO ÑAN:* la vialidad indígena en el noroccidente de Pichincha y el trasfondo aborigen del camino de Pedro Vicente Maldonado. (*Cultura/ Quito*, 8:24b, enero/abril 1986, p. 611–626, bibl.)

Exchange had long existed between the Yumbos of the Guayllabamba River system and Esmeraldas on the coast, and Quito in the highlands. In the 18th century Maldonado unsuccessfully attempted to replace the native footpath network with a carriage road.

688 Sánchez-Albornoz, Nicolás. La mita de Lima: magnitud y procedencia. (*Histórica/Lima*, 12:2, dic. 1988, p. 193–209, bibl., table)

History of the large mining *mitas* is now well known. Less studied are the local *mitas de plaza* for service in Spanish urban centers and surrounding fields. Here are important clues based on a document in the Archivo General de la Nación in Buenos Aires concerning operation of Lima's *mita* from 1575 to the mid-17th century.

Santamaría, Daniel J. Resistencia anticolonial y movimientos mesiánicos entre los chiriguanos del siglo XVIII. See item **2200.**

689 Santos, Fernando. Memorial del Capitán Don Pedro Bohórquez: segunda parte del manuscrito. (*Amazonía Peru.*, 8:14, 1987, p. 131–149)

Pt. 2 contains the transcription of report by Capt. Andrés Salgado de Araujo (for pt. 1, see *Amazonía Peruana*, 7:13, Sept. 1986). Here are excerpts from the 1650 cabildo sessions of San Miguel Arcángel de Salbatierra on the frontier of the Cerro de la Sal. Much information on nearby peoples.

690 Santos Granero, Fernando. Templos y herrerías: utopía y re-creación cultural en la Amazonía peruana, siglos XVIII-XIX. (*Bull. Inst. fr. étud. andin.*, 17:2, 1988, p. 1–22, bibl., map, photo, tables)

Solid survey of the 100 years (1742–1847) during which the Amuesha and Campa of the central *montaña* were able to remain independent. Stresses acquisition of the knowledge of iron-founding under Franciscan rule, and the association between iron production and religious rites that followed the expulsion of the Franciscans.

691 Sarmiento de Gamboa, Pedro. Historia de los Incas. Madrid: Miraguano Ediciones: Ediciones Polifemo, 1988. 191 p.: bibl. (Biblioteca de viajeros hispánicos; 4)

First peninsular ed. of a basic, quasi-first hand source on the Incas and their empire. Based on oral testimonies of knowledgeable informants. [M.T. Hamerly]

692 Shapiro, Judith. From Tupã to the land without evil: the Christianization of Tupi-Guarani cosmology. (*Am. Ethnol.*, 14:1, Feb. 1987, p. 126–139, bibl.)

Interpretive effort. Early Catholic missionaries among the Tupi-Guarani used existing native religious concepts to foster evangelization. In the present century the Tupi concept of an early paradise is being used by radical clergy to convert the Church hierarchy to support of socioeconomic change.

693 Shea, Daniel E. Preliminary discussion of prehistoric settlement pattern and relation to terracing in Achoma, Colca Valley, Arequipa, Peru. (*in* Congreso Internacional de Americanistas, *45th, Bogotá, 1985.* Arqueología de las Américas. Bogotá: Fondo de Promoción de la Cultura, 1988, p. 159–168, bibl., map)

Study based on extensive fieldwork. Author examines link between environment and terrace agriculture in the middle Colca Valley. Local economy was balanced, with part of Achoma production dedicated to puna pastoralism. Finds that Toledo settlement policy resulted in substantial disruption of valley economy, with Urinsaya residents suffering most.

694 Silva G., Osvaldo. El reino Lupaca y la complementaridad vertical en los Andes centrales. (*Dédalo*, 25, 1987, p. 87–98, bibl., map)

Another description of the "vertical economy" of the Lupaqa of the shore of Lake Titicaca, based on the 1566 *visita* of Garci Diez de San Miguel.

695 Silverman-Proust, Gail P. Cuatro motivos Inti de Q'ero. (*Bol. Lima*, 8:43, enero 1986, p. 61–76, bibl., graphs, ill., maps, tables)

Argues that contemporary Q'ero textile motifs carry symbolic concepts of space and time that may parallel those of the Inca period.

696 Szemiński, Jan. Cywilizacja, religia, naród: przypadek Tawantinsuyu [Civilization, religion, nation: the case of Tawantinsuyu]. (*in* Narody: jak powstaway i jak wybijały się na niepodlegość? [Nations: how did they come into being and how did they achieve their independence?] Edited by Marcin Kula. Warszawa: Państwowe Wydawnictwo Naukowe, 1989, p. 190–202)

Believes that the basis of government (i.e., *Incanato*) and religion were cohesive factors of Tawantinsuyu. Regards the latter as a single religious system and not as a combination of different, local cults; it eventually determined a specific form of Andean Catholicism. Perceives difference between *misti* and *runa* in Andean civilization as primarily religious. [M. Nalewajko]

697 Taylor, Anne Christine. La evolución demográfica de las poblaciones indígenas de la Alta Amazonía del siglo XVI al XX. (*Cultura/Quito*, 8:24b, enero/abril 1986, p. 507–518)

Laments sparse population data on Amazonian population, compared with that for coast and highland populations. Nevertheless, provides population estimates, with heavy mortality noted during epidemics of 1642, 1660, 1680, and 1756.

698 Taylor, Anne Christine. La invención del jívaro. (*in* Primer Simposio Europeo sobre Antropología del Ecuador: Memorias. Recopilación de Segundo E. Moreno Yáñez. Bonn: Instituto de Antropología Cultural de la Univ. de Bonn; Quito: Ediciones Abya-Yala, 1985, p. 255–267)

Essay on the evolution of the outsider's "stereotype" of the Jívaro.

699 Taylor, Gérald. Cultos y fiestas de la comunidad de San Damián, Huarochirí, según la *Carta Annua* de 1609. (*Bull. Inst. fr. étud. andin.*, 16:3/4, 1987, p. 85–96)

Transcription of Jesuit *Carta Annua* of 1609, today in the Order's archives in Rome, which refers to various native religious festivals. Includes excellent information on Pariacaca and Inaccha.

700 Tomasini, Alfredo. Contribución para una historia de los mocovi del Chaco Austral. (*Supl. Antropol.*, 22:1, junio 1987, p. 29–47, bibl.)

Study of one ethnic entity of the large Guaycuru language family, who were hunters and gatherers when the first Europeans arrived. With the acquisition of the horse there was a cultural transformation and they became warriors, only to be conquered by the modern Paraguayan State in 1870–84.

701 Urbano, Henrique. En nombre del Dios Wiracocha: apuntes para la definición de un espacio simbólico prehispánico. (*Allpanchis*, 20:32, 1988, p. 135–154, bibl.)

In a heated and vitriolic interpretive essay, author rejects the concept of Wiracocha as a Judeo-Christian creator god in the precolumbian Andes.

702 Uriarte, Manuel J. Diario de un misionero de Maynas. Iquitos, Perú: Monumenta Amazónica, 1986. 686 p.: bibl., index. (Monumenta amazónica B; 2)

Carefully-kept diary of Jesuit missionary recording events of 1750–69, with ethnographic content ranging from good to excellent. Includes catechism in Quechua and Omagua, baptism and confession for the Ticunas, and a brief doctrine in Yamea and Masamea.

703 Urton, Gary. La historia de un mito: Pacariqtambo y el origen de los indios. (*Rev. Andin.*, 7:1, 1989, p. 129–216, appendix, bibl., tables)

Thorough analysis of the many myths of origin of the Incas found in the accounts of the chronicles and in local evidence. Includes commentaries by Yuri Berezkin, Therese Bouysse-Cassagne and Thierry Saignes, Richard L. Burger, Pierre Duviols, Javier F. Flores Espinoza, Ana María Lorandi, Deborah A. Poole, José Sánchez Parga, and Lawrence E. Sullivan, as well as author's reply.

704 Urton, Gary. The history of a myth: Pacariqtambo and the origin of the Inkas. Austin: Univ. of Texas Press, 1990. 172 p.: bibl., ill., index.

Significant analysis of origin myths of the Incas and their importance in establishing and maintaining hegemony. At the local level, demonstrates how one family (Callapiña) manipulated myth to achieve personal status. Includes excellent presentation of the ayllu and moiety system as it functions in Pacariqtambo.

705   Useche Losada, Mariano. Colonización española e indígenas en el Alto Orinoco, Casiquiare y Río Negro. (*in* Congreso Internacional de Americanistas, *45th, Bogotá, 1985.* Etnohistoria e historia de las Américas. Bogotá: Ediciones Uniandes, 1988, p. 225–242, bibl., map, tables)

Introduction to the European penetration of the Upper Orinoco-Río Negro highlands and the nature of the native American response. Five nations—Spain, Portugal, the Netherlands, France, and Great Britain—made colonizing efforts in the area.

706   Valdivia Carrasco, Julio C. El imperio esclavista de los inkas. Lima: Editorial e Imprenta Desa, 1988. 107 p.: bibl. (Introducción al estudio de la historia del Perú; 1)

Argues that Inca developed a slave state which functioned well until the rule of Huayna Capac; the Spanish conquest brought feudalism to Peru.

707   Vega, Juan José and **Luis Guzmán Palomino.** El Inti Raymi incaico. (*Bol. Lima,* 8:45, mayo 1986, p. 49–65, bibl., ill.)

Detailed and comprehensive account of the origin and nature of the festival of Inti Raymi which celebrates the winter solstice. Based on the principal chronicles.

708   Viertler, Renate B. A formação da sociedade Bororo: mitologia e considerações etno-históricas. (*Rev. Antropol./São Paulo,* 29, 1986, p. 1–39, bibl., ill., table)

Important examination of the connection of the Bororo myth to social organiza-

tion. Funeral ritual in particular depicts the dual structure of society and the complexity of kin relationships.

Villasante, Mariella. Stratégies de redéfinition sociale et ethnique chez les Ashaninca de la forêt tropicale péruvienne. See *HLAS 51:939.*

709   Whitehead, Neil L. Lords of the tiger spirit: a history of the Caribs in Colonial Venezuela and Guyana, 1498–1820. Dordrecht, Holland; Providence, Rhode Island: Foris Publications, 1988. 250 p. (Caribbean series/Koninklijk Instituut voor Taal-, Land- en Volkenkunde; 10)

History of Caribs from lowland areas based on European accounts (they left no written record of themselves). Caribs relentlessly and violently resisted the *entradas* and missionary activity, finally succumbing to disease. Work lacks the scholarly sophistication of Andean ethnohistorical studies, perhaps as a result of limited sources. [K. Waldron]

710   Yafe, Jochanan Bar. Revitalización, mesianismo y nacionalismo: el movimiento tupamarista. (*Estud. Latinoam.,* 12, 1989, p. 173–210, tables)

Examines role of religious concepts, both Christian and native Andean, in the late 18th-century rebellion of Tupac Amaru.

711   Zuidema, R. Tom. Inca civilization in Cuzco. Translated by Jean-Jacques Decoster. Foreword by Françoise Héritier-Augé. Austin: Univ. of Texas Press, 1990. 101 p.: bibl.

Translation brings this finely-crafted condensation of the thought of a leading specialist to the general English-speaking public. Formidable attempt to enter and understand the structures of Inca time and space.

GENERAL HISTORY

JAMES D. RILEY, *Professor of History, The Catholic University of America*

RESEARCH ON GENERAL TOPICS during the late 1980s was shaped by three overlapping celebrations: the Columbus Quincentennial; the quincentennial of the birth of Bartolomé de Las Casas; and the bicentennial of the reign of Charles III.

Interest was high on issues related to Columbus himself, Spanish exploration in general, Iberian mentalities, the impact of Europe on the New World, and the character of late-Bourbon policy.

While (as always) the great majority of the works produced on these subjects were quite forgettable, the production included some notable contributions. In addition to the reissuance of the collected writings of Las Casas, the commemoration of his birth also produced a first rate biography by Pedro Borges (item **764**). A number of works focused on the issues that Las Casas raised and the general question of evangelization in the Americas. A collection of papers from a conference on Franciscans in the New World is worthy of note (item **782**), as are a collection organized by Susan Ramírez (item **812**) and an intriguing article on Fray Alonso de Maldonado by Carlos Sempat Assadourian (item **759**).

Columbus, specifically, and European explorations, in general, did not fare as well. Almost all of the works produced on these themes simply rehashed the old controversies or dealt with minor points. Sadly, no new biographies of the principal characters have yet appeared; this gap will hopefully be filled during the next biennium. About the only fresh approach to these questions was provided by David Henige (item **802**).

Work on other colonial topics was spotty. Few book-length contributions appeared, but colonial social history was strengthened by a very interesting collection of essays edited by Asunción Lavrin on *Sexuality and marriage in colonial Latin America* (Lincoln: Univ. of Nebraska Press, 1989; articles have been annotated individually below). Two pieces included in this book break new ground: Ann Twinam's essay dealing with concepts of honor among colonial elites (item **859**) and Richard Boyer's work on women's perceptions of their rights in marriage (item **767**).

Work on the 19th century centered on issues revolving around the Cortes of 1812 and commerce. The best book-length monograph was Frank Dawson's treatment of loans during the first decade of independence (item **874**), while the best article was an interpretative essay by William Glade (item **880**) on debates over tariffs in the early republics.

As always, issues related to diplomacy and international relations dominated the 20th-century section. Bill Albert's book on the impact of World War I (item **896**) and Paul Drake's on the impact of financial experts in shaping Latin America's economic growth (item **904**) are very well done. Those interested in labor history would be well advised to consult the essay by Emilia Viotti da Costa (item **903**) and its related commentaries (items **897, 913, 914,** and **916**) which provide an excellent overview of recent work in that area.

GENERAL

712 Abramson, Pierre-Luc. L'Etat et le pouvoir de l'Eglise en Amérique latine au XXe. siècle. (*in* Colloque de Lyon, *Lyon, France, 1985.* Actes: Etat et pouvoir; réception des idéologies dans le midi, l'antiquité et le temps modernes. Marseille, France: Presses universitaires d'Aix-Marseille, Faculté de droit et de science politique, 1986, p. 93–98)

Brief essay argues that the State had to import a culture with which to oppose the culture of Catholicism. The State chose French philosophical model on which to build a modernizing anti-clerical culture.

713 Anderle, Adám. Las relaciones entre etnia y nación en la historia de América Latina. (*Islas*, 87, mayo/agosto 1987, p. 3–17, tables)

Essay argues that the development of a nation's collective consciousness is fundamentally linked to the idea of progress promoted by capitalism, and thus Latin America is behind in the development of this consciousness. Sees parallels to Central and Eastern Europe in the Latin American experience.

714 Bonilla, Heraclio. Las consecuencias económicas de la independencia en hispanoamérica. (*Economía/Lima*, 11:22, dic. 1988, p. 133–143)

Brief, superficial article looks at commerce, markets, and capital in the late colonial and early republican periods.

715 Bosch García, Carlos. La transición en la historia general de America. (*Cuad. Am.*, 19:1, enero/feb. 1990, p. 108–118)

Decries fact that because of the immensity of the task, Latin American historians are not writing syntheses of continental history. Suggests in broad strokes themes that such a synthesis could cover.

716 Conversaciones Internacionales de Historia, 4th, Univ. de Navarra, Spain, 1988. Balance de la historiografía sobre Iberoamérica, 1945–1988: actas. Edición a cargo de Valentín Vázquez de Prada e Ignacio Olabarri Gortazar. Pamplona, Spain: Ediciones Univ. de Navarra, 1989. 770 p.: bibl., ill. (Col. histórica; 45)

Conference papers, most by distinguished European scholars, present analyses of historiography of different topics (mainly colonial). One intriguing aspect is the inclusion of discussions about the presentations. Copious bibliographies give insights into what European historians are reading and indicate the gulf between the English-speaking world of scholarship and the non-English-speaking world.

717 Curtin, Philip D. The rise and fall of the plantation complex: essays in Atlantic history. Cambridge, England; New York: Cambridge Univ. Press, 1990. 222 p.: bibl., ill. (Studies in comparative world history)

Useful interpretative essays focus on the evolution of sugar economies in the New World. Explores global background and context for the structure of plantation land use and labor systems as well as the causes of changes in the 18th and 19th centuries.

718 Españoles hacia América: la emigración en masa, 1880–1930. Recopilación de Nicolás Sánchez-Albornoz. Madrid: Alianza Editorial, 1988. 346 p.: bibl., ill. (Alianza América; 20)

Fifteen scholarly essays on Spanish immigration to America. First section provides examples of regional immigration to America and the second studies immigration to specific countries (Argentina, Brazil, Cuba, Puerto Rico and Mexico). Sánchez-Albornoz provides an overview.

719 Galloway, J.H. The sugar cane industry: an historical geography from its origins to 1914. Cambridge, England; New York: Cambridge Univ. Press, 1989. 266 p.: bibl., ill., index. (Cambridge studies in historical geography; 12)

Broad comparative study of the industry traces its beginnings in Southeast Asia to the introduction of cane in the islands of the Western Pacific in the early 20th century.

720 Granda Gutiérrez, Germán de. Lingüística e historia: temas afro-hispánicos. Valladolid, España: Univ. de Valladolid, Secretariado de Publicaciones, 1988. 274 p.: bibl. (Serie Lingüística y filología; 6)

Twenty-one essays by the author pertaining to linguistic analysis of Creole languages in the Hispanic Caribbean. Focuses on African cultural forms in Creole languages. Of interest for historians because it looks at slave culture going back to the 18th century.

Halperín Donghi, Tulio. El espejo de la historia: problemas argentinos y perspectivas hispanoamericanas. See item **2704.**

721 Halperín Donghi, Tulio. The state of Latin American history. (*in* Changing Perspectives in Latin American Studies: insights from six disciplines. Edited by Christopher Mitchell. Stanford: Stanford Univ. Press, 1988, p. 13–62)

Sees an increasing fragmentation and "erosion of disciplinary certainties" which makes current state of scholarship confusing and the future hard to predict. With this pessimistic introduction, author proceeds to a routine analysis of a few significant works in different geographical areas.

722 Hanke, Lewis. The delicate balance: a consideration of some of the forces and circumstances that should be reckoned with today in a discussion of "the place of native peoples in the Western World." (*Historia/Santiago*, 21, 1986, p. 379–401, bibl.)

Publication of a speech given in Alaska on question of whether special rights should be recognized for aboriginal populations and aboriginal cultures. Usefulness for Latin Americanists lies in the comparison of colonial debates over the rights of native cultures.

723 Hernán Baquero, Mario. Influencia de la historiografía francesa de los anales en la historiografía latinoamericana. (*Univ. Humaníst.*, 17:29, enero/junio 1988, p. 173–184, bibl.)

Very broad study of the influence of the Anales school in Latin American thought. Rather than talking of work influenced by it, discusses Latin American thinkers who supported the approach.

724 Johnson-Odim, Cheryl and **Margaret Strobel.** Conceptualizing the history of women in Africa, Asia, Latin America and the Caribbean, and the Middle East. (*J. Women's Hist.*, 1:1, Spring 1989, p. 31–62)

Explores literature on gender in the non-Western world. Concludes that there is a broad commonality to the construction of gender throughout the world, although there are differences on specifics.

725 Joseph, Gilbert M. On the trail of Latin American bandits: a reexamination of peasant resistance. (*LARR*, 25:3, 1990, p. 7–53, bibl.)

Argues that current literature focuses too narrowly in critiquing Hobsbawm's theories of social banditry and ignores innovative approaches to roots of peasant social action and mentality. Concludes that bandit studies will advance only as a more nuanced social history of the countryside emerges. This would focus on internal organization of the rural sector and link it to the outside world, examining the social composition of bandit groups as well as the development of national judicial systems. See also the commentary and debate on this article in LARR (26:1, p. 145–174).

Judge, Joseph and **James L. Stanfield.** The island of landfall. See *HLAS 51:2814*.

726 Krebs, Ricardo. El significado del dominio español en Indias. (*An. Univ. Chile*, 5:11, agosto 1986, p. 327–346)

Routine essay from a hispanophile perspective on the impact of the discovery and settlement of the New World.

727 La-ting Mei-chou shih Iun wen chi = Essays on Latin American history. Pei-ching: Tung fang ch' u pan she, 1986. 353 p.: tables

Collection of selected papers presented at the 2nd Symposium of the Chinese Society of Latin American History. Includes important articles on Sino-Latin American relations during different historical periods (e.g., "The earliest diplomatic relations between China and Latin American countries in the Ch'ing Dynasty"). [Mao Xianglin]

728 Lateinamerika: Geschichtsunterricht, Geschichtslehrbücher, Geschichtsbewusstsein. Edited by Michael Riekenberg. Frankfurt: M. Diesterweg, 1990. 172 p.: bibl. (Studien zur internationalen Schulbuchforschung; 66)

Articles by historians and teachers analyze Latin American history instruction in Latin America and Germany. Takes into account heterogeneity of historical interpretation in Latin American countries, but concludes that weak institutionalized foundation of historical research often results in use of history for ideological and political purposes. [M.L. Wagner]

729 Li, Ch'un-hui. La-ting Mei-chou yü Chung-kuo ti li shih kuan hsi [Historical relations between Latin America and China]. (*in* Li Ch'un-hui. La-ting Mei-chou shih kao [History notes of Latin America]. Pei-ching: Shang wu yin shu kuan, 1983, p. 314–368)

Chapter of pioneering work consists of textual research of and dispute over question of whether a Chinese monk reached the Americas before Columbus; trade relations between Latin America and China; question of Chinese laborers; modern diplomatic relations between China and Latin American countries. Author is noted historian, professor and chairman of China's Society of Latin American History. [Mao Xianglin]

730 Lo, Jung-ch'ü. Chung-kuo jen fa hsien Mei-chou chih mi: Chung-kuo yü Mei-chou Ii shih Iien hsi Iun chi [The myth of the Chinese discovery of the Americas: a collection of essays on the historical connections between China and Latin America]. Ch'ung-ch'ing: Ch'ung-ch'ing ch'u pan she, 1988. 232 p.: appendices, bibl., ill., maps, tables.

Well-researched, scholarly compilation of important essays on "the discovery of America by the Chinese." Author, a famous professor of history at Pei-ching Univ., refutes assertion that the Americas were first discovered by a Chinese monk in the 5th century AD and provides authoritative view of this century-long dispute in academic circles. Also includes as appendices key essays which present opposing views. [Mao Xianglin]

731 Mei-chou Hua ch'iao Hua jen shih [History of overseas Chinese and citizens of Chinese origin in the Americas]. Edited by Li Ch'un-hui and Yang Sheng-mao. Pei-ching: Tung fang ch'u pan she, 1990. 753 p.: ill., maps, tables.

First and only study of overseas Chinese published in China. Six chapters written by several noted Chinese historians examine early immigration to Latin America, Chinese contributions to the region's development, historical and cultural transition of overseas Chinese, and their present situation. Based on numerous archives, documentary sources, and field research. Highly recommended work for students of the history of overseas Chinese in Latin America. [Mao Xianglin]

732 Melgar Bao, Ricardo. El movimiento obrero latinoamericano: historia de una clase subalterna. Madrid: Alianza Editorial, 1988. 490 p.: bibl., index. (Alianza América; 19)

Comparative overview of the development of syndicalism, unionism, and workers' movements. Begins with mid 19th-century egalitarian movements, then discusses anarchism in the early 20th century, classic unionism during the 1920s, and union movements of the post-World War II era. Fascinating, thoughtful and well-organized.

733 Mörner, Magnus. La sociedad, siglos XVIII–XIX: balance de la historiografía. (in Conversaciones Internacionales de Histora, 4th, Pamplona, Spain, 1988. Balance de la historiografía sobre Iberoamérica, 1945– 1988: Actas. Pamplona, Spain: Ediciones Univ. de Navarra, Centro de Investigaciones de Historia Moderna y Contemporánea, 1989, p. 557–591)

Conference paper tracing development of social history in Latin America

emphasizes degree to which insights of the social sciences have affected historical methodologies.

734 Morse, Richard M. Las ciudades como personas. Traducción del ingles de Eduardo Passalacqua. (in Nuevas pespectivas en los estudios sobre historia urbana latinoamericana. Buenos Aires: Instituto Internacional de Medio Ambiente y Desarrollo (IIED) América Latina, 1989, p. 59–76)

Provocative essay argues that descriptive typologies of cities do little to allow us to understand the "personalities" of urban environments. Describes differences in personality of cities in North and South America.

735 Morse, Richard M. Ciudades "periféricas" como arenas culturales: Rusia, Austria, América Latina. Traducción de Ernesto Leibovich. (in Cultura urbana latinoamericana. Recopilación de Richard Morse y Jorge Enrique Hardoy. Buenos Aires: Consejo Latinoamericano de Ciencias Sociales, 1985, p. 39–62)

Compares culture of Buenos Aires, Rio de Janeiro, Paris, St. Petersburg and Vienna. Hypothesizes that a city's cultural and literary production is a reflection of its organization and society.

736 El Pacífico español de Magallanes a Malaspina. Edición de Carlos Martínez Shaw. Madrid: Ministerio de Asuntos Exteriores, Secretaría de Estado para la Cooperación Internacional y para Iberoamérica, Dirección General de Relaciones Culturales, 1988. 185 p.: bibl., ill.

Beautifully illustrated set of essays on the Spanish Pacific presence prepared for the Brisbane World Fair of 1988 by Spanish scholars. Teachers looking for visual materials to accompany lectures will do well to consult this volume.

737 Ramos, Carmen. The history of women in Latin America. (in Retrieving women's history: changing perceptions of the role of women in politics and society. Edited by S. Jay Kleinberg. Oxford, England; New York: Berg; Paris: UNESCO Press, 1988, p. 303–318)

Surveys literature on women highlighting gaps and research needs. Decries the fact that the study of women's history is still a province of research institutions and organized groups of women.

738 Scott, Rebecca Jarvis. Exploring the meaning of freedom: postemancipation societies in comparative perspective. (*HAHR*, 68 : 3, Aug. 1988, p. 408–428)

Survey of literature on post-emancipation societies. Sees a growing sophistication in research which draws from recent developments in colonial studies and studies of slave cultures regarding degrees of dependence and autonomy among subordinate populations.

739 Skoczek, Maria. Kolonizacja rolnicza a zmiany w rozmieszczeniu ludności w Ameryce Łacińskiej [Agricultural colonization and changes in the location of the population in Latin America]. Warszawa: Uniwersytetu Warszawskiego, 1989. 283 p.: maps, tables. (Rozprawy Uniwersytetu Warszawskiego, 0509–7177; 323)

History of agricultural colonization in Latin America since 16th century emphasizes 1950–80 period and concentrates on specific regions in Mexico, Colombia, Brazil, Peru, and Paraguay. Based on sources and the author's field work. [M. Nalewajko]

740 Slicher Van Bath, B.H. A summary of the study of Caribbean and Latin American history in the Netherlands, 1970–1987. (*Bol. Estud. Latinoam.*, 44, junio 1988, p. 19–28, bibl.)

Description of topics studied by Dutch historians.

741 Szuchman, Mark D. The middle period in Latin American history: values in search of explanations. (*in* The middle period in Latin America: values and attitudes in the 17th-19th centuries. Edited by Mark D. Szuchman. Boulder, Colo.: Lynne Rienner Publishers, 1989, p. 1–18)

This introduction to a collection of essays examines generations of Latin American historiography as reflections of "exemplar" and "Collective Behaviorist" models of historical analysis.

742 Tanzi, Héctor José. Historiografía americana. (*Rev. Hist. Am.*, 104, julio/dic. 1987, p. 65–112, bibl.)

Examination of the approaches and problems encountered in writing a general history of the Americas.

743 Valverde, José Luis and **José A. Pérez Romero.** Drogas americanas en fuentes de escritores franciscanos y dominicos. Granada, Spain: Univ. de Granada, 1988. 296 p.: bibl., index. (Estudios de la Cátedra de Historia de la Farmacia y Legislación Farmacéutica de la Univ. de Granada; 8)

Study of ethnopharmacology found in works by Franciscan and Dominican Chroniclers. Of 24 reports, 22 are from colonial missionaries and two from 20th century Dominican missionaries. Lists drugs and pharmaceuticals by category and provides the description of them given by the reporter.

744 Viajeros hispanoamericanos: temas continentales. Recopilación de Estuardo Núñez. Caracas: Biblioteca Ayacucho, 1989. 669 p.: bibl. (Biblioteca Ayacucho; 140)

Excerpts from 73 descriptions of various parts of the Americas by Hispanic American travelers during the 19th and 20th centuries.

COLONIAL

745 Abril Castelló, Vidal. Las Casas contra Vitoria, 1550–1552: la revolución de la duodécima Réplica, causas y consecuencias. (*Rev. Indias*, 47 : 179, enero/abril 1987, p. 83–101, bibl.)

Standard consideration of the Valladolid debates specifically referring to the clash with Vitoria's ideas regarding the use of force against the Indians.

746 Acosta, José de. Historia natural y moral de las Indias. Edición de José Alcina Franch. Madrid: Historia 16, 1987. 515 p.: bibl. (Crónicas de América; 34)

New edition of the text previously edited by Edmundo O'Gorman. Brief introduction provides intellectual context for the work.

747 Acosta-Solís, Misael. La ciencia iberoamericana durante la Conquista y la Colonia. (*Cultura/Quito*, 8 : 23, sept./dic. 1985, p. 141–199, bibl.)

Lengthy description of the development of interest in the natural history of the New World, particularly by 18th-century expeditions.

748 Albi de la Cuesta, Julio. El modelo borbónico para la defensa de las Indias.

(*Cuad. Hispanoam. Complement.*, 2, dic. 1988, p. 126–145)

Study of the effectiveness of the Bourbon plan for defense of America. Argues that basing its defense on militias was not unrealistic and proved no less successful than British and French strategies.

749 Altman, Ida. Emigrants and society: an approach to the background of colonial Spanish America. (*Comp. Stud. Soc. Hist.*, 30:1, Jan. 1988, p. 83–102, bibl.)

Argues that social and economic behavior of immigrants during the conquest period are only explicable in terms of their roots. Illustrates this fact by reference to Cáceres, Spain.

750 Alvarez Peláez, Raquel. El doctor Hernández: un viajero ilustrado del siglo XVI. (*Rev. Indias*, 37:180, mayo/agosto 1987, p. 617–629)

Examines what author considers a 16th-century scientific expedition, the journey of the Protomedicato sent by Philip II to the Indies. Unfortunately, only a few letters and no report on the journey have been discovered so author gives more of a broad description than actual details.

751 América después del descubrimiento: conmemoración del V Centenario. Madrid: Colegio Mayor Zurbarán, 1988. 152 p.: ill. (Humanismo y cultura; 7)

Text of discussion among Spanish academics on the following topics: the Church that went to America; human dignity in Indian law; the education of the Indian; contemporary views of America; culture and education in the colonization of New Spain and Peru; State and society in the 18th century; and the influence of the Canaries in the discovery.

752 La América española en la época de las luces: tradición, innovación, representaciones; coloquio franco-español, Maison des Pays Ibériques, Burdeos, 18–20 septiembre 1986. Madrid: Ediciones de Cultura Hispánica, 1988. 423 p.: bibl., ill. (Col. Ensayo)

Twenty-two conference papers by Spanish and French scholars, many summarizing their previously published work on the subject. Volume does contain some new monographic studies. For edition in original French, see item **753.**

753 L'Amérique espagnole à l'époque des Lumières: tradition, innovation, représentations; colloque franco-espagnol du CNRS, 18–20 septembre 1986. Paris: Editions du Centre national de la recherche scientifique; Presses du CNRS, diffusion, 1987. 375 p.: bibl., ill. (Collection de la Maison des pays ibériques; 32)

Rather weak collection of 22 essays which examine impact of the French Enlightenment on the Spanish empire. Explores Spanish political initiatives in America, the colonial economy, intellectual movements in the New World, and images of Spanish America in French thought. For Spanish translation, See item **752.**

754 Anadón, José. El Padre Acosta y la personalidad histórica del Hermano Lorenzo. (*Cuad. Am.*, 12:6, nov./dic.1988, p. 12–38)

Examines the historicity of Brother Lorenzo, a character Acosta uses as the protagonist in one of his works, heretofore considered a literary device. Author concludes Lorenzo was a historical figure whose activities became the basis for a general recapitulation of the Jesuit *relaciones* which is the real historical purpose of the work.

755 Andrés, Gregorio de. La biblioteca manuscrita del americanista Andrés González de Barcia, 1743, del Consejo y Cámara de Castilla. (*Rev. Indias*, 47:181, sept./dic. 1987, p. 811–831)

Inventory of unpublished manuscripts in the collection of Andrés González de Barcia, a noted collector of the 18th century whose materials went to the royal library.

756 Andrés Martín, Melquíades. Contribución dineraria de la diócesis de Badajoz al descubrimiento de América. (*Arch. Ibero-Am.*, 47:185/188, enero/dic. 1987, p. 3–55, photos)

Brief analysis of the accounts of Alonso de las Cabezas, treasurer of the Bula de la Santa Cruzada for the diocese of Badajoz. This treasury provided money contributed by Luis de Santangel to the first Columbus voyage.

757 Archivo General de Indias. Catálogo de las consultas del Consejo de Indias. v. 5, 1626–1636. Introducción y dirección de Antonia Heredia Herrera. Colaboración de Antonia Heredia Herrera, Javier Rubiales

Torrejón y María Dolores Vargas Zúñiga. Sevilla: Diputación Provincial, 1988? 1 v.: (V Centenario del descubrimiento de América; 5)

Vol. 5 of a continuing project includes 1,757 entries ordered by date with geographical, subject and onomastic indexes.

758 Archivo General de Indias. Catálogo de las consultas del Consejo de Indias. v. 8, 1644–1650. Introducción y dirección de Antonia Heredia Herrera. Colaboración de Antonia Heredia Herrera, Javier Rubiales Torrejón y María Dolores Vargas Zúñiga. Sevilla: Diputación Provincial, 1990. 1 v.: bibl., index. (V Centenario del Descubrimiento de América; 8)

Vol. 8 of a continuing reference work adds 2,500 more citations for the years described.

759 Assadourian, Carlos Sempat. Fray Alonso de Maldonado: la política indiana, el estado de damnación del Rey Católico y la Inquisición. (*Hist. Mex.*, 38:4, abril/junio 1989, p. 623–661)

Long petition on behalf of the Indians by a Franciscan argued that the king was damned for his failure to protect them. A very interesting introduction addresses the context of pro-Indian agitation among the friars as well as the petition and its consequences.

760 Ayala, Manuel José de. Diccionario de gobierno y legislación de Indias. Edición y estudios de Milagros del Vas Mingo. Madrid: Instituto de Cooperación Iberoamericana; Ediciones de Cultura Hispánica, 1988. 3 v.: bibl., ill., indexes.

Reedition of 1936 Altamira edition of work by colonial jurist. Vas Mingo has added very useful indexes.

761 Bauer, Arnold J. La cultura mediterránea en las condiciones del Nuevo Mundo: elementos en la transferencia del trigo a las Indias. (*Historia/Santiago*, 21, 1986, p. 31–53, bibl.)

Reviews traditional agricultural practices in the Americas and concludes that Mexican Indians resisted the cultivation of wheat because of the innovations it would have required, whereas in Peru, it was better accepted because it could fit into traditional agricultural patterns. Also looks at differing patterns of cultivation in Chile, Guadalajara and Cochabamba in the 18th century.

762 Bernabéu Albert, Salvador. Ciencia ilustrada y nuevas rutas: las expediciones de Juan de Lángara al Pacífico, 1765–1773. (*Rev. Indias*, 47:180, mayo/agosto 1987, p. 447–467, appendix)

Study of the role of scientifically-trained naval officers on the voyage of the frigate *Venus* to the Philippines, 1771–73.

763 Borges Morán, Pedro. Misión y civilización en América. Madrid: Alhambra, 1987. 296 p.: bibl. (Estudios; 36. Humanidades)

Interesting study of missionaries as "civilizers" of the Indians. Carefully analyzes what the missionaries tried to teach indigenous population and suggests that it was not exactly European or Hispanic values.

764 Borges Morán, Pedro. Quién era Bartolomé de las Casas. Madrid: Ediciones Rialp, 1990. 309 p.: bibl. (Libros de historia; 33)

Excellent biography of Las Casas emphasizes the complexity of his character. Makes the interesting observation that he was most effective when representing a group of like-minded individuals but least effective when pursuing personal objectives. He had great rhetorical gifts but little persuasive power because those who opposed him perceived him as arrogant.

765 Bosch García, Carlos. Sueño y ensueño de los conquistadores. México: Instituto de Investigaciones Históricas, Univ. Nacional Autónoma de México, 1987. 150 p.: bibl. (Serie Historia novohispana; 40)

Well-written but not very inventive essay on the destiny of the first generation of conquistadores asks what happened to their hopes and dreams.

766 Boyd-Bowman, Peter. La emigración extremeña a América en el siglo XVI. (*Rev. Estud. Extremeños*, 44:111, sept./dic. 1988, p. 601–621, maps, tables)

Statistical study of the origins, destinations, and motives of Extremedurans who came to the Americas prior to 1600.

767 Boyer, Richard. Women, *La Mala Vida*, and the politics of marriage. (*in* Sexuality and marriage in colonial Latin America. Edited by Asunción Lavrin. Lincoln, Neb.: Univ. of Nebraska Press, 1989, p. 252–286)

Examines norms found in confessional manuals for relations between married couples and what happened when relations broke down. Uses Inquisition records resulting from the complaints of women that they were subjected to *la mala vida*—the name given to a deterioration in marital relations.

768 Bradley, Peter T.*Crónicas de Indias:* some recent editions. (*Rev. Interam. Bibliogr.*, 38:4, 1988, p. 499–512)

Annotated bibliography of Spanish publications.

769 Camiroaga de la Vega, Alejandro. Cántabros en el descubrimiento, 1492–1542. Santander, Spain: Ediciones TANTIN, 1987. 151 p.: bibl., ill.

Brief descriptions of the activities of 188 inhabitants of northern Spain in the early conquest, culled from chronicles and reports.

770 Campomanes, Pedro Rodríguez. Reflexiones sobre el comercio español a Indias, 1762. Edición de Vicente Llombart Rosa. Madrid: Instituto de Estudios Fiscales; Centro de Publicaciones, Ministerio de Economía y Hacienda, 1988. 505 p.: bibl. (Clásicos del pensamiento económico español; 8)

Re-edition of classic 18th-century work includes a brief descriptive introduction.

771 Carli, Gianrinaldo. Delle lettere americane. Selezione, studio introduttivo e note di Aldo Albònico. Roma: Bulzoni Editore, 1988. 293 p.: facsims.

Facsimile reproduction of 1785 work which is part of a late 18th-century debate over capabilities of American Indians. Introduction provides context of debate.

772 Casado Arboniés, Francisco Javier *et al.* Fuentes locales y regionales para la historia de América: los archivos de Alcalá de Henares y Guadalajara. Alcalá de Henares, Spain: Servicio Municipal de Archivos y Bibliotecas, Comisión de Cultura, Ayuntamiento de Alcalá de Henares, 1989. 109 p.: bibl.

Description of four Spanish archives with material related to America: the Sección Histórica and the Archivo General de Administración de Estado of Alcalá de Hena-

res; the Jesuit Province of Toledo; and the Archivo Provincial y Municipal de Guadalajara. Descriptions of the holdings of the Sección Histórica and the Jesuit Province of Toledo are precise, the others, rather anecdotal.

773 Casas, Bartolomé de las. De regia potestate, o, Derecho de autodeterminación. Edición de Luciano Perena *et al.* Ed. crítica bilingüe de Luciano Pereña *et al.* Madrid: Consejo Superior de Investigaciones Científicas, 1984. 517 p.: bibl. (Corpus Hispanorum de pace; 8)

Critical bilingual edition (Spanish/Latin) of a fascinating work by Las Casas in which he argued as representative of the Indians of Peru against a proposed purchase by encomenderos of perpetuity of possession of their encomiendas. A long erudite introduction describes the work's theses and their significance.

774 Casas, Bartolomé de las. Obras completas. v. 9, Apologia. Edición de Angel Losada. Madrid: Alianza, 1988–1989. 1 v.: bibl.

Part of the series of Las Casas' complete works. Vol. 9 features the core of Las Casas' presentation at Valladolid. Although not a critical edition, the very useful introduction by Angel Losada gives the provenance of Las Casas' sources and analyzes his argument.

775 Casas, Bartolomé de las. Obras completas. v. 14, Diario del primer y tercer viaje de Cristóbal Colón. Edición de Angel Losada. Madrid: Alianza, 1988–1989. 1 v.: bibl.

A new critical edition with introduction by Consuelo Varela.

776 Castañeda Delgado, Paulino. Los memoriales del Padre Silva sobre predicación pacífica y repartimientos. Madrid: Consejo Superior de Investigaciones Científicas, Instituto Gonzalo Fernández de Oviedo, 1983. 402 p.: (Col. Tierra nueva e cielo nuevo; 6)

Reports by Fray Juan de Silva sent to King (1613–18) regarding treatment of Indians deal specifically with issues of evangelization without force and licitness of repartimiento and personal service. Includes a long introduction on these subjects.

777 Castro, Manuel de. Misioneros de la provincia de Castilla en América, siglos XVI y XVII. (*Arch. Ibero-Am.*, 47:185–188, enero/dic. 1987, p. 219–259)

Transcriptions of biographies of 16th- and 17th-century missionaries from Castile derived from a manuscript of 1684.

778 Cavallini de Arauz, Ligia. Elementos de paleografía hispanoamericana. San José: Editorial de la Univ. de Costa Rica, 1986. 240 p.: bibl., facsims.

Very useful paleographic handbook explains the historical development of writing styles in medieval Spain and Latin America. Provides excellent tables and exercises for beginners.

779 Chang, Chih-shan. Ko-lun-pu yü Chung-kuo [Columbus and China]. (*Shih chieh li shih*, 3, 1990, p. 48–55)

Chinese scholar on Columbus contributes this study to the quincentennial celebration. Argues that the earliest record on Columbus in Chinese appears in the book *Chih fang wai chi* written by Julio Aleni (1582–1645). Also reviews status of Columbian studies and publications in China. [Mao Xianglin]

780 Cioranescu, Alexandre. Una amiga de Cristóbal Colón: doña Beatriz de Bobadilla. Santa Cruz de Tenerife, Spain: Caja General de Ahorros de Canarias, 1989. 235 p.: bibl. (Servicio de Publicaciones de la Caja General de Ahorros de Canarias; 135. Investigación; 34)

Chatty and sympathetic biography of Beatriz de Bobadilla, wife of the Lord of the Canary Islands, and, according to contemporary gossip, the lover of Cristóbal Colón. This episode is dealt with only briefly.

781 Columbus, Christopher. Diario de navegación y otros escritos. Estudios preliminares de Joaquín Balaguer y Ramón Menéndez Pidal. Notas de Carlos Esteban Deive. Santo Domingo: Ediciones de la Fundación Corripio, 1988. 370 p., 6 leaves of plates: bibl., ill. (Biblioteca de clásicos dominicanos; 1. Los precursores; 1)

Another collection of the accounts of the Columbus voyages found in Spanish repositories.

782 Congreso Internacional sobre los Franciscanos en el Nuevo Mundo, 2nd, La

Rábida, 1987. Actas. Madrid: Editorial Deimos, 1988. 989 p., 4 p. of plates: bibl., ill., index.

Twenty-five conference papers, the vast majority representing new research or documentary description on Franciscan presence during 16th century. This is a solid and vital work for anyone interested in Franciscans during the 16th century.

783 Cuestionarios para la formación de las relaciones geográficas de Indias: siglos XVI–XIX. Edición de Francisco de Solano. Madrid: Consejo Superior de Investigaciones Científicas, Centro de Estudios Históricos, Depto. de Historia de América, 1988. 363 p.: bibl. (Col. Tierra nueva e cielo nuevo; 25)

Collection of 33 questionnaires sent to officials between 1530–1812 requesting information on local conditions is preceded by eight articles which analyze their content.

784 Domínguez Compañy, Francisco. Regulación municipal del trabajo libre de los oficios mecánicos en Hispanoamérica colonial. (*Rev. Hist. Am.*, 103, enero/junio 1987, p. 75–106, bibl.)

Traditional study of regulations governing artisans in colonial period.

785 Elcano, Juan Sebastián de *et al.* La primera vuelta al mundo. Madrid: Miraguano; Polifemo, 1989? 183 p. (Biblioteca de viajeros hispánicos; 5)

All of the narratives of the Magellan voyage except the Pigafetta memorial. Popular edition of work published elsewhere.

786 En el quinto centenario de Bartolomé de las Casas. Madrid: Ediciones Cultura Hispánica; Instituto de Cooperación Iberoamericana, 1986. 234 p.: bibl.

Group of very light lectures on various themes pertaining to Las Casas' work is forgettable except for a bibliography of all work by or about Las Casas.

787 Ezquerra Abadía, Ramón. Las principales colecciones documentales colombinas. (*Rev. Indias*, 48:184, sept./dic. 1988, p. 661–691)

Description of repositories of Columbian materials and various 19th- and 20th-century editions of their documents.

788 Feliciano Ramos, Héctor R. Las relaciones ilícitas de los británicos con los indios de los territorios españoles durante el siglo XVIII. (*Rev. Cent. Estud. Av.*, 2, enero/junio 1986, p. 22–33, ill., map)

Study of secret contacts between English officials and coastal tribes under Hispanic control from Darien to the Carolinas. Concludes that the Spanish were aware of the contacts but could do nothing about them.

789 Ferrer Benimeli, José A. Política americana del conde de Aranda. (*Cuad. Hispanoam. Complement.*, 2, dic. 1988, p. 71–94, photos)

Interesting article studies the thought of the Conde de Aranda regarding the question of reorganization of the New World kingdoms and the possibilities of independence. A common thread in his approach to the Family Pact of 1761, American Independence in 1776 and the French Revolution in 1794 was Anglophobia and a belief that the New World kingdoms had to be reorganized to recognize the inevitable pressures for independence.

790 Galera Gómez, Andrés. La aportación científica de la expedición Malaspina a la historia natural. (*Asclepio*, 39:2, 1987, p. 85–102, bibl.)

Discusses intellectual bases for the Malaspina expedition emphasizing the role of Antonio Pinedo y Ramírez.

791 García-Abasolo, Antonio. Mujeres andaluzas en la América colonial, 1550–1650. (*Rev. Indias*, 49:185, enero/abril 1989, p. 91–110, table)

Useful vignette of Cordoba's women migrating to the Indies in the 16th and 17th centuries. Based on Spanish archival sources. [A. Lavrin]

792 García Regueiro, Ovidio. América en la política de Estado de Carlos III. (*Cuad. Hispanoam. Complement.*, 2, dic. 1988, p. 25–52, facsims.)

Essay on diplomatic goals of Charles III in extending the empire into Louisiana, Alta California and the Pacific, and involvement in the North American Revolution.

793 Gil, Juan. Los armadores de Sebastián Caboto: un inglés entre italianos. (*Anu. Estud. Am.*, 45, 1988, p. 3–63)

Critical analysis of a contract between Cabot and his commercial backers in 1524 for the failed voyage to the Moluccas. Pro-

vides background to the commercial concessions sought in the 1525 Capitulación for that voyage as well as on the merchants, including one Englishman, who financed the exploration.

794 Gil, Juan. Mitos y utopías del descubrimiento. v. 2, El Pacífico. Madrid: Alianza, 1989. 1 v.: bibl., indexes. (Alianza universidad; 585)

Useful study of 16th-century Pacific voyages is based on rich sources. Mainly interested in the visions and objectives which impelled the voyagers and includes a brief epilogue that looks at the 18th century. Suggests that the Pacific voyages shared the spirit of adventure and dreams that motivated the Atlantic explorations detailed in vol. 1.

795 Gil, Juan. Sobre la vida familiar de Vicente Yáñez Pinzón. (*Rev. Indias*, 47:181, sept./dic. 1987, p. 745–754)

Gives biographical detail concerning the family of Columbus' navigator, in particular his wives.

796 Gil, Juan and **Consuelo Varela.** Temas colombinos. Sevilla: Escuela de Estudios Hispano-Americanos de Sevilla, 1986. 85 p.: bibl. (Publicaciones de la Escuela de Estudios Hispano-Americanos de Sevilla, 0210–5810; 324. Serie 1a, Anuario)

Four short essays on the Columbian enterprise. Three are useful: one considers the crew of the third voyage; the second examines Columbus' accounts of the voyages; and the third considers the chronicler of the second voyage.

797 Gil-Bermejo García, Juana. La Casa de Alba y América. (*Anu. Estud. Am.*, 45, 1988, p. 139–165)

Interesting small piece on the granting of monopolies, encomienda revenues, and other sinecures in the Indies to Spanish aristocrats as payment for services. The Dukes of Alba were major participants in this traffic.

798 Guerra, Francisco. El intercambio epidemiológico tras el descubrimiento de América. (*Asclepio*, 38, 1986, p. 117–137, bibl., tables)

Brief consideration of epidemic diseases prevalent in Spain and precolumbian America at time of the discoveries.

799 Guirao de Vierna, Angel. ¿Expediciones científicas o ciencia en las expediciones? Tres ejemplos clarificadores.
(*Rev. Indias*, 47:180, mayo/agosto 1987,
p. 469–488)

Examines purposes of the Malaspina,
Córdoba and Pérez expeditions of the late
18th century to determine whether or not
they could be considered "scientific" expeditions in the 18th-century meaning of that
term. Concludes that first two were scientific, the last was not.

800 Hampe Martínez, Teodoro. Oro, plata
y moneda de las Indias para el socorro
militar de Carlos V: una requisa de 1552.
(*Bol. Am.*, 30:38, 1988, p. 151–168, appendix, tables)

Discusses role which arriving New
World treasure played in 1552 in financing
military expenditures related to Hapsburg
foreign policy.

Hart, Catherine Pouperey. Relations de l'expedition Malaspina aux confins de l'empire
Espagnol: l'echec du voyage. See item **3317.**

801 Helmer, Marie. La Mission Nordenflycht en Amérique espagnole, 1788:
échec d'une technique nouvelle. (*Asclepio*,
39:2, 1987, p. 123–144, bibl., ill., map)

Studies technical mission headed by
Baron Timothy de Nordenflycht sent by
Charles III to Potosí to introduce recent sci-
entific and technological developments into
American mining practices. Examines why
the mission failed.

802 Henige, David. Text, context, inter-
text: Columbus' *Diario de a bordo* as
palimpsest. (*Americas/Francisc.*, 46:1, July
1989, p. 17–40)

Attempts to determine what in the
Diario was actually Columbus talking and
what was Las Casas as editor interpreting.
Also suggests which of Columbus' actual
thoughts were left out by Las Casas.

803 Higueras, María Dolores. NW coast of
America: iconographic album of the
Malaspina expedition; a study. Madrid: Mu-
seo Naval, 1991. 157 p.: bibl., ill.

Beautifully prepared catolog for an exhibition of the drawings and cartography of
the Malaspina expedition.

804 Hilton, Sylvia L. Apuntes sobre rivali-
dades internacionales y expediciones

españoles en el Pacífico, 1763–1794. (*Rev.
Indias*, 47:180, mayo/agosto 1987, p. 431–
446, bibl.)

Superficial review of European, particularly Spanish, involvement in the Pacific.

**805 Jornadas de Andalucía y América, 4th,
Univ. de Santa María de la Rábida,
Sevilla, Spain, 1984.** Andalucía y América
en el siglo XVIII: actas. Edición de Bibiano
Torres Ramírez y José Jesús Hernández Pa-
lomo. Sevilla: Escuela de Estudios Hispano-
Americanos de Sevilla, 1985. 2 v.: bibl., ill.
(Publicaciones de la Escuela de Estudios His-
pano-Americanos de Sevilla; 314)

Fifteen essays from 1984 congress include an interesting exploration of American
painting and silverwork found in Andalusian
Churches and the completion of churches by
native sons who immigrated to the Indies.
Also contains essays on Andalusians who
held high posts in the Indies and on literary
history.

806 Klein, Herbert S. and **Jacques A. Bar-
bier.** Recent trends in the study of
Spanish American colonial public finance.
(*LARR*, 23:1, 1988, p. 35–62, bibl.)

Valuable article analyzes the importance of recent works in quantitative colonial financial history for the broader field of
17th-and 18th-century studies.

807 Laet, Joannes de. Mundo Nuevo, o,
Descripción de las Indias Occidentales. Edición de Marisa Vannini de Gerule-
wicz. Caracas: Univ. Simón Bolívar, Instituto
de Altos Estudios de América Latina, 1988.
2 v. (1329 p.): bibl., ill.

Two-volume critical edition of a general natural and political history of the Western Hemisphere by a director of the Dutch
West Indies Company who gained his information from company sailors and settlers.
Based on 1640 French edition.

808 Lavrin, Asunción. Introduction: the
scenario, the actors, and the issues. (*in*
Sexuality and marriage in colonial Latin
America. Edited by Asunción Lavrin. Lincoln, Neb.: Univ. of Nebraska Press, 1989,
p. 1–43, facsims.)

Introduction to, and summary of, ten
essays on this unexplored theme. Examines
issues such as ecclesiastical and civil law,
varieties of sexual practices, marriage customs, relationship between honor and sex-

uality, efforts of Church and society to impose tight moral control on human behavior, divorce, and relations between the sexes. [E.B. Couturier]

809 Lavrin, Asunción. Misión de la historia e historiografía de la Iglesia en el período colonial americano. (*Anu. Estud. Am.*, 46, 1989, p. 11–44)

Useful study of changes in attitude toward the colonial Church as reflected in objectives of, and methodology employed by, historians beginning with the early chroniclers and continuing up to recent times. Emphasizes studies of institutional Church and treatment of the history of religious orders.

810 Lombardi, John V. Population reporting systems: an eighteenth-century paradigm of Spanish imperial organization. (*in* Studies in Spanish American population history. Edited by David J. Robinson. Boulder, Colo.: Westview Press, 1981, p. 11–23)

Argues census materials can be used more broadly by historians to reveal Spanish colonial self-image, imperial priorities, information on local social structures, etc.

811 Lucena Salmoral, Manuel. Hernán Cortés: la espada de Quetzalcóatl. Madrid: Anaya, 1988. 126 p. (Biblioteca ibero-americana; 37)

Brief biography of Cortés is based on standard sources and beautifully illustrated with paintings and photographs of places important to the story.

812 Macleod, Murdo *et al.* Indian-religious relations in colonial Spanish America. Edited by Susan E. Ramírez. Syracuse, N.Y.: Maxwell School of Citizenship and Public Affairs, Syracuse Univ., 1989. 102 p.: bibl., ill. (Foreign and comparative studies/Latin American series; 9)

Four essays on various aspects of Indian-Church relations in colonial Mexico, Chiapas and Paraguay. Topics include ecclesiastical authorities' view of Indians, an educated Indian's view of the Church, and the nature of missions and missionaries in Paraguay. Introductory and concluding essays by Susan Ramírez and Eric Van Young place the contributions in the larger context of colonial history. Originally a session at the American Historical Association, the essays hold together and make a worthwhile publication.

813 Marín Guzmán, Roberto. El espíritu de cruzada español y la ideología de la colonización de América. San José: Instituto Costarricense de Cultura Hispánica, 1985. 174 p., 14 p. of plates: bibl., ill.

Three unrelated essays treat the Spanish spirit of the Crusade, the functioning of the Bula de la Santa Cruzada in Costa Rica and the ideology of colonization. The first and last are purely derivative and the second is an uncritical description of the documents establishing the sales of the indulgences in Costa Rica.

814 Mauro, Frédéric. Sistema agrario y régimen de trabajo en América. (*Hist. Mex.*, 38:4, abril/junio 1989, p. 841–853, bibl.)

Short, simplistic essay linking labor systems to agrarian structures.

815 Miño Grijalva, Manuel. Capital comercial y trabajo textil: tendencias generales de la protoindustria colonial latinoamericana. (*HISLA*, 9, 1987, p. 59–79, bibl.)

Very useful survey of literature on role of merchant capital in colonial production of textiles. Argues that it was critical to the development of artisan industry because *obrajeros* and local artisans were incapable of judging market demands. The result was a "putting out" system which is an example of "protoindustry."

816 Miño Grijalva, Manuel. El obraje colonial. (*Rev. Eur.*, 47, dic. 1989, p. 3–19, bibl., maps, tables)

Useful comparative study of *obrajes* in the Andean region and New Spain focuses on different forms of production (wool and cotton), physical plants, labor, net value of enterprise, and changes in production. [A. Lavrin]

817 Miño Grijalva, Manuel. ¿Proto-industria colonial? (*Hist. Mex.*, 38:4, abril/junio 1989, p. 793–818)

Sophisticated analysis questions whether the European concept of protoindustrialization can be accurately applied to textile production in New Spain. Argues that while in some ways it can be applied to the period of Indian textile production between 1530–70, it is inapplicable to the late-colonial period.

818 Mires, Fernando. La colonización de las almas: misión y conquista en hispanoamérica. San José: Depto. Ecuménico de Investigaciones, 1987. 228 p.: bibl. (Col. universitaria)

Brief polemical essay regarding the uses of the mission in the process of Spanish occupation of the Americas.

819 Mires, Fernando. En nombre de la cruz: discusiones teológicas y políticas frente al holocausto de los indios; período de conquista. San José: Depto. Ecuménico de Investigaciones, 1986. 219 p.: bibl.

Interesting and balanced review of the theology behind the arguments of the participants in the debates over the nature and fate of the Indians. Contains little that is new, but information is assembled in a satisfying package.

820 Monge Martínez, Fernando. La honra nacional en las expediciones de Cook y Malaspina: una visión antropológica. (*Rev. Indias*, 47:180, mayo/agosto 1987, p. 547–558)

Considers the complex motivations for two major expeditions to determine whether they were purely scientific or had economic and military objectives. Concludes that a desire for prestige among European nations was the basic motive for launching them.

821 Morales Padrón, Francisco. Historia del descubrimiento y conquista de América. 5. ed. rev. y aum. Madrid : Gredos, 1990. 717 p.: bibl., ill. (Manuales)

Standard narrative history of the explorations and conquest to about 1550. General perspective is Hispanophile.

822 Muñoz Mendoza, Joaquín A. El indio americano y los Santos Tribunales: "la lógica de la locura." (*Ibero-Am. Arch.*, 14:4, 1988, p. 437–452, bibl.)

Essay argues that the Church in the New World was tranquil and that the Inquisition was rarely used against the Indians because Indians accepted the logic of their situation thus making repression and violence unnecessary.

823 Muro Orejón, Antonio. Los Cedularios Indianos, 1492–1638: fuentes de la *Historia del Consejo de Indias*, de Antonio de León Pinelo. (*Historia/Santiago*, 22, 1987, p. 233–247, bibl., table)

Rambling and generally weak published speech examines the work of 17th-century jurist, León Pinelo, particularly the usefulness of his extracts of decisions of the Council of the Indies.

824 Nava Rodríguez, María Teresa. En torno a la historiografía oficial indiana, 1764–1768: la bibliografía americanista y la primera comisión de Indias. (*Rev. Indias*, 49:185, enero/abril 1989, p. 111–133)

Examines work between 1764–67 of a committee charged by the royal government with writing an official history of America, and explains why they failed to accomplish their task.

825 New Iberian world: a documentary history of the discovery and settlement of Latin America to the early 17th century. v. 1, The conquerors and the conquered. v. 2, The Caribbean. v. 3, Central America and Mexico. v. 4, The Andes. v. 5, Coastlines, rivers, and forests. Edited, with commentaries, by John H. Parry and Robert G. Keith. New York: Times Books; Hector & Rose, 1984. 5 v.: bibl., ill., index.

Monumental compilation of English translations of segments of basic documents (both indigenous and Spanish) on discovery and settlement of the New World.

826 Pagden, Anthony. Spanish imperialism and the political imagination, 1513–1830. New Haven, Conn.: Yale Univ. Press, 1990. 184 p.: bibl.

Well-written series of essays on how Italian, Spanish and New World political theorists viewed the character and ideology of the Spanish Empire and what moral lessons they drew from its condition.

827 Pérez, Joseph. La revolución francesa y la independencia de las colonias hispanoamericanas. (*Cuad. Am.*, 6:18, nov./dic. 1989, p. 55–71)

Routine consideration of acceptance of French Enlightenment in late colonial period argues that all but a few elites rejected French thought; most were either disinterested or feared it.

828 Pérez Canto, María Pilar and C. Vázquez Rodríguez de Alba. El Consejo de Indias ante los decretos de Nueva Planta, 1714. (*Bol. Am.*, 30:38, 1988, p. 227–245)

Analysis of the response of members of the Council of the Indies to royal attempts to reform the body. The reforms were withdrawn because of internal political debate but author suggests that this failure was the ultimate cause of royal decision to bypass the institution.

829 Pérez Herrero, Pedro. Los comienzos de la política reformista americana de Carlos III. (*Cuad. Hispanoam. Complement.*, 2, dic. 1988, p. 53–70, appendix, tables)

Explores the purposes of reform of Charles III as expounded by the "modernist" group of ministers assisting him, particularly Campomanes and Gálvez.

830 Pérez Herrero, Pedro and **Pedro A. Vives.** Perfil bibliográfico de la América de Carlos III. (*Cuad. Hispanoam. Complement.*, 2, dic. 1988, p. 251–273)

Bibliography of works on effects of Charles III's reign in Americas.

831 Pietschmann, Horst. Estado y conquistadores: las capitulaciones. (*Historia/Santiago*, 22, 1987, p. 249–262, bibl.)

Reflection on character of the *capitulación*. Was it a *merced*, i.e., merely a grant of royal favor? Or was it a contract? Suggests that the nature changed over time with the tendency toward being *mercedes* because of crown efforts to avoid jurisdictional limitations on freedom of action.

832 Pietschmann, Horst. Grundzüge der Entwicklung des Bildungssystems im kolonialen Hispanoamerika. (*Z. Kult.austausch*, 38:3, 1988, p. 365–373, bibl.)

Favorable analysis of Spain's educational system in colonial America based primarily on secondary sources. States that system helped create an acculturated Indian elite which was in some instances absorbed by colonial society and acted as intermediary with Indian society. Education facilitated integration of different strata of society and contributed to change of criteria for ethnic hierarchy. Argues that educational system helped promote colonial society's search for identity despite its resistance to the society's values. [M.L. Wagner]

833 Pinto, Sonia. Fundamentos económicos de la sociedad de la conquista. (*Historia/Santiago*, 22, 1987, p. 263–285, bibl., tables)

Brief commentary and tables describing 120 individuals who paid the royal

quinto in Santiago between 1567–77, and 176 who did so in Lima.

834 Piossek Prebisch, Teresa. Las conquistadoras: presencia de la mujer española en América durante el siglo XVI. Argentina: T. Piossek Prebisch, 1989. 37 p.: bibl.

Brief but intriguing essay on the women who participated in the voyages of discovery and came among the *primeros pobladores*.

835 Puerto Sarmiento, F. Javier and **Antonio González Bueno.** Renovación sanitaria y utilidad comercial: las expediciones botánicas en la España ilustrada. (*Rev. Indias*, 47:180, mayo/agosto 1987, p. 489–500)

Brief description of Spanish Botanical expeditions of 1770s and 1780s.

836 Pumar Martínez, Carmen. Españolas en Indias: mujeres-soldado, adelantadas y gobernadoras. Madrid: Anaya, 1988. 125 p.: bibl., ill. (Biblioteca iberoamericana; 51)

General and superficial review of the migration of Spanish women to the New World contains beautiful illustrations.

837 Quiroz Norris, Alfonso W. La expropiación inquisitorial de cristianos nuevos portugueses en Los Reyes, Cartagena y México, 1635–1649. (*Histórica/Lima*, 10:2, dic. 1986, p. 237–303, appendix, bibl.)

Spanish version of previously annotated article (see *HLAS 50:925*).

838 Ramos Gómez, Luis Javier. Los lucayos, ¿guias náuticos de Colón en el primer viaje?: la navegación entre Guanahani y Samoet. (*Rev. Indias*, 49:185, enero/abril 1989, p. 11–26)

Addresses question of whether Columbus had Indian assistance in navigating the Caribbean. Concludes that he did, but also suggests that he was not immediately aware of Indian knowledge of the ocean.

839 Ramos Pérez, Demetrio et al. Hispanoamérica. v. 1. Caracas: Academia Nacional de la Historia de Venezuela, 1987. 1 v.: bibl., ill., indexes. (Historia general de América; 11: Período colonial)

Collaborative work by noted Spanish historians covers the 16th-century discoveries and early stages of settlement. Reflects an older scholarship and an institutional approach.

840 La Revolución Francesa y el mundo ibérico. Edición de Robert M. Maniquis, Oscar R. Martí y Joseph Pérez. Madrid: Sociedad Estatal Quinto Centenario; Turner, 1989. 732 p.: bibl. (Col. Encuentros: Serie Textos)

Collaborative analysis of the bibliography dealing with the impact of the French Revolution on the Iberian world. Contributions describe literature on specific subjects and continuing research problems.

841 Rípodas Ardanaz, Daisy. Popularidad de lo jurídico en los siglos coloniales: un examen de la literatura de la Arquidiócesis de Charcas. (*Rev. Hist. Am.*, 101, enero/junio 1986, p. 37–64, bibl.)

Examination of the offbeat topic of law and lawyers in popular opinion during colonial period as seen through pieces of colonial literature produced in the Archdiocese of Charcas.

842 Rodríguez Vicente, María Encarnación. Economía, sociedad y Real Hacienda en las Indias españolas. Madrid: Alhambra, 1987. 370 p.: bibl., ill. (Estudios; 33. Humanidades)

Collected articles on immigration and economic and fiscal topics focus on South America, mainly Peru.

843 Romano, Ruggiero. Algunas consideraciones sobre los problemas del comercio en Hispanoamérica durante la época colonial. (*Bol. Inst. Hist. Ravignani*, 3:1, 1989, p. 23–49, graphs, map, tables)

Unremarkable essay examines the rhythm and framework for commerce involving the New World.

844 Romano, Ruggiero. Kilka uwag na temat handlu w Ameryce hiszpańskiej w epoce kolonialnej [Some remarks on trade in Spanish America in the colonial period]. (*in* Narody: jak powstawały i jak wybijały się na niepodległość? [Nations: how did they come into being and how did they achieve their independence?]. Edited by Marcin Kula. Warszawa: Państwowe Wydawnictwo Naukowe, 1989, p. 112–145, graphs, maps, tables)

Essay written from a Spanish American perspective describes the development of the region's trade with Spain and Europe. Analyzes the slave trade and discusses interregional as well as local trade. Claims that, as a colonial subject, Latin America

could not rely on its master Spain for the supply of goods and slaves and had to secure them from other sources. [M. Nalewajko]

845 Sala Catalá, José. El agua en la problematica científica de las primeras metrópolis coloniales hispanoamericanas. (*Rev. Indias*, 49:186, mayo/agosto 1989, p. 157–281, photos)

Superficial and poorly organized examination of handling of problems of water supply, flooding, and sanitation related to initial foundations of Mexico City and Lima.

846 Sala Catalá, José. Crónica de Indias e ideología misional. (*Cuad. Am.*, 12:6, nov./dic. 1988, p. 39–59)

Surveys misson statements in 16th-century chronicles to describe the idea of America which informs them, in an attempt to discern the mentality of 16th-century Spain.

847 Sánchez Bella, Ismael. Hallazgo de la *Recopilación de las Indias* de León Pinelo. (*Jahrb. Gesch.*, 24, 1987, p. 135–177, appendix)

Describes the discovery of León Pinelo's legal manuscript which provided a preliminary to the *Recopilación* of 1680 and then compares the two.

848 Santa Cruz Gamarra, Nicomedes. El negro en Iberoamérica. (*Cuad. Hispanoam.*, 451/452, enero/feb. 1988, p. 7–46, bibl., photo)

Weak treatment of recent work on slavery in the Western Hemisphere oddly ignores almost everything published in English or published after 1981.

849 Seminario Interdisciplinar sobre Iberoamérica en el V Centenario del Descubrimiento. Descubrimiento y fundación de los reinos de Indias, 1475–1560: la huella de España en América. Coordinación de Gregorio González Roldán et al. Madrid: Colegio Oficial de Doctores y Licenciados de Madrid; Comisión Nacional Quinto Centenario del Descubrimiento de América, 1988. 387 p.: bibl.

Useful as a brief compilation of the thoughts of noted Iberian Americanists on various topics related to colonial period. Most papers deal with the 16th century.

850 Slicher van Bath, B.H. Indianen en Spanjaarden: een ontmoeting tussen twee werelden, Latijns Amerika 1500–1800 [Indians and Spanish: meeting of two worlds, Latin America 1500–1800]. Amsterdam: B. Bakker, 1989. 301 p.: bibl., ill.

In ten essays historian Slicher van Bath gives impressions of an encounter between two worlds, or better yet, of three continents: America, Europe, and Africa. He discusses the Spanish colonial system, the economy, and the role of the Church. The last article is an overview of the historiography of the period 1492–1820. [R. Hoefte]

851 Slicher van Bath, B.H. Real Hacienda y economía en Hispanoamérica, 1541–1820. Amsterdam: CEDLA, 1989. 182 p.: appendices, bibl., ill., maps, tables. (Latin America studies; 49)

Economic history of the period 1600–1780 by the influential historian Slicher van Bath. Analysis of economic activities in this period is based on the data complied by TePaske and Klein in *The Royal Treasuries of the Spanish Empire in America*. [R. Hoefte]

852 Solano, Francisco de. Ciudad y geoestrategia española en América durante el siglo XVIII. (*in* Nuevas perspectivas en los estudios sobre historia urbana latinoamericana. Buenos Aires: Instituto Internacional de Medio Ambiente y Desarrollo (IIED) América Latina, 1989, p. 41–58)

Compares purposes of 16th-and 18th-century settlements. 18th century cities were not born of the impulse to defend the conquest but with the purpose of populating empty spaces.

853 Solano, Francisco de. Viajes, comisiones y expediciones científicas españolas a ultramar durante el siglo XVIII. (*Cuad. Hispanoam. Complement.*, 2, dic. 1988, p. 146–156)

Broadly categorizes the various types of scientific expeditions organized by Spain in the 18th century by their form, goals, destination, and results.

854 Someda, Hidefuji. Las Casas den: shinsekai seifuku no shinmonsha [Biography of Las Casas: the inquisitor at the conquest of the New World]. Tokyo: Iwanami Shoten, 1990. 388 p.: bibl., maps.

One of the few excellent biographies of Bartolomé de las Casas written in Japanese. Vividly presents the life and struggles for justice by this Spanish Dominican friar,

making free use of original documents. [K. Horisaka]

855 Suárez, Santiago Gerardo. Las reales audiencias indianas: fuentes y bibliografía. Caracas: Academia Nacional de la Historia, 1989. 516 p.: bibl., index. (Biblioteca de la Academia Nacional de la Historia: Fuentes para la historia colonial de Venezuela; 200)

Useful annotated bibliography of sources for study of the Audiencias of the New World.

856 Taviani, Paolo E. Colón: genovés. (*Bol. Acad. Nac. Hist./Caracas*, 71:282, abril/junio 1988, p. 333–348, bibl.)

Analysis of the historiographical debate over Columbus' birthplace.

857 Thornton, John K. On the trail of voodoo: African Christianity in Africa and the Americas. (*Americas/Francisc.*, 44:3. Jan. 1988, p. 261–278, bibl.)

Provides evidence that what have been described as traditional African elements in black Christianity in the New World are actually vestiges of the syncretic Christianity legitimized by the Portuguese in 15th-century Angola.

858 Tibesar, Antonine. The king and the Pope and the clergy in the colonial Spanish-American empire. (*Cathol. Hist. Rev.*, 75:1, Jan. 1989, p. 91–109)

Published lecture on the relationship between Church and State in colonial Spanish America and its effect on religious practice.

859 Twinam, Ann. Honor, sexuality, and illegitimacy in colonial Spanish America. (*in* Sexuality and marriage in colonial Latin America. Edited by Asunción Lavrin. Lincoln, Neb.: Univ. of Nebraska Press, 1989, p. 118–155, graphs, tables)

Fascinating study of how premarital relations which resulted in illegitimate children were handled by the elite. Uses this information to explore concepts of honor among colonial elites. Based on petitions for *cédulas de gracia a sacar*.

860 Uzquiza González, José Ignacio. El espejo que humea: Cristóbal Colón. Madrid: Swan; Avantos & Hakeldama, 1990. 210 p.: bibl., ill. (Col. Torre de la Botica; 21)

Imaginative study of Columbus' character by a literary specialist uses Columbus' writings as the basis for the analysis.

861 Varela, Consuelo. El testamento de Amerigo Vespucci. (*Historiogr. Bibliogr. Am.*, 30:2, 1986, p. 3–20, appendix, photos)

Reproduces the last will and testament of the explorer, together with an analysis of its contents.

862 Vericat, José. A la búsqueda de la felicidad perdida: la expedición Malaspina o la interrogación sociológica del imperio. (*Rev. Indias*, 47:180, mayo/agosto 1987, p. 559–615)

Study of the Malaspina expedition from an interesting perspective comments on the ideology of the late 18th century which tried to resurrect a false metropolitan consciousness, and saw in the colonial period a lost arcadia. Believes expedition was sent as much to restore power and a sense of linkage in the colonies as to collect flora and fauna.

863 Vigil, Ralph H. *Oidores letrados* and the idea of justice, 1480–1570. (*Americas/Francisc.*, 47:1, July 1990, p. 39–54)

Discussion of the basic philosophy taught to judges concerning their role and the goals of the law. Argues that poor pay and ambition led many to ignore their strict duty and pursue personal objectives.

864 Vives, Pedro A. La América de Carlos III: geopolítica imperial para la era de las revoluciones. (*Cuad. Hispanoam. Complement.*, 2, dic. 1988, p. 7–24, bibl., photos)

Introductory essay for a special issue devoted to Charles III and the New World suggests ways in which Charles III brought modernity to the Americas and explores his geopolitical vision.

INDEPENDENCE AND 19TH CENTURY

865 Albi, Julio. Banderas olvidadas: el ejército realista en América. Madrid: Instituto de Cooperación Iberoamericana; Ediciones de Cultura Hispánica, 1990. 415 p.: bibl., ill. (Historia)

Examines the work of the Spanish armies in America during the Wars of Independence. Suffers from an overall lack of focus

which reduces it to little more than battle history.

866 Barbier, Jacques A. *Comercio Neutral* in Bolivarian America: La Guaira, Cartagena, Callao and Buenos Aires. (*in* América Latina en la época de Simón Bolívar. Edición de Reinhard Liehr. Berlin: Colloquium Verlag, 1989, p. 363–377, tables)

Argues that "the loss of political sovereignty merely ratified the verdict of commercial life." Tests belief that the economy of Northern South America had already shifted away from Spain before the Independence movements by looking at the degree to which neutral shipping was a major policy of late Spanish empire, even in times of peace.

867 Berruezo, María Teresa. La actuación de los militares americanos en las Cortes de Cádiz, 1810–1814. (*Rev. Estud. Polít.*, 64, abril/junio 1989, p. 235–258, table)

Minor piece examines involvement of military officers in the Cortes and concludes they were predominantly liberal in ideology.

868 Berruezo, María Teresa. El funcionariado americano en las Cortes gaditanas, 1810–1813. (*Cuad. Hispanoam.*, 460, oct. 1988, p. 35–69, facsims., tables)

Biographical detail on the twenty American representatives who occupied official posts. Most were lawyers, judges, or treasury officials.

869 Berruezo, María Teresa. La participación americana en las Cortes de Cádiz, 1810–1814. Prólogo de José Luis Abellán. Madrid: Centro de Estudios Constitucionales, 1986. 326 p. (Col. Pensamiento español contemporáneo; 7)

Biographical study of American representatives to the Cortes. Using their involvement in debates, describes each individually and summarizes the tendencies of the group.

870 Blancpain, Jean-Pierre. Origines et caractères des migrations germaniques en Amèrique latine au XIX siècle. (*Jahrb. Gesch.*, 25, 1988, p. 349–383)

Disjointed survey of various aspects of German immigration in the 19th century and the social character of their communities in the New World.

871 Bolívar en la cancillería mexicana. Prólogo de Leopoldo Zea. Recopilación y notas introductorias de Edgar Gabaldón Márquez. México: Secretaría de Relaciones Exteriores; Univ. Nacional Autónoma de México, 1983. 166 p.: bibl. (Archivo histórico diplomático mexicano: Cuarta época; 16)

Documents dated between 1822–30 from Mexican diplomatic archives refer to Simón Bolívar. Correspondents include Vicente Rocafuerte and Col. José Anastasio Torrens, a Mexican diplomat reporting on the Panama conference and conspiracies against Bolívar. Most documents are brief and quite negative.

872 Brading, Celia Wu. Plan de pacificación y comercial de Gran Bretaña en Hispanoamérica, 1842. (*Histórica/Lima*, 12:1, julio 1988, p. 75–99, appendix, bibl.)

Analysis of a proposal contained in a memorandum written by the British secretary for Foreign Affairs, Lord Aberdeen, arguing for the establishment of an informal British protectorate in South America. Includes the memorandum and the response to it from British representative in Peru.

873 Bushnell, David and **Neill Macaulay.** The emergence of Latin America in the nineteenth century. New York: Oxford Univ. Press, 1988. 335 p.: bibl., ill., index.

Textbook interpretation on socioeconomic developments rather than straight political narrative emphasizes collective interpretations, with separate chapters on Brazil and Mexico. Generally argues that liberalism did as well as any conceivable competing ideology to promote the evolution of Latin America.

874 Dawson, Frank Griffith. The first Latin American debt crisis: the city of London and the 1822–25 loan bubble. New Haven, Conn.: Yale Univ. Press, 1990. 281 p.: bibl., ill., index, maps.

Interesting study of investment boom of 1822–25 during which English investors sunk £56 million in Latin American stocks and bonds, only to lose most of it by 1830. Author sees parallels with the crisis of the early 1980s.

875 Fernández Cabrelli, Alfonso. La francmasonería en la independencia de Hispanoamérica. Montevideo: Ediciones América Una, 1988. 167 p., 41 p. of plates (some folded): bibl., ill., facsims.

Brief study of the Masonic order's role

in promoting Southern Cone Independence. Based on previous work by the author and others.

876 Ferrer Benimeli, José A. Las Cortes de Cádiz: América y la masonería. (*Cuad. Hispanoam.*, 460, oct. 1988, p. 7–34, facsims.)

Discusses role of Masons during the Cortes. Argues that they were not as significant as older literature declares.

877 Gándara Enríquez, Marcos. Espíritu y obra de las Cortes de Cádiz: su influencia en América y en Europa. (*Cultura/ Quito*, 8:23, sept./dic. 1985, p. 65–121)

Narrative of the work and ideological influence of the Cortes also describes the work of the Ecuadorian delegates. Slim reading of the secondary literature.

878 Gandía, Enrique de. Nueva historia de América: las épocas de libertad y antilibertad desde la independencia. Caracas: Academia Nacional de la Historia, 1986. 836 p. (Biblioteca de la Academia Nacional de la Historia: Estudios, monografías y ensayos; 76)

Reedition of 1946 history of Independence period contains nothing new.

879 Gerst, Thomas. Deutschland und das 400-jährige Jubiläum der Entdeckung Amerikas. (*Jahrb. Gesch.*, 25, 1988, p. 849–860)

Reviews how Germans reacted to the 4th centennial of the discovery in 1892. Influenced by nationalism and recent unification, the event was celebrated as a reflection of the greatness of European civilization. [G.M. Dorn]

880 Glade, William P. Commercial policy in early republican Latin America: a reassessment from the standpoint of global perspective. (*in* América Latina en la época de Simón Bolívar. Edición de Reinhard Liehr. Berlin: Colloquium Verlag, 1989, p. 379–396)

Very interesting consideration of background to debates over free trade. Suggests that neither liberal nor conservative approaches were particularly useful and thus bordered on irrelevancy as far as economic growth was concerned.

881 Jornadas de Andalucía y América, 5th, Univ. de Santa María de la Rábida, Sevilla, Spain, 1985. Andalucía y América en el siglo XIX: actas. Edición de Bibiano Torres Ramírez y José Jesús Hernández Palomo. Sevilla: Escuela de Estudios Hispano-Americanos, C.S.I.C., 1986. 2 v.: ill. (Publicaciones de la Escuela de Estudios Hispano-Americanos de Sevilla; 325)

Two volumes from 1985 conference. Most contributions in Vol. 1 are brief and of dubious value, but three monographic articles related to the 19th-century Caribbean are of interest. Vol. 2 contains twenty-two short but useful monographic articles on political and economic themes.

882 Jornadas de Historia de Occidente, 6th, Jiquilpan de Juárez, Mexico, 1983. Sexta Jornadas de Historia de Occidente: Simón Bolívar, 25–26 de agosto 1983. Jiquilpan de Juárez, Mexico: Centro de Estudios de la Revolución Mexicana Lázaro Cárdenas, 1984. 167 p.: bibl.

Publication of papers and commentaries from a conference honoring 200th birthday of Simón Bolívar. The contributions seem more politically than intellectually motivated.

883 Kahle, Günter. Friedrich Rasch und Carl Sowersby. (*Jahrb. Gesch.*, 27, 1990, p. 199–226, appendix)

Article on participation of approximately 300 German volunteers in Latin American wars of independence is interesting contribution to historiography, despite lack of primary sources due to unknown fate of volunteers. Appendix includes biographies of two German officers written by 19th-century German diplomat Albert Schumacher. Introduction and annotations by author. [M.L. Wagner]

884 López-Ocón, Leoncio Cabrera and Miguel Angel Puig-Samper. Los condicionantes políticos de la Comisión Científica del Pacífico: nacionalismo e hispanoamericanismo en la España Bajoisabelina, 1854–1868. (*Rev. Indias*, 37:180, mayo/agosto 1987, p. 669–682)

Looks at the political purpose and cultural implications of an 1862 scientific mission sent by the Ministerio de Fomento to South America. Sees it as an effort to counter growing US influence in region.

885 Madrid Alvarez, Juan Carlos de la. El viaje de los emigrantes asturianos a América. Prólogo de Francisco Erice. Gijón,

Spain: Silverio Cañada, 1989. 197 p.: bibl., ill. (Biblioteca histórica asturiana; 18)

Thorough archival study of the "middle passage" for Asturian immigrants in the 19th century considers the vessels, their crews, the conditions of the voyage, and the character of the immigrants themselves.

886 Mathew, W.M. Britain and the Bolivarian Republics, 1820–1850: *Interimperium* and the tariff. (*in* América Latina en la época de Simón Bolívar. Edición de Reinhard Liehr. Berlin: Colloquium Verlag, 1989, p. 397–421, table)

Discusses debates over tariffs and notes that trade with England was insignificant to England throughout the period even when it increased toward the end. Tariffs had no effect on this situation.

887 Moreno Alonso, Manuel. La política americana de las Cortes de Cádiz: las observaciones críticas de Blanco White. (*Cuad. Hispanoam.*, 460, oct. 1988, p. 71–89, facsims.)

Examines views on Spain's American policy held by Spanish Catholic priest who converted to Anglicanism and then Unitarianism in England. See also item **894.**

888 Mroziewicz, Robert. Dyplomacja USA wobec Ameryki Centralnej, 1822–1850 [US diplomacy towards Central America, 1822–1850]. Wrocław: Zakład Narodowy im. Ossolińskich, 1986. 183 p.: (Prace habilitacyjne)

Focuses on the rivalry with Great Britain that ended successfully for the US in the signing of the Clayton-Bulwer Treaty in 1850. Based principally on sources from the US State Dept. [M. Nalewajko]

889 Oribe Stemmer, Juan E. Freight rates in the trade between Europe and South America, 1840–1914. (*J. Lat. Am. Stud.*, 21:1, Feb. 1989, p. 23–59, appendix, graphs, tables)

Quantitive study of trends in cost of shipping for bulk and general cargoes concludes that there was a long-term trend to lower costs which predated shift from sail to steam.

890 Ortega y Medina, Juan Antonio. La manipulación historiográfica estadounidense del pasado histórico y arqueológico latinoamericano. (*Cuad. Am.*, 19:1, enero/feb. 1990, p. 119–136)

Evaluates work of 19th-century Latin Americanists in the US and concludes that they studied Latin America with sympathy and great cultural interest in an attempt to find common values or "an American essence."

891 Schneider, Jürgen. Sinopsis sobre el comercio exterior en Latinoamérica, 1810–1850. (*in* América Latina en la época de Simón Bolívar. Edición de Reinhard Liehr. Berlin: Colloquium Verlag, 1989, p. 489–502, tables)

Brief, outdated summation of research concerning foreign trade of early republics.

892 Schneider, Jürgen. Trade relations between France and Latin America, 1810–1850. (*in* América Latina en la época de Simón Bolívar. Edición de Reinhard Liehr. Berlin: Colloquium Verlag, 1989, p. 423–437, graph, tables)

Suggests that terms of trade were much more favorable to early Republics than previously believed. Based primarily on French statistics for trade.

893 Shulgovski, Anatoli. Jacobinos latinoamericanos: mito o realidad. (*Am. Lat./Moscú*, 2, 1990, p. 80–90, photos)

Superficial essay examines Jacobin tendencies in the Revolutions for Independence.

894 Varela Bravo, Eduardo. Blanco White, la tolerancia y las Cortes de Cádiz. (*Cuad. Hispanoam.*, 460, oct. 1988, p. 91–103)

Study of writings on toleration by a 19th-century Catholic priest who went to England and converted to Anglicanism. See also item **887.**

895 Zárate Toscano, Verónica. El testamento político de los diputados americanos en 1814. (*Anu. Estud. Am.*, 45, 1988, p. 343–382)

Analyzes petitions submitted by American delegates to the Cortes when it was dissolved upon the return of Ferdinand VII. While some presented requests for redress of conditions in their homelands, most requested personal favors.

20TH CENTURY

896 Albert, Bill and **Paul Henderson.** South America and the First World War: the impact of the war on Brazil, Argentina, Peru, and Chile. Cambridge; New York: Cambridge Univ. Press, 1988. 388 p.: bibl., index. (Cambridge Latin American studies; 65)

Excellent study of economic and financial impact of World War I on continent using Argentina, Brazil, Peru and Chile as examples. In general, tests whether wartime conditions promoted or hindered the processes of economic modernization and concludes that the general debate over whether strong foreign links had a positive or negative effect on development are misconceived or oversimplified.

897 Anderson, Perry. The common and the particular. (*Int. Labor Work. Class Hist.*, 36, Fall 1989, p. 31–36)

Response to essay by Emilia Viotti da Costa (see item **903**) supports her conclusions but refines her categories and examines how various historians deal with the problem of how experience is transformed into consciousness.

898 Avni, Haim. Antisemitism under democratic and dictatorial regimes: the experience of Latin American Jewry. Translated by Aryeh Rubinstein. Jerusalem: Shazar Library, Institute of Contemporary Jewry, Vidal Sassoon International Center for the Study of Antisemitism, Hebrew Univ. of Jerusalem, 1986. 58 p. (Study Circle on World Jewry in the Home of the President of Israel; 7)

Translation of a lecture and discussion in home of Israeli president. Compares antisemitic outbursts in Argentina, Mexico, Cuba, and Chile to suggest ways of restraining such sentiments and posits that concerns over virulent antisemitism in Latin America are misplaced.

899 Bethell, Leslie and **Ian Roxborough.** Latin America between the Second World War and the Cold War: some reflections on the 1945–8 conjuncture. (*J. Lat. Am. Stud.*, 20:1, May 1988, p. 167–189, bibl.)

Argues that the immediate post-war years were a critical conjuncture and determined the social and ideological struggles of the 1950s and 1960s. Centers on question of why democratic openings of the immediate post-war period closed so quickly.

900 Blancpain, Jean-Pierre. Des visées pangermanistes au noyautage hitlérien: le nationalisme allemand et l'Amerique latine, 1890–1945. (*Rev. hist./Paris*, 570, avril/juin 1989, p. 433–482)

Study of Pan-German nationalism in Latin America emphasizes period between 1890–1918. Concentrates on Imperial diplomacy and its impact on German immigrants to Latin America. Argues that Germany treated such persons better than other European nations treated their emigrants, and that German emigrants were not Pan-German nationalist simply because they maintained cultural ties to mother country. Believes that this stigma was attached because of allied propaganda during World War I.

901 Bushnell, David and **Lyle N. McAlister.** An interview with Lewis Hanke. (*HAHR*, 68:4, Nov. 1988, p. 654–674)

One of a series of interviews with notable historians published by *HAHR*.

902 Costa, Emília Viotti da. Estructuras versus experiencia: nuevas tendencias en la historia del trabajo y la clase trabajadora en Latinoamérica:¿Qué ganamos? ¿Qué perdemos? (*HISLA*, 11, 1988, p. 81–95, bibl.)

Spanish version of item **903**.

903 Costa, Emília Viotti da. Experience versus structures: new tendencies in the history of labor and the working class in Latin America: What do we gain? What do we lose? (*Int. Labor Work. Class Hist.*, 36, Fall 1989, p. 3–24, bibl.)

Suggests new studies represent a significant shift away from traditional approaches to labor history. Investigation now focuses on workers' culture and experience as opposed to leadership, structures, and ideology of labor movements. Calls for a synthesis of the traditional and more recent approaches so as not to reduce labor history to the "history of daily life." For responses and further discussion, see items **897, 913, 914,** and **916.**

904 Drake, Paul W. The money doctor in the Andes: the Kemmerer missions, 1923–1933. Durham, N.C.: Duke Univ. Press, 1989. 335 p.: bibl., ill., index.

Uses the financial mission of Edwin Kemmerer to Peru to illustrate how the use of technical experts illuminates the "origins, patterns and dynamics of inter-American financial relations." Drake is particularly interested in analyzing the effectiveness of this assistance and the real influence of these advisors in shaping growth of capitalism in these economies. Argues that the Kemmerer reforms were widely accepted and believes that they made enormous contributions to thought processes and basic institutions of banking and finance which survived the Depression. For political scientist's comment, see *HLAS 51:4436.*

905 Hernández Sánchez-Barba, Mario. Iberoamérica en el siglo XX: dictaduras y revoluciones. Madrid: Anaya, 1988. 127 p. (Biblioteca iberoamericana; 33)

Very brief popular history of the 20th century gives significant coverage to cultural and intellectual movements.

906 Jornadas de Andalucía y América, 6th, Univ. de Santa María de la Rábida, Sevilla, Spain, 1986. Andalucía y América en el siglo XX: actas. v. 1–2. Sevilla: Escuela de Estudios Hispano-Americanos, C.S.I.C., Univ. Hispanoamericana Santa María de la Rábida; Huelva: Diputación de Huelva, Caja Provincial de Ahorros de Huelva, 1987. 2 v.: bibl., ill. (Publicaciones de la Escuela de Estudios Hispano-Americanos de Sevilla ; 336 (no. general))

Two volumes of conference papers. Vol. 1 contains some good pieces on influences on colonial art and architecture, and vol. 2 has a useful study of immigration to Brazil and Cuba, 1880–1940.

907 Jornadas Internacionales sobre la Migración en América, 1st, Buenos Aires, 1983. La inmigración a América Latina: trabajos. México: Instituto Panamericano de Geografía e Historia, 1985. 176 p.: bibl., ill. (Serie Inmigración; 2)

Fifteen papers from a 1983 conference on immigration. Twelve relate to Argentine themes, one compares experience of difference regions, one refers to Brazil, and one deals with immigrants during the Wars of Independence.

908 Kaplan, Marcos *et al.* América Latina: história de meio século. Coordinação de Pablo González Casanova; tradução de Marcos Bagno e Ricardo Gonçalves R. Castro. Brasília: Editora UnB, 1988. 1 v.: (Pensamento latino-americano e caribenho)

Essays study political development of the Southern Cone countries (1925–75).

Quality varies but the contribution by Marcos Kaplan on Argentina is useful.

909 Knape, John. Anglo-American rivalry in post-war Latin America: the question of arms sales. (*Ibero-Am. Arch.*, 15:3, 1989, p. 319–350, bibl.)

Examines immediate post-war views of the two countries regarding arms sales using both Foreign Office and National Archives material. The British viewed US efforts to restrict sales on grounds of desire to restrict arms race as hypocritical. The British needed to sell surplus arms to earn hard currency, and ultimately they broke with US on this issue.

910 Ludwig, Walther. Ein deutscher Kaufmann in Südamerika, 1905–1911. (*Jahrb. Gesch.*, 27, 1990, p. 338–374)

Collection of 15 personal letters written to his family in Germany by Rudolf Ludwig, a young businessman who worked for a German firm in Bolivia prior to World War I. Interesting document of living and working conditions and of German/South American relations. Includes biography of author and annotations by editor. [M.L. Wagner]

911 Luna, Lola G. El video aplicado a la memoria de las mujeres latinoamericanas. (*Bol. Am.*, 30:38, 1988, p. 141–150)

Description of an oral history project to obtain information on women's movements in the 1970s.

912 Miller, Francesca. Latin American women and the search for social justice. Hanover: Univ. Press of New England, 1991. 324 p.: bibl., ill., index, maps.

General history of women in Latin America in the 20th century with the theme of social justice setting the tone of the work. A brief review of the colonial period precedes a survey of education, but the focus is on women in the political arena. The latter is understood as women's interaction with the social reality of the continent, either through traditional or non-traditional means. This informative synthesis is especially recommended for classroom use. [A. Lavrin]

913 Nash, June. Gender issues in Latin American labor. (*Int. Labor Work. Class Hist.*, 36, Fall 1989, p. 44–50)

Response to essay by Emilia Viotti da Costa (item **903**) examines question of women and labor. Argues that Viotti da Costa is wrong in asserting that approach of womens studies often diametrically opposes labor studies in analyzing the experience of workers.

Ruppin, Arthur. Los judíos en América del Sur. See item **2770**.

914 Spalding, Hobart A. Somethings old and somethings new. (*Int. Labor Work. Class Hist.*, 36, Fall 1989, p. 37–43)

Another response to Emilia da Costa's essay (item **903**). Agrees with her but dwells on questions of rejection of Marxist theories, movement toward a type of Hegelian Idealism, and a new activism among historians.

915 Universiṭah ha-ʿIvrit bi-Yerushalayim. Makhon le-Yahadut zemanenu. Latin American Division. Oral documents from Latin America. Jerusalem: Institute of Contemporary Jewry, Hebrew Univ. of Jerusalem, 1987. 79 p.: index.

Index of oral interviews available in the Oral History Division of Hebrew University's Institute of Contemporary Jewry. Describes general subjects covered.

916 Weinstein, Barbara. The new Latin American labor history: what we gain. (*Int. Labor Work. Class Hist.*, 36, Fall 1989, p. 25–30)

Response to essay by Emilia Viotti da Costa (item **903**). Agrees with her analysis but suggests that her recommendations are already being put into practice by mainstream historians. The only real break in labor history has been the rejection of Marxist view that the working class is the vanguard of the revolution.

917 Wickham-Crowley, Timothy P. Terror and guerrilla warfare in Latin America, 1956–1970. (*Comp. Stud. Soc. Hist.*, 32:2, April 1990, p. 201–237)

Surveys literature related to six case studies of contemporary insurgency to determine use of terror by both sides as a tactic to obtain support or demoralize the opposition.

918 Young, George F.W. German capital investment in Latin America in World War I. (*Jahrb. Gesch.*, 25, 1988, p. 215–239, tables)

Examines size and distribution of German investment in Latin America prior to World War I and its fate during and after the war. Argues that except for Brazil, Guatemala, and Peru, it was practically untouched during the war because of the sympathy of local communities.

919 **Zeuske, Max** and **Ulrich Strulik.** Die Geschichte der deutsch-lateinameri-

kanischen Beziehungen vom Ende des 19: Jahrhunderts bis 1945 im Spiegel der DDR-Historiographie. (*Jahrb. Gesch.*, 25, 1988, p. 807–830)

Focuses on German relations with Latin America, 1898–1945. [G.M. Dorn]

MEXICO
General

ASUNCION LAVRIN, *Professor of History, Howard University*
EDITH B. COUTURIER, *National Endowment for the Humanities*

920 **Acevedo Cárdenas, Conrado et al.** Historia de Tijuana: semblanza general. Coordinación de David Piñera Ramírez. Tijuana, Mexico: Centro de Investigaciones Históricas UNAM-UABC, 1985. 338 p.: bibl., ill., maps, tables.

Fragmented but useful survey of Tijuana in 27 chapters. Over two-thirds of the essays deal with the 20th century. [AL]

921 **Los archivos municipales de Tabasco.** Coordinación de Patricia Rodríguez Ochoa. Mexico: Sistema Nacional de Archivos; Gobierno del Estado de Tabasco; Archivo General de la Nación, Dirección de Desarrollo de los Sistemas Estatales de Archivos, 1987. 478 p., 1 folded leaf of plates: bibl., ill., map. (Serie Archivos estatales y municipales de México; 7)

Chronologically organized inventory of 17 municipal archives in the Tabasco state covers municipal activities in recent years. The Cabildo council meetings are recorded from 1850–1985, but most documents date from 1960s to the present. [AL]

922 **Associación México Japonesa.** Nichiboku koryûshi [The history of Japanese-Mexican relations]. Tokyo: PMC Shuppan, 1990. 1174 p.: bibl., ill., index.

First history of Japanese-Mexican relations written by seven members of Japanese *isseis* (first generation) and *nisseis* (second generation) living in Mexico. Consists of five parts: initial contacts, history of Japanese immigration, economic relations, cultural

exchanges, and 90th anniversary of Japanese immigration to Mexico. [K. Horisaka]

Butzer, Karl W. Cattle and sheep from Old to New Spain: historical antecedents. See *HLAS 51:2908.*

923 **Coloquio de Historia Regional, 1st, Pachuca, Mexico, 1986.** Memoria. Pachuca, Mexico: Univ. Autónoma del Estado de Hidalgo, 1986. 534 p., 17 leaves of plates: ill. (Serie Universitas; 1. Biblioteca conmemorativa)

Collection of 25 essays selected from over 80 papers presented at the Colloquium. Most deal with economic topics, but several are devoted to the discussion of archival sources and the concept of regional history. [AL]

924 **Cornelio Sosa, Roger Elías** and **Jaime Mireles Rangel.** Historia del movimiento obrero de Campeche, 1540–1990. Campeche, Mexico: Federación de Trabajadores de Campeche, 1990. 471 p.: bibl., ill.

Official history of the workers' federation in Campeche is of sociological interest. Largely elegiac, it claims no objectivity. [AL]

925 **Delpar, Helen.** Frank Tannenbaum: the making of a Mexicanist, 1914–1933. (*Americas/Francisc.*, 45:2, Oct. 1988, p. 153–171, bibl.)

Well-written essay about this colorful interpreter of the Mexican revolution. Delpar's delineation of Tannenbaum's political activities and his progress towards becoming a student of Mexican affairs is smooth and

engaging. Based on Tannenbaum's personal papers.[AL]

926 Documentos históricos mexicanos. Edición de Genaro García. Ed. facsimilar. México: Comisión Nacional para las Celebraciones del 175 Aniversario de la Independencia Nacional y 75 Aniversario de la Revolución Mexicana, 1985. 7 v.: ill., indexes. (La Biblioteca de obras fundamentales de la Independencia y la Revolución)

Reissue of collection first published between 1910–12 is a rich and useful source of information on the Mexican process of independence. Strong for the period 1808–1813, but includes few documents beyond 1813. [AL]

927 Elite, clases sociales y rebelión en Guadalajara y Jalisco, siglos XVIII y XIX. Edición de Carmen Castañeda García. Guadalajara, México: El Colegio de Jalisco: Gobierno de Jalisco, Depto. de Educación Pública, 1988. 130 p.: bibl., ill.

Four separate essays treat the relationship among class, occupation, status, and ethnicity. One work deals with rural rebellion in the first half of the 19th century. Although the book lacks internal coherence, its parts are thought-provoking and merit reading. [AL]

928 Encuentro de Historiadores, Antropólogos y Economistas: la Historia Morelense en la Investigación Social, _Cuernavaca, Mexico, 1983._ Morelos: cinco siglos de historia regional. Coordinación de Horacio Gutiérrez Crespo. San Angel, Mexico: Centro de Estudios Históricos del Agrarismo en México; Cuernavaca: Univ. Autónoma del Estado de Morelos, 1984. 464 p.: bibl., ill.

Collection of 25 essays on the history of Morelos state covers prehispanic times to the present. Agricultural production and politics are predominant themes although two sections deal with the sources and methodology of history, and medical and botanical themes. Useful overview contains quality essays. [AL]

929 Encuentro Nacional de Historiadores, _1st, México, 1979._ Movimientos populares en la historia de México y América Latina: memoria del Primer Encuentro Nacional de Historiadores. México: Univ. Nacional Autónoma de México, 1987. 603 p.: bibl.

Collection of 46 papers deals with popular and peasant movements, the state of historical research in Mexico, and problems in the teaching of history. [AL]

930 Florescano, Enrique. El nuevo pasado mexicano. México: Cal y Arena, 1991. 229 p.: bibl.

Comprehensive review of the historiography of Mexico in recent years (1969–80) includes major chronological periods and themes. The Mexican Revolution takes the lion's share in number of works and attention of the author. An evaluation of the present and future of Mexican historiography closes this useful guide and adds Florescano's personal view. The notes contain extensive bibliographical references. Commendable effort. [AL]

931 Garavaglia, Juan Carlos and **Juan Carlos Grosso.** Mexican elites of a provincial town: the landowners of Tepeaca, 1700–1870. (_HAHR_, 70:2, May 1990, p. 255–293, graphs, maps, table)

Thoughtful study of the landowning elite of the Tepeaca region. Authors deal with several echelons of landownership and carefully analyze the meaning of familial linkages and inheritance in the maintenance of socioeconomic status through several generations. Four family histories illustrate how maintaining social status was as important as achieving it. [AL]

932 Gutiérrez Casillas, José. Historia de la Iglesia en México. 2a ed., rev. y adicionada. México: Editorial Porrúa, 1984. 678 p., 17 leaves of plates: bibl., ill., index.

Second edition of a work first published in 1974 (see _HLAS 38:2439_). [AL]

933 Henkel, Willi. Die Konzilien in Lateinamerika. v. 1, Mexiko, 1555–1897. Mit einer Einführung von Horst Pietschmann. Paderborn, Germany: F. Schöningh, 1984. 1 v.: bibl., indexes, maps. (Konziliengeschichte: Reihe A, Darstellungen)

Vol. 1 concentrates on the provincial ecclesiastical councils. An especially interesting section is devoted to the Mexican _juntas_ of 1524–46 as prototypes for later synods. Henkel deals with each of the provincial councils of the Catholic Church first in the Viceroyalty of New Spain and later in independent Mexico. The work is based on the

actas and other documentation generated by the councils. [G.M. Dorn]

934 Historia de la cuestión agraria mexicana. v. 1, El siglo de la hacienda, 1800–1900 [de] Antonio García de León, Enrique Semo y Ricardo Gamboa Ramírez. v. 2, La tierra y el poder, 1800–1910 [de] Enrique Semo *et al.* v. 3, Campesinos, terratenientes y revolucionarios, 1910–1920 [de] Oscar Betanzos *et al.* v. 4, Modernización, lucha agraria y poder político, 1920–1934 [de] Enrique Montalvo, José Rivera Castro y Oscar Betanzos Piñón. México: Siglo Veintiuno Editores: Centro de Estudios Históricos del Agrarismo en México, 1988. 4 v.: bibl., ill.

First four volumes (of a projected nine) of an agrarian history of Mexico in the 19th and 20th centuries highlight landownership, labor, politics, etc., with the rural scene as the focus of each essay. Each volume contains several thematic essays written by different authors, and follows a broad chronological order. Most essays are syntheses of printed sources or secondary works. For vol. 7, see *HLAS 51:1856.* [AL]

935 Lecturas históricas del estado de Oaxaca. v. 1, Época prehispánica. v. 3, Siglo XIX. v. 4, 1877–1930. Recopilación de Marcus Winter y María de los Angeles Romero Frizzi. México: Instituto Nacional de Antropología e Historia, 1986–1990. 3 v.: bibl., ill., maps. (Col. Regiones de México)

Multivolume history of Oaxaca contains essays on key themes of the period authored by distinguished scholars. Despite fragmentation inherent to this organization, this is a valuable contribution to the history of Oaxaca state. For Vol. 2 see *HLAS 50:1020* [AL]

936 Lombardo de Ruiz, Sonia *et al.* Y todopor una nación: historia social de la producción plástica de la Ciudad de México, 1781–1910. Coordinación de Eloísa Uribe. 2. ed. México: Instituto Nacional de Antropología e Historia, 1987. 213 p.: bibl. (Col. científica; 164. Serie Historia)

Collection of essays on the development of high culture and art in Mexico from the late colonial period through the end of the Porfiriato. Essays attempt to link the political and economic situation of the nation with the artistic expression. Artesanal and "high" art are included. [AL]

Luzbetak, Louis J. If Junípero Serra were alive: missiological-anthropological theory today. See *HLAS 51:712.*

937 MacLeod, Murdo J. Death in western colonial Mexico: its place in village and peasant life. *(in* The middle period in Latin America: values and attitudes in the 17th-19th centuries. Edited by Mark D. Szuchman. Boulder, Colo.: Lynne Rienner Publishers, 1989, p. 57–73, tables)

Author examines burial records for four Guadalajara region villages between 1590–1800, highlighting causes of death and attitudes toward it. Compares conditions between the crises of the 1730s and the 1780s, and discusses various causes of mortality. [EBC]

938 Movimientos de población en el occidente de México. Coordinación de Thomas Calvo y Gustavo López Castro. Zamora, Michoacán: Colegio de Michoacán; México: Centre d'études mexicaines et centraméricaines, 1988. 372 p.: bibl., ill.

Papers from a 1986 conference cover all aspects of migration from prehispanic movements to the present. Leading scholars included are David Robinson, Jorge Durand, Nicole Pecheron, Thomas Calvo, Robert McCaa and Gail Mummert. [EBC]

939 Obregón Martínez, Arturo. Las obreras tabacaleras de la Ciudad de México, 1764–1925. México: Centro de Estudios Históricos del Movimiento Obrero Mexicano, 1982. 136 p.: bibl., ill. (La Formación histórica de la clase obrera en México. Cuadernos obreros; 25)

Brief history of the tobacco industry in Mexico City with useful information on women workers concentrates mostly on the second half of the 19th century. [AL]

940 Origen y evolución de la hacienda en México: siglos XVI al XX; memorias del simposio realizado del 27 al 30 de septiembre de 1989. Coordinación de María Teresa Jarquín Ortega *et al.* Toluca, México: Colegio Mexiquense A.C.: Univ. Iberoamericana; Instituto Nacional de Antropología e Historia, 1990. 263 p. : ill.

Record of continuing research on the history of haciendas includes materials about all parts of Mexico. Most of the contributions are based on primary sources. Covers a variety of topics such as debt peonage, *tien-*

das de raya, family history, *hacendados* and politics. [EBC]

941 Pacheco Ladrón de Guevara, Lourdes C. Fuentes para el estudio de Nayarit. Tepic, Mexico: [s.n], 1988. 2 v. (212 leaves): bibl.

Exhaustive bibliography on Nayarit state includes books, theses, newspapers, and documents from abroad. [AL]

942 Probert, Alan. En pos de la plata: episodios mineros en la historia hidalguense. Traducción de Lucía Vera Graciano. 1a ed. en español. Pachuca, Mexico: Compañía Real del Monte y Pachuca; SEMIP, 1987. 391 p.: bibl., ill., maps.

Translation of the major articles of a mining engineer and amateur historian who lived and worked in the Pachuca region between 1935–1948, and who spent many years researching its history. Includes material on Bartolomé de Medina, Romero de Terreros, and aspects of the history of the mining camps of Pachuca and Real del Monte. Useful and well-written compendium. [EBC]

943 Riot, rebellion, and revolution: rural social conflict in Mexico. Edited by Friedrich Katz. Princeton, N.J.: Princeton Univ. Press, 1988. 594 p.: bibl., index.

Collection of 17 essays on the historical phenomenon of peasant revolts in rural Mexico includes five essays on the colonial period and nine on the 19th and 20th centuries. Linkages among revolts and economic, political, and ethnic factors are aptly established by this exceptionally rich and scholarly collection. [AL]

944 Rosenzweig, Fernando *et al.* Breve historia del Estado de México. Toluca: El Colegio Mexiquense; Gobierno del Estado de México, 1987. 320 p.: bibl., ill.

General history of the state of Mexico. Four essays based on secondary sources highlight society and economy prior to the 19th century. Society, politics, and the economy are examined from the 19th century to 1940. For general audience. [AL]

945 Serrano Migallón, Fernando. Toma de posesión: el rito del poder. Presentación de Lorenzo Meyer. México: M.A. Porrúa, 1988. 189 p.:

Account of the ceremonies and speeches of those acceding to power focuses

on the 19th and 20th centuries. Includes a summary of presidential messages. [AL]

946 Simposio de Historiografía Mexicanista, 1988. Memorias. México: UNAM, Comité Mexicano de Ciencias Históricas; Gobierno del Estado de Mexico, 1990. 1 v.

Conference papers take a retrospective look at Mexican historiographical output since 1968. Essays by distinguished historians assess works written in that period by thematic and by chronological arrangement (i.e., historiography of the 19th century; historiography of art; regional historiography; historiography of labor; the Church; women; and so forth). Extremely useful for all academic levels. [AL]

947 Thomson, Guy P.C. Puebla de los Angeles: industry and society in a Mexican city, 1700–1850. Boulder, Colo.: Westview Press, 1989. 396 p.: bibl., ill. (Dellplain Latin American studies; 25)

Study of the city of Puebla stresses economy, political economy, and social structure. Strong in information on population, occupation, social stratification, and the economic profile of the city and its adjacent region for the period prior to independence. One-fourth of the book focuses on the industrial recovery of the city during the first three decades of independence. Well documented and useful study. [AL]

948 Torre Champsaur, Lucrecia de la; Teresa Matabuena Peláez and María Eugenia Ponce Alcocer. Catálogo de manuscritos: colección de la Biblioteca Francisco Xavier Clavigero de la Univ. Iberoamericana. México: Univ. Iberoamericana, 1990. 381 p.: ill., index.

Lavishly produced, richly illustrated, and annotated catalog of the colonial archives of Univ. Iberoamericana. Includes collections of sermons, foundations of *obras pias,* confraternity documents, and hacienda titles. [EBC]

949 Valdés Lakowsky, Vera. De las minas al mar: historia de la plata mexicana en Asia, 1565–1834. México: Fondo de Cultura Económica, 1987. 368 p., 4 folded leaves of plates: bibl., ill., index. (Sección de obras de historia)

Historical survey of the silver trade between New Spain and the Far East is strongest for the 18th and 19th centuries. Based on Mexican archival materials and printed sources. [AL]

950 Villa de Mebius, Rosa Helia. San Luis Potosí: una historia compartida. México: Instituto de Investigaciones José María Luis Mora, 1988. 583 p.: bibl., ill.

Historical synthesis of San Luis Potosí from 1824–1925 devotes special attention to cultural themes. [AL]

951 Visión histórica de la frontera norte de México. v. 1–2. Coordinación de David Piñera Ramírez. Mexicali, Mexico: Univ. Autónoma de Baja California, Centro de Investigaciones Históricas UNAM-UABC, 1987. 2 v.: bibl., ill., maps, ports.

Handsomely produced volumes contain fine illustrations and texts written by leading historians. Includes generous selections from the writings of contemporary protagonists. Vol. 1 begins with geography and concludes with a chapter on the events of 1846–48. Vol. 2 starts with the Wars of Independence and continues through the Porfiriato. Both volumes contain sections devoted to each of the northern states. [EBC]

952 Winter, Marcus *et al.* Historia de la cuestión agraria mexicana: estado de Oaxaca. v. 1, Prehispánico-1924. v. 2, 1925–1986. Coordinación de Leticia Reina y José Sánchez Cortés. México: Juan Pablos Editor, 1988. 2 v.: bibl., ill.

Essays on the "agricultural issues" in Oaxaca state from precolombian times to the present. Essays deal with ecological factors, system of agricultural production, landownership, labor, markets, and the conflicts and political issues raised by the evolution of these factors. The essay on 20th century issues uses oral history. Useful synthesis of available recent scholarship. [AL]

Colonial

ASUNCION LAVRIN, *Professor of History, Howard University*
EDITH B. COUTURIER, *National Endowment for the Humanities*

RESEARCH ON MEXICAN COLONIAL HISTORY continued to focus primarily on the central geographical core of the Viceroyalty of New Spain and, chronologically, on the 16th and the late 18th centuries. In the last biennium little was written on the southern areas, and Oaxaca and Yucatán monopolized the few works on that region. The northern areas of New Spain held their own in terms of historical attention as is noted below. Two main concerns of historians, the accessibility of documentary sources and the evaluation of the historiographical output of scholars, were served by the publication of several guides to archival materials, and by assessments of individual historians in scholarly meetings. Among the former are guides to the study of colonial agriculture (item **965**); the continuation of the guide to the notarial records of Monterrey (item **960**); the reissue of Genaro García's documentary sources on the independence (item **926**), and Sarabia Viejo's lengthy bibliography on colonial works (item **979**). The latter category was best represented by the publication of a retrospective on the historiography between 1960–90 in the *Memorias del Simposio de Historiografía Mexicanista*, an impressive collection of essays on a broad spectrum of themes. Enrique Florescano's studies on the nature of historical thought in Mexico and the historiography of the recent past are also worth noting (item **930**).

Monographs, rather than over-arching thematic coverage, were the predominant venue of expression. The search for illuminating details of regional or local history is based on the conviction that the nuances of time and locality need to be explored with methodological rigor in order to understand the variety of patterns developed throughout 300 years of colonial experience. Sweeping generalizations about some institutions are no longer applicable to the entire Viceroyalty, and discrete units of study seem to be establishing firmer grounds for future reinterpretations. The endeavors of local and regional historians are supported by the growing accessibility of regional archival sources and by the activities of local historical centers such as the Colegios de Michoacán and Guadalajara, to mention only two of several distinguished institutions. For examples of microregional studies see the works of Guy P.C. Thomson on Puebla (item 947) and Thomas Calvo on New Galicia (item 956). Emilio Duhau (item 963) and María de los Angeles Romero Frizzi (item 977) produced shorter but pithy regional essays. Also useful is a collection of papers focusing on Morelia (item 928). The collection of essays on Indian-Spanish economic and social relationships edited by Arij Ouweneel and Simon Miller (item 969) gathers a series of studies about the local circumstances of indigenous communities, thus fulfilling the current need to write a history focusing on the tensions of interests therein.

In addition to an interest in regional history there are also efforts to develop global histories such as the projected nine-volume study on 19th-20th-century agrarian problems (item 934), and a collection of essays edited by Friedrich Katz on rebellion and rural conflict (item 943). Slightly outdated by a delayed printing is a volume on the history of popular movements (item 929). Two other important syntheses were Gonzalbo Aizpuru's volumes on the history of education of Indians and Creoles in New Spain in which she provides grand overviews of these important topics (items 967). Regional global histories such as those of the state of Oaxaca (item 935) combine the excellence of monographic studies with a more encompassing focus.

Hacienda and landownership studies have ceded their former preeminence to studies of interethnic relations at the social and economic levels. Whether such relations describe antagonism and resistance, or long-term adaptation, their study encompasses a broad spectrum of human activities as central concerns. Good examples of such studies are the works of Lolita Gutiérrez-Brockington (item 1000); Grant Jones (item 1037); John K. Chance (item 1004); and the collection on Oaxaca edited by Leticia Reina (item 952). Significantly, these works also focus on the peripheral south. Among the few hacienda studies we must underline those of Arij Ouweneel (item 1058) which intends to revise the method of studying agricultural production. Also worth noting are a study by María del Carmen Velázquez (item 1093) and Mari-José Amerlinck's essay on the acquisition of haciendas by the Dominican Order (item 990).

Social and economic history are no longer separate categories and most historical works interweave them in their analysis. Examples of this approach are the following books: Louisa S. Hoberman's on 17th-century Mexico City merchants (item 1034); Virginia García Acosta's (item 1020); Agueda Jiménez's (item 1036); Manuel Miño Grijalva's (item 1053); and Juan Carlos Caravaglia and Juan Carlos Grosso's (item 931). More strictly geared to the study of economic processes are several works which concentrate on the late 18th century. The Bourbon period continues to serve as the treasure trove for economic, institutional and political history, given the abundance of documentation and the significance of changes undertaken throughout the end of the colonial period. Of special interest as a source for the study of economic thought is the edition of the economic writings of the secretaries of the Consulado de Veracruz by Ortiz de la Tabla (item 1049). Another important book in this category is the one by Pedro Pérez Herrero on credit and commerce (item **1061**). Margaret Chowning reviews the impact of *Consolidación* legislation in Michoacán in a model study of local economic history (item **1005**). Also of interest for economists is Vera Valdés' study of mining and the Pacific trade (item **949**). The Pacific basin still remains a neglected area in Mexican historiography but one compilation of studies attempts to redress this situation (item **975**). The technical aspects of the textile industry were highlighted by Miño Grijalva (item **973**). The academic debate on the use of statistical techniques to detect economic cycles has been enlivened by Arij Ouweneel's *The economic cycle in Bourbon Central Mexico* (item **1057**), which poses important questions on the analysis of economic cycles. Critiques by David Brading and others (item **999**) enlivened the discussion over the interpretation of mathematical data. Despite these works, the output in classic economic history was limited.

Vicente Rodríguez García's study of the Royal Exchequer's attorney, Ramón de Posada, points to the need to connect biography and politics (item **1070**). Also successful in this line of inquiry is Linda Arnold's prosopography of the late colonial bureaucracy (item **955**), and Couturier's essay on the entrepreneurial career of Pedro Romero de Terreros (item **1011**). Fray Servando Teresa de Mier was highlighted by a recent French publication (item **1052**). But the best re-examined figure of the colonial period was that of Hernán Cortés, the subject of a new biography (item **1047**) and of a conference in Spain that brought to light every possible detail in the life and thoughts of the conquistador (item **1008**).

Ecclesiastical history elicited considerable interest, perhaps as a result of a more intensive use of ecclesiastical records for social or mentalité studies, and their greater accessibility to researchers in recent years. Antonio Rubial García, who has been studying the Augustinian order for some time, has written a capable synthesis of the Order's move to New Spain (item **1073**). Also noteworthy is Manuel Ramos Medina's study of Carmelite nunneries in Mexico City (item **989**). Murdo MacLeod's study of the struggle of Church and State over the control of the indigenous population in 16th-century Chiapas revisits this important topic (item **971**). Others have been attracted by the recovery of the texts produced by historians of the past. We have now two editions of the 17th-century history of the Carmelite Order by Agustín de la Madre de Dios, a previously unpublished manuscript at the Univ. of Tulane (items **988** and **989**). The publication of the 1585 text of the *History of New Spain* by Fray Bernardino de Sahagún (item **1075**) is worth noting as another example of the interest in the reproduction of texts. Among other significant publications on the Church are the study of the ideology of the regular clergy by B. Connaughton (item **1009**), the study of *cofradías* by Alicia Bazarte (item **992**), and the comparative study of tithe collection in New Spain and Peru by Schwaller (item **1076**). The 1989 International Congress on Franciscans in the New World produced an important monograph on the role of the Order (item **1072**). The extensive study of the Inquisition by Solange Alberro (item **953**) stands apart. It is more an intriguing and appealing social history of New Spain than a history of the Inquisition itself. The intellectual content of the Jesuits' educational policies have been meticulously analyzed by Gonzalbo Aizpuru in a work that departs from traditional historiographical paths (item **966**). Works by Torre Villar on confessionals (item **982**), Victoria Cumming on the economic stake of the 16th century (item **1014**) and Richard Greenleaf on the process of inquisitorial visits are also serious contributions (item **1029**). The bibliographical compilation by Rubial García and García Ayluardo (item **978**) is useful.

Deserving mention among demographic works are the methodological analysis by David J. Robinson (item **1068**), a collection of works on western Mexico (item **938**), and Miguel Angel Cuenya on a Puebla parish (item **1012**). Cecilia Rabell reviews the contributions of several demographic works (item **976**) and the black sector of the population is examined in monographs by Patrick Carroll (item **957**) and Adriana Naveda (item **1055**).

Family and women's history have been enriched by several important works that discuss marriage and honor (Seed, item **980**), sexuality and the Church (Lavrin, item **970**) female philanthropy (Couturier, item **962**) family (Boyer and Calvo, item **767** and **1001**) and gender and witchcraft (Behar, item **993**). Works on *beatas* and models of religious lives broaden the thematic concern of ecclesiastical history (items **1069** and **1090**) and an unusual study on rape by Castañeda (item **1003**) adds criminality to the range of topics. [AL]

This has been an especially rich period in the broad category of social history of the northern regions of New Spain. Of particular note are works on labor history—perhaps those that are most important are studies by Susan Deeds on problems of forced labor in Nueva Vizcaya (item **1108**), Robert Jackson and Peter Stern on mining labor and the cyclical nature of labor needs (item **1112**), and Jiménez Pelayo on Indian communities in southern Zacetecas (item **1113**). Other important works in social history are those by Cynthia Radding on Sonora (item **1122**) and a collection of documents compiled by Carlos Manuel Valdés and Ildefonso Dávila (item **1131**). The debate over the canonization of Junípero Serra has enlivened the missionary history of the region, especially that of James Sandos (item **1128**), but note should also be taken of the transcription of a collection of documents from 1812 by Edward D. Castillo (item **1105**). An attempt by James E. Ivey (item **1111**) to date 17th-century missions in New Mexico indicates the lacunae that still remain in writing the history of the north. Works by José Cuello on the region include a study of the city of Saltillo in the late colonial period; a collection of his translated articles (item **1107**) makes an important contribution to the study of the region. Oakah L. Jones, one of the most productive contributors to the field of North and Borderlands history, contributes a history of Nueva Vizcaya (item **1114**). Another important account written about the North is the article by Cheryl Martin (item **1116**) which breaks new ground for the use of speech to investigate gender and race. Richard Nostrand, a geographer, adds to the new field of ecological history (item **1103**). Finally, one addition to the history of science in Baja California should be mentioned: Salvador Bernabeu Albert's study of mining in Baja California in the 1760s and 1770s provides a fresh vision of events (item **1103**). [EBC]

GENERAL

953 Alberro, Solange. Inquisition et société au Mexique, 1571–1700. México: Centre d'études mexicaines et centraméricaines, 1988. 489 p.: bibl., ill., index, tables. (Etudes mésoaméricaines, 0378–5726; 15)

Extensive and intensive study treats, in a series of essays and documentary appendices, the following themes: men who ran the Inquisition; institutions; crimes; heretics; and prisons. Book contains large number of case studies as well as analysis of the nature of the offenses and their relationship to the society of particular places such as Celaya and Zacatecas as well as to events in New Spain. Also published in Spanish translation by the Fondo de Cultura Económica (México, 1988). [EBC]

954 Alberro, Solange. Olvidar o recordar para ser: españoles, negros y castas en la Nueva España, siglos XVI-XVII. (*in* Simposio de Historia de las Mentalidades, *2nd, México, 1983*. La memoria y el olvido [see item **1081**,] p. 135–144)

The Inquisition had specific mechanisms to build a memory, states author, who proceeds to define how Africans in Mexico constructed a memory before the Holy Office. Loss of memory of first migrants before the Inquisition was compensated by the new memory built by some acculturated individuals. Essay compares their experience with that of other groups. [AL]

955 Arnold, Linda. Bureaucracy and bureaucrats in Mexico City, 1742–1835. Tucson: Univ. of Arizona Press, 1988. 202 p.: bibl., ill., index.

Study of the politics of bureaucratic appointments and the professionalization of the viceregal bureaucracy in the late 18th century. Surveys continuities and changes through the independence period and covers the Viceregal Secretariat, the Audiencia and the fiscal bureaucracy. A profile of bureaucratic careers enhances this work. [AL]

Assadourian, Carlos Sempat. La despoblación indígena en Perú y Nueva España durante el siglo XVI y la formación de la economía colonial. See item **2130.**

Borchart de Moreno, Christiana. Capital comercial y producción agrícola: Nueva España y la Audiencia de Quito en el siglo XVIII. See item **2084.**

956 Calvo, Thomas. La Nueva Galicia en los siglos XVI y XVII. Presentación de Carmen Castañeda. Guadalajara, México: Centro de Estudios Mexicanos y Centroamericanos: Colegio de Jalisco, 1989. 199 p.: ill., map.

Gathers 11 articles on the history of Guadalajara and Jalisco that had been published by the author in several journals and languages. Useful, despite the lack of thematic unity. [AL]

957 Carroll, Patrick James. Blacks in colonial Veracruz: race, ethnicity, and regional development. Austin: Univ. of Texas Press, 1991. 240 p.: bibl., ill., index, maps, tables.

In-depth study of African labor in the coastal region of Veracruz from inception of slave trade through first decade of Independence. Careful study that encompasses labor, social relations, Maroon towns, process of freedom, family life and the status of the Afro-Veracruzanos in Mexican society. Author's thesis is that race was an important

signifier in colonial society. Grounded on archival research. [AL]

958 Cartas de cabildos hispanoamericanos: Audiencia de México. Edición e introducción de Enriqueta Vila Vilar y María Justina Sarabia Viejo. Con la colaboración de Angeles Flores Moscoso y María Concepción Hernández-Díaz Tapia. Sevilla: Escuela de Estudios Hispano-Americanos, Consejo Superior de Investigaciones Científicas: Diputación Provincial de Sevilla, 1985. 1 v.: bibl., index, map. (Escuela de Estudios Hispano-Americanos; 310)

Guide to and description of each of the 650 *legajos* of the AGI's section of the Audiencia de México on municipal affairs before 1700. Organized by bishoprics, then by Spanish town and Indian pueblo, there is a brief summary and information on the resolution of the issue when available. Well-indexed. Model of useful tool for exploitation of the AGI. [EBC]

959 Cartografía histórica de la Nueva Galicia. Edición de Juan López. Guadalajara, México: Univ. de Guadalajara; Sevilla: Escuela de Estudios Hispano-Americanos de Sevilla, 1984. 421 p.: bibl., ill., maps.

Impressive collection of maps of New Galicia reproduced from the originals in several Mexican archives and European repositories. Maps range from mid-1570s to 1822, and from general maps of the region to close-ups of villages and buildings. Quality of reproduction is fair to good. Bibliographical annotations for each reproduction were carefully written by team of Spanish scholars. Very worthwhile publication. For geographer's comment see *HLAS 51:2911*.[AL]

960 Cavazos Garza, Israel. Catálogo y síntesis de los protocolos del Archivo Municipal de Monterrey. v. 4, 1756–1785. Monterrey, Mexico: Administración Municipal de Monterrey, 1983. 1 v.: index.

Vol. 4 consists of useful synoptic summary of all notarial deeds registered in Monterrey (1756–85). Contains 519 deeds recording powers of attorney, dowries, real estate sales, wills, etc. Smaller number of notarial deeds indicates period of economic stagnation. [AL]

961 Contreras Sánchez, Alicia del C. El palo del tinte: motivo de un conflicto entre dos naciones, 1672–1822. (*Hist. Mex.*, 37:1, julio/sept. 1987, p. 49–74, bibl.)

Recounts the story of "dye wood" production in Tabasco and Yucatán in the context of English and Spanish efforts to exploit and market the product as it became an important aspect of European textile manufacturing. [EBC]

962 Couturier, Edith. "For the greater service of God:" opulent foundations and women's philanthropy in colonial Mexico. (*in* Lady bountiful revisited: women, philanthropy, and power. Edited by Kathleen D. McCarthy. New Brunswick, New Jersey: Rutgers Univ. Press, 1990, p. 119–141)

Examines role of women as philanthropists in colonial Mexico. Covers dowries, convents and poor relief. Author underlines role of women as givers and as recipients and points out differences between men and women as donors. [AL]

963 Duhau, Emilio. Mercado interno y urbanización en el México colonial. México: Univ. Autónoma Metropolitana: Gernika, 1988. 306 p.: bibl., maps.

Duhau argues that a true urban history of New Spain must be based on the assumption that cities developed as a result of the internal economy of the Viceroyalty. Studies several provincial cities to explain their correlation with regional economies, and their role as mercantile centers. [AL]

964 Florescano, Enrique. Memoria mexicana: ensayo sobre la reconstrucción del pasado; época prehispánica-1821. México: Editorial J. Mortiz, 1987. 337 p.: bibl., ill. (Contrapuntos)

Surveys historical concepts of the past and ways of preserving them in colonial Mexico. Deals mostly with the indigenous experience, both prior to and after the conquest. Spanish historiography is surveyed only for the late colonial period. Based on printed sources. [AL]

965 Fuentes para el estudio de la agricultura colonial en la diócesis de Michoacán: series de diezmos, 1636–1810. Recopilación de Enrique Florescano y Lydia Espinosa. México: Instituto Nacional de Antropología e Historia, 1987. 2 v.: bibl., ill., indexes. (Col. Fuentes)

Tithes Series, roughly from mid-17th to mid-18th century, contains useful raw data. [AL]

966 Gonzalbo, Pilar. La educación popular de los jesuitas. México: Univ. Iberoamericana, Depto. de Historia, 1989. 247 p.: bibl.

Extended treatment of educational mission of Jesuits seeks to explain both their work among urban elites and their posts on the frontiers. Balanced account of strengths and weaknesses is based on careful reading of contemporary publications and manuscripts. [EBC]

967 Gonzalbo, Pilar. Historia de la educación en la época colonial: el mundo indígena. México: El Colegio de México, Centro de Estudios Históricos, 1990. 274 p.: bibl., index. (Serie Historia de la educación)

Thorough and well-documented study of all institutions founded for the education of Indian children in New Spain. Author also surveys informal education. Commendable synthesis. [AL]

968 Gonzalbo, Pilar. Historia de la educación en la epoca colonial: la educación de los criollos y la vida urbana. México: Colegio de México, Centro de Estudios Históricos, 1990. 395 p.: bibl., index, map. (Serie Historia de la educación)

Begins with 16th-century ideas about education and continues with the establishment and operation of the University. Emphasizes the work of Jesuit colleges and the training of clergy. Conclusions relate both strengths and weaknesses of the educational system to the problems of the society. Explores many sources. [EBC]

969 The Indian community of colonial Mexico: fifteen essays on land tenure, corporate organizations, ideology, and village politics. Edited by Arij Ouweneel and Simon Miller. Amsterdam: CEDLA, 1990. 321 p.: bibl., ill., maps. (Latin America studies; 58)

First part of this fine collection of essays discusses the formation of the landbase of the corporate community as well as the consolidation of Indian land tenure. Second part treats religious character of the Indian community and the economic position of the religious brotherhoods, ideology, and village politics. [R. Hoefte]

970 Lavrin, Asunción. Sexuality in colonial Mexico: a Church dilemma. (*in*

Sexuality and marriage in colonial Latin America. Edited by Asunción Lavrin. Lincoln, Neb.: Univ. of Nebraska Press, 1989, p. 47–95, facsims.)

Delivering more than title suggests, this article describes and analyzes sexual behavior, relations of power between men and women, and conflicts between ecclesiastical principles and human sexuality. Based on a wide selection of printed contemporary sources, such as guides for confessors, combined with legal and ecclesiastical sources dealing with relations between men and women. [EBC]

López Cervantes, Gonzalo and **Rosa María García García.** Ensayo bibliográfico del período colonial de México. See item **41.**

971 MacLeod, Murdo J. La espada de la Iglesia: excomunión y la evolución de la lucha por el control político y económico en Chiapas colonial, 1545–1700. (*Mesoamérica/Antigua,* 2:20, dic. 1990, p. 199–213)

Chronicles the long-term and inconclusive struggle for power among the Church, settlers and the Audiencia over Indian labor and tribute. Shifting allegiances of the Dominicans and the Bishop over secularization of doctrines complicated the picture. Based on archival sources. [AL]

972 Millares Carlo, Agustín. Cuatro estudios biobibliográficos mexicanos: Francisco Cervantes de Salazar, Fray Agustín Dávila Padilla, Juan José de Eguiara y Eguren, José Mariano Beristáin de Souza. México: Fondo de Cultura Económica, 1986. 462 p.: bibl., facsims. (Sección de obras de historia)

Erudite studies of four colonial intellectuals by the masterful pen of Millares Carlo. Each study has historical introduction and bibliographical essay. Relevant documents are attached to each. Highly recommended. [AL]

973 Miño Grijalva, Manuel. La manufactura colonial. Léon, México: Colegio del Bajío, 1985. 213 p.: bibl., ill. (Cuadernos de investigación; 3)

Book-length study of the textile industries of New Spain and Peru focuses on technical aspects of production. [AL]

974 Miño Grijalva, Manuel. La política textil en México y Perú en la época colonial: nuevas consideraciones. (*Hist. Mex.,* 38:2, oct./dic. 1988, p. 283–323, bibl.)

Traces the ups and downs of royal policies regulating the textile industry in two important colonial centers from the 16th through the late 18th century. Underlines the contradictory interests of the Crown and its subjects in the New World. Concludes that the demand for cheap textiles was so great that colonial industries never ceased to produce. [AL]

975 La presencia novohispana en el Pacífico insular: actas de las primeras jornadas internacionales celebradas en la Ciudad de México, del 19 al 21 de septiembre de 1989. Coordinación de María Cristina Barrón y Rafael Rodríguez-Ponga Salamanca. México: Univ. Iberoamericana; Embajada de España en México; Comisión Puebla V Centenario; Pinacoteca Virreinal, 1990. 210 p.: bibl., ill.

Includes papers on the linguistic effects of New Spain in the Pacific, army recruits, a biography of the Philippines governor, an expedition to Siam, the process of Christianization, the Philippines' trade, San Felipe de Jesús, and the Malaspina Expedition, among others. [EBC]

976 Rabell, Cecilia Andrea. La población novohispana a la luz de los registros parroquiales: avances y perspectivas de investigación. México: Instituto de Investigaciones Sociales, UNAM, 1990. 91 p.: bibl., ill. (Cuaderno de investigación social; 21)

Analytical synthesis of 11 demographic monographs published in the 1970s. Provides useful panorama of methodologies used and the results obtained by several demographers of New Spain. [AL]

977 Romero Frizzi, María de los Angeles. Economía y vida de los españoles en la Mixteca Alta, 1519–1720. México: Instituto Nacional de Antropología e Historia; Gobierno del Estado de Oaxaca, 1990. 636 p.: bibl., ill., maps. (Col. Regiones de México)

Unusual long-term study of the Spanish population in the Mixtec area is based on local archives. Author identifies the white population in the area and traces its pattern of occupation, mercantile activites, ownership of land, role in local government, credit ties, internal social stratification, etc. This amounts to a study of the regional elite in a predominantly agricultural area. Although lacking a final synthesis, this is an important and richly documented book. [AL]

978 Rubial García, Antonio and **Clara García Ayluardo.** La vida religiosa en el México colonial: un acercamiento bibliográfico. México: Univ. Iberoamericana, Depto. de Historia, 1991. 137 p.: bibl.

Compilation of all printed works on the colonial Church with short introductions to the two main divisions (works on the several ecclesiastical institutions, and printed sources for the study of religious orders and the secular Church). First section is subdivided into: "General Works;" "The Mendicant Orders;" "Feminine Institutions;" "The Secular Clergy;" "Hospitals;" "Inquisition;" "Confraternities;" and "Religiosity." Second section is arranged by religious orders, and includes works on the secular clergy, and documentary collections. Useful guide. [AL]

979 Sarabia Viejo, María Justina. Bibliografía de México en la época colonial. (*Historiogr. Bibliogr. Am.*, 30:2, 1986, p. 79–118)

Annotated bibliography of major themes of colonial history by Spanish scholar. [AL]

980 Seed, Patricia. To love, honor, and obey in colonial Mexico: conflicts over marriage choice, 1574–1821. Stanford, Calif.: Stanford Univ. Press, 1988. 322 p.:bibl., index.

Study of marriage options in central New Spain. Honor, love, and the will to marry are discussed before reviewing evolution of parental authority, ecclesiastical doctrine of free will in marriage, and couples' choices throughout the 17th and 18th centuries. Concludes that familial and royal policies of marital restriction prevailed against freedom of choice at the end of the colonial period, and that such change was partly due to the expansion of capitalism, carrying in itself a decline in the value of female honor. Based on archival sources. [AL]

981 Taylor, William B. The Virgin of Guadalupe in New Spain: an inquiry into the social history of Marian devotion. (*Am. Ethnol.*, 14:1, Feb. 1987, p. 9–33, bibl.)

Revisits history of the cult of the Virgin of Guadalupe to find out that her worship was officially promoted by colonial authorities. As a symbol of mediation between humans and God, Guadalupe appealed to Spaniards and Indians. Her worship did not become symbolic of Indian and rural areas—or national—until the independence period. Challenging interpretation of the subject. [AL]

982 Torre Villar, Ernesto de la. Aspectos sociales de los instrumentos de pastoral cristiana en Nueva España. (*Hist. Mex.*, 38:4, abril/junio 1989, p. 609–621)

Interesting study of several confessionals used in New Spain for the Christian catechesis of the population as a means to understand the pastoral message during the 16th and 17th centuries. [AL]

Torres Lanzas, Pedro. Catálogo de mapas y planos de México. See *HLAS 51:68.*

983 Uchmany, Eva Alexandra. Simón Váez Sevilla. (*Estud. Hist. Novohisp.*, 9, 1987, p. 67–93)

History of a part of the *converso* community in New Spain, Portugal, Italy, and Holland sheds light on the events of the 1640s in New Spain as well as on the Inquisitorial processes that led to the condemnation of a part of that community. [EBC]

984 Van Young, Eric. Haciendo historia regional: consideraciones metodológicas y teóricas. (*Anu. IEHS*, 2, 1987, p. 255–300)

Van Young addresses definitional problem of what is a region and discusses strengths and weaknesses of a regional approach to history with special reference to colonial Mexico. Presents regional typology based on market relations. [S.M. Socolow]

985 Yuste, Carmen. Francisco Ignacio de Yraeta y el comercio transpacífico. (*Estud. Hist. Novohisp.*, 9, 1987, p. 189–217)

Details commercial operations of Basque merchant Francisco Yraeta in the Philippine trade (1769–97). Based on private business correspondence supplemented by commercial agreements, this study was published as an essay in another form in 1985 (see *HLAS 50:1043*). Sheds light on aspects of family and commercial affairs still little understood by historians. [EBC]

CENTRAL AND SOUTH

986 Aguila, Yves. Albores de la seguridad social en México, 1770: la Concordia de la Manufactura de Tabacos. (*Jahrb. Gesch.*, 24, 1987, p. 335–352, tables)

Outlines the foundation and subsequent development of a workers' mutual benefit association in the Mexico City tobacco manufacturing plant. Author sees this association as a proto-union model. [AL]

987 Aguila, Yves. Innovación técnica y Estado en la Nueva España ilustrada. (*Asclepio*, 39:2, 1987, p. 297–315, bibl., photo)

Discussion of the fate of technical innovations in late-18th-century New Spain in the mining, tobacco and textile industries. Mechanization was resisted or ignored by authorities and workers. [AL]

988 Agustín de la Madre de Dios, Fray. Tesoro escondido en el Monte Carmelo mexicano: mina rica de exemplos y virtudes en la historia de los Carmelitas Descalzos de la Provincia de la Nueva España; descubierta cuando escrita por Fray Agustín de la Madre de Dios, religioso de la misma orden. Versión paleográfica, introducción y notas de Eduardo Báez Macías. México: Univ. Nacional Autónoma de México, Instituto de Investigaciones Estéticas, 1986. 453 p.: bibl., 2 facsims.

Consists of 17th-century history of the Carmelite Order in New Spain, edited and introduced by Eduardo Báez Macías. See also 1984 edition edited by Manuel Ramos Medina (item **989**). [AL]

989 Agustín de la Madre de Dios, Fray. Tesoro escondido en el Santo Carmelo Mexicano, mina rica de ejemplos y virtudes en la historia de los Carmelitas Descalzos de la Provincia de la Nueva España. Paleografía, notas y estudio introductorio de Manuel Ramos Medina. Presentación de Elías Trabulse Atala. México: PROBURSA; Depto. de Historia de la Univ. Iberoamericana, 1984. 432 p., 94 p. of plates: bibl., ill.

Beautifully printed and illustrated first edition of a manuscript located at Tulane Univ. and finished ca. 1655. This is the first chronicle of the Carmelite Order in Mexico. Capable introduction by Manuel Ramos Medina. For 1986 edition edited by Eduardo Báez Macías, see item **988**. For art historian's comment see *HLAS 50:196*. [AL]

990 Amerlinck de Bontempo, Mari-José. Conquista espiritual y económica: la formación de haciendas de frailes dominicos en Chiapas. (*Mesoamérica/Antigua*, 2:20, dic. 1990, p. 215–229)

Author analyzes the establishment of the Dominican Order as a landowner and tribute-collector in Chiapas and the antagonism the Order met with from settlers and the Audiencia. [AL]

991 Baudot, Georges. Política y discurso en la conquista de México: Malintzin y el diálogo con Hernán Cortés. (*Anu. Estud. Am.*, 45, 1988, p. 67–82)

Poetic and historic reconstruction of the life of Doña Marina (Malinche, Malintzin) that displays her momentous role in the conquest of Mexico and her life as the exemplar for the origins of mestizaje. [EBC]

992 Bazarte Martínez, Alicia. Las cofradías de españoles en la ciudad de México, 1526–1860. México: Univ. Autónoma Metropolitana, Unidad Azcapotzalco, División de Ciencias Sociales y Humanidades, 1989. 278 p.: ill. (Serie Humanidades)

Thoughtful examination of materials in the AGN Ramo de Cofradías y Archicofradías clarifies many areas of the history of confraternities including their rules, similiarities and differences, methods of selecting orphans, fiestas, services to the community, and loans. Includes special study of the Cofradía Santissimo Sacramento. [EBC]

993 Behar, Ruth. Sexual witchcraft, colonialism, and women's powers: views from the Mexican Inquisition. (*in* Sexuality and marriage in colonial Latin America. Edited by Asunción Lavrin. Lincoln, Neb.: Univ. of Nebraska Press, 1989, p. 178–206, facsims.)

Using Inquisition cases, Behar analyzes the relationship of women's subordinate position with their use of witchcraft both for protection and to gain relative amount of power. Participation by all classes in the society in the discourse of witchcraft provides window on the dynamics of class, ethnic, and sexual relationships. [EBC]

994 Berthe, Jean-Pierre. L'évangile et l'outil: le changement technique dans un village indien du Mexique au XVIe siècle. (*Tech. Cult.*, 11, jan./juin 1988, p. 65–82, appendix, bibl.)

Author uses Tiripitío as an example to survey introduction of European agricultural and manufacturing techniques as part of

Westernization process which Indians often had to adopt to meet economic demands. [AL]

995 Berthe, Jean-Pierre. Les Franciscains de la province mexicaine du Saint-Évangile en 1570: un catalogue de Fray Jerónimo de Mendieta. (*in* Enquêtes sur l'Amérique Moyenne. Mélanges offerts à Guy Stresser-Péan. Coordination de Dominique Michelet. México: Instituto Nacional de Antropología e Historia, Consejo Nacional para la Cultura y las Artes; Centre d'Etudes Mexicaines et Centraméricaines, 1989, p. 213–234, appendix)

Author analyzes the data provided by list of Franciscans in New Spain in 1570 to shed light on their knowledge of indigenous languages and their ability to indoctrinate millions of Indians living in the core of the Viceroyalty. [AL]

996 Berthe, Jean-Pierre. Le mercure et l'industrie minière mexicaine au XVIe siècle. (*in* Ciencia, vida y espacio en Iberoamérica. v. 2. Coordinación de José Luis Peset. Madrid: Consejo Superior de Investigaciones Científicas, 1989, p. 141–152, appendices)

Places introduction of mercury for the refinement of silver in Mexico no later than mid-1554. Attributes success of mining to that technique, which helped overcome a demographic decline in New Spain. [AL]

997 Booker, Jackie R. The Veracruz merchant community in late Bourbon Mexico: a preliminary portrait, 1770–1810. (*Americas/Francisc.*, 45:2, Oct. 1988, p. 187–199, bibl., tables)

Preliminary prosopographic study of the merchants of Veracruz in the late 18th century also includes information on the character of the merchandise, and marriage inclinations. [AL]

998 Borah, Woodrow. Unos documentos sobre las empresas cortesianas en Panamá y Acajutla, 1539–1540. (*Estud. Hist. Novohisp.*, 9, 1987, p. 9–18)

Transcription of several little-known letters related to Cortés' entrepeneurial activities on the Pacific Coast. [AL]

999 Brading, D.A. *et al.* Comments on "The Economic Cycle in Bourbon Central Mexico: a Critique of the *Recauda-*

ción del diezmo líquido en pesos," by Ouweneel and Bijleveld. (*HAHR*, 69:3, Aug. 1989, p. 531–557)

Three historians analyze and critique Ouweneel's and Bijleveld's study of economic cycles in Bourbon Mexico (see item **1057**). Lively academic exchange. [AL]

1000 Brockington, Lolita Gutiérrez. The leverage of labor: managing the Cortés haciendas in Tehuantepec, 1588–1688. Durham, N.C.: Duke Univ. Press, 1989. 245 p.: bibl., ill., maps, tables.

Uses 17th-century labor records from the Cortés estates on the Isthmus of Tehuantepec to show the importance of slavery in cattle production. Provides different vision of the operations of Marquesado del Valle estates. Significant review of comparative materials on labor and on hacienda production. [EBC]

1001 Calvo, Thomas. The warmth of the hearth: seventeenth-century Guadalajara families. (*in* Sexuality and marriage in colonial Latin America. Edited by Asunción Lavrin. Lincoln, Neb.: Univ. of Nebraska Press, 1989, p. 287–312, tables)

Informed by extensive archival research, theoretical piece considers the urban family and its relative stability. Article contributes to our understanding of a variety of issues such as legitimacy, demographic realities, wet-nursing, concubinage, etc. Finds "fluid marriage patterns" and a "flexible" family. [EBC]

1002 Canedo, Lino Gómez. Pioneros de la Cruz en México: Fray Toribio de Motolinía y sus compañeros. Presentación de Carlos Amigo Vallejo. Madrid: Editorial Católica, 1988. 221 p. bibl. (Biblioteca de autores cristianos: BAC popular; 90. Grandes evangelizadores de América)

Synthetic narrative of the historical role of the Franciscan order in the spiritual conquest of Mexico written for the nonspecialist. [AL]

1003 Castañeda García, Carmen. Violación, estupro y sexualidad: Nueva Galicia, 1790–1821. Guadalajara, México: Editorial Hexágono, 1989. 203 p.: bibl.

Interesting in-depth study of acts of rape recorded in New Galicia. Author focuses on the sociological profile of the victims and the perpetrators, underlining the role of the authoritiies and the social mores of the period. [AL]

1004 Chance, John K. Conquest of the Sierra: Spaniards and Indians in colonial Oaxaca. Norman: Univ. of Oklahoma Press, 1989. 233 p.: bibl., ill., index.

Historical survey of the Jurisdiction of Villa Alta, Oaxaca throughout the colonial period focuses on population, the economy, the Indian community's organization and the tension between the Indian and Spanish religions. Solidly researched work deftly combines analysis and synthesis and stands out as a model of regional ethnohistory. [AL]

1005 Chowning, Margaret. The Consolidación de Vales Reales in the Bishopric of Michoacán. (*HAHR*, 69:3, Aug. 1989, p. 451–478, tables)

Revisionist essay on the enforcement and economic effects of the Law of *Consolidación de Vales Reales.* Using Michoacán as a case study author concludes that middle class was not as hurt as previously assumed, and that the effects of the law on property-owning and credit were relatively mild. Based on archival sources. [AL]

1006 *Codex Ramírez: origen de los mexicanos.* Edición de Germán Vázquez. Madrid: Historia 16, 1987. 243 p.: bibl., ill. (Crónicas de América; 32)

Reissue of the *Codex Ramírez*—a history of the origin and beliefs of the Aztecs—following the 1878 first printing of the document. Preceded by study of the texts, especially the fragments that enhance the Texcocan participation, which reflects the editor's interpretation. [AL]

1007 Congreso Hernán Cortés y su Tiempo, *Guadalupe, Spain, 1985.* Actas. Mérida, Spain: V Centenario (1485–1985); Editora Regional de Extremadura, 1987. 2 v. (824 p.): bibl., ill., maps.

Hernán Cortés serves as the focus of 84 essays on 16th-century Spain—especially Extremadura—and on several key aspects of his role as conqueror of the Aztecs. Most contributions are on peninsular history. Worthy global view of the man and his times. [AL]

1008 Congreso Internacional sobre Hernán Cortés, *1st, Salamanca, Spain, 1985.* Actas. Edición preparada por Alberto Navarro

González. Salamanca, España: Ediciones Univ. de Salamanca, 1986. 640 p.: bibl., ill. (Acta Salmanticensia: Filosofía y letras; 185)

Consists of 35 essays presented at an international congress on Hernán Cortés (Salamanca, 1986). He is variously analyzed as a military man, diplomat, and politician. Other essays deal with the Mexican world at the time of the conquest, the impact of his figure on literature, and the consequences of the conquest. [AL]

1009 Connaughton, Brian. La Iglesia y la Ilustración tardía en la Intendencia de Guadalajara: el discurso ideológico del clero en su contexto social. (*Estud. Hist. Novohisp.,* 9, 1987, p. 159–188)

Author reviews writings of key members of Guadalajara's clergy to show how a reformist sector of the Church supported the socioeconomic reforms of the Bourbon kings. [AL]

1010 Cortés, Hernán. Historia de Nueva-España: escrito por su esclarecido conquistador Hernán Cortés. Aumentado con otros documentos y notas por el Ilustríssimo Señor Don Francisco Antonio Lorenzana. Bogotá, Colombia: Carvajal, 1988–1989. 2 v.: ill.

Facsimile edition of letters of Hernán Cortés, as reprinted in 1770 by Archbishop Francisco Antonio Lorenzana. [AL]

1011 Couturier, Edith. Family and fortune: the origins of an entrepreneurial career in eighteenth-century Andalucía and Querétaro: the case of Pedro Romero de Terreros, 1710–1740. (*in* Middle Atlantic Council for Latin American Studies, *9th, Richmond, Virginia, 1988.* MACLAS Latin American Essays. New Brunswick, N.J.: MACLAS; State Univ. of New Jersey, s.d., v. 2, p. 61–75)

Following the early career of Pedro Romero de Terreros, later Count of Regla, author documents key role of family ties to ensure a continuous line of successful administrators in entrepreneurial families. These ties were as beneficial to Spain as to New Spain. [AL]

1012 Cuenya Mateos, Miguel Angel. Evolución demográfica de una parroquia de la Puebla de los Angeles, 1660–1800. (*Hist. Mex.,* 36:3, enero/marzo 1987, p. 443–464, bibl., graphs, tables)

Useful demographic profile of a section of Puebla de los Angeles. Based on parish books, essay registers natural biological rhythms, but does not discuss migration. [AL]

1013 Cuevas Aguirre y Espinosa, Joseph Francisco de. México y su valle en 1748. México: Editorial Innovación, 1981. 71 p.

Facsimile edition of report on the water resources of the Valley of Mexico written by a general attorney and member of the city council in 1748. [AL]

1014 Cummins, Victoria Hennessey. The Church and business practices in late sixteenth century Mexico. (*Americas/Francisc.*, 44:4, April 1988, p. 421–440)

Author makes a case for the use of ecclesiastical sources for the study of business practices in late-16th-century Mexico. Using examples culled from such sources, Cummins illustrates how business transactions were carried out despite proscription of usury by the Church, and suggests how early banking began in New Spain. [AL]

1015 Durand-Forest, Jacqueline de. Hernández y la botánica mexicana. (*Caravelle*, 55, 1990, p. 53–64)

Delineates the life and work of Francisco Hernández, physician to Philip II and capable botanist of New Spain, whose original manuscripts have disappeared, but whose work was used by many others for 200 years. [AL]

1016 Eugenio Martínez, María Angeles. La defensa de Tabasco, 1600–1717. 2a ed. México: Consejo Editorial del Gobierno del Estado de Tabasco, 1981. 189 p. (Serie Historia; 30)

Study of the defense of the Tabasco region against pirates, corsairs and other intruders from 1600 to 1717, when Spain succeeded in consolidating its hold over the area. Detailed study based on archival sources. [AL]

1017 Farriss, Nancy M. Recordando el futuro, anticipando el pasado: tiempo histórico y tiempo cósmico entre los mayas de Yucatán. (*in* Simposio de Historia de las Mentalidades 2nd, *México, 1983*. La memoria y el olvido [see item **1081,**] p. 47–60, bibl.)

Complex but fascinating analysis of the understanding of time among the Mayas.

Cyclic and linear visions of history coexisted before and after the conquest and help explain the philosophical attitude of these people about the conquest and other colonial events. [AL]

1018 Garavaglia, Juan Carlos and Juan Carlos Grosso. El abasto de una villa novohispana: mercancías y flujos mercantiles en Tepeaca, 1780–1820. (*Anu. IEHS*, 2, 1987, p. 217–253, appendices, graphs, maps, tables)

Study of commercial flows to and from a medium sized market in the Puebla region based on *alcabala* figures. The authors believe that Tepeaca serves as an example of an average rural market and stress the complex network of exchange on which the colonial economy was based. For related piece, see item **1019.** [S.M. Socolow]

1019 Garavaglia, Juan Carlos and Juan Carlos Grosso. Marchands, *hacendados* et paysans à Tepeaca: un marché local mexicain à la fin du XVIIIe siècle. (*Ann. écon. soc. civilis.*, 44:3, mai/juin 1989, p. 553–580, graphs, maps)

Using *alcabala* records from 1776, this study underscores the important share of the local market in grains, livestock, salt, and peppers enjoyed by Indians, mestizos and poor Spaniards. At least for this local region, this work changes our views of the dominance of the hacienda on the local market. See item **1018** for related theme. [EBC]

1020 García Acosta, Virginia. Las panaderías, sus dueños y trabajadores: Ciudad de México, siglo XVIII. México: Centro de Investigaciones y Estudios Superiores en Antropología Social, 1989. 255 p.: bibl., ill. (Ediciones de la Casa Chata; 24)

Solid study of bread production in 18th-century Mexico City. Based mostly on archival sources, this work covers all aspects of bread production and consumption, such as distribution of raw materials, ownership of bakeries, credit and capital investment, manufacture and distribution. Useful for social historians. [AL]

1021 García-Lomas, Cristina. Las huestes de Hernán Cortés. (*in* Jornadas de historiadores americanistas, *1st, Santa Fe, España, 1987*. Actas: América; hombre y sociedad. Presentación de Joaquín A. Muñoz Mendoza. Granada, Spain: Diputación Provincial de Granada, 1988, p. 155–180)

Engaging essay on the nature of the men and the "army" they formed to follow Cortés. Such men exemplified the type of individuals who carried out the conquest of the New World. Author establishes that there was no professional "army" in the 1520s, and proceeds to analyze the sociological profile of Cortés' men, the behavior of the group, and the relationship between the captain and his men. [AL]

1022 Garner, Richard L. Further consideration of "facts and figments" in Bourbon Mexico. (*Bull. Lat. Am. Res.*, 6:1, 1987, p. 55–63, bibl., tables, graphs)

Garner interjects his calculations and opinions in an ongoing debate as to what was the result of the State's policy regarding silver production, inflation and the Spanish Crown's collection of revenue. For the specialist. [AL]

1023 *Gazeta de México*. Vol. A-1, enero-agosto 1784; Vol. A-2, agosto-dic. 1784; Vol. A-3, enero-julio 1785. Edición facsimilar. México: Rolston-Bain, 1983–1986. (Col. Documenta novae hispaniae)

Facsimile edition of important late colonial newspaper is useful for new collectors. [AL]

1024 Giraud, François. Una fuente de delincuencia en Nueva España: la ruptura familiar. (*Cristianismo Soc.*, 27:102, 1989, p. 33–38)

Brief essay indicates family tensions among orphans, relatives, and servants were key sources of delinquency in the late 18th century. [AL]

1025 Goldberg, Rita. Nuevos documentos y glosas cortesianos: Hernán Cortés y su familia en los archivos españoles. Madrid: J. Porrúa Turanzas, 1987. 198 p.: bibl., facsims., index. (Col. Chimalistac de libros y documentos acerca de la Nueva España; 47)

Consists of 16 documents found in three Spanish archives pertaining to Cortés, his two sons, wife, and grandaughters. Mostly letters and wills. Women's wills are noteworthy. [AL]

1026 González Claverán, Virginia. Un documento colonial sobre esclavos asiáticos. (*Hist. Mex.*, 38:3, enero/marzo 1989, p. 523–532)

Testimonial evidence concerning the

process of liberating "Chinese" (Filipinos) and New Mexicans enslaved in the so-called "Just War," a royal policy accepted and enforced in the second half of the 17th century. [AL]

1027 González Claverán, Virginia. Malaspina en Acapulco. Introducción de Javier Wimer. Prólogo de Elías Trabulse. Documentación de María Dolores Higueras. Madrid: Turner, 1989 217 p.: bibl., col. ill.

Beautifully illustrated and printed indepth narrative of Malaspina's survey of New Spain's western coast. [AL]

1028 González Claverán, Virginia. Un verano en el México de Revillagigedo, 1791. (*Hist. Mex.*, 38:2, oct./dic. 1988, p. 199–240, appendix, bibl.)

Summary and description of a diary kept by a member of the Malaspina Expedition. Includes material on scientific collections, the Acordada, Viceregal palace, religious institutions, hospitals, social life. Generously annotated. [EBC]

1029 Greenleaf, Richard E. The great Visitas of the Mexican Holy Office. (*Americas/Francisc.*, 44:4, April 1988, p. 399–420)

Richly documented and well written account of the 17th-century power struggle among the Mexican Inquisition, Bishop Palafox and the Jesuits. Essay's most important contribution is recounting Visitor Pedro Medina Rico's investigation of the Mexican Inquisition and its mishandling of ecclesiastical justice during the first half of the century. [AL]

1030 Grijalva, Juan de. Crónica de la Orden de N.P.S. Agustín en las provincias de la Nueva España: en cuatro edades desde el año de 1533 hasta el de 1592. México: Editorial Porrúa, 1985. 543 p.: bibl. (Biblioteca Porrúa; 85)

Reissue of the 1624 history of the Augustinian Order. Second edition was published 300 years later in 1924 (Mexico, Imprenta Victoria). At a distance of six decades, this reissue will be a welcome addition to libraries and a source of study for scholars. [AL]

1031 Gruzinski, Serge. La memoria mutilada: construcción del pasado y mecanismos de la memoria en un grupo otomí de la mitad del siglo XVII. (*in* Simposio de

Historia de las Mentalidades, *2nd, México, 1983*. La memoria y el olvido [see item **1081**,] p. 33–46]

Early 17th-century Otomi manuscript (i.e., *Relación anónima*) on the settlement of Querétaro gives different view than the official history. Author sees in this document an attempt to reconstruct history on favorable terms for the vanquished as well as an assimilation of subtle forms of the dominant culture. [AL]

1032 Hampe Martínez, Teodoro. La biblioteca del Virrey Don Martín Enríquez: aficiones intelectuales de un gobernante colonial. (*Hist. Mex.*, 36:2, oct./dic. 1986, p. 251–271, bibl.)

Descriptive essay on the books in the library of a late-16th-century Viceroy of both Mexico and Peru. [AL]

1033 Herrera Casasús, María Luisa. Presencia y esclavitud del negro en la Huasteca. México: M.A. Porrúa, 1989. 77 p.: bibl.

Brief descriptive survey of slavery in the Huastec region. Data was obtained from several archival sources of the late 18th century. [AL]

1034 Hoberman, Louisa Schell. Mexico's merchant elite, 1590–1660: silver, State, and society. Durham, N.C.: Duke Univ. Press, 1991. 352 p.: bibl., ill., maps.

The fruit of many years of archival investigation, this important book on 17th-century merchants enlightens us on many long-debated topics. Studies how merchants achieved their positions through trade, agriculture, and manufacturing as well as investment in urban real estate and public office. Other topics investigated include the politics of taxation and the struggles over interregional trade and the commercialization of sugar, cacao and wheat. Finds a congruence between Irving Leonard's vision of Baroque Mexico based on literary sources and the economic and social data. [EBC]

1035 Jiménez Codinach, Estela Guadalupe. En Londres de la insurgencia: en busca de las huellas de un emigrado novohispano, 1811–1816. (*in* Historia, antropología y política: homenaje a Angel Palerm. México: Alianza Editorial Mexicana, 1990, v. 2, p. 154–185, appendices, bibl., ill.)

Excellent description of the life of Fray Servando Teresa de Mier in London brings much new material to bear upon his biography and the life of the Mexican immigrant community in Europe. [EBC]

1036 Jiménez Pelayo, Agueda. Condiciones del trabajo de repartimiento indígena en la Nueva Galicia en el siglo XVII. (*Hist. Mex.*, 38:3, enero/marzo 1989, p. 455–470, bibl.)

Study of personal forced labor (i.e., repartimiento) in New Galicia in the 17th century. Author uses archival sources to compare first and second half of the century, concluding that while wage labor and repartimiento coexisted, the latter began to decline after 1690. [AL]

1037 Jones, Grant D. Maya resistance to Spanish rule: time and history on a colonial frontier. Albuquerque: Univ. of New Mexico Press, 1989. 365 p.: bibl., ill., index, maps, tables.

Study of the cultural dialogue between Spanish and Maya people in central Yucatán (1540s-mid 1600s). Jones follows the Spanish settlement of Bacalar and contrasts it with the Maya frontier, the point of contact between cultures. Confrontation of Catholic Christianity and Maya world views resulted in rebellions in mid 17th century, with eventual submissions, and Maya retreats from Spanish influence. History of these events is vividly accounted for in this readable and well researched work. [AL]

1038 Kellogg, Susan. Households in late prehispanic and early colonial Mexico City: their structure and its implications for the study of historical demography. (*Americas/Francisc.*, 44:4, April 1988, p. 483–494, table)

Argues for use of archival documents from various sources to assess the size and configuration of households in precolumbian Tenochtitlán-Texcoco. Supports such use for grasping human interaction in the household and adding a new dimension to population estimates. [AL]

1039 Klein, Herbert S. Familia y fertilidad en Amatenango, Chiapas, 1785–1816. (*Hist. Mex.*, 36:2, oct./dic. 1986, p. 273–286, bibl., tables)

Demographic analysis of a small Tzeltal community (1780–1810) points to early marriages and high fertility. Marriage and fertility patterns are compared to others in rural Mexico, North America, and Europe. [AL]

1040 Lipsett-Rivera, Sonya. Puebla's eighteenth-century agrarian decline: a new perspective. (*HAHR*, 70:3, Aug. 1990, p. 463–481, graphs, maps)

Ecological issues are found to be at the root of Puebla's 18th-century weakening as an exporter of agricultural commodities. Questions of land tenure and demography are also discussed in this well-argued account. Important contribution to 18th-century economic history. [EBC]

1041 Lira González, Andrés. Letrados y analfabetos en los pueblos de indios de la Ciudad de México: la historia como alegato para sobrevivir en la sociedad política.

Author uses legal suits of Indian towns close to Mexico City to explore the manner in which such official sources contribute to reaffirm and sometimes create a communal memory. [AL]

1042 Lizana, Bernardo de. Historia de Yucatán. Edición de Félix Jiménez Villalba. Madrid: Historia 16, 1988. 288 p. (Crónicas de América; 43)

Reissue of a 1633 history of the Franciscan Order in Yucatán contains little-known materials on Fray Diego de Landa and preconquest Mayas. [AL]

1043 Lohmann Villena, Guillermo. Notas sobre la presencia de la Nueva España en las cortes metropolitanas y de cortes en la Nueva España en los siglos XVI y XVII. (*Hist. Mex.*, 39:1, julio/sept. 1989, p. 33–40, bibl.)

Brief essay on the inconclusive attempts of the Mexico City Council to organize the local *cortes* and to pay tribute to the Crown for the privilege. Similar attempts to have American representatives in the Spanish *cortes* came to naught. Taxation implicit in the granting of such privilege killed the desire for it among new settlers. [AL]

1044 Luque Alcaide, Elisa. Colegio de la Caridad: primer establecimiento educativo para la mujer en el Mexico virreinal; estudio de sus constituciones. (*Anu. Estud. Am.*, 47:2, 1990, p. 3–25, suplemento)

Reprints in full the Constitutions of the School of La Caridad. Also includes preliminary study of the school, and educational objectives set by its regulations. [AL]

1045 Malvido, Elsa. Los novicios de San Francisco en la Ciudad de México: la edad de Hierro, 1649–1749. (*Hist. Mex.*, 36:4, abril/junio 1987, p. 699–738, bibl., tables)

Quantitative study of the social and geographic origins of Franciscan friars indicates the adjustments the Order made to offset the secularization of *doctrinas* in 1649. These changes contributed to the ability of the Order to participate in the evangelization of the North. Important continuation of Francisco Morales' previous work on earlier generations of Friars. [EBC]

1046 Marichal, Carlos. Las guerras imperiales y los préstamos novohispanos, 1781–1804. (*Hist. Mex.*, 39:4, abril/junio 1990, p. 881–907, bibl., table)

Informative essay on loans extracted from New Spain subjects by the Spanish Crown in the last 20 years of imperial control. All social classes were tapped for loans that were used for defense in Europe. The extent of taxation attests to the growing fiscal crisis in Spain. [AL]

1047 Martínez, José Luis. Hernán Cortés. México: Univ. Nacional Autónoma de México; Fondo de Cultura Económica, 1990. 1015 p.: bibl., ill., index. (Sección de obras de historia)

Latest biography of Cortés provides exhaustive information on the conqueror and historical works inspired by him, iconography, and an analysis of his ideas and character. Author maintains clinical objectivity about his subject. [AL]

1048 Mauriño Márquez, José Angel. Las congregaciones novohispanas: provincia de Tlanchinol, 1604. (*Anu. Estud. Am.*, 47:2, 1990, p. 27–69, suplemento, appendix, maps)

Describes process for organizing *reducciones* or consolidating indigenous populations during the Viceroyalty of the Marquis of Montesclaros (1603–05). Surveys one carried out in the area of Tlanchinolticpac. Includes documentary appendix. [AL]

1049 Memorias políticas y económicas del Consulado de Veracruz, 1796–1822. Edición y estudio preliminar de Javier Ortiz de la Tabla Ducasse. Sevilla, Spain: Escuela de Estudios Hispano-Americanos de Sevilla,

1985. 407 p.: bibl., index. (Escuela de Estudios Hispano-Americanos de Sevilla; 303)

Book contains economic writings of Vicente Basadre, José Donato de Austria, and José María Quirós, secretaries of the Consulado of Veracruz (1796–1822). Long-sought but not found by previous researchers, these writings shed light on economic theories and plans of three key late colonial economists. Introductory study aptly highlights the importance of these administrators and their writings. [AL]

1050 Méndez, María Agueda. Ilusas y alumbradas: ¿discurso místico o erótico? (*Caravelle*, 52, 1989, p. 5–15)

Survey of late 18th-century Inquisitorial cases of female pseudo-mystical experiences. Suggests heavy doses of eroticism underlying the beata's discourse. [AL]

1051 Menes Llaguno, Juan Manuel. Bartolomé de Medina: un sevillano "pachuqueño." Pachuca, Mexico: Univ. Autónoma del Estado de Hidalgo, 1986. 176 p.: bibl., ill. (Biblioteca conmemorativa)

Biography written by aficionado, based on primary materials, provides much information about the life and works of the man who brought the amalgamation process for refining silver to New Spain. [EBC]

1052 Mier Noriega y Guerra, José Servando Teresa de. Historia de la revolución de Nueva España. Coordinación de André Saint-Lu and Marie-Cécile Bénassy-Berling. Paris: Publications de la Sorbonne, 1990. 1 v.: index. (Serie Langues et Langages; 20)

New edition of Fray Servando Teresa de Mier's classic history of the Mexican War of Independence, with critical introductory study and copious annotations by a group of French researchers. Index and chronology help in guiding the reader through the original manuscript. Commendable effort. [AL]

1053 Miño Grijalva, Manuel. Obrajes y tejedores de Nueva España, 1700–1810. Madrid: Instituto de Cooperación Iberoamericana; Quinto Centenario; Instituto de Estudios Fiscales, Ministerio de Economía y Hacienda, 1990. 402 p.: bibl., ill., maps. (Monografías Economía quinto centenario)

Global history of 18th-century textile industry. Most of the material focuses on the late years of the century. Author posits that increasing commercialization of this industry relied mostly on artisanal labor in a few critical areas. Industry began to decline precipitously in first decade of the 19th century. Based on 1984 doctoral dissertation. [AL]

1054 Morilla Critz, José. Crisis y transformación de la economía de Nueva España en el siglo XVII: un ensayo crítico. (*Anu. Estud. Am.*, 45, 1988, p. 241–272)

Lucid and wide-ranging critique of the Borah-Chevalier hypothesis of a 17th-century depression is based on an impressive variety of secondary sources and published economic data. Author concludes that internal markets substituted for foreign commerce, and that both population and economic activity expanded during the century. [EBC]

Murphy, Michael E. Irrigation in the Bajío region of colonial Mexico. See *HLAS 51:2934.*

1055 Naveda Chávez-Hita, Adriana. Esclavos negros en las haciendas azucareras de Córdoba, Veracruz: 1690–1830. Xalapa, México: Univ. Veracruzana, Centro de Investigaciones Históricas, 1987. 189 p.: bibl., ill. (Col. Historias veracruzanas; 4)

Although Córdoba never had a large number of African slaves, this work provides solid information on all aspects of the slave trade, population, and labor in that city and its surrounding haciendas. Based on archival research. Brief but very useful. [AL]

1056 Ouweneel, Arij. The agrarian cycle as a catalyst of economic development in eighteenth-century central Mexico: the arable estate, Indian villages and proto-industrialization in the central highland valleys. (*Ibero-Am. Arch.*, 15:3, 1989, p. 399–417, bibl., facsim.)

Author suggests need to supersede concept of latifundia-minifundia in colonial landholding. Studies regional economy of central New Spain to show that rural production becomes tied to growth of the city in the 18th century, with the bond between production and markets becoming crucial. [AL]

1057 Ouweneel, Arij and Catrien C.J.H. Bijleveld. The economic cycle in Bourbon Central Mexico: a critique of the *Recaudación del diezmo líquido en pesos.* (*HAHR*, 69:3, Aug. 1989, p. 479–530, graphs, tables)

Massive but inclusive contribution to the continuing debate on economic conditions in 18th-century New Spain. Authors find tithe receipts inadequate as an index and they use 17 additional indicators including silver production, pulque revenue and monument building. Periods of crisis emerge from their data. For comments by D.A. Brading *et al.*, see item **999**. [EBC]

1058 Ouweneel, Arij. Schedules in hacienda agriculture: the cases of Santa Ana Aragón, 1765–1768, and San Nicolás de los Pilares, 1793–1795, Valley of Mexico. (*Bol. Estud. Latinoam.*, 40, June 1986, p. 63–97, ill., maps, tables)

Detailed short-term study of the management of two haciendas in the late 18th century uses schedules of harvest, labor, ecological factors, etc., to design a hypothetical model of agricultural production for future research. [AL]

1059 Padrones de Tlaxcala del siglo XVI y padrón de nobles de Ocotelolco. Edición de Teresa Rojas Rabiela. Paleografía, estudios introductorios, notas, cuadros, índices y glosarios de Marina Anguiano, Matilde Chapa y Amelia Camacho. México: Centro de Investigaciones y Estudios Superiores en Antropología Social, 1987. 383 p.: bibl., facsims., index., maps. (Col. Documentos; 1)

Synthesis of census of four Tlaxcalan towns ca. 1557 enumerates men, widows, diseases, and occupations. Tlaxcala City itself is not included. Two introductory studies place document in context. [AL]

1060 Pérez Herrero, Pedro. Los comerciantes del Consulado de México: la adecuación de sus mecanismos de control económico ante los cambios de la segunda mitad del siglo XVIII, el caso de las libranzas. (*Rev. Hist./Heredia*, 16, junio/julio 1987, p. 35–49, bibl.)

Study of the use of credit letters or promisory notes (*libranzas*) by consulado merchants as one of several strategies to retain their economic preeminence after the enactment of "Free Trade" regulations. [AL]

1061 Pérez Herrero, Pedro. Plata y libranzas: la articulación comercial del México borbónico. México: Centro de Estudios Históricos, Colegio de México, 1988. 362 p.: appendices, bibl., ill., index, plates, tables.

Lucid analysis of the development of the monetary system, the role of the Consulado of Mexico, and the policies of the government in the last half of the 18th century.

Important work uses both Spanish and Mexican materials. [EBC]

1062 Pescador C., Juan Javier. Devoción y crisis demográfica: la Cofradía de San Ygnacio de Loyola, 1761–1821. (*Hist. Mex.*, 39:3, enero/marzo 1990, p. 767–801, bibl., appendices)

Study of the financial administration of the Confraternity of San Ignacio in Mexico City. Underlines problems due to excessive payments for funeral rites in times of epidemics as well as loans to the Crown. [AL]

1063 Poole, Stafford. The last years of Archbishop Pedro Moya de Contreras, 1586–1591. (*Americas/Francisc.*, 47:1, July 1990, p. 1–38)

Detailed account of Archbishop Moya de Contrera's last years in Spain is an addenda to author's biography of the archbishop (see *HLAS 50:1083*). Contributes to our knowledge of the bureaucratic machine in the time of Philip II. [AL]

1064 Puebla, de la colonia a la revolución: estudios de historia regional. Puebla, México: Centro de Investigaciones Históricas y Sociales, Instituto de Ciencias de la Univ. Autónoma de Puebla, 1987. 391 p.: bibl., ill.

Papers from LASA's 11th Meeting (Mexico City, 1983). Includes contributions by Garavaglia and Grosso as well as David La France, among others, and is particularly strong on the 19th century. Valuable contribution to the historiography of this region. [EBC]

1065 Rabell, Cecilia Andrea and Neri Necochea. La mortalidad adulta en una parroquia rural novohispana durante el siglo XVIII. (*Hist. Mex.*, 36:3, enero/marzo 1987, p. 405–442, bibl., graphs, tables)

Methodologically interesting article concludes that the most accurate technique for estimating adult mortality can be found in the index of orphans listed in marriage registers. [EBC]

1066 La Rebelión del Indio Mariano: un movimiento insurgente en la Nueva Galicia, en 1801, y documentos procesales. Recopilación de Juan López. Guadalajara, México: Ayuntamiento de Guadalajara, 1985. 3 v.

Complete judicial dossier of an Indian insurgent plot in New Galicia is a documentary source for the study of popular rebellions. [AL]

1067 Relaciones geográficas del Arzobispado de México, 1743. Edición de Francisco de Solano. Madrid: Consejo Superior de Investigaciones Científicas, Centro de Estudios Históricos, Depto. de Historia de América, 1988. 2 v. (553 p.): bibl., ill., index. (Col. Tierra nueva e cielo nuevo; 28)

Excellent edition of the 1743 geographical description of the Archbishopric of Mexico is beautifully illustrated with maps of the *Ecclesiastical Atlas of the Archbishopric* (1767). Excellent source for the study of this region in mid-18th century. Very good demographic source. [AL]

1068 Robinson, David J. Migration in eighteenth-century Mexico: case studies from Michoacán. (*J. Hist. Geogr.*, 15:1, 1989, p. 55–68, ill., maps, tables)

Author analyzes value of and problems inherent to several colonial sources for the study of population migration. Stresses importance of migration in the history of 18th-century New Spain, underlining its connection with the process of marriage. Study uses a 10-parish mini-example to illustrate thesis, and is a heuristic piece rather than a complete monograph. [AL]

1069 Rodríguez Colodrero, Antonio. María Rita Vargas, María Lucía Celis: beatas embaucadoras de la colonia; de un cuaderno que recogió la Inquisición a un iluso, Antonio Rodríguez Colodrero, solicitante de escrituras y vidas. Prólogo, transcripción y notas de Edelmira Ramírez. México: UNAM, Coordinación de Humanidades, Dirección General de Publicaciones, 1988. 288 p.: bibl. (Biblioteca de letras)

Transcription of late 18th-century Inquisitorial investigation of a chaplain of the Convent of San Lorenzo, Mexico. The chaplain encouraged two women to believe they could achieve a life of religious perfection, and transcribed their confessions to him. They constitute the two "diaries" included here, along with the Inquisition's examination of the case. Complex source for the study of mentalities is ably introduced by Ramírez. [AL]

1070 Rodríguez García, Vicente. El Fiscal de Real Hacienda en Nueva España: Don Ramón de Posada y Soto, 1781–1793.

Oviedo, Spain: Publicaciones de la Univ. de Oviedo, 1985. 379 p.: ill.

Provides biographical sketch and follows the career of the attorney (*fiscal*) of the Royal Exchequer in New Spain. A powerful and knowledgeable royal officer, he was a crucial figure in the administration of New Spain between 1781–93. Author has used a vast array of archival sources to shed light on the man as well as on the institutional structure and activities of the Royal Exchequer. [AL]

1071 Rodríguez O., Jaime E. Two revolutions: France 1789 and Mexico 1810. (*Americas/Francisc.*, 47:2, Oct. 1990, p. 161–176, bibl.)

By comparing Mexico in 1810 with France in 1789 author seeks to elucidate similarities and differences between the two political revolts. For Rodríguez, the outcome in France was more positive insofar as it eliminated most of the privileges of the Old Regime, while Mexico retained many and did not succeed in establishing a strong State. [AL]

1072 Román Gutiérrez, José F. Situación de la Orden Franciscana en Nueva Galicia a principios del s. XVII. (*in* Congreso Internacional sobre los Franciscanos en el Nuevo Mundo, 3rd, La Rábida, Spain, 1989. Actas. Madrid: Editorial Deimos, 1988, p. 1179–1211, tables)

Assessment of the state of the Franciscan Order in New Galicia in early 17th century is based on internal reports of the Audiencia. Concludes that the order was in a reorganizational mode and had lost its earlier missionary zeal. [AL]

1073 Rubial García, Antonio. El convento agustino y la sociedad novohispana: 1533–1630. México: Univ. Nacional Autónoma de México, 1989. 343 p., 5 p. of plates: appendices, bibl., graphs, ill., index, maps, tables. (Serie Historia novohispana; 34)

Studies the transplant and rooting of the Augustinian Order in New Spain taking into consideration the human element, monastic organization, evangelizing work, and economic structure. Important chapter covers theme of assimilation of Mexican-born monks into the order. Useful synthesis is based largely on Spanish archival materials and primary printed sources. [AL]

1074 Rubial García, Antonio. Una monarquía criolla. México: Consejo Nacional para la Cultura y las Artes, 1990. 189 p.: bibl.

Uses abundant documentation of a conflict between Creoles and peninsulares over the Province of Santísimo Nombre de Jesús to place the conflicts over the *alternativa* in a broader social context. Contains many transcribed and annotated manuscript appendices which provide a flavor of life in 17th-century New Spain. [EBC]

1075 Sahagún, Bernardino de. Conquest of New Spain: 1585 revision. Reproductions of Boston Public Library Manuscript and Carlos María de Bustamante's 1840 edition. Translated by Howard F. Cline. Edited with an introduction and notes by S.L. Cline. Salt Lake City: Univ. of Utah Press, 1989. 672 p., 1 leaf of plates: bibl., ill.

Work contains the Boston copy of the 1585 revision of Bernardino de Sahagún's *Conquest of New Spain*, in Spanish and in English translation, and reproduces the first Spanish edition by Carlos María de Bustamante (1840). Introduction by editor S.L. Cline traces the history of the three documents. Valuable tool for research, although the technical quality of the reproductions of the manuscript and the 1840 edition leave much to be desired. [AL]

1076 Schwaller, John Frederick. Tithe collection and distribution in Mexico and Peru, circa 1600. (*Jahrb. Gesch.*, 26, 1989, p. 1–18, tables)

Compares the tithe collection and distribution in Mexico and Peru and finds significant differences between the two. [AL]

1077 Seed, Patricia. Marriage promises and the value of a woman's testimony in colonial Mexico. (*Signs*, 13:2, Winter 1988, p. 253–276)

Posits that between the 17th and 18th centuries there was a decline in the concepts of honor and female credibility in legal suits concerning engagements and loss of virginity. Author attributes the decline to the increasing reliance on the written word and surmises that all these facts made women more dependent on men and victims of double standards of morality. (For Spanish translation of article see *Cristianismo y Sociedad*, 27:102, 1989, p. 39–60.) [AL]

1078 Seed, Patricia. Memoria de la herencia étnica: lo élite criolla del siglo XVIII mexicano. (*in* Simposio de Historia de las Mentalidades, 2nd, *México, 1983*. La memoria y el olvido [see item **1081**,] p. 99–106, bibl.)

Author uses several cases of marriage dissent to explore how the memory of ethnic origins among the late 18th-century Mexican elite could be manipulated to suit personal and familial interests. Argues that class and power were more important than ethnicity. [AL]

1079 Seijas y Lobera, Francisco de. Gobierno militar y político del Reino Imperial de la Nueva España, 1702. Estudio, transcripción y notas de Pablo Emilio Pérez-Mallaína Bueno. México: Univ. Nacional Autónoma de México, 1986. 623 p.: bibl., ill. (Serie documental/Instituto de Investigaciones Históricas; 17)

First printing of rich and largely unknown description of Viceregal New Spain in the last decades of the 17th century. Original manuscript is in France. Author of report was a royal officer, traveler, and later exile in France with a keen eye and a critical mind. Preceded by an able study by Pérez-Mallaína, this work is a useful new historical source. [AL]

1080 Seminario de Historia de la Familia, *México, 1989*. Familias novohispanas: siglos XVI al XIX. Coordinación de Pilar Gonzalbo. México: Centro de Estudios Históricos, El Colegio de México, 1991. 399 p.: bibl., ill.

Papers presented at symposium on the history of the family (Mexico City, Oct. 1989). Includes interesting material on law, demography, the Church and marriage, kinship, and women. [EBC]

1081 Simposio de Historia de las Mentalidades, 2nd, *México, 1983*. La memoria y el olvido. México: Instituto Nacional de Antropología e Historia, Dirección de Estudios Históricos, 1985. 193 p.: bibl. (Col. científica; 144)

Consists of 14 papers and three comments delivered at symposium (Mexico City, 1983). Themes of remembrance and oblivion among precolumbian and colonial groups are deftly explored, providing political, ethnic, and social insights into the people's own vision of their past. Articles by the following authors are annotated separately in this volume: Serge Gruzinski (item **1031**); Andrés Lira (item **1041**); Nancy Farriss (item **1017**); Patricia Seed (item **1078**); and Solange Alberro (item **954**). [AL]

1082 Tanck Estrada, Dorothy. Aspectos políticos de la intervención de Carlos III en la Universidad de México. (*Hist. Mex.*, 38:2, oct./dic. 1988, p. 181–197, bibl.)

Author detects strong evidence of regalism in the appointment of professors to the university faculty, the foundation of a royal school for surgeons, and the growing tensions between the university and the Crown. [AL]

1083 Tanck Estrada, Dorothy. Castellanización, política y escuelas de indios en el Arzobispado de México a mediados del siglo XVIII. (*Hist. Mex.*, 38:4, abril/junio 1989, p. 701–741, bibl., tables)

Study of the evolution of an Indian language policy in New Spain. The secularization of Indian doctrines brought about an official policy to ban Indian languages and teach Spanish to children in parochial schools, a policy which met with little success. [AL]

1084 Tardieu, Jean-Pierre. Les jésuites et la pastorale des Noirs en Nouvelle-Espagne, XVIe siècle. (*Ibero-Am. Arch.*, 16:4, 1990, p. 529–544)

Author delineates the evangelization methods used by the Jesuits with their African and other slaves in 16th-century New Spain. [AL]

1085 Torre Villar, Ernesto de la. Diego Antonio Bermúdez de Castro en la historiografía novohispana. (*Hist. Mex.*, 39:2, oct./dic. 1989, p. 387–416, bibl.)

Capable analysis of one of the least-known historians of the city of Puebla. [AL]

1086 Trabulse, Elías. Los manuscritos perdidos de Sigüenza y Góngora. Mexico: El Colegio de México, 1988. 144 p.: bibl., index.

Exhaustive study of the fate of the library and manuscripts of Sigüenza. Includes evaluation of the contents and 18th- and 19th-century history of the collection. Fascinating yet depressing story. [EBC]

1087 Trabulse, Elías. La vida conventual de un científico novohispano. (*Hist.*

Mex., 38:4, abril/junio 1989, p. 743–769, bibl.)

Readable account of the internal problems of the Mercedarian Order in Mexico in the first half of the 17th century. [AL]

1088 Urquiola, José Ignacio. La formación del trabajo asalariado en las manufactureras textiles: 1570–1610. León, Mexico: El Colegio del Bajío, 1985. 45 leaves: bibl., tables. (Cuadernos de investigación)

Author examines 966 labor contracts from the early colonial period in Tlaxcala, Texcoco, and Querétaro, including both textile and other contracts. Data suggest that the average wage of an *obraje* worker had a rough equivalence to contemporary European wages for similar labor. [EBC]

1089 Valcárcel Martínez, Simón. Una aproximación a Francisco López de Gómara. (*Caravelle*, 53, 1989, p. 7–24, bibl.)

Brief but well written survey of the historical and literary merits of the works of Francisco López de Gómara, chaplain of Hernán Cortés and Renaissance historian of the conquest of the New World. [AL]

1090 Vallarta, Luz del Carmen. Voces sin sonido: José Eugenio Ponce de León y su modelo de mujer religiosa. (*Relaciones/Zamora*, 45, 1990, p. 33–61)

Sensitive analysis of one of the writings of 18th-century popular ecclesiastical author. Vallarta examines the conceptual framework of Ponce de León, and the model of religious life he drew from the lives of several religious women of Michoacán.

1091 Varela Marcos, Jesús. Los prolegómenos de la Visita de José de Gálvez a la Nueva España, 1766: Don Francisco de Armona y la instrucción secreta del Marqués de Esquilache. (*Rev. Indias*, 46:178, julio/dic. 1986, p. 453–470, bibl.)

Fascinating detective story describes sudden death of the Visitador Francisco de Armona and the initial efforts to promote a Visita General before the appointment of Gálvez. Describes relations of Esquilache and Cruillas. [EBC]

Vargas P., Ernesto and **Lorenzo Ochoa.** Navegantes, viajeros y mercaderes: notas para el estudio de la historia de las rutas fluviales y terrestres entre la costa de Tabasco-Campeche y tierra adentro. See *HLAS 51: 2949*.

1092 Vega, Josefa. Milicias y sociedad a finales del siglo XVIII: el caso de Michoacán. (*Rev. Indias*, 45 : 175, enero/junio 1985, p. 51–71)

Summary and analysis of the establishment of the provincial militias, based in part on the Archivo de Simancas records of men who served in Michoacán. Considers legislation, financing, *fuero militar*, sale of positions, and problems of promotion. Explains the Creole predominance, and the abundant possibilities for achieving noble status by entering a military order because of service in the militia. [EBC]

1093 Velázquez, María del Carmen. Hacienda de Señor San José Deminyo, 1780–1784. México: El Colegio de México, 1988. 142 p.: bibl., ill. (Jornadas; 112)

History of the administration of an hacienda in Hidalgo state is based on two-year account books. Includes information on labor and salaries. [AL]

1094 Vergara Hernández, María Josefa. Testamento. Querétaro, México: Dirección de Patrimonio Cultural, Secretaría de Cultura y Bienestar Social del Gobierno del Estado de Querétaro, 1987. 225 p. (Documentos de Querétaro; 3)

Transcript of the will and testamentary procedures of a late-18th-century female philanthropist. Sources go beyond the personal as the disposal of her will involved members of the family, charity institutions, and the sale of properties during the troubled years of the Wars of Independence. Unusual and useful source. [AL]

1095 Viesca Treviño, Carlos. Hechizos y hierbas mágicas en la obra de Juan de Cárdenas. (*Estud. Hist. Novohisp.*, 9, 1987, p. 37–50)

Author analyzes the work of this late 16th-century physician and assesses the state of medical art in New Spain and the opinion held by a representative of European science about indigenous witchcraft. [AL]

1096 Viqueira, Carmen. Los obrajes de paños de Nueva España ante la crisis demográfica del siglo XVI: ensayo en homenaje a Angel Palerm. (*in* Historia, antropología y política: homenaje a Angel Palerm. Coordinación de Modesto Suárez. México: Alianza Editorial Mexicana, 1990, v. 2, p. 128–153)

Analysis of the legislation on working conditions in 18th-century *obrajes* includes long quotations from relevant documents. Author contends that the desire of the Crown for silver and the need to subsidize it made authorities decide to agree to forced *obraje* labor in order to have cheap cloth for mine workers. [EBC]

1097 Viqueira Albán, Juan Pedro. ¿Relajados o reprimidos?: diversiones públicas y vida social en la Ciudad de México durante el Siglo de las Luces. México: Fondo de Cultura Económica, 1987. 302 p., 3 leaves of plates: bibl., ill., maps. (Seccion de obras de historia)

Author investigates popular culture in late colonial Mexico to determine whether mores were more "relaxed" in that period. Focuses on bullfighting, the theater, popular dances, drinking, etc. Viqueira argues that there was no such increased relaxation but a desire of the elite to restrain the growing forms of expression of popular counterculture. [AL]

1098 West, Delno C. Medieval ideas of apocalyptic mission and the early Franciscans in Mexico. (*Americas/Francisc.*, 45 : 3, Jan. 1989, p. 293–313)

Detailed study of the lineage of apocalyptic visions of the discovery of the Americas traces its roots to Franciscan spirituality, especially the reformed Franciscans of 15th-century Spain, and analyzes its presence in Columbus and Fray Pedro de Benavente (Motolinía). [AL]

1099 Wobeser, Gisela von. La Inquisición como institución crediticia en el siglo XVIII. (*Hist. Mex.*, 39 : 4, abril/junio 1990, p. 849–879, bibl., tables)

Informative study of the income and investments of the Inquisition, especially during the 18th century. Loans, liens, and credit policy changes are carefully described. Banking relationship between merchants and Inquisition funds in the early 19th century is of special interest. [AL]

1100 Wobeser, Gisela von. La política económica de la Corona española frente a la industria azucarera en la Nueva España, 1599–1630. (*Estud. Hist. Novohisp.*, 9, 1987, p. 51–66, bibl.)

Outlines the Crown's restrictive policy towards the sugar industry in New Spain. Reasons that policy was due to favoring Caribbean island production; preserving Indian labor for mining; and preventing the saturation of a limited market. [AL]

1101 Wright, David. Querétaro en el siglo XVI: fuentes documentales primarias. Mexico: Dirección de Patrimonio Cultural, 1989. 428 p.: bibl., indexes. (Col. Documentos; 13)

Extensive introduction serves as a brief history of Querétaro and the four sets of documents printed here in paleographic and modern transcriptions. Includes the *Relación Geográfica de 1582*, documents about the Tapias, and two 1564 documents about Jurica and Santa María Atongo. Annotated. [EBC]

1102 Zeitlin, Judith Francis. Ranchers and Indians on the Southern Isthmus of Tehuantepec: economic change and indigenous survival in colonial Mexico. (*HAHR*, 69:1, Feb. 1989, p. 24–60, maps, tables)

Author explores different ways by which Zapotecs, Zoques and Huaves adapted to colonialism, especially during the period 1580–1620. Focuses on ranching and land grants as economic elements exerting significant pressure for cultural adaptation, and discusses how the three groups responded to new labor and land-holding patterns and to what degree they succeeded in retaining their self-identity. [AL]

NORTH AND BORDERLANDS

1103 Albert, Salvador Bernabeu. Ciencia y minería en Baja California: el Informe de Joaquín Velázquez de León, 1771. (*Asclepio*, 39:2, 1987, p. 103–122, bibl.)

Brings wealth of material to this study of the 1760s and 1770s in Baja California. Also describes Gálvez Visita and mining prospects in the region. [EBC]

1104 Alhborn, Richard Eighme. The will of a New Mexico woman in 1762. (*N.M. Hist. Rev.*, 65:3, July 1990, p. 319–355, appendixes, ill., tables)

Study of the will of a Hispanic woman followed by appendixes identifying people, places, and artifacts itemized in the will. Useful glossary. Ahlborn aptly places this will in historical context for a readable account. [AL]

1105 The assassination of Padre Andrés Quintana by the Indians of Mission Santa Cruz in 1812: the narrative of Lorenzo Asisara. Translated, edited, and introduced by Edward D. Castillo. (*Calif. Hist.*, 68:3, Fall 1989, p. 117–125, facsims.)

Annotated translation of account of the murder of a friar raises questions about the alleged benevolence of Franciscan activities. Part of a critical body of material about Franciscan-Indian relations in California. [EBC]

1106 Cuello, José. The economic impact of the Bourbon reforms and the late colonial crisis of empire at the local level: the case of Saltillo, 1777–1817. (*Americas/Francisc.*, 44:3, Jan. 1988, p. 301–323, bibl.)

Clearly written and thoroughly researched examination of the effect on one municipality of new taxes levied as part of the Bourbon reforms. Original contribution to municipal government's reaction to these measures. [EBC]

1107 Cuello, José. El Norte, el noreste y Saltillo en la historia colonial de México. Traducción de Marco Antonio Silva *et al.* Saltillo, Mexico: Archivo Municipal de Saltillo, R. Ayuntamiento de Saltillo, 1990. 190 p.: bibl., maps.

Exceptionally valuable collection of essays, some published previously in English, are sharply critical of how Northern Mexico and Southwest US have been conceptualized in the past. One essay describes the variety of land tenure arrangements in the North, and notes the continuation of encomienda and peonage. Places the North within the context of developments in the history of New Spain. [EBC]

1108 Deeds, Susan M. Rural work in Nueva Vizcaya: forms of labor coercion on the periphery. (*HAHR*, 69:3, Aug. 1989, p. 425–449, map)

Analyzes the unique and complex process for continuation of the encomienda-repartimiento in a labor-scarce and poor economy. Article deals with conflicts between the missions and secular society as well as differences among Indian groups. New and thoughtful vision of old issues. [EBC]

1109 Gutiérrez, Ramón A. When Jesus came, the corn mothers went away: marriage, sexuality, and power in New Mexico, 1500–1846. Stanford, Calif.: Stanford Univ. Press, 1991. 424 p.: bibl., ill., maps.

Sensitive and complete history of colonial New Mexico is especially commendable for its interdisciplinary focus and extensive use of primary sources. Beyond its important contribution to social history, book clarifies much that was opaque previously. Delivers more than the title promises. [EBC]

1110 Herrera Leyva, Pedro. Diario de lo ocurrido a las milicias del Nuevo Reino de León al mando de su comandante el Capitán Don Pedro Herrera Leyva en sus operaciones contra los insurgentes. Edición de Isidro Vizcaya Canales. Monterrey, México: Archivo General del Estado de Nuevo León, 1985. 82 p.: bibl.

Diary of activites of Captain Pedro Herrera Leyva, a royal officer in charge of raising troops and carrying out operations against Mexican insurgents in New Leon, Coahuila and New Santander during 1811. Includes small collection of documents printed from archival sources. [AL]

1111 Ivey, James E. Another look at dating the Scholes manuscript: a research note. (*N.M. Hist. Rev.*, 64:3, July 1989, p. 341–347)

Reveals complex problems in determining the date of a list of 17th-century missions which was compiled between 1639–59. Indicates research still needing to be accomplished in the early history of New Mexico. [EBC]

1112 Jackson, Robert H. and **Peter Stern.** *Vagabundaje* and settlement patterns in colonial northern Sonora. (*Americas/Francisc.*, 44:4, April 1988, p. 461–481, tables)

New perspective on the history of a section of northern New Spain that emphasizes the role of a boom-and-bust mining economy and the floating population of men who worked in these mines and their relationship to the missions and presidios. [EBC]

1113 Jiménez Pelayo, Agueda. Haciendas y comunidades indígenas en el sur de Zacatecas: sociedad y economía colonial, 1600–1820. México: Instituto Nacional de Antropología e Historia, 1989. 228 p.: (Serie Historia Col. científica)

Thorough study of four key regions of southern Zacatecas. Author underlines im-

portance of landownership in this area and provides thorough study of patterns of ownership among Spaniards, Indians and *criollos*. Includes much detail on credit, pious deeds and sociopolitical relationships among landowners throughout this period. Based on archival research. [AL]

1114 Jones, Oakah L. Nueva Vizcaya: heartland of the Spanish frontier. Albuquerque: Univ. of New Mexico Press, 1988. 342 p.: appendices, bibl., ill., index, maps, tables.

Important contribution to the regional study of the northern frontier makes abundant use of archival materials and recent publications on the period. Lacks extensive analytic framework, and emphasizes administrative and military history. [EBC]

1115 Lecompte, Janet. Coronado and conquest. (*N.M. Hist. Rev.*, 64:3, July 1989, p. 279–304, facsims., map)

Well-reasoned article concludes that Coronado should be placed in the category of explorer rather than conqueror. Revisionist view of the expedition to New Mexico. [EBC]

1116 Martin, Cheryl English. Popular speech and social order in Northern Mexico, 1650–1830. (*Comp. Stud. Soc. Hist.*, 32:2, April 1990, p. 305–324)

Detailed study of the use of offensive epithets in popular speech draws examples from archival sources dealing with personal suits. Author ties use of words to gender and race. [AL]

1117 Mathes, W. Michael. The mythological geography of California: origins, development, confirmation and disappearance. (*Americas/Francisc.*, 45:3, Jan. 1989, p. 315–341, bibl.)

Thorough review of published primary and secondary sources claiming that California was an island. Attempts to explain persistence of the idea within the context of the history of the discoveries in the Pacific. [EBC]

1118 Morgado, Martin. *Non Recedet Memoria Ejus:* the story of Blessed Junípero Serra's Mission Carmel grave. (*Calif. Hist.*, 67:3, Sept. 1988, p. 150–167, facsims., photos)

Begins with account of Junípero Serra's death and continues with a history of the

Carmel mission following its 1834 secularization. This piece describes the various reinterments and examinations of the bones of Serra and includes an account of the preparatory steps in his canonization. [EBC]

1119 Nostrand, Richard L. The century of Hispano expansion. (*N.M. Hist. Rev.*, 62:4, Oct. 1987, p. 361–386, maps)

Important work by geographer based on census schedules and secondary sources contains valuable maps. Hypothesizes that New Mexico sheep-raisers settled many parts of the Southwest. Indicates conflicts and ecological problems between Anglo cattle-breeders and Hispanic sheep-herders. Also outlines Hispanic methods of village settlement. [EBC]

1120 Officer, James E. Hispanic Arizona, 1536–1856. Tucson: Univ. of Arizona Press, 1987. 462 p.: bibl., ill., index, maps.

History of the Sonora-Arizona region is especially detailed for the late 18th and early 19th centuries. Contains information about family history and demography, as well as an account of military and political events. [EBC]

1121 The Pueblo Indian revolt of 1696 and the Franciscan missions in New Mexico: letters of the missionaries and related documents. Translated, edited, and with an introduction by José Manuel Espinosa. Norman: Univ. of Oklahoma Press, 1988. 313 p.: bibl., ill., index.

Lengthy introduction places these translations dealing with the 1696 rebellion and the re-establishment of the Franciscan missions in the context of the history of New Mexico. Translations maintain the flavor of the originals. [EBC]

1122 Radding, Cynthia. "A la sombra de la sierra:" etnicidad y el naciente campesinado del Noroeste de Nueva España. (*HISLA*, 11, 1988, p. 13–44, bibl., graphs, tables)

Interesting and thoughtful effort to write the history of peasant communities in the provinces of Sonora and Tarahumara from the time of the Jesuits through the end of the colonial period. Uses quantitative and population materials in comparing communities with each other as well as with other geograhic areas. [EBC]

1123 Radding, Cynthia. Familias y comunidades campesinas en los altos de Sonora, siglo XVIII. (*Rev. Eur.*, 49, Dec. 1990, p. 79–106, bibl., maps, tables)

Examines impact of colonial labor and demographic policies on the indigenous communities and families of Sonora. Posits that the survival of the communities depended on access to different resources. While not conclusive, essay poses important questions and suggests answers. Based on archival sources. [AL]

1124 Río, Ignacio del. Proceso y balance de la reforma tributaria del siglo XVIII en Sonora y Sinaloa. (*in* Simposio de Historia y Antropología de Sonora, *13th, Hermosillo, Mexico, 1989.* Memoria. Coordinación de Juan Manuel Romero Gil. Hermosillo, Mexico: Instituto de Investigaciones Históricas, Univ. de Sonora, 1989, v. 1, p. 161–178)

Detailed and precise article on the establishment and collection of tributes among indigenous groups in Sonora and Sinaloa after Gálvez's visit in 1769. Author establishes the reluctance shown by Indians to pay taxes and the meager results obtained from actual collection. Based on archival sources. [AL]

1125 Rock, Rosalind Z. *"Pido y Suplico":* women and the law in Spanish New Mexico, 1697–1763. (*N.M. Hist. Rev.*, 65:2, April 1990, p. 145–159)

Uses 18th-century examples of women's legal suits to illustrate how they relied on existing laws to protect their interests and to survive in a hostile frontier environment. [AL]

1126 Sales, Luis de and **Antonio de los Reyes.** Noticias de la provincia de Californias [y] Observaciones sobre el obispado de Sonora. Valencia, Spain: Generalitat Valenciana; Comissío per al V$_0$ Centenari del Descobriment d'América, 1989. 419 p.: bibl. (Misioneros valencianos en Indias; 2)

Facsimile editions of work on California by Luis de Sales and notes on the Bishopric of Sonora by Antonio de los Reyes. [J.D. Riley]

1127 Salmón, Roberto Mario. A marginal man: Luis of Saric and the Pima Revolt of 1751. (*Americas/Francisc.*, 45:1, July 1988, p. 61–77, bibl.)

Analysis of leadership qualities and characteristics of Indian rebellions reveals unsuspected aspects of ethnic and tribal conflict. Describes various frontier types and their interaction while providing an original synthesis of 18th-century life in the North. Emphasizes Indian leader's life combined with a thoughtful account of the rebellion he led. [EBC]

1128 Sandos, James A. Junípero Serra's canonization and the historical record. (*Am. Hist. Rev.*, 93:5, Dec. 1988, p. 1253–1269)
Description and analysis of the methods used to present the historical record in Serra's canonization. Includes a summary of the historiography of the mission system and its critics. Argues that the canonization proceedings ignored evidence presented by Sherburne F. Cook and Indian activists. [EBC]

1129 Schilz, Thomas Frank and **Donald E. Worcester.** Spread of firearms among the Indian tribes on the Northern frontier of New Spain. (*Am. Indian Q.*, 11:1, Winter 1987, p. 1–10, bibl.)
Indian control over sources of guns from British and French traders as well as Spanish supplies delayed and at times stopped the advance of the Spanish frontier northward. Examines dilemmas of Spanish policy while providing new insight on the 18th-century history of Texas. [EBC]

1130 Shaler, William. Diario de un viaje entre la China y la costa noroeste de América efectuado en 1804. Traducción, edición y notas de Estela Guadalupe Jiménez Codinach. México: Univ. Iberoamericana, Depto. de Historia, 1990. 106 p.: bibl., ill., maps.
Abundantly annotated translation of journal written by New England merchant and businessman with an interest in the fur trade. Editor places his description of California in 1804 in its historic, economic, and political context. [EBC]

Trautmann, Wolfgang. Geographical aspects of Hispanic colonization on the northern frontier of New Spain. See *HLAS 51:2947.*

1131 Valdés, Carlos Manuel and **Ildefonso Dávila B.** Esclavos negros en Saltillo: siglos XVII–XIX. Saltillo, Mexico: R. Ayuntamiento de Saltillo; Univ. Autónoma de Coahuila, 1989. 159 p.: bibl., ill., index. (Documentos del Archivo Municipal)
Reviews 249 documents on slave population in the municipal archives of Saltillo dated 1659–1859. Authors transcribe 11 documents in full and synthesize the rest. Graphs on population of Saltillo and its vicinity according to the 1777 census, and the brief introduction by the authors make this modest work a useful if limited tool to document slavery in colonial Mexico. [AL]

Independence, Revolution, and Post-Revolution

DON M. COERVER, *Professor of History, Texas Christian University*
LINDA B. HALL, *Professor of History, University of New Mexico, Albuquerque*
BARBARA A. TENENBAUM, *Editor in Chief, Encyclopedia of Latin-American History*

INDEPENDENCE TO REVOLUTION

THE LAST BIENNIUM BROUGHT an embarrassment of riches for the 1810–1910 period with major advances in an array of fields. The flourishing trend of regional history previously noted in *HLAS 50* gained strength in the last biennium, particularly among Mexican scholars. Studies focusing on regional topics comprised over one third of the total contributions reviewed for this period, exclusive of collections of essays, and almost 60 percent of those were written by Mexican historians. Indeed, few foreign scholars resident outside Mexico chose to study regional topics, with the significant exceptions of Anderson and Chowning (items **1136** and **1156**).

Michoacán led the list with six contributions by the aforementioned Chowning, Guzmán (item **1173**), Lameiras (item **1188**), Ortiz Escamilla (item **1202**), and two by Sánchez Díaz (items **1215** and **1216**). Veracruz claimed its share of researchers with Blázquez Domínguez (item **1151**), the *Documentos gráficos para la historia de México* for the port city (item **1163**), González de la Lama (item **1169**), Jiménez Codinach (item **1182**), and Naveda Chávez-Hita (item **1200**). Pedro and Sosa Bracamonte (item **1152**), Konrad (item **1184**), and Urías Horcasitas (item **1225**) examined Yucatán while Aguirre (item **1132**) and the Centro de Investigaciones Históricas y Sociales, Instituto de Ciencias de la Univ. Autónoma de Puebla (item **1206**) looked at Puebla. There were also several noteworthy additions to the history of the northern frontier by the ubiquitous Cerutti for the Northeast (item **1209**), Almada Bay and Súarez Arguello for Sonora (items **1135** and **1221**), Falcón for Coahuila (item **1165**), and Garza Guajardo for Tamaulipas (item **1168**).

This biennium also saw increased interest in both the Catholic Church and Protestantism. On the former there are works by Dumas, (item **1164**), Rodríguez O. (item **1212**), Romero de Solís (item **1214**), and Vázquez (item **1230**); and on the latter, a study by Bastian (item **1249**). There were also new works on the army by Hanson (item **1175**), Hernández Chávez (item **1176**), Santoni (item **1217**), and Vázquez (item **1230**).

Examinations of the national and fiscal economy continued with major articles by Carmagnani (item **1155**) and Coatsworth (item **1157**); entrepreneurial activity received its due from Aguirre (item **1132**), Bernecker (item **1148**), Krause (item **1185**), Mentz (item **1194**), and Thomson (item **1223**); and agricultural history came to the fore with contributions from Aldana Rendón (item **1134**), González Navarro (item **1275**), Holden (item **1178**), Konrad (item **1184**), Kaerger (item **1183**), Lameiras (item **1188**), Nickel (item **1203**), and de Vos (item **1233**).

Diplomatic history was expanded with works by Díaz y de Ovando (item **1162**), Lamar (item **1187**), Pi-Suñer (item **1196**), and Valdés Lakowsky (item **1226**). Intellectual history made a striking comeback with entries by Barrera Bassols (item **1143**), Brading (item **1153**), Covo (item **1161**), Hale (item **1174**), del Río (item **1210**), Talavera Ibarra (item **1222**), and Urías Horcasitas (item **1225**); and Van Young's two articles added to the discussion of "mentalités." (items **1228** and **1227**).

Worthy of special individual note were contributions by González de la Lama on revolts in Veracruz (item **1169**), Guedea's lengthy article describing Indian volunteers and the royalist cause (item **1171**), Lugo Olín on demography (item **1190**), Moreno Corral for a striking contribution to history of science (item **1199**), Oliver on the 1833 cholera epidemic (item **1201**), Priego Ramírez for a masterful discussion of photography in Querétaro (item **1205**), Rodríguez O. *et al.*, for a collection of important essays from the Bourbon Reforms to the first centralist republic (item **1179**), Rojas Rabiela for a source book for history of attitudes toward Indians (item **1207**), Stevens' computer reassessment of Mexican instability (item **1220**), and Vaughn's magisterial look at education (item **1229**). Curiously, while the biennium overflowed with marvelous individual contributions, there was only one addition to an existing series, that of *Documentos gráficos para la historia de México: Veracruz, 1858–1914* (item **1163**, see also *HLAS 50:1146*) and no major series of note were initiated. [BAT]

REVOLUTION AND POST-REVOLUTION

Regional history continued as a major focus for research on the revolutionary period. An eight-volume document collection, *La revolución en Oaxaca, 1900–1930* (item **1323**), edited by Víctor Raúl Martínez, added greatly to the ease of researching in this area. Francisco Ruiz Cervantes also contributed a monograph on this subject (item **1325**). Other regional studies covering a longer time period included contributions by Pedro Echeverría V. on the Yucatán (item **1266**), Romana Falcón and Soledad García on Adalberto Tejeda in Veracruz (item **1270**), and the impressive multi-volume collection of essays on Jalisco published by the government of that state (item **1289**).

Interest in labor history also remained high. Another volume appeared in the series *La clase obrera en la historia de México* coordinated by Pablo González Casanova (item **1261**), with Jaime Tamayo covering the crucial organizational period of 1920–24. Durand Ponte covered a longer period (1938–52), but with a similar emphasis on relations between the state and the labor movement (item **1265**). The relationship between organized labor and the Mexican government came in for considerable criticism in the interpretative survey of the labor movement by Dan La Botz (item **1298**). Also worthy of note was *Cincuenta años de lucha obrera*, a lengthy ten-volume documentary history of the CTM published by the PRI (item **1260**).

By far the largest concentration of materials was in the area of agrarian movements, changing agrarian structures, and peasant studies. These were no longer concentrated entirely or even primarily on the years of the Revolution, but extended well into the post-revolutionary period. They included studies by Bartra (item **1248**), Brannon and Baklanov (item **1251**), Leal and Bornemann (item **1299**), Radding (item **1321**), and Gates (item **1273**); articles by Becker (item **1250**), Entrena Durán (item **1267**), González Navarro (item **1275**), and Lerner (items **1301** and **1302**); and David Nugent's useful edited work on rural revolt and its connection with US intervention (item **1326**).

Reprints of major works also figured prominently in the publications of the last biennium. José C. Valadés' ten-volume *Historia general de la revolución mexicana* (item **1340**) was one of the most significant works in this category as was the paperback edition of Alan Knight's *The Mexican Revolution* (item **1295**). The fundamental work on the revolutionary army by Juan Barragán Rodríguez was also reissued (item **1247**). Works by two prominent *carrancistas*—Isidro Fabela and Alfredo Breceda—were also reprinted (items **1268** and **1252**).

Border studies did not figure as prominently as in previous periods, but two major works did appear by veteran commentators. Oscar Martínez discussed border problems from the differing perspectives of the US, Mexico, and the border residents themselves (item **1313**) while Linda Hall and Don Coerver provided the first general survey of the border during the military phase of the Revolution (item **1283**).

Enrique Krauze's well-written and extensively illustrated *Biografía del poder* series (item **1297**) provided political biographies of some of the leading revolutionary figures: Porfirio Díaz, Francisco Madero, Emiliano Zapata, Pancho Villa, Venustiano Carranza, and Alvaro Obregón.

Two important works for understanding Mexico's continuing economic problems also appeared. Stephen Haber examined the "first wave" of Mexican industrialization and the characteristics of the industrial sector that emerged (item **1282**) while Alex Saragoza described the evolution of the "Monterrey elite" and its role in national political and economic affairs (item **1329**). While both studies covered only through 1940, they furnished important insights into Mexico's contemporary economic difficulties.

Two major new syntheses of the Mexican Revolution appeared from John M. Hart (item **1284**) and Hans Werner Tobler (item **1338**). Hart's volume focused most heavily on the development of the mass base for the Revolution while indicating that the Revolution itself did little to resolve the problems of those who fought it. Tobler's study looked principally at the 1920–40 period, emphasizing the regional diversity of the Revolution and its real but limited impact. [DMC and LBH]

INDEPENDENCE TO REVOLUTION

1132 Aguirre, Carmen. Personificaciones del capital: siete propriedades en la sociedad e industria textil de Puebla durante el siglo XIX. Puebla, Mexico: Centro de Investigaciones Históricas y Sociales, 1987. 60 p.: bibl., ill. (Cuadernos de la Casa Presno; 7)

Brief but useful examination of investment and impact of 7 entrepreneurial families in Puebla (Haro y Tamariz, Furlong, Torres, García Teruel, Marrón y Carballo, and the sociedades Benítez Hermanos and Velasco Hermanos).

1133 Aldana Rendón, Mario A. *et al.* De los Borbones a la Revolución: ocho estudios regionales. Coordinación de Mario Cerutti. Mexico: GV Editores: 1986. 265 p.: bibl., ill. (Ciencias sociales)

Includes 8 essays that concentrate mostly on the political and economic history of the Porfiriato in Yucatán, Jalisco, Pueblo, and Veracruz. Also includes an excellent study by Cerutti on war economies on the frontier from 1854–67.

1134 Aldana Rendón, Mario A. Proyectos agrarios y lucha por la tierra en Jalisco, 1810–1866. Guadalajara, Mexico: Gobierno de Jalisco, Secretaría General, Unidad Editorial, 1986. 289 p.: bibl. (Col. Historia: Serie Documentos e investigación; 21)

Monographic study of the land question in Jalisco during the critical years after Independence argues that struggle for land continued throughout the reform and the empire, disputing theories that Indians supported Maximilian and that dispossession came during the Restored Republic.

1135 Almada Bay, Ignacio. Pólvora, plomo y pinole: algunas consideraciones generales sobre Sonora alrededor de 1821. (*in* Simposio de Historia y Antropología de Sonora, *13th, Hermosillo, Mexico, 1989*. Memoria. Coordinación de Juan Manuel Romero Gil. Hermosillo, Mexico: Instituto de Investigaciones Históricas de la Univ. de Sonora, 1989, v. 1, p. 273–304, bibl., table)

Misleading title to an interesting summary of Sonoran history from 1760 to 1825 which contends that the history of the North requires different periodization from the more central areas. Points out that Sonora considered itself very much part of the Mexican Republic, despite frantic efforts to separate itself from Sinaloa.

Altamirano, Ignacio Manuel. Obras completas. v. 1–6. See item **3383.**

1136 Anderson, Rodney D. Race and social stratification: a comparison of working-class Spaniards, Indians, and *castas* in Guadalajara, Mexico in 1821. (*HAHR*, 68:2, May 1988, p. 211–243, bibl., map)

Makes the case that economic and social stratification at the time of Independence resulted from the rise of early commercial capitalism rather than colonial racial policy. Uses Guadalajara census of 1793 to argue that poor Spaniards often lived alongside poor Indians and mestizos and that all had tougher road to social mobility after Independence. Recommended.

1137 Anna, Timothy E. The Mexican empire of Iturbide. Lincoln: Univ. of Nebraska Press, 1990. 286 p.: bibl., index.

First biography in English of Mexico's only native emperor since Robertson (Durham, Duke Univ. Press, 1952). Argues that Iturbide's problems were similar to heads of State elsewhere in the region and that he abdicated because he had lost control over the army and did not wish to surrender power to Congress.

1138 Annino, Antonio. Pratiche creole e liberalismo nella crisi dello spacio urbano coloniale: il 29 novembre 1812 a Città del Messico. (*Quad. Stor.*, 69:3, dic. 1988, p. 727–763, maps)

Examines how powerful creoles seized the opportunity as representatives to the

1812 constitutent assembly in Cádiz by finding convincing legal grounds tofacilitate the legal transformation of a corporatist, tripartite society into an informally class-based one. Annino's Braudelian model of explanation is rooted in a vision of urban space that was central to the creole task as illustrated in the Mexico City cabildo elections of 1811, whose members would control the Mexican delegation to Cádiz. Using arguments that harked back to 16th century "natural law" conceptions of the "nation" and the State, creoles controlled the procedures, including bi-level elections and a host of prohibitions, sufficiently narrowing the electorate legally, thus allowing lawyers, ecclesiastics and landowners to take power, wed liberalism to decentralization, and fend off the centralized State tendency promoted by the Cádiz leaders. This strategy would provide the model for the legalization of creole control of *ayuntamientos* throughout Mexico following independence. Presents the core of an important argument concerning the philosophical and political sources of Mexican liberalism which the author promises to elaborate in future studies. [Vincent C. Peloso]

1139 Arauz, Juan Víctor. Guadalajara, iconografía del siglo XIX y principios del XX. Textos de Francisco Ayón Zester. Guadalajara, Mexico: Gobierno de Jalisco, Secretaría General, Unidad Editorial, 1988. 140 p.: ill.

Fascinating volume of photos detailing Guadalajara's appearance in the 19th and 20th centuries.

1140 Archer, Christon I. The young Antonio López de Santa Anna: Veracruz counterinsurgent and incipient caudillo. (*in* The human tradition in Latin America. Edited by Judith Ewell and William H. Beezley. Wilmington, Delaware: Scholarly Resources, 1989, p. 3–16, bibl.)

First effort to make sense of Santa Anna's early career depicts him as a good administrator of land reform in Veracruz at the end of the colonial period. His hunger for power led to adoption of the Independence cause under Iturbide in 1821. Also provides excellent sense of daily life of the royalist army as Mexico neared Independence.

1141 Arnold, Linda. La política de la justicia: los vencedores de Ayutla y la Suprema Corte Mexicana. (*Hist. Mex.*, 39:2, oct./dic. 1989, p. 441–473, bibl.)

Tries to demonstrate that Mexican judiciary started out independent, but that the Ley Juárez subsequently made it subservient to the executive. Argues that authoritarian presidency began as early as the Reform.

1142 Arrom, Silvia M. Popular politics in Mexico City: the Parián riot, 1828. (*HAHR*, 68:2, May 1988, p. 247–268, map)

Thoughtful discussion of pivotal riot in Mexico City concludes that, as a result of riots, elites decided to reject democracy as too dangerous and became willing to use more force to control the poor.

1143 El Bardo y el bandolero: la persecución de Santanón por Díaz Mirón. Recopilación de Jacinto Barrera Bassols. Puebla, Mexico: Univ. Autónoma de Puebla, 1987. 179 p.: bibl., map. (Col. Crónicas y testimonios; 5)

Insightful account of a fictional duel between deputy and literary figure Salvador Díaz Mirón (1853–1928) and Veracruz bandit Santana Rodríguez Palafox ("Santanón") with excellent commentary by Barrera Bassols. Provides useful glimpse of the Porfiriato in its last days.

1144 Bastian, Jean Pierre. Las sociedades protestantes y la oposición a Porfirio Díaz, 1877–1911. (*Hist. Mex.*, 37:3, enero/ marzo 1988, p. 469–512, bibl., tables)

Significant contribution shows the importance of Protestants to the movements against Díaz, especially Protestant support of Flores Magón and Francisco Madero.

1145 Bellingeri, Marco. Dal voto alle baionette: esperienze elettorali nello Yucatan costituzionale ed indipendente. (*Quad. Stor.*, 69:3, dic. 1988, p. 765–785)

Notes that the incessant "plans" issued in the 19th century shaped the dynamic of political legitimacy, reifying it in electoral institutions, themselves subject to overturn by "plans." Thus the legitimacy of temporary oligarchic factional victories could be declared. To illustrate, the author examines politics in Yucatán between the Cádiz declaration and the first military government (1829) formed in a locale where the oligarchy was able to unify behind candidates. Reviews the region's corporatist electoral tradition from the 17th century forward and analyzes the impact of the Cádiz Constitution on the cabildo of Mérida. Ends with a discussion of the mix of legality and force that shaped the electoral project developed by the Yucatán constituent assembly of 1823–1825. Effective use of municipal electoral records. [Vincent C. Peloso]

1146 Bellingeri, Marco. Formazione e circolazione della merce terra-uomo in Yucatán, 1880–1914. (*Quad. Stor.*, 65:2, agosto 1987, p. 599–614, graph, table)

Narrows a well-worked subject down to the question of the juridical status of Mayans and the possibility of the existence of modern slavery in the late-19th century in the northwestern portion of Yucatán. Focuses on foreign investment and repressed peasant labor in the sisal market, challenging the customary view that landowners were pro-imperialist and dependent upon foreign investors for funding and credit. Of the 29 landlords examined for the first two decades of the 20th century, author found most properties and projects to be funded by national sources. Brief but interesting study based on Yucatecan notarial and public registry materials. [Vincent C. Peloso]

1147 Bernecker, Walther L. Los alemanes en el México decimonónico: cuantificación, estructura socioprofesional, posturas político-ideológicas. (*Jahrb. Gesch.*, 25, 1988, p. 385–414)

Emphasizes sociological aspects of a group willing to adapt but not assimilate, acculturate or integrate into Mexican society in part because Germans clung to their Protestantism in a Catholic world.

1148 Bernecker, Walther L. Comercio y comerciantes extranjeros en las primeras décadas de la independencia mexicana. (*in* América Latina en la época de Simón Bolívar. Edición de Reinhard Liehr. Berlin: Colloquium Verlag, 1989, p. 87–114, tables)

Explains foreign commercial success by arguing that Mexicans lacked resources, exports, and entrepreneurial spirit. Shows that French edged out the British in retail sales, particularly of luxury goods.

1149 Bernecker, Walther L. Foreign interests, tariff policy and early industrialization in Mexico, 1821–1848. (*Ibero-Am. Arch.*, 14:1, 1988, p. 61–102, bibl., tables)

Supports Platt's assertion that Mexi-

can market for imports was far smaller than previously believed and was not responsible for the failure of Mexican industrialization. Tentatively falls back on old canard that Mexicans are not entrepreneurial people.

1150 Bertola, Elisabetta. La designazione dei candidati elettorali: la construzione di un compromesso nel Messico porfirista, 1876–1911. (*Quad. Stor.*, 69:3, dic. 1988, p. 929–939)

Study of the electoral process during Porfiriato uses the Porfirio Díaz archive in the AGN (Mexico) to explain the importance of *suplentes* elected at the state level in congressional contests. Presents interesting evidence, that contrary to conventional belief, such elections were not a farcical procedure but rather presented opportunities for the exercise of power by governors against the central authorities. Also makes clear that electoral procedures received fastidious attention. Questions the myth of centralized authority in every sphere of Porfirian rule. [Vincent C. Peloso]

1151 Blázquez Domínguez, Carmen. Veracruz liberal (1858–1860). Colaboración de Concepción Hernández Ramírez y Aurelio Sánchez Durán. México: Centro de Estudios Históricos, Colegio de México; Jalapa: Gobierno del Estado de Veracruz, 1986. 269 p., 20 p. of plates: bibl., ill., index, ports.

Straightforward narrative account of Veracruz during the War of the Reform, during which business apparently continued as usual despite limitations. Provides much new information on elections and the financing of both liberal and conservative sides.

1152 Bracamonte y Sosa, Pedro. Haciendas y ganado en el noroeste de Yucatán, 1800–1850. (*Hist. Mex.*, 37:4, abril/junio 1988, p. 613–639, bibl., tables)

Depicts life on Yucatecan haciendas for workers who remained there for access to land, water, food, and even religious solace. Despite corporal punishments and regimented lives, these workers did not join the Caste War of 1849.

1153 Brading, D.A. Liberal patriotism and the Mexican *Reforma*. (*J. Lat. Am. Stud.*, 20:1, May 1988, p. 27–48, bibl.)

Describes how Ignacio Ramírez and Ignacio Manuel Altamirano transformed the liberalism of Mora and his generation into classical republicanism by repudiating "creole nationalism" and substituting the legacies of the French Revolution and the 1810 insurgency itself. This ideology was then superseded by Justo Sierra's and Andrés Molina Enriquez's transmogrification of Benito Juárez and the evolution of the mestizo.

1154 Buisson, Inge. Die mexikanische Hacienda im Spiegel deutschsprachiger Veröffentlichungen des 19. Jahrhunderts. (*Jahrb. Gesch.*, 25, 1988, p. 789–805)

Valuable contribution analyzes reports and descriptions of the Mexican hacienda by 19th-century German residents and travelers who had spent time in Mexico. Though most descriptions claim objectivity, many are subjective and paint a rather negative picture. Several descriptions present valuable insights on agrarian conditions, while others are unique for their outside perspective on regional differences. Authors studied include I.W. Müller, Carl Sartorious, the Freiherr von Richthofen, Karle Koppe, and Hermann Paasche. [G.M. Dorn]

1155 Carmagnani, Marcello. El liberalismo, los impuestos internos y el estado federal mexicano, 1857–1911. (*Hist. Mex.*, 38:3, enero/marzo 1989, p. 471–496, bibl., graphs, tables)

Confusing but important study of internal taxation which came to comprise approximately one-third of the revenues of the national treasury during the Porfiriato. Argues that toward the end of the period, the Treasury Ministry had developed a true core of federal functionaries. Recommended.

1156 Chowning, Margaret. The management of Church wealth in Michoacán, Mexico, 1810–1856: economic motivations and political implications. (*J. Lat. Am. Stud.*, 22:3, Oct. 1990, p. 459–496, graphs, tables)

Thorough discussion of Church's economic role in key state shows that from 1845 on it divested itself of much of its real estate. Contends that liberal reforms aimed to reduce its political rather than economic role. Recommended.

1157 Coatsworth, John H. The decline of the Mexican economy, 1800–1860. (*in* América Latina en la época de Simón Bolívar. Edición de Reinhard Liehr. Berlin: Colloquium Verlag, 1989, p. 27–53, tables)

Argues that Mexico's economic decline from 1800–60 caused it to fall behind the US and made it more dependent on foreign trade. Includes lengthy analysis and sectoral tables of economy sector showing that agriculture was affected least, and livestock production most. Valuable addition to this debate.

1158 Congreso sobre la Insurgencia Mexicana, *Zamora, Mexico, 1984.* Repaso de la independencia: memoria del Congreso sobre la Insurgencia Mexicana, octubre 22–23 de 1984. Recopilación de Carlos Herrejón Peredo. Zamora, Mexico: El Colegio de Michoacán, 1985. 282 p.: bibl.

Includes eight papers on the Independence movements and commentary. Particularly noteworthy are Archer's contribution on the finances of the insurgency and De la Torre Villar's on secret societies.

1159 Costeloe, Michael P. Los generales Santa Anna y Paredes y Arrillaga en México, 1841–1843: rivales por el poder o una copa más. (*Hist. Mex.*, 39:2, oct./dic. 1989, p. 417–440, bibl.)

Detailed account of feud between two of the most important military figures of the period which author believes led to Paredes' revolt of 1844.

1160 Costeloe, Michael P. Generals versus politicians: Santa Anna and the 1842 Congressional elections in Mexico. (*Bull. Lat. Am. Res.*, 8:2, 1989, p. 257–274)

First look at the 1842 elections focuses on Santa Anna. Shows that popular sentiment clearly favored liberals even in the centralist period.

1161 Covo, Jaqueline. La idea de la revolución francesa en el congreso constituyente de 1856–1857. (*Hist. Mex.*, 38:1, julio/sept. 1988, p. 69–78, bibl.)

Using extensive quotations, dicusses impact of the French Revolution on the members of the 1856 Constitutent Congress.

1162 Díaz y de Ovando, Clementina. Crónica de una quimera: una inversión norteamericana en México, 1879. México: Coordinación de Humanidades, UNAM, 1989. 692 p., 2 leafs of plates: bibl., ill.

Lengthy and fully-documented account of the attempts of Díaz and Minister of Foreign Relations Manuel María Zamacona to avert war with the US by improving commercial relations. Includes an interesting discussion of US trade fair held in 1879.

1163 Documentos gráficos para la historia de México. v. 3, Veracruz, 1858–1914. Edición de Luis Gutiérrez Muñoz. México: Editora del Sureste, 1985–1988. 3 v.: bibl., ill., index.

Vol. 3 of a series of historical photos with introductions by Carmen Blázquez Domínguez and Berta Ulloa. For first two vols. see *HLAS 50:1146.*

1164 Dumas, Claude. El discurso de oposición en la prensa clerical conservadora de México en la época de Porfirio Díaz (1876–1910). (*Hist. Mex.*, 39:1, julio/sept. 1989, p. 243–256, bibl.)

Disjointed but thought-provoking look at the under-researched clerical opposition toward both the Jacobin and Positivist strands of Liberalism during the Porfiriato. Would have been better if author discussed single issue in depth instead of running the gamut from education to the Spanish-Cuban-American War.

Dunbar, Gary S. The compass follows the flag: the French scientific mission to Mexico, 1864–1867. See *HLAS 51:2918.*

1165 Falcón, Romana. La desaparición de jefes políticos en Coahuila: una paradoja porfirista. (*Hist. Mex.*, 37:3, enero/marzo 1988, p. 423–467, bibl.)

Interesting case study of Porfirian politics in Coahuila explains how regional interests used a revolt against Governor Garza Gaján to gain more power for themselves. Recommended.

1166 Foley, John Adrian; Jaime Olvera; and José Luis Ramírez Larios. Colima: una historia compartida. Coordinación de Servando Ortoll. México: Secretaría de Educación Pública: Instituto de Investigaciones José María Luis Mora, 1988. 432 p.: bibl., ill.

Eleven essays on the history of Colima in the 19th century. Topics include the establishment of the railroad, agrarian reform and relations between Church and State. [A. Lavrin]

1167 French, John D. Commercial foot soldiers of the Empire: foreign merchant politics in Tampico, Mexico, 1861–1866. (*Americas/Francisc.*, 46:3, Jan. 1990, p. 291–314)

Uses rarely-studied Tampico as a test case to dispute contention that foreign merchants suffered greatly by trading in Mexico. Shows how European and US merchants sought to win advantages for themselves during French blockade, only to reject them when it appeared that the Mexicans would win.

1168 Garza Guajardo, Celso. En busca de Catarino Garza: 1859–1895. Nuevo León, Mexico: Univ. Autónoma de Nuevo León, Centro de Información de Historia Regional, 1989. 362 p., 61 p. of plates: ill. (Serie Biblioteca de Nuevo León; 5)

Important work examines the history of Mexicans in Texas and political dissent during the Porifiriato. Includes full copy of the memoirs of a noted leader of a revolution of Mexicans in Texas and Tamaulipas, who fled to Central America where he penned "La Era de Tuxtepec en México" against Díaz.

1169 González de la Lama, Renée. Los papeles de Díaz Manfort: una revuelta popular en Misantla Veracruz, 1885–1886. (*Hist. Mex.*, 39:2, oct./dic. 1989, p. 475–521, appendices, bibl., maps, tables)

Brilliant analysis of an 1885–86 revolt in Veracruz which author attributes to Totonac Indian fears of losing their religious practices and customs that had been kept alive since the conquest. Discussed in the context of other regional rebellions over a 200-year span. Includes original documents and helpful maps. Highly recommended.

1170 González Navarro, Moisés. Kaerger: peonaje, esclavitud y cuasiesclavitud en México. (*Hist. Mex.*, 36:3, enero/marzo 1987, p. 527–562, bibl.)

Interprets Kaerger's description of Mexican agriculture (item **1183**) in light of that author's prejudices, and includes other more favorable portraits of Porfirian agriculture at the time. Fascinating and recommended.

1171 Guedea, Virginia. Los indios voluntarios de Fernando VII. (*Estud. Hist. Mod. Contemp. Méx.*, 10, 1986, p. 11–81)

Significant study of the behavior of the Indians of San Juan in Mexico City vis-à-vis the royalist cause. The community volunteered many times to fight for King Fernando VII, but its willingness to assist went unappreciated by royal officials in New Spain.

Author hints tantalizingly that the same Indians also volunteered for service with several insurgents as well.

Guide to the notarial records of the Archivo General de Notarias, Mexico City, for the year 1829. = Guía de los protocolos notariales del Archivo General de Notarias, Mexico, D.F., año 1829. See *HLAS 51:86.*

1172 **Gutiérrez Ibarra, Celia.** Cómo México perdió Texas: análisis y transcripción del *Informe secreto,* 1834, de Juan Nepomuceno Almonte. México: Instituto Nacional de Antropología e Historia, 1987. 146 p., 1 folded leaf of plates: bibl., index, maps. (Col. Fuentes)

Misleading title to a very useful group of documents including Almonte's *Informe,* complete with scholarly introduction. Recommended.

1173 **Guzmán Avila, José Napoleón.** Michoacán y la inversión extranjera, 1880–1911. Morelia, Mexico: Univ. Michoacana de San Nicolás de Hidalgo, Depto. de Investigaciones Históricas, 1982. 230 p.: bibl., ill. (Col. Historia nuestra; 3)

Interesting addition to the literature on the economic history of the Porfiriato examines the arrival of US capitalism to Michoacán in the form of railroads, mining, timber, and meat-packing.

1174 **Hale, Charles A.** The transformation of liberalism in late nineteenth-century Mexico. Princeton, N.J.: Princeton Univ. Press, 1989. 291 p.: bibl., index.

Detailed discussion of the central debates of Mexican positivists during the Porfiriato. Argues that Mexicans were more likely to follow Comptian philosophy than Spencerian, thus countering Zea's previous analysis. Winner of the Bolton prize for the best book of 1990.

1175 **Hanson, Lawrence Douglas Taylor.** Voluntarios extranjeros en los ejércitos liberales mexicanos, 1854–1867. (*Hist. Mex.,* 37:2, oct./dic. 1987, p. 205–237, bibl.)

Reports that Europeans and Americans joined the liberal side both for idealistic reasons and for good pay, but that Juárez was more apt to trust the Europeans given memories of 1848.

1176 **Hernández Chávez, Alicia.** Origen y ocaso del ejército porfiriano. (*Hist.*

Mex., 39:1, julio/sept. 1989, p. 257–296, bibl., tables)

Discussion of how Porfirians established the Guardia Nacional and the professional army while they concentrated on developing economic infrastructure. Argues that cuts in the army in 1896 led to its inability to protect the regime against rebels in 1910–11.

1177 **Hewitt, Harry P.** The Mexican Boundary Survey Team: Pedro García Conde in California. (*West. Hist. Q.,* 21:2, May 1990, p. 171–196, maps)

Valuable look at the creation of the US-Mexican border which corrects previous denigration of Mexican participation in the process.

1178 **Holden, Robert H.** Priorities of the State in the survey of the public land in Mexico, 1876–1911. (*HAHR,* 70:4, Nov. 1990, p. 579–607, tables)

Corrects misperception that survey companies took advantage of both the Porfirian State and the peasantry in measuring government lands in Chiapas, Chihuahua, Durango, Sinaloa, Sonora, and Tabasco. Demonstrates campesinos often won their complaints and kept their lands. Recommended.

1179 **The independence of Mexico and the creation of the new nation.** Edited by Jaime E. Rodríguez O. Los Angeles: UCLA Latin American Center Publications, Univ. of California; Irvine: Mexico/Chicano Program, Univ. of California, 1989. 374 p.: bibl., ill., index. (UCLA Latin American studies; 69)

Collection of 18 essays concerning Independence, the first 15 years after Independence and comparisons with the Mexican Revolution, the Brazilian experience, and the Porfiriato. Particularly noteworthy are TePaske on the royal treasury and Guedea on secret societies.

1180 **Jiménez Codinach, Estela Guadalupe.** *La Conféderation Napoléonnie:* el desempeño de los conspiradores militares y las sociedades secretas en la Independencia de México. (*Hist. Mex.,* 38:1, julio/sept. 1988, p. 43–68, bibl.)

Asserts the importance of secret societies in the Independence process in Mexico and all Latin America. Notes connection between the rise of military leaders throughout the region and the Napoleonic example.

1181 Jiménez Codinach, Estela Guadalupe. México en 1821: Dominique de Pradt y el Plan de Iguala. México: Ediciones El Caballito: Univ. Iberoamericana, Depto. de Historia, 1982. 197 p.: bibl., facsims. (Col. Fragua mexicana; 52)

Uses cross-textual analysis to argue that the writings of the Abbe de Pradt, especially *Des colonies et de la révolution actuelle de l'Amerique* (1817) had a decisive impact on the articulation of the *Plan de Iguala*. Although previously recognized by scholars, this link makes the case for the connection between European revolutionary thinking and that of the Mexican Independence movement.

1182 Jiménez Codinach, Estela Guadalupe. Veracruz, almacén de plata en el Atlántico: la casa Gordon y Murphy, 1805–1824. (*Hist. Mex.*, 38:2, oct./dic. 1988, p. 325–353, bibl., tables)

Uni-dimensional look at Veracruz as a port city through the relations between the merchant house of Gordon and Murphy and the Spanish and English governments during the years prior to Independence. Mentions but does not fully discuss the relevance of capital flight from Mexico to Great Britain during the period.

1183 Kaerger, Karl. Agricultura y colonización en México en 1900. Traducción de Pedro Lewin y Gudrun Dohrmann. Introducción de Roberto Melville. Mexico: Univ. Autónoma de Chapingo: Centro de Investigaciones y Estudios Superiores en Antropología Social, 1986. 349 p.: bibl., ill.

Translation of *Ladwirtschaft und Kolonisation im Spanischen Amerika*, very important work on Mexican agriculture. Includes much detail on the growing of sisal, cacao, tobacco, coffee, vanilla, rubber, cochineal and indigo as well as grains and livestock.

1184 Konrad, Herman W. Capitalismo y trabajo en los bosques de las tierras bajas tropicales mexicanas: el caso de la industria del chicle. (*Hist. Mex.*, 36:3, enero/marzo 1987, p. 465–505, bibl., graphs, tables)

Compact examination of the impact of harvesting chicle for chewing gum on the workers and the states of Yucatán and Quin-

tana Roo. Shows that foreigners, not Mexicans or the Mexican government, determined the growth and parameters of the industry and that workers received few benefits from their labors.

1185 Krause, Corinne A. Los judíos en México: una historia con énfasis especial en el período de 1857 a 1930. Traducción, presentación y notas de Ariela Katz de Gugenheim. México: Univ. Iberoamericana, Depto. de Historia, 1987. 290, 11 p. of plates: bibl., ill.

Translation of doctoral dissertation at Univ. of Pittsburgh provides valuable look at the Jewish community from 1857 to 1930. Very helpful for scholars of Mexican banking and industrialization.

1186 LaFrance, David G. The Mexican Revolution in Puebla, 1908–1913: the Maderista movement and the failure of liberal reform. Wilmington, Del.: Scholarly Resources Books, 1989. 299 p.:

Case study of the Maderista movement in Puebla contends that Madero failed to integrate all elements of Puebla's society into his governing coalition, eventually undermining his most loyal supporters by ignoring their demands for socioeconomic change.

1187 Lamar, Quiton Curtis. A diplomatic disaster: the Mexican mission of St. Anthony Butler, 1829–1834. (*Americas/ Francisc.* 45:1, July 1988, p. 1–17, bibl.)

Author contends that Butler, Poinsett's replacement as minister to Mexico, thought he would have a better chance to buy Texas from Foreign Minister Lucas Alamán than from his successors in the Santa Anna/Gómez Farías regime. Contribution to the "what ifs" of Mexican history.

1188 Lameiras, Brigitte B. de. Peasants and entrepreneurs in the Cienega de Chapala, Michoacán, Mexico. (*Agric. Hist.*, 3:2, Spring 1989, p. 62–76, graph, map, table)

Frightening tale of how Porfirian developmental decisions resulted in the drying up of the Cienega district and its resulting inability to grow subsistence crops like corn and wheat. Recommended.

1189 Lubienski, Johann. Der maximilianeische Staat: Mexiko 1861–1867; Verfassung, Verwaltung und Ideengeschichte.

Wien: Böhlau, 1988. 161 p.: appendix, bibl., ill., index. (Forschungen zur europäischen und vergleichenden Rechtsgeschichte; 4)

Brief analysis of reign of Emperor Maximilian based primarily on Austrian archival material. Focuses on Maximilian's ideas of constitution, administration, policy towards the Church, liberation of Indians, colonization, and mining. Appendix includes facsimiles of essential documents important for further research.[M.L. Wagner]

1190 Lugo Olín, Concepción. Tendencias demográficas de Cuautitlán, siglo XIX: fuentes y técnicas para su estudio. México: Instituto Nacional de Antropología e Historia, 1990. 111 p.: bibl., ill., map. (Serie Historia. Col. científica; 218)

Recommended study of demographic history techniques uses Cuautitlán, a pueblo in Mexico state, as a case study.

1191 Maison, Hippolite and **Charles Debouchet.** La colonización francesa en Coatzacoalcos. Xalapa, Mexico: Univ. Veracruzana, 1986. 165 p. (Col. UV rescate; 21)

Interesting study of the plans for a French colony in Coatzacoalcos in 1827 includes original letters concerning the project.

1192 Martínez, Xóchitl et al. Sultepec en el siglo XIX: apuntes históricos sobre la sociedad de un distrito minero. Coordinación de Brígida von Mentz. Zinacantepec, Mexico: Colegio Mexiquense; Lomas de Santa Fe: Univ. Iberoamericana, Depto. de Historia, 1989. 120 p.: bibl.

Includes six essays on mining territory of Sultepec in Mexico state from 16th to end of 19th century. Concluding essay by Von Mentz on late 19th century is extremely valuable.

1193 Meneses Morales, Ernesto. Tendencias educativas oficiales en México. v. 1, 1821–1911, la problemática de la educación mexicana en el siglo XIX y principios del siglo XX. v. 2., 1911–1934, la problemática de la educación mexicana durante la Revolución y los primeros lustros de la época posrevolucionaria. México: Editorial Porrúa; Centro de Estudios Educativos, 1983. 2 v.: bibl., ill., index.

Most comprehensive history of Mexican education to date. Vol. 1 is a massive study of the development of education in Mexico after Independence through the end

of the Porfiriato. Chronologically organized, the text provides a wealth of information on the philosophies underlying public education policies, their implementation, and the thought of distinguished educators. Vol. 2 covers the years of the Revolution with its important educational reforms. Thorough coverage of topic based on unpublished sources. Based on extensive research, this work will remain a standard source of information on the subject for many years. For education specialist's comment, see *HLAS 51: 2664.* [A. Lavrin]

1194 Mentz, Brígida von. Empresas y empresarios alemanes en México, 1821–1945. (*Jahrb. Gesch.,* 25, 1988, p. 1–31)

Very thorough discussion of German participation in the Mexican economy on the macro and micro level from Independence to the end of World War II. During the 19th century, Germans opted first for merchant opportunities, but during the late Porfiriato, firms in both Germany and Mexico invested in industry.

1195 The Mexican and Mexican American experience in the 19th century. Edited by Jaime E. Rodríguez O. Tempe, Ariz.: Bilingual Press/Editorial Bilingüe, 1989. 128 p.: bibl., index.

Six interesting essays on Mexico and the US Southwest discuss royalists in the Independence Wars, liberals and the Church, conservative thought, the treaty of Guadalupe Hidalgo, women in the 19th century Southwest, and post-colonial Mexico.

1196 México y España durante la república restaurada. Recopilación e introducción de Antonia Pi-Suñer. México: Secretaría de Relaciones Exteriores, 1985. 256, 9 p.: bibl. (Archivo histórico diplomático mexicano: Cuarta época; 24)

Collection of documents concerning the relations between Mexico and Spain, 1868–78 includes diplomatic reports for Mexican delegation in Spain. Important contribution to a neglected aspect of a very neglected period.

1197 Mier Noriega y Guerra, José Servando Teresa de. Obras completas. v. 4, La formación de un republicano. Edición de Jaime E. Rodríguez O. México: Univ. Nacional Autónoma de México, Coordinación de Humanidades, 1988. 1 v.: (Nueva biblioteca mexicana; 97)

Contains important writings from 1820 to 1822 with an excellent historical introduction by Jaime E. Rodríguez O.

1198 Moheno, César. Las historias y los hombres de San Juan. Zamora, Mexico: Colegio de Michoacán; México: CONACYT, 1985. 187 p.: bibl., ill.

Microhistory of the farming pueblo and parish of San Juan Parangaricutiro, near Uruapan, Michoacán from preconquest days to the present. Useful for students of Michoacán, but lacks statistics and maps.

1199 Moreno Corral, Marco Arturo. Odisea 1874, o, El primer viaje internacional de científicos mexicanos. México: Secretaría de Educación Pública; Fondo de Cultura Económica; Consejo Nacional de Ciencia y Tecnología, 1986. 142 p.: bibl., ill. (La Ciencia desde México; 15)

Interesting monograph on Mexican attempts to prove itself scientifically by sending five scientists to Japan to measure the planet Venus' trips across the sun. Important contribution to history of science.

1200 Naveda Chávez-Hita, Adriana and **González Sierra, José G.** Papantla. Jalapa, Mexico: Gobierno del Estado de Veracruz, Archivo General del Estado, 1990. 175 p.: bibl., ill.(some col.) (Veracruz, imágenes de su historia; 4)

Lavishly illustrated photo history of Papantla, Veracruz includes sensational shots of El Tajín before excavation.

1201 Oliver, Lilia Victoria. Un verano mortal: análisis demográfico y social de una epidemia de cólera; Guadalajara, 1833. Guadalajara, Mexico: Gobierno de Jalisco, Secretaría General, Unidad Editorial, 1986. 223 p.: bibl., ill. (Col. Historia: Serie Documentos e investigación; 22)

Study brimming with data on the cholera epidemic of 1833 in Guadalajara concludes unsurprisingly that the working class and the poor Indians were the hardest hit. Good beginning for a serious study of the epidemic nationwide.

1202 Ortiz Escamilla, Juan. El pronunciamiento federalista de Gordiano Guzmán, 1837–1842. (*Hist. Mex.*, 38:2, oct./dic. 1988, p. 241–282, bibl.)

Description of significant revolt in Michoacán in favor of federalism and the repeal of new taxes. While Mexico City was distracted with the Pastry War, the insurgents held sway, but once the larger struggle was concluded, General Paredes managed to defeat the rebels. Lacks maps and, more importantly, sociological analysis.

1203 Paternalismo y economía moral en las haciendas mexicanas del porfiriato. Edited by Herbert J. Nickel. Puebla, Mexico: Comisión Puebla, Gobierno del Estado; México: Univ. Iberoamericana, Depto. de Historia, 1989. 217 p.: bibl., ill.

Collaboration between the Univ. Iberoamericana and the Univ. de Bayreuth offers five essays on the nature of estate agriculture during the Porfiriato. Application of the theories of Scott and Thompson to the Latin American hacienda is particularly interesting. Emphasizes the difference in labor relations between regions. Good companion to Kaerger (see item **1183**).

1204 Penny, William T. Zaguán abierto al México republicano, 1820–1830. Traducción e introducción de Juan Antonio Ortega y Medina. México: Univ. Nacional Autónoma de México, 1987. 216 p., 32 p. of plates: bibl., ill. (Serie Historia moderna y contemporánea; 18)

Spanish translation of Penny's *A sketch of the customs and society of Mexico* . . . with very interesting introductory comments on travel literature and foreigners in Mexico during that period.

The political plans of Mexico. See *HLAS 51:3476*.

1205 Priego Ramírez, Patricia and **José Antonio Rodríguez.** La manera en que fuimos: fotografía y sociedad en Querétaro, 1840–1930. Querétaro, México: Dirección de Patrimonio Cultural, Gobierno del Estado de Querétaro, 1989. 199 p.: bibl., ills. (Col. Fotografía queretana)

Not simply a collection of photos, this survey studies the profession of photography in Querétaro as well. Recommended.

1206 Puebla, de la colonia a la revolución: estudios de historia regional. Puebla, Mexico: Centro de Investigaciones Históricas y Sociales, Instituto de Ciencias de la Univ. Autónoma de Puebla, 1987. 391 p.: bibl., ill.

Ten valuable and sophisticated essays focus on demographic and economic issues in the state from 1650–1913. Includes valuable essays by Cuenya on Poblano population from 1650–1850, Contreras Cruz on the growth of the city, and La France on Maderismo. Most papers were presented at the conference of the Latin American Studies Association (11th, México, 1983).

1207 Ramos, J.L. et al. El indio en la prensa nacional mexicana del siglo XIX: catálogo de noticias. Coordinación de Teresa Rojas Rabiela. México: SEP, 1987. 3 v. (Cuadernos de la Casa Chata; 137–139)

Compendium of articles on Indians from major and minor newspapers throughout Mexico, 1806–99. Vol. 1 covers nine newspapers; Vol. 2 focuses on *El Monitor Republicano*; and vol. 3 covers *El Universal* and also includes an index to the set. Very useful for understanding what urban Mexicans thought about Indians in other parts of the country.

1208 Ramos-Escandón, Carmen. Mujeres trabajadoras en el México porfiriano: género e ideología del trabajo femenino, 1876–1911. (*Rev. Eur.*, 48, junio 1990, p. 27–44, tables)

Shows that women entered industrial labor force more slowly than previously thought. The transition from artesanal work to mechanized activity gave substantial advantages to men, particularly in the textile and tobacco industries studied.

1209 Reséndiz Balderas, José et al. Monterrey, Nuevo León, el Noreste: siete estudios históricos. Coordinación de Mario Cerutti. Monterrey, México: Facultad de Filosofía y Letras, Univ. Autónoma de Nuevo León, 1987. 275 p.: bibl.

Seven valuable essays by various authors concerning the economic history of Nuevo León from 1821–1935. Includes material on the citrus industry, factory production, the relationship with North American capitalism, relations with the Lipanes (Indians of the Apache tribe), and on the military history of the region.

1210 Río, Ignacio del. Manuel Calero y Esteban Maqueo Castellanos: dos opiniones sobre la solución histórica del porfirismo. (*Estud. Hist. Mod. Contemp. Méx.*, 10, 1986, p. 137–154)

Brief discussion of how two intellectuals understood problems and contradictions for Mexico after Díaz. In studying Calero and Maqueo, author highlights the "horrible" choices awaiting those who saw stability as inevitably personified by one man and "democracy" as the threatening possibility that illiterate Indians might vote.

1211 Riot, rebellion, and revolution: rural social conflict in Mexico. Edited by Friedrich Katz. Princeton, N.J.: Princeton Univ. Press, 1988. 594 p.: bibl., index.

Recommended collection of 18 essays by Mexican, European, and US historians focuses on rural uprisings throughout Mexico. Includes six on the colonial period, six on the Revolution and four on the republic. Also contains interesting thematic piece by Coatsworth comparing Mexico with the rest of Latin America.

Rivas Mata, Emma; María Esther Jasso Sáenz; and **Gabriela Sánchez Vences.** Catálogo de la Colección Fondo reservado de la Biblioteca Manuel Orozco y Berra. See item **79.**

1212 Rodríguez O., Jaime E. The conflict between Church and State in early Republican Mexico. (*New World*, 2:1/2, 1987, p. 93–112)

Concise summary of relationship between Church and State from 1821–56 includes excellent account of struggle over Mexico's retention of the *patronato* after Independence.

1213 Romero, Héctor Manuel. Historia del transporte en la Ciudad de México: de la trajinera al metro. México: Secretaría General de Desarrollo Social, 1987. 157 p.: bibl., ill.

Fun survey of modes of transportation from precolumbian times to the present filled with interesting pictures and photographs. Recommended for social historians.

1214 Romero de Solís, José Miguel. Apostasía episcopal en Tamaulipas, 1896. (*Hist. Mex.*, 37:2, oct./dic. 1987, p. 239–282, bibl.)

Strange tale of supposed furor in Mexican Church over the resignation of profligate bishop of Tamaulipas in 1896. Interesting episode but few documents on the resulting "scandal."

1215 Sánchez Díaz, Gerardo; José Alfredo Uribe Salas; and José Napoleón Guzmán Avila. Michoacán: tres décadas de historia militar. (*Estud. Hist. Mod. Contemp. Méx.*, 11, 1988, p. 85–121)

Significant article on the military in Michoacán describes recruitment of both regular army and state militia, and the behavior of the state in several key historical episodes including the war with the US.

1216 Sánchez Díaz, Gerardo. El suroeste de Michoacán: economía y sociedad, 1852–1910. Morelia, Mexico: Univ. Michoacana de San Nicolás de Hidalgo, Instituto de Investigaciones Históricas; Asociación de Historiadores Latinoamericanos y del Caribe, 1988. 366 p., 29 leaves of plates: bibl., ill., maps. (Col. Historia nuestra; 8)

Complete study of the effects of the Reform laws on land holding and agricultural production in Michoacán. Essential for researchers of the economy during the Porfiriato. Needs more maps.

1217 Santoni, Pedro. A fear of the people: the civic militia of Mexico in 1845. (*HAHR*, 68:2, May 1988, p. 270–288)

Provides insights into political maneuvering at a critical time in the Mexican Republic by examination of the reluctance to establish a civilian military force.

1218 Seminario sobre la Formación del Capitalismo en México, 4th, Jalapa, Mexico, 1985. Los lugares y los tiempos: ensayos sobre las estructuras regionales del siglo XIX en México. Coordinación de Alejandra García Quintanilla y Abel Juárez. Monterrey, Mexico: Consejo Mexicano de Ciencias Sociales; Univ. Autónoma de Nuevo León; Jalapa, Mexico: Univ. Veracruzana; México: Editorial Nuestro Tiempo, 1989. 283 p.: bibl., ill. (Col. Desarrollo)

Begins with important essay by Mario Cerutti on recent contributions to regional history, 1850–1910. Continues with articles on landholding in Jalisco, Yucatán, Puebla, Jalapa, Nuevo León, and Tlaxcala, and concludes with pieces on the sugar industry in Morelos, pre-revolutionary Chihuahua, and the Yaqui in the Mexican Revolution.

1219 Sims, Harold. The expulsion of Mexico's Spaniards, 1821–1836. Pittsburgh, Pa.: Univ. of Pittsburgh Press, 1990. 277 p.: bibl., index. (Pitt Latin American series)

Argues that the various expulsions totalling approximately three-quarters of the Spanish community adversely affected the Mexican economy during the first 15 years after Independence. Winner of the MACLAS prize for best book of 1990.

1220 Stevens, Donald Fithian. Origins of instability in early republican Mexico. Durham: Duke Univ. Press, 1991. 184 p.: bibl., index.

Fascinating use of computer analysis of available biographical and other data to determine the reasons for Mexico's legendary instability from 1821–67. Finds that conflict was based on the disjuncture between liberal thought and traditional economic and social patterns. Recommended. Winner of the 1992 MACLAS prize for best book of 1991.

1221 Suárez Argüello, Ana Rosa. La leyenda de la riqueza de Sonora según los viajeros franceses. (*in* Simposio de Historia y Antropología de Sonora, 13th, Hermosillo, Mexico, 1989. Memoria. Coordinación de Juan Manuel Romero Gil. Hermosillo, Mexico: Instituto de Investigaciones Históricas de la Univ. de Sonora, 1989, v. 1, p. 259–272)

Argues that books written by French travelers in Sonora helped convince Napoleon III to establish an empire in Mexico. Although the books do exist, author presents no evidence of their impact in France.

1222 Talavera Ibarra, Pedro Leonardo. Eduardo Ruiz, o, El fausto de la Ciudad del Progreso. Morelia, Mexico: Univ. Michoacana de San Nicolás de Hidalgo, Coordinación de la Investigación Científica, 1985. 272 p.: bibl., ill., ports. (Col. Pluma decimonónica; 2)

Semibiography of a leading intellectual of the Porfiriato contains complete chronology, formidable bibliography, and facsimiles.

1223 Thomson, Guy P.C. Traditional and modern manufacturing in Mexico, 1821–1850. (*in* América Latina en la época de Simón Bolívar. Edición de Reinhard Liehr. Berlin: Colloquium Verlag, 1989, p. 55–85, tables)

Important contribution to the study of Mexican industrialization. Argues that warfare helped Mexican manfacturing because it kept foreign goods away, that cotton textiles did better than most believe, and that problems arose when manufacturers sought to control all stages of production rather than content themselves with mere profits. Recommended.

1224 Urbach, Monica. Mexico zwischen Republik und Monarchie: Europas Kampf um Mexico vom Interventionskrieg 1861 bis zum Ende des Maximilianischen Kaiserreiches 1867 in der Beurteilung der deutschen Presse, unter besonderer Berücksichtigung der "Allgemeinen Zeitung." Frankfurt; New York: P. Lang, 1987. 227 p., 1 leaf of plates: appendix, bibl. (Europäische Hochschulschriften: Reihe III, Geschichte und ihre Hilfswissenschaften, 0531–7320; 328)

Studies contemporary coverage by German newspapers of foreign intervention in Mexico. Appendix includes reprints of selected documents and statistical analysis of all reports on Mexico that appeared in *Allgemeine Zeitung.* [M.L. Wagner]

1225 Urías Horcasitas, Beatriz. Conciencia regional y poder central: ensayo sobre el pensamiento separatista yucateco en la primera mitad del siglo diecinueve. (*Estud. Hist. Mod. Contemp. Méx.*, 11, 1988, p. 59–83)

Shows how Yucatecan political thinkers saw separatism as an extension of liberal thought, but stopped far short of wanting to extend democracy to the Indians of their region.

1226 Valdés Lakowsky, Vera. Vinculaciones sino-mexicanas: albores y testimonios, 1874–1899. México: UNAM, Colegio de Historia, Facultad de Filosofía y Letras, 1981. 279 p.: appendices, bibl., ill. (Seminarios)

Discusses Chinese-Mexican relations up to 1899 supported by compilation of documents on the same theme and lengthy chronological comparisons. Concludes that even though both Ch'ing dynasty and Porfiriato sought recognition of their modernity through better relations, a failure to follow through negated their efforts.

1227 Van Young, Eric. Agustín Marroquín: the sociopath as rebel. (*in* The human tradition in Latin America. Edited by Judith Ewell and William H. Beezley. Wilmington, Delaware: Scholarly Resources, 1989, p. 17–38, bibl.)

Arresting example of how pathology became combined with political action in Hidalgo rebellion of 1810–11. Van Young shows that, far from Hobsbawm's social bandit, Marroquín committed "revolutionary" and other excesses for his own pleasure and financial gain.

1228 Van Young, Eric. The raw and the cooked: elite and popular ideology in Mexico, 1800–1821. (*in* The middle period in Latin America: values and attitudes in the 17th-19th centuries. Edited by Mark D. Szuchman. Boulder, Colo.: Lynne Rienner Publishers, 1989, p. 75–102)

Distinguishes between elite creole ideology concerning State-building after Independence and popular beliefs in messianism, particularly concerning the figures of Fernando VII and Ignacio Allende. Argues that for Indians, the community, not the State, was the viable entity. Interesting theoretical discussion.

1229 Vaughn, Mary Kay. Primary education and literacy in nineteenth-century Mexico: research trends, 1968–1988. (*LARR*, 25:1, 1990, p. 31–66)

Makes pathbreaking case for the centrality of education in understanding the history of society and culture in Mexico, examined in terms of the interaction between State, society, and economy. Bibliographical examples are weakest on the economy. Highly recommended.

1230 Vázquez, Josefina Zoraida. Iglesia, ejército y centralismo. (*Hist. Mex.*, 39:1, julio/sept. 1989, p. 205–234, bibl.)

Rambling discussion of the role of the Church in politics under federalism and centralism, concludes that historians place too much importance on role of the Church in the establishment of centralism and that the religious issue was used simply to rally popular support.

1231 Vázquez, Josefina Zoraida. Santa Anna y el reconocimiento de Texas. (*Hist. Mex.*, 36:3, enero/marzo 1987, p. 553–562, bibl.)

Introduces documents from Public Records Office showing British interest in obtaining Mexican recognition of Texas' independence. Just when Santa Anna indicated willingness to discuss the matter, however, Texas joined the US, thus precipitating the very crisis Britain had hoped to avoid.

1232 **Victoria, Guadalupe.** Guadalupe Victoria: correspondencia diplomática. Introducción de Hira de Gortari Rabiela. México: Secretaría de Relaciones Exteriores, 1986. 314 p. (Archivo histórico diplomático mexicano: Cuarta época, 26)

Significant group of documents shows Guadalupe Victoria in a new light—as a diplomat who worked with Lucas Alamán to try to negotiate a Spanish withdrawal from San Juan de Ulúa. Well-written introduction by Hira de Gortari Rabiela places incident in proper context.

1233 **Vos, Jan de.** Oro verde: la conquista de la Selva Lacandona por los madereros tabasqueños, 1822–1949. Villahermosa, Mexico: Gobierno del Estado de Tabasco, Instituto de Cultura de Tabasco; México: Fondo de Cultura Económica, 1988. 330 p., 16 p. of plates: bibl., ill. (Sección de obras de historia)

Excellent account of the history of the Lacandon mahogany forest and its ultimate "conquest" by lumbermen and woodcutters from Tabasco. Valuable for those interested in the region, global ecology, and natural resources. Important contribution.

Zorrilla, Luis G. Los casos de México en el arbitraje internacional. See *HLAS 51:4269.*

REVOLUTION AND POST-REVOLUTION

1234 **Abascal, Salvador.** Tomás Garrido Canabal: sin Dios, sin curas, sin iglesias, 1919–1935. México: Editorial Tradición, 1987. 279 p., 4 p. of plates: bibl., ill.

Predictably unflattering political portrait of revolutionary figure best known for his anti-clerical activities as governor of Tabasco. Narrative is long on anecdotes and short on footnotes.

1235 **Abramson, Pierre-Luc.** Cléricalisme et anticléricalisme dans le Méxique post-révoluionnaire, 1920–1940. (*Ibérica*, 3, 1981, p. 359–369)

Article asserts that the struggle between pro- and anti-clerical forces in the two decades immediately following the Mexican Revolution was essentially political rather than religious. The forces of the right used the emotional clerical issue to mount a counterrevolutionary attack on the new government. The government itself, in attacking the Roman Catholic Church, was seeking the stabilization of the new regime and the subordination, rather than the elimination, of the Church in Mexico.

1236 **Aguilar Camín, Héctor.** La revolución que vino del Norte. (*Rev. Univ./ Tabasco*, 9, sept. 1985, p. 18–40, photos)

Excellent general discussion in which author demonstrates that the unique experience of the Sonorans gave them a "northern viewpoint" different from that of the South and Center in regard to key issues such as the agrarian question, the working class, military affairs, state finances, and government involvement in the economy. Originally presented as a symposium paper in 1977.

1237 **Altamirano, Graziella** *et al.* —Y nos fuimos a la Revolución. Coordinación de Eugenia Meyer. México: Museo Nacional de la Revolución: Depto. del Distrito Federal, Instituto de Investigaciones Dr. José María Luis Mora, 1987. 109 p.: bibl., ill.

Brief but solid essay covers 1867–1917. Designed for the general reader, it includes numerous illustrations and an excellent ten-page chronology.

1238 **Anderle, Ádám** and **Monika Kozári.** A monarchia utolsó követe: Kánya Kálmán Mexikóban, 1914–1919 [El último embajador de la Monarquía austro-húngara: Kálmán Kánya en México entre 1914–1919]. Szeged, Hungary: JADE, 1990. 120 p.

Esboza la carrera política del distinguido diplomático húngaro, K. Kánya, el último Embajador austro-húngaro en México (1914–19). Publica una treintena de textos salvados de los archivos de Viena, Ciudad de México y la prensa mexicana contemporánea. La importancia del volumen es presentar una visión centroeuropea, de las postrimerías del imperio habsburgo, de la Revolución Mexicana y de las relaciones políticas entre los EE.UU. y la América Latina durante los años de la Primera Guerra Mundial. [L. Scholz]

1239 **Archivo de Historia Oral (Mexico).** Catálogo. v. 1–2. Coordinación de Salvador Rueda Smithers. Jiquilpan, Mexico: Archivo de Historia Oral, Centro de Estudios de

la Revolución Mexicana Lázaro Cárdenas, 1986–87. 2 v.

Guide to approximately 100 oral history interviews conducted with older residents of Jiquilpan, Michoacán. They cover the Porfiriato, the Mexican Revolution, and the post-revolutionary period, emphasizing such themes as daily life, work, commerce, political life, religion, the system of justice, and basic historical events from the political, economic and social perspective of the town.

1240 Aspectos del movimiento obrero en Oaxaca: fuentes. Recopilación de Francisco José Ruiz Cervantes y Anselmo Arellanes Meixueiro. Oaxaca, Mexico: Gobierno del Estado, Casa de la Cultura Oaxaqueña, 1987. 80 p.: facsim. (Col. Agua quemada)

Brief collection of documents relating to labor activities in the late 1920s.

1241 Avila Carrillo, Enrique et al. Historia del México contemporáneo. México: Ediciones Quinto Sol, 1985. 320 p.: bibl.

Analysis of the Mexican revolutionary period from 1910 through the end of the Maximato focuses on the struggle between social and economic groups. Based largely on secondary sources.

1242 Avila Palafóx, Ricardo. ¿Revolución en el Estado de México? México: Instituto Nacional de Antropología e Historia: Gobierno del Estado de México, 1988. 300 p.: bibl., ill., maps. (Serie Historia. Col. Divulgación)

Useful survey of state of Mexico 1900–20 uses statistical information on demography, agriculture and political culture to provide an accurate picture of that region. Author posits that the State of Mexico does not fit stereotyped models of pre-revolutionary Mexico. [A. Lavrin]

1243 Avila Ramírez, Margarita et al.

Manual de historia del México contemporáneo, 1917–1940. Coordinación de Alejandra Lajous. México: Instituto de Investigaciones Históricas, UNAM, 1988. 357 p.: bibl., ill.

Useful reference work organized around presidential administrations. Chap. 1 reviews the Constitution of 1917, while each of the following chapters is devoted to a president. Each chapter features a narrative overview of the period, a detailed chronology, a brief annotated bibliography, quotations from leading figures, and numerous (though uncaptioned) photographs.

1244 Backal, Alicia Gojman de. La acción revolucionaria mexicanista y el fascismo en México: los Dorados. (*Jahrb. Gesch.*, 25, 1988, p. 291–302)

Examination of an extreme right-wing group, known as the ARM or "Gold Shirts," noted for anti-semitism, anti-communism, and ultra-nationalism. Traces history of ARM from its foundation in 1933 to the death of its principal leader, Nicolás Rodríguez, in 1940. Movement ultimately failed because of the international situation and the popular support enjoyed by Cárdenas.

Baldridge, Donald Carl. Mexican petroleum and United States-Mexican relations, 1919–1923. See *HLAS 51:4216*.

1245 Baldwin, Deborah J. Diplomacia cultural: escuelas misionales protestantes en México. (*Hist. Mex.*, 36:2, oct./dic. 1986, p. 287–322, bibl.)

Analysis of the influence of Protestant missionary activity, especially in education, on political developments in the military phase of the Revolution. Since the Protestants were especially active in the North, most of the attention is devoted to their relationship with Carranza. The Revolution presented new opportunities for evangelizing, and the Protestant missionaries attempted to adjust to religious restrictions of the Constitution of 1917 rather than oppose them.

1246 Baldwin, Deborah J. Protestants and the Mexican Revolution: missionaries, ministers, and social change. Urbana: Univ. of Illinois Press, 1990. 203 p.:

Study of Protestantism and missionary activity as a phase of the Revolution rather than as denominational history. Author distinguishes between different roles of Protestant missionaries in Mexico versus Protestant ministers of Mexican nationality. Both groups almost unanimously supported the Revolution, particularly Carranza, although his strong nationalism served to widen the gap between the foreign missionaries and the Mexican ministers.

1247 Barragán Rodríguez, Juan. Historia del ejército y de la revolución constitucionalista. v. 1–2. Ed. facsim. Mexico: Comisión Nacional para las Celebraciones del 175 Aniversario de la Independencia Nacional y 75 Aniversario de la Revolución Mexicana, 1985. 2 v.: ill., index, ports. (Biblioteca de obras fundamentales de la Independencia y la Revolución)

Reprint of work first published in 1946. See *HLAS 12:2009.*

1248 Bartra, Armando. Los herederos de Zapata: movimientos campesinos posrevolucionarios en México, 1920–1980. México: Ediciones Era, 1985. 164 p.: (Col. Problemas de México)

Examines the evolution of State-directed agrarianism and the various responses to it by peasants movements. Argues against the view of a traditional peasantry meekly following the directions of the State.

1249 Bastian, Jean Pierre. El paradigma de 1789: sociedades de ideas y Revolución Mexicana. (*Hist. Mex.,* 38:1, julio/sept. 1988, p. 79–110, bibl.)

Good study of the intellectual background of the Mexican Revolution focuses on Masonic Lodges and the Porfiriato. Hypothesizes that political, social and religious organizations in Mexico before 1919 expressed a growing democratic movement parallel to that of France before 1789. [E.B. Couturier]

1250 Becker, Marjorie. Black and white and color: cardenismo and the search for a campesino ideology. (*Comp. Stud. Soc. Hist.,* 29:3, July 1987, p. 453–465)

Explores the differences in ideology between Michoacán cardenistas in state and national government and a group of Tarascan Indians living in the region of Lake Pátzcuaro. As the cardenistas came to understand the ideological concerns of the Indians, they were able to devise means of binding these rural people to the centralizing Mexican State. In this way, according to the author, the cardenistas replicated the system of social control formerly imposed by the old elite.

1251 Brannon, Jeffery and Eric N. Baklanoff. Agrarian reform & public enterprise in Mexico: the political economy of Yucatán's henequen industry. Foreword by Edward H. Moseley. Tuscaloosa, Ala.: Univ. of Alabama Press, 1987. 237 p.: bibl., ill., index, maps, tables.

Unflattering examination of the central government's efforts to promote, or at least preserve, the Yucatán's traditional henequen industry. While well-intentioned in its actions, the government ignored world market conditions, emphasized political rather than economic considerations, heavily subsidied the corrupt and inefficient ejidal sector, and promoted corruption.

1252 Breceda, Alfredo. México revolucionario. v. 2. Ed. facsimilar. México: Comisión Nacional para las Celebraciones del 175 Aniversario de la Independencia Nacional y 75 Aniversario de la Revolución Mexicana, 1985. 1 v. (La Biblioteca de obras fundamentales de la Independencia y la Revolución)

Reprint of a memoir, first published in 1941, of a major participant in the Carranza faction of the Mexican Revolution. Vol. 2 focuses on the year 1913.

1253 Cabrera Parra, José. Díaz Ordaz y el '68. México: Editorial Grijalbo, 1982. 195 p.

Short biographical study by a journalist of President Gustavo Díaz Ordáz focuses on his personality and governing style. Includes news reports of the 1968 student movement reprinted from *Excelsior.*

1254 Camp, Roderic Ai. *Camarillas* in Mexican politics: the case of the Salinas cabinet. (*Mex. Stud.,* 6:1, Winter 1990, p. 85–107)

Examination of the role played by *camarillas* (political cliques), "the cement of the Mexican political system." Author examines historical dimensions of contemporary *Camarillas,* identifying three different generations of the post-revolutionary political class. Most contemporary *camarillas* extend back to those of either Miguel Alemán or Lázaro Cárdenas. Salinas is unusual in that he has historical links to both of these *camarillas.*

1255 Candelas Villalba, Sergio. La Batalla de Zacatecas. Zacatecas, Mexico: Gobierno del Estado de Zacatecas, 1989. 160 p.: bibl., ill.

Solid narrative (with extensive illustrations) of the key Battle of Zacatecas in June 1914 which led to the overthrow of the Huerta regime. Concluding section contains biographies of principal participants. Publication commemorates the 75th anniversary of battle.

1256 Casasola, Agustín Víctor. Jefes, héroes y caudillos. Texto de Flora Lara Klahr. Selección y edición de Pablo Ortiz Monasterio. México: Fondo de Cultura Económica, 1986. 109 p.: ill. (Col. Río de luz)

Another excellent collection of photographs from INAH's Archivo Casasola, covering 1903–24. Accompanying text deals with history of photography and the contributions of the Casasolas, rather than with the subjects of the photos.

1257 Castillo, José R. del. Historia de la revolución social de México. México: Instituto Nacional de Antropología e Historia, 1985. 370 p.: facsims., indexes. (Col. Biblioteca del INAH)

Facsimile ed. of the original 1915 work included new indexes. Covers the last years of the Porfiriato through the Madero movement and the fall of Díaz. Unfortunately no information is provided about the author or the original circumstances of publication.

1258 Chen, Zhiyun. The 1910–1917 Mexican Revolution and the 1911 Chinese Revolution: a comparative study. (in Modernization and revolution in Mexico: a comparative approach. Edited by Omar Martínez Legorreta. Tokyo: The United Nations University, 1989, p. 138–150)

Three-part analysis of similarities and differences in social changes brought about by these two great revolutions examines: 1) Mexico and China on the eve of their revolutions; 2) the differing characteristics of these two revolutions; and 3) the influence of the revolutions on the modernization processes of both countries. Author is Senior Research Fellow of China's Institute of Latin American Studies and specializes in Mexico. [Mao Xianglin]

1259 Ciclo de Conferencias México: Revolución y Modernidad, *México, 1987.* Memoria. México: Partido Revolucionario Institucional, ICAP, 1987. 371 p.

Papers by public figures and leading academics from a conference organized by the PRI in 1987. Includes sections on historical roots and modernization, ideological pluralism, economics and society, international considerations, and reflections on the future.

1260 50 años de lucha obrera: historia documental. v. 1–10. México: Partido Revolucionario Institucional, Instituto de Capacitación Política, 1986. 10 v.

Documentary history of the Confederación de Trabajadores de México (CTM) focuses on national councils and meetings (1936–86). Vol. 1 contains short (6 p.) introduction to set, but individual volumes lack introductions or other background information. Arranged chronologically by year.

1261 La clase obrera en la historia de México. v. 7, En el interinato de Adolfo de la Huerta y el gobierno de Alvaro Obregón, 1920–1924 [de] Jaime Tamayo. Coordinación de Pablo González Casanova. México: Siglo Veintiuno Editores: Instituto de Investigaciones Sociales de la UNAM, 1987. 302 p.: bibl., ill.

Good account of labor organizations and labor-State relations during a key period of consolidation for both labor and government. This series organized around presidential administrations emphasizes political and institutional developments rather than social and economic aspects of working-class evolution. For other volumes see *HLAS 50:1228, HLAS 48:2128, HLAS 46:2185* and *HLAS 44:1844.*

1262 Collado, María del Carmen. La burguesía mexicana: el emporio Braniff y su participación política, 1865–1920. México: Siglo Veintiuno Editores, 1987. 174 p.: bibl., ill. (Sociología y política)

Study of the political and social activities of the Braniff family which became a major North American investor in Porfirian Mexico. Combines the history of the Braniff family with an analysis of Mexican history from 1865–1920. Author concludes that Thomas Braniff became an influential member of the Mexican bourgeoisie upon which the Díaz regime depended.

1263 Conferencia Nacional de Análisis Ideológico sobre la Revolución Mexicana, 1910–1985, *México, 1985.* Memoria. México: Comité Ejecutivo Nacional del PRI, 1985. 191 p.: ill., ports.

Collection of 16 essays, most by PRI officials, from a 1985 conference sponsored by the PRI's Executive Committee. Topics include: the fight for national sovereignty and democracy in Mexico; economic and social development; and cultural and political transformation. Highly nationalistic, pro-government assessment of the Revolution and the PRI.

1264 Delpar, Helen. Frank Tannenbaum: the making of a Mexicanist, 1914–1933. (*Americas/Franuisc.*, 45:2, Oct. 1988, p. 153–171, bibl.)

Examination of the career of the journalist/scholar whose writings made him one of the most important interpreters of the Revolution in its early decades.

1265 Durand Ponte, Víctor Manuel. La ruptura de la nación: historia del movimiento obrero mexicano desde 1938 hasta 1952. México: Univ. Nacional Autónoma de México, Instituto de Investigaciones Sociales, 1986. 214 p.: bibl.

Concentrates heavily on the effect that the cardenista period, with its ideology and symbolism, had on subsequent developments in the interaction between the Mexican State and the labor movement.

1266 Echeverría V., Pedro. La política en Yucatán en el siglo XX, 1900–1964. Mérida, Mexico: Maldonado Editores, 1985. 167 p.: bibl. (Col. Historia y sociedad; 1)

Brief survey of Yucatecan politics from the Porfiriato to 1964 in the context of national and world events. Topics include callismo and cardenismo in Yucatán, labor disputes, and union activities. Key theme is the subordination of local politics to the national government.

1267 Entrena Durán, Francisco. Los levantamientos cristeros en México: entre la "Guerra Santa" y la reivindicación agrarista. (*Rev. Indias*, 46:178, julio/dic. 1986, p. 593–607, bibl.)

Analysis of the economic and religious-symbolic roots of the Cristero Rebellion. According to the author, it was an expression of the antagonism between the rural people with their traditional religion and the new rationalistic and aggressive State.

1268 Fabela, Isidro. Historia diplomática de la Revolución Mexicana. Ed. facsimilar. Mexico: Comisión Nacional para las Celebraciones del 175 Aniversario de la Independencia Nacional y 75 Aniversario de la Revolución Mexicana, 1985. 2 v.: (La Biblioteca de obras fundamentales de la Independencia y la Revolución)

Reprint of 2 vol. work published in 1958–59. See *HLAS 22:3021* and *HLAS 24:3891*.

1269 Falcón, Romana. Esplendor y ocaso de los caciques militares: San Luis Potosí en la Revolución Mexicana. (*Mex. Stud.*, 4:2, Summer 1988, p. 265–293)

Author traces the political fortunes of the regional military leaders of San Luis Potosí from the dispersion of power between 1910–25 through the "golden age" of *cacicazgo* in the 1920s to the recentralization of power in the late 1930s. As might be expected, Saturnino Cedillo figures prominently in the narrative. See also *HLAS 50: 1238* for the author's *Revolución y caciquismo: San Luis Potosí, 1910–1938.*

1270 Falcón, Romana; Soledad García Morales; and María Eugenia Terrones. La semilla en el surco: Adalberto Tejeda y el radicalismo en Veracruz, 1883–1960. México: Colegio de México, Centro de Estudios Históricos; Jalapa: Gobierno del Estado de Veracruz, 1986. 411 p., 16 p. of plates: bibl., ill., index, ports.

Well-researched and well-written biography of Governor Adalberto Tejeda of Veracruz interweaves his life with the history of radical movements in the state. Tejeda is seen as a major figure linking national postrevolutionary governments and the various social and political groupings of Veracruz.

1271 Folgarait, Leonard. So far from Heaven: David Alfaro Siqueiros' "The March of Humanity" and Mexican revolutionary politics. Cambridge; New York: Cambridge University Press, 1987. 140 p., 33 p. of plates: bibl., ill., index. (Cambridge Iberian and Latin American studies)

Uses a deconstructionist approach to link the largest work by the last of the big three Mexican muralists with the political reality of PRI-led Mexico. For art historian's comment, see *HLAS 50:265.*

1272 French, William E. Mining and the State in twentieth-century Mexico. (*J. West*, 27:4, Oct. 1988, p. 85–93, ill.)

After an extensive discussion of the "enclave" nature of mining development during the Porfiriato, author surveys fluctuations in government policy toward the industry to the 1970s. The Revolution affected mining operations but did not reduce foreign domination of the industry, which actually increased during 1920s. Cárdenas increased government control of mining but resisted pressures for its nationalization. "Mexicanization" of mining finally took place in 1960s as a result of government fiscal incentives.

1273 Gates, Marilyn. Institutionalizing dependency: the impact of two decades of planned agricultural modernization on peasants in the Mexican State of Campeche. (*J. Dev. Areas*, 22:3, April 1988, p. 293–320)

Highly negative evaluation of three different models of State intervention in ejidal agriculture: frontier colonization, small irrigation projects, and large-scale resettlement. While the models differ greatly in concept and operation, they have several undesirable features in common: 1) disproportionate costs; 2) damage to fragile tropical ecosystems; and 3) further marginalization of the peasant. Covers mid-1960s to mid-1980s.

1274 Gilderhus, Mark T. Many Mexicos: tradition and innovation in the recent historiography. (*LARR*, 22:1, 1987, p. 204–213)

Reviews 11 books published between 1981–84 that cover Mexico's history from 1910–40. New themes discussed are relationships between foreign and local elites, the importance of feminist activities, and the regional and local development of the Mexican Revolution. [A. Lavrin]

1275 González Navarro, Moisés. El maderismo y la revolución agraria. (*Hist. Mex.*, 37:1, julio/sept. 1987, p. 5–27, bibl., table)

Analysis of the chaotic situation surrounding agrarian reform efforts during the Madero Administration. Madero tackled a number of different problems (agrarian credit, colonization, irrigation, the status of the ejido) but was hindered by congressional opposition, military resistance, and rural rebellions.

1276 González Salas, Carlos. Acercamiento a la historia del movimiento obrero en Tampico, 1887–1983. Ciudad Victoria, México: Univ. Autónoma de Tamaulipas, Instituto de Investigaciones Históricas, 1987. 214 p., 16 leaves of plates: bibl., ill.

Four-part work includes: 1) general introductory essay which reviews the labor movement in Tampico, 1887–1983; 2) memoirs of Ricardo Treviño Valustri, a partici-

pant in the labor movement who had been affiliated with the Magonista movement in San Antonio, Texas, joined the Casa del Obrero Mundial in 1916 or 1917 in Tampico, and later became a leader of the CROM; 3) lengthy discussion of rural and urban anarchism in Tampico; and 4) much shorter section discussing labor struggles of oil workers. Documents of interest are scattered throughout and are also included in a short appendix.

1277 González y González, Luis. La ronda de las generaciones: los protagonistas de la Reforma y la Revolución Mexicana. Mexico: SEP Cultura, 1984. 131 p. (Foro 2000)

Generational profile of 900 Mexican political and intellectual leaders from La Reforma to the Revolution. Examines origins, educational background, formative influences, political and cultural activities, and significance of each generation.

1278 Gracia García Cumplido, Guadalupe. Autobiografía, narraciones, documentos de y por el Dr. Guadalupe Gracia García Cumplido. Recopilación de Estela Gracia García Martínez. Mexico: Editores Mexicanos Unidos, 1982. 481 p.: ill., ports.

Memoir and papers of a physician involved in the Mexican Revolution provides valuable information on development of military's medical facilities during that conflict.

1279 Grayson, George W. Oil and Mexican foreign policy. Pittsburgh, Pa.: Univ. of Pittsburgh Press, 1988. 207 p.: bibl., ill., index, tables. (Pitt Latin American series)

Study of changes in Mexican foreign policy between 1977–87 as a function of the changing oil situation. Favorable oil prices in the late 1970s and early 1980s permitted Mexico to play an activist role as a regional leader. Declining oil prices after 1981 forced a retreat from activism and a more pragmatic foreign policy. For comments by international relations specialist see *HLAS 51:4232*.

1280 Guerrero Tarquín, Alfredo. Memorias de un agrarista. v. 1–2. México: Instituto Nacional de Antropología e Historia, 1987. 2 v.: ill., ports. (Serie Testimonios. Col. Divulgación.)

Memoirs of an agrarian leader in Guanajuato state covers 1913–38 and focuses on Guanajuato's Sierra Gorda. Begins with author's earliest recollections of the Revolution, continues with his active involvement in the agrarian movement at the age of 15, and includes both his active part in the war against the Cristeros and his passionate involvement with Cardenismo.

1281 Guevara Niebla, Gilberto. La democracia en la calle: crónica del movimiento estudiantil mexicano. México: Siglo Veintiuno Editores; Instituto de Investigaciones Sociales, UNAM, 1988. 312 p.: bibl. (Biblioteca México: actualidad y perspectivas)

Chronicle of the student movements at UNAM by a former student activist. Author places student movements in broader context of social conflict while providing details of the inner workings of UNAM.

Gutiérrez del Cid, Ana Teresa. Las relaciones de México con la Unión Soviética: una evaluación crítica. See *HLAS 51:4233*.

1282 Haber, Stephen H. Industry and underdevelopment: the industrialization of Mexico, 1890–1940. Stanford, Calif.: Stanford Univ. Press, 1989. 237 p.: bibl., index, map.

Examination of the structural development of Mexican industry focuses on the "first wave" of industrialization, arguing persuasively that the real roots of modern Mexican industrialization are to be found in the Porfiriato. Early Mexican industry soon developed an "inward-looking style" based on the "twin pillars" of imported technology and government protection. The industrial sector was characterized by concentration of ownership, low labor productivity, capital intensiveness, and lack of profitability. Based on "firm-level" sources rather than the usual macro-level official sources.

1283 Hall, Linda B. and Don M. Coerver. Revolution on the border: the United States and Mexico, 1910–1920. Albuquerque: Univ. of New Mexico Press, 1988. 205 p.: bibl., ill., index, maps, tables.

First general study of the US-Mexican border during the military phase of the Revolution. Topics covered include military activities, oil, mining, immigration, and trade. Based on extensive research in both Mexican and US archives.

1284 Hart, John Mason. Revolutionary Mexico: the coming and process of the Mexican Revolution. Berkeley: Univ. of California Press, 1987. 478 p.: bibl., index.

Major interpretative overview looks at the Mexican Revolution as a mass movement arising from unrest among popular classes and as nationalistic in action as well as rhetoric. Places considerable emphasis on economic ties between revolutionary leaders and American capitalists and the US impact on the revolutionary process. For related entries see items **1338, 1295,** and **1296.**

1285 Hellman, Judith Adler. Continuity and change in Mexico. (*LARR,* 23:2, 1988, p. 133–144)

Thoughtful essay on eight works discusses recent economic and political change in Mexico. Places major emphasis on the presidencies of Luis Echeverría (1970–76) and José López Portillo (1976–82), but some earlier material is also included.

1286 Herrera Pérez, Octavio. Historia gráfica de Tamaulipas. Fotografía de Carlos Santamaría Ochoa. Ciudad Victoria, Mexico: Instituto Tamaulipeco de Cultura, 1989. 409 p.: ill., photos.

Work ranges from the prehispanic period to the present. Each of four sections has a brief introduction. The illustrations, many in color, are well-captioned.

1287 Historia de la Revolución Mexicana. Edición de José T. Meléndez. México: Instituto Nacional de Estudios Históricos de la Revolución Mexicana, 1987. 2 v. in 1: ill.

Reprint in one vol. of work that originally appeared in 2 vols. (1936, 1940). Vol. 1 features individual chapters on Madero, Huerta, Villa, and Zapata. Vol. 2 is chronologically organized in terms of presidential administrations, from Carranza through Abelardo Rodríguez.

1288 Historia de Tijuana, 1889–1989: edición conmemorativa del centenario de su fundación. Coordinación de David Piñera Ramírez y Jesús Ortiz Figueroa. 2. ed. Tijuana, Mexico: Univ. Autónoma de Baja California, Centro de Investigaciones Históricas, UNAM-UABC, 1989. 2 v.: bibl., ill., maps.

Multi-authored work published to commemorate the centennial of Tijuana. Volumes are organized chronologically and topically and cover everything from geography to local cuisine. Extensive illustrations.

1289 Jalisco desde la Revolución. v. 1–12. Guadalajara, Mexico: Gobierno del Estado de Jalisco, Univ. de Guadalajara, 1987–1988. 12 v.: bibl., ill.

Multi-volume regional study of the Revolution in Jalisco. Vol. 1 covers the elections of 1910 to the Constitution of 1917, emphasizing political and military events and the growth and activities of various revolutionary and counterrevolutionary factions. Vol. 2 is a political history of the state focusing on relations between local leaders and national factions. Vol. 3 covers political institutionalization and centralization, 1928–1940. Vol. 4 discusses worker-peasant movements, particularly the Confederación de Agrupaciones Obreras Libertarias de Jalisco, Confederación Obrera de Jalisco, Confederación Nacional Católica del Trabajo, Los Mineros, El Sindicato Revolucionario de Inquilinos, the 1922 rent strike, and various peasant groups. Vol. 5 includes contributions on the oligarchy, workers, peasants, radical right, and students. Vol. 6 is a study of the Catholic Church's role in the era's politics. Vol. 7 studies education, including sections on Manuel M. Diéguez, the effects of the Revolution on traditional education, labor activities of the teachers, socialist education, development of the Univ. de Guadalajara, expansion of primary education, and the involvement of the state in development of a socialist perspective in education. Vol. 8 is organized in two parts: the first deals with such literary forms as the novel, poetry, and drama; the second looks at newspaper and periodical literature. Vol. 9 covers political developments 1940–1979, emphasizing the "political reform" of the 1970s and the condition of state finances, including extensive tables and appendices. Vol. 10 considers architectural development and changes from the Porfiriato until approximately 1970, with valuable tables on urbanization in Jalisco. Vol. 11 considers the development of educational institutions and teachers. Vol. 12 is a well-organized examination of literary and artistic developments between 1940–80, including brief biographies of a number of cultural figures.

1290 Jauffret, Eric. Révolution et sacrifice au Mexique: naissance d'une nation, 1910–1917. Paris: Editions du Cerf, 1986. 317 p., 16 p. of plates: bibl., ill., index. (Sciences humaines et religions, 0768–2190: Nouvelle série)

Comprehensive study of the myths of the Mexican Revolution focuses on four themes: 1) ideological divisions and trends; 2) the agrarian movement; 3) the heroic movement; and 4) the question of sacrifice. Uses precolumbian religion and the Roman Catholic faith as major points of departure for analysis.

1291 Jones, Errol D. The Mexican electrical industry: conflicts and issues. (*J. West*, 27:4, Oct. 1988, p. 75–84, ill.)

Survey of the Mexican electrical industry from the late Porfiriato to the present. The central role of electrical power in economic development and its domination by a small number of foreign companies made it an obvious target for regulation and eventual nationalization. When nationalization did come in 1960, it was at the request of the companies who sold out at good prices. CFE, the state agency that runs the industry, has played a key role in the debt problems of the country due to its borrowing to keep electrical rates low.

1292 Jore, Jeff. Pershing's mission in Mexico: logistics and preparation for war in Europe. (*Mil. Aff.*, 52:3, July 1988, p. 117–121, ill.)

Author examines the important role played by the Pershing Expedition in preparing the US Army and the US for World War I. Covers topics such as motorized transport, air operations, medical practices, use of railways, and personnel training and selection.

1293 Juanicó, Diana. Partidos, facciones políticas y elecciones: Tlaxcala en 1924. (*Hist. Mex.*, 37:1, julio/sept. 1987, p. 75–100, bibl.)

Examination of the "apparent paradox" between the decline of the Partido Liberal Constitucionalista at the national level in 1922–23 and its strength in Tlaxcala state in 1924 elections. After examining the political background to 1924 at both national and state levels, author explains the paradox in terms of the PLC's control of state government apparatus and the unwillingness of the central government under Calles to provoke a confrontation despite the PLC's lack of support for or from Calles.

1294 King, Robin. Propuesta mexicana de una moratoria de la deuda a nivel continental, 1933. (*Hist. Mex.*, 38:3, enero/marzo 1989, p. 497–522, bibl.)

Discussion of the Latin American debt situation of the 1930s makes frequent comparisons to the situation of the 1980s. Reviews the history of Mexican debt leading to Mexico's proposal for a debt moratorium at the 7th Inter-American Conference in 1933. The proposal was referred to a subcommittee that recommended the matter be taken up at a later conference which was never held. The diverse financial situations of the Latin American countries precluded a common front on the debt issue in the 1930s, just as it would in the 1980s.

1295 Knight, Alan. The Mexican Revolution. v. 1, Porfirians, liberals and peasants. v. 2, Counter-revolution and reconstruction. Lincoln: Univ. of Nebraska Press, 1990. 2 v.: bibl., indexes.

Paperback version of major work first published in 1986. See *HLAS 50:1255.*

1296 Knight, Alan. U.S.-Mexican relations, 1910–1940: an interpretation. La Jolla, Calif.: Center for U.S.-Mexican Studies, Univ. of California, San Diego, 1987. 149 p.: bibl. (Monograph series.)

Author rejects traditional views that US economic interests suffered major losses as a result of the Revolution and that a popularly-based economic nationalism threatened American interests. Instead, he believes American interests emerged from the Revolution more powerful than ever. For related items see **1338** and **1284.**

1297 Krauze, Enrique. Biografía del poder. t. 1, Porfirio Díaz, el místico de la autoridad. t. 2, Francisco I. Madero, místico de la libertad. t. 3, Emiliano Zapata, el amor a la tierra. t. 4, Francisco Villa, entre el ángel y el fierro. t. 5, Venustiano Carranza, puente entre siglos. t. 6, Alvaro Obregón, el vértigo de la victoria. t. 7, Plutarco E. Calles, reformador desde el origen. t. 8, Lázaro Cárdenas, general misionero. México: Fondo de Cultura Económica, 1987. 8 v. (Tezontle)

Well-balanced, extensively illustrated political biographies of prominent Mexican figures. For literary critic's comment see *HLAS 50:3103.*

1298 La Botz, Dan. The crisis of Mexican labor. New York: Praeger, 1988. 228 p.: bibl., index.

Interpretative history of Mexican labor movement during the 20th century by self-described supporter of "socialism from below." Author is highly critical of the relationship between organized labor and the State which he sees as a product of corruption and an outdated revolutionary nationalism. For political scientist's comment see *HLAS 51:3443.*

Lamborn, Alan C. and **Stephen P. Mumme.** Statecraft, domestic politics, and foreign policy making: the El Chamizal dispute. See *HLAS 51:4235.*

Leal, Juan Felipe and **Margarita Menegus Bornemann.** Inflación y revolución: el caso de las haciendas de Mazaquiahuac y El Rosario. See *HLAS 51:4590.*

1299 Leal, Juan Felipe and **Margarita Menegus Bornemann.** La violencia armada y su impacto en la economía agrícola del estado de Tlaxcala, 1915–1920. (*Hist. Mex.*, 36:4, abril/junio 1987, p. 595–642, bibl., map, tables)

Examines impact of armed conflict on the haciendas of northern Tlaxcala. The authors begin by discussing the confused military/political situation in the state, especially 1914–18, and the different agrarian structures in the region. Though little affected by revolutionary developments prior to 1914, the haciendas experienced major changes between 1914–18; some changed their production practices while others experienced "predatory cultivation" or ceased operations altogether. Confronted with growing chaos in the agricultural sector, the state government fixed prices, rationed goods, and attempted to halt the sale of agricultural products outside the state.

1300 León, Luis L. Crónica del poder: en los recuerdos de un político en el México revolucionario. México: Fondo de Cultura Económica, 1987. 479 p. (Vida y pensamiento de México)

Memoirs of a major participant in the Sonoran revolution and the Obregón and Calles Administrations. Covers personal and political events from the Porfiriato through 1934, focusing particularly on the question of post-revolutionary agrarian reform.

1301 Lerner, Victoria. La suerte de las haciendas: decadencia y cambio de propietarios, 1910–1920. (*Hist. Mex.*, 36:4, abril/junio 1987, p. 661–697, bibl.)

Analysis of the transfer of control and the decline of haciendas in the eastern part of San Luis Potosí state. Shifts in control reflected the dominant political faction at the time. While prior to 1914 these shifts took place within the Porfirian elite, between 1914–17 property transfers were in favor of the constitutionalist governor, General Juan Barragan Rodríguez, and his clients. The haciendas in the area, regardless of ownership, underwent a general economic decline that lasted into the 1920s and even the 1930s. See also item **1302.**

1302 Lerner, Victoria. Los zozobras de los hacendados de algunos municipios del oriente de San Luis Potosí, 1910–1920. (*Hist. Mex.*, 36:2, oct./dic. 1986, p. 323–365, bibl., tables)

Examination of the problems of the *hacendado* class in the eastern part of San Luis Potosí state, an area much affected by the activities of Saturnino Cedillo during the Revolution. Author focuses on three problem areas: 1) a shortage of capital that antedated the Revolution; 2) specific difficulties relating to the outbreak of the Revolution, such as transportation interruptions and rebel occupation of haciendas; and 3) the accumulation of back taxes due that made many *hacendados* debtors or insolvent. See also item **1301.**

1303 López, Chantal and **Omar Cortés.** El Partido Liberal Mexicano, 1906–1908. México: Ediciones Antorcha, 1986. 408 p.: ill.

Collection of documents, principally from the years 1906–07, includes letters, newspaper articles, and legal documents, interspersed with short essays by the editors.

1304 López Beltrán, Lauro. La persecución religiosa en México: Carranza, Obregón, Calles, Portes Gil. México: Tradición, 1987. 620 p.: bibl., ill., ports.

Catholic priest examines Church-State relations between 1917–29, focusing on the Cristero Rebellion, a term which he dislikes. Although the author is sympathetic to the Church, he is critical of all parties involved in the settlement of 1929. For related work see item **1315.**

1305 López Obrador, Andrés Manuel. Revolución y justicia. (*Rev. Univ./Tabasco*, 9, sept. 1985, p. 41–61, photos, tables)

Uneven account of the pursuit of "social justice" (worker-peasant causes) under revolutionary governments devotes much attention to the Porfiriato. Author puts the expected emphasis on the Cardenas Administration, but only briefly deals with the post-1940 period.

1306 Machado, Manuel A., Jr. Centaur of the north: Francisco Villa, the Mexican Revolution, and northern Mexico. Austin, Texas: Eakin Press, 1988. 211 p.: bibl., ill., index, ports.

Generally favorable biography of Villa focuses on his personality rather than his political program or ideology. Author portrays Villa as an "ardent though nonideological populist" and emphasizes the interaction between Villa and his northern environment. Written for a popular audience.

1307 Machado, Manuel A., Jr. Cows and conflict: the North Mexico cattle industry. (*J. West*, 27:4, Oct. 1988, p. 5–13, ill.)

Examination of the cattle industry in Northern Mexico and the impact of government policy on its development in the 20th century. With a longstanding connection to the US, cattle raisers in Northern Mexico resisted efforts by the central government to increase regulation, ranging from expropriation to restrictions on exports.

1308 Madero, Francisco I. Madero y los partidos Antirreeleccionista y Constitucional Progresista: a través de cartas, manifiestos, acuerdos y otros documentos. Recopilación de Chantal López y Omar Cortés. México: Ediciones Antorcha, 1988. 245 p.: bibl.

Collection of letters, manifestos, accords and other documents covering Feb. 1909—May 1911. Includes a brief introductory essay by compilers.

1309 Madero, Francisco I. The presidential succession of 1910. Translated by Thomas B. Davis. New York: P. Lang, 1990. 307 p. (American university studies: Series IX, History; 89)

Excellent translation of Madero's famed political tract. The text confirms the translator's view that "as a literary figure

Madero does not command our attention." Appendices include the Creelman interview and Madero's Plan of San Luis Potosí.

1310 Magaña, Gildardo and **Carlos Pérez Guerrero.** Emiliano Zapata y el agrarismo en México. Ed. facsimilar. México: Comisión Nacional para las Celebraciones del 175 Aniversario de la Independencia Nacional y 75 Aniversario de la Revolución Mexicana, 1985. 5 v.: facsims., ports. (La Biblioteca de obras fundamentales de la Independencia y la Revolución)

Commemorative edition originally published in 1937 (vols. 1 and 2), 1946 (vol. 3), and 1952 (vols. 4 and 5). Magaña authored vols. 1 and 2. After his death in 1939, the three remaining volumes were written by Carlos Pérez Guerrero who was selected for the task by the Frente Zapatista.

1311 Mahan, Elizabeth. Mass media and society in twentieth-century Mexico. (*J. West,* 27:4, Oct. 1988, p. 41–49, ill.)

Survey of the impact of mass media in shaping Mexican culture as it became more urbanized. While post-revolutionary governments recognized the importance of the mass media, State intervention was minimal and economic considerations were the primary influence in the evolution of the industry. The trend of favoring economic over cultural/political objectives led to a strong US influence on the mass media, despite Mexican ownership.

1312 Mares, David R. Mexico's foreign policy as a middle power: the Nicaragua connection, 1884–1986. (*LARR,* 23:3, 1988, p. 81–107, bibl.)

Uses Mexico's relationships with the US and Nicaragua as case studies to explore role of a "middle power" in international politics. Four periods are discussed: 1) Guatemala's threat to Nicaragua, 1882–88; 2) the conflict between the US and Nicaragua, 1906–10; 3) the Sandino era, 1925–29; and 4) the Sandinista period since 1979.

1313 Martínez, Oscar J. Troublesome border. Tucson: Univ. of Arizona Press, 1988. 177 p., 1 leaf of plates: bibl., ill., index, maps, tables. (Profmex monograph series)

Good overview of border problems from three different perspectives: 1) Mexico; 2) US; and 3) border inhabitants themselves. While conflict over border issues is a con-

stant theme at the national level, there is a great deal of cooperation at the local and regional levels. See also item **1283.**

Meneses Morales, Ernesto. Tendencias educativas oficiales en México. v. 2., 1911–1934, la problemática de la educación mexicana durante la revolución y los primeros lustros de la época posrevolucionaria. See *HLAS 51:2664.*

1314 Mraz, John. Some visual notes toward a graphic history of the Mexican working class. (*J. West,* 27:4, Oct. 1988, p. 64–74, ill.)

Brief, episodic overview of labor history during the Porfiriato and revolutionary period. Contending that graphic history has usually been "markedly officialist" in Mexico, author offers a number of alternative illustrations.

Mumme, Stephen P.; C. Richard Bath; and **Valerie J. Assetto.** Political development and environmental policy in Mexico. See *HLAS 51:3469.*

1315 Negrete, Marta Elena. Relaciones entre la Iglesia y el Estado en México, 1930–1940. México: El Colegio de México, Centro de Estudios Históricos; Univ. Iberoamericana, Depto. de Historia, 1988. 347 p.: bibl.

Study of Church-State relations in the urban area of the Archdiocese of Mexico and the Federal District. Author views the Church-State settlement of 1929 as a "political convenience" for both parties that led to renewed attacks on the Church after 1932. The split between Cárdenas and Calles forced the State to adopt a more conciliatory approach, leading to a modus vivendi by 1940. Extensive use of sources on both sides of issue. For related work see item **1304.**

1316 Niblo, Stephen R. Development without the people. (*J. West,* 27:4, Oct. 1988, p. 50–63, ill.)

Well-researched and provocative analysis of the shift in Mexico's development policy beginning in the 1940s. Author argues that Mexico's adoption of a US-style national income accounting system led to faulty evaluation of the success of the new policy and the postwar propriety associated with it. The policy aroused little opposition at the time and led the country into the "debt trap" of the 1980s which the author criticizes for its "socialization of costs and privatization of benefits."

1317 Nieto López, J. de Jesús. Diccionario histórico del México contemporáneo, 1900–1982. México: Alhambra Mexicana, 1986. 214 p.

Inexpensive paperback reference work with chronology is limited primarily to political events and personalities. Recent citations are most useful.

Paoli Bolio, Francisco José. Estado y sociedad en México, 1917–1984. See *HLAS 51:4605.*

1318 Paulsen, George E. Helping hand or intervention? Red Cross relief in Mexico, 1915. (*Pac. Hist. Rev.*, 57:3, Aug. 1988, p. 305–325)

Examination of the brief attempt (June-Sept., 1915) by the American Red Cross to engage in relief efforts. These efforts were largely frustrated by revolutionary factionalism, transportation problems, nationalism, and feared intervention. Carranza in particular felt that talk of the need for relief aid was an effort to justify intervention.

1319 Pérez de León, José. Reseña gráfica de la invasión americana: Veracruz 1914. Veracruz, Mexico: H. Ayuntamiento de Veracruz, 1987. 133 p.: bibl., ill.

After a brief (3 p.) introduction, the work consists exclusively of photographs. The shortage of narrative is partially compensated for by lengthy captions.

1320 Philip, George. Petroleum in Mexico. (*J. West*, 27:4, Oct. 1988, p. 26–32, ill.)

Overview of the oil industry from late Porfiriato to 1980s. Author views the history of the industry as an effort to reconcile the protection of national sovereignty with the pursuit of economic development. The economic crisis of the 1980s forced the adoption of a new "model" composed of greater financial accountability, a limited expert role, and a weakening of trade union power.

The political plans of Mexico. See *HLAS 51:3476.*

1321 Radding, Cynthia. Peasant resistance on the Yaqui Delta: an historical inquiry into the meaning of ethnicity. (*J. Southwest*, 31:3, Autumn 1989, p. 330–361, bibl.)

Account of peasant resistance in the lower Yaqui Valley of southern Sonora centers on the period 1880–1970. Traditional native landholding patterns were threatened by regional landowners, foreign land companies, and state and federal officials. Having often resorted to armed resistance in the past, after 1930 the indigenous population increasingly relied on political action

1322 Ramos-Escandón, Carmen. La industria textil y el movimiento obrero en México. México: Univ. Autónoma Metropolitana, División de Ciencias Sociales y Humanidades, Depto. de Filosofía-Historia, Area de Cultura, 1988. 103 p.: bibl. (Cuadernos universitarios; 39)

Brief study of the development of worker activism in the Mexican textile industry summarizes the growth of the industry from colonial times through the Mexican Revolution and examines labor organization and protest within the context of that growth.

1323 La Revolución en Oaxaca, 1900–1930. v. 1–8. Coordinación de Víctor Raúl Martínez Vásquez. Oaxaca, Mexico: Instituto de Administración Pública de Oaxaca, 1985. 8 v.: bibl., ill.

Multi-volume collection of documents published in connection with 75th anniversary of Revolution. Each volume has a brief introduction and numerous illustrations. Volumes are organized on a topical basis covering such items as the precursory movement, maderista activities, revolutionary state governments, business activities, education, political organizations, and the presidential succession struggle of 1919–20.

1324 Rudenko, B.T.; N.M. Lavrov; and M.S. Al'perovich. Cuatro estudios sobre la Revolución Mexicana. 2a ed. México: Ediciones Quinto Sol, 1984. 172 p.:

Four very general essays discuss the origins of the Mexican Revolution, the 1910–17 period, the historiography of Mexican/US relations, and "bourgeois" US writing on modern Mexican history.

1325 Ruiz Cervantes, Francisco José. La Revolución en Oaxaca: el movimiento de la soberanía, 1915–1920. México: Instituto de Investigaciones Sociales, Fondo de Cultura Económica, 1986. 223 p., 1 folded leaf of plates: bibl., map. (Sección de obras de historia)

Arguing the need to examine the revolutionary era in its regional diversity rather than under "the generic mantle of the Mexican Revolution," author focuses on the movement for "sovereignty" in Oaxaca state. The effort by the local dominant class to maintain control at times led to cooperation with the national anti-Carranza movements, beginning with Félix Díaz and ending in an accommodation with the new Obregón Administration. Useful chronological table and representative collection of documents.

1326 Rural revolt in Mexico and U.S. intervention. Edited by Daniel Nugent. La Jolla, Calif.: Center for U.S.-Mexican Studies, Univ.of California, San Diego, 1988. 285 p.: bibl. (Monograph series; 27)

Collection of essays approaches the analysis of rural revolt in three contexts: 1) the micro-historical context of the particular region; 2) the national-historical context of Mexico; and 3) the context of US-Mexican relations. Emphasizes northern Mexico but also includes essays on Oaxaca and Yucatán.

1327 Salas, Elizabeth. Soldaderas in the Mexican military: myth and history. Austin, Texas: Univ. of Texas Press, 1990. 163 p.: bibl., ill., index.

Excellent study of the changing role of the *soldadera* from precolumbian times to the present, with most of the emphasis on the 20th century. Author discusses both the reality and the cultural symbolism connected with women in the military. Based on a variety of sources including archival records, interviews, films, and recordings.

1328 Salazar Adame, Jaime *et al.* Historia de la cuestión agraria mexicana: Estado de Guerrero, 1867–1940. v. 2 México: Gobierno del Estado de Guerrero, 1987. 1 v.: bibl., ill.

Four detailed essays examine the agrarian movement in Guerrero from the Reforma to the Cárdenas Administration. Despite the campesino struggle against the process of land concentration that began with the Reform Laws, neither the Mexican Revolution nor *cardenismo* resulted in significant land reform.

1329 Saragoza, Alex. The Monterrey elite and the Mexican State, 1880–1940.

Austin: Univ. of Texas Press, 1988. 258 p.: bibl., ill., index, tables.

Blending political and economic analysis, author examines evolution of the Monterrey elite before, during, and after the Revolution. Emphasizes the singularity of the Monterrey group and its national role. Although this group maintained its regional autonomy during and immediately after the Revolution, by the 1940s, it had reached an accomodation with the central government. For sociologist's comment see *HLAS 51:4619.*

1330 Schneider, Ben Ross. Partly for sale: privatization and State strength in Brazil and Mexico. (*J. Interam. Stud. World Aff.*, 30:4, 1988/1989, p. 89–116)

Comparative study of privatization efforts in Brazil and Mexico emphasizes their similarities. Author views role of PRI in Mexico as the crucial difference, permitting the implementation of policies that would be "suicidal" for most Latin American governments. Statistically Mexico is a world leader in privatization, but its efforts in this area have involved "mostly state housekeeping" and were actually designed to make government intervention in the economy more effective.

1331 Schuler, Friedrich E. From multinationalization to expropriation: the German I.G. Farben concern and the creation of a Mexican chemical industry, 1936–1943. (*Jahrb. Gesch.*, 25, 1988, p. 303–320)

Examination of how I.G. Farben's drive to multinationalize and Mexico's desire to industrialize initially worked in harmony but later conflicted in the face of Mexico's nationalistic economic policies. After US entry into World War II, Mexico was able to nationalize Farben's assets without international repercussions—an action Mexico had been considering as early as 1938.

1332 Shao, Lixin. Reflections on democratic revolutions in Mexico and China. (*in* Modernization and revolution in Mexico: a comparative approach. Edited by Omar Martínez Legorreta. Tokyo: The United Nations University, 1989, p. 151–159)

Argues that both revolutions attempted to reconstruct the State and organize society according to bourgeois principles. Compares relative status of the revolutions in both countries, elaborating why one has taken the capitalist road while the other has embraced socialism after completion in 1940s. [Mao Xianglin]

1333 Sierra, Christine Marie. Mexicans in the United States: history, evolution, and transformation. (*LARR*, 24:2, 1989, p. 218–230)

Essay discusses eight works, principally on history, sociology, and politics of Mexicans and Mexican Americans in the US. Entries cover the 19th century to present, with a focus on the post-World War II period.

1334 Simposio sobre Historia Contemporánea de México, 1940–1984, 1st, México. Inventario sobre el pasado reciente. México: Dirección de Estudios Históricos, Instituto Nacional de Antropología e Historia, 1986. 362 p.: bibl. (Col. científica; 156)

Essays by distinguished Mexican scholars discuss Mexican history, 1940–1984, from five different points of view: 1) the Mexican political system; 2) political economy and the accumulation of capital; 3) mass media and culture; 4) Mexico and the US; and 5) social movements. Contributors include Carlos Monsiváis, Lorenzo Meyer, and Hector Aguilar Camín.

1335 Simposium sobre la Revolución en Michoacán, Morelia, Mexico, 1985. La Revolución en Michoacán 1900–1926. Morelia, Mexico: Univ. Michoacana de San Nicolás de Hidalgo; Museo Regional Michoacano, 1987. 156 p.: bibl., ill., ports.

Collection of nine essays covers a variety of themes and stages in the Revolution in Michoacán state. Topics range from the background of the Revolution to counter-revolutionary activities in the early 1920s. Includes a limited section of documents.

1336 Spalding, Rose J. Peasants, politics and change in rural Mexico. (*LARR*, 23:1, 1988, p. 207–219, bibl.)

Review of seven books and papers published 1982–85 stresses the developing sophistication of these studies. Focuses on "the structure of power and the distribution of resources," and notes that peasants are now seen as interacting extensively with the external society rather than existing in traditional isolation.

1337 Story, Dale. Industry, the State, and public policy in Mexico. Austin: Univ.

of Texas Press, 1986. 275 p.: appendices, bibl., ill., index, tables. (Latin American monographs; 66)

Author argues against placing Mexico in the "associated dependent development" category, maintaining that domestic capital has played an important role in development and that industrialists have enjoyed a high degree of freedom of action while simultaneously influencing government economic policy. For economist's comment see *HLAS 51:1895*.

1338 Tobler, Hans Werner. Die mexikanische Revolution: gesellschaftlicher Wandel und politischer Umbruch, 1876–1940. Frankfurt am Main: Suhrkamp, 1984. 655 p., 48 p. of plates: bibl., ill., index

Author focuses on the 1920–40 period, viewing the Revolution as real but limited in impact. The uniqueness and complexity of the Revolution are due to regional variations and the diversity of movements that converged to form "the Revolution." For related entry see item **1284.**

1339 Ulloa, Berta; María Larrazolo; and Abel Juárez. Veracruz, capital de la nación, 1914–1915. México: Centro de Estudios Históricos, Colegio de México; Gobierno del Estado de Veracruz, 1986. 189 p.: bibl., ill., index.

Highly detailed study uses extensive archival sources of the port city of Veracruz from Nov. 1914 until Oct. 1915. Book focuses mainly on the period during which Venustiano Carranza's government was in residence but also includes a brief discussion of the US occupation.

1340 Valadés, José C. Historia general de la Revolución Mexicana. Ed. conmemorativa del 75 aniversario de la Revolución Mexicana. México: SEP Cultura, Dirección General de Publicaciones; Ediciones Gernika, 1985. 10 v.: bibl., ill.

Reprint of classic work first published in 1963–65. See *HLAS 28:713, HLAS 30: 1460,* and *HLAS 32:1730.*

1341 Valdés, Dennis Nodín. Mexican revolutionary nationalism and repatriation during the Great Depression. (*Mex. Stud.,* 4:1, Winter 1988, p. 1–23)

Uses the state of Michigan as a case study to examine the impact of the Depression on the repatriation of resident *Mexica-*

nos along three lines: 1) connection between type of employment and repatriation; 2) role of governmental and private agencies in both the US and Mexico in repatriation; and 3) role of Mexican revolutionary nationalism in repatriation. Author finds that industrial workers were most likely to be affected by repatriation, and that Mexican nationalist sentiment supported the repatriation movement, and that US federal government took the lead in the repatriation drive.

1342 Vanderwood, Paul J. and **Frank N. Samponaro.** Border fury: a picture postcard record of Mexico's Revolution and U.S. war preparedness, 1910–1917. Albuquerque: Univ. of New Mexico Press, 1988. 293 p.: bibl., ill., index.

Examination of the turmoil along the US-Mexican Border based on picture postcards popular at the time. The authors place these images in historical perspective and examine the themes that emerge from them such as racial superiority and the growing interest in technology.

1343 Vanderwood, Paul J. The picture postcard as historical evidence: Veracruz, 1914. (*Americas/Francisc.*, 45:2, Oct. 1988, p. 201–225, bibl., photos)

Discussion in both general and specific terms of the use of the picture postcard, popular in the late 19th and early 20th centuries, as an historical source. For a broader examination, see Vanderwood and Samponaro, (item **1342**).

1344 Velázquez Estrada, Rosalía. Sublevación de Emiliano Zapata: 10 de marzo de 1911. México: Comisión Nacional para las Celebraciones del 175 Aniversario de la Independencia Nacional y 75 Aniversario de la Revolución Mexicana, 1985. 77 p.: bibl., ports. (Serie de cuadernos conmemorativos; 14)

Brief account of the initial *zapatista* revolt against Díaz, culminating in the *Plan de Ayala*. Bulk of the work is appendices, all taken from Gildardo Magaña's *Emiliano Zapata y el agrarismo en México* (see item **1310**).

CENTRAL AMERICA

STEPHEN WEBRE, *Professor of History, Louisiana Tech University*
RALPH LEE WOODWARD JR., *Professor of History, Tulane University*

MOST OF THE RESEARCH ON CENTRAL AMERICA continues to be focused on individual states, although two new histories of the entire region by Rodolfo Pastor (item **1363**) and James Dunkerley (item **1436**) are notable, as are Robert Naylor's two works on the British in Central America (items **1361** and **1474**). Thomas Schoonover provides a less comprehensive, but nevertheless useful overview of German economic interest in the isthmus (item **1496**). Costa Ricans remain preoccupied with coffee and Nicaraguans with Sandino and Sandinismo, but there was a new vitality evident in Honduras and some notable items were published on Guatemalan history. By contrast, the turmoil in El Salvador appears to have slowed serious historical study in that country.

The approaching Quincentennial of Columbus' first voyage has not yet drawn as much attention to the colonial period in Central America as it seems to have done elsewhere in the Americas, although there are some notable exceptions, such as Antonio Gutiérrez Escudero's popular biography of Pedro de Alvarado (item **1386**). The Costa Rican Quincentennial Commission began its celebration early, sponsoring a symposium in 1986 on colonial society in San José. Most of the important papers from this conference have now been published: papers on Costa Rica were published in a single volume of proceedings (item **1403**) and those on other topics appeared separately (items **1398, 1408,** and **1411**). Also appropriate to the commemoration are valuable essays on the long-term legacy of discovery and conquest for the native inhabitants by Richard N. Adams (item **1345**) and W. George Lovell (item **1360**).

Otherwise, scholarly activity on the colonial period remains slight, although of generally good quality. Several new local and community studies for Guatemala have appeared, including the Sorbonne dissertations of Michel Bertrand on Rabinal (item **1374**) and Jean Piel on San Andrés Sajcabajá (item **1364**), and new works by Jorge Luján Muñoz (item **1390**) and Julio César Pinto Soria (item **1398**) on the Central Valley. A number of shorter local studies are gathered together in the collection edited by Stephen Webre (item **1404**). Recent significant contributions to colonial economic history are the two studies of food production and consumption by Alfredo Castillero Calvo (items **1377** and **1378**) and José Antonio Fernández Molina's pioneering article on iron production (item **1381**).

For the national period, in addition to Dunkerley's impressive history of the 20th century noted above, a number of works during the past two years merit special notice. Historians, depending heavily upon oral sources, have been seeking the roots of labor militancy and political radicalism in the previously neglected 1920s and 1930s. Significant results so far include Jeffrey L. Gould's studies of Nicaraguan sugar workers and artisans (items **1446** and **1447**), Arturo Taracena Arriola's essays on Guatemalan anarchists and communists (items **1502** and **1503**), and Víctor Hugo Acuña Ortega's sensitive evocation of daily life and workplace culture among Costa Rica's radicalized shoemakers (item **1414**).

Several notable contributions to Guatemalan history are the work of North American scholars, among them Michael F. Fry (item **1439**), Virginia Garrard Burnett (items **1423** and **1424**), Jim Handy (items **1451, 1452, 1453,** and **1454**), and Paul Dosal (item **1434**). But the period also saw significant publications by Spaniard Jesús María García Añoveros (item **1440**) and Guatemalans Julio Castellanos Cambranes (items **1350** and **1426**) and Gisela Gellert and Julio César Pinto Soria (item **1355**). O. Nigel Bolland has once again enriched Belizean history, this time with a brief but erudite study on land and labor (item **1422**). Little has appeared on El Salvador, although two welcome contributions are Amílcar Figueroa's overview of the modern period (item **1438**) and Patricia Parkman's book on the end of the Hernández Martínez era (item **1479**).

An important development in Honduran historiography has been the return of Rodolfo Pastor to his native land. In addition to his general interpretative history, Pastor's works on San Pedro Sula (item **1362**) and the Honduran Sugar Company (item **1480**) are worthy contributions. The publication of Mario Argueta's fine biography of caudillo Tiburcio Carías Andino (item **1419**) is also a welcome event. For Nicaragua, the first two volumes of Alejandro Bolaños' long-awaited work on William Walker have appeared (item **1421**), standing almost alone amidst the heavy concentration on the 20th century among Nicaraguan studies. Finally, in Costa Rica, national and foreign scholars continue to add socioeconomic dimensions to traditional political accounts. Lowell Gudmundson's fine article on the formation of Costa Rica's smallholder coffee class (item **1448**) is a splendid example, as are Mario Samper Kutschbach's study of the social context of electoral politics (item **1493**) and Alberto Sáenz' book on Braulio Carrillo (item **1490**).

GENERAL

1345 Adams, Richard N. The conquest tradition of Mesoamerica. (*Americas/*

Francisc., 46:2, Oct. 1989, p. 119–136, table)
Informative and provocative discussion of race relations and their social, economic, and political consequences in Me-

soamerica. Adams suggests that nearly 500 years of conflicts between Indians, Spanish, and ladinos have left a heritage of fear, terror, economic exploitation, and political repression in the region.

1346 Araya Pochet, Carlos and **Priscilla Albarracín González.** Historia de régimen municipal en Costa Rica. San José: Instituto de Fomento y Asesoría Municipal; Editorial Univ. Estatal a Distancia, 1986. 147 p.: bibl.

Informative documented description of Costa Rican municipal government from the colonial *cabildos* to the problems associated with the management of the country's modern welfare state. Concentrates especially on the national period and the changes brought about by the 1948 revolution.

1347 Arellano, Jorge Eduardo. Reseña histórica de la Universidad de León, Nicaragua. 2a. ed. abreviada. León, Nicaragua: Editorial Universitaria, 1988. 183 p., 11 leaves of plates: bibl., ill.

Historical overview of Nicaragua's national university (inaugurated in 1816) emphasizes colonial antecedents and developments in the 19th century.

1348 Barillas, Edgar. El "problema del indio" en la época liberal en Centro América: el caso de Guatemala. (*Folk. Am.,* 45, enero/junio 1988, p. 73–98)

Traces "Indian problem" in Guatemala from conquest to present, showing remarkable continuity of attitudes between colonial and liberal periods. "Problem" has roots in racist assumptions and exploitative relationships. Even defenders of the Indians have seen them as obstacles to progress and expected them to work for Europeans and accommodate themselves to European ways.

1349 *Boletín del Archivo Histórico Arquidiocesano Francisco de Paula García Peláez.* Vol. 1, No. 1, julio 1988– . Guatemala: Archivo Histórico Arquidiocesano Francisco de Paula García Peláez.

Welcome event, symbolic of greater access to ecclesiastical records that historians have enjoyed under Guatemala City's new archbishop, Mons. Próspero Penados del Barrio. Under editorship of archives director Ramiro Ordóñez Jonama, *Boletín's* first number reproduces several interesting colonial documents, including a 1689 report on

parishes administered by Dominican friars, an early 19th-century account of *reducciones* on the Honduran frontier, and an 1814 census of Guatemala City's Sagrario parish.

1350 Castellanos Cambranes, Julio. Sobre los empresarios agrarios y el Estado en Guatemala. Guatemala: Centro de Estudios Rurales Centroamericanos (CERCA), 1988. 51 p. (Cuaderno; 1)

Traces economic motivations and political methods of the Guatemalan planter class from 16th century to beginning of 20th century. Argues that coffee oligarchs of the late 19th and early 20th centuries impeded development because they tended to operate primarily for their own self-interest at the expense of more general economic development of the country.

1351 Chang Sagastume, Germán Rolando. Monografía del Departamento de Izabal. Guatemala: s.n., 1989. 287 p.: bibl., ill.

Thorough, factual account of the history and geography of Guatemala's Caribbean coast province.

1352 Collado Herrera, Carmen. Nicaragua. México: Instituto de Investigaciones Dr. José María Luis Mora; Guadalajara, Mexico: Univ. de Guadalajara, 1988. 234 p.: bibl., ill. (América Latina)

Brief synthesis of Nicaraguan history from late 18th century to fall of dictator José Santos Zelaya in 1909. Includes detailed chronology and bibliography of secondary works.

1353 Creedman, Theodore S. Historical dictionary of Costa Rica. 2nd ed. Metuchen, N.J.: Scarecrow Press, 1991. 338 p.: bibl., maps. (Latin American historical dictionaries; 16)

Revised, corrected, and expanded second edition (for 1977 first ed., see *HLAS 40:2796*). Includes many new entries, particularly in the area of recent and current biography, and is now prefaced by a short historical chronology.

Cuadernos Centroamericanos de Historia. No. 1, enero/abril 1988– . See *HLAS 51:121*.

1354 Dutrénit, Silvia. El Salvador. México: Instituto de Investigaciones Dr. José María Luis Mora; Guadalajara, Mexico: Univ. de Guadalajara, 1988. 233 p.: bibl., ill., maps. (América Latina)

Brief, synthetic account traces history of El Salvador from early days of Spanish rule to end of 19th century.

Feldman, Lawrence H. Master list of historic, pre-1840, earthquakes and volcanic eruptions in Central America. See *HLAS 51:2845.*

Fowler, William R. Cacao, indigo, and coffee: cash crops in the history of El Salvador. See *HLAS 51:687.*

García, Claudio. Etnia, identidad nacional y Estado en Nicaragua. See *HLAS 51:2893.*

1355 Gellert, Gisela and **Julio César Pinto Soria.** Ciudad de Guatemala: dos estudios sobre su evolución urbana, 1524–1950. Guatemala: Centro de Estudios Urbanos y Regionales; Univ. de San Carlos de Guatemala, 1990. 80 p.: bibl., maps, tables.

Two pioneering essays on Guatemala's capital link the city's spatial evolution to its social composition and suggest a more sophisticated agenda for Central American urban history.

Geografía de Panamá: estudio introductorio y antología. See *HLAS 51:2899.*

1356 González Davison, Fernando. Sobre el Estado y la salud en Guatemala del período colonial a mediados del siglo XX. (*Polít. Soc./Guatemala*, 10, s.d., p. 13–55)

First installment of a promised series on health care in Guatemala offers little new information on health care in the colonial period or first half of the 19th century. It is a convenient survey of the topic, however, particulary in its effort to describe the relative ability of peasants to secure adequate Church or State medical assistance.

1357 Guillén, Diana. Costa Rica. México: Instituto de Investigaciones Dr. José María Luis Mora; Guadalajara, Mexico: Univ. de Guadalajara, 1988. 175 p.: bibl., ill. (América Latina)

Brief, synthetic account traces Costa Rica's historical development from the Bourbon Reforms of the 18th century to the emergence of the United Fruit Company at the close of the 19th century. Includes detailed chronology.

1358 Gutiérrez-Haces, María Teresa et al. Centroamérica: una historia sin retoque. Prólogo de Agustín Cueva. México: Sociedad Cooperativa Publicaciones Mexi-

canas; Instituto de Investigaciones Económicas, UNAM, 1987. 298 p.: bibl. (El Día en libros; 20)

Diverse collection of interpretative, scholarly essays on each of the Central American states. Each attempts to identify the salient historical characteristics of its respective state, with a focus on the 20th century. Authors include María Teresa Gutiérrez-Haces (Costa Rica), Berenice P. Ramírez López (El Salvador), Alfredo Guerra-Borges (Guatemala), Juan Aranciba Córdova (Honduras), Mario Salazar Valiente (Nicaragua), and Lucrecia Lozano (Nicaragua).

1359 Las instituciones costarricenses: de las sociedades indígenas a la crisis de la república liberal. Selección y coordinación de Jaime E. Murillo. San José: Editorial de la Univ. de Costa Rica, 1989. 460 p., 1 leaf of plates: bibl., ill., maps, tables.

Textbook for use in course on Costa Rican institutions contains much original research and interpretation. Includes essays by some of Costa Rica's brightest young scholars on the following topics: precolumbian societies; the conquest; colonial economy and agrarian structure; the rise of coffee and capitalist agriculture; the State and law; the military; education; liberalism; economic cycles and institutional change; social movements and the 1929 crisis; and the origins of liberal democracy.

1360 Lovell, W. George. Surviving conquest: the Maya of Guatemala in historical perspective. (*LARR*, 23:2, 1988, p. 25–57, tables)

Eloquent survey pays tribute to resilience of Guatemala's Maya Indians who have survived three "cycles of conquest:" 1) by Spain; 2) by world capitalism; and 3) by the State-sponsored terror of the 1980s. Author concludes that most recent cycle represents "yet another intrusion that Maya Indians somehow will respond to in ways that ensure meaningful group preservation" (p. 48). For geographer's comment, see *HLAS 51:2885.*

1361 Naylor, Robert A. Penny-ante imperialism: the Mosquito Shore and the Bay of Honduras, 1600–1914; a case study in British informal empire. Rutherford N.J.: Fairleigh Dickinson Univ. Press; London: Associated Univ. Presses, 1989. 315 p.: bibl., index, maps.

Thorough history of British involvement on the eastern coast of Central America synthesizes the diverse and scattered secondary literature and adds significant new research.

1362 Pastor Fasquelle, Rodolfo. Biografía de San Pedro Sula, 1536–1954. San Pedro Sula, Honduras: Centro Editorial, 1989. 483 p.: bibl., ill.

Sensitive and skillfully written narrative of the city of San Pedro Sula, Honduras, from its 1536 founding by Pedro de Alvarado through 1954. Includes brief overview of events from 1954 to the present. Well documented and perceptive, this work sets a new standard for Honduran regional histories.

1363 Pastor Fasquelle, Rodolfo. Historia de Centroamérica. México: Centro de Estudios Históricos, Colegio de México, 1988. 272 p.: bibl., ill., index.

Brief survey from precolumbian period to the present identifies the major themes in Central American history during both colonial and national periods with emphasis on colonial history.

1364 Piel, Jean. Sajcabajá: muerte y resurrección de un pueblo de Guatemala, 1500–1970. Traducción de Eliana Castro Ponlsen. México: Centre d'études mexicaines et centraméricaines, 1989. 456 p.

Encyclopedic community study examines demographic, cultural, economic, and political changes experienced by Quiché town in western Guatemalan highlands, from Spanish conquest (1524) to arrival of first motor truck (1964). Mass of factual data is impressive, but, given the length and complexity of the study, the lack of an introduction or conclusion is lamentable.

1365 Polo Sifontes, Francis. Historia de Guatemala: visión de conjunto de su desarrollo político-cultural. Guatemala: E. Guatemala, 1988. 287 p., 24 p. of plates: bibl., ill.

Textbook-like survey, roughly one-third of which is devoted to preconquest and conquest periods. The 20th century is treated in only 25 pages, and the period after 1951 receives no coverage at all.

1366 Revista de la Academia Guatemalteca de Estudios Genealógicos, Heráldicos, e Históricos. Vol. 9, 1987– . Guatemala: Academia Guatemalteca de Estudios Genealógicos, Heráldicos e Históricos.

Appearing irregularly over the years, this *Revista* has long been a treasure trove of odd facts enjoyed by historians, especially of the colonial period and the 19th century. Current number contains articles on well-known families such as the Arana, Valdés, and Varón de Berrieza, and, more importantly, a 1740 *Relación Geográfica* of the Chiquimula de la Sierra district.

1367 Toussaint Ribot, Mónica. Guatemala. México: Instituto de Investigaciones Dr. José María Luis Mora; Guadalajara, México: Univ. de Guadalajara, 1988. 166 p.: (América Latina)

Brief account of Guatemalan history from late colonial period to dictatorship of Manuel Estrada Cabrera (1898–1920). Detailed chronology lists events in relation to contemporary happenings in Mexico.

1368 Yankelevich, Pablo. Honduras. México: Instituto de Investigaciones Dr. José María Luis Mora; Guadalajara, México: Univ. de Guadalajara, 1988. 294 p.: bibl., ill. (América Latina)

Competent survey of Honduran history from the late 18th century to the Carías dictatorship of the mid-20th century emphasizes economic factors. Includes a detailed chronology comparing Honduran and Mexican history during the period 1742–1935.

COLONIAL

1369 Aguilar, Francisco. History of the foundation of the town of Chamiquín. Translated by Lawrence H. Feldman. Culver City, Calif.: Labyrinthos, 1988. 142 p.: bibl., ill., maps.

Chamiquín, in the Alta Verapaz, was the last northern frontier town founded in Guatemala before Independence. Translation of account written 1819–23 is accompanied by a more general description of province first published in English in 1841, and by a modern scholarly introduction. Rich in demographic and ethnographic data.

1370 Alvarenga Venutolo, Patricia. La composición de la producción agropecuaria en el Valle Central Costarricense: un estudio comparativo de las regiones de oriente y occidente, 1785–1805. (*Rev. Hist./Heredia*, 16, julio/dic. 1987, p. 53–83, bibl., tables)

Research in probate records permits reexamination of old problem of dual development in Costa Rica's Valle Central. Different kinds of merchant-producer relationships emerged in dynamic San José and conservative Cartago. The tobacco boom facilitated the divergence, but did not cause it.

1371 Alvarez Arévalo, Miguel. Manuscritos de Covalchaj. Paleografía de Luis Domingo Quiroa y Miguel Alvarez Arévalo. Guatemala: Museo Popol Vuh, Univ. Francisco Marroquín; Librería Marquense, 1987. 47 p.: bibl., ill. (Col. Documentos históricos; 1)

Descriptive summary of manuscripts held by Vicente family of Momostenango, Guatemala, which claims descent from Quiché nobility. Reveals persistence of *caciques* as privileged group throughout colonial period. Reproduces two important *títulos* (Casa de Ixquín Nijaib and Don Francisco Ixquín Nijaib) already known in other versions, and promises more installments in future.

1372 Arellano, Jorge Eduardo. Vida y muerte de León Viejo. (*Bol. Nicar. Bibliogr. Doc.*, 57, mayo/julio 1988, p. 13–20)

Brief historical sketch of old city of León, Nicaragua, from founding in 1524 to abandonment following earthquake of 1610. Treats important personalities since conquest, original layout of city, first buildings, and population.

1373 Bertrand, Michel. Les techniques agraires dans la région de Rabinal au XVIII siècle. (*Asclepio*, 39:2, 1987, p. 145–159, bibl., maps)

Isolated Rabinal region of Guatemala remained largely dependent on traditional crops and techniques of cultivation, but the 18th-century dynamic example of Dominican haciendas inspired spread of innovative practices, including irrigation and new cash crops.

1374 Bertrand, Michel. Terre et société coloniale: les communautés Maya-Quiché de la région de Rabinal du XVIe au XIXe siècle. México: Centre d'Études Mexicaines et Centraméricaines, 1987. 332 p.: bibl., maps, plates, tables. (Études mesoaméricaines; 14)

Revised version of author's 1983 Sorbonne thesis. In *Annales* tradition, study is model of global history at local level, examining demography, ethnicity, settlement patterns, land tenure, crops, agricultural techniques, *mentalités*, against background of topography, climate, and communications routes. Greatly condensed version in Spanish appears as Chapter 5 in item **1404.**

1375 Calvo Poyato, José. Francisco Hernández de Córdoba y la conquista de Nicaragua. (*Cuad. Hispanoam.*, 459, sept. 1988, p. 7–18)

Traditionalist account based on familiar sources helps identify key unresolved questions regarding Hernández de Córdoba's background, his expedition to Nicaragua, and his death at the hands of Pedrarias Dávila.

1376 Capítulos de las ordenanças reales. Prólogo de Jorge Luján Muñoz. Guatemala: Archivo General de Centroamérica, 1985. 72 p.

Operating rules of Audiencia of Guatemala, enacted in 1568. Brief introduction by noted legal historian Jorge Luján Muñoz emphasizes influence of Antonio de Mendoza's and Tello de Sandoval's reforms in New Spain. Fundamental document for study of colonial law and administration.

1377 Castillero Calvo, Alfredo. Niveles de vida y cambios de dieta a fines del período colonial en América. (*Anu. Estud. Am.*, 44, 1987, p. 427–476, appendix, bibl., maps, tables)

Important, innovative essay focuses on Panama City and Portobelo, but cites abundant comparative data from elsewhere in empire. Real increase in meat prices by end of 18th century meant decline in material standard of living. In temperate areas, wheat bread increased in dietary importance, but in tropical areas such as Panama, all classes spent increasingly larger shares of disposable income on beef, while consuming more pork, plantains, yucca, and, eventually, rice.

1378 Castillero Calvo, Alfredo. Subsistencias y economía en la sociedad colonial: el caso del Istmo de Panamá, siglos XVI y XVII. (*Rev. Hist./Heredia*, 18, julio/dic. 1988, p. 23–91, appendices, graphs, tables)

Valuable study of food production in colonial Panama by one of Central America's most talented historians devotes greatest attention to development of cattle industry. Beef was plentiful and cheap, and dominated the colonial diet in 16th and 17th centuries. By 1650, stockraising may have accounted for 97 percent of all land in production. As same author concludes in item **1377** however, situation changed dramatically by late 18th century.

1379 Chaclán Díaz, José. Biografía del Padre Dionisio Chunay, traductor del *Título de los señores de Totonicapan. (Antropol. Hist. Guatem.,* segunda época, 1985, p. 157–168)

Based on archival sources, sketches basic facts in life of Dionisio Chunay (1786–1837). Although Chunay is remembered primarily for Quiché manuscript he translated, his career illustrates possibilities open to high-born Indians, even in late-colonial Guatemala.

1380 Chinchilla Aguilar, Ernesto. Las encomiendas de Atitlán, Alotenango y San Miguel Uzpatlán. Guatemala: Editorial José de Pineda Ibarra, 1982. 95 p.: ill. (Biblioteca Guatemalteca de cultura popular 15 de septiembre: Duodécima serie; 111)

Two brief romanticized essays on preconquest and early colonial history of the Guatemalan *encomienda* towns cited in title. Author reproduces two relevant documents and promises more substantial work on *encomiendas* in future.

Davidson, William V. Geografía de los indígenas toles—jicaques—de Honduras del siglo XVIII. See *HLAS 51:2886.*

1381 Fernández, José Antonio. La producción de hierro en el Reino de Guatemala. (*Rev. Hist./Heredia,* no. especial, 1988, p. 83–137, appendices, bibl., graphs, maps, tables)

Detailed study of iron mining and refining in 18th-century Guatemala and El Salvador. Technology, fuel, and skilled labor were in such short supply that only an interruption in shipments from Spain could make investments in local iron production profitable.

1382 Fowler, William R. La población nativa de El Salvador al momento de la conquista española. (*Mesoamérica/Antigua,* 9:15, junio 1988, p. 79–116, bibl.)

Carefully structured and lucidly ex-

pressed argument uses three independent methods to estimate contact-era population of El Salvador. Author arrives at "conservative" final estimates of 700,000 to 800,000 for 1519 and 400,000 to 500,000 for 1524.

1383 García, Jesús María. Población y estado sociorreligioso de la Diócesis de Guatemala en el último tercio del siglo XVIII. Guatemala: Editorial Universitaria, Univ. de San Carlos, 1987. 243 p., 1 leaf of plates: bibl., map.

Detailed exegesis of manuscript record of *visita* made by Archbishop Pedro Cortés y Larraz to the parishes of Guatemala and El Salvador, 1768–70. Most exhaustive analysis yet of this familiar source, rich in data on population, economic activities, and popular religious and moral life in the late 18th century. Author claims to eschew interpretation, intending instead to "dejar que los documentos 'canten' por sí mismos" (p. 2).

1384 García, Jesús María. Presencia franciscana en la Taguzgalpa y la Tologalpa, La Mosquitia. (*Mesoamérica/Antigua,* 9:15, junio 1988, p. 47–78, bibl.)

Straightforward, richly detailed account of repeated unsuccessful Franciscan attempts to reduce and catechize the Mosquito Coast of Honduras and Nicaragua. Author attributes failures to lack of funds, shortage of missionaries, semi-nomadic target population, unattractive climate and terrain, and English competition.

González, Nancie L. Rumbo a Roatán. See *HLAS 51:690.*

1385 Greñas, Rosa. Costa Rica en la época del gobernador Don Juan de Ocón y Trillo. San José: Editorial Costa Rica, 1985. 314 p.: bibl., map.

Detailed narrative account of Costa Rican politics and society during the administration of an uninhibited and unpopular Spanish governor, 1604–12. Useful contribution to a little studied period.

1386 Gutiérrez Escudero, Antonio. Pedro de Alvarado: el conquistador del país de los quetzales. Madrid: Anaya, 1988. 128 p.: bibl., ill. (some col.). (Biblioteca iberoamericana; 66)

Beautifully illustrated biography of the *adelantado* of Guatemala. Based on familiar secondary sources and written in a popular tone, book is frank about Alvarado's short-comings. Good example of quincentennial-inspired literature.

1387 Hill, Robert M. Social organization by decree in colonial highland Guate-mala. (*Ethnohistory*, 36 : 2, Spring 1989, p. 170–198, bibl.)

Case studies of development of *par-cialidad*, or *chinamit*, in Sacapulas, Tecpán, and Totonicapán suggest that social organiza-tion in highland Indian communities was not so much a product of preconquest tradition or of wholesale European innovation, but of unique Spanish administrative responses to specific disputes arising in individual towns.

1388 Ibarra R., Eugenia. El intercambio y la navegación en el Golfo de Huetares (o de Nicoya) durante el siglo XVI. (*Rev. Hist./Heredia*, 17, enero/junio 1988, p. 35–67, bibl., maps)

Archaeological and documentary evi-dence supports this description of Costa Ri-can social and economic organization at time of Spanish contact. Author argues for strate-gic importance of Gulf of Nicoya for access to Central Valley and to trade routes linking Mesoamerican and South American regions.

1389 Lovell, W. George. Las enfermedades del Viejo Mundo y la mortandad indí-gena: la viruela y el tabardillo en la Sierra de los Cuchumatanes, Guatemala, 1780–1810. (*Mesoamérica/Antigua*, 9 : 16, dic. 1988, p. 239–285, maps, tables)

Detailed analysis of impact of epidem-ics in one remote region in the late colonial period. Repeated outbreaks of smallpox and typhus retarded the gradual recovery of the Indian population begun in the late 17th cen-tury. Official response, uneven but increas-ingly energetic, featured some evident suc-cesses, such as the vaccination campaign of 1805–1807.

1390 Luján Muñoz, Jorge. Agricultura, mer-cado y sociedad en el Corregimiento del Valle de Guatemala, 1670–80. Guate-mala: Univ. de San Carlos, 1988. 150 p.: bibl., ill. (Cuadernos de investigación; 2–88)

Significant study of wheat, maize, livestock, and sugar production in central valley of Guatemala in late 17th century emphasizes impact of growing urban market in Santiago, the *audiencia* capital. Demo-graphic recovery began earlier than in other

areas because of urban growth. Shift of In-dian communities to wheat production pre-vented bread shortages as urban demand expanded, but may have contributed to in-creasing volatility in maize market.

1391 Luján Muñoz, Jorge. El reino poko-mam de Petapa, Guatemala, hacia 1524. (*An. Acad. Geogr. Hist. Guatem.*, 62 : 60, enero/dic. 1986, p. 159–174, bibl., maps)

Useful survey of political organization of central Guatemalan highlands at time of conquest. Focuses on eastern Pokomam re-gion and suggests area was weakly organized but independent, although it may have been in process of succumbing to Cakchiquel con-trol when Spaniards arrived.

1392 MacLeod, Murdo J. Los indígenas de Guatemala en los siglos XVI y XVII: tamaño de la población, recursos y organiza-ción de la mano de obra. (*in* Población y mano de obra en América Latina. Compila-ción de Nicolás Sánchez-Albornoz. Madrid: Alianza Editorial, 1985, p. 53–67)

Rapid survey of colonial Central America's provinces from Soconusco to Costa Rica, noting their populations, chief economic resources and activities, systems of labor procurement, and degree of accul-turation of native inhabitants.

1393 Martínez, José Luis. Las Hibueras: des-peñadero de desgracias. (*Jahrb. Gesch.*, 24, 1987, p. 111–134)

Narrative account of Cortés' ill-fated expedition to Central America is based on the few contemporary sources available. [A. Lavrin]

1394 Martínez, Mario Felipe. Apuntamien-tos para una historia colonial de Tegu-cigalpa y su alcaldía mayor. Tegucigalpa: Edi-torial Universitaria, 1982. 171 p.: appendices, bibl., map. (Col. Letras hondureñas; 14)

Sophisticated municipal history of Te-gucigalpa's early years goes well beyond cus-tomary focus on architecture and patrician genealogy, but does not ignore them. Valu-able for occasional provocative theses, but especially for documentary appendices and frequent citations to manuscript sources found in Honduras, Guatemala, and Spain.

1395 Martínez, Mario Felipe. Los últimos días de Lempira y otros documentos:

el conquistador español que venció a Lempira. Tegucigalpa: Univ. Nacional Autónoma de Honduras, Editorial Universitaria, 1987. 113 p.: bibl. (Col. Documentos; 2)

Probanza of Rodrigo Ruiz, recorded at Mexico City in 1558 and located in AGI, Patronato, leg. 69. Editor asserts that document establishes historicity of Lempira, hero of Indian resistance to Spanish conquest of Honduras, and the identity of Ruiz as the previously unidentified Spanish soldier who killed him in battle.

1396 Mena García, María del Carmen. La autonomía legislativa en Indias: las Leyes de Burgos y su aplicación en Castilla del Oro por Pedrarias Dávila. (Rev. Indias, 49:186, mayo/agosto 1989, p. 283–353)

Publication and analysis of Pedrarias's 1521 ordinances for government of Castilla del Oro (Panama). As the chronological midpoint between the Antilles and New Spain experiences, early Panama merits greater attention to its legal and encomienda history than it has received to date.

1397 Mena García, María del Carmen. El traslado de la Ciudad de Nombre de Dios a Portobelo a fines del siglo XVI. (Anu. Estud. Am., 40, 1983, p. 71–102, map)

Overview of early urbanism in Panama, followed by episodic account of abandonment of Nombre de Dios in favor of Portobelo in 1590s. New site was to be healthier, more convenient, and easier to defend.

Newson, Linda. La población indígena de Honduras bajo el régimen colonial. See HLAS 51:2890.

1398 Pinto Soria, Julio César. El valle central de Guatemala, 1524–1821: un análisis acerca del origen histórico-económico del regionalismo en Centroamérica. Guatemala: Editorial Universitaria, Univ. de San Carlos, 1988. 65 p., 6 leaves of plates: bibl., ill., maps. (Col. Estudios universitarios; 31)

Important essay on early development of geographic regions in Central America emphasizes the dominant central valley of Guatemala. Covers much of the same ground as item **1390,** but includes a lucid discussion of development of hacienda complex in eastern half of region. Especially informative on Guatemalan sugar culture, heretofore little studied.

1399 Quirós Vargas, Claudia. Las actividades económicas de la provincia de Costa Rica, 1569–1610. (Rev. Hist./Heredia, 15, enero/junio 1987, p. 45–62, bibl., ill.)

Account of early Costa Rican economy stresses importance of commercial activities, including marketing of tribute surpluses, export of livestock to Panama, and shipbuilding and servicing activities at Nicoya and El Realejo. Author raises provocative questions concerning origins of Costa Rican society, but fails to support stated conclusions with specific evidence.

1400 Quirós Vargas, Claudia and **Margarita Bolaños Arquín.** Una reinterpretación del origen de la dominación colonial española en Costa Rica, 1510–1569. (Anu. Estud. Centroam., 52:1, 1989, p. 19–47, bibl., table)

Authors criticize traditional accounts of conquest and colonization as isolated episodes, stressing instead the regional context of the origin of Spanish society in Costa Rica's Central Valley. Exceptional nature of Costa Rican experience is the result of its formation at a time when the power of the Spanish State in Central America was already well established.

1401 Remesal, Antonio de. Historia general de las Indias Occidentales y particular de la gobernación de Chiapa y Guatemala. Edición y estudio preliminar de Carmelo Sáenz de Santa María. México: Editorial Porrúa, 1988. 2 v.: bibl., ill. (Biblioteca Porrúa; 89–90)

Handsome modern edition of Guatemala's first colonial chronicle, originally published in 1619. Among other things, Dominican author Remesal deserves credit for the earliest biography of Bartolomé de Las Casas which is included here. Editor Sáenz de Santa María has made a few changes to his valuable preliminary study since his edition of Remesal's work first appeared in the 1960s as vols. 175 and 189 of the Biblioteca de Autores Españoles.

1402 Rubio Sánchez, Manuel. Historia del Ejército de Guatemala. v. 1. Guatemala: Editorial del Ejército, 1987. 1 vol.: bibl., ill. (Col. Historia militar: Serie Documentos militares)

Account of early military history of Central America, from Spanish conquest to defense of isthmus against first foreign pirates. Weak as interpretative synthesis, but rich in narrative detail, as well as in citations to and lengthy quotations from primary sources.

1403 Simposio La Sociedad Colonial en Mesoamérica y el Caribe, *San José, 1986*. Costa Rica colonial: ponencias sobre Costa Rica. San José?: Comisión Costarricense V Centenario del Descubrimiento de América; Ediciones Guayacán, 1989. 289 p.: appendices, bibl., ill., maps, tables.

Papers on Costa Rican topics presented at important symposium (Univ. de Costa Rica, Dec. 1–3, 1986). Significant contributions include those of Eugenia Ibarra on conquest-era social structure; Elizet Payne on 17th-century artisans; Claudia Quirós and Margarita Bolaños on *mestizaje*, Elizabeth Fonseca on sugar cane cultivation; Patricia Alvarenga on provisioning Cartago; Ligia Carvajal and Guillermo Arroyo on *cofradías*, and Clotilde Obregón on early San José.

1404 La sociedad colonial en Guatemala: estudios regionales y locales. Edición de Stephen Webre. Traducción de Margarita Cruz de Drake *et al.* Antigua, Guatemala: Centro de Investigaciones Regionales de Mesoamérica; South Woodstock, Vt.: Plumsock Mesoamerican Studies, 1989. 272 p.: bibl., ill., index, maps, tables. (Serie monográfica, 0252–9971; 5)

Essays, most not previously published, on different aspects of Guatemalan society in colonial period, each with specific local or regional focus. Contributors are Anne C. Collins on missionization in the western highlands, Pilar Sanchiz Ochoa on social structure in the central valley, W. George Lovell on Indian labor in the Cuchumatán highlands, Julio César Pinto Soria on agrarian structure and settlement patterns, Michel Bertrand on rural society in the Baja Verapaz, Stephen Webre on economic activities of Santiago's municipal elite, and Inge Langenberg on urban structure and social change in Nueva Guatemala.

1405 Stone, Samuel Z. El surgimiento de los que mandan: tierra, capital y trabajo en la forja de las sociedades centroamericanas. San José: Centro de Investigación y Adiestramiento Político Administrativo, 1980. 79 p.: bibl., ill., map. (Estudios del Centro de Investigación y Adiestramiento Político Administrativo; 5)

Distinguished sociologist seeks roots of contemporary Central American reality, including Costa Rican distinctiveness, in the experience of the Spanish conquest.

1406 Suñe Blanco, Beatriz. Los franciscanos en Guatemala en el siglo XVI. (*Arch. Ibero-Am.*, 49: 193/194, enero/junio 1989, p. 153–165)

Brief survey of early history of Franciscan order in Guatemala. Missionization is seen as programmed acculturation, with early friars—pioneers of applied anthropology—partly responsible for shape of Indian culture and religion today.

1407 Vila Vilar, Enriqueta. Cimarronaje en Panamá y Cartagena: el costo de una guerrilla en el siglo XVII. (*in* Congreso Internacional de Americanistas, *45th, Bogotá, 1985*. Identidad y transformación de las Américas. Bogotá: Ediciones Uniandes, 1988, p. 118–125)

Communities of runaway slaves were particularly bothersome when they were near major transit points and could molest travelers and traders. Efforts to control them were expensive and not very effective.

1408 Vives, Pedro A. Intendencias y poder en Centroamérica: la reforma incautada. (*Anu. Estud. Centroam.*, 13:2, 1987, p. 37–47, bibl.)

Based on a review of secondary sources, Vives argues that Central American intendents acquired particular importance only from 1811 forward, but that by this time the original reformist content of the system had been considerably weakened. He also believes the intendencies adapted to the pre-existing struggle between the Guatemalan merchants, reformist officials, and provincial elites. Concludes that the intendency system was useful in propitiating a new political order, but failed to adequately restrict the Guatemalan merchant oligarchy.

1409 Ward, Christopher. Historical writing on colonial Panama. (*HAHR*, 69:4, Nov. 1989, p. 691–713)

Critical overview of existing literature identifies current needs, and appeals for recognition of colonial Panama as a field of opportunity for new researchers. Points out that "it is very rare to discover so much unstudied material of such a high level of importance" (p. 713).

1410 **Webre, Stephen.** Política y comercio en la Guatemala del siglo XVII. (*Rev. Hist./Heredia*, 15, enero/junio 1987, p. 27–41, bibl.)

Brief essay argues that the most important political issues in late 17th-century Central America were taxation and regulation of trade. Merchants constituted a powerful interest group which resisted imperial authority in these questions.

1411 **Webre, Stephen.** El trabajo forzoso de los indígenas en la política colonial guatemalteca: siglo XVII. (*Anu. Estud. Centroam.*, 13:2, 1987, p. 49–61, bibl.)

Review of political controversies surrounding exploitation of Indian labor in 17th-century Guatemalan agriculture reveals that royal commitment to protect Indian interests was weak and that local elites generally were able to obstruct enforcement of unpopular legislation.

1412 **Webre, Stephen.** Water and society in a Spanish American city: Santiago de Guatemala, 1555–1773. (*HAHR*, 70:1, Feb. 1990, p. 57–84, map, tables)

Study of municipal water system of colonial Santiago (modern Antigua Guatemala). Expansion of aqueducts and fountains responded more to technical limitations and elite priorities than to larger pattern of urban growth. Operations and maintenance demands strained primitive administrative and financial arrangements, but produced abundant records which can be useful to urban historians.

NATIONAL

1413 **Acuña Ortega, Víctor Hugo.** La ideología de los pequeños y medianos productores cafetaleros costarricenses, 1900–1961. (*Rev. Hist./Heredia*, 16, julio/dic. 1987, p. 137–159, bibl.)

Acuña relies on newspaper research to construct the political and social orientation of small- and medium-scale Costa Rican coffee growers. Conclusions emphasize the conflicting class interests of small growers and *beneficiadores* throughout the period, and point to the socioeconomic victories of these producers to explain Costa Rica's democratic tradition.

1414 **Acuña Ortega, Víctor Hugo.** Vida cotidiana, condiciones de trabajo y organización sindical: el caso de los zapateros en Costa Rica, 1934–1955. (*Rev. Hist./Heredia*, no. especial, 1988, p. 223–245)

Excellent oral history of Costa Rica's shoemakers who enjoyed a reputation for militance and led both the formation of the Communist Party and the creation of the modern labor movement. Industrialism and the social welfare state led to decline of shoemakers' union and their peculiar workplace culture.

1415 **Administraciones del coronel Joaquín San Martín.** Recopilación de Freddy Leistenschneider. San Salvador: Impr. Nacional, 1980. 64 p.: bibl., ports.

Documents and episodes from the public career of Honduran-born San Martín (1770–1854), Francisco Morazán's antagonist, who governed El Salvador twice (1832, 1833–1834) during troubled Federation period.

1416 **Alvarenga Venutolo, Patricia.** Las explotaciones agropecuarias en los albores de la expansión cafetalera. (*Rev. Hist./Heredia*, julio/dic. 1986, p. 115–132, bibl., tables)

Analysis of the impact of coffee production in the Heredia region of Costa Rica during the 1830s and 1840s includes a discussion of social structure and land tenure prior to introduction of coffee cultivation.

1417 **Alvarez Aragón, Rosa María.** Estudio sobre la conjura de Belén. (*Antropol. Hist. Guatem.*, segunda época, 1985 p. 83–98)

Brief overview, based on archival sources, of little-appreciated episode in Independence-era Guatemala. More anti-Spanish agitation existed in Central America than is generally acknowledged by the "peaceful break" school of Independence historiography, but a good deal less existed than that claimed by the "blood and martyrdom" school.

Arellano, Jorge Eduardo. Bosquejo ideológico de Augusto Sandino. See item **5343.**

1418 **Arévalo, Juan José.** Seis años de gobierno: informes, discursos, mensajes. v. 1. Guatemala: CENALTEX, Ministerio de Educación, 1987. 1 vol.

Vol. 1 of a collection of addresses and messages by Juan José Arévalo during his presidency of Guatemala covers 1945–48.

1419 Argueta, Mario. Tiburcio Carías: anatomía de una época, 1923–1948. Tegucigalpa: Editorial Guaymuras, 1989. 390 p.: bibl. (Col. Códices: Ciencias Sociales)

Detailed study of Tiburcio Carías, National Party leader and long-term president (1933–48) of Honduras. This balanced, thoroughly-researched work reviews Honduran political and economic development through much of the first half of the 20th century and includes a great many documents of the period. This biography is highly objective and analytical, making it one of the more important works on 20th-century Honduran history and justifying its selection for the 1988 Rafael Heliodoro Valle Prize.

1420 Arosemena, Justo. Fundación de la nacionalidad panameña. Selección, prólogo y cronología de Ricaurte Soler. Caracas: Biblioteca Ayacucho, 1982. 514 p.: bibl. (Biblioteca Ayacucho; 92)

Traces the development of the state of Panama in 19th century through the writings and other documents of Arosemena. Includes a detailed chronology relating the life and work of Justo Arosemena (1817–96) to events in Panama and the world.

1421 Bolaños Geyer, Alejandro. William Walker: the gray-eyed man of destiny. v. 1–2. Lake Saint Louis, Mo.: A. Bolaños-Geyer, 1988–1989. 2 vols.: bibl., ill., index, maps.

First two volumes of a projected three-volume work on life and times of William Walker by a long-time researcher on the Walker episode. Vol. 1 explores Walker's early life as a physician, lawyer, and journalist before becoming a soldier-of-fortune, and attaches special importance to his personality change following the death of his fiancée in New Orleans. Based heavily on Walker's own writings, including a psychoanalysis of his handwriting. Vol. 2 covers the filibusterer's career in California (1850–55), and gives special attention to his adventures in Sonora. Volume closes as Walker departs on first expedition to Nicaragua.

1422 Bolland, O. Nigel. Labour control and resistance in Belize in the century after 1838. (*Slavery Abolit.*, 7:2, Sept. 1986, p. 175–187, bibl.)

Based on archival research in Belize and London, Bolland suggests that although certain restraints on labor were lifted in 1830s, the most significant means of controlling the work force in 19th-century Belize, as in much of Central America and the Caribbean during this period, was to limit its access to land. Concludes that workers did not threaten capitalist control of land until unrest became widespread in the 1930s, finally altering the distribution of political and social power.

1423 Burnett, Virginia Garrard. God and revolution: Protestant missions in revolutionary Guatemala, 1944–1954. (*Americas/Francisc.*, 46:2, Oct. 1989, p. 205–223)

Describes expansion of Protestant influence during the Guatemalan Revolution (1944–54), integrating missionary reports, bulletins, and memoirs with research in Guatemalan government documents. Demonstrates considerable Protestant expansion under Arévalo government, but reveals difficulties for Protestant missionaries under the Arbenz administration which suspected them of being agents of US imperialism.

1424 Burnett, Virginia Garrard. Protestantism in rural Guatemala, 1872–1954. (*LARR*, 24:2, 1989, p. 127–142, bibl.)

Explores relationship between the Guatemalan State and Protestantism during the formative years before 1954, making the point convincingly that for much of its history Protestantism in Guatemala has been as much a vehicle for conveying political and social behaviors as it has been a form of religion. Well-researched article effectively demonstrates how the liberal governments of Guatemala (1871–1945) perceived Protestantism as a useful political tool and actively encouraged its missionary activities.

1425 Burns, E. Bradford. Patriarch and folk: the emergence of Nicaragua, 1798–1858. Cambridge, Mass.: Harvard Univ. Press, 1991. 307 p: bibl., index.

Important addition to the limited bibliography available on 19th-century Nicaragua. Author focuses on the "partriarchial family" as the principal institution both uniting and dividing elites during these years; on how elites' expectations for national development clashed with those of the "folk;" and on the causes and effects of foreign intervention. Based chiefly on published sources, in this book Burns continues the innovative use of popular literature, drama, and poetry as historical sources characteristic of his earlier work. Recommended. [D.J. McCreery]

1426 Castellanos Cambranes, Julio. Democratización y movimientos campesinos pro-tierras en Guatemala. Guatemala: Centro de Estudios Rurales Centroamericanos (CERCA), 1988. 32 p. (Cuaderno; 3)

Discusses peasant grievances regarding land tenure and land use and their 20th-century efforts to regain control of their land in Guatemala. Expresses doubt that present "democratization" process can have much success in restoring land to the peasants.

1427 Castillero Calvo, Alfredo. El café en Panamá: una historia social y económica, siglos XVIII–XX. Panamá: Ediciones Nari, 1985. 100 p.: bibl.

Careful, rather brief study of coffee production for both export and domestic consumption in Panama. Accurately titled as both a social and economic history.

1428 Cerdas Albertazzi, Ana Luisa and Gerardo A. Vargas Cambronero. La abolición del ejército en Costa Rica: hito de un cambio de democracia y paz. San José: Comisión Nacional de Conmemoraciones Históricas; Junta Administrativa de la Impr. Nacional, 1988. 105 p.: bibl., ill.

Commemorative publication marking 40th anniversary of the abolition of the regular army in Costa Rica, an event praised by the country's admirers at home and abroad. Celebratory study includes a general overview of the history of the military and of democratic practices in Costa Rica.

1429 Chandler, David Lee. Juan José de Aycinena: idealista conservador de la Guatemala del siglo XIX. Traducción de Victoria Vázquez, Marina Vázquez y Lucía Robelo Pereira. Antigua, Guatemala: Centro de Investigaciones Regionales de Mesoamérica; South Woodstock, Vt.: Plumsock Mesoamerican Studies, 1988. 304 p.: bibl., index. (Serie monográfica, 0252–9971; 4)

Translation of author's MA thesis reviews the career of one of the leading 19th-

century Central American conservative ideologues. Volume includes 20 of Aycinena's more important writings.

1430 Chandler, David Lee. Peace through disunion: Father Juan José de Aycinena and the fall of the Central American Federation. (*Americas/Francisc.,* 46:2, Oct. 1989, p. 137–157)

Details role of a major Guatemalan conservative cleric in breakup of the United Provinces of Central America.

1431 Conte Porras, Jorge. Antología de la Guerra Civil de los Mil Días, 1899–1902. v. 1. Panamá: Editorial Acuario, 1986. 1 vol.: bibl., ill. (Biblioteca José Domingo Espinar; 5–6)

Collection of documents, memoirs, and other personal accounts from Panama's Independence movement, 1899–1902. Volume includes a foreword by General Manuel Antonio Noriega, a discussion of liberal ideas in Colombia by Gerardo Molina, contemporary accounts of the war by Belisario Porras, and a description of the war's causes by Rafael Uribe Uribe.

1432 Coraggio, José Luis and Rosa María Torres. Transición y crisis en Nicaragua. Quito: Editorial El Conejo, 1987. 249 p. (Col. Ecuador/Hoy)

Based on numerous interviews in Nicaragua, authors examine difficult period of transition in Nicaragua under Sandinista rule from 1979 to 1986, considering military as well as socioeconomic changes in the country. Includes detailed chronology of events in Nicaragua during the period.

1433 Delgado, Jesús. Oscar A. Romero: biografía. Madrid: Ediciones Paulinas, 1986. 207 p. (Testigos; 5)

Sympathetic biography of San Salvador Archbishop Romero and an account of his 1980 assassination, written by his secretary.

1434 Dosal, Paul J. The political economy of Guatemalan industrialization, 1871–1948: the career of Carlos F. Novella. (*HAHR,* 68:2, May 1988, p. 322–357, graphs)

Carefully-researched study of the rise of Guatemala's major cement company and its relations with the government. An excellent case study, with considerable import for the larger economic and political history of 20th-century Guatemala.

1435 Dr. Rafael Angel Calderón Guardia, reformador social de Costa Rica. Recopilacíon de Mario Hidalgo Brenes con la colaboración de María del Rosario Calderón Fournier. México: Litografía e Impr. Borrasé, 1983. 270 p.: ill., ports.

Biography of Calderón Guardia (1900–70) includes several chapters on the social legislation initiated by his National Republican government (1940–44). Using documents relating to his career, the study dedicates considerable attention to Calderón's exile in Mexico in 1949, his return to Costa Rica in 1958, and his last years.

1436 Dunkerley, James. Power in the Isthmus: a political history of modern Central America. London; New York: Verso, 1988. 691 p.: bibl., index, maps.

Meticulously documented and detailed history of Central America in the 20th century also includes an excellent review chapter on the 19th century (1820–1910). Most complete general work yet published on 20th-century Central America is especially comprehensive on the political history of the five Central American states (Guatemala, El Salvador, Honduras, Nicaragua, and Costa Rica) since 1930. For political scientist's comment see *HLAS 51: 3504.*

1437 El Salvador at war: an oral history of conflict from the 1979 insurrection to the present. Edited by Max G. Manwaring and Court Prisk, with a preface by Edwin G. Corr. Washington: National Defense Univ. Press, 1988. 500 p.: ill.

Collection of interviews emphasizes the military and international aspects of the current conflict in El Salvador. Contains oral interviews and a few other documents, principally from US and Salvadoran military, political, and diplomatic sources. Valuable collection for the views that these men present, but unfortunately the work does not include oral testimony from peasants, urban workers, or the Salvadoran middle class. For political scientist's comment see *HLAS 51:3540.*

1438 Figueroa Salazar, Amílcar. El Salvador: elementos de su historia y sus luchas, 1932–1985. Caracas: Fondo Editorial Tropykos, 1987. 160 p.: bibl., ill. (Serie Ensayos)

Historical overview of El Salvador since the 1932 "massacre" emphasizes development of labor's conflict with capitalism,

and social roots of present crisis. Carefully documented work presents a sympathetic account of the struggle of the FMLN against both the Salvadoran elites and the US.

1439 Fry, Michael F. Política agraria y reacción campesina en Guatemala: la región de La Montaña, 1821–1838. (*Mesoamérica/Antigua,* 9:15, junio 1988, bibl., map)

Examines liberal agrarian policy and its effects on peasants in "La Montaña" region of eastern Guatemala. Basing his argument on extensive archival research, Fry claims that liberal land policy was an important cause of the Carrera Revolt of 1837.

1440 García, Jesús María. La reforma agraria de Arbenz en Guatemala. Madrid: Ediciones Cultura Hispánica, Instituto de Cooperación Iberoamericana, 1987? 423 p.: bibl., indexes.

Thorough, well-documented examination of the Guatemalan Revolution (1944–54) with particular emphasis on the 1952 agrarian reform law of President Jacobo Arbenz. García suggests that the revolution failed largely because of the opposition to agrarian reform.

1441 García, Miguel Angel. La imprenta en Honduras, 1828–1975. Tegucigalpa: Univ. Nacional de Honduras, Editorial Universitaria, 1988. 301 p.: ill. (Col. Letras hondureñas; 35)

Narrative chronology of origins and development of the printing industry throughout Honduras in the 19th and 20th centuries.

1442 General José Domingo Espinar. 2a ed. Panamá: Editorial Acuario, 1987. 170 p.: ill., port. (Biblioteca José Domingo Espinar; 2)

Collection of letters, decrees, and communiques issued by the Panamanian General José Domingo Espinar (1791–1865), with a very brief biographical sketch. Espinar served as private secretary to Simón Bolívar during the Wars of Independence, and in 1830 took part in an unsuccessful attempt to establish Panamanian independence from Colombia.

1443 Gil Pacheco, Rufino. Ciento veinticinco años del Banco Anglo Costarricense en la historia de Costa Rica, 1863–1988. San José: Editorial Univ. Estatal a Distancia, 1988. 502 p.: bibl., ill.

Detailed and technical, commemorative history of Costa Rica's oldest commercial bank should be of interest to economic and institutional historians.

1444 Gómez, Alejandro. Rómulo Betancourt y el Partido Comunista de Costa Rica, 1931–1935. Caracas: Fondo Editorial de Humanidades y Educación, Univ. Central de Venezuela, 1985. 219 p.: bibl. (Col. Estudio)

Detailed examination of Betancourt's involvement as a leading figure in the Costa Rican Communist Party of the early 1930s. Author sees more continuity than contradiction in the political career of the subsequent leader of the Venezuelan Acción Democrática.

González, Nancie L. Nueva evidencia sobre el origen de los caribes negros, con consideraciones sobre el significado de la tradición. See *HLAS 51:788.*

1445 González Davison, Fernando. El régimen liberal en Guatemala, 1871–1944. Guatemala: Editorial Universitaria, Univ. de San Carlos, 1987. 73 p.: bibl. (Col. Editorial Universitaria; 78)

Convenient overview of the Liberal Party governments in Guatemala from the Reforma of 1871 to the fall of Jorge Ubico in 1944. Especially useful are several sections that discuss the distinct character of the regimes of Presidents Manuel Lisandro Barillas (1885–91), José María Reina Barrios (1891–98), and Manuel Estrada Cabrera (1898–1920).

1446 Gould, Jeffrey L. The enchanted burro, bayonets and the business of making sugar: State, capital, and labor relations in the Ingenio San Antonio, 1912–1926. (*Americas/Francisc.*, 46:2, Oct. 1989, p. 159–188)

Investigates the capitalist expansion and modernization of the San Antonio Sugar Mill, Nicaragua's largest employer and most important revenue producer between 1912–36. Includes an excellent analysis of the social and political consequences of its operations and the relationship it engendered between the Granada conservative elite, the incipient Somocista faction of the Liberal Party, and the sugar mill workers.

1447 Gould, Jeffrey L. "Estábamos principiando:" un estudio sobre el movi-

miento obrero en Chinandega, Nicaragua, 1920–1949. (*Rev. Hist./Heredia*, 18, julio/dic. 1988, p. 93–159, table)

Comparative study of labor organization in two geographically adjacent but otherwise different environments: 1) the Ingenio San Antonio, Nicaragua's most highly developed capitalist enterprise; and 2) the town of Chinandega, where production remained concentrated in small artesanal activities. Emphasizes late 1940s and relies heavily on oral interviews.

1448 Gudmundson, Lowell. Peasant, farmer, proletarian: class formation in a smallholder coffee economy, 1850–1950. (*HAHR*, 69:2, May 1989, p. 221–257, map, tables)

Detailed investigation of inheritance patterns, land tenure, and class differences in the development of Costa Rica's coffee economy. Basing his study on an impressive array of national, departmental, and local records, Gudmundson plots emergence and consolidation by the mid-20th century of Costa Rica's petit bourgeois producers.

1449 Guerra, Tomás. José Figueres, una vida por la justicia social. Heredia, Costa Rica: Centro de Estudios Democráticos de América Latina, 1987. 292 p.: bibl., port.

Sympathetic biography of José Figueres—whom Guerra hails as the father of modern Costa Rica—places considerable focus on his early life, the formation of his political thought, and his role in regional and hemispheric affairs.

1450 Gutiérrez, Pedro Rafael. Este es Calderón: retrato de un luchador que decidió ser presidente. San José: Ediciones Lena, 1985. 136 p., 34 leaves of plates: index.

Highly favorable biography of Rafael Angel Calderón Fournier, published during his successful 1989–90 campaign for the presidency of Costa Rica, based largely on opinions of his friends and relatives. Also presents Calderón's political ideology.

1451 Handy, Jim. The Guatemalan Revolution and civil rights: presidential elections and the judicial process under Juan José Arévalo and Jacobo Arbenz Guzmán. (*Can. J. Lat. Am. Caribb. Stud.*, 10:19, 1985, p. 3–21)

Although allegations of fraud and civil rights violations plagued the Arévalo and Arbenz Administrations, Handy finds this "legend" of unconstitutional behavior not supported by the evidence. He argues that anti-Communist opposition first created this "legend" and, since 1954, has used it to justify the violence perpetrated against moderates and leftists in the succeeding three decades.

1452 Handy, Jim. "The most precious fruit of the revolution:" the Guatemalan agrarian reform, 1952–54. (*HAHR*, 68:4, Nov. 1988, p. 675–705)

Handy links 1954 overthrow of Jacobo Arbenz to the Guatemalan military's opposition to the 1952 agrarian reform law, arguing that conflict between peasant organizations and the military was a primary cause of Arbenz's fall.

1453 Handy, Jim. National policy, agrarian reform, and the corporate community during the Guatemalan revolution, 1944–1954. (*Comp. Stud. Soc. Hist.*, 30:4, Oct. 1988, p. 698–724)

Challenges the views of Robert Wasserstrom and Carol Smith regarding the breakdown of Guatemalan Indian corporate communities during the Guatemalan Revolution. Handy details the rural policies of the Revolution and concludes that, while there was substantial pressure on the structure of the corporate community, the period was also marked by intense community identification. Also a useful review of the literature on the question of the survival of Indian communities in 19th- and 20th-century Guatemala.

1454 Handy, Jim. *A sea of Indians:* ethnic conflict and the Guatemalan revolution, 1944–1952. (*Americas/Francisc.*, 46:2, Oct. 1989, p. 189–204)

Based on extensive contemporary sources, Handy focuses on Indian-ladino conflict. Concludes that unrest in the countryside fostered by a moderate agrarian reform law alarmed Guatemala's ladino minority and thereby contributed to the overthrow of the Revolution in 1954.

1455 Hernández, Alcides. El neoliberalismo en Honduras. 2a ed. Tegucigalpa: Editorial Guaymuras, 1987. 213 p.: bibl., ill. (Col. Códices: Ciencias Sociales)

Theoretical investigation of the monetary policies advocated by economist Milton Friedman and their effect on Honduran socio-

economic development during the Administration of Roberto Suazo Córdova (1982–86). Includes numerous trade statistics and economic indicators to discredit neoliberalism and to demonstrate its links to Latin American underdevelopment and dependency.

1456 Herrera Balharry, Eugenio. Los alemanes y el estado cafetalero. San José: Editorial Univ. Estatal a Distancia, 1988. 230 p., 18 p. of plates: bibl., ill.

Careful study of German immigrants' integration by marriage into Costa Rica's small ruling elite. Author's debt to sociologist Samuel Stone's work is evident.

1457 Hilje Q., Eugenia. Legislación agraria y apropiación de la tierra en Guanacaste: el caso de Cañas, 1884–1907. (*Rev. Hist./Heredia*, 17, enero/junio 1988, p. 69–97, bibl., map, tables)

Based on meticulous research in the Costa Rican National Archives, Hilje describes the development and economic exploitation of the Cañas region of Guanacaste. She is primarily concerned with Minor Keith's River Plate Company and its extensive land holdings, and suggests that the return of much of the company's lands in the early part of the 20th century was a consequence of a political and economic conflict with the Costa Rican agrarian elite.

1458 Howett, Charles F. Neighborly concern: John Nevin Sayre and the mission of peace and goodwill to Nicaragua, 1927–28. (*Americas/Francisc.*, 45:1, July 1988, p. 19–46, bibl.)

Reviews the journey of the 1927–28 peace mission to Nicaragua of John Nevin Sayre, an Episcopal priest, showing how mission was hampered by US State Dept. Based largely on Sayre's journal and other writings, author argues that US policy insisted on military victory and eschewed negotiated settlement.

1459 Instituto de Estudio del Sandinismo. Ahora sé que Sandino manda. Managua: Editorial Nueva Nicaragua, 1986. 327 p.: ill., index. (Col. Séptimo aniversario)

Traces the story of Augusto C. Sandino and his rebellion through excerpts from his writings and testimony of 114 campesinos and other representatives of the working classes.

1460 Jeifets, Lázar. ¡Manos fuera de Nicaragua! (*Am. Lat./Moscú*, 10, 1988, p. 85–93, bibl., ill., photos)

Describes the 1928 formation in Mexico of the "Manos Fuera de Nicaragua" Committee of the Anti-Imperialist League and documents its communist connections.

1461 Juliao Rosas, Víctor Nelson. Recuerdos de mi vida. S.l.: Impresiones K-Lin, 1987. 178 p.: ill., ports.

Autobiography of a Panamanian engineer, professor, politician, and diplomat focuses primarily on his diplomatic and political career (1950–60) and his involvement in three revolts against the military government of General Omar Torrijos after 1968.

1462 Laino, Domingo. El general comerciante. Asunción: Ediciones Cerro Corá, 1983. 199 p.: bibl.

Documents the Somoza family's links to agro-export, multinational companies, and international financial networks. This undisguised, poignant attack on the Somoza dynasty focuses on the exploitative and corrupt nature of the family's business practices.

1463 Leonov, Nikolaï Sergeevich. Omar Torrikhos: "Ia ne khochu voïti v istoriĭu, ĭa khochu voïti v zonu kanala" [Omar Torrijos: "I don't want to go down in history, I want to go down into the Canal Zone"]. Moscow: "Mezhdunar. otnosheniĭa," 1990. 240 p.: bibl., ill.

Soviet historian of 20th-century Latin America provides a political biography of Torrijos, whom the book's Moscow publisher calls the "Latin American David." Author draws on his personal acquaintance with Torrijos and on Panamanian and US sources to discuss the general's role in domestic and international politics, especially the Panama Canal Treaty. Touches on Torrijos' relations with Jimmy Carter, Daniel Ortega, Castro, Tito, Qaddafi, and others. Chap. 1 provides a "Brief History of the Struggle for the Canal." For general audiences. [B. Dash]

Leslie, Vernon. The Belize River boat traffic. See *HLAS 51:2851.*

1464 Luján Muñoz, Luis. J. Joaquín Pardo, forjador de la investigación histórica moderna en Guatemala. Guatemala: Archivo General de Centroamérica, 1984. 51 p.: bibl., ill., photos.

Brief biography and review of Pardo's work in developing the Guatemalan national archives includes a bibliography of Pardo's works and many photographs. Pardo (1905–64) directed the archives from 1935–64.

1465 Martínez, José de Jesús. Mi general Torrijos. San Salvador: Editorial Universitaria, Univ. de El Salvador, 1988. 355 p. (Col. Ave fénix)

Personal memoir and biography of Torrijos by an admirer.

1466 McCreery, David. Land, labor, and violence in highland Guatemala: San Juan Ixcoy (Huehuetenango), 1893–1945. (*Americas/Francisc.*, 45:2, Oct. 1988, p. 237–249, bibl.)

Case study of struggle between Indians and ladinos that arose with onset of coffee production discusses coercive and violent alteration of traditional society caused by the favoring of coffee cultivation over Indian subsistence farming.

1467 Mejía, Medardo. Historia de Honduras. v. 3. Tegucigalpa: Univ. Nacional Autónoma de Honduras, Editorial Universitaria, 1983. 1 vol. (Col. Realidad nacional; 15)

Vol. 3 of ongoing series focuses on the era of Francisco Morazán, from his election as governor of Honduras (1829) to his capture and execution (1842). Narrative episodes alternate with extensive reproduction of primary texts, but there is little attempt at interpretative synthesis.

1468 Mejía, Medardo. Historia de Honduras. v. 4. Tegucigalpa: Univ. Nacional Autónoma de Honduras, Editorial Universitaria, 1983. 1 vol. (Col. Realidad nacional; 19. Ediciones Nueva Universidad)

Vol. 4 of Mejía's continuing narrative deals with the mid-19th century, especially 1850–65, with particular attention to the governments of Trinidad Cabañas and Santos Guardiola. Includes chronology of origin and development of the "Olancho Factions" of the late 1860s, compiled by Justo Pérez. Primarily a compilation of historical documents with little analysis.

Miller, Hubert J. The Taracena Flores Collection in the Benson Latin American Collection at the University of Texas, relating to Church and State materials in Guatemala, 1945–1954. See *HLAS 51:65.*

1469 Molina Jiménez, Iván. Habilitadores y habilitados en el Valle Central de Costa Rica: el financiamiento de la producción cafetalera en los inicios de su expansión, 1838–1850. (*Rev. Hist./Heredia*, 16, julio/dic. 1987, p. 85–128, bibl., graphs, tables)

Detailed study of the *habilitación* system of credit in early 19th century, with particular emphasis on Costa Rica's integration into the world market and its rising dependency on English capital. Concludes that inherent in the relationship between *habilitador* and *habilitado* were two forms of exploitation: unequal exchange and extraction of economic surplus. However, Molina argues that it was not the middle-sized producer, but rather the campesino, the *jornalero*, and the *beneficio* worker—those that suffered most from the onerous terms of the agreement—who actually financed the expansion of coffee production.

1470 Molina Jiménez, Iván. El Valle Central de Costa Rica en la Independencia. (*Rev. Hist./Heredia*, julio/dic. 1986, p. 85–114, bibl.)

Well-organized essay reviews the literature on establishment of Independence in the Central Valley of Costa Rica, concluding that there is still much research to be done, especially on the economic and social history of the period. Molina suggests a number of historical questions that need answers.

1471 Morgan, Henry G. Vistas de Costa Rica. San José: Comisión del Centenario de la Democracia Costarricense; Imprenta Nacional, 1989. 105 p.

Fifty-six photographs of rural and urban scenes of Costa Rica taken by North American photographer Henry G. Morgan in 1892 show people, agricultural and industrial enterprises, public and private buildings, churches, transportation, etc.

1472 Natalini de Castro, Stefanía; María de los Angeles Mendoza Saborío; and Joaquín Pagán Solórzano. Significado histórico del gobierno del Dr. Ramón Villeda Morales. Tegucigalpa: Univ. Nacional Autónoma de Honduras, Editorial Universitaria, 1985. 220 p.: bibl. (Col. Realidad nacional; 10)

Sympathetic study of the Liberal Honduran government of Villeda Morales (1957–63) emphasizes the multi-class orientation of the Villeda Administration. Explains in great detail his attempt to implement middle-class reforms that, authors argue, inevitably led to the 1963 military coup.

1473 Navas Zepeda, Máximo. El rapto de Nicaragua: historia documentada de la intervención americana. S.l.: Instituto Histórico Nicaragüense, 1987. 202 p.: bibl., ill., index.

Collection of photos, biographical sketches, declarations, and treaties that trace US diplomatic and military intervention in Nicaragua and their sociopolitical impact on Nicaraguan society. Navas Zepeda, a pro-Contra Nicaraguan expatriate, berates US initiatives in Nicaragua from the early decades of this century through those of the Reagan Administration to explain the successes of the FSLN in the 1970s and 1980s.

1474 Naylor, Robert A. La influencia británica en el comercio centroamericano durante las primeras décadas de la independencia, 1821–1851. Antigua, Guatemala: Centro de Investigaciones Regionales de Mesoamérica; South Woodstock, Vt.: Plumsock Mesoamerican Studies, 1988. 314 p.: bibl., index, map, tables. (Serie monográfica; 3)

Careful and thorough investigation of the powerful British commercial role in Central America during the first three decades of Independence. Major contribution argues persuasively that commercial interests were the primary reason for Britain's dominant role in the region.

1475 The Nicaraguan Mosquitia in historical documents, 1844–1927: the dynamics of ethnic and regional history. Edited by Eleonore von Oertzen, Lioba Rossbach, and Volker Wünderich. Berlin: Dietrich Reimer Verlag, 1990. 486 p.: appendix, bibl., index, map.

Selected documents on Mosquito life and culture in the shadow of international rivalry. Major sources include correspondence of Patrick Walker (British consul at Bluefields, 1844–48), and materials drawn from Moravian mission publications and archives. Most documents are in English; materials in other languages (principally German) are not translated.

1476 Núñez Téllez, Carlos. La insurrección de Managua: el repliegue a Masaya.

Buenos Aires: Editorial Cartago, 1987. 140 p.: ill., ports.

Comandante of the Sandinista Revolution relates the story of the insurrection in the neighborhoods surrounding Managua and the tactical retreat to Masaya in 1979.

1477 Ortega, Miguel R. Morazán: laurel sin ocaso; biografía. v. 1. Tegucigalpa: Ediciones II Centenario, Fundación Morazánica Honduras, 1988. 1 vol.: bibl., ill.

First installment of laudatory, didactic biography, rich in reproductions of primary documents, some previously unpublished. Eccentric plan of three-volume work proposes to move backwards through time. Vol. 1 focuses on last years of Morazán's career as he might have reflected on them the night before his execution.

1478 Palmer, Steven. Carlos Fonseca and the construction of Sandinismo in Nicaragua. (*LARR*, 23:1, 1988, p. 91–109, bibl.)

Analyzes Sandinismo constructed by Carlos Fonseca as an ideology that attempted to provide leadership, meaning, and motivation for the Sandinista Revolution. Also comments on other works dealing with Fonseca and Sandinismo. For political scientist's comment see *HLAS 51:3592*.

1479 Parkman, Patricia. Nonviolent insurrection in El Salvador: the fall of Maximiliano Hernández Martínez. Tucson: Univ. of Arizona Press, 1988. 168 p.: bibl., ill., index.

Well-documented monograph examines the May 1944 strike led by the professional and economic elites of San Salvador that paralyzed El Salvador and forced Maximiliano Hernández Martínez to surrender power. For political scientist's comment see *HLAS 51:3551*.

1480 Pastor Fasquelle, Rodolfo. Memoria de una empresa hondureña. San Pedro Sula, Honduras: Compañía Azucarera Hondureña, 1988. 449 p.: ill.

Carefully-researched and informative narrative published by the Honduran Sugar Company on the occasion of its 50th anniversary. Not surprisingly—given its publisher and the author's family connections to the company—book is a sympathetic, though highly professional, treatment based on company records and interviews with key personnel. Well-written company histories of this quality are rare in Central America, so this is a most welcome contribution.

1481 Pozas, Víctor S. La revolución sandinista, 1979–88. Madrid: Editorial Revolución, 1988? 370 p.: bibl., ill.

Sympathetic account of the Sandinista Revolution from the fall of Somoza to the Esquipulas accords. Author, an admirer of the revolutionary process, saw the accords as a major turning point in the Central American struggle and particularly as a vindication of the legitimacy of FSLN rule. Obviously he could not foresee the revolutionaries' dismissal by the Nicaraguan electorate shortly thereafter.

1482 Presa Fernández, Julián. Historia de la Sociedad Española de Beneficencia de Guatemala. Guatemala: Talleres de Impre Offset Profesional, 1987. 498 p.: bibl., ill., ports.

Detailed chronological record of the religious, humanitarian, and patriotic activities and projects of an important organization of Spanish immigrants in Guatemala since its foundation in 1866.

1483 Quesada C., Juan Rafael. El nacimiento de la historiografía en Costa Rica. (*Rev. Hist./Heredia*, no. especial, 1988, p. 51–81, bibl.)

Explains that Costa Rica's sophisticated, highly developed tradition of historical inquiry was built on sound foundations by late-19th-century lawyers who carefully accumulated documentation for the practical purpose of defending territorial claims.

1484 Reina Valenzuela, José. José Trinidad Cabañas: estudio biográfico. Tegucigalpa: Ejército, 1984. 241 p.: bibl.

Rather eulogistic biography of the leading Morazanista Honduran military leader of the 19th century commemorates the centennial of his death in 1871. Following Morazán's death, Cabañas was involved in repeated attempts to restore the Central American Federation and to develop Honduras according to liberal modernization concepts.

1485 *Revista del Archivo Nacional.* Vol. 51, Nos. 1/12, 1987– . San José, Costa Rica: Imprenta Nacional.

Recent issue of venerable journal is devoted to Luz María Campos González's study "La Municipalidad de San José en la Formación del Estado de Costa Rica (1814–1841)." Based on extensive archival research, this thorough monograph transcends narrow limits of traditional municipal history to offer rich portrait of material and social fabric of urban life in early national San José.

1486 Ricord, Humberto E. Panamá en la Guerra de los Mil Días. Panamá: H.E. Ricord, 1989. 351 p.: bibl., ill.

Detailed political and military account of Panama's role in the Colombian civil war (1899–1902), which, according to author, represented "el punto decisivo en que se bifurca el destino histórico del pueblo panameño-colombiano" (p. 303).

1487 Rodríguez Sáenz, Eugenia and **Iván Molina Jiménez.** La formación de compañías económicas en el Valle Central de Costa Rica, 1824–1860: un avance tecnológico. (*Rev. Hist./Heredia*, no. especial, 1988, p. 139–155, graph, tables)

Study of formation and dissolution of partnerships (*sociedades* or *compañías*) in mid-19th-century Costa Rica, based on notarial records. Authors argue that such partnerships increased in 1840s, meeting the need for new forms of entrepreneurial organization imposed by expansion of capitalist agriculture.

1488 Rodríguez Sáenz, Eugenia. Las interpretaciones sobre la expansión del café en Costa Rica y el papel jugado por el crédito. (*Rev. Hist./Heredia*, 18, julio/dic. 1988, p. 163–186)

Useful overview of Costa Rican coffee historiography emphasizes contribution of professional historians working since the 1960s.

1489 Rubio Sánchez, Manuel. El mariscal de campo José Clara Lorenzana. Guatemala: Editorial del Ejército, 1987. 124 p.: bibl. (Col. Historia militar: Serie Mariscales de campo)

Second in author's series of biographies of 19th-century Guatemalan military leaders is largely a collection of documents highlighting the military and political career of José Clara Lorenzana (1796–1864), one of Rafael Carrera's most loyal and trusted field marshals.

1490 Sáenz Maroto, Alberto. Braulio Carrillo, reformador agrícola de Costa Rica. San José: Editorial de la Univ. de Costa Rica, 1987. 128 p.: bibl., port.

Sympathetic political biography of Costa Rican liberal leader Braulio Carrillo (1800–45) pays special attention to the agricultural, economic, and social policies initiated by Carrillo governments (1835–37 and 1838–42).

1491 Salas Víquez, José Antonio. La privatización de los baldíos nacionales en Costa Rica durante el siglo XIX: legislación y procedimientos utilizados para su adjudicación. (*Rev. Hist./Heredia*, 15, enero/junio 1987, p. 63–118, bibl., tables)

Careful study of the application of liberal economic philosophy to Costa Rican land tenure in 19th-century is based on archival research. Discusses specific procedures used to privatize uncultivated public lands, and problems arising in 20th century from application of these procedures. Includes statistical evidence.

1492 Salazar, Carlos. Memoria de los servicios prestados a la nación, 1908–1944. 2a ed. Guatemala: Grupo Literario Editorial RIN-78, 1987. 335 p. (Col. Rescate; 3)

New edition of a memoir first published in 1945 describes Salazar's years of public service to Guatemalan government. Provides intimate and detailed description of inner workings of Guatemalan government and of political manipulations and intrigues of international diplomacy during the first half of the 20th century.

1493 Samper Kutschbach, Mario. Fuerzas sociopolíticas y procesos electorales en Costa Rica. (*Rev. Hist./Heredia*, no. especial, 1988, p. 157–222, graphs, maps, tables)

Creative and sophisticated effort to blend political history ("from above") and social history ("from below") to understand origins of peculiar combination of attitudes and behavior accounting for resilience of civil society and electoral process in modern Costa Rica. Focuses on 1920s and 1930s as critical prelude to major realignment of political forces resulting in, and from, crisis of late 1940s.

1494 Samper Kutschbach, Mario. Uso de la tierra y unidades productivas al finalizar el siglo XIX: noroeste del Valle Central,

Costa Rica. (*Rev. Hist./Heredia*, 14, julio/dic. 1986, p. 133–177)

Informative and well-organized discussion of land use and organization of rural society in the period 1895–1904, as the agricultural frontier began to move beyond the Central Valley.

1495 Sandino, Augusto César. Sandino without frontiers: selected writings of Augusto César Sandino on internationalism, Pan-Americanism, and social questions. Essays by Carlos Fonseca Amador and Sergio Ramírez. Edited, annotated, and introduced by Karl Bermann. Translated by Karl Bermann *et al.* Hampton, Va.: Compita Pub., 1988. 138 p.: bibl., ill.

English translations of a selection of Sandino's letters and other writings that reflect his views on inter-American relations, internationalism, and social questions. Volume includes an introductory essay by Karl Bermann and a selection from *Viva Sandino* by Carlos Fonseca Amador. Two essays by Sergio Ramírez, "The Lad from Niquinohomo" and "The Relevance of Sandino's Thought," are especially enlightening on Sandino's career and its relation to modern Sandinismo in Nicaragua.

1496 Schoonover, Thomas. Germany in Central America, 1820s to 1929: an overview. (*Jahrb. Gesch.*, 25, 1988, p. 33–59, tables)

Boasting extensive German archival research, article explains German economic expansion in Central America to 1929 and links German political and economic interests on the isthmus to social problems unleashed by industrial capitalism in Germany.

1497 Schoonover, Thomas and Ebba Schoonover. Statistics for an understanding of foreign intrusions into Central America from the 1820s to 1930. (*Anu. Estud. Centroam.*, 15 : 1, 1989, p. 93–119, tables)

First of three planned installments includes introductory material on definitions, methodology, and provisional conclusions. Reports statistics gathered from a wide variety of sources on foreign investment, immigration, commercial firms, and trade (both export and import) for Central America as a whole and for each country individually.

1498 Solórzano, Juan Carlos. Rafael Carrera, ¿reacción conservadora o revolución

campesina?: Guatemala, 1837–1873. (*Anu. Estud. Centroam.*, 13 : 2, 1987, p. 5–35, bibl., map)

Challenges traditional historiography of orthodox Marxists and Liberals who claimed that Carrera's peasant uprising was orchestrated as an instrument of Guatemala's conservative or feudal elite. Article provides useful review of the historical literature on Carrera and reflects some research in primary sources as well.

1499 Stephens, Clyde. Bosquejo histórico del cultivo del banano en la provincia de Bocas del Toro, 1880–1980. Edición de Stanley Heckadon Moreno. Panamá: Impretex, 1987. 50 p.: ill., map, ports. (Revista panameña de antropología: Publicaciones especiales; 1)

Author, an entomologist with United Fruit Company, is also an accomplished amateur historian. Study traces development of banana industry on Atlantic coast of Panama from its origins to the present, and contains much of interest on early history of United Fruit, infrastructure development, impact on landscape, and changing patterns of labor supply. Many fine old photographs.

1500 Suñol, Julio C. Insurrección en Nicaragua: la historia no contada. 2a ed. San José: Editorial Costa Rica, 1982. 237 p.: bibl., facsims.

Costa Rican diplomat and journalist reconstructs events of 1978–79 that toppled the Somoza dynasty in Nicaragua on the basis of interviews with prominent Costa Rican politicians and FSLN comandantes and other Nicaraguan government officials. Perceptive contemporary memoir of the Nicaraguan Revolution.

1501 Surí Quesada, Emilio. Los cachorros andan sueltos. Managua: Editorial Vanguardia; La Habana: Editora Política, 1987. 207 p.: ill., ports.

Personal accounts of Sandinista soldiers fighting against the Contras. Although heavily biased and propagandistic against the US and the Contras, book has value for the social historian in its descriptive testimony by the people involved in the Contra war.

1502 Taracena Arriola, Arturo. Presencia anarquista en Guatemala entre 1920 y 1932. (*Mesoamérica/Antigua*, 9 : 15, junio 1988, p. 1–23, bibl.)

Survey of growth of anarchist thought

and activity in Guatemala following the dictatorship of Manuel Estrada Cabrera notes influences from other Latin American countries and the relationship of anarchists to the Guatemalan labor movement.

1503 Taracena Arriola, Arturo. El primer partido comunista de Guatemala, 1922–1932: diez años de una historia olvidada. (*Anu. Estud. Centroam.*, 15:1, 1989, p. 49–63)

Broader in scope than title implies, well-documented study examines working class organization and political activity in neglected 1920s decade which author calls "los únicos diez años de vida democrática que ha tenido Guatemala en lo que va de este siglo" (p. 62).

1504 Ulloa Mayorga, Juan Manuel *et al.* Apuntes de historia de Nicaragua. León, Nicaragua: Editorial Universitaria, Univ. Nacional Autónoma de Nicaragua, 1988. 234 p.: bibl.

Narrowly-focused textbook meant for use in university courses on history of Sandinista Revolution emphasizes period from the fall of José Santos Zelaya (1909) to the assassination of Anastasio Somoza (1956), and examines themes such as world capitalism, US imperialism, and the rise of Somoza.

1505 Vargas Coto, Joaquín. Crónicas de la época y vida de Don Ricardo. San José: Editorial Costa Rica, 1986. 403 p.

Admiring, anecdotal biography of Ricardo Jiménez Oreamuno, twice president of Costa Rica during "golden age" of coffee-based prosperity (1910–14 and 1924–28). Does not cover his third, Depression-era Administration (1932–36).

1506 Woodward, Ralph Lee. Economic development and dependency in nineteenth-century Guatemala. (*in* Crises in the Caribbean Basin. Edited by Richard Tardanico. Newberry Park, Ca.: Sage Publications, 1987, p. 59–78, bibl., tables)

Examination of origins of export-driven dependent development in Guatemala. Although author recognizes continuities underlying entire 19th century, he calls attention to Conservative period (1840–71) as potential example "for underdeveloped countries that wish to preserve traditional lifestyles within a framework of gradual modernization" (p. 73).

1507 Wünderich, Volker. *Dios hablará por el indio de las Segovias:* las bases sociales de la lucha de Sandino por la liberación nacional en Nicaragua, 1927–1934. (*Rev. Hist./Heredia*, 17, enero/junio 1988, p. 13–32, tables)

Examines nationalist nature of Sandino's struggle to achieve dignity, justice, and liberty in north-central Nicaragua. Pays particular attention to evidence that Sandino sought to improve the social and economic status of the Indian and working classes, but also suggests that Sandino's nationalist program encouraged cooperation with the Nicaraguan bourgeoisie and never supported expropriation of land from large holders.

THE CARIBBEAN, THE GUIANAS AND THE SPANISH BORDERLANDS

EDWARD L. COX, *Associate Professor of History, Rice University, Houston*
ANNE PEROTIN-DUMON, *Associate Visiting Professor of History, University of Virginia*
FRANCISCO SCARANO, *Professor of History, University of Wisconsin-Madison*
JOSE M. HERNANDEZ, *Adjunct Professor of History, Georgetown University*
ROSEMARIJN HOEFTE, *Deputy Head, Department of Caribbean Studies, Royal Institute of Linguistics and Anthropology*

THE BRITISH CARIBBEAN

SLAVERY AND SLAVE SOCIETY continue to attract the attention of most scholars of the British Caribbean, and, although no recently-published pieces fall into the "excellent" category, a few very important works did appear. By making use of the

1813–16 slave registration data for Trinidad, Meredith John's *The plantation slaves of Trinidad* (item **1667**) provides a marvelously interesting portrait gallery of plantation slavery in the early-19th century. Her conclusions of high mortality and low fertility rates for slaves confirm what has been intuitively suspected of the island and the British Caribbean as a whole, though they do not embrace or address Higman's projection of improved rates as emancipation approached (see *HLAS 48:2517b*). Armstrong's archaeological study of the Drax Hall Plantation (item **1513**) gives a fascinating, important glimpse of the material culture of workers on one Jamaican plantation during times of slavery and freedom. Hall has edited and provided a useful introduction to a revealing journal kept by a Jamaican planter (item **1652**) which significantly improves our knowledge and understanding of important aspects of slave life, slave management, the process of creolization, and the relationships between whites and slaves.

Campbell's book (item **1641**) is undoubtedly the most comprehensive and intellectually stimulating treatment to date on Maroons in Jamaica, while Beckles' and Watson's useful article "Social Protest and Labour Bargaining" (item **1632**) examines another aspect of slave resistance. Their argument that Barbadian slaves utilized bargaining power rather than revolutionary means to extract concessions aimed at improving their own material conditions is a sharp reminder of how slaves' experiences and patterns of behavior were likely to vary over time and under different conditions. Gaspar's "Slavery, Amelioration, and Sunday Markets in Antigua" (item **1756**) indicates that though reformers viewed amelioration as potentially beneficial for slaves, the slaves themselves reacted negatively toward the abolition of Sunday markets because it denied them a meaningful opportunity to trade and otherwise promote their own self-interests.

The free colored population is covered in two worthwhile publications. *An address to the Right Honourable Earl Bathurst, by a free mulatto* (item **1810**) is simultaneously a powerful articulation of the disabilities which the Trinidad group faced during a critical transitional period, and a moving appeal by a member of the body for redress. Sio's "Marginality and Free Coloured Identity in Caribbean Slave Society" (item **1690**) rightly reminds us of the need to reexamine the rank and file of this important group rather than relying too heavily on examples from the highly visible elite to portray the entire community as being assimilationist.

The resurgence of interest in Caribbean economic history, noted in previous volumes of the *Handbook,* is evident in some recent publications, two of which deserve special mention. Solow and Engerman have edited a volume of essays entitled *British capitalism and Caribbean slavery* (item **1525**) which reexamines Eric Williams' contributions to Caribbean economic history, especially his central thesis on the symbiosis of capitalism and slavery. Carrington's *The British West Indies during the American Revolution* (item **1642**) analyzes the British West Indian commercial and political developments (1770–87) and concludes that the economic decline of the islands began during the American Revolution when the islands lost access to British North American markets.

Important aspects of the post-emancipation society and labor system are addressed by a number of authors. Trotman's *Crime in Trinidad: conflict and control in a plantation society* (item **1849**) succinctly analyzes how planters criminalized certain aspects of Creole culture in order to maintain social control over the laboring population, while Mangru (item **1780**) provides a fruitful study of Guyanese planters' unsuccessful attempts to eliminate their financial responsibility for providing return passages to East Indians at the end of their indentureship. Shepherd's

"The Dynamics of Afro-Jamaican/East Indian Relations in Jamaica" (item **1597**) points to deteriorating relations between workers of these different ethnic groups especially during periods of economic depression.

The 20th-century nationalist movement has received coverage in three fine articles and a monograph. Magid's *Urban nationalism: a study of political development in Trinidad* (item **1933**) portrays disputes within the Port-of-Spain Town Council and the subsequent radicalization of political behavior as the forerunner of island-wide nationalism, while Basdeo (item **1874**) makes creditable use of class analysis in examining Trinidad's labor politics in the early 20th century when riots and protests against the colonial power were rampant throughout the British Caribbean. Palmer (item **1953**) addresses the uncertain search for racial identity in Jamaica where the presence of racial and class tensions facilitated government efforts to crush the Black Power ideology of the 1960s. Finally, Bennett (item **1876**) argues along a similar vein by detailing the continued racial tensions in Trinidad at the time of the outbreak of the "February Uprising." The government's belated recognition of the validity of the claims of the revolutionaries, however, placed an official seal on the latter's charges that full independence was a mere chimera in the presence of so many lingering aspects of colonialism and imperialism. [ELC]

FRENCH AND DANISH CARIBBEAN

Recent publications on the French Caribbean and French Guiana explore new avenues in addition to pursuing well-known topics. It is particularly encouraging that French Guiana history has grown to encompass new topics such as the bases of the region's colonial economy—first annatto-plantations (Saint-Martin, item **1593**) and then gold (Huyghues-Belrose and Bruleaux, item **1562**), her long history of slavery (item **1532**), and changes brought about by each World War (Huyghues-Belrose and Alexandre, items **1922** and **1859**).

The bicentennial of the French Revolution of 1789 has stimulated the study of this region's revolutionary period. Geggus provides an overview of the Haitian Revolution (item **1662**) and the Historical Society of Guadeloupe has reprinted one of the best narratives on the English Caribbean campaigns during the Revolutionary Wars (item **1697**). Interest in colonial Freemasonic lodges (items **1670** and **1649**) and the relationship between the French Islands and the Spanish Caribbean (item **1679**) has also generated new publications.

The late colonial period continues to attract many scholars, with urban history emerging as a new field of study in this Caribbean region. The growth of 18th-century colonial port cities is documented by Pérotin-Dumon (items **1580** and **1678**), Geggus (items **1659** and **1663**), Butel (items **1639** and **1640**) and Loupès (items **1672** and **1671**).

On sugar and slavery, topics with significance extending beyond the 18th century, the trend is towards syntheses such as Stein's *French sugar business* (item **1692**) and Renault and Daget's *Traite negrière* (item **1588**). A gap has also been filled by Saugera on the Atlantic French slave trade of the early 1800s (item **1829**).

The abolition of slavery continues to dominate the 19th-century history of the region: Schmidt examines its political significance in conjunction with the universal male suffrage proclaimed by the French Second Republic (item **1831**), and Buffon examines its implications for the national economy, given the indemnifications granted to former slave owners (item **1730**).

Perhaps the most creative studies, overlapping several centuries, deal with art and architecture. Bégot shows the limits to artistic creativity under colonial rule, a creativity which has blossomed over the past century of independent Haiti (items 1520 and 1521). Greene and Cissel (item 1554) and Bégot and Mousnier (item 1602) convey the architectural dimensions of colonial power and economy. Religious history, hitherto a neglected field, is emerging thanks to Lafleur's account of the 17th-century Protestant minority in the French Antilles (item 1614) and Hellström's study of the enlightened Protestant churches in the 19th-century Danish islands (item 1558).

Haitian political history dominates the 20th-century subsection: Hector traces the complex history of labor unions (item 1920); Bonnardot and Danroc have recorded the anti-Duvalierist voices of grassroots churches and political organizations (item 1889); and Pizetty-van Eeuwen analyzes Haiti's political destiny in light of the country's present hopes and difficulties (item 1583). [APD]

DUTCH CARIBBEAN

Recent work on the history of the Dutch Caribbean continues to focus on the study of slavery and Maroon society. It is remarkable, however, that anthropologists have written most of these historical works. Postma is one of only two representatives of the historian's guild mentioned in this *HLAS* essay covering 1988–90. His long-awaited account of *The Dutch in the Atlantic slave trade* (item 1683) is an eminent study which fills a huge gap in the literature.

Richard and Sally Price edited and introduced Stedman's classic *Narrative of a five years expedition against the revolted Negroes of Surinam* (item 1691). This splendid volume is based on Stedman's personal copy of the 1790 manuscript rather than on the edited version of 1796.

Anthropologists Thoden van Velzen and Van Wetering's 25 years research among the Ndjuka Maroons in Suriname are the basis of the fascinating *The Great Father and The Danger*, the first extensive study of the religious and social history of these Maroons (see *HLAS 51:842*). In an experimental work which is not always satisfying, Richard Price presents the successful struggle for freedom of the Saramaka Maroons by interweaving four historical voices (set in as many type styles) of the Saramakas, the Dutch, the missionaries, and Price himself as the mediating historian (item 1584).

In comparison to the historiography of the region as a whole, the Dutch Caribbean contribution is meager. In addition, most works on the history of the Antilles and Suriname lack a Caribbean context. Even though the quantity of historical works has grown appreciably during the last two decades, the same cannot be said of their quality. It is rather telling that this brief survey does not include publications on the Netherlands Antilles and Aruba. With the exception of Curaçao, the history of the Dutch Caribbean islands—Aruba, Bonaire, St. Maarten, Saba, and St. Eustatius—largely remains to be written. Goslinga has published three volumes on the Dutch in the Caribbean (item 1552), yet emphasizes political and economic developments. Topics such as the 20th-century social history, immigration, and the history of women have been barely touched. The compilation of an integrated inventory of all material available in Antillean, European, South and North American archives is sorely needed to facilitate and improve the quality of historical research. [RH]

PUERTO RICO

The current crop of Puerto Rican historical writings once again evinces the same focus on politics and culture observed in *HLAS 50*. The more exciting work builds upon the so-called New History, which in the 1970s and early 1980s tried to un-ravel the class dynamics of a colonial society thrust upon the world market as a staple producer. Current historiography widens this focus to capture a nuanced and complex picture of the relationship between social forces and the State, as well as between power and culture. Structural issues, especially those arising from export production, continue to claim substantial attention. But previously unexplored themes such as political discourse, urbanization, collective mentalities, social movements, plebeian solidarities and the formation of subaltern communities and popular culture have also begun to excite the imaginations of island historians.

Quintero Rivera's latest writings exemplify the organic connection between the New History and this *novísima historia* (*Newest* History). In the 1970s, his writings on class, colonialism, politics, and, more specifically, on the politics of la-bor, were a key component of the revisionist literature. Recently, however, he has turned his attention to different topics: to what he describes as the "camouflaged" imprint that Africans left on Creole culture (item **1585**). In this essay, Quintero Rivera offers fresh interpretations of the process of creolization. He boldly uses concepts and methods borrowed from musical studies and architecture, among others, to dissect these processes and to demonstrate African cultures' profound in-fluence in Puerto Rico. Other significant studies that look beyond socioeconomic history include Sepúlveda's stunning work on the capital city (item **1595**), his com-panion study of Cangrejos-Santurce co-authored by Jorge Carbonell (item **1594**), and Rivera-Belardo's "Los Problemas de la Expansión Urbana: San Juan de Puerto Rico, 1850–1898" (item **1819**).

Another way in which the latest writings have added to the socioeconomic literature of the past two decades is in the analysis of political alignments and ide-ologies. In this, Cubano's research has led the way. Her revised dissertation *El hilo en el laberinto: claves de la lucha política en Puerto Rico, siglo XIX* (item **1736**), skillfully combines economic and political history. It aptly recounts Arecibo's eco-nomic history of sugar and coffee, while making sense of various complex strands of elite politics: the tangled web of economic and social relations between import-export merchants and planters for example, which she argues cannot readily fit into a rigid conservative-liberal mold, and the colonial policies of the 1880s and 1890s, which helped to cement the Puerto Rican elite's adherence to Spanish sovereignty. Cubano addresses key historical questions even more directly in various other es-says: three are noteworthy for the clear and effortless manner in which they resolve crucial questions of imperial control and colonial acquiescence (items **1738, 1739,** and **1737**).

Believing, like Cubano, that notions of power and social order are not deter-mined by relations of production, Alvarez Curbelo has examined the contingent ways in which powerless groups constructed such conceptions. Two of her essays (items **1863** and **1714**) throw light upon how people translated grievances into po-litical ideologies, whether it was the proto-fascism of certain middle farmers in the 1920s and 1930s or the "moral economy of the crowd" evident in urban riots four decades earlier. In a similar vein, Baldrich studies how tobacco farmers mobilized against a corporate finance and marketing monopoly in the early 1930s (item **1871**), a movement that led to a successful growers strike in 1931–32. The book is theo-retically clear and sophisticated, a valuable addition to the literature on social movements in the Caribbean during the turbulent Depression era.

Twentieth-century political life is also the subject of Ferrao's solid work on Pedro Albizu Campos (item **1904**). A controversial work because its central issues have contemporary resonance, the book has opened up new vistas on nationalism—the character of its leadership, its motivations and programs. Ferrao delves deeper than previous scholars into the topic of Albizu Campos and his Nationalist Party devotees: who they were, what they actually believed in, and how important certain events during the 1930s—the Depression, of course, but also the Spanish Civil War and the neighboring Dominican Republic's Trujillo dictatorship—were to their formulation of a radical nationalist solution to Puerto Rico's vexing problems.

Finally, Picó's suggestive history of a free black community in the periphery of San Juan has advanced our understanding of the politics of resistance and evasion among the island's poor. *Vivir en Caimito* (item **1582**) weaves the community's story in with the tale of State and elite attempts to coerce people into work and social discipline, from the 18th century to the present. Picó argues that many generations of *caimiteños* have resisted encroachments on their freedom. While he explores only superficially the nature of community solidarity and consensus, and overlooks the inevitable fissures inside the community, the book is a passionately written reminder of the possibilities of doing history "from below" in the Puerto Rican context. [FAS]

CUBA, THE DOMINICAN REPUBLIC, AND THE SPANISH BORDERLANDS

The overall quality of the material received for review this biennium differs little from that of the works included in the previous *HLAS* volume. Authors continue to dwell on the same familiar topics providing only slight additional detail; articles and books have been as uncritical and panegyrical in tone as before; and, as a rule, they have continued to suffer from the lack of a solid base of research. In addition, Cuban historiography has not yet matured enough to rid itself from the theoretical preconceptions and political prejudices that have hampered it until now.

This is not to say that there are no exceptions that rise above the mass of average or below average publications. Indeed, there are nearly two dozen books and articles that were published during the last two years that have either filled historiographical gaps, broken new ground on certain subjects, or approached old problems from entirely new perspectives. Some are genuinely amusing, like Deive's piquant account of daily life in Hispaniola during the colonial period (item **1542**). Others, like Aguilar's short work (item **1510**), are an open invitation to the reader to philosophize about people and their historical destiny.

Among the articles are two that cannot be ignored. One is Moreno Fraginals' comparative study of slavery in Cuba and the Spanish Caribbean and in the English-speaking colonies (item **1674**). The other is the detailed discussion of the celebrated Martí-Roa dispute by Toledo Sande (item **1843**), a paradigm for exhaustive research and impartial treatment of a thorny subject.

Most of the noteworthy work appears in the 19th-century subsection: Jorge and Isabel Castellanos' commendable survey of the evolution of Afro-Cuban culture (item **1528**); Bergad's erudite study of sugar monoculture in Matanzas, Cuba (item **1723**); and Schwartz's monograph on the connection between patriot-brigands and Cuban independence (item **1832**). Lamore's analysis of Martí's view of "our America" (item **1774**) probably belongs in this category also, as does Paquette's book on the "Escalera" slave conspiracy in Cuba (item **1804**), written despite the fact that he was not permitted to examine Cuban records. As to Amigo's interpretation of Varela's philosophical thought (item **1718**), there is little doubt of its significance, since few have been as well equipped as he to pass judgment on the Cuban priest's eclecticism.

There are also works that deserve to be singled out in the other subsections. Such is the case of the other monographs by Deive (items **1651** and **1541**) and the various books by Vega (items **1988, 1990, 1992,** and **1991**). Of the books written or edited by Vega, however, none perhaps is as provocative as the collaborative volume on Dominican culture (item **1603**). Far more shocking, but nonetheless useful for understanding problems afflicting Cuban society, is Moore's angry examination of race in Cuba (item **1570**).

Finally, we should note among positive developments the appearance of scholarly works on the Catholic Church in both Cuba and the Dominican Republic, a subject which to date has received only spotty attention from historians. Balanced interpretations of the Church-State relationship in present-day Cuba have begun to see the light (item **1961**), and researchers have dipped into archival sources in procurement of hitherto unknown data with renewed enthusiasm. This tendency is best exemplified by Sáez's two-volume account of the activities of the Jesuits in the Dominican Republic (item **1969**). Also worthy of note is Maza's publication of documents relevant to the Cuban Church vis-à-vis the independence movement (item **1569**). Perhaps these auspicious efforts are an indication that similar projects will be undertaken in the future. [JMH]

GENERAL

1508 Abénon, Lucien-René. La Guadeloupe de 1671 à 1759: étude politique, économique et sociale. Paris: L'Harmattan, 1987. 2 v.: bibl., graphs, ill., index.

Traces the island's development from the beginning of royal rule emphasizing the early decades of 18th century. Argues that the impact of sugar and African slavery was felt later than previously assumed (1730 rather than 1680), as Guadeloupe retained a balance between sugar and subsistence agriculture. [APD]

1509 Abou, Antoine. L'école dans la Guadeloupe coloniale. Paris: Éditions caribéennes, 1988. 277 p.: bibl., tables. (Col. Lékôl)

Argues that primary and secondary schools, developed mainly in the 19th and 20th centuries, have transmitted conflicting values of colonial submission and individual autonomy. [APD]

1510 Aguilar, Luis E. Reflexiones sobre Cuba y su futuro. Miami, Fl.: Ediciones Universal, 1991. 155 p.: (Col. Cuba y sus jueces)

All those interested in Cuban history should read this insightful little book, which puts most Cuban dreams, biases, peculiarities, and emotions in historical perspective. For would-be Cuban revolutionaries and politicians it is required reading, regardless of their political persuasion. [JMH]

1511 Almodóbar, Carmen. Antología crítica de la historiografía cubana: epoca colonial. La Habana: Editorial Pueblo y Educación, 1986. 693 p.: bibl., ill.

Useful for the interesting comments, observations, and critical annotations by the author, rather than for the actual selections. [JMH]

1512 Archives Nationales (France). Etablissements pénitentiaires coloniaux, 1792–1952, série Colonies H: répertoire numérique. Par Sylvie Clair, Odile Krakovitch et Jean Préteux. Paris: Archives nationales, 1990. 107 p.: bibl.

Definitive research tool on archival series concerning more than 100,000 individuals sent to French colonial penitentiaries, including Cayenne (Devil's island). [APD]

1513 Armstrong, Douglas V. and **Elizabeth Jean Reitz.** The old village and the great house: an archaeological and historical examination of Drax Hall Plantation, St. Ann's Bay, Jamaica. Urbana: Univ. of Illinois Press, 1990. 400 p.: bibl., ill., index. (Blacks in the New World)

Important examination of slave settlement and ruins provides a detailed picture of a slave community on an important plantation in Jamaica. Contains extremely valuable information relating to size and layout of the houses of slaves and free persons, materials used in their construction, artifacts, and diet of inhabitants. [ELC]

1514 Azize Vargas, Yamila. Mujeres en lucha: orígenes y evolución del movimiento feminista. (*in* La mujer en Puerto Rico: ensayos de investigación. Edición de Yamila Azize Vargas. Río Piedras, Puerto Rico: Ediciones Huracán, 1987, p. 9–25)

Introduction to Puerto Rican feminist anthology traces the history of organized feminism in Puerto Rico as well as in the US and Europe. Places Puerto Rican feminism in the context of changes experienced by women on the island since before the Spanish conquest, emphasizing the sometimes contradictory effects of US colonial policies on women's lives. Describes Puerto Rican women's struggles to obtain the vote, yet argues that suffrage has not ended women's subordination. Calls for further feminist scholarship and feminist educational policies. (See also items **1515** and **1516.**) [FAS]

1515 Baerga Santini, María del Carmen. La articulación del trabajo asalariado y no asalariado: hacia una reevaluación de la contribución femenina a la sociedad puertorriqueña; el caso de la industria de la aguja. (*in* La mujer en Puerto Rico: ensayos de investigación. Edición de Yamila Azize Vargas. Río Piedras, Puerto Rico: Ediciones Huracán, 1987, p. 89–111)

Largely theoretical discussion of women and class formation in dependent capitalism, drawing on Feminist-Marxist theory as well as reports on female homeworkers in the Puerto Rican needlework industry during the 1930s. Argues that the examination of women and their paid and unpaid labor within the working class household necessarily leads to a broader definition of the Puerto Rican working class and a reevalution of working class consciousnes. (See also items **1514** and **1516.**) [FAS]

1516 Barceló Miller, María F. de. De la polilla a la virtud: visión sobre la mujer de la Iglesia jerárquica de Puerto Rico. (*in* La mujer en Puerto Rico: ensayos de investigación. Edición de Yamila Azize Vargas. Río Piedras, Puerto Rico: Ediciones Huracán, 1987, p. 49–88)

Uses published primary documents, particularly Puerto Rican bishops' letters, to argue that the notion of woman expressed by Church leaders changed from an image of sexual depravity at the end of the 18th century to one of virtue by the late 19th century. Changing political and socioeconomic conditions led the Church hierarchy to attempt to establish its authority over the family by idealizing matrimony, motherhood and feminine virtue. Such idealization did not in any way correspond to female emancipation. (See also items **1514** and **1515.**) [FAS]

1517 Baud, Michiel. German trade in the Caribbean: the case of Dominican tobacco, 1844–1940. (*Jahrb. Gesch.*, 25, 1988, p. 83–115, graph, table)

Well-researched study explores international trade and its consequences for a regional economy in the Caribbean. [JMH]

1518 Beckles, Hilary. A history of Barbados: from Amerindian settlement to nation-state. Cambridge; New York: Cambridge Univ. Press, 1990. 224 p.: bibl., ill., index, maps.

General work stresses centrality of slavery and plantation system to the island's history. Argues that modern-day civil rights demands represent a continuation of struggles for social equality, civil rights, and material betterment by blacks, free coloreds, and some whites during earlier periods. Useful corrective to previous historiography of island. [ELC]

1519 Bégot, Danielle. Au coeur du patrimoine, la destruction: l'exemple du patrimoine industriel antillais. (*in* Ville et campagne dans le monde antillais: Barbade, Cuba, Guadeloupe, Martinique, *Martinique, 1986*. Actes du colloque international des sciences historiques. Centre antillais de recherche et de documentation historiques. Martinique: Univ. des Antilles et de la Guyane, 1988, p. 87–102)

Skillfully describes the physical destruction of sugarmills in Martinique and Guadeloupe which have been displaced by banana industry. [APD]

1520 Bégot, Danielle. Imitation et créolité: une problématique des beaux-arts en espace créole insulaire; le cas des Antilles francophones, Martinique, Guadeloupe, Haïti, XVIII–XXe siècles. (*Etud. créoles*, 10, 1987, p. 118–143)

Incisive inquiry on the relative lack of

artistic creation in the French colonial Caribbean. Emphasizes the smallness of white population—the main consumer of art—and the psychological dimension of colonial dependency that imposed European artistic canons. [APD]

1521 Bégot, Danielle. Peinture et identité: l'imaginaire du paysage dans la peinture cubaine du XIXe siècle et dans la peinture haïtienne indigéniste. (*in* Cuba et les Antilles: actes du colloque de Pointe-à-Pitre. Organisé par le Centre interuniversitaire d'études cubaines et le Centre d'études et de recherches caraïbéennes; avant-propos par Alain Yacou. Talence, France: Presses Univ. de Bordeaux, 1988, p. 89–104)

Insightful comparative study of seven paintings from 19th- and 20th-century Haiti and Cuba. Shows the role of landscape painters, along with other forms of cultural expression, in articulating a search for national identity. [APD]

1522 Bégot, Danielle and Mireille Mousnier. Usines et habitations sucreries de Guadeloupe et de Martinique, XVIIe–XXe siècles: bilan de trois années d'un inventaire régional. (*in* L'architecture industrielle en France. Comité d'informations et de liaison pour l'archéologie, l'étude et la mise en valeur du patrimoine industriel. Paris: Ministère de la Culture, 1987, p. 9–52)

Exemplary study resulting from field research undertaken in 1983 traces three centuries of sugar-making technology and sugar culture in Martinique and Guadeloupe. For related article see item **1602.** [APD]

1523 Bergad, Laird W. ¿Dos alas del mismo pájaro? notas sobre la historia socioeconómica comparativa de Cuba y Puerto Rico. (*Hist. Soc./Río Piedras,* 1, 1988, p. 143–153)

Overview that recognizes "superficial" parallels between Cuban and Puerto Rican history while underscoring differences in economic history, class development, and political alignments. While some facts are misjudged or exaggerated in order to accentuate the intended contrast, essay is orginal and suggestive. [FAS]

1524 Beshoff, Pamela. Conversation with C.L.R. James. (*Jam. J.,* 19:1, Feb./Apr. 1986, p. 22–28, bibl., photo)

Eminent Caribbean historian and writer who was at the forefront of the campaign for Caribbean self-government and Pan-Africanism provides insightful reflections on his experience and thinking on a range of Caribbean and African developments. [ELC]

Black, Clinton Vane de Brosse. The history of Montego Bay. See *HLAS 51:2837.*

Bosch, Juan. Capitalismo tardío en la República Dominicana. See *HLAS 51:4672.*

1525 British capitalism and Caribbean slavery: the legacy of Eric Williams. Edited by Barbara L. Solow and Stanley L. Engerman. Cambridge; New York: Cambridge Univ. Press, 1987. 345 p.: bibl. (Studies in interdisciplinary history)

Series of essays evaluates the contributions of Williams to British Caribbean slave historiography. Authors conclude that issues raised and ideas advanced by Williams in 1944 are still very relevant to current studies of Caribbean economic history during slavery, though some refinement of his initial positions may be necessary. [ELC]

1526 Campbell, John. History of policing in Guyana. Georgetown, Guyana: Guyana Police Force, 1987. 245 p.: bibl., ill., index.

Institutional history of the police force (1839–1960s) provides insights into arrangements made for policing local communities and measures adopted for dealing with specific emergencies and instances of civil unrest in the present century. [ELC]

1527 Cartay Angulo, Rafael. Ideología, desarrollo e interferencias del comercio caribeño durante el siglo XVII. Caracas: Academia Nacional de la Historia, 1988. 286 p.: (Biblioteca de la Academia Nacional de la Historia: Fuentes para la historia colonial de Venezuela; 196)

Mercantilism is often viewed as an economic system adopted by the Spanish Empire after other European powers had already discarded it. Cartay examines this premise by analyzing the influence of leading 17th-century Spanish economists on the development of colonial mercantile structure, its major institutions, and royal efforts to monopolize trade. Concludes that Spanish policy evolved in reaction to immediate needs, not theory. Under attack from pirates and later from contraband trade, Spain ultimately failed to maintain a commercial empire. Although a one volume treatment of such a broad subject invariably has problems, Cartay's Spanish perspective amplifies a history usually told from English or Dutch points-of-view. [K. Waldron]

1528 Castellanos, Jorge and Isabel Castellanos. Cultura afrocubana. v. 1, El negro en Cuba, 1492–1844. Miami, Fla.: Ediciones Universal, 1988. 369 p.: bibl., ill.

Perhaps the best synthesis written thus far of the evolution of Afro-Cuban culture in colonial Cuba. For sociologist's comment see *HLAS 51:4673* [JMH]

Castellanos, Jorge and Isabel Castellanos. Geographic, ethnologic, and linguistic roots of Cuban blacks. See *HLAS 51:4674.*

1529 Catalogue du fonds local, 1883–1985. Fort-de-France, Martinique: Bibliothèque Schoelcher, 1987. 327 p.

List of French Caribbeana acquired over a century by best public library in the French Caribbean. [APD]

1530 Celma, Cécile. Les femmes au travail à la Martinique, XVII–XXe siècles: première approche. (*Doss. Outre-mer,* 82, primer trimestre 1986, p. 24–31)

Examines the presence of female workers and their involvement in social struggles throughout Martinican history. [APD]

1531 Los censos de población y vivienda en Cuba. v.1, Estimaciones, empadronamientos y censos de población de la época colonial y la primera intervención norteamericana. Havana: Instituto de Investigaciones Estadísticas, 1988. 1 v.: bibl., ill.

Useful study of the census compilations carried out in Cuba during the colonial period includes some pertinent materials published for the first time. [JMH]

1532 Centre guyanais d'études et de recherches. Deux siècles d'esclavage en Guyane française, 1652–1848. Coordination de Anne-Marie Bruleaux, Régine Calmont, Serge Mam-Lam-Fouck. Cayenne: Centre guyanais d'études et de recherches; Paris: L'Harmattan, 1986. 341 p.: bibl., ill. (Etudes & documents; 1)

Overview of French Guianese slavery shows that it developed away from major

transatlantic routes in areas surrounded by large tracts of forest ideal for runaways. Leroux's article presents archaeological evidence of 18th-century domestic slave culture in the hey-day of plantation society. Huyghues-Belrose discusses methodological issues in studying slaves' religion. [APD]

1533 Chapters in Barbados history. First series. Edited by P.F. Campbell. St. Ann's Garrison, Barbados: Barbados Museum and Historical Society, 1986. 152 p.: ill.

Extremely useful collection of articles, previously published in the Society's journal, dealing with various aspects of Barbados' early history. This basic reader, intended primarily for visitors and others interested in the island's local history, includes discussion of hotels, plantations, chapels, and paintings on the island. [ELC]

1534 Chomereau-Lamotte, Marie. A historical guide to Saint Pierre. Fort-de-France: Bureau du Patrimoine, Conseil régional de la Martinique, 1987. 96 p.: bibl., ill.

Drawing from the work of professional historians Adélaïde-Merlande and Chauleau, author evokes the wealthiest port city in the French Caribbean, which was devastated by the 1902 volcanic eruption. [APD]

1535 Costumes de femmes: traditions vestimentaires en Martinique de 1870 à 1940. Rédigé par Lyne-Rose Beuze et al. Fort-de-France: Bureau du patrimoine du Conseil régional de la Martinique, 1989. 47 p.: ill.

Handsome illustrations document traditional feminine clothing which is among the prettiest in the Caribbean.

1536 Cottias, Myriam. Mortalité et créolisation sur les habitations martiniquaises du XVIIIe au XIXe siècle. (*Population,* 44:1, jan./fév. 1989, p. 55–84, appendices, graphs, tables)

Longitudinal study based on 1,740 slaves from coffee and sugar plantations in Lamentin, Martinique (1766–1844) shows persistent high mortality which author interprets as an obstacle to creolization. For sociologist's comment see *HLAS 51:4682.* [APD]

1537 Cuba. Fuerzas Armadas Revolucionarias. Dirección Política Central. Historia de Cuba. La Habana: Editorial de Ciencias Sociales, 1985. 627 p.: bibl., ill. (Historia de Cuba)

Fifth reprinting of the Cuban history textbook produced and used by the Cuban armed forces. Covers the period from discovery to the 1933 revolution, and is admittedly, an unbalanced approach to the Cuban past. It is partial, omits troubled episodes, glosses over others and occasionally relies on "less than exhaustive research." According to its publishers it has no academic pretentions. [JMH]

1538 Cuban Studies. Vol. 17, 1987– . Pittsburgh, Pa.: Center for Latin American Studies, Univ. of Pittsburgh.

Includes four articles on "Sex, Gender, and Revolution," and two articles on Afro-Cubanism. The essay by Jorge and Isabel Castellanos is especially interesting. [JMH]

1539 De Gids. Vol. 7/8, No. 153, jul./aug. 1990– . Amsterdam: Mulenhoff.

Special issue of this famous journal devoted to the society and culture of the Netherlands Antilles and Aruba. More than 20 contributions contain poetry, prose, as well as social, political, and cultural analyses. [RH]

1540 De Gids. Vol. 10/11, okt./nov. 1990– . Amsterdam: Meulenhoff.

Double issue commemorates the 15th anniversary of Suriname's independence. The 32 contributions include essays on politics, history, culture, and society as well as short stories and poetry. An earlier edition of De Gids published in 1970 also focused on Suriname. [RH]

1541 Deive, Carlos Esteban. Los guerrilleros negros: esclavos fugitivos y cimarrones en Santo Domingo. Santo Domingo: Fundación Cultural Dominicana, 1989. 307 p.: bibl.

Excellent monograph uses previously unknown archival sources to cast new light on the life and culture of runaway slaves on Hispaniola. [JMH]

1542 Deive, Carlos Esteban. La mala vida: delincuencia y picaresca en la colonia española de Santo Domingo. Santo Domingo: Fundación Cultural Dominicana, 1988. 270 p.: bibl.

Delightful account of some of the less edifying aspects of daily life in the Dominican Republic during the colonial period. Well-written and impeccably researched. [JMH]

1543 Delabergerie, Guy. La Guyane à la Belle Epoque. Cayenne, French Guiana: Editions G. Delabergerie, 1986. 92 p.: ill.

Postcards recreate the *belle époque* in French Guiana. [APD]

1544 Derkx, Jo and **Irene Rolfes.** Suriname: a bibliography, 1980–1989. Leiden, The Netherlands: Dept. of Caribbean Studies, Royal Institute of Linguistics and Anthropology, 1990. 297 p.: (Caribbean bibliographies)

Survey covering the period 1980–89 contains 1,926 items on Suriname and Surinamese migrant communities. Includes monographs, essays, novels, poetry, youth literature, unpublished manuscripts, and an extensive index. [RH]

1545 Duarte Oropesa, José A. Historiología cubana. v. 1, Desde la era mesozoica hasta 1898. v. 2, Desde 1898 hasta 1944. v. 3, Desde 1944 hasta 1959. Miami, Fla.: Ediciones Universal, 1974–1989. 3 v.: bibl. (Col. Cuba y sus jueces)

Fairly conventional Cuban history despite the nationalistic and revolutionary interpretation professed by the author. Makes no major contribution to the factual knowledge of Spanish Cuba. [JMH]

1546 Dupuy, Alex. Haiti in the world economy : class, race, and underdevelopment since 1700. Boulder, Colo.: Westview Press, 1989. 245 p.: bibl., index. (Latin American perspectives series; 4)

Points to a combination of external and domestic causes for Haiti's underdevelopment. Argument elucidates no new conclusions. For sociologist's comment see *HLAS 51:4686.* [APD]

1547 Eguren, Gustavo. La fidelísima Habana. La Habana, Cuba: Editorial Letras Cubanas, 1986. 436 p.: bibl., ill., index.

Fascinating anthology of archival materials and contemporary accounts describes life and events in Havana from its foundation until the end of Spanish domination. [JMH]

1548 Fouchard, Jean. Regards sur l'histoire. Port-au-Prince, Haïti: H. Deschamps, 1988. 222 p.: bibl. (Regards sur le temps passé; 8)

Reprint of articles by a senior historian of Haiti. Includes study of advertisements for runaways that appeared in colonial newspapers, the basis for Fouchard's controversial thesis of *marronage* as the spark of the Haitian revolution. [APD]

Geggus, David. The Caribbean collections at the University of Florida: a brief description. See *HLAS 51:63.*

1549 Gjessing, Frederik C. and **William P. MacLean.** Historic buildings of St. Thomas and St. John. London: Macmillan Caribbean, 1987. 106 p.: ill., maps.

Specialists involved in the islands' preservation of historical buildings aptly document history and style of military, commercial, residential, religious and plantation buildings. [APD]

1550 Gonzalez, Nancie L. From cannibals to mercenaries: Carib militarism, 1600–1840. (*J. Anthropol. Res.*, 46:1, Spring 1990, p. 25–39, bibl.)

Important work addresses Carib warfare between the 16th and 19th centuries, with particular emphasis on the Black Caribs of St. Vincent and their descendents—the Garifuna of Central America. Argues that in response to European incursions, religion became separated from warfare, assuming increasing importance for cultural survival. While Europeans prevailed throughout most of region, the peculiar circumstances of St. Vincent facilitated survival of the Black Caribs. [ELC]

1551 González Vales, Luis E. El juicio de residencia como documento histórico. (*Bol. Centro Invest. Hist.*, 2, 1986/1987, p. 67–89)

Uses records from the ordinary *residencia* proceedings against Gabriel Gutiérrez de la Riva (governor and captain-general, 1700–03) to illustrate the usefulness of such documents for economic, social, and political history. [FAS]

1552 Goslinga, Cornelis Christiaan. The Dutch in the Caribbean and in Surinam, 1791/5–1942. Assen, Netherlands: Van Gorcum, 1990. 812 p.: bibl., ill., index, maps, tables. (Anjerpublikaties; 22)

Third and final volume in the The *Dutch in the Caribbean* series presents a flood of facts and figures on the period from the demise of the Dutch West India Company and the Society of Suriname to the announcement of a new colonial relationship. Based on archival records in the Netherlands and Curaçao. For previous volumes see *HLAS 50:1493* and *HLAS 34:1340.* [RH]

1553 Goveia, Elsa V. A study on the historiography of the British West Indies. Havana: J. Martí Pub. House, 1988. 232 p.: bibl.

Reissue of a pathbreaking historiographical work on the British Caribbean, with a penetrating foreword by a Caribbean historian. Examines various shifts in focus by different historians and pseudo-historians whose themes reflect the changing interests and perspectives of imperial powers. Book remains as relevant now as when it first appeared in 1956 (see *HLAS 19:3045.*) [ELC]

1554 Greene, Jerome A. and **William F. Cissel.** Fort Christiansvaern: Christiansted National Historic Site, Christiansted, Virgin Islands. Harpers Ferry, W. Va.: Harpers Ferry Center, National Park Service, US Dept. of the Interior, 1989. 218 p.: bibl., ill. (Historic furnishings report)

Excellent study of one of the best preserved US Virgin Islands colonial forts combines: 1) a history of its architecture, military organization and daily life under Danish rule; and 2) a compilation of printed and iconographic sources, mainly for 1830–55 (years of major activity) on regiments stationed, their weaponry, uniforms, furniture, etc. [APD]

Guanche, Jesus. Aportes canarios a la cultura campesina cubana. See *HLAS 51:4697.*

1555 Guerra Alemán, José. ¡Juro, pero no prometo!: biografía del general José Braulio Alemán y otros relatos de la guerra y la paz. México: Costa-Amic Editores, 1989. 415 p.

Journalistic account of the life and times of independence General José B. Alemán, who was also prominent in Cuban politics until 1930. Although the book is generally hagiographic in tone, it does include reprints of some useful documents. [JMH]

1556 Hall, N.A.T. The Danish West Indies: empire without dominion, 1671–1848. Virgin Islands: Division of Libraries, Museums and Archaeological Services, 1985. 35 p.: bibl. (Occasional paper; 8)

Very useful survey on Danish colonization in the Caribbean. [APD]

1557 Harricharan, John T. The Catholic Church in Trinidad, 1498–1852. Port of Spain, Trinidad: Inprint Carribbean, 1983. 1 v.: (An Inprint paperback)

General and somewhat superficial treatment of the history of the Catholic Church in Trinidad to the mid-19th century. Of some use for understanding the official position of the Church on the island. [ELC]

1558 Hellström, Jan Arvid. Åt alla christliga förvanter: en undersökning av kolonialförvaltning, religionsvård och samfundsliv på S:t Barthélemy under den svenska perioden, 1784–1878 [A study of colonial administration, support of, and care for religion and denominational life on St. Barthélemy during the Swedish period, 1784–1878]. Uppsala: Malmö, Sweden; Univ. of Uppsala, 1987. 360 p. (Studies on churches and denominations)

Well-researched study on a colonial church whose peculiarities reflected the uniquely cosmopolitan nature of St. Barthélemy. Swedish authorities not only supported their national church but also encouraged Catholic and Methodist schools, the latter educating free-coloreds and slaves. [APD]

1559 Hoefte, Rosemarijn. Suriname. Oxford, England; Santa Barbara, Calif.: Clio Press, 1990. 257 p.: index, map. (World bibliographical series; 117)

First annotated bibliography on Suriname. This selective survey contains 731 entries and covers the history, the ethnic, cultural and linguistic diversity of Surinamese society, and the current social, economic, and political problems. It is divided into 30 chapters and includes a 20-page introduction to the country. [RH]

1560 Holzberg, Carol S. Minorities and power in a black society: the Jewish community of Jamaica. Lanham, Md.: North-South Pub. Co., 1987. 289 p., 2 folded leaves of plates: bibl., ill.

Book focuses on small but relatively affluent and powerful Jewish community in Jamaica from 1600s through 1970s. Author details its history, religious traditions, cultural symbols, social organization, and how members exercise an extraordinary amount of political and economic influence as part of island's entrepreneurial elite. [ELC]

1561 Huisken, Jacobine; Friso Lammertse; and H.J. Scheepmaker. Curaçao, an island of monuments. The Hague, The Netherlands: Gary Schwartz/SDU, 1990. 1 v.

Nicely-illustrated architectural history of Curaçao and its monuments includes paintings, maps, and historical photographs. Several authors discuss the town's history as well as the present policy of preservation. [RH]

1562 Huyghues-Belrose, Vincent and Anne-Marie Bruleaux. L'orpaillage en Guyane: du siècle des lumières aux années folles. Cayenne, Guiana: Dép. de la Guyane, Direction des services d'archives, Service éducatif, 1988. 1 portfolio: bibl., ill., facsims., maps.

Intended primarily as educational material, this "dossier" of original documents with 10 p. of introduction, bibliography, glossary, and chronology constitutes an excellent synthesis on gold mining in French Guiana (1870–1910). [APD]

John, Ann Meredith. Plantation slave mortality in Trinidad. See *HLAS 51:4707.*

1563 Kirk, John M. Between God and the party: religion and politics in revolutionary Cuba. Tampa: Univ. of South Florida Press, 1989. 231 p.: bibl., ill., index.

Overview of four centuries of religion in Cuba, two-thirds of which is devoted to Church-State relations under Castro. The author's theological perspective is as controversial as his view of Castro's religious policy. The regime's discrimination against Catholics and other religious groups elicits only the mildest of criticism. [JMH]

1564 Krakovitch, Odile. Les femmes bagnardes. Paris: O. Orban, 1990. 301 p.: bibl., ill.

Author uses original sources to document lives of female convicts in 19th-century Cayenne (Devil's Island). [APD]

1565 Lafleur, Gérard. Bouillante en Guadeloupe: coeur de la Côte-sous-le-vent. Guadeloupe: G. Lafleur, 1988. 160 p.: bibl., ill., tables.

Well-researched and carefully-written monograph on one of the oldest settlements in Guadeloupe. [APD]

1566 Lafleur, Gérard. Saint-Martin, XVIIIe–XIXe siècles: étude socio-économique de la partie française de Saint-Martin; Saint

Martin, carrefour des Antilles. S.l.: G. Lafleur, 1990. 75 p.: bibl., ill., maps, tables.

Examination of white Protestant refugees from other Caribbean islands who settled this Caribbean frontier island in 1763, turning it into an active *entrepôt*. [APD]

1567 Laguerre, Michel S. Port-au-Prince 1860–1915: la construcción de una metrópolis caribeña. Traducción de Marta Savigliano. (*in* Cultura urbana latinoamericana. Recopilación de Richard Morse y Jorge Enrique Hardoy. Buenos Aires: Consejo Latinoamericano de Ciencias Sociales, 1985, p. 227–242)

Uses travelers' narratives to illustrate aspects of the urbanization of Port-au-Prince including: the centralization of political and intellectual resources; expansion of telephone and tramways; popular protest affecting political events; and the presence of foreign elite and native bourgeoisie educated in France. [APD]

1568 Lamore, Jean. La Havane: de la *porte du Nouveau Monde* à la grande ville des citoyens. (*in* La grande ville en Amérique Latine. Edition de Claude Bataillon et Jacques Gilard. Paris: Centre National de la Recherche Scientifique, 1988, p. 141–155, maps, tables)

Studies evolution of the city of Havana from its foundation by Spain to current efforts to stop its excessive growth. [JMH]

Madruga, José Manuel. Azúcar y haitianos en la República Dominicana. See *HLAS 51:4716.*

1569 Maza Miquel, Manuel. Clero católico y esclavitud en Cuba: siglos XVI al XIX; ensayo de sintesis. (*Estud. Soc./Santo Domingo,* 23:79/80, enero/julio 1990, p. 17–60, bibl.)

Excellent summary of the position of the Catholic clergy vis-à-vis the problem of slavery in colonial Cuba is based on printed sources. [JMH]

1570 Moore, Carlos. Castro, the Blacks, and Africa. Los Angeles: Center for Afro-American Studies, Univ. of California, 1988. 472 p.: bibl., index, ports. (Afro-American culture and society, 0882–5297; 8)

Significant contribution to the study of Cuba's internal evolution and foreign relations shows that racism has been and still is an inherent part of Cuban history. No analyst of Castro's African policy can ignore Moore's conclusions. For sociologist's comment see *HLAS 51:4417* [JMH]

Moore, Carlos. Race relations in socialist Cuba. See *HLAS 51:4721.*

1571 Mousnier, Mireille. L'habitation Anse Latouche: conservatoire du patrimoine industriel de la Martinique. (*in* Ville et campagne dans le monde antillais: Barbade, Cuba, Guadeloupe, Martinique; actes du colloque international des sciences historiques. Martinique: Centre antillais de recherche et de documentation historiques, Univ. des Antilles et de la Guyane, 1988, p. 129–142)

Fascinating description of buildings and equipment in one of Martinique's oldest plantations which was dedicated successively to sugar, manioc, cacao, indigo, a distillery and pottery. [APD]

Neira Vilas, Xosé. A prensa galega de Cuba. See *HLAS 51:4723.*

1572 Oostindie, Gert. Roosenburg en Mon Bijou: twee Surinaamse plantages, 1720–1870. Dordrecht, Holland; Providence, USA: Foris Publications, 1989. 548 p.: bibl., ill., index, maps. (Caribbean series/Koninklijk Instituut voor Taal-, Land- en Volkenkunde; 11)

Case study of a sugar and a coffee plantation focuses on the economic and agricultural development of the plantations as well as labor relations. Author also examines the world the slaves made and places his research in a Caribbean context. [RH]

1573 Ortega, Elpidio. Ensayo histórico y arquitectónico de la Ciudad de Montecristi. Santo Domingo: Museo del Hombre Dominicano, 1987. 437 p.: bibl., ill., maps. (Fundación Ortega Alvarez; 5)

Interesting combination of regional history, pre-colonial and colonial archaeology, and architectural cataloguing. Half of the book is devoted to a unique collection of photographs. [JMH]

Ortiz, Fernando. Los negros curros. See *HLAS 51:4725.*

1574 Paiewonsky, Isidor. Eyewitness accounts of slavery in the Danish West Indies: also graphic tales of other slave happenings on ships and plantations. St. Thomas, Virgin Islands: I. Paiewonsky, 1987. 166 p.: bibl., ill., index.

Original documents translated into English depict slavery in 18th- and 19th-century Danish colonial Virgin Islands. [APD]

1575 Péan, Marc. L'échec du firminisme. Port-au-Prince: H. Deschamps, 1987. 181 p.: bibl., ill.

Péan pursues his inquiry into Haiti's turbulent past by focusing on Anténor Firmin, a liberal who dominated politics at the turn of the century. [APD]

1576 Pérez, Louis A. Cuba: between reform and revolution. New York: Oxford Univ. Press, 1988. 504 p.: bibl., index, maps. (Latin American histories)

Survey of Cuban history with special emphasis on social and economic history. The discussion of events in terms of the reform/revolution dilemma tends to oversimplify the Cuban past. Includes an excellent bibliographical essay. [JMH]

1577 Pérez, Louis A. Lords of the mountain: social banditry and peasant protest in Cuba, 1878–1918. Pittsburgh, Pa.: Univ. of Pittsburgh Press, 1989. 267 p.: bibl., index. (Pitt Latin American series)

Unsuccessful attempt to apply Hobsbawm's social bandit model to Cuban historical realities. Oversimplifies some well-known Cuban revolts into class confrontations between an impoverished peasantry and oppressive capitalists. [JMH]

1578 Pérez, Louis A. Twenty-five years of Cuban historiography: views from abroad. (*Cuba. Stud.*, 18, 1988, p. 87–101, bibl.)

Excellent survey of historiographical trends in the literature published outside of Cuba since 1959 provides balanced overview of the most important works of the last 25 years. [JMH]

1579 Pérez Memén, Fernando. El arzobispo Fernando Carvajal y Rivera: un crítico de la política colonial española y otros ensayos históricos. Santo Domingo: Univ. Nacional Pedro Henríquez Ureña, 1985. 243 p.: bibl.

Includes six essays on the Dominican Catholic Church, most on the colonial period. Some use archival sources and the ap-

pendix reproduces important documents. [JMH]

1580 Pérotin-Dumon, Anne. Cabotage, contraband, and corsairs: the port cities of Guadeloupe and their inhabitants, 1650–1800. (*in* Atlantic port cities: economy, culture and society in the Atlantic world. Edited by Franklin W. Knight and Peggy K. Liss. Knoxville: Univ. of Tennessee Press, 1991, p. 58–86)

Examines the factors and rhythms of growth for two medium-sized colonial port cities in the French Caribbean. Author outlines commercial functions, patterns of urban settlement, urban planning and population composition to show the significance of port cities in the formation of Caribbean societies. [APD]

1581 Picó, Fernando. La demografía histórica y la historia de la Iglesia: perspectivas para la historia de la Iglesia Católica en Puerto Rico. (*Punto Coma*, 1:1, 1988, p. 37–41)

Summarizes some basic demographic trends in Puerto Rico and discusses how demography can be used to cast light on changing religious practices. Argues that these changes, as reflected in the parish records from which most historical demographic data is obtained, related to worsening living conditions for most Puerto Ricans during the 19th century. [FAS]

1582 Picó, Fernando. Vivir en Caimito. Río Piedras, Puerto Rico: Ediciones Huracán, 1989. 184 p.: bibl., ill. (Col. Semilla)

Traces the history of a community of free people of African descent from its 18th-century beginnings to the present, relying on family reconstitution methods to trace the history of whole families through several generations. Contains a brilliant exploration of how free blacks and mulattoes in Caimito constructed group identity and solidarity in opposition to an encroaching State. The 19th-century chapters, which constitute the book's core, provide valuable insights on issues such as the social marginality in an emerging plantation economy; the family and the demographic history of the free black group; peasant resistance to the State and to landowners; and the social meaning of race, among others. Unfortunately, neither intra-community conflict nor the actual class influences on the ever-encroaching State are adequately explored. For the 20th century, coverage of key issues (e.g., the family) is sparse. Nonetheless, this is a praiseworthy attempt to reconstruct the social history of a marginal community across more than two centuries. [FAS]

1583 Pizetty-Van Eeuwen, Yolande. Haiti ou la démocratie impossible? (*Ibero-Am.*, 18:1, 1988, p. 39–50)

Excellent synthesis of Haitian political history from 1804 up to its first (aborted) presidential elections of 1987. The analysis of the enormous challenges facing the country remains relevant. [APD]

1584 Price, Richard. Alabi's world. Baltimore: Johns Hopkins University Press, 1990. 444 p., 1 leaf of plates: bibl., ill., map. (Johns Hopkins studies in Atlantic history and culture)

Experimental evocation of the history of the Saramaka Maroons not only communicates the Saramaka past in their own terms, but adds several layers of interpretation and mediation. The voice of officials, missionaries, and of Price himself are in four distinct typeset styles. The study is based on oral histories and archival sources in the Netherlands. [RH]

1585 Quintero Rivera, Angel G. La música puertorriqueña y la contra-cultura domocrática: espontaneidad libertaria de la herencia cimarrona. (*Folk. Am.*, 49, enero/junio 1990, p. 135–167)

Provocative essay uses an analysis of popular musical styles to explore a concealed or "camouflaged" African influence in Puerto Rican culture. Argues that early colonial society outside San Juan was forged in opposition to the colonial State and the San Juan-based elite. These counter-plantation and anti-urban inclinations comprised a virtual "heritage of marronage" for the peasants, who were distinguished racially by an amalgam of African, European, and Amerindian elements and had developed an inclination for flight and itinerance. Concludes that the *jíbaro* musical tradition, which scholars once associated with a peasantry of nearly exclusive European stock, reveals a plethora of African stylistic and expressive elements upon closer scrutiny. [FAS]

1586 Quintero Rivera, Angel G. Patricios y plebeyos: burgueses, hacendados, artesanos y obreros; las relaciones de clase en el Puerto Rico de cambio de siglo. Río Piedras, Puerto Rico: Ediciones Huracán, 1988. 332 p.: bibl., ill. (Col. La Nave y el puerto)

Five suggestive essays on class, politics, and imperialism in 19th- and 20th-century Puerto Rico by a leading student of island history. The most stimulating piece, a long essay on the comparative social and political significance of San Juan and Ponce, blends perspectives from economic and social history with vistas gleaned from the study of private and public architecture, urban planning and design, and the intersection of elite and plebeian musical traditions. In the 1800s, Ponce rose to landed and commercial importance, overshadowing San Juan as the colony's most dynamic urban center. The transformation gave rise to a contest between the official "first city," the hub of a decadent colonial bureaucracy and a reactionary merchant establishment, and the signeurial "second city," home to a patrician bourgeoisie and vibrant, if at times accommodating, plebeian groups. Other essays explore the party alignments of sugar planters after the US invasion of 1898; the making of the working class and its participation in electoral politics 1900–34; the history of sociological ideas and writing in Puerto Rico; and debates surrounding an earlier collection of essays, *Conflictos de clase y política en Puerto Rico* (Río Piedras, Puerto Rico: Ediciones Huracán, 1976). Allows reader to survey the evolution of theoretically-minded historiography on Puerto Rico over span of two decades. [FAS]

1587 Reddock, Rhoda. Women and the slave plantation economy in the Caribbean. (*in* Retrieving women's history: changing perceptions of the role of women in politics and society. Edited by S. Jay Kleinberg. Oxford, England; New York: Berg, Paris: UNESCO Press, 1988, p. 105–132, table)

Refreshing and stimulating analysis of how slave women's productive capacity, particularly in Trinidad, was manipulated to serve needs of planter class. Argues that by shifting responsibility for food production and other labor to women slaves, and by encouraging selective aspects of European conjugal family system, planters relegated slave women to marginal societal status. [ELC]

1588 Renault, François and **Serge Daget.** Les traites négrières en Afrique. Paris: Karthala, 1985. 235 p.: bibl., ill., maps. (Hommes et sociétés)

Best overview written in French of the Atlantic slave trade by two specialists who piece together the Caribbean and African parts of the process. Useful bibliography. [APD]

1589 *Répertoire des recherches latino-américanistes en France: réportoire de institutions et des chercheurs.* Toulouse, France: Centre national de la recherche scientifique, 1988. (Réseau documentaire Amérique latine; 3)

Lists current research projects by topic and author. Includes index for geographical areas and research institutions. [APD]

1590 Resistance and rebellion in Suriname: old and new. Edited by Gary Brana-Shute. Williamsburg, Va.: Dept. of Anthropology, The College of William and Mary, 1990. 310 p.: bibl., maps, tables. (Studies in Third World Societies)

Collection of ten essays by anthropologists, historians, and a political scientist on selected topics that are crucial for understanding the past and present of Suriname. The editor surveys sources in a bibliographic essay covering the most important literature published since World War II. [RH]

1591 Ricardo, José G. La imprenta en Cuba. La Habana: Editorial Letras Cubanas, 1989. 357 p.: bibl., ill. (Giraldilla)

Useful and comprehensive historical account of publishing in Cuba. [JMH]

Rouse-Jones, Margaret D. Recent research in the history of Trinidad and Tobago: a review of the journal and conference literature, 1975–1985. See item **49.**

1592 Ruhomon, Peter. Centenary history of the East Indians in British Guiana: 1838–1938. Foreword by Sir Gordon Lethem. Georgetown, Guyana: East Indians 150th Anniversary Committee, 1988. 312 p.: ill., index.

Reprint of work originally published in 1947 is based primarily on government documents. Author argues that East Indian immigration was the salvation of the colony after the 1838 abolition of slavery and that Indians themselves proved to be most valuable assets to colony through their pioneering involvement in rice and cattle industries.

Useful though somewhat unbalanced work. [ELC]

1593 Saint-Martin, José M. Le sang de l'arbre: le roucou dans l'économie de la Guyane et des Antilles du XVIIe siècle à nos jours. Paris: Editions caribéennes, 1989. 255 p.: bibl., ill., tables.

First monograph on the *annatto*, a native American dye plant grown mainly on French Guianese plantations and used by the European textile industry until the 19th century. Written by an economist. [APD]

1594 Sepúlveda Rivera, Aníbal and Jorge Carbonell. Cangrejos-Santurce: historia ilustrada de su desarrollo urbano, 1519–1950. San Juan: Carimar, 1987. 85 p.: bibl., facsims., ill., maps, photos, tables.

Brief general history of a Puerto Rican community located just outside San Juan. Conceived primarily as a contribution to the history of urban design and architecture, book traces the rise and fall of Santurce in relation to broader forces affecting the development of the San Juan area. Initially a community of freedmen and escaped slaves from neighboring foreign colonies, Cangrejos-Santurce gradually grew in the late 19th and early 20th centuries into a suburban dependency of the capital, and then into the downtown area of a sprawling metropolis. Book is tastefully illustrated and elegantly written and provides a compelling glimpse into the cycles of growth, stagnation, and decline which have characterized the history of this satellite-cum-core of an urban community. [FAS]

1595 Sepúlveda Rivera, Aníbal. San Juan: historia ilustrada de su desarrollo urbano, 1508–1898. San Juan: Carimar, 1989. 335 p.: bibl., facsims, ill., maps, photos, tables.

Beautifully illustrated history of Puerto Rico's capital city from its founding in the early 16th century to the end of the Spanish period is based on author's dissertation. Focuses on urban design and architecture, with considerable attention paid to military construction. Social history is not slighted, however. The result is a highly readable survey equally accessible to laymen and scholars. Like its companion volume on Cangrejos-Santurce (see item **1594**), book is notable for its thoughtful design and printing. [FAS]

1596 Serbín, Andrés. Etnicidad, clase y nación en la cultura política del Caribe de habla inglesa. Caracas: Academia Nacional de la Historia, 1987. 477 p.: bibl., index. (Biblioteca de la Academia Nacional de la Historia: Estudios, monografías y ensayos; 93)

Useful study, based on secondary sources, focuses on the impact of ethnic and racial forces on colonial and postcolonial societies of the Anglophone Caribbean. Includes discussion of history of race and ethnicity in the region, presents tentative methodologies for analyzing ethnicity, and shows importance of ethnic and class considerations in the formation of political parties and the working of the political system. [ELC]

1597 Shepherd, Verene A. The dynamics of Afro-Jamaican/East Indian relations in Jamaica, 1845–1945: a preliminary analysis. (*Caribb. Q.*, 32:3/4, Sept./Dec. 1986, p. 14–26)

Departing from traditional pattern of examining majority-minority relations in Caribbean, this study is a fruitful attempt to understand subordinate group relationship in a plural society. Concludes that economic depression led to worsening relations between Jamaica's East Indian and Black populations, especially when jobs and/or wage levels were threatened by the other's presence or perceived actions. [ELC]

1598 Sonesson, Birgit. La emigración española a Puerto Rico: ¿continuidad o irrupción bajo nueva soberanía? (*in* Españoles hacia América: la emigración en masa, 1880–1930. Edición de Nicolás Sánchez-Albornoz. Madrid: Alianza Editorial, 1988, p. 296–321)

Overview of Spanish immigration to Puerto Rico during the last decades of Spanish rule and the first 30 years of US sovereignty. In contrast to Cuba, where Spaniards continued to pour in after independence in 1902, the establishment of American rule in Puerto Rico all but terminated peninsular settlement there. Uses census data to discuss immigrant profiles (demographic and occupational characteristics) and settlement patterns 1897–1930. Bulk of the discussion concerns the period before 1910, since net Spanish immigration was insignificant thereafter. [FAS]

1599 Tesauro de datos históricos: índice compendioso de la literatura histórica de Puerto Rico, incluyendo algunos datos inéditos, periodísticos y cartográficos. Preparado en la Oficina del Indice Histórico de Puerto Rico, bajo la dirección de Aldofo de Hostos. Río Piedras, Puerto Rico: Editorial de la Univ. de Puerto Rico, 1990. 1 v.: bibl.

Reprint of painstakingly compiled 1948 index to published primary sources, with individual notations for persons, places, events, institutions, and themes in Puerto Rican history. The first volume published covers the letters A though E (which comprises the three volumes published originally). Other volumes are promised, consisting of data already indexed by Hostos, the late archaeologist and official historian of the Government of Puerto Rico. Of significant use to researchers, although the index has not been updated and therefore lacks references to latest collections of printed primary sources. [FAS]

1600 Thompson, Alvin O. Colonialism and underdevelopment in Guyana, 1580–1803. Bridgetown, Barbados: Carib Research & Publications, 1987. 299 p.: bibl., ill., index.

Useful survey of Dutch period in three colonies that now comprise Guyana. Examines roots of Guyanese economic dependency by focusing on administrative techniques and structure of Dutch settler society, as well as wider European and Atlantic activities affecting colonies up to their capture and cession to the British. [ELC]

Tomich, Dale W. White days, black days: the working day and the crisis of slavery in the French Caribbean. See *HLAS 51:4741.*

1601 Tyson, George F.; Laverne E. Ragster; and Myron Jackson. The St. Thomas Harbor: a historical perspective; a collection of articles. St. Thomas, Virgin Islands: St. Thomas Historical Trust, 1986. 62 leaves: bibl., ill., maps, tables.

Local historians bring the history of this once bustling colonial entrepôt up to the present. [APD]

1602 Usines et habitations-sucreries: trois siècles de patrimoine industriel martiniquais. Rédigé par Mireille Mousnier and Danielle Bégot. Fort de France: Bureau du patrimoine du Conseil régional de la Martinique, 1987. 66 p.: ill.

Initially conceived as a catalog for an exhibit on Martinique's old sugar mills. Provides useful information on techniques and engines involved in the sugar-making process. For related article see item **1522.** [APD]

1603 Vega, Bernardo *et al.* Ensayos sobre cultura dominicana. 2a ed. Santo Domingo: Fundación Cultural Dominicana: Museo del Hombre Dominicano, 1988. 255 p.: bibl., ill.

Strongly recommended essays on the cultural roots of the Dominican Republic by some of its most noted scholars. [JMH]

1604 Watts, David. The West Indies: patterns of development, culture, and environmental change since 1492. Cambridge; New York: Cambridge Univ. Press, 1987. 609 p.: bibl., ill., index, maps. (Cambridge studies in historical geography; 8)

General treatment of interrelation between environment, population, land use patterns, and economy in the Caribbean, especially during era of slavery. Author argues that in light of largely illusory gains and mixed results of sugar cultivation over past five centuries, region should reassess its land use policy and develop strategies for environmental protection. [ELC]

Whitehead, Neil L. Lord of the tiger spirit: a history of the Caribs in colonial Venezuela and Guyana, 1498–1920. See *HLAS 51:850.*

EARLY COLONIAL

1605 Caron, Aimery. Sainte-Croix française. (*Bull. soc. hist. Guadeloupe,* 79/82, 1989, p. 3–29, bibl.)

Treats the French settlement of Saint Croix (1650–96), which initiated European colonization and deforestation of the island. [APD]

1606 Castillo Meléndez, Francisco. La defensa de la isla de Cuba en la segunda mitad del siglo XVII. Sevilla: Excma. Diputación Provincial de Sevilla, 1986. 458 p., 16 leaves of plates: bibl., ill. (Publicaciones de la Excma. Diputación Provincial de Sevilla: Sección Historia: Serie V Centenario del descubrimiento de América; 8)

First-rate scholarly account of Spain's efforts to defend Cuba from the aggressions of its European rivals during the period of imperial decline. Largely based on archival material. [JMH]

1607 Castillo Meléndez, Francisco. Población y defensa de la isla de Cuba, 1650–1700. (*Anu. Estud. Am.,* 44, 1987, p. 1–87, appendices, bibl.)

Excellent demographic study of colonial Cuba during the 17th century shows the close relationship between defense needs and the demographic policies of the Crown. Uses secondary sources and considerable archival materials. [JMH]

1608 Deagan, Kathleen. El impacto de la presencia europea en La Navidad—La Española. (*Rev. Indias,* 47:181, sept./dic. 1987, p. 713–732, facsims., maps, photo, tables)

Important scholarly contribution focuses on the cultural changes which the first contact with Columbus and his men brought on the Arawak Indians of Hispaniola. [JMH]

Dreyfus, Simone. Historical and political anthropological inter-connections: the multilinguistic indigenous polity of the "Carib" islands and mainland coast from the 16th to the 18th century. See *HLAS 51:777.*

1609 Ewen, Charles Robin. Spanish colonial adaptation to the New World: current research at Puerto Real, Haiti. (*Bull. Bur. natl. ethnol.,* 2, 1985, p. 103–109, bibl., tables)

Seventeenth-century ceramics found on early Spanish settlements throw light on gender-differentiated acculturation processes. Aboriginal Arawakan ceramics, most likely used by females domestically, are twice as numerous as those of European origin. [APD]

1610 Exquemelin, A.O. Boucaniers et flibustiers des Antilles. Fort-de-France: Désormeaux, 1986. 164 p. (Col. Les Grands romans des Antilles-Guyane)

New edition of famous 17th-century narrative on buccaneers and freebooters in the Caribbean. [APD]

1611 Fuente García, Alejandro de la. A alforria de escravos em Havana, 1601–1610: primeiras conclusões. (*Estud. Econ./ São Paulo,* 20:1, jan./abril 1990, p. 139–159, bibl., graphs, tables)

Well-researched and useful article, but covers too short a period to be truly significant.

1612 García del Pino, César and **Alejandro de la Fuente García.** Introducción a la cultura en Cuba en los siglos XVI y XVII: elementos para un nuevo enfoque. (*Rev. Bibl. Nac. José Martí*, 31:2, mayo/agosto 1989, p. 5–33, table)

Valiant effort to show that Cuba was not a cultural backwater during the 16th and 17th centuries, as is commonly believed. [JMH]

Hall, Douglas. In miserable slavery: Thomas Thistlewood in Jamaica, 1750–86. See *HLAS* 51:793.

1613 Helminen, Juha Pekka. ¿Eran caníbales los caribes?: Fray Bartolomé de las Casas y el canibalismo. (*Ibero-Am.*, 19:1, 1989, p. 45–56)

Brief discussion of Fray Bartolomé de las Casas' attitude concerning the cannibalism of some precolumbian Indians. [JMH]

1614 Lafleur, Gérard. Les protestants aux Antilles françaises du Vent sous l'Ancien régime. (*Bull. soc. hist. Guadeloupe*, 71/74, 1987, p. 1–305, bibl., ill., tables)

Shows French and Dutch Protestant minorities helped expand the French Caribbean. Traces their exodus to British America after they were excluded from French possesions in 1685–87. [APD]

1615 López Cantos, Angel. Fiestas y juegos en Puerto Rico: siglo XVIII. San Juan, Puerto Rico: Centro de Estudios Avanzados de Puerto Rico y el Caribe, 1990. 376 p.

Comprehensive study of elite and popular diversions—legal and clandestine—in 18th-century Puerto Rico, chiefly based on archival sources from Seville. Describes a variety of activities, from religious festivals, feasts held to celebrate the crowning of a new monarch, and bullfights, to illegal gambling. Although conceptually unsophisticated, represents a useful departure for persons interested in issues of elite and popular culture in early Spanish colonial times. [FAS]

1616 López Cantos, Angel. Miguel Enríquez: una aproximación a su vida. (*Rev. Hist./San Juan*, 3:5/6, 1987, p. 7–29)

Fullest biographical account yet of the almost mythical mulatto corsair, whose wealth and fame provoked the envy and wrath of the San Juan-based white elite. Author regards him as "the most important Puerto Rican of the Hispanic period." While

he may not deserve such hyperbole, his rise from relatively obscure origins to the position of banker to the island's royal exchequer is a story worth examining for its social and economic implications. As this study shows, Seville's Archivo General de Indias contains abundant documents with which to study the intersection of race, class, and status in the 18th century; Enríquez's life history is a compelling starting point. [FAS]

1617 Meier, Johannes. Die anfänge der Kirche auf den Karibischen Inseln: die Geschichte der Bistümer Santo Domingo, Concepción de la Vega, San Juan de Puerto Rico und Santiago de Cuba von ihrer Entstehung (1511/22) bis zur Mitte des 17. Juhrhunderts. Immensee, Switzerland: Neue Zeitschrift für Missionswissenschaft, 1991. 313 p.: bibl., index, plates.

Author analyzes the first century and a half of various Catholic dioceses in the Spanish Caribbean. Based partly on archival sources and the relevant secondary sources, Meier traces this early period of evangelization from the misssionary point of view. A useful contribution. [G.M. Dorn]

1618 Moreau, Jean-Pierre. Guide des trésors archéologiques sous-marins des Petites Antilles: d'après les archives anglaises, espagnoles et françaises des XVIe, XVIIe et XVIIIe siècles. Clamart, France: J.-P. Moreau, 1988. 276 p.: bibl., indexes, maps. (Col. d'histoire maritime et d'archéologie sous-marine, 0985–8172)

Of interest to underwater archaeologists of the Lesser Antilles, this guide offers a short history of each island, a list of shipwrecks as identified by the author in major European colonial repositories, and a survey of relevant literature in maritime history. For archaeologist's comment see *HLAS* 51:445.

1619 Pichardo, Hortensia. La fundación de las primeras villas de la isla de Cuba. La Habana: Editorial de Ciencias Sociales, 1986. 89 p., 14 p. of plates: bibl., ill. (Historia de Cuba)

Rigorous attempt to correct traditional errors concerning the date and place of the foundation of Cuba's first cities. Flawless use of archival sources. [JMH]

1620 Picot-Bermond, Evelyne. Mirage ou réalité économique: les armements pour les "Indes" à Bordeaux dans la deuxième moitié du XVIe siècle. (*Bull. Cent. hist. atl.*, 5, 1990, p. 127–135)

Provides valuable data on maritime enterprises from the French Atlantic port of Bordeaux to West Africa and the Caribbean since 1541. [APD]

1621 Quinn, David B. Bermuda in the age of exploration and early settlement. (*Bermud. J. Archaeol. Marit. Hist.*, 1, 1989, p. 1–23, maps)

Points out that, though located along the route to the New World, Bermuda's hazardous reefs and isolated location discouraged settlement. Eventual English settlement in 1609 followed half-hearted 16th-century attempts by Spaniards and French. Even then, colonists' preference for the mainland hindered Bermuda's eventual growth. [ELC]

1622 Silva Gotay, Samuel. La Iglesia y la esclavitud en América Latina y el Caribe. (*Cristianismo Soc.*, 27 : 102, 1989, p. 77–95, bibl.)

Examines attitude of Catholic Church toward Indian slavery in the Caribbean and compares the way Anglican, Non-Conformist and Catholic churchmen dealt with black slaves in the Anglo-Caribbean. Although some Catholic churchmen argued against slavery, the pro-slavery arguments were accepted by the majority. Anglican clerics did little work among slaves and, during the 18th century, Non-Conformist clergy concentrated on converting slaves while accepting the institution. Prior to 1807 only the Quakers rejected slavery *per se*. [J.D. Riley]

1623 Sued Badillo, Jalil. Beatriz: india, cubana, cimarrona. (*Caribb. Stud.* 21 : 1/2, enero/junio 1988, p. 192–214, bibl.)

Fascinating portrait of the person who could very well have been the first political exile in Cuban history. Based on archival documentation. [JMH]

1624 Varela, Consuelo. La Isabela: vida y ocaso de una ciudad efímera. (*Rev. Indias*, 47 : 181, sept./dic. 1987, p. 733–744)

Summarizes what historical sources tell us about the first city founded by Columbus in the New World, and points to a possible contradiction between historical and archaeological findings. [JMH]

1625 Wilson, Samuel M. Hispaniola: Caribbean chiefdoms in the age of Colum-

bus. Tuscaloosa: Univ. of Alabama Press, 1990. 170 p.: bibl., ill., index, maps.

Scholarly study of the multi-village chiefdoms that Spanish discoverers found in the Caribbean is based mostly on the letters, accounts, journals, etc. produced by the Spaniards in the 15th and 16th centuries. [JMH]

LATE COLONIAL AND FRENCH REVOLUTIONARY PERIOD

1626 Abénon, Lucien-René and **Jacques Cauna.** La Révolution aux Caraïbes. Sous la direction de Liliane Chauleau et Bernard Lehembre. Paris: Nathan, 1989. 224 p.: bibl., ill.

Standard account of the revolutionary process in the French Caribbean. [APD]

1627 Anduse, Roland. Ignace, premier rebelle guadeloupéen. (*in* De la Révolution française aux révolutions créoles et nègres. Sous la direction de Michel L. Martin et Alain Yacou. Paris: Editions Caribéennes, 1989, p. 105–121)

Refreshing interpretation of one leading figure in Guadeloupe revolt of 1802. [APD]

1628 Anduse, Roland. Joseph Ignace, le premier rebelle: 1802, la révolution antiesclavagiste guadeloupéenne. France: Editions Jasor, 1989. 303 p.: bibl., ill.

Popularized version sees Guadeloupe slave revolt of 1802 as a prologue to the island's independence. [APD]

1629 Araúz, Celestino Andrés. La acción ilegal de los holandeses en el Caribe y su impacto en las Antillas y Puerto Rico durante la primera mitad del siglo XVIII. (*Rev. Rev. Interam.*, 14 : 1/4, Winter/Spring 1984, p. 67–79)

Article examines Dutch illicit trade in the Caribbean during the first half of the 18th century. Leading role is played by Curaçaoans who smuggled both slaves and goods. Based on archival research in Spain, this essay is part of the two-volume study *El contrabando holandés en el Caribe durante la primera mitad del siglo XVIII* (see *HLAS 50:1880*). [RH]

1630 Auguste, Claude Bonaparte and **Marcel B. Auguste.** L'expédition Leclerc,

1801–1803. Port-au-Prince: Imprimerie Henri Deschamps, 1985. 345 p., 2 p. of plates: ill.

Account of the French expedition of 1804 to confront Haitian resistence meticulously documents military operations, their costs and casualties. Departs from standard treatment. [APD]

1631 Bangou, Henri. La Révolution et l'esclavage à la Guadeloupe, 1789–1802: épopée noire et génocide. Paris: Messidor, Editions Sociales, 1989. 200 p.: bibl., ill. (Histoire. 1789–1989; 21)

Author is political figure of the island who sees the revolutionary mobilization for racial equality as a milestone of the 20th-century *négritude* movement.

1632 Beckles, Hilary and **Karl Watson.** Social protest and labour bargaining: the changing nature of slaves' responses to plantation life in eighteenth-century Barbados. (*Slavery Abolit.*, 8:3, Dec. 1987, p. 272–293, table)

Balanced analysis of slave responses to slavery in 18th-century Barbados examines reasons for the relatively few attempts at insurrection on that island. Authors contend that slaves fully realized the difficulty of radically changing their material conditions through revolutionary means, and thus utilized bargaining power to extract concessions from their masters. [ELC]

1633 Bégot, Danielle. La révolution de Saint-Domingue à travers les peintres haïtiens. (*in* De la Révolution française aux révolutions créoles et nègres. Sous la direction de Michel L. Martin et Alain Yacou. Paris: Editions Caribéennes, 1989, p. 151–182)

Analyzes major works by painters from Le Cap, Haiti's northern capital, on historic events that took place in their region. Emphasizes limits of the historic inspiration drawn from the French Revolution, a bookish culture foreign to their life experience. [APD]

1634 Bléchet, Françoise. La correspondance de Sonthonax, commissaire délégué par le Directoire à Saint-Domingue, adressée à Toussaint-Louverture. (*in* La période révolutionnaire aux Antilles: images et résonances. Fort-de-France: Groupe de recherche et d'étude de littératures et civilisations de

la Caraïbe et des Amériques noires, 1987, p. 75–89)

Sonthonax's correspondence housed at the Bibliothèque nationale (Paris) sheds interesting light on his action as commissioner sent by French revolutionary authorities to Haiti/Saint-Domingue in the 1790s. [APD]

1635 Brana-Shute, Rosemary. Approaching freedom: the manumission of slaves in Suriname, 1760–1828. (*Slavery Abolit.*, 10:3, Dec. 1989, p. 40–63, table)

Author approaches manumission less as a legal phenomenon and more as a social process, since personal relationships could lead to such a legal change. Study is based on a systematic sample of 943 letters of petition which led to one-third of all manumissions in Suriname between 1760–1826. [RH]

1636 Bruley, Georges. Les Antilles pendant la Révolution française. Paris: Éd. caribéennes, 1989. 141 p.

Letters of a former planter of St. Dominigue, first published in 1890, document the *mentalité* of many white patriots in the French Caribbean who held the mulattoes responsible for all disturbances. [APD]

1637 Buchet, Christian. La lutte pour l'espace caraïbe et la façade atlantique de l'Amérique centrale et du sud, 1672–1763. Paris: Libr. de l'Inde, 1991. 2 v. (1297 p.): ill.

Systematic study, based on archival research, of European naval campaigns in the Caribbean which were dominated by Franco-British rivalry and their competition for Spanish possessions. Particular attention is given to logistical capabilities and problems: shipbuilding, soldiers' and sailors' recruitment, provisioning, sanitary conditions, and expeditions' leadership. Comparative examination of Dutch, English, French and Spanish navies shows that unsanitary conditions during the transatlantic passage and tropical disease were by far the first cause for casualties. In the 1740s, the English reorganized their methods, relying increasingly on North American logistical support and manpower to give them the advantage in the Seven Years War (1756–1763). See also item **1638.** [APD]

1638 Buchet, Christian. La Royal Navy et les levées d'hommes aux Antilles, 1689–1763: difficultés recontrées et modalités évolutives. (*Hist. écon. soc.*, 4, 1990, p. 521–543)

Article focuses on changes successfully introduced by English naval expeditions to the Caribbean. Complements Buchet's detailed *La lutte pour l'espace caraïbe* (see item **1637**). [APD]

1639 Butel, Paul. L'investissement immobilier des blancs et des gens de couleur dans les villes de Saint-Domingue à la veille de la Révolution: l'exemple du Cap Français et de Port-au-Prince. (*in* La période révolutionnaire aux Antilles: images et résonances. Fort-de-France: Groupe de recherche et d'étude des littératures et civilisations de la Caraïbe et des Amériques noires, 1987, p. 101–114)

Shows extensive speculation in construction and real estate by white and free-. colored persons derived from strong commerce-based growth in colonial Haiti's two main port-cities. [APD]

1640 Butel, Paul. Le modèle urbain à Saint Domingue au XVIIIo siècle: l'investissement immobilier dans les villes de Saint-Domingue. (*in* Franco-Irish Seminar of Social and Economic Historians, *4th, Dublin, 1984*. Cities and merchants: French and Irish perspectives on urban development, 1500–1900. Dublin: Dept. of Modern History, Trinity College, 1986, p. 149–163, map, tables)

Examines the rapid urban growth (1740–80) in Le Cap, the French Caribbean's first port city. Uses original research to show active speculation in real estate and construction, as well as official policy for urban development. Along with Loupès' work (item **1672**), charts important new directions. [APD]

1641 Campbell, Mavis Christine. The Maroons of Jamaica, 1655–1796: a history of resistance, collaboration & betrayal. Granby, Mass.: Bergin & Garvey, 1988. 296 p.: bibl., ill., index, maps.

Discusses origins of Jamaican maroons, their relationship with colonial authorities, and the internal dynamics of their societies. Traces their resistance to and later cooperation with authorities, their betrayal and ultimate suppression, after which they were shipped to Nova Scotia and then to Sierra Leone. [ELC]

1642 Carrington, Selwyn H.H. The British West Indies during the American Revolution. Dordrecht, Holland; Providence, USA: Foris Publications, 1988. 222 p.: bibl., ill., index. (Caribbean series/Koninklijk Instituut voor Taal-, Land- en Volkenkunde; 8)

Examination of commercial relations between British Caribbean and North America during American Revolution. Author assesses impact of Revolution on islands, and concludes that islands' economic decline started only during the war when they lost their central role in the North Atlantic Commercial System. [ELC]

1643 Cauna, Jacques. Le cimetière intérieur de Port-au-Prince: un site historique franco-haïtien. (*Bulletin/Paris*, 40, 1989, p. 4–8, ill.)

Brief research report on Haitian site linked to French revolutionaries reveals little-known connections between the French and Haitian Revolutions. See also Cauna's related article, "Billaud-Varenne et Haïti, ses dernières années, sa mort et sa sépulture" (*Cahiers du centre d'histoire et de généalogie des Isles d'Amérique*, 28, 1989, p. 190–195). [APD]

1644 Cauna, Jacques La revolution à Port-au-Prince, 1791–1792, vue par un bordelais. (*Ann. Midi*, 101 : 185/186, jan./juin 1989, p. 169–200)

A merchant and coffee planter from Bordeaux chronicles early revolutionary politics in Haiti-St. Domingue. See also *HLAS 50:1567*. [APD]

1645 Chatillon, Marcel. Images de la Révolution aux Antilles: catalogue de l'exposition. Organisée dans le cadre de la commémoration du bicentenaire de la Révolution. Basse-Terre: Société d'histoire de la Guadeloupe, 1989. 69 p.: ill.

Catalog of an exhibit organized for the bicentennial of the French Revolution displays little-known iconography on the theme of slavery and freedom. [APD]

1646 Chauleau, Liliane. La ville de Saint-Pierre sous la Révolution française. (*in* La période révolutionnaire aux Antilles: images et résonances. Fort-de-France: Groupe de recherche et d'étude des litérature et civilisations de la Caraïbe et des Amériques noires, 1987, p. 115–134)

Describes main French Caribbean port

city as an active arena for revolutionary politics. [APD]

1647 Cherubini, Bernard. Les Acadiens en Guyane française: des colons exemplaires pour une colonisation en dillettantes, 1762–1772. (*Bull. Cent. hist. atl.*, 5, 1990, p. 157–196, tables)

Well-researched article on several thousand French Canadians from Nova Scotia who, after seeking refuge in France, were recruited as new settlers for Guiana. Their success as small farmers raising cattle in Kourou and Sinnamary regions was eclipsed by the tragic failure of another colonizing expedition organized by French minister Choiseul. [APD]

1648 Cohen, Robert. Jews in another environment: Surinam in the second half of the eighteenth century. Leiden; New York: E.J. Brill, 1991. 350 p.: bibl., index. (Brill's series in Jewish studies, ISSN 0926–2261; 1)

Interdisciplinary study of the impact of environment on Jewish life and the modification of traditional values and modes of behavior. The author discusses migration, mobility, demography, economic structures, and the cultural and intellectual community. Based on archival sources in Paramaribo, Amsterdam, Leiden, The Hague, and Waltham, Mass. [RH]

Colloque international pluridisciplinaire sur la période révolutionnaire aux Antilles, *Fort-a-France et Pointe-à-Pitre, 1986.* Proceedings: la période révolutionnaire aux Antilles: images et résonances; littérature, philosophie, histoire sociale, histoire des idées. See item **4874.**

1649 Combes, André. La franc-maçonnerie aux Antilles et en Guyane française. (*in* La période révolutionnaire aux Antilles: images et résonances. Fort-de-France: Groupe de recherche et d'étude des litératures et civilisations de la Caraïbe et des Amériques noires, 1987, p. 155–180)

Survey of about 40 French Caribbean masonic lodges flourishing at the end of the *ancien régime.* They disappeared in 1790 only to be re-formed at the end of the decade. [APD]

1650 *Conjonction: Revue franco-haïtienne.* Vol. 181, 1989– . Spécial bicentenaire de la Révolution française. Port-au-Prince: Bulletin de l'Institut français d'Haiti.

Contains biographical vignettes on French revolutionary figures (Billaud-Varenne, Sonthonax, and Camille Desmoulins) whose destiny led them to Haiti. [APD]

1651 Deive, Carlos Esteban. Los refugiados franceses en Santo Domingo, 1789–1801. Santo Domingo: Univ. Nacional Pedro Henríquez Ureña, 1984. 218 p.

Important scholarly study of the fate of French refugees in Saint-Dominique at the time of the slave uprising of 1791. [JMH]

1652 The Diary of a Westmoreland planter. Pt. 1, Thomas Thistlewood in the vineyard, 1750–51. Pt. 2, The vinyard slaves. Pt. 3, Conclusion: Above all others: Phibbah. Edited by Douglas Hall. (*Jam. J.*, 21:3, Aug./Oct. 1988, p. 16–29; 21:4, Nov./Jan. 1989, p. 2–16; 22:1, Feb./April 1989, p. 57–64; facsims., ill., photos)

Edited version, with commentary by one of Jamaica's leading historians, of journal kept by Thomas Thistlewood during his residence on Jamaica from 1750 to his death in 1786. An Englishman, Thistlewood had gone to Jamaica to seek his fortune. The Jamaican portions of his diary record his experiences in various capacities on the island, but chiefly in the management of slave labor on plantations in the southeastern portion of the island. Extremely valuable for the faithful detailing of his observations of local flora and fauna, experiences with slaves, aspects of slave life and culture, his own adjustment to life in the slave society, and detailed treatment of his relationship with selected female slaves. [ELC]

1653 Doléances des peuples coloniaux à l'Assemblée nationale constituante, 1789–1790. Choix de textes par Monique Pouliquen; avant-propos par Jean Favier. Paris: Archives nationales, 1989. 164 p.: bibl., ill.

Welcome publication of 23 pleas and memoranda sent by white and free colored colonists to the National Constituent Assembly. Selected and introduced by a specialist, the documents aptly illustrate the range of issues the colonial question brought into the metropolitan revolutionary process. [APD]

1654 Dorsinville, Roger. Toussaint Louverture, ou, La vocation de la liberté. 2e éd. Montreal: Editions du CIDIHCA;

Flushing, N.Y.: Haitian Book Centre, 1987. 269 p.: bibl., index, map.

This biography by a senior Haitian intellectual is biased in favor of the Haitian revolutionary figure. For first edition see *HLAS 28:808*. [APD]

1655 Elisabeth, Léo. Gens de couleur dans les Iles du Vent, 1789–1793. (*Rev. fr. hist. Outre-mer*, 76:282/283, 1989, p. 75–95)

Treats the participation of free coloreds and slaves in the revolution in the French Lesser Antilles. Focusing on the case of Martinique, author argues that their political mobilization may have preceded rather than followed that of the whites. [APD]

1656 Feliciano Ramos, Héctor R. El comercio de contrabando en la costa sur de Puerto Rico, 1750–1778. (*Rev. Rev. Interam.*, 14:1/4, Winter/Spring 1984, p. 80–99)

Voluminous 1769 report on smuggling along the southern littoral provides a fascinating glimpse into trading circuits, agents, and methods of this illegal business. Argues that networks of complicity and silence protected smugglers and their agents from the authorities' reach and, whenever possible, obstructed the execution of justice when they were caught. Concludes that over time smuggling networks had evolved into a stable system of relationships resembling capitalist commerce. [FAS]

1657 Feliciano Ramos, Héctor R. El contrabando inglés en el Caribe y el Golfo de México, 1748–1778. Sevilla: Excma. Diputación Provincial de Sevilla, 1990. 414 p., 10 leaves of plates: bibl., maps. (Publicaciones de la Excma. Diputación Provincial de Sevilla: Sección Historia: Serie V centenario del descubrimiento de América; 10)

Well-researched study enhances our knowledge of British contraband trade in the Caribbean. [JMH]

1658 García del Pino, César. Insurrecciones en Cuba en el primer tercio del siglo XVIII. (*Univ. La Habana*, 235, 1989, p. 225–230)

Well-researched study, but mistakes local for full-fledged insurrections. [JMH]

1659 Geggus, David. El desarrollo urbano de Saint Domingue en el siglo XVIII. Traducción de Mónica Soria. (*in* Nuevas perspectivas en los estudios sobre historia urbana latinoamericana. Buenos Aires: Instituto Internacional de Medio Ambiente y Desarrollo (IIED) América Latina, 1989, p. 195–222, graphs, tables)

Discusses sources available and methodological issues for the study of colonial Haitian urban development. Examines administrative, religious, and military functions; forms of sociability; and physical and demographic growth of urban centers. Shows that hierarchy between urban centers stemmed from volume of trade. [APD]

1660 Geggus, David. Les esclaves de la Plaine du Nord à la veille de la Révolution française: les équipes de travail sur une vingtaine de sucreries: pt. 4. (*Rev. Soc. haïti.*, 43:149, dic. 1985, p. 16–42, tables)

Pt. 4 and new addition to author's ongoing study of slaves in the Plaine du Nord sugar plantations on the eve of the 1791 uprising (See *HLAS 48:2430*). Two conclusions differ from Debien's previous study: 1) average number of slaves per plantation is 150–200, with males only slightly exceeding women; and 2) significant presence of Creole slaves. Brings forth significant differences within labor-force: skilled workers are predominantly male and Creole; two-thirds of field workers are African and women. [APD]

1661 Geggus, David. The French and Haitian revolutions, and resistance to slavery in the Americas: an overview. (*Rev. fr. hist. Outre-mer*, 76:282/283, 1989, p. 107–124)

Survey of slave movements in the Caribbean during the revolutionary era underlines role of free coloreds and discusses the impact of the French revolution. [APD]

1662 Geggus, David. The Haitian Revolution. (*in* The modern Caribbean. Edited by Franklin W. Knight and Colin W. Palmer. Chapel Hill, N.C.: Univ. of North Carolina Press, 1989, p. 21–50)

Describes unique situation of France's wealthiest sugar island in 1789, distinguishing the main political and military phases of the Revolution. Examines complex relationships between social groups and assesses the outcome of the process but refutes stereotyped and ideology-laden interpretations. [APD]

1663 Geggus, David. The major port towns of Saint-Domingue in the later eighteenth century. (*in* Atlantic port cities:

economy, culture and society in the Atlantic world. Edited by Franklin W. Knight and Peggy K. Liss. Knoxville: Univ. of Tennessee Press, 1991, p. 87–116)

Overview of 13 port towns of colonial Haiti involved in international trade discusses demographic estimates on the basis of available sources. Last section deals with the urban beginnings of the Haitian revolution. [APD]

1664 Geggus, David. Racial equality, slavery and colonial secession during the Constituent Assembly. (*Am. Hist. Rev.,* 94:5, 1989, p. 1290–1308)

Standard account of the colonial policy developed by France's First National Assembly under the pressure of events in the Caribbean colonies. [APD]

1665 Hoogbergen, Wim S.M. The Boni Maroon wars in Suriname. Leiden; New York: E.J. Brill, 1990. 254 p.: bibl., index, maps.

English translation—slightly condensed—of the definitive history of the Maroon wars. For annotation of the Dutch original see *HLAS 50:1582.* [APD]

1666 Isert, Paul Erdmann. Voyages en Guinée dans les îles Caraïbes en Amérique. Introduction et notes de Nicoué Losjou Gayibor; avant-propos de Claude Hélène Perrot. Paris: Karthala, 1989. 269 p., 16 p. of plates: bibl., ill., maps. (Relire)

Letters originally published in 1793 by a physician employed by a Danish slave-trading company. Last two letters offer unique testimonies on trade and port cities in Danish (today US) Virgin Islands, Martinique, and Guadeloupe at the end of the 18th century. [APD]

1667 John, A. Meredith. The plantation slaves of Trinidad, 1783–1816: a mathematical and demographic enquiry. Cambridge; New York: Cambridge Univ. Press, 1988. 259 p.: bibl., ill., index.

Uses mathematics and demographic techniques to examine slave registration data (1813–16) in attempt to portray plantation slavery in Trinidad. Concludes that high mortality and moderate fertility up to 1816 support generally-held view that outside sources of labor were necessary for plantation slavery to continue. [ELC]

1668 Kuitenbrouwer, Maarten. Afwijking en tolerantie bij slavenhandel en negerslaverij, 1600–1863 (Deviance and tolerance concerning slave trade and negro slavery). (*in* Een schijn van verdraagzaamheid: afwijking en tolerantie in Nederland van de zestiende eeuw tot heden. Edited by Marijke Gijswit-Hofstra. Hilversum, The Netherlands: Verloren, 1989, p. 211–235)

Study of the slave trade compares Dutch involvement with that of other countries, Britain in particular, and to other forms of trade and labor. Also discusses the official policy and public opinion in The Netherlands concerning this topic. [RH]

1669 Lafleur, Gérard. Bouillante et la Révolution française. (*in* De la Révolution française aux révolutions créoles et nègres. Sous la direction de Michel L. Martin et Alain Yacou. Paris: Editions Caribéennes, 1989, p. 81–95)

Examination of the Revolution in a small *commune* of Guadeloupe concludes that it accelerated social change initiated long before. [APD]

1670 Ligou, Daniel. Les "isles" aux origines du rite ancien et accepté: quelques notes sur la maçonnerie des hauts grades dans l'Amérique française à la fin du XVIIIe siècle. (*in* La période révolutionnaire aux Antilles: images et résonances. Fort-de-France: Groupe de recherche et d'étude des littératures et civilisations de la Caraïbe et des Amériques noires, 1987, p. 419–436)

Diffusion of rites shows that French colonial masonry had active links with French metropolitan lodges as well as with North American ones. [APD]

1672 Loupès, Philippe. Le modèle urbain a Saint-Domingue au XVIIIe siècle: la maison et l'habitat au Cap Français et à Port-au-Prince. (*in* Franco-Irish Seminar of Social and Economic Historians, *4th, Dublin, 1984.* Cities and Merchants: French and Irish perspectives on urban development, 1500–1900. Edited by P. Butel and L.M. Cullen. Dublin: Dept. of Modern History, Trinity College, 1986, p. 165–179, tables)

Initial results of research project on Haitian colonial cities complements Butel's article (item **1640**). Documents residential architecture including materials used, the function of rooms, and architectural style. [APD]

1673 Malas Quesada, Berta de. La clase obrera cubana: surgimiento y primeros pasos. (*Univ. La Habana*, 234, 1989, p. 59–74, bibl., tables)

Amateurish attempt to trace the origins of the Cuban labor movement during the colonial period. [JMH]

1674 Moreno Fraginals, Manuel. Peculiaridades de la esclavitud en Cuba. (*Islas*, 85, sept./dic. 1986, p. 3–12)

Brilliant, though somewhat partial, explanation of why slavery tended to be less abusive in Cuba and other Spanish Caribbean colonies than in the English-speaking colonies. [JMH]

1675 Nemours, Alfred. Toussaint Louverture fonde à Saint-Domingue la liberté et l'égalité: avec des documents inédits. 2ème éd. Port-au-Prince: Editions Fardin, 1988. 104 p.: bibl., ill.

Letters from Haiti's founding father provide insight on his political thought and action. [APD]

1676 Oldendorp, C.G.A. C.G.A. Oldendorp's history of the Mission of the Evangelical Brethren on the Caribbean islands of St. Thomas, St. Croix, and St. John. Edited by Johann Jakob Bossart; English edition and translation by Arnold R. Highfield and Vladimir Barac. Ann Arbor, Mich.: Karoma Publishers, 1987. 737 p.: bibl., ill., index.

English translation of Oldendorp's observations of 18th-century Moravian activity on the Virgin Islands. Despite the title, work is especially useful for contemporary insights of master-slave relationships, and some of the perceived customs, habits, and language of slaves. [ELC]

1677 Peña Batlle, Manuel Arturo. La Isla de la Tortuga: plaza de armas, refugio y seminario de los enemigos de España en Indias; estudio de algunas de las causas primeras y más importantes que determinaron la declinación del imperio español en América. 3. ed. Santo Domingo: Editora Taller, 1988. 271 p.: bibl., map.

Reviews the role of the pirates and buccaneers from Tortuga Island in the decline of the Spanish Empire. Largely based on printed sources. [JMH]

1678 Pérotin-Dumon, Anne. Commerce et travail dans les villes coloniales des Lumières: Basse Terre et Pointe-à-Pitre, Guadeloupe. (*Rev. fr. hist. Outre-mer*, 75:278, 1988, p. 31–78)

Deals with the commercial functions, urban development and occupational structure of the two main port cities on an 18th-century sugar island. Includes new findings on: 1) coastal trade and contraband as characteristically interrelated activities for a secondary port in the Atlantic trade system; 2) enlightened colonial administration active in urban planning; 3) the origins of Guadeloupe's present urban structure, with different administrative and commercial centers; and 4) occupational structure similar to other 18th-century Atlantic port cities (including large female labor force). Last section deals with major privateering activity, 1793–1810. Appendix contains detailed 1797 occupational list for both towns. [APD]

1679 Pérotin-Dumon, Anne. Révolutionnaires français et royalistes espagnols dans les Antilles. (*Rev. fr. hist. Outre-mer*, 76:282/283, 1989, p. 125–158)

Shows how relationships between the French Lesser Antilles and their Spanish neighbors from Cuba, Puerto Rico, Trinidad and Venezuela were altered, continued, or expanded during the French Revolution. Provides new data on active economic relationships which channeled French propaganda to Spanish America after 1795, and on French presence in Trinidad and Puerto Rico during the English offensive of 1797. [APD]

1680 Pluchon, Pierre. Toussaint-Louverture: un révolutionnaire noir d'ancien régime. 2nd. ed. Paris: Fayard, 1989. 654 p.: bibl., index, maps.

Augmented version of 1979 edition (see *HLAS 44:2538*), this is the best study available on the Haitian revolutionary leader. [APD]

1681 Portuondo Zúñiga, Olga. El Departamento Oriental visto a través de los padrones, 1756–1766. (*Santiago*, 64, marzo 1987, p. 115–126, tables)

Useful demographic study of eastern Cuba in the late 18th century is based on printed and archival sources. [JMH]

1682 Portuondo Zúñiga, Olga. Nicolás Joseph de Ribera. La Habana: Editorial de Ciencias Sociales, 1986. 201 p.: bibl. (Palabra de Cuba)

Interesting information about a prominent member of Cuba's mid-18th-century colonial patriciate. Transcribes his two known works. [JMH]

1683 Postma, Johannes. The Dutch in the Atlantic slave trade, 1600–1815. Cambridge; New York: Cambridge Univ. Press, 1990. 428 p.: appendices, bibl., index, maps, tables.

Important analysis of Dutch participation in the transatlantic slave trade examines the acquisition of slaves in Africa, their treatment, their mortality during the sea voyage, and the profitability of the trade. The study is based on Dutch archival data. [RH]

1684 Price, Richard. Representations of slavery: John Gabriel Stedman's "Minnesota" manuscripts. Minneapolis, Minn.: Associates of the James Ford Bell Library, Univ. of Minnesota, 1989.

In a lecture introducing Stedman's "Minnesota" manuscripts, Price assesses their significance and recounts the history of editing the 1988 version of Stedman's *Narrative . . .* which led Richard and Sally Price to Suriname, Germany, The Netherlands, and England. Lecture draws upon the introduction to the aforementioned edition of the *Narrative . . .* (see item **1691**). [RH]

1685 Price, Richard. Subsistence on the plantation periphery: crops, cooking, and labour among eighteenth-century Suriname Maroons. (*Slavery Abolit.*, 12:1, May 1991, p. 107–127, tables)

Study of subsistence activities (making and tending gardens, hunting and fishing, preparing food) of Saramaka Maroons. The author argues that most routine subsistence tasks of men and women were and are embedded in complex webs of social and cultural meaning. Based on missionary diaries, Dutch military and colonial reports, and oral history. [RH]

1686 Rigau Pérez, José G. Las expediciones botánicas a Puerto Rico de Sessé, 1796, Baudin y Ledru, 1797, y Plée, 1823. (*Hómines*, 11, marzo 1987/feb. 1988, p. 9–33)

Summarizes three expeditions to Puerto Rico and concludes that while they brought no economic or technical benefits to the island they are useful for historians, particularly in illustrating the importance of corsairs in Puerto Rican history. [FAS]

1687 Rossignol, Philippe and **Bernadette Rossignol.** De Saint-Affrique à Bordeaux en passant par la Guadeloupe. (*Bull. Cent. hist. atl.*, 5, 1990, p. 137–156)

Traces origins and ascent of planter's dynasty in colonial French Caribbean. [APD]

1688 Roux, Antoine de. La ville du Fort Royal de la Martinique: Naissance et développement aux XVIIème et XVIIIème siècles. (*Bull. Cent. hist. atl.*, 4, 1988, p. 185–218)

Specialist traces origins and development of a "new town" founded by the king in a deep sheltered bay. Contains important iconography. [APD]

1689 Sevilla Soler, María Rosario. Inmigración y cambio socio-económico en Trinidad, 1783–1797. Sevilla: Escuela de Estudios Hispanoamericanos, Consejo Superior de Investigaciones Científicas, 1988. 238 p.: bibl., ill. (Publicaciones de la Escuela de Estudios Hispano-Americanos de Sevilla, C.S.I.C.; 337)

Superficial treatment of the socioeconomic history of Trinidad during its final years as a Spanish colony. Based largely on official archival records in Spain, the study credits large-scale migration to the island around 1780 for its subsequent transformation. Author argues that this prosperity ironically was a major factor in Spain's eventually losing the island to the British. [ELC]

1690 Sio, Arnold A. Marginality and free coloured identity in Caribbean slave society. (*Slavery Abolit.*, 8:2, Sept. 1987, p. 166–182)

Long overdue attempt to redirect questions raised and conslusions made about free coloreds calls for renewed investigations of rank and file before making overly broad generalizations about group's assimilation tendencies based on actions of small established elite. Contends that some evidence suggests the group was more radical than previously thought. [ELC]

1691 Stedman, John Gabriel. Narrative of a five years expedition against the revolted Negroes of Surinam: transcribed for the first time from the original 1790 manuscript. Edited, and with an introduction and notes, by Richard Price and Sally Price. Baltimore: Johns Hopkins Univ. Press, 1988. xcvii, 708 p.: bibl., ill. (some col.), plates.

Beautifully produced volume based on Stedman's personal copy of the manuscript rather than on the heavily edited first published edition. Text is presented intact and discusses the campaigns against the Maroons; flora and fauna; plantation life; and Stedman's romance with the slave Joanna. The commentary by Price and Price appears separately in the introduction, the notes, and two appendices. For ethnologist's comment see *HLAS 51:837*. (See also item **1684**.) [RH]

1692 Stein, Robert Louis. The French sugar business in the eighteenth century. Baton Rouge: Louisiana State Univ. Press, 1988. 185 p.: bibl., index.

The best synthesis in English on the giant Caribbean sugar industry at the end of the 18th century. Demonstrates sugar's contribution to French economic development which was based primarily on commerce rather than on industry. (French ports reexported much of the sugar to Europe.) Solidly documents: 1) slave labor force, their work, and methods for growing and refining sugar on plantations; and 2) sugar export, distribution and consumption. [APD]

1693 Tarrade, Jean. Les colonies et les principes de 1789: les assemblées révolutionnaires face au problème de l'esclavage. (*Rev. fr. hist. Outre-mer*, 76:282/283, 1989, p. 9–34)

New research on national assemblies of revolutionary France explains gap between their colonial policy and egalitarian principles, as the latter threatened the interests of some members' constituencies. [APD]

1694 Thibau, Jacques. Le temps de Saint-Domingue: l'esclavage et la Révolution française. Paris: J.-C. Lattès, 1989. 384 p.: bibl., index, map.

Journalistic account of events linking the French and Haitian revolutions emphasizes the slavery issue but misses important literature in English. [APD]

1695 Thoby, Béatrice. L'ile de la Guadeloupe sous la Révolution: inventaire analytique des volumes Guadeloupe; mars 1763-fructidor an IV. Nantes, France: Centre des Archives diplomatiques, 1989. 28 p.

Research tool provides access to French diplomatic series recently opened to the public dealing with Guadeloupe during the French Revolution. [APD]

1696 Valous, Camille de. Avec les *rouges* aux Iles-du-Vent: souvenirs du chevalier de Valous, 1790–1793; pendant la Révolution française. Présentation de Jacques Adélaïde-Merlande. Paris: Ed. Caribéennes, 1989. 217 p.

Reprint of memoirs, originally published in 1930, of an aristocrat who operated in the Caribbean during the revolutionary era. Unreliable at times. [APD]

1697 Willyams, Cooper. An account of the campaign in the West Indies in the year 1794. Basse-Terre, Guadeloupe: Société d'histoire de la Guadeloupe, 1990. 211 p.: bibl., ill., maps. (Bibliothèque d'histoire antillaise; 12)

Handsome reprint of the best narrative source on the English campaign in the Lesser Antilles. A chaplain on board the admiral ship depicts the dramatic setback that followed the sweeping conquest of the French islands. [APD]

SPANISH BORDERLANDS

1698 Emerson, Ann P. Standards of nutrition in a St. Augustine Hospital, 1783–1821. (*Fla. Hist. Q.*, 65:2, Oct. 1986, p. 145–162, bibl., photo)

Interesting evaluation, according to modern standards, of the hospital diets used in the St. Augustine hospital during the period. Uses considerable archival material. [JMH]

1699 Ewen, Charles Robin. Apalachee winter. (*Archaeology*, 42:3, May/June 1989, p. 37–39, photos)

Preliminary report on the archaeological findings at Hernando de Soto's winter encampment in what is now downtown Tallahassee. [JMH]

1700 Hann, John H. Apalachee counterfeiters in St. Augustine. (*Fla. Hist. Q.*, July 1988, p. 52–67, bibl.)

Annotated translation of the record of a criminal investigation carried out in St. Augustine in 1695 to determine if two young Apalachee visitors were guilty of counterfeiting activity. Casts light on Indian acculturation, Spanish labor recruitment practices, and the mission's influence. [JMH]

1701 Hann, John H. Summary guide to Spanish Florida missions and *visitas* with churches in the sixteenth and seventeenth centuries. (*Americas/Francisc.*, 46:4, April 1990, p. 417–513)

Well-documented scholarly catalog of the mission centers and outstations of Spanish Florida. [JMH]

1702 Hann, John H. Twilight of the Mocamo and Guale aborigines as portrayed in the 1695 Spanish visitation. (*Fla. Hist. Q.*, 66:1, July 1987, p. 1–24)

Carefully researched and written portrait of the Indians that lived in the coastal missions of Georgia and northern Florida before their destruction in 1702. [JMH]

1703 Hoffman, Paul E. A new Andalucia and a way to the Orient: the American Southeast during the sixteenth century. Baton Rouge: Louisiana State Univ. Press, 1990. 353 p.: bibl., index, maps.

Pathbreaking account of the role that geographic legends played in the exploration of the American Southeast during the 16th century is clearly written and solidly researched. [JMH]

1704 Lyon, Eugene. Pedro Menéndez's strategic plan for the Florida Peninsula. (*Fla. Hist. Q.*, 67:1, July 1988, p. 1–14, bibl.)

Careful study of Menéndez's imperial vision and his policy of geographic outreach. [JMH]

1705 Midlo Hall, Gwendolyn. Raza y libertad: la manumisión de los esclavos rurales de la Luisiana bajo la jurisdicción del Capitán General de Cuba. (*Anu. Estud. Am.*, 43, 1986, p. 365–376, bibl.)

Establishes that the cases of "coartación" were relatively few in rural Louisiana when the territory was under Spanish domination. Based on archival sources. [JMH]

1706 Poitrineau, Abel. Demography and the political destiny of Florida during the second Spanish period. (*Fla. Hist. Q.*, 66:4, April 1988, p. 420–443, bibl., table)

Carefully written and well-researched article shows how East Florida was doomed by stagnation during the second Spanish period owing to the lack of immigration from Hispanic countries. [JMH]

1707 Rasico, Philip D. The Minorcan population of St. Augustine in the Spanish census of 1786. (*Fla. Hist. Q.*, 66:2, Oct 1987, p. 160–184, bibl.)

Supplements Lockey's well-known study of the St. Augustine census of 1876. The article is followed by a translation into English of the Census' section on the so-called Minorcans. [JMH]

19TH CENTURY

1708 Abad, Diana. Documentos del Partido Revolucionario Cubano. Pt. 3–4. (*Univ. La Habana*, 233, 1988, p. 155–162; 234, 1989, p. 103–124)

Documents and comentary concerning the conspiratorial work of Cuban revolutionary societies in Key West in 1892 and Jose Martí's participation in such activities. [JMH]

1709 Abad, Diana. Para un estudio del Partido Liberal-Autonomista. (*Univ. La Habana*, 233, 1988, p. 105–124)

Interpretive essay reassesses the historical role of Cuba's Autonomist party (1878–98), characterized as an enemy of independence and essentially counterrevolutionary. [JMH]

1710 Adelaide-Merlande, Jacques. Travail libre et travail servil: Antilles et Guyane françaises, 1840–1848. (*Bull. soc. hist. Guadeloupe*, 75/78, 1988, p. 3–16)

Shows number of wage-earners increased among free coloreds and slave labor force on the eve of emancipation. [APD]

1711 Allahar, Anton L. Merchants, planters, and merchants-become-planters: Cuba, 1820–1868. (*NS*, 10:19, 1985, p. 73–93, bibl.)

Studies the conflicting interests of industrially-minded planters and merchants, on the one hand, and the traditional class of medium-sized planters, on the other, in late-19th century Cuba. [JMH]

1712 Allahar, Anton L. Slaves, slave merchants and slave owners in 19th-century Cuba. (*Caribb. Stud.* 21:1/2, enero/junio 1988, p. 158–191, bibl., tables)

Maintains that dependency on slavery and Spanish slave merchants' capital were the major factors that prevented the modernization of the Cuban sugar industry in the 19th century. Interpretative essay written from a sociological perspective. [JMH]

1713 Almodóbar, Carmen. Vicente García en la historiografía cubana, 1873–

1958: anotaciones al margen. (*Santiago*, 67, dic. 1987, p. 73–96)

Fair assessment of Cuban historical literature on the controversial figure of General Vicente García. Unfortunately, it overlooks what has been published outside of Cuba on the subject. [JMH]

1714 Alvarez Curbelo, Silvia. El Motín de los Faroles y otras luminosas protestas: disturbios populares en Puerto Rico, 1884. (*Hist. Soc./Río Piedras*, 2, 1989, p. 120–146)

Applies ideas derived from E.P. Thompson's "moral economy of the crowd" and George Rudé's depiction of pre-industrial "food riots" to a series of popular protests in San Juan in 1894 which were prompted by a subsistence crisis with both structural and conjunctural origins. Ably describes the process by which anti-monopoly protests were accorded ideological and political meaning. [FAS]

1715 Alvarez Estévez, Rolando. General José Lacret Morlot: ensayo biográfico. La Habana: Editorial de Ciencias Sociales, 1983. 171 p., 22 p. of plates: bibl., ill., ports. (Biografía)

Despite the author's narrow perspective, this reasonably well-researched study of the controversial military and political career of one of the leaders of the Cuban independence movement fills a gap in Cuban historiography. [JMH]

1716 Alvarez Gutiérrez, Luis. La diplomacia bismarckiana ante la cuestión cubana, 1868–1874. Prólogo de Manuel Espadas Burgos. Madrid: Consejo Superior de Investigaciones Científicas, Centro de Estudios Históricos, Depto. de Historia Contemporánea, 1988. 423 p.:

Culls information from German and other European archives about Bismark's cautious diplomacy in the face of the tensions generated by Cuba's first war of independence. Casts light on a largely unexplored subject. Curiously, no Cubans are mentioned among its sources. [JMH]

1717 Alvarez López, Luis. Secuestro de bienes de rebeldes: estado y sociedad en la última dominación española, 1863–1865. Santo Domingo: Instituto Tecnológico de Santo Domingo, 1987. 43 p.: bibl., ill.

Brief analysis of the Dominican rebellion against Spanish domination in the 1860s and the Spanish policy of sequestration of rebel property. Makes adequate use of archival material. [JMH]

1718 Amigó Jansen, Gustavo. La posición filosófica del Padre Félix Varela. Miami, Fla.: Editorial Cubana, 1990. 251 p.: bibl.

Essential for the correct interpretation of Varela's philosophical thought. The author adds a solid philosophical background to a thorough study of Varela's life and works. [JMH]

1719 Argüelles Espinosa, Luis Angel. La abolición de la esclavitud a través de algunos diarios habaneros de la época: 1880 y 1886. (*Anu. Estud. Am.*, 43, 1986, p. 241–257, bibl.)

Underlines the importance of the press as a source to learn the position of political parties active in Cuba during the period vis-à-vis the abolition of slavery. [JMH]

1720 Armas, Ramón de. José Martí: la verdadera y única abolición de la esclavitud. (*Anu. Estud. Am.*, 43, 1986, p. 333–351, bibl.)

Echoes José Martí's opinion that the abolition of slavery in Cuba was really the result of the wars for independence. [JMH]

1721 Barcia, María del Carmen. Táctica y estrategia de la burguesía esclavista de Cuba ante la abolición de la esclavitud. (*Anu. Estud. Am.*, 43, 1986, p. 111–126, bibl.)

Analyzes the "abolition-without-financial-ruin" strategy of Cuban slave owners during the second half of the 19th century. Uses archival materials from Cuban and Spanish sources. [JMH]

1722 Bergad, Laird W. Cuban rural society in the nineteenth century: the social and economic history of monoculture in Matanzas. Princeton, N.J.: Princeton Univ. Press, 1990. 425 p.: bibl., ill., index.

Regional history with major impact on national history. Crucial for the evaluation and reinterpretation of the role of slavery in colonial Cuba. Excellent and indispensable point of departure for future research. Based solidly on new archival data. [JMH]

1723 Bergad, Laird W. The economic viability of sugar production based on slave labor in Cuba, 1859–1878. (*LARR*, 24:1, 1989, p. 95–113, bibl., tables)

Important contribution challenges thesis that abolition in Cuba resulted from slavery's increasing inefficiency or lack of viability, suggesting instead that it was caused by non-economic factors. [JMH]

1724 Betances, Ramón Emeterio. Cuba en Betances. Selección e introducción de Emilio Godínez Sosa. La Habana: Editorial de Ciencias Sociales, 1985. 438 p.: (Palabra de Cuba)

Compilation of articles, letters, and other documents written by the Puerto Rican exile who represented the Cuban independence movement in France for many years; includes much unpublished and little-known material. Despite title, it also covers Puerto Rican men and events. [JMH]

1725 Betances, Ramón Emeterio. Les écrits de Betances dans le XIXe siècle, 1875–1878: *Les Antilles pour les antilliens.* Direction de Léone Goldstein. Paris: Équipe de Recherche de l'Univ. de Paris VIII, 1987. 99 p. (Histoire des Antilles Hispaniques; 3)

Useful compilation of Betances' early Parisian writings on Caribbean politics and society at the time of the Ten Years' War in Cuba. Introduction skillfully places Betances' life and thought in the context of Parisian internationalist politics and of broader Caribbean events. [FAS]

1726 Betances, Ramón Emeterio. La manigua en París: correspondencia diplomática de Betances. Recopilación de Félix Ojeda Reyes. San Juan, Puerto Rico: Centro de Estudios Avanzados de Puerto Rico y El Caribe; Centro de Estudios Puertorriqueños, Hunter College, City Univ. of New York, 1984. 158 p.: ill.

Transcribes letters written by Betances to leaders of the Cuban independence movement (1892–98), most culled from Cuban archives. Book includes a short biography of Betances. [JMH]

1727 Bonnin, María Isabel. Los contratos de refacción y el decaimiento de la hacienda tradicional en Ponce, 1865–1880. (*Bol. Centro Invest. Hist.*, 3, 1987/1988, p. 123–150)

An analysis of harvest underwriting contracts (*contratos de refacción*) between sugar planters and Ponce-based merchant financiers during a period of low prices and market disruptions. Argues that merchants took advantage of their access to international connections and credit, a devalued local currency, and their political preeminence to gain ground on their debtors. Ultimately, though, the 1870s depression bankrupted the majority of the merchants, including many who themselves had become planters by foreclosing on planter debt. [FAS]

1728 Boutin, Raymond. Les esclaves du Moule au XIXe siècle: naissances, mariages et décès. (*Bull. soc. hist. Guadeloupe,* 75/78, 1988, p. 17–26)

In Guadeloupe's most populated *commune,* slaves still comprised 80 percent of the population by the mid-19th century. [APD]

1729 Boutin, Raymond. La violence en Guadeloupe au XIXe siècle. (*CARE,* 13, 1988, p. 9–31)

Court records document enduring forms of violence in a colonial society shifting from slavery to freedom. [APD]

1730 Buffon, Alain. L'indemnisation des planteurs après l'abolition de l'esclavage. (*Bull. soc. hist. Guadeloupe,* 67/68, 1986, p. 53–74, tables)

Examines the economic, political, and legal aspects of compensations awarded to planters when slavery was abolished. Research in tax records, census, and notary archives yields new data on property value represented by slaves on the eve of abolition as well as credit arrangements granted to former slave owners afterwards. [APD]

1731 Champagnac, Philip and Yolande Champagnac. La ley penal y su aplicación. (*Anu. Estud. Am.,* 43, 1986, p. 143–170, appendix, bibl.)

Useful contribution traces the antecedents of the 1845 law against the slave trade and explains that law's ineffectiveness. [JMH]

1732 Coradin, Jean. Histoire diplomatique d'Haïti, 1804–1843. Port-au-Prince: Edition des Antilles, 1988. 1 v.:

Brief summary of Haiti's early diplomatic history emphasizes the continuing threat France posed to the new nation and its isolation in the hemisphere. [APD]

1733 Cottias, Myriam. Trois-Ilets de la Martinique au XIXe siècle: essai d'étude d'une marginalité démographique. (*Population*, 40:4/5, juillet/oct. 1985, p. 675–697)

A study of 926 individuals in the decades prior to the abolition of slavery shows marriage to be an insignificant variable in slave society demography. [APD]

1734 Cox, Edward. The free coloureds and slave emancipation in the British West Indies: the case of St. Kitts and Grenada. (*J. Caribb. Hist.*, 22:1/2, 1988, p. 68–87)

Makes ample use of archival sources to explain clearly the divergent attitudes of Grenada's and St. Kitts' free coloreds toward slavery and its abolition. [JMH]

1735 Craton, Michael. Continuity not change: the incidence of unrest among ex-slaves in the British West Indies, 1838–1876. (*Slavery Abolit.*, 9:2, Sept. 1988, p. 144–170)

Useful reevaluation and synthesis of literature on labor relations in British Caribbean during 19th century concludes that as planters sought to maintain control over workers in post-emancipation period, ex-slaves drew on their experience of resistance during slavery to demand better working conditions. Argues that labor disturbances in Barbados, Jamaica, and Guyana should be seen as continuation of slave unrest before 1838. [ELC]

1736 Cubano, Astrid. El hilo en el laberinto: claves de la lucha política en Puerto Rico, siglo XIX. Rio Piedras, Puerto Rico: Ediciones Huracán, 1990. 166 p.: graphs, maps, tables.

Thoroughly researched study of planter and merchant politics in late-19th-century Puerto Rico traces the development of an export-oriented elite in the coastal city of Arecibo. Bulk of evidence for the latter decades comes from the ledgers and account books of Roses & Compañía, a trading firm. Author skillfully traces the broader implications for island history and argues compellingly that planters and merchants, especially the more successful ones, adapted reasonably well to the recessive economic conditions prevalent after 1870. They diversified their businesses and took advantage of favorable Spanish monetary and fiscal policies which transferred the brunt of the economic crisis to the plebeian sectors. Thus, most business groups continued to support the maintenance

of Spanish colonialism, even though some adhered to an autonomist, liberal vision of the colonial relationship with Spain. [FAS]

1737 Cubano, Astrid. Paz pública y propiedad territorial: la discusión sobre política agraria en Puerto Rico, 1880–1889. (*Bol. Centro Invest. Hist.*, 5, 1990, p. 11–36)

Penetrating discussion of the 1880s formulation of a "conservative" agrarian discourse in favor of protectionism and State encouragement of a stable, secure peasantry. Since the leading ideologues of this movement were high government officials and other prominent pro-Spanish elements, author believes that their disavowal of an open export-agricultural economy oriented toward the US market signalled a rift between the most powerful elements of the landowning elite (especially sugar planters) and the colonial State. [FAS]

1738 Cubano, Astrid. La política de la élite mercantil y el establecimiento del régimen autonómico en Puerto Rico, 1890–1898. (*Bol. Centro Invest. Hist.*, 3, 1987/1988, p. 151–173)

Important essay provides a framework for understanding party politics in Puerto Rico during the final two decades of Spanish rule, based on an analysis of the ties between parties and social classes. Uses private documents of a large trading firm (Roses & Cía.) in the port city of Arecibo to analyze the large merchants' connection to the Partido Incondicional, the powerful conservative party. The party was not monolithic, however, as its left wing favored controlled reforms in the colonial system. Views factionalism within the Autonomist Party as reflection of an incremental rift between landed groups and urban popular classes. [FAS]

1739 Cubano, Astrid. Sugar trade and economic elites in Puerto Rico: response to the sugar crisis in the Arecibo region, 1878–1898. (*Hist. Soc./Río Piedras*, 2, 1989, p. 70–89)

Provocative account of strategies pursued by sugar planters in the important district of Arecibo to stabilize their fortunes during the lean years of the 1880s and 1890s. Suggests that several tactics were available to the sugar barons to increase their incomes, including: 1) modernizing processing-mill technology; 2) obtaining preferential treatment in mortgage foreclosures; and 3) shifting much of the burden of the declining economy to middle-sized cane farmers and improvished workers. Suggests that sugar planters were not generally disgruntled with the Spanish colonial regime because it gave them preferential treatment and, through its regressive monetary policy, made the working classes pay disproportionately for the devaluation in island wealth. [FAS]

1740 De Verteuil, Anthony. Sylvester Devenish and the Irish in nineteenth century Trinidad. Port of Spain, Trinidad: Paria Pub. Co., 1986. 157 p.: bibl., ill., index, ports.

Non-scholarly history provides useful and interesting data about individual families, chiefly that of Sylvester Devenish, and details of their involvement in local affairs. [ELC]

Díaz Uribe, Amparo. El siglo de solidaridad. See item **2345.**

1741 Duarte, Juan Pablo. Escritos. Recopilación de Mariano Lebrón Saviñón. Santo Domingo: Publicaciones ONAP, 1982. 142 p.: bibl. (Col. Ensayos; 6)

Useful anthology of Dominican national hero's writings is preceded by a short biography. [JMH]

1742 Duharte Jiménez, Rafael. La esclavitud en la ciudad de Santiago de Cuba durante el siglo XIX. (*Santiago*, 64, marzo 1987, p. 127–137, tables)

Provides interesting data about the economic activity of domestic slaves in the city of Santiago de Cuba in the 19th century. Based on archival sources and periodicals of the time. [JMH]

1743 Durnerin, James. La abolición del patronato en Cuba en 1886: los debates en Madrid. (*Anu. Estud. Am.*, 43, 1986, p. 185–199, bibl.)

Focuses on the political dabates that paved the way in Spain for the elimination of the last vestiges of slavery in Cuba. [JMH]

1744 Emancipation I: a series of lectures to commemorate the 150th anniversary of emancipation. Edited by Alvin O. Thompson. Barbados: Dept. of History, Univ. of the West Indies; National Cultural Foundation, 1986. 108 p., 1 leaf of plates: bibl., ill.

Book consists of seven lectures that cover: West Africa in the period of the slave trade; the slave trade to Barbados; the nature of slave society; sugar plantation agriculture; slaves' struggle for freedom; amelioration and emancipation; and post-emanicipation adjustments. Especially useful for understanding history of slavery in Barbados. [ELC]

1745 La esclavitud en Cuba. Edición del Instituto de Ciencias Históricas. La Habana: Editorial Academia, 1986. 279 p.: bibl., ill.

Various articles, including a study by José L. Franco, examine aspects of slavery in Cuba. Four essays are devoted to bibliography and evaluation of source materials. [JMH]

1746 Estévez, Felipe J. El perfil pastoral de Félix Varela. Miami, Fla.: Ediciones Universal, 1989. 38 p.: ill. (Col. Cuba y sus jueces)

Excellent introduction to one of the lesser known aspects of Varela's life. [JMH]

1747 Estrade, Paul. La colonia cubana de París, 1895–1898: el combate patriótico de Betances y la solidaridad de los revolucionarios franceses. La Habana: Editorial de Ciencias Sociales, 1984. 383 p., 6 p. of plates: bibl., ill. (Historia de Cuba)

Documents the conspiratorial activities of Cuban emigrés in Paris during the 1895–98 War of Independence. Scholarly, but written from a Marxist perspective. Recognizes the contribution of Marta Abreu, but is too critical of other wealthy exiles. [JMH]

1748 Estrade, Paul. Jose Martí, militante y estratega. La Habana: Editorial de Ciencias Sociales: Centro de Estudios Martianos, 1983. 164 p.: bibl. (Col. de estudios martianos)

Six scholarly essays on various aspects of Martí's political activities and ideas are worth reading despite Marxist perspective. [JMH]

1749 Fallope, Josette. Résistance d'esclaves et ajustement au système: le cas de la Guadeloupe dans la première moitié du XIXe siècle. (*Bull. soc. hist. Guadeloupe*, 67/68, 1986, p. 31–52)

Responses of slaves to their condition ranged from passive resistance to open rebellion in the decades preceding the emancipation in Guadeloupe. [APD]

1750 Figueredo, Fernando. La revolución de Yara: 1868–1878; conferencias. Prólogo de Pedro Martínez Freire. Introducción de Juan M. Portuondo. Ed. facsimilar. Miami, Fla.: Editorial Cubana, 1990. 330 p.: bibl., port.

New edition of this classic of Cuban historiography continues to be indispensable for the study of Cuba's first War of Independence. [JMH]

1751 Fornet-Betancourt, Raúl. José Martí y el problema de la raza negra en Cuba. (*Cristianismo Soc.*, 27:102, 1989, p. 97–108)

Analyzes Martí's best-known writings on racial problems and concludes that his position was based on conviction rather than political expediency. [JMH]

1752 García-Carranza, Araceli. Análisis crítico de la *Biobibliografía del Padre Félix Varela y Morales*. (*Rev. Bibl. Nac. José Martí*, 31:3, sept./dic. 1989, p. 33–44)

Required reading for all interested in Varela's life and thought. [JMH]

1753 García Cisneros, Florencio. El león de Santa Rita: el general Vicente García y la Guerra de los Diez Años, Cuba, 1868–1878. Miami, Fla.: Ediciones Universal, 1989. 231 p. (Col. Cuba y sus jueces)

Unconvincing effort to vindicate General Vicente García, a prominent figure in the first Cuban War of Independence generally seen as divisive and unruly. Mostly based on printed sources, book is hagiographic in tone. [JMH]

1754 García Rodríguez, Gervasio L. Economía y trabajo en el Puerto Rico del siglo XIX. (*Hist. Mex.*, 38:4, abril/junio 1989, p. 855–879, bibl.)

Succinct overview of issues concerning rural labor in 19th-century Puerto Rico. Excellent discussion of laborers' attitudes toward work, which author regards as the double legacy of pre-industrial (peasant) society and of slavery. With evidence drawn from contemporary testimonies, confirms workers' proclivity for itinerance and migration, which made constancy of work attendance difficult and challenged the elites' and the State's capacity for social control. [FAS]

1755 García Rodríguez, Gervasio L. Las primeras actividades de los Honrados Hijos del Trabajo, 1873–1898. (*Bol. Centro Invest. Hist.*, 5, 1990, p. 179–247)

In-depth study of the earliest Puerto Rican workers' organizations. Under strict prohibition to strike or otherwise impede "free commerce," workers initially founded social and cultural associations, sometimes in apparent imitation of elite institutions. From such initial cohesiveness and solidarity arose more deliberate resistance organizations—newspapers, clubs, mutual aid societies, and unions—during the final years of the Spanish period. Based on a thorough scrutiny of newspapers and other printed primary sources. [FAS]

1756 Gaspar, David Barry. Slavery, amelioration, and Sunday markets in Antigua, 1823–1831. (*Slavery Abolit.*, 9:1, May 1988, p. 1–28, map, tables)

Author makes very persuasive argument for reexamining slave response to amelioration. Shows that Antiguan slaves resented abolition of Sunday markets because it denied them important opportunity for local trade. A resultant 1831 disturbance highlighted dilemmas encountered through divergent interests of masters, slaves, and colonial authorities in the critical transitional period. [ELC]

1757 Gilmore, John. The toiler of the Sees: a life of John Mitchinson, Bishop of Barbados. Bridgetown, Barbados: Barbados National Trust, 1987. 112 p.: bibl., ill.

Biography of Mitchinson, who served as Anglican Bishop of Barbados during the late 19th century. His involvement in the religious and educational life of Barbados and the Windward Islands provides useful insights into British Caribbean society during this critical period. [ELC]

1758 Gómez, Máximo. Iconografía de Máximo Gómez. (*Islas*, 85, sept./dic. 1986, p. 149–167, bibl., photos)

Reprints an iconographic study of General Máximo Gómez first published in 1917, including a number of interesting pictures taken after the inauguration of the Cuban republic. [JMH]

Gómez Abreu, Nery and **Manuel Martínez Casanova.** Contribución al estudio de la presencia de las diferentes etnías y culturas africanas en la región central de Cuba: zona de Placetas, 1817–1886. See *HLAS 51:786.*

1759 Grosson Serrano, José Luis. José Martí: raíces valencianas de un gran pensador americano. (*Anu. Centro Estud. Martianos*, 10, 1987, p. 215–222)

Partial reconstruction of Martí's family background is harbinger of more serious research to follow. [JMH]

1760 Guerra Díaz, Carmen. Acerca de la relación azúcar-esclavitud en la región cienfueguera. (*Islas*, 89, enero/abril 1988, p. 26–40, tables)

Studies the peculiar development of sugar and slavery in south central Cuba. [JMH]

1761 Guerra Díaz, Carmen and **Ivonne Núñez Parra.** Notas para el estudio de la esclavitud en la antigua región de Villa Clara. (*Islas*, 84, mayo/agosto 1987, p. 3–29, bibl., graphs, tables)

Useful study of the development of the sugar industry and slavery in central Cuba during the 19th century uses some archival sources. [JMH]

1762 Guerrero Cano, María Magdalena. Santo Domingo, 1795–1865. Cádiz, Spain: Servicio de Publicaciones de la Univ. de Cádiz, 1986. 286 p.: bibl.

Well-researched study draws on Dominican and Spanish sources to portray the annexation of the Dominican Republic by Spain in 1865 as the result of an intrigue between the Captain General of Cuba, Francisco Serrano, and the Dominican General, Pedro Santana. Interesting and useful. [JMH]

1763 Gutiérrez Félix, Euclides. Perfil militar dominicano de Máximo Gómez. Santo Domingo: Editora Alfa y Omega, 1986. 54 p.: bibl., ill.

Interesting study of Gómez's guerrilla tactics from the perspective of Dominican military history. [JMH]

Haraksingh, Kusha. Control and resistance among Indian workers: a study of labour on the sugar plantations of Trinidad, 1875–1917. See *HLAS 51:794.*

1764 Hernández Sandoica, Elena. El transporte por mar y la acción del Estado en la España del Siglo XIX: Cuba y Filipinas en la concurrencia naviera por la subvención oficial. (*Hispania/Madrid*, 47:167, sept./dic. 1987, p. 977–999)

Scholarly study traces the origin of the monopoly that *Transatlántica Española* acquired over shipping lines between Spain and the remnants of its colonial empire in the 19th century. [JMH]

1765 Heureaux, Ulises. La correspondencia del presidente Heureaux—Lilís. t. 1, 1882. Selección y notas de Juan Daniel Balcácer. Santo Domingo: Editora Universitaria-UASD, 1987. 1 v.: (Publicaciones de la Univ. Autónoma de Santo Domingo; 580: Col. Archivo histórico; 4)

Useful contribution transcribes the correspondence of the dictator extant in the Dominican national archives. Vol. 1 of projected six volumes covers Gen. Heureaux's 1882 correspondence. He served as president in 1882, 1887–88, 1888–89, 1892–93, and 1898–99. [JMH]

1766 Hoefte, Rosemarijn. De betovering verbroken: de migratie van Javanen naar Suriname en het rapport-Van Vleuten, 1909 [The magic spell is broken: the migration of Javanese to Suriname and the Van-Vleuten Report, 1909]. Dordrecht, Holland; Providence R.I.: Foris Publications, 1990. 131 p.: bibl., ill. (Caribbean series/Koninklijk Instituut voor Taal-, Land- en Volkenkunde; 12)

Abridged and edited version of this unpublished report by Dutch East Indian government official H. Van Vleuten on the condition of Javanese contract laborers. Introduction describes the history and culture of the Javanese in Suriname, the background of Van Vleuten, and compares his report to other contemporary accounts. [RH]

Hoffmann, León-François. Esclavitud y tensiones raciales en Haití a través de la literatura. See item **4879.**

1767 Hostos, Eugenio María de. Hostos: ensayos inéditos. Selección y anotación de Emilio Godínez Sosa. Síntesis biográfica de Loida Figueroa. Río Piedras, Puerto Rico: Editorial Edil, 1987. 84 p.

Collection of articles on Cuba's future that Hostos wrote for a newspaper published by Cuban emigrés in Paris in 1896. Most were not published because they reached the editors after publication had been suspended. [JMH]

1768 Ibarra, Jorge. Crisis de la esclavitud patriarcal cubana. (*Anu. Estud. Am.*, 43, 1986, p. 391–417, bibl., table)

Useful effort describes planters of

Eastern Cuba at the time of the outbreak of the first Cuban War of Independence. Draws comparisons with the situation in Brazil and Puerto Rico. [JMH]

1769 José Martí, antimperialista. Selección del Centro de Estudios Martianos. La Habana: Editorial de Ciencias Sociales, 1984. 545 p.: bibl. (Col. de estudios martianos)

More than a dozen studies, by as many authors, on Martí's well-known criticism of US politics and society presents an unbalanced picture of Marti's views. [JMH]

1770 Kinsbruner, Jay. Caste and capitalism in the Caribbean: residential patterns and house ownership among the free people of color of San Juan, Puerto Rico, 1823–46. (*HAHR*, 70: 3, Aug. 1990, p. 433–461, graphs, tables)

Uses census data from Puerto Rico's capital city for the period 1823–46 to challenge the familiar thesis that the "caste system," with color ascriptions as key markers, had eroded since the early colonial period. Suggests the primacy of caste considerations in selection of marriage partners but not in residential arrangements. Unexpectedly, describes San Juan as less segregated than cities in other slave societies and as "a place of opportunity for freee people of color," despite the alleged survival of strict caste lines. An interesting study, but one hampered by fragmentary data and the lack of an explanatory framework. Much has been written recently on the revival of island slavery in the early 19th century, but author does not relate his findings on San Juan to island-wide developments regarding slavery and race. Regrettably, neither does he attempt to bring the city's socioeconomic conditions (e.g., its extreme population density) and history (e.g., the preeminence of military functions) to bear upon observed demographic patterns. [FAS]

La Rosa Corzo, Gabino. Los cimarrones de Cuba. See *HLAS 51: 4708.*

1771 La Rosa Corzo, Gabino. Sobre marcas de esclavos en Cuba. (*Bol. Mus. Hombre Domin.*, 15: 21, 1988, p. 59–69, facsims.)

Very informative article is based on the description made of captured runaway slaves so that they could be identified by their owners. [JMH]

1772 Labarre, Roland. La conspiración de 1844: un complot por lo menos dudoso y una atroz maquinación. (*Anu. Estud. Am.*, 43, 1986, p. 127–141, bibl.)

Well-written and tightly reasoned essay casts doubts about the reality of the slave conspiracy of *The Ladder* which shook colonial Cuba in 1844. Uses some material from French archives, but is largely based on secondary sources. [JMH]

1773 Labrada Rodríguez, Eduardo. La prensa camagüeyana del siglo XIX. Santiago de Cuba: Editorial Oriente, 1987. 199 p.: bibl., ill.

Carefully-researched local history is often relevant to national developments. [JMH]

1774 Lamore, Jean. José Martí et l'Amérique. t. 2, Les expériences hispano-américaines. Paris: L'Harmattan, 1988. 2 v.: bibl., ill., index. (Recherches & documents: Amérique latine)

Scholarly contribution focuses on Martí's experiences in Cuba, Mexico, Guatemala, and Venezuela as the basis of his view of "our America," his term for Spanish America as a united and multi-racial whole. [JMH]

1775 Larin, Evgeniĭ Aleksandrovich. Kuba kontŝa XVIII-pervoĭ treti XIX veka [Cuba from the end of the 18th to the first third of the 19th century]. Moskva: Nauka, 1989. 270 p.: bibl., ill.

Documented and scholarly history of Cuba (1810–99). [R.V. Allen]

1776 Lecuyer, Marie-Claude. Immigration blanche à Cuba: l'expérience galicienne, 1853–1855. Paris: Équipe de Recherche, Univ. Paris VIII, 1987 69 p. (Histoire des Antilles Hispaniques; 4)

Well-researched account of the importation of over 1,700 Galician workers into Cuba in mid-19th century. The affair and its investigation by the Spanish parliament sheds light on slave labor in the island and the development of abolitionism in Spain. [JMH]

1777 Lepkowski, Tadeusz. La présence polonaise dans l'histoire d'Haïti et des Haïtiens. (*Estud. Latinoam.*, 11, 1988, p. 141–195, bibl., ill., photos, tables)

Of the Poles who had fought with Haitians for their independence, 400 survivors settled in the south of the island. This is a fascinating account of this minority and its descendants. [APD]

1778 Luque de Sánchez, María Dolores. Con pasaporte francés en el Puerto Rico del siglo XIX, 1778–1850. (*Bol. Centro Invest. Hist.*, 3, 1987/1988, p. 95–122)

Traces French settlement and influence in Puerto Rico from the end of the 18th century to the eve of the US invasion. Uses consular correspondence and documents regarding foreign settlement found in Puerto Rican archives, as well as published documents, monographs, and articles. French immigrants "conquered" the island culturally, and Corsican merchants were vital in providing credit for the 19th-century Puerto Rican economy. [FAS]

1779 Maluquer De Motes Bernet, Jordi. Abolicionismo y resistencia a la abolición en la España del siglo XIX. (*Anu. Estud. Am.*, 43, 1986, p. 311–331, bibl.)

Shows the relationship between colonial interests and the political groups that blocked the abolition of slavery in Spain during the 19th century. Uses archival and printed sources. [JMH]

1780 Mangru, Basdeo. Abolishing the return passage entitlement under indenture: Guianese planter pressure and Indian government response. (*Caribb. Q.*, 32:3/4, Sept./Dec. 1986, p. 1–13)

Succinct analysis of pressures exerted by Guyanese planters and their representatives in England to eliminate their financial liability of providing for return to India of indentured workers. Although the Indian government, desirous to promote emigration, made concessions, it refused to agree to elimination of entitlements. [ELC]

1781 Marie-Sainte, Edouard. Jean-Baptiste Jammes: docteur médecin et maire de Goyave au XIXe siècle. (*Bull. soc. hist. Guadeloupe*, 69/70, 1986, p. 1–147, ill., maps, tables)

Biography of notable physician in a small commune conveys the social climate surrounding the abolition of slavery in Guadeloupe. [APD]

Marrero, Leví. Cuba, economía y sociedad. vol. 14, Azúcar, ilustración, y conciencia, 1763–1868. See *HLAS 51:4718.*

1782 Marte, Roberto. Cuba y la República Dominicana: transición económica en el Caribe del siglo XIX. Santo Domingo: Univ. APEC, 1988. 439 p.: bibl., ill.

Draws a parallel between the economies of Cuba and the Dominican Republic during the second half of the 19th century. The author passed over the Cuban archives. [JMH]

1783 Martí, José. Manifiesto de Montecristi: el Partido Revolucionario Cubano a Cuba. Ed. facsimilar. La Habana: Editorial de Ciencias Sociales, 1985. 174 p.: ill.

New facsimile edition of the famous manifesto signed by José Martí and General Máximo Gómez at the beginning of the 1895–98 Cuban War of Independence. Includes facsimiles of the drafts of the document. [JMH]

1784 Martínez Vergne, Teresita. The liberal concept of charity: *beneficencia* applied to Puerto Rico, 1821–1868. (*in* The middle period in Latin America: values and attitudes in the 17th-19th centuries. Edited by Mark D. Szuchman. Boulder, Colo.: Lynne Rienner Publishers, 1989, p. 167–184)

Examines the establishment of municipal welfare boards (*juntas de beneficencia*) in Puerto Rico after 1821 as a part of the liberal thrust to pass to the state certain social functions formerly performed by the Church. Relates the operation of the *juntas* to other state initiatives in areas such as the regulation of work, the persecution of vagrancy, the founding of schools, and the provision of direct social assistance.

1785 Martínez Vergne, Teresita. Politics and society in the Spanish Caribbean during the nineteenth century. (*in* The modern Caribbean. Edited by Franklin W. Knight and Colin A. Palmer. Chapel Hill, N.C.: Univ. of North Carolina Press, 1989, p. 185–202)

Summarizes the vicissitudes of nationalism in the region during the 19th century but neglects to cover historical development of it. [JMH]

1786 May, Robert E. The southern dream of a Caribbean empire, 1854–1861. Athens: Univ. of Georgia Press, 1989. 304 p., 1 leaf of plates: bibl., ill., index, map.

Historians interested in the North American side of the activities of Narciso López and other Cuban agitators in mid-19th century must consult this book. Nearly two decades after its first printing, it is still an indispensable research tool. For first edition see *HLAS 36:2187*. [JMH]

1787 Maza Miquel, Manuel. El alma del negocio y el negocio del alma: testimonios sobre la Iglesia y la sociedad en Cuba, 1878–1894. Santiago, República Domincana: Pontificia Universidad Católica Madre y Maestra, 1990.

Transcribes, annotates, and comments on ten previously unpublished documents relevant to the history of Catholicism in late-19th-century Cuba. Required reading for all interested in the subject. [JMH]

1788 Mendoza Lorenzo, Leidy. Estudio sobre el Cabildo de Congos Reales "San Antonio" de Trinidad. (*Islas*, 85, sept./dic. 1986, p. 49–73, appendixes, bibl., ill.)

Interesting and informative description of an association of slaves and free persons of Bantu origin, organized in Trinidad, central Cuba. Relates changes the group underwent due to a variety of cultural influences, including the Revolution. [JMH]

1789 Miranda Francisco, Olivia. La bibliografía sobre Félix Valera. (*Rev. Bibl. Nac. José Martí*, 30:1, enero/abril 1988, p. 5–34, bibl.)

Marxist-Leninist critique of the literature on Varela includes books and articles published outside Cuba. [JMH]

1790 Miranda Francisco, Olivia. El pensamiento de Félix Varela: coherencia y sistematicidad en sus ideas filosóficas, políticas y sociales. (*Univ. La Habana*, 232, 1987, p. 15–40, facsims.)

Purports to show from a Marxist perspective how Varelas' thought is simply the point of departure of a process of ideological radicalization which was to culminate in the Cuban Revolution. [JMH]

1791 Molinar Castañeda, Israel. Las sublevaciones de esclavos en Matanzas. (*Islas*, 85, sept./dic. 1986, p. 24–48, tables)

Uses printed and archival sources to sketch slave uprisings that occured in the province of Matanzas prior to the 1844 "Ladder Conspiracy." [JMH]

1792 Montbrun, Christian and **Maurice Rose.** L'habitation sucrerie Bellevue-Laplaine, Murat, au XIXe siècle: contribution à l'étude du patrimoine industriel marie-galantais. Marie-Galante: Ecomusée de Marie-Galante, 1988. 65 p.: ill.

Documents the history of a sugarmill in Marie-Galante, Guadeloupe's sugar-producing administrative dependency. At the peak of its activity, the slave labor force was predominantly female and one-third of it was unproductive. [APD]

1793 Mount, Graeme S. Friendly liberator or predatory aggressor?: some Canadian impressions of the United States during the Spanish-American War. (*NS*, 11:22, 1986, p. 59–70)

Thoughtful and well-reasearched analysis of the pro-US Canadian public opinion during the Spanish-American War. [JMH]

1794 Navarro García, Jesús Raúl. Reto educativo y expansión económica: el caso de Puerto Rico, 1820–1840. (*Rev. Hist./San Juan*, 7, enero/dic. 1988, p. 18–80)

History of mid-19th-century colonial educational policies in Puerto Rico and their effects. Despite some reforms and initiatives, education at primary, secondary, and advanced levels was inadequate and elitist. Failure of the colonial state to establish a university on the island, whether due to lack of funds or for fear of creating a potentially subversive cultural institution, adversely affected the formation of a professional class. Even for the island elite, establishing educational institutions was not a priority. [FAS]

1795 Nelson, William Javier. The crisis of liberalism in the Dominican Republic, 1865–1882. (*Rev. Hist. Am.*, 104, julio/dic. 1987, p. 19–29, bibl.)

Concludes that Dominican liberalism failed due to the lack of a literate and well-informed electorate. [JMH]

1796 Nelson, William Javier. The Haitian political situation and its effect on the Dominican Republic: 1849–1877. (*Americas/Francisc.*, 45:2, Oct. 1988, p. 227–249)

Blames the whimsical decisions made by France, Britain, and the US for the troubled and conflict-ridden relations between Haiti and the Dominican Republic. Uses secondary sources. [JMH]

1797 Núñez Jiménez, Antonio. Marquillas cigarreras cubanas. S.l.: Comisión Nacional Cubana del Medio Milenio del

Encuentro de Dos Mundos, 1989. 139 p.: bibl., ill.

Beautifully printed collection of the colorful designs used by Cuban cigar and cigarette manufacturers in the 19th century to distinguish their products. [JMH]

1798 Offner, John. Washington mission: Archbishop Ireland on the eve of the Spanish-American War. (*Cathol. Hist. Rev.*, 73:4, Oct. 1987, p. 562–575)

Relates Archbishop Ireland's last-minute attempt to prevent war between the US and Spain in 1898. Suffers from lack of background materials on the Vatican's attitude towards Cuba's independence. [JMH]

1799 Ojeda Reyes, Félix. Colonialismo sindical o solidaridad internacional?: las relaciones entre el movimiento obrero puertorriqueño y el norteamericano en los inicios de la Federación Libre, 1898–1901. (*Rev. Cienc. Soc./Río Piedras*, 26:1/4, enero/dic. 1987, p. 311–343)

Seeks to elucidate the earliest ties between the Puerto Rican and American labor movements. Issue is controversial because of the strong annexationist (pro-statehood) leanings of the island's top labor leadership after 1920, which has raised questions about the origins of worker admiration for the US. Using previously unexplored documents of American labor organizers and the US labor press, as well as insular sources, shows that the initial links were multifaceted and the drive to establish them, for the most part, reciprocal. Suggests that on both sides, workers and their organizations displayed an interest in forging ties, not out of labor-union colonialism on the part of the AFL and other US organizations, but out of genuine concern for the workers' conditions. In this emerging relationship, Puerto Rican labor leaders were not passive spectators or bystanders. [FAS]

1800 Opatrný, Josef. Antecedentes históricos de la formación de la nación cubana. Praga, Czechoslovakia: Univ. Carolina, 1986. 254 p.: bibl., ill. (Ibero-americana pragensia: Supplementum; 3/1984)

Sensible, although fragmentary, view of the formation of the Cuban nationality leaves out many fundamental aspects of Cuba's evolution. [JMH]

1801 Ortiz Cuadra, Cruz Miguel. Crédito y azúcar: los hacendados de Humacao

ante la crisis del dulce. (*Rev. Oriente*, 2, dic. 1986, p. 7–69)

Careful study of the economic and social history of sugar planting in an often overlooked area of Puerto Rico. the humid eastern lowlands. Uses notarial and parish records to reconstruct the plantation sector, its structure and evolution. Facing growing indebtedness, *hacendados* creatively diversified their operations and transferred risk to others, especially farmers who were willing to grow cane for sale to mill owners. Underscores the planters' pervasive reliance on merchant credit. Detailed histories of some sugar properties, short planters, and family histories help the reader glean information on financial and social networks established by local landowners. [FAS]

1802 El Padre Varela: pensador, sacerdote, patriota. Edición de Roberto Esquenazi-Mayo. Washington: Georgetown Univ. Press, 1990. 103 p.:

Includes essays by some of the most knowledgeable students of Varela's life and thought. [JMH]

1803 Papeles de Santo Domingo. Dirección de María Teresa de la Peña Marazuela con la colaboración de María Teresa Díez de los Ríos y María Angeles Ortega Benayas. Madrid: Ministerio de Cultura, Dirección General de Bellas Artes y Archivos, 1985. 379 p.: facsims., ill., index. (Archivo Histórico Nacional: Sección de ultramar)

Lists the materials extant in the Spanish National Historical Archive on the Dominican Republic's colonial border disputes and the period of the Spanish annexation. [JMH]

1804 Paquette, Robert L. Sugar is made with blood: the conspiracy of La Escalera and the conflict between empires over slavery in Cuba. Middletown, Conn.: Wesleyan Univ. Press, 1988. 346 p., 24 p. of plates: bibl., ill., index.

Traces the origin and development of the famous "Ladder Conspiracy" in Cuba (1844), maintaining that it was a series of overlapping conspiracies of whites, free people of color, and slaves. An outstanding work that reflects complete familiarity with the available bibliography and sources. [JMH]

1805 Pérez, Louis A. The first Cuban revolution, 1895–1898: an unfinished

agenda. (*Rev. Rev. Interam.*, 14:1/4, Winter/
Spring 1984, p. 133–153)

It is as easy to agree with the central
thesis of the article as it is to challenge some
facets of its interpretative infrastructure. Required reading for anyone interested in the
subject. [JMH]

1806 Pérez, Louis A. The meaning of the
Maine: causation and the historiogra-
phy of the Spanish-American War. (*Pac. Hist.
Rev.*, 58:3, Aug. 1989, p. 293–322)

Sharp reappraisal of the causal explanations of the Spanish-American War conclu-
sively shows that the significance of the explosion of the *Maine* has been overstated.
[JMH]

1807 Pérez Murillo, María Dolores. Aspectos demográficos y sociales de la isla
de Cuba en la primera mitad del siglo XIX.
Cádiz, Spain: Servicio de Publicaciones,
Univ. de Cádiz, 1988? 308 p., 1 folded leaf of
plates: bibl., ill.

Much of the material compiled by the
author is well known, but she makes some
significant contributions, especially in the
area of peninsular immigration. [JMH]

**1808 Pérez-Prendes y Muñoz de Arracó, José
Manuel.** La revista *El Abolicionista*
1865–1876 en la génesis de la abolición de la
esclavitud en las Antillas Españolas. (*Anu.
Estud. Am.*, 43, 1986, p. 215–240, appendix,
bibl., tables)

Examines the role that this periodical
played in the anti-slavery movement in Spain
as well as the work of the abolitionist leader
Rafael María de Labra. [JMH]

1809 Pérez Vega, Ivette. El efecto económico, social y político de la emigración
de Venezuela en el sur de Puerto Rico, Ponce,
1810–1830. (*Rev. Indias*, 47:181, sept./dic.
1987, p. 869–885)

Relies principally on local sources to
sketch a composite picture of Venezuelan
immigration to the southern city of Ponce at
the time of the Spanish American Independence Wars. Demonstrates the immigrants'
elite origin and their ability to climb the social hierarchy in the host colony, particularly
through involvement in sugar planting, the
slave trade, and general plantation commerce. A substantial number of immigrants
were also welcomed into the Spanish bureaucracy. Posits that, in general, this privileged

immigrant group had a positive economic effect on the island. [FAS]

Petras, Elizabeth McLean. Jamaican labor migration: white capital and black labor, 1850–
1930. See *HLAS 51:4727.*

1810 Philip, John Baptista. An address to
the Right Hon. Earl Bathurst by a free
mulatto. Port-of-Spain, Trinidad: Paria Pub.
Co., 1987. 311 p.: bibl.

Reprint of 1824 address by Trinidadian
to Secretary of State for the Colonies outlines difficulties under which free coloreds
on the island labored and sought redress.
Very important publication covers a volatile
period when free coloreds throughout the
Caribbean were clamoring for change. [ELC]

1811 Planas Viñals, Concepción. Presencia
y sentido de la Liga General de Trabajadores Cubanos. (*Univ. La Habana*, 234,
1989, p. 87–101)

Informative but sectarian sketches of
the development of *La Liga* as an embryonic
attempt at centralizing the leadership of the
Cuban labor movement. [JMH]

1812 Poey Baró, Dionisio. Apuntes sobre la
participación de José Martí en el movimiento revolucionario cubano durante los
años 1882 y 1883. (*Anu. Centro Estud. Martianos*, 9, 1986, p. 269–283)

Focuses on the conspiratorial activities of the Cuban emigrés in New York and
the gradual development of Martí's political
strategy. [JMH]

1813 Poumier Taquechel, María. El suicidio
esclavo en Cuba en los años 1840.
(*Anu. Estud. Am.*, 43, 1986, p. 69–86, bibl.)

Scholarly and competent study emphasizes the high rate of suicide among the
slaves in Cuba and underlines the different
meaning of suicide for recently arrived and
for those who had undergone some degree of
acculturation. [JMH]

1814 Poyo, Gerald Eugene. With all, and
for the good of all: the emergence of
popular nationalism in the Cuban communities of the United States, 1848–1898. Durham, N.C.: Duke Univ. Press, 1989. 182 p.:
bibl., ill.

Original contribution to the study of
Cuban nationalism as it evolved among the
exiled communities in the US. Some of the
author's conclusions are not fully docu-

mented; he also tends to overemphasize the ascendancy of the exiles over the independence movement. [JMH]

1815 Puig-Samper, Miguel Angel and **Francisco Pelayo.** Darwin en Cuba: el transformismo en la *Revista de Cuba.* (*Rev. Indias,* 49 : 186, mayo/agosto 1989, p. 423–435)

Interesting insight into the scientific history of Cuba based largely on primary sources. [JMH]

1816 Ramos Mattei, Andrés A. Las centrales olvidadas: formación de capital y los cambios técnicos en la industria azucarera puertorriqueña, 1873–1880. (*Hist. Soc./Río Piedras,* 1, 1988, p. 81–98)

Modernization and centralization of the Puerto Rican sugar industry predated the US invasion of 1898. Puerto Rican and European entrepreneurs established the first modern, centralized sugar factories during the 1870's in response to charging market conditions. Puerto Rican sugar entrepreneurs should be seen as the partners, rather than the victims, of American capital after 1898. [FAS]

1817 Ramos Zúñiga, Antonio. Las armas del ejército mambí. La Habana: Editora Política, 1984. 182 p.: bibl., ill.

Interesting study of the weapons most commonly used by the Cuban liberating army during the Wars of Independence. Largely based on printed sources. [JMH]

1818 Las relaciones Gómez-Carrillo. (*Islas,* 85, sept./dic. 1986, p. 179–199, bibl.)

Reprints some of the letters that General Máximo Gómez addressed to General Francisco Carrillo (1884–99) published for the first time in 1971 by Hortensia Pichardo. Important for the study of the Cuban independence movement. [JMH]

Ripoll, Carlos. Martí: democracy and antiimperialism. See item **5357.**

1819 Rivera-Belardo, Benjamín. Los problemas de la expansión urbana: San Juan de Puerto Rico, 1850–1898. (*in* Nuevas perspectivas en los estudios sobre historia urbana latinoamericana. Buenos Aires: Instituto Internacional de Medio Ambiente y Desarrollo (IIED) América Latina, 1989, p. 263–279, map, table)

Important essay uses previously unexplored archival materials to discuss demographic and social problems caused by San Juan's unprecedented growth in the final half of the 19th century.

1820 Robles Muñoz, Cristóbal. La oposición al activismo independentista cubano. (*Hispania/Madrid,* 48 : 168, enero/abril 1988, p. 227–288, appendix)

Recounts efforts made by Spain (1878–98) to prevent Cuban rebels from using the US as a base for hostile activities. Relates Spanish suspicions about the US and underlines the differences between the attitude of federal and local authorities. Despite scholarly apparatus, overlooks some of the most important instances of American interference with rebel activity. [JMH]

1821 Robles Muñoz, Cristóbal. Paz en Santo Domingo, 1854–1865: el fracaso de la anexión a España. Madrid: Centro de Estudios Históricos, Consejo Superior de Investigaciones Científicas, 1987. 256 p.: bibl. (Monografías; 4)

Balanced account of the annexation of the Dominican Republic by Spain based on printed and archival sources. [JMH]

1822 Rodríguez, Pedro Pablo. La primera invasión. La Habana: Unión de Escritores y Artistas de Cuba, 1987. 149 p.: bibl.

Sensible study of one the least known campaigns conducted by General Máximo Gómez during the first Cuban War of Independence, the Ten Year's War. [JMH]

1823 Roldán de Montaud, Inés. La hacienda en Cuba durante la Guerra de los Diez Años, 1868–1880. Prólogo de César Albiñana García-Quintana. Madrid: Instituto de Cooperación Iberoamericana; Sociedad Estatal Quinto Centenario; Instituto de Estudios Fiscales, 1990. 321 p.: bibl. (Monografías Economía quinto centenario)

Excellent study of the questionable methods used by the Spanish treasury to finance the expenses of the first Cuban War of Independence. [JMH]

1824 Ronning, C. Neale. José Martí and the emigré colony in Key West: leadership and state formation. New York: Praeger, 1990. 175 p.:

Informative summary of what is known about Martí's style of leadership and the techniques and qualities which he displayed while organizing the 1895–98 Cuban War of Independence. Useful and serious study. [JMH]

1825 Ruiz, Ernesto. Máximo Gómez: selección bibliográfica y documental. La Habana: Editorial Academia, 1986. 98 p.

Lists and annotates 592 bibliographical items by General Gómez or related to him extant in Cuba's National Archive and the José Martí National Library. Useful. [JMH]

1826 San Miguel, Pedro. El mundo que creó el azúcar: las haciendas en Vega Baja, 1800–1873. Río Piedras, Puerto Rico: Ediciones Huracán, 1989. 1 v. (Col. semilla)

Well-researched study of the economic and social history of a coastal sugar district in Puerto Rico during the final decades of slavery reveals the pervasive exploitation of African slaves in sugar production. Uses documents from the *municipio* of Vega Baja to analyze in detail the demographic and social profile of the principal working groups, in the broader context of changes in the agrarian structure. Contains an especially insightful discussion of peasant attitudes toward work, the State's role in the formation of a fragmentary labor market, and the free population's resistant adaptation to estate labor. [FAS]

1827 Sánchez Dotres, María Mercedes. Las reales juntas superiores gubernativas de medicina y cirugía y de farmacia: origen, estructura y funciones. (*Univ. La Habana*, 234, 1989, p. 75–86)

Covers a significant chapter of history of the medical and pharmaceutical professions in Cuba. Based almost entirely on primary sources. [JMH]

1828 Sanguily, Manuel. Manuel Sanguily frente a la dominación yanqui. Recopilación de Rafael Cepeda. La Habana: Editorial Letras Cubanas, 1986. 390 p., 27 p. of plates: ill., facsims., ports.

Valuable collection of 66 newspaper articles published by the great champion of Cuban nationalism, Manuel Sanguily, at the time of Cuba's first intervention by the US. Carefully edited and preceded by a highly professional introduction. [JMH]

1829 Saugéra, Eric. Pour une histoire de la traite française sous le Consulat et

l'Empire. (*Rev. fr. hist. Outre-mer,* 76:282/283, 1989, p. 203–229)

Superbly researched article surveys sources and methodological issues on the French slave trade which, banned since 1793, was resumed in 1800, essentially oriented toward the Caribbean market. Fills a gap in research. [APD]

1830 Scarano, Francisco A. Labor and society in the nineteenth century. (*in* The modern Caribbean. Edited by Franklin W. Knight and Colin A. Palmer. Chapel Hill, N.C.: Univ. of North Carolina Press, 1989, p. 51–84)

Draws parallels between the post-emancipation labor situation in Cuba and Puerto Rico and in the British West Indies. The contrastive analysis helps to set the peculiarities of the Spanish colonies in bold relief. [JMH]

1831 Schmidt, Nelly. Le problème de l'ordre colonial après la Révolution de 1848: le cas des colonies françaises des Caraïbes. (*in* Société d'Histoire de la Révolution de 1848 et des Révolutions du XIXe siècle. Maintien de l'ordre et polices en France et en Europe au XIXe siècle. Paris: Creaphis, 1987, p. 103–116)

Rather than social disturbances or economic dislocation, the abolition of slavery resulted in problems of law enforcement for the police in Martinique and Guadeloupe. The political context of the French revolution of 1848 gave particular emphasis to an emergent political participation. [APD]

1832 Schwartz, Rosalie. Lawless liberators: political banditry and Cuban independence. Durham, N.C.: Duke Univ. Press, 1989. 297 p.: bibl., ill., index.

Well-researched and carefully written portrait of the patriot brigands who operated in the Cuban countryside after the first War of Independence. The cause-and-effect scenario structured by the author incorporates most of the nuances of reality and is quite convincing. [JMH]

1833 Scott, Rebecca Jarvis. La dinámica de la emancipación y formación de la sociedad pos-abolicionista: el caso cubano en perspectiva comparativa. (*Anu. Estud. Am.,* 43, 1986, p. 87–98, bibl.)

Maps out future research concerning the abolition of slavery in Cuba and its possible connection with the subsequent emergence of a rural proletariat and the social composition of the liberating army which fought in the 1895–98 war. [JMH]

1834 Serrano, Carlos. Anarchisme et indépendance nationale à Cuba à la fin du XIXe siècle. Saint-Denis, France: Equipe de recherche de l'Univ. de Paris VIII Histoire des Antilles hispaniques, 1986. 95 p. (Histoire des Antilles hispaniques; 1)

Brief summary of the attitude of Cuban anarchists vis-à-vis the movement for political emancipation. Reprints a number of useful documents. [JMH]

1835 Serrano Monteavaro, Miguel Angel. Fernando Villaamil: una vida entre la mar y el dolor; la Guerra de Cuba. Prólogo de Pascual O'Dogherty. Madrid: Arnao, 1988. 658 p.: bibl.

Portrait of the life and times of a Spanish officer who fought and died at the Santiago de Cuba naval battle in 1898 is partially based on primary sources. Author's knowledge of Cuban history is a bit scanty. [JMH]

1836 Sevilla Soler, María Rosario. Las Antillas y la independencia de la América Española, 1808–1826. Madrid: Consejo Superior de Investigaciones Científicas, Escuela de Estudios Hispano-Americanos, 1986. 183 p.: bibl. (Publicaciones de la Escuela de Estudios Hispano-Americanos de Sevilla; 315)

Adds a few details to our knowledge of the situation in the Antilles during the Spanish-American Wars of Independence. Focuses primarily on Cuba. Draws mostly from secondary sources although it also uses some archival materials. [JMH]

1837 Sevilla Soler, María Rosario. La intervención norteamericana en Cuba y la opinión pública andaluza. (Anu. Estud. Am., 43, 1986, p. 469–516, bibl.)

Documents reaction of the Spanish press to the US intervention in Cuba in 1898 as reflected by four newspapers in Seville. [JMH]

1838 Sonesson, Birgit. La Real Hacienda en Puerto Rico: administración, política y grupos de presión, 1815–1868. Madrid: Instituto de Cooperación Iberoamericana; Sociedad Estatal Quinto Centenario; Instituto de Estudios Fiscales, 1990. 418 p.: bibl., ill., map. (Monografías Economía quinto centenario)

Fundamental study of Puerto Rico's fiscal and commercial history is based on portions of the author's doctoral dissertation. Coverage is much broader than the title indicates: it is as much a study of the changing structures and flows of foreign commerce and of the working of the State as a social agent, as it is an institutional history of the Spanish colony's royal exchequer. Pays special attention to the social composition and political interventions of export-import merchants. Provides valuable insight into the political and ideological conflicts attendant upon the island's integretion into the world market as a producer of sugar, coffee, and tobacco. Documentary appendix reproduces-final reports of several island intendants, the chief fiscal executives, written 1836–52. [FAS]

1839 Suárez Díaz, Ada. El antillano: biografía del Dr. Ramón Emeterio Betances, 1827–1898. San Juan, Puerto Rico: Centro de Estudios Avanzados de Puerto Rico y el Caribe: Revista Caribe, 1988. 301 p.: bibl., ill.

Most detailed biography yet of the great Puerto Rican revolutionary. Based on author's 1964 doctoral dissertation, it provides detailed description and analysis of Betances's life and writings until about 1880. The final two decades—including his efforts on behalf of the Cuban insurrection—are covered much less throughly. [FAS]

Szlajfer, Henryk. Capitalist development in nineteenth century Latin America: one model only? an example of Haiti and Paraguay. See item **2836.**

1840 Taffin, Dominique. Des miasmes et des races: les officiers de santé de la marine et le monde colonial antillais. (Ultramarines, 1, juin 1990, p. 3–11)

Until 1880, navy physicians were exclusively in charge of health policy and sanitary conditions in the French Caribbean. The tropical environment shaped their views in the debate on contagious disease that stirred their profession between 1815–50. [APD]

1841 Taffin, Dominique. Maladies et médecine à la Guadeloupe au XIXe siècle. (in Position des thèses. Paris: Ecole nationale des Chartes, 1985, p. 139–148)

Prior to microbiology, medical knowledge focused on environmental and racial factors. Author identifies major endemic and contagious tropical diseases that affected the island's population during the 19th century. Also describes medical profession and practice, government health policy, and sanitary institutions. [APD]

1842 Thésée, Françoise. Auguste Plée, 1786–1825, un voyageur naturaliste: ses travaux et ses tribulations aux Antilles, au Canada, en Colombie. Paris: Editions caribéennes, 1989. 219 p., 8 p. of plates: bibl., ill., maps. (Collection Kòd yanm)

Well-researched study on a French scientific expedition to the Caribbean in the 1820s. Plée brought back rich information on flora and fauna and numerous drawings and notes on the social and political situation (particularly for Puerto Rico). [APD]

1843 Toledo Sande, Luis. "A pie y llegaremos:" sobre la polémica Martí-Roa-Collazo. (*Anu. Centro Estud. Martianos*, 9, 1986, p. 141–212)

Exhaustive treatment of Martí's famous dispute with Raúl Roa's grandfather. Definitive point of departure for subsequent discussion of the topic. [JMH]

1844 Toledo Sande, Luis. Contra los cegadores de la luz: a propósito de las crónicas de José Martí sobre el sacerdote Edward McGlynn. (*Univ. La Habana*, 232, 1987, p. 71–82)

Emphasizes Martí's tempered anticlericalism in order to connect it with Liberation Theology and Castro's attitude toward religion. [JMH]

1845 Toledo Sande, Luis. José Martí contra *The New York Herald: The New York Herald* contra José Martí. (*Anu. Centro Estud. Martianos*, 10, 1987, p. 21–72)

Accuses *The New York Herald* of having deliberately mutilated the printed version of the manifesto that Martí sent to that newspaper shortly before his death in combat in Cuba. Biased and unconvincing, the author knows little about American journalism and the difficulties of rendering Martí's prose into English. [JMH]

1846 Tomich, Dale W. *Liberté ou Mort:* republicanism and slave revolt in Martinique, February 1831. (*Hist. Workshop*, 29, Spring 1990, p. 85–91)

In the 1831 uprising at St. Pierre, Martinique, slave wage-earners adapted symbols and rhetoric from the French insurrection of 1830. [APD]

1847 Tomich, Dale W. Slavery in the circuit of sugar: Martinique and the world economy, 1830–1848. Baltimore, Md.: Johns Hopkins Univ. Press, 1990. 353 p.: bibl., ill. (Johns Hopkins studies in Atlantic history and culture)

Attempts to illuminate changes in the 19th-century sugar and slavery system of Martinique by placing them within the context of a changing world economy. [APD]

1848 Tornero, Pablo. Emigración, población y esclavitud en Cuba, 1765–1817. (*Anu. Estud. Am.*, 44, 1987, p. 229–280, bibl., graphs)

Interesting information on white immigration during the period, but the treatment of black immigration and slavery is at times superficial and simplistic. [JMH]

1849 Trotman, David Vincent. Crime in Trinidad: conflict and control in a plantation society, 1838–1900. Knoxville, Tenn.: Univ. of Tennessee Press, 1986. 345 p.: bibl., index.

Study of relationship between crime and the political economy of Trinidad's multi-ethnic 19th-century society. Argues that planters pursued their economic interests and maintained their social and political hegemony over the laboring population by criminalizing various aspects of creole culture and instituting laws very reminiscent of the slavery era. [ELC]

1850 Valdés, Antonio José. Antonio José Valdés: ¿historia de Cuba o historia de La Habana? Selección e introducción de Hortensia Pichardo. La Habana: Editorial de Ciencias Sociales, 1987. 158 p.: (Palabra de Cuba)

Portrait of one of Cuba's earliest historians includes a critical analysis of his work and the reproduction of some of its most salient passages. [JMH]

1851 Valdés Carreras, Oscar. *El Habanero:* precursor; *Patria:* soldado. (*Univ. La Habana*, 233, sept./dic. 1988, p. 87–102)

Parallel between the revolutionary ideas of Félix Varela and José Martí as reflected in the newspapers which they founded. Author's interpretation of Varela's attitude toward US is debatable. [JMH]

1852 Varela, Félix. Letters to Elpidio. Edited by Felipe J. Estévez. New York: Paulist Press, 1989. 344 p.: bibl., index. (Sources of American spirituality)

First translation into English of one of the fundamental works of a man who was one of the founding fathers of Cuban nationalism and of New York Catholicism. Excellent English version is fully annotated and followed by a most complete bibliography on Varela and his writings. Important contribution. [JMH]

1853 Vas Mingo, Milagros del. El derecho de patronato en los proyectos abolicionistas cubanos. (*Anu. Estud. Am.*, 43, 1986, p. 171–184, bibl.)

Examines the juridical antecendents of the *patronato* in Cuba, which is seen as the culmination of a process initiated by the various legislative proposals for the abolition of slavery. [JMH]

1854 Vázquez, Manuel Salvador and **Carmen Menéndez de León.** Higiene y enfermedad del esclavo en Cuba durante la primera mitad del siglo XIX. (*Anu. Estud. Am.*, 43, 1986, p. 419–445, bibl.)

Study of the living conditions of slaves employed in the Cuban sugar industry during the colonial period. Uses some archival sources, but it is largely based on secondary materials. [JMH]

1855 Vila Vilar, Enriqueta. Intelectuales españoles ante el problema esclavista. (*Anu. Estud. Am.*, 43, 1986, p. 201–214, bibl.)

Examines a number of Spanish publications in order to show that Spanish intellectual circles generally remained indifferent to the problem of Cuban slavery. [JMH]

20TH CENTURY

1856 Abou, Antoine. L'enseignement technique à la Guadeloupe jusqu'en 1950. (*Bull. soc. hist. Guadeloupe*, 67/68, 1986, p. 75–92, table)

Traces the island's current economic problems to flawed organization of vocational training since 1920s. [APD]

Los abuelos: historia oral cubana. See *HLAS* 51:4666.

1857 Acosta, Ivonne. La mordaza: Puerto Rico, 1948–1957. Río Piedras, Puerto Rico: Editorial Edil, 1987. 238 p.: bibl., ill.

Thorough study of political repression in Puerto Rico during the first ten years of Luis Muñoz Marín's governorship uses a variety of sources to demonstrate US complicity in the persecution of nationalist and communist dissidents. Places the repression in the context of hemispheric and Cold War confrontations. [FAS]

1858 Adkin, Mark. Urgent fury: the battle for Grenada. Lexington, Mass.: Lexington Books, 1989. 391 p., 12 p. of plates: bibl., ill., index. (Issues in low-intensity conflict series)

Analysis and discussion of the 1983 US-led invasion of Grenada which toppled the military government installed following a coup in which the Prime Minister and countless other Grenadians were killed. Also casts some light on the island's political history in the period preceding the coup. [ELC]

1859 Alexandre, Rodolphe. La Guyane sous Vichy. Préface de Gaston Monnerville. Paris: Editions caribéennes, 1988. 186, 4 p. of plates: bibl., ill., tables.

Uses original sources to document French Guiana during World War II, emphasizing: 1) rise of *France libre* movement challenging collaborationist colonial authorities; 2) reconversion from export to subsistence economy; and 3) increased cultural lethargy due to isolation. [APD]

1860 Alfonso, Jorge. Puños dorados: apuntes para la historia del boxeo en Cuba. Santiago de Cuba: Editorial Oriente, 1988. 233 p.: ill.

Modest attempt to sketch the history of professional and amateur boxing in Cuba. [JMH]

Almeida Bosque, Juan. Presidio. See item 3628.

1861 Almodóbar, Carmen. Historiografía realizada en Cuba después de la revolución "Castrista," 1959–1984. (*Rev. Indias*, 49:185, enero/abril 1989, p. 173–191)

Written from the ideological perspective prevailing in present-day Cuba. [JMH]

1862 Alofs, Luc and **Leontine Merkies.** Ken ta Arubiano?: sociale integratie en na-tievorming op Aruba [Who is Aruban?: Social integration and nation building in Aruba]. Leiden, The Netherlands: Caraïbische Afd., Koninklijk Instituut voor Taal-, Land- en Volkenkunde, 1990. 232 p.: bibl., ill., map. (Antillen working papers; 15)

First anthropological study of the po-litical movement striving for a separate status for Aruba. Based on interviews and ar-chival research in Aruba, authors focus on the cultural identity of the Arubans and rela-tions between different population groups living on the island. [RH]

Alva Castro, Luis. Haya de la Torre. v. 2, Pere-grino de la unidad continental. See item **2441.**

1863 Alvarez Curbelo, Silvia. Un discurso ideológico olvidado: los agricultores puertorriqueños. (*Bol. Centro Invest. Hist.,* 2, 1986/1987, p. 141–160)

Articles and opinions published in *El agricultor puertorriqueño* during the 1920s are considered in the international context of a growing popular disillusionment with lib-eral ideology and reflect the growing appeal of fascist ideology to agricultural producers who comprised the Asociación de Agricul-tores and joined the Alianza Puertorriqueña after its founding in 1924. Puerto Rican farm-ers expressed anti-American and anti-indus-trial sentiments and sought to maintain an agrarian society. [FAS]

1864 Alvarez Tabío, Pedro. Diario de la guerra: diciembre de 1956-febrero de 1957. La Habana: Oficina de Publicaciones del Consejo de Estado, 1986. 336 p., 1 leaf of plates: ports.

Covers the first few weeks of Castro's anti-Batista struggle in the Sierra Maestra. Largely based on Guevara's and Raúl Castro's personal diaries. [JMH]

1865 Alvarez Tabío, Pedro. Diario de la guerra. Buenos Aires: Editorial An-tarca, 1987. 262 p. (Col. latinoamericana de Antarca)

Sympathetic reconstruction of the first eleven weeks of Castro's guerrilla campaign in the Sierra Maestra. Readable and useful re-print of accounts published by *Granma* in 1979. [JMH]

1866 Anderle, Adám. El reformismo en Cuba: apuntes metodológicos. (*Lat.am. Stud.,* 23, 1987, p. 59–70)

Informative discussion of the little-known Cuban *Aprista* party. [JMH]

1867 Annino, Antonio. 1959: el colapso del populismo en Cuba. (*Lat.am. Stud.,* 23, 1987, p. 71–91)

Explores the political agenda and ulti-mate failure of moderate elements who sup-ported Castro early in 1959. [JMH]

1868 Armas, Emilio de. Juan Marinello: crí-tico de la poesía martiana. (*Anu. Cen-tro Estud. Martianos,* 10, 1987, p. 202–214)

Laudatory reappraisal of Marinello's well-known study of Martí's poetry. [JMH]

1869 Baerga Santini, María del Carmen. Women's labor and domestic unit: in-dustrial homework in Puerto Rico during the 1930s. (*Cent. Estud. Puertorriq. Bull.,* 2:7, Winter 1989/1990, p. 33–39, bibl.)

Interpretative essay ascribes to female homeworkers in the needle industry a key role in the social reproduction of the Puerto Rican working class during the Depression. Women markedly increased their participa-tion in this industry in the 1930s. An ex-ploitative piece-rate system and reliance on unpaid family labor allowed home needle-work to reproduce gender roles and thus women's general subordination. Argues that home-based needlework coexisted casually with the performance of domestic chores and thus did not alter the gender-division of labor in society. Though suggestive, the discussion of domestic paid labor and its broader impli-cations is much too abbreviated and simpli-fied. See also item **1515.** [FAS]

Báez Evertsz, Franc. Braceros haitianos en la República Dominicana. See *HLAS 51:4669.*

1870 Balaguer, Joaquín. Memorias de un cortesano de la "era de Trujillo." Santo Domingo: Editora Corripio, 1988. 477 p.: ill.

Source book of great importance for the contemporary history of the Dominican Republic. [JMH]

Balaguer, el hombre del destino: recopilación de documentos, apuntes y datos para la bio-grafía del Presidente Joaquín Balaguer. See *HLAS 51:3644.*

1871 Baldrich, Juan José. Sembraron la no siembra: los cosecheros de tabaco puertorriqueños frente a las corporaciones tabacaleras, 1920–1934. Río Piedras, Puerto Rico: Ediciones Huracán, 1988. 194 p.: bibl., ill. (Col. Semilla)

Important study of agrarian protest and resistance in 20th-century Puerto Rico analyzes the orgins and development of organized resistance by local growers, many of them large landowners, to US corporate control over tobacco financing and marketing. The growers' actions culminated in 1932 with a successful campaign against planting which reduced island production by more than 80 percent. Theoretically-informed study underscores the potential for further research on social movements and forms of resistance in contemporary Puerto Rico. [FAS]

1872 Balfour, Sebastian. Castro. London; New York: Longman, 1990. 184 p.: bibl., maps. (Profiles in power)

More than a personal biography, book examines the historical conditions that enabled Castro to seize and maintain power. Author argues that the source of Castroism is the Cuban revolutionary tradition rather than Marxism-Leninism. [JMH]

1873 Baptista Gumucio, Mariano. ¿La venganza del Che? (in Bolívar volviera. La Paz: Editorial e Imprenta Artística, 1988, p. 91–102, ill.)

Provides interesting detail and information on the "unlucky end" of Bolivians that participated in the counter-guerrilla campaign against Che Guevara ending in his capture and death. Practically all of the following have since died in accidents or been killed or crippled by gunshot wounds: René Barrientos, Alfredo Ovando, Juan José Torres, Joaquín Zentano Anaya, Andrés Selich Chop, Mario Terán, Roberto Quintanilla, Gary Prodo, Zacarías Monje, Arnaldo Saucedo Parada, Antonio Arguedas, and Luis García Meza. [Ed.]

1874 Basdeo, Sahadeo. Indian participation in labour politics in Trinidad, 1919–1939. (Caribb. Q., 32:3/4, Sept./Dec. 1986, p. 50–65)

Important examination of Indian involvement in trade union activity in Trinidad argues that Adrian Cola Rienzi used class analysis of society to bridge racial gap existing between Indians and Blacks. Under

his leadership, trade unions won from British government "legislative demands which Cipriani, Roodal, and Butler had toiled so assiduously to achieve in the 1920s and early 1930s." [ELC]

1875 Benjamin, Jules R. Interpreting the U.S. reaction to the Cuban revolution, 1959–1960. (Cuba. Stud., 19, 1989, p. 145–165)

One of the most balanced interpretations written thus far of the immediate US response to the challenge of the Cuban Revolution. Especially accurate in pointing out the weaknesses of previous interpretations. [JMH]

1876 Bennett, Herman L. The challenge to the post-colonial State: a case study of the February revolution in Trinidad. (in The modern Caribbean. Edited by Franklin W. Knight and Colin A. Palmer. Chapel Hill, N.C.: Univ. of North Carolina Press, 1989, p. 129–146)

Cogent examination of factors contributing to revolution in post-independence Trinidad concludes that revolutionary leaders grossly underestimated continued racial fissures on the island, while rightly attacking lingering evidence of colonialism and imperialism within an independent nation. Movement, though crushed, achieved some gains when government belatedly acted to redress situation. [ELC]

1877 Blanco, Salvador Jorge. Archipiélago de intereses. Santo Domingo?: Dirección General de Información, Publicidad y Prensa de la Presidencia, 1986. 333 p.

Speeches by a Dominican president may be useful for writing the history of his Administration. [JMH]

1878 Bonilla, Frank and Ricardo Campos. Industry and idleness. New York: Centro de Estudios Puertorriqueños, Hunter College, City University of New York, 1986. 106 p.: bibl.

Four provocative essays are authored individually or jointly by leading duo of specialists on Puerto Rican political economy. They show convincingly that the conditions of the island and of communities of Puerto Rican descent in the US are closely interrelated. Some predictions about future patterns of migration and politics have come true while others have not. [FAS]

1879 Bosch, Juan. Póker de espanto en el Caribe. Santo Domingo: Editora Alfa y Omega, 1988. 217 p.

Venerable Dominican writer and politician gives his opinion about the origin and development of dictatorships in the Caribbean. He bases his conclusions on four case studies: Trujillo, Somoza, Pérez-Jiménez and Batista. [JMH]

1880 Cassá, Roberto. Movimiento obrero y lucha socialista en la República Dominicana: desde los orígenes hasta 1960. Santo Domingo: Fundación Cultural Dominicana, 1990. 620 p.

Revised and improved master's thesis makes extensive use of primary sources. [JMH]

1881 Castor, Suzy. L'occupation américaine d'Haïti. Port-au-Prince: Société haïtienne d'histoire, 1988. 272 p.

Standard interpretation of the US occupation in Haiti as a case study in imperialism. [APD]

1882 Castro, Fidel Análisis histórico de la Revolución Cubana: informe central al Primer Congreso del PCC. La Habana: Editorial de Ciencias Sociales, 1982. 82 p.: ill.

Castro's personal interpretation of Cuba's revolutionary history. [JMH]

1883 Castro, Fidel. Fidel en Holguín. Recopilación de Hiram Pérez Concepción, Irene Bolmey Pavón y Angeles Aguilera Montejo. La Habana: Editora Política, 1984. 248 p., 34 p. of plates: ill.

Speeches made by Castro in the Holguín province include journalistic information about his activities in the region. [JMH]

1884 Castro, Fidel. In defense of socialism: four speeches on the 30th anniversary of the Cuban Revolution. Edited by Mary-Alice Waters. New York: Pathfinder, 1989. 142 p.: bibl., ill.

Unambiguous confirmation of Castro's commitment to socialism. [JMH]

1885 Castro García, Angelina. Estampas del Museo Bacardí. La Habana: Gente Nueva, 1984. 71 p.: bibl., ill.

Brief description of the historical and artistic collection housed in the Bacardí Museum in Santiago de Cuba. [JMH]

1886 Che 20 anos depois. Organização de Flávio Koutzii e José Corrêa Leite. São Paulo: Busca Vida, 1987. 239 p.: bibl., ill. (Col. Sempre viva)

Non-scholarly essays and other writings on Che Guevara, many of them by participants in the Latin American revolutionary movements of the 1960s. [JMH]

1887 Che, sierra adentro. Recopilación de Froilán Escobar y Félix Guerra. La Habana: Editora Política, 1988. 366 p.: bibl., ill. (Enero)

Recounts Guevara's exploits as a guerrilla as told by those who knew him. [JMH]

1888 Chmara, Michał. Ideologia rewolucji kubańskiej, 1959–1970 [The ideology of the Cuban Revolution, 1959–1979]. Poznań, Poland: Uniwersytet im. Adama Mickiewicza w Poznaniu, 1991. 152 p.: bibl. (Seria Socjologia; 0554–8225: 17)

Historical and sociological study of the most original and creative period of the Cuban Revolution (1959–1970). Author interprets this stage as an attempt to integrate into a new whole various motifs from Latin American, North American, and European tradition. Stresses the Cuban Revolution's opposition to both dependent capitalism and post-Stalinist socialism in European countries. [M. Nalewajko]

1889 La chute de la maison Duvalier: 28 novembre 1985–7 février 1986; textes pour l'histoire. Rassemblés par Martin-Luc Bonnardot et Gilles Danroc. Avant-propos de Paul Blanquart. Paris: Karthala; Montréal: Editions Cidihca, 1989. 319 p., 16 p. of plates: bibl., ill.

Texts issued by grassroots organizations and unions in the months preceding the departure of Jean-Claude Duvalier, translated from Creole. Invaluable source for future historians. [APD]

1890 Clark, Juan. Cuba: mito y realidad; testimonios de un pueblo. Miami, Fl.: Saeta Ediciones, 1990. 1 v.

Bound to become one of the classical statements of the anti-Castro view of the Cuban Revolution. The chapters on the emergence of a "new-class" in revolutionary Cuba are especially recommended. [JMH]

1891 Clerc, Jean-Pierre. Fidel de Cuba. Paris: Ramsay, 1988. 493 p.: bibl., index. (Document)

Yet another premature attempt to produce a biography of Castro. [JMH]

1892 Contour, Solange. Saint-Pierre, Martinique. t. 1, La ville et le volcan avant 1902. t. 2, La catastrophe et ses suites. Paris: S. Contour, 1988. 2 v.: bibl., ill.

Postcards and excerpts from contemporary testimonies evoke the life of the port city on the eve of its total destruction by the volcanic eruption of 1902.

1893 Córdova, Efrén. El trabajador cubano en el estado de obreros y campesinos. Miami, Fla.: Ediciones Universal, 1990. 219 p.: bibl. (Col. Cuba y sus jueces)

Assessment of labor conditions inside Cuba by an exiled Cuban expert is based on information supplied by the Cuban press and interviews with exiled workers. [JMH]

1894 Crahan, Margaret E. Catholicism in Cuba. (*Cuba. Stud.*, 19, 1989, p. 3–24)

Discussion of the current state of Catholicism in Cuba. Surprisingly, the author devotes little space to the 1986 National Ecclesial Encounter and to Castro's statements to Frei Betto (1985) about discrimination against Catholics. [JMH]

1895 Cronología, 25 años de revolución. Edición de Carina Pino-Santos Navarro. La Habana: Editora Política, 1987. 394 p.

Extends the chronology published in 1983 to include the first quarter century of the Revolution, maintaining the tendentious character of the original work and including many trivial events. [JMH]

1896 Cuba after thirty years: rectification and the Revolution. Edited by Richard Gillespie. London; Savage, Md.: F. Cass, 1990. 188 p.: bibl., index.

Collection of generally commendable articles written on the 30th anniversary of the Cuban Revolution. Alistair Hennessy's "wider view" of the event is especially recommended. [JMH]

1897 The Cuban military under Castro. Edited by Jaime Suchlicki. Introduction by James A. Morris. Coral Gables, Fla.: Institute of Interamerican Studies, Univ. of Miami; North-South Center, 1989. 197 p.: bibl.

Informative and useful essays explore the history of the Cuban military institution: its evolution; its current mission and doctrine; the shifts in civil-military relations since 1980; and the impact and influence of the Soviet Union. [JMH]

1898 Cupull, Adys. Julio Antonio Mella en los mexicanos. México: Ediciones El Caballito, 1983. 118 p. (Col. Fragua mexicana; 74)

Collection of statements by Mexicans who knew Mella that adds very little to what is already known. Focuses on circumstances of his violent death. [JMH]

Dávila Santiago, Rubén. El derribo de las murallas: orígenes intelectuales del socialismo en Puerto Rico. See item **5347.**

Dávila Santiago, Rubén. El pensamiento social obrero a comienzos del siglo XX en Puerto Rico. See item **5348.**

1899 Désinor, Carlo A. L'affaire Jumelle. Port-au-Prince: L'Imprimeur II, 1987. 208 p.: ports. (Col. Dossiers contemporains)

This companion to Désinor's study on Fignolé (item **1900**) further illuminates the political crisis that lead to the rise to power of François Duvalier in 1957. Focuses on President Magloire's elimination of Clément Jumelle, a former member of his cabinet considered his eventual successor to the presidency. [APD]

1900 Désinor, Carlo A. Daniel Fignolé. v. 1, Un espoir vain. Port-au-Prince: L'Imprimeur II, 1986. 1 v. (Col. Dossiers contemporains)

Biography of a politician who played a crucial role in Haitian politics 1946–57 by organizing the popular sectors of Port-au-Prince. Written by member of MOP, the populist party founded by Fignolé (See also item **1899**.) [APD]

1901 The Dutch Caribbean : prospects for democracy. Edited by Betty Nelly Sedoc-Dahlberg. New York: Gordon and Breach, 1990. 333 p.: bibl., ill., index, maps, tables. (Caribbean studies, 0275–5793; 5)

Uneven collection of 14 essays on the recent history and the political future of the Netherlands Antilles, Aruba, and Suriname. The quality of the articles on Suriname is disappointing. The Netherlands Antilles and Aruba receive better treatment, particularly with regard to the forecasts for the constitutional future of the islands. [RH]

1902 Estades Font, María Eugenia. Los intereses estratégico-militares de Estados Unidos en Puerto Rico a principios del

siglo XX. (*Bol. Centro Invest. Hist.*, 3, 1987/
1988, p. 175–187)

Draws on Alfred Mahan's emphasis on
naval dominance and control over strategic
waterways as keys to imperial expansion to
argue that military and geopolitical considerations led the US to take and maintain
control over Puerto Rico. [FAS]

1903 Ferguson, James. Papa Doc, Baby Doc:
Haiti and the Duvaliers. Oxford, England; New York: B. Blackwell, 1988. 204 p.,
8 p. of plates: bibl., ill., index.

Historical analysis of the Duvaliers'
dictatorship (1957–86), with special emphasis on the final three-month crisis. Second
edition includes section on aftermath of Du-
valierism (1987–88). [APD]

1904 Ferrao, Luis Angel. Pedro Albizu Campos y el nacionalismo puertorriqueño.
Río Piedras: Editorial Cultural, 1990. 367 p.:
bibl., ill., index.

Most rigorous examination yet of the
Nationalist movement in Puerto Rico during
the height of its militancy and political importance in the 1930s. Study is based on author's doctoral dissertation and places the development of Nationalist ideology and party
strategy in the context of insular social conflicts, relations with the US metropole, and
international events such as the Spanish
Civil War. Its greatest contribution resides in
a painstaking analysis of Albizu's and the
Nationalists' ideology, the organization and
workings of the party, and its internal fissures. For these, author relies on a thorough
review of newspapers and other printed documents, and on party documents not ordinarily consulted by scholars. Like other revisionist writings on the subject, this work has
stirred up heated controversy among inde-
pendence-minded intellectuals and activists
on the island. [FAS]

1905 Franqui, Carlos. Vida, aventuras y de-
sastres de un hombre llamado Castro.
Barcelona, España: Planeta; Caracas: Editorial Planeta Venezolana, 1988. 480 p.: ill.
(Documento; 243)

Personal and unconventional assessment of the achievements and failures of the
Castro regime is an interesting but limited
contribution to the literature. [JMH]

1906 Galván, William. Ercilia Pepín, una
mujer ejemplar. Santo Domingo: Edi-

tora Universitaria, UASD, 1986. 213 p.: bibl.,
ill., ports. (Publicaciones de la Univ. Autónoma de Santo Domingo; 502: Col. Educación
y sociedad; 29)

Laudatory biographical sketch of the
well-known Dominican educator is well researched. [JMH]

1907 Gama, Raymond and **Jean-Pierre Sain-
ton.** Mé 67: mémoire d'un événement.
Pointe-à-Pitre, Guadeloupe: Sociéte guadeloupéenne d'édition et de diffusion, 1985.
263 p.: ill.

Groupe d'Organisation Nationale de
la Guadeloupe (GONG) sympathizers write
on the role played in Pointe-à-Pitre riots of
1967 by the Guadeloupe underground pro-
independence organization formed in 1963.
[APD]

1908 García-Carranza, Araceli and **Josefina
García Carranza.** Bibliografía cubana
del comandante Ernesto Che Guevara. La
Habana: Biblioteca Nacional José Martí,
Depto. de Investigaciones Bibliográficas,
1987. 473 p.: bibl., indexes.

Lists the items by Guevara or on Guevara extant in Cuba's José Martí National Library. [JMH]

1909 García-Carranza, Araceli and **Josefina
García-Carranza.** Biobibliografía de
Carlos Rafael Rodríguez. La Habana: Editorial Letras Cubanas, 1987. 300 p.: bibl.,
indexes.

Provides useful background information for one of the most important figures of
Castro's Cuba. [JMH]

1910 García-Carranza, Araceli. Biobibliogra-
fía de Emilio Roig de Leuchsenring.
Prólogo de Julio Le Riverend. La Habana:
Ministerio de Cultura, Biblioteca Nacional
José Martí, 1986. 2 v. (xiii, 627 p.):

Lists the considerable literary and historical output of one of the most prolific figures of Cuban historical revisionism. Also
includes an excessively detailed chronology
of his life. [JMH]

1911 García Pérez Castañeda, Angel and
Piotr A. Mironchuk. Los soviets obreros y campesinos en Cuba. La Habana: Editorial de Ciencias Sociales, 1987. 227 p., 16 p.
of plates: bibl., ill. (Historia de Cuba)

Interesting study of the soviets organized by Cuban workers and peasants during

the 1933 Revolution. Significant contribution given the paucity of information on the subject. [JMH]

1912 Geyer, Georgie Anne. Guerrilla prince: the untold story of Fidel Castro. Boston : Little, Brown, 1991. 445 p., 8 p. of plates: bibl., ill., indexes.

Certainly not a definitive biography of Castro, but it does concentrate on his personal life, unlike other attempts on the subject. Also introduces to the English-speaking public some formerly unknown details of the Cuban leader's evolution. [JMH]

Gómez García, Carmen. Acerca de la periodización del pensamiento social de Carlos Baliño, el primer marxista cubano. See item **5350.**

1913 Gómez Treto, Raúl. La Iglesia Católica durante la construcción del socialismo en Cuba. San José: Comisión de Estudios de Historia de la Iglesia en Latinoamérica; Depto. Ecuménico de Investigaciones, 1987. 125 p.: (Col. Historia de la Iglesia y de la teología)

Non-scholarly work traces the evolution of the Catholic Church under the Castro regime. Tendentious in the choice and interpretation of facts, it frequently reflects the official government perspective. For sociologist's comment see *HLAS 51:4696.* [JMH]

González Díaz, Emilio. Luchas políticas y democracia en Puerto Rico, 1968–1985. See *HLAS 51:3670.*

1914 Grobart, F. Un forjador eternamente joven. La Habana: Gente Nueva, 1985. 75 p., 24 p. of plates: ill.

Collection of articles sheds some light on the life and times of one of the founding fathers of the Cuban Communist Party. [JMH]

1915 Guérin, Daniel. Les Antilles décolonisées. Introduction par Aimé Césaire. Paris: Présence africaine, 1986. 188 p.: bibl., map.

Reedition of a classic (Buenos Aires, 1959) in anti-colonialist literature of the 1950s. [APD]

1916 Guerrero, María Luisa. Elena Mederos, una mujer con perfil para la historia. Washington: Of Human Rights; Miami, Fla.: Ediciones Universal, 1991. 315 p., 8 p. of plates: bibl., ill. (Col. Cuba y sus jueces)

Based largely on personal reminiscences, with limited scholarly apparatus. Readable and informative, this work certainly could serve as the nucleus of a more thoroughly researched future biography. [JMH]

1917 Guerrero, Miguel. Enero de 1962: ¡el despertar dominicano! Santo Domingo: Ediciones Mograf, 1988. 276 p., 21 p. of plates: bibl., ill., ports. (Col. Historia y cultura)

Interesting and well-written account of the events that led to the creation of the Council of State in the Dominican Republic in Jan. 1962. [JMH]

1918 Guevara, Ernesto. Che Guevara and the Cuban Revolution: writings and speeches of Ernesto Che Guevara. Edited by David Deutschmann. Sydney, Australia: Pathfinder/Pacific and Asia, 1987. 413 p., 48 p. of plates: bibl., ill., index.

Selection of Guevara's articles, speeches, and letters, a number of which appear in English for the first time. Entirely new translation includes useful annotations. [JMH]

1919 Guevara Lynch, Ernesto. Aquí va un soldado de América. Buenos Aires: Sudamericana/Planeta, 1987. 170 p., 15 p. of plates: ill.

Second part of Che Guevara's biography by his father covers approximately until the 1955 Guevara-Castro meeting in Mexico. Based on the guerrilla leader's correspondence with his family and closest Argentine friends. Interesting for intimate details of his personality and political opinions. [JMH]

1920 Hector, Michel. Syndicalisme et socialisme en Haïti: 1932–1970. Port-au-Prince: Impr. H. Deschamps, 1989. 226 p., 3 folded leaves of plates: ill.

Excellent study of political parties and unions (1932–70) distinguishes three periods: 1) beginning of communist movement which led to appearance of the first unions, 1932–46; 2) period of joint development of party and union, 1946–57; and 3) the dictatorship of François Duvalier from 1957–70, initially marked by relatively free expression for parties and unions followed by episodic and violent political struggles as unions were suppressed. [APD]

Helg, Aline. Race in Argentina and Cuba, 1880–1930: theory, policies, and popular reaction. See item **2707**.

Henkin, Alice H. *et al.* Human rights in Cuba: report of a delegation of the Association of the Bar of the City of New York. See *HLAS 51:4698.*

1921 Herek, Gregory M.; Irving L. Janis; and Paul Huth. Quality of U.S. decision making during the Cuban missile crisis: major errors in Welch's reassessment. (*J. Confl. Resolut.,* 33:3, Sept. 1989, p. 446–459, bibl.)

Esoteric discussion of opposing views about the quality of decision-making during the Cuban missile crisis is not very enlightening. [JMH]

Hurbon, Laënnec. Comprendre Haïti: essai sur l'Etat, la nation, la culture. See *HLAS 51:4703.*

1922 Huyghues-Belrose, Vincent. La Guyane pendant la Grande Guerre, 1914–1918: dossier pédagogique. Sous la direction de d'Anne-Marie Bruleaux. Cayenne, Guyane: Archives départementales de la Guyane, 1985. 27 p.: bibl., ill.

Presents 23 original documents that show the impact of World War I on French Guyanese convicts, gold-diggers, and Amerindians. Includes introduction and bibliography. [APD]

1923 Jolibois, Gérard. L'exécution des frères Coicou. Port-au-Prince: Impr. Le Natal, 1986. 332 p.: ill.

As popular unrest and liberal uprising built up in Haiti (1907–08), President General Nord-Alexis, otherwise regarded as an honest man, ordered an indiscriminate repression of his opponents, among them Coicou, a popular *chansonnier.* [APD]

1924 Kelshall, Gaylord. The U-boat war in the Caribbean. Port of Spain, Trinidad: Paria Pub. Co., 1988. 496 p., 25 p. of plates: ill.

History of the Caribbean theater during World War II by a military officer in the Trinidad Coast Guard provides useful information on an often-neglected aspect of U-boat activity in the Atlantic. [ELC]

1925 Knight, Franklin W. Cuba: politics, economy, and society, 1898–1985. (*in* The modern Caribbean. Edited by Franklin W. Knight and Colin A. Palmer. Chapel Hill,

N.C.: Univ. of North Carolina Press, 1989, p. 169–184)

Unsuccessful attempt to compress nearly a century of Cuban history into 16 pages, almost half of which are devoted to the Casto Revolution. The result is a largely unbalanced and somewhat distorted view of Cuba's evolution. [JMH]

1926 Korol, Claudia. El Che y los argentinos. Buenos Aires: Ediciones Dialéctica, 1988. 281 p.: bibl., ill. (Col. Testimonial)

Useful non-scholarly work treats little-known aspects of Argentine history connected with Guevara's life and activities. [JMH]

1927 Kukovecz, György. Nación y progreso en Cuba: dos aspectos de una crisis revolucionaria entre 1930 y 1959. (*Lat.am. Stud.,* 23, 1987, p. 43–57)

Interpretive essay from a Marxist perspective shows the interrelationship between the 1933–35 revolutionary cycle and the one that began in 1959. [JMH]

1928 Lajara Burgos, Luis Homero. ¿Por qué se produjo la revolución del 24 de abril del año 1965? Santo Domingo: Taller, 1987. 333 p., 1 leaf of plates: ports.

Unpretentious narrative of the 1965 Dominican Revolution and the ensuing US intervention is non-scholarly, but informative and interesting. [JMH]

1929 Lazo Pérez, Mario. Recuerdos del Moncada. La Habana: Editora Política, 1987. 191 p.: bibl., ill.

Although the author did participate in the Moncada attack, most of his reminiscences cover the subsequent events. [JMH]

1930 Lebedinsky, Mauricio. Cuba y el Che. Buenos Aires: Dialéctica, 1988. 151 p.: bibl. (Col. Política y sociedad)

Tendentious analysis of the Cuban Revolution on its 30th anniversary, with special emphasis on the role played by Che Guevara. [JMH]

1931 Levi, Darrell E. Michael Manley: the making of a leader. Athens: Univ. of Georgia Press, 1990. 349 p., 16 p. of plates: bibl., ill.

Readable biography of Jamaican politician and current prime minister is devoted largely to Manley's public life and career as a trade union organizer in the 1950s and his involvement in politics especially after 1962 when he articulated his belief in democratic socialism. Well-documented, though somewhat sympathetic to Manley. Extremely useful for understanding contemporary Jamaican politics. [ELC]

1932 Luzón, José Luis. Economía, población y territorio en Cuba, 1899–1983. Madrid: Ediciones Cultura Hispánica del Instituto de Cooperación Iberoamericana, 1987. 341 p.: bibl., ill.

Shows how economic changes have affected the growth of Cuba's population and its geographical distribution. Maintains that despite the Revolution, many of the old demographic patterns persist. [JMH]

1933 Magid, Alvin. Urban nationalism: a study of political development in Trinidad. Gainesville: Univ. Presses of Florida: Univ. of Florida Press, 1988. 294 p.: bibl., index, maps.

Examines dispute in early 1900s between Port-of-Spain's elected municipal council and the island's appointed government. The former's dissolution and replacement by appointed body contributed to the emergence of opposition parties and radicalization of political process. Author concludes that this urban activity was major stimulus for growth of anticolonial activity, nationalism, and independence. [ELC]

1934 Maillard, Jean-Claude. Éléments pour une histoire de l'industrie bananière en Guadeloupe: les développements récents de l'exportation antillaise et l'effort de renouvellement du transport bananier, 1953–1980. (*Bull. soc. hist. Guadeloupe,* 67/68, 1986, p. 3–30, bibl., tables)

Documents impressive growth of banana industry in Martinique and Guadeloupe from 1950–80: shipping companies introduced cold rooms and containers and the State made considerable effort to improve the port facilities and road network. [APD]

1935 Martínez Díaz, Dina. La última opción reformista: el Partido del Pueblo Cubano—Ortodoxos. (*Univ. La Habana,* 233, 1988, p. 133–147)

Analyzes the role played in Cuba in the late forties and early fifties by the strident reformism of the political party founded by Eduardo Chibás. Journalistic account inspired by a distorted view of reality and a preconceived theoretical framework. [JMH]

1936 Medin, Tzvi. Cuba: the shape of revolutionary consciousness. Translated by Martha Grenzback. Boulder, Colo.: L. Rienner Publishers, 1990. 191 p.: bibl.

Thought-provoking analysis of the process whereby Castro and other leaders grafted Marxism-Leninism on Cuban revolutionary consciousness. Helps to explain how the anti-Batista insurrection was transformed into a socioeconomic upheaval. [JMH]

1937 Medland, William J. The Cuban missile crisis of 1962: needless or necessary. New York: Praeger, 1988. 167 p.

Useful review of the various historical interpretations of the crisis. Unfortunately, the author's rather balanced conclusions ignore long-term consequences for Cuba and Latin America. [JMH]

1938 Meel, Peter. Money talks, morals vex: The Netherlands and the decolonisation of Suriname, 1975–1990. (*Rev. Eur.,* 48, junio 1990, p. 75–98, bibl.)

Probably the best analysis of political and economic relations between Suriname and The Netherlands, 1975–90, focuses on the 1980s when the military regime and its violation of human rights put these relations under severe pressure. [RH]

1939 Meléndez, Edgardo. La crisis del movimiento anexionista en Puerto Rico, 1924–1952. (*Rev. Cienc. Soc./Río Piedras,* 26:1/4, enero/dic. 1987, p. 9–69)

Dense study of the statehood movement during a period in which its social base was narrowing and its ideology becoming more conservative. Devises a complicated explanatory framework for this "crisis" within the statehood movement. Part of the article develops a finely nuanced analysis of the politics of sugar, including a detailed account of the ideology of groups associated with the vital sugar industry, from the mass of poor, dependent *colonos,* to the large central-mill owners. Nonetheless, not all the main points are compellingly made, and at times it is difficult to follow the main line of argument. [FAS]

1940 Meléndez, Edgardo. The social basis for annexationism in Puerto Rico and the emergence of the New Progressive Party, 1952–1968. (*Hómines,* 11, marzo 1987/feb. 1988, p. 49–81)

Attributes the rise of the New Progressive Party out of the PER to the eclipse of the reactionary sugar elite by the industrial bourgeoisie during the 1950s. Led by Luis Ferré, the industrial bourgoisie built a socially reformist statehood movement with wider appeal among middle and lower sectors. Notes statehood was particularly appealing to Federal employees and US army veterans in Puerto Rico. [FAS]

1941 Mencía, Mario. Tiempos precursores. La Habana: Editorial de Ciencias Sociales, 1986. 356 p.: bibl. (Historia de Cuba)

Compilation of newspaper and magazine articles covers Castro's revolutionary activity before the landing of the Granma expedition in 1956. Informative and useful, although noticeably biased and hagiographic. [JMH]

1942 Minà, Gianni. Il racconto di Fidel. Prefazione di Gabriel García Márquez. Traduzione di Claudio M. Valentinetti. Milano, Italia: A. Mondadori, 1988. 314 p. (Ingrandimenti)

Lengthy interview touches upon every conceivable subject, from foreign policy, human rights, and Europe to the economy, domestic policies, and Cuban society. At the same time, Castro manages to interject his views on culture, religion, medicine, and sports, and to talk about Guevara and his concept of the new man. [JMH]

1943 Mintz, Sidney W. Taso, trabajador de la caña. Introducción de Francisco A. Scarano. Río Piedras, Puerto Rico: Ediciones Huracán, 1988. 1 v. (Clásicos Huracán; 4)

First Spanish-language edition of an anthropological classic. Mintz interweaves the life story of Eustaquio Zayas Alvarado (Don Taso) with expert commentary, allowing readers to explore the making of a rural proletarian community in the Puerto Rican sugar lowlands. Although some of the recorded interviews on which the original English-language translation was based have been deleted, the omissions are barely noticeable. In any case, the ability to read Don Taso's own words more than compensates for the lost passages. Introduction places this work and Mintz's related writings on Puerto Rican society and culture in the context of a developing island historiography of social classes and workers' struggles. [FAS]

1944 Morales Carrión, Arturo. La crisis económica de 1913 y sus consecuen-

cias ideológicas. (*Bol. Centro Invest. Hist.*, 5, 1990, p. 153–178)

Lecture given in 1987 at the inauguration of the Univ. of Puerto Rico's doctoral program in history was published posthumously. Offers an overview of Puerto Rican reaction to President Woodrow Wilson's 1912 advocacy of duty-free entry of foreign sugar into the US. Island producers, having based their newfound prosperity on free access to the US market, and on the tariff protection accorded there to their sugar, lobbied vigorously in Washington and San Juan against the Underwood Tariff. Explores the connection between the threat to the sugar industry, the outbreak of World War I, and the onset of colonial reforms leading to the Jones Act of 1917. [FAS]

1945 Morizot, Frédéric. Grenade, épices et poudre: une épopée caraïbe. Préface de Jean Ziegler. Paris: L'Harmattan, 1988. 385 p., 16 p. of plates: bibl., ill. (Col. Monde antillais, recherches et documents)

History of rise and fall of Grenada Revolution by a Frenchman who was in charge of implementing an agricultural assistance program on the island 1980–85. Particularly rich on island events after 1979. Author implies that internal disagreements among leaders largely determined final denouement. [ELC]

1946 Morley, Morris H. Imperial state and revolution: the United States and Cuba, 1952–1986. Cambridge; New York: Cambridge Univ. Press, 1987. 571 p.: bibl., index.

Controversial and highly debatable reinterpretation of US-Cuban relations during the period in light of the Marxist-inspired construct of the imperial State. [JMH]

1947 Los movimientos sociales en el Caribe. Coordinación de Gérard Pierre-Charles. Santo Domingo: Editora Universitaria, 1987. 389 p.: bibl., ill., maps. (Publicaciones de la Universidad Autónoma de Santo Domingo; 575. Colección Estudios sociales; 4)

Includes special studies of the Dominican labor and peasant movemments, an interview with Juan Bosch about the 1984 popular uprising, and an essay on political activities of Cuban women (1959–80). [JMH]

1948 Naranjo Orovio, Consuelo. Cuba, otro escenario de lucha: la guerra civil y el exilio republicano español. Madrid: Consejo Superior de Investigaciones Científicas, Centro de Estudios Históricos, Depto. de Historia de América, 1988. 336 p.: bibl., ill. (Col. Tierra nueva e cielo nuevo; 24)

Dispassionate study of the controversies caused in Cuba by the Spanish Civil War. Well-researched, but suffers from insufficient coverage of the Cuban background. [JMH]

1949 Naranjo Orovio, Consuelo. Cuba vista por el emigrante español a la Isla, 1900–1959: un ensayo de historia oral. Madrid: Consejo Superior de Investigaciones Científicas, Centro de Estudios Históricos, Depto. de Historia de América, 1987. 164 p., 4 leaves of plates: bibl., ill. (Anexos de Revista de Indias; 3)

Given the number of immigrants interviewed by the author (209 out of hundreds of thousands), the study should be regarded as a mere approach to the problem. [JMH]

1950 Naranjo Orovio, Consuelo. Transterrados españoles en las Antillas: un acercamiento a su vida cotidiana. (*Anu. Estud. Am.*, 44, 1987, p. 521–548, bibl.)

Informative study of the vicissitudes of life of the Spanish refugees who came to the Dominican Republic in 1939. [JMH]

1951 Negrón Portillo, Mariano. Las turbas republicanas, 1900–1904. Río Piedras, Puerto Rico: Ediciones Huracán, 1990. 1 v.

Most thorough analysis yet of the social origins and ideas of Puerto Rican annexationists during the transition to American rule. Regards the US takeover as a critical juncture in which, for the first time, plebeian sectors actively participated in the country's political life. [FAS]

1952 Okuneva, M.A. La clase obrera en la Revolución Cubana. Edición de I.R. Grigulévich. La Habana: Editorial de Ciencias Sociales; Editorial Progreso, 1988. 143 p.: bibl.

Unconvincing attempt to demonstrate that the working class was the leading force in the Cuban Revolution. [JMH]

1953 Palmer, Colin A. Identity, race and black power in independent Jamaica. (*in* The modern Caribbean. Edited by Franklin W. Knight and Colin A. Palmer. Chapel Hill, N.C.: Univ. of North Carolina Press, 1989, p. 111–128)

Careful and judicious treatment of black Jamaicans' search for racial identity, from 1944 universal adult suffrage to 1960s independence period. Argues that official government and middle class reaction, especially to Black Power ideology imported from the US, points to racial and class strains which suggest that a secure, confident racial identity is not yet forged.[ELC]

1954 La parole des anciens est la mémoire du peuple. v. 1, Pè Jeanton. Directeurs Jérôme Cléry et Laurent Farrugia. Basse-Terre, Guadeloupe: OMC, 1980. 1 v.: ill.

Witty 82-year-old man from Basse-Terre recalls his many jobs and love affairs, and shares his views on politics. Valuable oral source. [APD]

1955 Peña Gómez, José Francisco. Construcción de la democracia: agosto 16 de 1978-agosto 15 de 1982. v. 4. Edición de Sara Peralta de Rathe. Santo Domingo: Editora Corripio, 1986. 1 v. (Col. Pensamiento político; 4)

Useful collection of political articles by the author, a key figure in the Dominican Revolutionary Party. [JMH]

1956 Persons, Albert C. Bay of Pigs: a firsthand account of the mission by a U.S. pilot in support of the Cuban invasion force in 1961. Foreword by Joseph L. Shannon. Jefferson, N.C.: McFarland, 1990. 162 p.: index, maps.

Observations, comments, and reminiscences by one of the American pilots who participated in the ill-fated attempt. Squarely attributes the fiasco to the timidity, irresolution, and indecisiveness of President Kennedy and his Administration. Indispensable source book. [JMH]

1957 Pierre, Pressoir. Témoignages, 1946–1976: l'espérance déçue. Port-au-Prince: Impr. H. Deschamps, 1987. 285 p.: ill.

Haitian military officer in exile bears witness to the repressive nature of the Duvalierist regime (1957–86). [APD]

1958 Pividal, Francisco. Los tres días de Fidel en Caracas: hace treinta años. Caracas: Biblioteca de la Univ. Central de Venezuela, 1989. 52 p.: ill. (Col. Rectorado)

Step-by-step account of Castro's brief visit to Venezuela in Jan. 1959 is partial, but reliable and informative. [JMH]

1959 Portuondo, Yolanda. Guillermo Sardiñas, el sacerdote comandante. La Habana: Editorial Cultura Popular, 1987. 257 p.: bibl., ill. (Testimonio)

Quasi-official biography of the first priest that joined Castro's guerrillas in the mountains is based on oral testimony from relatives, friends, and associates. [JMH]

1960 Prado Salmón, Gary. Como capturé al Che. Barcelona, Spain: Ediciones B, Grupo Zeta, 1987. (Serie Reporter)

Useful account reveals a number of details about Guevara's capture by Bolivian troops in 1967. [JMH]

1961 Quigley, Thomas E. The Catholic Church in Cuba. (in Catholicism and politics in communist societies. Edited by Pedro Ramet. Durham: Duke Univ. Press, 1990, p. 296–312)

Sober-minded appraisal of Church-State relations in present-day Cuba corrects some of the distortions that characterize conventional interpretations of the Church's failed relationship with the Revolution. [JMH]

Ramos, Marcos Antonio. Protestantism and revolution in Cuba. See *HLAS 51:4730.*

1962 Ramos Mattei, Andrés A. La emigración puertorriqueña hacia el Caribe, 1899–1901. (*Hist. Soc./Río Piedras*, 3, 1990, p. 60–77)

Worsening economic conditions at the end of the 19th century, compounded by the US invasion and military rule, motivated migration by Puerto Rican workers to other parts of the Caribbean and even to Hawaii. Mostly descriptive account relies on newspaper articles, government reports, and secondary sources. [FAS]

1963 Ramsoedh, Hans. Suriname 1933–1944: koloniale politiek en beleid onder gouverneur Kielstra [Suriname 1933–1944: colonial politics and policy under Governor Kielstra]. Delft, The Netherlands: Eburon, 1990. 255 p.: bibl., ill., index.

Study of the Administration of Governor J.C. Kielstra (1933–44) which marked a distinct watershed in the history of Suriname. Kielstra broke with policy of assimilation designed to promote the Dutch language and culture in Suriname. Author looks at reasons underlying this break in policy, its

consequences, and reactions to it. Originally a dissertation (Rijksuniv. Utrecht, The Netherlands, 1990), this monograph includes English summary. [R. Hoefte]

1964 Rey Díaz, Ana Angélica. Conrado, primer maestro mártir. La Habana: Editora Política, 1987. 55 p.: bibl., ill.

Biographical sketch of a rural teacher killed by anti-Castro guerrillas is hagiographic in tone and substance. [JMH]

1965 Rivera, Eulalie R. Growing up on St. Croix: recollections of a Crucian girlhood, including a selection of best-loved Virgin Islands spirituals, a description of a tea meeting, and some of the games we played. Frederiksted, St. Croix: E.C. Rivera, 1987. 64 p.: ill.

Memoirs of a retired schoolteacher evoke the island's popular culture before World War II. [APD]

1966 Rodríguez Castro, María Elena. Tradición y modernidad: el intelectual puertorriqueño ante la década del treinta. (*Bol. Centro Invest. Hist.*, 3, 1987/1988, p. 45–65)

Describes attempts by elite Puerto Rican intellectuals to create a nationalist, unifying discourse that would reassert the hegemony they perceived their class to be losing in the face of rapid change, modernization, and North American domination. Argues that intellectuals of the early 20th century utilized ideals of family and household that emerged from the patriarchal hacienda milieu in their efforts to organize their own class and, ultimately, the image of the nation they purported to represent. Based on autobiographical accounts, other writings by the intellectuals themselves, and articles published in the intellectual journal *Indice.* [FAS]

1967 Rojas, Marta. El juicio del Moncada. 4. ed., amplida y rev. La Habana: Editorial de Ciencias Sociales, 1988. 357 p., 38 p. of plates: ill., index. (Ediciones políticas)

Detailed and sympathetic account of the trial of Castro and his companions after the Moncada attack. Readable, but of journalistic quality. [JMH]

1968 Rosa, Gilberto de la. Petán: un cacique en la era de Trujillo. Santiago, República Dominicana: UCMM, 1988? 154 p.: bibl., ill. (Col. Estudios; 121)

Describes the domination by one of dictator Trujillo's brothers over the town of Bonao. Relies on printed sources, personal interviews, and some unpublished materials. [JMII]

1969 Sáez, José L. Los jesuítas en la República Dominicana. v. 1, Los primeros veinticinco años, 1936–1961. v. 2, Hacia el medio siglo, 1962–1986. Santo Domingo: Museo Nacional de Historia y Geografía; Archivo Histórico de las Antillas, 1988–1990. 2 v.: bibl., index.

Covers the 20th century, a very important period of Jesuit history in the Dominican Republic. Exhaustively researched work is fairly objective, but could benefit from additional background material and a more thorough discussion of some important events. [JMH]

1970 Sánchez Bermúdez, Juan Alberto. La presencia villareña en la insurrección de agosto de 1931. (*Islas*, 87, mayo/agosto 1987, p. 124–133, bibl.)

Brings to light little known ramifications of the 1931 revolt against Machado's dictatorship. [JMH]

1971 Sanders, Andrew. British colonial policy and the role of Amerindians in the politics of the nationalist period in British Guiana, 1945–68. (*Soc. Econ. Stud.*, 36:3, Sept. 1987, p. 77–98, bibl.)

Superficial and uncritical treatment of Amerindians' political behavior in Guyana (1945–68). Argues that their unique legal status in Guyanese society led them to oppose nationalistic parties, candidates, and policies during a critical period of the nation's history. [ELC]

1972 Santamaría, Haydée. Haydée habla del Moncada. La Habana: Editorial de Ciencias Sociales, 1978. 119 p.: ill. (Ediciones políticas)

Eyewitness account of Castro's attack on the Moncada military barracks on July 26, 1953 by one of Castro's closest companions at the time. [JMH]

1973 Sarabia, Nydia. Moncada, biografía de un cuartel. La Habana: Editorial de Ciencias Sociales, 1984. 98 p., 32 p. of plates: bibl., ill. (Historia de Cuba)

Provides interesting information on the Moncada military barracks, the target of Castro's renowned attack in 1953. [JMH]

1974 Sarracino, Rodolfo. El grupo Rockefeller actua: entreguismo e injerencia anglo-yanqui en la década del treinta. La Habana: Editorial de Ciencias Sociales, 1987. 233 p., 5 p. of plates: bibl., ill. (Economía)

Marxist perspective on aspects of US-Cuban economic relations in the late thirties. Also studies importance of British interference at that time. [JMH]

1975 Saunders, D. Gail. The 1937 riot in Inagua, The Bahamas. (*Nieuwe West-Indische Gids*, 62:3/4, 1988, p. 129–145, bibl., map)

Overview of disturbances on southern Bahamian island at time when labor riots were rampant throughout the BWI. Argues that this local incident resulted from personal vendetta among rival employers, but failed to develop into political or labor riot because of absence of committed leadership and unpoliticized state of local population. [ELC]

1976 Scarano, Francisco A. El colonato azucarero en Puerto Rico, 1873–1934: problemas para su estudio. (*Hist. Soc./Río Piedras*, 3, 1990, p. 143–167)

Treats the formal aspects of the proliferation of cane farmers (*colonos*) in Puerto Rico after the island's incorporation into the US tariff system in 1900. Argues that for many small and medium-sized farmers, the American tariff subsidized their participation in the sugar sector, the country's most dynamic. While the relationship between *colonos* and the mills were always marred by conflict, there was also a potential for patronage and cooperation. [FAS]

1977 Schrils, J.M.R. Een democratie in gevaar: een verslag van de situatie op Curaçao tot 1987 [A democracy in danger: a report on the situation in Curaçao until 1987]. Assen, The Netherlands: Van Gorcum, 1990. 291 p.: bibl., index.

Sociohistorical analysis of Curaçao as a product of its past is based on interviews and secondary literature and hovers between investigative journalism and social science. This Curaçaoan historian questions the prospects for democracy due to the existing economic, political, constitutional, and bureaucratic problems. [RH]

1978 Selva Alvarez, William A. Girón: testimonio de una victoria; Frente Norte.

La Habana: Editorial de Ciencias Sociales, 1987. 195 p., 8 p. of plates: ill. (Testimonio)

Yet another version of Castro's victory at Bay of Pigs by one of the participants. Focuses on aspects of the action overlooked in other narratives. [JMH]

1979 Sheppard, Jill. Marryshow of Grenada: an introduction. Foreword by Beverley Steele. Grenada; Barbados, West Indies: Letchworth Press, 1987. 62 p.: bibl., ill.

Useful biography of Grenadian journalist and Caribbean statesman stresses his role in the campaign for representative government for the region. Author aims to demolish some of the myths surrounding Marryshow and to give a more accurate impression of the man. [ELC]

1980 Smith, Lois M. and **Alfred Padula.** Women workers in Socialist Cuba, 1959–1988: progress and problems. (*Ibero-Am.*, 18:2, 1988, p. 33–56, bibl., tables)

Sympathetic appraisal of the efforts made by the Revolution to incorporate women into the work force recognizes the many contradictions and problems yet to be solved. [JMH]

1981 Tablada Pérez, Carlos. Ernesto "Che" Guevara: hombre y sociedad. Buenos Aires: Editorial Antarca, 1987. 295 p.: bibl.

Excessively laudatory work focuses on the details of Guevara's economic thought. [JMH]

1982 Taylor, Frank F. Revolution, race, and some aspects of foreign relations in Cuba since 1959. (*Cuba. Stud.*, 18, 1988, p. 19–41, bibl.)

Maintains that the apparent integration of blacks into the Revolution results not from any active domestic policy but rather because of the spillover effects of Cuba's African foreign policy. [JMH]

1983 Taylor, Henry. My political memoirs. Nassau, Bahamas: H. Taylor, 1987? 410 p.: ill., ports.

Written from what the author calls his first-hand knowledge, book recounts his experiences and some of the political history of the Bahamas. The author formed one of the first political parties, served in numerous elective and appointive governmental capacities, and attained the position of deputy governor-general. [ELC]

1984 Tellería Toca, Evelio. Los congresos obreros en Cuba. La Habana: Editorial de Ciencias Sociales, 1984. 593 p.: bibl., ill. (Historia de Cuba)

Faithfully reflects the official line on workers' congresses throughout Cuba's history. Some congresses are simply excluded. [JMH]

1985 Tirado Avilés, Amílcar. Notas sobre el desarrollo de la industria del tabaco en Puerto Rico y su impacto en la mujer puertorriqueña, 1898–1920. (*Cent. Estud. Puertorriq. Bull.*, 2:7, Winter 1989/1990, p. 18–29, photos)

Describes the operation of American Tobacco Company subsidiaries in Puerto Rico and their rationale for the employment of women in large-scale, quasi-industrial tobacco production. Explains how the tobacco workforce was segmented by gender, with men accomplishing the most skilled and better-paid tasks. Uses printed union documents and labor newspapers to trace the history of labor organizing among women tobacco workers. Includes poignant testimonies by women unionists who articulated a mature labor-union mentality and class consciousness. [FAS]

1986 Torriente, Loló de la. Testimonio desde dentro. La Habana: Editorial Letras Cubanas, 1985. 494 p.

Personal reminicences of a Cuban intellectual are particularly relevant to the events of the 1920s and 1930s. [JMH]

1987 Torriente Brau, Pablo de la. El periodista Pablo: crónicas y otros textos, 1930–1936. Selección, prólogo y notas de Víctor Casaus. La Habana: Editorial Letras Cubanas, 1989. 494 p. (Giraldilla)

Selected newspaper articles by a prominent student leader of the thirties. [JMH]

Trinidad and Tobago: the independence experience, 1962–1987. See *HLAS 51:2045.*

1988 Unos desafectos y otros en desgracia: sufrimientos bajo la dictadura de Trujillo. Recopilación de Bernardo Vega. Santo Domingo: Fundación Cultural Dominicana, 1986. 284 p.: ill., index, ports.

Facsimiles of documents from dictator Trujillo's personal archives concern Dominicans who were regarded as disaffected or who were in disfavor with the government. Arranged chronologically and preceded by explanatory introductions in each case. [JMH]

1989 Uribe O., Hernán. Operación Tía Victoria. México: Editorial Villicaña, 1987. 189 p.: ill. (Testimonios)

Tells the story of how Guevara's Bolivian diary reached Cuba. Allegedly, corrects and amplifies the disclosures previously made by the Bolivian Minister, Antonio Arguedas. [JMH]

1990 Vega, Bernardo. Nazismo, fascismo y falangismo en la República Dominicana. Santo Domingo: Fundación Cultural Dominicana, 1985. 415 p.: bibl., ill., index, ports.

Sober reappraisal, based on exhaustive archival research, of the possible connections between the Trujillo regime and the Axis powers, not excluding the shadow cast by Spanish *falangismo*. Does away with the myths and generalized beliefs that have obscured the field until now. [JMH]

1991 Vega, Bernardo. Trujillo y el control financiero norteamericano. Santo Domingo: Fundación Cultural Dominicana, 1990. 652 p.: bibl., index, ports.

Solidly-researched work shows that, contrary to what many believed thus far, the dictator Trujillo really mishandled the problem of the Dominican debt. Makes extensive use of archival sources in the US and Dominican Republic. [JMH]

1992 Vega, Bernardo. Trujillo y Haití. Santo Domingo: Fundación Cultural Dominicana, 1988. v. 1: bibl., ill.

Carefully written and amply researched account of the massacre of Haitians carried out in 1937 on orders of Dominican dictator Rafael L. Trujillo. Projected vol. 2 will deal with its consequences, and vol. 3 with Dominican-Haitian relations after 1939. Highly recommended. [JMH]

1993 Weissman, Muriel McAvoy. The correspondence of Henry Cabot Lodge and J.D.H. Luce, 1898–1913. (*Hist. Soc./Río Piedras*, 1, 1988, p. 99–122)

Personal correspondence between the Massachussetts Senator and the Boston businessman shows how the latter used his family connections to establish himself in the Puerto Rican sugar industry and to influence US policy in favor of Puerto Rican sugar interests. Throws valuable light on the financial and political aspects of US-based plantation interests. [FAS]

1994 Williams, J. Randolf. Peaceful warrior: Sir Edward Trenton Richards. Hamilton, Bermuda: Camden Editions, 1988. 375 p., 28 p. of plates: bibl., ill., index.

Biography of Bermudan politician and statesman who eventually became the island's second Government Leader and first Premier. Author stresses the critical role he played in promoting integration in Bermuda and furthering local participation in political affairs (1948–76). [ELC]

1995 Wright, Ann. Intellectuals of an unheroic period of Cuban history, 1913–1923: the *'Cuba Contemporánea'* Group. (*Bull. Lat. Am. Res.*, 7:1, 1988, p. 109–122)

Excellent study of a little-known period of Cuba's intellectual history, although it approaches the subject from the narrow perspective of Castro's brand of nationalism. [JMH]

SPANISH SOUTH AMERICA
General

Bizzarro, Salvatore. Historical dictionary of Chile. See item **2561.**

1996 Demélas, Marie-Danielle and **Yves Saint-Geours.** La vie quotidienne en Amérique du Sud au temps de Bolivar: 1809–1830. Paris: Hachette, 1987. 251 p.: bibl., ill., maps.

Not altogether successful attempt to depict daily life in Spanish South America on the eve of and during the Wars of Independence. Worthwhile for new data culled from variety of Old and New World archives as well as for authors' occasional inspired interpretations. [MTH]

1997 Hampe Martínez, Teodoro. El Padre Vargas Ugarte y su aportación a la historiografía de Perú Colonial. (*Rev. Hist. Am.,* 104, julio/dic. 1987, p. 141–167, bibl.)

Able summary of career and publications of the extraordinarily productive Peruvian historian and Jesuit, Rubén Vargas Ugarte, who rescued from neglect and illuminated much of the history of Viceroyalty of Peru at large as well as of Peru proper. [MTH]

1998 Historia general de la Iglesia en América Latina. v. 8, Perú, Bolivia y Ecuador. Salamanca: Ediciones Sígueme; CEHILA, 1987. 1 v.: bibl., ill., index. (El Peso de los días; 19)

Vol. 8 of a projected 12-volume history of Christianity in Latin America covers Peru, Bolivia, and Ecuador. Chapters on the Catholic Church in Peru (Fernando Aliaga Rojas for colonial period and Jeffrey Klaiber for national period) and in Bolivia (Josep M. Barnada for both colonial and national periods) are detailed and well-documented. Those on the Church in Ecuador by José Mariá Vargas are superficial. Includes three chapters on Protestantism in Bolivia by Mortimer Arías. A laudable work destined to become a standard reference. [MTH]

Jaramillo Medina, Carlos. Evolución histórica de la ciudad de Cuenca. See *HLAS 51:3021.*

1999 Petrov, Dimitŭr and T͡Svetan Nikolov. Bŭlgari v I͡Uzhna Amerika. Sofii͡a: Partizdat, 1988. 185 p., 8 p. of plates: ill. (Istorichesko chetivo)

Useful study of Bulgarian emigration to South America. [R.V. Allen]

Colonial Period

MICHAEL T. HAMERLY, *Associate Professor of Library Science, University of Guam*
SUSAN M. SOCOLOW, *Professor of History, Emory University*
KATHY WALDRON, *Citibank International, Miami*

BY THE TIME *HLAS 52* APPEARS, the quincentennial of 1492 will have come and gone. One of the legacies of 1992 is the exceptionally large number of recently published studies on the Iberian world. Regardless of how substantive the works in question prove to be, their sheer volume is impressive. Altogether we have included over 300 items on colonial Spanish South America this biennium—more than half again as many citations as in any previous *Handbook*. Inevitably we have annotated some older items that heretofore eluded us. At the same time we have not yet seen all of the new studies. Not only has much been published of late, but there is more to come.

Overshadowed by 1992 but not altogether overlooked was 1986. The two hundred and fiftieth anniversary of the earth measuring expedition of the 1730s prompted: 1) a 1985 colloquium in Paris, the proceedings of which were published (item **2004**); 2) a new, critical edition of Jorge Juan and Antonio de Ulloa's *Discurso y reflexiones políticas . . .* or *Noticias secretas de América* (item **2019**); 3) a 1986 congress in Quito, whose papers do not appear to have been published; and 4) an excellent book on *Los caballeros del punto fijo* (item **2015**).

GENERAL

There was a substantial increase in the number of general colonial studies and source materials on Spanish South America, not that any of them had anything to do with 1492 *per se*. Almost all of the new general works are highly specialized, as are the colony-specific books and articles. Some will welcome this development; others will not. But what few of us welcome is the increasing lack of clarity: cutting-edge historians should be able to write for the general literate public, not just for the specialists.

Peter T. Bradley gave us a readable account of foreign interlopers in the Pacific in the 1600s (item **2001**); José Miguel Oviedo a lovely coffee table book on the Incas and their conquerors (item **2006**); Arturo Alvarez a new edition of that gem of an early travel account, Diego de Ocaña's truly fascinating *Viaje fascinante . . .* (item **2005**); and Franklin Pease a new edition of Raúl Porras Barrenechea's basic *Los cronistas del Perú* (see *HLAS 50:724*). Other significant studies include: Laura Escobari de Querejazu's thesis on trade between Upper Peru and neighboring colonies (see *HLAS 50:724*); Carlos Daniel Malamud Rikles' book on French trade with Peru during the War of the Spanish Succession (item **2017**); the essays in *Reform and insurrection in Bourbon New Granada and Peru* (item **2021**); and Pablo Emilio Pérez-Mallaína and Bibiano Torres Ramírez's major monograph on the South Sea Fleet (item **2018**).

VENEZUELA

Output on colonial Venezuela increased, but not by very much. Publications of the Academia Nacional de la Historia continue to proliferate. For colonial Venezuela and Nueva Granada, the topics being covered are more diverse, and the level of scholarship has improved since the last biennium. Studies of the 16th and 17th centuries tend to concentrate on the conquerors and the conquered. Especially interesting and somewhat novel are Neil Whitehead's book on the Caribs in colonial Venezuela and Guyana (item **709**) and Susana Romero de Febres' article on the discourse employed in Oviedo y Baños' 1723 account of the conquest (item **2044**). Of several volumes of newly reproduced maps, one is well done (item **2030**). Two others (items **2033** and **2046**), the first reiterating Venezuelan claims to former British Guiana, are marred by poor graphics.

Regional studies continue to enlarge our understanding of the complexities of the colony. Scholarship on the llanos is still dominated by Miquel Izard who has synthesized many of his earlier studies in a new book (item **2037**) which focuses on the *llanero* as a social bandit. Mariano Useche Losada offers important new perspectives on the high llanos (item **2049**), emphasizing the importance of pacification by missionaries and soldiers, and attempting a more complete study of, and a more integral approach to, the plains area examined. He succeeds admirably in that attempt.

Andean towns and districts are also being scrutinized, beginning with Lucas Guillermo Castillo Lara's exhaustive book on San Cristóbal in the 1500s (item **2029**). Mérida has also received considerable attention. In addition to Milagros Contreras Dávila's institutional study (item **2031**), see Roberto Picón-Parra's genealogical study of the town fathers (item **2042**) and Nelly Velázquez's exciting "La Participación del Indígena en la Formación de los Circuitos Económicos en la Provincia de Mérida" (item **2050**).

Given all the ground-breaking local and regional studies that have been done, more thematic and interpretive essays would not be remiss. One such study is Robert J. Ferry's superior *The colonial elite of early Caracas* (item **2034**). Ferry employs the methodology of family reconstitution to demonstrate that the elite of the capital maintained its status and wealth over two centuries primarily through strategic marriages.

Institutions and bureaucrats, especially the Audiencia of Caracas and its members, continue to attract attention. While the new edition of Mario Briceño-Iragorry's biography of José Francisco de Heredia (item **2027**) is far from definitive, the noted Audiencia scholar Alí Enrique López Bohórquez provides a useful interpretation of the regent's political philosophy (item **2038**). There is also an interesting account of the major *visita* of the Audiencia undertaken in the twilight of the colonial period (item **2025**). Surprisingly enough, the history of the Audiencia of Caracas remains to be written, although Guillermo Morón examines the role of the Audiencia in the formation of modern Venezuela (item **2041**).

The Caracas Company also continues to attract attention, but scholars of Venezuela have expanded the discussion of commerce to include other nations. Morón's revisionist study of the impact of the Compañía Guipuzcoana on the political as well as economic life of the colony is well worth reading (item **2040**). Ramón Aizpurua Aguirre argues that illicit trade via Curaçao and the French Caribbean continued to link Venezuela to Europe despite crown and Company efforts to halt contraband (items **2022** and **2024**), an interpretation shared by Marielena Capriles who examines trade with the Danes via San Tomás (item **2028**).

Three other studies are especially noteworthy: Kathy Waldron treats us to a stunning piece on sexuality and society in the late colonial period (item **2051**) and Aizpurua Aguirre's "La insurrección de los negros . . . " (item **2023**) reexamines the Coro slave revolt of 1795 in light of social and economic variables, which serves as a lead-in to Izard's historiographic essay on historians of independence movements of Venezuela and Nueva Granada (item **2061**).

NUEVA GRANADA

The amount of work produced during the 1980s oscillated too greatly to determine whether or not there has been a real increase in productivity. At least one Christopher Columbus piece appeared, a reexamination of Amerigo Vespucci's claim to have discovered Tierra Firme first (item **2053**).

Two major trends may be said to characterize recent scholarship on colonial Colombia. The first is an increasingly prevalent interpretation of scientific experimentation as an emulation of the Enlightenment in the Old World and as a cornerstone for the intellectual origins of the independence movement. Thomas Gomez expands upon the achievements of José Celestino Mutis (see *HLAS 50: 1909, HLAS 50:1910, HLAS 50:1912, HLAS 50:1916,* and *HLAS 50:1918)* by relating them to those of the *fiscal* Francisco Antonio Moreno y Escandón and the Archbishop Viceroy Antonio Caballero y Góngora (item **2057**). Mario Acevedo Díaz reviews the life of Juan Eloy Valenzuela in the new edition of the latter's diary of the Royal Botanical Expedition (item **2074**), Jeanne Chenu examines the work of the much studied Francisco José de Caldas (item **2055**), and Tulio Ospina studies the career of Juan Antonio Mon y Velarde, the far-from-overlooked Governor of Antioquía and later President of Quito (item **2065**). These essays place the Age of Reason and its New World advocates within a Colombian context of scientific achievement, intellectual flourishing, and educational reform. The facsimile edition of the *Flora de la Real Expedición Botánica del Nuevo Reino de Granada* (Madrid: Ediciones Cultura Hispánica, 1953-) is still in progress; 16 volumes have appeared as of 1989.

The second trend involves the redefinition of regionally oriented historiography into more wide ranging thematic studies, building on the pioneering work of Jaime Jaramillo Uribe, Germán Colmenares, Ann Twinam and other socioeconomic historians. No one better represents this trend than the prolific Hermes Tovar Pinzón, herein represented by three articles (items **2069, 2071,** and **2072**) and a revised and augmented edition of his *Hacienda colonial y formación social* (item **2070**). Breaking with the tradition of narrowly focused regional studies, Tovar Pinzón focuses on the colony at large and long term economic trends.

Other significant economic studies are those of Thomas Gomez, Angela Inés Guzmán, Gilma Mora de Tovar, and Arlene Urdanet Q. and Luz Maracaibo. Gomez delineates the emergence of the Río Magdalena transportation network and analyzes its impact on the native population in the 1500s (item **2058**); Guzmán links early encomiendas to the formation of towns, especially in Santander (item **2060**). Turning to the late colonial period, Mora de Tovar details the social as well as economic consequences of the establishment of the royal *aguardiente* monopoly (items **2063** and **2064**). Urdanet and Maracaibo examine the supplanting of the Magdalena route by the Cúcuta alternative (item **2073**).

Not surprisingly, local histories continue to loom large as exemplified by Eduardo Lemaitre's able one-volume summary of his four-volume history of Cartagena (item **2062**). Other towns such as Honda are beginning to receive attention too (item **2075**).

There are no new demographic studies to report and very little in the way of social history *per se.* Finally, historians of colonial Colombia mourn the deaths of Germán Colmenares, Juan Friede, and Guillermo Hernández de Alba. Colmenares gave us many major monographs in the *Annales* tradition. Working almost to his death, he also produced a new, more reliable edition of the viceregal *relaciones* (item **2056**). Friede enriched the ethnohistory of his native country more than any other scholar, while Hernández de Alba published prolifically on Antonio Nariño and on Mutis, especially source materials.

QUITO

There has been a significant increase in the quality and an unprecedented increase in the quantity of work being done on the former Presidency of Quito. There are nearly four times as many publications on colonial Ecuador in this *Handbook* as in volumes 46 and 50, and about twice as many as in volumes 44 and 48. Other indicators of the robustness of current Ecuadorian historiography are the spawning of two new historical journals, *Miscelánea Histórica Ecuatoriana* (Quito: Museos del Banco Central del Ecuador, 1988-) and *Revista Ecuatoriana de Historia Económica* (Quito: Banco Central del Ecuador, 1987- ; see *HLAS 51:2207*), and the appearance of two major guides to Church archives in Cuenca (items **2080** and **2089**).

The most important publication of the last few years is the multi-authored, multi-volume, truly new *Nueva historia del Ecuador* (item **2114**). Almost all of the recent studies, including the essays in the *Nueva historia del Ecuador,* are highly specialized. With few exceptions, the most notable being María Luisa Laviana Cuetos' "Un Proceso por Brujería en la Costa . . . " (item **2100**) and María Elena Porras' *Gobernación y Obispado de Mainas* (item **2120**), the majority of the specialized studies focus on either northern or southern highlands. Especially interesting are Chantel Caillavet's examination of the domestic manufacture of textiles in the northern *corregimiento* of Otavalo in the 1500s and 1600s (item **2088**), and Iveline Lebret's book on daily life in the same *corregimiento* in the 1700s (item **2101**). Equally important are Christiana Borchart de Moreno's essay on one of the most important and powerful merchants and landowners of the capital (item **2084**), and Luis J. Ramos Gómez's resurrection of the 1737 imbroglio between the President and the Cabildo of Quito (item **2122**). A welcome development is the critical reexamination of early and late colonial riots and rebellions in the capital in light of new evidence and concerns: e.g., see Bernard Lavalle on the tax riots of 1592/1593 (item **2099**); Kenneth K. Andrien and Anthony McFarlane on the tax riots of 1765 (items **2079, 2108,** and **2107**); and Scarlett O'Phelan on the rebellion of 1809 (item **2197**).

There are eight works on the southern highlands. Insofar as Cuenca and its district are concerned, Claudio Cordero Espinosa, Lucas Achig Subía, and Adrián Carrasco Vintimilla's "La Región Centro-Sur" is exceptionally well informed and highly informative (item **2090**). The most interesting studies on Loja and its province are Susana Aldana Rivera's article on trade between southern Ecuador and northern Peru in the late 1700s (item **2077**) and María Concepción Bravo Guerreira's essays on prehispanic and colonial Loja (item **2087**). The size and movement of the population of the Presidency of Quito at large is becoming better known as exemplified by the able summaries of Francisco Javier Ortiz de la Tabla Ducasse (item **2116**) and Martin Minchom (item **2110**).

PERU

There was an appreciable increase in historical output on colonial Peru. Specialization has become the hallmark of Peruvian historiography. The only popular accounts are biographies of Pizarro (item **2141**), Almagro (item **2159**), and Túpac Amaru (item **2171**); the only work that embraces the whole of the colonial period is Serena Fernández Alonso's review of Spanish scholarship (item **2144**). The overwhelming majority of the new and recent studies treat a particular place as well as period.

Interest in the conquest years appears to have diminished. More importantly, the work being done on the early colonial period is much more interesting than it used to be. The most exciting of the new studies are Sabine G. MacCormack's thoughtful and thought provoking "Atahualpa y el Libro" (item **2166**), Antonio San Cristóbal and Edmundo Guillén Guillén's debunking of Pizarro's skeleton (item **2178**), and Paul Stewart's well wrought article on the Battle of Salinas (item **2180**). The middle colonial period is no longer ignored. Approximately one fifth of the articles and books on colonial Peru annotated in this *Handbook* study in whole or in large part one or more aspects of the 17th century. The only study *per se* of the "forgotten century," however, is Luis Miguel Glave's reexamination of the "general crisis" of the 1600s (item **2150**).

Nonetheless, far more work continues to be done on the late colonial period. Nearly one third of the annotations treat the 1700s and/or the early 1800s. Among the most interesting are Kendall W. Brown's article on mercury mining at Huancavélica (item **2133**), David P. Cahill's study of the illegal continuation of the forced sale of goods to Indians after the abolition of the *reparto* (item **2135**), Luis Durand Flórez's major monograph on Cusco after Túpac Amaru (item **2142**), and John T.S. Melzer's study of bread prices in Lima in the early 1800s (item **2169**). The best of the new studies on the Indian uprisings of the 1780s are Scarlett O'Phelan Godoy's case study of the impact of the Túpac Amaru rebellion on the merchant elite of Cusco (item **2172**) and Ward Stavig's methodologically sophisticated study of socioeconomic conditions in rural Cusco on the eve of the rebellion (item **2179**).

Only a few demographic studies appeared. The most important are Carlos

Sempat Assadourian's comparative analysis of the post-conquest decline of the Indian populations of Mexico and Peru (item **2130**) and Ann M. Wightman's major monograph on Indian migrants in and around Cusco (item **2186**). Social history was somewhat more abundant. The most interesting items are David P. Cahill's revisionist study of the Arequipa tax riots of 1780 (item **2136**), Lyn Lowry's preliminary findings on the use of religion as a means to control urban Indians (item **2164**), Juan Marchena Fernández's report on "The Social World of the Military in Peru and New Granada" (item **2167**), and Nancy Van Deusen's working paper on institutions for the care of women (item **2185**). There were many contributions to the economic history of the colonial period, all of them of value. The most novel and, coincidentally, important contributions to the ecclesiastical history of Lower Peru are Manuel Burga's essay on the economic as well as religious significance of chaplaincies (item **2134**) and Donald L. Gibbs's pioneering study of the economic activities of nuns and friars in Cusco (item **2149**). Another unusual as well as significant piece on Church history is Fernando Iwasaki Cauti's comparative study of early Christian evangelization in Peru and Japan (item **2157**). Historians of ideas will find much of interest this time around, especially in the contributions of Pedro Guibovich Pérez (item **2151**) and Teodoro Hampe Martínez (items **2152, 2153, 2154,** and **2155**).

Peru also lost one of its better historians, Alberto Flores Galindo. Two of his most important books deal substantially with the colonial period: *Aristocracia y plebe* (San Isidro, Peru: Mosca Azul Editores, 1984), an examination of the effects of colonialism and ethnic domination on the society and political culture of colonial Lima; and *Buscando un inca* (see *HLAS 50:2212*), a far ranging work that spans the history of Peru from the Spanish conquest through the turbulent 1980s.

ALTO PERU

At first glance the quincentennial does not appear to have resulted in a noticeable increase in output on colonial Bolivia. However, of the 14 works annotated, eight are books, and all eight make a major contribution to the historiography of Upper Peru. Not surprisingly, three have to with Potosí: Peter Bakewell's biography of the silver baron Antonio López de Quiroga (item **2188**); Josep María Barnadas' biography of the quicksilver wizard Alvaro Alonso Barba (item **2189**); and Rose Marie Buechler's study of Bourbon efforts to bolster the flagging industry and therefore the flow of silver from the red mountain (item **2190**). The pasts of other towns and regions are also being delineated and illuminated: e.g., see José María García Recto's prize winning dissertation on Santa Cruz de la Sierra (item **2193**); Brooke Larson's solid monograph on Cochabamba (item **2196**); and Roberto Querejazu Calvo's chatty account of his native Chuquisaca/La Plata/Charcas/Sucre (item **2198**).

As for the six articles, all are based on original research; all are well written; all have something new to say; and all reflect the diversity and sophistication increasingly characteristic of the historiography of Upper Peru. At the risk of being invidious, especially interesting are Luis Miguel Glave's "Mujer Indígena, Trabajo Doméstico y Cambio Social . . ." (see *HLAS 50:639*) and Ann Zulawski's "Social Differentiation, Gender, and Ethnicity" (item **2202**). Unfortunately, laying hands on all of the work that is being done in and on Bolivia continues to be a problem. Fortunately, however, Herbert S. Klein admirably synthesizes almost all of the old and new studies in the second edition of his *Bolivia: the evolution of a multi-ethnic society* (New York: Oxford University Press, 1992; see *HLAS 44:183* for first edition).

CHILE

Chile has long been known for the maturity and sophistication of its historiography, but for some time its output has been modest at the best, at least on the colonial period. It is gratifying therefore to note that work on colonial Chile has increased dramatically. This *Handbook* features 29 items of significance, a number more than twice as large as usual; only four of these are reprints of older works. Although welcoming this revitalization of Chilean historiography, at the same time we lament the loss of Gonzalo Izquierdo Fernández, Eugene H. Korth, and Rolando Mellafe. Primarily a student of the national period, Izquierdo produced a new general history of Chile shortly before his death (item **2214**). Korth will be remembered for his *Spanish policy in colonial Chile* (*HLAS 32:2290*) and, together with Della M. Flusche, for *Forgotten females* (*HLAS 48:1624*). Mellafe advanced the study of population and social history of Latin America at large, in many ways and in many works, not the least of which are his last two books, *Historia social de Chile y América* (*HLAS 50:844*) and with René Salinas Meza, *Sociedad y población rural en la formación de Chile actual: La Ligua, 1700–1850* (item **2220**).

The other important historical demographic works are the well edited *Visita general de la Concepción y su Obispado* from the 1760s (item **2224**) and Gabriel Guarda's publication and study of the 1749 *Visita* of Valdivia and its district (item **2213**). The most interesting economic studies are Guillermo Bravo Acevedo's microanalysis of the *obraje* of Melipilla (item **2204**) and Marcello Carmagnani's quantitative analysis of the origins of Spanish estates in and around Santiago, available in Spanish as well as in Italian (item **2205**). Turning to social history, Isabel Cruz de Amenábar's piece on "Trajes y Moda . . . " is fascinating (item **2207**); Adela Dubinovsky's revisionist study of the slave trade demonstrates that there is far more to be learned about this already well worked topic (item **2208**); and Della Flusche ably exemplifies how much can be reconstructed of family histories in her latest book (item **2210**).

Three more examples of how variegated as well as vigorous the historian's craft has become in and on Chile will have to suffice. Guarda has given us another one of his monumental guides, a vademecum of nearly every parish church, chapel, and oratory built through 1826 (item **2212**). Ramón Soriano treats us to a fresh reading of *El cautiverio feliz* (item **2226**). And Gustavo Valdés Bunster revives the trial and tribulations of a 17th-century notary who lost everything, including the clothes on his back, for having poked fun publicly at the governor (item **2228**).

RIO DE LA PLATA

Output on colonial Argentina, Uruguay, and Paraguay has also increased, albeit not as dramatically as that on colonial Ecuador or Chile. The history of trade continues to elicit serious study. The port city receives the most attention, but there are also several works which provide a much needed examination of trade and transport in the interior. Among the more interesting of the recent works on Buenos Aires are: Zacarías Moutoukias' article on commerce and society in the 1600s (item **2284**) and his book on *Contrabando y control colonial en el siglo XVII* (item **2283**); José María Mariluz Urquijo's article on trading companies in the mid-1700s (item **2273**); and Jerry W. Cooney's article on the emergence of porteño merchants as equal partners with their European counterparts in the Atlantic trading community (item **2242**). As for the inland provinces, see especially: Klaus Muller's quantitative study of the economic history of Tucumán (item **2286**); Miguel A. Rosal's article on overland traders with the interior (item **2293**); and Claudia Wentzel's piece on river trade between the interior and the port city (item **2308**).

Perhaps the hottest topic in recent Río de la Plata historiography is the nature of the economy and society of the pampas, the debate having been renewed in the Anglo-American world by Ricardo Salvatore and Jonathan C. Brown in "Trade and Proletarianization in Late Colonial Banda Oriental: Evidence from the Estancia de Las Vacas, 1791–1805" (item **2298**) and Samuel Amaral in "Rural Production and Labour in Late Colonial Buenos Aires" (item **2233**), and in the Iberian world by Carlos A. Mayo, Samuel Amaral, Juan Carlos Garavaglia, and Jorge Gelman in *Anuario del IEHS* (item **2276**). Gelman critiques Salvatore and Brown in the Nov. 1989 *HAHR* (item **2261**) to which they respond in the same issue (item **2297**). And Garavaglia and Gelman renew the fray in *El mundo rural rioplatense a fines de la época colonial* (item **2257**).

Lyman L. Johnson raises important issues regarding the economy and society of Buenos Aires and, by implication, of other Spanish American cities and towns in his path-breaking essays on apprenticeship (item **2267**), on military expenditures (item **2266**), and on working class property (item **2268**). Susan Socolow also breaks new ground on urban society in her fascinating "Acceptable Partners: Marriage Choice in Colonial Argentina, 1778–1810" (item **2302**). José Carlos Chiaramonte and Mariluz Urquijo make important contributions to the intellectual background of the 18th century and the extent to which the Enlightenment affected Río de la Plata (items **2241** and **2274**).

There are several significant new studies on colonial Paraguay. Especially noteworthy are Cooney's ongoing contribution to the study of Paraguayan trade during the late colonial period (item **2243**) and James S. Saeger's discussion of Jesuit missions among the Guaycuruans (item **2294**). Regional scholars who have made stimulating contributions to the history of the Jesuit missions throughout the Platine include Mariluz Urquijo on Father José Cardiel (item **2238**) and Rafael Carbonell de Masy on the black robes as rural developers (item **2237**). Gastón Gabriel Doucet's meticulous study of encomiendas in Tucumán during the early colonial period is also important (item **2245**).

GENERAL

2000 Bradley, Peter T. The loss of the flagship of the Armada del Mar del Sur, 1654, and related aspects of viceregal administration. (*Americas/Francisc.*, 45:3, Jan. 1989, p. 383–403)

Detailed analysis of loss of *Jesús María* off Chanduy in 1654, especially of the successful efforts to recover her silver. Insightful for aspects of sailing practices, salvage operations, and viceregal trade. [MTH]

2001 Bradley, Peter T. The lure of Peru: a study of maritime intrusion into the South Sea, 1598–1701. New York: St. Martin's Press, 1990. 242 p.: bibl., index, maps.

Ably-told story of Dutch, English, and French incursions into the Southern Pacific during the 17th century and of the Peruvian viceroys' sporadic but not altogether ineffectual, efforts to defend their vast realms. Includes new data. Based on accounts of the interlopers and Old and New World archival sources. [MTH]

2002 Bradley, Peter T. Vicisitudes del comercio entre Perú y España en la época del virrey Conde de Alba de Liste, 1655–1661. (*Rev. Indias*, 46:178, julio/dic. 1986, p. 403–419, bibl.)

Delineates the causes for discontinuing the annual fleet of *galeones* to the Isthmus of Panama. Well-written and researched but slights other scholarship on the subject. [MTH]

2003 Castillo Mathieu, Nicolás del. Las flotas de galeones a Tierra Firme,

1650–1700. (*Anu. Estud. Am.*, 47:2, 1990, p. 83–129, suplemento)

Summarizes the voyages of the 18 fleets dispatched to Portobelo and Cartagena in the second half of the 17th century. Based on research notes of the late-Colombian historian Pastor Restrepo. [MTH]

2004 Colloque international La Condamine, Paris, 1985. Proceedings. México: IPGH, 1987. 119 p.: bibl.

Published proceedings of the 1985 international colloquium on the French scientist and explorer Charles Marie de la Condamine and other French members of the earth-measuring expedition of 1735–43. Also includes papers on Pedro de Maldonado and Antonio de Alcedo. [MTH]

2005 Diego, *de Ocaña*. A través de la América del Sur. Edición de Arturo Alvarez. Madrid: Historia 16, 1987. 256 p.: bibl. (Crónicas de América; 33)

Abridgement of a little-known gem of an early travel account—published in its entirety only once as *Viaje fascinante por la América hispana . . .* (Madrid: Studium, 1969)—by the Jeronimite, Diego de Ocaña, who journeyed through Lower and Upper Peru, Chile, New Spain, and other parts of Spanish America between 1599 and 1608, recording and drawing what he heard and saw. Unfortunately, this edition lacks Ocaña's watercolors and sketches. [MTH]

2006 La edad del oro. Edición de José Miguel Oviedo. Barcelona, Spain: Tusquets/Círculo, 1986. 377 p.: bibl., ill.

Novel, lavishly illustrated anthology on the Incas and their conquest by the Spaniards. Compiler has thematically strung together excerpts from chroniclers and early travelers, creating more of a coffee table book than a scholarly work. Approach is intriguing and reproductions of the illustrations are exceptionally well-done. [MTH]

2007 Escobari de Querejazu, Laura. Producción y comercio en el espacio sur andino en el siglo XVII: Cuzco-Potosí, 1650–1700. La Paz: Embajada de España en Bolivia, 1985. 218 p., 12 p. of plates: bibl., ill. (Col. Arzans y Vela)

Original, quantitative study of local production and intercolonial trade in the Peruvian/Bolivian Altiplano during the second half of the 17th century. Includes chapter on

traffic between Alto Perú and the Río de la Plata. Exceptionally important licentiate thesis based on extensive research in Spain, Peru, Bolivia, and Argentina. [MTH]

2008 La Expedición Malaspina, 1789–1794. v. 1, Circunstancia histórica del viaje [de] Ricardo Cerezo Martínez. Madrid: Ministerio de Defensa, Museo Naval; Barcelona: Lunwerg, 1987? 1 v.: bibl., ill., indexes, maps, ports.

Inaugural volume in projected 12-volume set on the most important of Spain's 18th century voyages of discovery and exploration in the Pacific, the Malaspina Expedition. Cerezo Martínez reviews other 18th-century, especially Spanish, expeditions in the Pacific, introduces the members of the Malaspina Expedition, highlights the records resultant from the expedition, and outlines the voyages and encounters of the *Atrevida* and the *Descubierta*. Handsomely bound and printed, magnificently illustrated, and well-indexed. [MTH]

2009 Fisher, John Robert. The effects of *comercio libre* on the economies of New Granada and Peru: a comparison. (*in* Reform and insurrection in Bourbon New Granada and Peru. [see item **2021**] p. 147–163, tables)

Statistical study of the differential impact of the free trade legislation of 1778–89 on what are now Colombia, Ecuador, and Peru. Revisionist in findings and offers suggestions for further research. [MTH]

2010 Fisher, John Robert. El impacto del comercio libre en el Perú, 1778–1796. (*Rev. Indias*, 48:182/183, enero/agosto 1988, p. 401–420, tables)

Quantitative reexamination of the impact of the 1778 *Reglamento de comercio libre* on trade between Spain and the Viceroyalty of Peru. [MTH]

2011 González Casasnovas, Ignacio. La minería andina en la época colonial: tendencias y aportaciones en la historiografía actual, 1966–1987. (*Rev. Indias*, 48:182/183, enero/agosto 1988, p. 613–633, bibl.)

Lucid review of considerable work that has been done on history of mining and related topics in Andean region, since the 1966 seminal work of Alvaro Jara, *Tres ensayos sobre la economía minera hispanoamericana*. [MTH]

2012 Hampe Martínez, Teodoro. La biblioteca del Arzobispo Hernando Arias de Ugarte: bagaje intelectual de un prelado criollo, 1614. (*Thesaurus*, 42 : 2, mayo/agosto 1987, p. 337–361)

Arias, a Creole, studied in Salamanca from 1577–83 before returning to America as an *oidor* in Panama, Charcas, and Lima. In 1607 he took vows and later became bishop of Quito and Bogotá. His strong background in civil and canon law is reflected in the inventory of the 417 works which comprised his library. A more complete biography of this interesting judge turned cleric would be welcome. [KW]

2013 Hampe Martínez, Teodoro. La división gubernativa, hacendística y judicial en el Virreinato del Perú, siglos XVI-XVII. (*Rev. Indias*, 48 : 182/183, enero/agosto 1988, p. 59–85, maps)

Excellent delineation of periodically redefined administrative, fiscal, and judicial districts into which the Viceroyalty of Peru was divided in the 16th and 17th centuries. Includes a useful series of maps. [MTH]

2014 Heredia, Edmundo A. Las relaciones internacionales hispanoamericanos en los prolegómenos de la emancipación. (*Res Gesta*, 16/17/18, julio/dic. 1984-enero/dic. 1985, p. 9–17)

Discusses Spanish foreign policy at the end of the colonial period, especially as it affected Spanish America. Concentrates on how foreign policy alternatives were restricted after the Napoleonic invasions, focusing on England and the US. [SMS]

2015 Lafuente, Antonio and Antonio Mazuecos. Los caballeros del punto fijo: ciencia, política y aventura en la expedición geodésica hispanofrancesa al virreinato del Perú en el siglo XVIII. Barcelona: Ediciones el Serbal; Madrid: CSIC, 1987. 256 p.: bibl., ill., index, maps, ports. (Libros del buen andar; 20)

Lavishly illustrated, well researched and written book about earth-measuring expedition of 1730s and 1740s. Discusses dispute over whether earth bulged at poles or equator, the Audiencia of Quito as perceived by French academicians and Spanish naval lieutenants who comprised the expedition, the collective and individual activities of expedition members, and of course Juan and Ulloa themselves. Major contribution to history of natural science and Age of Enlightenment in Europe and South America. [MTH]

2016 Lucena Giraldo, Manuel. Ciencia para la frontera: las expediciones españolas de límites, 1751–1804. (*Cuad. Hispanoam. Complement.*, 2, dic. 1988, p. 157–173, appendix, photo)

Reviews four 18th-century expeditions dispatched by the crown to the interior of South America to establish and demarcate the boundaries between Spain's and Portugal's colonies. Includes some new data on Amazon Commission of 1780–1804. [MTH]

2017 Malamud Rikles, Carlos Daniel. Cádiz y Saint Malo en el comercio colonial peruano, 1698–1725. Cádiz, Spain: Diputación Provincial de Cádiz, 1986. 364 p.: bibl., ill. (Serie Descubrimiento; 3)

Quantitative study of short-lived, but significant, commercial incursion by France into Viceroyalty of Peru during War of Spanish Succesion and reign of Philip V. This important, original work adds appreciably to our knowledge of trade and contraband in the southern Pacific during the early 1700s. [MTH]

2018 Pérez-Mallaína Bueno, Pablo Emilio and Bibiano Torres Ramírez. La armada del Mar del Sur. Sevilla, Spain: Escuela de Estudios Hispano-Americanos de Sevilla, C.S.I.C., 1987. 363 p., 15 leaves of plates: bibl., ill., index. (Escuela de Estudios Hispano-Americanos de Sevilla, C.S.I.C.,; 329)

Most comprehensive account to date of the *Armada del Mar del Sur* examines organization and regulation of the fleet, its crews, the ships that comprised the Armada, costs, the role of the fleet in defense of the Viceoyalty of Peru, and the actions it saw. Well-researched but neglects Ecuadorian and Peruvian sources. [MTH]

Porras Barrenechea, Raúl. Los cronistas del Perú, 1528–1650, y otros ensayos. See *HLAS 50:724.*

2019 Ramos Gómez, Luis Javier. Epoca, génesis y texto de las "Noticias secretas de América," de Jorge Juan y Antonio de Ulloa. v. 1, El viaje a América, 1735–1745, de los tenientes de navío Jorge Juan y Antonio de Ulloa, y sus consecuencias literarias. v. 2, Edición anotada del texto original de las

Noticias secretas de América, de Jorge Juan y Antonio de Ulloa. Madrid: Consejo Superior de Investigaciones Científicas, Instituto Gonzalo Fernández de Oviedo, 1985. 2 v.: bibl. (Tierra nueva e cielo nuevo; 16–17)

Vol. 1 overviews earth-measuring expedition of 1735–43, conditions and events (especially those discussed by Juan and Ulloa) in Spanish South America (particularly Ecuador and Peru), and careers and writings of the two naval lieutenants. Vol. 2 is a "critical" edition of complete text of *Discurso y reflexiones políticas sobre el estado presente de los reinos del Perú . . .* , better known as *Noticias secretas de América.* This edition should be preferred over all others. Unfortunately, however, it is not indexed. [MTH]

2020 Ramos Gómez, Oscar Gerardo. Sebastián de Benalcázar: conquistador de Quito y Popayán. Madrid: Anaya, 1988. 126 p.: bibl., ill. (Biblioteca iberoamericana; 88)

Popular biography of one of the major *conquistadores,* the founder of Quito and Popayán. Readable and profusely illustrated, but not particularly informative. [MTH]

2021 Reform and insurrection in Bourbon New Granada and Peru. Edited by John Robert Fisher, Allan J. Kuethe, and Anthony McFarlane. Baton Rouge: Louisiana State Univ. Press, 1990. 356 p.: bibl., index., maps.

Anthology of ten original essays on late colonial Colombia, Ecuador, and Peru, all of which advance new perspectives and suggest venues for further research, especially on economic and political developments. For essays on Ecuador and Peru, see items **2009, 2136, 2167,** and **2108.** [MTH]

Tanzi, Héctor José. El continente antártico y la Tierra del Fuego en el siglo XVI. See *HLAS 51:3088.*

VENEZUELA

2022 Aizpurua Aguirre, Ramón. El contrabando en la provincia de Venezuela en tiempos de la Compañía Guipuzcoana, 1730–1784. (*Rev. Rev. Interam.,* 14:1/4, Winter/Spring 1984, p. 4–19)

Historians question whether or not the arrival of the Compañía ended Venezuela's notorious contraband trade, thus alienating those involved and turning them against royal control. This article examines commerce between Curaçao and Amsterdam as a reflection of the contraband trade and argues that goods passing through Curaçao to Europe originated in Venezuela, an interesting point which needs further examination. Here, the author concludes that the Compañía reduced but could not eliminate contraband, especially during European wars which disrupted normal legal Caribbean commerce. [KW]

2023 Aizpurua Aguirre, Ramón. La insurrección de los negros de la serranía de Coro de 1795: una revisión necesaria. (*Bol. Acad. Nac. Hist./Caracas,* 71:283, julio/sept. 1988, p. 705–723)

Carefully-argued call for reinterpretation of the 1795 Coro slave revolt as a pre-independence movement influenced by revolutionary thought of France and Saint-Domingue. The author suggests that the revolt was a reaction to local socioeconomic factors such as the imposition of the *alcabala* and slave hostility to certain white owners. This is one of the few articles on slavery in colonial Venezuela to stress local conditions of work, health, master-slave relations and other factors critical for understanding slave resistance. [KW]

2024 Aizpurua Aguirre, Ramón. Las mulas venezolanas y el Caribe oriental del siglo XVIII: datos para una historia olvidada. (*Bol. Am.,* 30:38, 1988, p. 5–15)

Mule exports, an understudied topic, provided significant revenues to llanero ranchers despite royal efforts to limit the trade. Illicit cargoes to the French Caribbean helped consolidate ties between the two areas which later allied during the independence movements. [KW]

2025 Albornoz de López, Teresa. La visita de Joaquín Mosquera y Figueroa a la Real Audiencia de Caracas, 1804–1809: conflictos internos y corrupción en la administración de justicia. Caracas: Academia Nacional de la Historia, 1987. 294 p. (Biblioteca de la Academia de la Historia: Fuentes para la historia colonial de Venezuela; 195)

Exhaustive study by the *oidor* of the Mexican Audiencia visiting the Caracas court concluded that corruption was rampant. Despite the charges, no corrective action occurred as events in Spain obscured colonial administrative affairs. The visitador alienated powerful Venezuelan interests but still went on to a distinguished career in the Council of Indies before becoming a Regent of Spain in 1812. The major part of the volume is documents. An analysis of the failing of the court rather than just the judges would have enhanced this work. [KW]

2026 Baños y Sotomayor, Diego de. Sínodo de Santiago de León de Caracas de 1687. Madrid: Centro de Estudios Históricos del Consejo Superior de Investigaciones Científicas; Salamanca: Instituto de Historia de la Teología Española de la Univ. Pontificia de Salamanca, 1986. 560 p.: (Tierra nueva e cielo nuevo; 19: Sínodos americanos; 5)

Facsimile of 1848 edition, since out of print. In 1687, Bishop Diego de Baños y Sotomayor convened a diocesan synod, the third in the province's history, to reformulate Church doctrine and comply with the dictates of the Council of Trent. The most significant rulings stated certain rights of Indians and slaves and noted the obligations of slaveowners and encomenderos. The privileges of the regular clergy were reduced in favor of the seculars, and civil authority was constricted in specific matters believed to be the purview of the Church. The vigorous activity of the Bishop was opposed by Governor Diego de Maldonado who tried but failed to prevent publication of the synod's rulings. A good introduction places the synod in perspective and provides insight into the Church/civil conflict. [KW]

2027 Briceño-Iragorry, Mario. El Regente Heredia, o, La piedad heróica. Caracas: Academia Nacional de la Historia, 1986. 207 p.: bibl., index. (Biblioteca de la Academia Nacional de la Historia: Fuentes para la historia colonial de Venezuela; 184)

Hagiographic but useful reedition of 1947 biography (see *HLAS 15:1635*) of José Francisco de Heredia, Caracas Audiencia regent 1812–17 and father of the Cuban poet. During the military campaigns of Monteverde and Boves, Heredia tried to pressure the legal system to ensure humane treatment for imprisoned patriots. For related article on Heredia, see item **2038**. [KW]

2028 Caprilles de Prada, Maríaelena. Las relaciones entre Venezuela y la Isla de San Tomás durante los siglos XVIII y XIX. (*Bol. Acad. Nac. Hist./Caracas*, 71:282, abril/junio 1988, p. 423–441, bibl.)

The Danes colonized San Tómas in 1666 as a source of sugar, indigo, and cotton. The island also served as a base for the slave trade. Trade with Venezuela linked European production to Barinas tobacco, especially when European wars cut normal trade patterns to Spain and permitted legal free commerce. Better organized and more statistical analysis of trade data would enhance this preliminary work and determine the importance of this trade route. [KW]

2029 Castillo Lara, Lucas Guillermo. Elementos historiales del San Cristóbal colonial: el proceso formativo. Caracas: Biblioteca de Autores y Temas Tachirenses, 1987. 648 p.: bibl., index. (Biblioteca de Autores y Temas Tachirenses; 91)

Exhaustive history of 16th century San Cristobal, an Andean town in southwest Venzuela at the mid-point between Bogotá and Caracas with divided loyalties and conflicting economic interests. Indian grievances and local disputes form the core of this volume by Venezuela's leading regional historian. Interesting chapter on *hacendado-corregidor* conflict escalated to the Audiencia reveals small-town concerns. Castillo Lara's series of books now provides the basis for a comprehensive history of the province. No scholar is better suited to synthesize the excellent regional histories. Also published by Academia Nacional de la Historia (Caracas, 1987). [KW]

2030 El continente de papel: Venezuela en el Archivo de Indias. Recopilación y selección de Federico Vegas *et al.* Caracas: Ediciones Fundación Neumann, 1984. 151 p.: ill., maps.

Beautiful reproductions of 82 figures and maps of Venezuela, found in the AGI in Seville. The diagrams include maps of towns and religious, military, and civil constructions from the entire colonial period. Each plate is accompanied by a documentary explanation of its significance. [KW]

2031 Contreras Dávila, Milagros. Evolución político-administrativa de Mérida, 1558–1909. (*Bol. Acad. Nac. Hist./Caracas*, 70:279, julio/set. 1987, p. 719–743, bibl.)

Evolution of Mérida from a corregimiento to a province is a case study of the early rivalry between the Audiencias of Santo Domingo and Santa Fe and internecine cabildo disputes. By 1777 the area was juridically tied to Santo Domingo but militarily under the Intendancy of Caracas. Local cabildos continously objected to realignments, primarily seeking the least effective point of royal control to evade taxes and any unwelcome legislation. Such squabbles among institutions are often misunderstood if not placed in the larger historical context of competing economic regions. Important for understanding later regionalism of Venezuela. [KW]

2032 Documentos para el estudio de los esclavos negros en Venezuela. Selección y estudio preliminar de Ermila Troconis de Veracoechea. 2a ed. Caracas: Academia Nacional de la Historia, 1987. 390 p.: (Biblioteca de la Academia Nacional de la Historia: Fuentes para la historia colonial de Venezuela; 103)

Reedition of the 1969 volume. Carefully selects 95 documents on slavery from the 16th-18th centuries. Slaves comprised nearly one-third of the population yet petitions for new importations abounded as the Creoles claimed labor shortages. The fear of slave revolts and the Crown's inability to control contraband imports are evident throughout the documents. The selection adds to the already extensive literature on slavery. [KW]

2033 Donís Ríos, Manuel Alberto. Evolución histórica de la cartografía en Guayana y su significación en los derechos venezolanos sobre el Esequibo. Caracas: Academia Nacional de la Historia, 1987. 487 p.: ill. (Biblioteca de la Academia Nacional de la Historia: Fuentes para la historia colonial de Venezuela; 191)

Analysis of 50 colonial maps attempt to prove Spain's discovery and colonization of Guayana and by implication, Venezuela's claim to the still-disputed Essequibo territory. Argues that Berrio's 1595 map was later copied by Raleigh to claim the area for England. Subsequent Dutch and French incursions were commercial, not colonizing, ventures which did not displace Spain. Analysis ends with 1817 since later periods are already studied. Poor reproduction of maps mars detailed history of strategically important zone. [KW]

2034 Ferry, Robert J. The colonial elite of early Caracas: formation & crisis, 1567–1767. Berkeley: Univ. of California Press, 1989. 342 p.: bibl., ill., index.

Superior monograph based upon meticulous analysis of hacienda censuses of 1684, 1720, and 1744, household census of Caracas of 1759, and notarial records. Ferry reconstructs elite family structure and marriage strategies to demonstrate "generational transfer of agricultural wealth" over two centuries. Unlike other parts of Spanish America, the Caracas elite retained its status and wealth even as farming shifted from wheat to cacao and labor from Indian to African slave to free laborer. Ferry reinterprets the 1749 León revolt against the Guipuzcoana Company as a crisis for the elite. Threatened by immigrant smallholders, the elite first supported, then withdrew from, the León faction in recognition of their own interests, finally making peace with a strengthened royal authority. A different conclusion would have been possible had the study gone beyond 1767. [KW]

2035 Hacienda y comercio de Venezuela en el siglo XVII, 1601–1650. Dirección de Eduardo Arcila Farías. Caracas: Banco Central de Venezuela, 1986. 304 p.: bibl., ill. (Col. histórico-económica venezolana; 22. Serie Proyecto hacienda pública colonial venezolana; 5.)

Vol. 5 in continuing series (see *HLAS 48:2639*) by Venezuela's most famous colonial economic historian is filled with useful public revenue and shipping statistics. Arcila Farías has dispelled forever the idea that the 17th century was insignificant for Venezuela. His exacting archival research shows that royal officials collected seven times the tax revenues after 1650 than before, and demonstrates that Caracas was the fourth largest revenue provider out of all the colonies. The introduction of cacao in the 1640s was so successful that it soon comprised 78 per cent of all exports, creating a near monopoly controlled by a powerful Creole merchant group. Valuable addition to the series. [KW]

2036 Humbert, Jules. La ocupación alemana de Venezuela en el siglo XVI: período llamado de los Welser, 1528–1556. Traducción de Roberto Gabaldón. Caracas: Academia Nacional de la Historia, 1983. 118 p.: (Biblioteca de la Academia Nacional de la Historia: Fuentes para la historia colonial de Venezuela; 157)

Humbert wrote several histories on Venezuela in the first quarter of this century. The Academia published one work in 1976 and now presents a new translation of the original 1906 volume. Archival material from Sevilla and London are combined with German sources to provide a more balanced account than the Welsers normally receive. Humbert, nevertheless, concludes that the Germans failed to colonize the region as contracted with Spain. The search for gold and quick riches cost them their franchise. [KW]

2037 Izard, Miquel. Orejanos, cimarrones y arrochelados. Barcelona: Hospitalet de Llobregat; Sendai, 1988? 126 p.: ill.

General synthesis of Izard's articles on *llaneros* extends time horizon to Federal Wars. Conflicts between small and large ranchers involved royal forces in calming violent regional revolts which presaged the civil war aspect of Venezuelan independence. After Carabobo, rural unrest continued as *llaneros* remained outside new political institutions and resisted efforts of elite domination. Half bandit, half insurgent, the *llanero* continued opposing centralized government, even under Gómez. [KW]

2038 López Bohórquez, Alí Enrique. *Idea del gobierno eclesiástico y civil de la España Ultramarina:* obra inconclusa del Oidor Decano Regente José Francisco Heredia. (*Bol. Acad. Nac. Hist./Caracas,* 69:275, julio/sept. 1986, p. 665–675)

Useful overview of the life of Heredia, Caracas Audiencia regent, 1812–17. Heredia proposed to write a treatise on the civil and ecclesiastic government of the Spanish empire at a time when he witnessed the dissolution of that empire. Caught in the revolutionary turmoil and embittered by events, Heredia outlined his work, but never completed it. For related article on Heredia, see item **2027**. [KW]

2039 Miller, Gary M. Bourbon social engineering: women and conditions of marriage in eighteenth-century Venezuela. (*Americas/Francisc.,* 46:3, Jan. 1990, p. 261–290)

Case study of 242 marriages among a total of 485 military officers serving in Venezuela between 1750–1810. The Crown regulated its officer class' choice of marriage partners to prevent financial hardship and maintain the status of the officer class. Most were middle-class who married peers of their own choice. Dowries were required but widows had access to Montepío Militar pensions which provided security. Miller overstresses the differences between military wives and other women with respect to their duties and privileges as females. This close look at a small group is informative and invites comparison with a larger cohort. [KW]

2040 Morón, Guillermo. La Provincia de Venezuela en el siglo XVIII y la Compañía Guipuzcoana de Caracas. (*Bol. Acad. Nac. Hist./Caracas,* 71:284, oct./dic. 1988, p. 973–984)

Attempt to reinterpret the role of the Compañía Guipuzcoana in solidifying national boundaries, promoting commerce, and strengthening the economy. This preeminent historian postulates that prosperity of the Province attracted Spanish merchants who sought to capitalize on vigorous trade and agriculture. Venezuelan sense of nationality predated the Compañía, instead of being formed by it, and then reemerged in the early 19th-century to achieve independence. Unusual interpretation but well worth further consideration. [KW]

2041 Morón, Guillermo. La Real Audiencia de Caracas: unidad política de Venezuela. (*Bol. Acad. Nac. Hist./Caracas,* 69:275, julio/sept. 1986, p. 579–590)

Philosophical approach to identify the Venezuelan nation-state's origins in the Audiencia of Caracas, 1786–1810. The country's most prominent historian argues that the Audiencia's jurisdiction united seven disparate regions to form the basis of the nation. A national identity was born from the juridical unification of the regions and the implementation of one legal code and judicial system. Thoughtful but not entirely convincing. [KW]

2042 Picón-Parra, Roberto. Fundadores, primeros moradores y familias coloniales de Mérida, 1558–1810. Caracas: Academia Nacional de la Historia, 1988. 2 v.: bibl. (Biblioteca de la Academia Nacional de la Historia: Fuentes para la historia colonial de Venezuela; 197–198)

Brief sketches of 124 prominent men who founded Mérida, including the leaders Rodríguez Suárez and Maldonado. Genealogical approach reveals that few original families survived the first century but new migrants established lineages which endured. Factions developed based upon the distribution of land and Indians as well as personal feuds. Useful, but criteria for inclusion are not clear. [KW]

2043 Rojas, Reinaldo. Contribución de Federico Brito Figueroa a la comprensión histórica de Venezuela colonial. (*Rev. Afr. Medio Oriente*, 5:2, 1988, p. 79–108, bibl.)

Useful summary of a distinguished Marxist historian's work. The themes of indigenous and African slavery, land tenure, and class formation are core subjects of the historian's major publications spanning 40 years. Uncritical view detracts from an otherwise informative article. [KW]

2044 Romero de Febres, Susana. Aproximación al sentido de la Historia de Oviedo y Baños como un hecho de lenguaje. Caracas: Academia Nacional de la Historia, 1984. 154 p.: bibl., ill., indexes. (Biblioteca de la Academia Nacional de la Historia: Estudios, monografías y ensayos; 53)

Interesting textual analysis of Oviedo y Baños' *Historia* written in 1723. The intense polemic about the authenticity of the *Historia* continues but Romero takes a unique approach, dissecting the language of discourse. She concentrates on the dialogue between Spanish conqueror and Indian chief to reveal the cultural assumptions of the narrator, an 18th-century Creole, as he relates an historic encounter. Recent works in Mexico and Peru paved the way for this type of study. This is the first Venezuelan attempt, and it succeeds. [KW]

2045 Ruiz, Gustavo Adolfo. Organización educativa durante la colonia. (*Bol. Acad. Nac. Hist./Caracas*, 69:275, julio/sept. 1986, p. 737–754, bibl., table)

Reviews development of education in the colony. Reliance on secondary sources and a legalistic approach mar the study since it is well-known that *ordenanzas* were often not enforced. What is striking is the lack of schools and universities in Venezuela so late into the colonial era. [KW]

2046 Salazar-Quijada, Adolfo. La toponimia venezolana en las fuentes cartográficas del Archivo General de Indias. Caracas: Academia Nacional de la Historia, 1983. 723 p.: bibl., maps. (Biblioteca de la Academia Nacional de la Historia: Estudios, monografías y ensayos; 40)

Reproduces 75 key geographic maps of rivers, regions, and towns of colonial Venezuela taken from the AGI in Sevilla. The toponymy of each map is provided, but this edition is not as complete as the 1968 *Catálogo* of Julio González (See HLAS 33:5380) which contains 273 maps and plans from the AGI. The poor quality of the reproductions mars the usefulness of the book. [KW]

2047 Sanz Tapia, Angel. Refugiados de la Revolución Francesa en Venezuela, 1793–1795. (*Rev. Indias*, 47:181, sept./dic. 1987, p. 833–867)

Excellent analysis of official Venezuela's reaction to influx of royalist French refugees from the Caribbean. Governor Carbonell, fearing contamination of his province by revolutionary ideas, sought quick removal of refugees to Spain. The author argues that historians overemphasize French revolutionary influence on Venezuelan independence, perhaps a valid point but not one proven here. [KW]

Tosta, Virgilio. Historia de Barinas. v. 2, 1800–1863. See item **2333.**

2048 Troconis de Veracoechea, Ermila. Historia de las cárceles en Venezuela, 1600–1890. Caracas: Academia Nacional de la Historia, 1983. 224 p.: bibl., ill. (Biblioteca de la Academia Nacional de la Historia: Estudios, monografías y ensayos; 28)

More than just a history of jails, the author describes colonial attitudes toward crime and punishment, providing case studies of homicide, adultery, rape, and other acts. Stresses civil rather than ecclesiastic authority in maintaining order, noting that the late-18th-century proliferation of jails in regional towns reflected the growing complexity of the society. It was not until the Guzmán Blanco era that political prisoners appeared in abundance; during the Gómez era Venezuelan jails became notorious. [KW]

2049 Useche Losada, Mariano. El proceso colonial en el alto Orinoco-Río Negro: siglos XVI a XVIII. Bogotá: Fundación de Investigaciones Arqueológicas Nacionales, Banco de la República, 1987. 208 p., 5 leaves of plates: bibl., ill.

The high llanos in southern Venezuela which border Brazil and Colombia proved inhospitable to settlement until mid-1700s when missionaries finally established permanent bases. Book's unique scope spans three centuries and several regions, concluding that the lack of a centralized administration and European competition for control explain the evolution of the frontier region. Comprehensive, well-researched study of a complicated geopolitical zone. [KW]

2050 Velázquez, Nelly. La participación del indígena en la formación de los circuitos económicos en la Provincia de Mérida: siglo XVII. *(Bol. Acad. Nac. Hist./Caracas,* 70:279, julio/set. 1987, p. 765–773, bibl., map)

Preliminary analysis of trade routes in Mérida and the Lake Maracaibo district. *Resguardos de indios* and religious *reducciones* concentrated Indians into towns which formed nuclei of colonial trade, exporting tobacco and importing iron, oil, and wine from Castile. The indigenous role in trade patterns is examined using anthropological and historical sources in a creative blend of the two disciplines. [KW]

2051 Waldron, Kathy. The sinners and the bishop in colonial Venezuela: the *visita* of Bishop Mariano Martí, 1771–1784. *(in* Sexuality and marriage in colonial Latin America. Edited by Asunción Lavrin. Lincoln, Neb.: Univ. of Nebraska Press, 1989, p. 156–177)

Utilizing data on male and female relationships in Bishop Martí's diary of his extraordinarily comprehensive *visita* as warp, and her own extensive knowledge of the time and place as weft, Waldron weaves a well-worked analysis of the ways in which men and women interacted sexually and as social partners in late colonial Venezuela. [MTH]

2052 Zubillaga Perera, José María. Procerato caroreño. Caracas: Academia Nacional de la Historia, 1986. 275 p.: bibl., ill. (Biblioteca de la Academia Nacional de la Historia: Estudios, monografías y ensayos; 74)

Reedition of 1928 book gives brief biographies of 51 patriots from Carora, the *llano* city in the path of warring armies. No

doubt Carora contributed to the royalist cause as well, but the author is determined to eulogize his native city's inhabitants and their place in history. [KW]

NUEVA GRANADA

2053 Camargo Pérez, Gabriel. Colombia, 1497, primer arribo español a Tierra Firme: la verdad de Amérigo Vespucci. Bogotá: Instituto Colombiano de Cultura Hispánica, 1985. 70 p., 14 leaves of plates: ill.

Examines the veracity of Vespucci's claim to have discovered *Tierra Firme* in 1497, one year before Columbus. Author analyzes the explorer's letters and maps against contemporary works to judge Vespucci's journey and claims to distances traveled. Although interesting, this study is not likely to settle the competition between fans of the two explorers. [KW]

2054 Cartas de los obispos de Cartagena de Indias durante el período hispánico, 1534–1820. Recopilación de Gabriel Martínez Reyes. Medellín, Colombia: Editorial Zuluaga, 1986. 698 p.: bibl., index, maps. (Academia Colombiana de Historia Eclesiástica: Serie mayor)

Cartagena had 43 Spanish bishops during the colonial period. It became the bishopric see in 1534, only one year after its foundation, and exerted extensive regional influence. Volume contains 245 letters carefully selected for their social commentary. The author provides a brief biography of each bishop and summarizes the longer letters. Especially noteworthy are correspondence of Bishop M.A. de Benavides, imprisoned by the Inquisition in 1687, and the pastoral of royalist Bishop G.J. Rodríguez denouncing Bolívar. [KW]

2055 Chenu, Jeanne. Du bon usage d'instruments imparfaits: science et technique dans le Vice-Royaume du Nouvelle Grenade, deuxième moitié du XVIII siècle. *(Asclepio,* 39:2, 1987, p. 255–272, bibl.)

Francisco José de Caldas, a Creole mathematician from Popayán, experimented with barometers and thermometers to discover a new way to measure topographical elevations for a map of the Viceroyalty completed in 1802–04. His discovery was recognized by his contemporaries, earning him fame on both sides of the Atlantic. Caldas' achievements are part of the scientific enlightenment in New Granada awakened by Mutis and others. [KW]

2056 Colmenares, Germán. Relaciones e informes de los gobernantes de la Nueva Granada. Bogotá: Fondo de Promoción de la Cultura del Banco Popular, 1989. 3 v.: bibl., ill. (Biblioteca Banco Popular; 134–136)

Three vols. of *Relaciones* by viceroys cover 1729 to 1818. This work corrects and supplements the 1869 and 1910 publications, the only previous attempts at producing all the viceregal *Relaciones*. The new edition adds the *Relación* of Gil y Lemos, the *Apuntes* of Silvestre, a description by Moreno y Escandón, and charts omitted earlier. The almost century-long detailed reviews of all aspects of late colonial government are an invaluable source. Useful introduction by one of Colombia's leading scholars. [KW]

Fisher, John Robert. The effects of *comercio libre* on the economies of New Granada and Peru: a comparison. See item **2009**.

2057 Gomez, Thomas. Ciencias y técnicas en la formación de las élites ilustradas en Nueva Granada, 1760–1810. (*Asclepio*, 39:2, 1987, p. 239–253, bibl.)

Argues that Moreno y Escandón (*fiscal*), Caballero y Góngora (archbishop/viceroy), and Mutis (scientist) were all philosophers who promoted the scientific method and educational reform. Their effect on New Granada's society indirectly promoted a sense of nationalism among young followers who later became the intellectuals of the independence movement. A theoretical antidote to the overly-detailed recent studies of the famous botanical expedition. [KW]

2058 Gomez, Thomas. L'envers de l'Eldorado: économie coloniale et travail indigène dans la Colombie du XVIème siècle. Toulouse, France: Association des publications de l'Université Toulouse-Le Mirail, 1984. 353 p.: bibl., ill. (L'Université de Toulouse-Le Mirail. Série A; 51)

Important research on use of encomienda Indians to develop transport system along the Magdalena River and its tributaries, the primary route connecting interior towns with the coast and a unique river network in the New World. The autonomy of the encomenderos allowed extreme exploitation of the native population, leading to destruction of Indian communities. Depopulation is not as well-studied as elsewhere, so extent of demographic decline relative to other areas is not established. River system failed to provide sustained access which explains economic isolation, but not necessarily stagnation of the colony. [KW]

2059 Gutiérrez, José Fulgencio. Galán y los comuneros: estudio histórico-crítico. 2a ed. Bogotá: Caja de Crédito Agrario, Industrial y Minero, 1982. 518 p.: (Col. Biblioteca Caja Agraria; 13)

Verbose but interesting reedition of the 1939 history of José Antonio Galán based on secondary sources. Myths and legends are incorporated with fact to produce a colorful story. Gutiérrez clearly sees a link between the 1780 comunero revolt and the 1810 independence movement, concluding finally that "Galán was the revolution."

2060 Guzmán, Angela Inés. Poblamiento y urbanismo colonial en Santander: estudio de 10 pueblos de la región central. Bogotá: Univ. Nacional de Colombia, Centro Editorial, 1987. 236 p.: bibl., ill., maps. (Col. popular de la Univ. Nacional de Colombia)

Important study includes 68 maps and graphs of ten towns in central Santander. Demonstrates how encomiendas formed basis of original Spanish towns which, along with Indian pueblos, evolved into an urban network. Dense indigenous population and modest landholdings produced a more democratic society of urban artisans and merchants closely tied to small scale agricultural production. Political hierarchy of towns shifted over time and in reaction to economic conditions. [KW]

Historia de Antioquia. See item **2352**.

2061 Izard, Miquel. Nueva Granada. (*in* La Revolución Francesa y el mundo ibérico. Edited by Robert Maniquis, Oscar Martí, Joseph Pérez. Madrid: Sociedad Estatal Quito Centenario; Turner, 1989, p. 527–575)

Historiographical essay groups major intellectual approaches to independence into four categories: 1) the romantics such as Yáñez, Baralt, Restrepo, Austria and González; 2) the positivists such as Alvarado, Arcaya, Fortoul, Vallenilla Lanz, and Zumeta; 3) the materialists such as Irazábal, Brito Figueroa, Ramos, Moncada, Fals Borda, and Izard; and 4) the academicians like Carrera Damas, Forero, Madariaga, and Lievano Aguirre. Sections on economy and society, ideology, and revolts round out this review of most studies of 18th-century New Granada. Izard reacts to official histories which deliberately distort, romanticize, and obscure the past. He then raises a series of questions for future students, categorizing the early 19th century into three periods: 1) the civil war, 1810–15; 2) the colonial war, 1815–21; and 3) the republic, 1821–30. The most important and complete essay to appear in years. [KW]

2062 Lemaitre, Eduardo. Breve historia de Cartagena de Indias, 1501–1901. Bogotá: Cámara de Representantes, 1986. 262 p.: bibl., ill., index, ports. (Col. Pensadores políticos colombianos)

Master historian of Cartagena condenses his four larger volumes (see *HLAS 48:2674*) into one compact readable volume. Claims history of the city is the history of the nation, at least for much of the colonial period, an overstated claim. Of general use for scholars. [KW]

Marchena Fernández, Juan. The social world of the military in Peru and New Granada: the colonial oligarchies in conflict, 1750–1810. See item **2167.**

2063 Mora de Tovar, Gilma Lucía. Aguardiente y conflictos sociales en la Nueva Granada durante el siglo XVIII. Bogotá: Univ. Nacional de Colombia, Centro Editorial, 1988. 242 p.: bibl., ill., maps.

Outstanding study of Bourbon efforts to transform production and sale of aguardiente into a State-run monopoly. Price controls infuriated local producers while *alcaldes* resented royal officials usurping power. 18th-century revolts culminating in that of the *Comuneros* of 1781 are directly linked to resistance to the monopoly. Use of Spanish and Colombian archives and regional studies enhances an excellent study. [KW]

2064 Mora de Tovar, Gilma Lucía. El comercio de aguardientes catalanes en la Nueva Granada, siglo XVIII. (*Bol. Am.*, 30:38, 1988, p. 209–225, tables)

Excellent case study of how free trade law of 1787 allowed Catalan grape aguar-

diente exports to overwhelm local cane liquor producers. Tax records reveal a rapid decline in local sales as the more competitive Catalan producers flooded the market. Peninsular merchants profited handsomely while royal revenues tied to the local monopoly declined. Important because it mirrors the larger economic relationship between colony and metropolis. See also author's book on the same topic, item **2063.** [KW]

2065 Ospina, Tulio. El regenerador de Antioquia: Mon y Velarde. (*Repert. Hist. Acad. Antioq. Hist.*, 38:251, 1988, p. 145–169)

Governing the province as *oidor* from 1785–89, Mon y Velarde increased revenues fourfold, revived mining and agriculture, established schools, and encouraged commerce. He later presided over the Audiencia of Quito. The long term effects of the *oidor's* administrative talents are ignored, as are his successes in creating institutional changes. [KW]

2066 Poblamientos en la provincia de Santa Marta: siglo XVIII. Recopilación de José María de Mier. Bogotá: Colegio Máximo de las Academias de Colombia; Libreros Colombianos, 1987. 3 v.: bibl., index. (Historia de Colombia según sus protagonistas)

Well-indexed compilation of 224 documents relating to the *poblador* and *maestro de campo* of Santa Marta, José Fernando de Mier. With some exceptions, selections are well-chosen for their information on Indians, trade, population growth, and settlement of the region. Mier led *entradas* against Chimilas, defended the coast from English attacks, and pacified the region. [KW]

2067 Silvestre, Francisco. Relación de la Provincia de Antioquia. Transcripción, introducción y notas de David J. Robinson. Medellín, Colombia: Secretaría de Educación y Cultura de Antioquia, 1988. 632 p.: bibl., index, maps. (Ediciones especiales; 4)

This *relación*, written 1786–97, has been rarely used despite its accessability at the Univ. of Texas since 1937. Robinson hopes to change this by publishing it in its entirety with a lengthy, thorough introduction. Silvestre, a *peninsular* with strong Creole ties, served as governor of Antioquia 1782–85, devoting much energy to reviving gold mining and developing strategies for royal revenues. Descriptions of agriculture, commerce, mining and *Real Hacienda* are of great interest to historians. [KW]

2068 Torres y Velasco, Gabriel de. Ordenes militares del último gobernador español en Cartegena de Indias, 1820–1821. Bogotá: Litografía Arco, 1986. 82 p.: facsims.

Transcription and facsimile edition of the last Spanish governor's military orders for Cartagena. Gabriel de Torres capitulated in Sept. and sailed for Santo Domingo on Oct. 10, 1821 with many royalist families. The orders reveal the desperate military position of the Spanish forces and the valiant effort of the governor to protect the remnants of the army after defeat in what had been bitter fighting. [KW]

2069 Tovar Pinzón, Hermes. Fuentes y archivos históricos de los esclavos negros en la sociedad colonial de la Nueva Granada. (*in* Simposio sobre Bibliografía del Negro en Colombia, *1st, Bogotá, 1983.* El negro en la historia de Colombia. Fondo Interamericano de Publicaciones de la Cultura Negra de las Américas, UNESCO, F.C.I.F., p. 111–120)

Concise review of major archives in Colombia notes that the Archivo Histórico Nacional de Bogotá is richest for the colonial period. Good place for students to begin before undertaking archival research. [KW]

2070 Tovar Pinzón, Hermes. Hacienda colonial y formación social. Barcelona, Spain: L'Hospitalet de Llobregat; Sendai Ediciones, 1988? 285 p.: bibl.

Well-written revision of author's 1980 work includes two new chapters on haciendas' links to internal markets and wage structure and profitability. Extremely detailed work with graphs and maps of specific 18th-century haciendas. Five sections cover land occupation, labor relations, descriptions of sample haciendas, salaries and investments, and internal and international markets. Land concentration dispossesed Indians of their ancestral holdings while oversupply of labor led to pauperization of the rapidly developing free work force. Salaried *peones,* not unduly tied to the land, entered the market economy while *hacendados* received returns in excess of those obtained from other investments. Concludes most *hacendados* were astute managers who succeeded. [KW]

2071 Tovar Pinzón, Hermes. Orígenes y características de los sistemas de terraje y arrendamiento en la sociedad colonial durante el siglo XVIII: el caso neogranadino. (*in* Peones, conciertos y arrendamientos en América Latina. Edición de Jan Bazant *et al.* Bogotá: Univ. Nacional de Colombia, 1987, p. 122–153, maps, tables)

Important introduction to rental system employed by wealthy *hacendados* who leased lands to renters in exchange for services, goods, and cash. Author demonstrates how system supplemented *hacendado* income, passed crop failure risks to renters and exploited laborers. The rental system was used extensively to bring new lands under cultivation, especially for coffee production, which formed the basis for a large part of the 19th-century agricultural system. This talented historian challenges others to expand upon his initial research. [KW]

2072 Tovar Pinzón, Hermes. Problemas de la estructura rural antioqueña en la segunda mitad del siglo XVIII. (*Ibero-Am. Arch.,* 13:3, 1987, p. 363–441, appendices)

Important, well-researched *antioqueña* history by leading colonialist. Rather than concentrate on the crisis in mining sectors, the article focuses on agriculture, especially post-1780 land tenure patterns. The reformist government of Mon y Velarde distributed Crown holdings in the highlands to the lower classes, thereby encouraging migration from overpopulated and economically moribund lowlands. Modest holdings were parceled out to families based upon need once royal officials identified uneven land distribution as a cause of regional decay. Combines demographic data with land records for excellent results. [KW]

2073 Urdanet Q., Arlene and **Luz Maracaibo.** San José de Cúcuta en el comercio marabino del siglo XIX. (*Bol. Am.,* 30:38, 1988, p. 247–258, table)

When transport on the Magdalena began to be unreliable and slow, an alternative route via Cúcuta developed. Maracaibo claimed jurisdiction quickly, believing that control of the town would allow it to surpass Cartagena as the major port of the Atlantic. Trade prospered along the new route, tying Cúcuta to the fortunes of the lake city. Useful overview and interesting idea for a more in-depth study. [KW]

2074 Valenzuela, Eloy. Primer diario de la Real Expedición Botánica del Nuevo Reyno de Granada: comprende desde el día 29 de abril de 1783, hasta el día 8 de mayo de 1784. Prólogos de Enrique Pérez Arbeláez y Mario Acevedo Díaz. 2a ed. Bogotá: Ministerio de Educación Nacional, Instituto Colombiano de Cultura Hispánica, 1984. 458 p., 17 leaves of plates: ill.

Good introduction to a tedious text. Valenzuela, a priest, scientist, and doctor, accompanied Mutis on the famous Botanical Expedition before assuming pastorship of Bucaramanga in 1786. As the parish priest, he lived through the revolution, evolving from royalist to patriot to survive until he was killed by robbers in 1834. No doubt Valenzuela led a fascinating life but it is not revealed here. [KW]

2075 Velandia, Roberto. La villa de San Bartolomé de Honda. v. 1, Epocas de la conquista y la colonia. Bogotá: Editorial Kelly, 1989. 1 v.: bibl., ill.

First of multivolume work on the city of Honda which controlled access to the strategic Magdalena river. Founded at the site where rapids divided the river into its upper and lower branches, the town was a natural port of transit for people and commerce. Traffic from the coast moved inland along the waterways and then overland from Honda to Bogotá. Although based upon extensive archival work, poor organization of material mars the study of this important regional city. [KW]

2076 Vila Vilar, Enriqueta. Cimarronaje en Panamá y Cartagena: el costo de una guerrilla en el siglo XVII. (*Caravelle*, 49, 1987, p. 77–92)

Compares the costs of military excursions against runaway slave communities in Panama and Cartagena. Heavy use of slave labor produced revolts and rebel towns which Spanish authorities tried to eliminate. The cost of subduing rebels was high according to historic accounting books. The author equates the rebels to latter-day *guerrilleros*, a misleading comparison since no evidence of political consciousness among the *cimarrones* is presented. [KW]

QUITO

2077 Aldana Rivera, Susana. Esbozo de un eje de integración: el comercio Piura-Loja-Cuenca, siglo XVIII tardío. (*Rev. Arch. Nac. Hist. Azuay*, 8, 1989, p. 108–129, bibl.)

Pioneering study of trade between southern Ecuador and northern Peru in the late 18th century. Mostly based on original research in Piura and Trujillo. [MTH]

2078 Anda Aguirre, Alfonso. La trata de los negros en Loja. (*Cultura/Quito*, 8:22, mayo/agosto 1985, p. 197–215)

Research note on black slaves in colonial Loja, especially on sales thereof. [MTH]

2079 Andrien, Kenneth J. Economic crisis, taxes and the Quito insurrection of 1765. (*Past Present*, 129, Nov. 1990, p. 104–131, graphs, table)

Places the rebellion of 1765 in its economic context. Based on Ecuadorian as well as Spanish and Colombian sources. See also McFarlane's study of the political and social aspects of the insurrection (item **2107**). [MTH]

2080 Archivo de la Curia Arquidiocesana de Cuenca. Catálogo del Archivo de la Curia Arquidiocesana de Cuenca. v. 1, Diezmos y economía. Preparado por Martha Maldonado Samaniego y Lucía Villavicencio de Burbano. Cuenca, Ecuador: Banco Central del Ecuador, Centro de Investigación y Cultura, 1989. 1 v.

Inaugural vol. of catalog of the episcopal archives of Cuenca, a major repository important for the study of the history of the coast and the southern highlands. [MTH]

2081 Arias, Hugo. La economía de la Real Audiencia de Quito y la crisis del siglo XVIII. (*in* Nueva historia del Ecuador. Edición de Enrique Ayala Mora. Quito: Corporación Editora Nacional, 1989, v. 4, p. 187–229, ill., maps, tables)

Examines impact of the mining "crisis" in Lower and Upper Peru on Quito and the northern Audiencia's economic responses thereto. Also examines the impact of the Bourbon reforms. [MTH]

2082 Benavides Vega, Carlos. Sinopsis histórica del siglo XVII. (*in* Nueva historia del Ecuador. Edición de Enrique Ayala Mora. Quito: Corporación Editora Nacional, 1989, v. 4, p. 105–137)

Sketches economic and social as well as cultural and political developments in the 17th century. [MTH]

2083 Benítez, Silvia and **Gaby Costa.** La familia, la ciudad y la vida cotidiana en el período colonial. (*in* Nueva historia del Ecuador. Edición de Enrique Ayala Mora. Quito: Corporación Editora Nacional, 1989, v. 5, p. 187–230, ill.)

Laudable attempt to synthesize the disparate literature about daily life and family in the highlands as well as on the coast throughout the colonial period. [MTH]

2084 Borchart de Moreno, Christiana. Capital comercial y producción agrícola: Nueva España y la Audiencia de Quito en el siglo XVIII. (*Anu. Estud. Am.*, 46, 1989, p. 131–172, tables)

Reconstructs the career of Carlos Araújo, a major merchant and landowner in late colonial Quito. Briefly compares Araújo to two of the richest merchants of coeval Mexico (Rodríguez de Pedroso and Castañiza). This is a pioneering and significant essay, given the paucity of historical studies on the elite of the Ecuadorian highlands. [MTH]

2085 Borchart de Moreno, Christiana and **Segundo Moreno Yáñez.** La historia socioeconómica ecuatoriana del siglo XVIII: análisis y tendencias. (*Rev. Indias*, 49:186, mayo/agosto 1989, p. 379–409, bibl.)

Critical yet objective review of literature on economic history of the 18th century examines what has been and needs to be done on mining, the agricultural sector, textile manufacturing, trade, population and urban development, elites, and the Bourbon reforms. [MTH]

2086 Borchart de Moreno, Christiana. Origen y conformación de la hacienda colonial. (*in* Nueva historia del Ecuador. Edición de Enrique Ayala Mora. Quito: Corporación Editora Nacional, 1989, v. 4, p. 139–166, map, tables)

Excellent summary of what is known about the origins of haciendas in the northern and central highlands in the 1500s by the leading authority on the early history of landed estates in Ecuador. [MTH]

2087 Bravo, Concepción. Un proceso de regionalización precoz en el Virreinato del Perú: el caso de Loja, siglos XVI-XIX. (*Rev. Indias*, 48:182/183, enero/agosto 1988, p. 23–58)

Two essays on what is now Loja prov. in southern Ecuador. The first delineates the ethnohistory of the region prior to its subjugation by the Incas. The second examines various aspects of the demographic, economic, and social history of Loja and its district during the colonial period. [MTH]

2088 Caillavet, Chantal. La artesanía textil en la época colonial: el rol de la producción doméstica en el norte de la Audencia de Quito. (*Cultura/Quito*, 8:24b, enero/abril 1986, p. 521–530, bibl.)

Brief but fascinating article on the manufacture for sale of cotton textiles at home, mostly by Indian women, in the northern highlands. Such cottage industries are an overlooked sector of the colonial economy. [MTH]

2089 Catálogo del archivo del Cabildo Eclesiástico de Cuenca. Dirección de Juan Chacón Z. Quito: Centro de Investigación y Cultura, Banco Central del Ecuador, 1986. 324 p.

Calendar of the geographically as well as chronologically extensive holdings of Archives of Ecclesiastical Chapter of Cuenca as inventoried by research team headed and trained by Juan Chacón Zhapán. Useful research guide. [MTH]

Colloque international La Condamine, *Paris, 1985.* Proceedings. See item **2004.**

2090 Cordero Espinosa, Claudio; Lucas Achig Subía; and **Adrián Carrasco.** La región centro-sur. (*Rev. Arch. Nac. Hist. Azuay*, 5, 1985, p. 13–52)

Cogent outline of the demographic, economic, political, and social characteristics of and cycles in what are now the provinces of Cañar and Azuay. Includes a stimulating research agenda. [MTH]

2091 Documentos para la historia de la Villa de Gualaceo. Colección de Max Romeo Arízaga y Arízaga. Cuenca, Ecuador: Publicaciones y Papeles, 1983. 210 p.: bibl., ill.

Miscellaneous sources for the history of Gualaceo, a town in the southern highlands of Ecuador. [MTH]

2092 Estupiñán-Freile, Tamara. Testamento de Don Francisco Atagualpa. (*Misc. Hist. Ecuat.*, 1, 1988, p. 8–67, appendix, bibl., facsims., photos)

Publishes in facsimile and transcription with explanatory notes the last will and testament (1582) and the codicil thereto (1583) of Francisco Topatauchi, the most important of Atahualpa's sons in the region of Quito. Includes extensive appendix on the urban and rural properties of the *auqui* (native lord). [MTH]

2093 Figueroa, Francisco de et al. Informes de jesuitas en el Amazonas, 1660–1684. Francisco de Figueroa, Cristóbal de Acuña y otros. Iquitos, Peru: Monumenta Amazónica, 1986. 365 p.: bibl. (Monumenta amazónica B; 1)

First vol. in "Misioneros" subset of "Monumenta amazónica" series. Convenient and well-indexed anthology of chronicles on 17th-century Jesuit activities in the Upper Amazon Basin. Includes accounts by two of the greatest chroniclers of the missions, Cristóbal de Acuña (1641) and Francisco de Figueroa (1661), and basic sources on proselytization of the area, its historical ethnography and geography. For ethnohistorian's comment, see *HLAS 50:634.* [MTH]

2094 Guerra Brava, Samuel. La cultura en la época colonial. (*in* Nueva historia del Ecuador. Edición de Enrique Ayala Mora. Quito: Corporación Editora Nacional, 1989, v. 5, p. 137–161, ill.)

Competent overview of intellectual life during the colonial period. [MTH]

2095 Guerra Brava, Samuel. La iglesia en los siglos de coloniaje hispánico. (*in* Nueva historia del Ecuador. Edición de Enrique Ayala Mora. Quito: Corporación Editora Nacional, 1989, v. 5, p. 57–86, ill.)

Well-written and thoughtful summary of what is known and what remains to be clarified or researched regarding the role of the Catholic Church in the Spanish conquest of Ecuador and in the politics and government, the economy, society, and the culture of the colonial period. [MTH]

2096 Jácome, Nicanor. Economía y sociedad en el siglo XVI. (*in* Nueva historia del Ecuador. Edición de Enrique Ayala Mora. Quito: Corporación Editora Nacional, 1988, v. 3, p. 123–160, ill., tables)

Praiseworthy attempt to summarize and interpret what is known regarding the economy and society of Ecuador in the 16th century. [MTH]

2097 Jurado Noboa, Fernando. Los Larrea: burocracia, tenencia de la tierra, poder político, crisis, retorno al poder y papel en la cultura ecuatoriana. Quito: Sociedad Ecuatoriana de Amigos de la Genealogía, 1986. 239 p.: bibl., ill., tables, ports. (Col. Amigos de la Genealogía; 22)

Genealogical study of the Larrea, one of the leading families of Ecuador since the late 17th century. Includes biographical data on the more outstanding members of the clan (e.g., the late historian Carlos Manuel Larrea). [MTH]

Lafuente, Antonio and **Antonio Mazuecos.** Los caballeros del punto fijo: ciencia, política y aventura en la expedición geodésica hispanofrancesa al virreinato del Perú en el siglo XVIII. See item **2015.**

2098 Landázuri Camacho, Carlos. De las guerras civiles a la insurreción de las alcabalas, 1537–1593. (*in* Nueva historia del Ecuador. Edición de Enrique Ayala Mora. Quito: Corporación Editora Nacional, 1988, v. 3, p. 161–210, ills.)

"New approach" review of political developments of the 1500s. [MTH]

2099 Lavalle, Bernard. La rebelión de las alcabalas, Quito, julio de 1592-abril de 1593: ensayo de interpretación. (*Cultura/Quito,* 9:26, sept./dic. 1986, p. 41–93, appendix)

Most detailed, sophisticated, and well-researched study to date of the sales tax rebellion of 1592–93. [MTH]

2100 Laviana Cuetos, María Luisa. Un proceso por brujería en la costa ecuatoriana a fines del siglo XVIII: la Punta de Santa Elena, 1784–1787. (*Anu. Estud. Am.,* 46, 1989, p. 93–129)

Informative analysis of 1780s investigation of witches, sorcerers, and native healers in the Peninsula of Santa Elena. [MTH]

2101 Lebret, Iveline. La vida en Otavalo en el siglo XVIII. Traducción de Patricia Tauber y Tamara Estupiñán. Otavalo, Ecuador: Instituto Otavaleño de Antropología, 1981. 368 p.: bibl., ill. (Serie Historia. Col. Pendoneros; 22)

Consists of four terse chapters on the corregimiento of Otavalo and childhood, marriage, and death there during the 18th century. Contains a substantial appendix of notarial sources (p. 115–368) transcribed by Yolanda Andrade de Nicolalde. [MTH]

2102 Maier S., Jorge. Historia postal de Quito, 1534–1864. (*Cultura/Quito,*

8:23, sept./dic. 1985, p. 223–258, appendix, facsims., tables)

Reconstructs the history of postal service in Quito during the colonial and early national periods. Reproduces post marks from 1770 through 1864. [MTH]

2103 Marchán Romero, Carlos. Economía y sociedad durante el siglo XVIII. (*Cultura/Quito*, 8:24a, enero/abril 1986, p. 55–76, tables)

Revisionist review of economic and social developments as well as problems in the Presidency of Quito and its component regions during the 1700s. Previews author's apparently yet to be published *Economía y sociedad en la Real Audiencia de Quito durante el siglo XVIII*. Also appears in vol. 4 of *Nueva historia del Ecuador* (Quito: Corporación Editora Nacional, 1989). [MTH]

2104 Maroni, Pablo; Andrés de Zárate; and Juan Magnin. Noticias auténticas del famoso Río Marañón y misión apostólica de la Compañía de Jesús de la Provincia de Quito en los dilatados bosques de dicho río, escribíalas por los años de 1738, un misionero de la misma compañía, Pablo Maroni; Seguidas de las Relaciones de los P.P.A. de Zárate y J. Magnin (1735–1740). Edición crítica, introducción e índices de Jean-Pierre Chaumeil. Iquitos, Peru: IIAP-CETA, 1988. 565 p., 2 folded leaves of plates: bibl., index, maps. (Monumenta amazónica B; 4)

Vol. 4 in "Misioneros" subset of "Monumenta amazónica" series, a set that belongs on the shelves of all students of the Upper Amazon Basin. Vols. 2 and 3, which I have not seen, reprint Uriarte's *Diario de un misionero de Maynas* and Amich's *Historia de las misiones del Convento de Santa Rosa de Ocopa*. This tome consists primarily of Maroni's 1738 *Noticias auténticas*. [MTH]

2105 Martín Cuesta, José. Jaén de Bracamoros. v. 4, Historia y evangelización del siglo XVII. Lima: Librería Studium, 1988. 466 p.: bibl., ill., index.

Traditional, well-reasearched history of the city and province of Jaén de Bracamoros in the 17th century covers only political and ecclesiastical events. For vols. 1–3 see *HLAS 48:2706.* [MTH]

2106 Martínez de la Vega, Eduardo. D. Pedro Franco Dávila: un sabio naturalista

guayaquileño. (*Rev. Hist. Am.*, 102, julio/dic. 1986, p. 125–141)

Succinct sketch of the *guayaquileño* who founded and was the first director of what became the Museo Nacional de Ciencias Naturales in Madrid. Researchers should also consult María de los Angeles Calatayud Arinero, *Catálogo de documentos del Real Gabinete de Historia Natural, 1752–1786* (3 vols., Madrid: Consejo Superior de Investigaciones Científicas, 1987). [MTH]

2107 McFarlane, Anthony. The "rebellion of the barrios:" urban insurrection in Bourbon Quito. (*HAHR*, 69:2, May 1989, p. 283–330)

Detailed reexamination of the rebellion of 1765 sheds considerable light on a revolt that has long been touted as an early stirring for independence but which heretofore has not been studied in depth. See also item **2108.** [MTH]

2108 McFarlane, Anthony. The rebellion of the *barrios:* urban insurrection in Bourbon Quito. (*in* Reform and insurrection in Bourbon New Granada and Peru. [see item **2021**] p. 197–254, map)

Earlier but not substantially different version of item **2107.** One of McFarlane's most important contributions is his analysis of the composition and role of the crowd. [MTH]

2109 Mejía Lequerica, José. José Mejía, primer botánico ecuatoriano. Introducción y selección de Eduardo Estrella. Quito: Ediciones ABYA-YALA, 1988. 99 p.: facsims., ill., ports. (Col. Historia de las ciencias; 1)

Publishes seven letters of Mejía, six of them for the first time, plus his heretofore unknown *Plantas quiteñas* in facsimile and in transcription. Significant sources for the history of natural science in Ecuador. Contains excellent introduction. [MTH]

2110 Minchom, Martin. La evolución demográfica del Ecuador en el siglo XVII. (*Cultura/Quito*, 8:24b, enero/abril 1986, p. 459–480, graphs, tables)

Able exposition on the state and movement of the population of Ecuador, especially of the highlands, during the 18th and early 19th centuries (the "XVII" in the title is a "typo") by a leading scholar of colonial Ecuadorian demography. For earlier contributions by Minchom see *HLAS 48:1672* and *HLAS 48:2707*. [MTH]

2111 Miño Grijalva, Manuel. La economía de la Real Audiencia de Quito. (*in* Nueva historia del Ecuador. Edición de Enrique Ayala Mora. Quito: Corporación Editora Nacional, 1989, v. 4, p. 47–103, graph, maps, tables)

Reviews demographic and economic developments of the 17th century, arguing that the economy was not nearly as prosperous as traditional historiography maintains. Until the agrarian sector of the 1600s is studied, however, the discussion is moot. [MTH]

2112 Moreno Yáñez, Segundo. La Colección Documental Bernardo Mendel y su importancia en la historiografía ecuatoriana. (*Anu. Estud. Am.*, 46:1, 1989, p. 35–50, suplemento)

Describes manuscript holdings on Ecuador of the Lilly Library at Indiana University. Of particular interest are 22 *legajos* originally pertaining to the diocesan archives of Quito. [MTH]

2113 Moreno Yáñez, Segundo. La sociedad indígena y su articulación a la formación socioeconómica colonial en la Audiencia de Quito. (*in* Nueva historia del Ecuador. Edición de Enrique Ayala Mora. Quito: Corporación Editora Nacional, 1989, v. 5, p. 93–136)

Important statement on the impact, especially economic, of the colonial State on and of cultural changes in Indian societies, by a leading authority on the postconquest history of ethnic groups of the sierra. [MTH]

Moreno Yánez, Segundo E. Sublevaciones indígenas en la Audiencia de Quito: desde comienzos del siglo XVIII hasta finales de la colonia. See *HLAS 50:690*.

2114 Nueva historia del Ecuador. v. 3, Conquista y primera etapa colonial. v. 4, Segunda y tercera etapa colonial. v. 5, Perspectiva general de la colonia. Edición de Enrique Ayala Mora. Quito: Corporación Editora Nacional: Grijalbo, 1983–1989. 3 v.: bibl., ill., plates, tables.

Truly a "new" history of Ecuador. Almost all of the vol. editors and authors are professionally-trained men and women in their 30s, 40s, and 50s, versed in demographic, economic, ethnohistorical, and social as well as current approaches to cultural or intellectual and political history. Vols. 1–2 are dedicated to the "época aborigen" and vols. 6–15 to the independence and national periods. For noteworthy contributions to vols. 3, 4, and 5, see items **2081, 2082, 2083, 2086, 2094, 2095, 2096, 2098, 2111, 2113, 2121,** and **2124.** For vol. 9, see item **2429.** [MTH]

2115 Ontaneda Pólit, Max. Eugenio de Santa Cruz y Espejo: examen de su obra. Quito: Ediciones Abya-Yala, 1988. 168 p.: bibl.

Refreshing reexamination of the writings of the much-touted and much-misunderstood Eugenio Espejo rightly maintains that the mestizo medic has been mythicized. [MTH]

O'Phelan, Scarlett. Por el rey, religión y la patria: las juntas de gobierno de 1809 en La Paz y Quito. See item **2197.**

2116 Ortiz de la Tabla Ducasse, Javier. La población tributaria del Ecuador colonial. (*Cultura/Quito*, 8:24b, enero/abril 1986, p. 447–458)

Excellent summary of the increasingly more complete picture of the state and movement of the native population of Ecuador during the colonial period. Evidence indicates that the Indians of the highlands of Ecuador did not experience nearly as drastic a decline as their counterparts in Mexico or neighboring Peru. Why this should have been the case remains to be established, however. [MTH]

2117 Paladines, Carlos. Ciencia y pensamiento moderno en la Audencia de Quito. (*Cultura/Quito*, 8:24a, enero/abril 1986, p. 77–92)

Novel contribution to the history of ideas in Ecuador outlines work of "precursor" of scientific method in Quito, the virtually forgotten Juan Magnin, a professor of canon law at the Univ. de San Gregorio and author of *Milliet en armonía cón Descartes* (1746?). [MTH]

2118 Pesillo: documentos para su historia. Recopilación de Piedad Peñaherrera de Costales y Alfredo Costales Samaniego. Quito: Ediciones Abya-Yala, 1987. 174 p.: ill.

Anthology of documents relating to major hacienda near Quito consists mostly of *visita* and census materials. Includes national period sources. [MTH]

2119 Pimentel Carbo, Julio. Caminos y medios de transporte en nuestro primer siglo colonial. Guayaquil, Ecuador: Comisión Permanente para la Defensa del Patrimonio Nacional, 1985. 35 p.: bibl., maps.

Textually accurate, but cartographically-erroneous sketch of routes and modes of transportation between the coast, especially the port cities, and the highlands in the 16th century. Drawn from standard sources. [MTH]

2120 Porras P., María Elena. Gobernación y Obispado de Mainas: siglos XVII y XVIII. Quito: Ediciones ABYA-YALA: Taller de Estudios Históricos, 1987. 136 p., 5 folded leaves of plates: bibl., ill., maps.

Institutional study of Governorship and Diocese of Maynas, established by royal decrees in 1617 and 1802, respectively. Lackluster but well-researched. [MTH]

2121 Quintero L., Rafael. El Estado colonial. (*in* Nueva historia del Ecuador. Edición de Enrique Ayala Mora. Quito: Corporación Editora Nacional, 1989, v. 5, p. 7–56, ill.)

Stimulating reexamination of economic, political, and social structures of colonial Ecuador. [MTH]

2122 Ramos Gómez, Luis Javier. Un ejemplo de la lucha por el poder en Quito. (*Cultura/Quito*, 8:24a, enero/abril 1986, p. 117–132)

Adds a new chapter to political history of the capital city by rescuing from archival oblivion a 1737 struggle between the presidents of the Audiencia and the Cabildo over who should serve as *alcaldes ordinarios de primer y segundo voto* that year. At issue was who would control municipal government, the Crown's man or the local elite. [MTH]

Ramos Gómez, Luis Javier. Epoca, génesis y texto de las "Noticias secretas de América," de Jorge Juan y Antonio de Ulloa. v. 1, El viaje a América, 1735–1745, de los tenientes de navío Jorge Juan y Antonio de Ulloa, y sus consecuencias literarias. v. 2, Edición anotada del texto original de las *Noticias secretas de América*, de Jorge Juan y Antonio de Ulloa. See item **2019.**

Ramos Gómez, Oscar Gerardo. Sebastián de Benalcázar: conquistador de Quito y Popayán. See item **2020.**

2123 Requena, Francisco. Diario del viaje al Japurá. Estudio preliminar de Michèle Cohen. (*Anu. Estud. Am.*, 40:2, 1988, p. 3–68, map)

Major ethnohistorical and historical/geographical source of the late 1700s on the Upper Amazon Basin. Prefaced by a pithy preliminary study. [MTH]

2124 Salomon, Frank. Crisis y transformación de la sociedad aborigen invadida, 1528–1573. (*in* Nueva historia del Ecuador. Edición de Enrique Ayala Mora. Quito: Corporación Editora Nacional, 1988, v. 3, p. 91–122, ill.)

Important statement on the native peoples of Ecuador during the conquest and early colonial period by the leading authority on the subject. [MTH]

2125 Salomon, Frank. Indian women of early colonial Quito as seen through their testaments. (*Americas/Francisc.*, 44:3, Jan. 1988, p. 325–341, bibl.)

Superb analysis of social, economic and ethnohistorical data gleaned from careful reading of colonial wills. Model essay demonstrates how much remains to be learned from surviving sources about postconquest Indian society in Ecuador. For ethnohistorian's comment, see *HLAS 50:748.* [MTH]

2126 Terán, Rosemarie. Los proyectos del imperio borbónico en la Real Audiencia de Quito. Quito: Ediciones ABYA-YALA; Taller de Estudios Históricos, 1988. 114 p.: bibl., ill.

Licentiate thesis on administrative reforms attempted and implemented by Bourbons in Audiencia of Quito. Prosaic but adds some new data to the discussion, mostly culled from Archives of the Ministry of Foreign Affairs. See also Terán's "Sinopsis histórica del siglo XVIII" in *Nueva historia del Ecuador* (item **2114**). [MTH]

2127 Tyrer, Robson Brines. Historia demográfica y económica de la Audiencia de Quito: población indígena e industria textil, 1600–1800. Quito: Banco Central del Ecuador, 1988. 325 p.: bibl., ill. (Biblioteca de historia económica; 1)

Spanish version of well-known doctoral dissertation on Indian population and textile industry of the highlands in the 1600s and 1700s. Somewhat dated but still a benchmark study. For economist's comment, see *HLAS 51:2212.* [MTH]

PERU

2128 Aldana, Susana. Empresas coloniales: las tinas de jabón en Piura. Piura, Peru: Centro de Investigación y Promoción del Campesinado; Lima: Instituto Francés de Estudios Andinos, 1989? 193 p., 5 leaves of plates: bibl., ill. (Col. Travaux de l'IFEA; 47. Historia Regional; 1)

Quantitative study of soap trade in Viceroyalty of Peru and prosopographic study of the soap makers. The center of soap manufacturing was Piura. Major contribution to economic and regional history of northern Peru. [MTH]

2129 Assadourian, Carlos Sempat. Acerca del cambio en la naturaleza del dominio sobre las Indias: la mit'a minera del Virrey Toledo; documentos de 1568–1571. (*Anu. Estud. Am.,* 46, 1989, p. 3–70)

Reexamines the extent to which Toledo or his superiors were ultimately responsible for the imposition of the mining *mita* in Upper and Lower Peru. Maintains that Cardinal Espinosa, if not Philip II himself, "encomendó al virrey la mit'a minera como el único instrumento eficaz para conseguir el objetivo de aumentar fuertemente los ingresos de la Hacienda Real." [MTH]

2130 Assadourian, Carlos Sempat. La despoblación indígena en Perú y Nueva España durante el siglo XVI y la formación de la economía colonial. (*Hist. Mex.,* 38:3, enero/marzo 1989, p. 419–453, bibl.)

Comparative study of the postconquest collapse of Indian populations in Mexico and Peru and the economic causes and consequences thereof. The author is an authority on the early economic history of the Andes. [MTH]

2131 Biedma, Manuel *et al.* La conquista franciscana del Alto Ucayali. Selección, introducción y notas de Julián Heras y Antonine Tibesar. Iquitos, Perú: CETA: IIAP, 1989. 292 p.: bibl., index. (Monumenta amazónica B; 5)

First complete edition of Franciscan accounts of the abortive evangelization of the Indians of the Upper Ucayali in the late 1600s. Includes historical and geographic "introductions" by Tibesar and Heras, respectively. [MTH]

2132 Brenot, Anne-Marie. Pouvoir et profits au Pérou colonial au XVIIIe siècle: gouverneurs, clientèles et ventes forcées. Paris: Éditions L'Harmattan, 1989. 529 p.: appendices, bibl., facsims., tables. (Col. Recherches et documents Amérique Latine)

Covers much the same ground as Alfredo Moreno Cebrián's *El coregidor de indios y la economía peruana del siglo XVIII* (Madrid, 1977) on which Brenot relies heavily (see *HLAS 42:2707*). The "novelty" and importance of Brenot's works lies in her detailed analysis of "voyageurs européens au Pérou au XVIIIie siècle" (p. 1–108). [MTH]

2133 Brown, Kendall W. La crisis financiera peruana al comienzo del siglo XVIII: la minería de plata y la mina de azogues de Huancavelica. (*Rev. Indias,* 48:182/183, enero/agosto 1988, p. 349–381, tables)

Reexamines relationship between the financial crisis of the late 1600s and early 1700s—resulting, in large part, from a decline in silver production in Lower and Upper Peru—and early Bourbon attempts to boost silver production in the Altiplano by reviving mercury production at Huancavelica. Includes new archival data. [MTH]

2134 Burga, Manuel. The triumph of colonial Christianity in the central Andes: guilt, good conscience, and Indian piety. (*in* The middle period in Latin America: values and attitudes in the 17th-19th centuries. Edited by Mark D. Szuchman. Boulder, Colo.: Lynne Rienner Publishers, 1989, p. 33–55, graphs, tables)

Draws on *capellanía* records in the Archivo Arzobispal de Lima to examine the economic, ethnic, and ecclesiastical significance of religious mortgages in 16th and 17th century Peru. Novel analysis of sources; contains thought-provoking interpretations. [MTH]

2135 Cahill, David P. Repartos ilícitos y familias principales: el sur andino, 1780–1824. (*Rev. Indias,* 48:182/183, enero/agosto 1988, p. 449–473)

Pioneering essay on implications of

the illegal continuation of the forced sale of goods, especially textiles, among Indians, mestizos, and castes during the late colonial period. Also examines effects of the abolition of the *reparto* and other economic developments on the leading families of Cusco. [MTH]

2136 Cahill, David P. Taxonomy of a colonial "riot": the Arequipa disturbances of 1780. (*in* Reform and insurrection in Bourbon New Granada and Peru [see item **2021,**] p. 255–291)

Revisionist study of the tax riots of Jan. 1780 focuses on social aspects such as the composition and actions of the crowd as well as the economic causes of the protests. [MTH]

2137 Charney, Paul J. El indio urbano: un análisis económico y social de la población india de Lima en 1613. (*Histórica/Lima,* 12:1, julio 1988, p. 5–33, bibl., graphs, ill.)

Brief analysis of 1613 census of the Indian population of Lima is somewhat simplistic and marred by typographical errors, especially in the tables and bibliography.

2138 Cisneros, Luis Jaime and **Pedro Guibovich Pérez.** Juan de Espinosa Medrano, un intelectual cuzqueño del seiscientos: nuevos datos biográficos. (*Rev. Indias,* 48:182/183, enero/agosto 1988, p. 327–347)

Drawing on archival research in Peru and Spain, Cisneros and Guibovich correct many mistakes in the biographies of Espinosa Medrano and add considerably to our knowledge of this exceptionally literate priest. This prolific writer does not appear to have been a musician or a composer as heretofore believed. [MTH]

2139 Dargent Chamot, Eduardo. La moneda peruana en el siglo XVII: reflejo de una crisis. Lima: Univ. de Lima, Facultad de Ciencias Humanas, 1988. 134 p.: bibl. (Cuadernos de historia; 7)

Diachronic study of the mints of Lima and Potosí during the 17th and first half of the 18th centuries includes documentary appendix. [MTH]

2140 Dargent Chamot, Eduardo. La primera ceca de Lima, 1568–1692 [sic]. (*Rev. Indias,* 48:182/183, enero/agosto 1988, p. 161–186)

Well-researched and richly detailed descriptive account of the first mint in Lima (1568–1592). [MTH]

2141 Díaz-Trechuelo Spínola, María Lourdes. Francisco Pizarro: el conquistador del fabuloso Perú. Madrid: Anaya, 1988. 126 p.: bibl., ill. (Biblioteca iberoamericana; 21)

Skeletal biography of the conqueror of Peru. [MTH]

2142 Durand Flórez, Luis. Criollos en conflicto: Cuzco después de Túpac Amaru. Lima: Univ. de Lima, 1985. 254 p., 5 leaves of plates: bibl., ill.

Most extensive study to date of political developments in Cusco between the defeat of Túpac Amaru in 1782 and the Ubalde and Aguilar conspiracy of 1805. Focuses primarily on conflict between Creoles and peninsulars (e.g., between Bishop Moscoso and Intendant Mata Linares) and includes chapters on concurrent events in southern Peru and in Upper Peru. [MTH]

La edad del oro. See item **2006.**

Escobari de Querejazu, Laura. Producción y comercio en el espacio sur andino en el siglo XVII: Cuzco-Potosí, 1650–1700. See item **2007.**

2143 Fernández Alonso, Serena. Medidas reformistas en torno a la minería peruana: la creación del estanco de la pólvora. (*Rev. Indias,* 48:182/183, enero/agosto 1988, p. 383–399)

Sketches the extension of gunpowder monopoly to Peru in 1786 and its allegedly beneficial impact on silver mining in the Andes. [MTH]

2144 Fernández Alonso, Serena. El Perú colonial a través de la historiografía española. (*Rev. Indias,* 50:188, enero/abril 1990, p. 213–226)

Critical review of the relatively few but substantial contributions by Spanish historians to Peru's recovery of its colonial past. [MTH]

Fisher, John Robert. The effects of *comercio libre* on the economies of New Granada and Peru: a comparison. See item **2009.**

Fisher, John Robert. El impacto del comercio libre en el Perú, 1778–1796. See item **2010.**

2145 García Vera, José Antonio. Aduanas, comerciantes y nación mercantil, Trujillo, 1796–1836. (*Rev. Indias*, 48:182/183, enero/agosto 1988, p. 435–447, tables)

Research notes on merchants and traders in late-18th and early-19th-century Trujillo. [MTH]

2146 Gaytan Pajares, Evelio. Repercusión de la rebelión de Tupac Amaru en Cajamarca. (*Bol. Lima*, 8:48, nov. 1986, p. 53–58)

Publishes and comments on reaction by corregidor of Cajamarca to possible local "adhesión a Túpac Amaru." [MTH]

2147 *Gazeta de Lima de 1793 a junio de 1794: Gil de Taboada y Lemos.* Recopilación, prólogo y apéndices de José Durand. Lima: COFIDE, Oficina de Asuntos Culturales, 1983. 421 p.: ill.

Photofacsimile edition of *Gacetas de Lima* issued in 1793 and 1794. For the only other two volumes of *Gacetas* apparently reproduced to date (vols. 2 and 3) see *HLAS 50:1948*. A welcome reissue of an important late colonial source. [MTH]

2148 Gerbi, Antonello. Il mito del Perù. A cura di Sandro Gerbi. Milano, Italy: F. Angeli, 1988. 359 p., 5 p. of plates: bibl., ill. (Saggi di storia; 5)

This series of essays by the late (1904–76) Italian intellectual historian who was exiled to Peru in the Mussolini years is in three parts. Pt. 1 introduces and analyzes the impact of the discovery and conquest of Peru upon European legends and the Black Legend, and traces the impact of Peruvian silver upon European attitudes toward wealth as seen in the writings of European thinkers. Ends with a discussion of the model of the "stoic, socially disciplined Inca" myth in the 18th- and 19th-century European debates on liberalism and democracy. Concludes that Manco Capac, the "Romulus of Cuzco," had become the "Spartacus of the Sierra." In Pt. 2, Gerbi speculates on the descriptions of early conquest era travelers as a vehicle for his own dissection of the Hegelian *mot* on the New World as "immature." Essays in Pt. 3 illustrate aspects of the continuing dialogue between the Old World and the New on the sources and meaning of "barbarism" and "civilization." Provocative and witty, work is based on prodigious reading in key sources and is organized and presented by his son. [V. Peloso]

2149 Gibbs, Donald L. The economic activities of nuns, friars, and their *conventos* in mid-colonial Cuzco. (*Americas/Francisc.*, 45:3, Jan. 1989, p. 343–362, bibl.)

Pioneering study of the economic activities of nuns and friars in Cuzco. Well researched, analyzed, interpreted, and written account compensates for inaccessability to scholars of most convent archives in Peru by drawing on notarial records. [MTH]

2150 Glave Testino, Luis Miguel. El Virreinato Peruano y la llamada "crisis general" del siglo XVII. Lima: Univ. de Lima, Depto. Académico de Ciencias Humanas, 1986. 59 p.: bibl., ill. (Cuadernos de historia; 2)

Dense paper on the alledged crisis of the 17th century. Both an evaluation of what has been written on 17th-century Viceroyalty of Peru, especially on what are now Peru and Bolivia, and a working paper on Glave's ongoing research on economic and social aspects thereof. Repays close reading. [MTH]

2151 Guibovich Pérez, Pedro. Unanue y la Inquisición de Lima. (*Histórica/Lima*, 12:1, julio 1988, p. 49–59, appendix, bibl.)

Brief essay on Unanue's ambivalent attitude towards the Inquisition, especially its role as censor of books. [MTH]

2152 Hampe Martínez, Teodoro. Una biblioteca cuzqueña confiscada por la Inquisición. (*Anu. Estud. Am.*, 45, 1988, p. 273–315, appendices)

Lists and analyzes holdings of Agustín Valenciano de Quiñones, a 16th-century lawyer and *vecino* of Cuzco who was arrested and investigated by the Holy Office as a possible heretic. Apparently Quiñones' library constituted the most extensive collection of legal materials in the Viceroyalty, at least in the 1500s. Also published in *Revista Andina* (5:2, dic. 1987, p. 526–564). [MTH]

2153 Hampe Martínez, Teodoro. La biblioteca del virrey Don Martín Enríquez: aficiones intelectuales de un gobernante colonial. (*Bol. Lima*, 8:48, nov. 1986, p. 43–51, bibl., photo)

Analyzes the library holdings of a 16th-century viceroy of New Spain and Peru in order to determine his intellectual formation and interests. [MTH]

2154 Hampe Martínez, Teodoro. La difusión de libros e ideas en el Perú colonial: análisis de bibliotecas particulares, siglo XVI. (*Bull. hisp.*, 89:1/4, 1987, p. 55–84)

Laudable attempt to establish which works were widely read and ideas generally held by literati of 16th-century Peru. Based on analysis of holdings of 14 private libraries, on almost all of which Hampe has published separately. [MTH]

2155 Hampe Martínez, Teodoro. Libros profanos y sagrados en la biblioteca del tesorero Antonio Dávalos, Lima, 1583. (*Rev. Indias*, 46:178, julio/dic. 1986, p. 385–402, bibl.)

Identifies and analyzes the 75 books that Antonio Dávalos brought with him from the mother country in 1583. [MTH]

Hampe Martínez, Teodoro. El Padre Vargas Ugarte y su aportación a la historiografía de Perú Colonial. See item **1997.**

2156 Iwasaki Cauti, Fernando. Ambulantes y comercio colonial: iniciativas mercantiles en el virreinato peruano. (*Jahrb. Gesch.*, 24, 1987, p. 179–211)

Pioneering study on the scale and significance of smalltime, mostly under-the-table dealers, especially stall vendors, hucksters, and peddlers, in colonial Lima. [MTH]

2157 Iwasaki Cauti, Fernando. La evangelización en Perú y Japón durante el siglo XVI: modelo comparativo de dos políticos de evangelización. (*Rev. Indias*, 48:182/183, enero/agosto 1988, p. 147–160)

Working paper on similarities and differences in Catholic Church's early efforts to proselytize the peoples of Peru and Japan. [MTH]

2158 Lang, Mervyn. El derrumbe de Huancavelica en 1786: fracaso de una reforma borbónica. (*Histórica/Lima*, 10:2, dic. 1986, p. 213–226, bibl.)

Reexamines the causes and consequences of the collapse of the Santa Barbara mercury mine on Sept. 25, 1786. [MTH]

2159 Larraín Valdés, Gerardo. Dios, sol y oro: Diego de Almagro y el descubrimiento de Chile. Santiago: Editorial Andrés Bello, 1987. 329 p.: bibl., ill.

Quasi-popular, semischolarly biography of the ill-fated partner of Pizarro who

discovered Chile reads easily and is more or less factually accurate. [MTH]

2160 Lassegue Moleres, Juan Bautista. Guía del investigador en el Archivo Arzobispal del Cuzco. Lima: Fondo del Libro del Banco Industrial del Perú, 1981. 76 p.: ill.

Delineates history and holdings of the Archdiocesan Archives of Cusco. [MTH]

2161 Lohmann Villena, Guillermo. Los Fernández de Córdoba: un linaje preponderante en el Perú en los siglos XVI y XVII. (*Anu. Estud. Am.*, 45, 1988, p. 167–240)

Genealogical study of an eminent family in 16th-and 17th-century Perú includes data on careers of important family members. [MTH]

2162 Lohmann Villena, Guillermo. El licenciado Francisco Fernández de Córdoba, 1580–1639: un poeta, historiador y apologista de los criollos en el Perú virreinal. (*Rev. Indias*, 48:182/183, enero/agosto 1988, p. 285–325)

Thoroughly-researched biography of the author of *Perú en armas* (1624). Important contribution to regional as well as intellectual history of the middle colonial period. Fernández de Córdoba held the post of corregidor of Huamanga and other local offices. [MTH]

2163 Lohmann Villena, Guillermo. Notas sobre la situación socioeconómica de los libertos en Lima durante el Virreinato. (*Historia/Santiago*, 22, 1987, p. 71–89, bibl.)

Research notes on the social life and economic activities of freedmen in colonial Lima. [MTH]

2164 Lowry, Lyn. Religión y control social en la colonia: el caso de los indios urbanos de Lima, 1570–1620. (*Allpanchis*, 20:32, 1988, p. 11–42, bibl.)

Preview of work in progress on the role of Catholicism in the reformation of Indian life in early colonial Lima. Especially concerned with the use of religion as means of social control. [MTH]

2165 Lucena Giraldo, Manuel. Entre las fidelidades: un catálogo ilustrado de las producciones peruanas. (*Rev. Indias*, 48:182/183, enero/agosto 1988, p. 637–649)

Publishes with sketchy introduction an anonymous late-18th-century "Catalogo de algunas producciones naturales ya conoci-

das y de otras que se encuentran en el Perú
... " attributed by Lucena to José María
de Lecuanda, the controversial nephew of
Bishop Martínez Compañón. Part of the apparently substantial "Discurso preliminar en
que se manifiesta el patrimonio y recursos
del Perú. . . . " [MTH]

2166 MacCormack, Sabine G. Atahualpa y
el libro. (*Rev. Indias*, 48 : 184, sept./
dic. 1988, p. 693–714, facsims.)

MacCormack insightfully contends
that the "sacred" book Valverde handed Atahualpa during the fatal encounter at Cajamarca played contradictory roles in the
accounts of the conquest. It was of monumental importance in Spanish eyes since the
Inca's "rejection" of the "word" justified the
conquest, but of no significance whatsoever
in the Andean view as the book was a non-
object. [MTH]

Malamud Rikles, Carlos Daniel. Cádiz y
Saint Malo en el comercio colonial peruano,
1698–1725. See item **2017**.

Mannheim, Bruce. La memoria y el olvido en
la política lingüística colonial. See item
3330.

2167 Marchena Fernández, Juan. The social
world of the military in Peru and New
Granada: the colonial oligarchies in conflict,
1750–1810. (*in* Reform and insurrection in
Bourbon New Granada and Peru [see item
2021,] p. 54–95, tables)

Able summary of recent findings, especially those of Marchena himself, on social
history of the late colonial militia and regular army in Peru proper and New Granada.
[MTH]

**2168 Medrano, José Miguel and Carlos Ma-
lamud.** Las actividades de los Cinco
Gremios Mayores en el Perú: apuntes preliminares. (*Rev. Indias*, 48 : 182/183, enero/
agosto 1988, p. 421–433)

Pioneering essay on commercial activities of the *Cinco Gremios Mayores* of
Madrid in Arequipa and Lima—the two colonial cities in which the peninsular company
maintained a presence. [MTH]

2169 Melzer, John T.S. The rise in the price
of wheat for the "bakery in the Street
of the Fishmarket" in the city of Lima, 1812–
1821. (*Account. Hist. J.*, 15 : 1, Spring 1988,
p. 89–118, bibl., facsims., tables)

Important study shows what happened

to prices of basic commodities during the
independence period. One of the very few
pieces on prices in Lima. See also *HLAS
50 : 1950* and item **2478**. [MTH]

Miño Grijalva, Manuel. La manufactura colonial. See item **973**.

Miño Grijalva, Manuel. La política textil en
México y Perú en la época colonial: nuevas
consideraciones. See item **974**.

2170 Mogrovejo Rosales, Jerry. La fracasada
rebelión de 1565: un documento histórico. (*Bol. Lima*, 9 : 52, julio 1987, p. 13–19,
bibl.)

Literal transcription of the April 16,
1565 minutes of the town council of Cusco
regarding an unrealized uprising of Indians of
Jauja, Huánuco, and Huamanga. Includes
prefatory notes. [MTH]

2171 Moreno Cebrián, Alfredo. Túpac
Amaru: el cacique inca que rebeló los
Andes. Madrid: Anaya, 1988. 127 p.: bibl., ill.
(Biblioteca iberoamericana; 75)

Popular biography of the leader of the
Indian rebellion of 1780–82 is lavishly illustrated. [MTH]

2172 O'Phelan, Scarlett. Aduanas, mercado
interno y élite comercial en el Cusco
antes y después de la Gran Rebelión de 1780.
(*Apuntes/Lima*, 19, segundo semestre 1986,
p. 53–72, bibl., maps, tables)

Case study of the impact of Bourbon
reforms and of the Tupac Amaru rebellion of
1780 on the merchant elite of Cusco focuses
on the interests of its five most prominent
members. Based on custom-house records.
[MTH]

2173 Pärssinen, Martii. Otras fuentes escritas por los cronistas: los casos de
Martín de Morúa y Pedro Gutiérrez de Santa
Clara. (*Histórica/Lima*, 13 : 1, julio 1989,
p. 45–65, bibl.)

Exemplifies but does not demonstrate
the extent to which Morúa and Gutiérrez
borrowed from earlier chroniclers (especially
Román y Zamora and Diego Fernández), a
consideration that must be taken into account when relying on one or the other as
independent and therefore corroborative
sources. [MTH]

**Pérez-Mallaína Bueno, Pablo Emilio and Bi-
biano Torres Ramírez.** La armada del Mar del
Sur. See item **2018**.

2174 Puente Brunke, José de la. Los oidores en la sociedad limeña: notas para su estudio, siglo XVII. (*Temas Am.*, 7, 1990, p. 8–13)

Explores the ways Audiencia officials played a major role in local society by examining incidents in the lives of four 17th-century *oidores* as examples. [MTH]

2175 Puente Brunke, José de la. Política de la Corona en torno a las ecomiendas peruanas, 1670–1750. (*Histórica/Lima*, 11:2, dic. 1987, p. 181–206, appendix, bibl.)

Delineates the multifaceted policy of the Crown towards the remaining 53 encomiendas in the established colony. Based on peninsular sources, especially as found in the AGI. See also item **2176**. [MTH]

2176 Puente Brunke, José de la. Las "tercias de encomiendas" en el Virreinato del Perú: en torno a la política fiscal de la Corona en el siglo XVII. (*Rev. Indias*, 48:182/183, enero/agosto 1988, p. 187–205)

Diachronic study of royal policy on imposition and collection of encomienda tax in Peru, specifically of the retention of one-third of encomienda rents, beginning in 1615. [MTH]

Pumar Martínez, Carmen. Pedro de Valdivia: fundador de Chile. See item **2223**.

2177 Ramos, Gabriela. Las manufacturas en el Perú colonial: los obrajes de vidrios en los siglos XVII y XVIII. (*Histórica/Lima*, 13:1,julio 1989, p. 67–106, bibl., tables)

Pioneering study of the manufacture of glass, especially bottles for wine and liquor, in the 1600s and 1700s. Apparently the production of glass was centered in the Ica vally. See also the author's earlier *Economía de una hacienda-vidrería colonial* (Lima, 1984). [MTH]

Ramos Gómez, Luis Javier. Epoca, génesis y texto de las "Noticias secretas de América," de Jorge Juan y Antonio de Ulloa. v. 1, El viaje a América, 1735–1745, de los tenientes de navío Jorge Juan y Antonio de Ulloa, y sus consecuencias literarias. v. 2, Edición anotada del texto original de las *Noticias secretas de América*, de Jorge Juan y Antonio de Ulloa. See item **2019**.

2178 San Cristóbal Sebastián, Antonio and **Edmundo Guillén Guillén.** La ficción del esqueleto de Pizarro. Estudio antropoló-

gico de C. Arturo del Pozo Flórez. Lima: Univ. Ricardo Palma, 1986. 283 p., 2 leaves of plates: bibl., ill.

Demonstrates that the remains found in 1977 during repairs to the Cathedral of Lima and placed on display in 1985 in the Chapel of the Kings as the skeleton of Pizarro could not possibly be that of the conqueror of Peru, notwithstanding the claims of the Instituto Nacional de Cultura. From mummy to skeleton! What next? Or, how many Francisco Pizarros were there? [MTH]

Sarmiento de Gamboa, Pedro. Historia de los Incas. See item **691**.

Schwaller, John Frederick. Tithe collection and distribution in Mexico and Peru, circa 1600. See item **1076**.

2179 Stavig, Ward. Ethnic conflict, moral economy, and population in rural Cuzco on the eve of the Tupac Amaru II rebellion. (*HAHR*, 68:4, Nov. 1988, p. 737–770, tables)

Multivariate analysis of demographic, economic, and social conditions in pre-1780 rural Cusco, specifically in the *partidos* of Quispicanchis and Canas y Canchis. Important contribution to the growing body of increasingly sophisticated literature on grass-roots history of the Andes. [MTH]

2180 Stewart, Paul. The battle of Las Salinas, Peru, and its historians. (*Sixt. Century J.*, 19:3, Fall 1988, p. 407–433)

Probably as definitive and dispassionate an account of what actually happened at the Battle of Salinas (1538) and its significance in the affairs of the early colony as the sources permit. Also an eloquent historiographical essay. [MTH]

2181 Tardieu, Jean-Pierre. L'Action pastorale des Jésuites auprès de la population noire de Lima, XVIe-XVIIe s. (*Arch. Hist. Soc. Iesu*, 58:116, Iul./Dec. 1989, p. 315–327)

Cogent review of Jesuit efforts to proselytize and protect black slaves in 16th- and 17th-century Lima. [MTH]

2182 Tardieu, Jean-Pierre. Le marronnage à Lima, 1535–1650: atermoiements et répression. (*Rev. hist./Paris*, 564, oct./déc. 1987, p. 293–319, map)

Original study of runaway slaves and communities of refugee blacks in the vicinity of Lima during the early colonial period focuses on local efforts to cope with *cimarrones*. [MTH]

2183 Ten, Antonio E. Ciencia e ilustración en la Universidad de Lima. (*Asclepio*, 40:1, 1988, p. 187–221, bibl.)

Informative, insightful analysis of the study and teaching of science at San Marcos during the Age of the Enlightenment. [MTH]

2184 Unanue, José Hipólito. Guía política, eclesiástica y militar del Virreynato del Perú para el año de 1793. Edición, prólogo y apéndices de José Durand. Lima: Oficina de Asuntos Culturales, COFIDE, 1985. 475 p.: ill., index, port.

Welcome photofacsimile reprint of one of the most important sources on the state of Peru in the late 18th century, Unanue's well-known but scarce *guía de forasteros* of 1793. Includes an onomastic index, complied by Alicia Castañeda de Gutiérrez, and statistical updates from the 1794, 1795, 1796, and 1797 editions. [MTH]

2185 Van Deusen, Nancy. Dentro del cerco de los muros: el recogimiento en la época colonial. Lima: Centro de Documentación sobre la Mujer, 1987. 38 p.: (Cuadernos culturales. Serie I, La mujer en la historia)

Working paper on institutions for the care of unmarriageable, widowed, and "fallen" women in colonial Lima. [MTH]

2186 Wightman, Ann M. Indigenous migration and social change: the *forasteros* of Cuzco, 1570–1720. Durham, N.C.: Duke Univ. Press, 1990. 315 p.: bibl., index, map, tables.

Quantitative study of the origins, nature, significance, and impact of migrant Indians in Cusco and its district during the middle colonial period is unfortunately marred by poor exposition, especially the chapters that present author's statistical analysis and interpretations. Nonetheless, the most significant work on *indios forasteros* in the Viceroyalty of Peru since Nicolás Sánchez-Albornoz's work (see *HLAS 42: 2811*). [MTH]

2187 Xerez, Francisco de. Verdadera relación de la conquista del Perú. Edición de Concepción Bravo. Madrid: Historia 16, 1985. 206 p.: bibl., map. (Crónicas de América; 14)

Critical edition of a standard chronicle of the Spanish conquest of Peru is based on the original printing of 1534. Includes the "Relación Sámano," the authorship of which is sometimes attributed to Xerez but remains in doubt, and the "Crónica de Diego Trujillo." Bravo's introductions are excellent. For ethnohistorian's comment, see *HLAS 50:805*. [MTH]

ALTO PERU

2188 Bakewell, P.J. Silver and entrepreneurship in seventeenth-century Potosí: the life and times of Antonio López de Quiroga. Albuquerque: Univ. of New Mexico Press, 1988. 250 p.: bibl. ill., index.

Bakewell's second major work on the history of the Red Mountain and the men who exploited and were exploited by her (see also *HLAS 48:2766*). Expands upon his earlier study of López de Quiroga, the leading miner of 17th-century Potosí (see *HLAS 38:3154*). [MTH]

2189 Barnadas, Josep M. Alvaro Alonso Barba, 1569–1662: investigaciones sobre su vida y obra. La Paz: Biblioteca Minera Boliviana, 1986. 283 p.: appendix bibl., ill. (Biblioteca Minera Boliviana; 3)

Well researched study of Alonso Barba and his *Art of Metals* (1640) which described for the first time the process of refining silver through the use of quicksilver. Includes substantial documentary appendix (p. 135–262). [MTH]

2190 Buechler, Rose Marie. Gobierno, minería y sociedad: Potosí y el "renacimiento" borbónico, 1776–1810. 1a ed. en castellano, rev., corr. y aum. La Paz: Biblioteca Minera Boliviana, 1989. 2 v. (xxi, 544 p.): (Biblioteca Minera Boliviana; 5)

Revised, corrected and augemented edition in Spanish of *Mining society of Potosí* (Syracuse, N.Y.: Syracuse Univ., 1981), a detailed, painstaking, and sophisticated study of the economy and society of Potosí during the late colonial period, especially of the mercury guild (Gremio de Azogueros) and impact on it of the Bourbon reforms. Major contribution to the history of late colonial Bolivia. [MTH]

2191 Cañedo-Argüelles Fábrega, Teresa. Efectos de Potosí sobre la población indígena del Alto Perú: Pacajes a mediados del siglo XVII. (*Rev. Indias*, 48:182/183, enero/agosto 1988, p. 237–255, bibl., tables)

Examines the impact of the *mita* or labor draft for Potosí on the demography and economy of the Indian population of Pacajes in the mid-17th century, drawing on period sources in the AGI. [MTH]

2192 Cangiano, María Cecilia. Curas, caciques y comunidades en el alto Perú: Chayanta a fines del siglo XVIII. Tilcara, Argentina: Proyecto ECIRA, Sección Antropología Social, ICA, Facultad de Filosofía y Letras, UBA-MLAL, 1987. 55 p.: bibl., maps. (Documentos de trabajo: Serie Historia andina; 1)

Working paper on Pacajes (one of the five provinces of the Intendancy of Potosí) examines its native rulers, Indian communities, and Catholic priests during the late 18th century. [MTH]

Dargent Chamot, Eduardo. La moneda peruana en el siglo XVII: reflejo de una crisis. See item **2139.**

Durand Flórez, Luis. Criollos en conflicto: Cuzco después de Túpac Amaru. See item **2142.**

Evans, Brian M. The structure and distribution of the Indian population of Alto Peru in the late seventeenth century. See *HLAS* 51:3078.

2193 García Recio, José María. Análisis de una sociedad de frontera: Santa Cruz de la Sierra en los siglos XVI y XVII. Sevilla, Spain: Diputación Provincial de Sevilla, 1988. 534 p.: bibl., ill. (Publicaciones de la Exma. Diputación Provincial de Sevilla: Sección Historia: V centenario del descubrimiento de América; 9)

Prize-winning doctoral dissertation on the Dept. of Santa Cruz de la Sierra in the 16th and 17th centuries examines demographic, economic, social and political events. Major contribution to the regional as well as colonial history of Bolivia. [MTH]

2194 Gato Castaño, Purificación. La promoción social en el Alto Perú: el colegio para huérfanas de Charcas a finales del siglo XVIII. (*Rev. Indias*, 48:184, sept./dic. 1988, p. 735–763)

Describes the establishment of schools for girls (not just for orphans and the daughters of whites but also for Indian girls) by José Antonio de San Alberto, Bishop of Córdoba (1778–83) and Archbishop of La Plata (1782–1804), in Córdoba, Catamarca, Sucre, and Cochabamba. [MTH]

Glave Testino, Luis Miguel. El Virreinato Peruano y la llamada "crisis general" del siglo XVII. See item **2150.**

Gordillo C., José M. and Robert H. Jackson. Mestizaje y proceso de parcelización en la estructura agraria de Cochabamba: el caso de Sipe-Sipe en los siglos XVIII-XIX. See item **2540.**

2195 Historia de Tarija: corpus documental. Dirección de Cristina V. Minutolo de Orsi. Tarija, Bolivia: Prefectura del Depto. de Tarija : Univ. Autónoma Juan Misael Saracho, 1986–87. 4 v.: ill., maps, ports.

Four-volume compilation of 594 sources on the history of the city and dept. of Tarija. All but one of the documents date from the 18th or 19th centuries. The exception is a letter of 1590. [MTH]

2196 Larson, Brooke. Colonialism and agrarian transformation in Bolivia: Cochabamba, 1550–1900. Princeton, N.J.: Princeton Univ. Press, 1988. 375 p.: bibl., ill., index, tables.

Although Larson touches upon 19th-century developments in her concluding chapter, this solid work is primarily a study of the economy and society of the Cochabamba region during the colonial period. An engaging and significant contribution to the agrarian history of all Spanish America and to the history of colonial Bolivia in particular. [MTH]

Mira, Guillermo C. La provisión de azogue en el virreinato del Río de la Plata. See item **2279.**

2197 O'Phelan, Scarlett. Por el rey, religión y la patria: las juntas de gobierno de 1809 en La Paz y Quito. (*Bull. Inst. fr. étud. andin.*, 17:2, 1988, p. 61–80, graphs, map)

Revisionist as well as comparative study of the beginnings of the movement for independence in what would become Bolivia and Ecuador. Illuminates the origin, composition, and downfall of both *juntas*. [MTH]

2198 Querejazu Calvo, Roberto. Chuquisaca, 1539–1825. Sucre, Bolivia: Impr.

Universitaria, 1987. 740 p., 12 leaves of plates: bibl., ill.

Detailed but chatty account of the city of four names (Chuquisaca/La Plata/Charcas/Sucre) during colonial and independence periods. Well-researched although sparse in citations. Author is a lawyer, native son, and scion of a distinguished family. [MTH]

2199 Saguier, Eduardo R. La penuria de agua, azogue y mano de obra en el origen de la crisis minera colonial: el caso de Potosí a fines del siglo XVIII. (*HISLA*, 12, 1988, p. 69–81, bibl.)

Argues that a lack of sufficient water, labor, and mercury plus the decline in ore yield were responsible for the mining crisis of the late 1700s and early 1800s. Covers some of the same ground as Buechler (item **2190**) but not in nearly as much depth. [MTH]

2200 Santamaría, Daniel J. Resistencia anticolonial y movimientos mesiánicos entre los chiriguanos del siglo XVIII. (*Anuario/Rosario*, 13, 1988, p. 169–198)

Discusses two messianic movements that broke out among the Chiriguanos in 1778. Santamaría sees the movements as anticolonial actions reaffirming Chiriguanio identity yet at the same time related to internal transformations of indigenous society. [SMS]

2201 Vázquez Machicado, José. Catálogo descriptivo del material del Archivo de Indias referente a la historia de Bolivia: Sevilla, 1933. La Paz: Ministerio de Educación y Cultura, Instituto Boliviano de Cultura, 1989. 525 p.: ill.

The basic guide to holdings of the Audiencia of Charcas, Buenos Aires, and Lima *fondos* of the Archivo General de Indias on colonial Bolivia. Compiled nearly 60 years ago, the catalog has had only limited availability. [MTH]

2202 Zulawski, Ann. Social differentiation, gender, and ethnicity: urban Indian women in colonial Bolivia, 1640–1725. (*LARR*, 25:2, 1990, p. 93–113)

Cogent reexamination of the roles played by urban Indian women and the extent to which they were subject to discrimination and exploitation. For related article by Glave, see *HLAS 50:639.* [MTH]

CHILE

2203 Astudillo Tapia, Francisco J. and **Carlos S. Ruiz-Tagle Vial.** Historia general de Quilpué. Santiago: Editorial Universitaria, 1986. 159 p.: bibl., ill.

Popular history of Quilpué in central Chile by native sons. [MTH]

Bazán Dávila, Raúl. El patrimonio territorial que recibimos del Reino de Chile. See *HLAS 51:3138.*

2204 Bravo Acevedo, Guillermo. El obraje de Melipilla en el siglo XVII. (*Cuad. Hist.*, 7, julio 1987, p. 119–135, maps, tables)

Microeconomic study of a colonial enterprise, the textile factory of Melipilla (1605–1660), established to produce uniforms for the Ejército Permanente de la Frontera. [MTH]

2205 Carmagnani, Marcello. Le terre dei conquistatori: le origini della proprietà fondiaria nella regione di Santiago del Cili, 1559–1599. (*Quad. Stor.*, 65:2, agosto 1987, p. 453–466, tables)

Detailed, quantitative analysis of the origins of Spanish properties, especially *chacras*, in and around Santiago is based on notarial registers. For version in Spanish, see *HISLA*, vol. 10, 1987, p. 3–14. [MTH]

2206 Cavieres Figueroa, Eduardo. San Felipe en la política fundacional del siglo XVII: espacio urbana y conflicto de intereses. (*Cuad. Hist.*, 7, julio 1987, p. 77–98, map, tables)

Informative study of the origins and early years of San Felipe de Aconcagua is particularly concerned with why the "city" was such a backwater and therefore so slow to grow. [MTH]

2207 Cruz de Amenábar, Isabel. Trajes y moda en Chile 1650–1750: jerarquía social y acontecer histórico. (*Historia/Santiago*, 21, 1986, p. 177–214, bibl.)

Data-rich article on dress by sex and class during the mid-colonial period taken from author's *Arte y sociedad en Chile, 1650–1750* (Santiago: Ediciones Univ. Católica, 1986). Unfortunately not illustrated. [MTH]

2208 Dubinovsky, Adela. El tráfico de esclavos en Chile en el siglo XVIII. (*Cuad.*

Hispanoam., 451–452, enero/feb. 1988, p. 110–160, bibl., photos, ill.)

Revisionist analysis of the traffic in and liberation of slaves in the 18th century includes new archival data. Among other findings, author asserts that far more female blacks were imported than historians have maintained. [MTH]

2209 Ferrando Keun, Ricardo. Y así nació la frontera: conquista, guerra, ocupación, pacificación, 1550–1900. Santiago: Editorial Antártica, 1986. 623 p.: bibl., ill., index, ports. (Biblioteca Francisco de Aguirre; 70)

Detailed, diachronic study of the episodic conquest and eventual settlement of southern Chile. [MTH]

2210 Flusche, Della M. Two families in colonial Chile. Lewiston, N.Y.: E. Mellen Press, 1989. 244 p.: bibl., index. (Latin American studies; 2)

Well-researched case studies of two important families during early colonial period, the patrician Irarrázaval and the nouveaux riches Toro Mazote. Important contribution to the growing historiography of the familiy in Spanish America. [MTH]

2211 Ghigliazza, Raimundo. Historia de la Provincia dominicana de Chile. t. 2. Santiago: Salesianos, 1985. 2 v.: bibl., index.

Vol. 1 of this classic history of the Dominican order in early colonial Chile was published in 1898. Vol. 2 originally appeared in *El mensajero del rosario* between 1919 and 1923 and therefore has been difficult to consult until now. At long last, vol. 2 had been issued separately with added notes and onomastic indexes to both volumes by Ramón Ramírez. Regrettably vol. 1 does not appear to have been reissued. As useful today as when it first appeard. [MTH]

2212 Guarda, Gabriel. Centros de evangelización en Chile, 1541–1826. Santiago: Pontificia Univ. Católica de Chile, 1986. 186 p.: bibl., index. (Anales de la Facultad de Teología, 0069–3596; 35, cuaderno único)

Another of Guarda's exquisitely-detailed, exhaustively researched vademecums. Includes nearly every parish church, chapel, and oratory erected throughout Chile during the entire colonial period (2,736 structures), and is replete with locations, dates, and types of construction. [MTH]

2213 Guarda, Gabriel. La vista del fiscal Dr. Don José Perfecto de Salas al Gobierno de Valdivia y el censo de su población, 1749. (*Historia/Santiago*, 21, 1986, p. 289–354, bibl., tables)

Publishes and analyzes 1749 nominative list of the inhabitants of Valdivia and its jurisdiction. An important historical demographic source and study. [MTH]

2214 Izquierdo Fernández, Gonzalo. Historia de Chile. t. 1. Santiago: Editorial Andrés Bello, 1989. 1 v.: bibl., ill.

Vol. 1 in announced set of three on the history of Chile from prehistoric times through 1970. Intended as a high school and university text, coverage is somewhat superficial, at least for the colonial period. [MTH]

2215 Jara, Alvaro. Trabajo y salario indígena, siglo XVI. Santiago: Editorial Universitaria, 1987. 214 p.: bibl., ill. (Col. Imagen de Chile)

Reprints two standard works by one of Chile's leading historians on Indian labor in the 16th century: 1) "Los Asientos de Trabajo y la Provisión de Mano de Obra para los Noencomenderos en la Cuidad de Santiago, 1586–1600," which originally appeared in *Revista Chilena de Historia y Geografía,* (125, 1967); and 2) *El salario de los indios y los sesmos del oro en la tasa de Santillán* (see *HLAS 24:3723*). Includes a new introduction. [MTH]

Larraín Valdés, Gerardo. Dios, sol y oro: Diego de Almagro y el descubrimiento de Chile. See item **2159.**

2216 Lorenzo, Santiago. Concepto y funciones de las villas chilenas del siglo XVIII. (*Historia/Santiago*, 22, 1987, p. 91–105, bibl.)

Examines the social, religious, military, and economic roles the State intended for the new towns founded in the 18th century. [MTH]

2217 Mariluz Urquijo, José María. Las notas inéditas de Ramón Martínez de Rozas a la Real Ordenanza de Intendentes de 1782. (*in* Congreso del Instituto Internacional de Historia del Derecho Indiano, *7th, Santiago, 1987.* Actas. p. 135–161)

After a brief discussion about Martínez de Rozas, adviser to Ambrosio O'Higgins, Governor of Chile and later Viceroy of

Peru, the author analyzes and reproduces Martínez's marginal notes to the Intendancy legislation. Many of the notes, written in the 1790s, served as a personal update of the original Intendancy plan. [SMS]

2218 Mazzei de Grazia, Leonardo. Fundación y supresión de la primera audiencia de Chile: Concepción, 1567–1575. (*Rev. Indias*, 49:185, enero/abril 1989, p. 27–89)

Detailed review of the short-lived first Audiencia of Chile is based on author's doctoral thesis. [MTH]

2219 Mazzei de Grazia, Leonardo and **Arnoldo Pacheco Silva.** Historia del traslado de la ciudad de Concepción. Concepción, Chile: Editorial de la Univ. de Concepción, 1985. 169 p.: bibl., ill.

Well-documented, detailed analysis of the 1764 relocation and reconstruction of Concepción precipitated by the annihilation of the city during the earthquake of 1751 and necessitated by the repeatedly demonstrated shortcomings of the city's previous site. [MTH]

2220 Mellafe R., Rolando and **René Salinas Meza.** Sociedad y población rural en la formación de Chile actual: La Ligua, 1700–1850. Santiago: Univ. de Chile, 1988. 366 p.: bibl., ill.

Quantitative study of the economy and population of the city and district of La Ligua in the 18th and first half of the 19th century. Most important work on the historical demography of Chile since Robert McCaa's *Marriage and fertility in Chile* (see *HLAS 46:3107*).

2221 Mellén Blanco, Francisco. Manuscritos y documentos españoles para la historia de la Isla de Pascua: la expedición del capitán D. Felipe González de Haedo a la Isla de David. Madrid, Spain: Biblioteca CEHOPU, 1986? 351 p.: bibl., ill.

Exhaustively researched but poorly articulated work on 1770 exploration of Easter Island, following its "discovery" in 1767 by a Spanish pilot. Includes many primary sources in appendix, perhaps the most interesting of which is the long-presumed lost logbook of the pilot of the González de Haedo expedition. [MTH]

2222 Millar Carvacho, René. El obispo Alday y el Probabilismo. (*Historia/Santiago*, 22, 1987, p. 189–212, bibl.)

Demonstrates that Alday was an advocate of the doctrine of probabilism and maintains that he sympathized, at least implicity, with the expelled Jesuits and their teachings. [MTH]

2223 Pumar Martínez, Carmen. Pedro de Valdivia: fundador de Chile. Madrid: Anaya, 1988. 126 p.: bibl., ill. (Biblioteca iberoamericana; 67)

Popular, profusely illustrated biography of the "founder" of Chile. [MTH]

Ramírez Rivera, Hugo Rodolfo. Galería geográfica de Chile: Fray Joseph Francisco Xavier de Guzmán y Lecaroz. See *HLAS 51:3167*.

2224 Sala, José de la. Visita general de la Concepción y su obispado por Fray Pedro Angel de Espiñeyra, su meritísimo prelado, 1765–1769. Estudio preliminar, transcripción y notas de Jorge Pinto Rodríguez. Chillán, Chile: Ediciones Instituto Profesional de Chillán, 1986. 163 p., 2 leaves of plates: bibl., ill., facsims., ports. (Serie Estudios de la región; 2)

Publishes the extensive inspection of the Diocese of Concepción undertaken in the 1760s by Bishop Espiñeyra. Sala was the secretary and notary of the *visita*. An important historical, demographical, and geographic source as well as a revealing statement on the component parishes of the diocese and their parishioners. Solid introduction by Pinto Rodríguez. [MTH]

2225 Salinas C., Maximiliano. Presença africana na religiosidade colonial do Chile. (*in* Escravidão negra e história da Igreja na América Latina e no Caribe. Edição da Comissão de Estudos de História da Igreja na América Latina (CEHILA). Petrópolis, Brazil: Editora Vozes Ltda., 1987, p. 199–213, table)

Essay on the impact of Catholicism on black beliefs and religious practices. [MTH]

2226 Soriano, Ramón. El *Cautiverio feliz* de Francisco Nuñez de Pineda y Bascuñán: cuadro de costumbres, ficción novelesca y crítica política de la guerra de Arauco y de los funcionarios del Reino de Chile. (*Anu. Estud. Am.*, 44, 1987, p. 3–21, suplemento)

Even old works have something new to tell us when viewed from a fresh perspective as Soriano aptly demonstrates in his eminently readable analysis of Núñez de Pineda's thoughts. Topics include the legal philosophy and political organization of the Araucanians who held him captive, the state of the Spanish colony of Chile, and the reforms Núñez de Pineda thought the colony needed if it were to survive and prosper. [MTH]

2227 Urbina B., Rodolfo. La distribución de solares en las villas chilenas del siglo XVII. (*Cuad. Hist.*, 7, julio 1987, p. 99–118, ill., tables)

Analyzes distribution and occupancy of lots in towns founded during the 18th century. Based on coeval maps, *matrículas de vecinos*, and notarial records. [MTH]

2228 Valdés Bunster, Gustavo. Un juicio político en el siglo XVII: el caso Miranda Escobar, 1630–1632. Santiago: Pehuén, 1986. 92 p.: bibl., facsims.

Brief but fascinating study of the tribulations of the notary Miguel de Miranda Escobar who was apprehended, tried, tortured, found guilty, and exiled for having satirized Governor Francisco Laso de la Vega in publicly circulated verses. Miranda Escobar was also deprived of office and stripped of all his belongings, including the clothing he was wearing. [MTH]

2229 Vargas Cariola, Juan Eduardo. Antecedentes sobre las levas en Indias para el ejército de Chile en el siglo XVII, 1600–1662. (*Historia/Santiago*, 22, 1987, p. 335–356, bibl., tables)

Working paper on an unstudied aspect of the Indian wars in Chile: the extent to which colonial authorities had to rely on conscripts, and the geographic origins of those drafted. Apparently, Lima and Quito provided the majority of recruits, at least in the 1600s. [MTH]

2230 Vicuña Mackenna, Benjamín. El primer y el último crimen de la Quintrala. Prólogo de Carlos Ruiz-Tagle. Santiago: Editorial Universitaria, 1987. 104 p.: (Col. Fuera de serie)

Macabre but true story of the infamous 17th-century *encomendera* Catalina de los Ríos y Lisperguer who poisoned her own father and capriciously put lovers as well as slaves to death. Pt. 1, *Los Lisperguer y la Quintrala*, first appeared in 1877 and has been reprinted many times. Pt. 2, *El último de los cuarenta asesinatos de Doña Catalina*

de los Ríos (1884), is here reprinted for the first time. [MTH]

2231 Vivar, Jerónimo de. Crónica de los reinos de Chile. Edición de Angel Barral Gómez. Madrid: Historia 16, 1988. 366 p.: (Crónicas de América; 41)

Scholarly acceptable version of the *Crónica y relación copiosa y verdadera de los reynos de Chile*, a basic source on the conquest and early history of Chile. The text has been modernized and numerous explanatory notes added. [MTH]

RIO DE LA PLATA

2232 Aguilar Piñal, Francisco. La oración fúnebre del arzobispo de La Plata en las honras de Carlos III, 1789. (*Cuad. Hispanoam. Complement.*, 2, dic. 1988, p. 237–242)

Brief biography of José Antonio de San Alberto is followed by an analysis of funeral oration delivered by this royalist archbishop. Unfortunately the text itself is not reproduced. [SMS]

2233 Amaral, Samuel. Rural production and labour in late colonial Buenos Aires. (*J. Lat. Am. Stud.*, 19:2, Nov. 1987, p. 235–278)

Quantitative study of a late colonial *estancia* finds that the Clemente López Osornio landed property was run as a profit-making venture. Contrary to what many historians have postulated, Amaral maintains that haciendas in the Río de la Plata were not acquired primarily for purposes of prestige. [MTH]

2234 Armani, Alberto. Philosophers' dreams and historical reality in the Jesuit "state" of Paraguay, XVII and XVIII centuries. (*Lat.am. Stud.*, 14, 1984, p. 21–41)

Discussion of Jesuit missions of Paraguay as an example of an ideal "Republic" as presented in 17th- and 18th-century European literature, especially in the writings of Muratori and Peramas. [SMS]

2235 Berberián, Eduardo E. Crónicas del Tucumán, siglo XVI. Córdoba, Argentina: Comechingonia, Revista de Antropología e Historia, 1987. 297 p.: bibl., index, maps. (Conquistadores de Indias; 1)

Author attempts to unite the most significant chronicles or fragments of chronicles in order to piece together the early history of Tucumán, the period of conquest and establishment of cities. Each selection is preceded by a brief description of the chronicle and its author. [SMS]

2236 Cadena de Hessling, María Teresa. Enciclonoa: enciclopedia ilustrada del noroeste. v. 1, Historia de Salta. Cartografía de Alicia Fraga de Cuenca y Alejandro Quevedo. Fotografías de Julio César Rodríguez. Salta, Argentina: Ediciones Puna, 1984. 1 v.: bibl., ill.

Vol. 1 of a two-volume history of Salta from colonial times to the present is amply illustrated with maps, drawings, and photographs. Also features chronological charts comparing Salta to nearby provinces, the rest of Spanish America, and Spain. [SMS]

2237 Carbonell de Masy, Rafael. Las reducciones como estrategia del desarrollo rural. (*Supl. Antropol.*, 21:2, dic. 1986, p. 41–66)

Analysis of Jesuit missions from the viewpoint of rural development theory. Author divides mission production into that earmarked for the Jesuit order and that for the Indians themselves. Finds that although the missions engaged in some external commerce, they were primarily involved in agricultural production for their own consumption. Interesting article suggests that Jesuit practices encouraged rural development by clearly fixing their goals, making normative behavior clear, and allowing Indian participation in the development process. Finds that the Jesuits encouraged exchange of technical information among the missions, and were committed to the idea of fixed price to benefit the common good. [SMS]

2238 Cardiel, José. Compendio de la historia del Paraguay, 1780. Estudio preliminar de José María Mariluz Urquijo. Buenos Aires: Fundación para la Educación, la Ciencia y la Cultura, 1984. 212 p.:

Modern edition of an 18th-century history of Paraguay by the Jesuit missionary José Cardiel. An eyewitness to his order's expulsion, Cardiel wrote about the circumstances leading up to this cataclysmic event and about the Indian missions. Mariluz Urquijo provides a fine introduction to Cardiel

and to the tortuous politics which began with the 1750 Treaty of Madrid and ended with the Jesuits being banished from Spanish America. [SMS]

2239 Cardiel, José. Las misiones del Paraguay. Edición de Héctor Sáinz Ollero. Madrid: Historia 16, 1989. 204 p.: bibl., ill. (Crónicas de América; 49)

Another of the writings of Jesuit missionary José de Cardiel (1704–81) who as a missionary in Paraguay and subsequently in exile in Europe wrote at length on the life of and history of the Guarani missions. The work is preceded by a fine essay reviewing Cardiel's life and work. [SMS]

2240 Cauzzi, Teresa. Intervención de la primera Audiencia de Buenos Aires en los casos de arribadas de barcos. (*Res Gesta*, 14/15, julio/dic. 1983—enero/junio 1984, p. 28–34, table)

After reviewing legislation that gave the Audiencia jurisdiction over ships involved in contraband trade, Cauzzi looks at the mid-17th-century Audiencia's actions, finding Audiencia members and other government officials more involved in illegal trade than its suppression. Gives details on 21 ships which escaped prosecution during the 1661–72 period. [SMS]

2241 Chiaramonte, José Carlos. La ilustración en el Río de la Plata: cultura eclesiástica y cultura laica durante el Virreinato. Buenos Aires: Puntosur Editores, 1989. 366 p.: (La Ideología argentina)

Chiaramonte sees attempts to implant Enlightenment ideas in 18th-century Río de la Plata as a difficult and conflictive process because of the basic contradiction in the very idea of a Catholic Enlightenment. Interesting addition to late colonial intellectual history looks at such *porteño* thinkers as Juan Baltasar Macial, Manuel José de Lavarden, Hipólito Vieytes, and Pedro Cerviño, and provides a lengthy selection of documents drawn from their writings. [SMS]

2242 Cooney, Jerry W. Oceanic commerce and Platine merchants, 1796–1806: the challenge of war. (*Americas/Francisc.*, 45:4, April 1989, p. 509–524)

Based on primary and secondary sources (including the little-used *escribanía de marina*), Cooney challenges the traditional interpretation of the "neutral trade"

Spain was forced to give her colonies after she became enmeshed in conflict between England and France. Instead of seeing the merchants of Buenos Aires as passively dependent on newly arriving neutral traders, Cooney argues that between 1797–1804 the merchants of Buenos Aires created their own merchant marine, became deeply involved in international commerce, and were transformed into equal partners in the Atlantic mercantile community. Author underlines *porteño* participation in the slave trade from Africa and Mauritius, local construction of ships as well as purchase of foreign vessels, the founding of a maritime insurance company in Buenos Aires and a deep water port at Ensenada de Barragán, and a bustling trade with Brazil, England, Havana and Germany. Although he fails to recognize that this commerce was created and sustained by a specific subset of *porteño* merchants, this is a solid and important article. [SMS]

2243 Cooney, Jerry W. A riverborne society: life and labor on the *Carrera del Paraguay, 1776–1811. (SECOLAS Ann.,* 20, March 1989, p. 5–19)

Lively description of the effects of riverine transport on the culture of Asunción, the northern terminus of this system, and surroundings areas. Focuses on the building and maintenance of ships, the river journey itself, and daily life and culture of those who moved the agricultural products and raw material of Paraguay down river. [SMS]

2244 Corominas, Jorge. Matrimonios de la Catedral de Tucumán, 1727–1765. Buenos Aires: Fuentes Históricas y Genealógicas Argentinas, 1987. 54 p.:

Complete transcription of the oldest surviving marriage register from San Miguel de Tucumán is a valuable source for historical demography. [SMS]

2245 Doucet, Gastón Gabriel. Los réditos de Quilpo: funcionamiento de una encomienda cordobesa a fines del siglo XVI, 1595–1598. *(Jahrb. Gesch.,* 23, 1986, p. 63–119, tables)

Based on the detailed accounts of a "personal service" encomienda, Doucet describes how an encomienda functioned, its income and expenditures, and the resources which an *encomendero* could use to his or her profit and advantage. Covers the use of

an agent (or *poblero*) to administer the encomienda, tribute payments by the Indians to the *encomendero,* the use of Indian labor for agricultural and pastoral activities and for personal service, as well as the religious services paid for by the *encomendero.* Solid study stresses the survival of the encomienda into the late 16th century and the fact that *encomenderos* controlled both land and labor. [SMS]

2246 Durán, Margarita. De la colonia al Vaticano II: historia de la catequesis en el Paraguay. Bogotá: Consejo Episcopal Latinoamericano (CELAM), 1987. 108 p.: bibl. (Col. V Centenario; 14)

Brief history of the process of catechism in Paraguay from 16th to 20th centuries. [SMS]

2247 Durán, Margarita. Presencia franciscana en el Paraguay. v. 1, 1538–1824. Asunción: Univ. Católica, 1987. 1 v.: bibl., ill. (Biblioteca de estudios paraguayos; 19)

Based on documents in the National Archives of Paraguay and the Curia, Durán studies the multiple activities of Franciscans in Paraguay, including their urban convents and hospices, as well as their missionary activities among the Guarani before and after the expulsion of the Jesuits. Includes information on individual Franciscan missionaries and bishops. [SMS]

2248 Ensinck, Oscar Luis. Propios y arbitrios del Cabildo de Buenos Aires: 1810–1812. *(Res Gesta,* 16/17/18, julio/dic. 1984—enero/dic. 1985, p. 1–9)

Detailed discussion of the income and expenditures for the city of Buenos Aires during the early independence period. Lacks analytic framework. [SMS]

2249 Ezquerra Abadía, Ramón. El madrileño Felipe de Cáceres, Gobernador del Paraguay. *(Rev. Indias,* 47:179, enero/abril 1987, p. 39–82, bibl.)

Biography of a 16th-century Madrid-born *conquistador* and governor of Paraguay. Set against the intrigues and raucous politics of 16th-century Asunción, Cáceres rose to power as an opponent of Governor Cabeza de Vaca, governing the colony from Dec. 1568 to July 1572, when he was arrested on charges of Lutheranism and sent to Spain for an Inquisition trial. [SMS]

2250 Fernández de Burzaco y Barrios, Hugo. Aportes biogenealógicos para un padrón de habitantes del Río de la Plata. v. 1. Buenos Aires: R.J. Pellegrini e Hijo Impresiones, 1986. 1 v.: bibl., port.

Vol. 1 covers letters A and B of a massive genealogical *fichero* compiled by the late Fernández de Burzaco. Entries include information on place and date of birth, marriage, and children for male heads of household who lived in the Río de la Plata area from the 16th to the 19th century. Drawn from a wide variety of archival sources. [SMS]

2251 Frakes, Mark A. Governor Ribera and the War of Oranges on Paraguay's frontiers. (*Americas/Francisc.*, 45:4, April 1989, p. 489–508, map)

Discussion of the 1801 War of Oranges during which the Napoleonic conflict in Europe boiled over to hostilities along the northern frontier of Paraguay with the Portuguese. The author believes the war was important for Paraguay because it revealed the necessity for militia reform and reorganization. It also marked an end to the late colonial northward expansion of the Río de la Plata Viceroyalty. An interesting addition to the literature. [SMS]

2252 Frias, Susana R. Aporte vasco a la población argentina anterior a la "Gran Inmigración." (*Bol. Inst. Am. Estud. Vascos*, 38:151, oct./dic. 1987, p. 164–170; 39:152, enero/marzo 1988, p. 15–21, bibl.)

Discussion of Basque immigration from late 16th to middle of 19th century. Frías finds that the Rio de la Plata was atypical because of the relatively large percentage of Basques in the population from the 17th century onward. The article mentions successful Basque immigrants who married into the local elite. Interesting but could be stronger. [SMS]

2253 Fuente, Ariel de la. Aguardiente y trabajo en una hacienda catamarqueña colonial: La Toma, 1767–1790. (*Anu. IEHS*, 3, 1988, p. 91–121, tables)

Author studies one hacienda during two periods in the late 18th century (1767–69 and 1783–90) to trace changes in the work force from slave to free market labor. He points out the relatively larger economic capacity of haciendas owned by religious corporations, and underlines the negative effects of the Bourbon reforms for the Catamarca region. [SMS]

2254 Gallardo, Guillermo. Acerca de Juan de Garay y la fundación de Buenos Aires. (*Bol. Acad. Nac. Hist./B. Aires*, 53, 1980, p. 289–295, bibl.)

Nit-picking article on the birthplace of Buenos Aires' founder and the original name of the city. [SMS]

2255 Galmarini, Hugo Raúl. Los prisioneros realistas en el Río de la Plata: breve historia de sus desventuras. (*Rev. Indias*, 47:179, enero/abril 1987, p. 103–122, bibl.)

Brief discussion of Spanish (and some French) prisoners taken by the revolutionary government 1810–20. The author finds that in general these prisoners were mistreated, although a few privileged individuals were able to protect themselves. Continues Galmarini's work on the first decade of independence. [SMS]

2256 Garavaglia, Juan Carlos. El campesinado paraguayo y las rebeliones comuneras. (*Supl. Antropol.*, 21:2, dic. 1986, p. 7–23, bibl., tables)

Uses a heavy dose of Marxist terminology (modes of production, units of production, exploitation, and hegemony) to argue that the *comunero* rebellions served as a catalyst in the change from an economy based on production by Indians held in encomienda to one based on peasant production. Analyzes rural census data from 1714–21 for information on the size of the domestic group, sex ratios, widowhood, number of soldiers, percentages of slaves and of *indios originarios*, and ownership of livestock and land, in an attempt to understand the emerging peasantry as economic actors. [SMS]

2257 Garavaglia, Juan Carlos and Jorge Gelman. El mundo rural rioplatense a fines de la época colonial: estudios sobre producción y mano de obra. Buenos Aires: Fundación Simón Rodríguez; Editorial Biblos, 1989. 83 p.: bibl., ill. (Cuadernos Simón Rodríguez; 17)

Two articles by scholars who are among a group reexamining the economic history of rural Buenos Aires. Garavaglia's article, "Producción Cerealera y Producción Ganadera en la Compaña Porteña: 1770–1820" is an enlarged and somewhat reworked version of his *HAHR* article based on *diezmo* figure (*HLAS 48:2810*). The Gelman piece, "Sobre Esclavos, Peones, Gauchos y Campesinos: el Trabajo y los Trabajadores en una Estancia Colonial Rioplatense," continues his analysis of the Estancia de las Vacas records (see items **2261** and **2262**). [SMS]

2258 Garavaglia, Juan Carlos. Reflexiones en torno a la yerba mate (*Ilex Paraguariensis*). (*Supl. Antropol.*, 22:1, junio 1987, p. 7–27)

Applying the ideas of French anthropologist Louis Lewin about the role of caffeine-rich substances in human society, Garavaglia focuses on the social contexts of maté consumption, the moral attack on maté, the failure of yerba maté in Europe and the medicinal claims made for the product. [SMS]

2259 Garavaglia, Juan Carlos. Soldados y campesinos: dos siglos en la historia rural del Paraguay. (*Supl. Antropol.*, 21:1, junio 1986, p. 7–71, graphs, tables)

Thought-provoking essay describes the impact of frontier conditions and changes in the economy on rural inhabitants from colonial times through the republican period. Based on an analysis of the partial censuses of Tebikuary (1714), La Cordillera (1721), Pirayú (1780), and Santa Tecla (1813).

2260 Gelman, Jorge. Economía natural-economía monetaria: los grupos dirigentes de Buenos Aires a principios del siglo XVII. (*Anu. Estud. Am.*, 44, 1987, p. 89–107, appendix, bibl.)

Study of the principal economic activities undertaken by the Buenos Aires elite during the first half of the 17th century. Gelman underlines the growing importance of commerce, smuggling, the slave trade, and credit networks, all concentrated in the hands of a small group of locally-resident merchants and high-ranking bureaucrats. The result was the monetization of the city's economy, the victory of this group (the *confederados*) over the descendants of the original founders of the city (the *benemeritos*), and the growing control by the *confederados* of the rural economy. Gelman's attempt to link these developments to the question of the relationship of a "monetized economy" to a so-called "natural economy" is somewhat problematic. [SMS]

2261 Gelman, Jorge. New perspectives on an old problem and the same source:

the gaucho and the rural history of the colonial Río de la Plata. (*HAHR*, 69:4, Nov. 1989, p. 715–731, tables)

Critique of the Salvatore and Brown article, "Trade and proletarianization in late colonial Banda Oriental" (item **2298**), argues that very different conclusions about the nature of the economy and the labor force can be drawn from the same source, the correspondence of the *Estancia de las Vacas*. Gelman suggests that the *estancia* reacted as other small producers did to the periodic closing of the Atlantic trade, increasing the production of hides to maintain a minimum income. Furthermore he challenges Salvatore's and Browns's picture of a willful, lazy, fluctuating labor force by arguing that peons' response to the *estancia's* demand for labor was influenced by the growth of wheat cultivation which drew from the same labor pool at specific times of year. Gelman concludes that labor was provided by a peasant (rather than gaucho) labor force which had several employment alternatives. See item **2297** for rejoinder by Salvatore and Brown. [SMS]

2262 Gelman, Jorge. Una región y una chacra en la campaña rioplatense: las condiciones de la producción triguera a fines de la época colonial. (*Desarro. Econ.*, 28:112, enero/marzo 1989, p. 577–600, tables)

Gelman continues his work based on *Estancia de las Vacas* records, adding *diezmo* information to his sources. Stressing the complex nature of rural society, this article looks at wheat production in the Colonia region concentrating on labor force and grain production. Gelman finds a large number of producers, ranging from *estancieros* and *chacra* owners to renters and squatters. Most production was between 11 and 40 *fanegas* per year. Wheat cultivation was marked by strong seasonality, and a large demand occured only in the January harvest season. Labor was expensive. Furthermore the low yields and low prices paid in Buenos Aires produced little or no profit. "Large" producers had little incentive to expand production, but small producers, making use of family labor, were able to survive in spite of a series of obstacles. Important article with interesting implications for the study of women's labor in the rural sector. [SMS]

2263 Gelman, Jorge. Sobre el carácter del comercio colonial y los patrones de inversión de un comerciante en el Río de la

Plata del siglo XVIII. (*Bol. Inst. Hist. Ravignani*, 3:1, 1989, p. 51–69, tables)

Continuing his work on colonial commerce based on the records of Domingo Belgrano Pérez, Gelman presents a detailed analysis of one merchant's activities during three sample periods. Stresses that *porteño* merchants not only diversified investments, but had a wide variety of markets and products to counterbalance their highly risky trade. Solid study. [SMS]

2264 Historia de Nicolás I, Rey del Paraguay y Emperador de los Mamelucos. Madrid: Ediciones A. Machado, 1986? 96 p.: ill. (Biblioteca Antonio Machado de Obras Raras y Curiosas; 5)

Lavish edition of the spurious "history" of Nicolás I, the self-proclaimed king who, in conjunction with the Jesuits, supposedly led the Guarani uprisings (*guerra guaranitica*) of 1752–53. This history which circulated through Europe and America was used by the Spanish Crown to fuel anti-Jesuit sentiment. [SMS]

2265 Itatí (Argentina). Cabildo. Actas del Cabildo de Itatí: desde el 7 de febrero de 1793 hasta el 24 de diciembre de 1798. Prólogo de Alberto A. Rivera. Corrientes, Argentina: Instituto de Investigaciones Geohistóricas, 1980. 104 p. (Documentos de geohistoria regional; 1)

Transcription of the rather brief *Cabildo* sessions held in the town of Itati (Corrientes) covers the years 1793–98 and supplements *Acuerdos del Viejo Cabildo de Itati* (1930). An interesting document reflecting the concerns and jurisdiction of an Indian community. [SMS]

2266 Johnson, Lyman L. Los efectos económicos y políticos del gasto militar en el Buenos Aires colonial. (*HISLA*, 9, 1987, p. 41–57, bibl., tables)

Looks at Bourbon military policy concentrating on the social and economic effects of growing expenditures aimed at strengthening Buenos Aires' strategic position. While military expenditures affected the regional economy, Johnson points out that military recruitment and salary remained problems throughout much of the period, and were remedied only after the first British invasion. He sees the British invasion as a turning point in the city's level of militarization, also

producing a change in organizational style and leadership of the militia. Suggests that military expenditures tended to fuel consumption rather than production, and that they were closely linked to rising cost of skilled and unskilled labor and rising consumer prices. [SMS]

2267 Johnson, Lyman L. The role of apprenticeship in colonial Buenos Aires. (*Rev. Hist. Am.*, 103, enero/junio 1987, p. 7–30, bibl., tables)

Solid discussion of the manner in which apprenticeship, a method of artisan recruitment, functioned in late-18th-century Buenos Aires. Johnson depicts the city as a racially and ethnically hierarchical society in which guilds never existed legally. By close analysis of the extant apprenticeship contracts found in the Archivo General de la Nación in Argentina, he finds that the use of formal apprenticeships varied greatly from industry to industry, but that, on the whole, apprentices tended to be unprotected, poorly disciplined *casta* boys who, it was feared, would fall into crime if not provided with a structured environment. [SMS]

2268 Johnson, Lyman L. The scale and composition of wealth held by the working class of colonial Buenos Aires. (*in* Rocky Mountain Council on Latin American Studies, *36th, Fort Collins, Colo., 1988.* Proceedings. Las Cruces, N.M.: Center for Latin American Studies, New Mexico State Univ., p. 43–54, tables)

Working paper on heretofore ignored topic; the kind and scale of movable and immovable property accumulated by the artisan class in late-colonial Buenos Aires and the extent to which these alternative sources of income supplemented wage earnings. [MTH]

2269 Jornadas de Historia de Salta, 1st, Salta, Argentina, 1982. Actas. Edición del Complejo Museo Histórico del Norte, Asociación Amigos del Cabildo. Salta, Argentina: Aráoz Anzoátegui Impresores, 1984. 313 p.: bibl., ill.

Series of micro-studies by both established and younger scholars on the history of Salta, concentrating on the colonial period. Topics considered include: subsistence during the first 100 years of the city's existence; early encomiendas; the Cabildo; the frontier; and criminal justice. [SMS]

2270 Labor de investigación, 1982: Universidad Nacional de Córdoba, Facultad de Filosofía y Humanidades, Instituto de Estudios Americanistas "Doctor Enrique Martínez Paz." Córdoba, Argentina: Dirección General de Publicaciones, 1984. 257 p.: bibl., facsims., tables.

Seven articles dealing with the history of Córdoba include two of special interest to colonialists: 1) "La Aplicación del Derecho de Doble Almojarifazgo en Córdoba" by Norma Clara Galván de Somoza; and 2) "Pueblos, Capillas y Lugares de la Antigua Provincia de Córdoba del Tucumán, Según el Censo de 1778" by Dora Estela Celton de Peranovich and Emiliano Endrek. The degree to which academic life has been politicized in Argentina is reflected in a rather bizarre disclaimer at the beginning of the publications which mentions that these articles were written before the return of democracy in 1983, and that the editorial commission in place in 1984 does not necessarily subscribe to the same ideas. [SMS]

2271 Maeder, Ernesto J.A. Un evangelizador criollo: Roque González de Santa Cruz, 1576–1628. (*Criterio/Buenos Aires,* 61:2010, julio 1988, p. 332–337, bibl.)

Biography of a Creole-born Jesuit missionary recently elevated to sainthood by Pope John Paul II. González de Santa Cruz served in missions among the Guaycurus and Guaraníes before being killed in 1628 during an Indian uprising in the town of Caaró. [SMS]

2272 Mariluz Urquijo, José María. La *Gazeta* de Buenos Ayres, 1764. (*Invest. Ens.,* 38, 1988, p. 449–483)

Places the creation of a newspaper in Buenos Aires within context of the general Enlightenment growth of a Spanish press, and the growing need of *porteños* (especially merchants) to have good information about world events. Reproduces handwritten *Gazeta,* published three times between June and Sept. 1764. [SMS]

2273 Mariluz Urquijo, José María. Proyección y limites del comercio vasco en el Río de la Plata. (*in* Jornadas sobre el comercio vasco con América en el siglo XVIII y la Real Compañía Guipuzcoana de Caracas en el II Centenario de Carlos III, *Bilbao, Spain, 1988.* Los vascos en América: Actas. Bilbao, Spain: Laida, 1988, p. 107–133)

Concentrating on the period prior to "free trade," Mariluz Urquijo discusses the ways in which Basque merchants tied to the Buenos Aires trade were able to press their demands in Madrid. Article spotlights the *Compañía de Buenos Aires,* a trading company founded in 1752 by three Basque merchants closely tied to Spanish officialdom to monopolize trade between Cádiz and Buenos Aires. [SMS]

2274 Mariluz Urquijo, José María. El Virreinato del Río de la Plata en la época del Marqués de Avilés, 1799–1801. 2a ed. Buenos Aires: Plus Ultra, 1987. 670 p.: (Col. del V centenario)

New and expanded edition of a carefully detailed study of the economic, intellectual, cultural, military, and civil problems and policies during the Viceregal administration of the Marqués de Avilés. Mariluz believes that this period is one in which Enlightenment ideas made major inroads into *porteño* intellectual circles. A basic and important study. [SMS]

2275 Martínez de Sánchez, Ana María. Contribución al estudio de los abastos en América durante el período hispánico: el abasto de carne a la ciudad de Córdoba, 1783–1810. (*Jahrb. Gesch.,* 23, 1986, p. 189–207, table)

Description of the various mechanisms adopted to insure a steady supply of meat to the Córdoba market; yearly and seasonal variations in the supply; the Cabildo's efforts to control prices; and the groups involved in the production, processing and sale of the commodity. [SMS]

2276 Mayo, Carlos A.; Samuel Amaral; Juan Carlos Garavaglia; and Jorge Gelman. Polémica: gauchos, campesinos y fuerza de trabajo en la campaña rioplatense colonial. (*Anu. IEHS,* 2, 1987, p. 23–70)

Another chapter in the on-going and important discussion on the nature of the rural work force in colonial Buenos Aires. Mayo opens the debate by pointing out a central contradiction: that the rural economy was plagued by both a shortage of labor and an excess of unemployed (*vagos*). He argues that direct access to cattle, land, and housing allowed the rural population to survive without working. Amaral, basing his work on the account books of the López de Osonio *estan-*

cia counters that the problem was one of seasonal and unstable labor demand rather than supply. He sees the countryside as populated by people who worked as seasonal laborers in order to survive. Garavaglia changes the focus of the debate slightly, pondering whether the countryside was populated by *gauchos* or *campesinos.* He stresses the large number of wheat cultivators, and the existence of a migratory rural population who provided supplementary labor during the harvest season. Although he underlines regional variation, he finds few *gauchos.* Gelman tends to agree with Mayo on the question of direct access to land, but like Amaral, accents the seasonal demands on labor. He also argues that the *estancias* had nothing to gain from stabilizing their work force. [SMS]

2277 Mayo, Carlos A. Sociedad rural y militarización de la frontera en Buenos Aires, 1737–1810. (*Jahrb. Gesch.*, 24, 1987, p. 251–263)

Responding to increased Indian raids between 1737–85, the colonial government attempted to militarize the frontier. Interesting article investigates resistance of local frontier population to attempts to organize them into an effective militia. Mayo suggests that rural itinerant behavior, combined with a demand for labor, made it easy to escape militia service, while the seasonal needs of cattle raising and farming fed the hostility of the rural population. [SMS]

2278 Michieli, Catalina Teresa. La región de Cuyo y sus naturales a través de la crónica de Gerónimo de Bibar y su confrontación con otras fuentes. Los indígenas de la Punta de los Venados a la llegada de los españoles. San Juan, Argentina: Univ. Nacional de San Juan, Facultad de Filosofía, Humanidades y Artes, Instituto de Investigaciones Arqueológicas y Museo, 1984. 39 p.: bibl. (Publicaciones; 10)

First article briefly discusses a 16th-century chronicle describing Francisco de Villagra's discovery of the Cuyo region. Michieli finds this chronicle especially useful because of its detailed information on flora, fauna and indigenous people of the region. The second piece revises two theories on the origin of the indigenous groups native to the region around Punta de los Venados. Author suggests that neither the *huarpes* nor the *co-*

mechingones theories are correct, and draws on evidence in 16th-century chronicles to suggest that these Indians were related to Pampas tribes. [SMS]

2279 Mira, Guillermo C. La provisión de azogue en el virreinato del Río de la Plata. (*Cuad. Hispanoam. Complement.*, 2, dic. 1988, p. 209–222, photo)

After a lengthy discussion of the Bourbon reforms in general and the Viceroyalty of Río de la Plata in particular, the author discusses the mercury supply for Potosí. He sees the shift from mercury supplied from Huancavelica to that supplied by Almadén as part of Viceroy Cevallos' program to break Potosí's dependence on Peru. Concentrates on Superintendent Sanz's problems with supply, price, and distribution of this crucial metal against a background of viceregal political wrangling. Interesting article, but contains no footnotes and only one bibliographic citation. [SMS]

2280 Moreno Alonso, Manuel. Las cosas de España y la política americana de Carlos III en Inglaterra: las observaciones del conde de Malmesbury durante la crisis de las Malvinas. (*Cuad. Hispanoam. Complement.*, 2, dic. 1988, p. 95–114)

Analysis of the 1768–70 Anglo-Spanish crisis over the Falkland (Malvinas) Islands as reported by a young English diplomat in Madrid, James Harris, future Count Malmesbury. Author sees this episode as illustrative of Bourbon foreign policy as well as English perceptions of that policy and of Spain in general. [SMS]

2281 Mörner, Magnus. Experiencia jesuíta en el Paraguay: los hechos y los mitos, lo corriente y lo peculiar. (*Lat.am. Stud.*, 14, 1984, p. 65–79, bibl., map)

Additional comments and reflections on Mörner's earlier path-breaking work on the Jesuit missions. He presents a seven-part chronology of the "Jesuit State," while stressing the need to understand their enterprise within the framework of Jesuit history and colonial Latin American history. Interesting article. [SMS]

2282 Moutoukias, Zacarías. Burocracia, contrabando y autotransformación de las elites: Buenos Aires en el siglo XVII. (*Anu. IEHS*, 3, 1988, p. 213–248)

Study of the relationship between the local commercial elite and Crown representatives during a period of widespread illicit trade argues that corruption on the part of local officials alone fails to explain the trade, that the Crown benefited enormously from this trade, and that high ranking soldiers, magistrates and merchants were closely intertwined. Also argues that the *navios de registro*, the *situado* and the participation of magistrates and military officers in the economic life of the colony were all interrelated in a logical system. [SMS]

2283 Moutoukias, Zacarías. Contrabando y control colonial en el siglo XVII: Buenos Aires, el Atlántico y el espacio peruano. Buenos Aires: Centro Editor de América Latina, 1988. 217 p.: bibl., ill. (Bibliotecas universitarias: Historia)

Interesting and important book focuses on the economic relations of Buenos Aires, the interior provinces, and Europe, as well as the role of the city as a center of bureaucracy, and the relationship between the city's commecial structure and its political one. Moutoukias uses a wealth of statistical information garnered from archives in Spain and Holland to suggest that, although silver production of Alto Perú linked Buenos Aires and Tucumán with the mines, this relationship was more complex and more elastic than previously has been assumed. Buenos Aires became more than a simple exporter of metals; it also played an important role in importing European goods and African slaves for growing regional markets. Moutoukias also stresses the overlapping relationship between commerce, the rural sector, and the State, a relationship which defined *porteño* society until the period of Independence and resulted in prosperity and demographic growth for the city and its surrounding regions. [SMS]

2284 Moutoukias, Zacarías. Power, corruption, and commerce: the making of the local administrative structure in seventeenth-century Buenos Aires. (*HAHR*, 68:4, Nov. 1988, p. 771–801, appendix, tables)

Important study argues that the late-17th-century Spanish Crown financed its administrative and military structure in Buenos Aires from legal, semi-legal and illegal commerce. Moutoukias documents the entrance of large numbers of Dutch ships into the port, ostensibly seeking "refuge." He outlines a system of regular and structured contraband trade aided and abetted by a corps of Crown authorities who themselves engaged in commerce and were allied to the city's commercial elite. [SMS]

2285 Moyano, Hugo. La organización de los gremios en Córdoba: sociedad artesanal y producción artesanal, 1810–1820. Córdoba, Argentina: Centro de Estudios Históricos, 1986. 243 p.: bibl., ill.

After a brief discussion of the creation of urban guilds in late-18th-century Córdoba, Moyano looks at the demographic structure of both urban and rural artisan groups as well as production of export goods such as ponchos, blankets, soap, and military provisions. Moyano finds both urban and rural labor forces during this period to be overwhelmingly young and female. [SMS]

2286 Müller, Klaus. Comercio interno y economía regional en Hispanoamérica colonial: aproximación cuantitativa a la historia económica de San Miguel de Tucumán, 1784–1809. (*Jahrb. Gesch.*, 24, 1987, p. 265–334, graphs, tables)

Basing his analysis primarily on *alcabala* records, Müller discusses the role of Tucumán as an intermediary in the Buenos Aires-Alto Perú traffic, a producer of goods (cotton and woolen goods, cattle, mules, horses, wheat and fruit) for a variety of markets, and a supplier of local markets. This interesting study of commerce questions the importance of the applicability of a dependency model to the general economic development of the region. [SMS]

2287 Oddo, Vicente. Santiago del Estero: orígenes de un hagiogeotopónimo y de la ciudad que el mismo nombra. Santiago del Estero, Argentina: Editorial El Liberal, 1987. 171 p.: bibl., ill.

After reviewing the importance of the name "Santiago" (St. James) in European and Spanish culture, this rather superficial volume discusses the origin of the name of the city of Santiago del Estero. [SMS]

2288 Olivares, Itamar. José Ramón Milá de la Roca: un "afrancesado" du Río de la Plata. (*Caravelle*, 51, 1988, p. 5–21)

Discussion of Milá de la Roca, an important Montevideo merchant and *saladero* owner and his ties during the decade of the 1790s to the French Pacific Ile Bourbon (Mauritius) and later to France itself. The author sees Milá, who later went to Napoleonic Spain as a deputy to the Bayonne Assembly, as representative of a frustrated Creole bourgeoisie influenced by French liberal ideas. [SMS]

2289 Otero Clotet, Orlando. Tomás de Rocamora, fundador de pueblos. Buenos Aires: F.A. Colombo, 1983. 85 p., 1 folded leaf of plates: bibl., facsims., ill.

Standard biography of Rocamora, an American-born military officer instrumental in setting up Spanish settlements in the Gualeguay Grande region (present-day Entre Ríos) in the 1780s. Reproduces several documents. [SMS]

2290 Palermo, Miguel Angel. La innovación agropecuaria entre los indígenas pampeano-patagónicos: genesis y procesos. (*Anu. IEHS*, 3, 1988, p. 43–90, maps)

Traces the rapid changes in both domestic animals and cultigens, and the important transformations produced in the economy and society of the autonomous tribes of the Pampas and the Patagonian region. Palermo stresses that these tribes were not forced to adopt these innovations, but rather chose them. These choices tied the Indian economy to that of the Spaniards through the exchange of animals for manufactured goods and imported primary materials. [SMS]

Prieto, María del Rosario. Relación entre clima, condiciones ambientales y asentamientos humanos en la provincia de Mendoza en los siglos XVI, XVII y XVIII. See *HLAS 51:3123.*

2291 Rivarola Paoli, Juan Bautista. Organización hacendística en la época colonial. (*Hist. Parag.*, 23, 1986, p. 159–214, tables)

Detailed article explains the organization, terminology, and various funds collected by the Asunción treasury. Useful basic information for understanding the revenues collected by this branch of the royal fisc. [SMS]

2292 Rodríguez Molas, Ricardo E. Esclavitud africana, religión y origen étnico. (*Ibero-Am. Arch.*, 14:2, 1988, p. 125–147, bibl.)

Author concentrates on African groups belonging to three principal "nations"— Bantu, Guinea-Sudanese, and Sudanese— found in 18th- and 19th-century Buenos Aires, and the survival of their cultures. Most of the data for this article are from 19th-century sources, but strangely there is no mention of the work of George Reid Andrews. [SMS]

2293 Rosal, Miguel Angel. Transportes terrestres y circulación de mercancias en el espacio rioplatense, 1781–1811. (*Anu. IEHS*, 3, 1988, p. 123–159, graphs, tables)

Study of land transport based on a sample of commercial manifests looks at total traffic over the various routes linking Buenos Aires to the interior, the number of carts and mules involved, and the speed of the system. Rosal also attempts to calculate the amount of capital invested in overland shipping. He suggests that many of those involved in moving goods were not professional carters, but rather country folk and small merchants who filled in a growing demand for transportation. [SMS]

2294 Saeger, James S. Eighteenth-century Guaycuruan Missions in Paraguay. (*in* Indian-religious relations in colonial Spanish America. Edited by Susan E. Ramírez. Syracuse, N.Y.: Maxwell School of Citizenship and Public Affairs, Syracuse Univ., 1989, p. 55–86)

In-depth look at the Guaycuruan missions founded in Paraguay 1760–82. The Guaycuruans (also called Mbayas) were a people native to the northeastern Chaco who were eventually forced into missions because of ecological damage to their food sources. Saeger details the founding of these late Jesuit missions and discusses the complex process of acculturation. Suggests that the Guaycuruans adapted too well to Spanish society, passing from their missions to rural Hispanic society. Also included is a comparison of these missions with the more successful Guaycuruan reductions of Santa Fé. An important and interesting article. [SMS]

2295 Saguier, Eduardo R. Economic impact of commercial capital on credit transactions: Buenos Aires in the early seventeenth century. (*Anu. Estud. Am.*, 44, 1987, p. 109–139, bibl., appendix)

Study of economic cycles caused by both external and internal factors in the first half of the 17th century, and the effect of these cycles on cash and commercial and mortgage credit. Saguier stresses the paradox that in times of peace and prosperity, Buenos Aires suffered from a shortage of coin as trade drained silver from the port, while during periods of commercial stagnation, there was an oversupply of cash. He underlines the correlation between credit transactions and general economic prosperity as reflected in other measures such as carts traveling to the interior and the hiring of Indian labor. [SMS]

2296 Saguier, Eduardo R. Economic impact of Indian inmigration and commercial capital on the formation of a colonial labor force: the case of Buenos Aires in the early seventeenth century. (*Rev. Hist. Am.*, 101, enero/junio 1986, p. 65–104, bibl., tables)

After a detailed overview of the historiography on the demand for Indian labor, and the resultant salary or wage relations, Saguier examines early-17th-century Indian migration to Buenos Aires, the "social relations of production" into which these migrants were placed, and the impact of this system on the survival of the encomiendas of the interior provinces. He argues that wages paid to Indians were neither feudal nor capitalist income, but rather an intermediate type ruled by the interest rate on commercial capital. Regardless of what these wages represented, Saguier concludes that the ability to earn wages made Buenos Aires an attractive place to migrate. [SMS]

2297 Salvatore, Ricardo Donato and **Jonathan C. Brown.** The old problem of gauchos and rural society. (*HAHR*, 69:4, Nov. 1989, p. 733–745)

Rejoinder to Gelman's critique (item **2261**) asserts that Gelman: 1) overestimates the demand for labor during the wheat harvest; 2) misunderstands the capitalist relationship of the *estancia* to the market; 3) minimizes the shortage of labor in the rural economy; 4) overlooks the varied production of the colonial *estancia* which continually balanced labor demands; and 4) wrongly transforms itinerant gauchos into a stable peasantry. Authors see the lack of repeat

workers and the need for slaves as permanent workers as proof that the *estancia* suffered from a too small work force because gauchos insisted on maintaining their cultural independence. They argue that rural people were not entirely creatures of the economic system, but could in turn shape that system and their own lives. A most interesting debate. [SMS]

2298 Salvatore, Ricardo Donato and **Jonathan C. Brown.** Trade and proletarianization in late colonial Banda Oriental: evidence from the *Estancia de Las Vacas*. (*HAHR*, 67:3, Aug. 1987, p. 431–459)

Although the absentee owners of the *Estancia de Las Vacas* sought to impose regular work hours and production quotas, the gauchos successfully resisted attempts at labor rationalization. According to the authors, the vagaries of the world market for hides favored the gauchos' preference for leisure, independence, and rustling. In brief, owners had to accept local conditions or face profit-depleting opposition. [MTH]

2299 Santiago, Rafael de. Fortificaciones de la Bahía e Isla de Maldonado. (*Bol. Hist. Ejérc.*, 271/274, 1986, p. 67–152, appendix, ill., map, photos)

Traces the Maldonado fort from the earliest glimmerings of the idea of fortifying the mouth of the Río de la Plata around present-day Punta del Este in 1751, through the construction of the fort, to the last mention of the military bastion in 1826. Interested solely in military and defense aspects of the project and includes a lengthy transcription of documents. A map showing the fort's relationship to Montevideo would have been helpful. [SMS]

2300 Silva, Hernán. El comercio ilícito en el Río de la Plata. (*Todo es Hist.*, 260, feb. 1989, p. 70–81, bibl., ill., maps, photos)

Concentrates on illegal commerce during the Viceregal period. Based largely on secondary sources. Although illicit trade continued after 1776, Silva's contention that smuggling supplied Buenos Aires with low-priced articles of mass consumption attractive to the urban poor is somewhat overstated. [SMS]

2301 Simposio sobre las Tres Primeras Décadas de las Misiones Jesuíticas de Guaraníes, 1609–1642, *1st, Posadas, Argen-*

tina, 1979. Actas. Posadas, Argentina?: Ediciones Montoya, 1986. 202 p.: bibl., map.

Seventeen short papers deal with the early Jesuit missions in Argentina, Paraguay, Uruguay, and Brazil. Contributions tend to concentrate on specific mission settlements. [SMS]

2302 Socolow, Susan Migden. Acceptable partners: marriage choice in colonial Argentina, 1778–1810. (*in* Sexuality and marriage in colonial Latin America. Edited by Asunción Lavrin. Lincoln, Neb.: Univ. of Nebraska Press, 1989, p. 209–251, facsims., tables)

Superior analysis of late colonial lawsuits regarding choice of spouse in Buenos Aires and Córdoba. At issue were the social, usually the "racial," and/or economic status of the protested partner. Parents had the legal right to forbid children to marry a particular partner, and offspring had the right to challenge through the courts parental rejection of the betrothed. [MTH]

2303 Socolow, Susan Migden. Los cautivos españoles en las sociedades indígenas: el contacto cultural a través de la frontera argentina. (*Anu. IEHS*, 2, 1987, p. 99–136, tables)

After a discussion of the taking of human captives along the frontier during the 18th and early 19th centuries, author analyzes the list of captives freed by Rosas during his campaign of 1833 to elucidate who was seized and why. Women made up the largest group of prisoners and were always an object of Indian raids, while males were usually only captured at a young age. [SMS]

2304 Soler, Amadeo P. Sebastián Gaboto, el primer argentino. Rosario, Argentina: Editorial Amalevi, 1984. 222 p.: bibl., ill.

Biography of 16th-century naval captain and explorer, founder of the ill-fortuned fort of *Sancti Spiritus*, first Spanish settlement in the Río de la Plata. Soler sets the life of Gaboto against the politics and intrigues of the court of Charles V. An urban history of Puerto Gaboto is appended to this study. [SMS]

2305 Storni, P. Hugo. Consideraciones sobre el *Catálogo de los Jesuitas de la pro-*

vincia del Paraguay, Cuenca del Plata, 1585–1768. (*Lat.am. Stud.*, 14, 1984, p. 9–19)

Brief description of Storni's catalog of Jesuits in Paraguay followed by a rather unsophisticated attempt at a quantitative analysis of these men over a 200 year period. Included in the Paraguayan region was much of present-day Argentina, Bolivia, Uruguay, and Chile, as well as regions of Brazil. [SMS]

2306 Velázquez, Rafael Eladio. Poblamiento del Paraguay colonial. (*Estud. Parag.*, 14:1/2, dic. 1986, p. 167–182)

Concentrating on Spaniards, non-missionized Guaraníes and mestizos, Velázquez divides the population history of Paraguay into three periods: 1) the conquest era of expansion ending in 1621; 2) the 17th-century period of demographic crisis which ended with the *comunero* revolt of 1721; and 3) the 18th-century period of demographic expansion caused by both natural increase and immigration. [SMS]

2307 Villegas, Juan. Oficios, mano de obra y trabajos en el puerto de Montevideo, 1774–1775. Montevideo: Instituto de Estudios Genealógicos del Uruguay, 1985. 54 p.

Brief study based on receipts issued by the *administración de correos* of Montevideo, the agency responsible for provisioning mail boats arriving from La Coruña, presents some wage and price data. Ninety-seven receipts for a variety of services are reproduced in the appendix. [SMS]

2308 Wentzel, Claudia. El comercio del litoral de los ríos con Buenos Aires: el area del Paraná 1783–1821. (*Anu. IEHS*, 3, 1988, p. 161–210, tables)

Study of commerce between regions bordering the Paraná river and Buenos Aires underlines both the growing importance of this region during the Viceregal period and the effect of Independence on trade. Uses commercial manifest to examine overall trade, as well as four regions: Paraguay, Corrientes, Santa Fé and Paraná. Finds that while trade increased overall, during the period 1760–90 a wide variety of products were exported from the region, while after 1790 trade tended to be more concentrated in *yerba maté*, tobacco, hides, and other cattle products. [SMS]

19th and 20th Centuries
Venezuela

WINTHROP R. WRIGHT, *Professor of History, University of Maryland, College Park*

VENEZUELAN HISTORIANS HAVE FINALLY ABANDONED the patron saints of national independence as a major focus of their attention. The move away from the cult of heroes has encouraged a new generation of Venezuelans to treat a rich variety of post-1830 topics, including questions related to the nation's troubled agro-export economy and her difficult political history.

Two works on the labor policies of commercial farming demonstrate the high level of historical analysis now given to agriculture and labor. The first, by Gastón Caravello and Josefina Ríos de Hernández (item **2315**), explains the long decline in the role of haciendas in the export economy, which the authors attribute to an inability to control their labor forces. The second, by Aníbal Arcondo (item **2309**) shows that coffee producers failed to attract labor because of their unwillingness to offer incentives. Morella Barreto's guide to labor newspapers from 1846–1937 (item **2310**) complements these studies.

Thanks to the ongoing efforts of Ramón J. Velásquez, Mary Floyd's excellent dissertation on the Guzmán Blanco Administration has appeared in Spanish translation (item **2319**). Three other works on 19th-century politics merit attention. Nikita Harwich Vallenilla (item **2320**) has masterfully challenged Germán Carrera Damas' emphasis upon the cult of Bolívar in an analysis of the origins of the "official history" taught at Venezuelan secondary schools during the 19th century. Similarly, Domingo Irwin G. (item **2322**) has written a provocative study of the different types of caudillos and caudillism found in Venezuela. A short biographical sketch of Codazzi's military/political career in Barinas (item **2329**) offers another insight into Venezuelan politics during the 19th century.

Works on the 20th century offer an equally broad and rich list of topics. Susan Berglund (item **2311**) and Ermila de Veracoechea (item **2336**) have provided comprehensive studies of immigration, the former dealing with the post-World War II period, the latter giving an overview of policies during the entire national period. Like Berglund, Margarita López Maya (item **2325**) has turned to unused archival material to give a statistical analysis of voting patterns during the elections of 1946 and 1947, patterns which proved essential in legitimizing Acción Democrática's rise to power through an open system of voting. Winthrop R. Wright (items **2338** and **2337**) has provided two studies of racial attitudes, one which focuses on a racial incident in 1945, the other a larger study of changing racial and national images since the colonial era. In an essay on Venezuelan positivism and modernity, Harwich Vallenilla offers a philosophical analysis of the contributions of the positivists to the evolution of modern Venezuela (item **5364**).

Trinidadian historian Kelvin Singh has made two significant contributions to Venezuelan history through the use of Trinidadian and British records, as well as US and Venezuelan archives. His well-documented study of attempts by 19th-century Venezuelan rebels to launch attacks from Trinidad (item **2331**) not only illustrates a basic cause of tension between Britain and Venezuela, but also underlines Venezuela's weakness at the negotiating table. Singh's other work (item **2330**) points out the ineffectiveness of the López Contreras Government to follow Mexi-

co's lead in establishing real control of the nation's petroleum reserves and is a well-balanced picture of the post-Gómez political scene in Venezuela.

2309 Arcondo, Aníbal. Oferta de trabajo y expansión agraria: la agricultura venezolana del período de Guzmán Blanco, 1873–1889. (*in* Población y mano de obra en América Latina. Recopilación de Nicolás Sánchez-Albornoz. Madrid: Alianza Editorial, 1985, p. 299–311)

Analyzes why coffee producers complained of lack of workers during harvest periods. Suggests inelasticity did exist, but that harvest rather than prices determined need for labor. Wages seldom reflected market value of coffee, whether in good times or bad. In latter, producers wanted to cut wages drastically, but gave no large incentives in good times.

2310 Barreto, Morella. Un siglo de prensa laboral venezolana: hemerografía obrero-artesanal, 1846–1937. Caracas: Monte Avila Editores; Instituto Autónomo Biblioteca Nacional y de Servicios de Bibliotecas, 1986. 341 p., 8 p. of plates: bibl., facsims., indexes.

Useful guide to newspapers dedicated to workers' and artisans' causes includes brief citations of specific articles and notes on presses and their directors. Helpful research tool.

Berglund, Susan and **Humberto Hernández Calimán.** Los de afuera: un estudio analítico del proceso migratorio en Venezuela, 1936–1985. See *HLAS 51:4768.*

2311 Berglund, Susan. . . . Y los últimos serán los primeros: la inmigración masiva en Venezuela, 1945–1961. (*in* Población y mano de obra en América Latina. Recopilación de Nicolás Sánchez-Albornoz. Madrid: Alianza Editorial, 1985, p. 313–326)

Brief study of post-World War II immigration data shows that the relatively small numbers of immigrants to Venezuela came predominantly from Spain, the Canary Islands, Italy, and Portugal. Attributes the disproportionate presence of immigrants among management and skilled professions to better education and technical skills.

2312 Betancourt, Rómulo. Hombres y villanos. 1a ed. venezolana. Caracas: Grijalbo, 1987. 347 p.: ill. (Grijalbo/testimonios)

Short essays in which Betancourt describes his impressions of various individuals. The villains include Juan D. Perón, Jorge Ubico, Maximiliano Hernández Martínez, Francisco Franco, and Benito Mussolini. Among the good are Gandhi, Mossadegh, Pablo Casals and Andrés Eloy Blanco.

2313 Blanco-Fombona, Rufino. Ensayos históricos. Prólogo de Jesús Sanoja Hernández. Selección de Rafael Ramón Castellanos. Caracas: Biblioteca Ayacucho, 1981. 542 p. (Biblioteca Ayacucho;36)

Convenient compilation of Blanco Fombona's writings on historical topics. Once an influential member of Venezuela's intellectual and social elites, he wrote much of his works in exile during the Castro/Gómez period.

2314 Blink, M.J. van den. Olie op de golven: de betrekkingen tussen Nederland, Curaçao en Venezuela gedurende de eerste helft van de twintigste eeuw. Amsterdam: De Bataafsche Leeuw, 1989. 119 p.

Study of relations between the Netherlands/Curaçao and Venezuela during the Vicente Gómez period, which saw the growth of the oil industry, with Venezuelan oil refined in Curaçao. The author focuses on both the diplomatic and economic ties between Venezuela on the one hand and Curaçao and the Netherlands on the other. [R. Hoefte]

Brito Figueroa, Federico. La aristocracia del dinero en Venezuela actual, 1945–1985. v. 1. See *HLAS 51:4769.*

2315 Carvallo, Gastón and **Josefina Ríos de Hernández.** Mano de obra en la agricultura de exportación venezolana. (*in* Población y mano de obra en América Latina. Recopilación de Nicolás Sánchez-Albornoz. Madrid: Alianza Ediorial, 1985, p. 279–297)

Explains decline of haciendas in agro/export commercial farming during the late-19th and early-20th centuries. Good discussion of forms of payment and the basic split between plantation (export) and *conuco* (family subsistence) farming. Shows that by 1929 Venezuela was no longer a major exporter, largely because forms of coercion by

which *hacendados* controlled labor had collapsed. In contrast, *conucos* survived as family units.

Congreso de Historia del Negro en el Ecuador y Sur de Colombia, 1st, Esmeraldas, Ecuador, 1988. Actas. See item **2416.**

Cunill Grau, Pedro. Geografía del poblamiento venezolano en el siglo XIX. See *HLAS 51:2968.*

2316 Documentos británicos relacionados con el bloqueo de las costas venezo-lanas. Caracas: Instituto Autonómo Biblioteca Nacional; Fundación para el Rescate del Acervo Documental Venezolano, 1982. 714 p.

Spanish translations of British Foreign Office documents concerning the blockade of Venezuela in 1902.

2317 Fernández Heres, Rafael. La instrucción pública en el proyecto político de Guzmán Blanco: ideas y hechos. Caracas: Academia Nacional de la Historia, 1988. 190 p.: bibl., index. (Biblioteca de la Academia Nacional de la Historia: Estudios, monografías y ensayos; 95)

Reviews Guzmán Blanco's attempts to introduce obligatory public education in 1870, and his efforts to support public higher education. Well-researched work based upon primary sources sheds light on Venezuelan liberals of the Guzmán era. Discusses the use of education not only to foster Venezuelan development, but also to create a Venezuelan state of mind under the influence of liberalism and positivism.

2318 Fiebig-von Hase, Ragnhild. Lateinamerika als Konfliktherd der deutsch-amerikanischen Beziehungen, 1890–1903: vom Beginn der Panamerikapolitik bis zur Venezuelakrise von 1902/03. v. 1. Göttingen, Germany: Vandenhoeck & Ruprecht, 1986. 1 v.: bibl. (Schriftenreihe der Historischen Kommission bei der Bayerischen Akademie der Wissenschaften; 27)

Thorough study of Germany's relations with Latin America at the turn of the 20th century focuses mostly on Venezuela and Brazil. Methodically explores the export of capital, emigration from Germany to Latin America, and evolving policies. Germany never lost sight of the looming US presence in the hemisphere and the threat it presented to German interests in the area. [G.M. Dorn]

2319 Floyd, Mary. Guzmán Blanco: la dinámica de la política del septenio. Caracas: Instituto Autónomo Biblioteca Nacional: Fundación para el Rescate del Acervo Documental Venezolano, 1988. 264 p.: bibl. (Venezuela vista por autores extranjeros)

Spanish translation of author's PhD dissertation on the *septenio* period (1870–77) makes good use of Guzmán Blanco papers housed at the Fundación Boulton.

2320 Harwich Vallenilla, Nikita. La génesis de un imaginario colectivo: la enseñanza de la historia de Venezuela en el siglo XIX. (*Bol. Acad. Nac. Hist./Caracas,* 71:282, abril/junio 1988, p. 349–387, bibl.)

Analysis of the history taught at secondary schools during the 19th century, and the genesis of an "official" history that escaped the various ideologies then shaping intellectual currents. Interesting and worthy addition to Venezuelan historiography challenges Germán Carrera Damas' emphasis upon the cult of Bolívar as the major byproduct of such education.

Harwich Vallenilla, Nikita. Venezuelan positivism and modernity. See item **5364.**

2321 Un informe sobre los motilones, 1915. (*Bol. Arch. Hist. Miraflores,* 28:125, julio 1987/junio 1988, p. 143–148)

In 1915 G.W. Murray of the Colón Development Company Ltd. wrote two letters to President Gómez urging a pacific approach to dealing with the Motilon Indians of western Venezuela. He described the Motilones as hard working, highly civilized peoples, not given to savagery as usually dipicted by the criollos who encroached on their territories.

Iribertegui, Ramón. Amazonas, el hombre y el caucho. See *HLAS 51:2976.*

2322 Irwin G., Domingo. Unas definiciones de caudillo y caudillismo. (*Bol. Acad. Nac. Hist./Caracas,* 71:284, oct./dic. 1988, p. 1019–1034, bibl.)

Interesting essay on different types of caudillos and *caudillismo* found in Venezuela. Between 1830–46 the caudillo Páez acted as President to maintain the republican form of government through State powers. The ascension (1846–48) of Monagas introduced a decade of autocratic or despotic caudillism, which was followed by an era of anarchistic caudillism, with no national caudillo in charge of the lesser caudillos. Thoughout the 19th century, caudillos of various types were the dominant and fundamental political agents of social control.

Izard, Miquel. Orejanos, cimarrones y arrochelados. See item **2037.**

2323 Un juicio presidencial sin antecedentes, 1908. (*Bol. Arch. Hist. Miraflores,* 28 : 125, julio 1987/junio 1988, p. 75–112)

Transcripts of a hearing in 1909 concerning Gómez's accusation that Gen. Cipriano Castro ordered his assassination in Dec. 1908.

2324 El Lápiz. Mérida, Venezuela: Instituto Autónomo Biblioteca Nacional, Sala Tulio Febres Cordero; Consejo de Publicaciones de la Univ. de los Andes, 1985. (Libros de la Univ. de los Andes: Col. autores y escritores merideños; 1)

Copies of *El Lápiz* published in Mérida between 1885–96 contain wealth of information on history, customs, ethnography, and other aspects of Mérida, as well as "little known facts and curiosities for reader's enjoyment and enlightenment." Tulio Febres Cordero edited and published the newspaper. Also includes apendices of letters to Don Tulio from many of his contemporaries.

Liehr, Reinhard. La deuda exterior de la Gran Colombia frente a Gran Bretaña, 1820–1860. See item **2362.**

Llambí, Luis. Small modern farmers: neither a peasant nor fully-fledged capitalists?: a theoretical and historical discussion. See *HLAS 51:4778.*

2325 López Maya, Margarita. Las elecciones de 1946 y 1947. (*Bol. Acad. Nac. Hist./Caracas,* 70:278, abril/junio 1987, p. 431–450, bibl., tables)

Statistical analysis of voting in the elections of 1946 and 1947 based on previously unavailable data from the archives of Consejo Supremo Electoral. Shows that the 1946 system of colored ballots allowed illiterates to vote, that a suprisingly high percentage of eligible voters participated in both elections, and that Acción Democrática legitimately won through an open system of voting.

2326 Medina Angarita, Isaías. Gobierno y época del presidente Isaías Medina Angarita. v. 1–2, El pensamiento oficial, 1941–1945. v. 3–6, El debate parlamentario, 1941–1945. v. 7–8, Los partidos políticos, 1941–1945. v. 9–17, Opinión política a través de la prensa, 1941 1945. Caracas: Congreso de la República, 1987. 17 v.: index. (Pensamiento político venezolano del siglo XX; 33–49: Documentos para su estudio; 2a etapa, t. 9, v. 17–33. Ediciones conmemorativas del bicentenario del natalicio del Libertador Simón Bolívar)

Political documents from newspapers, congressional debates and other sources, some not previously open to the public. The volumes treat all aspects of Medina's political agenda, including valuable material from the Dirección Civil y Política of the Federal District government and from the political archives of the Ministry of Interior Relations. Very useful guides to rich data about a little-studied politician.

2327 La oposición liberal en Oriente: editoriales de El Republicano, 1844– 1846. Recopilación, introducción y notas de Manuel Pérez Vila. Caracas: Academia Nacional de la Historia, 1981. 157 p. (Biblioteca de la Academia Nacional de la Historia: Serie Fuentes para la historia republicana de Venezuela; 27)

Selection of editorials by Blas Bruzual, veteran of the independence struggle who joined liberals in calling for change. While not attacking Páez personally, Bruzual opposed the oligarchy and the Ley de 10 de Abril, and called for a 6 percent ceiling on loans by a "truly national" bank.

2328 Pineda, Rafael. 100 años de fotografía en el Orinoco-Guayana. Caracas: C.V.G. Electrificación del Caroní, 1984. 260 p., 1 leaf of plates: ill.

Poor-quality reproductions mar an otherwise extraordinary collection taken from archives of pioneer 19th-century and early-20th-century photographers who worked in the Guayana frontier region. A good text accompanies this excellent visual recreation of the past on one of Venezuela's underpopulated sections. Covers a wide variety of subjects, from mining to upper class society.

2329 Ruiz-Guevara, J.E. Codazzi en Barinas. Barinas, Venezuela: Centro de Estudios Históricos del Estado Barinas, 1984. 290 p.: bibl., ill.

Short biographical sketch of Codazzi's military/political career in Barinas includes copies and reproductions of his annual statements as governor to the provincial assemblies of 1846 and 1847. Good insights into complexities of mid-19th-century Venezuelan politics.

Santander y los sucesos políticos de Venezuela, 1826. v. 1–2. See item **2410.**

2330 Singh, Kelvin. Oil politics in Venezuela during the López Contreras Administration, 1936–1941. (*J. Lat. Am. Stud.*, 21:1, Feb. 1989, p. 89–104)

Major oil companies opposed the liberal policies of López Contreras and pushed both the Venezuelan and US governments to repress popular movements by raising the specter of communism and tying themselves to right-wing military opposition. The companies reluctantly met conditions of reform, but refused to recognize unions. Author concludes that López's vacillation cost Venezuela an opportunity to gain real control of its petroleum reserves, as did Mexico. He also suggests that high government officials, including López, took payments from the oil companies in lieu of pressing Venezuelan claims, but his evidence is shaky.

2331 Singh, Kelvin. Trinidad as a base for Venezuelan insurgency, 1870–1888. (*Rev. Rev. Interam.*, 14:1/4, Winter/Spring 1984, p. 47–65)

Well-documented account of several attempts by Venezuelan rebels to mount incursions in Orinoco and eastern Venezuela from Trinidad during the Guzmán Blanco era. Based on British and Trinidadian sources, the article also discusses other exile activities in Port-of-Spain as well as British and Venezuelan efforts to reach an accord and ease tensions. Venezuela's weakness, nonetheless, rendered it impotent in negotiations with the British.

2332 Testimonios del periodismo trujillano. t. 1–8. Recopilación de Luis González. Valera, Venezuela: Editorial Venezuela, 1985–87. 2 v.: bibl., facsims.

Reproductions of newspapers published in the state of Trujillo 1921–44. Editor's comments on newspapers, their editors, and their positions, attitudes, and interests covers wide range of topics, showing views of contemporary "provincial Venezuelans" who kept in touch with the world through AP and National Press in Caracas and Maracaibo.

2333 Tosta, Virgilio. Historia de Barinas. v. 2, 1800–1863. Caracas: Academia Nacional de la Historia, 1987. 1 v.: (Biblioteca de la Academia Nacional de la Historia: Fuentes para la historia colonial de Venezuela; 194.)

Comprehensive second vol. of history of Barinas, the rich cattle and agricultural province left impoverished after the Independence and Federal Wars ruined trade and caused depopulation. Recovery was marred by competition between conservative and liberal caudillos throughout the mid-19th century. Barinas faired well when the strongman it supported became president but faltered when power shifted. Local institutions failed to develop since national politics predominated and most top officials, including governors, were appointed by the president. Much more than a regional history, Tosta's analysis covers national politics and competing alliances which affected Barinas and the rest of the nation. For first vol., see *HLAS 50:1903.* [KW]

Troconis de Veracoechea, Ermila. Historia de las cárceles en Venezuela, 1600–1890. See item **2048.**

2334 Vargas, José María. Obras Completas. v. 1, pt. 1–2, Anatomía, v. 2, Cirugía, v. 3, Informes científicos, v. 4, Trabajos históricos, v. 5, p. 1–2, Presidencia de la Dirección General de Instrucción Pública, v. 6, Traducciones. Recopilación y notas de Blas Bruni Celli. 2a ed. Caracas: Congreso de la República, 1986. 6 v.: ill.

Scientific and political papers of Venezuela's second president.

2335 Vargas, José María. El universo de un hombre justo: textos escogidos. Traducción y selección de Blas Bruni Celli. Caracas: Comisión Nacional del Bicentenario del Natalicio del Doctor José Vargas; Ministerio de Educación, 1986. 435 p., 12 leaves of plates: facsims., ports. (Bicentenario del doctor José Vargas, 1786–1986; 5. Ediciones del Ministerio de Educación)

Bicentennial collection of writings, letters, and speeches of Vargas recognizes him as a public servant, educator, and intellectual, as well as a politician and short-time president of the republic.

2336 Veracoechea, Ermila de. El proceso de la inmigración en Venezuela. Caracas: Academia Nacional de la Historia, 1986. 336 p.: bibl., index. (Biblioteca de la Academia Nacional de la Historia: Fuentes para la historia republicana de Venezuela; 41)

Comprehensive review of government immigration policies begins with brief chapters on the colonial era, but concentrates on the post-1830 national period. Good source of information on the changing attitudes of elites toward race, as well as toward work and development. Though not a ground-breaking immigrant history, the book ably outlines major movements of immigrant groups, chronicles the expectations of several generations of Venezuelans, and contains useful statistical data.

2337 Wright, Winthrop R. Café con leche: race, class, and national image in Venezuela. Austin: Univ. of Texas Press, 1990. 1 v.: bibl.

Analyzes race prejudice in recent Venezuelan history through newspapers, magazines, public documents, and scholarly studies. After emphasizing Venezuela's unique denial of Africa in a heavily African-influenced culture, study explores the persistence of colonial castes into the mid-19th century Federal Wars. Also scrutinizes how Venezuela's elite created a defensive image of itself which is reflected in the nation's immigration policy, public statements, and studies by novelists and other intellectuals. Argues that myth of racial democracy only crumbled when race became a middle-class issue for Acción Democrática (AD) after which a new governing elite restated it in defense of the national image. Reveals many problems of historical study of race consciousness among elites in multi-ethnic, multi-cultural Latin America. Discerning, careful analysis of a subject that has heretofore been elusive to grasp and difficult to explain. [V. Peloso]

2338 Wright, Winthrop R. The Todd Duncan affair: Acción Democrática and the myth of racial democracy in Venezuela. (*Americas/Francisc.*, 44:4, April 1988, p. 441–459)

A 1945 racial incident serves as focus for review of Venezuelan attitudes toward race at mid-century. Traces the origins of the "myth of racial democracy" in Venezuela and its political implications. Members of Acción Democrática furthered their cause as champions of all Venezuelans by openly adopting racial democracy as part of their movement's popular platform. Conservatives also advocated policies of non-discrimination, but were slow to put rhetoric into political action.

Colombia and Ecuador

JANE M. RAUSCH, *Professor of History, University of Massachusetts-Amherst*

THE BOOM IN COLOMBIAN HISTORIOGRAPHY noted in the last two reporting periods has flourished unabated, producing many superb documentary collections and general interpretations. For the independence and early national eras, attention has focused on Francisco de Paula Santander; in 1986 the Fundación Francisco de Paula Santander was established to prepare for the celebration of the 150th anniversary of his death in 1990 and the 200th anniversary of his birth in 1992. Charged with locating, organizing, and editing studies of the events in which the "Man of Laws" was a major actor, the Fundación has begun to publish modern, critical editions of Santander's correspondence, diaries, and other documents. Nine volumes in this multi-volume collection are listed below under the heading "Santandereana." All contain scholarly introductions that place the documents in historical context and are supplemented with indexes, maps, and bibliographies. Because of these features, they supersede older collections such as the *Archivo Santander* (Bogotá, 1913–32) and make available new materials formerly buried in obscure archives. The Fundación has also published Lozano Esquivel's biography of Santander (item **2398**), but both in scope and analytic depth it is surpassed by the massive study written by the former director of the Archivo Nacional, Pilar Moreno de Angel (item **2399**).

For Colombian history since 1840, a welcome development is a trend toward historical synthesis. Two multi-volume general histories that cover events from conquest to the 1980s have taken their places beside the Academia Historia de Colombia's *Historia extensa*. The eight-volume *Historia de Colombia* (item **2353**) edited by the late Guillermo Hernández de Alba features appealing texts composed by scholars for a popular audience, while the eight-volume *Nueva historia de Colombia* under the editorship of Jaime Jaramillo Uribe is directed more toward researchers: vols. 1–2 reprint the *Manual de historia de Colombia* published by Colcultura between 1978–80 and vols. I-VI (items **2367—2372**), contain especially prepared essays by two dozen "new historians" who, besides summarizing political events from 1886 to 1986, cover topics ranging from international relations and social movements to the history of Colombian science and urban social life. Both sets can be supplemented by Orlando Melo's unique two-volume anthology of eyewitness accounts of key events from colonial times to the present (item **2383**) and the more pedestrian *Forjadores de Colombia contemporánea* -biographical sketches of 81 individuals whom Carlos Perozzo regards as influential in the formation of Colombian culture and history (item **2379**). Also worthy of mention is Alfredo Iriarte's *Breve historia de Bogotá*, an engrossing abridgement of a three-volume social and cultural history published in 1988 to mark the 450th anniversary of the city's founding (item **2357**).

Synthesis is taking place on a regional level as well: *Historia de Antioquia* (item **2352**) is encyclopedic in breadth with 49 essays on all aspects of Antioqueñan life up to 1950; Ortiz Mesa discusses political strife in the province between 1850–80 (item **2373**); Valencia Llanos (item **2391**) and Colmenares (item **2344**) analyze Cauca during the 19th century; Pasto is represented by a magnificent album of photographs taken 1880–1945 (item **2377**); *El Caribe colombiano* (item **2378**) brings together eight important but previously hard-to-find journal articles on the Caribbean region; two works are on the history and culture of El Quindío (items **2349** and **2364**); and Mosquera Mosquera's exposé of discrimination against Chocó's population reveals the awakening of black consciousness (item **2366**), a phenomenon underscored by the proceedings of the Primer Simposio sobre Bibliografía del Negro en Colombia (item **2386**) and of the Congreso de Historia del Negro en el Ecuador y Sur de Colombia (item **2416**).

A portrait of Colombian society in the late 19th century can be gleaned from the 32 sketches on topics covering sports to politics assembled by Londoño Vélez to mark the centennial of the Constitution of 1886 (item **2363**). It is complemented by a facsimile edition of a volume commemorating the centennial of Bolívar's birth published by the Colombian Senate in 1883 (item **2355**). Outstanding among other 19th-century entries are two studies of the Catholic Church: Fernán González examines Church-State relations between 1820–60 to understand why Colombian developments differ from those in other Latin American countries (item **2350**), and Pinilla Cote investigates the activities of the first papal representative to New Granada, Monseñor Cayetano Baluffi (item **2380**).

Turning to the 20th century, the publication of the papers of political leaders reported in *HLAS* 50 continues with a new edition of the speeches and letters of Alfonso López Pumarejo (item **2365**). James D. Henderson has written a stimulating analysis of the ideas of the controversial Conservative caudillo, Laureano Gómez (item **2351**). *Don Manuel: Mister Coffee* is a two-volume collection of testimonials to and reports by Manuel Mejía, one of the architects of Colombia's coffee economy (item **2346**). Other contributions on economic themes include Michael Jiménez's essay on Cundinamarcan coffee haciendas (item **2361**), two studies of labor relations in Antioquia (items **2359** and **2374**), and Povedo Ramos' concise survey of the rise and decline of Colombian railroads (item **2381**).

Finally, the Violencia retains its fascination as a research topic. Quintero Ospina reviews the Gaitán assassination and concludes that Juan Róa Sierra acted alone (item **2382**); two journalists have written biographies of guerrilla fighters (items **2340** and **2388**), and Olga Behar has compiled testimonies from more than 50 protagonists in the civil strife that dragged on between 1948–85 (item **2341**). It is evident from these new works that Ilse Cohnen's list of 257 books and articles published before July 1987 on the Violencia (item **2343**) will soon have to be updated.

A yearning for synthesis is also apparent in Ecuadorian historiography. Enrique Ayala Mora has edited two essay collections that systematically review national history (items **2422** and **2429**). The Banco Central is reissuing the works of Gabriel Cevallos García, one of Ecuador's most distinguished 20th-century historians. Among them are his *Historia del Ecuador*, a university textbook written in 1967, and his more philosophical *Reflexiones sobre la historia del Ecuador* first published in 1960 (items **2413** and **2414**). There is also a new edition of Pedro Fermín Cevallos' six-volume history published originally in Lima in 1870 (item **2412**).

Noteworthy among 19th-century entries are Linda Alexander Rodríguez's analysis of political developments between 1830–1925 that stresses the interplay between regionalism, authoritarianism, militarism and personalism (item **2433**) and Tamara Estupiñán-Freile's family history of latifundista Nicolás Martínez (item **2419**). For the 20th century, Canadian anthropologist Blanca Muratorio breaks new ground with her social and economic history of the Alto Napo (item **2428**). By juxtaposing the oral testimony of Rucuyaya Alonso, a Quechua rubber collector, with data drawn from written sources, Muratorio presents the history of this upper Amazon region from an Indian point of view and demonstrates how historians can utilize anthropological methodologies to expand their understanding of the past.

COLOMBIA

2339 Agudelo Giraldo, Guillermo. Los arzobispos de Bogotá que he conocido: medio siglo en la historia eclesiástica colombiana, 1928–1984. Bogotá?: La Impr., 1987? 429 p.: bibl., ill., ports.

Apologetic review of careers of four Colombian archbishops by a priest who knew them personally. Based on published sources, book places their activities within context of universal Church and includes brief biographies of five popes who served between 1939–84. Not definitive, but worth consulting.

2340 Alape, Arturo. Tirofijo: las vidas de Pedro Antonio Marín, Manuel Marulanda Vélez. Bogotá: Planeta, 1989. 399 p.: bibl., ill. (Col. Documento)

Biography of Manuel Marulanda Vélez, a.k.a. Pedro Antonio Marín, or "Tirofijo," guerrilla leader of the "independent republic" of Marquetalia on the border between Tolima and Huila who defied the National Front in the early 1960s. Includes extensive bibliography on La Violencia.

2341 Behar, Olga. Las guerras de la paz. Bogotá: Planeta, 1985. 406 p.: map. (Autores colombianos)

Journalist investigates recurring civil

strife (1948–85) through personal testimonies of more than 50 protagonists including former presidents, cabinet ministers, military officers, and guerrilla members of FARC, M-19, EPL, ADO, and ELN. Behar introduces each statement, but her interpretations do not make use of preconceived theories. Valuable primary material for students of La Violencia.

2342 Carrizosa de López, María. Estudio sobre las tendencias del liberalismo en Colombia, 1930–1945. (*Univ. Humaníst.*, 17:29, enero/junio 1988, p. 7–44, bibl.)

Traces the development and clash between "centrist" Liberals led by Eduardo Santos and "leftist" Liberals directed by Alfonso López Pumarejo. Primarily a study in political theory and action, rather than broadly-based history.

2343 Cohnen, Ilse Valerie. La Violencia in Kolumbien. (*Jahresbibliogr. Bibl. Zeitgesch.*, 59, 1987, p. 347–369)

Lists 257 books and articles dealing with La Violencia published in US, Europe, and Colombia before July 1987. Items are arranged in two basic categories—politics and literature—but are not annotated.

2344 Colmenares, Germán. Popayán: continuidad y discontinuidad regionales en la época de la independencia. (*in* América Latina en la época de Simón Bolívar. Edición de Reinhard Liehr. Berlin: Colloquium Verlag, 1989, p. 157–181)

Draws on archival materials to analyze the complicated social, political, and economic factors emanating from the War of Independence that brought about the decline of Popayán and the emergence of important new urban centers in Cauca.

2345 Díaz Uribe, Amparo. El siglo de solidaridad. (*Am. Lat./Moscú*, 2:110, feb. 1987, p. 46–56, photos)

Surveys interaction between Colombians and Cubans during Enlightenment, Wars of Independence, Ten Years War, and War of Thousand Days. Briefly sketches careers of Manuel del Socorro Rodríguez and Pedro Romero (Cubans who played important roles in Colombia); and of José Fernández Madrid, Manuel Ancízar, and Avelino (Colombians who contributed to cause of Cuban independence). Popularly written, but intriguing topic.

2346 Don Manuel: Mister Coffee. Bogotá: Fondo Cultural Cafetero, 1989. 2 v.: bibl., ill.

Manuel Mejía (1887–1958), as head of the Federación Nacional de Cafeteros, promoted the Fondo Nacional del Café and the Inter-American Treaty on Coffee Exports. In Vol. 1, ten associates assess his contributions to development of the coffee industry. Vol. 2 contains Mejía's reports to coffee congresses, interviews, and laws, decrees and treaties related to coffee. Essays are anecdotal rather than scholarly. Useful for 20th-century economic history.

2347 Flórez Gallego, Lenín; Adolfo Atehortúa C.; and Humberto Vélez R. Estudios sobre la Regeneración. Cali, Colombia: Impr. Departamental del Valle, 1987. 123 p.: bibl., ill.

Three scholarly essays: 1) Vélez R. considers the Regeneration as a historiographic, historical, and political phenomenon; 2) Flórcz Gallego compares development of Cauca with that experienced by Uruguay and Mexico; and 3) Atehortúa C. analyzes elite formation in Buga.

2348 Fonseca Galán, Eduardo. Los combatientes del Llano, 1949–1953. Bogotá: s.n., 1987. 264 p.: ill.

Frank, clear, authentic account of Liberal guerrillas in the Llanos from 1949–53, by principal participant. Autobiographic survey of causes and stages of revolt, organization of the guerrilla bands, behavior of commanders, triumphs and defeats. Originally written in 1953. Key source for understanding La Violencia.

Friedemann, Nina S. de and **Jaime Arocha.** De sol a sol: génesis, transformación y presencia de los negros en Colombia. See *HLAS 51:4748.*

2349 Gómez Aristizábal, Horacio et al. El Quindío y Colombia en el siglo XXI: la creación del Departamento del Quindío y su verdadera historia; estudios polémicos sobre El Quindío; homenaje a Armenia con motivo de sus 100 años de fundación. Bogotá: Editorial Kelly, 1989. 361 p., 10 p. of plates: ill.

Sixteen essays (eleven by Gómez Aristizábal) dcal with history and culture of Armenia and Dept. of Quindío. Important primarily as expression of regional identification.

Gómez L., Augusto. Llanos orientales: colonización y conflictos interétnicos, 1870–1970. See item **617.**

2350 González, Fernán E. Iglesia y Estado en Colombia durante el siglo XIX (1820–1860). Bogotá: Centro de Investigación y Educación Popular, 1985. 44 p.: bibl. (Documentos ocasionales; 30)

Stimulating analysis of Church-State relations considers both international context and heterogenity within Colombian clergy and political parties. Author's periodization suggests Colombian Church-State conflicts follow pattern distinct from rest of Latin America. Excellent introduction to complex topic.

2351 Henderson, James D. Conservative thought in twentieth century Latin America: the ideas of Laureano Gómez. Athens, Ohio: Ohio Univ., Center for Latin American Studies, 1988. 217 p.: bibl., index. (Monographs in international studies: Latin America series; 13)

Stimulating analysis of ideas of Laureano Gómez (1889–1965), fiery leader of traditional Conservatives and president 1949–53. Identifies Catholic, liberal, positivist, romantic, and nationalistic elements of his thought. Assesses his role in Colombian history and within the evolution of Latin American conservatism in 20th century. Objective assessment of a major political actor long obscured by polemic and controversy.

2352 Historia de Antioquia. Edición de Jorge Orlando Melo. Bogotá: Editorial Presencia, 1988. 544 p.: bibl., ill. (some col.).

Encyclopedic volume contains 49 short essays by competent scholars on all aspects of Antioqueñan history, politics, society, economy, and culture from preconquest to 1950, as well as an extensive bibliography. Comprehensive, up-to-date, and lavishly illustrated. Excellent starting place for research topics on Antioquia.

2353 Historia de Colombia. Recopilación de Guillermo Hernández de Alba. Bogotá: Salvat Editores Colombia, 1987. 8 v.: bibl., ill. (some col.).

Guillermo Hernández de Alba assembled an impressive team of scholars to produce this eight-volume history marking the 500th anniversary of the discovery of America. Written for non-academics, texts are objective, clear, and interesting, without being simplistic. All volumes are illustrated with sections on art, music, education, and social movements, and concise summaries of political developments. Includes short bibliographies and some extracts from original documents. Excellent popular history.

2354 Holton, Isaac Farwell. La Nueva Granada: veinte meses en los Andes. Traducción de Angela de López. Bogotá: Banco de la República, 1981. 635 p., 1 folded leaf of plates : ill., indexes, map. (Archivo de la economía nacional; 40)

Spanish translation of the original 1857 English ed. by US chemistry professor from Middlebury College who traveled through Colombia in 1850, recording his impressions in a detailed account with a unique perspective. Holton found the countryside enchanting but hopelessly backward in agricultural development and scientific improvement. A classic. [K. Waldron]

2355 Homenaje de Colombia al Libertador Simón Bolívar en su primer centenario, 1783–1883. Edición de Manuel Ezequiel Corrales. Ed. facsimilar, 2a ed. Bogotá: Plaza & Janés; Senado de la República; Academia Colombiana de Historia, 1983. 446 p.

The Academia Colombiana de Historia sponsored this facsimile edition of a volume commissioned in 1883 by the Colombian Senate to mark the centennial of Bolívar's birth. The massive book contains all the laws passed in Bolívar's honor in 1882 and 1883 by Congress and the nine individual states, texts of municipal *acuerdos*, records of public ceremonies, essays, poems, and periodical articles celebrating the Liberator's role in Colombian history. Brief introductions by Carlos Holguín Sardi and Germán Arciniegas provide historical context for assessing the significance of 1883 celebration. Interesting as a stage in Bolívar's apotheosis and as an overview of Colombian intellectual and political culture in 1883.

2356 Ibáñez, Pedro M. and **Eduardo Posada.** Crónicas de Bogotá. Bogotá: Academia de Historia de Bogotá; Tercer Mundo Editores, 1989. 4 v. (Historia. Biblioteca Popular de Cultura Colombiana)

Reprinting of second ed. published in 1952. Vols. 1–3 cover Bogotá's history from 1538–1818. Vol. 4, completed by Eduardo Posada after Ibáñez's death in 1919, carries the narrative to the end of 19th century with installation of the telephone and inauguration of the trolley. Anecdotal, but based on primary sources.

2357 Iriarte, Alfredo. Breve historia de Bogotá. Bogotá: Fundación Misión Colombia; Editorial Oveja Negra, 1988. 262 p.

Skillful abridgement of three-volume social and cultural history, two-thirds of which covers 1810–1958, was published in 1958 to mark Bogotá's 450th anniversary. Lacks footnotes and bibliography, but was prepared by scholars. Written in popular style with emphasis on daily life. Especially fascinating for anyone who has ever lived in Bogotá.

2358 Jaramillo, Carlos Eduardo. El guerrillero de "El Paraíso:" General Tulio Varón Perilla, 1860–1901. Bogotá: Ediciones Contraloría General del Tolima, 1987. 200 p.: bibl., ill.

Definitive military biography of Tulio Varón, legendary Liberal *guerrillero* from Tolima, who fought in wars of 1895 and 1899–1902. Draws on periodicals and national and regional archives, and includes 17 relevant documents, helpful illustrations, and extensive bibliography.

2359 Jaramillo A., Ana María and Jorge Bernal M. Sudor y tabaco: trayectoria de una unidad. Medellín, Colombia: Gráficas ALON'S, 1988. 274 p., 32 p. of plates: bibl., ill.

Uses oral and written sources to document history of the workers at Colombiana de Tabaco in Antioquia, and of their union, Sintracoltabaco, established in 1938. Intended as a contribution to the history of labor organization, includes analysis of strikes of 1967 and 1982.

2360 Jaramillo Uribe, Jaime. Temas americanos y otros ensayos. Bogotá: Ediciones Uniandes; Tercer Mundo Editores, 1989. 264 p.: bibl., map. (Ensayos de historia social; 2. Historia)

Seventeen stimulating essays prepared for various academic functions (1976–86). Most were previously unpublished and relate to social and cultural history or history of ideas. Seven focus specifically on Colombia and range from a brief history of Bogotá to an analysis of political ideas in the 1930s.

2361 Jiménez, Michael F. Traveling far in grandfather's car: the life cycle of central Colombian coffee estates: the case of Viotá Cundinamarca, 1900–1930. (*HAHR*, 69:2, May 1989, p. 185–219, tables)

Analyzes collective histories of major coffee haciendas in Viotá to show that patterns of land utilization and labor contracts were a rational response to limits imposed on agrarian entrepreneurship during consolidation of export capitalism. Effectively challenges the widely-held notion that latifundia were the enemy of modernity.

Lemaitre, Eduardo. Breve historia de Cartagena de Indias, 1501–1901. See item **2062.**

2362 Liehr, Reinhard. La deuda exterior de la Gran Colombia frente a Gran Bretaña, 1820–1860. (*in* América Latina en la época de Simón Bolívar. Edición de Reinhard Liehr. Berlin: Colloquium Verlag, 1989, p. 465–488, graphs)

Examines fiscal history of Colombia, Venezuela, and Ecuador to determine reasons for and consequences of growth of Latin American foreign debt in early national period. Drawing on published and archival sources, rejects "dependency" or "informal imperialism" models and emphasizes gap between industrializing economies of Europe and decapitalized economies of South America.

2363 Londoño Vélez, Santiago. Colombia 1886: programa centenario de la constitución: Biblioteca Luis Angel Arango, julio-septiembre 1986, Bogotá. Bogotá: Banco de la República, 1986. 124 p.: bibl., ill. (some col.).

Thirty-two sketches of aspects of Colombian life in the late 19th century were written to mark the centenary of the Constitution of 1886. Topics range from politics to sports, and include trade, travel, roads, education, Church, literature, etc. Well-written introduction to Regeneration Era is based on primary sources and profusely illustrated.

2364 Lopera Gutiérrez, Jaime. La colonización del Quindío: apuntes para una monografía del Quindío y Calarcá; primer centenario de Calarcá, 1886–1986. Bogotá: Banco de la República, 1986. 200 p.: bibl., ill., maps. (Col. bibliográfica Banco de la República. Historia Colombiana.)

Traces history of Quindío from precolumbian times to 1953. Considers Antioqueñan colonization, development of coffee industry, and impact of migrations on social and economic composition of region. Modest contribution to regional history is based on secondary materials.

2365 López Pumarejo, Alfonso. Alfonso López Pumarejo, polemista político. Presentación de Alfonso López Michelsen. Bogotá: Instituto Caro y Cuervo, 1986. 339 p., 3 p. of plates: ill., indexes.

Collection of 17 speeches and 14 messages, letters, and telegrams spanning 1929–59 and organized in three sections: Colombian Politics; International Politics; and Economic and Social Problems. López Michelsen's introduction and Ardila Duarte's biographical sketch provide context for the documents.

Molano, Alfredo. Selva adentro: una historia oral de la colonización del Guaviare. See *HLAS 51:4753.*

2366 Mosquera Mosquera, Juan de Dios. Las comunidades negras de Colombia: pasado, presente y futuro. Pereira, Colombia: Movimiento Nacional por los Derechos Humanos de las Comunidades Negras de Colombia, 1985. 165 p.: bibl., map.

Exposé of institutional and cultural discrimination against blacks with special attention to Chocó and the Pacific Coast. Calls on black youth to redress these wrongs by building a national organization to forge ideological and ethnic cohesion within black community. Polemical but historically accurate.

2367 Nueva historia de Colombia. v. I, Historia política, 1886–1946. Dirección de Jaime Jaramillo Uribe. Bogotá: Planeta, 1989. 1 v.: bibl., ill.

This objective and up-to-date multivolume work provides excellent, informative summaries for both researchers and general public. In Vol. I, 13 essays by nine scholars are arranged chronologically. Topics include federalism, Constitution of 1886, the War of the Thousand Days, separation of Panama, Quinquenio, Ospina and Abadía, Olaya Herrera, López Pumarejo, and Eduardo Santos. See below for vol. II-VI.

2368 Nueva historia de Colombia. v. II, Historia política, 1946–1986. Dirección

de Jaime Jaramillo Uribe. Bogotá: Planeta, 1989. 1 v.: bibl., ill.

Fifteen essays by eight scholars arranged chronologically. Topics include Ospina Pérez, April 9, 1948, Laureano Gómez, Rojas Pinilla, La Violencia, National Front, Lleras Camargo and Valencia, Lleras and Pastrana, third parties, contemporary military history, and Church and State (1886–1985).

2369 Nueva historia de Colombia. v. III, Relaciones internationales; movimientos sociales. Dirección de Jaime Jaramillo Uribe. Bogotá: Planeta, 1989. 1 v.: bibl., ill.

Fourteen informative essays by nine scholars. Topics include foreign policy 1930–86, boundary negotiations, Colombia and Latin America 1886–1930, England and Colombia 1880–1930, the banana conflict, working class 1886–1980, agrarian question 1900–85, and 20th-century colonization.

2370 Nueva historia de Colombia. v. IV, Educación y ciencia; luchas de la mujer; vida diaria. Dirección científica de Jaime Jaramillo Uribe. Bogotá: Planeta, 1989. 1 v.: bibl., ill.

Fifteen essays by as many scholars cover status of women, education 1880–1980, history of Colombian science in general and specifically astronomy, historiography, philosophy, economic thought, sociology, anthropology, medicine, land and cattle techniques, and urban daily life.

2371 Nueva historia de Colombia. v. V, Economía, café, industria. Dirección de Jaime Jaramillo Uribe. Bogotá: Planeta, 1989. 1 v: bibl., ill.

Fifteen essays by twelve scholars survey history of three great processes of the Colombian economy in the 20th century: 1) development of coffee; 2) evolution of industry; and 3) demographic growth. Also covers struggles of coffee peasants 1930–46.

2372 Nueva historia de Colombia. v. VI, Literatura y pensamiento; artes; recreación. Dirección de Jaime Jaramillo Uribe. Bogotá: Planeta, 1989. 1 v.: bibl., ill.

Fifteen essays on topics generally overlooked by historians. Includes literature and thought 1886–1930, journalism, art, architecture, theater, cinema, classical and popular music, regional humor, sport, and chess.

Ocampo López, Javier. Los orígenes ideológicos de Colombia contemporánea. See item **5373.**

2373 Ortiz Mesa, Luis Javier. Aspectos políticos del federalismo en Antioquia, 1850–1880. Medellín, Colombia: Univ. Nacional de Colombia, Seccional de Medellín, 1985. 119 p.

Argues that the Revolution of 1851 polarized Conservatives and Liberals and crystalized their ideological differences. Analyzes elections between 1850–80, legislation passed, the religious question, and nature of party loyalties. A solid, carefully-footnoted monograph.

Ortiz Sarmiento, Carlos Miguel. Estado y subversión en Colombia: La Violencia en El Quindío, años 50. See *HLAS 51:4755.*

2374 Osorio Ochoa, Iván Darío. Historia del sindicalismo antioqueño, 1900–1986. Bogotá?: Instituto Popular de Capacitación, 1987? 260 p.

Survey of activities of key labor unions, federations, and strikes in Antioquia (1900–86) is based on research in public and union archives. Encyclopedic but disjointed compendium of facts.

2375 Ospina, Gloria Inés. España y Colombia en el siglo XIX: los orígenes de las relaciones. Madrid: Ediciones Cultura Hispánica, Instituto de Cooperación Iberoamericana, 1988? 207 p.: bibl., index.

Doctoral thesis, written at the Univ. Complutense de Madrid, examines 19th-century bilateral relations. Draws on archival documents located in Madrid, Bogotá, Paris, and Washington. Clearly-written contribution on neglected topic.

2376 Otálora de Corsi, Rosa María. José Eusebio Otálora. Tunja, Colombia: Publicaciones de la Academia Boyacense de Historia, 1984. 298 p.: ill. (Biblioteca de la Academia Boyacense de Historia: Serie Obras fundamentales; 2)

Otálora (1828–84) was a Radical committed to modernization. While president of Boyacá he promoted iron and railroad industries. Chastized by other Liberals for his support of Núñez, he was accused of improprieties while serving as President of the Republic between 1882–84. This biography by his great-granddaughter draws on family documents; reprints Otálora's *Mi defensa o replica obligada* written on April 12, 1884; and includes introductory essay by Javier Ocampo López. Unique portrait of a neglected figure.

Palacios, Marco. Estado y clases sociales en Colombia. See *HLAS 51:4756.*

2377 Pasto a través de la fotografía: Pasto 450 años. Recopilación de Carmen Helena Perini y María Eugenia Díaz del Castillo. Bogotá: Banco de la República, 1986? 120 p.: ill. (some col.).

Fascinating collection of 400 photos taken between 1880 and 1945, first assembled by Banco de la República for an exposition in 1985 includes scenes of people, places, political and natural events, and popular diversions.

2378 Pedraja Tomán, René de la et al. El Caribe colombiano: selección de textos históricos. Recopilación y prólogo de Gustavo Bell Lemus. Barranquilla, Colombia: Ediciones Uninorte, 1988. 227 p.: bibl., maps. (Col. Caribe)

Eight perceptive essays by Colombian and North American scholars dealing with 19th- and 20th-century developments, previously published in three hard-to-find journals: *Desarrollo y Sociedad, Anuario Colombiano de Historia y de Cultura,* and *Boletín Cultural y Bibliográfico.* Prologue presents incisive overview of Caribbean historiography. Valuable addition to any research library.

2379 Perozzo, Carlos; Renán Flórez; and Eugenio de Bustos Tovar. Forjadores de Colombia contemporánea: los 81 personajes que más han influido en la formación de nuestro país. v. 1–2. Bogotá: Planeta, 1986. 2 v.: indexes, ports.

Biographical sketches of 81 individuals who left their mark on Colombian history and culture. Vol. 1 features persons born between 1506 and 1873; Vol. 2 covers 1879–1942. Includes *conquistadors,* independence heroes, politicians, intellectuals, and artisans, but only two women—Policarpa Salavarrieta and Manuela Sáenz. Handy reference work.

2380 Pinilla Cote, Alfonso María. Del Vaticano a la Nueva Granada: la internunciatura de monseñor Cayetano Baluffi en

Bogotá, 1837–1842, primera en Hispano-américa. Bogotá: Fundación para la Conmemoración del Bicentenario del Natalicio y el Sesquicentenario de la Muerte del General Francisco de Paula Santander, 1988. 418 p., 5 leaves of plates: bibl., indexes, maps, port. (Biblioteca de la Presidencia de la República)

Handsome edition of doctoral thesis written at Gregorian Univ. (Rome, 1953) uses Colombian and Vatican primary sources to investigate Baluffi's important role in New Granadan domestic affairs and relations with the Vatican. Major contribution to Church-State history.

2381 Poveda Ramos, Gabriel. Nuestra historia ferroviaria. (*Rev. Antioq. Econ. Desarro.*, 21, 1986, p. 6–19, maps, photos, tables)

Concise historical survey covering the construction, economic importance, and demise of Colombian railroads. Argues that railroads still have role to play in economy. Well-written introduction to the topic.

2382 Quintero Ospina, Tiberio. El asesinato de Gaitán, y otros procesos famosos. Bogotá: Editorial ABC, 1988. 329 p.: ports.

To mark 40th anniversary of Gaitán's assassination, a former penal law professor and Supreme Court judge examines circumstances surrounding event and concludes that Juan Roa Sierra acted alone. Author reviews three other sensational crimes: 1) the murder of Alfredo Forero Vanegas by Nepomuceno Matallana Matallana in May 1951; 2) the alleged crimes for which José Raimundo Russi was executed on July 15, 1851; and 3) the Lindbergh kidnapping case of March 1932. Interesting approach to Colombian social history.

Los radicales del siglo XIX: escritos políticos. See item **5374.**

2383 Reportaje de la historia de Colombia: 158 documentos y relatos de testigos presenciales sobre hechos ocurridos en 5 siglos. v. 2, Desde la rebelión de Mosquera hasta la época actual. Selección y presentación de textos de Jorge Orlando Melo. Bogotá: Planeta, 1989. 1 v.: ill.

More than 40 chronologically-arranged eyewitness accounts of key events in Colombian history, from Cordovez Moure's description of General Obando's death in 1861 to a newspaper report of 1989 national soccer

match. Brief introductions by Orlando Melo suggest context and significance of each document. Engrossing collection assembled to give lay people as well as scholars "a more complex and varied vision of the history of the country."

2384 Restrepo Restrepo, Jorge Alberto and **Manuel Rodríguez Becerra.** La actividad comercial y el grupo de comerciantes de Cartagena a fines del siglo XIX. Bogotá: Facultad de Administración de Empresas, Univ. de los Andes, 1987. 62 p. (Monografías; 6)

Well-written and researched essay demonstrates that despite Cartagena's decline, 19th-century commerce was important enough to allow merchants to become the local elite. Describes key economic activities and profiles influential merchants. Concludes that merchants became effective entrepreneurs.

2385 Safford, Frank. Commercial crisis and economic ideology in New Granada, 1825–1850. (*in* América Latina en la época de Simón Bolívar. Edición de Reinhard Liehr. Berlin: Colloquium Verlag, 1989, p. 183–206)

Expansion of theme first introduced in author's book *The ideal of the practical* (Austin: Univ. of Texas Press, 1976). Argues that economic crisis of 1825–45 encouraged members of the elite to support development of import-substitution manufacturing and to advocate a protectionist policy. Analyzes causes for collapse of protectionist strategy.

Shulgovski, Anatoli. La comuna de Bogotá y el socialismo utópico. pts. 1–2. See item **5375.**

2386 Simposio sobre Bibliografía del Negro en Colombia, 1st, Bogotá, 1983. El negro en la historia de Colombia: fuentes escritas y orales. Bogotá: Fondo Interamericano de Publicaciones de la Cultura Negra de las Américas, UNESCO, Fundación Colombiana de Investigaciones Folclóricas, 1983. 191 p.

Substantial essays by 10 distinguished scholars on subjects including oral tradition, poetry, colonial and national history, and contemporary Colombia. Contains detailed bibliographies of black history sources in national and regional archives. Essential for any study dealing with blacks in Colombian history.

2387 Sowell, David. La teoría y la realidad: The Democratic Society of Artisans of Bogotá, 1847–1854. (*HAHR*, 67:4, Nov. 1987, p. 611–630, bibl.)

Re-examination of membership, ideology, and political impact of the Democratic Society of Artisans. Concludes that group was not motivated by "socialism" as previously asserted, but by opposition to lower tariffs. Based on meticulous research in the Archivo del Congreso.

2388 Téllez, Pedro Claver. Crónicas de la vida bandolera: historia de los bandidos colombianos más famosos del siglo XX. Bogotá: Planeta, 1987. 265 p.: ill. (Col. Documento)

Short, narrative sketches of ten famous Colombian bandits from the War of the Thousand Days to the *narcotraficantes* of the 1980s. Author draws on personal experiences and interviews to provide a journalist's perspective on La Violencia.

2389 Torres Almeida, Jesús Clodoaldo. Manuel Murillo Toro, caudillo radical y reformador social. Bogotá: Ediciones El Tiempo, 1984. 450 p., 1 leaf of plates: appendices, bibl., ill. (Ediciones El Tiempo; 3)

Solid but unexciting biography based on wide range of published sources argues that Murillo Toro (1816–80) was "the most notable and genial statesman of Colombian radicalism and social reform of the nineteenth century." Appendices contain three documents and excerpts from previously-published works on Murillo.

2390 Uribe de Hincapié, María Teresa and **Jesús Maria Alvarez G.** Poderes y regiones: problemas en la constitución de la Nación Colombiana, 1810–1850. Medellín, Colombia: Univ. de Antioquia, Depto. de Publicaciones, 1987. 300 p.: bibl.

Meticulously researched analysis of political and economic processes in first half of 19th century that led to reforms of 1850s. Clear narrative based on careful synthesis of published primary and secondary sources; pays special attention to Antioqueñan developments. Essential reading for scholars seeking to understand the early national period.

2391 Valencia Llano, Alonso. Estado soberano del Cauca: federalismo y regeneración. Bogotá: Banco de la República, 1988. 297 p.: bibl. (Historia colombiana. Col. bibliográfica)

Superb history of Cauca (1863–86) is

based on careful review of *informes* of provincial presidents and governors, regional press, and personal correspondence in national and regional archives. Examines political and economic developments and role of *caudillos* Mosquera, Trujillo, and Payán. Originally a master's thesis done at Univ. del Valle. Required reading for scholars interested in Federation Era as well as in regional history.

2392 Varela, Teresa de. Diego Luis Córdoba: biografía. Colombia: Impr. Fondo Rotatorio Policía Nacional, 1987. 236 p.: bibl., ill.

Biography of Córdoba (1907–64), called "the last Liberal-Marxist-Catholic" who represented the Dept. of Chocó in Congress for 30 years. Contains random bits of information on Chocó and on the contribution of Afro-Colombians to Colombian development. Interesting primarily as evidence of awakening black ethnic identity.

2393 Vázquez Carrizosa, Alfredo. Colombia y Venezuela: una historia atormentada. 2a ed. corr. y aum. Bogotá: Tercer Mundo Editores, 1987. 481 p., 1 folded leaf of plates: bibl., map. (Relaciones internacionales)

Survey of Colombian-Venezuelan relations (1821–1980) emphasizes efforts to negotiate a common boundary and settle claims over Gulf of Venezuela. Author—a professor of international law and former Colombian minister of foreign relations—has added to this second edition a prologue and final chapter updating the status of the dispute to 1988. Vázquez Carrizosa blames Venezuela's politization of an essentially juridical problem for the breakdown of talks and worsening relations during Barco Administration.

2394 Violence in Colombia: the contemporary crisis in historical perspective. Edited by Charles W. Bergquist, Ricardo Peñaranda, and Gonzalo Sánchez G. Wilmington, Del.: SR Books, 1992. 1 v. (Latin American silhouettes)

Fourteen essays (four published previously in Spanish) provide the English reader with an up-to-date synthesis of recent research on the antecedents of La Violencia, its characteristics during 1946–66, and its effects on current conditions. Contributors consider the roles played by drug mafia, guerrillas, paramilitary right, agrarian and labor movements, class conflict, and economic development. Excellent introduction to a fundamental 20th-century theme.

Visión sociocultural del negro en Colombia. See *HLAS 51:4763.*

Zamosc, León. The agrarian question and the peasant movement in Colombia: struggles of the National Peasant Association, 1967–1981. See *HLAS 51:4767.*

SANTANDEREANA

2395 Acevedo Latorre, Eduardo. Colaboradores de Santander en la organización de la república. Prólogo de David Bushnell. 2a ed. rev. Bogotá: Fundación para la Conmemoración del Bicentenario del Natalicio y el Sesquicentenario de la Muerte del General Francisco de Paula Santander, 1988. 487 p., 1 leaf of plates: bibl., ill., indexes. (Biblioteca de la Presidencia de la República)

Short biographies of key bureaucrats in the governments of Gran Colombia and New Granada. Originally published in 1944. Includes excerpts from ministerial reports, correspondence, and other documents, as well as lists of principal laws and decrees. This second ed. is indexed by person, place, theme. Bushnell calls it a "Who's Who" of the era.

2396 Conte Bermúdez, Héctor. Vida del General José Domingo Espinar. (*Lotería,* 371, marzo/abril 1988, p. 52–105)

Documents relating to the career of Espinar (b. 1791), a Panamanian-born engineer, doctor, and soldier who distinguished himself as Jefe de Estado Mayor of the Colombian armies in Peru in the 1820s. Author argues that Espinar has been unfairly neglected by historians. Includes material from national archives of Panama and Colombia.

2397 Legación a la América meridional, 1821–1824: siglo XIX. Recopilación de José María de Mier. Bogotá: Colegio Máximo de las Academias de Colombia; Libreros Colombianos, 1987. 3 v.: bibl., index. (Historia de Colombia según sus protagonistas)

As diplomatic representative of Gran

Colombia (1821–24), Joaquín Mosquera negotiated treaties with Peru, Chile, and Rio de la Plata, promoting unity among the newly-created South American nations. Mier reprints documents related to these activities, assembled from Colombian archives and previously-published collections. Documents are arranged chronologically and indexed by individuals and places, with introductory essay to establish historical context. Valuable source for researchers.

2398 Lozano Esquivel, Alvaro. Santander, 1792–1840. Bogotá: Fundación para la Conmemoración del Bicentenario del Natalicio y el Sesquicentenario de la Muerte del General Francisco de Paula Santander, 1988. 355 p., 1 leaf of plates: bibl., indexes, map. (Biblioteca de la Presidencia de la República)

Journalist utilizes Santander's correspondence and standard secondary works to portray him as "builder, hero and martyr of our country . . . the maximum symbol of Colombian liberty and independence." Useful summary of his life but not a definitive biography.

2399 Moreno de Angel, Pilar. Santander. Bogotá: Planeta, 1989. 795 p.: bibl.

In this massive biography, the director of the Archivo Nacional draws on wide range of manuscripts and published sources to present Santander as an extraordinary soldier, statesman, bibliophile, lover of arts and letters, and principal architect of Colombian democracy. Lacks introduction, but is well-written and researched. Most profound study of Santander to date.

2400 Paredes Ferrer, Alvaro. La Guerra de 1830. Bogotá: Univ. Central, 1985. 238 p.: bibl. (Pensamiento latinoamericano; 4. Historia de las guerras civiles colombianas; 1)

Disjointed analysis of conditions leading to defeat of Bolivarism and triumph of Obando, Azuero, and Santander. Based on contemporary periodicals and secondary works but omits reference to Bushnell's *The Santander regime.* First of projected series of books sponsored by Univ. Central dealing with 19th-century civil wars.

2401 Proceso seguido al General Santander: por consecuencia del acontecimiento de la noche del 25 septiembre de 1828 en Bogotá. Presentación de Germán Mejía Pavony.

Bogotá: Fundación para la Conmemoración del Bicentenario del Natalicio y el Sesquicentenario de la Muerte del general Francisco de Paula Santander, 1988. 401 p., 5 leaves of plates: bibl., ill., indexes (Biblioteca de la Presidencia de la República)

Documents relating to Santander's trial for events of September 25, 1828, his imprisonment in Cartagena, and preparations for exile, plus analysis of trial published by Julio Barriga Alarcón as his thesis in 1943. Editor's introduction concludes that Santander was found guilty for political rather than legal reasons. Indexed by name, place, and theme. Outstanding source material.

2402 Sáenz, Manuela. Manuela Sáenz: epistolario. Estudio y selección de Jorge Villalba F. Quito: Banco Central del Ecuador, Centro de Investigación y Cultura, 1986. 232 p., 10 leaves of plates: bibl., ill., indexes. (Col. Epistolarios; 1)

Sixty letters written by Sáenz (1830–53), most previously unpublished and many addressed to General Juan José Flores. Includes letter to Daniel O'Leary describing attempted assassination of Bolívar. Introductory essays give historical context and genealogical background. Indexed by place and person.

2403 Santander, Francisco de Paula and **Simón Bolívar.** A los colombianos: proclamas y discursos, 1819–1840. Recopilación y notas de Luis Horacio López Domínguez. Bogotá: Fundación para la Conmemoración del Bicentenario del Natalicio y el Sesquicentenario de la Muerte del General Francisco de Paula Santander, 1988. 427 p.: bibl., ill., indexes, ports. (Biblioteca de la Presidencia de la República)

Proclamations and speeches by Bolívar and Santander organized chronologically by decade: 1810–20, 1820–30, and 1830–40. Three-quarters of texts were written by Bolívar and sent to Santander for publication. López Domínguez's introduction provides historical context.

2404 Santander, Francisco de Paula and **Simón Bolívar.** Cartas Santander-Bolívar. v. 1–4. Bogotá: Fundación para la Conmemoración del Bicentenario del Natalicio y el Sesquicentenario de la Muerte del General Francisco de Paula Santander, 1988. 4 v.: bibl., indexes, maps. (Biblioteca de la Presidencia de la República)

Four (of five planned) volumes of correspondence between Santander and Bolívar (1813–28). Vol. 1 covers April 24, 1813– Feb. 5, 1820; Vol. 2, Feb. 8-Oct. 1, 1820; Vol. 3, Oct. 1, 1820-Dec. 31, 1822; and Vol. 4, Jan. 8, 1823-June 21, 1825. Letters are arranged chronologically. Each volume is indexed by person, place, and subject, and contains a specially-prepared map indicating sites where letters were written. Vol. 1 has introductory essay by Germán Arciniegas.

2405 Santander, Francisco de Paula. Diarios de campaña, libro de órdenes, y reglamentos militares, 1818–1834. Introducción de Roberto Ibáñez Sánchez. Bogotá: Fundación para la Conmemoración del Bicentenario del Natalicio y el Sesquicentenario de la Muerte del General Francisco de Paula Santander, 1988. 281 p., 14 leaves of plates: bibl., indexes. (Biblioteca de la Presidencia de la República)

Documents concerning Santander's participation in Venezuelan armies and his organization of the Army of the Vanguard, the Liberation Campaign, and laws regulating the army and navy of the Republic of Colombia. Introductory essay by Roberto Ibáñez Sánchez. Excellent reference tool includes glossary of military terms, maps, and sketches of period uniforms.

2406 Santander, Francisco de Paula. Escritos autobiográficos, 1820–1840. Bogotá: Fundación para la Conmemoración del Bicentenario del Natalicio y el Sesquicentenario de la Muerte del General Francisco de Paula Santander, 1988. 293 p.: bibl., facsims., indexes. (Biblioteca de la Presidencia de la República)

New edition of three previously published works: *El General Simón Bolívar en la campaña de la Nueva Granada de 1819; Memorias sobre el origen, causas y progresos de las desavenencias entre el presidente de la República de Colombia, Simón Bolívar, y el vice-presidente de la misma, Francisco de Paula Santander, escritas por un colombiano en 1829;* and *Apuntamientos para las memorias sobre Colombia y la Nueva Granada por el General Santander, 1837.* Introductory essay by Guillermo Hernández de Alba. Valuable source material.

2407 Santander, Francisco de Paula. Santander en Europa. v. 1–5. 2nd. ed. Bogotá:

Fundación para la Conmemoración del Bicentenario del Natalicio y el Sesquicentenario de la Muerte del General Francisco de Paula Santander, 1989. 5 v.: facsims., indexes. (Biblioteca de la Presidencia de la República)

Documents related to Santander's travels in Germany, Belgium, France, England, Switzerland, and the US while in exile (1829–32). Vols. 1 and 2 present a new edition of his *Diario* first edited by Rafael Martínez Briceño and published in 1963. Vols. 3 and 4 contain 407 letters, many previously unpublished, written by Santander to colleagues, friends, and family during this period. Vol. 5 is a directory of persons and places visited. Introductions by Virgilio Barco and Mario Germán Romero point out that these documents reveal the intimate Santander—his pleasures, fears, and interior life.

2408 Santander, Francisco de Paula. Santander y los ejércitos patriotas. t. 1, 1811–1891. t. 2, 1819. Recopilación de Andrés Montaña. Presentación de Camilo Riaño. Bogotá: Fundación para la Conmemoración del Bicentenario del Natalicio y el Sesquicentenario de la Muerte del General Francisco de Paula Santander, 1989. 2 v.: bibl., indexes. (Biblioteca de la Presidencia de la República)

Documents related to Santander's military activities are arranged chronologically. Vol. 1 covers April 1, 1811-Jan. 19, 1819; vol. 2 covers Jan. 19-July 26, 1819, and deals exclusively with Casanare. In his introduction Camilo Riaño argues that the nickname "Man of Laws" has obscured Santander's military prowess and that these documents will enable a more precise assessment of this facet of his career.

2409 Santander, Francisco de Paula. Santander y los empréstitos de la Gran Colombia, 1822–1828. v. 1. Bogotá: Fundación para la Conmemoración del Bicentenario del Natalicio y el Sesquicentenario de la Muerte del General Francisco de Paula Santander, 1988. 1 v.: bibl, ill. (Biblioteca de la Presidencia de la República, Administración Virgilio Barco)

Twenty-six documents concerning negotiation of British loan of 1824 are complemented by statements of Santander, Francisco Montoya, and Manuel José Hurtado justifying their actions. Preliminary essay provides historical context. Indispensable.

2410 Santander y los sucesos políticos de Venezuela, 1826. v. 1–2. Presentación de Javier Ocampo López. Bogotá: Fundación para la Conmemoración del Bicentenario del Natalicio y el Sesquicentenario de la Muerte del General Francisco de Paula Santander, 1988. 2 v.: ill. (Biblioteca de la Presidencia de la República)

Documents related to "La Cosiata" or the rebellion of Páez in 1826. Includes *actas* of the municipalities and correspondence of Páez, Santander, Bolívar, Soublette, Escalona, Peñalver, J.M. Restrepo, and Urdaneta. Introduction suggests that these documents help explain the multiple causes for the collapse of Gran Colombia and the rise of national states.

ECUADOR

Benites Vinueza, Leopoldo. Ecuador, drama y paradoja. See *HLAS 51:4787.*

2411 Carrión, Benjamín. García Moreno: el santo del patíbulo. 2a ed. Quito: Editorial El Conejo, 1984. 746 p. (Col. Ecuador/ historia)

Facsimile reprint of first ed. published in Mexico (1959) draws on Freudian concepts to present a hostile portrait of García Moreno. Adam Szászdi has described the work as "overdrawn libel, in which the author's unjustified pretence to erudition leads him to errors of the grossest sort" (see HAHR, 44:4, 1964, p. 524).

2412 Cevallos, Pedro Fermín. Historia del Ecuador. v. 5–6. Ambato, Ecuador: Ilustre Municipio de Ambato, 1985. 2 v.: port. (Biblioteca Letras de Tungurahua; 9–10)

Cevallos published first ed. of his 6-volume history in Lima (1870) and the second ed. in Guayaquil (1886–89). Volumes under review are faithful reprinting of second ed., with new title. Vol. 5 narrates political events between 1830–45. Vol. 6 describes administration, industry, economy, religion, population, and geographic regions of the republic between 1859–87.

2413 Cevallos García, Gabriel. Historia del Ecuador: texto. Cuenca, Ecuador: Banco Central del Ecuador, Centro de Investigación y Cultura, 1987. 645 p. (Obras completas; 3)

This second ed. of text published in 1967 for use in Ecuadorian universities is part of Banco Central's project to publish complete works of Cevallos in 11 volumes. No revisions were made to this edition which provides solid survey of Ecuadorian history to 1966.

2414 Cevallos García, Gabriel. Reflexiones sobre la historia del Ecuador. Estudio introductorio de José María Vargas. Quito: Banco Central del Ecuador; Corporación Editora Nacional, 1987. 2 v.: bibl. (Biblioteca básica del pensamiento ecuatoriano; 35–36)

Reprint of seminal study first published in 1960. Introductory essay by José María Vargas for this edition places the work and author in the context of Ecuadorian historiography. Vol. 1 analyzes classic histories of Juan de Velasco, Pedro Fermín Cevallos, and Federico González Suárez. Vol. 2 discusses Quito's role in Ecuadorian history.

2415 Cevallos García, Gabriel. Temas históricos ecuatorianos. Cuenca, Ecuador: Banco Central del Ecuador, Centro de Investigación y Cultura, 1987. 2 v.: bibl. (Obras completas; 1–2)

Reissue of collection originally published between 1944–78 by influential historian. Vol. 1 includes bio-bibliography and six essays on the colonial era including well-known "Para entender bien el Ecuador." Eight essays in vol. 2 concern García Moreno, Eloy Alfaro, and "Las ideas liberales en el Ecuador." Banco Central intends to reprint the remainder of Cevallos' writings in nine additional volumes.

2416 Congreso de Historia del Negro en el Ecuador y Sur de Colombia, 1st, Esmeraldas, Ecuador, 1988. Actas. Coordinación de Rafael Savoia. Quito: Centro Cultural Afro-Ecuatoriano, Depto. de Pastoral Afro-Ecuatoriano, 1988. 272 p.: bibl., ill.

Proceedings of 1988 conference held in Esmeraldas. Topics include archaeology, colonial and national history, blacks in Guayaquil, slave trade in Sierra region, noble black slaves, and *cimarronismo* in Colombia. Important contribution to history of blacks in Latin America.

Cordero Espinosa, Claudio; Lucas Achig Subía; and Adrián Carrasco. La región centrosur. See item **2090.**

2417 Corkill, David and David Cubitt. Ecuador, fragile democracy. London: Latin American Bureau, 1988. 139 p.: bibl., ill.

Succinct, well-informed survey of political, economic and social developments in contemporary Ecuador emphasizes developments of the 1970s and 1980s. [M.T. Hamerly]

Documentos para la historia de la Villa de Gualaceo. See item **2091.**

2418 Estupiñán, César Névil. Nuestro Vargas Torres. Esmeraldas, Ecuador: Ediciones de la Univ. Técnica Luis Vargas Torres, 1987. 301 p.: bibl., ill., ports.

Eulogistic biography of Liberal officer from Esmeraldas who led some of Eloy Alfaro's forces against Veintimilla's dictatorship in 1882 and who was captured and executed in 1887. Argues that Vargas Torres was an outstanding Liberal who would have been president had he survived.

2419 Estupiñán-Freile, Tamara. Una familia republicana: los Martínez Holguín. Quito: Museos del Banco Central del Ecuador, 1988. 382 p.: appendices, bibl., ill., photos.

Carefully researched "tesis de grado" in history at Pontificia Univ. Católica uses family, local, and provincial archival materials to create a biography of Nicolás Martínez (1821–87), his wife Adelaida Holguín (1840–1921), and their 11 children. Analyzes development and organization of their enormous estate, "Lyria." Lavish edition with many photographs.

2420 Gimeno, Ana. Juan José Flores en España: algunos antecedentes de la tentativa de expedición del ex-presidente del Ecuador en 1846. (*Cultura/Quito*, 9:25, mayo/agosto 1986, p. 23–45)

Discusses efforts of Flores to convince Spain to mount an expedition to Ecuador in 1846 to re-establish a monarchy. Based on materials in Spanish archives. Interesting analysis of Flores' monarchical views.

2421 Godard, H.R. El período cacaotero en el Ecuador, 1890–1925, y sus repercusiones en Guayaquil, nuevo centro de gravedad del país. (*Rev. Geogr./Quito*, 26, dic. 1987, p. 139–172, bibl., graphs, photos, tables)

Geographer examines demographic, social, and economic expansion of Guayaquil during the cacao boom. Concludes that the "weight" of history, economic orientations, and geographic location has forged two mentalities: the "closed" space of Quito and the "open" space of Guayaquil that fosters a more flexible social system. Scholarly piece worth reading.

2422 La historia del Ecuador: ensayos de interpretación. Edición de Enrique Ayala Mora. Quito: Corporación Editora Nacional, 1985. 403 p.: bibl. (Biblioteca de historia ecuatoriana; 10)

Stimulating essays by 19 scholars and writers systematically explore Ecuador's history. Editor's introduction gives brilliant overview of Ecuadorian historiography from Velasco to 20th-century socialist interpretations. Required reading for anyone interested in interpretations of Ecuador's past.

Jurado Noboa, Fernando. Los Larrea: burocracia, tenencia de la tierra, poder político, crisis, retorno al poder y papel en la cultura ecuatoriana. See item **2097.**

Lara, Jorge Salvador. Notas acerca del pensamiento de los próceres quiteños de 1809. See item **5380.**

Liehr, Reinhard. La deuda exterior de la Gran Colombia frente a Gran Bretaña, 1820–1860. See item **2362.**

2423 Luna Tamayo, Milton. Orígenes del movimiento obrero de la sierra ecuatoriana: el Centro Obrero Católico. (*Cultura/Quito*, 9:26, sept./dic. 1986, p. 285–315)

Traces efforts of Church, militant Conservatives, and Quito artisans to build a national Catholic workers' organization. Case history of the Centro Obrero Católico from its foundation in 1906 to the emergence of the Confederación Ecuatoriana de Obreros Católicos in 1938.

Maier S., Jorge. Historia postal de Quito, 1534–1864. See item **2102.**

Márquez Bararatta, Raúl. Investigación documental sobre la formación político-administrativa y otros documentos socio-económicos de la Provincia de El Oro. See *HLAS 51:4799.*

2424 Moncayo, Abelardo. Pensamiento político. Guayaquil, Ecuador: Depto.

de Publicaciones de la Facultad de Ciencias Económicas de la Univ. de Guayaquil, 1983. 152 p. (Biblioteca Ecuatoriana; 48)

Brief biography of Moncayo (1877–1939), a Liberal economist who reformed Ecuador's financial system in the late 1920s. Includes six documents and offers insight into a little-studied era.

2425 Moscoso C., Martha. Comunidad, autoridad indígena y poder republicano en el siglo XIX. (*Rev. Andin.*, 7:2, dic. 1989, p. 481–499)

During the 19th century indigenous authorities in Cuenca served as intermediaries between white-mestizo republican authorities and Indian communities. The communities accepted the republic and its tax and labor impositions as long as these remained within customary boundaries. Article based on primary sources. [N.P. Jacobsen]

2426 Muñoz, Leonardo J. Testimonio de lucha: memorias sobre la historia del socialismo en el Ecuador. Introducción de Enrique Ayala Mora. Quito: Corporación Editora Nacional; Ediciones La Tierra, 1988. 151 p.: ill., ports. (Col. Testimonios; 1)

Recollections of pioneer figure in evolution of Ecuadorian Socialist Party transcribed from tape recorded a year before his death in 1988. Provides information on founding and activities of the party, with rich analysis of the 1930s and 1940s. Excellent introduction by Enrique Ayala Mora.

2427 Muñoz Borrero, Eduardo. En el Palacio de Carondelet: del presidente Flores al presidente Febres Cordero, 1830–1985. 2a ed. Quito: Artes Gráficas Señal, 1985. 704 p.: bibl., ill.

Brief sketches of 28 constitutional presidents, 19 supreme *jefes*, and 23 provisional governments that ruled Ecuador between 1830 and 1985, by corresponding member of the Academia Nacional de Historia. Second ed. differs from the 1981 ed. by addition of four-page entry on León Febres Cordero, president from 1981–84. Interesting introduction to role of executive branch.

2428 Muratorio, Blanca. Rucuyaya Alonso y la historia social y económica del Alto Napo, 1850–1950. Quito: Ediciones Abya-Yala, 1987. 341 p., 14 p. of plates: bibl., ill. (some col.).

Canadian anthropologist presents two simultaneous accounts of history of the Tena-Archidona zone of Napo Province in Ecuador's Upper Amazon region. The first is the personal narrative, translated into Spanish from Quechua, of Rucuyaya Alonso, ex-*cargador*, gold washer, rubber collector, and Shell Oil employee, who recounts the history of the Upper Amazon as told to him by his father and grandfather and as he himself experienced it. The second is author's careful synthesis of region's history based on written sources. Stresses ongoing resistance of natives to white abuse and economic exploitation, and discusses Indian reaction to competing Protestant and Catholic missionaries. Based on six years of field research. Skillful, fascinating, and convincing.

2429 Nueva historia del Ecuador. v. 9. Edicion de Enrique Ayala Mora. Quito: Corporación Editora Nacional; Grijalbo, 1988. 1 v.: bibl., ill. (some col.), graphs.

Well-designed textbook consisting of essays by six leading scholars who examine aspects of the 1895–1925 era. Topics include international perspective, cacao boom, evolution of political conflicts, culture, daily life, and origins of labor movements. Superb, clearly written introduction to crucial period in national history. For volumes 3, 4, and 5, see item **2114.**

2430 Pérez Concha, Jorge. Carlos Concha Torres: biografía de un luchador incorruptible. Quito: Editorial El Conejo, 1987. 224 p.: bibl. (Col.Ecuador/biografías)

Biography of Concha Torres (1864–1919), *caudillo* of Esmeraldas, who supported the slain Eloy Alfaro and led a rebellion in Sept. 1913 against Alfaro's successor, Leonidas Plaza Gutiérrez. Based on archival materials and secondary sources.

2431 Pérez Concha, Jorge. De la goleta Alcance al cañonero Calderón. v. 1–2. Guayaquil, Ecuador: Instituto de Historia Marítima, Armada del Ecuador, 1987. 2 v.: bibl., ill., ports.

Twenty-eight episodes in Ecuador's naval history. Vol. 1 covers 1818–1914, including Flores' naval expedition of 1852, the defense of Guayaquil against Spain in 1864, and War of the Pacific battles. Vol. 2 covers 1912–41 and includes navy's role in 1932

war with Colombia and the 1941 Peruvian invasion. Cites some sources, but style is popular rather than scholarly.

Pesillo: documentos para su historia. See item **2118.**

2432 Pineo, Ronn F. Reinterpreting labor militancy: the collapse of the cacao economy and the general strike of 1922 in Guayaquil, Ecuador. (*HAHR*, 68:4, Nov. 1988, p. 708–736)

Argues persuasively that Ecuadorian labor history did not follow same trends observed in Argentina or Chile. Shows that general strike of 1922 was not led by foreign anarchists but by local workers responding to lower standard of living due to collapse of cacao export economy. This PhD research draws on varied periodical and primary materials.

2433 Rodríguez, Linda Alexander. La política en el Ecuador, 1830–1925. (*Cultura/Quito*, 9:26, sept./dic. 1986, p. 285–315)

Concise summary of political developments stresses interplay of regionalism, authoritarianism, militarism, and personalism. Perceptive analysis is based on sure command of published and archival sources.

2434 Saint-Geours, Yves. La evolución demográfica del Ecuador en el siglo XIX. (*Cultura/Quito*, 8:24b, enero/abril 1986, p. 481–492, bibl., graphs, tables)

Concise summary of demographic trends by director of French Institute of Andean Studies in Lima. Lists sources for population statistics and divides data into three periods: 1780–1830, 1830–70, and 1870–1930. Demonstrates that Ecuador experienced real, sustained growth after 1860, unlike some other South American countries.

2435 Tobar Donoso, Julio. La invasión peruana y el Protocolo de Río: antecedentes y explicación histórica. Quito: Banco Central del Ecuador, 1982. 559 p., 2 folded leaves of plates: maps. (Col. histórica; 2)

As Ecuadorian foreign minister, Tobar Donoso signed the Río Protocol in 1942 which settled the boundary dispute with Peru but was widely regarded by Ecuadorians as a cowardly surrender of territory. He defended his actions in a classic work published in 1945 but until now out of print. For this second edition the Banco Central has reproduced the original book, adding an introduction to explain the historical context.

2436 Van Aken, Mark J. King of the night: Juan José Flores and Ecuador, 1824–1864. Berkeley: Univ. of California Press, 1989. 382 p.: bibl., ill., index, maps.

Best-written and most thoroughly-researched study to date of Juan José Flores, three-time president of Ecuador, and his endeavours to establish a monarchy in his adopted country. Highly-informative and enlightening, but somewhat lacking in biographical coverage. [M.T. Hamerly]

2437 Villegas Domínguez, Rodrigo. Historia de la Provincia de Imbabura. Ibarra, Ecuador: Centro de Ediciones Culturales de Imbabura, 1988. 296 p.: bibl. (Monografía de Imbabura; 1)

Well-written survey of provincial history from preconquest to 1987, one-half of which deals with post-independence period. The first of four projected volumes in this series that will deal with the history of Imbabura.

Peru

NILS P. JACOBSEN, *Associate Professor, University of Illinois, Urbana-Champaign*

IN SPITE OF THE INCREASINGLY DIFFICULT CONDITIONS for scholarly work in Peru, published research on the country's republican history has continued at an impressive clip, although a good share of the output within Peru follows political conjunctures. Some of the perennial favorite subjects, especially work on the War of the Pacific and the reformist military regime of 1968–80, have drawn less interest compared to the preceding reporting periods, but APRA and its leaders have seen a further rise in historical publications, as the party held national power for the first time from 1985–90. The output of works on national and regional heroes as well as local histories, written for a broad public distant from the ivory tower, has continued unabated with its markedly different methodological and discursive canons.

Publications by professional historians inside and outside of Peru evince uncertainty about methods and paradigms. Straight-forward dependency or orthodox Marxist interpretations of Peru's republican history are becoming rarer among professional historians, but retain popularity in politically inspired historiography. Structuralist economic and social history publications remain numerous. Peruvianists have been comparatively slow in combining such themes with approaches focusing on culture, ideologies and mentalities, as well as political power constellations. Social and political movements received much attention in the present reporting period. The focus in this area is gradually expanding beyond the history of organized labor and peasant uprisings to include other forms of urban and rural protest movements and associations. But most topics which we suggested in *HLAS 50* as urgently needing attention, such as demographic history, the history of the bureaucracy and military during the century after independence, the history of taxation, the history of gender roles, and the evolution of public health, continue to be neglected.

The most ambitious Peruvian publication project of the 1980s, the complete works of Victor Andrés Belaunde (items **2447, 2448, 2450, 2451,** and **2449**) began to appear in print in our reporting period. Thus the works of the country's most influential conservative thinker, who based his vision of a Catholic Peruvian identity on an interpretation of post-conquest history, will become as accessible as the writing of his great socialist and populist counterparts, Mariátegui and Haya de la Torre. Most publications on Haya in this period were part of a concerted effort by the Peruvian Aprista Party during the presidency of Alan García to popularize and aggrandize the party's contributions to the nation's development; these works suffer from an uncritical hagiographic bias (e.g., see item **2482**). But Alva Castro's documentary editions (items **2440** and **2441**) have made available important contemporary influences on Haya's thought and political activities between the 1930s and 1960, and on APRA's appeal in other parts of Latin America. Autobiographies and reprints of earlier publications by other APRA leaders and militants (items **2514, 2521,** and **2461**) further our understanding of doctrinal and political struggles in the party. The volume edited by Bonilla and Drake (item **2444**) provides important analyses on the transformation of the party between the 1960s and mid-1980s, as well as early evaluations of the García Administration. The greatest strides in deciphering Peru's republican history have been made by a spate of publications on the early post-independence period, an era whose historiography until recently was as obscure as its chaotic politics. Paul Gootenberg has provided us with a lucid, if controversial framework for making sense of those politics, emphasizing coalition building around foreign trade issues and the political economy of chronic fiscal deficits (items **2477** and **2479**). Celia Wu (item **2455**) further demonstrates the ties between Peru's foreign relations and the domestic struggles between caudillos, as well as the difficulty of defining the Peruvian nation and the concomitant early rise of rather empty national hero worship. Villanueva Urteaga (item **2526**), Remy (item **2504**), Hünefeldt (item **2484**) and Contreras (item **2463**) offer new information and sophisticated interpretations of changing political and social constellations on the local and regional levels in the southern and central sierra, demonstrating the complex struggles between Creoles, mestizos and the local peasantry. New studies on the era's economic development (e.g., Quiroz's article in item **2486** and Burga, item **2458**) highlight the regional, sectoral, and even communal diversity of conjunctures.

Essays by Aguirre (item **2445**) and Hünefeldt (item **2484**) offer major reinterpretations of the final phase of black slavery in post-independence Peru, suggesting that the system was undergoing a rapid decomposition by the actions of the slaves themselves, either through marronage and banditry or through working for wages, contractual manumission and litigation. Our understanding of labor conditions on the coast after the abolition of slavery has been much advanced through a number of articles and monographs. Cecilia Méndez (item **2495**) shows the economic rationale behind the reliance on coolies and prison labor in the extraction of guano and how the workers struggled to improve their miserable working conditions. Humberto Rodríguez Pastor (item **2506**) has given us a balanced and sympathetic portrait of the coolies, highlighting the contrast between harsh labor conditions and their cultural autonomy. Michael Gonzales (item **2476**) offers a sophisticated analysis of the crucial transition period of coastal labor regimes between the 1870s and 1890s, underscoring the central role played by various categories of Chinese workers even after the end of the coolie trade. Peter Kammann's major scholarly work (item **2487**) documents how much the wages and living conditions of north coast sugar workers improved between the 1920s and 1960s and how it was the specific group interests of certain worker categories, more than the pernicious influence of APRA ideology, that turned their movement conservative by the 1950s.

In Peruvian urban labor history we now see sophisticated studies that combine an analysis of labor regimes and working conditions with an analysis of the labor movement itself. Francisco Quiroz (item **2503**) shows the ideological and organizational limitations of Lima's artisans at the crucial moment when Peru adopted free trade in the 1850s. Luis Tejada (item **2520**) presents detailed information on the crucial bakery sector of Lima's industries around 1900, covering entrepreneurs, labor processes, working conditions, and the unresolved conflicts in the radicalizing union of bakery workers. The testimony of the pioneering organized textile workers from the 1930s, collected by Derpich and Israel (item **2467**), provides crucial insights into the everyday life and early union activities during the Depression years. For rural society, the contributions to the volume by Aguirre and Walker (item **2445**) have considerably recast our image of banditry and criminality, demonstrating the ties of rural unrest to political struggles on the national level, the stark conflicts within local groups of peasants and rural workers, the lack of social goals for most bandit activity, and perversion of indigenista rhetoric into racist stereotypes of the Indian, used by authoritarian policy-makers to legitimize measures of social control. William Stein's minute analysis of the Atusparia uprising of 1885 (items **2517** and *HLAS 50:767*) demythologizes this important movement by pointing to the strategic involvement of urban groups.

Purely economic historical studies, beyond those already mentioned for the early republican era, have been relatively scant during this reporting period. However, we should mention Gootenberg's important study on prices between the 1820s and 1870s (item **2478**), an invaluable tool for further economic analyses. Luna's article (item **2492**) suggests that for brief periods German business activity in Peru may have been rather more important than hitherto thought, even before the 1930s.

The political history of the confusing middle decades of the 20th century is beginning to receive more attention. In his suggestive synthesis Geoffrey Bertram (item **2452**) downplays the role of APRA and speaks of a variety of experimental political models, in a situation in which old and new forces, oligarchic, liberal and populist parties, the military and regionalist movements could never impose their will on power contenders for long. Orazio Ciccarelli (item **2462**) comes to similar conclusions about the Benavides regime (1933–39) which, despite sympathies for Italian fascism, ultimately followed pragmatic policies to insure regime stability. In a thorough analysis of economic policy-making during the brief reformist era of 1945–48, Mirella García (item **2473**) also diagnoses the weakness of specific interest groups, the instability of the ruling coalition, and pure ineptness as the causes for the downfall of the Bustamante Administration.

The severe and ongoing crisis of the last decade is beginning to attract serious historical study and reflection. Expressing views widely held among social scientists, Steve Stein and Carlos Monge (item **2515**) trace the crucial juncture between the demise of the "patrimonial state," the growing economic crisis, and the rise of new, more autonomous social and political movements since the military regime of 1968–80. In the first thorough historical study of the Sendero Luminoso insurrection, Gustavo Gorriti (item **2480**) emphasizes the misunderstandings and indecisiveness of Peru's political elites, intellectuals, and military and intelligence apparatus to account for the stunning early successes of Sendero's clandestine revolutionary movement.

This reporting period saw further important publications on the history of church and missionary activity in republican Peru. Jeffrey Klaiber (item **2489**) has given us the first comprehensive history of the Catholic Church and its lay movements since independence, a judicious and balanced account which is sure to remain a reference work for years to come. Pilar García Jordan (item **2474**) continues to chronicle Church-State relations during the 19th and early 20th centuries. And Rosa del Carmen Bruno-Jofre (items **2457** and **2456**) has undertaken to elucidate the impact of mainline Protestant groups on Peruvian society, a topic whose importance will surely grow in the future.

An important new source for 19th-century Peruvian history, selections from the diaries of the German-born merchant Heinrich Witt (item **2530**), is rich in information on a broad range of topics covering more than half a century. Research on the 19th century will also be made easier by Estuardo Núñez's thorough compendium of travel literature, a major reference tool (item **2497**).

Finally, I would like to mention the last book-length publication of Alberto Flores Galindo (item **2470**), whose premature death leaves a great void in Peruvian historiography. In this collection of essays Flores Galindo once again demonstrated the enormous range of his interests and knowledge, and his concern for connecting historical scholarship to the serious issues facing Peru today. It is to be hoped that the open historiographical debate to which he contributed so much can be sustained against the enormous odds which confront all historians working on Peru today.

2438 A la gloria del gran almirante del Perú, Miguel Grau, en el sesquicentenario de su natalicio, 1834/1984. 3a ed. numerada, corr. y ampliada. Lima: Secretaría del Ministro de Marina, 1984. 441 p.: ill.

Luxurious commemorative volume contains biographical essays, eulogies, poems, and inaugural speeches about Peru's most famous naval officer, written between the 1860s and the present. Letters, reports and other documents written by Grau himself are also included. Latest in a string of hagiographic publications about the "hero of Angamos," the book may serve to trace the construction of military's nationalist sentiment.

2439 Altuve Carrillo, Leonardo. Introducción a Choquehuanca y otros temas bolivarianos. Caracas: Los Gabrieles, 1987. 76 p.: bibl., ill.

Work includes episodes of Bolívar's life, mostly concerning Peru: the state of research on José Domingo Choquehuanca, scion of a family of Southern Andean nobility who in 1825 pronounced a famous speech in praise of Bolívar, and a section on Simón Rodríguez, Bolívar's "teacher," in his old age.

2440 Alva Castro, Luis. Haya de la Torre. v. 1, Peregrino de la fraternidad boliva-riana: Haya de la Torre en Chile. Lima: s.n., 1988. 1 v.: ill.

Contemporary newspaper accounts of Haya's trip to Chile in April 1946, on the occasion of a congress of Latin American-socialist parties. In speeches and interviews Haya stressed need for Latin American political and economic integration.

2441 Alva Castro, Luis. Haya de la Torre. v. 2, Peregrino de la unidad continental. Lima: Fondo Editorial V.R. Haya de la Torre, 1990. 1 v.: ill.

Facsimile reproduction of publications and manifestos by Partido Aprista Cubano and articles from newspapers and periodicals (*Patria, Futuro, Bohemia*) close to the party or allied political groups covering 1934–59. There are many articles by Haya in these Havana publications, including one praising Fidel Castro and the Cuban Revolution.

2442 Amayo, Enrique. La política británica en la Guerra del Pacífico. Lima: Editorial Horizonte, 1988. 282 p.: bibl., ill. (Historia; 6)

England supported Chile during the War of the Pacific because the governments of both countries and their strongest business lobbies supported free trade. Author seeks to invigorate notion of the War as an episode in Britain's free trade imperialism.

Analyzes the interests of British, Chilean, and Peruvian businessmen concerning nitrates between 1876–91, and British diplomacy in support of economic interests. Based on incomplete and opinionated readings of diplomatic correspondence and newspapers.

2443 Anrup, Roland. El taita y el toro: en torno a la configuración patriarcal del régimen hacendario cuzqueño. Stockholm: Depto. de Historia, Univ. de Gotemburgo: Instituto de Estudios Latinoamericanos, Univ. de Estocolmo, 1990. 280 p.

Psychoanalytical portrayal of the relation between *hacendados* and labor tenants on Cusco estates during the 20th century. Author suggests that the former labor tenants' lack of interest in the success of agrarian reform cooperatives resulted from their disorientation, since they had lost the father figure of the *hacendado*. Based on extensive interviews and estate records.

2444 El APRA, de la ideología a la praxis. Edición de Heraclio Bonilla y Paul W. Drake. Lima: Centro Latinoamericano de Historia Económica y Social; San Diego: Center for Iberian and Latin American Studies, Univ. of California, 1989. 402 p.: bibl., ill.

Sixteen essays by prominent historians, social scientists and businessmen from Peru and the US, some of which retrace the history of APRA from the 1920s through 1985. Most offer an early evaluation of APRA'S first three years in power under President Alan García (1985–1990), focusing on relations between the party and the military and various business groups, economic policies, the foreign debt problem, and social policies. As a whole the essays question whether a populist project designed in the first third of the century is still viable for the 1980s.

2445 Bandoleros, abigeos y montoneros: criminalidad y violencia en el Perú, siglos XVIII-XX. Edición de Carlos Aguirre *et al.* Lima: Instituto de Apoyo Agrario, 1990. 393 p.: bibl., map. (Serie Tiempo de historia; 7)

Eleven innovative essays on various aspects of rural banditry, livestock theft, marronage and politically active rural bands from the late colonial period through the 1970s, based on primary archival and ethno-graphical research. Several contributions draw into doubt Hobsbawm's notion of social banditry. In the early independence period bandit and maroon groups close to Lima influenced the movement towards abolition of slavery and intervened in the struggles between liberals and conservatives (Aguirre, Walker). The relation of bandits to their communities varied greatly according to the land tenure regime, ethnic structures, and commercial patterns (Orlove, Langer). Between the 1920s and 1950 indigenista emphasis on a continued and strong Indian cultural and social identity became perverted by jurists into positivist and racist notions of Indian criminal predisposition requiring a "normalization" through special Indian codes that sought to integrate the Indians into the westernized national society (Poole).

2446 Basombrío Iglesias, Carlos and Wilson Sagástegui Lozada. El movimiento obrero: historia gráfica. v. 6, 1968–76: tiempos de reforma. Lima: Tarea, 1987? 1 v.: ill., facsims.

Compilation of valuable photographs, cartoons and newspaper headlines on strikes, labor union organizations and ideology from the first phase of the revolutionary military regime, accompanied by brief, popular texts of an orthodox Marxist bent. For vol. 5, see *HLAS 50:2190.*

2447 Belaúnde, Víctor Andrés. Obras completas. v. 1, primera serie, El proyecto nacional. El Perú antiguo y los modernos sociólogos y otros ensayos. Introducción de Raúl Porras Barrenechea *et al.* Epílogo de Pedro Planas Silva. Lima: Comisión Nacional del Centenario, 1987. 330 p.: bibl., ill., index.

First volume in this major monographic series planned for publication of Belaúnde's complete works: monographs, dispersed articles and correspondence in some 35 volumes. One of the most influential intellectuals of 20th-century Peru, Belaúnde's work spans six decades (1906–66) and covers a range of disciplines, including philosophy, religion, history, ethnography, literature, jurisprudence, and international relations. The edition combines a topical and chronological scheme. The first part of this series, 5 vols. subtitled *El proyecto nacional*, brings together Belaunde's publications concerned with Peru's national identity. This volume contains early works (1904–23), among them his positivist bachelor's thesis on philosophy of law, and four works on Peru's prehispanic civilizations. For other volumes in this series, see items **2448, 2450, 2451,** and **2449.**

2448 Belaúnde, Víctor Andrés. Obras completas. v. 2, primera serie, El proyecto nacional. Meditaciones peruanas. Introducción de Jorge Basadre *et al.* Epílogo de Fernando Iwasaki C. Lima: Comisión Nacional del Centenario, 1987. 459 p., 1 folded leaf of plates: bibl., ill., index.

Third ed. of work originally published in 1933 is a collection of essays written between 1907–23. Editors have included six short texts not found in the second edition. Written mostly in the heat of contemporary political and social debates, essays contain Belaúnde's notions of democracy, his critique of national institutions and politics, early ideas on indigenismo and university reform, and a critique of Italian fascism written in 1923 when Belaúnde had fully converted to Catholic social reform doctrines.

2449 Belaúnde, Víctor Andrés. Obras completas. v. 3, primera serie, El proyecto nacional. La realidad nacional. Introducción de Luis Alberto Sánchezy Antonio Espinosa Laña. Epílogo de Hugo Neyra. Lima: Comisión Nacional del Centenario, 1987. 306 p.: bibl., ill., index.

Sixth ed. of the work restores the complete text of the first ed. of 1931, including the chapters criticizing Leguia's *Oncenio,* withdrawn by Belaúnde himself in subsequent editions. The work constitutes Belaúnde's answer to Mariategui's *Seven interpretive essays on Peruvian reality,* and contains his Christian, semicorporatist vision of the nation.

2450 Belaúnde, Víctor Andrés. Obras completas. v. 4, primera serie, El proyecto nacional. El debate constitucional. Introducción de José de la Riva Agüero *et al..* Epílogo de Eduardo Benavides Torres. Lima: Comisión Nacional del Centenario, 1987. 488 p.: bibl., ill., index.

Belaúnde's speeches in the Constitutional Congress of 1931–32 and an essay on the economic and political evolution of Peru 1914–39. Of special importance are his speeches on voting rights, decentralization, the "Indian problem," freedom of the press,

Church-State relations, and the functional senate.

2451 Belaúnde, Víctor Andrés. Obras completas. v. 5, primera serie, El proyecto nacional. Peruanidad. Introducción de Aurelio Miró Quesada S. *et al.* Epílogo de César Pacheco Vélez. Lima: Comisión Nacional del Centenario, 1987. 488 p.: bibl., ill., index.

Sixth ed. of the work, originally published in a much briefer version in 1942 is largely organized chronologically, with half the chapters treating colonial culture. Book constitutes Belaúnde's most complete expression of his Christian, ethnically-integrated vision of the Peruvian nation.

2452 Bertram, Geoffrey. Peru, 1930–1960. (*in* The Cambridge history of Latin America. Edited by Leslie Bethell. Cambridge: Cambridge Univ. Press, 1991, v. 8, p. 385–450)

Highly original synthesis focuses on economic and demographic trends and the political system. Stresses the fragmented and experimental character of Peruvian politics, downplaying the struggle between APRA, the military, and the oligarchy.

Böhm, Günter. Inmigración de judíos de habla alemana a Chile y Perú durante el siglo XIX. See item **2563.**

2453 Bonfiglio, Giovanni. Introducción al estudio de la inmigración europea en el Perú. (*Apuntes/Lima,* 18, 1986, p. 93–127, appendix, bibl., tables)

Outline of Peruvian immigration policy and demography of European immigration to Peru since mid-19th century.

2454 Bonilla, Heraclio. Peru and Bolivia from Independence to the War of the Pacific. (*in* The Cambridge History of Latin America. Edited by Leslie Bethell. Cambridge: Cambridge Univ. Press, 1985, v. 3, p. 539–582)

Accomplished synthesis of the two republics' economic, social and political evolution 1820s-83 by a prominent representative of the dependency approach. Bonilla stresses the failures of the outward-looking economic development between the 1840s-70s (based on guano exports for Peru and silver and nitrates for Bolivia) to produce a substantive advance towards integrated internal markets benefitting all social groups.

2455 Brading, Celia Wu. Generals and diplomats: Great Britain and Peru, 1820–40. Translated and edited by D.A. Brading. Cambridge: Centre of Latin American Studies, Univ. of Cambridge, 1991. 125 p.: (Cambridge Latin American miniatures, 0266–7541; 3)

Four separate essays deal with British-Peruvian relations and the struggles between military caudillos during the early post-independence period. Suggests the difficulties of defining a Peruvian nation, the large influence of "foreign" military leaders, both from neighboring countries and from Europe, the tensions between cautious Foreign Office policies and the more interventionist stance of British Chargés d'Affaires, consuls, and commanders of the naval squadron, and the early foundation of the cult of nationalist military heroes such as Felipe Santiago Salaverry.

2456 Bruno-Jofré, Rosa del Carmen. Methodist education in Peru: social gospel, politics, and American ideological and economic penetration, 1888–1930. Waterloo, Canada: Canadian Corp. for Studies in Religion; Wilfrid Laurier Univ. Press, 1988. 223 p.: (Comparative ethics series: 2)

Despite the small numbers of their pupils, Methodist and other Protestant schools in Peru helped shape the middle-class work ethic and influenced many reformist politicians who taught or studied there. They also promoted "imperialist capitalism." Based on primary research.

2457 Bruno-Jofré, Rosa del Carmen. Social Gospel, the Committee on Cooperation in Latin America and the APRA: the case of the American Methodist Mission, 1920–1930. (NS, 9:18, 1984, p. 75–110)

Methodist missionaries in Peru, espousing a religious version of North American pragmatism, combined ethnocentricity and cultural imperialism with support for reformist political movements. Haya and early APRA maintained lively contacts with Protestant missionaries.

2458 Burga, Manuel. El Perú Central, 1770–1860: disparidades regionales y la primera crisis agrícola republicana. (in América Latina en la época de Simón Bolívar. Edición de Reinhard Liehr. Berlin: Colloquium Verlag, 1989, p. 227–310, graphs, tables)

Careful study of tithe payments for coastal and highland region of the bishopric of Lima documents stagnation of coastal agriculture between 1820s-60s, while central highlands underwent growth based on integration of mining, livestock estates, and peasant crop agriculture. Author draws broad conclusions about contrary phases of Hispanic and Indian agricultural production.

2459 Cahill, David P. Una visión andina: el levantamiento de Ocongate de 1815. (Histórica/Lima, 12:2, dic. 1988, p. 133–159, bibl.)

After presenting a broad overview of the growing repression of Cusco's Indian communities during the decades after the Tupac Amaru rebellion, the author details a hitherto overlooked local peasant uprising linked to the Creole-lead Pumacahua rebellion. While the movement's popular base called for expulsion or extermination of all whites, the leaders primarily sought to keep the mita and tribute abolished for good.

2460 Campos, Ignacio. Coloquios de Haya de la Torre. Selección y notas de Luis Alva Castro Bogotá: Tercer Mundo Editores, 1988. 2 v. (371 p.) (Col. Pensamiento político latinoamericano)

Reedition of some of Campos' popular transcriptions of Haya's lectures and debates with students and party members in the APRA headquarters during the early 1960s covers a broad sweep of historical, philosophical, social, and political issues. Printed for the first time are Campos' digests of some of Haya's major works.

2461 Chanduví Torres, Luis. El APRA por dentro: lo que hice, lo que vi, y lo que sé, 1931–1957. Lima: Tall. Gráf. Copias e Impresiones, 1988. 551 p.: bibl., ill.

Minute report of former APRA militant about plots, uprisings, assassinations and underground activities planned or carried out by the party or groups within it between 1931–48. Author, petty officer in the army who was eager for an APRA-led social revolution by coup, was imprisoned repeatedly for his activities. Originally captivated by Haya de la Torre's charisma and rhetoric, by 1948 he was persuaded that Haya was a coward and that Haya, together with much of the political leadership of the party, boycotted the militants' conspiratorial plans. Based on personal diaries and interviews with fellow activists, the book contains new information especially on revolutionary activity in Trujillo during 1931–32 attack on the O'Donovan barracks and the Oct. 3, 1948 military uprising.

2462 Ciccarelli, Orazio. Fascism and politics in Peru during the Benavides Regime, 1933–39: the Italian perpective. (*HAHR*, 70:3, Aug. 1990, p. 405–432)

While Benavides maintained close military and commercial relations with Italy, he never embraced fascism. After 1937, with mounting pressures from the US and growing domestic nationalism, he pragmatically balanced ties with Axis and Allied powers. In Peru's extremely complex and fragmented political and ideological struggles of the 1930s, both fascism and liberal-democratic ideals were often proclaimed merely for tactical reasons. Italian diplomats, on whose reports the article is based, at times exaggerated the fascist leanings of Benavides who remained a pragmatic politician.

2463 Contreras, Carlos. Estado republicano y tributo indígena en la Sierra Central en la post-Independencia. (*Histórica/Lima*, 13:1, julio 1989, p. 9–44, bibl., tables)

Careful analysis of *indígena* and *casta* tax lists of 1835 and 1846 leads author to suggest a changed relation of the individual peasant to the State in Central Peru since 1820s. By mid-19th century, colonial corporate Indian communities were being transformed into voluntary associations of individual peasant families.

2464 Cornejo Polar, Jorge. Estado y cultura en el Perú republicano. Lima: Univ. de Lima, Depto. Académico de Ciencias Humanas, 1987. 142 p.: bibl. (Cuadernos de historia; 3)

Chronological synopsis of the central government's policies toward cultural issues, 1821–1985. Author diagnoses lack of coherence between such policies and the pluralistic cultural aspirations of the Peruvian people, especially the various Indian cultural communities.

2465 Cotler, Julio. Peru since 1960. (*in* The Cambridge history of Latin America. Edited by Leslie Bethell. Cambridge: Cambridge Univ. Press, 1991, v. 8, p. 451–508)

Synthesis of regimes and politics in Peru from 1960 through the presidency of Alan García (1985–90).

2466 Cueto, Marcos. Excelencia científica en la periferia: actividades científicas e investigación biomédica en el Perú, 1890–1950. Lima: Grupo de Análisis para el Desarrollo, 1989. 230 p.: bibl., ill.

One of the first scholarly monographs on Peruvian scientific history focuses on high-altitude physiology, but presents a model for the conditions of scientific research in poor peripheral countries in general. The success of high-altitude physiological studies since the 1930s was due to the natural environment, foreign foundation support, and contacts with international scientific networks. Important work based on extensive research.

2467 Derpich, Wilma and Cecilia Israel. Obreros frente a la crisis: testimonios años treinta. Lima: Fundación Friedrich Ebert, 1987. 114 p.: ill.

Testimony collected in 1985 from 15 pioneer communist, socialist and Aprista textile workers describes living conditions, union organizing, and strike and protest movements during the 1930s. Tends to stress the solidarity between unions of different ideological orientation, importance of the economic crisis of 1929–32 for labor organization, and the fact that even those without formal employment found means to feed their families (in contrast to the present crisis).

2468 Drake, Paul W. La Misión Kemmerer al Perú: asesores e inversionistas norteamericanos durante la Gran Depresión, 1930–33. (*HISLA*, 9, 1987, p. 3–39, bibl., tables)

Pushed by US banking interests which held a great part of Peru's foreign debt, Sánchez Cerro invited Kemmerer and his team to propose fiscal, monetary and banking reforms for Peru in hopes of receiving new foreign loans. While the Commission's monetary and banking proposals were rapidly enacted (and subsequently relaxed or subverted), the suggested budgetary and taxation reforms were shelved under presure from broad coalition of business, bureaucratic, professional and political-ideological groups, when prospects for new loans had vanished. Abandonment of the gold standard in 1932 signaled victory for the traditional export interests against importers, industrialists and the foreign bankers. Kemmerer's influence, nonetheless, remained visible both in the banking institutions he had created and in the free convertibility of the currency. An important article, based on painstaking research.

2469 Favre, Henri. Perú: Sendero Luminoso y horizontes ocultos. México: Univ. Nacional Autónoma de México, 1987. 32 p.: (El Perú de hoy)

Important early interpretation of Sendero Luminoso (the French original appeared in 1984), in which the author refutes any links of the movement to Indian millenarianism. Instead he sees it as a desperate, westernizing, integrationist movement led by declassé mestizo intellectuals in the context of failing economic and social structures, heightened tensions due to the mobilization of poor peasants in the Sierra, and the collapse of oligarchic politics. For political scientist's comment, see *HLAS 51:3775.*

2470 Flores Galindo, Alberto. Tiempo de plagas. Lima: El Caballo Rojo, 1988. 255 p.

Collection of journalistic and scholarly articles written during the 1980s on topics ranging from Andean utopia during the colonial period to biographical sketches on Francisco García Calderón and Eudocio Ravines, to issue of political strategy in the 1920s and the 1960s, to contemporary massacres and violence in Peru. Written with great insight, elegance, and extraordinary clarity, pieces are essential for understanding how Flores Galindo combines historical research with political commitment, and how, in the face of Peru's present hopelessness, he steadfastly clings to a hope for a brighter future.

2471 Garavito Amézaga, Hugo. El Perú liberal: partidos e ideas políticas de la Ilustración a la República Aristocrática. Lima: Ediciones El Virrey, 1989. 262 p.:

Conventional overview of political ideas and party programs from the Bourbon reforms until 1895. Author considers liberal doctrines, although increasingly fragmented, as dominant in 19th-century Peru.

2472 Garavito Amézaga, Hugo. El santo hereje: Mariano Amézaga y el radical-ismo anticlerical en el Perú del XIX. Lima: Ediciones El Virrey, 1986. 106 p.

Discusses the life and publications of a combative free-thinker and early radical anti-*civilista* of some notoriety between the 1860s-80s.

2473 García, Mirella. Coyuntura y política económica populista en la postguerra, 1945–1948. (*Apuntes/Lima,* 18, 1986, p. 140–151)

When Bustamante and the Frente Democrático Nacional took power in 1945, their economic program was totally undetermined, disputed between industrialists and APRA. APRA's parliamentary block, together with rising popular mobilization, pushed Bustamante increasingly towards populist economic policy. Incompetence in managing foreign exchange controls, failure to contract foreign loans, and the subsequent fiscal shortfall lead to the collapse of this policy and dissatisfaction of both industrialists and popular groups. Export interests had been the primary losers in Bustamante's economic policies, but industrialists remained politically too weak to push the government towards policies explicitly favoring industrialization.

2474 García i Jordan, Pilar. Estado moderno, Iglesia y secularización en el Perú contemporáneo, 1821–1919. (*Rev. Andin.,* 6:2, 1988, p. 351–401, bibl., tables)

Broad overview of Church-State relations in the century after Independence. Liberal governments of the guano era and Civilistas of the Aristocratic Republic gradually achieved secularization of Peru's public sphere, while using the clergy to the State's advantage. Economically, and in terms of manpower, the Church reached its nadir in the 1870s. After the War of the Pacific it became more and more active as a modern pressure group expressing interests of the hierarchy and of regional conservative elites.

2475 García i Jordan, Pilar. Iglesia y vida cotidiana en el Perú finisecular: conflictos alrededor de la religión, el matrimonio y la muerte. (*Bol. Am.,* 30:38, 1988, p. 63–75, bibl.)

Between 1885–1915 the Peruvian Congress passed legislation establishing civil marriage, freedom of worship, and liberalizing burial of non-Catholics. The Catholic hierarchy and lay associations fought these measures both on doctrinal grounds and because they claimed that they undermined Catholicism as the only glue holding together Peru's national society.

2476 Gonzales, Michael. Chinese plantation workers and social conflict in Peru in the late 19th century. (*J. Lat. Am. Stud.*, 21:3, Oct. 1989, p. 385–424, bibl.)

During the profound economic and political crisis between the mid-1870s and mid-1890s coastal agriculture survived due to Chinese laborers who worked under a system of "debt peonage" at wages considerably below market rates. The Chinese protested to improve their working conditions and, especially in the cotton-growing regions, *hacendados* lost control of the labor market. Chinese labor contractors mediated between free Chinese and estate owners. Important article to understand transition to *enganche* and tenancy on coastal estates.

2477 Gootenberg, Paul Eliot. Between silver and guano: commercial policy and the state in post-independence Peru. Princeton, N.J.: Princeton Univ. Press, 1989. 234 p.: bibl., index, map.

Peruvian merchants forged a broad "nationalist" coalition that successfully fought liberalization of trade between mid-1820s and mid-1840s and formed the social foundation of caudillist regimes. The coalition collapsed with the rise of guano revenues and growing dependence of Peruvian merchants on foreign traders. Important study based on broad research in contemporary publications is especially good on finances of caudillo regimes and theoretical issues of dependency and nationalism.

2478 Gootenberg, Paul Eliot. *Carneros y Chuño:* price levels in nineteenth-century Peru. (*HAHR*, 70:1, Feb. 1990, p. 1–56, appendix, tables)

First major study of food prices, consumer price indexes for food, textiles and rents, and inflation rates for Lima between 1830s and early 1870s. Also incorporates work by other scholars on the period between 1790s-1830s. In addition to dispersed published price lists, Gootenberg found valuable purchase records for various hospitals. Author's indexation appears highly reliable, as it was subjected to carefully constructed

deflators and weights. The data confirms the integration of Peru's coastal economy into the world market. The guano era appears as an age of declining real wages. An important study.

2479 Gootenberg, Paul Eliot. Los liberales asediados: la fracasada primera generación de librecambistas en el Perú, 1820–1850. (*Rev. Andin.*, 6:2, 1988, p. 403–450, bibl.)

Author further elaborates his notion that the foreign and domestic free traders in Peru lost politically against a broad nationalist coalition between 1820s-52. English version appeared in *Guiding the invisible hand: economic liberalism in Latin American history* (New York: Prager, 1988).

2480 Gorriti Ellenbogen, Gustavo. Sendero: historia de la guerra milenaria en el Perú. v. 1. Lima: Editorial Apoyo, 1990. 1 v.:

Major account of the most serious insurrection in Peru since the Tupac Amaru rebellion, written by a judicious and well-informed journalist. First of three volumes covers 1979–82, the period in which Sendero Luminoso prepared its "people's war" which carried Sendero to its early, stunning successes. The book focuses on ideology, organization, and planning of Sendero, as well as on the politics of Peruvian security forces' reaction. Contains the most complete account of Sendero's actions, based on little-known or secret government reports, Sendero publications, and interviews. Gorriti demonstrates the utter misunderstanding and imprudent reaction by Peruvian politicians, intellectuals, and security forces to this novel and most serious threat to the country's citizens and institutions. While opinionated and weak on certain aspects, the book is compulsory reading for understanding the progress of Peru's most recent civil war.

2481 Hampe Martínez, Teodoro. Historia de la Pontificia Universidad Católica del Perú, 1917–1987. Lima: Pontificia Univ. Católica del Perú, Fondo Editorial, 1989. 220 p., 1 folded leaf of plates : bibl., ill., index.

First synthesis of the history of this influential center of higher learning. Based on research in the university archives, the volume focuses on institutional aspects.

2482 Haya de la Torre, Víctor Raúl. Después de mi muerte, la victoria: 20 reportajes, 1 testimonio. Lima: Okura Editores, 1985. 270 p.: ill.

Twenty interviews, newspaper reports, and periodical reports with or on Haya de la Torre, and his own brief memoir of his asylum in the Colombian embassy in Lima. While selected to show the Aprista leader at his best, the directness of the interviews still allows important glimpses into shifting political positions and his complex, ambiguous attitude to many issues.

2483 Historia general del Perú: la independencia. Edición de Virgilio Roel. Lima: Editorial Gráfica Labor, 1988. 663 p.

Elaborating on his previous works, author seeks to underscore the Peruvian people's struggle for independence since the late-18th century. Achievement of independence is viewed as the passage from monopolistic capitalism to liberal capitalism. Using rather superficial notions of Marxist analysis and relying on an outdated bibliography, the author nevertheless presents a detailed and encompassing account of campaigns, insurrections, policies and ideologies during the process towards independence, as well as Peru's shifting economic and social structures between the 1780s and 1820s.

2484 Hünefeldt, Christine. Jornales y esclavitud: Lima en la primera mitad del siglo XIX. (*Economía/Lima,* 10:19, junio 1987, p. 35−57, bibl.)

Many slaves in Lima worked for wages outside of their masters' households and used their savings to purchase freedom for themselves and their families, thereby contributing to the dissolution of the city's slavery regime. Based on court records, the author demonstrates diverse constellations and negotiations between slaves and masters.

2485 Hünefeldt, Christine. Poder y contribuciones: Puno, 1825−1845. (*Rev. Andin.,* 7:2, dic. 1989, p. 367−407, bibl., tables)

Analysis of the complex interplay between local authorities, priests, military, the central government, and community peasants in the Peruvian Altiplano during the post-independence decades. Often the district governors were too weak to impose their designs on the peasantry, which repeatedly succeeded in escaping the payment of the head tax. Based on extensive archival research.

2486 Independencia y revolución, 1780−1840. Recopilación de Alberto Flores Galindo. Lima: Instituto Nacional de Cultura, 1987. 2 v. (331 p.): bibl., ill. (Col. El Libro popular peruano: Serie Ciencias humanas y filosofía)

Important essays, most previously published, offer a broad perspective on politics, society and economy of the era between the Tupac Amaru rebellion and the post-Independence civil wars. Fontana suggests that the American colonies' contribution to Madrid's revenues were important and irreplaceable in the short run and that the American colonial market was crucial for the economy of some Spanish ports and their hinterlands. Malamud analyzes the slow discomposition of the trade to Peru and other colonies of a major Spanish merchant house in Cádiz, in which the Goyeneche family was a shareholder. Flores Galindo offers a complex model of the Peruvian Independence process, 1780−1825, seeking to determine whether it was a social revolution: the ruling class, Peru's peninsular aristocracy of merchants and large landowners, was overthrown; some of the popular classes, especially the Indian peasantry, were mobilized and pursued revolutionary goals, but they could not achieve power because they were too splintered. O'Phelan Godoy's important article seeks to establish that between 1809−14 there were a number of important rebellions aiming at autonomy from Spain whose ideas had been germinating since the 1730s. These movements were defeated because they increasingly expressed only Southern Andean regional aspirations. Quiroz offers a panorama of the regional economic development in the post-Independence era: the major winners were a new group of merchants involved in the guano trade since the early 1840s, who loaned money to the State. Bonilla suggests a strong continuity of economic policies and mechanisms of domination between the late colonial era and the post-Independence decades, with the critical difference that after 1821 no fraction of the dominant class was strong enough to impose its will on the State. Basadre offers a magisterial discussion about the reasons for failure of the Confederation between Peru and Bolivia, the fragility of Peru's national unity, and 19th-century debates about this issue.

2487 Kammann, Peter. Von der Landarbeiterbewegung zur Angestelltengewerkschaft: soziale Protestbewegungen im Tal des Chicama, Peru 1909–1968. Frankfurt am Main: Haag + Herchen, 1990. 719 p.: bibl., maps.

The labor movement on large north coast sugar estates shifted from a radical social movement of semi-proletarian migrant workers of peasant origin, artisans, and new factory workers in 1921 to conservative unions of a labor aristocracy of skilled workers and white-collar employees willing to co-operate with management by the 1960s. The increasing subservience to the political goals of APRA was not the main reason for this; rather it followed the impressive gains of select groups of workers in material well-being, living conditions, and job security. Painstakingly reconstructs levels of real wages, food subsidies, organization of strikes and other labor actions, and union's political ties. The most thorough, long-range study on the subject, using massive documentary evidence not employed to date.

2488 Kapsoli Escudero, Wilfredo and **Wilson Reátegui Chávez.** El campesinado peruano: 1919–1930. Lima: Univ. Nacional Mayor de San Marcos, 1987. 216 p.: bibl., ill.

Marxist perspective of the social and economic conditions of Peru's rural population during Leguia regime, from workers and sharecroppers on the coast to Indian community peasantry. Most informative on government policies and peasant movements. For related work, see *HLAS 44:2934.*

2489 Klaiber, Jeffrey L. La Iglesia en el Perú: su historia social desde la independencia. Lima: Pontificia Univ. Católica del Perú, Fondo Editorial, 1988. 530 p.: bibl.

First book-length history of the Catholic Church in Peru between Independence and the late 20th century. Gradually losing State support during the 19th century, the Church passed through a phase of militantly reasserting its rights and doctrines of the pre-Independence period. The 20th-century Church fostered a political lay movement that sought to address the problems arising from rapid social change and secularization. Since the 1950s the Church has become increasingly involved in all aspects of society, independent of the State. From a North American perspective of the separation of Church and State and the congregational orientation of the Church, the author discusses the role of Catholicism in the constitution of a Peruvian nation. Indispensable reference work on Church organization and lay movements during the past century.

2490 Klaren, Peter. The origins of modern Peru, 1880–1930. (in The Cambridge history of Latin America. Edited by Leslie Bethell. Cambridge: Cambridge Univ. Press, 1986, v. 5, p. 587–640)

Delicately interwoven synthesis of political, economic, social and cultural history stresses the deep crisis of the War of the Pacific, and the modernizing effects of export-led growth, as well as the social change it wrought. As the main beneficiary of economic expansion, the *civilista* oligarchy came to dominate politics, and proved unwilling to carry out sufficient reforms to accomodate increasingly mobilized middle class and popular sectors.

2491 Lukin, B.V. En los orígenes de las relaciones ruso-peruanas. (*Am. Lat./ Moscú*, 1:109, 1987, p. 71–77, photos)

Since the 1778 translation into Russian of Marmontel's work on the Incas, a lively interest in Peru has developed among Russian scientists and men of affairs, leading to several commercial and scientific expeditions during the early 19th century. Author ignores Western scholarship on the subject.

2492 Luna, Pablo F. El Perú y el Imperio Alemán antes de la Primera Guerra Mundial. (*Jahrb. Gesch.*, 25, 1988, p. 189–214, tables)

German economic influence in Peru in the Wilhelmian era focused on commerce, banking, and shipping, and much less on direct investment. During 1906–12 the Banco Alemán Transatlántico played an important role in negotiation of Peruvian government loans. Based on French diplomatic correspondence and US trade publications, articles also includes tables on foreign banks in Peru, breakdown of imports by commodity groups and country of origin, and lists of major German merchant houses.

2493 Macha Bardales, Adolfo. La defensa en las diferentes etapas históricas del Perú: apuntes de las conferencias dictadas en el CAEM por Adolfo Macha Bardales,

1984–1985. Lima: Centro de Altos Estudios Militares, 1985. 129 p.

Discussion of various military campaigns, from Inca empire to the War of the Pacific, and the underlying power constellation between contending forces. Concludes that the Andes are the Peruvian heartland, and only the military strategies that centered on this region have been successful. To improve its military strength Peru needs to develop its national identity, becoming integrated politically, socially, economically, and culturally.

2494 Markham, Clement Robert. Markham in Peru: the travels of Clement R. Markham, 1852–1853. Edited by Peter Blanchard. Austin: Univ. of Texas Press, 1990. 148 p.: bibl., ills., maps.

Hitherto unpublished account of the travels on Peru's coast and the Southern Highlands by the foremost 19th-century British authority on Peru. While especially attentive to antiquities, Markham provides much detail on agriculture, daily life, and social customs. As always, author's text is marked by his sympathy for the Peruvian people, from his upper-class hosts to slaves and Indian peasants.

Martínez Riaza, Ascención. Función de la prensa en los orígenes del liberalismo peruano: la opinión pública ante la independencia. See item **5391.**

2495 Méndez, Cecilia. La otra historia del guano: Perú, 1840–1879. (*Rev. Andin.*, 5:1, julio 1987, p. 7–81, bibl., map, tables)

Prison laborers and Chinese coolies were preferred for the extraction of guano because they were cheaper than free workers. Different categories of laborers forged an "isolated mass" type of community on the guano islands, with few conflicts between each other. Chinese coolies, the most important group of laborers, resisted the harsh conditions of work and life, gaining some improvements both through their own actions and through international protests. Study is based on archival research and includes commentaries from other historians.

2496 Miller, Rory. La oligarquía costera y la república aristocrática en el Perú, 1895–1919. (*Rev. Indias*, 48:182/183, enero/agosto 1988, p. 551–566)

Control over national politics exer-cised by the coastal export oligarchy from 1895–1919 was more fragile than generally assumed. Parties remained personalistic and clientile groups from the same socioeconomic class often clashed over issues of local control. Further elaborates author's revisionist ideas first developed in a 1982 article (see *HLAS 46:2995*).

2497 Núñez, Estuardo. Viajes y viajeros extranjeros por el Perú: apuntes documentales con algunos desarrollos histórico-biográficos. Lima: Tall. Gráf. P.L. Villanueva, 1989. 751 p.: bibl., index.

Useful guide to the foreign travel literature on Peru from the 16th to the 20th century is most complete for the 18th and 19th centuries. Seeks to portray different genres of travel literature. Volume contains brief biographical sketches of many travelers, incomplete references to the history of their publications, and a chronological table of all travelers.

2498 Peñaloza Jarrín, José Benigno. Los inmortales de Junín y Pasco: hechos épicos regionales desde la prehistoria hasta 1885. Lima: Editorial Médicos Asesores, 1985. 439 p., 51 leaves of plates: bibl., ill., facsims.

Narrative history of Junín and Pasco departments is mostly based on published sources. Detailed accounts of military campaigns during Wars of Independence, La Breña campaign during the War of the Pacific, as well as on the life of Daniel Carrión (1857–85), epidemiologist and native of Junín. Many contemporary documents are printed in their entirety.

2499 Perú promesa. Edición de César Pacheco Vélez. Lima: Univ. del Pacífico, 1988. 354 p.: bibl., ill.

Lavishly produced and illustrated handbook on all aspects of Peruvian history, society, politics, economy and culture. Some 50 prestigious contributers offer brief information and reflect on contemporary Peru, its social problems, history, and prospects for the future.

2500 Pons Muzzo, Gustavo. El coronel Francisco Bolognesi y el expansionismo chileno. Lima: Asoc. Editorial Bruño, 1987. 308 p., 8 p. of plates: bibl., ill.

Laudatory biography of Francisco Bolognesi, a Peruvian officer who died unsuccessfully defending Arica during the War of the Pacific. Military historians might find this useful.

2501 Portal, Magda et al. Flora Tristán, una reserva de utopía. Lima: Centro de la Mujer Peruana Flora Tristán: Tarea, 1985. 127 p.: bibl. (Col. Peruanicemos el Perú)

Essays about the reception of Tristán's writings in Peru (Magda Portal), the psychological, sociological, and political aspects of her *Peregrinaciones de una paria* (Denys Cuche), Tristán's political activities in France (Daniel Armogathe and Jacque Grandjonc), a comparison of Tristán and George Sand (Stephane Michaud), and Tristán's feminist utopia (Maritza Villavicencio).

2502 Prado, Jorge del. Cuatro facetas de la historia del PCP. Lima: Ediciones Unidad, 1987. 323 p., 16 p. of plates: appendices, ill., ports.

Official contributions to history of Peru's orthodox Communist Party since the 1920s by its long-time Secretary General. Most valuable are brief biographical sketches of 17 important party activists, as well as contemporary documents on the purges of "deviationists" (such as Eudocio Ravines) from 1940s to 1970s.

2503 Quiroz, Francisco. La protesta de los artesanos, Lima-Callao, 1858. Lima: Univ. Nacional Mayor de San Marcos, Facultad de Ciencias Sociales, 1988. 1 v. .: appendices.

Militant protests by artisans from Callao and Lima against importation of construction material show the internal divisions among popular classes. At the time, few artisan groups had programs that went beyond protectionism and popular education. Based on primery research, work includes valuable appendices of artisan petitions and government communiqués.

2504 Remy, María Isabel. La sociedad local al inicio de la República: Cusco, 1824–1850. (*Rev. Andin.*, 6:2, 1988, p. 451–484, bibl., tables)

After independence, the vague intermediary position of mestizo inherited from the colonial regime continued in Cusco, but due to political pressures, mestizos slowly gained fiscal advantages. With the abolition of the *contribución de indígenas* in 1854, mestizos become the strongest group in pro-vincial society, the social basis for *gamonalismo* ready to expropriate peasant community lands. Based on tax records and the correspondence of Cusco's prefects.

2505 Rieu-Millán, Marie Laure. Rasgos distintivos de la representación peruana en las Cortes de Cádiz y Madrid, 1810–1814. (*Rev. Indias*, 48:182/183, enero/agosto 1988, p. 475–515, tables)

On balance the Peruvian deputies in Cádiz tended to be more conservative than representatives of other American regions, especially on social issues. Nevertheless, they sought to advance the interest of their provinces and routinely voted with the other American deputies. Well-researched essay lays out the views of the Peruvian deputies on a wide range of issues.

2506 Rodríguez Pastor, Humberto. Hijos del Celeste Imperio en el Perú (1850–1900): migración, agricultura, mentalidad y explotación. Lima: Instituto de Apoyo Agrario, 1989. 317 p.: bibl., ill.

Most important work about Chinese immigrants in Peru since Stewart's *Chinese bondage in Peru* (Durham, N.C.: Duke Univ. Press, 1951). Coolies were "semi-slaves," severely limited in their freedom during the period of indenture on the estates, yet received a wage. The legal frame of the contract was largely respected and after its termination they procured better labor conditions. Treatment on the sugar and cotton plantations was harsh, but *hacendados* did not interfere with the Chinese cultural practices. Between the late-1870s and mid-1890s the Chinese remained the crucial labor force for Peru's coastal agriculture, under a variety of labor regimes. Growing numbers of Chinese went to the cities, entering trades. Although vilified by racism and competition, many maintained their culture and still managed upward social mobility.

2507 Romero, Fernando. Grau, biografía lírica. Lima: Dirección General de Intereses Marítimos, Ministerio de Marina, 1984. 140 p., 56 p. of plates: ill.

Although written without any critical distance to subject, author gives a vivid and realistic picture of the political and cultural circumstances shaping the life of Peru's foremost military hero, Admiral Miguel Grau (1834–79), killed at the Battle of Angamos during the War of the Pacific.

Romero, Fernando. El negro en el Perú y su transculturación lingüística. See *HLAS 51: 1227.*

2508 Rubio Fataccioli, Alberto. Sebastián Lorente y la educación en el Perú del siglo XIX. Prólogo de Carlos Daniel Valcárcel. Lima: Editorial Allamanda, 1990. 261 p.: bibl., ill.

Discusses the considerable influence of Lorente (1813–84) on Peruvian educational institutions and thought. A heterodox liberal Spaniard who came to Peru in 1842, Lorente worked to free Peruvian schools and university education from colonial, scholastic orientations and was an early proponent of equal access to learning for women and popular classes. Includes a list of Lorente's numerous publications.

2509 Sánchez, Luis Alberto. La vida del siglo. Recopilación, prólogo y notas de Hugo García Salvattecci. Cronología y bibliografía de Marlene Polo Miranda. Caracas: Biblioteca Ayacucho, 1988. 445 p.: bibl., ill. (Biblioteca Ayacucho; 135)

Selections from Luis Alberto Sánchez's prolific writings on Peruvian and Latin American literature, history, and politics, and from his important essays interpreting the evolution of Peru's culture. Selections stress the author's view of Peru as a young and conflictive mestizo culture in the process of formation. Volume contains a biographical sketch of the author and a bibliography of his works.

2510 Sánchez Olivencia, Fernando. Callao: pasado, presente, futuro. Lima: Okura Editores, 1989. 286 p.: bibl., ill.

Typical provincial monograph covers natural history, ethnography, economy, and social and political structure of Callao, together with a basic historical account centered on events and famous persons. Valuable statistics on 20th century.

2511 Santillana Cantella, Tomás Guillermo. Los viajes de Raimondi. Lima: Occidental Petroleum Company of Peru, 1989. 222 p., 13 leaves of plates: ill., maps.

Useful travelog based on all of Antonio de Raimondi's publications concerning his journeys through Peru from 1850s to early-1870s is arranged in chronological sequence.

2512 Seminario Permanente de Investigación Agraria, 3rd, Cusco, Peru, 1989. Perú: el problema agrario en debate. Edición de Alberto Chirif, Nelson Manrique y Benjamín Quijandría. Lima: Seminario Permanente de Investigación Agraria; Cusco: Centro de Estudios Rurales Andinos Bartolomé de las Casas, 1990. 482 p.: bibl., ill.

Proceedings of *Seminario Permante de Investigación Agraria*, (3rd, Cusco, 1989). Includes important contributions by historians, anthropologists, economists, and sociologists from Peru and Europe on agrarian history, contemporary rural development, and the agrarian problem of the Amazon lowlands. Topics include land tenure, commodity and credit markets, capital accumulation, peasant economy, rural violence, State policies, and class formation.

2513 Seminario sobre Poblaciones Inmigrantes, 1st, Lima, 1986. Actas. t. 2. Lima: Consejo Nacional de Ciencia y Tecnología, 1987–1988. 1 v.: bibl., ill.

Essays on African, Chinese, Japanese, and European immigrant groups in Peru from colonial era to present, some of which present new research. Topics include slavery, indentured servants, immigrant occupational specialization, social control and resistence, and cultural survival. Important especially on Chinese and Japanese immigrants. For t. 1, see *HLAS 51:4835.*

2514 Seoane, Manuel. Páginas del Cachorro. Edición de Luis Alva Castro. Lima,: EMI, 1988. 267 p.: ill.

Newspaper articles by leading APRA politician and professional journalist published 1954–55 while in exile in Santiago cover everything from Peruvian and Latin American politics and economies to football and literature. Written in a lively, incisive and often humorous style, articles offer impressionistic glimpses into hopes and visions of Seoane, who remained a politician dedicated to social reform.

2515 Stein, Steve and Carlos Monge. La crisis del estado patrimonial en el Perú. Lima: Instituto de Estudios Peruanos; Coral Gables, Fla.: Univ. de Miami, 1988. 250 p.: bibl. (Serie Ideología y política; 5)

Authors analyze the breakdown of the patrimonial State in Peru between the military regime (1968–80) and Belaúnde's second term (1980–85), when Peruvian society had become socially polarized and the State had lost any influence and contact with civil society. Popular reactions spanned the gamut from an enormous upsurge of individual violence to the new phenomenon of autonomous popular organizations largely unwilling to accept authoritarian, clientelistic dependence on established institutions or powerful individuals. Sendero Luminoso represents the negation of this new popular autonomy. The volume contains vivid testimonies of the crisis by inhabitants of Lima's *barriadas*.

2516 Stein, William W. and **Renato Alarcón G.** José Carlos Mariátegui y Waldo Frank: dos amigos. (*Anu. Mariateg.*, 1 : 1, 1989, p. 161–184)

Documents the surprising respect and friendship which Mariátegui held for Frank between 1925 and his death, despite the latter's vague and insipidly spiritual anti-imperialist stance.

2517 Stein, William W. El levantamiento de Atusparia: el movimiento popular ancashino de 1885; un estudio de documentos. Lima: Mosca Azul Editores, 1988. 365 p.: bibl.

The Atusparia rebellion of 1885, although ignited by the reintroduction of the Indian head tax, was sustained by a broad coalition of Indians, mestizos, and whites, both rural and urban residents, all pursuing different goals. Rebellion was also entangled with the struggle between generals Iglesias and Cáceres for political control of the country. Exhaustive study with lengthy quotes from contemporary documents and modern authors.

2518 Taussig, Michael. Cultura del terror—espacio de la muerte: el informe Putumayo de Roger Casement y la explicación de la tortura. (*Amazonía Peru.*, 14, 1987, p. 7–36, bibl.)

As part of his efforts to explore the dialectic between colonialism and Western culture, author "analyzes the report which Roger Casement submitted to the British Foreign Office in 1912 about Indian abuse in the Putumayo rubber fields. Through this, Taussig establishes the elements which constitute the culture of terror. These, far from being a negation of civilization, are built on the same images of savagery and underworld,

of paradise and utopia, inextricably linked in occidental culture." For anthropologist's comment see *HLAS 51:920.*

2519 Taylor, Lewis. Economía y sociedad en la provincia de Hualgayoc, 1870–1900. (*Rev. Indias*, 48 : 182/183, enero/agosto 1988, p. 567–592, maps, tables)

Broad and informative overview of production, trade, social structure, land tenure, and labor regimes in a province of the Northern Sierra. Author finds both peasants and estate owners highly integrated into regional and national markets, a great degree of mobility of agricultural workers, and a rapid advance of rural proletarianization, especially due to population growth.

2520 Tejada, Luis. La cuestión del pan: el anarcosindicalismo en el Perú, 1880–1919. Lima: Instituto Nacional de Cultura; Banco Industrial del Perú, 1988. 418 p.: bibl., ill.

Panoramic study of Lima's bakeries, technical and social aspects of their labor process, their entrepreneurs and workers, and the organization and politics of the bakery workers' union, *La Estrella del Perú*, the first to embrace anarchism in the country. Pt. 2 of the book deals with the union movement, stressing the complex and inconclusive struggles between mutualists and anarchosyndicalists within the union.

2521 Townsend Ezcurra, Andrés. 50 años de aprismo: memorias, ensayos y discursos de un militante. Lima: Editorial e Impr. DESA, 1989. 355 p., 12 p. of plates: ill.

In his brief memoirs, a leading APRA politican between the 1930s and his expulsion in 1981 intertwines his own trajectory with that of the party and the Peruvian political system. Seeks to show that throughout his political career he remained a "democratic leftist," closely following the leadership and doctrines of Haya de la Torre. Essays offer political and ideological discussions and biographic sketches of leading politicians and intellectuals from Peru and other Latin American countries.

2522 Trachtenberg Siederer, León. La inmigración judía al Perú, 1848–1948: una historia documentada de la inmigración de los judíos de habla alemana. Lima: Tall. Gráf. de Tipo-Offset SESATOR, 1987. 322 p.: bibl., ill., facsims., ports.

History of Jewish institutions and their prominent members is especially valuable for coverage of 1930–48 and the activities of the community to aid European Jewish refugees, though hampered by the antisemitism of Peruvian officials. Loaded with facts, the book at times reads like a protocol.

2523 Valdizán Gamio, José. Historia naval del Perú. v. 4. Lima: Ministerio de Marina, Dirección General de Intereses Marítimos, 1987. 1 v.: bibl., ill., index.

Vol. 4 in a narrative history of the ships and men of the Peruvian navy covers 1866–77.

2524 Velarde Herrera, Mateo Francisco. Crónicas de Islay y Mollendo. Peru: s.n., 1987? 185 p.

Drawn from newspaper articles and local archives, book chronicles a wealth of information, especially for 1850–1930, on local events and institutions in southern Peru's most important port.

2525 Vilar, Pierre et al. Peruanistas contemporáneos: temas, métodos, avances. v. 1. Edición de Wilfredo Kapsoli Escudero. Lima: CONCYTEC, 1988. 1 v.:

Pt. 1 contains wide-ranging and informative interviews by the editor with six prominent French historians and social scientists on their biographies, research methodologies, and interpretations of past and contemporary Peruvian society, arts, and letters. Pt. 2 contains six brief articles on education in 19th-century Peru, the rebellion of Atusparia, Sendero Luminoso, Messianism and contemporary Peruvian politics, and Protestant education in Peru.

2526 Villanueva Urteaga, Horacio. Gamarra y la iniciación republicana en el Cuzco. Lima: Fondo del Libro del Banco de los Andes, 1981. 357 p., 4 leaves of plates: bibl., ill.

Exhaustive and thoroughly-researched study of the Administration of Agustín Gamarra as first prefect of republican Cusco, 1825–27, touching on everything from public finance to Church-State relations, infrastructure investments, public education, and the onset of electoral politics. Author portrays Gamarra as an activist with rather liberal ideas but an authoritarian style of rule, who ultimately failed to pull Cusco out of its economic crisis. Important documents are cited in their entirety.

2527 Walker, Charles. El estudio del campesinado en las ciencias sociales peruanas: avances, limitaciones y nuevas perspectivas. (*Allpanchis*, 21:33, 1989, p. 161–205, bibl.)

Critical appraisal of some recent anthropological and historical work on Andean peasantry. Suggests the need to interrelate political role of peasants and ideological currents with everyday resistance against exploitation.

2528 Walker, Charles. El uso oficial de la selva en el Perú Republicano. (*Amazonía Peru.*, 14, 1987, p. 61–89, bibl., tables)

Based on secondary literature, the author presents an overview of government policies towards the Peruvian Amazon and how they related to the region's socioeconomic development from the early postindependence period to the mid-20th century. Throughout this period politicians have used the *selva* as an escape hatch for problems on the coast or in the Andes, and thus have repeatedly failed to design policies addressing the real problems of the region.

2529 Werlich, David P. Admiral of the Amazon: John Randolph Tucker, his confederate colleagues, and Peru. Charlottesville: Univ. Press of Virginia, 1990. 353 p., 18 p. of plates: bibl., ill., index.

Thoroughly researched and elegantly written account of the life of a Virginian navy officer, briefly appointed Commander of the joint Peruvian-Chilean navy squadron in the war against Spain (1866), and head of the Peruvian hydrographic commission charting the headwaters of the Amazon and its tributaries (1867–74). While much of the cartographic work of the commission has been lost, the route pioneered by Tucker and his Confederate colleagues for central Andean-Amazonian communication (the Pichis trail), remained important for decades.

2530 Witt, Heinrich. Diario y observaciones sobre el Perú, 1824–1890. Selección y prólogo de Pablo Macera. Traducción de Kika Garland de Montero. Lima: Oficina de Asuntos Culturales, COFIDE, 1987. 552 p.: ill., indexes.

A volume certain to become a classic source on 19th-century Peru. Extracted from the massive diaries of a German-born merchant who spent more than 65 years in Peru as manager of Gibbs' Lima office and as successful independent businessman, patriarch of an extended oligarchic family, well-connected in Peru's highest social and political circles. The volume offers precise information on economic matters (trade, mining, agriculture and textile workshops), on the foreign business community, on religious festivities, and on the workings of politics and friendship connections in Peru's highest social spheres. Written in a graceful style, the hallmark of Witt's observations lies in his acerbic and frankly critical portrayal of contemporary figures, the cause for the long delay of publication. This selection includes extensive material on Lima and on numerous regions and towns from Cajamarca to Arica.

Bolivia and Chile

WILLIAM F. SATER, *Professor of History, California State University, Long Beach*

BOLIVIA

THE LATEST SCHOLARSHIP ON BOLIVIA has produced some interesting works. Abecia's three-volume diplomatic history, for example, is a comprehensive synthesis of this often neglected topic (item **2531**). Tristan Platt studies the reaction of Bolivia's Indian population to the white/mestizo society's attempt to control them (item **2549**). Erick Langer explains how Indians resisted, sometimes violently, the efforts of rapacious *hacendados* to reduce their already limited rights or to alter traditional landlord-tenant relations (item **2542**). Works by Albó, Jackson, and Dandler and Torrico analyze more modern aspects of the agrarian problem (items **2533, 2541,** and **2538**).

Since Bolivia's politics have often confounded scholars, Malloy and Gamarra's study of the 1964–85 period is especially welcome (item **2545**). Their joint efforts not only provide information on that turbulent epoch, but also explain why the military found it easier to depose the MNR than to govern.

Che Guevara's abortive campaign to topple the La Paz government is described from two opposing points of view: a combination memoir/analysis written by Gen. Gary Prado, a participant in the campaign against Che Guevara (item **2551**); and the diary of Harry Villegas (item **4850**), one of Guevara's compatriots. Military historians will also profit from Lechín's painstaking study (item **2544**) of one phase of Bolivia's participation in the Chaco War.

Various general works have appeared, most of which are so ideological or superficial that they do not enhance our knowledge of Bolivia. Although lacking innovation, Pacheco Loma's work (item **2547**) provides a fleshed out chronology of the most recent events. A more worthy effort is Crespo's biography (item **2537**) of the ill-fated President Hernando Siles, who ruled in the late 1920s. A compilation of speeches by the equally star-crossed Gen. Juan José Torres furnishes a new perspective on a particularly controversial period in Bolivia's history (item **2552**).

CHILE

The Catholic Church has attracted scholarly attention. Aliaga (item **2558**) chronicles the Church's impact on Chilean society from the colonial period to the present; Moreno (item **2595**) shows how the clergy influenced the union movement. Pinochet de la Barra's biography of Cardinal Silva Henríquez (item **2602**) is useful for understanding the attitude of the hierarchy during the Frei-Allende-Pinochet periods.

Rodríguez's work on the creation and functioning of the army's service corps during the War of the Pacific is excellent (item **2607**); it addresses a very important but often neglected aspect of military history. The Estado Mayor's latest volume (item **2597**), with its lavish pictures of the various uniforms, insignia, and medals, provides a splendid supplement to the existing multi-volume history of the Chilean army.

Chile's diplomatic history, particularly relations with the US, also has emerged as a topic of interest. Marambio's volume (item **2587**) is an exhaustive study of the *Macedonian* claims, one of Chile's more contentious, if not long lived, diplomatic disputes. Jensen's densely written and extremely biased two-volume exposition (item **2581**) on US interaction with the Allende regime tends to plough already tilled ground. Clearly the most innovative diplomatic study is Meneses' work (item **2592**) which shows how Chile's naval and maritime needs influenced Santiago's relations with Washington.

Material on the activities of specific immigrant groups proves quite interesting. Böhm (item **2563**) and Sater (item **2610**) show that Chile neither welcomed nor accepted Jewish immigrants socially. Waldmann (item **2620**) demonstrates that decades passed before German settlers, sure of their cultural superiority, blended into local Chilean society. Scholars interested in ethnic history must consult Corvalán's impressive study of the impact of the Yugoslav community on Chile's north (item **2568**); Mayo's description of the activities of the first English residents (item **2590**); and Blancpain's entertaining analysis of the impact of French culture and institutions on Chile's culture and elites (item **2562**).

Economic history will benefit from Sergio Villalobos' book which, much to the *dependistas'* dismay, shows that protectionism, not Free Trade, influenced the Moneda's policies (item **2618**). In a similar vein, José del Pozo argues that the Radical presidents used the State to stimulate Chile's economic development (item **2605**). As Marcos Mamalakis ably indicates, however, government economic intervention sometimes aggravated rather than relieved economic problems (item **2586**). Thomas O'Brien's splendid article on the Guggenheims' ill-fated *salitre* venture amply demonstrates that private businessmen also failed to achieve their goals (item **2598**).

The study tracing the activities of organizations dedicated to enfranchising Chilean women will also interest historians (item **2574**). Méndez and Ramón study how the Chilean cities changed in response to foreign influence and to accommodate increasing population (items **2591** and **2606**).

The collaborative effort of Iván Jaksíc and Sol Serrano provides valuable material on the formation and growth of the Univ. de Chile (item **2580**). Ibáñez's historiographical article on the influences of Catholicism and Hispanism on Mario Góngora, will interest intellectual historians (item **2578**).

Two works merit special attention: Blakemore's bibliographical study constitutes a splendid addition to our knowledge of Chile (item **9**); and the latest volume of Vial's interesting, as well as entertaining, multi-volume history (item **2617**) provides a needed overview of a critical period in Chile's historical development.

BOLIVIA

2531 Abecia Baldivieso, Valentín. Las relaciones internacionales en la historia de Bolivia. 2a ed. rev. y aum. La Paz: Editorial Los Amigos del Libro; Academia Nacional de Ciencias de Bolivia, 1986. 3 v.: bibl., ill., index.

Traces the history of Bolivia's foreign relations from its colonial past to the present. Well-researched and employing a variety of sources, the author ably explains his nation's difficulties with its neighbors, noting how domestic politics affected La Paz's foreign policy. Emphasizes Bolivia's relations with Argentina and Brazil, its participation in ALALC, as well as the perpetual problem: the quest for a port.

2532 Aguirre Lavayén, Joaquín. 1884: pacto de tregua, Guerra del Pacífico; documentos reservados inéditos; actas, Junta Constitutiva de 1884; correspondencia privada de Nataniel Aguirre. La Paz: Editorial Los Amigos del Libro, 1987. 330 p. (Col. Historia)

An interesting work containing many of the private papers and correspondence of Nataniel Aguirre, an important 19th-century Bolivian politician. Excellent source for discovering more about Bolivia's participation in the War of the Pacific and its subsequent attempts to extricate itself from the conflict with Chile.

2533 Albó, Xavier. From MNRistas to Kataristas to Katari. (in Resistance, rebellion, and consciousness in the Andean peasant world, 18th to 20th centuries. Edited by Steve J. Stern. Madison: Univ. of Wisconsin Press, 1987, p. 379–419, bibl.)

The demand for agrarian reform continued after the 1952 Revolution. The failure to satisfy this need led to the creation of the largely Aymara supported Katarismo movement. Katarismo, which is based in La Paz—the same area that produced Tupac Katari—emphasizes the need for a return to communal landholding more than the Cochabamba based Quechuas, who tend to rely on the State and State-owned enterprises for support.

Albó, Xavier. Una nación con 40 naciones. See *HLAS 51:983.*

2534 Arnade, Charles W. Bolivian history. La Paz: Editorial Los Amigos del Libro, 1984. 231 p.: maps.

English-language study of Bolivia from the colonial period to the early 1960s, apparently written more than 20 years ago, does provide an overview but uses few primary sources. Jaime Flores has written an appendix bringing the study up to 1982.

Baptista Gumucio, Mariano. ¿La venganza del Che? See item **1873.**

2535 Bieber, León E. Bolivia, 1825–1850: aislamiento internacional y economía nacional. (in América Latina en la época de Simón Bolívar. Edición de Reinhard Liehr. Berlin: Colloquium Verlag, 1989, p. 341–360, tables)

Geographical isolation and a lack of both foreign investment and valuable resources led to the collapse of Bolivia's mining sector. The inability to develop a viable export sector led to depopulation and the destruction of infant industries, which, in turn, handicapped Bolivia's economic growth. Interesting article provides a useful overview of Bolivia's early history.

2536 Birbuet España, Miguel. Recuerdos de la campaña de 1879: manuscrito inédito. La Paz: Ediciones ISLA, 1986. 80 p.

Interesting memoir of a soldier who participated in Bolivia's first, and almost only, campaign, during the War of the Pacific. Gives valuable Bolivian perspective.

2537 Crespo, Alfonso. Hernando Siles, el poder y su angustia. La Paz: Empresa Editora Siglo, 1985. 360 p.: bibl., ill., index.

Treats life and regime of Hernando Siles who, like so many of Bolivia's presidents, ruled only a short time (1926–30). Siles was the father of Hernán Siles, who subsequently twice served as president. While clearly biased, the volume provides insights into Bolivia and includes information on the nation's economic, political, and intellectual development on the eve of the Chaco War.

Crespo R., Alberto *et al.* Siporo: historia de una hacienda boliviana. See *HLAS 51:2354.*

2538 Dandler, Jorge and **Juan Torrico A.** From the National Indigenous Congress to the Ayopaya Rebellion: Bolivia, 1945–1947. (in Resistance, rebellion, and consciousness in the Andean peasant world, 18th to 20th centuries. Edited by Steve J. Stern. Madison: Univ. of Wisconsin Press, 1987, p. 334–378, bibl., map)

The 1945 National Indigenous Congress became a vehicle for Bolivian peasants to express their discontent with their working conditions. The return of brutal working conditions, the fear that the old system would remain intact, and the collapse of the peasant movement following Vilarroel's death, led the peasants of Ayopaya to rebel in

1947. Based on many interviews, this is a very valuable study of peasant discontent.

Estudios sobre Gabriel René Moreno: homenaje al sesquicentenario del nacimiento de Gabriel René Moreno, 1986. See item **5394.**

2539 Gallego, Ferran. Un caso de populismo militar latinoamericano: la gestión de David Toro en Bolivia. (*Ibero-Am. Arch.*, 14:4, 1988, p. 473–503, bibl.)

David Toro, who ruled 1936–37, fell from power because: 1) he failed to win the military's support; 2) he could not revive Bolivia's Depression-devastated economy; and 3) he failed to create a sound political base. Narrative study lacks depth.

2540 Gordillo C., José M. and **Robert H. Jackson.** Mestizaje y proceso de parcelización en la estructura agraria de Cochabamba: el caso de Sipe-Sipe en los siglos XVIII-XIX. (*HISLA*, 10, 1987, p. 15–37, bibl., maps, tables)

Quantitative answers for the district of Sipe-Sipe to some of the questions posed by Larson in her recent book, *Colonialism and agrarian transformation in Bolivia: Cochabamba, 1550–1900* (item **2196**). Examines when, where, and to what extent fragmentation of land holding occured after independence, on the one hand, and what happened to the make-up of the peasantry on the other. [M.T. Hamerly]

Historia de Tarija: corpus documental. See item **2195.**

La inmigración japonesa en Bolivia: estudios históricos y socio-económicos. See *HLAS 51:4846.*

2541 Jackson, Robert H. The decline of the hacienda in Cochabamba, Bolivia: the case of the Sacaba Valley, 1870–1929. (*HAHR*, 69:2, May 1989, p. 259–281, appendix, maps, tables)

Competition with foreign and domestic procedures, the loss of local markets, high interest rates, and the division of land, led to a collapse of the hacienda system in the Cochabamba Valley during the late 19th to 20th centuries. Rather than remain on their land, owners sold their property to peasants. Consequently, when the MNR initiated its program of agrarian reform, it discovered that the hacienda system was not prevalent in Cochabamba.

2542 Langer, Erick Detlef. Economic change and rural resistance in southern Bolivia, 1880–1930. Stanford, Calif.: Stanford Univ. Press, 1989. 269 p.: bibl., index.

In an effort to profit from farming, late 19th-century Bolivian landlords encroached upon communal lands and increased exploitation of the Indian workforce. The Indians of Yamparez, Cinti, Azero, and Tomina provinces resisted these incursions, sometimes violently. Splendidly researched, and based upon a wealth of primary and secondary sources, this is a premier study.

2543 Langer, Erick Detlef. Mano de obra campesina y agricultura comercial en Cinti. (*Hist. Boliv.*, 2:3, 1983, p. 71–93)

Penetrating analysis of the attempts of two Bolivian haciendas to alter traditional economic relationships with their peasants in order to increase profitability and to modernize agriculture. Extensively based on archival sources, provides an interesting view of the clash of cultures.

2544 Lechín Suárez, Juan. La batalla de Villa Montes: estudio crítico. Barcelona: Técnicos Editoriales Asociados; Cochabamba, Bolivia: Editorial Los Amigos del Libro, 1988. 2 v.: bibl., ill.

Extremely well documented and analytical study of Bolivia's involvement in the Chaco War (1934–35). Very useful synthesis for military historians.

Lehm Ardaya, Zulema and **Silvia Rivera Cusicanqui.** Los artesanos libertarios y la ética del trabajo. See *HLAS 51:4851.*

2545 Malloy, James M. and **Eduardo Gamarra.** Revolution and reaction: Bolivia, 1964–1985. New Brunswick, N.J.: Transaction Books, 1988. 244 p.: bibl., index.

In the 1960s, the Bolivian army became involved in politics after the MNR fragmented, creating a political vacuum. Limitations in the nation's political and economic system, however, handicapped the military's ability to rule. Essential work for the specialist; comprehensively traces political events in Bolivia (1964–85). For political scientist's comment see *HLAS 51:3752.*

2546 Medio siglo de vida judía en La Paz. 2da. ed., corr. La Paz: Círculo Israelita, 1987. 326 p.: ill., ports.

While not scholarly, this work offers

some understanding of the nature of Bolivia's small Jewish colony. Mainly refugees from Hitler's Germany, these individuals have created various social, educational, and charitable institutions to serve the needs of a community which has diminished in size.

Mitre, Antonio. El monedero de los Andes: región económica y moneda boliviana en el siglo XIX. See *HLAS 51:2364.*

Osborne, Harold. Bolivia, a land divided. See *HLAS 51:108.*

2547 Pacheco Loma, Misael. Resumen de la historia de Bolivia. 2a edic., rev. y complementada. Oruro, Bolivia: Offset Alea Ltda., 1984. 744 p., 1 leaf of plates: bibl., ill., ports.

One-volume factual account of Bolivia's history from precolumbian period to the early 1980s is a valuable source of information about the modern period. Not analytical.

2548 Perfiles de Oruro: antología. v.1. Recopilación de Elías Delgado Morales. Oruro, Bolivia: Offset Alea Ltd., 1987. 1 v.: ill., ports. (Serie Biblioteca orureña)

Series of uneven essays dealing with various aspects of the development of Oruro lacks factual material or focus and serves little purpose.

2549 Platt, Tristan. The Andean experience of Bolivian liberalism, 1825–1900: roots of rebellion in 19th-century Chayanta, Potosí. (*in* Resistance, rebellion, and consciousness in the Andean peasant world, 18th to 20th centuries. Edited by Steve J. Stern. Madison: Univ. of Wisconsin Press, 1987, p. 280–323, bibl., map, table)

Bolivia's Indians were not merely passive instruments or quiescent. In order to protect their interests they formed political alliances and even rebelled against the government. The author uses a variety of secondary and archival materials to argue his point convincingly.

2550 Platt, Tristan. Le calendrier économique des indiens de Lipez en Bolivie au XIXe siècle. (*Ann. écon. soc. civilis.*, 42:3, mai/juin 1987, p. 549–576, bibl., tables)

Platt shows that Indians selectively entered the market economy. Generally their decision coincided with the requirements brought on by the arrival of certain festival days or to meet personal needs, such as having to pay taxes. A highly original work, utilizing traditional archival material and interdisciplinary techniques.

2551 Prado Salmón, Gary. La guerrilla inmolada: la campaña del Ché en Bolivia; testimonio y análisis de un protagonista. Santa Cruz, Bolivia: Editorial Punto y Coma, 1987. 297 p., 15 leaves of plates: bibl., ill., maps.

Careful military analysis of the counter-guerrilla campaign directed against Che Guevara in 1965 by participant in campaign provides extensive background information. Invaluable for specialist in military history.

Seiferheld, Alfredo M. Economía y petróleo durante la Guerra del Chaco: apuntes para una historia económica del conflicto paraguayo-boliviano. See item **2835.**

2552 Torres González, Juan José. En defensa de mi nación oprimida. La Paz: Ediciones ISLA, 1985. 338 p.

Series of speeches by the former leftist president who came to power in 1970. Excellent source for understanding his regime, his thinking, and his policies.

Uribe O., Hernán. Operación Tía Victoria. See item **1989.**

2553 Valencia Vega, Alipio. Historia política de Bolivia. v. 2. La Paz: Librería Editorial Juventud, 1985? 1 v.:

Vol. 2 of a multi-volume political history. Factual, uninspired, and based largely on secondary sources, it provides few surprises and little insight into the period preceding the revolutionary process in Bolivia.

2554 Vargas Salinas, Mario. El "Che": mito y realidad. Caracas: SEPA Editores, 1987. 114 p.: ill.

Memoirs of a young captain who participated in the campaign against Che. Interesting but lacking in depth.

2555 Vázquez-Viaña, Humberto. Antecedentes de la guerrilla del Che en Bolivia. Stockholm: Univ. of Stockholm, Institute of Latin American Studies, 1986. 81 p.: bibl. (Research paper series)

Narrative attempts to explain the political reasons why Che selected Bolivia as a site from which to launch his revolution.

2556 **Villegas, Harry** Materiales sobre la guerrilla de Ñancahuazú. v. 1, Diario de Pombo. Recopilación de María Garcés. Quito: Editorial El Mañana, 1986. 1 v.

Reprint of diary first published in *El Diario* of La Paz, in 1969. Harry Villegas arrived in Bolivia prior to Che, participated in the abortive campaign, and, unlike others, managed to survive. Quite useful for learning about the guerrilla perspective.

2557 **Zambrana Yáñez, Manuel.** Historia de Bolivia y la realidad nacional. Cochabamba, Bolivia: Impr. Oquer, 1987. 316 p.:

Highly slanted and truncated study of Bolivia virtually ignores the post-1880 period. Author argues that Bolivia is a semicolonial nation which is economically exploited by the system of world capitalism.

CHILE

2558 **Aliaga Rojas, Fernando.** La Iglesia en Chile: contexto histórico. 2a ed. Santiago: Pontificia Univ. Católica de Chile, 1986. 244 p.: bibl.

Traces the evolution of the Church as it was forced to deal with an increasingly secular society. Useful because it demonstrates how the Church modernized its teaching as well as created new institutions to deal with social and economic problems. Provides a wealth of needed information on various internal changes in the Chilean Church, including important synods. Tends to stress the pre-1930 period.

Amayo, Enrique. La política británica en la Guerra del Pacífico. See item **2442.**

Astudillo Tapia, Francisco J. and **Carlos S. Ruiz-Tagle Vial.** Historia general de Quilpué. See item **2203.**

2559 **Barros Ortiz, Tobías.** Recogiendo los pasos. v. 2, Testigo militar y político del siglo XX. Santiago: Editorial Planeta Chilena, 1988. 565 p.: ill. (Espejo de Chile; 2)

The author, a professional army officer, observed and participated in the 1924 and 1925 coups which brought down the Parliamentary period and returned Alessandri to power. Posted to train with the *Reichswehr*, he subsequently served as Chile's ambassador to Hitler's Germany and later as president of CORFO. Given the author's age and

his proximity to power, this anecdotal work offers useful insights about some of the most important events in Chile's history.

2560 **Bauer, Arnold J.** Industry and the missing bourgeoisie: consumption and development in Chile, 1850–1950. (*HAHR*, 70:2, May 1990, p. 227–253, tables)

Using largely secondary sources, some outdated and others suspect, author unsuccessfully attempts to explain Chile's limited industrialization and failure to develop a bourgeoisie. Unconvincingly argues that Chile developed both industries and a bourgeoisie but that they are not easily seen.

2561 **Bizzarro, Salvatore.** Historical dictionary of Chile. 2nd ed., rev., enl., and updated. Metuchen, N.J.: Scarecrow Press, 1987. 583 p.: bibl., maps (Latin American historical dictionaries; 7)

Updated and revised edition includes biographical information as well as explanations on significant events in Chilean history. While valuable because it includes a wealth of information on the post-1970 period, the author tends to become extremely ideological when describing the Allende and Pinochet regimes.

2562 **Blancpain, Jean-Pierre.** Cultura francesa y francomanía en América Latina: el caso de Chile en el siglo XIX. (*Cuad. Hist.*, 7, julio 1987, p. 11–52, ill.)

Entertaining analysis of the impact of French culture and institutions on Chilean culture and elites.

2563 **Böhm, Günter.** Inmigración de judíos de habla alemana a Chile y Perú durante el siglo XIX. (*Jahrb. Gesch.*, 25, 1988, p. 455–493)

German Jews arrived in Chile and Peru soon after these nations became independent, becoming involved in commerce, mining, and the professions. Although Chile was more tolerant than Peru, most Jews who settled in Chile converted to Catholicism, sometimes under duress, in order to become accepted socially. Well-researched essay by one of the premier authorities on a generally neglected topic.

2564 **Calm, Lillian.** El Chile de Pío IX, 1824. Santiago: Editorial Andrés Bello, 1987. 236 p.: bibl., ill., index.

Diary of Juan María Mastai Ferretti

who, before becoming Pope Pius IX, lived in Chile in 1824. Includes biography of Mastai as well as a description of his Pontificate and copies of his correspondence, some of which concerns Chile. Concludes with seven interviews with prominent Chilean historians explaining various facets of Chilean society during Mastai's stay.

2565 Campos Harriet, Fernando. Los últimos años de O'Higgins. (*An. Univ. Chile*, 5:11, agosto 1986, p. 317–325, bibl., photo)

O'Higgins became romantically involved with Rosario Puga who gave birth to his son Demetrio in 1818. Article describes O'Higgins' life on the Peruvian hacienda of Montalván where the former Supreme Director remained, with Demetrio, until his death in the 1840s.

Cánepa, Gina. Folletines históricos del Chile independiente y su articulación con la novela naturalista. See item **3407.**

2566 Carrera Verdugo, José Miguel. Diario del brigadier general D. José Miguel Carrera Verdugo. Santiago: Academia de Historia Militar, 1986. 3 v.: ill.

Reprint of the diary of one of the progenitors of Chilean independence covers 1810–15. Consists of three volumes: a facsimile of the original document; a transcription of this information; and a copy which is edited in order to be more clear.

2567 Collier, Simon. Gobierno y sociedad en Chile durante la "República Conservadora," 1830–1865. (*Bol. Inst. Hist. Ravignani*, 3:1, 1989, p. 115–126)

Valuable overview demonstrates that Chile's conservatives ruled through the measured application of force and the use of extra-legal practices, such as bribery. The combination of these two methods produced a government characterized more by efficiency than brutality, and which guided Chile through its formative years.

2568 Corvalán Masson, Marcelo. Presencia eslava en el norte de Chile: testimonios para una historia. Antofagasta, Chile: Univ. de Antofagasta, 1988? 398 p., 11 leaves of plates: bibl., ill., ports.

Extremely well-done study on the influential Yugoslav colony which settled in Chile's north provides extensive information

not only on prominent Yugoslavs but also on their economic activities and their sociocultural institutions. Essential for understanding both the development of Chile's north as well as this important ethnic group's contribution.

2569 Donoso Vergara, Guillermo. La lucha en Talca. (*Rev. Chil. Hist. Geogr.*, 153, 1985, p. 59–94)

Extremely tedious narrative, devoid of analysis, recounts the reaction of Talca's press to Santa María's legislation to secularize Chile (1883–84).

2570 Drpić, Zvonimir Martinić. La intervención norteamericana en la Guerra del Pacífico: el caso de Hurlbut y Blaine visto por la diplomacia italiana. (*Cuad. Hist.*, 7, julio 1987, p. 53–75, table)

Based on Chilean secondary sources and archives, this essay provides Italy's perspective on the War of the Pacific.

2571 Estrada Turra, Bartolomero. Los relatos de viajeros como fuente histórica: visión de Chile y Argentina en cinco viajeros ingleses, 1817–1835. (*Rev. Indias*, 47:180, mayo/agosto 1987, p. 631–666)

Employing the works of five English travelers, author notes the usefulness of their observations for understanding Argentina and Chile. He warns, however, that historians should use these sources with discretion because the foreign authors, for a variety of reasons—including an inability to speak the language well—often lacked objectivity.

2572 Fabres Villarroel, Oscar. Don Maximiano Errázuriz Valdés, 1895–1950: un caballero en nuestro tiempo; el educador, el político y el hombre de trabajo; comentarios y reflexiones sobre su vida. Santiago: Salesianos, 1985. 121 p.

Highly laudatory biography of conservative politician, diplomat, and educator.

Ferrando Keun, Ricardo. Y así nació la frontera: conquista, guerra, ocupación, pacificación, 1550–1900. See item **2209.**

2573 Garrido de Vargas, Eugenia. Cuando Valparaíso se asomó al siglo XIX. (*Atenea/Concepción*, 453/454, 1986, p. 203–229, bibl., ill.)

Relying upon the works of approximately twenty Europeans and Americans, the author describes early 19th-century Valparaíso, its social customs and life, and educational institutions. Also discusses the impact of the sea in the port's development. Serves as a useful overview.

2574 Gaviola Artigas, Edda et al. Queremos votar en las próximas elecciones: historia del movimiento femenino chileno, 1913–1952. Santiago: Centro de Análisis y Difusión de la Condición de la Mujer, 1986. 101 p.: bibl., ill.

Traces the development of the women's movement (1913–52). Describes changes in Chilean women's economic, legal, and political status culminating in the first presidental election in which they could vote. Beginning in the northern *salitreras*, the women's movement became more powerful, leading to the formation of feminist organizations which, in turn, agitated successfully for the granting of suffrage to women and their eventual participation in the political process.

2575 Gross, Patricio. Un acercamiento a los planes de transformación de Santiago de Chile, 1875–1985. (*in* Nuevos perspectivas en los estudios sobre historia urbana latinoamericana. Buenos Aires: Instituto Internacional de Medio Ambiente y Desarrollo (IIED) América Latina, 1989, p. 305–325)

Beginning in the late 19th century, municipal officials, the Chilean legislature, and later various government agencies, often using the work of foreign consultants and Europeans examples, developed various plans to modernize Santiago. Because it provides a brief history of some important legislation, urban historians will find this article useful.

2576 Guerrero Yoacham, Cristián. La misión de Vicuña Mackenna a los Estados Unidos, 1865–1866. (*Atenea/Concepción*, 453/454, 1986, p. 239–275, facsims., ill., photos)

Describes the attempts of Benjamín Vicuña Mackenna to obtain military supplies and win US support for Chile during its confrontation with Spain. Based largely upon Vicuña's papers, Guerrero explains in detail Vicuña's efforts and his eventual disillusionment with the US.

Guzmán Brito, Alejandro. Portales y el derecho. See item **5398.**

2577 Hirsch-Weber, Wolfgang. Grundbesitz und herrschaft im vorindustriellen

Chile. (*Ibero-Am. Arch.*, 13:4, 1987, p. 455–543, tables)

Compares Chile's *inquilinaje* system, which the author blames for limiting Chile's agrarian sector, with two German institutions: the *Grundherrschaft* and *Gutsherrschaft*. Despite many hardships, author argues that *inquilinos* suffered less than their rural German counterparts. Although some of the author's conclusions are debatable (he seems unaware of the more brutal aspects of Chilean rural life), the work does provide some points of comparison.

2578 Ibáñez Santa Maria, Adolfo. Estatismo y tradicionalismo en Mario Góngora. (*Historia/Santiago*, 22, 1987, p. 5–23, bibl.)

Believing that it protected the human element in individuals and the State, Mario Góngora favored a statist government which stressed *hispanidad*, nationalism, and *indigenismo* in preference either to Liberalism or an authoritarian state. Provides insights into the thinking of one of Chile's foremost historians.

2579 Infante Díaz, Florencio. Presencia de la Iglesia en la Guerra del Pacífico. Santiago: Estado Mayor General del Ejército, 1986. 247 p.: bibl., ports. (Biblioteca militar; 70–75)

Series of brief biographical sketches of various military chaplains who served in the War of the Pacific with samples of their sermons and the diary of a naval chaplain as well. Limited perspective but nonetheless useful for the military historian.

Jaksic, Ivan. Academic rebels in Chile: the role of philosophy in higher education and politics. See item **5399.**

2580 Jaksic, Ivan and **Sol Serrano.** In the service of the nation: the establishment and consolidation of the Universidad de Chile, 1842–79. (*HAHR*, 70:1, Feb. 1990, p. 139–171, tables)

Responding to the needs of a modernizing nation, the Univ. de Chile began to train professionals as well as individuals who could contribute technical skills to the country. Slowly the university's graduates entered the nation's mainstream, using their knowledge to accelerate the process of change. An important study for understanding Chile's intellectual development.

2581 Jensen, Poul. The garotte: the United States and Chile, 1970–1973. Aarhus C, Denmark: Aarhus Univ. Press, 1988. 2 v., 606 p.: bibl., ill., index.

Based largely on US sources, author accuses Washington of opposing Allende's election, sabotaging his regime, and engineering his overthrow. Sometimes densely-written, it provides a comprehensive albeit extremely ideological view of this critical period.

2582 Kellenbenz, Hermann. Eduardo Wilhelm Berckemeyer, mercader hamburgués en Valparaíso, 1837–1838. (*Historia/Santiago*, 22, 1987, p. 25–45, bibl., tables)

Précis of the diary of a German who visited Chile in 1837–38. Includes a biography of Berckemeyer as well as some information on ship movements into and out of Valparaíso.

2583 Kellenbenz, Hermann. Relaciones consulares entre las ciudades hanseáticas y Chile: el caso de Valparaíso hasta los años de 1850. (*Jahrb. Gesch.*, 25, 1988, p. 117–140)

Utilizing commercial houses located throughout Latin America, Hanseatic nationals began to trade with Chile as early as 1818. Soon German merchants had established other commercial outlets, particularly in Valparaíso. Diplomatic relations followed in the 1830s. Traces the activities of Baltic Germans, such as Berckemeyer and Kindermann, who became involved in commerce with Latin America and particularly Chile.

Lavrin, Asunción. Women, labor, and the left: Argentina and Chile, 1890–1925. See item **2722.**

2584 Leaman de la Hoz, Félix. Historia urbana de Chillán, 1835–1900. Chillán, Chile: Ediciones Instituto Profesional de Chillán, 1985. 142 p.: (Serie Estudios de la región; 1)

Based on wealth of primary sources, the author describes Chillán during the 19th century. Provides information on the city's economic development, charitable institutions, police, the creation of a transportation network, as well as describing the area's economic development and the political impact of civil wars of 1851, 1859, and 1891. Well-done work on local history for one of the more important towns in Chile's Central Valley.

2585 Maldonado Prieto, Carlos. Körner y la intervención alemana: acerca de la presencia militar del imperialismo alemán en Chile, 1886–1900. (*Estud. Latinoam.*, 11, 1988, p. 123–140, bibl.)

Using a limited number of sources, author attempts to explain the impact of the Prussian officer, Emil Körner, on the Chilean army. Employs a Marxist focus to repeat what is already known: that Körner had an enormous impact and that he hoped to modernize Chile's army by introducing German weapons and military institutions.

2586 Mamalakis, Markos. The notion of the State in Chile: six topics. (*Historia/Santiago*, 22, 1987, p. 107–115, bibl.)

Interesting and innovative work by a respected scholar addresses the nation's economic problems by focusing on specific issues. Although inspired by the best of intentions, the Chilean State created institutions which essentially benefitted the middle-class and sometimes the rich. Consequently, State-owned economic enterprises aggravated the very social conditions State intervention sought to cure by absorbing funds to employ the middle-class. Chile must, in the future, provide incentives to those who produce, rather than protect certain economic classes.

2587 Marambio Cabrera, Augusto. La cuestión del *Macedonian* en las relaciones de Chile con Estados Unidos de América y Bélgica, 1819–1863. Santiago: Editorial Jurídica de Chile; Editorial Andrés Bello, 1989. 147 p., 7 p. of plates: bibl., ill.

Discusses the *Macedonian* claims, a dispute over damages to an American vessel which consumed the energies of American and Chilean diplomats for decades. Perhaps the definitive work on this tedious topic which happily has ceased to preoccupy diplomats and scholars.

2588 Martínez, Pedro Santos. La inmigracion en Chile: el caso de los colonos vascos, 1882–1883. (*Historia/Santiago*, 22, 1987, p. 287–311, bibl.)

Santiago hoped to entice immigrants to settle in Chile. A group of Basques did embark for Chile but upon learning of conditions in Chile, and encouraged by the Uruguayan government, they stayed in Uruguay rather than continuing their journey. This incident provoked serious discussion over how the government could entice foreigners to people Chile's virgin lands.

2589 Martinic Beros, Mateo. Nogueira el pionero. Punta Arenas, Chile: Ediciones de la Univ. de Magallanes, 1986. 173 p.: bibl., ill., ports.

Well-researched biography of Jose Nogueira, a Portuguese merchant who built a financial empire in the Punta Arenas area. Of interest to students of the economic development of Chile's south.

2590 Mayo, John. The British community in Chile before the nitrate age. (*Historia/Santiago*, 22, 1987, p. 135–150, bibl., table)

The first English immigrants to Chile settled mainly in Valparaíso or the northern mining area. Initially serving as an intermediary between London and Santiago, the British did not become significant in Chile until after the War of the Pacific. Very useful study of an economically powerful ethnic group.

Mellafe R., Rolando and **René Salinas Meza.** Sociedad y población rural en la formación de Chile actual: La Ligua, 1700–1850. See item **2220.**

2591 Méndez Beltrán, Luz María. Paisaje y costumbres recreativas en Chile: Valparaíso en el siglo XIX. (*Historia/Santiago*, 22, 1987, p. 151–188, bibl., ill., tables)

With urbanization and European immigration, Valparaíso's urban landscape changed: immigrants brought new plants; the city's recreational activities expanded; new types of gardens appeared; and traditional plazas became parks for cultural events. Tracing the changing impact of urban culture on the relationship between space and people in the 19th century, this valuable study will benefit the urban and social historian.

2592 Meneses Ciuffardi, Emilio. El factor naval en las relaciones entre Chile y los Estados Unidos, 1881–1951. Santiago: Ediciones Pedagógicas Chilenas, Librería Francesa, 1989. 229 p.: bibl., ill. (Col. Histo-Hachette)

Highly innovative work discusses how naval matters influenced Chile's diplomatic relations with the US. After its 1891 Revolu-

tion, Chile's naval power began a slow decline, forcing Santiago to reach an accommodation with Washington.

2593 Millán, Gabriel F. Alessandri: Don Arturo, perspectiva y retrato, legado y vigencia. Santiago: Impr. y Litografía Marinetti, 1985. 121 p.: bibl., ill., ports.

Spotty work ostensibly studies the life and impact of Alessandri. More laudatory than analytical, it will not interest the specialist.

2594 Montes, Hugo. Evocación de Jaime Eyzaguirre. Santiago: Academia Chilena de la Lengua, 1985. 29 p.: (Cuadernos del centenario de la Academia Chilena de la Lengua)

Short biography of Jaime Eyzaguirre. Although brief, it includes a good bibliography.

2595 Moreno Beauchemin, Ernesto. Historia del movimiento sindical chileno: una visión cristiana. Prólogo de Raúl Silva Henríquez. Santiago: Instituto Chileno de Estudios Humanísticos, 1986. 140 p.:

Argues that the Roman Catholic Church strongly influenced the Chilean union movement from the onset. Although initially only parish priests and laymen advocated reforms, the hierarchy subsequently backed this movement for change. The author argues that the Church actually anticipated many of the needs of the movement. Criticizes Christian union leaders for failure to take control of the movement.

2596 Moreno Martín, Armando. La expedición naval española del navío *Asia* y del bergantín *Aquiles:* 1824–1825. (*Rev. Chil. Hist. Geogr.*, 153, 1985, p. 95–116, map, photo)

Uninspired narrative describes the mutiny aboard two Spanish naval vessels, the *Aquiles* and *Asia* which sailed from the South Pacific. The *Asia* traveled to Mexico and the *Aquiles* to Chile.

2597 Nuestros uniformes. Edición de Enrique Valdés Puga, Virgilio Espinoza Palma, Edmundo González Salinas. Ilustraciones de Julio Berrios Salazar. Santiago: Estado Mayor General del Ejercito, 1986. 306 p.: ill. (Historia del Ejército de Chile; 11) (Col. Biblioteca militar)

Lavishly illustrated work describes the

various uniforms worn by Chilean armed forces and depicts officers' and enlisted men's insignia, unit badges, and military decorations. Includes the legislation and regulations describing and authorizing various uniforms, insignia, and decorations. Part of a larger series on the Chilean army which is an essential for military historians.

2598 O'Brien, Thomas F. "Rich beyond the dreams of avarice:" the Guggenheims in Chile. (*Bus. Hist. Rev.*, 63:1, Spring 1989, p. 122–159)

Well-researched and interesting study traces the Guggenheim family's nitrate ventures which culminated in the ill-fated COSACH experiment. Although normally well-organized and skilled, the Guggenheims failed to consider the devastating effects of the Great Depression. Excellent analysis of the American firm's involvement in Chile's mining sector and its attempt to introduce new technology into the *salitreras.*

2599 O'Higgins, Bernardo. Manifiesto que hace a las naciones el director supremo de Chile de los motivos que justifican su Revolución y la declaración de su Independencia. Recopilación de Hugo Rodolfo E. Ramírez Rivera. Ed. facsimilar a plana y renglón. Santiago: Ediciones de la Revista Libertador O'Higgins, 1985. 30 p.: 1 port., bibl. (Biblioteca del Instituto O'Higginiano de Chile; 1. Serie Fuentes de la Emancipación)

Facsmile copy of O'Higgins' original statement justifying Chile's movement for independence.

2600 Ortiz, Eduardo. Un caso de retorno a los cuarteles: Chile, 1932. (*Opciones*, 15, 1989, p. 141–154)

Describes the transfer of power from General Bartolomé Blanche to civilians following the overthrow of the Socialist Republic. Although relying mainly on secondary sources, article fills a void.

2601 Palacios, Nicolás. Raza chilena: libro escrito por un chileno y para los chilenos. Ed. facsimilar según la ed. original de 1904, 3a ed. Santiago: Ediciones Colchagua, 1987. 743 p.: facsim., index, ports.

Reprint of the famous 1904 book which argued that Chileans were a fusion of the Araucanian Indian and the Spanish Goths. A biography of Palacios and an essay explaining his "philosophy" are also included.

El pensamiento socialista en Chile: antología, 1893–1933. See item **5402.**

2602 Pinochet de la Barra, Oscar. El Cardenal Silva Henríquez: luchador por la justicia. Santiago: Editorial Salesiana, 1987. 248 p., 16 p. of plates: ports.

Laudatory biography of Cardinal Silva Henríquez, leader of Chile's Catholic Church. While based on sources which cannot be verified, the work does provide some understanding of the Cardinal's activities during the Allende and the Pinochet regimes.

2603 Pinto, Sonia. Benjamín Vicuña Mackenna y la historia regional. (*Cuad. Hist.*, 7, julio 1987, p. 147–153)

Based on Vicuña Mackenna's histories of Santiago and Valparaíso, his author attempts to demonstrate Vicuña Mackenna's interest in regional history and nationalism.

2604 Ponce Molina, Homero. Historia del movimiento asociativo laboral chileno. v. 1. Santiago: Editorial ALBA, 1986. 1 v.: bibl., indexes.

Studies Chile's labor unions and various professional groups. Traces their creation and the enabling legislation while attempting to place the process within the context of Chile's historical development. Although lacking analysis, provides useful information.

2605 Pozo, José del. Los gobiernos radicales en Chile frente al desarrollo, 1938–1952. (*Caravelle*, 53, 1989, p. 37–64)

The economic policies of Chile's Radical presidents did not represent an abrupt change from earlier governments. Radical governments, however, did establish the precedent for energetic State intervention in the economy, particularly in the area of planning and implementation, and they were willing to tolerate more inflationary fiscal policies. Useful overview of an often neglected period of Chilean historiography.

2606 Ramón, Armando de and **Patricio Gross.** Medio ambiente urbano en Santiago de Chile: 1891–1918. (*in* Cultura urbana latinoamericana. Recopilación de Richard Morse y Jorge Enrique Hardoy. Buenos Aires: Conscjo Latinoamericano de Ciencias Sociales, 1985, p. 243–264)

Describes various projects to beautify Santiago as well as create and expand its sewer and transportation systems and establish police protection. Preliminary results of an ongoing project which will interest social historians.

2607 Rodríguez Rautcher, Sergio. Problemática del soldado durante la Guerra del Pacífico. Santiago: Estado Mayor General del Ejército, 1986? 187 p.: bibl., ill., ports. (Col. Biblioteca militar; 70–1)

Splendid volume studies the supply and administration of the Chilean army during the War of the Pacific. Author provides information on their pay, equipment and rations, and the system of military justice which regulated their lives. Work offers valuable information on how the Chilean army functioned during this crucial war and contains an extensive bibliography on the War of the Pacific.

2608 Rojas Flores, Jorge. El sindicalismo y el estado en Chile 1924–1936. Santiago: J. Rojas Flores, 1986. 113 p., 1 folded leaf of plates: bibl., ill. (Col. Nuevo siglo.)

The Ibáñez government supported the unionization of various industries more to guarantee social peace and production than to advance the interest of the working class. Leftists such as the Anarchists and Commuists, however, refused to participate in these unions, arguing for the creation of an independent union, free of government domination.

2609 Rojas Mix, Miguel. Un dia en Santiago al terminar la época colonial: ensayo iconográfico. (in La grande ville en Amérique Latine. Edition de Claude Bataillon et Jacques Gilard. Paris: Centre National de la Recherche Scientifique, 1988, p. 29–52, bibl., facsims.)

Misleadingly titled essay examines Santiago de Chile as it was in the second half of the 19th century, and argues that the social structure of the capital remained "colonial" throughout the 1800s. The illustrations are telling. [M.T. Hamerly]

2610 Sater, William F. Labor, immigration, and the *cuestión social*. (*Historia/Santiago*, 22, 1987, p. 313–323)

Some Chileans advocated immigration to compensate for a labor shortage following the War of the Pacific. While Northern Europeans were welcomed, Jews, Italians, and Chinese were not. Some argued that Chile would not need immigrants if the government improved living conditions so that enough poor would live long enough to join the workforce.

2611 Schaepman, Kees. Chili. Amsterdam: Koninklijk Instituut voor de Tropen; Novib; SDU Uitg., 1989. 68 p.: bibl., ill., maps. (Landen)

Brief, but fine introduction to the history, political system, economy, and culture of Chile, intended for a general public. Emphasizes the Allende period and the political and economic situation under Pinochet. [R. Hoefte]

2612 Serrano, Sol. De la academia a la especialización: la Universidad de Chile en el siglo XIX. (*Opciones*, 13, enero/abril 1988, p. 9–34, bibl.)

Studies the creation and expansion of the Univ. de Chile in the 19th century. Also touches on such ancillary issues as the nature of the university, its administration, student population, and role of the State in the educational and degree granting process. Extremely useful for understanding intellectual history.

2613 Silva G., Osvaldo. Aspectos de las campañas de 1879: el testimonio de los actores. (*Cuad. Hist.*, 7, julio 1987, p. 155–174, bibl.)

Author uses excerpts from already published sources, as well as one manuscript, to explain military life during the War of the Pacific. Ineresting, but not particularly informative for the specialist.

2614 Stemplowski, Ryszard. La diplomacia alemana frente a la República Socialista de Chile de 1932. (*Jahrb. Gesch.*, 25, 1988, p. 259–271)

Based on German diplomatic sources, this article provides a brief summary of Germany's policies toward the Socialist Republic. More of a summary than a detailed analysis, it does provide some valuable archival information.

2615 Torres Marín, Manuel. Quintanilla y Chiloé: la epopeya de la constancia. Santiago: Editorial Andrés Bello, 1985. 103 p., 4 p. of plates : bibl., ill.

Traces the activities of Royalist army officer who, following the defeat at Chacabuco, defended Chiloé and the South. Work describes the efforts of the Chileans to dislodge the Spaniards. Quintanilla subsequently returned to Spain and led an uneven military career, dying in relative obscurity.

2616 Valdivieso Ariztía, Rafael. Testigos de la historia. Prólogo de Hermógenes Pérez de Arce. Santiago: Editorial A. Bello, 1985. 141 p.: bibl., index.

Compilation of articles on various important political and diplomatic figures provides brief observations about certain issues in Chilean history. Although these articles have appeared in the press, they do offer interesting insights into some important issues.

Valenzuela, Julio Samuel. Democratización vía reforma: la expansión del sufragio en Chile. See *HLAS 51:4943.*

2617 Vial Correa, Gonzalo. Historia de Chile, 1891–1973. v. 3, Arturo Alessandri y los golpes militares, 1920–1925. Santiago: Editorial Santillana del Pacífico, 1987. 1 v.: bibl., ill., index.

Vol. 3 of a multi-volume study traces Chile's development 1891–1973. Studies the rise of Alessandri and the coups which brought down the Parliamentary Regime and created modern Chile. Argues that the 1925 coup occured because the sociopolitical system lacked viability. Vial not only mentions the events preceding Alessandri's 1924 overthrow, but the subsequent incidents: the emergence of the middle class; the writing of the 1925 Constitution; separation of Church and State; and Don Arturo's struggle with Ibáñez. The author, moreover, attempts to provide some insights into Chilean society, its mores, and values. Although not relying extensively on primary sources, this is an essential study which all historians interested in Chile will read with pleasure and ignore at their peril.

Villalobos R., Sergio. Origen y ascenso de la burguesía chilena. See *HLAS 51:4947.*

2618 Villalobos R., Sergio and **Rafael Sagredo B.** El proteccionismo económico en Chile, siglo XIX. Santiago: Instituto Profesional de Estudios Superiores Blas Cañas, 1987. 206 p.: (Col. Sociedad, tiempo y cultura)

This book puts to rest the idea that economic liberalism reigned supreme in Chile. Protectionism enjoyed more currency as the legislature and the government instituted tariffs to protect fledgling industries, while *laissez faire* economic doctrines enjoyed only a brief spurt of popularity during the mid-century. Beginning in the 1870s, Chile again turned to protectionist legislation to help local industry. Seminal study which should interest economic historians while depressing the followers of Andre Gunder Frank.

2619 Vitale, Luis. Chile en la época del exilio de Sarmiento. (*Todo es Hist.,* 255, sept. 1988, p. 73–77, bibl., ill., photo)

Presumably focusing on Sarmiento's exile in Chile, the author spends most of his time describing social, political, and economic conditions in Chile. Uses the chance to criticize Sarmiento for supporting the Montt Administration. Written for a popular audience, the work contains little of significance.

2620 Waldmann, Peter. Conflicto cultural y adaptacion paulatina: La evolución de las colonias de inmigrantes alemanes en el sur de Chile. (*Jahrb. Gesch.,* 25, 1988, p. 437–453)

Because they arrived in groups, lived in an isolated area of the country, were better educated, and possessed largely Protestant value systems, German immigrants tended not to adopt Chilean customs or to mix with the local population. With the passage of years, however, German-Chileans adopted local customs while retaining a sense of ethnic identity. Interesting work on this important ethnic group.

Argentina, Paraguay, and Uruguay

JOSEPH T. CRISCENTI, *Professor of History, Emeritus, Boston College*

HISTORICAL WRITINGS IN THIS BIENNIUM continued the pattern noted in previous years. Works on the 20th century continue to exceed those on the 19th: nearly two-thirds of the publications annotated below focus on the 20th century, and two-thirds of these on the post-1930 years. Women historians are more in evidence than in the past, and they too prefer the 20th century to the 19th; their presence is most noticeable among Argentine historians, least among the Paraguayans. There has been a pronounced increase in contributions from foreign scholars, primarily concentrating on the 20th century. A smaller but nonetheless significant group is exploring numerous facets of Paraguayan history. Scholars interested in statistical data continue to encounter incomplete and unreliable census data, incomplete sets of accounting records, and poorly defined terms. Census takers and ledger keepers were not very meticulous, and like the lawyers they dealt with, some used ambiguous and contradictory language. A large number of reference works appeared.

ARGENTINA

For the past few years our understanding of Argentine political and economic developments between 1810–70 has been undergoing subtle changes as more documents become available and established interpretations are questioned. García-Godoy has assembled and has had translated an impressive collection of documents related to San Martín (item **2775**). The recently released Quiroga papers reveal the economic conditions that existed among the Interior Provinces and the nature of their relations with the Province of Buenos Aires (item **2711**). Two sets of documents for the Rosas period (items **2767** and **2647**) illustrate the strain placed on the limited financial resources of the Province of Buenos Aires by the need to protect itself from the Indians on its southern and northern flanks and from a neighboring province, and its dependence on outside sources for horses for its own army. The memoirs of the famous Mariquita Sánchez describe economic conditions during the Rosas Administrations from another perspective (item **2796**).

The reasons for the independence movement and its goals are subject to constant review. In a challenging article Saguier theorizes that the Revolution of 1810 was a by-product of the economic and social changes wrought by fluctuations in the commercial cycle (item **2773**). The program of the *saavedristas* still is subject to dispute, but not that of the *morenistas*. Dürnhöfer republished Manuel Moreno's "Plan de Operaciones" and his version of the US Constitution (item **2670**). Salas notes that some revolutionaries favored a modified version of the English constitutional model (item **2774**). Dürnhöfer and Goldman (item **2691**) agree that the *morenistas* were Jacobins. González Bernaldo believes that the patriots created and governed an abstract State, and that their *patria* was the city of Buenos Aires (item **2692**). Chiaramonte (item **2654**) concedes that the legal documents of the period are characterized by ambigious and contradictory language, and attributes the creation of the Argentine nation to political decisions. Galmarini observes in another connection that the law often failed to reflect reality (item **2680**). Chiaramonte does not believe that a national sentiment existed prior to 1810, and Pomer (item **2748**) found none prior to 1870. Indeed, Pomer sees the "national state" as the artificial creation of a small porteño element that was influenced by European ideas (item **2749**). That they failed to create national unity, as Merchensky (item **2731**) maintains, could be attributed to the presence of the three federalist movements described by Torres Molina (item **2785**). The force for unity in the littoral might have been the financial dependence of the upriver provinces on Buenos Aires that Chiaramonte suggests existed (item **2653**).

An excellent general economic history of the pre-1870 years will be found in Cuccorese and Panettieri (item **2661**). Halperín Donghi assesses the potential consequences that the opening of Buenos Aires to free trade had (item **2702**). Bidut de Salas describes altogether too briefly the business world of three merchants located in Rosario and the importance of Rosario as a port prior to 1850 (item **2645**). Sábato studies the changes that took place in the free labor market of the city and province of Buenos Aires with the arrival of foreign investments (item **2771**). Cortés Conde's brilliant study of the monetary and banking system that existed after 1862 suggests, by implication, that the nonexistence of a national monetary system or a single national currency was not an obstacle to economic progress in the provinces prior to that date (item **2659**). Minutolo de Orsi details the political and economic maneuvering of the *revolucionarios a sueldo* (item **2736**). Duarte unravels the complex relationship that existed between a presidential election and a revolutionary force in a province bordering a foreign country (item **2669**). Guerrino assesses the health of the soldiers and Indians (item **2698**).

Luna connects the pre- and post-1870 years in a sweeping survey of the growth and evolution of Argentine democracy from 1852–83 (item **2728**). An analysis of the Pellegrini Administration's handling of the financial problems of 1890–92 is found in Richmond's study (item **2760**). Bordi de Ragucci assembles the ideas of del Valle (item **2648**). Díaz Araujo (item **2668**) finds the cause for the Semana Trágica in the application of ideas acquired by European immigrants in industrial Europe to pre-industrial Argentina. Sabsay and Etchepareborda write an insightful history of the Yrigoyen and Alvear Administrations (item **2772**). Alén Lascano concentrates on the faction within the Unión Cívica Radical that helped Justo overthrow the Yrigoyen government (item **2621**). The views of one of Justo's partisans, Federico Pinedo, are summarized by Cirigliano (item **2656**). Selections from the Justo archives are now available (item **2626**). García and Rodríguez Molas have compiled documents that help clarify the military period that Justo inaugurated (item **2708**). Bou (item **2649**) discusses the European influences on the formation of the Popular Front, Ciria (item **2655**) the popular culture of the peronist years, and Reyes (item **2759**) the short life of the Labor Party. In a volume edited by Di Tella and Watt (item **2629**), experts describe British and US relations with Argentina and conditions inside the country. Greenberg highlights the intramural battles within the US Dept. of State over an American policy (item **2697**), while González de Oleaga stresses the Argentine policy of Spain (item **2693**). Quijada shows that the Spanish community in Buenos Aires was pro-Franco (item **2752**).

In a retrospective essay, Quiroga attributes the years of political instability that followed the overthrow of Perón to clashes between the industrial and agricultural interests (item **2753**). Rodríguez Lamas (item **2765**) and to some extent Smulovitz (item **2777**) instead stress the divisions within Argentine society and the unwillingness to compromise. Babini (item **2634**) testifies to the existence of a crisis within the Unión Cívica Radical, and Arévalo (item **2627**) to one in the Communist party. Bergstein documents the role of the Communist party in Córdoba in the *cordobazo* of 1969 (item **2642**). Orsolini (item **2744**) and Gasparini (item **2683**) substantially agree in their analysis of the Montonero program and its activities. Verbitsky (item **2764**) publishes the journalistic articles of the Montonero intellectual Rodolfo Walsh, and Nudelman (item **2622**) the speeches of Alfonsín. Halperín Donghi (item **2703**) summarizes the explanations advanced for the decade of terror (1973–80).

An economic history of the post-1870 years that incorporates the results of recent research remains to be written. A valuable study of the agrarian credit system was prepared by Castillo and Tulchin (item **2652**). Tulchin (item **2786**) argues that foreign market demands and the ability of the entrepreneur to meet them influenced the nature of social organizations. Vedoya notes that elimination of the Indian problem permitted modernization of the pastoral industry (item **2788**). His research convinced Míguez (item **2734**) that the agricultural sector is dynamic and adaptable to changing demands and technology. Guy found that modernization of a sugar refinery did not assure success (item **2700**). Gerbal de Blacha (item **2687**) and Rosenzvaig (item **2768**) study the sugar industry in the Argentine Northwest. Two studies (items **2730** and **2623**) illustrate the pro-agricultural policies of the government in the 1930s, and another (item **2783**), the shift to a pro-industrial policy in the 1940s. Interestingly, Lattuada found that the liberal conservative parties and the large landowners then endorsed similar programs (item **2721**).

In labor history Korzeniewicz (item **2718**) finds more evidence that the labor force did adjust to changing labor conditions in the 1880s and 1890s, while Falcón (item **2675**) seeks to identify the views of the laborer on labor issues at the turn of the century. López tells the story of the short-lived Federación Obrera Regional Argentina (item **2727**). Zorrilla (item **2797**) and Godio (item **2689**) find significant differences between the labor leaders of 1910 and those of the peronist era. The role of the labor bureaucracy is studied by Pozzi (item **2751**).

The essays in Armus (item **2635**) provide an excellent introduction to urban history. In his important study of the middle cities, Scobie devotes more attention than others to cities outside the littoral (item **2776**). Lynch (item **2729**) succinctly describes the essential features of Buenos Aires in mid-19th century, and Osculati (item **2758**) embellishes that picture. Szuchman, the leading US authority on Argentine cities, subjects the city of Buenos Aires to microscopic examination (items **2778, 2781,** and **2779**). Health and labor conditions, and social and cultural activities in the city after 1875 are discussed in a series of conference papers (items **2714, 2715,** and **2716**). Hardoy studies conditions in Rosario between 1858–1910 (items **2706** and **2705**). Ternavasio examines the effects of the Sáenz Peña law of 1912 on municipal elections (item **2784**). Vidaurreta calls attention to the composition of the population in two *entrerriano* cities (items **2794** and **2792**).

The Comisión de Estudios sobre Inmigración has published a useful collection of the laws, decrees, and administrative rulings that were in effect between 1876 and 1941 (item **2628**). Devoto diagnoses the Italian community in the city of Buenos Aires between 1830–80, and the activities of mutual aid societies (items **2664** and **2665**). Favero explains why the mutual aid societies were unsuccessful with their elementary schools (item **2677**). Nascimbene compares the illiteracy rate among the Italian and Spanish immigrants with the native population with significant results (item **2738**). Cacopardo and Moreno (item **2650**) find that the Italian immigrant who arrived after 1907 differed from his predecessor in important ways. What the immigrant faced and could expect is well illustrated in the family correspondence edited by Baily (item **2743**). Gradenigo calls attention to the Italian soldier in Argentina and Uruguay (item **2696**).

Studies of Jewish immigration to Argentina rely more on interviews than on documentation. An exception is the highly recommended study of the Jewish community by Mirelman (item **2737**). Ruppin reports his observations on Jewish assimilation, anti-Semitism, and Jewish agricultural colonies (item **2770**). Wolff (item **2717**) assesses Jewish contributions to the development of Argentina, while Kowalska (item **2719**) settles some issues about the Polish Jew. Jackisch (item **2713**) and Rojer (item **2766**) describe the German-speaking community and German Jews.

Contributions to Church history in the last biennium focus on the reaction of the Church to the heavy influx of immigrants and the incipient industrialization. Auza points out that some clergymen and Catholic laymen were not indifferent to the plight of the working class (item **2631**). The hierarchy was silent, Zubillaga states, because it could not agree on a strategy (item **2798**). Instead, Salesian priests and other Italian missionaries took an active interest in furthering the spiritual and material welfare of the immigrant. In Córdoba, the Church stressed religious education and sermons on Catholic doctrine first, and later, the improvement of the material welfare of the worker (items **2646, 2724,** and **2725**).

Contributions to women's history in the last biennium have been meager. Auza found that women in the 19th century were preoccupied with educational and cultural issues (item **2632**). Lavrin explains that anarchists and socialists changed their views of women as more women entered the work force (item **2722**). Guy describes the socialist approach to the prostitution issue (item **2701**). Bianchi finds that Eva Perón was not really interested in women's issues (item **2643**). Recalde describes the conditions women faced at work and at home (item **2757**).

Numerous reference works appeared during the last biennium. There are bibliographical guides to the provincial library in San Juan (item **2644**), to books and articles by or about Ricardo Rojas (item **2685**), to books, articles, and miscellaneous publications on the Unión Cívica Radical (item **2684**), to the materials and publications on Perón and peronism in the Hoover Institution (item **2709**), and to the works written by the followers of Yrigoyen (item **2787**). An index prepared in 1857 to the records of the Spanish Embassy in Rio de Janiero is now available (item **2694**), as well as a biographical dictionary containing the names of Irishmen who were in Argentina prior to the 20th century (item **2657**). Vidaurreta indicates where collections of *entrerriano* newspapers may be found (item **2790**). Post-1943 educational policy is analyzed by Leonard (item **2723**). Vera de Flachs presents a well-rounded history of education in the Province of Córdoba (item **2789**). Halperín Donghi re-published some of his former articles and papers (item **2704**). Middlebrook presents a history of the Malvinas/Falklands War (1982) from the viewpoint of the Argentine military (item **2732**). The Comité Internacional de Ciencias Históricas has published an assessment of all scholarly publications on Argentina written 1958–86 (item **2658**).

PARAGUAY

The pre-1870 history of Paraguay continues to receive scholarly attention. Romero (item **2833**) has published a collection of documents on the Francia era, and Vargas Peña (item **2838**) has translated a rare book attributed to Vicente Pazos Kanki purportedly detailing Francia's little-known foreign policy objective to help Spain reconquer America. Fournial (item **2814**) sheds light on the influence of the French Revolution on Francia, while Cooney (see *HLAS 50:2079*) calls attention to a rival of Francia. Church-State relations before 1862 are skillfully analyzed by Heyn Schupp (item **2822**). Garavaglia (item **2259**) studies the effects of frontier conditions on the rural population, and Martínez Cuevas (item **2824**) looks at the grazing industry. Whigham sketches British efforts to open trade with Francia's Paraguay (item **2842**).

Baptista's suggestive but undocumented biography of Elisa Lynch indicates that more research is needed on this subject (item **2807**). Both Ganson (item **2818**) and Granada (item **2821**) pay tribute to the heroic Paraguayan women. Reber challenges the prevalent notion that the Paraguayan War caused the nation to lose most of its population (item **2831**).

For the post-1870 period there are several important contributions. Two doctoral candidates in the US have published their dissertations: Caballeros Aquino on the policies of Bernardino Caballero (item **2809**), and Miranda on the Stroessner regime (item **2826**). Seiferheld consulted US diplomatic papers to learn why the governments of Federico Chávez and Epifanio Méndez Fleias fell (items **2835** and **2805**). The meddling of foreign governments in the domestic affairs of Paraguay and the rise of rebel groups is amply documented by Miranda (item **2826**). In two studies, Abente identifies the domestic international factors that contributed to the fall of the Liberal party in 1936 (items **2800** and **2801**). Labor history benefits from the studies of Gaona (item **2819**) and Barboza (item **2808**).

The outpouring of works on the Chaco War continues, but there are encouraging signs that military history will be written with the professional soldier in mind. Works by Tufari Recalde (item **2837**) and Vittone (item **2841**) are serious efforts at writing military history. At the unit level, both Saldívar (item **2834**) and Escobar Rodas (item **2812**) have written impressive accounts. Ramos (item **2830**) provides useful biographies of the generals and colonels he knew. That professional soldiers can differ on strategy, politics, and administrative procedures is made apparent in Alemán (item **2802**) and Franco (item **2816**). The reasons for the military's dissatisfaction with the peace treaty are fully explained in Escobar (item **2811**) and Granada (item **2821**). Both writers and Seiferheld (item **2835**) evaluate the importance of oil as a cause for the war and an obstacle to peace. Cooney and Whigham interview Harris Gaylord Warren, the leading US historian of Paraguay (item **2810**). Kallsen published a bibliographical guide to literature on Asunción (item **2823**).

URUGUAY

Among the impressive additions to the historical literature of Uruguay are a volume in the Archivo Artigas documentary collection (item **2845**), an interpretation of Uruguayan culture (item **2847**), and instructive materials on the origins and development of the Jewish community in Uruguay (item **2864**).

The historical period that received the most attention was that following the Revolution of 1870. The Archivo Artigas volume and the documents unearthed in Spain by Vidal Rossi (item **2878**), reinforce the clarion call of Ramírez and others for a reappraisal of Artigas. Fernández Cabrelli (item **2855**) examines the role of the Masons in the independence period. In an important study, Santiago discusses the growth of an anti-militaristic element in the Blanco (National) Party (item **2874**).

In the post-1870 years the careers and political programs of several Colorado and Blanco leaders have been subjected to scholarly review. Reyes Abadie argues persuasively for a new appraisal of Lorenzo Latorre and his administration (item **2869**), and in a study of the family of Aparicio Saravia (item **2853**), he illustrates the influence family loyalty can have on a family with different national origins and party affiliations. Garat (item **2858**) focuses not only on the career of Luis A. de Herrera and the evolution of his ideas, but also on the intra-party challenges to his leadership. The interesting retrospective reflections of Wilson, member of a dissident party wing, on the goals and politics of the National Party were taped shortly before he died (item **2857**). Abal Oliú defends the claim of the National Party that it took the initiative in sponsoring social legislation (item **2843**). The opposite viewpoint is upheld by Anastasia and others (item **2844**), who have carefully analyzed what Batlle y Ordóñez wrote in his newspaper before becoming president. The conclusion that Barrán reaches in two scholarly studies (items **2846** and **2848**) is that the two parties shared essentially the same principles, and this conclusion Abal Oliú (item **2843**) reluctantly accepts.

One of the reasons for the social legislation, as Rial implies (item **2870**), was the economic dislocation that existed at the beginning of the century. Additional economic and political problems appeared with the first World War and the Great Depression of 1929, and were a factor in bringing about the revolutions of 1933 and 1973. Only sporadic studies of the period appeared during this biennium. Castellanos (item **2851**) deemphasizes the economic situation and attributes the Revolution of 1933 to the alleged effects of the "simultaneous double vote law" of 1910. This interpretation finds scant support in Oddone's analysis of party politics prior to 1933 (item **2865**). The policies adopted by the Terra dictatorship to solve the problems it had inherited failed to win wide support. Ruiz describes the growing disenchantment with it among leftist elements, and the formation of the Popular Front (item **2873**). The socialist preaching of Vivián Trías (item **2877**) reached a growing audience, and Nardone organized the rural middle class into a political force (see *HLAS 46:3424*.) A decade later the "Tupamaros" or Movimiento de Liberación Nacional appeared. Fernández Huidobro (item **2856**) describes its origins and activities. The relations of the Tupamaros with the armed forces and their involvement in the *golpe* of 1973 are explained in Caula and Silva (item **2852**). A thoughtful assessment of the Tupamaro movement is presented by Alberto Sendic (item **2876**).

Several immigrant accounts appeared in the last biennium. Oxman interviewed the survivors of a Jewish agricultural colony that failed (item **2866**). Raicher records the Jewish reactions to both Uruguay and Israel (item **2859**). Seluja introduces the Lebanese of Uruguay (item **2875**), while Medina Pintado focuses on the German community there (item **2862**). Rodríguez Villamil contributes to women's history (item **2872**). Finally, three Uruguayan historians were honored during the biennium: Pivel Devoto (item **2879**), Carlos Real de Azúa (item **2867**) and Apolant (item **2854**).

ARGENTINA

2621 Alén Lascano, Luis C. Yrigoyenismo y antipersonalismo: surgimiento en el gobierno de Alvear. Buenos Aires: Centro Editor de América Latina, 1986. 139 p.: (Biblioteca Política argentina; 164)

Describes the origins of the divisions within the Unión Cívica Radical which appeared at the party convention of 1922, and the formation during the Alvear Administration of the alliance between conservatives and disaffected Radicals which led to the Revolution of 1930.

2622 Alfonsín, Raúl. El poder de la democracia. Recopilación y edición de Ricardo Nudelman. Buenos Aires: Ediciones Fundación Plural, 1987. 232 p.: ill., ports.

Reproduces five speeches Alfonsín made 1985–87. Includes commentaries.

2623 Alvarez, Norberto. Crisis y caminos: intereses sectoriales e intervención del Estado en el origen de la red caminera argentina, 1930–1943. (*Anu. IEHS*, 1, 1986, p. 229–253, tables)

Demonstrates that Argentina initiated a vigorous road building program in 1932 in response to the world economic crisis. Aims were to create jobs for the unemployed, to provide automobile owners with a national road network, and to increase the income of the agrarian sector by giving it an alternative to the railroad with its high freight rates and by providing isolated areas an opportunity to contribute to Argentine exports. Describes in detail the terms of the Ley Nacional de Vidalidad of Sept. 30, 1932.

2624 Alzugaray, Rodolfo A. Ramón Carrillo, el fundador del sanitarismo nacional. Prólogo de Fermín Chávez. Buenos Aires: Centro Editor de América Latina, 1988. 2 v., 231 p. (Biblioteca Política argentina; 225–226)

Biography of the first Minister of Public Health, an office created in 1946. European-educated and an ardent Peronist, Carrillo was primarily interested in improving health conditions in Argentina.

2625 Archetti, Eduardo P. Ideología y organización sindical: las ligas agrarias del norte de Santa Fe. (*Desarro. Econ.*, 28 : 111, oct./dic. 1988, p. 447–461, bibl.)

Analysis of the social organization of the Ligas Agrarias in northern Santa Fe prov., and especially of the Santa Cecilia colony. The Ligas Agrarias were a product of the Rural Movement of Catholic Action, in which rural youth predominated, and of the Juventud Cooperativista organized by the Unión Agrícola of Avellaneda. The ideology of the colonists, originally from Friuli, was molded by the clergy. Based on field work in Santa Cecilia colony in 1973–74.

2626 Archivo del General Justo: la Presidencia. Recopilación de Fernando García Molina y Carlos A. Mayo. Buenos Aires: Centro Editor de América Latina; M. Cancellaro, 1987. 2 v. (208 p.): bibl. (Biblioteca Política argentina; 192–193)

Selection of documents written between Jan. 1, 1931 and Sept. 6, 1936 which focuses on the economic and political problems faced by the Justo Presidency. Police and intelligence reports predominate. Selections in vol. 2 cover trade with Paraguay, the Chaco War, the Roca mission to London, economic relations with Brazil and the US, and the World Economic Conference of 1933.

2627 Arévalo, Oscar. Historia del Partido Comunista. (*Todo es Hist.*, 250, abril 1988, p. 6–35, bibl., facsims., photos)

Summary description of the divisions within the Argentine Communist Party from its origins to 1983. The connection between the internal debates and changing conditions in Argentina and the world is clearly indicated.

2628 Argentina. Comisión de Estudios sobre Inmigración. Sistema migratorio argentino: exposición cronológica de la política de inmigración en Argentina. Buenos Aires: Comisión de Estudios sobre Inmigración, 1986. 252 p.: bibl.

Collection of laws, decrees, and administrative rulings affecting immigration that were implemented 1876–1941.

Argentina. Ejército. Informe oficial del Ejército Argentino: conflicto Malvinas. v. 1., Desarrollo de los acontecimientos. v. 2., Abreviaturas, anexos y fuentes bibliográficos. See *HLAS 51:4444.*

2629 Argentina between the Great Powers, 1939–46. Edited by Guido Di Tella and D. Cameron Watt. Pittsburgh, Pa.: Univ. of Pittsburgh Press, 1990. 212 p.: bibl., index, maps. (Pitt Latin American series)

Ten thought-provoking essays, revisionist in nature, by Alec Campbell, Warren F. Kimball, Joseph S. Tulchin, Carlos Escudé, Mario Rapoport, Ronald C. Newton, Callum A. MacDonald, Stanley E. Hilton, Guido Di Tella, and John Major. Comments by Paul B. Goodwin on the Rapoport essay and H.S. Ferns on the Newton essay should be read, as should the introduction by D. Cameron Watt.

2630 Argentina, historia y contemporaneidad. Moscú: Redacción Ciencias Sociales Contemporáneas, 1986. 191 p.: bibl. (Serie América Latina, estudios de científicos soviéticos; 30)

Collection of short articles on Argentine history, Argentine-USSR relations, and contemporary Argentine economic, political, and social problems. Especially noteworthy are: Viacheslav Gamutilo's "Estudio de Argentina en la URSS;" L. Sheinbaum's "Peculiaridades de la Formación de la Nación;" and A. Stróganov's "La Lucha de los Trabajadores por la Democracia y la Soberanía Nacional."

Armus, Diego and **Jorge Enrique Hardoy.** Entre el conventillo y la casa propia: notas sobre la vivienda popular en el Rosario del novecientos. See *HLAS 51:4957.*

2631 Auza, Néstor Tomás. Aciertos y fracasos sociales del catolicismo argentino. v. 1, Grote y la estrategia social. v. 2, Mons. de Andrea. v. 3, El proyecto episcopal y lo social. Buenos Aires: Editorial Docencia, 1987–1988. 3 v.: bibl., ill.

Pioneer study of the reaction of the Argentine Catholic Church between 1890–1945 to the nation's multiplying social problems corrects many opinions on Catholic activities during the period, and presents a reasonable explanation for the inertia of the hierarchy. This product of over 20 years of research is based essentially on the Catholic press and journals because the Church and Catholic associations either failed to keep documentary records or refused to make them available. In fact, one bishop openly recommended that documents describing Catholic activities be destroyed, and many

Catholic laymen did so. Fourth and final vol. of the study was not seen. Reference work.

2632 Auza, Néstor Tomás. Periodismo y feminismo en la Argentina, 1830–1930. Buenos Aires: Emecé Editores, 1988. 316 p.: bibl., facsims., index.

Examines the contents of twelve *porteño* literary periodicals written by women. Concludes that the feminist movement in the 19th century did not demand equal civil and political rights with men but centered on educational and cultural issues.

2633 Avni, Haim. Argentina and the Jews: a history of Jewish immigration. Translated from Hebrew by Gila Brand. Tuscaloosa: Univ. of Alabama Press, 1991. 267 p.: bibl., ill., index. (Judaic studies series)

Excellent introduction to Jewish immigration to Argentina.

2634 Babini, Nicolás. Frondizi, de la oposición al gobierno: testimonio. Buenos Aires: Editorial Celtia, 1984. 320 p.: bibl., ill., index.

A collaborator of Frondizi thoughtfully recalls the leadership crisis within the Unión Cívica Radical, suggesting why the UCR Intransigente failed to become a party and why Frondizi disappointed his followers. Based on Babini's recollections and notes in his personal archives. Interesting.

2635 Barrancos, Dora *et al.* Mundo urbano y cultura popular: estudios de historia social argentina. Recopilación de Diego Armus. Buenos Aires: Editorial Sudamericana, 1990. 361 p.: (Col. Historia y cultura)

Collection of 13 essays makes a notable contribution to Argentine urban history.

2636 Barrionuevo Imposti, Víctor. Historia de Río Cuarto. v. 2, El autonomismo cordobés y el rosismo. Buenos Aires: TIPENC, 1986–88. 1 v.: bibl., ill., index.

Well-documented history emphasizes relations with the Indians and political history. Based on provincial and municipal archives of Córdoba.

2637 Bartolomé, Leopoldo J.; Danuta Łukasz; and Ryszard Stemplowski. Sowianie w argentyńskim Missiones 1897–1977: zbiór studiów [Slavs in Argentine missions, 1897–1977]. Warszawa: Państwowe

Wydawnictwo Naukowe, 1991. 277 p.: maps, tables.

Five studies by four historians and one anthropologist describe the number and location of Polish and Ukrainian settlements in Argentina. Also discusses typical settlers' farms, organization of education for Polish immigrants, and the contemporary community of Apóstoles. Interesting, multidisciplinary approaches are based on printed sources, archives, and participant observation. [M. Nalewajko]

2638 Bauer, Alfredo. La Asociación Vorwärts y la lucha democrática en la Argentina. Introducción de Emilio J. Corbière. Buenos Aires: Editorial Legasa, 1989. 155 p.: bibl., ill. (Ensayo crítico)

Attempts to reconstruct the history of the Verein Vorwärts, founded in Buenos Aires in 1882 by German Marxists and socialists fleeing persecution in their homeland. Members contributed to the development of labor unions and leftist political organizations, including the Argentine Socialist Party. The Verein archives and library were lost. Useful introduction to the subject.

2639 Bayer, Osvaldo *et al.* Gli Italiani fuori d'Italia: gli emigrati italiani nei movimenti operai dei paesi d'adozione, 1880–1940. Cura di Bruno Bezza. Introduzione di V. Traxler. Conclusioni di L. Della Briotta. Milano, Italy: F. Angeli, 1983. 922 p.: (Quaderni di Affari sociali internazionali; 7)

Contains the following interesting essays on Italians in the Rio de la Plata: Torcuato S. Di Tella, "Argentina: un'Australia italiana? L'impatto dell'emigrazione sul sistema politico argentino;" Carlos Filgueira and Juan Rial, "Gli immigrati italiani nella costruzione del 'welfare state' in Uruguay all'inizio del secolo;" Osvaldo Bayer, "L'influenza dell'immigrazione italiana nel movimento anarchico argentino;" María de Luján Leiva, "Il movimento antifascista italiano in Argentina (1922–1945);" and Eugenia Scarzanella, "L'industria argentina e gli immigrati italiani: nascita della borghesia industriale bonaerense." All contributions are well-documented, some relying more than others on Italian archives and monographic studies, and all make an important contribution to the history of Italian immigration.

2640 Béjar, María Dolores. Otra vez la historia política: el conservadorismo bonaerense en los años treinta. (*Anu. IEHS*, 1, 1986, p. 199–227)

Straightforward political analysis of the Partido Conservador of Buenos Aires prov., its internal factions, its relations with the other political parties, and its efforts to retain control of the provincial government. The party had a weak structure as a result of absorbing the Partido Provincialista in 1930, and this accounted for many of its problems. See item **2649** for a broader view of the contemporary scene.

2641 Benvenuto, Daniel. La poética de la industria: vida y obra de Francisco Prati. Buenos Aires: Editorial Fraterna, 1990. 127 p., 24 p. of plates: ill.

Restrained but laudatory story of the achievements of an Italian industrial engineer who immigrated to Argentina, Francisco Prati (1887–1974). Prati, a confirmed optimist, was involved in many industries, especially in textiles and paper. Author uses his grandfather's files.

2642 Bergstein, Jorge. El "cordobazo:" memorias, testimonios, reflexiones. Buenos Aires: Editorial Cartago, 1987. 138 p.:

A prominent Communist, then secretary of the Communist party in Córdoba prov., recalls his role and that of his party in organizing the general strike of May 29–30, 1969, and in resisting government forces in the violent clash known as the "cordobazo." Includes excerpts from the recollections of six Córdoba communists taped during a roundtable in May, 1974, and considerable discussion of the non-communist Agustín Tosco of Luz and Fuerza and of political groups in Córdoba. Aim of the author is to contribute to an ongoing analysis within the party of its policies and activities after the military coup of 1966.

Bertoncello, Rodolfo *et al.* The dynamics of Argentine migration, 1955–1984: democracy and the return of expatriates. See *HLAS 51:4961.*

2643 Bianchi, Susana. Peronismo y sufragio feminino: la ley electoral de 1947. (*Anu. IEHS*, 1, 1986, p. 255–296)

Maintains that in 1947 Eva Perón engaged in a needless campaign for a law giving women the right to vote because she wanted to identify the political rights of women with peronism; to show that she alone was responsible for women receiving the right to vote; and to legitimatize her political influence. She only deviated briefly from the traditional view of women. Based on the speeches Eva addressed to women between Jan.-Sept. 1947.

2644 Bibliografía sarmientina. Recopilación de Gabriel Eduardo Brizuela y Lydia Edith Gómez. San Juan, Argentina: Sistema Provincial de Archivos, Subsecretaría de Ciencia y Técnica, Ministerio de Educación y Cultura, 1989. 34 p.

Lists titles of 238 books that appeared 1888–1988 that are available in San Juan.

2645 Bidut de Salas, Vilma E. Los comerciantes "del Rosario," 1810–1850. (*Todo es Hist.*, 23:273, marzo 1990, p. 64–78, bibl., facsims.)

Briefly describes the operations of three merchants located in Rosario. These case histories illustrate the effects of the civil wars and the Anglo-French blockades on individual merchants who dealt with both Montevideo and Buenos Aires and the role of merchants as lenders to individuals, as general merchandisers, and as tax payers. The port of Rosario received products from the interior provinces as well as from overseas. Based on the manuscript collection of the Museo Histórico Provincial, Rosario.

2646 Bischoff, Efraín U. La Córdoba que vio Esquiú. Córdoba: Dirección del Patrimonio Cultural, 1983. 42 p.

Brief description of the response by Bishop Mamerto Esquiú of Córdoba (1881–82) to liberal reforms affecting the Church and of his effort to reinvigorate Catholicism in the province.

2647 Bonura, Lina and **Elena Bonura.** El sentido común en el poder: Rosas y los problemas de su tiempo. Buenos Aires: Impr. Sellarés, 1986. 195 p.

Unedited documents describe the effects of fiscal austerity in 1830 and 1831 on relations with the Indians, on border security, and on a military campaign.

2648 Bordi de Ragucci, Olga N. Aristóbulo del Valle en los orígenes del radicalismo. Buenos Aires: Centro Editor de América Latina, 1987. 128 p.: (Biblioteca Política argentina; 188)

Semi-biography corrects many aspects

of the life and ideology of del Valle. Del Valle left no archives, but his speeches and debates in the Senate strongly suggest that he was influenced by Domingo F. Sarmiento and Vicente Fidel López.

2649 Bou, Marilú. 1936: el fraude, el Frente, el fascismo. (*Todo es Hist.*, 237, feb. 1987, p. 8–25, bibl., photos)

Maintains that contemporary events in Europe, especially in Spain, indirectly influenced the formation of the Popular Front in Argentina in 1936. Complements Béjar's article (item **2640**).

Buchrucker, Cristian. La "tentación fascista" en la Argentina. See item **5418**.

2650 Cacopardo, María Cristina and **José Luis Moreno.** Características demográficas y ocupacionales de los migrantes italianos hacia Argentina, 1880–1930. (*Stud. Emigr.*, 31:75, set. 1984, p. 277–293, bibl., graphs, tables)

Available Argentine and Italian statistics indicate that after 1907 Italian immigrants, primarily single men, were no longer predominantly farmers but day laborers, artisans, businessmen, and professionals. Compares Argentine and Italian fertility and mortality rates.

2651 Calvera, Leonor. Camila O'Gorman, o, El amor y el poder. Buenos Aires: Editorial Leviatán, 1986. 161 p.: (Temas argentinos)

Story of two famous lovers who lived at a time when women were beginning to challenge the legal and societal view that they had no rights and were subordinate to men.

Cárdenas, Isabel Laura. Ramona y el robot: el servicio doméstico en barrios prestigiosos de Buenos Aires, 1895–1985. See *HLAS* 51:4968.

2652 Castillo, Hugo F. and **Joseph S. Tulchin.** Dèveloppement capitaliste et structures sociales des régions en Argentine: 1880–1930. (*Ann. écon. soc. civilis.*, 41:6, nov./déc. 1986, p. 1359–1384, map, tables)

Statistical analysis of the bank drafts issued by the Banco de la Nación 1910–29 suggests how the agrarian credit system used during a boom in exports influenced activity in each of the socio-economic regions of Argentina. Authors recognize that there are other banks in Argentina that finance agricultural activities (they mention the Banco de la Provincia de Buenos Aires as an example), but they assume that the Banco de la Nación is representative of the entire banking system. Calls attention to the need to study the credit policies of the other banks, and especially of the foreign banks.

Centenario de Río Gallegos. See *HLAS* 51:3100.

2653 Chiaramonte, José Carlos. Finanzas públicas de las provincias del Litoral, 1821–1841. (*Anu. IEHS*, 1, 1986, p. 159–198, bibl., tables)

Concludes from an examination of the pertinent laws and a limited number of accounting records from Entre Ríos and Santa Fe provinces that the autonomy of these provinces was not complete because of their dependence on Buenos Aires for subsidies and loans, whereas the available records for Corrientes prov. suggest that it was financially independent of Buenos Aires and therefore could oppose it. Worthwhile study despite the paucity of accounting records available to the author.

2654 Chiaramonte, José Carlos. Formas de identidad en el Río de la Plata luego de 1810. (*Bol. Inst. Hist. Ravignani*, 3:1, 1989, p. 71–92)

Essayist concludes from an analysis of the ambiguous and often contradictory language found in the legal documents written in the first half of the 19th century that the formation of the Argentine nation was the result of political decisions made during the period and not of a national sentiment that antedated the independence movement. Pathbreaking study.

2655 Ciria, Alberto. Elite culture and popular culture in Argentina, 1930–1955. (*Rev. Interam. Bibliogr.*, 37:4, 1987, p. 501–516, bibl.)

Eminent cultural historian calls attention to the growing professionalization that took place in certain areas of popular entertainment prior to the rise of Perón and to its manifestations in the popular culture of the Peronist years. Suggests areas in need of research.

2656 Cirigliano, Antonio Angel. Federico Pinedo: teoría y práctica de un liberal.

Buenos Aires: Centro Editor de América Latina, 1986. 157 p.: bibl. (Biblioteca Política argentina; 163)

Sympathetic analysis of the economic and political ideas of the socialist Minister of Finance in the Justo Administration who showed no concern for the laborers despite the economic crisis. Does not include a discussion of his role in the Castillo Administration.

Clementi, Hebe. El miedo a la inmigración. See *HLAS 51:4971.*

2657 Coghlan, Eduardo A. Los irlandeses en la Argentina: su actuación y descendencia. Apéndice sobre heráldica irlandesa por Félix F. Martin y Herrera. Buenos Aires: Librería Alberto Casares, 1987. 963 p., 13 leaves of plates: ill., index.

Biographical dictionary contains the names of Irishmen who arrived in Argentina during the colonial period and the 19th century. Basic reference work is the result of over 30 years of research.

2658 Comité Internacional de Ciencias Históricas. Comité Argentino, 1988. Historiografía argentina, 1958–1988: una evaluación crítica de la producción histórica nacional. Buenos Aires: Comité Internacional de Ciencias Históricas, Comité Argentino, 1990. 625 p.:

Valuable assessment of scholarly publications on Argentina includes critical essays on the following subjects: colonial history; economic history; social history; intellectual history; political history; agrarian history; architectural history; demographic history; and history of foreign affairs.

2659 Cortés Conde, Roberto. Dinero, deuda y crisis: evolución fiscal y monetaria en la Argentina, 1862–1890. Buenos Aires: Editorial Sudamericana, Instituto Torcuato di Tella, 1989. 256 p.: (Col. Historia y sociedad)

Economic historian describes some previously overlooked characteristics of the monetary and banking system that existed during a crucial transition period. Focuses attention on the circulating medium (monetary base), the role of bank deposits, and the expansion of credit. Finds that the circulating medium was not always created by the government, that there was no uniform currency in Argentina, that two monetary markets existed, and that paper money was not the only currency used in domestic transactions. Attributes the crisis of 1873–76 to the monetary policies of the Banco de la Provincia de Buenos Aires and the Banco Nacional, and that of 1890 to monetary factors and to capital flight. Uses records of the Banco de la Provincia de Buenos Aires and the Banco Nacional. Major work.

2660 Cortés Conde, Roberto. Historia económica: nuevos enfoques. (*Bol. Acad. Nac. Hist./B. Aires,* 60, 1987, p. 101–117)

Survey of the tendencies that have influenced the writing of economic history in Argentina from the mid-19th century to the "new economic history" and the current "new institutional economic history." Ends with a plea for historians to study basic economics, mathematics, and statistics, and for economists to broaden their knowledge of the past and to learn to use the sources and techniques of the historian.

2661 Cuccorese, Horacio Juan and **José Panettieri.** Argentina: manual de historia económica y social. v. 1, Argentina criolla. Buenos Aires: Ediciones Macchi, 1983. 1 v.:

Two outstanding Argentine economic historians present a general introduction to the economic history of Argentina to 1876. Text calls attention to different interpretations and includes short bibliographies at the end of each chapter. Basic reference work.

2662 Delich, Andrés et al. El movimiento estudiantil de Perón a Alfonsín. Coordinación de Mario Toer. Buenos Aires: Centro Editor de América Latina, 1988. 2 v. (238 p.) (Biblioteca Política argentina; 229–230)

In interviews and seminars several leaders in the student movement between 1946–84 recall and reflect upon the characteristics and central issues of the student political movements they witnessed. They discuss the evolution of student objectives, the decline of the old and the emergence of new representative student bodies, the intrusion of national political parties in student politics, and the emergence of democratic student organizations.

2663 Deutsch, Sandra McGee. Counterrevolution and human rights abuses in Argentina: an historical perspective. (*in* Pacific Coast Council on Latin American Studies. *12th, San Diego, Calif., 1985.* Proceedings.

San Diego: San Diego State Univ., 1986, p. 119–130)

Author finds many parallels between the activities and goals of the Liga Patriótica Argentina and those of the post-1976 government in Argentina.

2664 Devoto, Fernando J. Los orígenes de un barrio italiano en Buenos Aires a mediados del siglo XIX. (*Bol. Inst. Hist. Ravignani*, 3:1, 1989, p. 93–114, tables)

Spanish version of item **2665.**

2665 Devoto, Fernando J. The origins of an Italian neighborhood in Buenos Aires in the mid XIX century. (*J. Eur. Econ. Hist.*, 18:1, Spring 1989, p. 37–64, appendix, tables)

Discussion of Italians in Buenos Aires 1830–70. In *La Boca* neighborhood half the population was Italian, primarily Ligurians from Varazze and Recco. Most were illiterate and engaged in the internal coastal trade. Based on Argentine and Italian census records, article illustrates the chain migration mechanism and corrects earlier versions of Italian migration. For version in Spanish, see item **2664.**

2666 Devoto, Fernando J. La primera élite política italiana de Buenos Aires, 1852–1880. (*Stud. Emigr.*, 26:94, giugno 1989, p. 168–194)

Essay on the formation of the first elite by liberal peninsulars, merchants, and intellectuals in the Italian community of Buenos Aires. Describes the initial conflict between monarchists and republicans, followed by the clash between clericals and anti-clericals, the growing anti-Italian sentiment among native Argentines and the leaders of other foreign communities, the effort to build a national ethnic identity among immigrants, the membership of the *Unione e Benevolenza*, and the Italian Masonic lodges. Calls attention to areas in need of research. Very thoughtful piece that should be read by all those interested in Italian immigration to Argentina.

2667 Devoto, Fernando J. Las sociedades italianas de ayuda mutua en Buenos Aires y Santa Fe: ideas y problemas. (*Stud. Emigr.*, 31:75, set. 1984, p. 320–342, tables)

Examination of the available records from 1876–1914 of four mutual aid societies—one in the Federal Capital, two in Buenos Aires prov., and one in Santa Fe prov.—reveals that both urban and rural societies were often of Mazzinian persuasion, attracted primarily artisans and laborers, and were led by middle-class professionals and merchants from northern Italy.

2668 Díaz Araujo, Enrique. La semana trágica de 1919: precedida por un estudio de los antecedentes de la inmigración y rebelión social. Mendoza, Argentina: Facultad de Filosofía y Letras, Univ. Nacional de Cuyo, 1988. 2 v.

Revisionist attempt to reconstruct events that took place during the "Semana Trágica" attributes the agitation of the period primarily to European immigrants who applied ideas they had acquired in industrial Europe to pre-industrial Argentina. Clarifies some issues.

2669 Duarte, María Amalia. Presencia de los exiliados de Entre Ríos en 1872. (*Bol. Acad. Nac. Hist./B. Aires*, 60, 1987, p. 155–166)

Fascinating account of the interrelationship between Mitre's peace mission to Rio de Janeiro, President Sarmiento's negotiations with Ricardo López Jordán, Argentine presidential elections, and Argentine fears that López Jordán would launch another revolution with Brazilian support.

2670 Dürnhöfer, Eduardo O. Moreno, el origen de la República: sus reveladores manuscritos inéditos. Buenos Aires: Escuela de Guerra Naval, 1985. 199 p.

Leading authority on Moreno summarizes his own well-documented contributions toward a better understanding of Moreno and his ideas. Contains unedited works of Moreno.

2671 Ejército argentino: cronología militar argentina, 1806–1980. Buenos Aires: Comando en Jefe del Ejército, 1982. 432 p.: bibl., ill., indexes, maps, ports.

Describes strength, composition, and deployment of troops engaged in battle in Argentina and Uruguay, indicating when sources disagree or are incomplete. Little attention given to milita units in Buenos Aires prov. and none to those in other provinces. Includes list of soldiers who died in struggle against subversion. Well illustrated.

2672 Enciclopedia de Entre Ríos. v. 1, Historia, época colonial. v. 2, Historia, desde fines del s. XVIII a mediados del s. XIX. v. 3, Historia, desde 1854 hasta 1978. Paraná, Argentina: Arozena Editores, 1978. 3 v.: bibl., ill., indexes.

Three vols. reviewed here present an excellent survey of provincial history from prehistoric times to 1977. All contributors are prominent provincial scholars who have worked in national archives and provincial archives of Entre Ríos and Santa Fe. Numerous illustrations.

2673 Epelbaum de Weinstein, Ana. Bibliografía sobre judaísmo argentino. v. 4, El movimiento obrero judío en la Argentina. Buenos Aires: Centro de Documentación e Información sobre Judaísmo Argentino Marc Turkow, 1987. 2 v.: bibl., indexes.

Concentrates on Jewish manual labor in the Federal Capital and Greater Buenos Aires from the end of the 19th century to 1939. Includes Edgardo Bilsky's, "Etnicidad y Clase Obrera: la Presencia Judía e el Movimiento Obrero Argentino," and interviews with 13 Jewish laborers (8 Polish, 2 Russian, 1 Ukrainian, and 2 unidentified). Concludes that Jewish labor movement had its own personality and subculture.

2674 Estampas informales de Buenos Ayres, 1865: relatos y dibujos de un viajero escocés que visita Buenos Aires y se radica en estancias del campo porteño, partido de Chascomús; descripción de costumbres, gauchos, carretas, diligencias, plantas y animales. Estudio preliminar y notas de Carlos Antonio Moncaut. Buenos Aires: Editorial El Aljibe, 1983. 116 p., 32 p. of plates: ill. (Col. Pampa virgen; 2)

Translation of an anonymous work that appeared in Edinburgh in 1868. The writer had lived in Chascomús, a town and district settled by Irishmen and Scotchmen. The editor's introduction quotes extensively from another rare work written by a resident in the area. It is especially interesting for its description of itinerant teachers among the English-speaking colonists. The sketches by the anonymous author and his comments about the scenes they depict make this a valuable travel account.

Estrada Turra, Bartolomero. Los relatos de viajeros como fuente histórica: visión de Chile y Argentina en cinco viajeros ingleses, 1817–1835. See item **2571.**

2675 Falcón, Ricardo. El mundo del trabajo urbano, 1890–1914. Buenos Aires: Centro Editor de América Latina, 1986. 141 p.: bibl. (Biblioteca Política argentina; 153)

Discusses the origins of the urban labor class and seeks to determine the attitude of the worker toward his employer, other workers, labor organizations, and the State. Concentrates on industrial, construction, and transportation workers in Buenos Aires. Appendix contains excerpts from labor press.

2676 Farcuh, Diana Elena. La "conciliación" santafesina de 1890 y la intervención de Nicasio Oroño. (*Res Gesta,* 16/17/18, julio/dic.1984—enero/dic. 1985, p. 36–43)

Brief description of the conflict between the newly elected governor of Santa Fe and his predecessor, and the successful mediation efforts of the Argentine president.

2677 Favero, Luigi. Le scuole delle società italiane di mutuo soccorso in Argentina, 1866–1914. (*Stud. Emigr.,* 31:75, set. 1984, p. 343–380, tables)

Significant discussion of the reasons for the rise and decline of elementary schools run by mutual aid societies. Though serving an educational need, they never enjoyed the wholehearted support of the Italian community because they seemed to conflict with the objectives of the societies. They declined in importance as public and Catholic schools were built, and as Italian children were integrated into Argentine society. Extensive use of Argentine and Italian statistics.

2678 Fernández, Virginia Ester. El N.E. de Mendoza durante el siglo XIX: el proceso de apropiación de los medios de producción por parte de un grupo dominante. (*Rev. Hist. Am.,* 107, enero/junio 1989, p. 119–133, bibl., maps)

Important examination of the process whereby rural descendants of the Huarpe Indians were dispossessed by 1908 of the land they had owned and worked since colonial times. Finds evidence that disproves the notion that the rural population failed to resist the seizure of their lands or to alter their defensive legal tactics. No one had a written title to the disputed land, and over time the position taken by the official mediators—and there were several—evolved from defending the Indian claims to asserting the claims of the State and favoring the intruders.

2679 Fonseca Figueira, José Antonio da. David Jewett, una biografía para la historia de las Malvinas. Prólogo de Laurio H. Destéfani. Buenos Aires: Sudamericana/Planeta, 1985. 191 p.: bibl., ill.

Very well documented biography of Jewett based on research conducted in three countries corrects earlier biographies and presents new data. Indispensable reading for those interested in the privateers of Buenos Aires prior to 1825, Argentine claims to the Falkland Islands (Malvinas), and the Brazilian navy.

Fortuna, Juan Carlos. Las bases de un desarrollo social diferente: estructura productiva y trabajo. See *HLAS 51:5012.*

2680 Galmarini, Hugo Raúl. Los españoles de Buenos Aires después de la Revolución de Mayo: la suerte de una minoría desposeída del poder. (*Rev. Indias,* 46:178, julio/dic. 1986, p. 561–592, bibl.)

Argues convincingly that a significant segment of the peninsular Spanish community—not just those who possessed wealth or social prestige or had married into the right families—was not affected by the anti-Spanish legislation passed 1810–19. There were numerous exemptions and the enforcement of the legislation was uneven. Anti-Spanish feeling did exist among the common people.

2681 Gálvez de Tiscornia, Lucía. La Iglesia en la Argentina: cuatro siglos de conflictos y entendimientos. (*Todo es Hist.,* 238, marzo 1987, p. 8–43, bibl., photos)

Thoughtful and balanced summary of Church-State relations from the first settlement of Buenos Aires to 1982. Notes the colonial bishops' excessive use of their power to excommunicate, and the political divisions within the clergy in the post-independence period. Excellent introduction to the subject.

2682 Garibaldi, Italo Américo. Los genoveses en Buenos Aires: la fe y el trabajo. Buenos Aires: Talleres Publimpres, 1983. 159 p., 24 p. of plates: ill.

Undocumented work is divided into two parts: 1) a history of the Genovese parish of La Guardia de Bernal; and 2) a partial listing of the Genovese settlers, their descendants and their activities. Includes a discussion of Genovese parishes in Buenos Aires, Rosario, and Arroyo Seco.

2683 Gasparini, Juan. Montoneros: final de cuentas. Buenos Aires: Puntosur Editores, 1988. 264 p.: bibl., ill.

Ex-Montonero and prisoner of the army for 20 months describes the origins, alliances, ideas, and activities of the Montoneros, and criticizes its leadership, especially Mario Firmenich, for ineptitude and poor judgment. Four annexes contain Montonero documents, plus a typical Montonero organizational chart. Often anecdotal. Substantially corroborates Mario H. Orsolini, *Montoneros: sus proyectos y sus planes* (see item **2744**).

2684 Giacobone, Carlos Alberto and **Edit Gallo.** Manual bibliográfico sobre la Unión Cívica Radical. Prólogo de César Jaroslavsky. Buenos Aires: Compañía Impresora Argentina, 1989. 460 p.

Bibliographic guide to books, periodical and newspaper articles, and miscellaneous publications on the UCR. Basic reference work includes 2,535 entries listed alphabetically by author, each fully described so the researcher can easily locate them. Reproduces tables of contents to describe book entries.

2685 Giacobone, Carlos Alberto and **Edit Gallo.** Ricardo Rojas, político: ensayo biblio-hemerográfico. Prólogo de Melchor Cruchaga. Buenos Aires: Unión Cívica Radical, Biblioteca, Archivo Histórico y Centro de Documentación, Comité de la Provincia de Buenos Aires, 1991. 1127 p.: appendix.

Bibliographical guide to books and periodical and newspaper articles by or on Ricardo Rojas written 1903–89. The 487 entries are listed chronologically. Basic reference work.

2686 Girbal de Blacha, Noemí M. and **María Silvia Ospital.** Elite, cuestión social y apertura política en la Argentina, 1910–1930: la propuesta del Museo Social Argentino. (*Rev. Indias,* 46:178, julio/dic. 1986, p. 609–625, bibl.)

Brief description of the content and themes of articles published in the *Boletín* of the Museo. Among topics discussed were the condition of women in Argentina, cooperatives, education, mutual aid societies, the family, and immigration. Members of the Museo regarded themselves as the intellectual elite of Argentina, and acted as a pressure group. They began as moderates and progressives, and gradually became reactionary.

2687 Girbal de Blacha, Noemí M. Estado, modernización azucarera y comportamiento empresario en la Argentina, 1876–1914: expansión y concentración de una economía regional. (*Anu. Estud. Am.*, 45, 1988, p. 383–417)

Outlines the process whereby the sugar industry became the basis of the northwest regional economy with Tucumán prov. at its center. Stresses the nature and consequences of the interdependence that existed between the provincial government, the national government, and the compact group of Argentine and foreign investors in the sugar industry.

2688 Girbal de Blacha, Noemí M. Política agrícola de los gobiernos radicales en Argentina, 1916–1930: fuentes para la investigación. (*Rev. Interam. Bibliogr.*, 37:2, 1987, p. 160–189, bibl.)

Annotated bibliography of publications on the agricultural policies of the Argentina government. Preceded by a suggestive introductory essay by the compiler.

2689 Godio, Julio. El movimiento obrero argentino, 1943–1955: nacimiento y consolidación de una hegemonía nacionalista-laboralista. Buenos Aires: Editorial Legasa, 1990. 299 p.: bibl. (Omnibus)

Peronist sociologist examines the formation of the modern labor class in Argentina and the influence of peronism on its development. Concludes that labor leaders were motivated by peronism and not by any socialist ideology, had learned to act as a pressure group within the government, and were unprepared to replace Perón's economic model with one of their own.

2690 Goldar, Ernesto. El enigma de Taco Ralo. (*Todo es Hist.*, 273, marzo 1990, p. 6–28, photos)

Chronicles the confusion that followed the arrest and trial of an armed band of young "peronist leftist" guerrillas captured at Taco Ralo on Sept. 19, 1968. They belonged to the Fuerzas Armadas Peronistas, which was influenced by Fidel Castro, Ernesto Guevara, and Juan D. Perón, who was expected to return and solve all problems. A year later they called themselves "montoneros."

2691 Goldman, Noemí. Los "jacobinos" en el Río de la Plata: modelo, discursos y prácticas, 1810–1815. (*Cuad. Am.*, 3:5, sept./oct. 1989, p. 157–178)

Analysis of the views of Mariano Moreno, Juan José Castelli and Bernardo Monteagudo on the Revolution of 1810. Concludes that *morenistas* held the same philosophical and political principles as the Jacobins.

2692 González Bernaldo, Pilar. Producción de una nueva legitimidad: ejército y sociedades patrióticas en Buenos Aires entre 1810 y 1813. (*Cuad. Am.*, 3:5, sept./oct. 1989, p. 134–156)

Challenges the traditional view of the contest between *saavedristas* and *morenistas* as one between moderates and Jacobins. Maintains that *saavedristas* represented the locally organized volunteer army formed to defend Buenos Aires during the English invasions of 1806–07, and *morenistas* the militant revolutionaries. The volunteer army was somewhat democratic in organization, was not an instrument of the militant revolutionaries, and was another local power base for the elite. It claimed legitimacy because it was recognized by the colonial *cabildo*. Consisting of citizen-soldiers, it was identified with popular sovereignty and the *Patria*, defined as the city of Buenos Aires and the Revolution. Their officers claimed to be the interpreters of the popular will. After March 1811, these officers and the militant revolutionaries turned the citizen-soldier into the citizen-subject of an abstract State which they governed as their representatives but without their assent. Significant.

2693 González de Oleaga, Marisa. La alianza Franco-Perón: una aproximación crítica desde la perspectiva de la dependencia, 1946–1951. (*Hispania/Madrid*, 48: 169, mayo/agosto 1988, p. 625–689, graphs, tables)

Uses Spanish archives to analyze the relationship between the governments of Franco and Perón. Argues that the aim of the former was to establish its legitimacy, and of the latter to become a continental power with an important role on the world scene, and to reduce its economic dependency on others, especially Great Britain, by encouraging industrialization. Discusses the propaganda and other activities of the Spanish Embassy in Argentina, the terms of the commercial pacts the two governments signed

between 1946–49, and the projected Confederation of Hispanic States. Polemical.

2694 González Pizarro, José Antonio. Itinerario de la documentación diplomática española proveniente de América en el siglo XIX: a propósito de la remisión de los fondos de la legación en el Brasil correspondiente a los años 1809–1851. (*Rev. Indias*, 49:185, enero/abril 1989, p. 205–216, tables)

Reproduces index prepared by N. Potestad in 1859 to the records of the Spanish Embassy in Rio de Janeiro that were sent to Spain and were eventually deposited in the Archivo Histórico Nacional. The documents refer to the independence movement in the viceroyalties of Río de la Plata and Peru.

2695 Gordillo, Mónica R. El movimiento obrero ferroviario desde el interior del país, 1916–1922. Buenos Aires: Centro Editor de América Latina, 1988. 121 p.: bibl., ill. (Biblioteca Política argentina; 227)

Well-documented study of the early struggles of *La Fraternidad* to protect the jobs of its members and to obtain recognition as a union. Describes the place of the railroad workers among other organized workers.

2696 Gradenigo, Gaio. Italianos entre Rosas y Mitre. Buenos Aires: Ediciones Ediliba, 1987. 330 p.: bibl., ill.

History of the military units formed by Italians in Argentina and Uruguay 1837–80 notes the crucial, if not decisive, role Italian infantrymen had in important battles. Sympathetic description of Garibaldi.

2697 Greenberg, Daniel J. From confrontation to alliance: Peronist Argentina's diplomacy with the United States, 1945–1951. (*Can. J. Lat. Am. Caribb. Stud.*, 12:24, 1987, p. 1–23, appendix)

Examines the evolution in Argentine-US relations, with the former desiring to maintain its traditional policy of neutrality and acquire equipment; and the latter determined to unite the hemisphere under its leadership against first the Axis and then the Soviet Union and communism, and to further its economic interests. Highlights personality conflicts and disagreements within the US State Dept. over Argentine policy and efforts to influence Argentine domestic politics. State Dept. documents suggest that Perón, with the hope of acquiring military equipment, sought to placate the US by continuing the denazificaction policy of the Farrell government and by favoring American business interests. Compare with the slightly different version of Argentine-US relations and Perón's policies in Rapoport's *Gran Bretaña, Estados Unidos y las clases dirigentes argentinas: 1940–1945* (*HLAS 44:3346*) and Newton's "The United States, the German-Argentines, and the myth of the Fourth Reich, 1943–47," (*HLAS 50:2396*).

2698 Guerrino, Antonio Alberto. La medicina en la conquista del desierto. Buenos Aires: Círculo Militar, 1984. 124 p.: bibl., ill. (Biblioteca del oficial; 718)

Examination of health conditions among Indians and the Argentine soldiers who confronted them, and brief biographies of a select number of doctors who served in the Argentine armies.

2699 Gutiérrez, Juan María. Colección Doctor Juan María Gutiérrez: archivo-epistolario. v. 6. Buenos Aires: Biblioteca del Congreso de la Nación, 1988. 1 v.: index.

Correspondence received by Juan María Gutiérrez between Nov. 1859 and July 1861 sheds light on conditions in Buenos Aires, the Argentine Confederation, and Chile. For vol. 1, see *HLAS 46:3259*.

2700 Guy, Donna J. Refinería Argentina, 1888–1930: límites de la tecnología azucarera en una economía periférica. (*Desarro. Econ.*, 28:111, oct./dic. 1988, p. 353–373, tables)

Fascinating story based on company records of the vain efforts of Argentine capitalists, using modern equipment, to monopolize the manufacture of refined sugar in a peripheral sugar market. The Refinería Argentina mill was located in Rosario, Santa Fe.

2701 Guy, Donna J. White slavery, public health, and the socialist position on legalized prostitution in Argentina, 1913–1936. (*LARR*, 23:3, 1988, p. 60–80, bibl.)

Carefully delineates the theories that influenced the Socialist approach to prostitution, the different views on white slavery and legalized prostitution, and the reasons why some efforts to end prostitution failed. Concentrates on the city of Buenos Aires.

2702 Halperín Donghi, Tulio. La apertura mercantil en el Río de la Plata: impacto global y desigualdades regionales,

1800–1850. (in América Latina en la época de Simón Bolívar. Edición de Reinhard Liehr. Berlin: Colloquium Verlag, 1989, p. 115–138)

Thoughtful and well-balanced assessment of the impact that the opening of free trade in Buenos Aires had on the city and on the Argentine provinces. Notes the lack of sufficient data to determine the effects of free trade on the different regions, but finds that available evidence fails to support the dependency theory or the notion that the opening of Buenos Aires to international trade led to the economic decline of the provinces.

2703 Halperín Donghi, Tulio. Argentina's unmastered past. (*LARR*, 23:2, 1988, p. 3–24, bibl.)

Important examination of how Argentine intellectuals, literary figures, and journalists explain years of terror (1973–80). Some seek historical parallels, others pretend all was normal, and still others try to understand the motives of the right and the military, and to account for the failure of the Montoneros. Also assesses the role of antisemitism.

2704 Halperín Donghi, Tulio. El espejo de la historia: problemas argentinos y perspectivas hispanoamericanas. Buenos Aires: Editorial Sudamericana, 1987. 294 p.: (Col. Historia y cultura)

Collection of scholarly papers that were published or presented at international conferences 1976–86, and that make a notable contribution to the history of ideas in Spanish America, especially Argentina. Some of the essays have been revised for the present volume.

2705 Hardoy, Jorge Enrique. La administración del crecimiento y del desarrollo urbano: Rosario entre 1890 y 1910. (*Rev. Indias*, 49:185, enero/abril 1989, p. 135–171)

Comprehensive description of the governmental structure of Rosario and of the changes the city experienced as a result of the influx of immigrants and the need to provide them with housing and public services. Detailed analysis of the city budget and sources of income. Government was in the hands of a commercial and financial elite composed primarily of natives of the city. Based on the provincial census of 1887, the national census of 1895, the municipal censuses of 1900, 1906, and 1910, and published municipal records.

2706 Hardoy, Jorge Enrique. La vivienda obrera en una ciudad en expansión: Rosario entre 1858 y 1910. (in Cultura urbana latinoamericana. Recopilación de Richard Morse y Jorge Enrique Hardoy. Buenos Aires: Consejo Latinoamericano de Ciencias Sociales, 1985, p. 63–94, ill., tables)

Uses census data to detail the growth of Rosario, stressing the quality of housing for the labor force and immigrants.

2707 Helg, Aline. Race in Argentina and Cuba, 1880–1930: theory, policies, and popular reaction. (in The idea of race in Latin America, 1870–1940. Edited by Richard Graham. Austin: Univ. of Texas Press, 1990, p. 37–69, photos)

Examines the racial ideas of three Argentines (Domingo F. Sarmiento, Carlos Octavio Bunge, and José Ingenieros) and two Cubans (Francisco Figueras and Fernando Ortiz Fernández). Argues convincingly that Creole elites in both countries, influenced by the scientific racism prevalent in Europe, favored the white race over Indians and blacks, and expected European immigration to "whiten" their nations, and education to unify them. Faced with conditions different from those in Argentina, Cuban intellectuals hoped their blacks and mulattoes would give up their black culture or give way to whites. Later, in reaction to developments, Argentines applied their racist ideas to ethnic groups, especially to Russian Jews, and the Cubans, to Haitians or Jamaican blacks in Cuba.

2708 La hora de la espada, 1924–1946. Recopilación de Alicia S. García y Ricardo E. Rodríguez Molas. Prólogo de Ricardo A. Rodríguez Molas. Buenos Aires: Centro Editor de América Latina, 1988. 3 v. (289 p.): bibl. (Textos y documentos: el autoritarismo y los argentinos. Biblioteca política argentina; 200–202.)

Enlightening anthology of documents related to the military revolutions that took place between 1930–43. In the prologue, Rodríguez Molas traces the prevalence of a military tradition in Argentine culture.

2709 Horvath, Laszlo. Peronism and the three Perons: a checklist of material on peronism and on Juan Domingo, Eva, and Isabel Perón, and their writings, in the Hoover Institution library and archives and in the Stanford University Libraries. Stanford, Calif.: Hoover Institution, Stanford Univ. 1988. 192 p.: (Hoover Press bibliography; 71)

Guide to books, pamphlets, offprints, and archival materials on Perón and peronism in the Hoover Institution and Stanford Univ. Libraries.

2710 Ingleses en Buenos Aires y otros documentos sobre inmigración a la Argentina en 1873. Recopilación de Alberto Kleiner. Buenos Aires: Libreros y Editores del Polígono, 1983. 137 p.

Contains information obtained from all immigrants arriving from Paraguay; the reports of immigration commissions in Buenos Aires, Córdoba, and Rosario; and a list of those who obtained shipping tickets. All the documents were prepared in the Ministerio del Interior. Among the immigrants were 370 Englishmen, 144 Germans, 15 Poles, 4 Russians, 2 Frenchmen, and 3 Italians.

2711 Instituto de Historia Argentina Doctor Emilio Ravignani. Archivo del brigadier general Juan Facundo Quiroga. v. 4. Introducción de Ricardo R. Caillet-Bois. Buenos Aires: Univ. de Buenos Aires, Depto. Editorial, 1988. 1 v. (Documentos para la historia argentina; 47)

Addition to a valuable collection includes 232 documents for 1826 and 142 documents for 1827. Topics mentioned in the correspondence include the Banco de Rescates, Banco Nacional, the military, war with Brazil, the national government, mining, and conditions in the provinces of Catamarca, San Juan, and Córdoba. For vol. 2 see *HLAS 25:3583.*

Isaacson, José *et al.* Pensar la Argentina. See item **5423.**

2712 Isuani, Ernesto Aldo and **Hugo Mercer.** La fragmentación institucional del sector salud: pluralismo o irracionalidad? Buenos Aires: Centro Editor de América Latina, 1988. 104 p.: (Biblioteca Política argentina; 241)

Surveys public and private health systems that existed from 1880–1983, emphasizing the lack of coordination between the two systems. Originally appeared in *Boletín Informativo Techint* (No. 244, 1986).

2713 Jackisch, Carlota. El nazismo y los refugiados alemanes en la Argentina,

1933–1945. Buenos Aires: Editorial de Belgrano, 1989. 306 p.:

Detailed study of the immigration to Argentina of German Jews and political opponents of Nazism, the Nazi organizations they found there, and the reaction of the Argentine government to Nazi activities in the German community. Based on German diplomatic and other government archives. Significant study.

2714 Jornadas de Historia de la Ciudad de Buenos Aires, 2nd, 1988. La salud en Buenos Aires. Buenos Aires: Instituto Histórico de la Ciudad de Buenos Aires, 1988. 473 p.

Thirty-two essayists discuss public health facilities and conditions, doctors, and medical practices in the city of Buenos Aires after 1875. Of special interest are: Leandro Gutiérrez and Ricardo González, "Salud y Orden Social: Buenos Aires, 1880–1914;" Néstor Tomás Auza, "La Política Municipal en el Sector Industrial y Sus Derivaciones en el Saneamiento Urbano y la Salud Pública, 1900–1920;" Julio Angel Luqui Lagleyze, "Reseña de los Estudios de Médicos en la Ciudad de Buenos Aires;" Wenceslao N. Domínguez, "Cómo se Crea y Cómo se Destruye la Medicina en Buenos Aires;" Olga M. García de D'Agostino, "La Municipalidad, el Hospital General de Hombres y las Hermanas de la Caridad."

2715 Jornadas de Historia de la Ciudad de Buenos Aires, 3rd, 1988. El trabajo en Buenos Aires. Buenos Aires: Instituto Histórico de la Ciudad de Buenos Aires, 1988. 554 p.: bibl.

Twenty-six essays on workers and working conditions in the city of Buenos Aires. Of special interest are: M. Guerín and M. Alonso, "El Sistema Laboral en la Ciudad de Buenos Aires Durante la Primera Mitad del Siglo XIX;" Néstor Tomás Auza, "La Política del Estado en la Cuestión Obrera al Comenzar el Siglo XX: el Departamento Nacional del Trabajo, 1907–1912;" S. Rato de Sambuccetti, "El Trabajo en Buenos Aires en 1890: Precios y Salarios Según una Fuente Inglesa;" María S. Colombo, "Las Luchas Obreras en el Teatro Nacional, 1915–1930: Luchas Sociales y Huelgas;" Héctor Recalde, "La Higiene y el Trabajo, 1870–1930."

2716 Jornadas de Historia de la Ciudad de Buenos Aires, 4th, 1988. La historia a través de la literatura. Buenos Aires: Instituto Histórico de la Ciudad de Buenos Aires, 1988. 380 p.: bibl., ill.

Nineteen young essayists either describe how Argentine writers presented various aspects of the city of Buenos Aires in their literary works or report the results of their own historical research. Of special interest are: Raquel Goldenberg, "El Grupo de Florida y el Periódico *Martín Fierro:* su Trascendencia Popular;" María Victoria Juan, "La Prostitución en Buenos Aires a través de las Obras Literarias, 1890–1930;" Néstor Tomás Auza, "La Large Lucha por una Conquista Laboral: la Ley de la Silla, 1907–1935;" Miguel A. Guerín *et al.*, "La Estructura Ocupacional de Buenos Aires y la Confirmación de una Elite Urbana, 1744;" and M.A. Rosal, "Afroporteños Propietarios de Terrenos y Casas, 1750–1810."

2717 Judíos & argentinos: judíos argentinos. Investigación y concreción de Martha Wolff y Myrtha Schalom. Dirección de Manrique Zago. Buenos Aires: M. Zago Ediciones, 1988. 288 p.: bibl., ill.

Well-illustrated introduction to Jewish contributions to the economic and cultural development of Argentina, and to the diverse origins of Jews who settled in the country.

2718 Korzeniewicz, Roberto P. Labor unrest in Argentina, 1887–1907. (*LARR*, 24:3, 1989, p. 71–98, bibl., tables)

Significant study based on new data calls attention to the mobility of the labor force, the effect of technological innovation, increased management control of production, and changes in the organization of the labor market on different groups of workers. Views the 1880s and 1890s as a transitional period for labor.

2719 Kowalska, Marta. La emigración judía de Polonia a la Argentina en los años 1918–1939. (*Estud. Latinoam.*, 12, 1989, p. 249–272, tables)

Comprehensive study of the immigration and settlement of Polish Jews in Argentina. Author consulted the correspondence and reports of the Polish Legation in Buenos Aires.

2720 Lähteenmäki, Olavi and **Reino Kero.** Colonia Finlandesa: uuden Suomen perustaminen Argentiinaan 1900-luvun alussa Colonia Finlandesa: the founding of New Finland in Argentina in the beginning of the 19th century. Helsinki: SHS, 1989. 282 p.: bibl., ill. (Historiallisia tutkimuksia, 0073–2559; 154)

Well-researched account of a colony of Swedish-speaking Finns who established a settlement in the Misiones territory in 1906. The motivation for emigration was political and economic. Many emigrants were not used to farm labor and encountered numerous difficulties in trying to adjust to life in Northern Argentina. Valuable contribution. [Renata V. Shaw]

2721 Lattuada, Mario J. Política agraria del liberalismo-conservador, 1946–1985. Buenos Aires: Centro Editor de América Latina, 1987. 139 p.: bibl., ill. (Biblioteca Política argentina; 187)

Compares agrarian policies advocated by liberal conservative parties and the large landowners on the pampa, and concludes they are similar. Realizes that there are numerous small liberal conservative parties; for the purposes of this study, the author built a model liberal conservative party.

2722 Lavrin, Asunción. Women, labor, and the left: Argentina and Chile, 1890–1925. (*J. Women's Hist.*, 1:2, Fall 1989, p. 88–116)

Important study compares the reaction of Argentine and Chilean anarchists and socialists to the increasing number of women in the urban work force. Concludes that views on women in the labor force, the working woman's health and moral standards, birth control, feminism, women in mutualist societies and labor organizations, and gender relations were all developed gradually. Careful and well-documented analysis.

2723 Leonard, Virginia W. Politicians, pupils, and priests: Argentine education since 1943. New York: P. Lang, 1989. 456 p.: bibl., map (American university studies: Series xxii, Latin American studies; 2)

Solid study of educational policy after 1943 calls attention to the influence of the Church, the growth of private education, and the failure of the educational system to further the development of democratic values and institutions.

2724 Liebscher, Arthur F. Institutionalization and evangelization in the Argentine Church: Córdoba under Zenón Bustos, 1905–1919. (*Americas/Francisc.*, 45 : 3, Jan. 1989, p. 363–381, bibl.)

Well-documented description of the efforts of Zenón Bustos to combat secularist influences and anticlericalism in a diocese characterized by religious indifference, lack of religious training, and a shortage of priests. He encouraged priests to abstain from politics, to rely on lay catechists to further religious education, and to preach Catholic doctrine and morality. Based on the archives of the Archbishopric of Córdoba.

2725 Liebscher, Arthur F. Toward a pious republic: Argentine social Catholicism in Córdoba, 1895–1930. (*J. Church State*, 30 : 3, Autumn 1988, p. 549–567)

Significant study describes the efforts of the Church in Córdoba prov. to reverse the decline in its prestige by undertaking to win the allegiance of the working-class by initiating and supporting measures that would improve its material well-being and strengthen its adherence to Catholic social values. Based on research in Jesuit and archdiocesan archives.

2726 Longo, Rafael E. Buenos Aires 1886: el último año de la gran aldea. Buenos Aires: F. Blanco, 1986. 140 p., 1 folded leaf of plates: bibl., ill., indexes.

Brief description of each *barrio* and parish in the city as they existed in 1886. Includes a short bibliography at the end of each chapter.

2727 López, Antonio. La FORA en el movimiento obrero. Buenos Aires: Centro Editor de América Latina; M. Canellaro, 1987. 2 v. (215 p.): (Biblioteca Política argentina; 175–176)

Well-documented review of the aims and accomplishments of the Federación Obrera Regional Argentina (FORA) while it was dominated by the anarchists. Contains extracts from 211 documents and articles by Emilio López Arango, Diego Abad de Santillán, and E.G. Gilimón.

2728 Luna, Félix. Fuerzas hegemónicas y partidos políticos. Buenos Aires: Editorial Sudamericana, 1988. 165 p.:

Prominent historian thoughtfully traces the development of Argentine democracy from its embryonic appearance (1852–80) through its "fragile and vulnerable" years

(1880–83) to the present collection of political parties, none of which enjoys preponderant influence. Anticipates the appearance of new minority parties, and with proper political leadership, the gradual prefection of Argentine democracy. Essay well-worth reading.

2729 Lynch, John. Foreign trade and economic interests in Argentina, 1810–1850. (*in* América Latina en la época de Simón Bolívar. Edición de Reinhard Liehr. Berlin: Colloquium Verlag, 1989, p. 139–155, tables)

Insightful and succinct description of the economic characteristics of the city of Buenos Aires.

Mainwaring, Scott. The State and the industrial bourgeoisie in Perón's Argentina, 1945–1955. See *HLAS 51 : 4982.*

2730 Malgesini, Graciela. ¿Subsidio o sustracción?: el control de cambios y los productores cerealeros en los años '30. (*Anu. IEHS*, 1, 1986, p. 121–155, tables)

Thesis asserts that the purposes of the foreign exchange policies of the 1930s was to provide the numerous and different interests in the cereal sector with a subsidy and to shield them from price fluctuations in international markets. Finds that devaluation or revaluation of the peso did not necessarily affect the buying power of groups within the cereal sector. Efforts to protect the agricultural sector led the government to fix prices, build grain elevators, and encourage the use of the latest technology. Significant work.

2731 Merchensky, Marcos. Proyectos y protagonistas en la historia argentina. Buenos Aires: Hachette, 1985. 183 p.

Pt. 1, a posthumously published essay, argues that efforts after the Revolution of 1810 to create national unity and an economically independent Argentina failed because they did not affect the economic and social structure. Pt. 2 contains articles written for *Clarín* (Buenos Aires), 1972–80. Author represented Buenos Aires prov. in the Argentine Congress, 1973–76.

2732 Middlebrook, Martin. The fight for the "Malvinas": the Argentine Forces in the Falklands War. London; New York: Viking, 1989. 321 p., 22 p. of plates: bibl., ill., index, maps.

Military history of the Falkland/Malvinas War as seen by the Argentine armed forces emphasizes combat readiness of the units involved, the problems they faced, and their activities in the field. In 1987, with the aid of an interpreter, the author questioned 65 army and navy officers and enlisted men. Also consulted translations of published accounts by Air Force officers. Corrects many press accounts, rumors, and, especially, army news releases that appeared during the war. The courage of the Argentine soldier is apparent from the narrative, but the armed forces were ill-prepared to carry out their mission.

2733 Míguez, Eduardo José. La expansión agraria de la pampa húmeda, 1850–1914: tendencias recientes de sus análisis históricos. (*Anu. IEHS*, 1, 1986, p. 89–119, bibl.)

Author reviews recent literature on agricultural developments in 19th-century Argentina, especially in Buenos Aires prov., and concludes that the tendency is to attribute the prevalence of large estates to economic variables rather than to institutional factors. The image of a traditional and conservative "oligarchy" has given way to one that emphasizes its ability to adapt to the changes brought about by the integration of Argentina in the world market.

2734 Míguez, Eduardo José. Las tierras de los ingleses en la Argentina, 1870–1914. Buenos Aires: Editorial de Belgrano, 1985. 348 p.: bibl. (Col. Conflictos y armonías en la historia argentina)

Concludes from an analysis of agrarian property owned by British individuals and private companies that the agrarian sector was very dynamic, constantly adapting itself to changing demand and new technology. Well-documented contribution to Argentine agricultural economic history. Author's 1981 Oxford dissertation is entitled *British interests in Argentine land development, 1870–1914: a study of British investment in Argentina.*

2735 Minsburg, Naúm. Capitales extranjeros y grupos dominantes argentinos: análisis histórico y contemporáneo. Prólogo de Eric Alfredo Calcagno. Buenos Aires: Centro Editor de América Latina, 1987. 2 v.: (Biblioteca Política argentina; 196–197)

Studies the impact on Argentina of the cyclical rise and fall in the importation of foreign capital, especially of the marked tendency of multinational firms to periodically review and even change their investment strategies, and to form "tacit" alliances with the dominant Argentine class. Notes that the national administrations after 1958 encouraged the influx of foreign capital, and that one result of this policy is that the growing external debt has created another form of dependence. In vol. 2 author analyzes the conduct of several international companies located in Argentina as well as that of Argentine companies which have connections with foreign firms.

2736 Minutolo de Orsi, Cristina V. Revolucionarios a sueldo. Buenos Aires: Editorial de Belgrano, 1985. 454 p., 4 leaves of plates: bibl., ill. (Col. Testimonios contemporáneos)

Well-documented account of political and military activities in Buenos Aires prov. and interior provinces between the fall of Rosas and the opening of the General Constitutional Congress in Santa Fe. Very revelatory of the political maneuvering that took place and desire of Urquiza (but not of *porteños*) to obtain national organization and a constitution without a war.

2737 Mirelman, Victor A. Jewish Buenos Aires, 1890–1930: in search of an identity. Detroit, Mich.: Wayne State Univ. Press, 1990. 300 p., 8 p. of plates: bibl., ill., index.

Comprehensive study of Jewish immigration to and settlement in the city of Buenos Aires calls attention to the diversity within the Jewish community in terms of origins, degree of secularization, Zionism, adaptation to Argentina, and occupations. Notes the role of Jews in the local economy. Well-documented and highly recommended work originally appeared in Spanish as *En búsqueda de una identidad: los inmigrantes judíos en Buenos Aires, 1890–1930* (Buenos Aires: Milá, 1988).

Most, Benjamin A. Changing authoritarian rule and public policy in Argentina, 1930–1970. See *HLAS 51:3948.*

2738 Nascimbene, Mario C.G. Analfabetismo e inmigración en la Argentina:

el caso italiano. (*Stud. Emigr.*, 31:75, set. 1984, p. 294–304, tables)

Compares the level of illiteracy found among Italian and Spanish immigrants and the local population 1895–1914 and finds regional differences.

2739 Nevares, Guillermo F. de. Cómo se desintegró el Virreinato del Río de la Plata y se consolidó el Brasil. Buenos Aires: Plus Ultra, 1987. 148 p.: bibl., maps. (Col. Esquemas históricos; 37)

Study of the Viceroyalty of Río de la Plata in the two decades following independence argues that the area disintegrated politically because: 1) the movement which produced the May 1810 Revolution lacked clear objectives and a political program; 2) Buenos Aires attempted to dictate to the rest of the region; and 3) a vacuum was created by the Revolution which no political authority could fill. The author argues that this region would have survived intact had a monarchy emerged, a solution proposed by several of the political actors of the period. [S.M. Socolow]

2740 Newton, Ronald C. Los Estados Unidos, los germano-argentino y el mito del Cuarto Reich, 1943–1947. (*Rev. Hist. Am.*, 105, enero/junio 1988, p. 111–146)

Summarizes the efforts of Hitler's Germany to organize the German-Argentine communities, without ever clarifying the Germans' objectives, and efforts of the US, especially after 1945, to eliminate German economic competition in Argentina. Based on diplomatic archives of Germany, Great Britain, and the US.

2741 Newton, Ronald C. The "Nazi menace" in Argentina, 1931–1947. Stanford, Calif.: Stanford Univ. Press, 1992. 1 v.: bibl.

The culmination of over a decade of research in Argentine, British, and German archives and libraries, this well-written and balanced study dissects the German community and the extent of German economic penetration in Argentina. Examines the plans of the competing agencies of the Third Reich and Nazi party to influence the Argentines, the Argentine government, and resident Germans, and the defensive measures taken by the Third Reich to defend its foothold in Argentina from both Great Britain and especially the US. Makes clear that the US did not understand Argentina, or German objectives there, but that the British did. A model study of diplomacy in action.

2742 Ollier, María Matilde. Orden, poder y violencia, 1968–1973. Buenos Aires: Centro Editor de América Latina, 1989. 2 v. (261 p.): (Biblioteca Política argentina; 273–274)

Reconstructs Argentine history from 1968–73 essentially on the basis of the newspaper *Clarín* and weekly magazine *Primera Plana*. Expansion of the author's *El fenómeno insurreccional y la cultura política, 1969–1973* (Buenos Aires, 1986).

2743 One family, two worlds: an Italian family's correspondence across the Atlantic, 1901–1922. Edited by Samuel L. Baily and Franco Ramella. Translated by John Lenaghan. New Brunswick, N.J.: Rutgers Univ. Press, 1988. 251 p.: bibl., ill., index.

Letters exchanged between members of the Sola family of Biella and Valdengo, Italy, and Buenos Aires reveal often overlooked aspects of the immigration process: the reasons for emigrating; the strong sense of family and attachment to the community; and expectations of family members. Introductory essay describes both the Sola family and the historical experience of the Biellesi with their sons departing and newcomers arriving. Should be read by those interested in immigration history.

2744 Orsolini, Mario H. Montoneros: sus proyectos y sus planes. Buenos Aires: Círculo Militar, 1989. 121 p.: bibl., ill. (Biblioteca del oficial; 740: Serie de actualización militar)

Argentine intelligence army officer succinctly presents his analysis of the ideology, political aims, strategic plans, pre-election plans for 1983, and the tactics of the Montoneros to 1989. Only one source is cited, but others presumably include publications and documents collected by the intelligence service. Especially interesting is the implication that Montoneros infiltrated or had sympathizers in the UCR and the Alfonsín government. Should be read.

Ortiz, Amalia A. Louro de. Los decretos alemanes de 1938 y la política inmigratoria argentina de esa época. See *HLAS 51:4989.*

2745 Páez de la Torre, Carlos. Historia de Tucumán. Buenos Aires: Plus Ultra, 1987. 758 p.:

Excellent, well-documented introduction to the political, economic, and cultural history of the province.

Panettieri, José. Argentina: historia de un país periférico, 1860–1914. See *HLAS* 51:2469.

2746 Pelosi, Hebe Carmen and **María Isabel de Ruschi Crespo.** La prensa católica: incidencia de la primera asamblea de los católicos argentinos. (*Res Gesta*, 16/17/18, julio/dic. 1984—enero/dic. 1985, p. 17–24)

One of the objectives of the First Assembly of Argentine Catholics that met in 1884 was the creation of a Catholic press, which led to the founding of *El Pueblo* (April 1, 1900). Authors analyze its views on Catholic and non-Catholic schools 1900–03.

2747 Pereira, Enrique and **Rodolfo Miguel Parente.** Cuando los tenientes coroneles eran radicales. Santa Fe, Argentina: Centro de Publicaciones de la Univ. Nacional del Litoral, 1990. 45 p.:

Very brief biographies of about 65 lieutenant colonels who were members of the UCR. Aim is to show that the UCR has always had supporters in the army.

2748 Pomer, León. Cinco años de guerra civil en la Argentina, 1865–1870. Buenos Aires: Amorrortu Editores, 1985. 298 p.:

Attributes the rebellions within Argentina during the Paraguayan War to the absence of a nationalist spirit and to the disappearance of the colonial order. Critical of older historians of the period.

2749 Pomer, León. El Estado nacional argentino. (*Rev. Hist. Am.*, 105, enero/junio 1988, p. 53–88)

Essayist maintains that in Argentina the "national state" preceded the "nation," and created it. A function of the "national state" was to prepare the nation for participation in the world system by creating a nationalist spirit and a political bureaucracy. The intellectuals and the educated, representing civilization, were alone to govern, and would impose order on the rural population. Idea of a "national state" originated with a small group of *porteños* who were influenced by European ideas.

2750 Potash, Robert A. Alfonsín's Argentina in historical perspective. Amherst: Univ. of Massachusetts, Latin American Studies Program, 1988. 26 p.: (Occasional papers series; 21)

Thoughtful appraisal of Alfonsín's response to conditions in a divided Argentina.

2751 Pozzi, Pablo A. Argentina, 1976–1982: labour leadership and military government. (*J. Lat. Am. Stud.*, 20:1, May 1988, p. 111–138, bibl., ill.)

Describes the shifting alliances within a labor bureaucracy that feared the loss of its control over the rank-and-file workers, and that negotiated or collaborated with a dictatorship interested in weakening the labor movement. Concludes that the efforts of the labor bureaucracy to preserve its power and to restrain the workers prevented the regime from achieving its labor objectives.

2752 Quijada, Mónica. Los españoles de la Argentina ante la Guerra Civil Española: las instituciones de la comunidad. (*in* Inmigración, integración y imagen de los latinoamericanos en España, 1931–1987. Madrid: Servicio de Publicaciones de la OEI, 1988, p. 77–97)

Analysis of Spanish diplomatic reports and correspondence suggests that the oldest and most prestigious Spanish groups, following the lead of the Argentine upper class, favored the Franco movement but not its ideology. Their associations officially adopted a policy of neutrality toward the Civil War even though the membership was pro-government. The small bourgeoisie, laborers, and others who belonged to the regional centers established after 1900 endorsed the Republic and did so publicly. In all groups, the regional origin of the Spanish immigrants was a factor that influenced their views of the Civil War.

2753 Quiroga, Hugo. Estado, crisis económica y poder militar, 1880–1981. Buenos Aires: Centro Editor de América Latina, 1985. 122 p.: (Biblioteca Política argentina; 105)

Essayist attributes political instability since the 1950s to the divergence in interests of industry and agriculture, to the dependence of industry on agricultural exports to produce the foreign exchange needed to finance its needs, and to the perceived need to reorganize the economic and social structure of Argentina to recover its export capacity and participate in the world market. The military will be part of the new political order.

2754 Ramella de Jefferies, Susana T. El radicalismo bloquista en San Juan, 1916–1934. San Juan: Gobierno de la Provincia de San Juan, 1986. 511 p.: bibl., ill.

Well-researched monograph calls attention to the progressive legislation passed under the aegis of Governor Federico José Cantoni (1923–25, 1932–35), and to the destructive effects of federal interventions. Years elapsed before the social legislation sponsored by Cantoni and his followers was imitated at the national level.

2755 Ramos, Jorge Abelardo. Breve historia de las izquierdas en la Argentina. Buenos Aires: Editorial Claridad; Editorial Heliasta, 1990. 2 v.: (Col. Breve historia)

Corrected second ed. of *Historia del stalinismo en la Argentina* (Buenos Aires: Ediciones Rancagua, 1974), in which a leftist nationalist critic looks at the Argentine Communist Party.

2756 Recalde, Héctor. La higiene y el trabajo: 1870–1930. Buenos Aires: Centro Editor de América Latina, 1988. 2 v. (196 p.) (Biblioteca Política argentina; 216–217)

Three essays that appear in vol. 1 describe the sanitary and hygenic conditions that existed in the work place and in the city of Buenos Aires. Factors affecting the health of women and children receive special attention. Vol. 2 contains extracts from works written by contemporaries describing health conditions in the city of Buenos Aires in 1910. Two of the essays also appear in item **2715.**

2757 Recalde, Héctor. Mujer, condiciones de vida, de trabajo y salud. Buenos Aires: Centro Editor de América Latina, 1988–1989. 2 v. (245 p.): bibl. (Biblioteca Política argentina; 244, 248)

Excellent discussion of the factors affecting women in the work place and at home, 1870–1980.

2758 *Revista de la Junta de Estudios Históricos de Mendoza*. Segunda Epoca, No. 11, T. 1, 1987– . Mendoza, Argentina: La Junta de Estudios Históricos de Mendoza.

Journal includes the following worthwhile articles: García-Godoy, "Los Estudios y la Formación Intelectual de Tomás Godoy Cruz;" Laria, "La Obra Educativa de Sarmiento;" Moreno Martin, "Dos Documentos Interesantes sobre las Relaciones de O'Brien y Rosas;" and Osculati, "Buenos Aires, San Luis y Mendoza Visto por el Viajero Italiano Gaetano Osculati en 1834."

Rey Balmaceda, Raúl C. Acerca de la "migración golondrina" en la República Argentina. See *HLAS 51:4993.*

2759 Reyes, Cipriano. La farsa del peronismo. Buenos Aires: Sudamericana/Planeta, 1987. 187 p.

An active member of the Labor Party seeks to account for its decline.

2760 Richmond, Douglas W. Carlos Pellegrini and the crisis of the Argentine elites, 1880–1916. New York: Praeger, 1989. 206 p.: bibl., ill., index.

Sympathetic study of President Pellegrini's response to the financial crisis of 1890–92, and his relations with Julio A. Roca. Author sees similarities between the problems Argentina faced in the 1880s-90s and today.

2761 Ripa, Julián I. Inmigrantes en la Patagonia. Buenos Aires: Ediciones Marymar, 1987. 164 p. (Col. Patagonia)

Story of 14 settlers in Patagonia is based on interviews with the immigrants themselves or with members of their families. Variety of nationalities are represented.

2762 Roca, C. Alberto. La jurisprudencia: ciencia común a argentinos y orientales, 1810–1870. (*Bol. Acad. Nac. Hist./B. Aires,* 54/55, 1981/1982, p. 145–160)

Calls needed attention to the interrelationship that existed between the legal professions of Argentina and Uruguay. Argentine and Uruguayan lawyers borrowed legal principles from each other and initiated or completed their legal studies, practiced law, or taught law in each others' country. Graduates of the Colegio del Uruguay, Entre Ríos, received their law degrees in Montevideo and not in Córdoba. Lawyers in both countries were influenced by French legal works.

2763 Rocha, Aurora Alonso de. Señoras y señoritas: un aporte a la historia de las mujeres bonaerenses. (*Todo es Hist.*, 259, enero 1989, p. 6–28, bibl., ill., photos)

Contains a series of brief anecdotes describing women who lived in the Azul-Olavarría district between 1894–1935, selections from the local press, and a discussion of the writer Herminia Brumana (1901–54), the first feminist born in the area.

2764 Rodolfo Walsh y la prensa clandestina, 1976–1978. Edición de Horacio Verbitsky. Buenos Aires: Ediciones de la Urraca, 1985. 141 p.: ill. (Col. El Periodista de Buenos Aires)

Incomplete collection of the underground publications of the Montonero Rodolfo J. Walsh. Contains items known to the press but generally ignored, such as: "La Escuela de Mecánica de la Armada: Historia de la Guerra Sucia en la Argentina;" "Carta Abierta de un Escritor a la Junta Militar;" news bulletins of the Agencia de Noticias Clandestina (ANCLA); bulletins of the Cadena Informativa; "Un Ensayo sobre San Martín;" and the letters of Rodolfo J. Walsh. The editor has contributed an interesting essay on the extent of military censorship of the press between 1955–78.

2765 Rodríguez Lamas, Daniel. La revolución libertadora. Buenos Aires: Centro Editor de América Latina, 1985. 160 p.: (Biblioteca Política argentina; 117)

Careful analysis of the divisions that appeared within the armed forces, the political parties, and the labor unions between the overthrow of Perón in 1955 and the election of Frondizi to the presidency in 1958.

2766 Rojer, Olga Elaine. Exile in Argentina, 1933–1945: a historical and literary introduction. New York: P. Lang, 1989. 250 p.: bibl., ill., index. (American university studies: Series XXII: Latin American studies; 3)

Excellent introduction to the experience of German-speaking exiles living in Argentina.

2767 Rosas, Juan Manuel José Domingo Ortiz de. Correspondencia inédita entre Juan Manuel de Rosas y Manuel José García. Recopilación de Juan Carlos Nicolau. Tandil, Argentina: Depto. de Historia, Instituto de Estudios Histórico-Sociales, Univ. Nacional del Centro de la Provincia de Buenos Aires, 1989. 72 p.: (Cuadernos de investigación)

Publishes the letters Juan Manuel Rosas wrote to the Ministro de Hacienda, Manuel José García, 1825–33. Subjects discussed are Indian relations, payment of the militiamen, and negotiations with General José María Paz and General Estanislao López. There are 53 letters, all found in the relevant *legajos* in the Archivo General de la Nación, Buenos Aires.

2768 Rosenzvaig, Eduardo. Historia social de Tucumán y del azúcar: del ayllú a la encomienda; de la hacienda al ingenio. Tucumán, Argentina: Univ. Nacional de Tucumán, 1987. 2 v.: bibl. (Publicación; 1399)

Surveys provincial economic and social history in terms of the following cycles: 1) the corn cycle; 2) the conquest cycle; 3) the Potosí cycle; 4) the mule and cart transportation cycle; 5) the hide cycle (1820–50); 6) the primitive sugar production cycle (1850–76); 7) the manufactured sugar production cycle and the formation of the modern sugar mill labor class (1876–96); and 8) the cycle of sugar crises (1896–1930). Exhaustive examination of the sugar industry from 1850–1930 appears in vol. 2.

2769 Rosoli, Gianfausto. Le organizzazioni cattoliche italiane in Argentina e l'assistenza agli emigrati italiani, 1875–1915. (*Stud. Emigr.*, 31:75, set. 1984, p. 381–408)

Excellent introduction to the Italian Catholic organizations that developed in response to Italian mass immigration to Argentina. Emphasizes cultural, economic, and educational activities of the Salesian priests, and the work of the institute "Italica Gens," a federation of missionary congregations interested in Italian immigrants in America. Priests encouraged the formation of cooperatives, labor and credit unions, mutual aid societies, the Popular Italian Party, Mass in Italian, the retention of an Italian identity, and the 1912 farm strike. Based on ecclesiastical archives in Italy and Argentina. "Italica Gens" is an example of Italian Catholic activism that deserves more research.

2770 Ruppin, Arthur. Los judíos en América del Sur. Introducción de Boris Vainstock. Buenos Aires: Círculo Benei Akiva, 1986. 151 leaves: bibl., ill.

Brief treatment of Jewish immigration to Argentina, Brazil, Chile and Uruguay based on interviews with Jewish settlers in those countries in 1935. Compares agricultural colonies in Argentina with those in Palestine. Discusses Jewish assimilation and antisemitism. Author was director of Jewish colonization in Palestine.

2771 Sábato, Hilda. Trabajar para vivir o vivir para trabajar: empleo ocasional y escasez de mano de obra en Buenos Aires, ciudad y campaña, 1850–1880. (*in* Población y mano de obra en América Latina. Recopilación de Nicolás Sánchez-Albornoz. Madrid: Alianza Editorial, 1985, p. 149–184, tables)

Important article examines the development of a free labor market in the city and province of Buenos Aires at a time when there was a shortage of labor, little employment stability, and a large supply of unskilled occasional workers. The introduction of capitalism did not immediately displace the traditional forms of labor. Good introduction to author's *Capitalismo y ganadería en Buenos Aires: la fiebre del lanar, 1850–1890* (Buenos Aires, 1989).

2772 Sabsay, Fernando Leónidas and **Robert Etchepareborda.** El Estado liberal democrático. Buenos Aires: Editorial Universitaria de Buenos Aires; Córdoba: Ediciones Macchi, 1987. 444 p.:

Sociopolitical history of the two Yrigoyen Administrations and of that of Alvear, based in part on the testimony of many of the participants, on the reports of the American ambassador in Buenos Aires, and on the legislation proposed by the Unión Cívica Radical. Interspersed throughout the text are interesting observations on some of the scholarly works that examine aspects of the period. Important interpretative study that is sympathetic to Yrigoyen.

2773 Saguier, Eduardo R. Polémicas en torno a la gestación de una sociedad de clases: una hipótesis para el caso de Buenos Aires. (*Historiogr. Bibliogr. Am.*, 30:2, 1986, p. 31–68, bibl.)

After analyzing theories that have been advanced to find colonial causes of the independence movement, author presents his own hypothesis that crises caused by fluctuations in the commercial cycles over three centuries, and especially in the 18th, resulted in economic, demographic, and social changes that led to the events of May, 1810, in Buenos Aires. Very comprehensive review of the controversial literature on the subject. Does not end the debate but is well worth reading.

2774 Salas, Rubén Darío. Los proyectos monárquicos en el proceso de la independencia argentina, 1810–1820. (*Ibero-Am. Arch.*, 15:2, 1989, p. 193–231, bibl.)

Presents strong evidence that the revolutionaries wanted to replace the Spanish monarchy in South America with a monarchy or monarchies that incorporated some features of the English constitutional model—but without sacrificing authoritarian and centralist principles—and that there were colonial antecedents for some of their monarchical ideas. Less convincing is assertion that they did not think of a republic.

2775 San Martín, José de. The San Martín papers. Edited by Christián García-Godoy. Translated by Barbara Huntley and Pilar Liria. Washington: Full Life; San Martín Society, 1988. 627 p.: bibl., ill., index, ports.

Contains English translations of a well-selected collection of documents which shed light on important moments in the life of San Martín and extracts from works in which his contemporaries describe him. Good introduction to San Martín for classroom use.

2776 Scobie, James R. Secondary cities of Argentina: the social history of Corrientes, Salta, and Mendoza, 1850–1910. Completed and edited by Samuel L. Baily. Foreword by Ingrid Winther Scobie. Stanford, Calif.: Stanford Univ. Press, 1988. 276 p., 12 p. of plates: bibl., ill., index, maps.

Attributes these secondary cities' failure to develop economically to their location, their dependency on Buenos Aires, their inability to attract European immigrants, and their small middle class. Notable contribution to Argentine urban history.

Senkman, Leonardo. La política migratoria argentina durante la década del treinta: la selección étnica. See *HLAS 51:4997.*

2777 Smulovitz, Catalina. Oposición y gobierno: los años de Frondizi. Buenos Aires: Centro Editor de América Latina, 1988. 2 v. (179 p.): (Biblioteca Política argentina; 213–214)

Concludes from a careful analysis of the evidence that the confrontational politics of the Unión Cívica Radical del Pueblo, the

Unión Cívica Radical Intransigente, and the peronists led to the military overthrow of the Frondizi government in 1962. Feels that the coup could have been avoided if Argentina had had a party system, and if Frondizi had shown a willingness to consult or negotiate with the opposition parties or members of his own party.

Socolow, Susan Migden. Los cautivos españoles en las sociedades indígenas: el contacto cultural a través de la frontera argentina. See item **2303.**

Stoetzer, O. Carlos. Raíces intelectuales de la Constitución argentina de 1853. See item **5435.**

2778 Szuchman, Mark D. A challenge to the patriarchs: love among the youth in nineteenth-century Argentina. (*in* The middle period in Latin America: values and attitudes in the 17th-19th centuries. Edited by Mark D. Szuchman. Boulder, Colo.: Lynne Rienner Publishers, 1989, p. 141–165)

Uses the concept of love among young *porteños* and *porteñas* to study the effect of the revolutionary political ideology of freedom and independence on parental authority in marriage selection, the timing of marriage, and the attitude of judicial and ecclesiastical authorities toward rebellious children.

2779 Szuchman, Mark D. Childhood education and politics in nineteenth-century Argentina: the case of Buenos Aires. (*HAHR*, 70:1, Feb. 1990, p. 109–138)

Impressive analysis of the political and nonpolitical objectives that influenced the type of education children in the city of Buenos Aires received in primary schools. See also item **2780.**

2780 Szuchman, Mark D. In search of deference: education and civic formation in nineteenth-century Buenos Aires (*SECOLAS Ann.*, 18, March 1987, p. 5–22)

Interesting discussion of elementary public schools and the evolution in liberal thinking on the role of education. Essentially concentrates on the 1810–36 period. Should be read alongside Carlos Newland's essay "La educación primaria privada bajo el gobierno de Rosas (1835–1852)," which appeared in *La Nación*, Buenos Aires, on Dec. 4 and 11, 1988. See also Szuchman's related article (item **2779**).

2781 Szuchman, Mark D. Order, family, and community in Buenos Aires, 1810–1860. Stanford, Calif.: Stanford Univ. Press, 1988. 307 p.: bibl., ill., index.

Seeks to identify the behavior and ideas of the *gente decente* and the *gente de pueblo,* and the effects of the former's attempts to reestablish law and order on population growth and family structure in the city of Buenos Aires. Pioneer study that deserves careful study.

2782 Tabakian, Eva. Los armenios en la Argentina. Buenos Aires: Editorial Contrapunto, 1988. 210 p.: bibl., ill.

Brief introduction to the Armenian community based on interviews with its leading members.

2783 Tecuanhuey Sandoval, Alicia. La revolución de 1943: políticas y conflictos rurales. Buenos Aires: Centro Editor de América Latina, 1988. 126 p.: bibl., ill. (Biblioteca Política argentina; 215)

Maintains that the agricultural policies in force 1943–46 favored industrialization over agricultural development in the rural areas of the pampa.

2784 Ternavasio, Marcela. El régimen municipal frente al problema de la democratización del sistema político: Argentina, 1912–1920. (*Cuad. CLAEH*, 14:2, 1989, p. 123–142)

Examines the electoral process at the municipal level and the functioning of municipalities, especially in the province of Santa Fe, to determine the impact of the Sáenz Peña law of 1912 on the political system. Concludes that only those who paid municipal taxes had the right to vote in municipal elections and that municipal autonomy was limited to administrative matters. "Local elites" administered the municipalities, while political issues were left to the national and provincial governments.

2785 Torres Molina, Ramón. Unitarios y federales en la historia argentina. Buenos Aires: Editorial Contrapunto, 1986. 134 p.: bibl. (Col. La Historia revisada)

Argues that between 1810–30 there were three federalist movements: 1) that of Artigas in the littoral; 2) that of Güemes in Salta; and 3) that of Quiroga in the interior provinces. These popular movements arose, the author maintains, because the central government was unable to fight for independence and to establish an economically independent nation.

2786 Tulchin, Joseph S. La relación entre trabajo y capital en la Argentina rural, 1880–1914. (*HISLA*, 3, 1984, p. 79–97, appendices, bibl., tables)

Argues that the social organization and the mode of production in the different pampa export regions were based on the ability of the entrepreneur to meet the demands of foreign markets. Carefully distinguishes between capital intensive and labor intensive areas, and between areas of large and small landowners. Analysis based on census of 1914.

2787 Unamuno, Miguel. La primera gran represión. (*Todo es Hist.*, 248, feb. 1988, p. 6–33, bibl., ill., photos)

Bibliographic essay describes some of the works written by followers of Hipólito Yrigoyen telling of their arrest, torture, or persecution during the regime of General José Félix Uriburu. Briefly refers to military attempts to overthrow Uriburu, to journalists who attacked Yrigoyen and supported Uriburu, and to an indifferent Supreme Court.

Vapnarsky, César A. Pueblos del norte de la Patagonia, 1779–1957. See *HLAS 51:3134.*

2788 Vedoya, Juan Carlos et al. La campaña del desierto y la tecnificación ganadera. Buenos Aires: Editorial Universitaria de Buenos Aires, 1981. 266 p., 1 folded leaf of plates: bibl., ill. (Lucha de fronteras con el indio; no. especial)

Excellent study examines the conquest of the desert which opened the way for the State and private interests to modernize the pastoral industry, especially in Buenos Aires prov., thereby furthering its integration into the world markets.

2789 Vera de Flachs, María C. and **Norma Dolores Riquelme de Lobos.** La educación primaria en Córdoba, 1930–1970: crecimiento y contradicciones. Córdoba: Junta Provincial de Historia de Córdoba, 1987. 166 p.: bibl., ill. (Cuadernos de historia; 7)

Comprehensive history of education in the province discusses the educational theories applied, regional variations in fiscal support for schools and in student atten-

dance, specialized schools, and the absence of a permanent corps of teachers. Notes that schools were administered by the federal government, the provincial government, or the municipality.

2790 Vidaurreta, Alicia. Cinco épocas en el periodismo de Entre Ríos, Argentina, 1819–1900. (*Rev. Interam. Bibliogr.*, 38:4, 1988, p. 517–527)

Valuable description of the newspapers published in Entre Ríos prov., and a guide to the existing collections of each journal.

2791 Vidaurreta, Alicia. Conflictos entre política y grupos de presión: Argentina y los aliados del Pacífico, 1872–1883. (*Rev. Hist. Am.*, 105, enero/junio 1988, p. 7–44)

Close analysis of the diplomatic relations of Argentina and Brazil with Bolivia, Chile, and Peru. Argentina legally was neutral during the War of the Pacific, but it did not stop trade with Bolivia and Peru.

2792 Vidaurreta, Alicia. Estructura socio-económica, demográfica y ocupacional de Concepción del Uruguay en 1869. (*Rev. Indias*, 47:179, enero/abril 1987, p. 123–156, bibl., ill., maps, tables)

Excellent description of the Dept. of Concepción del Uruguay, Entre Ríos, stresses its economic and population growth, and the characteristics of its population in 1869.

2793 Vidaurreta, Alicia. La muerte en Buenos Aires: 1871. (*Rev. Indias*, 49:186, mayo/agosto 1989, p. 437–460, tables)

Examines the effects of the yellow fever and smallpox epidemics in the city of Buenos Aires, the unsanitary conditions that existed there, and the reactions of national and municipal governments to the crisis. Available parish records indicate that the epidemics reached their peak in May and June, 1871, and that no social class was spared.

2794 Vidaurreta, Alicia. La población de La Paz en 1869. (*Estud. Parag.*, 13:1/2, dic. 1985, p. 413–429, tables)

Compares the statistics presented in the first Argentine census of 1869 with the original manuscripts, arriving at a more precise figure, and concludes that the Dept. of La Paz, Entre Ríos, had a very young population. The original manuscripts also contain errors, such as classifying people as *estanci-*

eros when they were *chacareros, arrendata-rios,* or *medianeros.*

Waisman, Carlos H. La ideología del naciona-lismo de derecha en Cabildo, 1973–1983. See *HLAS 51:5003.*

Waisman, Carlos H. Reversal of development in Argentina: postwar counterrevolutionary policies and their structural consequences. See *HLAS 51:5004.*

2795 Wirth, Juan Carlos F. Camila Nievas, una mujer entrerriana extraordinaria. Santa Fe, Argentina: Librería y Editorial Col-megna, 1984. 78 p.: port. (Col. Entre Ríos; 34)

Camilia Enriqueta Nievas de Capde-villa was for 40 years the director of the Instituto Magnasco of Gualeguaychú, Entre Ríos. This is an introduction to Camilia Nieva and the rarely used collection at the Instituto Magnasco. Contains the best assortment of 19th-century *Entrerriano* newspapers.

2796 Zavalía Lagos, Jorge A. Mariquita Sán-chez y su tiempo. Buenos Aires: Plus Ultra, 1986. 284 p.: (Col. Las Mujeres)

Published memoirs of Mariquita Sán-chez include some of her letters from the family archives. Sheds light on the economic conditions and politics of her time.

2797 Zorrilla, Rubén H. Líderes del po-der sindical. Buenos Aires: Ediciones Siglo Veinte, 1988. 202 p.: bibl. (Col. Temas argentinos)

Author interviewed or reconstructed the biographies of 91 union leaders active be-tween 1910–83 to determine their back-grounds, their occupational history, their so-cial mobility, their religious beliefs, and the social group to which they belonged. Unlike in 1910, he concludes, the labor leaders of the peronist period were well-educated, prop-erty owners, natives, Catholic, and reformers rather than revolutionaries.

2798 Zubillaga, Carlos. Sincronía de un fra-caso: la primera democracia cristiana en Argentina y Uruguay, 1902–1924. (*Cuad. CLAEH,* 14:2, 1989, p. 107–121)

Describes the different approaches of the Argentine and Uruguayan ecclesiastical hierarchies to the conflict between capital and labor, the former endorsing the German model of the *Círculos de Obreros,* the latter the French model, and the labor legislation

proposed by the Christian Democrats within these groups. Christian Democrats formed their own organizations in 1902 when they broke with the conservatives over tactics. Marked the end of neocorporatism in both countries.

2799 Zuleta Alvarez, Enrique; Mario Gui-llermo Saraví; and Enrique Díaz Araujo. Homenaje a Julio Irazusta. Mendoza, Argen-tina: Editorial Diario la Tarde, 1984. 118 p.: bibl., ill.

Laudatory introduction to the contri-butions and significance of Julio Irazusta (1899–1982), one of the founders of the "re-visionist" school of historiography and of the "nationalist" political movement.

PARAGUAY

2800 Abente, Diego. Foreign capital, eco-nomic elites and the State in Paraguay during the Liberal Republic, 1870–1936. (*J. Lat. Am. Stud.,* 21:1, Feb. 1989, p. 61–88, tables)

Significant article describing the post-1870 economic changes that took place in Paraguay, the rotating importance of the landowning, mercantile, and commercial elites, the rise of a political elite at the ex-pense of the mercantile elite, and the influ-ence of foreign capital. Insightful observa-tions on the Revolution of 1904.

2801 Abente, Diego. The Liberal Republic and the failure of democracy in Para-guay. (*Americas/Francisc.,* 45:4, April 1989, p. 525–546)

Attributes the end of the Liberal Re-public (1870–1936) to the internationaliza-tion of the political arena, the creation of a professional army, the development of clien-telistic political parties unwilling to cooper-ate, and to the failure to fulfill the aspira-tions of the middle classes.

2802 Alemán, Adolfo G. El soldado prohi-bido. Asunción: Editora Litocolor, 1990. 264 p., 5 p. of plates: bibl.

Impressive attempt to rehabilitate Luis Irrazábal, who twice defended Nanawa against Bolivian attacks during the Chaco War, was twice considered for the presidency, and who indirectly contributed to the revolu-tion of Feb. 17, 1936. Calls attention to the rivalry within the armed forces, to the still unstudied influence of Chilean army officers on Paraguayans who studied in their academies, and to the ideas of Irrazábal and his mentor, Gen. Manlio Schenoni Lugo. Uses that part of his military files that Irrazábal failed to destroy in 1955.

2803 Anuario del Instituto de Investigaciones Históricas Dr. José Gaspar Rodríguez de Francia. Año 1, No. 1, mayo 1979– . Asunción: El Instituto de Investigaciones Históricas Dr. José Gaspar Rodríguez de Francia.

In short essays Blas Garay reviews the works of Pedro Somellera (actually a reprint of a 1943 article), Matilde Meza de Gómez comments on Julio Llanos' *El Dr. Francia,* and Harmodio Efraín Brizuela calls attention to the friendly relations that existed between Church and State ùnder Francia. In a fascinating article, Thomas L. Whigham stresses the economic importance of Misiones to both Paraguay and the Corrientes prov. between 1820–34.

2804 Argentina, Estados Unidos e insurrección en Paraguay: documentos de inteligencia, político-militares y artículos de prensa. Recopilación de Anibal Miranda. Asunción: RP Ediciones/Miranda, 1988. 246 p.

Collection of official correspondence and press articles written between March, 1958 and March, 1960 stresses US, Argentine, Brazilian, Venezuelan, Cuban, and Russian involvement in the internal affairs of Paraguay, and the revolutionary plans of the Movimiento 14 de Mayo and the Frente Unido de Liberación Nacional (FULNA).

2805 El asilo a Perón y la caída de Epifanio Méndez: una visión documental norteamericana. Edición de Alfredo M. Seiferheld y José Luis de Tone. Asunción: Editorial Histórica, 1988. 237 p.: bibl., ill., ports. (Serie Documentos para la historia)

Presents in translation a selected group of reports sent by the US Embassy in Asunción to the US Dept. of State from Jan., 1955 to April, 1956. Three important events occurred during this period: 1) the overthrow of Juan D. Perón and his flight to Paraguay; 2) the unification of the Colorado Party as a result of the Argentine revolution; and 3) the fall of Epifanio Méndez Fleytas.

2806 Avila, Manuel Agustín. Sinopsis de la Guerra del Chaco: semblanzas e intimidades de la epopeya. Asunción: M.A. Avila, 1987. 444 p., 17 p. of plates: maps.

Pt. 1 contains brief biographies of the officers who commanded army and navy units during the Chaco War. Pt. 2 seeks to reconstruct the military campaigns of 1933 on the basis of operation orders and intelligence reports. Contains situation maps for several battles.

Ayala, Eligio. Evolución de la economía agraria en el Paraguay: ensayo escrito en Berna, Suiza, de junio a julio de 1915. See *HLAS 51:2378.*

2807 Baptista, Fernando. Elisa Lynch, mulher do mundo e da guerra. São Paulo: Civilização Brasileira em convênio com o Instituto Nacional do Livro, Fundação Nacional Pró-Memória, 1986. 600 p., 4 p. of plates: bibl., ports.

Sympathetic biography of Elisa Lynch focuses on her influence on the political decisions of Francisco Solano López, her involvement in his military activities, her participation in the cultural and social life of Asunción, and her concern for the modernization of Paraguay. Portrays Solano López as a patriot and stubborn man of principle. Impressive revisionist study with an excellent bibliography, though marred by the absence of documentation.

2808 Barboza, Ramiro Los sindicatos en el Paraguay: evolución y estructura actual. Asunción: Centro Interdisciplinario de Derecho Social y Economía Política: Librería El Lector, 1987. 565 p.: bibl. (Serie Investigaciones/CIDSEP; 4)

Close examination of existing labor laws, the strengths and weaknesses of the labor movement, and the organization and activities of the principal labor unions. Good reference work.

Benítez, Justo Pastor. Ensayos sobre el liberalismo paraguayo. See *HLAS 51:3978.*

Bourgade La Dardye, Emmanuel de. El Paraguay 1889: antigua crónica de un viaje al presente. See *HLAS 51:3179.*

2809 Caballero Aquino, Ricardo. La Segunda República Paraguaya, 1869–1906: política, economía y sociedad. 2a. ed.

Asunción: Arte Nuevo Editores, 1985. 298 p.: bibl., ill., index. (Serie Historia; 5)

Analysis of the political and economic policies of Bernardino Caballero, 1880–94, stresses the sale of public lands and the resort to public loans. Translation of *The economic reconstruction of Paraguay in the postwar of the Triple Alliance: politics and property in the era of General Caballero, 1869–1904* (PhD dissertation, Univ. of Illinois, 1980).

2810 Cooney, Jerry W. and **Thomas Lyle Whigham.** An interview with Harris Gaylord Warren: from the borderlands to Paraguay. (*Americas/Francisc.*, 45:4, April 1989, p. 443–460, bibl.)

The "father of Paraguayan studies in the United States" discusses his career, assesses Paraguayan historians, and suggests areas in need of research. An earlier version of this interview appears in *Revista Paraguaya de Sociología* (Asunción, 22:64, 1985).

2811 Escobar, Ramiro. El calvario de la patria: la mutilación del Chaco paraguayo. Asunción: El Gráfico, 1988. 555 p.: ill.

Presents a close examination of the diplomatic negotiations to end the Chaco War that began with the armistice of June 12, 1935, and resulted in the peace treaty of July 9, 1938. Accuses the Liberal Party, influenced by the mediating powers Argentina, Brazil, and the US, of giving Bolivia the rich oil and agricultural lands Paraguay held in the Chaco. Praises the conduct of Colonel Rafael Franco and his Administration. Extensive quotations from primary and secondary sources are incorporated into the text.

2812 Escobar Rodas, Cecilio. Mis verdades sobre algunas batallas de la Guerra del Chaco. Asunción: Gráficas Zamphirópolos, 1988. 309 p.: ill.

Interesting account of the contributions to Paraguayan victories made by an infantry reconnaissance platoon operating behind enemy lines. The author, commander of the platoon, seeks to correct the version of his activities and those of his division published by Col. Carlos J. Fernández.

2813 El estado general de la nación durante los gobiernos liberales. v. 1. Asunción: Archivo del Liberalismo, 1988. 1 v.: ports.

First of projected three volumes of documents contains the annual presidential

addresses to Congress from April 1, 1905 to April 1, 1924.

Ferreira Pérez, Saturnino. Proceso político del Paraguay, 1936–1942: una visión desde la prensa. v. 1, 1936–1942. v. 2, 1943–1947. v. 3, La Revolución de '47. v. 4, 1947–1949. See *HLAS 51:3982.*

2814 Fournial, Georges. José Gaspar Rodríguez de Francia, l'incorruptible des Amériques. Paris: Messidor/Editions sociales, 1985. 231 p.: bibl., ill. (Histoire. 1789–1989; 12)

Well-written and sympathetic account of Francia and his government stresses the influences of the French Revolution and especially of Robespierre's thinking on Francia's conduct.

2815 Francia, José Gaspar Rodríguez de. Cartas y decretos del dictador Francia. v. 1–2. Recopilación de Alfredo Viola. Asunción: Univ. Católica, 1989–1990. 2 v. (Biblioteca de estudios paraguayos; 31, 37)

Contains a selection of correspondence and decrees written between Oct. 6, 1814, and Dec. 31, 1818, and found in the Bareiro Collection. Documents touch upon the Indian invasions of the northern borders, Artigas in Misiones, trade with the Portuguese, efforts to purchase armaments, and the resettlement of peaceful Indians within the country.

2816 Franco, Rafael. Memorias militares. t. 1, Vanguardia, Boquerón, Saavedra, Gondra, acciones de julio, Campo Vía, el armisticio. Asunción: Nueva Edición, 1988. 1 v.: ill.

An ex-president of Paraguay (1936–37) describes his role and observations in the Chaco War from 1932 to the Battle of Campo Vía (Sept. 11, 1933). Critical of Gen. Estigarribia as a military strategist and leader. Memoirs were written in 1958 and published posthumously.

Friesen, Martin W. Neue Heimat in der Chacowildnis. See *HLAS 51:3181.*

2817 Galeano Perrone, Horacio. Paraguay: ideología de la dependencia. Asunción: Ediciones La República, 1986. 134 p. (Ediciones la República; 9)

Polemical work critical of the influence liberal ideas have had on Paraguayan development 1870–1970. Sees liberalism as the ideological instrument of imperialism.

2818 Ganson, Barbara J. Following their children into battle: women at war in Paraguay, 1864–1870. (*Americas/Francisc.*, 46:3, Jan. 1990, p. 335–371, map)

Comprehensive description of the roles women had in Paraguayan society before and during the Paraguayan War.

2819 Gaona, Francisco. Introducción a la historia gremial y social del Paraguay. v. 2. Asunción, Editorial Arandú, 1987. 1 v. bibl., facsims., ports.

Labor leader outlines Paraguayan labor history 1904–29, reproducing numerous documents and newspaper articles. Posthumous work. Vol. 1 appeared in 1967.

2820 Gondra, César and **Víctor I. Franco.** El General Patricio Escobar. Asunción: Arte Nuevo Editores, 1990. 192 p.: bibl., ill. (Serie Historia; 6)

Contains two sympathetic accounts of Escobar, one by the historian Franco, the other by a personal friend of many years, César Gondra. Escobar served under Solano López during the Paraguayan War, and was Paraguayan president 1886–90. The two national parties were founded during his Administration.

2821 Granada, Antonio. Historia del R.I. 20, Acá Yuasá. v. 2, Protocolo de paz; Tratado de paz. Asunción: Dirección de Publicaciones Militares, 1988. 1 v.: ill.

Criticizes Paraguayan diplomats for giving Bolivia land that the Paraguayan army had won and held when the peace treaty ending the Chaco War was signed on July 21, 1938. Feels they were responding to pressure from US oil companies. Calls attention to the women heros of the war. Vol. 1 was not seen.

2822 Heyn Schupp, Carlos Antonio. Iglesia y Estado en el Paraguay durante el gobierno de Carlos Antonio López, 1841–1862. Asunción: Univ. Católica Nuestra Señora de la Asunción, 1982. 331 p.: (Biblioteca de estudios paraguayos; 3)

Well-documented analysis of Church-State relations emphasizes canon law and Paraguayan law. Stresses continuity between Francia and López Administrations, and Vatican policy of cooperation with them without acknowledging the authority of the State over the Church. Appendix includes unedited documents (p. 244–331)

2823 Kallsen, Margarita. Asunción, 450 años de su fundación, 1537–1987: bibliografía. Prólogo de Roberto Quevedo. Asunción: Cromos, 1987. 67 p.: indexes. (Serie Bibliografía paraguaya, 0257–7070; 6)

Bibliography of books, pamphlets, journals, and journalistic articles that refer to Asunción. The 523 items are organized alphabetically by title.

Lechín Suárez, Juan. La batalla de Villa Montes: estudio crítico. See item **2544.**

2824 Martínez Cuevas, Efraín. La ganadería en el Paraguay: desde la conquista hasta la Guerra Grande. Asunción: La Rural Ediciones, 1987. 229 p.: bibl., ill., ports.

Sound analysis of the existing literature on the origins and development of the pastoral industry to 1867. Notes absence of reliable statistical data.

2825 McNaspy, Clement J. and **Fernando María Moreno.** Los jesuitas en el Paraguay: recuerdos de los últimos 60 años, 1927–1987. Asunción: Compañia de Jesús en el Paraguay, 1988. 42 p.: bibl., ill.

Short but interesting chronicle of Jesuit activities in Paraguay.

2826 Miranda, Carlos R. The Stroessner era: authoritarian rule in Paraguay. Boulder, Colo.: Westview Press, 1990. 177 p.: bibl., index, map.

Well-written analysis of the authoritarian Stroessner regime attributes its endurance to the political tradition of Paraguay. Provides an excellent introduction to Paraguayan politics.

2827 Pesoa, Manuel. Fundadores del Partido Liberal. Asunción: Archivo del Liberalismo, 1990. 603 p.: ill.

Brief but informative biographical sketches of the founders of the Liberal Party.

2828 Plá, Josefina. Españoles en la cultura del Paraguay. Prólogo de Francisco Corral. Asunción: Depto. Cultural de la Embajada de España en Asunción: Editorial Araverá, 1985. 427 p.: bibl., ill. (Serie Ensayos; 2)

Survey of Spanish contributions to all aspects of Paraguayan culture (art, music, theater, literature, journalism, etc.) from the colonial period to 1985. Includes an anthology of extracts from the works of Spanish writers who lived in Paraguay, but omits references to the religious work of the missionaries. Plá's historical essay adds immeasurably to the value of the book.

2829 Ramos, Alfredo. Concepción 1947: la revolución derrotada. Asunción: Editorial Histórica, 1985. 202 p.: maps.

Rebel officer recalls the military operations conducted by the revolutionaries, and concludes that the principal reason for the defeat of the revolution was the military ineptitude of his colleagues. Includes recollections of Col. Carlos J. Fernández on the events of April, 1947 and of Col. Federico W. Smith. Written while in exile between 1950–54, and maintains that Communist Party played a minor role in the revolution.

2830 Ramos, Alfredo. Semblanzas militares. Asunción: CRITERIO-Ediciones, 1987–1988. 2 v.: ports.

Biographical sketches of professional army officers, mostly of the combat arms, written by a professional soldier who knew them. In addition to Estigarribia, 13 generals and 13 colonels are described.

2831 Reber, Vera Blinn. The demographics of Paraguay: a reinterpretation of the Great War, 1864–70. (*HAHR*, 68:2, May 1988, p. 290–319, graphs, map, tables)

Well-reasoned convincing analysis of the available Paraguayan data and comparisons with the experience of other areas suggest that, during the War of the Triple Alliance, Paraguay lost between 8.7 and 18.5 percent of its prewar population, not the usually-quoted figure of over 50 percent.

2832 Regalsky, Andrés Martín. El Banco Francés del Río de la Plata y su expansión en el Paraguay. (*Estud. Parag.*, 14:1/2, dic. 1986, p. 281–310, tables)

Brief description of the efforts of a private Argentine bank founded by French firms in Buenos Aires and Paris, as well as others involved in Franco-Argentine trade, to expand into Paraguay. Bank participated in the founding of the Banco Paraguayo and the Banco de la República, and extended credit to private banks in Asunción and to the Paraguayan government.

2833 Romero, Roberto A. Dr. José Gaspar Rodríguez de Francia: ideólogo de la independencia del Paraguay; historia. Asunción: A.R. Impresiones, 1988. 178 p.: bibl., ill.

Collection of documents pertaining to the Francia era.

2834 Saldívar, Julio P.M. Historia del Regimiento Batallón 40: su creación y organización, acciones en que participó, sus jefes y oficiales, los cadetes y sargentos, la tropa de la aguerrida unidad. Asunción: Dirección de Publicaciones, Fuerzas Armadas, 1985. 150 p.: ill.

History of a distinguished infantry regiment composed of students, laborers and foreigners such as the White Russian volunteers. Description of the regiment from its organization in Aug. 1932 to Aug. 1933 is based on the notes kept by its first commander. The author himself joined the unit in Aug. 1933. Unit played a crucial role in the capture of Yrendagüé (Dec. 8, 1934).

2835 Seiferheld, Alfredo M. Economía y petróleo durante la Guerra del Chaco: apuntes para una historia económica del conflicto paraguayo-boliviano. Asunción: Instituto Paraguayo de Estudios Geopolíticos e Internacionales; Lector, 1983. 535 p.: bibl., ill. (Col. histórica; 4)

Primarily discusses the wartime economic policies of Paraguay and Bolivia, and to a lesser extent, Bolivian-Paraguayan oil policies as a cause of the Chaco War.

2836 Szlajfer, Henryk. Capitalist development in nineteenth century Latin America: one model only? an example of Haiti and Paraguay. (*Lat.am. Stud.*, 14, 1984, p. 147–180, bibl.)

Theoretical discussion compares Paraguayan and Haitian plans in the first half of the 19th century to develop an autonomous economy. The success of Paraguay and the failure of Haiti is attributed to the reaction of the "popular classes," the peasantry and urban poor, toward the costs of accumulating capital.

2837 Tufari Recalde, Pablo E. La Guerra del Chaco: antecedentes históricos y conducción político-estratégica del conflicto. Asunción: Dirección de Publicaciones, Fuerzas Armadas, 1987. 205 p.: bibl., ill., maps.

Emphasizes the development and execution of a strategic plan for the conduct of the war, which began with no plans or preparations worked out in advance by Paraguay. Excellent military maps show the disposition of military elements during various phases of the war.

2838 Vargas Peña, Benjamín. Secreta política del dictador Francia. Buenos Aires: Editorial Nueva Etapa, 1985. 356 p.: bibl.

Contains a translation of an anonymous work attributed to Vicente Pazos Kanki and published in London (1828) plus a group of documents that allegedly shed light on the activities of José Agustín Tort and the secret instructions he received from Francia. Thesis is that Francia was willing to help Spain reconquer America.

2839 Velilla Laconich de Arréllaga, Julia and **Alfredo M. Seiferheld.** Los ecos de la prensa en 1887: una propuesta de conciliación política. Asunción: Editorial Histórica, 1987. 169 p.: bibl., ill.

Reproduces a selection of articles that appeared in the five journals that existed in Asunción between June and Dec. 1887. Articles focus on the party struggles and violence of the period. In a preliminary essay the authors call for a conciliation of the political parties, noting that members of the Colorado and Liberal parties have successfully worked together in the same government since 1887.

2840 Viola, Alfredo. La esclavitud en la época del Dr. Francia. (*Estud. Parag.*, 14: 1/2, dic. 1986, p. 145–166)

Rapid review of the legal status of black and mulatto slaves in the Francia period.

2841 Vittone, Luis. La Guerra del Chaco. Paraguay: s.n., 1986. 3 v.: ill.

Meticulous and well-documented military history of the Chaco War describes and analyzes the operational plans, the tactics employed, and the troop maneuvers for each of the seven campaigns into which the war is divided. Excellent maps show the disposition of troop elements and their military objectives. Recommended for classes in military tactics.

2842 Whigham, Thomas. Some reflections on early Anglo-Paraguayan commerce.

(*Americas/Francisc.*, 44: 3, Jan. 1988, p. 279–284, bibl.)

Brief description of British attempts to open trade with Paraguay prior to 1842.

URUGUAY

2843 Abal Oliú, Estela and **Isabel Ezcurra Semblat.** El Partido Nacional y la cuestión social. Montevideo: CELADU, 1988. 193 p.: bibl., ill.

Outlines the principles upheld by the Partido Nacional from its founding to the present, including its positions on social issues. Asserts that the Partido Nacional and not the Colorado Party was the original sponsor of many pieces of social legislation passed between 1903–30, and that both parties reflected the ideas of their times. Fails to settle the debate over which party should be credited for the social legislation of the period.

2844 Anastasia, Luis V. et al. Batlle y *El Día*, 1886–1903. Montevideo: Fundación Prudencio Vázquez y Vega; Munich: Fundación Hanns Seidel, 1988. 252 p.: bibl.

Analyzes editorials and articles that appeared in *El Dia*, which became the official organ of the Colorado Party on Dec. 19, 1889. Reveals the political, social, and economic ideas Batlle y Ordóñez held before he became president of the Republic. Extensive reproductions of editorials and articles.

2845 Archivo Artigas. t. 22. Montevideo: Comisión Nacional Archivo Artigas, 1989. 438 p.: indexes.

After years of inactivity, the Comisión Nacional Archivo Artigas has resumed publication of its important collection of documents on the Artigas years. Latest vol. covers 1815–16 and includes correspondence with Artigas, the *cabildo* and governor of Montevideo, and others, plus a few judicial papers. Contents shed little light on military affairs, but much more on the efforts of Artigas to enforce fiscal integrity in the government and to further the economic development of Uruguay.

2846 Barrán, José Pedro and **Benjamín Nahum.** La derrota del batllismo, 1916. Montevideo: Ediciones de la Banda Oriental, 1987. 156 p.: bibl. (Batlle, los estancieros y el Imperio Británico; 8)

Close analysis of the election results of July 30, 1916 leads authors to conclude that the Uruguayan people had voted for a conservative but democratic government and against a continuation of the social reform movement.

2847 Barrán, José Pedro. Historia de la sensibilidad en el Uruguay. v. 1, La cultura bárbara, 1800–1860. v. 2, El disciplinamiento, 1860–1920. Montevideo: Ediciones de la Banda Oriental; Facultad de Humanidades y Ciencias, 1989–90. 2 v.: bibl. (Historia y presente; 4–5)

Cultural history of Uruguay focuses on the attitudes of people toward life as revealed by daily activities and their reaction to the world around them. The analysis relies essentially but not exclusively on news items in the press and journal articles. Superb introduction to Uruguayan civilization 1800–1920.

2848 Barrán, José Pedro. Lucha política y enfrentamiento social, 1913–1916. Montevideo: Ediciones de la Banda Oriental, 1986. 271 p.: bibl. (Batlle, los estancieros y el Imperio Británico; 7)

Well-researched work asserts that although political parties adhered to the same principles in 1904 and 1916, in the latter year they were seen by contemporaries to have acquired a socioeconomic content. The political parties were using and exaggerating the existing social tensions for their own purposes.

2849 Boix, Alberto. La inmigración uruguaya en España, 1970–1985. (*in* Inmigración, integración e imagen de los latinoamericanos en España, 1931–1987. Madrid: Servicio de Publicaciones de la OEI, 1988, p. 9–23, appendix)

Interviews with 21 middle-class Uruguayans living in Madrid reveal that they left home in search of a better economic future without an accurate knowledge of conditions in Spain or Europe, but attracted to Spain by the rise of democracy there. The politically persecuted—political leaders, union leaders, artists, and intellectuals—arrived essentially after 1976, but many were not readily absorbed. Disenchanted with political and economic conditions in Spain, they returned to Uruguay with the reestablishment of democracy. Interviewees came primarily from Montevideo.

2850 Caetano, Gerardo and **José Pedro Rilla.** El joven Quijano, 1900–1933: izquierda nacional y conciencia crítica. Montevideo: Ediciones de la Banda Oriental, 1986. 239 p.: bibl., facsims., ports. (Temas del siglo XX; 38)

Analysis of Quijano's ideas, political activities, and reflections on the contemporary scene is based on the journalistic articles and editorials he wrote 1924–33. Quijano founded the Agrupación Nacionalista Demócrata Social within the Partido Nacionalista.

2851 Castellanos, Alfredo Raúl. El pluralismo uruguayo, 1919–1933: el dislocamiento de los partidos. Montevideo: CLAEH, 1987. 2 v. (335 p.): bibl. (Serie Investigaciones; 52–53)

Argues that the principal cause for the March 31, 1933 revolution was not the world economic crisis of 1929, but the effect on the traditional political parties of a July 11, 1910 law. This law created the "simultaneous double vote," by which each voter was to vote simultaneously for his political party and for the candidate of his choice. The purpose of the law was to assure minority representation. Based on Montevideo newspapers.

2852 Caula, Nelson and **Alberto Silva.** Alto el fuego: FF.AA. y Tupamaros. Montevideo: Monte Sexto, 1986. 292 p.: bibl., ill. (Col. Polémica)

Reexamines events of 1972 that led to the *golpe* of 1973 in an attempt to rehabilitate the Movimiento de Liberación Nacional. Anecdotal account of the alleged secret negotiations between the Tupamaros and the armed forces in 1972, and the breaking of their truce agreement. Much of the information was obtained in interviews conducted between 1982–86 with leading contemporaries. See *HLAS 51:4001* for political scientist's comment.

Chasteen, John Charles. Trouble between men and women: machismo on nineteenth-century *estancias*. See item **2883.**

Costa Bonino, Luis. Wilson Ferreira Aldunate y la lógica nacionalista. See *HLAS 51:4003.*

2853 Crónica de Aparicio Saravia. v. 1–2. Prólogo y dirección de Washington Reyes Abadie. Montevideo: Ediciones El Nacional, 1989. 2 v.: ill.

Biography of the Blanco leader of the revolutions of 1896–97 and 1903–04, written with the aid of his descendents for the benefit of party members. Saravia also participated in a revolution led by his Brazilian-born brother in Rio Grande, 1892–94. He had brothers active in both Uruguayan political parties. Contains extensive quotations from published sources, and photographs from the Saravia family collection. Excellent introduction to the man and his goals.

2854 Feria, Rosa M. Juan Alejandro Apolant: alemán, historiador uruguayo; la historia como una ciencia exacta. (*in* Seminar on the Acquisition of Latin American Library Materials, *31st, Berlin, 1986.* Intellectual migrations: transcultural contributions of European and Latin American emigrés. Madison: SALALM Secretariat, Memorial Library, Univ. of Wisconsin, 1987, p. 203–210, bibl.)

Brief biography of a distinguished historian of Uruguay best known for his *Génesis de la familia uruguaya* (Montevideo, 1975) and *Operativo Patagonia: historia de la mayor aportación demográfica masiva a la Banda Oriental.* (Montevideo, 1970). Based on documentary sources, both are basic reference works based on documentary sources of interest to sociologists, demographers, and genealogists.

2855 Fernández Cabrelli, Alfonso. Presencia masónica en la Cisplatina. Montevideo: América Una, 1986. 213 p.: ill.

Studies influence of Masons on Uruguayan developments to 1828. Indirectly demonstrates that Masonic lodges did not behave strictly as Masonic lodges but as a temporary collection of individuals with a common political goal. Includes transcriptions from some short-lived Montevideo newspapers.

2856 Fernández Huidobro, Eleuterio. Historia de los tupamaros. t. 1, Los orígenes. t. 3, El MLN. Montevideo: Tae Editorial, 1986–1987. 2 v.

In vol. 1 a Tupamaro intellectual describes the origins and evolution of the Tupamaros 1962–64. This minority group attracted members from the Socialist Party and the *Movimiento de Apoyo al Campesino,* and saw agrarian reform as the answer to Uruguay's economic crisis. Vol. 3 covers

1966–72 and reveals that Tupamaros were members of other leftist organizations. Explains the reorientation and reconstruction of Tupamaro organization after the failure of its attempted bank robbery (Dec. 1966). Its growth plan stressed military armed struggle for a socialist revolution, based on labor and student unions. Vol. 2 was not seen for annotation.

2857 Ferreira Aldunate, Wilson. Wilson Ferreira Aldunate: eligiendo recuerdos. Entrevista de María Esther Gilio. Montevideo: Ediciones Trilce, 1986. 119 p., 4 p. of plates: ports. (Col. Espejos)

In a taped interview (no date is indicated), Ferreira comments on the political events he witnessed, the ideas of Luis Alberto de Herrera, US policy in Latin America, Argentine politics, the goals of the National Party, and military dictatorships.

2858 Garat, Carlos M. and Mirtha E. Garat de Marín. Herrera: semblanza de un patriota. Montevideo: Depto. de Investigaciones Históricas del Movimiento Nacional Luis A. de Herrera, 1989. 411 p.: bibl., ill.

Two members of the Partido Nacional follow Herrera's political career and the development of his ideas through his speeches and journalistic articles in the 20th century. Excellent description of the intra-party rivalries and the challenges within the party to Herrera's leadership. Carlos Garat was a confidant of Herrera in the 1950s.

Gradenigo, Gaio. Italianos entre Rosas y Mitre. See item **2696.**

2859 Historia viva: memorias del Uruguay y de Israel. Entrevistas y documentación de Rosa Perla Raicher. Edición de Haim Avni, Rosa Perla Raicher y David Bankier. Jerusalem: Instituto de Judaísmo Contemporáneo, Univ. Hebrea de Jerusalem, 1989. 234 p.: facsims.

Collection of brief interviews with present and former members of the Jewish community in Uruguay provides glimpses of community activities and the reaction of some Uruguayan Jews to Israel.

2860 Historias de vida de inmigrantes judíos al Uruguay. Estudio introductorio y recopilación de Teresa Porzecanski. Montevideo: Kehilá, Comunidad Israelita del Uruguay, 1986. 244 p.

Excellent introduction to the various origins and ideologies of the Jews who migrated to Uruguay. Most came from the Central Mediterranean (Sephardins), Eastern Europe (Ashkenazis), or Central and Western Europe. Here, 16 Jewish immigrants recall the events that led them to emigrate from their homeland and describe life in their new Jewish communities. Revealing commentaries on the process of integration and acculturation.

2861 Lorier, Eduardo. Historia de Florida. Montevideo: Ediciones de la Banda Oriental, 1989. 1 v.

Excellent history of an important Uruguayan dept. includes extensive bibliography.

2862 Medina Pintado, María del Carmen. La presencia alemana en el Uruguay, 1850–1930. Montevideo: HEGIL-Impresos, 1988. 282 p.: bibl., maps.

Brief but excellent overall review of German settlements and activities in Uruguay is based on numerous private archives as well as German and Uruguayan national archives and interviews.

2863 Melogno Vélez, Fabián. Biografía del Coronel Ventura Alegre. (*Bol. Hist. Ejérc.*, 275/278, 1989, p. 155–165, bibl., maps)

Brief biography of an Uruguayan who was an officer in both the Argentine and Peruvian armies during the Wars of Independence.

2864 Nemirovsky, Israel. Albores del judaísmo en el Uruguay. Montevideo: Impresora Cordón, 1987. 288 p.

Member of the Liberal Zionist Party, son of a rabbi who arrived in Montevideo in 1914, describes the gradual development of Jewish institutions and organizations in Uruguay, and the appearance of Jewish religious practices. Semi-autobiographical account; portions of it appeared earlier in *Semanario Hebreo*, Montevideo.

2865 Oddone, Juan Antonio. El Uruguay en los años treinta: la crisis política y sus protagonistas. Montevideo: Univ. de la República, Facultad de Humanidades y Ciencias, Depto. de Publicaciones, 1988. 41 p.: (Avances de investigación)

Brief analysis of the electoral campaign of 1930 and of party politics up to the Terra revolution of March 31, 1933. Author consulted the British diplomatic files.

2866 Oxman, Ramón. La colonia 19 de Abril: una experiencia de colonización agraria judía en el Uruguay. Montevideo: Ediciones del Nuevo Mundo, 1987. 68 p.: bibl., ill. (Cuadernos uruguayos; 5)

Account of a Jewish agricultural colony established in 1915 and abandoned for economic reasons in 1935. Based in part on the recollections of the original settlers from Poland (Galicia), Russia, and Romania (Bessarabia).

2867 Real de Azúa, Carlos et al. Vigencia de Carlos Real de Azúa. Montevideo: Centro de Informaciones y Estudios del Uruguay; Ediciones de la Banda Oriental, 1987. 131 p.: (Estudios sobre la sociedad uruguaya; 9)

Tribute to an outstanding Uruguayan historian contains selections from his publications and articles by seven distinguished scholars who appraise the man and his work.

2868 Reyes Abadie, Washington. Breve historia del Partido Nacional. Montevideo: Ediciones de la Banda Oriental, 1989. 239 p. (Ediciones de la Banda Oriental; 139)

Useful introduction to the history of the Partido Nacional is replete with quotations from the works of party members, only some of which are attributed.

2869 Reyes Abadie, Washington. Coronel Lorenzo Latorre: personalidad, vida, obra. Montevideo: Círculo Militar General Artigas, 1986. 215 p.: bibl., ill.

Argues forcefully for a favorable assessment of Latorre and his Administration. Quotes extensively without indicating sources.

2870 Rial, Juan. Población y mano de obra en espacios vacíos: el caso de un pequeño país: Uruguay, 1870–1930. (*in* Población y mano de obra en América Latina. Recopilación de Nicolás Sánchez-Albornoz. Madrid: Alianza Editorial, 1985, p. 185–219, tables)

Argues that the building of a modern infrastructure in the Rio de la Plata region and the introduction of capitalism adversely affected the socioeconomic structure of Uruguay and created the problem of structural underemployment. The size of the Uruguayan economy conditioned the labor market and limited demand. The aim of legislation passed after 1908 was to increase demand for labor. Based on imprecise and unreliable census statistics of 1889 and 1908 (there was no other national census until 1963). It is unclear that contemporary politicians would agree with author.

2871 Risso, Juan Ignacio. El viaje continúa: vida y leyenda del piloto-agrimensor genovés, Juan Risso, en el Uruguay, 1808–1861. Montevideo: Ediciones Liris, 1986. 73 p.: bibl., ill.

Life of Juan Risso, an Italian immigrant who arrived in Montevideo in 1830, is based in part on the family archives.

Roca, C. Alberto. La jurisprudencia: ciencia común a argentinos y orientales, 1810–1870. See item **2762.**

2872 Rodríguez Villamil, Silvia and **Graciela Sapriza.** Feminism and politics: women and the vote in Uruguay. (*in* Retrieving women's history: changing perceptions of the role of women in politics and society. Edited by S. Jay Kleinberg. Oxford, England: UNESCO Press, 1988, p. 278–297)

Discusses the early differences between feminists and women workers, the views of political parties on women's issues, and the social and political factors that contributed to women obtaining the vote.

2873 Ruiz, Esther and **Juana Paris.** El Frente en los años '30. Montevideo: Proyección, 1987. 165 p.: (Col. Historia; 3)

Uses the newspapers published in Montevideo and the interior cities to trace the growth of opposition to the Terra dictatorship among leftist elements and the formation of the Popular Front.

2874 Santiago, Rafael de. Blancos o nacionalistas?: 1852–1876, una época de definición. Montevideo: M. Pesce Impresos, 1987. 159 p.

Traces the growth within the Blanco Party of a resistance to the use of military force to achieve party objectives.

2875 Seluja, Antonio. Los libaneses en el Uruguay. Montevideo: A.D. Seluja Cecín, 1989. 224 p.: bibl., ill.

First study of the Lebanese in the Uruguayan republic is based essentially on the recollections of living Lebanese, and consists primarily of biographical sketches of the Lebanese who settled in Montevideo. Anecdotal, but reveals economic, social, and cultural activities of Lebanese community.

2876 Sendic, Alberto. Movimiento obrero y luchas populares en la historia uruguaya. Montevideo: Movimiento de Independientes 26 de Marzo en Uruguay, 1985. 144 p.

Essayist reviews the conduct of the Tupamaros, a militant leftist socialist faction, and concludes that the urban worker cannot affect profound structural changes without the cooperation of the rural classes and socialist movements elsewhere in the world. Author is related to Raúl Sendic, the Tupamaro leader.

2877 Trías, Vivián. Los caudillos, las clases sociales y el imperio. Prólogo de José E. Díaz. Montevideo: Ediciones de la Banda Oriental, 1988. 305 p.: (Selección de obras de Vivián Trías; 1. Serie ensayos históricos.)

Contains some articles the socialist thinker wrote for *El Sol* in the 1950s, his "Raíces, Apogeo y Frustración de la Burguesía Nacional" and "Las montoneras y el Imperio Británico." As a socialist thinker Trías is regarded by some as the successor of Marxist José Carlos Mariátegui.

2878 Vidal Rossi, Edith. Más datos de Artigas. Canelones, Uruguay: Tall. Gráficos Vanguardia, 1987. 94 p.: ill.

Reproduces 15 Spanish documents written 1817–20 which discuss Artigas, Portuguese occupation of the Banda Oriental del Uruguay, and events in Buenos Aires. Documents are located in the Archivo Histórico Nacional, Madrid.

2879 Vidaurreta, Alicia. An interview with Juan E. Pivel Devoto. (*HAHR*, 69:1, Feb. 1989, p. 1–22, bibl.)

The dean of Uruguayan historians describes his background, his political activities, his work as museum director, and his historical writings. His published documentary collections and his historical studies have contributed significantly to a better understanding of the 19th century in the Río de la Plata.

BRAZIL

MARSHALL C. EAKIN, *Associate Professor of History, Vanderbilt University*
ALIDA METCALF, *Associate Professor of History, Trinity University*
CARL A. HANSON, *Assistant Professor, Trinity University*

THE SCHOLARLY OUTPUT OF BRAZILIAN HISTORIANS has mushroomed since the last volume of the *Handbook*. The celebration of the centennials of abolition (1988) and of the proclamation of the Republic (1989) have been accompanied by the publication of a significant number of works on slavery, the Empire, and the Republic. Works on the 19th and 20th centuries greatly outnumber those on the colonial period. Labor history, family and women's history, social histories of urban and rural communities, and regional histories continue to gain in popularity. Meanwhile, biographies of military, political, and religious figures appear with regularity. Bethell's two edited volumes of selected articles from the *Cambridge history of Latin America* are an indispensable set of essays and bibliographies for the colonial and national periods (items **2911** and **2981**).

In the colonial period, historians are focusing more on social history and less on political and economic history. Laura de Mello e Souza's account (item **2963**) of popular religion in colonial Brazil is a work of major importance which shows the continuing influence of European, particularly French, historiography on Brazilian historians. Marcílio's book on Ubatuba, São Paulo (item **2932**), based solidly in historical demography, likewise breaks new ground in Brazilian family and regional history. Requirements for purity of blood and the aspirations of a powerful family collide in Cabral de Melo's fine study of Filipe Pais Barreto (item **2934**). Excellent studies of slavery continue to appear, focusing on family life, the slave trade, urban slavery, and runaway slave communities. The lives of women in the colonial period are explored in a number of works. Monteiro's contributions on Indian slavery in 17th-century São Paulo (items **2940** and **2939**) fill major lacunae in colonial historiography, while John Hemming's *Amazon frontier* (item **2889**) is required reading for the history of Indians in Brazil from the mid-18th century to 1910. The more traditional political and biographical approaches to the colonial period are evident in Lazzari Leite's account of the Pernambuco uprising in 1817 (item **2926**) and Piazza's study of José da Silva Paes (item **2951**).

A virtual flood of works have appeared on slavery and Afro-Brazilians, many published with the help of government subsidies. Although too often these are Masters theses that would have made better articles than books, a number are important studies. For the colonial period, the Africanist Joseph Miller's book (item **2938**) is an important work for Brazilian historians because of his superb knowledge of the African side of the slave trade. Algranti's reconstruction of the policing of slaves in Rio de Janeiro (item **2905**), Lara's examination of slave violence in that city (item **2925**), and the *Estudos Econômicos* issue on the demography of slavery (item **2914**), represent the best work on the colonial period. For the national period, Reis' work on the Malê slave revolt in Salvador and his edited volume of essays (items **2897** and **2886**), Gebara on the transition from slave to free labor (item **3020**), and Schwarcz and Azevedo on white attitudes toward blacks (items **3095** and **2971**) are noteworthy. Mattoso, Klein, and Engerman (item **3064**) examine slave prices in the 19th century. Carvalho (item **2881**) looks at slaves and crime using court records in mid-19th-century Pernambuco, while Machado (item **3058**) provides a similar type of analysis for Campinas and Taubaté. Trochim (item **3111**) looks at one organization of blacks attempting to promote social and economic reform in the late 19th century. Kiple (item **2892**) is an excellent piece of medical history linking beriberi and slave infant mortality.

The lives of women are the subject of several new works which promise to completely revise traditional images of Brazilian women, though here, as with studies of slavery, São Paulo and Rio de Janeiro are over-represented. Graham's excellent study places domestic servants in the world of the late 19th-century city (item **3028**). Contributions by Dias (item **3001**) and Soihet (item **3105**) likewise are fine studies that look at poor women in 19th-century São Paulo and turn-of-the-century Rio de Janeiro. Leite (item **2997**) contains accounts showing foreign travelers' perceptions of Brazilian women. Gama (item **3019**) is a brief but interesting biography of an early feminist, while Besse (item **2976**) studies wife-beating in early 20th-century São Paulo. French and Pedersen (item **3013**) discuss the female labor force in the late 1940s. Metcalf (item **2937**) and Nazzari (items **2943** and **2944**) look at women, the family, and property in colonial São Paulo. Samara (item **3091**) and Silva (item **2962**) discuss marriage and divorce in the colonial period respectively. Patai's illuminating accounts of contemporary Brazilian women's lives is highly recommended (item **2982**).

In the national period, a number of significant works have appeared on the Empire. Barman's political history (item **2974**) moves from late colony to mid-19th century. Carvalho, Graham, and Pang published major books on the nature of the imperial political system (items **2990, 3027,** and **3080**). Works by Souza (item **3107**), Marson (item **3062**), and Magalhães (item **3061**), analyze the regional revolts of the early Empire.

The Old Republic continues to receive a great deal of attention, especially from social historians interested in immigrants and workers, and from political historians. Alvim (item **2967**), Lesser (item **3048**), Luebke (item **3056**), Trento (item **3110**), and Kula (item **3035**) focus on Italian, German, Polish, Russian, and Jewish immigants. Casalecchi (item **2992**), Levi-Moreira (item **3049**), Prado (item **3084**), Lima (item **3054**), and Lessa (item **3047**) examine politics and political parties during the Old Republic. A spate of books have appeared on the Contestado revolt, although none is especially good.

Carone (item **2986**), Góes (item **3022**), Decca (item **2999**), Andrade (item **2968**), Blass (item **2977**), and Ribeiro (item **3088**) have written key works on labor during the Old Republic. Gomes (item **3023**) contains an essential bibliography on studies of the working class in Rio de Janeiro. Weinstein's article (item **3114**) is an excellent analysis of industrialists, the State, and labor policies in the 1930s and 1940s, while French (item **3012**) studies industrial workers in the 1940s.

The historiography of the post-1930 period leans heavily toward politics. Fonseca analyzes the economic discourse of Vargas (item **3010**). Works by Furtado (item **3017**) and Falcão (item **3007**) are autobiographical memoirs. Barbosa's study of Kubitschek (item **2973**), a collection of articles on Castelo Branco (item **2993**), Cláudio Lacerda's book on Carlos Lacerda (item **3037**), and Luthero Vargas' work on Getúlio Vargas (item **3113**) are among the recent works on prominent political figures. French analyzes Adhemar de Barros and the rise of postwar populism (item **3014**). Carneiro provides an important study of anti-semitism during the 1930s and 1940s (item **2985**). Santos (item **3094**) examines the military coup of 1964, while Heller (item **3031**) gives a detailed account of repression in Paraná during the military regime. Drosdoff (item **3003**) analyzes the Médici government, while Carone (item

2988) and Frederico (item 3006) look at labor during the military republic. Kinzo contributes a detailed examination of the official opposition party (MDB), and Reis Filho (item 3085) provides an interesting collection of interviews and photographs focusing on those who opposed military rule.

Giovanetti (item 3021), Sodré (item 3104), Falcão (item 3008), Carone (item 2988), and Oliveira (item 3077) look at the role of communists and the left, especially the Partido Comunista Brasileiro. Gorender's work is both a personal and historical look at the struggles of the left (item 3024), and Gomes contains some fascinating interviews with leftist militants (item 2979).

Several important studies on the free peasants, subsistence farming, and smallholders in the colonial and national periods have appeared. As noted above, Marcílio's work on colonial São Paulo is especially valuable (item 2932). Palacios (item 2949), Castro (item 2994), Dias (item 3001), Oliveira (item 3076), and Souza-Martins (item 3063) are important contributions in this poorly studied field. Holloway (item 3032) provides a very fine study of the social history of *capoeira* gangs in 19th-century Rio de Janeiro. Libby (item 3052) and Lanna (item 3041) have written pioneering studies on the economy of Minas Gerais in the 19th century and during the Old Republic.

In the field of economic history, Fritsch's work is an indispensable survey of the economic history of the Old Republic (item 3015). McDowall (item 3065) and Eakin (item 3005) provide the first full-length studies of foreign corporations operating in Brazil. Langer's article on the computer industry (item 3040) and Dean's on agricultural research (item 2998) are both fine articles in the little studied area of the history of science and technology. Turazzi's work is an unusual examination of the efforts to impose scientific management techniques in Rio de Janeiro industries at the turn of the century (item 3112).

Cobbs' article on Rockefeller (item 2996) and Albert's comparative study of Latin American nations' during the First World War (item 896) are among the few good works on foreign relations. Sevcenko's comparison of São Paulo and Rio de Janeiro (item 3097), and Carvalho's article on turn-of-the-century Rio de Janeiro (item 2989) are two solid essays on urban history.

The range, depth, and sheer number of recent publications on Brazilian history speaks to the increasing sophistication of historical work in Brazil. The coverage of some fields and regions still remains uneven, and many works, particularly those by young scholars, are published prematurely. Brazilian historians show themselves to be influenced by intellectual currents from around the world as well as driven by the problems faced at home. A strong contribution to Brazilian historiography continues to be made by North American scholars. The Morse interview (item 2978) explores the development of Brazilian historical studies, especially in the US. But as the entries that follow make clear, Brazilians clearly dominate the scholarly production, as well as the scholarly agenda, of Brazilian history.

GENERAL

2880 Alvim, Zuleika M.F. O imigrante italiano e a luta pelo trabalho familiar. (*An. Mus. Paul.*, 34, 1985, p. 145–179)
Excerpt from *Brava gente!* (see item 2967).

2881 Carvalho, Marcus J.M. de. "Quem furta mais e esconde:" o roubo de escravos em Pernambuco, 1832–1855. (*Estud. Econ./São Paulo*, 17: número especial, 1987, p. 89–110, bibl.)
Interesting analysis of little-studied phenomenon of theft of slaves uses court

records to show that number of thefts rose as end of slave trade approached in 1840s. Emphasizes that successful thefts required some cooperation by slaves, which gave slaves some power to ameliorate their situation.

Catálogo das dissertações e teses dos cursos de pós-graduação em História, 1973–1985. See item **31.**

O Catálogo de manuscritos da CEDEAM. See *HLAS 51:61.*

2882 Chacon, Vamireh. História dos partidos brasileiros: discurso e práxis dos seus programas. 2a. ed., rev. e aum. Brasília: Editora Univ. de Brasília, 1985. 739 p., 10 leaves of plates: bibl. (Col. Temas brasileiros; 5)

Revised and expanded edition of this very important and useful survey of political parties since the 1830s brings material up to the mid-1980s. A fundamental work for those interested in political parties in Brazil.

2883 Chasteen, John Charles. Trouble between men and women: machismo on nineteenth-century *estancias.* (*in* The middle period in Latin America: values and attitudes in the 17th-19th centuries. Edited by Mark D. Szuchman. Boulder, Colo.: Lynne Rienner Publishers, 1989, p. 123–140)

Theorizes that machismo developed among the people of the estancias in the Rio Grande do Sul as compensation for their failure to live up to their own Azorean code of sexual ethics.

Crawford, Leslie. El gaucho de España vino: ¿de dónde gaúcho? See *HLAS x52.*

2884 Donato, Hernâni. Dicionário das batalhas brasileiras. São Paulo: Instituição Brasileira de Difusão Cultural, 1987. 542 p.: bibl. (Biblioteca Estudos brasileiros; 15)

Useful reference source lists battles in chronological and alphabetical order, briefly describing each. Includes slave rebellions, Indian-European struggles, internal battles, and external conflicts. Written for a popular audience.

2885 Drescher, Seymour. Brazilian abolition in comparative perspective. (*HAHR,* 68:3, Aug. 1988, p. 430–460, tables)

Very useful comparative history highlights two striking characteristics of Brazilian abolition: 1) inability of a powerful planter class to mobilize against abolition; and 2) the *ad hoc* nature of the Brazilian abolitionist movement. Categories of comparison are demographic, economic, social, ideological, and political.

2886 Escravidão e invenção da liberdade: estudos sobre o negro no Brasil. Organização de João José Reis. Fotografias de Holanda Cavalcanti. São Paulo: Editora Brasiliense; Conselho Nacional de Desenvolvimento Científico e Tecnológico, 1988. 323 p., 16 p. of plates: bibl., ill.

Anthology of 13 articles, both new and previously published, divided into two parts: 1) "Life under Slavery" and 2) "Oppression, Resistance, and the Invention of Liberty." Brief introduction provides context for studies that range from early 18th century to 1980.

2887 Feres, João Bosco. Propriedade da terra: opressão e miséria; o meio rural na história social do Brasil. Amsterdam: CEDLA, 1990. 657 p.: bibl., ill. (Latin America studies; 56)

Detailed study of the role of the countryside in the social history of Brazil. Pt. 1 is a historical reconstruction based on secondary sources. Pt. 2 is a case study of agricultural modernization and its social consequences in southwest Paraná. [R. Hoefte]

2888 Freyre, Gilberto. Ferro e civilização no Brasil. Recife, Brazil: Fundação Gilberto Freyre; Rio de Janeiro: Editora Record, 1988. 467 p.: bibl.

Series of essays displays the idiosyncratic and insightful style of Freyre. The theme of iron and steel loosely ties these essays together.

2889 Hemming, John. Amazon frontier: the defeat of the Brazilian Indians. Cambridge, Mass.: Harvard Univ. Press, 1987. 647 p., 22 p. of plates: bibl., ill., index.

Beginning with the 1755 law which freed Indians from slavery and ending with the inauguration of the Indian Protection Service in 1910, this sequel to author's well-known *Red gold: the conquest of the Brazilian Indians (HLAS 42:1648)* covers the history of the contact, conquest, and decimation of numerous indigenous tribes in the 18th and 19th centuries. Comprehensive and well-documented, this book explains the demographic and cultural catastrophe that left less than one million tribal Indians in Brazil by 1910. For anthropologist's comment see *HLAS 51:877.*

2890 História e sexualidade no Brasil. Coordenação de Ronaldo Vainfas. Rio de Janeiro: Graal, 1986. 212 p.: bibl., ill. (Biblioteca de história; 17)

Volume contains ten essays on sexuality in the Brazilian past. Three of the six essays on the colonial period investigate Inquisition records for inferences on sexual beliefs, practices, and morality. Essays for the 19th century address illegitimacy and Church control over sexuality, the social control of prostitution, and the morality of poor women.

2891 Janotti, Maria de Lourdes Monaco and **Suely Robles Reis de Queiroz.** Memória da escravidão em famílias negras de São Paulo. *(Rev. Inst. Estud. Bras., 28, 1988, p. 77–89, graph)*

Description of project carried out in 1987–88 to collect oral histories of black families descended from slaves in the state of São Paulo.

2892 Kiple, Kenneth F. The nutritional link with slave infant and child mortality in Brazil. *(HAHR, 69:4, Nov. 1989, p. 677–690)*

Excellent piece of investigative medical history which establishes that beriberi was endemic in Brazil among the slave population due to a diet based largely on dried beef and manioc flour. Argues that beriberi was a major killer of slave infants and children and bears "much of the blame for the failure of Brazil's slave population to grow by natural means."

2893 Kossoy, Boris. Album de photographias do Estado de São Paulo,1892: estudo crítico. Tradução para o ingles de Annette Jenniffer Baughan. São Paulo: Companhia Brasileira de Projetos e Obras; Livraria Kosmos Editora, 1984. 175 p.: bibl., ill.

Wonderful collection of photographs from the late 19th century accompanied by a brief introductory essay.

2894 Levine, Robert M. Turning on the lights: Brazilian slavery reconsidered

one hundred years after abolition. *(LARR, 24:2, 1989, p. 201–217, bibl.)*

Comprehensive review essay of 14 major works on slavery and abolition occasioned by the centenary of the abolition of slavery in 1988. Provides excellent introduction to the wealth of material recently published on slavery in Brazil.

2895 Modern Brazil: elites and masses in historical perspective. Edited by Michael L. Conniff and Frank D. McCann. Lincoln: Univ. of Nebraska Press, 1989. 305 p.: bibl., ill. (Latin American studies series)

Short essays that serve as good introductions to studies of regional and national economic and political elites, the military, immigrants, urban labor, mass communications, and elite perceptions of the masses.

2896 Queiroz, Suely Robles Reis de. Rebeldia escrava e historiografia. *(Estud. Econ./São Paulo, 17: número especial, 1987, p. 7–35, bibl.)*

Review essay focuses on the emergence of the theme of slave resistance in Brazilian historiography. Queiroz discusses contributions to the study of Brazilian slavery by Clovis Moura, João José Reis (see *HLAS 50:2728*), Leila Mezan Algranti (item **2905**), Stuart Schwartz (item **2960**), and others.

2897 Reis, João José. O levante dos malês na Bahia: uma interpretação política. *(Estud. Econ./São Paulo, 17: número especial, 1987, p. 131–149, bibl.)*

Argues that the 1835 slave revolt in Bahia, despite ethnic and cultural overtones, was a political act as well as a class struggle.

2898 Rodrigues, José Honório. História viva. São Paulo: Global, 1985. 176 p.: bibl., index. (Global universitária: História)

Collection of previously published essays, mostly from newspapers. This is not one of this eminent historian's more important volumes.

2899 Rodrigues, José Honório. Vida e história. São Paulo: Editora Perspectiva, 1986. 277 p. (Col. Debates; 197)

Collection of essays by one of Brazil's most famous historians deals with the history of Rio de Janeiro, Brazilian historiography, and foreign historians.

2900 Samara, Eni de Mesquita. A história da família no Brasil. *(Rev. Bras. Hist., 9:17, set. 1988/fev. 1989, p. 7–35, bibl.)*

Brief review of the development of a history of the family and women in Brazil is accompanied by extensive 260-item bibliography drawn from studies of women and the family published in the last 20 years.

2901 Silva, Maria Beatriz Nizza da. A história da mulher no Brasil: tendências e perspectivas. (*Rev. Inst. Estud. Bras.*, 27, 1987, p. 75–91)

Useful review of the state of women's history in Brazil as of 1987 documents the early role of the Fundação Carlos Chagas in promoting women's history. Author emphasizes influence of historical demography, family history, and everyday life on historians searching for the role of women in the past.

2902 Tavares, Luis Henrique Dias. O capitalismo no comércio proibido de escravos. (*Rev. Inst. Estud. Bras.*, 28, 1988, p. 37–52)

Argues that the slave trade to Brazil continued illegally after the 1830s because the capitalist system needed it, and that the trade ended in 1860s when capitalism had advanced beyond the need for slaves. Weak argument based largely on secondary sources.

2903 Westphalen, Cecília Maria. Martius, o Instituto Histórico e a história regional do Brasil. (*Jahrb. Gesch.*, 25, 1988, p. 695–703)

Short essay on famous article by German naturalist Martius, "How the History of Brazil Should be Written." Sketches origins of the Instituto Histórico e Geográfico Brasileiro, the contest for which Martius wrote his essay in the 1840s, and his argument for a regional approach to Brazilian history.

COLONIAL

2904 Algranti, Leila Mezan. Criminalidade escrava e controle social no Rio de Janeiro, 1810–1821. (*Estud. Econ./São Paulo*, 18: número especial, 1988, p. 45–79, bibl., graphs, tables)

Based on records of police arrests 1810–21, article examines nature and changing pattern of criminality in Rio de Janeiro. Punishment grew more severe during the period as the slave population grew larger and more restive. Praiseworthy synthesis of primary and secondary sources.

2905 Algranti, Leila Mezan. O feitor ausente: estudo sobre a escravidão urbana no Rio de Janeiro. Petrópolis, Brazil: Vozes, 1988. 223 p., 15 p. of plates: bibl., ill., facsims. (História brasileira; 9. Col. Negros em libertação; 5)

Interesting and well-written study of slavery in Rio de Janeiro during the residence of King João VI. Author asks how slavery succeeded in an urban environment where slaves worked largely unsupervised at thousands of tasks throughout the city. Quantitative analysis of individuals sent to prison, 80 percent of whom were slaves, illustrates that the city police, as an organ of the State, took over the role of overseer and controlled the slave population.

2906 Alves Filho, Ivan. Memorial dos Palmares. Rio de Janeiro: Xenon, 1988. 208 p.: bibl. (Col. Memória viva; 2)

Well-researched study argues that the establishment of Palmares in the late 16th century marked the beginning of class struggle in Brazil. Endnotes and bibliography offer valuable leads for further work on the fortified *quilombos* of the Brazilian interior.

2907 Bellini, Ligia. A coisa obscura: mulher, sodomia e inquisição no Brasil colonial. São Paulo: Editora Brasiliense, 1989. 101 p.: bibl.

Initially a master's thesis, this short book focuses on confessions and denunciations of lesbianism during the 1592 visit of the Inquisition to Bahia and Pernambuco. Covers much of the same ground as Vainfas (see item **2965**).

2908 Bosi, Alfredo. Vieira, ou a cruz da desigualdade. (*Novos Estud. CEBRAP*, 25, out. 1989, p. 28–49)

Based primarily on Antônio Vieira's sermons, this essay provides interesting insights into the great Jesuit's thinking, particularly his ideas on economics, social justice, and slavery. Interesting contribution to the extensive literature on Vieira.

2909 Brasil, história econômica e demográfica. Organização de Iraci del Nero da Costa. São Paulo: Instituto de Pesquisas Econômicas, 1986. 322 p.: bibl., ill. (Série Relatórios de pesquisa; 27)

Anthology of new and previously published studies focuses on period from 1750–1888. Contains much useful quantitative information and a degree of coherence greater than is usually found in anthologies.

2910 Carreira, António. A Companhia Geral do Grão-Pará e Maranhão. São Paulo: Companhia Editora Nacional, 1988. 2 v.: bibl., ill. (Brasiliana: Grande formato; 25–26)

Two-volume history of the Grão-Pará e Maranhão monopoly created by the Marquês de Pombal. In vol. 1 analysis shows that the company transported a variety of agricultural products from Maranhão and Pará to Lisbon, and manufactured goods from Lisbon to Africa and Maranhão and Pará. Transcribed documents in vol. 2 include act establishing the company, petitions of merchants against the company, lists of slaves and of the agricultural and manufactured goods transported on the ships, and rolls of the stockholders, merchants, and clients of the company.

2911 Colonial Brazil. Edited by Leslie Bethell. Cambridge; New York: Cambridge Univ. Press, 1987. 398 p.: bibl., ill., index, maps.

This collection of essays by leading scholars first appeared in vols. I and II of the *Cambridge History of Latin America* (see HLAS 48:1808). Convenient and authoritative work with index, brief preface, and a "Note on Currency and Measurement."

2912 Costa, Iraci del Nero da and Nelson Hideiki Nozoe. Elementos da estrutura de posse de escravos em Lorena no alvorecer do século XIX. (*Estud. Econ./São Paulo*, 19:2, maio/agosto 1989, p. 319–345, bibl., tables, graphs)

In-depth quantitative analysis of demography and economics of slaveholding based on the 1801 census of the town of Lorena, São Paulo. Much variation in slave demography can be explained by size of estates on which slaves lived.

2913 Diffie, Bailey W. A history of colonial Brazil, 1500–1792. Malabar, Fla.: R.E. Krieger Pub. Co., 1987. 515 p.: bibl., ill., index.

Posthumously published work by a prominent student of Luso-Brazilian history surveys the era from discovery to the Inconfidencia Mineira. Emphasizes economic evolution of the colony. Includes chapter on music and literature, and a bibliography compiled by Mario Rodriguez. Lacks footnotes.

2914 Estudos Econômicos. Vol. 17, No. 2, maio 1987– . Demografia da Escravidão. São Paulo: Instituto de Pesquisas Econômicas.

Thematic issue which focuses on slave trade and demography of slavery. Of special interest are Herbert Klein's introductory essay; Alida Metcalf's analysis of Santana de Parnaíba; and Iraci Costa, Robert Slenes, and Stuart Schwartz on the slave family. An important, well-integrated journal issue.

2915 Ferlini, Vera Lúcia Amaral. Terra, trabalho e poder: o mundo dos engenhos no Nordeste colonial. São Paulo: Editora Brasiliense; Brasília: Conselho Nacional de Desenvolvimento Científico e Tecnológico, 1988. 271 p.: bibl., ill.

History of the sugar industry in 17th-century Brazilian northeast covers some of the same ground as Schwartz, *Sugar plantations in the formation of Brazilian society* (see *HLAS 48:3422a*). Author contends that sugar industry benefited the Portuguese State and a commercial elite. Plantation owners did not garner fabulous wealth, but were more than adequately compensated with cheap land and control over slave and free labor, which allowed them to dominate colonial society.

2916 Gebara, Ademir. Escravidão: fugas e controle social. (*Estud. Econ./São Paulo*, 18: número especial, 1988, p. 103–146, bibl.)

Based largely on published legislation, this article focuses on mechanisms of social control. Slave flight and urban context of slavery are also discussed.

2917 Girão, Valdelice Carneiro. As oficinas ou charqueadas no Ceará. Fortaleza, Brazil: Secretaria de Cultura e Desporto, 1984. 154 p.: bibl., maps.

Based on a master's thesis written at the Univ. Federal de Pernambuco, this brief but well-researched study examines the dried-beef industry in the Brazilian Northeast. Volume is especially useful for its discussion of the establishment of processing facilities and expansion of the export trade during latter half of the 18th century.

2918 Guimarães, Carlos Magno. Uma negação da ordem escravista: quilombos em Minas Gerais no século XVIII. São Paulo:

Icone Editora, 1988. 171 p.: bibl. (Col. Malungo: Ensaios)

Book focuses on runaway slave communities (*quilombos*) and the men commissioned to capture runaway slaves (*capitães de mato*) in 18th-century Minas Gerais. As the slave population grew in the mining areas, *quilombos* formed. To counteract their spread, an increasing number of men, 15 percent of whom were themselves freed slaves, received commissions as *capitães de mato* to hunt the fugitive slaves. Useful addition to the literature on slave resistance.

2919 Hemming, John. How Brazil acquired Roraima. (*HAHR*, 70:2, May 1990, p. 295–325, maps)

Article reconstructs 18th-century history of the northern Amazon. Hemming explores history of the many Indian tribes and the disastrous Portuguese influence on them, in addition to explaining how Portugal claimed Roraima. Luck and enterprise gave Portugal Roraima, which was closer to the Dutch colony at Guiana and to Spanish Venezuela.

2920 Higgins, Kathleen J. Masters and slaves in a mining society: a study of eighteenth-century Sabará, Minas Gerais. (*Slavery Abolit.*, 2, 1990, p. 58–73)

Very interesting study of slavery in Minas Gerais shows that slaves had considerable autonomy in their daily life and successfully bargained for control of major aspects of the master-slave relationship. The particular conditions of mining society created the possibility for greater slave autonomy, but this autonomy lessened as the region moved away from mining at the end of the 18th century. Important contribution to study of colonial slavery.

2921 Hirano, Sedi. Pré-capitalismo e capitalismo. São Paulo: Hucitec, 1988. 274 p.: bibl. (Estudos históricos)

Book takes up the theoretical question: "was Brazil a society of castes, estates, or classes?" Author reviews work of noted Brazilian intellectuals and finds no common consensus. Diversity of interpretations attests to difficulty of fitting the Brazilian experience into models of historical development formulated for Europe.

2922 Holanda, Sérgio Buarque de. O Extremo Oeste. São Paulo: Brasiliense;

Secretaria de Estado da Cultura, 1986. 172 p.: bibl., ill.

Posthumous publication (begun in 1976 and left unfinished by author) explores westward movement of people from São Paulo who were driven by a struggle against poverty, not a search for glory. Author returns to many of the themes he raised in *Monções* and *Caminhos e fronteiras*, such as Indian slavery, roads and tracks, methods of war, conflict with Indian tribes, and the politics of claiming the Brazilian west.

2923 Horch, Rosemarie Erika. Alexandre Rodrigues Ferreira: um cientista brasileiro do século XVIII. (*Rev. Inst. Estud. Bras.*, 30, 1989, p. 149–159)

Once described as the Brazilian Humboldt, Ferreira spent years on expeditions studying flora and fauna. Brief but useful portrait of an important New World scientist is based solely on secondary sources. Correctly notes need for further study of Ferreira's life and research.

2924 Kuznesof, Elizabeth Anne. A família na sociedade brasileira: parentesco, clientelismo e estrutura social, São Paulo, 1700–1980. (*Rev. Bras. Hist.*, 9:17, set. 1988/fev. 1989, p. 37–63)

Author traces evolution of the elite Brazilian family in São Paulo from the 17th through the 19th century. Kuznesof argues that vertically-integrated family clan gave way to a smaller family in which horizontal linkages among families of the same social class became more important.

2925 Lara, Silvia Hunold. Campos da violência: escravos e senhores na Capitania do Rio de Janeiro, 1750–1808. Rio de Janeiro: Paz e Terra, 1988. 389 p.: bibl. (Col. Oficinas da história)

Well-documented study reexamines question of violence as an inherent component of slavery. Data are used to show various ways in which master and slave interacted in a paternalistic and commercial context.

2926 Leite, Glacyra Lazzari. Pernambuco 1817: estrutura e comportamentos sociais. Prefácio de Manuel Correia de Andrade. Recife, Brazil: Fundação Joaquim Nabuco; Editora Massangana, 1988. 275 p.: bibl. (Série Estudos e pesquisas; 52)

Author places 74-day rebellion against

Portuguese royal authority in Pernambuco in the context of the northeastern economy, social structure, and political ideas of late 18th century. Argues that while the rebellion signaled discontent with the Portuguese colonial system, it did not advocate far-reaching change.

2927 Lewkowicz, Ida. Herança e relações familiares: os pretos forros nas Minas Gerais do século XVIII. (*Rev. Bras. Hist.,* 9:17, set. 1988/fev. 1989, p. 101–114, tables)

Analysis of inventories and wills of free blacks in 18th-century Minas Gerais illustrates that family lives of free blacks did not differ markedly from those of the rest of the free population: free blacks owned slaves; provided dowries for their daughters; requested masses for their souls; and attempted to influence the devolution of family property through inheritance.

2928 Lima, Lana Lage da Gama. O Santo Ofício e a moralização do clero no Brasil colonial. (*Vozes,* 83:6, nov./dez. 1989, p. 693–703)

Focuses on clerics who solicted women during confession. Women would reveal this to other confessors, who passed word to the Inquisition. The confessional thereby afforded inquisitors a means of policing clerical morality and extending their authority, even to remote regions.

2929 Lipiner, Elias. Gaspar da Gama: um converso na frota de Cabral. Rio de Janeiro: Editora Nova Fronteira, 1987. 276 p.: bibl., ill., facsims., ports.

Chronicles the contributions of Jews and New Christians to the expansion of Portuguese empire in the 15th and 16th centuries. Despite persecution of Jews during reign of Manuel I, the king relied on Jews and New Christians as important links between Portugal and the Orient. One such figure was Gaspar da Gama, who accompanied Cabral on his 1500 sortie for India.

2930 Lopes, Eliane Marta Santos Teixeira. Colonizador-colonizado: uma relação educativa no movimento da história. Belo Horizonte, Brazil: Editora UFMG, 1985. 259 p.: bibl., ill. (Série Teses)

Examines political and social environment in Minas Gerais during 18th century, using a loose Marxian framework. Concludes by stressing Crown's use of education to subject the unruly populace of the captaincy. Adequately researched, but sources are not well digested.

2931 Luna, Francisco Vidal. Estrutura de posse de escravos e atividades produtivas em Jacareí, 1777 a 1829. (*Rev. Inst. Estud. Bras.,* 28, 1988, p. 23–35, graphs, tables)

Quantitative analysis of slaveholders and slaves in three manuscript censuses of Jacareí, São Paulo, as coffee cultivation spread in early 19th century. Like articles in *Demografia da Escravidão* (item **2914**), it provides important local data that challenge conventional assumptions about slavery in São Paulo.

2932 Marcílio, Maria Luiza. Caiçara: terra e população; estudo de demografia histórica e da história social de Ubatuba. São Paulo: Edições Paulinas; CEDHAL, 1986. 244 p.: bibl., ill. (Col. Raízes)

Pioneering study of social history and historical demography of a Brazilian fishing and farming community from late 18th to mid-19th century focuses on themes of land ownership, inheritance, and subsistence and cash-crop farming, as well as on demographic history of the population. Work is particularly useful for light it sheds on survival strategies and family lives of "free poor" or peasant population of late colonial Brazil.

2933 Meireles, Denise Maldi. Guardiães da fronteira: Rio Guaporé, século XVIII. Petrópolis, Brazil: Vozes, 1989. 213 p.: bibl., ill., maps.

Examines Portuguese activity on Brazil's western frontier. Spanish missions, Portuguese fortifications, and beleaguered Indians comprise the main subjects. Contains useful maps and artists' renderings of indigenous peoples.

2934 Mello, Evaldo Cabral de. O nome e o sangue: uma fraude genealógica no Pernambuco colonial. São Paulo: Companhia das Letras, 1989. 363 p.: bibl., index.

Excellent study shows how powerful Brazilian families dealt with fetish for purity of blood, lack of which would have threatened to undercut their social ambitions. In this case, story involves genealogical coverup. Mello skillfully traces roots of the Pais Barreto and other clans, while illuminating impinging events, particularly the War of the Mascates.

2935 Mendonça, Marcos Carneiro de. Século XVIII: século pombalino do Brasil. Rio de Janeiro: Xerox, 1989. 801 p.: bibl. (Biblioteca reprográfica Xerox; 29)

Posthumously published, volume brings together 392 documents selected from archival collections and printed sources. Documents date from 1623 to ca. 1780 and illuminate matters of colonial administration, diplomacy, and economics. Valuable essay introduces this convenient and important compilation.

2936 Metcalf, Alida C. Between the kingdom and the wilderness: the *mentalité* of settlers in colonial São Paulo. (*in* The middle period in Latin America: values and attitudes in the 17th-19th centuries. Edited by Mark D. Szuchman. Boulder, Colo.: Lynne Rienner Publishers, 1989, p. 103–121)

Discusses how concepts of kingdom (*reino*), town (*vila*), and wilderness (*sertão*) shaped the "mental map" of people of Santana de Parnaíba, São Paulo.

2937 Metcalf, Alida C. Women and means: women and family property in colonial Brazil. (*J. Soc. Hist.*, 24:2, Winter 1990, p. 277–298, graph, table)

Interesting and richly detailed analysis of female property owners (single, married, and widowed) in colonial Santana de Parnaíba, São Paulo, and their ability to exercise rights to family property in a patriarchal society. Highlights contradition between their legal rights to property and their lack of a public voice.

2938 Miller, Joseph Calder. Way of death: merchant capitalism and the Angolan slave trade, 1730–1830. Madison, Wis.: Univ. of Wisconsin Press, 1988. 770 p.: bibl., ill., index.

Ambitious book weaves together economic, social, and demographic history to reconstruct complex interactions between Africans, Luso-Africans, Brazilians, Portuguese, Asians, and British involved in 18th-century slave trade from Luanda, Angola. Of particular interest are Miller's discussions of the functioning of this global trade, the African perceptions of slavery, the complicated power relationships between parties at each stage of the trade, financing of the trade, and the devastating mortality rate of slaves. Miller suggests that of the slaves originally captured in Africa, only half ever reached Brazil; after three to four years only one-third still remained alive.

2939 Monteiro, John M. Distribuição da riqueza e as origens da pobreza rural em São Paulo, século XVIII. (*Estud. Econ./São Paulo*, 19:1, jan./abril 1989, p. 109–130, bibl., tables)

Based on analysis of late 17th-century tax lists (*donativo real*), article investigates rural society and distribution of wealth in São Paulo. Contrary to prevailing view of 17th-century São Paulo as poor and without great distinctions of wealth, author finds significant inequality among free population, with the majority living barely above subsistence and hardly better than the Indian slaves who labored on estates of wealthy families.

2940 Monteiro, John M. From Indian to slave: forced native labour and colonial society in São Paulo during the seventeenth century. (*Slavery Abolit.*, 9:2, Sept. 1988, p. 105–127)

Excellent overview of Indian slavery in São Paulo's formative 17th century which contrasts with traditional histories of the period. Monteiro focuses on Indians captured from their tribal homelands who became the laborers of the colonists of São Paulo. Author investigates ambiguous legal status of the Indians (legally free but in reality enslaved) as well as relations between masters and slaves and slave resistance.

2941 Montenegro, João Alfredo de Sousa. Padre Mororó: o político e o jornalista. Fortaleza, Brazil: Associação Cearense de Impr., 1985. 122 p.

Biography of leading proponent of republicanism in Ceará ties his liberalism to reforms of the Pombaline era and details his contribution to journalism, particularly establishment of the *Diário do Governo do Ceará*. Typographical errors notwithstanding, study stands as a useful intellectual portrait.

2942 Mott, Luiz Roberto de Barros. Escravidão, homossexualidade e demonologia. São Paulo: Icone Editora, 1988. 151 p.: bibl. (Col. Malungo. Ensaios)

Collection of essays focuses on social outcasts of colonial Brazil: slaves, heretics, and homosexuals. Mott uses Inquisition trials to discuss witchcraft, sexual crimes (prostitution, homosexuality, bigamy, incest), and religious syncretism.

2943 Nazzari, Muriel. Dotes paulistas: composição e transformações, 1600–1870. (*Rev. Bras. Hist.*, 9:17, set. 1988/fev. 1989, p. 87–100, graphs, tables)

Through an extensive analysis of dowries granted in 17th, 18th, and 19th-century São Paulo, Nazzari documents a shift in the role and function of the dowry. In the 17th century daughters received large dowries which contained productive property such as slaves, while in the 19th century dowries were smaller and favored goods for consumption. This change resulted from the declining authority of the family patriarch and the changing roles of families.

2944 Nazzari, Muriel. Parent and daughters: change in the practice of dowry in São Paulo, 1600–1770. (*HAHR*, 70:4, Nov. 1990, p. 639–665, tables)

Detailed study clearly documents two important but disregarded aspects of marriage in São Paulo: 1) marriage and family relationships changed over time; and 2) parents favored daughters over sons. In this and a related article (item **2943**), Nazzari provides a major addition to family and women's history in colonial Latin America.

2945 Novais, Fernando A.; John R. Hall; and Luís Carlos Soares. Brazil and the world system. Edited with an introduction by Richard Graham. Austin: Univ. of Texas Press, 1991. 123 p.: bibl., index. (Critical reflections on Latin America series)

Brings together three theoretical pieces on colonial Brazilian economic and political history. Excellent translation of Fernando Novais' work provides English-speaking readers with the theoretical framework of his *Portugal e Brasil na crise do antigo sistema colonial* (see *HLAS 44:3526*). John Hall writes on the patrimonial character of colonial Brazil, while Luís Carlos Soares explicates the concepts of the slave mode of production, dependency theory, and the notion of a Brazilian nation in the works of prominent Brazilian historians.

2946 Novinski, Anita. Jewish roots of Brazil. (*in* The Jewish presence in Latin America. Edited by Judith Laikin Elkin and

Gilbert W. Merkx. Boston: Allen & Unwin, 1987, p. 33–44)

Brief overview of New Christians in colonial Brazil argues that although New Christians found wealth and social mobility in Brazil, they remained a marginalized and persecuted group. Despite the sustained numbers and considerable skills of New Christians, the Inquisition's obsession with eradicating Judaism prevented the survival of a Jewish culture in Brazil.

2947 Nunes, Maria Thetis. Sergipe colonial. v. 1. Rio de Janeiro: Tempo Brasileiro; Aracaju, Brazil: Univ. Federal de Sergipe, 1989. 1 v.: bibl., ill.

Vol. 1 of a survey history contains 11 thematic chapters which focus on the socioeconomic life of the captaincy. A well-researched but not so well-synthesized study.

2948 Oliveira, Elza Régis de. A Paraíba na crise do século XVIII: subordinação e autonomia, 1755–1799. Prefácio de Rosa Maria Godoy Silveira. Fortaleza, Brazil: Banco do Nordeste do Brasil, Escritório Técnico de Estudos Econômicos do Nordeste, 1985. 174 p.: bibl., ill. (Série Documentos do Nordeste; 6)

Book examines subordination of Paraíba to Pernambuco in second half of 18th century. Pombaline policies for cutting costs and streamlining bureaucracy appended Paraíba to Pernambuco but did little to solve economic problems of Paraíba. After restoration of the captaincy of Paraíba in 1799, the legacy of dependence on Pernambuco proved difficult to break.

2949 Palacios, Guillermo. Campesinato e escravidão: uma proposta de periodização para a história dos cultivadores pobres livres no Nordeste oriental do Brasil, c. 1700–1875. (*Dados*, 30:3, 1987, p. 325–356, bibl.)

Analysis of the peasants of the Northeast focuses on the place of free laborers in an agricultural society dominated by slavery. Role of the free poor changed over time as once autonomous peasants became subordinated to large planters. Offers framework for understanding this process as well as the emergence of popular revolts.

2950 Peregalli, Enrique. Recrutamento militar no Brasil colonial. Campinas, Brazil: Editora da UNICAMP, 1986. 184 p.: bibl., ill., maps. (Teses)

Cast in a dependency-theory mold, this well-documented study focuses on recruitment in São Paulo during latter half of 18th century. Attention is paid to supply, payment, promotion of recruits, and popular resistance to military service. Concludes by listing deleterious effects of recruitment born of the process of capital accumulation.

2951 Piazza, Walter Fernando. O Brigadeiro José da Silva Paes: estruturador do Brasil meridional. Florianópolis, Brazil: Editora da UFSC; Edições FCC; Rio Grande, Brazil: Editora da FURG, 1988. 172 p.: bibl., ill.

Based primarily on archival research, study provides new details on life and career of the renowned engineer and colonial official. Especially useful is chapter on Pais' fortification of the island of Santa Catarina.

2952 Priore, Mary del. A maternidade da mulher negra no período colonial brasileiro. São Paulo: Univ. de São Paulo, Centro de Estudos de Demografia Histórica da América Latina (CEDHAL), 1989. (Estudos CEDHAL; 4)

After a short introduction, author presents a unique document: a treatise on childbirth written by a Portuguese doctor in Pernambuco in late 17th century.

2953 Proença, Maria Cândida. A independência do Brasil: relações externas portuguesas, 1808–1825. Lisboa: Livros Horizonte, 1987. 135 p.: bibl. (Col. Horizonte histórico; 12)

Slim volume focuses on how political decisions were made in Portugal 1808–25, and notes the limited maneuverability of Portuguese political leaders given the antagonistic positions of powerful groups in Brazil, Portugal, and Great Britain. Because of their ignorance of changing economic relationships, Portuguese leaders stubbornly resisted a moderate political approach to Brazil. They paid for their errors with the complete independence of Brazil and an even greater Portuguese dependence on Britain.

2954 Queiroz, Maria Luiza Bertulini. A Vila do Rio Grande de São Pedro, 1737–1822. Prefácio de João José Planella. Rio Grande, Brazil: Editora da Fundação Univ. do Rio Grande, 1987. 191 p.: bibl., ill., facsims., maps, tables.

Detailed portrait of a heterogenous and fluid community on Brazil's southern-most frontier is of special interest for data provided in numerous tables.

2955 Ramos, Donald. Slavery in Brazil: a case study of Diamantina, Minas Gerais. (*Americas/Francisc.*, 45 : 1, July 1988, p. 47–59, bibl., tables)

Based on a register of slaves, Ramos finds that mortality for slaves employed in the diamond mines was extremely high, although not as high as historians have supposed. Runaway rates for slaves also registered high. Both rates varied by ethnic groups of slaves: Angolan slaves had highest mortality while Sabaru slaves were most likely to run away.

2956 Rodríguez-Pantoja Márquez, Miguel et al. José de Anchieta: vida y obra. Edición de Francisco González Luis. La Laguna, Spain: Ayuntamiento de San Cristóbal de La Laguna, 1988. 482 p.: bibl., ill., index. (Publicaciones del Excmo. Ayuntamiento de San Cristóbal de La Laguna)

Spanish-language collection of seven essays on Padre Anchieta stands as a valuable addition to literature on the pioneer Jesuit. An anthology of his texts follows the essays.

2957 Russell-Wood, A.J.R. Prestige, power, and piety in colonial Brazil: the Third Orders of Salvador. (*HAHR*, 69 : 1, Feb. 1989, p. 61–89)

For the men and women who joined the "Third Orders" or the lay brotherhoods of St. Francis, St. Dominic, and the Carmelites in colonial Brazil, the orders marked their social status; provided a focus for religious participation; guaranteed Christian burial; and encouraged charitable acts. Screened according to purity of blood, members represented the white, Old Christian population of the colony.

2958 Schäffer, Dagmar. Portuguese exploration to the West and the formation of Brazil, 1450–1800: catalogue of an exhibition. Providence: J.C. Brown Library, 1988. 86 p.: ill.

Catalog written to accompany exhibition of John Carter Brown Library's holdings of rare manuscripts pertaining to Portuguese navigation and colonization in Brazil. First formal introduction to the Brazilian collection consists of annotations of nine catalog sections, each introduced with a brief historical narrative, and good annotations of 102 items from exhibition.

2959 Schwartz, Stuart B. The formation of a colonial identity in Brazil. (*in* Colonial identity in the Atlantic World 1500–1800. Edited by Nicholas Canny and Anthony Pagden. Princeton: Princeton Univ. Press, 1987, p. 15–50)

Explores emergence of a Brazilian identity primarily among those of Portuguese descent in Brazil. Argues that earliest manifestation of "separateness" from Portugal occurred in the peripheries (São Paulo and Maranhão) and was expressed in action rather than thought. Colonial self-awareness emerged later in the core areas where ties to Portugal were stronger.

2960 Schwartz, Stuart B. Mocambos, Quilombos e Palmares: a resistência escrava no Brasil colonial. (*Estud. Econ./São Paulo*, 17: número especial, 1987, p. 61–88, bibl., ill., table)

Updated, Portuguese-language version of author's 1970 (see *HLAS 34:2964b*) article on runaway slave communities in Brazil. Useful addition to studies of *quilombos* and slave resistance in colonial Brazil.

2961 Schwartz, Stuart B. The voyage of the vassals: royal power, noble obligations and merchant capital before the Portuguese restoration of independence, 1624–1640. (*Am. Hist. Rev.*, 96:3, June 1991, p. 735–762)

Though focused primarily on the Iberian Peninsula, this article stands as an impressive synthesis of documentary and published sources on an especially complex and turbulent era in Luso-Brazilian history. Must reading for its discussion of conflict between noble and bourgeois interests.

2962 Silva, Maria Beatriz Nizza da. Divorce in colonial Brazil: the case of São Paulo. (*in* Sexuality and marriage in colonial Latin America. Edited by Asunción Lavrin. Lincoln, Neb.: Univ. of Nebraska Press, 1989, p. 313–340)

Revised version of a chapter in author's 1984 book *Sistema de casamento no Brasil colonial* (São Paulo: Editora da Univ. de São Paulo), article investigates 88 petitions for divorce in ecclesiastical court of São Paulo. Women who had been severely mistreated by their husbands initiated most divorce cases, but by end of 18th century divorce by mutual consent became more common. Interesting for its portrayal of marriage in colonial society.

2963 Souza, Laura de Mello e. O diabo e a Terra de Santa Cruz: feitiçaria e religiosidade popular no Brasil colonial. São Paulo: Companhia das Letras, 1986. 396 p.: bibl.

Major work on social history of colonial Brazil uses ecclesiastical and Inquisitional sources to investigate popular religious phenomena from late 16th through 18th centuries. Focusing on Bahia, Minas Gerais, and Maranhão, author illustrates how Indian, African, and Portuguese traditions of magic, sorcery, witchcraft, and healing, as well as beliefs in the devil, the saints, heaven, and hell, became part of the culture of colonial Brazil. Richly informed by the work of European historians and extensively documented with material from Inquisition and ecclesiastical archives, this book is first serious study of the *mentalité* in colonial Brazil.

2964 Trevisan, Amélia Franzolin. Casa Branca, a povoação dos ilhéus. São Paulo: Edições Arquivo do Estado, 1982. 156 p.: bibl., ill. (Col. Monografias; 4)

Originally a Univ. of São Paulo dissertation, study provides much useful information on Azorean settlement of the *freguesia* of Nossa Senhora das Dores de Casa Branca.

2965 Vainfas, Ronaldo. Sodomia, mulheres e inquisição: notas sobre sexualidade e homossexualismo feminino no Brasil colonial. (*An. Mus. Paul.*, 35, 1986/1987, p. 233–249, tables)

Study of the 29 women who confessed to or who were accused of lesbianism in the 1591 Inquisitorial visit to Bahia. Author uses these cases, unusual in the annals of the Inquisition, to explore issues of female sexuality and morality in colonial Brazil.

Whitehead, Peter James Palmer and **M. Boeseman.** A portrait of Dutch 17th-century Brazil: animals, plants, and people by the artists of Johan Maurits of Nassau. See *HLAS 51:3327*.

NATIONAL

2966 Addor, Carlos Augusto. A insurreição anarquista no Rio de Janeiro. Rio de Janeiro: Dois Pontos Editora, 1986. 219 p.: bibl.

Unrevised version of master's thesis written in 1985 at Univ. Federal Fluminense on 1918 anarchist uprising in Rio de Janeiro. After a discussion of the literature on the insurrection and anarchism in Brazil from 1900–20, final third of book analyzes the insurrection and its impact, relying largely on the *Jornal do Brasil* and anarchist publications.

2967 Alvim, Zuleika M.F. Brava gente!: os italianos em São Paulo, 1870–1920. São Paulo: Brasiliense, 1986. 189 p., 1 folded leaf of plates: bibl., ill.

Social history of Italian immigration to São Paulo looks at the immigrants' lives in Italy, in passage, and in the Brazilian city and countryside. Using excellent research work from Italian and Brazilian archives, emphasizes resistance of immigrants to oppressive social conditions.

2968 Andrade, Silvia Maria Belfort Vilela de. Classe operária em Juiz de Fora: uma história de lutas, 1912–1924. Juiz de Fora, Brazil: Editora da Univ. Federal de Juiz de Fora, 1987. 201 p., 10 p. of plates: bibl., ill.

Solid study of formation of an industrial working class in Minas Gerais focuses on three major strikes (1912, 1920, 1924) in the major industrial center of Minas in the early 20th century.

O Apostolado positivista e a República. See item **5403.**

Araújo, José Carlos Sousa. Igreja Católica no Brasil: um estudo de mentalidade ideológica. See item **5404.**

2969 Arquivo Histórico do Rio Grande do Sul. Coletânea de documentos de Bento Gonçalves da Silva, 1835–1845. Porto Alegre, Brazil: Arquivo Histórico do Rio Grande do Sul; Estado do Rio Grande do Sul, Comissão Executiva do Sesquicentenário da Revolução Farroupilha, 1985. 335 p.: ill., indexes.

Correspondence of one of the major figures in the *Farroupilha* (Ragamuffin) War in southern Brazil.

2970 O Arquivo José Américo e a revolução de 30: reprodução de cópias telegráficas, cartas, ofícios e notas diversas. Coordenação de Ana Isabel de Souza Leão Andrade. João Pessoa, Brazil: Fundação Casa de José Américo, 1985. 225 p.: ill., index, ports.

Reproduces telegrams, letters, and notes from the collection of one of the key political figures in the 1930 revolution. Most of the documents are very brief and not very revealing.

2971 Azevedo, Celia Maria Marinho de. Onda negra, medo branco: o negro no imaginário das elites; século XIX. Prefácio de Peter Eisenberg. Rio de Janeiro: Paz e Terra, 1987. 267 p.: bibl. (Col. Oficinas da história; 6)

Excellent analysis of elite perceptions of blacks in 19th-century Brazil demonstrates prevalence of racism among both pro-slave and abolitionist elites. Places emphasis on blacks, slave and free, as historical actors. Solid revisionist critique of studies of race relations by São Paulo "school" in the 1960s.

2972 Azzi, Riolando. A Igreja e os migrantes. v. 1, A imigração italiana e os primórdios da obra escalabriniana no Brasil, 1884–1904. São Paulo: Edições Paulinas, 1987. 1 v.: bibl.

Detailed history of the Congregation of Missionaries of St. Charles in southern Brazil places work of these Italian missionaries within the context of Italian immigration to Brazil and efforts of the Vatican to reform the Brazilian Catholic Church in late 19th century. Material is drawn primarily from the Scalabrinian archives in Rome.

2973 Barbosa, Francisco de Assis. Juscelino Kubitschek: uma revisão na política brasileira: formação e ascensão: com 20 ilustrações. v. 1. Rio de Janeiro: Editora Guanabara, 1988. 320 p.: bibl., ill.

New edition of first volume of projected three-volume biography begins with arrival of Kubitschek's great-grandfather to Brazil in early 19th century and ends with Revolution of 1932. The distinguished author is working on vol. 2 which will cover period from 1932 to end of Kubitschek's presidency.

2974 Barman, Roderick J. Brazil: the forging of a nation, 1798–1852. Stanford, Calif.: Stanford Univ. Press, 1988. 334 p.: bibl., index, maps.

Traditional political history emphasizes the role of external factors in the creation of the nation-state, and the struggle to consolidate the Brazilian nation from the 1820s to the 1850s. The most comprehensive survey of Brazilian history in the first half of the 19th century in English.

2975 Benevides, Maria Victoria de Mesquita. O PTB e o trabalhismo: partido e sindicato em São Paulo, 1945–1964. São Paulo: Editora Brasiliense; CEDEC, 1989. 171 p.: bibl.

Solid survey of struggles for control of PTB in São Paulo by supporters of Getúlio Vargas, Jânio Quadros, and Ademar de Barros. Brief and fairly general study has minimal scholarly apparatus.

2976 Besse, Susan K. Crimes of passion: the campaign against wife-killing in Brazil, 1910–1940. (*J. Soc. Hist.*, 22:4, Summer 1989, p. 653–666)

Argues that middle-class reformers' desire to impose modern, hygienic standards of sex and family life and to legitimate hierarchical nuclear family lay behind campaign to punish wife-killers. Analysis is qualitative rather than quantitative.

2977 Blass, Leila Maria da Silva. Imprimindo a própria história: o movimento dos trabalhadores gráficos de São Paulo no final dos anos 20. São Paulo: Edições Loyola, 1986. 127 p.: bibl. (Col. Brasil dos trabalhadores; 5)

Brief study of workers' movement in the printing industry during 1920s is based primarily on sources in the Arquivo Edgard Leuenroth. Emphasizes efforts of workers to organize and of dominant classes to combat organization.

2978 Bomeny, Helena Maria Bousquet. Uma entrevista com Richard Morse. (*Estud. Hist./Rio de Janeiro*, 3, 1989, p. 77–93)

Fascinating interview with one of the foremost US historians of Latin America provides wonderful insights into how Latin America is studied in the US.

2979 Boni, Elvira et al. Velhos militantes: depoimentos. Coordenação de Angela Maria de Castro Gomes. Colaboração de Dora Flaksman e Eduardo Navarro Stotz. Rio de Janeiro: J. Zahar, 1988. 204 p., 8 p. of plates: ill. (Antropologia social)

Fascinating set of interviews with four former militants in working-class movements in early 20th century.

2980 Borges, Vavy Pacheco. Tenentes, tenentismo, tenentismo versus oligar-

quia: reflexões para uma revisão historiográfica. (*An. Mus. Paul.*, 34, 1985, p. 105–143)

Valuable review of historiography of *tenentes* movement examines important writings by Brazilians and North Americans.

2981 Brazil: empire and republic, 1822–1930. Edited by Leslie Bethell. Cambridge, England; New York: Cambridge Univ. Press, 1989. 353 p.: bibl., ill.

Originally published as parts of vols. 3 and 5 of *Cambridge History of Latin America* (1985–86), this is an indispensable source for state of the discipline, with sections by Bethell, José Murilo de Carvalho, Richard Graham, Emília Viotti da Costa, Warren Dean, and Boris Fausto. Invaluable bibliographies, especially for advanced undergraduates and graduate students.

2982 Brazilian women speak: contemporary life stories. Interviews edited and translated by Daphne Patai. New Brunswick, N.J.: Rutgers Univ. Press, 1988. 398 p.: bibl., index.

Using richly detailed oral histories, Patai weaves a fascinating account of life in modern Brazil. Extensive notes and short introductions provide essential background information on race, religion, politics, work, family life, and sexuality. Excellent for classroom use.

2983 Cabral, Francisco Pinto. Plácido de Castro e o Acre brasileiro. Brasília: Thesaurus, 1986. 147 p., 1 folded leaf of plates: bibl., ill.

Simplistic and hagiographic account of the central military figure in the annexation of Acre at the beginning of the 20th century.

2984 Campos, Cristina Hebling. O sonhar libertário: movimento operário nos anos de 1917 a 1921. Campinas, Brazil: Pontes Editores; Editora da Univ. Estadual de Campinas, 1988. 189 p.: bibl., ill.

Diffuse and superficial analysis of anarchist labor movement in Rio de Janeiro and São Paulo (1917–21) is based on secondary sources and newspapers.

2985 Carneiro, Maria Luiza Tucci. O antisemitismo na era Vargas: fantasmas de uma geração, 1930–1945. Prefácio de Antonio Candido. São Paulo: Editora Brasiliense, 1988. 590 p.: bibl., ill.

Important and controversial analysis

of antisemitism in Brazilian politics and society argues that nationalism served as a mask for antisemitism that appeared in politics and in xenophobia of the era. Based on archival research, makes extensive use of periodical literature and interviews.

2986 Carone, Edgard. Classes sociais e movimento operário. São Paulo: Editora Atica, 1989. 309 p.: bibl. (Série Fundamentos; 40)

Study of the labor movement in the 1920s emphasizes role of the Brazilian Communist Party (PCB). Traditional labor history sticks close to the documents.

2987 Carone, Edgard. Literatura e público. (*Rev. Novos Rumos*, 3:8/9, 1988, p. 117–135)

Analysis of four notebooks in the Astrojildo Pereira Archive in Milan concerning distribution of leftist literature in Brazil during 1920s and 1930s. Interesting look at the kinds of literature that were available for the left.

2988 Carone, Edgard. Movimento operário no Brasil. v. 3, 1964–1984. São Paulo: DIFEL, 1984. 1 v.: bibl. (Corpo e alma do Brasil; 56, 59)

Third and final volume in series on Brazilian labor movement contains documents from groups that emerged out of the Brazilian Communist Party (PCB) and other leftist groups (VPR, POLOP, AP, and Trotskyists). Final section on 1980s focuses principally on the Partido dos Trabalhadores (PT).

2989 Carvalho, José Murilo de. Pueblo y política en Río de Janeiro en el cambio de siglo. Traducido del portugués por Luciana Daelli. (*in* Nuevas perspectivas en los estudios sobre historia urbana latinoamericana. Buenos Aires: Instituto Internacional de Medio Ambiente y Desarrollo (IIED)-América Latina, 1989, p. 91–123, tables)

Sophisticated and stimulating essay discusses seeming lack of political participation by the masses in Rio de Janeiro. Places city's population in comparative perspective and turns to sociological theories to explain differences from other major cities in Europe, North America, and Latin America.

2990 Carvalho, José Murilo de. Teatro de sombras: a política imperial. Rio de Janeiro: IUPERJ; São Paulo: Vértice, 1988. 196

p.: appendices, bibl., graphs, ill., tables. (Formação do Brasil; 4)

Thought-provoking and important study deals with the functioning of political power in the Empire by focusing on imperial finances, abolition, land policy, the Council of State, and electoral politics. For political scientist's comment see *HLAS 51:4036.*

2991 A Casa do Pinhal. Editado por Margarida Cintra Gordinho. São Paulo: Editora C.H. Knapp, 1985. 179 p.: bibl., ill. (some col.).

Beautifully-produced volume with lavish photographs celebrates the bicentennial of the Pinhal *fazenda* of the elite Arruda Botelho family near São Carlos, São Paulo. Exceptional, if uncritical, documentation of elite life on an evolving *paulista* coffee *fazenda*.

2992 Casalecchi, José Enio. O Partido Republicano Paulista: política e poder, 1889–1926. São Paulo: Editora Brasiliense, 1987. 325 p.: appendices, bibl., ill.

Valuable source on the party (PRP) that controlled state politics in São Paulo during the First Republic. Chapters on structure and organization of the party and appendices on political leaders are especially useful. Based largely on research in newspapers.

2993 Castello Branco: testemunhos de uma época. Organização e prefácio de Luiz Viana Filho. Revisão de Alberto de los Santos. Brasília: Editora da Univ. de Brasília, 1986. 116 p. (Col. Temas brasileiros; 61)

Series of brief essays by friends and associates remembering General Humberto Castelo Branco emphasizes his personality rather than his political or military career. Includes essays by Lincoln Gordon and Vernon Walters, among others.

2994 Castro, Hebe Maria Mattos de. Ao sul da história. São Paulo: Editora Brasiliense, 1987. 190 p.: bibl., graphs, map, tables.

Important work on a poorly-studied topic: smallholders and peasants. This analysis (largely based on wills) of the *município* of Capivary in 19th-century Rio de Janeiro province emphasizes relative autonomy of *lavradores* prior to decline of slavery in late 19th century.

2995 Castro, Hebe Maria Mattos de. Beyond masters and slaves: subsistence agriculture as survival strategy in Brazil during the second half of the nineteenth century. (*HAHR*, 68:3, Aug. 1988, p. 462–489, tables)

Case study of the *município* of Nossa Senhora da Lapa da Capivary, Rio de Janeiro, uses notarial records. After comparing Capivary with other cases, author maintains that "the ease of access [for free labor] to alternative survival strategies, made possible by the abundance of land, determined the persistence of slavery in the Southeast, and not the other way around."

2996 Cobbs, Elizabeth A. Entrepreneurship as diplomacy: Nelson Rockefeller and the development of the Brazilian capital market. (*Bus. Hist. Rev.*, 63:1, Spring 1989, p. 88–121, photos, tables)

Examines a mutual fund (Fundo Crescinco) started by Rockefeller in Brazil to promote economic development through expansion of private enterprise. Argues that the effort reflects liberal assumptions about the importance of the middle class in economic and political development. Interesting analysis of entrepreneurship as an extension of diplomacy is grounded in private business archives and interviews in Brazil and US.

2997 A condição feminina no Rio de Janeiro, século XIX: antologia de textos de viajantes estrangeiros. Organização de Miriam Moreira Leite. São Paulo: Editora HUCITEC; Instituto Nacional do Livro; Fundação Nacional Pró-Memória, Brasília, 1984. 191 p.: bibl., ill. (Col. Estudos históricos)

Selections from travel accounts are organized around topics of kinship, preparation for adult life, work activities, and social life. Interesting introductory essay and bibliography. Excellent resource for those interested in Brazilian women's history.

2998 Dean, Warren. The green wave of coffee: beginnings of tropical agricultural research in Brazil, 1885–1900. (*HAHR*, 69:1, Feb. 1989, p. 91–115)

Fine analysis of the creation and early travails of the Agronomic Institute of the State of São Paulo shows how Brazil missed the opportunity to become a leading center for research on coffee production, to make production more profitable, and to promote regional economic and social development.

2999 Decca, Maria Auxiliadora Guzzo. A vida fora das fábricas: cotidiano operá-

rio em São Paulo, 1920/1934. Rio de Janeiro: Editora Paz e Terra, 1987. 135 p.: bibl. (Col. Oficinas da história; 3)

Interesting study of the daily life of workers in São Paulo focuses is on housing, salaries, cost of living, hygiene, leisure, and the workers' press.

3000 Derengoski, Paulo Ramos. O desmoronamento do mundo jagunço. Florianópolis, Brazil: FCC Edições, 1986. 166 p.: bibl., ill., photos, ports.

Journalistic and superficial account of the Contestado revolt in Santa Catarina and Paraná in early 20th century.

3001 Dias, Maria Odila Leite da Silva. Quotidiano e poder em São Paulo no século XIX: Ana Gertrudes de Jesus. Prefácio de Ecléa Bosi. São Paulo: Brasiliense, 1984. 198 p., 8 p. of plates: bibl., ill.

Fine social history of roles of women, especially of the lower classes, in 19th-century São Paulo makes excellent use of local archival documents, travel accounts, and secondary sources.

3002 Dillenburg, Sérgio Roberto. A imprensa em Porto Alegre de 1845 a 1870. Porto Alegre, Brasil: Editora Sulina, 1987. 59 p.: bibl. (Col. Estante de comunicação social; 17)

Primarily a catalog and description of the newspapers published in Porto Alegre during this period.

3003 Drosdoff, Daniel. Linha dura no Brasil: o governo Médici, 1969–1974. São Paulo: Global, 1986. 175 p.: bibl.

Journalistic account of the Médici presidency is based on interviews, press accounts, and secondary sources.

3004 Drummond, José Augusto. O movimento tenentista: intervenção militar e conflito hierárquico, 1922–1935. Rio de Janeiro: Graal, 1986. 344 p.: bibl., ill. (Biblioteca de ciências sociais; 30)

Study by a political scientist argues that the *tenente* movement in the 1920s and 1930s produced a grave political division in the hierarchy of the Brazilian military. This split prevented the military from acting decisively in national politics during the period. Emphasis is more on analysis of the military and its internal dynamics than on historical processes.

3005 Eakin, Marshall C. British enterprise in Brazil: the St. John d'el Rey Mining Company and the Morro Velho Gold Mine, 1830–1960. Durham, N.C.: Duke Univ. Press, 1989. 334 p., 8 p. of plates: bibl., ill., index.

Study of one of the most successful foreign companies ever to operate in Brazil. First half of book analyzes the company, and the second half its impact on the surrounding community and region. Extensive use of company, local, and regional archives.

3006 A esquerda e o movimento operário, 1964/1984. v. 1, A resistência à ditadura, 1964–1971. Organização de Celso Frederico. São Paulo: Editora Novos Rumos, 1987. 1 v.

Valuable collection of documents deals with relations between diverse leftist groups and workers' movements, emphasizing urban workers and the city of São Paulo. Most of these documents are not readily available in any other form.

3007 Falcão, Armando. Tudo a declarar. Rio de Janeiro: Editora Nova Fronteira, 1989. 435 p., 8 p. of plates: ill.

Memoir by former Minister of Justice under Presidents Juscelino Kubitschek and Ernesto Geisel provides important insider account of politics in Brazil since the 1930s.

3008 Falcão, João. O Partido Comunista que eu conheci: 20 anos de clandestinidade. Rio de Janeiro: Civilização Brasileira, 1988. 460 p.: ill., ports.

Important memoir of key figure in the Communist Party covers period from late 1930s to late 1950s. Very detailed insider account is augmented by material from dozens of interviews by the author with former activists.

3009 Félix, Loiva Otero. Coronelismo, borgismo e cooptação política. Porto Alegre, Brazil: Mercado Aberto, 1987. 198 p.: bibl., maps. (Série Documenta; 23)

Analyzes *coronelismo* system in Rio Grande do Sul from 1880s to 1930s, arguing that Julio de Castilho and Borges de Medeiros constructed a form of *coronelismo* in Rio Grande do Sul marked by the pastoral military traditions of the State and by positivism. Based on intensive research in state archives.

3010 Fonseca, Pedro Cezar Dutra. Vargas: o capitalismo em construção, 1906–1954. São Paulo: Editora Brasiliense, 1989. 482 p.: bibl.

Analysis of the construction of capitalism in Brazil from the perspective of discourse analysis focuses on Getúlio Vargas. Rather than measuring economic results, Fonseca analyzes economic thought, emphasizing the "bourgeois revolution" that Brazil experienced in first half of the 20th century.

3011 Foot, Francisco. Trem fantasma: a modernidade na selva. São Paulo: Companhia das Letras; Editora Schwarcz, 1988. 291 p., 16 p. of plates: bibl., ill.

Brilliant and evocative cultural analysis of myth, history, and material progress focuses on ill-fated Madeira-Mamoré railway in early 20th-century Brazil.

3012 French, John D. Industrial workers and the birth of the Populist Republic in Brazil, 1945–1946. (*Lat. Am. Perspect.*, 16:4, Fall 1989, p. 5–27, bibl.)

Argues that "the events of 1945–1946 are best seen as a radical break with the past marked by the dramatic entry of the urban working class into Brazilian political life." Believes that the labor movement was not an "ineffectual creation of the corporatist state," but an important political force. Interpretative essay based on 1985 dissertation.

3013 French, John D. and Mary Lynn Pedersen. Women and working-class mobilization in postwar São Paulo, 1945–1948. (*LARR*, 24:3, 1989, p. 99–125, bibl., tables)

Employs "a community study method to investigate women's grass-roots participation in politics and labor mobilization" in postwar greater São Paulo. Argues that women made important breakthroughs by becoming active in working-class politics, shattering stereotypes, and contributing to radical, labor, and feminist movements.

3014 French, John D. Workers and the rise of Adhemarista populism in São Paulo, Brazil. (*HAHR*, 68:1, Feb. 1988, p. 1–44, bibl., map, tables)

Detailed analysis of the prominent postwar populist Adhemar de Barros emphasizes his political opportunism and lack of clear goals. Argues that emergence of populist politics of Barros and others was made possible by mass enfranchisement of working class in 1945 under Getúlio Vargas.

3015 Fritsch, Winston. External constraints on economic policy in Brazil, 1889–1930. Pittsburgh, Penn.: Univ. of Pittsburgh Press, 1988. 265 p.: (Pitt Latin American series)

Important work by an economist argues that the role of the São Paulo elite in the formulation of national economic policy has been overstated.

3016 Fukushima, Masanori. Eleitores e migrações internas no Brasil: o caso paranaense, 1900–1984. Curitiba, Brazil: s.n., 1988. 485 p.: bibl., ill.

Highly quantitative analysis of migration in Paraná uses a sample of nearly 10,000 voter registration cards. Emphasizes internal migration as a form of integration. Long on descriptive statistics and short on historical analysis.

3017 Furtado, Celso. A fantasia desfeita. São Paulo: Paz e Terra, 1989. 206 p.

Fascinating memoir by one of contemporary Brazil's most important intellectual and political figures. Insider's look at efforts in late 1950s and early 1960s to develop northeastern Brazil, especially through the Superintêndencia do Desenvolvimento do Nordeste (SUDENE) which Furtado headed.

3018 Gagliardi, José Mauro, O indígena e a república. São Paulo: Editora Hucitec; Editora da Univ. de São Paulo; Secretaria de Estado da Cultura de São Paulo, 1989. 310 p.: bibl., ill., maps. (Estudos brasileiros; 25)

Solid study of the origins of the Serviço de Proteção aos Indios in 1910 and its work in the 1910s and 1920s emphasizes role of positivists in the formation and development of government policy toward Indians.

3019 Gama, Lélia Vidal Gomes da. Elvira Komel: uma estrela riscou o céu. Belo Horizonte, Brazil: Secretaria de Estado da Cultura, 1987. 114 p., 13 leaves of plates: bibl., ill., ports. (Publicações BPELB)

Brief but interesting study of an early feminist leader active in Minas Gerais in the 1920s and 1930s.

3020 Gebara, Ademir. O mercado de trabalho livre no Brasil, 1871–1888. São Paulo: Brasiliense, 1986. 221 p.

Interesting analysis of policy debates and laws on slavery presents insights into the mentality of the Brazilian political elite and the peaceful demise of slavery.

3021 Giovannetti Netto, Evaristo. A bancada do PCB na Assembléia Constituinte de 1946. São Paulo: Editora Novos Rumos, 1986. 210 p.: bibl.

Diffuse analysis of role of the Brazilian Communist Party in the Constitutional Assembly of 1946. Based primarily on *anais* of the Assembly and on newspapers, this work was originally a doctoral dissertation.

3022 Góes, Maria da Conceição Pinto de. A formação da classe trabalhadora: movimento anarquista no Rio de Janeiro, 1888–1911. Rio de Janeiro: J. Zahar; Fundação José Bonifácio, 1988. 110 p.: bibl.

Brief analysis of anarchist labor movement in turn-of-the-century Rio de Janeiro is based on newspapers and secondary sources. Argument that anarchists failed because they did not understand the complexity of Brazilian working-class culture is not convincing.

3023 Gomes, Angela Maria de Castro and **Marieta de Moraes Ferreira.** Industrialização e classe trabalhadora no Rio de Janeiro: novas perspectivas de análise. (*ANPOCS BIB,* 24, 1987, p. 11–40, bibl.)

Invaluable review essay surveys works on industrialization and the formation of the working class in Rio de Janeiro. Emphasizes the First Republic and contains a great bibliography.

3024 Gorender, Jacob. Combate nas trevas: a esquerda brasileira; das ilusões perdidas à luta armada. São Paulo: Editora Atica, 1987. 255 p., 32 p. of plates: bibl., ill., ports. (Série Temas; 3: Brasil contemporâneo)

Analysis of the left in Brazilian politics, principally in the 1960s, by one of the most important communist intellectuals and militants in the postwar period.

3025 Gorender, Jacob; Manuela Carneiro da Cunha; and **Muniz Sodré.** Escravos brasileiros do século XIX na fotografia de Christiano Jr. Organização de Paulo Cesar de Azevedo e Mauricio Lissovsky. São Paulo: Ex Libris, 1988. 77 p. of plates: ill.

Interesting series of photographs taken 1864–66 by photographer Christiano Junior in his Rio de Janeiro studio. Many were intended as postcards to depict the "exotic" people of Brazil to Europeans. Although posed, the photographs provide important information on the daily lives of slaves (see also item **3050**).

3026 Graf, Márcia Elisa de Campos. De agredidos a agressores: um estudo sobre as relações sociais entre senhores e escravos no Paraná do século XIX. (*Estud. Econ./São Paulo,* 18: número especial, 1988, p. 147–166, bibl., tables)

Largely based on material from Paraná newspapers between 1871–88, article emphasizes brutality of slave masters and resistance of slaves.

3027 Graham, Richard. Patronage and politics in nineteenth-century Brazil. Stanford, Calif.: Stanford Univ. Press, 1990. 382 p.: bibl., ill.

Outstanding study of nature and functioning of power in imperial Brazil stresses that patronage is the key to understanding the political system.

3028 Graham, Sandra Lauderdale. House and street: the domestic world of servants and masters in nineteenth-century Rio de Janeiro. Cambridge, England; New York: Cambridge Univ. Press, 1988. 212 p.: bibl., ill., index. (Cambridge Latin American studies; 68)

Important effort to reconstruct lives of free and slave domestics and their relations with their masters. Creative use of traditional and non-traditional sources for 1860–1910 period.

3029 Greenfield, Gerald Michael. Recife y la gran sequía. Traducción de Ernesto Leibovich. (*in* Cultura urbana latinoamericana. Recopilación de Richard Morse y Jorge Enrique Hardoy. Buenos Aires: Consejo Latinoamericano de Ciencias Sociales, 1985, p. 203–226)

Analyzes impact of massive migration of rural folk from countryside into Recife during Great Drought of 1877–79. Draws parallels between urban social problems created by this migration, and modern migrations of the poor into the major cities of contemporary Brazil.

3030 Groot, Kees de. De Brazilianen: geschiedenis van 1889 tot nu. Muiderberg, The Netherlands: D. Coutinho, 1991. 199 p.: bibl., ill., index, map.

Fine introduction to the making of modern Brazil. Brief historical introduction precedes study of effect of economic transformations and growth on society, popular culture, and politics. Final chapters are devoted to the process of democratization and the current economic problems. [R. Hoefte]

3031 Heller, Milton Ivan. Resistência democrática: a repressão no Paraná. Rio de Janeiro: Editora Paz e Terra; Curitiba, Brazil: Secretaria de Estado da Cultura do Paraná, 1988. 683 p., 10 p. of plates: bibl., ill.

Volume put together by journalist recounts in detail repression in Paraná under the military regime in the 1960s and 1970s. Gives succinct overview of the regime and includes nearly 100 pages of documents, primarily the institutional acts of the military regime.

3032 Holloway, Thomas H. *A Healthy Terror*: police repression of *capoeiras* in nineteenth-century Rio de Janeiro. (*HAHR,* 69:4, Nov. 1989, p. 637–676, tables)

Excellent and judicious social history of *capoeira* gangs utilizes police records. Emphasizes expansion of State authority and differing interpretations of actions of *capoeira* gangs—as simple criminal activity or as the creative response of the oppressed to their oppressors.

3033 Ianni, Octavio. O colapso do populismo no Brasil. 4a. ed., rev. Rio de Janeiro: Civilização Brasileira, 1988. 190 p.: bibl.

Reissue of controversial work that first appeared in 1968 (see *HLAS 31:7306a*). Attempts to explain collapse of democratic politics and military coup of 1964 within context of "structural dependency." Ianni's definition of populism has been criticized as too broad and vague.

Kinzo, Maria D'Alva Gil. Legal opposition politics under authoritarian rule in Brazil: the case of the MDB, 1966–79. See *HLAS 51:4069.*

3034 Komissarov, Boris Nikolaevich. Peterburg—Rio-De-Zhaneĭro: stanovlenie otnosheniĭ, 1808–1828 = St. Petersburg—Rio de Janeiro: formação das relações 1808–1828. Leningrad: Izd-vo Leningradskogo universiteta, 1987. 241 p.: bibl., index.

Draws on primary sources from archives in the Russian Diplomatic History Dept. of the Ministry of the Interior and other archives throughout the former Soviet Union, as well as on Brazilian documents and extensive diplomatic correspondence.

Few Russian historians have addressed this early period in Brazil's political and economic relations with Russia and Western Europe. Includes extensive notes, lengthy name index, and topical table of contents in Russian and Portuguese. [B. Dash]

Kowarick, Lúcio. The subjugation of labour: the constitution of capitalism in Brazil. See *HLAS 51:5052.*

3035 Kula, Witold; Nina Assorodobraj-Kula; and Marcin Kula. Writing home: immigrants in Brazil and the United States, 1890–1891. Edited and translated by Josephine Wtulich. Boulder, Colo.: East European Monographs; New York: Columbia Univ. Press, 1986. 698 p.: bibl., ill. (East European monographs; 210)

Fascinating collection of letters, 73 of which are from Polish immigrants to Brazil. All of these letters were confiscated by Russian Tsarist censors and never reached their destination. Introduction does fine job of placing immigrants' letters in historical context of late 19th-century Eastern Europe.

3036 Labaki, Amir. 1961, a crise da renúncia e a solução parlamentarista. São Paulo: Brasiliense, 1986. 174 p., 8 p. of plates: appendix, bibl., ill.

Journalistic narrative of the political crisis set off by resignation of Jânio Quadros. Weak analysis, but appendix includes key documents such as the resignation letter and speech, and actions by military ministers.

3037 Lacerda Paiva, Cláudio. Carlos Lacerda, 10 anos depois. Rio de Janeiro: Editora Nova Fronteira, 1987. 330 p.

Collection of articles and interviews by and about Carlos Lacerda covers his political career in the 1960s. Compiled by his nephew as a supplement to the *Depoimento* (see *HLAS 42:3681*), the presentation is hagiographic.

3038 Lacombe, Américo Jacobina and Vicente Costa Santos Tapajós. Organização e administração do Ministerio da Justiça no Império. Brasília: Ministério da Justiça; Fundação Centro de Formação do Servidor Público, 1986. 322 p.: bibl. (História administrativa do Brasil; 12)

Valuable reference work forms part of a long-standing multi-volume project.

3039 Langa Laorga, María Alicia. España ante la independencia de Brasil. (*His-*

pania/Madrid, 49:172, mayo/agosto 1989, p. 573–596, bibl.)

Interesting analysis of the rarely-studied topic of Spain's reaction to Brazilian independence focuses on three issues: 1) Spain's refusal to recognize the independence of its own former colonies; 2) the dispute over the Banda Oriental; and 3) Spanish support for Dom Miguel in Portugal.

3040 Langer, Erick Detlef. Generations of scientists and engineers: origins of the computer industry in Brazil. (*LARR,* 24:2, 1989, p. 95–111, bibl.)

Excellent examination of the failures and fortuities in the 1950s and 1960s that led to creation of a national computer industry in the 1970s and 1980s. Concludes that few Third World countries have the ability and resources to achieve similar technological and scientific successes.

3041 Lanna, Ana Lúcia Duarte. A transformação do trabalho. Campinas, Brazil: Editora da UNICAMP, 1988. 124 p.: bibl. (Teses)

Contrasts transition from slavery to free labor in Minas Gerais with São Paulo. Shows how Minas solved its labor needs internally without need for immigrants, and emphasizes that problems faced in coffee production were shortages of capital and credit rather than of labor.

3042 Lauerhass, Ludwig. Getúlio Vargas e o triunfo do nacionalismo brasileiro. Belo Horizonte, Brazil: Editora Itatiaia; São Paulo: Editora da Univ. de São Paulo, 1986. 182 p., 30 p. of plates: bibl., ill., ports. (Col. Reconquista do Brasil; 2a. sér.,99)

Examination of Brazilian nationalism from 1880s to 1930s. Argues that Vargas transformed nationalism from an issue for intellectuals to a matter for the State, especially during the *Estado Novo,* and that nationalism was the most distinct characteristic of the Vargas regime. Translation of a 1972 doctoral dissertation.

3043 Leacock, Ruth. Requiem for revolution: the United States and Brazil, 1961–1969. Kent, Ohio: Kent State Univ. Press, 1990. 317 p.: bibl.

Survey of US/Brazil relations stresses influence of "American anticommunist ideology" in the 1960s. Despite subtitle, book focuses primarily on the period 1961–64.

3044 Leite, Miriam Moreira. Mulheres e famílias. (*Rev. Bras. Hist.*, 9:17, set. 1988/fev. 1989, p. 143–178, bibl., facsims.)

Interesting but unfocused survey of travel accounts written by women who visited Brazil in the 19th century. Valuable compilation.

3045 Lenharo, Alcir. A civilização vai ao campo: sindicialismo e cooperativismo rural a partir da década de 30. (*An. Mus. Paul.*, 34, 1985, p. 7–19)

Sketchy analysis of articles in *Estado do Mato Grosso* which discuss efforts to colonize land and form cooperatives from the 1930s to the 1950s.

3046 Leonzo, Nanci. A historiografia brasileira anti-republicana: a obra de Eduardo Prado. (*Rev. Inst. Estud. Bras.*, 27, 1987, p. 103–112)

Brief attempt to revise traditional view of one prominent intellectual and literary figure of the 1890s known for his opposition to the New Republic. Argues rather unconvincingly that Prado was more anti-republic than monarchist, and more liberal than anti-republic.

3047 Lessa, Renato. A invenção republicana: Campos Sales, as bases e a decadência da Primeira República brasileira. Rio de Janeiro: IUPERJ; São Paulo: Vértice, 1988. 173 p.: bibl., ill. (Formação do Brasil; 3)

Sophisticated and stimulating analysis of the pivotal role of President Campos Sales in the construction of the republican political order at the turn of the century.

3048 Lesser, Jeff H. Continuity and change within an immigrant community: the Jews of São Paulo, 1924–1945. (*Luso-Braz. Rev.*, 25:2, Winter 1988, p. 45–58)

Shows how long-standing divisions among Ashkenazic Jews were exacerbated in São Paulo by economic and political factors in Brazil in the 1940s. Stresses need to look at diversity within immigrant groups in Brazil rather than seeing them as a unified community.

3049 Levi-Moreira, Silvia. Ideologia e atuação da Liga Nacionalista de São Paulo, 1917–1924. (*Rev. Hist./São Paulo*, 116, jan./junho 1984, p. 67–74)

Brief description of the formation, goals, composition, and demise of a short-lived nationalist association.

3050 Levine, Robert M. Faces of Brazilian slavery: the *cartes de visite* of Christiano Junior. (*Americas/Francisc.*, 47:2, Oct. 1990, p. 127–160)

Analyzes the photographs of slaves in 19th-century Rio de Janeiro taken by Brazilian photographer Christiano Junior (see item **3025**) and discusses difficulties of using photographs as historical sources. Includes 20 full-page b/w reproductions.

3051 Libby, Douglas Cole. Proto-industrialization in a slave society: the case of Minas Gerais. (*J. Lat. Am. Stud.*, 23:1, Feb. 1991, p. 1–35, graph, map, table)

Valuable study blames local merchant class for failure to shift directly to factory-based industry. Strong ties to the entrenched slave system discouraged this group from taking advantage of available opportunities.

3052 Libby, Douglas Cole. Transformação e trabalho em uma economia escravista: Minas Gerais no século XIX. São Paulo: Editora Brasiliense, 1988. 404 p.: bibl., ill., maps, port.

Best study available of the *mineiro* economy in the 19th century. Revisionist analysis of labor and industry (iron and steel, textiles, and mining) emphasizes the dynamism and growth of the *mineiro* economy in the transition from slavery to free labor.

Libertários no Brasil: memória, lutas, cultura. See item **5408.**

3053 Lima, Oliveira O Império brasileiro, 1821–1889. Belo Horizonte, Brazil: Itatiaia; São Paulo: Editora da Univ. de São Paulo, 1989. 182 p.: bibl. (Col. Reconquista do Brasil; 2a. sér.,155)

New edition of one of the classic histories of the empire (first published in 1927) by a prominent diplomat and historian.

3054 Lima, Sandra Lúcia Lopes. O oeste paulista e a república. São Paulo: Edições Vértice, 1986. 110 p.: bibl., ill. (Formação do Brasil; 1)

Short and somewhat superficial study of the views of paulista coffee planters is based on an analysis of newspapers and parliamentary debates. Focuses on issues of credit, transport, and labor.

3055 Love, Joseph L. Of planters, politics, and development. (*LARR*, 24:3, 1989, p. 127–135)

Commentary on article "Coffee Planters, Politics, and Development in Brazil" by Mauricio Font (LARR, 22:3, 1987). Love believes Font overstates relative autonomy of the State and the degree of conflict between planters and the State. He stresses need for empirical research on relationship between coffee capital and industrialization.

3056 Luebke, Frederick C. Germans in Brazil: a comparative history of cultural conflict during World War I. Baton Rouge: Louisiana State Univ. Press, 1987. 248 p.: bibl., ill., index.

Important work on persons of German origin in Brazil, although work has been criticized for not delving deeply enough into German archival sources.

3057 Lyra Filho, João. Visconde de Itaboraí: a luneta do Império. Rio de Janeiro: Gráfica Portinho Cavalcanti, 1985? 255 p.: ill., ports.

Very traditional political biography of one of the major figures of the Empire. No scholarly apparatus.

3058 Machado, Maria Helena Pereira Toledo. Crime e escravidão: trabalho, luta e resistência nas lavouras paulistas, 1830–1888. São Paulo: Editora Brasiliense, 1987. 134 p.: bibl., port.

Interesting study using trial records of slave crimes in Campinas and Taubaté makes excellent use of local archival materials.

3059 Machado, Maria Helena Pereira Toledo. Trabalho, compensação e crime: estratégias e contra-estratégias. (Estud. Econ./São Paulo, 18: número especial, 1988, p. 81–102, bibl., table)

Chapter excerpted from Machado's book (see item **3058**).

3060 Maciel, Cleber da Silva. Discriminações raciais: negros em Campinas, 1888–1921. Campinas, Brazil: Editora da UNICAMP, 1987. 209 p.: bibl., ill. (Tempo e memória; 1: Série campiniana)

Competent but not very revealing examination of situation of blacks in Campinas in the aftermath of slavery emphasizes race relations.

3061 Magalhães, Domingos José Gonçalves de. Memória histórica e documentada da revolução da província do Maranhão desde

1839 até 1840. (Novos Estud. CEBRAP, 23, março 1989, p. 14–66)

Reprint of classic account of the Balaiada revolt first published in 1848.

3062 Marson, Izabel Andrade. O império do progresso: a Revolução Praieira em Pernambuco, 1842–1855. São Paulo: Editora Brasiliense, 1987. 487 p : bibl., ill.

Long and interesting study of the historiography of the Praieira Revolt in mid-19th-century Pernambuco argues that pre-1930 historians saw revolt primarily as a challenge to the "progress" of the Empire, while post-1930 historians have reversed the analysis to view revolt as an attempt to progress beyond the "backward" social order of the period.

3063 Martins, Jose de Souza. Del esclavo al asalariado en las haciendas de café, 1880–1914: la génesis del trabajador volante. (in Población y mano de obra en América Latina. Recopilación de Nicolás Sánchez-Albornoz. Madrid: Alianza Editorial, 1985, p. 229–257)

Very theoretical and abstract analysis of transition from slavery to wage labor, more specifically to the *colono libre*, in the coffee regions of Brazil.

3064 Mattoso, Kátia M. de Queirós; Herbert S. Klein; and **Stanley L. Engerman.** Trends and patterns in the prices of manumitted slaves: Bahia, 1819–1888. (Slavery Abolit., 7:1, May 1986, p. 59–67, tables)

Analysis of slave prices based on sample of 5,779 "letters of freedom" from Bahia shows rising prices until about 1860 and then declining prices until abolition in 1888. Prices in 1880s were still above 1830s levels.

3065 McDowall, Duncan. The light: Brazilian Traction, Light and Power Company Limited, 1899–1945. Toronto, Canada; Buffalo, N.Y.: Univ. of Toronto Press, 1988. 459 p., 25 p. of plates: bibl., ill.

First scholarly, book-length study of a foreign company operating in Brazil. This Canadian utilities firm was the largest foreign corporation in Brazil in the first half of 20th century. Makes extensive use of company archives, but does not cover history of company since 1945.

3066 Meade, Teresa. "Living worse and costing more:" resistance and riot in

Rio de Janeiro, 1890–1917. (*J. Lat. Am. Stud.*, 21:2, May 1989, p. 241–267)

Explores deterioriating living conditions of the working poor, the many spontaneous protests, and city's first general strike in 1917, as Rio underwent beautification for the elite.

3067 Migot, Aldo Francisco. História de Carlos Barbosa. Caxias do Sul, Brazil: Editora da Univ. de Caxias do Sul; Porto Alegre, Brazil: Escola Superior de Teologia e Espiritualidade Franciscana, 1989. 671 p.: bibl., ill., map. (Col. Imigração italiana; 98)

Thick and encyclopedic local history of a *município* in Rio Grande do Sul settled by European, especially Italian, immigrants.

3068 Miranda, Alcibiades. Contestado. Curitiba, Brazil: Instituto Histórico, Geográfico e Etnográfico Paranaense, 1987. 229 p., 1 leaf of plates: port. (Estante paranista; 28)

Heretofore unpublished account of Contestado rebellion written in the 1930s by Brazilian army colonel who participated in the fighting against the rebels.

Monbeig, Pierre. Pioneiros e fazendeiros de São Paulo. See *HLAS 51:3279.*

3069 Moraes, João Quartim de; Wilma Peres Costa; and Eliézer Rizzo de Oliveira. A tutela militar. São Paulo: Edições Vértice, Editora Revista dos Tribunais, 1987. 104 p.: bibl. (Grande Brasil, veredas; 3)

Three short essays by social scientists on role of the military in Brazilian politics. One essay deals with the military and the First Republic, and two others examine the military and the New Republic in the 1980s. The last two in particular are not of much use to the historian. For political scientist's comment see *HLAS 51:4084.*

3070 Morais, Evaristo de. Da monarquia para a república, 1870–1889. Prefácio de Evaristo de Moraes Filho. 2a. ed. Brasília: Editora Univ. de Brasília, 1985. 131 p.: bibl., facsims. (Col. Temas brasileiros; 57)

New edition of a famous account of the end of the Empire that was originally published in 1936.

3071 Nascimento, Anna Amélia Vieira. Dez freguesias da cidade do Salvador: aspectos sociais e urbanos do século XIX. Salvador, Brazil: Fundação Cultural do Estado da Bahia, 1986. 204 p.: bibl., ill.

Very informative quantitative analysis of the city of Salvador from 1760–1870 is heavily influenced by French historical methodology. Based largely on city census of 1855.

3072 Netto, Luiz Roberto Por debaixo dos panos: a máquina policial e o problema da infância desvalida na cidade de São Paulo, 1910–1930. (*Rev. Bras. Hist.*, 9:17, set. 1988/fev. 1989, p. 129–141, bibl., graph)

Looks at police detention of minors in São Paulo as a means of social control. Long on theorizing and moral indignation; short on specific information.

Nevares, Guillermo F. de. Cómo se desintegró el Virreinato del Río de la Plata y se consolidó el Brasil. See item **2739.**

3073 Neves, Tancredo. Tancredo Neves: sua palavra na história. Organização de Lucília de Almeida Neves Delgado. São Paulo?: Fundação Presidente Tancredo Neves, 1988. 345 p.: bibl., ill., ports.

Collection of key speeches of one of the most important political figures in Brazil during past 40 years.

3074 Octávio, José. Violência e repressão no Nordeste, 1825/32. Prefácio de Décio Freitas. João Pessoa, Brazil: Governo do Estado da Paraíba, 1985. 81 p.: bibl. (Col. IV centenário; 11)

Very brief and sketchy survey of forms of violence and repression in Recife during early 19th century.

3075 Oliveira, Betty Antunes de. Centelha em restolho seco: uma contribuição para a história dos primórdios do trabalho batista no Brasil. Rio de Janeiro: B.A. de Oliveira, 1985. 466 p.: bibl., facsims., ill., index, maps, ports.

Very detailed account claims that first Baptist church in Brazil was founded by Confederate expatriates in Santa Barbara, São Paulo, in 1870s. Very rich documentation on families and individuals in Santa Barbara and Americana in late 19th century. Self-published volume inspired by author's own personal ties to the community and her religious beliefs.

3076 Oliveira, Flávia Arlanch Martins de. Famílias proprietárias e estratégias de poder local no século passado. (*Rev. Bras. Hist.*, 9:17, set. 1988/fev. 1989, p. 65–85)

Looks at land ownership, and at intermarriage among powerful and their control of local politics in small city of Jaú in the interior of São Paulo state in mid-19th century. Minor case study that is not very revealing.

3077 Oliveira, Marcos Aurélio Guedes de. O PCB, a democratização e a reação conservadora, 1943–1948. (*Rev. Novos Rumos,* 3:10/11/12, 1988, p. 177–224, bibl.)

Analysis of tactics and politics of the PCB is based on published sources.

3078 Oliveira, Maria Coleta F.A. de and Felícia R. Madeira. Población y fuerza de trabajo: el caso de la cafeicultura en el oeste paulista. (*in* Población y mano de obra en América Latina. Recopilación de Nicolás Sánchez-Albornoz. Madrid: Alianza Editorial, 1985, p. 259–278, tables)

Suggestive analysis of family demography in São Paulo coffee regions seeks reasons behind declining fertility rate in Brazil during past few decades. Asks good questions and makes some important suggestions for research.

3079 Pandolfi, Dulce Chaves and Mário Grynszpan. Da Revolução de 30 ao Golpe de 37: a depuração das elites. Rio de Janeiro: Fundação Getúlio Vargas, Centro de Pesquisa e Documentação de História Contemporânea do Brasil, 1987. 48 leaves: bibl.

Short piece examines complex and shifting political alliances in Brazilian politics (1930–37). Emphasizes that the coup in 1937 was not the inevitable outcome of the Revolution of 1930.

3080 Pang, Eul-Soo. In pursuit of honor and power: noblemen of the Southern Cross in nineteenth-century Brazil. Tuscaloosa: Univ. of Alabama Press, 1988. 341 p.: bibl., index, maps.

Important and richly detailed study of imperial nobility emphasizes power of this elite in 19th-century Brazil.

3081 Petersen, Sílvia Regina Ferraz. A mulher na imprensa operária gaúcha do século XIX. (*Rev. Hist./Porto Alegre,* 1, 1986/1987, p. 83–110, appendix)

Looks at the treatment of women and at women's issues in the working-class press; concludes that despite denunciations of capitalist oppression, the question of patriarchal relations is not addressed. Includes numerous direct quotes from newspapers.

3082 Piccolo, Helga Iracema Landgraf. O discurso político na Revolução Farroupilha. (*Rev. Hist./Porto Alegre,* 1, 1986/1987, p. 39–53, bibl.)

Description of major objectives of leaders of the Farroupilha as seen through political statements. Very little analysis.

3083 Pinaud, João Luiz Duboc et al. Insurreição negra e justiça: Paty do Alferes, 1838. Rio de Janeiro: Expressão e Cultura; Ordem dos Advogados do Brasil, 1987. 135 p.

Multidisciplinary analysis by two lawyers and three social scientists of a slave rebellion in Santa Catarina in 1838. Records of the judicial process are transcribed and take up about one-third of the text. Excellent source for study of slave rebellions in 19th-century Brazil.

3084 Prado, Maria Ligia Coelho. O Partido Democrático de São Paulo: adesões e aliciamento de eleitores, 1926–1934. (*Rev. Hist./São Paulo,* 117, julho/dez. 1984, p. 71–85)

Uses correspondence from party archives to show methods and problems of recruitment. Emphasizes "incongruence" between liberal discourse of participation for the masses and control of party by a small elite.

3085 Reis Filho, Daniel Aarão and Pedro de Moraes. 1968, a paixão de uma utopia. Rio de Janeiro: Espaço e Tempo, 1988. 220 p.: bibl., photos. (Col. Pensando o Brasil; 9)

Depicts student movement in Brazil in 1968 through photographs and interviews with activists. Short essay introduces volume and discusses student movement in Brazil, placing it in the context of movements in Europe and US in 1968. Unfortunately, photographs are rarely labeled and interviews are not analyzed.

3086 Reitz, Raulino. Alto Biguaçu: narrativa cultural tetrarracial. Florianópolis, Brazil: Editora Lunardelli; Editora da UFSC, 1988? 581 p., 2 p. of plates: bibl., ill. (some col.).

Encyclopedic volume by amateur local historian of the *município* of Antônio Carlos in Santa Catarina is of limited use as reference tool for those interested in history of the region.

3087 Revolução de 32: a fotografia e a política. Rio de Janeiro: Edição Funarte, 1982. 60 p.: bibl., photos.

Nice collection of photographs of 1932 revolt of São Paulo against the central government, with very brief introductory essays.

3088 Ribeiro, Maria Alice Rosa. Condições de trabalho na indústria têxtil paulista, 1870–1930. São Paulo: Editora Hucitec; Editora da UNICAMP, 1988. 207 p.: bibl. (Economia & planejamento: Série Teses e pesquisas)

Well-documented study of textile industry in São Paulo state concentrates on working conditions in the factories.

3089 Ridings, Eugene W. Pre-modern interest groups and government: Brazil in the nineteenth century. (*Americas/Francisc.*, 46:3, Jan. 1990, p. 315–333)

Discusses how interest groups among planters and industrialists in 19th-century Brazil influenced government decision-making and public opinion.

3090 Rodrigues, José Honório. História da história do Brasil. v. 2, t. 1, A historiografia conservadora. v. 2, t. 2, A metafísica do latifúndio: o ultra-reacionário Oliveira Viana. São Paulo: Companhia Editora Nacional, 1988. 2 v. (Brasiliana: Grande formato; 23–24)

Completed shortly before author's death in 1987, these volumes continue *História da história do Brasil, v. 1, Historiografia colonial* published in 1979 (see *HLAS* 42:3603). Invaluable guide to Brazilian historiography in the 19th and 20th centuries by one of Brazil's greatest historians.

3091 Samara, Eni de Mesquita. Estratégias matrimoniais no Brasil do século XIX. (*Rev. Bras. Hist.*, 8:15, set. 1987/fev. 1988, p. 91–105)

Author investigates marriage patterns in 19th-century São Paulo using wills and manuscript census returns, and finds a high rate of single adults, many of whom lived in common law marriages or impermanent unions. Elite families sheltered their daughters and controlled them more than did the poorer classes. The reality of marriage and women's lives was more complex than has been thought previously.

3092 Santin, Silvino. A imigração esquecida. Porto Alegre, Brazil: Escola Superior de Teologia e Espiritualidade Franciscana; Caxias do Sul, Brazil: Editora da Univ. de Caxias, 1986. 95 p.: bibl., ill. (Col. Imigração italiana; 76)

Brief and not very sophisticated local history of Italian immigrant colony of Silveira Martins founded in 1877 near Santa Maria, Rio Grande do Sul.

3093 Santos, Sydney M. G. dos. André Rebouças e seu tempo. Petrópolis, Brazil: Ed. Vozes, 1985. 580 p.: bibl., ill.

Thorough but not very sophisticated biography of this notable black engineer and abolitionist was written by professor of engineering. Emphasizes technical accomplishments of Rebouças.

3094 Santos, Wanderley Guilherme dos. Sessenta e quatro: anatomia da crise. São Paulo: Vértice, 1986. 195 p.: bibl., ill. (Grande Brasil, veredas; 1)

Argues that Brazilian political system collapsed in 1964 not because of the consistent implementation of any program, but because of a paralysis in decision-making caused by a fragmentation in power resources accompanied by ideological radicalization, fragile political coalitions, and government instability. Originally written as a dissertation in political science at Stanford University. Stimulating analysis.

3095 Schwarcz, Lilia Moritz. Retrato em branco e negro: jornais, escravos e cidadãos em São Paulo no final do século XIX. São Paulo: Cia. das Letras, 1987. 284 p., 32 p. of plates: bibl., facsims., ill.

Useful study reconstructs attitudes of whites toward blacks through analysis of the portrayal of blacks in newspapers of São Paulo (1870–1900).

3096 Seitenfus, Ricardo Antônio Silva. O Brasil e o III Reich, 1933–1939. (*Jahrb. Gesch.*, 25, 1988, p. 273–289, tables)

Schematic analysis of relations between Brazil and Germany in 1930s emphasizes cultural influences of Germany on Brazil, trade, and fascist and anti-communist influences.

3097 Sevcenko, Nicolau. Río de Janeiro y San Pablo: desarrollo social y cultural comparativo, 1900–1930. Traducido del inglés por Eduardo Passalacqua. (*in* Nuevas perspectivas en los estudios sobre historia urbana latinoamericana. Buenos Aires: Instituto Internacional de Medio Ambiente y Desarrollo (IIED) América Latina, 1989, p. 149–167)

Comparison of urban growth of Rio de Janeiro and São Paulo in early 20th century contrasts the planned changes in Rio imposed by the government with the unplanned, largely privately sponsored, growth of São Paulo. This interesting comparison is not systematically explored.

3098 Silva, Hélio. O primeiro século da República. Rio de Janeiro: J. Zahar Editor, 1987. 171 p.: index.

Concise, synthetic political history of Brazil from 1889 proclamation of the Republic to 1987.

3099 Silva, Jandira M.M. da; Elvo Clemente; and Eni Barbosa. Breve histórico da imprensa sul-rio-grandense. Porto Alegre, Brazil: Companhia Rio Grandense de Artes Gráficas, 1986. 343 p.: bibl., index.

Valuable reference tool for the study of the press in southern Brazil. Has a thorough listing and description of the newspapers published in the region since early 19th century.

3100 Silva, Joaquim Norberto de Souza e. Investigações sobre os recenseamentos da população geral do Império e de cada província de per si tentados desde os tempos coloniais até hoje. Resumo histórico dos inquéritos censitários realizados no Brasil: recenseamento do Brasil, 1920. Ed. fac-similada São Paulo: Instituto de Pesquisas Econômicas, 1986. 251 p.

Facsimile edition of two important works on Brazilian censuses, one that originally appeared in 1870 and the other in 1920. Unfortunately, the edition has no introduction or analysis of the two works, which makes them less useful to the non-specialist.

3101 Silva, José Wilson da. O tenente vermelho. Porto Alegre, Brasil: Tchê!, 1987. 246 p.: facsims., ports.

Account by lieutenant in Brazilian army who worked with João Goulart and Leonel Brizola before and after 1964 coup claims that Goulart, Brizola, and Darcy Ribeiro received one million dollars from Cuba while in exile in Uruguay to fund a guerrilla

movement aimed at toppling the military regime. Short on details and sources.

3102 Silva, Marilene Rosa Nogueira da. Negro na rua: a nova face da escravidão. São Paulo: Editora Hucitec, 1988. 166 p.: bibl., ill. (Estudos históricos)

Originally a master's thesis, brief study of slavery in 19th-century Rio de Janeiro emphasizes the *escravo ao ganho*. Based on secondary sources and archival research. Karasch's work is far superior (see *HLAS 50:2521*).

3103 Skidmore, Thomas E. Racial ideas and social policy in Brazil, 1870–1940. (*in* The idea of race in Latin America, 1870–1940. Edited by Richard Graham. Austin: Univ. of Texas Press, 1990, p. 7–36, photos)

Largely drawn from his book *Black into White* (see *HLAS 38:4129*), which deals with racial views of the Brazilian elite during the First Republic. Chapter also briefly discusses racial ideas since 1940s.

3104 Sodré, Nelson Werneck. A intentona comunista de 1935. Porto Alegre, Brazil: Mercado Aberto, 1986. 118 p.: bibl. (Série Revisão; 26)

Brief, synthetic treatment of failed uprising by Brazilian Communist Party (PCB) in 1935 is written for general audience. Argues that PCB misjudged political conditions and attempted a revolution in a situation where revolutionary conditions did not exist. Concludes that *intentona* has been turned into a propaganda tool of conservative, anticommunist groups and the military.

3105 Soihet, Rachel. Condição feminina e formas de violência: mulheres pobres e ordem urbana, 1890–1920. Rio de Janeiro: Forense Universitária, 1989. 394 p.: bibl.

Richly documented study based on more than 300 criminal processes in Rio de Janeiro deals with topics such as prostitution, abortion, violence, and perceptions of women's role in society.

3106 Souza, Frederecindo Marés de. O Presidente Carlos Cavalcanti e a revolta do Contestado. Curitiba, Brazil: Instituto Histórico, Geográfico e Etnográfico Paranaense, 1987. 263 p., 5 leaves of plates: bibl., ill. (some col.). (Estante paranista; 29)

Amateurish and unfinished manuscript on role of the president of Paraná during the Contestado rebellion in early 20th century. Published posthumously.

3107 Souza, Paulo Cesar. A Sabinada: a revolta separatista da Bahia, 1837. São Paulo: Editora Brasiliense, 1987. 252 p.: appendix, bibl., ill.

Most complete study available on one of the major social rebellions that threatened the unity of the Brazilian Empire in early 19th century integrates social and political history of the revolt. Long appendix reproduces some key documents.

3108 Szmrecsányi, Tamás. Crecimiento y crisis de la industria azucarera brasileña, 1914–39. (*HISLA*, 11, 1988, p. 45–79, bibl., tables)

Dry and heavily quantitative analysis of sugar production statistics. Tables make up half the article.

3109 Tavares, Aurélio de Lyra. Aristides Lobo e a república. Rio de Janeiro: J. Olympio Editora, 1987. 187 p.: appendix, bibl., ports. (Col. Documentos brasileiros; 205)

Admiring and very traditional biography of key figure (from Paraíba) in the proclamation of the Republic in 1889, by a former general (also from Paraíba). Lots of interesting documents are reproduced but no specific sources cited.

3110 Trento, Angelo. Do outro lado do Atlântico: um século de imigração italiana no Brasil. Tradução de Mariarosaria Fabris e Luiz Eduardo de Lima Brandão. São Paulo: Nobel, 1989. 574 p.: bibl.

Pt. 1 of this very important work deals with Italian immigrants to Brazil up to 1920 and was originally published in Italy. Pt. 2 covers the period 1920–60, and includes extensive bibliography and listing of Italian-language Brazilian publications ordered chronologically.

3111 Trochim, Michael R. The Brazilian Black Guard: racial conflict in post-abolition Brazil. (*Americas/Francisc.*, 44:3, Jan. 1988, p. 285–300, bibl.)

Analysis based primarily on newspaper articles of a black organization seeking to promote social and economic reform. Argues that the Black Guard failed because of its support for the monarchy and its attacks on Republicans who came to power in 1889.

Good case study of racial conflict and of efforts at black political organization in 19th-century Brazil.

3112 Turazzi, Maria Inez. A euforia do progresso e a imposição da ordem: a engenharia, a indústria e a organização do trabalho na virada do século XIX ao XX. Rio de Janeiro: Núcleo de Publicações COPPE; São Paulo: Editora Marco Zero, 1989. 160 p.: bibl.

Interesting study of engineers and industrialists attempting to implement principles of scientific management in Rio de Janeiro at beginning of the 20th century. Good use of unusual source materials.

3113 Vargas, Luthero. Getúlio Vargas: a revolução inacabada. Rio de Janeiro: Bloch Editores, 1988. 405 p.: appendix, bibl.

Biography of Getúlio Vargas by his son draws on previous accounts and author's own reflections. This effort to "set the record straight" offers a historical account by someone within the Vargas family who was also a political activist.

Vianna, Sérgio Besserman. As relações Brasil-Estados Unidos e a política econômica do segundo governo Vargas. See *HLAS* 51:4482.

3114 Weinstein, Barbara. The industrialists, the State, and the issues of worker training and social services in Brazil, 1930–50. (*HAHR*, 70:3, Aug. 1990, p. 379–404)

Excellent analysis of role of industrial leadership in creating and promoting worker training and social services stresses strong role played by industrialists vis-à-vis the State, the limits of their power, and their ambivalence toward State power. Draws heavily on business and political archives.

3115 Whately, Maria Celina. O café em Resende no século XIX. Rio de Janeiro: J. Olympio Editora, 1987. 99 p.: bibl., ill.

Brief and serious effort to reconstruct history of a *município* in the state of Rio de Janeiro that was an early focus of coffee production in 19th century. Based primarily on archival documentation and newspapers.

3116 Wiesebron, Marianne L. Antônio Silvino: cangaceiro do nordeste. (*Caravelle*, 53, 1989, p. 93–112)

Overview (in French) of the life of famous rural bandit in northeastern Brazil at turn of the century. Based on a French doctoral thesis that draws on newspapers and literary sources. Good narrative with very little in-depth analysis.

JOURNAL ABBREVIATIONS

Account. Hist. J. The Accounting Historians Journal. Academy of Accounting Historians. University, Alabama.

Agric. Hist. Agricultural History. Agricultural History Society. Univ. of Calif. Press. Berkeley.

Allpanchis. Allpanchis. Instituto de Pastoral Andina. Cusco, Peru.

Am. Ethnol. American Ethnologist. American Ethnological Society. Washington.

Am. Hist. Rev. American Historical Review. American Historical Assn., Washington.

Am. Indian Q. American Indian Quarterly. Southwestern American Indian Society; Fort Worth Museum of Science and History. Hurst, Tex.

Am. Lat./Moscú. América Latina. Academia de Ciencias de la Unión de Repúblicas Soviéticas Socialistas. Moscú.

Amazonía Peru. Amazonía Peruana. Centro Amazónico de Antropología y Aplicación Práctica, Depto. de Documentación y Publicaciones. Lima.

Americas/Francisc. The Americas. Academy of American Franciscan History. Washington.

An. Acad. Geogr. Hist. Guatem. Anales de la Academia de Geografía e Historia de Guatemala. Guatemala.

An. Inst. Invest. Estét. Anales del Instituto de Investigaciones Estéticas. Univ. Nacional Autónoma de México. México.

An. Mus. Paul. Anais do Museu Paulista. São Paulo.

An. Univ. Chile. Anales de la Universidad de Chile. Santiago.

Ann. écon. soc. civilis. Annales: économies, sociétés, civilisations. Centre national de la recherche scientifique de la VIe Section de l'École pratique des hautes etudes. Paris.

Ann. Midi. Annales du Midi. Edouard Privat Editeur. Toulouse, France.

ANPOCS BIB. Boletim Informativo e Bibliográfico de Ciências Sociais: BIB. Associação Nacional de Pós-Graduação e Pesquisa em Ciências Sociais. Rio de Janeiro.

Antropol. Hist. Guatem. Antropología e Historia de Guatemala. Instituto de Antropología e Historia de Guatemala. Guatemala.

Antropológica. Antropológica. Fundación La Salle de Ciencias Naturales; Instituto Caribe de Antropología y Sociología. Caracas.

Anu. Antropol. Anuário Antropológico. Tempo Brasileiro. Rio de Janeiro.

Anu. Centro Estud. Martianos. Anuario del Centro de Estudios Martianos. Centro de Estudios Martianos. La Habana.

Anu. Estud. Am. Anuario de Estudios Americanos. Consejo Superior de Investigaciones Científicas; Univ. de Sevilla, Escuela de Estudios Hispano-Americanos. Sevilla, Spain.

Anu. Estud. Centroam. Anuario de Estudios Centroamericanos. Univ. de Costa Rica. San José.

Anu. IEHS. Anuario IEHS. Univ. Nacional del Centro de la Provincia de Buenos Aires, Instituto de Estudios Histórico-Sociales, Argentina.

Anu. Inst. Invest. Hist./Asunción. Anuario. Instituto de Investigaciones Históricas Dr. José Gaspar Rodríguez de Francia. Asunción.

Anu. Mariateg. Anuario Mariateguiano. Empresa Editora Amauta. Lima.

Anuario/Rosario. Anuario. Univ. Nacional de Rosario, Escuela de Historia. Argentina.

Apuntes/Lima. Apuntes. Univ. del Pacífico, Centro de Investigación. Lima.

Arbor. Arbor. Consejo Superior de Investigaciones Científicas. Madrid.

Arch. Hist. Soc. Iesu. Archivum Historicum Societatis Iesu. Roma.

Arch. Ibero-Am. Archivo Ibero-Americano. Revista de Estudios Históricos. Los Padres Franciscanos. Madrid.

Archaeology. Archaeology. Archaeology Institute of America. Cambridge, Mass.

Asclepio. Asclepio. Consejo Superior de Investigaciones Científicas, Instituto Arnau de Vilanova de Historia de la Medicina, Archivo Iberoamericano de Historia de la Medicina y Antropología Médica. Madrid.

Atenea/Concepción. Atenea. Univ. de Concepción. Chile.

Bermud. J. Archaeol. Marit. Hist. Bermuda Journal of Archaeological and Maritime History. Bermuda Maritime Museum.

Bol. Acad. Nac. Hist./B. Aires. Boletín de la Academia Nacional de la Historia. Buenos Aires.

Bol. Acad. Nac. Hist./Caracas. Boletín de la Academia Nacional de la Historia. Caracas.

Bol. Am. Boletín Americanista. Univ. de Barcelona, Facultad de Geografía e Historia, Depto. de Historia de América. Barcelona.

Bol. Antropol. Am. Boletín de Antropología Americana. Instituto Panamericano de Geografía e Historia. México.

Bol. Arch. Hist. Arq. Boletín del Archivo Histórico Arquidiocesano Francisco de Paula García Paláez. Guatemala.

Bol. Arch. Hist. Miraflores. Boletín del Archivo Histórico de Miraflores. Presidencia de la República, Secretaría General. Caracas.

Bol. Centro Invest. Hist. Boletín del Centro de Investigaciones Históricas. Facultad de Humanidades, Univ. de Puerto Rico. Río Piedras.

Bol. Estud. Latinoam. Boletín de Estudios Latinoamericanos y del Caribe. Centro de Estudios y Documentación Latinoamericanos. Amsterdam.

Bol. Hist. Ejérc. Boletín Histórico del Ejército. Montevideo.

Bol. Inst. Am. Estud. Vascos. Boletín del Instituto Americano de Estudios Vascos. Instituto Americano de Estudios Vascos. Buenos Aires.

Bol. Inst. Hist. Ravignani. Boletín del Instituto de Historia Argentina y Americana Dr. Emilio Ravignani. Facultad de Filosofía y Letras, Univ. de Buenos Aires. Buenos Aires.

Bol. Lima. Boletín de Lima. Revista Cultural Científica. Lima.

Bol. Mus. Hombre Domin. Boletín del Museo del Hombre Dominicano. Santo Domingo.

Bol. Mus. Para. Goeldi. Boletim do Museu Paraense Emílio Goeldi. Nova série: antropologia. Conselho Nacional de Desenvolvimento Científico e Tecnológico, Instituto Nacional de Pesquisas da Amazônia. Belém, Brazil.

Bol. Nicar. Bibliogr. Doc. Boletín Nicaragüense de Bibliografía y Documentación. Biblioteca, Banco Central de Nicaragua. Managua.

Bull. Bur. natl. ethnol. Bulletin du Bureau national d'ethnologie. Bureau national d'ethnologie. Port-au-Prince, Haiti.

Bull. Cent. hist. atl. Bulletin du Centre d'histoire des espaces atlantiques. Talence-Cedex, France.

Bull. hisp. Bulletin hispanique. Univ. de Bordeaux; Centre national de la recherche scientifique. Bordeaux, France.

Bull. Inst. fr. étud. andin. Bulletin de l'Institut français d'études andines. Lima.

Bull. Lat. Am. Res. Bulletin of Latin American Research. Society for Latin American Studies. Glasgow, Great Britain.

Bull. Soc. hist. Guadeloupe. Bulletin de la Société d'histoire de la Guadeloupe. Archives départementales avec le concours du Conseil général de la Guadeloupe. Basse-Terre, W.I.

Bulletin/Paris. Bulletin. Association France-Haïti. Paris.

Bus. Hist. Rev. Business History Review. Harvard Univ. Graduate School of Business Administration. Boston, Mass.

Calif. Hist. California History. California Historical Society. San Francisco.

Can. J. Lat. Am. Caribb. Stud. Canadian Journal of Latin American and Caribbean Studies. Univ. of Ottawa. Ontario, Canada.

Caravelle. Caravelle. Cahiers du monde hispanique et luso-brésilien. Univ. de Toulouse, Institute d'études hispaniques, hispano-americaines et luso-brésiliennes. Toulouse, France.

CARE. CARE. Centre Antillais de Recherches et d'Etudes. Editions Caribéennes, Paris.

Caribb. Q. Caribbean Quarterly. Univ. of the West Indies. Mona, Jamaica.

Caribb. Stud. Caribbean Studies. Univ. of Puerto Rico, Institute of Caribbean Studies. Río Piedras, Puerto Rico.

Cathol. Hist. Rev. Catholic Historical Review. American Catholic Historical Assn.; The Catholic Univ. of America Press. Washington.

Cent. Estud. Puertorriq. Bull. Centro de Estudios Puertorriqueños Bulletin. Hunter College, City University of New York. New York.

Church Hist. Church History. American Society of Church History, Univ. of Chicago. Ill.

Comp. Stud. Soc. Hist. Comparative Studies in Society and History. Society for the Comparative Study of Society and History; Cambridge Univ. Press. London.

Conjonction. Conjonction. Bulletin de l'Institut français d'Haïti. Port-au-Prince.

Cristianismo Soc. Cristianismo y Sociedad. Junta Latinoamericana de Iglesia y Sociedad. Montevideo.

Criterio/Buenos Aires. Criterio. Editorial Criterio. Buenos Aires.

Cuad. Am. Cuadernos Americanos. Editorial Cultura. México.

Cuad. CLAEH. Cuadernos del CLAEH. Centro Latinoamericano de Economía Humana. Montevideo.

Cuad. Hispanoam. Cuadernos Hispanoamericanos. Instituto de Cultura Hispánica. Madrid.

Cuad. Hispanoam. Complement. Cuadernos Hispanoamericanos: Los Complementarios. Instituto de Cooperación Iberoamericana. Madrid.

Cuad. Hist. Cuadernos de Historia. Univ. de Chile, Facultad de Humanidades y Educación, Depto. de Ciencias Históricas. Santiago.

Cuba. Stud. Cuban Studies. Univ. of Pittsburgh, Center for Latin American Studies. Pittsburgh, Penn.

Cultura/Quito. Cultura. Banco Central del Ecuador. Quito.

Dados. Dados. Instituto Universitário de Pesquisas. Rio de Janeiro.

Dédalo. Dédalo. Univ. de São Paulo, Museu de Arqueologia e Etnologia. São Paulo.

Desarro. Econ. Desarrollo Económico. Instituto de Desarrollo Económico y Social. Buenos Aires.

Doss. Outre-mer. Les Dossiers de l'Outre-Mer. Centre National de Documentation des Departments d'Outre-Mer (CENADDOM). Talence, France.

Economía/Lima. Economía. Pontificia Univ. Católica del Perú, Depto. de Economía. Lima.

Estud. Cult. Maya. Estudios de Cultura Maya. Centro de Estudios Mayas, Univ. Autónoma de México. México.

Estud. Econ./São Paulo. Estudos Econômicos. Univ. de São Paulo, Instituto de Pesquisas Econômicas. São Paulo.

Estud. Hist. Mod. Contemp. Méx. Estudios de Historia Moderna y Contemporánea de México. Univ. Nacional Autónoma de México. México.

Estud. Hist. Novohisp. Estudios de Historia Novohispana. Univ. Nacional Autónoma de México, México.

Estud. Hist./Rio de Janeiro. Estudos Históricos. Associação de Pesquisa e Documentação Histórica. Rio de Janeiro.

Estud. Latinoam. Estudios Latinoamericanos. Polska Akademia Nauk, Instytut Historii. Varsovia.

Estud. Parag. Estudios Paraguayos. Univ. Católica Nuestra Señora de la Asunción. Asunción.

Estud. Soc./Santo Domingo. Estudios Sociales. Centro de Investigación y Acción Social de la Compañia de Jesús. Santo Domingo.

Ethnogr.-Archäol. Z. Ethnographisch-Archäologische Zeitschrift. Deutscher Verlag Wissenschaften. Berlin.

Ethnohistory. Ethnohistory. American Society for Ethnohistory. Duke Univ., Durham, N.C.

Ethnol. Pol. Ethnologia Polona. Polish Academy of Sciences, Institute for the History of Material Culture. Wrocław, Poland.

Ethnos. Ethnos. Statens Etnografiska Museum. Stockholm.

Etnía. Etnía. Museo Etnográfico Municipal Dámaso Arce. Municipalidad de Olavarría, Provincia de Buenos Aires. Olavarría, Argentina.

Etud. créoles. Etudes créoles. Comité international des études créoles. Montréal.

Etud. ibér. ibéro-am. Etudes ibériques et ibéro-americaines. Annales de la Faculté des lettres et sciences humaines de Nice. Nice, France.

Fla. Hist. Q. The Florida Historical Quarterly. The Florida Historical Society. Jacksonville, Fla.

Folk. Am. Folklore Americano. Instituto Panamericano de Geografía e Historia, Comisión de Historia, Comité de Folklore. México.

Gids. De Gids. Meulenhoff. Amsterdam.

HAHR. Hispanic American Historical Review. Conference on Latin American History of the American Historical Assn.; Duke Univ. Press. Durham, N.C.

HISLA. HISLA. Lima.

Hispania/Madrid. Hispania. Instituto Jerónimo Zurita, Consejo Superior de Investigaciones Científicas. Madrid.

Hist. Boliv. Historia Boliviana. Cochabamba.

Hist. écon. soc. Histoire, économie et sociéte. Editions C.D.U. et S.E.D.E.S., Paris.

Hist. Mex. Historia Mexicana. Colegio de México. México.

Hist. Parag. Historia Paraguaya. Anuario de la Academia Paraguaya de la Historia. Asunción.

Hist. Relig. History of Religions. Univ. of Chicago. Chicago, Ill.

Hist. Soc./Río Piedras. Historia y Sociedad. Depto. de Historia, Univ. de Puerto Rico. Río Piedras, Puerto Rico.

Hist. Workshop. History Workshop. Ruskin College, Oxford Univ., England.

Historia/Santiago. Historia. Univ. Católica de Chile. Instituto de Historia. Santiago.

Histórica/Lima. Histórica. Pontificia Univ. Católica del Perú, Depto. de Humanidades. Lima.

Historiogr. Bibliogr. Am. Historiografía y Bibliografía Americanista. Escuela de Estudios Hispano-Americanos de Sevilla. Sevilla, Spain.

Hómines. Hómines. Univ. Interamericana de Puerto Rico. San Juan.

Ibérica. Ibérica. Cahiers ibériques et ibéro-américains de l'Univ. de Paris-Sorbonne. Paris.

Ibero-Am. Ibero-Americana. Scandinavian Assn. for Research on Latin America (NOSALF). Stockholm.

Ibero-Am. Arch. Ibero-Amerikanisches Archiv. Ibero-Amerikanisches Institut. Berlin.

Int. Labor Work. Class Hist. International Labor and Working Class History. Study Group on International Labor and Working Class History. New Haven, Conn.

Invest. Ens. Investigaciones y Ensayos. Academia Nacional de la Historia. Buenos Aires.

Islas. Islas. Univ. Central de Las Villas. Santa Clara, Cuba.

J. Anthropol. Res. Journal of Anthropological Research. Univ. of New Mexico. Albuquerque, N.M.

J. Caribb. Hist. Journal of Caribbean History. Caribbean Universities Press. St. Lawrence, Barbados.

J. Church State. Journal of Church and State. J.M. Dawson Studies in Church and State, Baylor Univ., Waco, Tex.

J. Confl. Resolut. The Journal of Conflict Resolution. Univ. of Michigan, Dept. of Journalism. Ann Arbor, Mich.

J. Dev. Areas. The Journal of Developing Areas. Western Illinois Univ. Press. Macomb, Ill.

J. Eur. Econ. Hist. The Journal of European Economic History. Banco di Roma. Rome.

J. Hist. Geogr. Journal of Historical Geography. Academic Press. London; New York.

J. Interam. Stud. World Aff. Journal of Interamerican Studies and World Affairs. Institute of Interamerican Studies, Univ. of Miami. Coral Gables, Fla.

J. Lat. Am. Lore. Journal of Latin American Lore. Univ. of California, Latin American Center. Los Angeles, Calif.

J. Lat. Am. Stud. Journal of Latin American Studies. Centers or Institutes of Latin American Studies at the Universities of Cambridge, Glasgow, Liverpool, London, and Oxford. Cambridge Univ. Press. London.

J. Soc. Hist. Journal of Social History. Carnegie Mellon Univ., Pittsburgh, Pa.

J. Southwest. Journal of the Southwest. Southwest Center, Univ. of Arizona. Tucson.

J. West. Journal of the West. Manhattan, Kan.

J. Women's Hist. Journal of Women's History. Indiana Univ. Press. Bloomington, Ind.

Jahrb. Gesch. Jahrbuch für Geschichte von Staat, Wirtschaft und Gesellschaft Lateinamerikas. Köln, Germany.

Jahresbibliogr. Bibl. Zeitgesch. Jahresbibliographie Bibliothek für Zeitgeschichte. Bernard & Graefe Verlag. Koblenz, Germany.

Jam. J. Jamaica Journal. Institute of Jamaica. Kingston.

LARR. Latin American Research Review. Latin American Research Review Board. Univ. of New Mexico, Albuquerque, N.M.

Lat. Am. Perspect. Latin American Perspectives. Univ. of California. Newbury Park, Calif.

Lat.am. Stud. Lateinamerika Studien. Univ. Erlangen-Nürnberg, Sektion Lateinamerika. Nürnberg, Germany.

Lotería. Lotería. Lotería Nacional de Beneficencia. Panamá.

Luso-Braz. Rev. Luso-Brazilian Review. Univ. of Wisconsin Press. Madison, Wis.

Mesoamérica/Antigua. Mesoamérica. Centro de Investigaciones Regionales de Mesoamérica. Antigua, Guatemala.

Mex. Stud. Mexican Studies/Estudios Mexicanos. Univ. of California, Berkeley.

Mil. Aff. Military Affairs. American Military Institute. Washington.

Misc. Hist. Ecuat. Miscelánea Histórica Ecuatoriana: Revista de Investigaciones Históricas de los Museos del Banco Central del Ecuador. Museos del Banco Central del Ecuador. Quito.

N.M. Hist. Rev. New Mexico Historical Review. Historical Society of New Mexico; Univ. of New Mexico. Albuquerque, N.M.

New World. New World: A Journal of Latin American Studies. New World Inc., New Orleans, La.

Nieuwe West-Indische Gids. Nieuwe West-Indische Gids. Martinus Nijhoff. The Hague.

Novos Estud. CEBRAP. Novos Estudos CEBRAP. Centro Brasileiro de Análise e Planejamento. São Paulo.

NS. NS/NorthSouth/NordSud/NorteSur/NorteSul. Canadian Assn. of Latin American Studies. Univ. of Ottawa.

Nuevo Texto Crít. Nuevo Texto Crítico. Dept. of Spanish and Portuguese. Stanford Univ., Calif.

Numen. Numen. International Assn. for the History of Religions. Leiden, The Netherlands.

Opciones. Opciones. Centro de Estudios de la Realidad Contemporánea, Academia del Humanismo Cristiano. Santiago.

Pac. Hist. Rev. Pacific Historical Review. Univ. of California Press. Los Angeles and Berkeley, Calif.

Past Present. Past and Present. London.

Polít. Soc./Guatemala. Política y Sociedad. Univ. de San Carlos de Guatemala, Instituto de Investigaciones Políticas y Sociales. Guatemala.

Population. Population. Institut national de'Etudes démographiques. Paris.

Punto Coma. Punto y Coma. Univ. del Sagrado Corazón. Santurce, Puerto Rico.

Quad. Stor. Quaderni Storici. Facoltà di Economia e Commercio, Institúto de Storia e Sociologia. Ancona, Italy.

Relaciones/Zamora. Relaciones. El Colegio de Michoacán. Zamora, Mexico.

Repert. Hist. Acad. Antioq. Hist. Repertorio Histórico de la Academia Antioqueña de Historia. Medellín, Colombia.

Res Gesta. Res Gesta. Instituto de Historia, Facultad de Derecho y Ciencias Sociales, Univ. Católica Argentina. Rosario, Argentina.

Rev. Acad. Guat. Estud. Geneal. Revista de la Academia Guatemalteca de Estudios Genealógicos, Heráldicos, e Históricos. Guatemala.

Rev. Afr. Medio Oriente. Revista de Africa y Medio Oriente. Centro de Estudios de Africa y Medio Oriente. La Habana.

Rev. Andin. Revista Andina. Centro Bartolomé de las Casas. Cusco, Perú.

Rev. Antioq. Econ. Desarro. Revista Antioqueña de Economía y Desarrollo. Fundación para la Investigación y la Cultura. Medellín, Colombia.

Rev. Antropol./São Paulo. Revista de Antropologia. Univ. de São Paulo, Faculdade de Filosofia, Letras e Ciências Humanas; Associação Brasileira de Antropologia. São Paulo.

Rev. Arch. Nac. Revista del Archivo Nacional. San José, Costa Rica.

Rev. Arch. Nac. Hist. Azuay. Revista del Archivo Nacional de Historia, Sección del Azuay. Casa de la Cultura Ecuatoriana, Núcleo del Azuay. Cuenca, Ecuador.

Rev. Bibl. Nac. José Martí. Revista de la Biblioteca Nacional José Martí. La Habana.

Rev. Bras. Hist. Revista Brasileira de Historia. ANPUH. São Paulo.

Rev. Cent. Estud. Av. La Revista del Centro de Estudios Avanzados de Puerto Rico y el Caribe. Centro de Estudios Avanzados de Puerto Rico y el Caribe. San Juan.

Rev. Chil. Hist. Geogr. Revista Chilena de Historia y Geografía. Sociedad Chilena de Historia y Geografía. Santiago.

Rev. Cienc. Soc./Río Piedras. Revista de Ciencias Sociales. Univ. de Puerto Rico, Colegio de Ciencias Sociales. Río Piedras, P.R.

Rev. Crít. Lit. Latinoam. Revista de Crítica Literaria Latinoamericana. Latinoamericana Editores. Lima.

Rev. Estud. Extremeños. Revista de Estudios Extremeños. Diputación de Badajoz, Institución de Servicios Culturales. Badajoz, Spain.

Rev. Estud. Polít. Revista de Estudios Políticos. Instituto de Estudios Políticos. Madrid.

Rev. Eur. Revista Europea de Estudios Latinoamericanos y del Caribe = European Review of Latin American and Caribbean Studies. Center for Latin American Research and Documentation; Royal Institute of Linguistics and Antropology. Amsterdam.

Rev. fr. hist. Outre-mer. Revue française d'histoire d'Outre-mer. Société de l'histoire des colonies françaises. Paris.

Rev. Geogr./Quito. Revista Geográfica. Instituto Geográfico Militar del Ecuador, Depto. Geográfico. Quito.

Rev. Hist. Am. Revista de Historia de América. Instituto Panamericano de Geografía e Historia, Comisión de Historia. México.

Rev. Hist./Heredia. Revista de Historia. Univ. Nacional de Costa Rica, Escuela de Historia. Heredia, Costa Rica.

Rev. hist./Paris. Revue historique. Presses Universitaires de France. Paris.

Rev. Hist./Porto Alegre. Revista de Historia. Univ. Federal de Rio Grande do Sul. Porto Alegre, Brazil.

Rev. Hist./San Juan. Revista de Historia. Asociación Histórica Puertorriqueña. San Juan.

Rev. Hist./São Paulo. Revista de História. Univ. de São Paulo, Faculdade de Filosofia, Letras e Ciências Humanas, Depto. de História. São Paulo.

Rev. Indias. Revista de Indias. Consejo Superior de Investigaciones Científicas, Instituto Gonzalo Fernández de Oviedo. Madrid.

Rev. Inst. Estud. Bras. Revista do Instituto de Estudos Brasileiros. Univ. de São Paulo, Instituto de Estudos Brasileiros. São Paulo.

Rev. Interam. Bibliogr. Revista Interamericana de Bibliografía. Organization of American States. Washington.

Rev. Junta Estud. Hist. Mendoza. Revista de la Junta de Estudios Históricos de Mendoza. Mendoza, Argentina.

Rev. Mus. Paul. Revista do Museu Paulista. São Paulo.

Rev. Novos Rumos. Revista Novos Rumos. São Paulo, Brazil.

Rev. Oriente. Revista de Oriente. Colegio Universitario de Humacao, Univ. de Puerto Rico. Humacao, Puerto Rico.

Rev. Rev. Interam. Revista/Review Interamericana. Univ. Interamericana. San Germán, P.R.

Rev. Soc. haïti. Revue de la Société haïtienne d'histoire et géographie. Port-au-Prince.

Rev. Univ./Tabasco. Revista de la Universidad. Univ. Juárez Autónoma de Tabasco. Villahermosa, Mexico.

Santiago. Santiago. Univ. de Oriente. Santiago, Cuba.

SECOLAS Ann. SECOLAS Annals. Southeastern Conference on Latin American Studies; West Georgia College. Carrollton, Ga.

Shih chieh li shih. Shih chieh li shih [World History]. Chung-kuo she hui k'o hsüeh ch'u pan she [Institute of World History Studies]. Pei-ching.

Shupihui. Shupihui. Centro de Estudios Teológicos de la Amazonia. Iquitos, Peru.

Signs. Signs. The Univ. of Chicago Press. Chicago.

Sixt. Century J. The Sixteenth Century Journal. Sixteenth Century Journal Publishers. Kirksville, Mo.

Slavery Abolit. Slavery and Abolition. Frank Cass & Co., Ltd., London.

Soc. Econ. Stud. Social and Economic Studies. Univ. of the West Indies, Institute of Social and Economic Research. Mona, Jamaica.

Sociologus. Sociologus. Berlin.

Stud. Emigr. Studi Emigrazione. Centro Studi Emigrazione. Roma.

Supl. Antropol. Suplemento Antropológico. Univ. Católica de Nuestra Señora de la Asunción, Centro de Estudios Antropológicos. Asunción.

Tech. Cult. Techniques & Culture. Maison des Sciences de l'Homme. Paris.

Temas Am. Temas Americanistas. Univ. de Sevilla, Escuela de Estudios Hispanoamericanos, Seminario de Historia de América. Spain.

Thesaurus. Thesaurus. Instituto Caro y Cuervo. Bogotá.

Tlalocan. Tlalocan. Instituto de Investigaciones Antropológicas, Instituto de Investigaciones Históricas, Univ. Autónoma de México. México.

Todo es Hist. Todo es Historia. Buenos Aires.

Ultramarines. Ultramarines: bulletin des amis del archives d'Outre-mer. Institut d'histoire del pays d'outre-mer. Aix-en-Provence, France.

Univ. Humaníst. Universitas Humanística. Pontificia Univ. Javeriana, Facultad de Filosofia y Letras. Bogotá.

Univ. La Habana. Universidad de La Habana. Habana.

Vozes. Vozes. Editôra Vozes. Petrópolis, Brazil.

West. Hist. Q. The Western Historical Quarterly. Western History Assn.; Utah State Univ., Logan, Utah.

Z. Kult.austausch. Zeitschrift für Kulturaustausch. Institut für Auslandsbeziehungen. Stuttgart, Germany.

LANGUAGE

MICHAEL D. POWERS, *Translation Division, Ebon Research Systems*

FOLLOWING A RECENT TREND, many worthy studies have been produced in the last few years on a wide variety of linguistic issues. In Portuguese, lexical and dialectical/sociolinguistic studies prevail (44 percent and 20 percent respectively). In Spanish, in addition to many lexical and dialectical/sociolinguistic studies (22 percent and 20 percent respectively), there were a large number of morphological and syntactic studies (19 percent). In both Spanish and Portuguese, a great deal of research has been done on European adstrata (17 percent) and African indigenous and Amerindian substrata (19 percent). Finally, in addition to these studies which examine such influences on the Spanish and Portuguese languages, studies have been completed on different Creole languages as well.

SPANISH
General and Bibliography

3117 Araya, Guillermo *et al.* Estudios lingüísticos en memoria de Gastón Carrillo-Herrera. Edición de Leopoldo Sáez-Godoy. Bonn: Romanisch-Historischer Verlag in Kommission, 1983. 152 p.: bibl., port.

Ten studies written in honor of hispanist Carrillo-Herrera. One, a study of a dictionary of Americanisms by Araya, refers to the classics (Malaret, 1925; Santamaría, 1942; Morinigo, 1966; and Nieves, 1973), and argues that a comprehensive dictionary of this nature should contain three dimensions simultaneously: etymological, historical, and current usage. Other contributors to this work include well-known linguists Juan Lope-Blanch, André Martinet, and Leopoldo Sáez-Godoy.

3118 Bernal Leongómez, Jaime. Tres momentos estelares en lingüística. Bogotá: Instituto Caro y Cuervo, 1984. 294 p.: bibl., ill. (Publicaciones del Instituto Caro y Cuervo: Series minor; 25)

Well-organized review of three major periods in the history of linguistics: 1) traditional grammar, including the Greeks up through the 17th-century Port Royal French school; 2) 19th-century comparative grammar which contributed to proto-Indo-European studies as well as to the scientific method; and 3) 20th-century linguistics, including structuralism and generative transformationalism.

3119 Congreso Nacional de Lingüística, 2nd, San Juan, Argentina, 1981. Actas. t. 4, pt. 2. San Juan, Argentina: Univ. Nacional de San Juan, Facultad de Filosofía, Humanidades y Artes, 1985. 1 v.: bibl., index, tables

Thirty-three brief, interesting, and well-documented studies on various aspects of linguistics generally related to Argentina.

3120 Cuervo, Rufino José. Epistolario de Rufino José Cuervo con Alfred Morel-Fatio, Gaston Paris y otros hispanistas de lengua francesa. Edición, introducción y notas de Mario Germán Romero. Bogotá: Instituto Caro y Cuervo, 1987. 389 p., 29 leaves of plates: bibl., ill. (Publicaciones del Instituto Caro y Cuervo: Archivo epistolar colombiano; 19)

Nineteenth book published on the letter writing of Rufino José Cuervo deals with his correspondence with certain French Hispanists. Letters span a 25-year period (1882–1907).

3121 Discursos académicos. v. 1. Presentación de Pedro Pablo Barnola. Edición, notas bio-bibliográficas e índices de Horacio

Jorge Becco. Caracas: Academia Venezolana Correspondiente de la Española, 1983. 1 v.: bibl., indexes.

Consists of 52 speeches (21 on language, 24 on literature, and seven on poetry) read by founding members of the Academia Venezolana Correspondiente de la Española, with corresponding replies.

3122 Encuentro Nacional de Lingüística, 4th, Mérida, Venezuela, 1983. Actas. Coordinación de Lourdes Pietrosemoli, Enrique Obediente, y Elsa Mora de González. Mérida, Venezuela: Univ. de los Andes, Facultad de Humanidades y Educación, Depto. de Lingüística, 1984. 141 p.: bibl., ill.

Twenty diverse linguistic works deal with sociolinguistic issues (manipulation in political speech, methodological considerations for social stratification, bilingual education in Venezuela, worldwide discrimination against Esperanto); generative and/or syntactic topics (word order in Spanish, linguistic theory, generative syntax); and other subjects (semantics, semiotics, etc.).

3123 García González, José and **María E. Díaz Gámez.** Bibliografía de trabajos de diploma sobre el español de Cuba en la Universidad Central de las Villas, 1971–85. (*Islas*, 84, mayo/agosto 1987, p. 186–192, bibl., index, tables)

Provides raw number of studies in different domains and indicates whether they covered Cuba in general or only the central area of the country; then lists the 45 titles. Includes subject index.

3124 Lázaro Mora, Fernando A. La presencia de Andrés Bello en la filología española. Salamanca, Spain: Ediciones Univ. de Salamanca, 1981. 277 p.: bibl. (Acta Salmanticensia: Studia philologica Salmanticensia: Anejos: Estudios; 3)

Thorough analysis shows how Bello's linguistic ideas have provided a perennial stimulus for Hispanists. Concludes that Bello's influence on the article, pronoun, and verb have withstood the test of time and earned him the undeniable position of master of the Spanish language.

3125 El lenguaje: un enfoque multidisciplinario. Tucumán, Argentina: Centro de Estudio del Lenguaje, 1985. 160 p., 2 p. of plates: bibl., ill.

Covers 14 diverse themes: defining language; language and communication; language and speech; language and philosophy; semantics; language and culture; phonetics and phonology; neurological language problems in the adult; language development; language and psychiatry; neurological language problems in the child; auditive problems and language formation; language problems and treatment in the child and adult; and speech problems and their treatment.

3126 Mora Monroy, Siervo. La enseñanza del español en Colombia: legado metodológico de Luis Flórez. Bogotá: Instituto Caro y Cuervo, 1988. 160 p.: bibl. (Publicaciones del Instituto Caro y Cuervo: Series Minor; 30)

Author presents statements of the late distinguished master of Colombian linguistics Dr. Luis Flórez concerning teaching of Spanish as a first language, drawn from diverse publications. Valuable source for anyone interested in writing texts for teaching of Spanish as a native language.

3127 Rivas Dugarte, Rafael Angel et al. Bibliografía sobre el español del Caribe hispánico. Prólogo de Iraset Páez U. Caracas: Instituto Universitario Pedagógico de Caracas, Departamento de Castellano, Literatura y Latín; Centro de Investigaciones Lingüísticas y Literarias Andrés Bello, 1985. 294 p.: index.

Well-organized bibliography covers circum-Caribbean area, with major emphasis on Venezuela, Puerto Rico, Cuba, and Atlantic portion of Colombia. Index divides studies thematically for each country, as follows: bibliographies; dialectical and sociolinguistic studies; phonetic and phonological; lexical and lexicographic; morphological and syntactic; psycholinguistic; and African, indigenous, and European substratums. For bibliographer's comment see *HLAS 50:39.*

3128 Rojas Jiménez, Oscar. Andrés Bello y el idioma castellano. Caracas: Ediciones de la Presidencia de la República, 1981. 101 p.: port.

Discusses contribution to America of Bello's famous grammar. Also touches on Bello's politics, poetic works, and defense of the Spanish language, as well as on archaisms, neologisms, and corruption of the language.

Phonology

Argüello, F.M. Arcaísmos fonéticos en el español y el quechua hablados en la región andina del Ecuador. See item **3133.**

Boyd-Bowman, Peter. Brotes de fonetismo andaluz en México hacia fines del siglo XVI. See item **3182.**

3129 Cedergren, Henrietta et al. Estudios sobre la fonología del español del Caribe. Recopilación de Rafael A. Núñez Cedeño, Iraset Páez Urdaneta y Jorge M. Guitart. Caracas: Ediciones La Casa de Bello, 1986. 178 p.: bibl., ill., index. (Col. Zona tórrida; 4: Estudios lingüísticos)

Ten studies on Caribbean phonological variation: implosive /r/ in Panamanian Spanish; phonological theories and dialects of Hispanic Caribbean; global rules in phonology of Cuban Spanish; a multidimensional model of Caribbean phonology and dialectology; social value of certain varieties of /s/ in Cartagena, Colombia; syllabic organization and implications for analysis of Caribbean Spanish; grammatical conditioning and phonological variation of a Puerto Rican dialect; implosive /r/ in a Puerto Rican dialect; disappearance of syllable final /s/ at lexical level in Dominican speech; and sociolinguistic aspects of the elision of the /d/ in Caracan Spanish.

3130 Costa Sánchez, Manuel. Observaciones sobre la realización de la n como velar en la región central de Cuba. (*Islas*, 86, enero/abril 1987, p. 77–91, bibl.)

Article deals with pronunciation of the velar in implosive position in central Cuba. Although in standard Spanish pronunciation nasals are homorganic, and thus through regressive assimilation the nasal is velarized when it precedes the unvoiced and voiced velar consonants (c and g respectively), study indicates that in central Cuba nasal is velar before all consonants regardless of their point of articulation.

Lipski, John M. /s/ in the Spanish of Nicaragua. See item **3195.**

3131 Lope Blanch, Juan M. La labiodental sonora en el español de México. (*Nueva Rev. Filol. Hisp.*, 36:1, 1988, p. 153–170)

Historical and descriptive study of the conflicting reports regarding the voiced fricative bilabial.

3132 Ruiz Hernández, J. Vitelio and Eloína Miyares Bermúdez. El consonantismo en Cuba: los laboratorios de fonética. La Habana: Editorial de Ciencias Sociales, 1984. 139 p.: bibl., ill. (Lingüística)

Scientific study completed in Prague, in which speech representative of western Cuba was analyzed through reading of written samples designed to test aspiration or elimination of phoneme /s/ and pronunciation of liquids /l/ and /r/ in different environments. Study shows that upon receiving "treatment," transposition of /l/ and /r/ was more successfully corrected than pronunciation of /s/.

Dialectology

3133 Argüello, F.M. Arcaísmos fonéticos en el español y el quechua hablados en la región andina del Ecuador. (*Orbis/Louvain*, 33:1/2, 1984, p. 161–170, bibl., tables)

Relates the Quechua substratum influence and the archaic pronunciations originating from the conquerers and colonizers which are characteristic of the Spanish spoken in the region.

3134 Benvenutto Murrieta, Pedro Manuel. Quince plazuelas, una alameda y un callejón: Lima en los años de mil ochocientos ochenta y cuatro a ochenta y siete: fragmentos de una reconstrucción basada en la tradición oral. Lima: Fondo del Libro Banco Industrial del Perú, 1983. 449 p., 16 p. of plates: bibl., ill., indexes.

Second part of this book deals with language and is subdivided into two parts: 1) Peruvianisms studied or classified by Juan de Arona (1883) and Ricardo Palma (1897 and 1903); and 2) Peruvianisms not studied or classified by Arona or Palma. Author admits that this study is not scientific, and points out need for a new vocabulary to replace Arona's classic based on data from 1860.

Cardona Santana, Héctor Rubén et al. Léxico del habla culta de San Juan de Puerto Rico. See item **3162.**

Chiossone, Tulio. Apuntaciones lexicológicas. See item **3163.**

3135 Coen, Arrigo. Para saber lo que se dice. v. 1. México: Editorial Domés, 1986. 1 v.: index.

Provides data on etymology and usage,

together with several other interesting facts, on Mexican Spanish. Author's credentials are impressive.

Díaz Montero, Aníbal. Del español jíbaro: vocabulario. See item **3187.**

3136 Díaz Seijas, Pedro. Bajo el signo creador de la lengua. Caracas: Academia Venezolana, 1985. 76 p. (Col. Logos)

First of a collection of essays dedicated to lexicographical aspects of popular Venezuelan speech contains few footnotes and no bibliography. Glossary of *venezolanismos* includes *arrime, boche, achicano, corozo, chico, lapa, mingo, turco, zamuro.* Author is director of the academy that published the work.

3137 Donni de Mirande, Nélida Esther *et al.* El español de Rosario: estudios sociolingüísticos. Rosario, Argentina: Facultad de Derecho y Ciencias Sociales del Rosario, Instituto de Historia, Centro de Lingüística Hispánica, 1987. 178 p.: bibl. (Estudios; 1)

Six sociolinguistic articles on the Spanish spoken in Rosario, Argentina. Themes include variation of final -s in second person singular preterite, gender and number of nouns, uses of the gerund in different socioeconomic strata, interrogative structures in informal speech, and Anglicisms in sporting terminology.

3138 Elizaincín, Adolfo and **Graciela Barrios.** Algunas características del español rural uruguayo: primera aproximación. (*Iberoromania,* 30, 1989, p. 63–69, bibl.)

Concludes that what makes rural Uruguayan Spanish so interesting is that it varies between non-frontier rural Spanish and Uruguayan dialectical Portuguese, with the latter providing the best of all laboratories for studying languages in contact.

3139 Estudio sobre el problema idiomático fronterizo. Montevideo: Academia Nacional de Letras, Comisión para el Estudio del Español en la Zona Fronteriza, 1982. 59 p.: bibl., ill.

Study of language usage along the Uruguay-Brazil frontier divided into five sections: 1) historical antecedents of penetration of Portuguese language into Uruguay; 2) Portuguese-language penetration into Uruguay via electronic media; 3) analysis of Uruguayan scholastic data; 4) languages in contact in the US, Canada, and France; and 5) some possible solutions to the "problem." The Comisión para el Estudio del Español en la Zona Fronteriza takes the position that the national language should be preserved in the frontier areas, a nationalistic reaction to be expected from a country bordered by a more powerful neighbor speaking a different language.

Fontanella de Weinberg, María Beatriz. El español bonaerense: cuatro siglos de evolución lingüística. See item **3189.**

3140 Fontanella de Weinberg, María Beatriz. Mantenimiento y cambio de lengua entre los italianos del sudoeste bonaerense. (*Stud. Emigr.,* 31:75, set. 1984, p. 305–319, bibl.)

Analyzes principal factors that determine linguistic behavior of Italian immigrants in Buenos Aires province, explaining that the rapid language change achieved by these immigrants is due to knowledge of Italian, differences among Italian dialects, and closeness of Italian to Spanish.

3141 Forum Callao: Historia y Cultura, 1st, Lima?, 1988. El Callao y los chalacos. Edición de Humberto Rodríguez Pastor y Francisco Quiroz. Lima: Consejo Nacional de Ciencia y Tecnología, 1988. 90 p.: bibl., ill.

Analyzes effects of the ethno-cultural mixture of the Spaniards with the indigenous population on the language and toponyms of the port of Callao. Some of the words analyzed are *callao, chalaco, chucuto,* and *pitipit.* Includes a list of works cited and a bibliography.

García Carrillo, Antonio. El español en México en el siglo XVI: estudio lingüístico de un documento judicial de la Audiencia de Guadalajara, Nueva España, del año 1578. See item **3185.**

3142 Garza Cuarón, Beatriz. El español hablado en la ciudad de Oaxaca, México: caracterización fonética y léxica. México: Colegio de México, 1987. 169 p., 2 folded leaves of plates: bibl., ill., index, maps. (Serie Estudios de dialectología mexicana; 2)

Important contribution to phonetic and lexical use of Spanish in Oaxaca, Mexico, is organized phonetically and lexically, and includes index of specific words.

Granda Gutiérrez, Germán de. Los esclavos del Chocó: su procedencia africana, siglo

XVIII, y su posible incidencia lingüística en el español del área. See item **3191**.

3143 El habla culta de la ciudad de Buenos Aires: materiales para su estudio.
v. 1. Buenos Aires: Univ. Nacional de Buenos Aires, Facultad de Filosofía y Letras, 1987. 1 v.

Provides data for analysis of learned speech through recording interviews and formal speeches.

3144 Kühl de Mones, Ursula. La partícula "de." Montevideo: Dirección General de Extensión Universitaria, División Publicaciones y Ediciones, 1980. 67 p.: bibl.

Based on questionnaire designed by author and references to classics (Kany, 1969; Seco, 1959), work describes usage of particle *de* in Montevideo, Uruguay. Concludes that there is a tendency to eliminate *de* after some intransitive verbs and adjectives, and between nouns, particularly in order to form compound words.

3145 Lipátova, Olga I. Acerca de algunas particularidades de la lengua española en Cuba. (*Santiago*, 67, dic. 1987, p. 35–45)

Among the more interesting aspects of this article on expressions peculiar to Cuban Spanish is the description of metaphorical use of adjectives such as *asesina* and *abusadora* with positive connotations.

3146 Lope Blanch, Juan M. Estudios sobre el español de Yucatán. México: Instituto de Investigaciones Filológicas, Univ. Nacional Autónoma de México, 1987. 137 p.: bibl. (Publicaciones del Centro de Lingüística Hispánica; 24)

Eight previously published essays on the Spanish of the Yucatán by a master linguist. Themes include phonetic, lexical, and etymological aspects.

López Morales, Humberto. Indices de mortandad léxica en Puerto Rico: afronegrismos. See item **3197**.

3147 Mántica, Carlos. El habla nicaragüense y otros ensayos. San José: Libro Libre, 1989. 310 p.: appendices, bibl. (Serie Raíces)

Includes author's complete works on Nicaraguan Spanish, previously published in various publications. Two appendices follow text: 1) 85 pages of Nicaraguan Nahuatlisms; and 2) Nahuatl place-names. First is quite informative, explaining meanings such as *an-*

dar por los aguacates ("to be totally out of place").

3148 Márquez Carrero, Andrés. Geografía lingüística del Estado Mérida: zonas dialectales. Mérida, Venezuela: Centro de Investigaciones Lingüísticas Julio César Salas, Facultad de Humanidades y Educación, Univ. de los Andes; Gobernación del Estado Mérida, 1985. 69 p.: bibl., ill., maps. (Publicación de la Gobernación del Estado Mérida; 38)

Extracted from author's thesis (Spain, 1972), book's principal objective is to describe speech of state of Mérida, Venezuela. Lists 68 terms, with usage of Spain compared to that of Mérida. Work is of some lexical interest.

3149 Martorell de Laconi, Susana and **Iride Rossi de Fiori.** Estudios sobre el español de la ciudad de Salta: dialectológicos y filológicos. v. 1. Salta, Argentina: Ediciones Roma, 1986. 1 v.: bibl.,ill.

One of the studies proceeding from the project on learned speech headed by Lope Blanch, launched by the *Simposio del Programa Interamericano de Lingüística y Enseñanza de Idiomas* held at Indiana University (Bloomington, Indiana, 1964). Analyzes the speech of Salta, Argentina, and should be considered within the context of the other studies completed for this project since 1964.

Megenney, William W. Black rural speech in Venezuela. See item **3198**.

3150 Montes Giraldo, José Joaquín. Estudios sobre el español de Colombia. Bogotá: Instituto Caro y Cuervo, 1985. 441 p.: bibl., ill., maps. (Publicaciones del Instituto Caro y Cuervo; 73)

Collection of large number of studies on Colombian Spanish published in *Thesaurus* from 1956 to mid-1980s. Includes general regional studies as well as phonetic, morphological, syntactical, semantical, and lexical contributions. Valuable study unites diverse topics under theme of Colombian Spanish.

Ríos Quiroga, Luis. Nuestro idioma popular en *La chaskañawi*: estudio lexicológico. See item **3175**.

3151 Rosell, Avenir. Del habla uruguaya: apuntes de lexicografía. Montevideo: Arca, 1987. 135 p.: bibl., index.

Excellent contribution to study of

Uruguayan speech. Contains extensive bibliography of nearly 200 entries, including several from 1980s. Succinct but valuable contribution analyzes more than 350 terms of variants, drawn from literary texts of the most varied type.

3152 Rossi de Fiori, Iride; Estela Ballone de Martínez; and Susana Martorell de Laconi. Algunas particularidades de la lengua oral de la ciudad de Salta. 3a ed. Salta, Argentina: Ediciones Roma; Univ. Católica de Salta, 1985. 30 p.: bibl.

Describes and systematizes certain characteristics of spoken language of city of Salta. Classifies recorded samples under criteria of morphological, syntactical, and phonetic, and offers conclusions on various tendencies on morphological, morpho-syntactic, semantic, and phonetic levels. Succinct, concise study.

Ruiz Hernández, J. Vitelio and Eloína Miyares Bermúdez. El consonantismo en Cuba: los laboratorios de fonética. See item **3132**.

3153 Studies in Caribbean Spanish dialectology. Edited by Robert M. Hammond and Melvyn C. Resnick. Washington: Georgetown Univ. Press, 1988. 145 p.: bibl., ill. (Romance languages and linguistics series)

Thirteen papers on following themes: sociolinguistic variation of liquids in word final position; linguistic factors for subject position in Caracas; vocalic nasalization in Caracas; Spanish imperative intonation; Hispanic-African contacts in equatorial Africa; bilingualism and linguistic attitudes in Puerto Rico; interference and markedness, and their role in a foreign accent; infinitive with an expressed subject in Spanish; compensatory vocalic lengthening in Cuban Spanish; phonology of liquids; some historical and legal aspects of bilingualism in colonial Hispanic America; a syntactic change in Caracas; and a social history of the term *mestizo* in the Caribbean.

3154 Thun, Harald; Carlos E. Forte; and Adolfo Elizaincín. El atlas lingüístico diatópico y diastrático del Uruguay (ADDU): presentación de un proyecto. (*Iberoromania*, 30, 1989, p. 26–62, appendices)

Very credible attempt to make a linguistic atlas of Uruguay by utilizing relevant past work and designing a questionnaire in both Spanish and Portuguese. Raises interesting methodological concerns.

Valdés Acosta, Gema. Algunos fenomenos semánticos en los remanentes africanos del centro de Cuba. See item **3179**.

Valdés Bernal, Sergio. La evolución de los indoamericanismos en el espanõl hablado en Cuba. See item **3204**.

3155 Villegas Duque, Néstor. Apuntaciones sobre el habla antioqueña en Carrasquilla. v. 3–4. Manizales, Colombia: Impr. Departamental, 1987. 2 v.: bibl. (Biblioteca de escritores caldenses)

Vols. 3 and 4, published posthumously, include Americanisms, regionalisms, and Colombianisms, as well as phrases used exclusively in Antioquia. However, everything included is used in Antioquia. Over 100 sources, all of which are more than 20 years old, include Cuervo, Flórez (1957), González (1942), etc.

3156 Williamson, Rodney. El habla de Tabasco: estudio lingüístico. México: Colegio de México, Centro de Estudios Lingüísticos y Literarios, 1986. 272 p.: bibl., maps. (Serie Estudios de dialectología mexicana; 1)

Based on 1978 Ph.D. thesis, study describes phonetic, morphological, and lexical attributes of Spanish of the state of Tabasco, Mexico. Employs sociolinguistic categories (age, sex, etc.) and compares results with other Spanish dialects of Mexico. Attention is given to loan words from Nahuatl, Maya, Chontal, and Zoque. [L. Campbell]

Lexicon

3157 Alfaro Echevarría, Luis; Gloria Méndez Cruz; and Mercedes Garcés Pérez. Observaciones sobre el léxico de la industria azucarera en la región central de Cuba. (*Islas*, 86, enero/abril 1986, p. 70–76, bibl.)

Authors point out importance of having standardized vocabulary so as to eliminate differences between official and popular use, variations caused by geographical and sociocultural factors, and polysemantic lexical items resulting in ambiguities. Explains approximately 30 terms which do not appear in the Cuban Science Academy's *Vocabulario de la cana de azucar*, but which are employed throughout Cuba by all personnel who work at sugar plants.

3158 Alvar, Manuel. Léxico del mestizaje en Hispanoamérica. Madrid: Ediciones Cultura Hispánica, Instituto de Cooperación Iberoamericana, 1987. 223 p.: bibl., ill.

Extremely well-documented lexical etymologies of 100 terms. Very valuable contribution for understanding mestizo lexicon in Spanish America.

3159 Alvarez Osben, Alberto. Diccionario de términos contables, comerciales y computacionales. 2a ed. Valparaíso, Chile: Ediciones Universitarias de Valparaíso, Univ. Católica de Valparaíso, 1987. 674 p.: bibl., ill.

Second edition of 1973 original is much improved for four reasons: 1) contains 1,004 accounting terms, a significant increase; 2) includes 640 of the most frequent computer terms; 3) provides 7,961 synonyms of given terms plus English equivalencies; and 4) main entries are given in German also. Definitions and alphabetical listing of terms are only in Spanish.

3160 Arévalo, Oscar et al. Breve diccionario político. México: Editorial Cartago, 1981. 141 p.: bibl.

Brief political dictionary is useful guide for terms commonly found in the media, conferences, books, etc. Main reference for work was *Pequeño diccionario político* (1969) by I.V. Liojin and M.E. Struve.

3161 Ascaso Liria, Alfonso and **Manuel Casals Marcén.** Vocabulario de términos meteorológicos y de ciencias afines. Madrid: Sección de Publicaciones del I.N.M., 1986. 408 p.: bibl.

Synthesis of diverse sources includes definitions from various polyglot vocabularies drawn from the World Meteorological Organization; however, primary source for work is American Meteorological Society's *Glossary of Meteorology.* Pertinent terms from the Real Academia Española's *Diccionario de la lengua española* are unchanged. Aims to be of use to both high school graduates and professionals.

3162 Cardona Santana, Héctor Rubén et al. Léxico del habla culta de San Juan de Puerto Rico. Coordinación de Humberto López Morales. San Juan: Academia Puertorriqueña de la Lengua Española, 1986. 254 p.: appendices, bibl., ill.

Study proceeds from project on learned speech launched by *Simposio del Programa Interamericano de Lingüística y Enseñanza de Idiomas* held at Indiana University (Bloomington, Indiana, 1964). Study combines four different lexical studies on specific domains, and is divided into following headings: the human body; food; clothing; family, life cycle, and health; social life and pastimes; city and commerce; transportation and travel; communication; newspapers, cinema, television, radio, theater, and circus; foreign trade and national politics; unions and cooperatives; occupations; finance; education; religion; meteorology; chronological time; terrain; vegetation and agriculture; and animals and livestock. Valuable contribution to study of variation in learned vocabulary selection in San Juan.

3163 Chiossone, Tulio. Apuntaciones lexicológicas. Caracas: Consejo de Profesores Universitarios Jubilados, UCV, 1986. 243 p.

Gives interesting comparison between words used for body parts in Venezuela and those used in Colombia and Honduras. Takes words beginning with letter "t" from the Real Academia Española's *Diccionario de la lengua española* and notes differences in their meaning in Venezuela. Makes reference to classification of some words as both "Venezuelanisms" *and* "Uruguayanisms, and points out that some words which have the same meaning in both Mexico and Venezuela are not so presented in Santamaría's *Diccionario de americanismos* nor in the Real Academia Española's *Diccionario.* Specifies which words listed in the *Diccionario de Venezolanismos* by María Josefa Tejera are actually Americanisms.

3164 Comisión Nacional de Valores (Mexico). Glosario de términos bursátiles. México: Comisión Nacional de Valores; Dirección General de Administración y Finanzas, 1987. 246 p.: bibl.

Alphabetical list in English of 761 terms gives equivalent term and succinct definition in Spanish. Includes two indexes to terms (English to Spanish and vice versa).

Díaz Montero, Aníbal. Del español jíbaro: vocabulario. See item **3187.**

Díaz Seijas, Pedro. Bajo el signo creador de la lengua. See item **3136.**

3165 Estrada, Leonel. Arte actual: diccionario de términos y tendencias. Colaboración de María Isabel de Molina y María Luisa E. de Vélez. Diseño y diagramación de Alberto Sierra. Medellín, Colombia: Editorial Colina, 1985. 247 p.: bibl., ill. (some col.).

Dictionary of technical terms relative to contemporary plastic arts includes more than 1,000 terms with most definitions consisting of 100 words or less. Also contains more than 100 pictures, more than half in color. Professor Detlef M. Noak of the Superior School of Arts in Berlin highly recommends this work for its conciseness, completeness, documentation, and diversity.

3166 García Díaz, Rafael. Diccionario técnico, inglés-español. México: Editorial Limusa, 1986. 540 p.

Provides Spanish equivalencies for engineering terms used in English. Includes thousands of terms, with detailed meaning discrimination, from all fields of technology, technical professions, sciences, thermodynamics, physics, and civil, mechanical, chemical, and electrical engineering. Particularly detailed in areas of metallurgical and mining engineering. Important tool for technical translations from English to Spanish.

3167 Gobello, José. Diccionario de voces extranjeras usadas en la Argentina. Buenos Aires: Fundación Federico Guillermo Bracht, 1988. 223 p.: bibl.

Interesting contribution to etymologies of foreign terms in Argentine Spanish.

Gottheim, Vera L. Dicionário prático de economia, finanças e comércio: português-inglês-alemão-espanhol. See item **3224**.

3168 Haensch, Günther. Der Wortschatz des amerikanischen Spanisch und seine Erfassung in lexikographischen Inventaren. (*Iberoromania*, 30, 1989, p. 1–25)

Historical panorama of lexicography in Spanish America reveals that first glossaries were annexes to historical treatments for the purpose of explaining difficult words to natives. These annexes provide evidence that differentiation in the lexicon of Spanish America has existed since the 17th century. Author criticizes a number of the existing dictionaries of Americanisms in Spanish America and calls for a new methodological approach.

López Morales, Humberto. Indices de mortandad léxica en Puerto Rico: afronegrismos. See item **3197**.

3169 Macazaga Ordoño, César. Los nahuatlismos de la Academia: textos y enmiendas. México: Editorial Innovación, 1987. 101 p.

Lists 465 Nahuatlisms included in the Real Academia Española's *Diccionario de la lengua española* and their respective commentaries. Alongside the commentaries, Macazaga Ordoño, author of specialized dictionaries on the Nahuatl culture, gives his opinions as to etymology of the terms and the accurateness of the Real Academia Española's definitions. For example, he disagrees with the definition for "avocado" which, according to the Academia, is always shaped like a pear and must be eaten with salt. Interesting contribution for understanding the influence of Nahuatl on Spanish.

3170 Marois, Roger et al. Estudio comparativo de los terminos franceses, ingleses, españoles y portugueses relativos a las técnicas de decoración de la cerámica prehistórica. (*Bol. Antropol. Am.*, 12, dic. 1985, p. 115–128, bibl., ill., tables)

Article standardizes lexical items in Spanish, Portuguese, French, and English concerning technical aspects of decoration of prehistoric pottery. Bibliography cites 17 publications: 10 in English, three in French, three in Spanish, and one in Portuguese.

3171 Montero, María Luisa. Vocabulario de Benito Lynch. Colaboración de Silvia N. Trentalance de Kipreos. Buenos Aires: Academia Argentina de Letras, 1986. 214 p.: port. (Serie Estudios lingüísticos y filológicos; 2)

Study of recorded vocabulary used by an author whose style is characterized by his peculiar and expressive use of language and dialog. Study was unanimously awarded the prize for a "complete vocabulary of a modern or classic author, Spanish or Spanish-American" by the Real Academia Española.

3172 Moreno de Alba, José G. Minucias del lenguaje. México: Océano, 1987. 160 p.

Provides 45 prescriptive and 50 descriptive rules for vocabulary usage. Prescriptive section gives some insight on current usage in Mexico. Extensive references to Real Academia Española's *Diccionario de la lengua española* (1984) and to many well-known linguists (Rosenblatt, Zamora Vicente, etc.).

3173 Muvdi, Elías E. Apuntes de español—a propósito de la vigésima edición del Diccionario Académico. Bogotá: Ediciones Tercer Mundo, 1984. 356 p.: bibl., index.

Consists of two parts: 1) study of certain words and phrases, and other grammatical considerations; and 2) suggestions for the Real Academia Española. Interesting contribution that sheds additional light on Colombian Spanish.

3174 Nazoa, Aníbal. La palabra de hoy. Caracas: Fondo Editorial Salvador de la Plaza, 1981. 368 p. (Serie roja: Literatura)

This enjoyable book employs double entendre in giving popular etymologies for 360 terms. Author has great sense of humor and makes reference to Greek, Anglo-Saxon, and other languages in his etymologies.

3175 Ríos Quiroga, Luis. Nuestro idioma popular en *La chaskañawi*: estudio lexicológico. Sucre, Bolivia: Ediciones Radio Loyola, 1984. 101 p.: index.

Gives context and explanation for 559 lexical items of popular speech of inhabitants of a section of Bolivia through analysis of third edition of novel *La chaskañawi* by Medinaceli. Analyzes expressions through reference to *Diccionario vivo del pueblo*. Interesting study, although no differentiation is made between widely-used regionalisms (e.g., *chola*) and more restricted terms (e.g., *viracochas*).

3176 Rodríguez, Tino. Primer diccionario de sinónimos del lunfardo: la palabra en movimiento. Buenos Aires: Editorial Atlántida, 1987. 355 p.: bibl.

Extensive bibliography enhances value of this dictionary of slang.

Rosell, Avenir. Del habla uruguaya: apuntes de lexicografía. See item **3151.**

Semantics

3177 Boisset Mujica, Guacolda. Origen y significado del vocablo *Vichuquén*. Santiago: Editorial América; Librería Chile Ilustrado, 1985. 27 p.: bibl., ill.

Author points out that *Vichuquén* is not only the name of a lagoon, but also that of a very old village which at times is combined with a neighboring village of the same name. Brief, well-documented study.

3178 Mora Monroy, Siervo. Algunos usos de los términos del color en el español de Colombia. (*Thesaurus*, 44:2, mayo/agosto 1989, p. 441–450, bibl.)

Interesting contribution discusses connotations of each color within its context.

3179 Valdés Acosta, Gema. Algunos fenomenos semánticos en los remanentes africanos del centro de Cuba. (*Islas*, 85, sept./dic. 1986, p. 104–113, bibl.)

Describes semantic phenomena of Bantu origin currently present in Spanish of central Cuba, and explains that these remnants, because of their slave origins, were sociolinguistically disparaged. Charles Kany's *American-Spanish semantics* is used as reference for explaining several semantic shifts.

Syntax

Kühl de Mones, Ursula. La partícula "de." See item **3144.**

Lope Blanch, Juan M. La estructura de la cláusula en el habla culta de Bogotá. See item **3196.**

3180 Mestre Varela, Gema *et al.* Observaciones en torno a la subordinación modal y a la comparativa. (*Islas*, 86, enero/abril 1987, p. 92–101, bibl.)

Authors conclude that *como* followed by a noun makes up a single component for the subordinate sentence, whereas when *como* is followed by *si* or *cuando*, it carries the connotation of a conditional or temporal relationship respectively.

3181 Profesor Candial. Los duendes del habla: aciertos, errores y dudas en nuestro lenguaje habitual. Buenos Aires: Corregidor, 1985. 227 p.

Using the Real Academia Española as a source, provides prescriptive treatment of correct usage, errors, and doubts of the language. Author's qualifications are: humanities teacher, journalist, humorist, and meteorologist. No bibliography.

Diachronic

Argüello, F.M. Arcaísmos fonéticos en el español y el quechua hablados en la región andina del Ecuador. See item **3133.**

3182 Boyd-Bowman, Peter. Brotes de fonetismo andaluz en México hacia fines del siglo XVI. (*Nueva Rev. Filol. Hisp.*, 36:1, 1988, p. 75–88, map, facsim.)

Weakening and loss of consonants was abundant in the 16th-century Spanish of Guatemala and Mexico, if the books published at that time were at all phonetic. This factor correlates positively with patterns of immigration of Andalusian settlers to lowlands of Spanish America.

3183 Bravo García, Eva María. El español del siglo XVII en documentos americanistas. Sevilla, Spain: Ediciones Alfar, 1987. 133 p.: bibl. (Alfar/universidad; 25)

Based on 70 documents written between 1607 and 1631. Describes the Spanish of 17th-century America and the documentary sources used for the work; then presents a linguistic study in the following areas: accentuation and pronunciation, use of capital letters, phonological analysis, phonetic evolution, morphosyntaxis, and lexicon. Author concludes that: 1) punctuation and use of capital letters seemed arbitrary; 2) orthography was not standardized; 3) phonological use of sibilants and progressive assimilation of vibrant to the following lateral was characteristic; 4) non-essential articles, conjunctions, and prepositions were eliminated; and 5) vocabulary was legal and administrative.

3184 Briceño Perozo, Mario. La obligación de enseñar el castellano a los aborígenes de América. Caracas: Academia Venezolana de la Lengua, 1987. 123 p.: bibl., ill. (Col. Logos; 4)

Historical treatment with footnotes studies teaching of Spanish to indigenous peoples from 16th-18th centuries, and pertinent decrees.

3185 García Carrillo, Antonio. El español en México en el siglo XVI: estudio lingüístico de un documento judicial de la Audiencia de Guadalajara, Nueva España, del año 1578. Sevilla, Spain: Ediciones Alfar, 1988. 137 p.: bibl. (Alfar/universidad; 28: Serie Investigación y ensayo)

Linguistic study based on analysis of an Archivo General de Indias judicial text from the 1578 Audencia de Guadalajara treats phonetic-phonological, morphosyntactic, and lexical/semantic aspects, analyzed in light of Andalusian influence existing at that time. Interesting contribution from specialist in this area. Approximately 50 good sources are listed in bibliography.

Sociolinguistics

3186 Camps Iglesias, Alina M. and **María Teresa Noroña Vilá.** Aproximación al estudio de la toponimia cubana. La Habana: Academia de Ciencias de Cuba, Instituto de Literatura y Lingüística, s.d. 79 p.: bibl., ill.

Outlines steps followed up to present concerning Cuban place-names. Concludes that place-names communicated a social need such as the economic, political, and/or social means of life, the stage of development, or the history of the locale. Interesting bibliography includes Soviet as well as Spanish and Latin American studies of the theme.

3187 Díaz Montero, Aníbal. Del español jíbaro: vocabulario. 3a ed., aum. y corr. Santurce, P.R.: Editorial Díaz-Mont, 1984. 172 p.: bibl.

Language used by author in his short stories reflects dialect used in remote parts of Puerto Rico. Work is valuable counterpart to literature devoted to "habla culta," and author's succinct definitions help preserve a dying vocabulary.

Donni de Mirande, Nélida Esther *et al.* El español de Rosario: estudios sociolingüísticos. See item **3137.**

Encuentro Nacional de Lingüística, 4th, Mérida, Venezeuela, 1983. Actas. See item **3122.**

3188 Figueroa Lorza, Jennie. Connotaciones socio-económicas en las respuestas del léxico de la alimentación. (*Thesaurus*, 42:3, sept./dic. 1987, p. 647–673)

Interesting article in which author explains that people's ways of expressing what they regularly eat helps to classify them socioeconomically.

3189 Fontanella de Weinberg, María Beatriz. El español bonaerense: cuatro siglos de evolución lingüística. Buenos Aires:

Hachette, 1987. 174 p.: bibl. (Col. Hachette universidad: Lengua-lingüística-comunicación)

Examines overall evolution of Spanish in Buenos Aires from 1580–1980, giving analyses and conclusions for each of the past four centuries. Offers sociolinguistic radiation from upper social strata to lower as reason for spread of palatalization of sibilants during 20th century, citing large number of terms from French and English (both prestige languages) through which this palatalization has taken place.

3190 Fundamentos lingüísticos para una política idiomática en la comunidad hispanohablante: seminario internacional celebrado en conmemoración del bicentenario del nacimiento de Don Andrés Bello, Santiago, 1981. Santiago: Univ. de Chile, 1983. 93 p.: bibl.

Includes six of the presentations given at an international seminar on linguistic fundamentals for formulating a language policy in the Spanish-speaking community. Seminar was an effort to determine the destiny of Spanish as a general language of culture for the extensive geographic area encompassed by the Spanish-speaking community. World-renowned sociolinguists such as Fontanella de Weinberg, Foster, and Roca-Pons participated.

3191 Granda Gutiérrez, Germán de. Los esclavos del Chocó: su procedencia africana, siglo XVIII, y su posible incidencia lingüística en el español del área. (*Thesaurus,* 42: 1, enero/abril 1988, p. 65–80)

African linguistic influence on the Spanish of the Chocó area of Colombia includes change of /d/>/r/ and replacement of /k/ with /?/. Nigerian linguistic influence can be seen through pronunciation of glottal movement (/kp/, /gb/). Also covers some morphosyntactic similarities and possible influence such as double negation.

3192 Granda Gutiérrez, Germán de. Los estudios lingüísticos afrohispanoamericanos, 1975–1985. (*Beitr. Roman. Philol.,* 26:2, 1987, p. 267–289)

Valuable contribution gives good overview of possible African language influences on Spanish, based on extensive research in this area completed from 1975–85. Expanded version of paper presented at International

Congress on the Spanish in America (2nd, 1986).

3193 Granda Gutiérrez, Germán de. Situación actual de los estudios lingüísticos afrohispanoamericanos. (*Thesaurus,* 42: 1, enero/abril 1987, p. 60–94)

Interesting overview of research in Afro-Hispanic linguistics.

3194 Lipski, John M. The origin and development of *lan/nan* in Afro-Caribbean Spanish. (*Beitr. Roman. Philol.,* 26:2, 1987, p. 291–300)

Very detailed study states that *lan/nan* appears consistently only in Cuban and Puerto Rican *bozal* (born in Africa and speaking little or no Spanish) Spanish after beginning of 19th century. Concludes that it is unlikely that *lan/nan* is an evolution of a putative West African Portuguese subject pronoun.

3195 Lipski, John M. /s/ in the Spanish of Nicaragua. (*Orbis/Louvain,* 33: 1/2, 1984, p. 171–181, map, tables)

Author concludes that aspiration or loss of /s/ has penetrated all social strata in Nicaragua.

3196 Lope Blanch, Juan M. La estructura de la cláusula en el habla culta de Bogotá. (*Thesaurus,* 43: 2/3, mayo/dic. 1988, p. 296–309, tables)

Study of data recorded for learned speech in Bogotá parallels the findings for other Latin American capitals since the same three syntactic features predominate in all: 1) subordinate clauses are more common than other types; 2) most frequent type of subordination is adverbial; and 3) causative subordination is most frequent type of adverbial subordination.

3197 López Morales, Humberto. Indices de mortandad léxica en Puerto Rico: afronegrismos. (*Nueva Rev. Filol. Hisp.,* 36:2, 1988, p. 733–751, appendices, tables)

Study indicates no social correlates according to sociocultural level or sex. Some variation based on generational level is shown, apparently due to a lack of penetration of lexical items.

Macazaga Ordoño, César. Los nahuatlismos de la Academia: textos y enmiendas. See item **3169.**

Mannheim, Bruce. La memoria y el olvido en la política lingüística colonial. See item **3330.**

3198 Megenney, William W. Black rural speech in Venezuela. (*Neophilologus,* 73:1, Jan. 1989, p. 52–61, bibl., map)
Barlovento, a geographical area southeast of Caracas heavily influenced by the slave trade, is analyzed for African substratum influence in three contexts: illness and remedies; short stories; and music and dance. Sub-Saharan influence in these three domains is first discussed at the lexical level through etymologies; then phonological interchange of /r/, /i/, and /d/ is explained as a possible African creole substratum trait.

3199 Obregón Muñoz, Hugo. Hacia la planificación del español de Venezuela y la determinación de una política lingüística. Caracas: Centro de Investigaciones Lingüísticas y Literarias Andrés Bello, Depto. de Castellano, Literatura y Latín, Instituto Universitario Pedagógico de Caracas, 1983. 81 p.: bibl., ill.
Study examines three subjects: 1) problems related to Venezuelan language policy based on scientific data; 2) need to define language policy, with some specific proposals; and 3) didactic observations directed primarily to educators. Work complements the now standard contributions of learned speech or *habla culta.*

3200 Política lingüística na América Latina. Organização de Eni Pulcinelli Orlandi. Campinas, Brazil: Pontes Editores, 1988. 191 p.: bibl., ill. (Linguagem/crítica)
Nine essays dealing with diverse themes including African influence on colloquial Cuban Spanish, indigenous languages, the teaching of foreign languages, and important linguistic topics in Mexico, Paraguay, Uruguay, and Bolivia.

3201 Rodríguez de Montes, María Luisa. Algunos quechuismos en el *Alec:* posibles quechuismos en el muisca y en el español de la primitiva zona de asentamieto muisca. (*Thesaurus,* 42:1, enero/abril 1987, p. 95–121, map)
The Quechua influence proposed in this study is supported by historical, linguistic, and archaeological documentation. Interesting contribution.

3202 Rojas Nieto, Cecilia. Las construcciones coordinadas sindéticas en el español hablado culto de la ciudad de México. México: Univ. Nacional Autónoma de México, Instituto de Investigaciones Filológicas, 1982. 271 p.: bibl. (Publicaciones del Centro de Lingüística Hispánica; 16)
Study based on data collected in Mexico City from questionnaire drafted at the *Simposio del Programa Interamericano de Lingüística y Enseñanza de Idiomas* held at Indiana University (Bloomington, Indiana, 1964). Investigation was limited to coordinating conjunctions *y, ni, o, pero,* and *sino.* Includes extensive bibliography.

3203 Silva Téllez, Armando. Punto de vista ciudadano: focalización visual y puesta en escena del graffiti. Bogotá: Instituto Caro y Cuervo, 1987. 86 p., 12 p. of plates: bibl., ill. (Publicaciones del Instituto Caro y Cuervo: Series minor; 29)
Interesting study of the relatively modern phenomenon of graffiti produced from data collected in Bogotá between 1978–82. Gives reasons for graffiti, followed by their social causes in parentheses: marginality (communication); anonymity (ideological); art (aesthetic); speed (instrumental); precariousness (economic); and impetuosity (social).

Studies in Caribbean Spanish dialectology. See item **3153.**

Valdés Acosta, Gema. Algunos fenomenos semánticos en los remanentes africanos del centro de Cuba. See item **3179.**

3204 Valdés Bernal, Sergio. La evolución de los indoamericanismos en el español hablado en Cuba. La Habana: Editorial de Ciencias Sociales, 1986. 185 p.: bibl., ill. (Lingüística)
Focuses on interesting processes through which indigenous speech was incorporated into Spanish in the spoken Spanish of Cuba, rather than on etymology of terms. Points out eastern provinces of Cuba conserved a greater number of indigenous terms than did other provinces. Interesting bibliography includes a number of Czechoslovakian sources.

3205 Valdés Bernal, Sergio. Las lenguas indoamericanas y el español hablado en Cuba. (*Am. Indíg.,* 48:2, abril/junio 1988, p. 403–417, bibl.)

Describes Arawak and Carib migrations and those of the Nahuatl and Maya-speaking peoples to illustrate certain linguistic terms as well as characteristics of the Spanish now spoken in Cuba. Points out Carib and Arawak lexicon is most widespread, and thus infers that the Taino and Lucayo must have been dominated by some of the Carib groups. Lists terms such as *cacique, guajiro,* and *papaya* as indigenous borrowings.

Williamson, Rodney. El habla de Tabasco: estudio lingüístico. See item **3156.**

PORTUGUESE
General and Bibliography

3206 Encontro de Lingüística e Literatura, 1st, Serra Talhada, Brazil, 1981. Anais. Recife, Brazil: Grupo de Estudos Lingüísticos do Sertão; Secretaria de Educação de Pernambuco, DDN, DEPLAN, Divisão de Avaliação e Pesquisa, 1982. 121 p.: bibl., ill.

Lectures cover three main areas: linguistics, Portuguese linguistics, and literature. Wide variation in quality of papers, some having no bibliographies.

3207 Ferreira, Carlota et al. Diversidade do português do Brasil: estudos de dialectologia rural e outros. Salvador, Brazil: Centro Editorial e Didático da UFBA, 1988. 235 p.: bibl., ill.

Collection of lectures, articles, papers, etc. written by professors and researchers of the Portuguese language at the Univ. Federal da Bahia. Includes two main themes: 1) rural dialectological studies concerned with speech in Bahia and the linguistic atlas of Sergipe; and 2) other research, including doctor/patient communication, the teaching of Portuguese in Brazil, subject/verb agreement in Brazilian Portuguese, role of relative pronouns in written Portuguese, etc.

Phonology

3208 Silveira, Regina Célia Pagliuchi da. Estudos de fonologia portuguesa. São Paulo: Cortez Editora, 1986. 254 p.: bibl., ill. (Série Gramática portuguesa na pesquisa e no ensino; 11)

Comprises a number of Portuguese

phonological studies and serves as basis for study of Brazilian phonemes.

3209 Wanke, Eno Theodoro. A ortografia que nos atormenta: reflexões e dados sobre o problema ortográfico e sugestões para a desburocratização da escrita. 2a. ed. Rio de Janeiro: Editora Codpoe, 1987. 48 p.: bibl.

Urges spelling reform for Portuguese so that written language is phonetic. Points out confusion of /s/ and /z/, /x/ and /ch/, /ss/ and /c/, and /s/ or /x/ before /t/. Work is a guide to improving spelling; does not address social issues involved in language change rejection. However, the suggestions do make sense.

Dialectology

Aragão, Maria do Socorro Silva de et al. Linguagem religiosa afro-indígena na grande João Pessoa. See item **3238.**

3210 Azevedo, Thales de. A francesia baiana de antanho. Salvador, Brazil: Univ. Federal da Bahia, Centro de Estudos Baianos, 1985. 42 p. (Centro de Estudos Baianos; 110)

"Contamination" of vocabulary and expressions via foreign influence seems to be the theme of this brief study. Not a scientific survey; no bibliography.

Callou, Dinah Maria Isensee. Variação e distribuição da vibrante na fala urbana culta do Rio de Janeiro. See item **3239.**

Elizaincín, Adolfo and **Graciela Barrios.** Algunas características del español rural uruguayo: primera aproximación. See item **3138.**

3211 Elizaincín, Adolfo; Luis Ernesto Behares; and Graciela Barrios. Nos falemo brasilero: dialectos portugueses en Uruguay. Montevideo: Editorial Amesur, 1987. 126 p.: bibl., maps. (Col. Análisis)

Linguistic description of Portuguese dialects of Uruguay, based on data collected from different areas of the country during 1979 and 1980. Presents thorough analyses, and includes nominal and verbal phrases and syntax. Useful study for researchers interested in linguistic influence of a powerful country on a weaker neighboring country speaking a different language.

Estudio sobre el problema idiomático fronterizo. See item **3139.**

Ferreira, Carlota et al. Diversidade do português do Brasil: estudos de dialectologia rural e outros. See item **3207**.

3212 Ferreira, Carlota and Suzana Alice Cardoso. Dois estudos sobre o léxico dos "falares baianos." Salvador, Brazil: Univ. Federal da Bahia, Centro de Estudos Baianos, 1985. 36 p.: bibl., maps. (Centro de Estudos Baianos; 114)

Two lexical studies of "Bahian speech," i.e., speech of the states of Bahia and Sergipe and part of the state of Goiás. Both are based on linguistic atlases, one published in 1963 and the other completed in 1978, though not yet published.

Matos, Francisco Gomes de. The sociolinguistics of Brazilian Portuguese. See item **3242**.

Questionário básico de trabalho campo [i.e. de campo] lingüístico: revisão crítica do questionário do Atlas lingüístico de Antenor Nascentes. See item **3243**.

Stawinski, Alberto Victor. Dicionário vêneto sul-rio-grandense—português: com breves noções gramaticais do idioma vêneto sul-rio-grandense. See item **3237**.

Thun, Harald; Carlos E. Forte; and Adolfo Elizaincín. El atlas lingüístico diatópico y diastrático del Uruguay (ADDU): presentación de un proyecto. See item **3154**.

Lexicon

3213 Belchior, Elysio de Oliveira. Vocabulário de termos econômicos e financeiros. Rio de Janeiro: Civilização Brasileira, 1987. 397 p.: bibl.

Gives basic definitions of approximately 1,500 economic and financial terms. Based on about 600 references, approximately 20 of which were published in the 1980s.

3214 Bueno, Francisco da Silveira. Grande dicionário da língua portuguesa-Lisa. São Paulo: Editora Lisa, 1987. 625 p., 14 p. of plates: col. ill.

Valuable contribution by one of the most respected Brazilian lexicographers.

3215 Dicionário de economia. Consultoria de Paulo Sandroni. São Paulo: Editora Best Seller, 1987. 459 p. (Os Economistas)

Lists approximately 2,000 economic terms in monolingual format. Definitions vary from a few sentences to several hundred words. No information given on selection process, authorship, etc. Lacks bibliography.

3216 Dicionário de informática: inglês-português. 4a. ed. Rio de Janeiro: Livros Técnicos e Científicos Editora; Sociedade dos Usuários de Computadores e Equipamentos Subsidiários, 1985. 687 p.

English lexical entries are translated into Portuguese, followed by succinct definitions in Portuguese. Useful tool for those involved with computer science.

3217 Dicionário de termos botânicos ilustrado. Redação de Domingo Alzugaray e Cátia Alzugaray. São Paulo: Três Livros e Fascículos, 1984. 88 p.: ill. (some col.).

Well-organized, easy-to-use illustrated botanical dictionary.

3218 Dicionário de termos militares: português-inglês, inglês-português. Brazil: Estabelecimento General Gustavo Cordeiro de Farias, 1983. 252 p.

English-Portuguese/Portuguese-English dictionary of military terms. Objectives and methodology are not explained.

3219 Duarte, Sérgio Guerra. Dicionário brasileiro de educação. Rio de Janeiro: Antares; Nobel, 1986. 175 p.

In addition to universal teaching terminology, includes legal elements unique to Brazil. Author is leading figure in educational research in Brazil.

3220 Ehlers, Edel Helga Kick and Gunter Ehlers. Dicionário alemão-português de economia e direito = Deutsch-portugiesisches Wörterbuch für Wirtschaft und Recht. São Paulo: E.H.K. Ehlers, 1981. 424 p.

Mono-directional German-Portuguese dictionary of economics and law alphabetized according to German terms. No definitions or grammatical information included.

3221 Ehlers, Edel Helga Kick and Gunter Ehlers. Dicionário português-alemão de economia e direito = Portugiesisch-deutsches Wörterbuch für Wirtschaft und Recht. São Paulo: E.H.K. Ehlers, 1982. 505 p.

Mono-directional Portuguese-German dictionary of economics and law alphabetized according to first term of the Portuguese phrases included. No definitions are given. The only grammatical information provided is gender of German nouns.

Ferreira, Carlota and **Suzana Alice Cardoso.** Dois estudos sobre o léxico dos "falares baianos." See item **3212.**

3222 Fraenkel, Benjamin B. Glossário inglês-português de termos médicos: termos médicos-termos correlatos, expressões idiomáticas, 3,500 verbetes, 103 páginas. Rio de Janeiro: Distribuidora, Livraria e Editora Revinter, 1987. 122 p.

Dictionary contains many terms which are non-medical and even unrelated to field of medicine, making its value dubious. Author is a civil engineer.

3223 Glossário de geologia estrutural e tectónica: com a correspondente terminologia em inglês e francês. Elaboração de Peter Rideg. Revisão de Alfredo J.S. Bjornberg. São Paulo: Associação Brasileira de Geologia de Engenharia, 1981. 32 p.: appendices, indexes. (Glossário de termos técnicos de geologia de engenharia.)

Lists 284 geological engineering terms with equivalencies in English and French, followed by succinct, approximately 50-word definitions in Portuguese. Main section is followed by two appendices arranged alphabetically in English and French, and cross-referenced back to dictionary and definitions section.

3224 Gottheim, Vera L. Dicionário prático de economia, finanças e comércio: português-inglês-alemão-espanhol. São Paulo: Editora Atica, 1987. 503 p.

Quadri-directional dictionary in Portuguese, English, German, and Spanish lists a few thousand of the most commonly used professional terms in economics and finance. Equivalencies given in target languages; multiple equivalencies given where appropriate.

3225 Guerra, Antônio Teixeira. Dicionário geológico, geomorfológico. 7a. ed., rev. e atualizada. Rio de Janeiro: Secretaria de Planejamento e Coordenação da Presidência da República, Fundação Instituto Brasileiro de Geografia e Estatística, 1987. 446 p., 1 folded leaf of plates: ill.

Dictionary intended primarily for the layman to provide understanding and appreciation of physical geography.

Hall, Joan; Ruth Alice McLeod; and **Valerie Mitchell.** Pequeno dicionário xavánte-português, português-xavánte. See item **3241.**

Heckler, Evaldo; Sebald Back; and **Egon Ricardo Massing.** Dicionário morfológico da língua portuguesa. v. 5. See item **3234.**

3226 Lederman, Isaac. Dicionário técnico de eletrônica inglês-português. São Paulo: Icone Editora, 1986. 125 p. (Col. Ciência e tecnologia ao alcance de todos)

Dictionary covers most common English-language terminology used in field of electronic technology. Entries are followed by equivalencies and definitions in Portuguese.

Luft, Celso Pedro. Dicionário prático de regência verbal. See item **3235.**

3227 Magliocca, Argeo. Glossário de oceanografia. São Paulo: Nova Stella; EDUSP, 1987. 355 p.: bibl., ill.

Standardizes Brazilian oceanographic terminology. Following glossary, hundreds of English-language terms and their Portuguese equivalencies are given. Includes extensive bibliography listing many publications from the 1970s and 1980s. Valuable contribution for accurate communication of Brazilian oceanographic terms.

3228 Martins, Amadeu. Glossário inglês-português de termos de engenharia costeira. Rio de Janeiro: Empresa de Portos do Brasil, 1981. 191 leaves: bibl., ill.

Listing approximately 1,100 terms, glossary is first attempt to list some of the most commonly used terms in coastal engineering. Main source is *Waves, tides, currents and beaches: glossary of terms and list of standard symbols* by Robert L. Wiegel (1953).

Matos, Francisco Gomes de. The sociolinguistics of Brazilian Portuguese. See item **3242.**

3229 Michaelis dicionário prático da língua portuguesa. Apresentação de Antônio Houaiss. São Paulo: Melhoramentos, 1987. 1043 p.

Dictionary written with linguistic rigor by qualified researchers, scientists, and technicians. Excellent contribution worthy of scholarly attention.

3230 Miranda, Nicanor. Dicionário de parônimos. Belo Horizonte, Brazil: Editora Itatiaia, 1989. 184 p. (Col. Argos; 5)

Portuguese words similar or identical in pronunciation but different in meaning are explained in great detail. Valuable as a tool for selecting the correct term.

3231 Rabaça, Carlos Alberto and **Gustavo Guimarães Barbosa.** Dicionário de comunicação. São Paulo: Editora Atica, 1987. 637 p.: bibl., ill.

Updates 1978 edition particularly in areas of cybernetics, informatics, television and telecommunication. Extensive bibliography includes some references from the 1980s.

Stawinski, Alberto Victor. Dicionário vêneto sul-rio-grandense—português: com breves noções gramaticais do idioma vêneto sul-rio-grandense. See item **3237.**

Tibiriçá, Luiz Caldas. Dicionário de topônimos brasileiros de origem tupi: significação dos nomes geográficos de origem tupi. See item **3244.**

3232 Toledo, Flávio de and **B. Milioni.** Dicionário RH de administração de recursos humanos. 2a. ed. rev. e aum. Curitiba, Brazil: Associação Brasileira de Recursos Humanos; São Paulo: Cardápio, 1983. 117 p. (Col. Cardápio; 2)

Monolingual dictionary lists terms related to personnel (human resources) and organizational behavior, followed by concise bilingual dictionaries (Portuguese-English and English-Portuguese) with roughly 600 entries in each language.

Syntax

3233 Everett, Daniel L. Anaphoric indices and inalienable possession in Brazilian Portuguese. (*Linguist. Inq.*, 20:3, Summer 1989, p. 491–497)

Generative transformational study done to determine how inalienably possessed NPs in Brazilian Portuguese differ from both pronouns and anaphors.

3234 Heckler, Evaldo; Sebald Back; and **Egon Ricardo Massing.** Dicionário morfológico da língua portuguesa. v. 5. São Leopoldo, Brazil: Univ. do Vale do Rio dos Sinos, Gráfica UNISINOS, 1985. 1 v.

Morphological dictionary in the strict structural sense.

3235 Luft, Celso Pedro. Dicionário prático de regência verbal. São Paulo: Editora Atica, 1987. 544 p.: bibl.

Thorough analysis of Portuguese verbs based on approximately 50 studies (mostly books), 16 of which were published in the 1970s and 1980s. Lists thousands of verbs, touching on transitivity, evolution, and prepositions used when introducing a following infinitive. Valuable contribution for understanding syntactic consequences of verbs on contemporary Brazilian Portuguese.

3236 Pessoa, Regina Maria. Manifestações da negação em portugues: a negação implícita. (*Alfa*, 29, 1985, p. 97–100, bibl.)

Examines some of the ways in which negation is expressed in Portuguese, both at the deep and surface levels. Tests pattern proposed for Spanish by Roberto Ibáñez in *Negation im Spanischen* (1972) and evaluates its adequacy for Portuguese.

Diachronic

3237 Stawinski, Alberto Victor. Dicionário vêneto sul-rio-grandense—português: com breves noções gramaticais do idioma vêneto sul-rio-grandense. Caxias do Sul, Brazil: EDUCS, 1987. 321 p.: bibl.

Dictionary of *vêneto*, a dialect developed from Italian immigrants and spoken in the southern mountain chain of Rio Grande do Sul in the 19th century. Work has great historical and cultural interest. Lexicographer has extensive knowledge of romance languages

Sociolinguistics

3238 Aragão, Maria do Socorro Silva de et al. Linguagem religiosa afro-indígena na grande João Pessoa. João Pessoa, Brazil: Fundação Casa de José Américo, 1987. 104 p.: bibl., ill.

Concludes that dominant source of African and indigenous religious language used in Greater João Pessoa is Sudanese (143 terms), while Bantu languages combined account for only 45 terms, and Tupi, 25.

Bernardes, Carmo. Memórias do vento. See item **4524.**

3239 Callou, Dinah Maria Isensee. Variação e distribuição da vibrante na fala urbana culta do Rio de Janeiro. Rio de Janeiro: PROED, Univ. Federal do Rio de Janeiro, 1987. 194 p.: bibl. (Teses)

Linguistic parameters of the vibrant in learned speech of Rio de Janeiro is divided into word initial, intervocalic, syllable final, and end of word. Data utilized are drawn from previously-conducted research on learned speech of Rio. Work is sociolinguistic study "a la Labov" in which social correlations are statistically established. Extensive bibliography.

3240 Castro, Sílvio. Italiano e italianismos em Antônio de Alcântara Machado. (Lett. Am., 2:9/10, autunno 1981, p. 155–172)

Examples of Italian text and codeswitching between Italian and Portuguese are given from the works of this Brazilian Modernist author.

3241 Hall, Joan; Ruth Alice McLeod; and Valerie Mitchell. Pequeno dicionário xavánte-português, português-xavánte. Brasília: Summer Institute of Linguistics, 1987. 491 p.

Objectives of this bi-directional Portuguese-Shavante dictionary are: 1) to provide an opportunity for Portuguese speakers to communicate with Shavante speakers; 2) to provide Shavante speakers with opportunity to learn Brazil's national language; 3) to provide a written record of rich lexicon of Shavante; and 4) to provide a source of information for those interested in indigenous languages. In their preface, authors explain that Shavante has four kinds of words: verbs, nouns, adjectives, and words with a prepositional function.

3242 Matos, Francisco Gomes de. The sociolinguistics of Brazilian Portuguese. (LARR, 23:2, 1988, p. 252–257)

After giving a brief overview of the status of Brazilian Portuguese in American universities, author evaluates Chamberlain and Harmon's A dictionary of informal Brazilian Portuguese and Bortoni-Ricardo's The urbanization of rural dialect speakers: a sociolinguistic study in Brazil. Concludes that the former is an accurate reference tool for

learning the informal spoken variety of Brazilian Portuguese; and that Bortoni-Ricardo's work is a valuable contribution to sociolinguistics, particularly on the qualitative and quantitative aspects of languages in their social and cultural aspects.

Política lingüística na América Latina. See item **3200.**

3243 Questionário básico de trabalho campo [i.e. de campo] lingüístico: revisão crítica do questionário do Atlas lingüístico de Antenor Nascentes. Organização de Mônica Rector. Rio de Janeiro: Fundação Casa de Rui Barbosa, 1983. 187 p.: bibl.

Provides data from the pioneering work proposed by Antenor Nascentes to be used as a basis for further linguistic research. The 30-page introduction explains how the proceedings of the Simposio del Programa Interamericano de Lingüística y Eseñanza de Idiomas held at Indiana University (Bloomington, Indiana, 1964) are used as a resource for the work. Extensive data provided make this a valuable contribution.

Stawinski, Alberto Victor. Dicionário vêneto sul-rio-grandense—português: com breves noções gramaticais do idioma vêneto sul-rio-grandense. See item **3237.**

3244 Tibiriçá, Luiz Caldas. Dicionário de topônimos brasileiros de origem tupi: significação dos nomes geográficos de origem tupi. São Paulo: Traço Editora, 1985. 197 p.: bibl.

Valuable contribution for understanding Brazilian toponyms of Tupi origin. Author is an expert on indigenous languages and on Tupi habits and beliefs. This is the complete and definitive work on this subject.

CREOLE

3245 Archer, Marie-Thérèse. Créologie haïtienne: latinité du créole d'Haïti: créole étudié dans son contexte ethnique, historique, linguistique, sociologique et pédagogique. Port-au-Prince: Impr. Le Natal, 1987. 622 p.: bibl. (Livre du maître; 1)

Covers diverse subjects related to Creole (origin of the language; Haitian culture; influence of the Spaniards, Africans, French, and British; non-Latin creole; vocabulary and other linguistic topics). In conclusion author warns against foreign university "brain washing" which does not reflect authentic Haitian culture.

3246 Gibson, Kean. The habitual category in Guyanese and Jamaican creoles. (*Am. Speech*, 63:3, Fall 1988, p. 195–202, bibl.)

Refutes Bickerton's contention (in *Dynamics of a Creole system*, 1975) that one morpheme is used in the Guyanese basilect, and by extension in the Jamaican basilect, for both the habitual and progressive meanings.

Granda Gutiérrez, Germán de. Lingüística e historia: temas afro-hispánicos. See item **720.**

3247 Huttar, George L. A Creole-Amerindian pidgin of Suriname. West Indies: Published for the Society for Caribbean Linguistics by the School of Education, Univ. of the West Indies, 1982. 13 p.: bibl. (Occasional paper; 15)

Overview of the Djuka language spoken by "Bush Negroes" and of the Oyana and Trio languages spoken by indigenous peoples in the southeast corner of Suriname. Based on De Goeje's (1908) observations and author's own fieldwork of the 1970s. Concludes that pidgin language used between Djuka and Oyana and Trio speakers for trade purposes has remained fairly stable, with segmental phonology deriving mostly from an earlier form of Djuka while clause-level syntax follows mainly a Cariban, possibly Trio, pattern.

3248 Joseph, Yves J. Le creole dans les sciences: problemes et perspectives. (*Bull. Bur. natl. ethnol.*, 2, 1985, p. 25–41, tables)

Interesting article concerning role of Creole, a mainly spoken language, and its suitability for communicating abstract notions of science and technology, using as examples some terms from marine science. Concludes by suggesting creation of a technical and scientific lexical committee on Creole for the purposes of filling lexical voids and dealing with emerging new realities within science and technology.

3249 Lauriette, Gérard. Le créole de la Guadeloupe: nègres-marrons. Pointe-à-Pitre: G. Lauriette, 1981. 84 p.: ill.

Interesting study of Guadeloupe Creole is divided into three sections: 1) ortho-

graphy according to semi-literate Creole speakers; 2) etymological orthography; and 3) phonetic orthography. Also gives meaning of some current Creole expressions.

3250 Mendes, John. Cote ce Cote la: Trinidad & Tobago dictionary. Illustrated by Wayne Berkeley and John Mendes. Trinidad: Syncreators, 1985. 200 p., 6 p. of plates: ill.

This dialect is a unique mixture of British English, Spanish, French, East Indian, Arabic, and Chinese languages. Dictionary translates terms and phrases into standard English. Very interesting, with expressions such as "cockroach have no right in fowl party." (Not previously annotated by *HLAS*.)

JOURNAL ABBREVIATIONS

Alfa. Alfa. Univ. de São Paulo, Faculdade de Filosofia, Ciências e Letras. Marília, São Paulo.

Am. Indíg. América Indígena. Instituto Indigenista Interamericano. México.

Am. Speech. American Speech. Columbia Univ. Press. New York.

Beitr. Roman. Philol. Beiträge zur Romanischen Philologie. Rütten & Loening. Berlin.

Bol. Antropol. Am. Boletín de Antropología Americana. Instituto Panamericano de Geografía e Historia. México.

Bull. Bur. natl. ethnol. Bulletin du Bureau national d'ethnologie. Bureau national d'ethnologie. Port-au-Prince, Haiti.

Iberoromania. Iberoromania. Max Niemeyer Verlag. Tübingen, Germany.

Islas. Islas. Univ. Central de Las Villas. Santa Clara, Cuba.

LARR. Latin American Research Review. Latin American Research Review Board. Univ. of New Mexico, Albuquerque, N.M.

Lett. Am. Letterature d'America. Bulzoni Editore. Roma.

Linguist. Inq. Linguistic Inquiry. MIT Press. Cambridge, Mass.

Neophilologus. Neophilologus. H.O. Tjeenk Willenk, etc. Groningen, The Netherlands.

Nueva Rev. Filol. Hisp. Nueva Revista de Filología Hispánica. El Colegio de México. México.

Orbis/Louvain. Orbis. Centre international de dialectologie générale. Louvain, Belgium.

Santiago. Santiago. Univ. de Oriente. Santiago, Cuba.

Stud. Emigr. Studi Emigrazione. Centro Studi Emigrazione. Roma.

Thesaurus. Thesaurus. Instituto Caro y Cuervo. Bogotá.

LITERATURE

SPANISH AMERICA
General

SARA CASTRO-KLAREN, *Professor of Hispanic and Italian Studies, The Johns Hopkins University, with the assistance of Marcy Schwartz.*

IN THE LAST THREE YEARS there has been an extraordinary increase in the number of works in literary criticism. These have been published in both specialized journals and as books printed all over the Spanish- and Portuguese-speaking worlds, the US, France, and even Russia.

Although books and articles on the writers of the "boom" continue to appear, their focus has changed. Instead of analyzing individual texts and styles, these studies now concentrate on retrospectives or interviews with a widening circle of writers, not necessarily members of the "boom" but of the same literary generation. Critical studies such as Pedro Lastra's *Relecturas hispanoamericanas* (item **3271**), Ana María Barrenechea's *El espacio crítico en el discurso literario* (item **3254**) and Jaime Giordano's *La edad de la náusea* (item **3263**) exemplify a growing sophistication in the critical appreciation and theoretical analysis of texts. Nevertheless, it would be fair to say that the most novel and interesting material produced in the last three years involves historical studies. More and more efforts are being directed towards understanding the development of Latin American literature as a conflicting, heterogenous, complex, and highly creative historical process. Two main approaches are used to explore it: regional studies and global designs.

The two outstanding works on the region produced in the last few years are Roberto Márquez's essay on Caribbean literary production (item **3277**) and Richard Jackson's comprehensive and up-to-date discussion of Caribbean literatures within the context of a "humanistic enthnopoetics" (item **3269**). Márquez's essay pioneers the way for the interdisciplinary and integrated study of linguistically and socially heterogenous materials, a project that was called for at the UNESCO-sponsored group meeting held in Campinas, Brazil, in 1983. Although not a participant in either the Campinas or the Caracas meeting led by Angel Rama, Márquez has mastered the French, English and Spanish affluents of Caribbean culture as they redefine themselves while meeting and mixing in the ocean of African culture. Equally useful, if not as insightful as Márquez's essay, are those that attempt to revise our received understanding of "indigenismo." Both René Prieto's study of "new indigenismo," which emphasizes the self-creativity of Indian myth, song, and language as literary formations of the present (item **3282**), and López-Martínez's study, which traces the changing role of religion in the creation of cultural identities (item **3264**), offer an important over-hauling of "indigenismo." Within this circuit of interaction between European cultural formations, their journey to this hemisphere, and the indigenous response to invasion and displacement, Cornejo Polar's strongly theoretical account of the conflictive and yet creative linguistic and socio-political realities that emerge in the Andes is perhaps a "tour-de-force" (item **3259**).

However, the novel and dominant trend in this *Handbook* is represented by essays and books on literary history. Worthy of note are works by Ana Pizarro (item **3273**) and Beatriz González Stephan (item **3266**). They both have published partial results of a project involving at least 10 scholars whose work is generally associated with the school of socio-criticism. To date, the most valuable effort at rethinking the history of Latin American writing with due attention to its heterogeneity and uneven developments has been Beatriz González's exhaustive bibliography on the histories of Latin American literature.

On the whole, the field is passing through a period of assimilation of the theoretical revolution of the last quarter of a century, utilizing a diversity of approaches to works once considered canonical *literary* texts. Although their volume remains constant, both feminist studies and socio-criticism continue to reorient the field towards what North American academic circles define as "cultural studies."

3251 Ainsa, Fernando. The invention of America: imaginary signs of the discovery and construction of Utopia. (*Diogenes/Philosophy*, 145, Spring 1989, p. 98–111)

Shows that separation between discovery and invention has not been always possible within the discourse of European expansion in the Western Hemisphere. Unlike the well-known historical source work done by Edmundo O'Gorman in his seminal *La invención de América* (1961, see *HLAS 25: 3013*), Ainsa tries to link the function of the imaginary to the foundation of Utopia. He writes that ". . . it is not an exaggeration to say that the first *idea* of America was inspired by the images that preceded its discovery" (p. 103). Ainsa links the *idea* of America to the European myth of the Golden Age. On the whole, this article adds little to the well-documented, provocative, and yet-to-be-superseded book by O'Gorman.

3252 Arango L., Manuel Antonio. Origen y evolución de la novela hispanoamericana. Bogotá: Tercer Mundo Editores, 1988. 543 p.: bibl. (Crítica literaria)

Solid review of the traditional periodization of the development of the novel in Latin America advances thesis that the novel is not only the most "representative" genre of Spanish American writing, but also that it serves as chief advocate and vehicle for social change. Differs from established notion that *El periquillo sarniento* (1816) was the first Spanish-American novel, and proposes *El desierto prodigioso y el prodigio del desierto* by Pedro de Solís y Valenzuela (1624–1711) instead. Welcome addition to the field that fills the need for a new *alternative*, authoritative history (chronology) of the Spanish-American novel. Highly recommended as a guide to individual authors, periods, and cultural context for specific texts.

3253 Araújo, Helena. La scherezada criolla: ensayos sobre escritura femenina latinoamericana. Bogotá: Centro Editorial, Univ. Nacional de Colombia, 1989. 258 p.: bibl., ill.

Thoughtful inquiry into writing by women in Latin America challenges standard views. Attributes notion of women having greater talent (weakness?) for conceptualization in terms of metaphorical and analogical thought due to their subject status. Highly influenced by French feminists. Points out need to reconceptualize women within social and symbolic orders in which they participate with as much contingent freedom as other social beings. Pt. 2 contains information on women writers translated into French. Wide-ranging, solid, and illuminating work covers at least 30 major women writers in detail. Recommended.

3254 Barrenechea, Ana María. El espacio crítico en el discurso literario. Buenos Aires: Kapelusz, 1985. 76 p.: bibl. (Col. La Comunicación verbal)

Brief and readable essays in which Barrenechea returns to her long-standing interest in the fantastic. Examines in illuminating detail the fantastic within the framework of speech act theory, and also includes innovative essays on "La Ilustre Fregona" by Cervantes and Unamuno's novelistic experiments. Although apparently disparate in subject matter, the book is an excellent example of coherence in methodology and theory. Recommended reading for those in search of methodology.

3255 Barylko, Jaime et al. Pluralismo e identidad: lo judío en la literatura latinoamericana. Buenos Aires: Milá, 1986. 268 p. (Ensayos)

Collection drawn from papers of 1986 conference examines Jewish themes of identity, repression, exile, and treatment of Israel in Latin American literature. Participants include important Argentine writers and intellectuals such as Sosnowski, Constantini, Goloboff, Kamenszain, and Steimberg. This significant forum is worth consulting in conjunction with Sosnowski's *La orilla inminente* (see *HLAS 50:3530*), Naomi Lindstrom's recent *Jewish issues in Argentine literature* (item **3942**) and Senkman's journal *Noah* (Jerusalem).

Bastos, María Luisa. Relecturas: estudios de textos hispanoamericanos. See item **3913**.

A bibliographical guide to Spanish American literature: twentieth-century sources. See item **27**.

3256 Calviño Iglesias, Julio. Historia, ideología y mito en la narrativa hispanoamericana contemporánea. Madrid: Ayuso, 1987. 294 p.: bibl., ill.

Fairly comprehensive analysis of the novels of dictatorship. Covers *El señor presidente, Yo el supremo, El recurso del método*, and *El otoño del patriarca*. Intelligent discussion of levels of mythic and historical meaning, although in a style somewhat obscured by jargon and a conceptually-packed vocabulary.

3257 Carballo, Emmanuel. Protagonistas de la literatura hispanoamericana del siglo XX. México: Coordinación de Difusión Cultural, Dirección de Literatura, UNAM, 1986. 206 p. (Textos de humanidades)

Interviews (1958–76) with writers on the political left such as Cortázar, Benedetti, Galeano, and others. Provides revealing commentary on intellectual history, politics, and developments in Latin America. Carballo focuses discussion not only on the writers'

lives but on their ideas and anlayses of Latin America in those years.

3258 Cobo Borda, Juan Gustavo. Visiones de America Latina. Bogotá: Tercer Mundo Editores, 1987. 310 p.: bibl. (Crítica)

Es esta la quinta recopilación de trabajos críticos que publica el autor. El conjunto es, en realidad, miscelánico: ensayos, artículos críticos, entrevistas de él y sobre él, notas de arte, etc. Hay páginas muy valiosas en la primera parte, pero no todo escapa a su efímera intención periodística. [J.M. Oviedo]

3259 Cornejo Polar, Antonio. Indigenist and heterogeneous literatures: their dual sociocultural status. (*Lat. Am. Perspect.*, 16:2, Spring 1989, p. 12–28, bibl.)

Excellent and clearly organized essay despite dense theoretical prose presents important framework for considering and appreciating how conflicting cultural, linguistic, and sociopolitical realities form Latin American literature. Concentrates on Andean literature but includes references to colonial chronicles and other "heterogeneous" indigenist literature "situated in the conflictive junction of two societies and two cultures." Cites Mariátegui, Jitrik, Rama, and begins and ends with Arguedas.

3260 Cortázar, Julio et al. Exilio: nostalgia y creación. Recopilación de Alberto Garrido. Mérida, Venezuela: Dirección de Cultura de la Univ. de los Andes, 1987. 92 p.: bibl.

Collection of interviews and lectures by Cortázar, Benedetti, Cardenal, Galeano, Skármeta, Jitrik, Droguett, and Britto García, drawn from a 1979 Venezuelan conference on "The Latin American Exile in the 1970s." Various talks emphasize exile as a positive, dynamic, creative experience. More interesting as a historical and biographical document than for its theoretical or critical content.

Cuentos judíos latinoamericanos. See item **3823**.

The Faber book of contemporary Latin American short stories. See item **4918**.

3261 Feal, Rosemary Geisdorfer. Women writers into the mainstream: contemporary Latin American narrative. (*in* Philosophy and literature in Latin America: a critical assessment of the current situation. Edited by Jorge J. E. Gracia and Mireya Camurati. Albany, N.Y.: State Univ. of New York Press, 1989, p. 114–124)

Attempts to link Borges, the Boom, and the writing of fiction by women. Points out that while "Boom" stars, such as García Márquez and Vargas Llosa living at the time in Barcelona, ridiculed the idea of "intellectual women," ". . . women writers were producing extremely good literature (Clarice Lispector), as they had been in Latin America long before the intellectual acclaim" (p. 119) brought on by the "Boom." Credits feminist literary critics for having taught colleagues to read and evaluate against the grain of officially established hierarchies. Fails, however, to describe, contend, or analyze the actual position or re-positioning of women writers into the mainstream or canon.

3262 Gálvez Acero, Marina. La novela hispanoamericana contemporánea. Madrid: Taurus, 1987. 180 p.: bibl. (Historia crítica de la literatura hispánica; 33)

Solid introductory study of the "new novel" of the "Boom." Starting with the 1940s, author gives historical overview of movements and the literary market, along with several chapters on novelistic theory, the fantastic, and "magic realism." Includes helpful bibliography of criticism and theory on the genre and its historical development.

3263 Giordano, Jaime. La edad de la náusea: sobre narrativa hispanoamericana contemporánea. Santiago: Instituto Profesional del Pacífico; New York: Distribución, J. Giordano, 1985. 252 p.: bibl. (Monografías del maitén; 3)

Collection of essays offers introspective and innovative panorama on Latin American narrative from Arlt to current novelists such as Luis Rafael Sánchez, Pacheco, and Cabrera Infante. Of particular interest are two essays: 1) on levels of writing, in which author discusses temporal relativity in three different generations of 20th-century narrative; and 2) on spatial subjectivity in Arlt. Provides far-reaching and well-grounded conclusions about the development of literary generations and their language.

3264 Gómez-Martínez, José Luis. La novela indigenista en la toma de consciencia de la identidad iberoamericana. (Torre, 3:9, enero/marzo 1989, p. 1–10)

This overview of the indigenist novel from late 19th century (Cumandá, Aves sin nido) through the 1950s (Arguedas' Los ríos profundos) concentrates on the changing role of religion in Latin American cultural identity. Organized chronologically, full of pertinent references, this article uses these novels to provide background on the emergence of Liberation Theology in the region's cultural consciousness. See also item **3280**.

3265 González Echevarría, Roberto. Colón, Carpentier y los orígenes de la ficción latinoamericana. (Torre, 2:7, julio/sept. 1988, p. 439–452)

Advances thesis that the current acknowledgment by writers such as García Márquez, Vargas Llosa, and Fuentes of the origins of the Latin American novel in the "crónicas de Indias" belies the fact that all novels wish to pass for history. The "crónicas" themselves were not written/read as history. Also proposes that it was Alejo Carpentier who discovered "the formula" that made possible the transformation of American history into novelistic discourse. Abovementioned writers recognize the filiation of their work with the "crónicas" as well as the shared "idealizaciones de fundación," and are regarded by author as disciples of Carpentier. His works evoke "ecos de lo ya nombrado," rendering absurd the much bandied about but simplistic notion that Colombus' arrogance was to act as if nothing before him had a name or belonged to the symbolic. Rigorous, extremely well-informed, strongly theoretical work. Highly recommended.

3266 González Stephan, Beatriz. Contribución al estudio de la historiografía literaria hispanoamericana. Caracas: Academia Nacional de la Historia, 1985. 214 p. (Biblioteca de la Academia Nacional de la Historia. Estudios, monografías y ensayos; 59)

Two-part, exhaustive, well-organized, extremely useful bibliography on the history of Latin American literature. Pt. 1 is a long essay on its historiography which notes neglect of literary history since textual studies gained unquestioned priority in early 1960s. Argues that our current concept of literary history is extremely vague. Points out that most comprehensive studies avoid the word "history" and call attention instead to notions such as "atlas," "sketch," "panorama." Most studies tend to "dehistorizar la comprensión del material literario, asumir el rol de verdaderos museos." Pt. 2 makes concrete proposals for the writing of a new literary history through 1) an examination of the vastness of literary production; 2) an analysis of existing literary histories; and 3) the writing of a comparative and comprehensive literary history that emerges out of the study of national histories as a system of plural literary conglomerates. Valuable contribution to an important problem. Should be read in conjunction with Ana Pizarro's work (item 3273).

3267 Gutiérrez Girardot, Rafael. Aproximaciones. Bogotá: Procultura, Presidencia de la República, 1986. 157 p.: bibl. (Nueva biblioteca colombiana de cultura)

In somewhat dense prose author offers intellectual and philosophical history of culture. Insightful chapter on Modernism traces the movement's emergence amid European secularization and urban expansion. Another important essay analyzes problems of periodization in Latin American literature.

3268 Hozven, Roberto. Pedro Henríquez Ureña: el maestro viajero. (*Rev. Iberoam.*, 54:142, enero/marzo 1988, p. 291–320)

Illuminating essay offers excellent interpretative introduction to Henríquez Ureña's work and thought. Provides comprehensive synthesis of this critic's recognition of differences within Latin American culture and language, and discusses three of his most important ideological and theoretical contributions: 1) "pluma libre," or the practice of writing for the public in a popular spirit; 2) formation of a dialectical style vs. a trivial or conventional one; and 3) his role as the "maestro viajero."

3269 Jackson, Richard L. Black literature and humanism in Latin America. Athens, Ga.: Univ. of Georgia Press, 1988. 166 p.: bibl., index.

Well-organized, comprehensive, up-to-date study constitutes a significant contribution to both black literature and Latin American literature. Examines black Latin American literature from the perspective of "humanistic ethnopoetics." Rather than treating such works in an isolated context or as a sub-canon, Jackson connects issues of ethnic authenticity and "civilization vs. barbarism" in black literature with broader literary Americanism. Reviews Afrocriollo movement, and concludes with two chapters on very recent black novelists (e.g., Carlos Guillermo Wilson, Quince Duncan, Jorge Artel).

3270 Jitrik, Noé. La vibración del presente: trabajos críticos y ensayos sobre textos y escritores latinoamericanos. México: Fondo de Cultura Económica, 1987. 183 p.: bibl. (Col. Tierra firme)

Essays on Borges, Lezama's *Paradiso*, Segovia, Arlt, Julieta Campos, and others. Analyzes dynamics of *Paradiso* as example of sway between sense and non-sense, rupture and chaos. Jitrik's essay on Rulfo's world of ciphered silences and symbols is one of the most incisive psychoanalytical approaches to this author's work. Echoes Paz's proposition concerning absence of critical thinking in Latin America as part of the Spanish failure to develop critical thought. Attempts to distinguish between "criticism" and "opinion," and to situate criticism within the realm of "scientific" or rational inquiry into a systematic production of meaning. Essays continue Jitrik's inquiry into discourse theory already presented in two of his previous books: *Producción literaria y producción social* (1975) and *La memoria compartida* (1982).

Kul'tura Latinskoĭ Ameriki: problema natsional'nogo i obshcheregional'nogo; sbornik stateĭ [Latin American culture: the problem of nationality and regionality; a collection of articles]. See item 290.

Landscapes of a new land: fiction by Latin American women. See item 4923.

3271 Lastra, Pedro. Relecturas hispanoamericanas. Santiago: Editorial Universitaria, 1987. 139 p.: bibl. (Col. El Saber y la cultura)

Refreshing collection of essays concentrates on intertextuality and "scriptural strategies," or how writing is conceived, constructed, and produced. Texts range from colonial period and Modernism to contemporary narrative and poetry. Discusses less-recognized writers (e.g., Enrique Lihn, Juan Emar) and lesser-known works by "Boom" writers.

3272 Liscano, Juan. National identity in Latin American literature. (*Diogenes/ Philosophy*, 138, Summer 1987, p. 41–60)

Insightful critical article discusses

how influence of Latin American literature on world culture was limited by the constraints of European literary forms. Cites literary examples from 19th-20th centuries, and stresses search for an "American essence," the pursuit of identity through racial mix, colonial history, and indigenous idealism. Concludes that Latin America continues to incorporate and project European cultural sensibilities.

3273 La literatura latinoamericana como proceso. Coordinación de Ana Pizarro. Buenos Aires: Bibliotecas Universitarias, Centro Editor de América Latina, 1985. 147 p.: bibl. (Lengua y literatura)

Concise essays by sophisticated Marxist-oriented critics (e.g., Angel Rama, Ana Pizarro) discuss social "imaginary" of Latin American letters, literary historiography, and the problematics of periodization in attempting to formulate a literary history of Latin American writing. Essays represent a sampling from a 1983 conference. (See also item **3281.**

Lives on the line: the testimony of contemporary Latin American authors. See item **4925.**

3274 Lopes, Edward and **Eduardo Peñuela Cañizal.** O mito e sua expressão na literatura hispano-americana. São Paulo: Livraria Duas Cidades, 1982. 157 p.: bibl., ill. (Col. O Baile das quatro artes)

Collection of essays with a consistent focus covers García Márquez, Borges, Cortázar, Paz, and avant-garde poets. Studies attempt to investigate "myth," or "essa vida contemporaneidade de toda historia americana," which Borges labels the autobiographical past of new countries. By recognizing the mythic narrative style of non-Western components of Latin American literature, these critics (e.g., Lopes and Cañizal) correctly attribute the avant-garde quality of writers such as Miguel Angel Asturias to an indigenous narrative heritage. Uses Proppian and semiotic analytical methodology to explain mythic narrative as an integral but variable component of technical innovations identified with the recent Latin American novel. Highly recommended for all those interested in the symbiotic relation between the realistic and mythic modes of representation.

3275 Losada Guido, Alejandro. La literatura en la sociedad de América Latina. München, Germany: W. Fink, 1987. 279 p.: bibl. (Beiträge zur Soziologie und Sozialkunde Lateinamerikas; 27)

Losada's last theoretical study elaborates his view of literature as praxis, or social practice and the process of production. This dense but organized and comprehensive study stresses the plurality of Latin American literatures, and constructs a model to account for the different regional modes of production that determine literary "systems" or periods as they emerge from the larger process of social development.

3276 Lustig, Wolf. Christliche Symbolik und Christentum im spanischamerikanischen Roman des 20. Jahrhunderts. Frankfurt am Main; New York: P. Lang, 1989. 595 p.: bibl. (Europäische Hochschulschriften: Reihe XXIV, Ibero-romanische Sprachen und Literaturen, 0721–3565; 29)

Surveys and analyzes Christian symbolism in the Spanish-American novel in the 20th century. Author singles out works by Carlos Dorguett, Roa Bastos, Eduardo Caballero Calderón, Vicente Leñero, Manuel Rojas, and José Manuel Vergara, among others. Lustig maintains that Alejo Carpentier's novels can be read as a sort of inventory of Spanish America's Christian heritage. Insightful, ambitious and careful study, based on a wide array of source materials. [G.M. Dorn]

3277 Márquez, Roberto. Nationalism, nation, and ideology: trends in the emergence of a Caribbean literature. (in The modern Caribbean. Edited by Franklin W. Knight and Colin A. Palmer. Chapel Hill, N.C.: Univ. of North Carolina Press, 1989, p. 293–340)

Lucid and insightful essay on the cultural vitality of Caribbean literature that incorporates references from English, French, and Spanish narrative and poetry. Includes excellent discussion of mid-19th-century narratives, and comments on Guillén, Carpentier, and Luis Rafael Sánchez. Concentrates on the fusion of European and African culture in metaphors that reveal the tension of a colonial, multi-cultural context.

3278 Márquez Rodríguez, Alexis. El barroco literario latinoamericano. (*Casa Am.*, 30:177, nov./dic. 1989, p. 58–72)

Introduction to conflicting interpretations of the Baroque in Latin American contemporary literature compares theories of Sarduy, Carpentier, Paz, and Fuentes. Article lacks application of these theories to examples in narrative and poetry. Compares the Baroque as a traditional, historic, European style with the more contemporary view of the Baroque as a constant, integral element of Latin American cultural identity.

Myth and the imaginary in the New World. See *HLAS 51:147.*

3279 Noya, Fumiaki. Ekkyousuru Latin America [Latin America crosses the borders]. Tokyo: PARCO Shuppan, 1989. 271 p.: photos.

Collection of literary criticism and essays on Latin American modern literature by the leading Japanese critic in the field. Noya reveals the universality of Latin American novels disseminated beyond their borders by reviewing works by Borges, García Márquez, Paz, etc. Essays on the influence of Latin American novelists upon Japanese modern writers are especially suggestive. [K. Horisaka]

3280 Pinillos, Nieves. Repercusión de la teología de la liberación en la narrativa iberoamericana. (*Cuad. Am.,* 12:6, nov./dic. 1988, p. 60–68)

Brief account of historic and ideological impulses behind Liberation Theology lead into Pinillos's examination of the social material in the Latin American novel. Liberation Theology is especially relevant to what she characterizes as "urban" and "guerrilla" novels. Article examines role of the priest in seven novels by Prada Oropeza, Canal Ramírez, Uzín, Pérez-Esclarín, Gómez Cerdá, Apuleyo Mendoza, and Argueta. (See also item **3264**.)

3281 Pizarro, Ana. Cultura e integración: un proyecto de historia literaria. (*Integr. Latinoam.,* 14:149/150, sept./oct. 1989, p. 53–63, bibl.)

Continues project to define and establish a history of Latin American literature begun in item **3273**. Advances thesis that since the Enlightenment, the nations of Iberoamerica have undergone a common history exemplified by the idea of integration. Explores the idea of integration in Latin America by delving into the thought of Miranda,

Bolívar's *Carta de Jamaica,* Martí's *Nuestra America,* and Henríquez Ureña's inaugural attempt to systematize the notion of a common literature in *Las corrientes literarias en América hispana* (1945). Describes current categories for this future project: 1) relations of cultural blocks (e.g., indigenous-Spanish, Spanish-Brazilian); 2) a definition of literature beyond the notion of "belles lettres;" 3) the adoption of an interdisciplinary methodology and field of discourse; and 4) the pursuit of a comparative approach.

3282 Prieto, René. La representación del indio en la novela hispanoamericana: corrientes de ayer, expresión artística de hoy. (*Insula,* 44:512/513, agosto/sept. 1989, p. 18–21)

Broad, carefully organized, and well-documented introduction to the "new indigenist" novel. This new literary form presents the *mestizo* or *indio* as a bridge between two cultures, and offers the *indio's* world through myth, song, and language rather than from an exoticized, European perspective. Focuses mostly on Peruvian narrative from the late 19th century through Arguedas, but also refers to Argentine, Mexican, and Guatemalan texts.

3283 Rama, Angel. La crítica de la cultura en América Latina. Selección y prólogos de Saúl Sosnowski y Tomás Eloy Martínez. Cronología y bibliografía de la Fundación Internacional Angel Rama. Caracas: Biblioteca Ayacucho, 1985. 402 p.: bibl. (Biblioteca Ayacucho; 119)

Includes Rama's (b. 1962, d. 1983) major essays. Less a critical edition, as is customary with Biblioteca Ayacucho, than a tribute to the deceased critic. Emphasizes ideas such as the undeniable and determining presence of ideology in all writing, most especially in places where it is considered least likely "to determine" the (i.e., the ethereal modernist text, the "literatura desinteresada"). Rama's thematic essays such as "La Ciudad Escrituraria," "Autonomía Literaria Americana," and "Indagación de la Ideología en la Poesía" show their enduring value for students of Latin American cultural formations. They also exemplify how a Marxist approach to literary studies, so widespread from the 1960s on, opened creative perspectives for understanding cultural processes in Latin America. Highly recommended for those not familiar with Rama's contribution to the study of contemporary Latin American urban cultures. Two prologues provide useful sketches of Rama as an intellectual and stylist.

3284 El realismo mágico en el cuento hispanoamericano. Edición de Angel Flores. México: Premià, 1985. 274 p.: bibl., ill. (La Red de Jonás: Estudios; 18)

Overview of the emergence of magic realism in Latin American narrative, with a brief but insightful historic introduction to European literary realism, followed by Flores' 1954 essay on magic realism. Concise, suggestive essays by an array of critics apply these broad theoretical outlines to short stories by Lugones, Cortázar, Carpentier, Rulfo. Includes text of stories.

Rey de Guido, Clara. Contribución al estudio del ensayo en Hispanoamérica. See item **5310.**

Short stories by Latin American women: the magic and the real. See item **4932.**

3285 Terteriàn, Inna Artashesovna. Chelovek mifotvoriàshchiĭ: o literature Ispanii, Portugalii i Latinskoĭ Ameriki [The myth-creator: on the literature of Spain, Portugal, and Latin America]. Sostaviteli Il'ià Moiseevich Fradkin i S.L. Kozlov. Moskva: Sov. pisatel', 1988. 560 p.: bibl., ill.

Stimulating anthology of scholarly articles by long-time member of Moscow University's Philology Dept., recently deceased, is mostly devoted to Latin America, including Brazil (p. 278–557). Focuses on social thought and cultural distinctiveness as revealed through literature. For scholarly and general audiences. [B. Dash]

3286 Ugalde, Sharon Keefe. Process, identity, and learning to read: female writing and feminist criticism in Latin America today. (*LARR*, 24:1, 1989, p. 222–232)

Review essay examines four collections of studies and interviews with Latin American women writers: *La sartén por el mango* (1984), *Revista Iberoamericana* (v. 51, 1985), *Women as myth and metaphor* (1985), and *Women's voices from Latin America: interviews with six contemporary authors* (1985). Points to great variety of authors, critics, styles, genres, periods, and critical strategies which attest to vigor of fem-

inist studies. Notes that strongly theoretical material is to be found in the essays by Josefina Ludmer, Sara Castro-Klarén, Marta Traba, and Rosario Ferré, included in *La sartén por el mango.* Ugalde's review states that some qualified generalizations can be made about the present state of feminist criticism: 1) learning to re-read; 2) unstable parameters; 3) deconstruction of oppressive stereotypes; 4) creation of an authentic feminine image. Good guide to women's literature produced in the last decade.

3287 A unidade diversa: ensaios sobre a nova literatura hispano-americana. Organização de Eduardo de Faria Coutinho. Rio de Janeiro: Editora Anima; Brasília: INL, 1985. 211 p.: bibl.

Misleading title. Collection of essays on various Spanish-American writers: García Márquez, Roa Bastos, Julio Cortázar, and some old-fashioned topics such as "o sentimento trágico do ser mexicano." Each essay is by a different critic. On the whole, the criticism repeats or ignores what has been abundantly established in the existing critical literature on these writers.

3288 Urrello, Antonio. Verosimilitud y estrategia textual en el ensayo hispanoamericano. Tlahuapan, Mexico: Premià, 1986. 146 p.: bibl. (La Red de Jonás: Estudios; 26)

Incisive review of the essay's experimental and self-reflective orientation as a generic form. Theoretically post-modern, Urrello takes up the question of verosimilitude, assuming that its relation with the real is at best a matter of simulation. Gauging and measuring the referential strategy, the book includes several worthwhile and refreshing essays on *Facundo, Ariel, Siete ensayos,* and *Amor perdido.* Strongly recommended for those reading and teaching non-fictional prose and/or other referential discourse.

Women's fiction from Latin America: selections from twelve contemporary authors. See item **4935.**

3289 You can't drown the fire: Latin American women writing in exile. Edited by Alicia Partnoy. Pittsburgh, Pa.: Cleis, 1988. 258 p.: bibl.

Much has been made of and by the

Latin American writer "in exile," and the definition has been stretched to encompass any residence outside one's country of birth. Here there is a reappropriation of the term "in exile" for the voices of women such as Rigoberta Menchú, Domitila Barrios, América Sosa, Mercedes Sosa, María Tila Uribe, and Irene Martínez, women who have lived the exile of relentless political oppression and bodily abuse. These selections make riveting reading. These testimonials, in conjunction with the selections chosen from the texts of other women writers, portray an articulate, combative, and gifted corpus of texts produced by feminist and politically-engaged contemporary Spanish-American writers. Excellent reading. Especially recommended as a counterpoint to the more widely-distributed translations of the few male writers circulating in the international book distribution networks. Translations are uneven, but on the whole the portrait of the *engagé* woman comes through clearly. For comment on translation see item **4936**.

Colonial Period

ALVARO FELIX BOLAÑOS, *Assistant Professor of Spanish, Tulane University*

LOS ESTUDIOS DE LAS LETRAS del período colonial hispanoamericano en los últimos años han seguido incrementándose y comienzan a demostrar una mayor precisión de criterios de análisis, un creciente consenso en la metodología y un interés en nuevos temas y autores. Entre los rasgos sobresalientes en la mayoría de estos estudios están la orientación interdisciplinaria, la superación de la noción de "literatura," o la precaria unidad "historia/ficción," en el estudio de textos cuyo propósito no es estético ni su composición incluyó incursiones dentro de la imaginación literaria como sucede con las llamadas "crónicas de Indias." Esta noción se tiende a reemplazar por la de "discurso," más amplia y versátil en la explicación de la naturaleza frecuentemente híbrida de estos textos. Además de la conformada por los trabajos aquí reseñados, otra prueba del fortalecimiento de esta tendencia la han ofrecido recientes congresos como "Reflections of Social Reality: Writing in Colonial Latin America" (Amherst, Mass., 19–21 abril, 1990) y "the University of New Mexico Conference on Hispanic Culture and Society: Revising the Encounter" (Albuquerque, 13–14 feb., 1992) en donde han sido escasas las ponencias sobre "literatura" propiamente dicha.

Comienza a imponerse también el examen de las obras en contextos culturales más amplios. Margarita Zamora ubica al Inca Garcilaso en la tradición intelectual del Humanismo renacentista para explicar la composición de *Comentarios reales* (en uno de los estudios quizás más importantes de esta década, item **3357**) y A. Colombí-Monguió tiene en cuenta la tradición intelectual del barroco europeo para explicar el valor de *Miscelánea Austral* (item **3309**). Rolena Adorno considera factores históricos y culturales en las Indias y en España para la mejor comprensión de discursos de resistencia amerindios y moriscos dentro del mismo contexto colonizador español (item **3291**). Se nota un incremento de estudios de la alteridad o las representaciones del "otro," sea americano o europeo, en los textos escritos durante el encuentro de América y Europa (items **3290, 3310** y **3342**); igualmente se nota el abandono de perspectivas eurocentristas en la valoración de los textos y la creciente utilización del concepto de "colonialismo" (items **3333, 3337** y **3360**) en el análisis de las estructuras verbales que componen las obras sobre el Nuevo Mundo.

Críticos como Rolena Adorno (items **3293, 3291** y **3294**), Walter Mignolo (item **3332**) y Margarita Zamora (item **3356**), continúan ofreciendo trabajos precisando aspectos metodológicos fundamentales que ayudarán muchísimo a una futura generación de estudiosos de estas letras coloniales. Se ha generalizado la tendencia a la relectura, más crítica y menos ideológica, de viejos textos. *Naufragios* de Alvar Núñez Cabeza de Vaca es objeto de aproximaciones saludablemente imaginativas e interdisciplinarias (se señalan Sylvia Molloy, item **3335** y E. Pupo-Walker, item **3346**); Cristóbal Colón propició dos artículos fundamentales que esclarecen la compleja naturaleza de su discurso y la presencia activa de Las Casas en él (items **3341** y **3358**); Hernán Cortés, Bernal Díaz y el mismo Las Casas fueron objetos de incisivos exámenes desmantelando personajes mitificados y cuestionando estrategias textuales de sus escritos consideradas antes inamovibles (items **3299, 3311** y **3292**).

Los estudios sobre los llamados discursos de resistencia, generalmente de escritores indígenas o mestizos, siguen concentrándose en la formidable obra de Guamán Poma de Ayala. Mercedes López-Baralt articula el análisis estuctural con el método etnohistórico en un monumental trabajo sobre este cronista amerindio (item **3327**). Raquel Chang-Rodríguez une a Guamán Poma con los menos conocidos cronistas (también peruanos) Titu Cusi Yupanqui y Joan de Santa Cruz Pachacuti en un trabajo que resalta el aporte amerindio al cuerpo de los primeros textos hispanoamericanos (item **3304**), y W. Mignolo examina las ambigüedades discursivas de la obra del mestizo mexicano Diego Muñoz Camargo (item **3334**).

El tema del barroco americano ha tenido interesantes aproximaciones en acuerdo con las perspectivas anotadas. García Morales (item **3313**) y Moraña (item **3336**), por ejemplo, examinan textos barrocos como manifestaciones textuales del poder colonizador español. B. Pastor, en una tesis audaz plantea el origen de la actitud barroca en América en una carta desengañada de Lope de Aguirre del siglo XVI (item **3344**). Sor Juana Inés de la Cruz continúa siendo objeto de excelentes aportes en reacción y en complementación del formidable trabajo de O. Paz. F. Luciani (item **3329**), por ejemplo, desautoriza la objetividad del retrato de la monja ofrecido por el poeta mexicano, mientras que A. Alatorre (item **3295**) hace un extraordinario y utilísimo estudio de la carta de Sor Juana al jerarca de la iglesia que más se opuso a su actividad intelectual, su confesor, el jesuita Núñez. Esta amplia monografía es a la vez un estudio de la personalidad y la biografía intelectual del confesor, del contexto de la literatura religiosa que propició el ataque a la monja, y de las relaciones de ésta con Núñez.

Además de las incursiones en Sor Juana, el estudio de textos por mujeres ha tenido desarrollos sólidos y de gran calidad en otro artículo de A. Colombí-Monguió reivindicando el genio poético de una autora peruana del siglo XVII (item **3308**), y en los descollantes edición y estudio de textos inéditos de monjas españolas e hispanoamericanas de E. Arenal y S. Schlau (item **3371**), con los cuales comienzan a llenar un vacíó y plantean fundamentales perspectivas de estudio de las letras femeninas.

El carnero de Rodríguez Freyle ha recibido rigurosas monografías como la de D. William Foster (item **3312**) quien rechaza la noción de "protonovela" y ofrece varias alternativas de estudio, y la de S. Herman (item **3318**) ofreciendo claves para la comprensión de la voz "carnero" en el contexto de su composición. Esta obra ha adquirido actualidad también a través de la primera edición de *El carnero de Mede-*

llín, obra escrita a imitación de *El carnero* por Antonio José Benítez entre el siglo XVIII y XIX. (item **3362**). Fray Servando Teresa de Mier ha sido estudiado con una rigurosa, saludable y ya necesaria actitud crítica en sólidos trabajos como el de R. Jara (item **3323**) y Kathleen Ross (item **3350**) quienes buscan un fraile menos mítico, más humano y complejo e inscrito en un sistema discursivo más definido. Entre los estudios de autores y obras nuevos se destaca la contribución de C.P. Hart sobre la relación del viaje a América y Oceanía de Alessandro Malaspina en el siglo XVIII al servicio de España (item **3317**), con el cual llama la atención sobre nuevas fronteras de estudio.

Finalmente hay que mencionar el gran incremento en ediciones de textos inéditos y las reediciones de otros como respuesta a la ampliación del público lector de estas obras. Debemos destacar la primera y muy cuidadosa edición completa de la *Suma y narración de los incas* de Juan de Betanzos por M. del C. Martín Rubio (item **3363**) que proporciona un material exquisito para el estudio de un texto indigenista del siglo XVI de gran importancia; y E. Núñez ha publicado unas *Obras selectas* de Pablo de Olavide (item **3368**), incluyendo novelas y textos políticos de reforma agraria y universitaria inéditos hasta la fecha que servirán para una más justa valoración de este autor peruano del período de la Ilustración.

El panorama positivo que ofrecemos en los estudios y ediciones de los textos del período colonial en los dos últimos años seguramente continuará en los dos años siguientes dadas la demostración de la importancia de las letras de este período colonial, la precisión de metodologías de estudio y, en especial la conmemoración de los 500 años de la llegada de Cristóbal Colón a América.

INDIVIDUAL STUDIES

3290 Adorno, Rolena. Arms, letters and the native historian in early colonial Mexico. (*in* 1492–1992: re/discovering colonial writing. Edited by René Jara and Nicholas Spadaccini. Minneapolis, Minn.: The Prisma Institute, 1989, p. 201–224)

Descarta el modelo de Todorov sobre "el otro" en *The conquest of America* y adopta el modelo de Michel de Certeau en *Heterologies* para examinar la obra del historiador nativo mexicano Fernando Alva Ixttlixochitl (descendiente de reyes de Texcoco). Según Adorno, en ella se manipulan estrategias de la cultura militar europea para exaltar la cultura militar de los guerreros prehispánicos ante un auditorio español, invirtiendo así el esquema bárbaro indígena, civilizado español. Importante esfuerzo para precisar un modelo de estudio de la alteridad en los discursos coloniales.

3291 Adorno, Rolena. La ciudad letrada y los discursos coloniales. (*Hispamérica*, 16:48, 987, p. 3–24)

Con base en la metáfora de la "ciudad letrada" de Angel Rama (como un conjunto de prácticas escriturales con las que se afirma el poder colonizador), Adorno propone un derrotero de investigación de las letras coloniales basado en las relaciones entre esa "ciudad" y los discursos marginados por ella. Desarrolla ejemplos de los discursos rebeldes de un autor morisco en España (Francisco Núñez Muley) y un indígena en Perú (Guamán Poma de Ayala). Sólida y clarificadora visión de conjunto de la colonización española contra sus minorías peninsulares (moros, judíos) y las mayorías americanas (los indios). Buena bibliografía sobre historia y teoría.

3292 Adorno, Rolena. Discourses on colonialism: Bernal Díaz, Las Casas, and the twentieth-century reader. (*MLN*, 103:2, March 1988, p. 239–258)

Perspicaz y bien documentado artículo que encuentra las razones del discurso de Bernal no en su debate contra Gómara como historiador mentiroso y Cortés como héroe acaparador de fama—como tradicionalmente se ha visto—sino en un debate con Las Casas y la ofensiva de la corona contra la encomienda. Bernal ya no es un simple héroe de la conquista sino como un encomendero defendiendo sus intereses. Excelente contribución a la revisión de penegíricos como el de Bernal en busca de versiones más objetivas y complejas en las letras del período colonial.

3293 Adorno, Rolena. Nuevas perspectivas en los estudios literarios coloniales hispanoamericanos. (*Rev. Crít. Lit. Latinoam.*, 14:28, 1988, p. 11–28, bibl.)

Evaluación de los nuevos enfoques y metodologías de los estudios textuales del período colonial hispanoamericano en los últimos años. La sustitución de la noción de "literatura" (práctica de escritura limitada a lo estético y eurocentrista) por la de "discurso" (que incluye voces silenciadas), la importancia de la cuestión de "el otro" (sujeto policultural, multilingüe y colonizado), y, en general, el estudio de las prácticas culturales en el contexto de la colonización, son rasgos característicos de las nuevas perspectivas. Trabajo imprescindible para todo estudioso de las letras coloniales. Extensa bibliografía.

3294 Adorno, Rolena. El sujeto colonial y la construcción cultural de la alteridad. (*Rev. Crít. Lit. Latinoam.*, 14:28, 1988, p. 55–68)

Breve pero formidable discusión sobre los procesos de construcción del concepto de "el otro" en los discursos caballerescos, históricos y filosófico-políticos de ambos sujetos coloniales, colonizador y colonizado. Con base en el modelo epistemológico de la similitud y la oposición, tanto el sujeto europeo como el nativo no solamente se conocen a sí mismos sino, fundamentalmente, se diferencian jerárquicamente del "otro." Util precisión de modelos de estudio de las letras coloniales. Amplia y excelente bibliografía.

Aguirre, Mirta. Estudios literarios. See item 3626.

3295 Alatorre, Antonio. La Carta de Sor Juana al P. Núñez, 1682. (*Nueva Rev. Filol. Hisp.*, 35:2, 1987, p. 591–673, bibl.)

Extenso y riguroso estudio de la carta en que la monja confronta a su confesor (Antonio Núñez de Miranda) quien entorpecía su actividad intelectual y en la que explícitamente declara su independencia espiritual. Descubierta en 1980 por A. Tapia Méndez (quien la publicó en 1981). Incluye una nueva edición crítica y comentada del texto. Alatorre explora circunstancias de las

vidas y estructuras intelectuales de Núñez y Sor Juana, así como el contexto cultural, social y bibliográfico, que explican esta apología de la monja. Copiosa, nueva e interesante bibliográfia. El trabajo identifica a Núñez como el principal instigador de Sor Juana y revela un amplio círculo de intelectuales-clérigos y seglares—que la apoyaban, en oposición a la idea común de toda la comunidad masculina en su contra.

3296 Andreu, Alicia G. Garcilaso y Bernal: interpretaciones interpretadas. (*Histórica/Lima*, 12:2, dic. 1988, p. 117–132, bibl.)

Examen de las evaluaciones de la labor de intérpretes entre conquistadores e indígenas de la Malinche y Felipillo expresadas respectivamente por Bernal en *Historia verdadera* y Garcilaso el Inca en *Comentarios reales*. La superioridad del castellano sobre las lenguas indígenas explica el fracaso de Felipillo, según Garcilaso; el éxito de la Malinche, exaltado por Bernal, supone una opinión positiva de la lengua mexicana del conquistador. Ambos escritores, según Andreu, reconocen la violencia sobre el "otro" del poder del lenguaje. Utiliza concepto de colonización y subyugación del otro a través de la palabra de Todorov.

3297 Barrera, Trinidad. Problemas textuales de *Los naufragios* de Alvar Núñez Cabeza de Vaca. (*Historiogr. Bibliogr. Am.*, 30:32, 1986, p. 21–30)

Edición corregida de un tercer texto autógrafo (el más antiguo) que relata los hechos de los 16 capítulos iniciales de *Naufragios* de Cabeza de Vaca y su contraste con su primera edición (Madrid, 1870) y la versión más amplia de 1555. En comentarios iniciales, Barrera supone que el autor de este texto fue el escribano de la expedición y que después de morir éste, fue rescatado y aprovechado por Alvar Núñez para la versión final. Discutible, aunque interesante, hipótesis. Buen aporte al estudio de la obra de Cabeza de Vaca y buena muestra de los problemas inherentes a la edición de estos textos historiográficos de la época.

3298 Belda, Francisco. La lengua de Francisco de Miranda en su *Diario*. Caracas: Academia Nacional de la Historia, 1985. 118 p.: bibl. (El Libro menor; 69)

Importante aunque breve trabajo demostrando la persistente deshispanización del lenguaje de Miranda. Examina las descuidadas ortografía y sintaxis y la abundancia de galicismos, anglicismos e italianismos en el léxico de su *Diario* de viajes escrito entre 1771–88. Belda sugiere que este alejamiento del espíritu hispánico influyó en su fracaso político en Venezuela. Analiza cada expresión en su contexto a manera de glosario.

3299 Benítez-Rojo, Antonio. Bartolomé de las Casas: entre el infierno y la ficción. (*MLN*, 103:2, March 1988, p. 259–288)

Brillante artículo utilizando la tesis de Freud sobre lo "Unheimliche" (lo insólito o sobrenatural en el relato), para analizar dos digresiones de Las Casas en su *Historia de las Indias* y señalar la omisión de la rebelión de los negros de los trapiches en uno de ellos. Según Benítez-Rojo, la culpabilidad del fraile por la esclavización del negro le llevó a silenciar el tema y a sustituirlo por símbolos en un relato de ficción. En esta omisión encuentra el origen de la literatura del Caribe. Aunque a veces lucubra un poco y abusa de extranjerismo, la tesis es audaz y bien demostrada.

3300 Benso, Silvia. La conquista di un testo: il *Requerimiento*. Roma: Bulzoni, 1989. 185 p.; (Letterature iberiche e latino-americane; 19)

Excelente examen del *Requerimiento* como texto jurídico de dominación, coerción y silenciación española del sujeto indígena. El análisis va del campo jurídico e histórico al literario al considerarlo como modelo ideal en la imaginación colectiva de la relación entre la cultura hispana y la indígena en el momento de la conquista.

3301 Bolaños, Alvaro Félix. El primer cronista de Indias frente al *mare magno* de la crítica. (*Cuad. Am.*, 20:2, marzo/abril 1990, p. 42–61, bibl.)

Señala dos tendencias problemáticas de muchos críticos sobre la vida y la obra de Gonzalo Fernández de Oviedo desde el siglo XVI hasta hoy, el libelo y el panegírico. Precisa ejemplos de errores y exageraciones sobre este autor que, a pesar de haber sido corregidos, siguen repitiéndose en muchos críticos hoy demostrando una confusión y laxitud en el manejo de la extensa bibliografía sobre los temas oviedianos.

3302 Carreño, Antonio. *Naufragios*, de Alvar Núñez Cabeza de Vaca: una retó-

rica de la crónica colonial. (*Rev. Iberoam.*, 53:140, julio/sept. 1987, p. 449–516)

El título desorienta un poco, porque es un examen de los mecanismos retóricos, lingüísticos y epistemológicos de aprehensión de la realidad americana en diversas relaciones del descubrimiento y conquista de América (de Colón, Bernal Díaz, Garcilaso, Cabeza de Vaca y otros) y su incorporación dentro del horizonte intelectual europeo. En el caso de *Naufragios*, señala el carácter híbrido entre la retórica de la historia, la crónica, el memorial, y la novela picaresca. Amplia y especializada bibliografía destacando el contexto cultural europeo.

3303 Cevallos, Francisco Javier. Don Alonso de Ercilla and the American Indian: history and myth. (*Rev. Estud. Hisp.*, 23:3, 1989, p. 1–20, bibl.)

Confronta la noción de que Ercilla es un defensor de los indígenas y la consideración de *La araucana* como crónica u obra histórica. Explica la exaltación de los araucanos como un tópico de un poema épico-renacentista dentro de la ideología española para resaltar la hazaña de los españoles. Excelente artículo, bibliografía actualizada.

3304 Chang-Rodríguez, Raquel. La apropiación del signo: tres cronistas indígenas del Perú. Tempe: Center for Latin American Studies, Arizona State Univ., 1988. 132 p.: bibl., ill., index.

Examen de estructura discursiva de resistencia y ubicación en contexto cultural de las relaciones del Perú virreinal de Titu Cusi Yupanqui, Joan de Santa Cruz Pachacuti, y Guamán Poma de Ayala. Basándose en la noción de las crónicas de autores europeos del siglo XVI como semilla de la narrativa hispanoamericana actual, se propone destacar la olvidada contribución amerindia a ese origen. Examina tensión en estos textos producto de asimilación de dos conceptos del tiempo histórico: el cronológico europeo y el cíclico andino. Importante contribución al estudio de autores marginados por el canon tradicional. Buena bibliografía.

3305 Chang-Rodríguez, Raquel. Rebelión y religión en dos crónicas indígenas del Perú de ayer. (*Rev. Crít. Lit. Latinoam.*, 14:28, 1988, p. 175–193, bibl.)

Sólido análisis de las estrategias del discurso subversivo de la *Relacion . . .* de

Titu Cusi Yupanqui y *Primer nueva cró-nica* . . . de Guamán Poma al narrar la rebelión de Manco Inca contra los españoles en 1536. Ambos cronistas—valiéndose de la historia y la teología americanas y europeas—justifican la rebelión del Inca acusando a los españoles de transgredir el patrón de reciprocidad andino (maltratando al Inca generoso) y el dogma católico (idolatrando el oro) para destacar su mayor dignidad ante los españoles y la ilegitimidad del control político de éstos. Buena bibliografía y buen aporte al análisis de los discursos de resistencia coloniales.

3306 Chang-Rodríguez, Raquel. Santo Tomás en Los Andes. (*Rev. Iberoam.*, 53 : 140, julio/sept. 1987, p. 559–567, ill.)

Análisis del discurso de resistencia de dos cronistas indígenas a través de la leyenda sobre la evangelización prehispánica de uno de los 12 apóstoles en los Andes presente en *Relación de antigüedades deste reyno del Pirú* (1613) de Joan de Santacruz Pachacuti y *Primer nueva corónica y buen gobierno* (1615) de Guamán Poma de Ayala. Según demuestra la autora, ambos cronistas desarrollan este mito para dejar sin piso una de las justificaciones de la conquista de los españoles—la evangelización—y cuestionar su presencia en las Indias. Valioso aporte.

3307 Cisneros, Luis Jaime and **Pedro Guibovich Pérez.** Un raro opúsculo del Lunarejo. (*Lexis*, 13 : 1, 1989, p. 95–115)

Reedición y comentarios del poco conocido *Discurso* (ejemplar de la Biblioteca Nacional de Santiago de Chile, con correcciones de erratas), en que J. de E. Medrano, "El Lunarejo," expuso en 1664 sus opiniones críticas sobre el sistema de concursos y ascensos en la jerarquía eclesiástica. Ofrece, según los autores, nuevos datos sobre su biografía que se le escaparon a J.T. Medina, y una muestra desconocida de su "prosa sobria." Contiene datos generales sobre su biografía intelectual. De interés para especialistas.

3308 Colombí-Monguió, Alicia de. Doña Francisca de Briviesca y Arellano: la primera mujer poeta del Perú. (*Anu. Let.*, 24, 1986, p. 413–425)

Entusiasta hipótesis sobre la identidad de la autora de uno de los sonetos preliminares de la *Miscelánea Austral* (1602) a quien

se identifica con Doña Francisca, esposa del autor Diego Dávalos y Figueroa. Explicación y valoración del soneto en contraste con la "adocenada y burda retórica" de los poemas de los hombres. Impugnación de la crítica tradicional que duda de la autoría femenina de este poema. Meritorio y bien documentado aporte al estudio de las letras femeninas del período.

3309 Colombí-Monguió, Alicia de. *Verba significans, res significantur:* libros de empresas en el Perú virreinal. (*Nueva Rev. Filol. Hisp.*, 36 : 1, 1988, p. 345–364)

Apología de *Miscelánea Austral* de Dávalos y Figueroa equiparándola con obras de la intelectualidad europea de la época. Examen riguroso de su materia emblemática (rueda de la fortuna, fénix, águila, etc.). La síntesis entre el Humanismo renacentista y el mundo peruano en esta obra la inscriben, según Colombi-Monguió, dentro de una larga y sofisticada tradición europea del pensamiento analógico y simbolista, y dentro del espíritu mismo de las letras del Renacimiento y el barroco. Erudito y coherente artículo.

3310 Conley, Tom. Montaigne and the Indies: cartographies of the New World in the *Essais*, 1580–88. (*in* 1492–1992: re/discovering colonial writing. Edited by René Jara and Nicholas Spadaccini. Minneapolis, Minn.: The Prisma Institute, 1989, p. 225–262, bibl.)

Examen de la atención de Montaigne a la conquista española de las Indias en su contexto histórico y cultural. Con base en la tesis de la alteridad de Michel de Certeau, demuestra que Montaigne hace una lectura crítica de sus fuentes—el cronista López de Gómara traducido al francés por M. Fumée en 1569, cosmógrafos como André Thevet y como Jean Léry—invirtiendo los términos de valoración del Nuevo Mundo en los que "barbarismo" se asocia a la moderación y moralidad que los europeos no tienen. Buena bibliografía.

3311 Díaz Balsera, Viviana. Estrategias metatextuales de Hernán Cortés, autor de la conquista de México. (*Neophilologus*, 73 : 2, April 1989, p. 218–229, bibl.)

Sólido y atractivo examen de las estrategias de persuasión de la *Segunda carta de relación* con las que Cortés legitimiza su empresa ilegal. Analizando los distintos discursos que la componen (historiográfico renacentista, retórica judicial), Díaz concluye que es el receptor de la carta (Carlos V) y no el referente (los hechos en México), lo que origina el texto quedando la "realidad" sujeta a la textualidad y la retórica. Pertinente y actualizada bibliografía.

3312 Foster, David William. Notes toward reading Juan Rodríguez Freyle's *El carnero;* the image of the narrator. (*Rev. Estud. Colomb.*, v. 1, 1986, p. 1–15)

Utilizando a F. Jameson, Foster examina la unidad del texto—propiciada por las estrategias del narrador y las espectativas del lector—la cual se deriva de la mutua dependencia del marco de 100 años de historia del Nuevo Reino (1536–1636) y las interpretaciones morales de los hechos. Rechaza las lecturas que buscan protonovelas o historia y propone tres alternativas: 1) la establecida por la humanista de las crónicas de Indias del siglo XVI; 2) la de interpretación moral de los eventos cotidianos (medieval tardía); y 3) la moderna que busca conjugar elementos dispares en un todo de acuerdo con las espectativas del público lector. Imprescindible para el estudioso de la obra de Rodríguez Freyle.

3313 García Morales, Alfonso. Las *Fiestas de Lima, 1632*, de Rodrigo de Carvajal y Robles. (*Anu. Estud. Am.*, 44, 1987, p. 141–171, bibl.)

Detallado examen de esta relación versificada (temáticas, formas poéticas, etc.) de la celebración en Lima en 1626 del nacimiento del príncipe Baltasar Carlos en el contexto de la cultura del siglo XVII. Con base en las tesis de Maravall y A. Bonet sobre el barroco como un variado conjunto de medios para preservar el sistema social, García Morales concibe la obra como típica del barroco en su representación ilusoria y artificiosa de la realidad y en acuerdo con el ejercicio del poder de la corona española y el virreinato. Buena bibliografía y sólida aproximación al estudio del barroco y los discursos de la colonización.

3314 Gimbernat de González, Ester. Apeles de la re-inscripción: a propósito del *Poema heroico* de Hernando Domínguez Camargo. (*Rev. Iberoam.*, 53:140, julio/sept. 1987, p. 569–579, bibl.)

Breve y perceptivo examen de la presencia latente de emblemas en el Canto IV del Libro II del poema para señalar la interacción de símbolos poéticos y visuales, convenciones y erudición típicas de la cultura del siglo XVII, y el sutil cuestionamiento del autor de las pautas artísticas contrarreformistas.

González Echevarría, Roberto. Colón, Carpentier y los orígenes de la ficción latinoamericana. See item **3653.**

3315 González Echevarría, Roberto. Reflexiones sobre *Espejo de paciencia* de Silvestre de Balboa. (*Nueva Rev. Filol. Hisp.*, 35:2, 1987, p. 571–590, bibl.)

Sugestivo y rigurso estudio de los esfuerzos de varias generaciones de críticos cubanos por encontrar en *Espejo* el origen de la literatura cubana. Demuestra que este esfuerzo (de corte romántico) responde a necesidades ideológicas de buscar una literatura de fundación en épocas de crisis social y cultural, y que lo que ven estos autores como cubanismos o exotismos criollistas en el poema, no es más que un rasgo genérico de la abundancia y la exuberancia desordenada del arte barroco. Para la versión inglesa, ver *HLAS 50: 2967.*

3316 González Stephan, Beatriz. The early stages of Latin American historiography. (*in* 1492–1992: re/discovering colonial writing. Edited by René Jara and Nicholas Spadaccini. Minneapolis, Minn.: The Prisma Institute, 1989, p. 291–322, bibl.)

Estudio de las clasificaciones, reflexiones y opiniones sobre la producción literaria e historiográfica desde el Descubrimiento hasta el siglo XIX con el propósito de destruir la noción de la inferioridad de Hispanoamérica. Concluye que ya existían en esa época clasificaciones integrales de los distintos discursos del período colonial, lo cual es base para solidificar una cultura propia de Hispanoamérica. Propone un estudio no eurocentrista que corrija la distorsión de la práctica cultural hispanoamericana y la omisión de caracteres distintivos de lo americano. Excelente trabajo, amplia bibliografía.

3317 Hart, Catherine Pouperey. Relations de l'expedition Malaspina aux confins de l'empire Espagnol: l'echec du voyage. Longueuil: Editions du Preambule, 1987. 170 p.: bibl.

Importante estudio de la relación de la

navegación a América y Oceanía entre 1789–94 (de espíritu enciclopedista para la exploración e inventario del planeta) del marino italiano Alessandro Malaspina al servicio de la corona española. Examina contextos intelectual, político, geográfico de la expedición, y la concepción y estrategias de representación históricas del texto. Fundamental trabajo de divulgación de textos olvidados y de la emergente área de estudio de las relaciones del período colonial de viajes marinos. Buena bibliografía.

3318 Herman, Susan. Toward solving the mystery of the placement of the name *Carnero* on Juan Rodríguez Freile's history. (*Rev. Estud. Hisp.*, 23:3, 1989, p. 37–52)

Bien documentado aporte al esclarecimiento del significado de la expresión "carnero" (osario, archivo, cuaderno, viejo tipo de imprenta) a través del examen de su utilización en los manuscriptos existentes entre los siglos XVII y XIX. La autora propone como significado "the morgue" (archivo de papeles de futura referencia) por ser usado en el Siglo de Oro español.

3319 Herrera, Arnulfo. Los modelos de un poeta novohispano: Francisco de Terrazas y el petrarquismo. (*An. Inst. Invest. Estét.*, 59, 1988, p. 223–237)

Detallado análisis y explicación del poema "Dejad las Hebras de Oro Ensortijado" de Terrazas. Demuestra que la imitación de Terrazas del modelo petrarquista no responde a una falta de originalidad sino al ejercicio consciente de la práctica de la escritura de poesía de los poetas de los siglos XVI y XVII quienes respetaban mucho la tradición establecida. Aunque es más un artículo sobre poesía española, es un buen ejemplo de los problemas de estudio planteados por los poetas novohispanos del período.

3320 Herrera Zapién, Tarsicio. Buena fe y humanismo en Sor Juana: diálogos y ensayos; las obras latinas; los sorjuanistas recientes. México: Editorial Porrúa, 1984. 275 p.

Colección de cinco ensayos sobre la influencia de la poesía clásica en Sor Juana, y uno en respuesta—impugnación del Octavio Paz sorjuanista. Examina las conexiones de la Décima Musa con Homero, Virgilio, Marcial, Horacio y Catulo, y su posición en las lenguas latina y modernas. Importante desarrollo de un nuevo enfoque en el estudio de esta poesía. Muy influido por el gran trabajo de O. Paz.

3321 Higgins, James. Orígenes coloniales de la poesía peruana. (*Rev. Indias*, 48: 182/183, enero/agosto 1988, p. 593–611)

Util esquema crítico del desarrollo de la poesía peruana desde el siglo XVI hasta el XX examinando poetas como Dávalos y Figueroa, Terralla Landa, Rosas de Oquendo, Caviedes, Mariano Melgar y su legado en poetas contemporáneos (González Prada, C. Vallejo, J.M. Eguren, Leoncio Bueno, A. Cisneros, M. Florán). En estos últimos han persistido los temas del desarraigo frente al medio, la protesta popular, la búsqueda de identidad y la sátira social, según Higgins. Reproduce poemas comentados. La bibliografía se limita a historias de la literatura y antologías.

3322 Invernizzi, Lucía. *Naufragios* e *Infortunios*: discurso que transforma fracasos en triunfos. (*Rev. Chil. Lit.*, 29, abril 1987, p. 7–22, bibl.)

Artículo un tanto difuso, aunque con buenos planteamientos. Señala las técnicas retóricas típicas del discurso judicial apologético del fracaso con las que Cabeza de Vaca y Sigüenza y Góngora convierten sus textos en sustitutos de la hazaña malograda y en instrumentos de persuasión. El relato de Alvar Núñez triunfa en la formación de un hombre nuevo (a través de la gran experiencia) y fracasa en la afirmación de los sueños imperiales; Sigüenza presenta un relato conservador en el que representa al criollo cortesano y su defensa de los valores tradicionales del imperio. Buena bibliografía.

3323 Jara, René. The inscription of creole consciousness: Fray Servando Teresa de Mier. (*in* 1492–1992: re/discovering colonial writing. Edited by René Jara and Nicholas Spadaccini. Minneapolis, Minn.: The Prisma Institute, 1989, p. 349–379, bibl.)

Muy buen artículo que examina el desarrollo del discurso criollo en el México del período colonial hacia la formación de la conciencia de independencia política, y la contribución de Fray Servando a través de la revitalización de los mitos de Quetzalcóatl y Guadalupe en la formación de una identidad mexicana en un contexto cristiano. Es casi una historia de las diferentes actitudes del criollo ante la negación de su origen, identidad y existencia durante los siglos de la colonia. Buena bibliografía.

3324 Johnson, Julie Greer. *El Nuevo Luciano* and the satiric art of Eugenio Espejo. (*Rev. Estud. Hisp.*, 23 : 3, 1989, p. 67–85, bibl.)

Examina la sátira literaria en *El Nuevo Luciano de Quito* (1779) de Espejo en el contexto de su pensamiento ilustrado, su lucha anticolonialista y las influencias literarias clásicas y españoles que muestra. Amplios detalles de su biografía, su formación intelectual y su marco histórico. Util aproximación a un autor que se le estudia más por sus contribuciones como político.

3325 Johnson, Julie Greer. Traveling in eighteenth-century Spanish America: the evaluation of a disgruntled Spaniard. (*SECOLAS Ann.*, 20, March 1989, p. 40–47, bibl.)

Breve pero preciso e ilustrativo examen del nivel satírico utilizado por Carrió en la composición de *El lazarillo de ciegos caminantes* en que distorsiona el género del libro de viajes e involucra el nivel anti-heroico picaresco. La sátira, según arguye Johnson, se origina en la decepción del autor ante el fracaso de su misión como agente modernizador de las colonias, lo cual lo lleva a señalar su deterioro y la obstaculización del progreso de parte de negros, nobles, clérigos, oficiales y en particular los indios. Atención a la confección literaria de los personajes Carrió y Concolorcorvo como agentes de este propósito satírico. Buena bibliografía.

3326 Leal, Luis. The first American epic: Villagrá's *History of New Mexico*. (*in* Pasó por aquí: critical essays on the New Mexican literary tradition, 1542–1988. Edited by Erlinda Gonzales-Berry. Albuquerque: Univ. of New Mexico Press, 1989, p. 47–62)

Bien documentada e informativa exposición y valoración del carácter y contenido del poema histórico de Gaspar Pérez de Villagrá (1555–1620) titulado *Historia de la Nueva México* (1610) que relata la expedición y conquista de Nuevo México de Cristóbal de Oñate en 1596. Leal incluye noticias sobre el autor, los personajes históricos, la historia bibliográfica del texto original español, su traducción inglesa (*History of New Mexico*, Los Angeles, 1933), y una útil evaluación de

la crítica que ha recibido este importante y casi olvidado poema.

3327 López-Baralt, Mercedes. Icono y conquista: Guamán Poma de Ayala. Madrid: Hiperión, 1988. 483 p.: bibl., ill., port. (Libros Hiperión; 102)

Basada en elementos teóricos de M. Weber y Lotman, en que los signos lingüístico e icónico forman la mínima unidad de cultura, López-Barat examina la relación jerárquica del texto y la imagen en la *Nueva corónica* para precisar la dialéctica entre resistencia cultural y aculturación en el contexto colonial. Pone énfasis en la función de retórica e ideología en las relaciones entre el emisor y el receptor de la obra. Orientación interdisciplinaria que explora posibilidades teóricas de la semiótica cultural articula el análisis estructural con el método etnohistórico. Formidable trabajo.

3328 López-Baralt, Mercedes. La metáfora como *translatio:* del código verbal al visual en la crónica ilustrada de Guamán Poma. (*Nueva Rev. Filol. Hisp.*, 36 : 1, 1988, p. 379–389, appendix, bibl., ill.)

Estupendo análisis comparativo de dos ilustraciones de *Nueva corónica y buen gobierno* con base en elementos teóricos de la semiótica de la imagen de Bernardette Bucher. Según López-Baralt, la primera ilustración es una representación mimética de la opresión de un indio bajo el régimen incaico, la cual complementa la segunda en la que el término comparado desaparece dejando una metáfora (en latín *translatio*) que denuncia la opresión del pueblo indígena bajo el régimen hispano. Se inicia con claro y útil recuento de estudios de semiótica de la ímagen desde el siglo XVI hasta hoy.

3329 Luciani, Frederick. Octavio Paz on Sor Juana Inés de la Cruz: the metaphor incarnate. (*Lat. Am. Lit. Rev.*, 15 : 30, July/Dec. 1987, p. 6–25)

Cuestiona la objetividad de la representación de la figura de Sor Juana que Octavio Paz expone en *Sor Juana Inés de la Cruz o las trampas de la fe* (ver *HLAS 46:5057*). Según Luciani no existen bases textuales indiscutibles para un retrato de la monja y en él Paz impone su propia visión artística, su autoridad y su prestigio de crítico y poeta, como garantía de su validez. La imagen de Sor Juana que surge de esta biografía es, para

Luciani, una conjuración imaginativa de las especulaciones de Paz. Imprescindible para el sorjuanista y para un punto de vista distinto al del poeta y crítico mexicano de esta autora.

3330 Mannheim, Bruce. La memoria y el olvido en la política lingüística colonial. (*Lexis*, 13 : 1, 1989, p. 13–45, bibl.)

Bosquejo histórico sobre la política lingüística contra la mayoría indígena hablante del Quechua surperuano, primero del imperio español, después de la República en el Perú desde el siglo XVI hasta hoy. Las dos estrategias de asimilación de los quechua parlantes (la suave o "liberal" y la violenta o "hispanista") utilizadas por los gobernantes españoles, señala Mannheim, todavía se emplean hoy ya que las condiciones de dominación política y económica colonial persisten. Riguroso y bien documentado y con buena bibliografía. De interés para historiadores y lingüistas.

3331 Merrim, Stephanie. The apprehension of the new in nature and culture. (*in* 1492–1992: re/discovering colonial writing. Edited by René Jara and Nicholas Spadaccini. Minneapolis, Minn.: The Prisma Institute, 1989, p. 165–199, bibl.)

Interesante dilucidación de tres discursos del bagage cultural de Oviedo en su exposición de lo novedoso americano en el *Sumario:* 1) el de la etnografía clásica (especialmente Plinio); 2) el de los libros de caballerías (a través de su experiencia con *Don Claribalte*); y 3) el religioso y didáctico-moral (que considera la naturaleza como expresión del poder grandioso de Dios, y su concepción edificante de la historia). Su experiencia con estos discursos y su obsesión con lo maravilloso y terrible de América le permiten a Oviedo, según Merrim, articular lo imaginativo, lo misceláneo y lo fidedigno en su proceso de conquista intelectual de América. Imprescindible aporte.

3332 Mignolo, Walter. Anáhuac y sus otros: la cuestión de la letra en el Nuevo Mundo. (*Rev. Crít. Lit. Latinoam.*, 14 : 28, 1988, p. 29–53, bibl., ill.)

Examen de transcripciones y traducciones hechas por Sahagún de conversaciones entre frailes franciscanos y nobles indígenas hacia 1524. Reconstruye la situación comunicativa entre estas dos culturas y evidencia

la imposibilidad de entenderse y aceptarse. También reformula los objetivos y el objeto de estudio de las llamadas "letras coloniales" del Nuevo Mundo incluyendo una pluralidad lingüística (rompiendo la limitación al castellano) y una oralidad primaria de las culturas precolombinas. Explora la percepción del "otro" de una cultura que reflexiona sobre sí misma, sea la amerindia o la europea. Artículo fundamental en la determinación de metodología y terminología de estudio de discursos coloniales.

3333 Mignolo, Walter. Literacy and colonization: the New World experience. (*in* 1492–1992: re/discovering colonial writing. Edited by René Jara and Nicholas Spadaccini. Minneapolis, Minn.: The Prisma Institute, 1989, p. 51–96, bibl.)

Explora desde una perspectiva semiótica el choque de dos capacidades de erudición en el contexto colonial hispanoamericano: 1) la alfabética de los europeos, que tiraniza, deforma y erradica; y 2) la pictoideográfica de los indígenas. Provee útiles herramientas conceptuales y terminológicas para el estudio de los discursos colonizadores en los primeros años del encuentro de América y Europa.

3334 Mignolo, Walter. El mandato y la ofrenda: la descripción de la ciudad y provincia de Tlaxcala, de Diego Muñoz Camargo, y las *Relaciones de Indias*. (*Nueva Rev. Filol. Hisp.*, 35 : 2, 1987, p. 451–484, bibl., ill.)

Examen de la obra de este mestizo mexicano enviada a Felipe II en 1558 en relación con dos modelos discursivos distintos que le sirven de base: 1) la "Instrucción o Memoria" (que ejerce el mandato) y 2) la historiografía humanista (que permite la ofrenda al Rey). La convivencia de estos discursos en la *Descripción* implican una libre interpretación del mandato y una ambigüedad discursiva muy interesante, según Mignolo. Orientación semiológica. Incluye edición de la "Instrucción y Memoria" oficial de 1577.

3335 Molloy, Sylvia. Alteridad y reconocimiento en los *Naufragios* de Alvar Núñez Cabeza de Vaca. (*Nueva Rev. Filol. Hisp.*, 35 : 2, 1987, p. 425–449, bibl.)

Imaginativo y detallado análisis de las transformaciones de la identidad de Alvar Núñez frente a dos alteridades cambiantes: la de los indios y la de los españoles. La inversión del propósito de la expedición de "conquistar y gobernar" a "informar y convencer" obliga al cronista del fracaso a distinguir su individualidad y resaltar la magnitud de su propia hazaña, lo cual afecta la construcción y estructura del relato. Referencia sólo a bibliografía esencial más reciente. Artículo típico del creador literario.

3336 Moraña, Mabel. Barroco y conciencia criolla en Hispanoamérica. (*Rev. Crít. Lit. Latinoam.*, 14:28, 1988, p. 229–251, bibl.)

Rechaza el estudio del barroco en el Nuevo Mundo con una perspectiva etnocentrista que lo reduce a una reproducción pálida de modelos europeos (peninsulares). Propone un análisis que considere el barroco en el contexto de la reproducción de formas de significado que legitimizan formas de dominación imperial y en cuyo seno aparecen las primeras evidencias de una conciencia social diferenciada en el seno de la sociedad criolla. Estas características, según ella, se proyectan sobre el desarrollo posterior de la literatura hispanoamericana. Excelente artículo de radical posición anticolonialista.

3337 Moraña, Mabel. *El periquillo sarniento* y la ciudad letrada. (*Rev. Estud. Hisp.*, 23:3, 1989, p. 113–125, bibl.)

Utilizando aportes teóricos de A. Rama y Foucault sobre el poder y las urbes examina *El periquillo* como instrumento crítico narrativo de desmonte ideológico y de penetración del ámbito del poder impuestos por el espacio urbano en el contexto de la dominación imperial. Estupendo trabajo siguiendo la senda propuesta antes por R. Adorno.

3338 Myers, Kathleen. History, truth and dialogue: Fernández de Oviedo's *Historia general y natural de las Indias* (Bk XXXIII, Ch LIV). (*Hispania/Teachers*, 73:3, Sept. 1990, p. 616–625, bibl.)

Análisis del diálogo entre Juan Cano, veterano conquistador, y Fernández de Oviedo, sobre la "noche triste," en el contexto de la teoría y práctica de la interpretación histórica realizada por este cronista. Myers demuestra que en este diálogo el autor recoge la tradición historiográfica del humanismo italiano y explora métodos propios del siglo XVI en la búsqueda de la "verdad" histórica, al mismo tiempo que critica versiones anteriores de la conquista de México (como la de Cortés) y propone un método preciso para el discurso histórico sobre el Nuevo Mundo. Admirable dilucidación de las técnicas de composición de la narración histórica de este cronista.

3339 Orjuela, Héctor H. Estudios sobre literatura indígena y colonial. Bogotá: Instituto Caro y Cuervo, 1986. 286 p.: bibl. (Publicaciones del Instituto Caro y Cuervo; 76)

Reúne seis ensayos sobre textos y temas colombianos y uno sobre Sor Juana. Los estudios sobre la epopeya indígena "Yurupay" (comparable al *Popol Vuh*) y los poetas F.A. Vélez Ladrón de Guevara y F. Alvarez de Velasco y Zorrilla son contribuciones fundamentales al estudio de obras y autores colombianos olvidados. Los estudios sobre Fernández de Oviedo y el del *Desierto prodigioso y prodigio del desierto*, son muy discutibles, pues en el primero arguye que con el cronista comenzó la literatura colombiana y en el segundo que con esta obra se inició la novela de este país.

3340 Ortega, Julio. El cronista indio Guamán Poma de Ayala y la conciencia cultural pluralista en el Perú colonial. (*Nueva Rev. Filol. Hisp.*, 36:1, 1988, p. 365–377, bibl.)

Interesante y claro examen de la dimensión semiótica cultural del texto y la escritura de la *Nueva corónica y buen gobierno*. Esclarece la diversidad estructural interna de la obra. Para Ortega, Guamán Poma propone un programa cultural con base en un plurilingüismo y un pluralismo cultural que permite el respeto y la coexistencia de todas las culturas, perserva y da cuenta de la identidad cultural andina y denuncia su abuso y destrucción de parte de los españoles. Pone énfasis en su calidad de archivo de diversas voces de las que el autor es intérprete y divulgador. Excelente artículo con buena bibliografía.

3341 Ortega, Julio. El Inca Garcilaso y el discurso de la abundancia. (*Rev. Chil. Lit.*, 32, nov. 1988, p. 31–43)

Análisis de la reproducción del tópico del *locus amoenus* (legado del discurso clásico) y su transformación en el *lugar abundante* (legado del discurso viajero) en el *Dia-*

rio de Colón y su influjo en *Comentarios reales* del Inca. Para Ortega, el sistema de registro de la exuberancia y gran fecundidad de la naturaleza de Indias iniciado por Colón está sometido por el Inca a un sistema de verificación que sostiene la racionalidad de tal discurso de la abundancia con el cual reivindica la historia de su patria. Muy buen ejemplo de análisis del discurso historiográfico colonial. El mismo artículo con pequeña variación aparece en *Revista de Crítica Literaria Latinoamericana* (14:28, 1988, p. 101–115).

3342 Palencia-Roth, Michael. La ley de los caníbales: Cartagena y el Mar Caribe en el siglo XVI. (*in* De ficciones y realidades: perspectivas sobre literatura e historia colombianas. Recopilación de Alvaro Pineda Botero y Raymond L. Williams. Bogotá: Tercer Mundo Editores, 1989, p. 123–136, bibl.)

Estudio de las imágenes del Nuevo Mundo y el Nuevo Hombre americano bajo el término "caribe" en la documentación oficial española sobre América y la cartografía europea. La predisposición de los conquistadores a encontrar monstruos en las nuevas tierras facilitó la clasificación de los aborígenes entre antropófagos y no antropófagos como estrategia de colonización. Propone la exploración de este aspecto de la caracterización de América como clave para la comprensión de la historia de la dominación de una cultura sobre otra. Excelente bibliografía.

3343 Pasquariello, Anthony M. Theatre in colonial Spanish America: religious and cultural impact. (*Hisp. J.,* 10:1, Fall 1988, p. 27–38, bibl.)

Bien documentada reseña histórica demostrando que la actividad teatral en los Virreinatos de México, Perú y Río de la Plata en el período colonial era tan nutrida y sofisticada como la de España. Destaca el respaldo de los religiosos de esta actividad en el siglo XVI (por su labor evangélica) y su oposición a ella una vez adquirió una orientación secular y su complejidad de industria artística en los grandes centros urbanos de la colonia. Util para historiadores y estudiantes del teatro.

3344 Pastor, Beatriz. Lope de Aguirre, El Loco: la voz de la soledad. (*Rev. Crít. Lit. Latinoam.,* 14:28, 1988, p. 159–173)

Examen del episodio histórico del rebelde Lope de Aguirre y de la reacción de sus contemporáneos en sus discursos historiográficos y literarios en los que se le reduce a loco y traidor, se le aísla de su contexto político-social y se escamotea así la crisis de la sociedad colonial implicada en esta rebelión. El discurso de crítica y rebeldía de Aguirre, según Pastor, presenta rasgos típicos del desengaño del barroco que hacen de esta carta a Felipe II un texto precursor del barroco español en América. Excelentes percepciones entorpecidas a veces por la disipación de su exposición.

3345 Pastor, Beatriz. Silence and writing: the history of the conquest. (*in* 1492–1992: re/discovering colonial writing. Edited by René Jara and Nicholas Spadaccini. Minneapolis, Minn.: The Prisma Institute, 1989, p. 121–163, bibl.)

Pastor niega la objetividad de discursos europeos como el de Colón y Cortés por su definición autoritaria y unívoca de la historia de la conquista, pues supone la omisión y escamoteo de las voces de protesta en el contexto de la opresión colonialista (caso de la Malinche, por ejemplo). Propone, entonces, una lectura que atienda a esos silencios. Aunque demuestra muy bien lo primero, no queda clara su estrategia para la lectura de esas voces suprimidas. Incluye examen de otros discursos de protesta y fracaso (Cabeza de Vaca) y crítica al orden colonial (Ercilla) y sus limitaciones para la expresión de las voces aborígenes de protesta.

Paz, Octavio. Sor Juana, or, the traps of faith. See item **5022.**

3346 Pupo-Walker, Enrique. Los *Naufragios* de Alvar Núñez Cabeza de Vaca: notas sobre la relevancia antropológica del texto. (*Rev. Indias,* 47:181, sept./dic. 1987, p. 755–776, bibl.)

Destaca la doble riqueza testimonial de *Naufragios* útil para estudios antropológicos de las comunidades prehispánicas del sur de EE.UU.: la objetividad y la modernidad de las observaciones de Núñez (sobre costumbres, economía, herramientas, etc.) y la dimensión paradójica de su shamanismo (pretendiendo evangelizar a los indios confirma las supersticiones de ellos). Utiliza conceptos de la antropología cultural de Lévi-Strauss, M. Elaide, E.B. Taylor, Franz Boas, etc. con orientación interdisciplinaria, es de interés para estudiosos de la antropología, la etnografía y el discurso hispano del siglo XVI. Amplia bibliografía.

3347 Rabasa, José. Utopian ethnology in Las Casas's *Apologética*. (*in* 1492–1992: re/discovering colonial writing. Edited by René Jara and Nicholas Spadaccini. Minneapolis, Minn.: The Prisma Institute, 1989, p. 263–289, bibl.)

Propone una lectura alternativa de esta obra del dominico sin proyectar nociones modernas sobre un discurso del siglo XVI. Examina dos estrategias utópicos del discurso antropológico de Las Casas: los conceptos del "noble salvaje" y el "jardín edénico," en que el indio americano es más digno de emulación que "el otro" del modelo clásico instaurado por el Renacimiento. Desarrolla la noción de la otredad y desmantela aquella de la superioridad de Occidente sobre los indígenas americanos. Gran aporte con buena bibliografía.

3348 Reedy, Daniel. "Que hay una peste . . . en Quito:" el sarampión como materia científica y poética en la obra de Bermejo y Roldán y de Caviedes. (*in* Congreso del Instituto Internacional de Literatura Iberoamericana, *26th, New York, 1987*. Memorias: la historia de la literatura iberoamericana. Edición, recopilación y prólogo de Raquel Chang-Rodríguez y Gabriella de Beer. Hanover, New Hampshire: Ediciones del Norte, 1989, p. 67–76)

Este interesante artículo explica cómo el mismo tema vulgar de una peste de sarampión estimula la escritura de un texto médico, *Discurso de la enfermedad sarampión* (1694) del protomedico Bermejo y Roldán, y otros poéticos (dos romances satíricos y un soneto laudatorio de Caviedes) en el Virreinato del Perú a fines del siglo XVII. Contrasta la actitud malévola (en unas composiciones) y benévola (en otra), de Caviedes frente a los médicos y destaca los importantes aportes de Bermejo y Roldán a la medicina universal.

3349 Rodríguez-Arenas, Flor María. La narración indígena en las crónicas de Indias: un caso en la *Miscelánea antártica*. (*Rev. Crít. Lit. Latinoam.*, 14:28, 1988, p. 197–213)

Interesante examen de un relato incaico prehispánico de tema amoroso y guerrero inserto en la crónica *Miscelánea Antártica* (1577–86). Destaca los rasgos de la fuente oral indígena sobre los que Miguel Cabello de Balboa, su autor, impuso su punto de vista europeo-etnocentrista. Con base en buena información etnográfica sobre los Incas, la autora intenta reconstruir la fuente oral indígena que presenta mitos centrales de la cosmogonía incaica, los cuales no pueden ser entendidos desde una perspectiva eurocentrista.

3350 Ross, Kathleen. A natural history of the Old World: the *Memorias* of Fray Servando Teresa de Mier. (*Rev. Estud. Hisp.*, 23:3, 1989, p. 87–99)

Cuestionamiento de lecturas romantizadas de las *Memorias* que buscan en Fray Servando un héroe (Rodríguez Monegal, A. Reyes, O'Gorman) indicando sus conexiones con las historias naturalistas de españoles del siglo XVI sobre América (en particular Las Casas) y su tensión entre los discursos narcisista y político. Otro excelente aporte a la desmitificación de héroes en las letras coloniales.

3351 Saint-Lu, André. Aspectos de la manera narrativa en la *Historia* de Fray Antonio de Remesal. (*An. Acad. Geogr. Hist. Guatem.*, 62:60, enero/dic. 1986, p. 147–157)

Llama la atención sobre la credulidad de críticos e historiadores modernos ante la *Historia de la provincia de San Vicente de Chiapa y Guatemala* de Remesal, la cual compara detenidamente con una de sus fuentes, la relacion de Fray Tomás de la Torre, dedicada al viaje de un grupo de dominicos con Fray Bartolomé de las Casas de España a Chiapas. Resalta la libre e imaginativa elaboración del texto de Remesal (escenificaciones, dramatizaciones, invenciones de discursos y circunstancias, omisiones). Poca consistencia de terminología literaria. Bibliografía primaria; poca bibliografía secundaria.

3352 Sáinz de Medrano, Luis. Historia y utopía en Fernández de Lizardi. (*in* Congreso del Instituto Internacional de Literatura Iberoamericana, *26th, New York, 1987*. Memorias: la historia de la literatura iberoamericana. Edición, recopilación y prólogo de Raquel Chang-Rodríguez y Gabriella de Beer. Hanover, New Hampshire: Ediciones del Norte, 1989, p. 77–83, bibl.)

Destacando similitudes de dos textos de Fernández de Lizardi (artículo periodístico de 1814 y pasaje de *El periquillo sarniento* 1816) que describen conglomerados imaginarios en islas remotas con la obra *Utopía* de Tomás Moro, demuestra que el autor mexicano continúa la tradición utópica hispanoamerica "de Colón, Zumárraga, el Inca Garcilaso" que anhela una sociedad perfecta en América. Aunque queda clara la inclusión de Fernández entre los utopistas hispanoamericanos no ocurre lo mismo con el concepto de "Historia" en este contexto.

3353 Schulman, Iván A. Espejo/*speculum: El espejo de paciencia* de Silvestre de Balboa. (*Nueva Rev. Filol. Hisp.*, 36:1, 1988, p. 391–406)

Elementos teóricos de Lezama Lima, E. Said y O. Paz le sirven a Schulman aquí para rechazar la lectura tradicional del *Espejo de paciencia* (1608) que lo considera como un prototipo del poema heroico lleno de carencias y deformaciones. Propone una nueva en que descifren los códigos planteados por el concepto "espejo" como reflexión compleja de una sociedad inestable en formación y que revele un poema no conformista ni tradicional que rechaza el centro metropolitano, prefiere el periférico-mundonovista, y prefigura la independencia. Buen ensayo.

3354 Surtz, Ronald E. Pastores judíos y Reyes Magos gentiles: teatro franciscano y milenarismo en Nueva España. (*Nueva Rev. Filol. Hisp.*, 36:1, 1988, p. 333–344)

Exploración de criterios ideológicos que determinaron los temas del teatro misionero de los franciscanos en el siglo XVI en México que indentifican a los indios con los gentiles del Nuevo Testamento y a su conversión masiva con la inminencia de Juicio Final. Esto demuestra en los frailes, según Surtz: 1) la superposición de interpretaciones sociológicas antes que teológicas del Evangelio en sus composiciones dramáticas; y 2) la justificación del *status quo.* Excelente bibliografía. Útil para especialistas.

Valcárcel Martínez, Simón. Una aproximación a Francisco López de Gómara. See item **1089.**

3355 Williams, Jerry. The early Mexican stage: censorship and conflict. (*Rev. Estud. Hisp.*, 23:3, 1989, p. 21–35, bibl.)

Examen de varios casos de censura de la actividad teatral en el siglo XVI de parte de las autoridades civiles y eclesiásticas. Señala la inconsistencia y contradicción entre los organismos censores que poco efecto

tuvieron sobre los dramaturgos y sus obras. Rico en datos históricos.

3356 Zamora, Margarita. Filología humanista e historia indígena en *Los comentarios reales.* (*Rev. Iberoam.*, 53:140, julio/sept. 1987, p. 547–558)

Considera el discurso histórico de *Comentarios reales* como un proyecto filológico típico del Humanismo renacentista que se propone rescatar el texto original (oral) incaico—malinterpretado por historiadores anteriores del Perú—en un esfuerzo más hermenéutico que historiográfico. Ubica a Garcilaso en el contexto de la revolución exegética humanista que se proponía rescatar textos originales a través de un buen conocimiento de la lingüística y el contexto histórico de ellos. Inportantísima precisión de perspectivas de análisis de la obra del Inca y del resto de cronistas de la época. Excelente bibliografía.

3357 Zamora, Margarita. Language, authority, and indigenous history in the *Comentarios reales de los incas.* Cambridge; New York: Cambridge Univ. Press, 1988. 209 p.: (Cambridge Iberian and Latin American studies)

Con base en el análisis del discurso y una aproximación interdisciplinaria examina los numerosos modelos retóricos (del humanismo renacentista) utilizados por el Inca para revindicar la historia del Imperio Inca ante el lector europeo del siglo XVII: historiografía tradicional, filología y hermenéutica humanistas, discurso utópico, etc. Uno de los mejores estudios de los últimos años sobre las letras coloniales hispanoamericanas. Amplia bibliografía.

3358 Zamora, Margarita. "Todas son palabras del Almirante:" Las Casas y el *Diario* de Colón. (*Hisp. Rev.*, 57:1, Spring 1989, p. 25–41, bibl.)

Con base en teorías del discurso literario (Bakhtin, Kristeva, Genette, etc.) Zamora señala que el "libro de la primera navegación" no es una trascripción del texto colombino original sino una re-escritura utilitarista que responde al interés ideológico del fraile. Excelente artículo. Corta pero pertinente bibliografía.

3359 Zapata, Roger A. Guamán Poma: indigenismo y estética de la dependencia en la cultura peruana. Minneapolis, Minn.:

Institute for the Study of Ideologies and Literatures, 1989. 218 p.: bibl., ill. (Series towards a social history of Hispanic and Luso-Brazilian literatures)

Considerando el texto como un instrumento de lucha indígena anticolonial se estudian tres aspectos: 1) la imagen del mundo colonial a través de motivos arquetípicos (búsqueda del padre, mundo al revés, peregrino); 2) aprehensión de cultura europea en defensa de la indígena; y 3) vigencia de dependencia colonialista en el Perú de hoy. Buena contribución al estudio de este cronista y de estrategias discursivas de resistencia en el período colonial.

3360 Zavala, Iris M. Representing the colonial subject. (*in* 1492–1992: re/discovering colonial writing. Edited by René Jara and Nicholas Spadaccini. Minneapolis, Minn.: The Prisma Institute, 1989, p. 323–348)

Examen de la representación del sujeto colonial desarrollado por un discurso imperialista en historias, relaciones, romances, narrativa de ficción e iconografía desde el siglo XVI hasta el XVIII. Se enfoca en la manera como los indígenas americanos y las generaciones producto de la mezcla de razas experimentaron su propia imagen como negativa en contraste con la imagen de los colonizadores. Basado en fuentes documentales de México. Buen aporte al estudio de los discursos colonialistas y sus estrategias.

TEXTS, EDITIONS, ANTHOLOGIES

3361 Ayrolo Calar, Gabriel de. Laurentina. Ed. fac-similar com transcrição paleográfica. Recife, Brazil: Pool Editorial, 1983. 341 p., 1 leaf of plates: ill., port.

Edición moderna de poema épico (Cádiz, 1624) en octavas rimas celebrando la victoria naval de Fadrique de Toledo y de San Lorenzo contra holandeses en el estrecho de Gibraltar en 1621. Aunque el tema no es hispanoamericano, sí lo es el autor (n. México) quien sigue tradición de exaltación de varones españoles como la representada por Lobo Lasso de la Vega en su *Mexicana* (1594).

3362 Benítez, José Antonio. *Carnero*, y miscelánea de varias noticias, antiguas y modernas, de esta villa de Medellín. Transcripción, prólogo y notas de Roberto Luis Ja-

ramillo. 1. ed. crítica. Medellín: Ediciones Autores Antioqueños, 1988. 545 p.: bibl., facsims., ill., maps. (Ediciones Autores antioqueños; 40)

Primera edición de una crónica de la Ciudad de Medellín, Colombia (1541–1840), escrita (1769–1840) a imitación de *El carnero* de Rodríguez Freile, aunque sin la gracia y calidad narrativa de éste. Narra hechos del descubrimiento y conquista, pormenores jurídicos, civiles, religiosos, criminales; incluye comentarios de los hechos—a veces moralizantes—y copias de evidencias documentales (cartas, impresos, documentos legales). Amplio estudio preliminar sobre marco histórico y biografía de Benítez. Importante aporte al estudio de la historiografía hispanoamericana de antes y después de la independencia.

3363 Betanzos, Juan de. Suma y narración de los incas. Prólogo, transcripción y notas de María del Carmen Martín Rubio. Estudios preliminares de Horacio Villanueva Urteaga, Demetrio Ramos Pérez y María del Carmen Martín Rubio. Madrid: Atlas, 1987. 410 p.: bibl., facsims.

Primera edición completa de la *Suma* (1551). Antes se conocían sólo 18 capítulos (de 34) editados por primera vez por M. Jiménez de la Espada (1880). Trata del origen y conquista del Imperio Inca hasta la rebelión de Manco Inca. Transcripción respeta sintaxis original del autor español quechua hablante quien transcribe directamente fuentes orales indígenas. Sobresale el estudio de D. Ramos sobre estructura, técnica e interpretación del mundo incaico de la obra de Betanzos. Fundamental contribución al estudio del discurso colonial afecto a cultura indígena y el discurso etnográfico.

3364 Chambaud Magnus, Jaime. Directoras de escena novohispanas del siglo XVII. (*Lat. Am. Theatre Rev.*, 23:1, Fall 1989, p. 111–117)

Breve pero importante nota destacando dos documentos notariales del siglo XVII en la Nueva España (publicados por el *Boletín del Archivo General de la Nación*) que revelan la existencia de dos mujeres directoras teatrales y sus esfuerzos para trabajar y sobrevivir en un ambiente hostil dominado por un sistema y unos colegas masculinos: 1) Ana María de los Angeles, "quizás la primera directora de la colonia" (p. 114); y

2) María de Celi, directora por "más de doce años" (p. 116). Llama la atención sobre las grandes posibilidades de investigación de la olvidada y numerosa "*intelligentsia* femenina novohispana" (p. 117).

3365 Domínguez Camargo, Hernando.
Obras. Prólogo de Giovanni Meo Zilio. Caracas: Biblioteca Ayacucho, 1986. 582 p.: bibl. (Biblioteca Ayacucho; 121)

Edición crítica del *Poema heroico* sobre San Ignacio de Loyola, con poesías y prosa de este autor neogranadino, basado en la edición de R. Torres Quintero (Instituto Caro y Cuervo, 1960). Prólogo con biografía, estructura ideológica y estilística del *Poema*, y estudio comparativo de estilo y técnicas entre poemas de Góngora y Camargo. El estudio demuestra que Camargo no es simplemente un imitador de Góngora, sino un poeta que logra una simbiosis y un sincretismo poético con las formas gongoristas, llevándolas a su máxima expresión en América.

3366 Espinosa Medrano, Juan de. Apologético. Selección, prólogo y cronología de Augusto Tamayo Vargas.Traducción del latín de Rafael Blanco Varela. Caracas: Biblioteca Ayacucho, 1982. 421 p.: bibl. (Biblioteca Ayacucho; 98)

Selección de obras literarias: *Apologético en favor de Don Luis de Góngora, Panegírica declamación por la protección de las ciencias y los estudios*, selección de sermones de *La novena maravilla*, dos obras teatrales, *El hijo pródigo* y *Amar su propia muerte*, y el "Prefacio" a *Filosofía tomista* sobre la igualdad de americanos y españoles. Incluye estudio preliminar sobre el barroco, su relación con El Lunarejo y noticias sobre los textos selectos. Amplia cronología, pero poco rigor en precisión de criterios de la edición. Buen aporte a la divulgación de este importante autor del conceptismo y el culteranismo del siglo XVII en América.

3367 Letras de la Audiencia de Quito: período jesuítico. Selección, prólogo y cronología de Hernán Rodríguez Castelo. Caracas: Biblioteca Ayacucho, 1984. 393 p. (Biblioteca Ayacucho; 112)

Selección de textos históricos y literarios hagiográficos, ascético-místicos, relatos misionales, poesía lírica (incluye poesías completas de J. Bautista Aguirre) y oratoria sagrada de clérigos ecuatorianos de los siglos XVII y XVIII. Prólogo exalta la historia y literatura de Quito, dando noticias sobre obras y autores seleccionados. Mínima cronología.

3368 Olavide, Pablo de. Obras selectas. Estudio preliminar, recopilación y bibliografía de Estuardo Núñez. Lima: Banco de Crédito del Perú, 1987. 864 p., 31 p. of plates: bibl., facsims., ill., indexes, ports. (Biblioteca clásicos del Perú; 3. Biblioteca peruana; 3.)

Selección de obras narrativas, dramáticas, poéticas y de reflexión incluyendo textos descubiertos recientemente (novelas y textos políticos de reforma agraria y universitaria). Amplio estudio preliminar reivindicando la modernidad de Olavide como autor preocupado por difusión popular de arte escénico, narrador y estadista planificador de orden social y educativo. Contiene útiles cronología, bibliografía anotada e índices onomástico y toponímico. Excelente contribución a la mejor comprensión de este autor ilustrado.

3369 Sigüenza y Góngora, Carlos de. Infortunios de Alonso Ramírez. Edición de Lucrecio Pérez Blanco. Madrid: Historia 16, 1988. 145 p.: (Crónicas de América; 42)

Edición basada en tres anteriores de este siglo (Espasa Calpe 1951, Porrúa 1960, Cordillera 1967) sin agregarles nada fundamental excepto modificaciones formales. Abundantes notas históricas, geográficas y semánticas. Amplia introducción que caracteriza la obra como la primera novela hispanoamericana, recubierta de didactismo. Apéndice diserta sobre las conexiones de la obra con *El Periquillo sarniento*. Presa de la dualidad historia/ficción, o historia al servicio de la ficción, la edición se empeña en hacer leer la obra como una novela.

3370 Tapia Méndez, Aureliano. Autodefensa espiritual de Sor Juana. Monterrey, Mexico: Univ. Autónoma de Nuevo León, Dirección General de Investigaciones Humanísticas, 1981. 98 p.: ill.

Primera edición de la "Carta de la Madre Juana Inés de la Cruz Escrita al R.P.M. Antonio Núñez"(1861), descubierta por Tapia en 1980. Incluye noticias sobre la personalidad del destinatario, y comparación del texto con el de la "Respuesta a Sor Filotea." Ilustrativas disertaciones sobre el choque de la Monja con el rígido confesor.

3371 Untold sisters: Hispanic nuns in their own works. Edited by Electa Arenal and Stacey Schlau. Translated by Amanda Powell. Albuquerque: Univ. of New Mexico Press, 1989. 450 p.: bibl., ill., index.

Selección de textos (cartas, autobiografías, poemas, etc.) de monjas españolas e hispanoamericanas del Renacimiento y el Barroco, en español moderno seguidos de su traducción al inglés. Sugestivo estudio preliminar intentando determinar lo que es propio del lenguaje, historia, literatura y crítica de la mujer y que ha sido y sigue siendo textualmente invisible. Cap. 5 y 6 dedicados a monjas del Perú y la Nueva España, respectivamente. Sólida contribución a la divulgación de su historia social, cultural e intelectual en España e Hispanoamérica. Buena bibliografía. For comments on translation see item **4933**.

MISCELLANEOUS

3372 Abbott, Don Paul. Aztecs and orators: rhetoric in New Spain. (*Texte*, 8/9, 1989, p. 353–365, bibl.)

Breve, sólido e informativo artículo sobre el estudio y cultivo de la retórica (nativa y del Renacimiento humanista) en el contexto del encuentro de las culturas azteca y europea en el México del siglo XVI. Establece tres pasos en su desarrollo: 1) el registro de los Franciscanos de la retórica azteca prehispánica; 2) el intento de enseñanza de la retórica humanista a los indígenas con propósitos evangélicos; y 3) la posterior enseñanza restringida de esta retórica europea a la élite de españoles y criollos que acaba con el pluralismo cultural iniciado por los franciscanos. Buena bibliografía.

3373 Ainsa, Fernando. De la historia a la ficción: mito y utopía de la ciudad de los Césares. (*in* Congreso del Instituto Internacional de Literatura Iberoamericana, *26th, New York, 1987.* Memorias: la historia de la literatura iberoamericana. Edición, recopilación y prólogo de Raquel Chang-Rodríguez y Gabriella de Beer. Hanover, New Hampshire: Ediciones del Norte, 1989, p. 41–54)

Breve pero importante trabajo se propone explicar las vicisitudes de la leyenda de esta ciudad perdida en la región austral americana a través de varios discursos (histórico, legendario, utópico y novelesco) desde el siglo XVI hasta el XX. Expone su desarrollo

desde los hechos históricos que le dieron origen, los aportes de la utopía humanista del renacimiento en sucesivas versiones y la independización del tema en el terreno novelesco. Importante aporte bibliográfico de documentos casi olvidados y estudios poco conocidos.

3374 Arrom, José Juan. Carlos de Sigüenza y Góngora: relectura criolla de los *Infortunios de Alonso Ramírez.* (*Thesaurus*, 42:1, enero/abril 1987, p. 23–46)

Author sustains that the *Infortunios* is more literary than historical in character. Finds a likely precedent for Sigüenza's work in the 16th-century European travel-adventure novel. Study includes comparative analysis of *Infortunios* and José Acosta's *Peregrinación de Bartolomé Lorenzo.* Important concepts and critical views. [D. Reedy]

3375 Arrom, José Juan. Juan Méndez Nieto: el traslado al Nuevo Mundo del cuento humorístico medieval. (*Thesaurus*, 40:1, enero/abril 1985, p. 1–16)

Divulgación de un autor olvidado del período colonial, el médico español J.M. Nieto (1530–1611) quien escribió un relato autobiográfico, *Discursos medicinales* (1607), lleno de anécdotas jocosas y festivas que demuestran un agudo conocimiento de la naturaleza humana. Arrom reproduce y analiza dos relatos que tienen lugar en la Isla Española identificando motivos recurrentes en la tradición narrativa medieval y encontrando en ellos anticipos de la literatura hispanoamericana del siglo XX. (Editor's Note: previous appearance of this item in *HLAS 50:2954* was an *errata*; annotation referred to item **3374**.)

3376 Colahan, Clark. Chronicles of exploration and discovery: the enchantment of the unknown. (*in* Pasó por aquí: critical essays on the New Mexican literary tradition, 1542–1988. Edited by Erlinda Gonzales-Berry. Albuquerque: Univ. of New Mexico Press, 1989, p. 15–46)

Sugestiva exposición de contenido y características generales de las relaciones sobre la exploración de la región de Nuevo México en el siglo XVI (Cabeza de Vaca, Fray M. de Niza, P. de Castañeda, H. Gallegos, A. de Espejo y Fray F. de Escobar). En el registro de lo legendario y desconocido los autores recurren a imágenes y técnicas de la literatura renacentista de ficción, según Colunan, quien evalúa los aportes (etnográficos, naturalistas, literarios, etc.) de cada relación y las ubica en el contexto histórico (mexicano y español) y cultural (humanista) que las determinó. Util para interesados en historiografía de ese período y esa región. Buena bibliografía.

3377 Goíc, Cedomil. Historia y crítica de la literatura hispanoamericana. v. 1, Epoca colonial. Barcelona: Editorial Crítica, Grupo Editorial Grijalbo, 1988. 1 v.: bibl., index. (Páginas de filología)

Representativa y cuidadosa selección de textos críticos (escritos 1922–85) en orden cronológico y temático sobre géneros, escritores, obras y temas destacados de la literatura hispanoamericana entre el Descubrimiento y la Independencia. Una evaluación del panorama de la crítica correspondiente, con énfasis en tendencias y criterios en auge, introduce cada capítulo. Excelente y útil bibliografía fundamental. Guía para estudiantes, profesores y especialistas de esta área de estudio.

3378 González Stephan, Beatriz. La historiografía literaria hispanoamericana: agenda para problemas de la literatura nacional. (*Rev. Estud. Colomb.*, 4, 1987, p. 29–33)

Confronta la noción decimonónica de las historias literarias que asimilan el concepto de "literatura" al de "nación" con base en un propósito voluntarista del nacionalismo político post-independentista. Examina las contradicciones de este proyecto que busca orígenes auténticos mientras niega el legado español, y que son producto de una "obturación de carácter ideológico" que ha llevado conclusiones falsas: "inmadurez" de Latinoamérica, naturaleza "nueva" de sus realidades, etc. De interés para estudiosos de las historias literarias y sus estructuras epistemológicas.

3379 Merkl, Heinrich. Die Sor Juana-Forschung des deutschen Sprachraums seit 1930. (*Iberoromania*, 26, 1987, p. 49–66)

Critical analysis of post-1930 German interpretations of Sor Juana focuses on two studies written during the Nazi era which were examples of intellectual resistance against regime. Merkl argues that Karl Vossler and Ludwig Pfandl indirectly criticized

regime: 1) Vossler emphasized Sor Juana's closeness to enlightenment and distance from racist and antisemitic ideology of the Siglo de Oro) and 2) Pfandl's interpretation of Sor Juana's neurosis which did not affect her art disagreed with the Nazi polemic toward the "Jewish Science" of Freud. Both critics were ignored in German research after WWII because of their emigration and German uneasiness with psychoanalytical interpretations. [M.L. Wagner]

3380 Merrim, Stephanie. Civilización y barbarie: Prescott como lector de Cortés. (*in* Congreso del Instituto Internacional de Literatura Iberoamericana, *26th, New York, 1987.* Memorias: la historia de la literatura iberoamericana. Edición, recopilación y prólogo de Raquel Chang-Rodríguez y Gabriella de Beer. Hanover, New Hampshire: Ediciones del Norte, 1989, p. 87–96)

Contradictoria imagen de un Moctezuma bárbaro, tirano, pusilánime y efeminado por excesos sensuales que ofrece tendenciosamente Hernán Cortés en su segunda carta, es retomada, según demuestra Merrim, por Prescott en su *History of the conquest of Mexico* para presentar una semi-cultura azteca condenada por su "refinamiento inútil." Con este ejemplo, la autora señala dos instancias (una del siglo XVI y otra del XIX) en el desarrollo de una de las metáforas culturales más utilizadas en los estudios de la cultura latinoamericana: civilización vs. barbarie. Excelente trabajo.

Ortega, Julio. Crítica de la identidad: la pregunta por el Perú en su literatura. See item **3717.**

3381 Urbano, Henrique. Crónicas, papeles y autores: publicaciones y estudios recientes de los siglos XVI, XVII y XVIII. (*Rev. Andin.*, 5:2, dic. 1987, p. 581–599)

Breve pero útil bibliografía anotada (35 entradas) de ediciones y estudios sobre obras y autores del período colonial de la región andina, en especial el Perú, publicados 1980–87. Aunque llama la atención sobre importantes e imprescindibles textos para el estudiante y el especialista, dista de ser representativa y de dar una idea precisa de lo escrito en la década del 80 sobre estos temas. Las reseñas (algunas de un párrafo, otras de varias páginas) frecuentemente caen en excesos encomiásticos o denigrantes que desdicen de sus méritos.

19th Century: Spanish American Literature Before Modernism

WILLIAM H. KATRA, *Department of Spanish, University of Wisconsin-Eau Claire*

WITHOUT A DOUBT THE MOST memorable benchmark of the biennium was the 100th anniversary of the death of Domingo F. Sarmiento (1811–88), Argentina's great romantic writer, journalist, educator, constitutionalist, and statesman. While many of Sarmiento's beliefs and acts will always be the source of controversy, even his most stalwart opponents are humbled by his immense and multifaceted contributions. The invitation by the Argentine government to co-sponsor academic gatherings in honor of this great Latin American was eagerly embraced by a number of institutions: The Library of Congress in Washington, Boston College, The Univ. of Ottawa, and the Univ. of California at Berkeley, as well as several Argentine universities. However, only the Univ. Nacional de Comahue in Neuquén succeeded in publishing its conference proceedings (item **3427**) before our *HLAS* deadline.

Sarmiento's first of many claims to fame was as a writer, a fact that did not escape the editorial committees of several important journals who organized special issues commemorating his achievements in this field. Some of the finest critical material written to date about the man and his multifaceted writings, can be found in these special issues: *Cuadernos Hispanoamericanos* item **3412**), *Revista Iberoamericana* (item **3440**), and *Todo es Historia* (item **3450**). Given the large number of such essays in these journals, and in spite of their consistently high quality, it has not been possible to annotate all of them individually in this HLAS chapter.

Another notable trend among critical writings of this biennium has been a return to Latin America's most renowned writers of the 19th century, seeking either unexplored aspects of their *oeuvre,* or applying new critical approaches. After Sarmiento, the individual writers that attracted the most attention were José Martí (10 items), Andrés Bello (8 items), and José Hernández (4 items).

An entirely different trend has been the reissue of several old works, now largely forgotten, that nevertheless deserve a place in the cultural history of their countries or regions. These works can be roughly divided into two categories: 1) those whose initial impact was limited on account of regional as opposed to metropolitan theme or distribution; and 2) those whose popularity declined with the emergence of new literary tastes. Mexico has been especially active in this enterprise of literary archaeology, with the republication of works by Leduc (item **3395**), Peón y Contreras (item **3398**), Castra (item **3389**), Carpio (item **3388**), and F. Calderón (item **3385**). Similar editions feature female writers: Ecuador's Palmyra Franco Villagómez (item **3391**), and Colombia's Soledad Acosta de Samper (item **3382**).

And finally, three critical works deserve special mention here as perhaps the most outstanding of the biennium: David William Foster's *The Argentine generation of 1880: ideology and cultural texts* (item **3417**); Adolfo Prieto's *El discurso criollista en la formación de la Argentina moderna* (item **3438**); and Oscar Rivera-Rodas' *La poesía hispanoamericana del siglo XIX: del romanticismo al modernismo* (item **3441**). These three works, which exhibit entirely different critical methodologies, have in common an innovative focus and a profound understanding of the historical and sociological contexts out of which literary expression emerges.

PROSE FICTION AND POETRY

3382 **Acosta de Samper, Soledad.** Una nueva lectura. Bogotá: Ediciones Fondo Cultural Cafetero, 1988. 401 p.: bibl.

Printing of five narrative works from an 1869 publication with a detailed bibliography and valuable critical essays by M. Ordóñez, L. Guerra-Cunningham, and G. Otero Muñoz.

3383 **Altamirano, Ignacio Manuel.** Obras completas. v. 1–6. México: Secretaría de Educación Pública, 1986. 6 v.

Six fine volumes with appropriate 10-page introductions by S. Reyes Nevares, M. Ochoa Campos, J.L. Martínez, and J.J. Blanco. Altamirano was a fiery liberal modernizer who struggled as a military official, politician, historian, journalist, and poet.

3384 **Batres Jáuregui, Antonio.** José Batres Montúfar: su tiempo y sus obras, 1809–1909. Guatemala: Editorial José de Pineda Ibarra, 1982. 251 p.: bibl., port. (Biblioteca guatemalteca de cultura popular 15 de septiembre; 118: duodécima serie)

Long 1906 introduction focusing mainly on author's writings precedes selections from *Tradiciones de Guatemala* and *Poesías líricas.*

3385 **Calderón, Fernando.** Obras poéticas: parnaso mexicano, 1844. Edición, presentación y apéndices de Fernando Tola de Habich. México: Premià, 1986. 630 p.: bibl., ill. (Libros del bicho)

Long preface emphasizing diverse critical opinions introduces facsimile edition of Calderón's (1809–45) *Obras poéticas* of 1844. Also includes the drama *Muerte de Virginia* (70 p.) and various poems.

3386 **Campo, Estanislao del.** Fausto: su prefiguración periodística. Edición, estudio y notas por Angel José Battistessa. Buenos Aires: Academia Argentina de Letras, 1989. 143 p., 5 leaves of plates: bibl., ill. (Biblioteca de la Academia Argentina de Letras: Serie Estudios académicos; 28)

Contains a 30-page introduction treating the poem's journalistic origins.

3387 **Caro, Miguel Antonio.** Anécdotas y poesías satíricas de Miguel Antonio Caro. Edición, introducción y notas de Guillermo Hernández Peñalosa. Bogotá: Instituto Caro y Cuervo, 1988. 299 p.: bibl., index. (Serie La Granada entreabierta; 47)

Anecdotes about Caro by about 50 writers, followed by a fine scholarly edition of *Poesía satírica.*

3388 **Carpio, Manuel.** Poesía. Edición, presentación y apéndices de Fernando Tola de Habich. Xalapa, Mexico: Univ. Veracruzana, 1987. 596 p.: bibl., facsims. (Col. UV rescate; 23)

Nine editions before 1900 attest to the popularity of the predominantly religious work of this Veracruz poet (1791–1860). Facsimile of 1860 edition has long prologue that incorporates a history of critical judgments.

3389 **Castera, Pedro.** Las minas y los mineros; Querens. Edición, introducción y notas de Luis Mario Schneider. 1a ed. B.E.U. México: Coordinación de Humanidades, Univ. Nacional Autónoma de México, 1987. 237 p.: bibl. (Biblioteca del estudiante universitario; 104)

Castera (1848–1906), known primarily for his sentimental novel *Carmen* (1882), also wrote realistic stories based on his experiences in the mines of San Luis de Potosí and Zacatecas. L.M. Schneider describes the novel *Querens* as " . . . the first Latin American novel in which hypnotism and esoteric energy provide the motive and foundation for artistic creation."

3390 **Chocano, José Santos.** Obras escogidas. Selección, prólogo y notas de Luis Alberto Sánchez. Lima?: Occidental Petroleum Corporation of Peru, 1988. 605 p.

Excellent edition except for the fact that the long 1951 prologue has not been updated or supplemented to take into account recent criticism.

3391 **Franco Villagómez, Palmyra.** Soledad: novela costumbrista del siglo XIX. Quito: Editorial Casa de la Cultura Ecuatoriana, 1985. 293 p.

Little-known novel by one of Ecuador's finest female writers at turn of the century.

3392 **Gómez de Avellaneda y Arteaga, Gertrudis.** Tradiciones. Selección y prólogo de Mary Cruz. La Habana: Editorial Letras Cubanas, 1984. 358 p. (Biblioteca básica de literatura cubana)

Prologue provides good general introduction.

3393 Hidalgo, Bartolomé. Obra completa. Prólogo de Antonio Praderio. Montevideo: Ministerio de Educación y Cultura, 1986. 245p.: (Biblioteca Artigas: Col. de clásicos uruguayos; 170)

En su enjudioso prólogo, Praderio reconstruye la biografía de Hidalgo y examina la autoría de textos. Clasifica la obra de Hidalgo en categorías: 1) obras cultas, que incluye nueve poemas y 2) obras populares o gauchescas, de autoría difícil de establecer por haberse publicado sin firma del autor. [M. García Pinto]

3394 Hostos, Eugenio María de. Obra literaria selecta. Selección, prólogo, bibliografía y cronología de Julio César López. Caracas: Biblioteca Ayacucho, 1988 362 p.: bibl. (Biblioteca Ayacucho; 136)

Short critical introduction, chronology, and select bibliography reinforce the anthology which concentrates on Hostos as a literary creator.

3395 Leduc, Alberto. Fragatita y otros cuentos. México: Instituto Nacional de Bellas Artes; Tlahuapan, Mexico: Premià, 1984. 95 p.: ill. (La Matraca; 2a ser., 26)

Consists of 15 stories by the Querétaro regionalist, emphasizing the psychological threat of encroaching modernization.

3396 Martí y el Uruguay: crónicas y correspondencia. Montevideo: Univ. de la República, Facultad de Humanidades y Ciencias, Depto. de Publicaciones, 1988. 107 p.

Short essays by R. de Armas and M. Benedetti precede several long articles by Martí dealing mainly with the US and published in Montevideo's *La Opinión Pública*, as well as several letters written to E. Estrazulas over the same period.

3397 Montalvo, Juan. El espectador. Ambato, Ecuador: Ilustre Municipio de Ambato, 1987. 370 p., 7 p. of plates: ports. (Biblioteca Letras de Tungurahua; 19)

Reprint of 1886 classic includes solid prologue.

3398 Peón y Contreras, José. José Peón y Contreras. Recopilación e introducción de Enrique Montalvo Ortega. México: Senado de la República, 1987. 291 p.: bibl., port. (Serie Los Senadores)

Includes one act of a drama and several poems by Yucatan's most renowned 19th-century writer, along with short reviews by Gutiérrez Nájera and Martí.

3399 Peza, Juan de Dios. Perucho, nieto de periquillo. México: INBA, SEP Cultura; Tlahuapan, Mexico: Premià Editora, 1986. 343 p.: ill. (La Matraca; 2a ser., 12)

First publication in book form of this *novela de entregas* which appeared in *El Mundo* (1895–96). Covers rise and fall of Emperor Maximillian.

3400 Ramos, Julio. Tres artículos desconocidos de José Martí. (*Rev. Iberoam.*, 55 : 146/147, enero/junio 1989, p. 235–247)

Commentary followed by texts published in *La Nación* of Buenos Aires (1883–84).

3401 Teja, Ada María. La poesía de José Martí entre naturaleza e historia: estudios sobre la antítesis y la síntesis. Cosenza, Italy: Marra Editore, 1990. 288 p.: bibl., indexes.

Most thoroughly documented study of Martí's poetry, essays, and letters highlights the synthesis and antithesis in Martí's thought, as his belief in polarity and tension between opposites (love/death, homeland/woman, "shipwreck"/reconstruction, nature/history), and how such oppositions point toward a synthesis. Best example of the latter is Martí's own dual role as poet and revolutionary.

LITERARY CRITICISM AND HISTORY

3402 Apter Cragnolino, Aída. Ortodoxia naturalista, inmigración y racismo en *En la sangre* de Eugenio Cambaceres. (*Cuad. Am.*, 14 : 2, marzo/abril 1989, p. 46–55)

Short, well-grounded ideological essay about the 1886 novel *En la sangre*. Apter Cragnolino regards it as a racist denunciation of Italian immigration and as a warning to Argentina's traditional families about the threat posed by the foreign influx.

3403 Arceo de Konrad, Candelaria. Justo Sierra Méndez: sus cuentos románticos y la influencia francesa. México: Instituto de Investigaciones Filológicas, Centro de Estudios Literarios, Univ. Nacional Autónoma de México, 1985. 133 p.: bibl. (Letras del siglo XIX)

Well-documented study emphasizes Gautier's influence on Sierra's short stories.

3404 Aristizábal, Luis H. Las tres tazas: de Santafé a Bogotá, a través del cuadro de costumbres. (*Bol. Cult. Bibliogr.*, 25 : 16, 1988, p. 60–79, bibl., photos)

Focuses on works of José María Vergara y Vergara (1831–72) and of several other *costumbrista* writers. Essay, illustrated with photos, traces transition of Bogotá from moribund colonial village to the "Athens of South America."

3405 Azeves, Angel Héctor. José Hernández, el civilizador. La Plata, Argentina: Depto. de Historia, Facultad de Humanidades y Ciencias de la Educación, Univ. Nacional de La Plata, 1986. 169 p.: bibl.

Depicts Hernández's politics as a consistent expression of Juan Bautista Alberdi's predictions.

3406 Biagini, Hugo Edgardo. Filosofía americana e identidad: el conflictivo caso argentino. Buenos Aires: Editorial Universitaria de Buenos Aires, 1989. 342 p.: bibl. (Temas)

Biagini's familiarity with a wide-ranging bibliography makes this study an important background reading for students of Sarmiento and Alberdi, and is especially relevant for researching the latter's little-studied fictional allegory *Peregrinación de luz del día*. Other rigorously discussed topics of interest to the scholar of 19th-century literature are Krausism, positivism, and the Argentine Generation of 1880. For philosopher's comment, see item **5417.**

Bonafoux y Quintero, Luis. Ultramarinos. See item **3637.**

3407 Cánepa, Gina. Folletines históricos del Chile independiente y su articulación con la novela naturalista. (*Hispamérica*, 17 : 50, 1988, p. 23–34)

Según la tesis del ensayo, la unidad ideológica de los folletines históricos del siglo XIX es la difusión de los valores patrióticos a la manera como eran entendidos por la mentalidad liberal, laica y librecambista de la época, valores que constituirán la matriz cultural y cívica de Chile y que serán reformulados bajo la dictadura militar. [J. Promis]

3408 Carrascosa-Miguel, Pablo. Rafael Pombo y el verso semilibre hispa-noamericano: aportación al estudio de su poesía a través del análisis métrico. (*Thesaurus*, 43 : 1, enero/abril 1988, p. 12–46, tables)

Describes and quantifies verses written by one of Colombia's foremost 19th-century poets. Demonstrates that Modernism's metric versatility and innovation had its precursors in the romantic period.

3409 Crema, Edoardo. Estudios sobre Andrés Bello. Estudio preliminar de Oscar Sambrano Urdaneta. Caracas: La Casa de Bello, 1987. 343 p.: bibl. (Anexos a las obras completas de Andrés Bello; 7)

Compilation of Crema's (1892–1974) most important works on Bello: "Los Dramas Psíquicos y Estéticos;" "A Través del Romanticismo;" and "Trayectoria Religiosa."

3410 La crítica de la literatura mexicana en el siglo XIX, 1836–1894. Edición de Fernando Tola de Habich. México: Coordinación de Difusión Cultural, Dirección de Literatura, Univ. Nacional Autónoma de México; Univ. de Colima, 1987. 144 p.: bibl., ill. (La crítica literaria en México; 2)

Anthology features literary criticism, as opposed to literary theory or history. Includes essays by J.M. Heredia, Conde de la Cortina, M. Gutiérrez Nájera, and I.M. Altamirano.

3411 Cruz, Mary. Las tragedias de la avellaneda. (*Rev. Lit. Cuba.*, 5 : 8, enero/julio 1987, p. 5–34)

These five dramas (1844–49) treat historical themes drawn from Medieval Spain and the Bible. Dramas effectively present politico-religious ethical dilemmas against a historical backdrop, and are among the most outstanding "tragedies" of Latin American literature.

3412 Cuadernos Hispanoamericanos. Los Complementarios. No. 3, abril 1989– . Madrid: Insituto de Cooperación Iberoamericana.

Issue dedicated to Sarmiento (1811–1888). Essays include: L. Pomer, "Sarmiento: el Caudillismo y la Escritura Histórica;" A. Rodríguez Pérsico, "Sarmiento y la Biografía de la Barbarie;" M.C. Graña, "La Utopía como Analogon;" W. Katra, "El Estilo Ensayístico de Sarmiento;" and H. Biagini, "Sarmiento y la Problemática Española."

3413 Díez Canedo, Aurora. Dos novelas históricas del siglo XIX en el sureste de

México: *Lágrimas del corazón* y *Antón Pérez*. (*in* Literatura, relato popular y religiosidad en el Sureste de México. México: Centro de Investigaciones y Estudios Superiores en Antropología Social, 1985, p. 1–32, bibl.)

Although lacking in critical perspective, essay does discuss two little-known historical novels that treat the 1863–65 French invasion as viewed from Chiapas and Tabasco.

3414 Durán Luzio, Juan. Secuencias paralelas en "La Compuerta Número 12," de Baldomero Lillo. (*Rev. Chil. Lit.*, 31, abril 1988, p. 63–79)

"Intertextual" reading of 1904 short story classic points out the similarities between this naturalistic rendering of descent of Chilean worker and his son into the coal mines, and Zola's *Germinal* and Dante's *Inferno*.

3415 Durán Luzio, Juan. Significación contextual de *Martín Rivas* de Alberto Blest Gana. (*Rev. Crít. Lit. Latinoam.*, 13:26, 1987, p. 43–54)

In the tradition of Balzac, this historical novel situates the fictional action against backdrop of events of 1850–61. Period was marked by "abysmal" separation of social classes and struggle of progesssive groups to remove representatives of the traditional order from political power.

3416 Ferrari, Américo. Manuel González Prada entre lo nuevo y lo viejo. (*Rev. Iberoam.*, 55:146/147, enero/junio 1989, p. 307–325)

Minúsculas (1901) and *Exóticas* (1911) gather González Prada's poems written much earlier: they exemplify his experimentation with verse form and admiration for the stylistic canons of Spanish classics. *Trozos de vida* (posthumous, 1918) attests to the "señera, altiva e intransigente" personality of Peru's great thinker in the months before his death.

3417 Foster, David William. The Argentine generation of 1880: ideology and cultural texts. Columbia, Mo.: Univ. of Missouri Press, 1990. 204 p.: bibl., index.

Formidable study that views literary narratives as constituting "semiotic transformations of the ideological and socio-cultural structures" of Argentina before the turn of the century. Includes authoritative readings of Mansilla's *Una excursión a los indios ranqueles*, Miguel Cané's *Juvenilia*, Fray Mocho's *Memorias de un viligante*, and J.V. González's *Mis montañas*. Other chapters consider the ideological impact of texts by E. Gutiérrez, F. Ramos Mejía, L.V. López, E. Wilde, J. Martel, E. Cambaceres, and others.

3418 García Marruz, Fina. En torno al *Ismaelillo*. (*Anu. Centro Estud. Martianos*, 10, 1987, p. 73–111)

Eloquent examination of three aspects of this work: 1) image of child-love in Martí's poems prior to *Ismaelillo*; 2) possible origin, and relation to text, of the *viñetas*—or simple drawings—found in the work's first edition; and 3) possible influence of Anacreonte's nine poems, translated by Martí from the Greek, on Martí's image of "suffering love."

3419 García Molina, José Antonio. Presencia indígena en la poesía de Juan Cristóbal Nápoles Fajardo. (*Santiago*, 65, junio 1987, p. 187–204)

Studies leading Cuban poet of the *siboneyista* tradition and how he recreated and embellished the spiritual presence of the extinct Caribbean Indian.

3420 Gómez Ocampo, Gilberto. Entre *María* y *La vorágine*: la literatura colombiana finisecular, 1886–1903. Bogotá: Fondo Cultural Cafetero, 1988. 205 p.: bibl. (Ediciones Fondo Cultural Cafetero; 20)

Focuses on the period 1886–1902, with studies on R. Núñez, M.A. Caro, J. de Dios Uribe, J.M. Vargas Vila, S. Acosta de Samper, C. Sota Borda). Offers exemplary scholarly study of literary works written in a time of "power, authority, and the dead weight of tradition."

3421 Gotschlich Reyes, Guillermo. Grotesco y tragicomedia en *El ideal de un calavera* de Alberto Blest Gana. (*Rev. Chil. Lit.*, 29, abril 1987, p. 119–148)

Análisis de la manera como el autor se apropia de categorías estéticas románticas para colocarlas al servicio de su proyecto literario de retratar constructivamente la sociedad chilena de su época. [J. Promis]

3422 Guerra-Cunningham, Lucía. Mercedes Cabello de Carbonera: estética de la moral y los desvíos no-disyuntivos de la

virtud. (*Rev. Crít. Lit. Latinoam.*, 13:26, 1987, p. 25–41)

Solid study of two themes: 1) Cabello de Carbonera's moralizing and edifying vision in her essays on literary criticism; and 2) ideological interpretation of her novel *Blanca Sol* (1894) about the Peruvian bourgeoisie (1860–80) which reveals the contradictions of her liberal perspective flavored by conservative and Catholic values.

3423 Halperín Donghi, Tulio. José Hernández y sus mundos. Buenos Aires: Editorial Sudamericana; Instituto Torcuato di Tella, 1985. 344 p.: bibl. (Col. Historia y sociedad)

Definitive study of the political thought and career of Hernández (1860–86), despite the critic's sometimes impenetrable prose.

3424 Hidalgo Paz, Ibrahím. Facetas inexploradas del "Manifiesto de Montecristi." (*Anu. Centro Estud. Martianos*, 9, 1986, p. 41–78, tables)

Critical *tour-de-force* based on exhaustive examination of existing drafts and versions of Martí's important document as well as relevant criticism. Focuses on Martí's revolutionary strategy (1894–95) and his advanced ideas on preparing the citizenry for both the military struggle and post-liberation society.

3425 Housková, Anna. Tipo de la novela mundonovista. (*Rev. Crít. Lit. Latinoam.*, 13:26, 1987, p. 67–85)

Housková proposes a typology of the *mundonovista* novel, often called regional or *criollo* novels, of the late 19th and early 20th centuries. Well-documented study includes analysis of plot, time, space, polarities, and discussion of the individual in *La vorágine, Doña Bárbara, Don Segundo Sombra*, and *Zurzulita*.[S. Castro-Klarén]

3426 Jorge, Elena. José Martí, el método de su crítica literaria. La Habana: Editorial Letras Cubanas, 1984. 281 p.: bibl. (Col. Crítica)

Excellent chronological treatment that highlights Martí's literary and critical ideas in relation to intellectual trends of his time.

3427 Jornadas Internacionales Domingo Faustino Sarmiento. Neuquén, Argentina: Depto. de Letras, Facultad de Humanidades, Univ. Nacional del Comahue, 1988. 353 p.: bibl.

Includes 15 essays, the most notable being those by N. Jitrik, J. Sazbón, E. Romano, and N. Rosa.

3428 Ludmer, Josefina. En el paraíso del infierno: el *Fausto* argentino. (*Nueva Rev. Filol. Hisp.*, 35:2, 1987, p. 695–719)

Solid analysis, despite verbosity and jargon, of why this poem constitutes a "break" with preceding works in the gauchesque tradition. Emphasizes how parody, exclusion of political issues, liberation from journalism, and separation from the oral tradition account for *Fausto's* "absolutely *literary*" nature.

3429 Marinello, Juan. Obras martianas. Selección y prólogo de Ramón Losada Aldana. Cronología y bibliografía de Trinidad Pérez y Pedro Simón. Caracas: Biblioteca Ayacucho, 1987. 409 p.: bibl. (Biblioteca Ayacucho; 130)

Martí's most authoritative and penetrating critic celebrates the poet's life and works in this impressive anthology.

3430 Martínez Almánzar, Juan Francisco. Enriquillo: ídolo de barro. Santo Domingo: Editora Fuente, 1986. 220 p.: bibl., ill., ports.

Revisionist, historical study of the indigenous chieftain explores the mythic dimensions of Galván's protagonist.

3431 Méndez de la Vega, Luz. La mujer en las obras de José Milla. (*Univ. San Carlos Guatem.*, 2:13, 1982, p. 3–36)

Secondary female characters in novels of Guatemala's most accomplished *costumbrista* writer provide invaluable sociological insights (e.g., women's unhappy marriages, moral sanctions against "sexually-liberated" widows or spinsters, etc.).

3432 Montero, Oscar. Las ordalías del sujeto: *Mi museo ideal* y *Marfiles viejos* de Julián del Casal. (*Rev. Iberoam.*, 55:146/147, enero/junio 1989, p. 287–306)

Contradicts common image of del Casal as exotic dandy and object of condescension by focusing on two series of sonnets in which the poet looks back admiringly on his continent's past values and offers a prophetic vision for its future.

3433 Murillo Rubiera, Fernando. Andrés Bello: historia de una vida y de una obra. Estudio preliminar de Pedro Grases. Caracas: Casa de Bello, 1986. 493 p., 17 p. of plates: bibl., ill., index, ports. (Anexos a las obras completas de Andrés Bello; 1)

Studies development of Bello's thought in relation to his life. Provides excellent critical chapters on Bello's contributions in education, language, philosophy, and law. Includes index and bibliography.

3434 Padrón Toro, Antonio. J.A. Pérez Bonalde: un hombre de hoy. Cumaná, Venezuela: Univ. de Oriente, 1980. 141 p.: bibl., port.

Largely a biographical study of the creator of "Poema del Niágara."

3435 Paz Castillo, Fernando et al. Significación histórica y vigencia moderna de la obra de Andrés Bello: literatura y lingüística. Caracas: Casa de Bello, 1987. 730 p.: bibl. (Anexos a las obras completas de Andrés Bello; 4)

Important studies by R. Caldera, F. Paz Castillo, P.P. Barnola, P. Grasas, A. Alonzo, A. Rosenblat, S. Gili Gaya, and A. Espinosa Pólit.

3436 Pedreáñez Trejo, Héctor. La versificación hispanoamericana premodernista. Estudio preliminar de Ignacio Herrero Fuentes. Caracas: Ediciones del Congreso de la República, 1985. 288 p.: bibl., ill., ports.

Spotty history of Latin American versification (60 p.) followed by short, solid essays on Bello and González Prada.

3437 Pérus Coinet, Françoise. María de Jorge Isaacs, o la negación del espacio novelesco. (*Nueva Rev. Filol. Hisp.*, 34:2, 1987, p. 721–751, bibl.)

Careful but verbose comparison of the novel *María* with Chateaubriand's *El genio del cristianismo*. However, Pérus Coinet fails to develop the fertile idea of the *vacío*—or "empty," "negated" narrative space—resulting from the novel's tragic character and its exaltation of an idyllic Christian setting.

3438 Prieto, Adolfo. El discurso criollista en la formación de la Argentina moderna. Buenos Aires: Editorial Sudamericana, 1988. 241 p.: bibl. (Col. Historia y cultura)

Ground-breaking sociological study of "reception" of pulp fiction published as pamphlets or in press installments (1880–1910). Reveals much about a new mass society resulting from massive immigration and public education. Vulgar, pseudo-gaucho, anti-social themes played a paradoxical role in assimilating immigrants to the established social order.

3439 Ramos, Julio. Saber decir: literatura y modernización en Andrés Bello. (*Nueva Rev. Filol. Hisp.*, 35:2, 1987, p. 675–694, bibls.)

Excellent comparative analysis demonstrates points of convergence and divergence in the thought of Hostos, Saco, and Sarmiento. Also discusses how Bello's emphasis on grammar and eloquence was not a defense of traditionalism—as interpreted by Sarmiento and repeated by critics—but an attempt to "organically" draw together dispersed American states and incorporate them into a modernizing world order.

3440 *Revista Iberoamericana.* Vol. 54, No. 143, abril/junio 1988– . Pittsburgh: Instituto Internacional de Literatura Iberoamericana, Univ. de Pittsburgh.

Special issue devoted to the centennial of Sarmiento's death (1888) was edited by Beatriz Sarlo. Includes important contributions by R. González Echevarría, S. Molloy, E. Garrels, A.M. Barrenechea, L.A. Romero, A. Prieto, N.P. Sacks, A. Rodríguez Pérsico, W. Katra, J. Ramos, D. Sorensen Goodrich, W.J. Nowak, and M.G. Nouzeilles.

3441 Rivera-Rodas, Oscar. La poesía hispanoamericana del siglo XIX: del romanticismo al modernismo. Madrid: Alhambra, 1988. 354 p.: bibl. (Humanidades; 35. Estudios)

Important critical study which does not consider the poets in question as "isolated and privileged presences;" rather, it examines their works as leading "to the evolutionary process of modernity." Highlights Heredia, Bello, Ros de Olano, Caro, Gutiérrez González, Zaldumbide, Pombo, Gutiérrez Nájera, del Casal, Silva, Darío, and Jaimes Freyre.

3442 Rodríguez R., Angela Rocío. Las novelas de Don Tomás Carrasquilla: un aporte a la historia de la novela en Colombia. Prólogo de Antonio Restrepo A. Medellín, Colombia: Ediciones Autores Antioqueños, 1988. 342 p.: bibl., ill. (Ediciones Autores Antioqueños; 47)

Extensive treatment of major publications by Carrasquilla is heavy on hagiography and light on criticism.

3443 Sacoto, Antonio. Juan Montalvo, el escritor y el estilista. v. 1–2. Cuenca, Ecuador: Casa de la Cultura Ecuatoriana Benjamín Carrión, Núcleo del Azuay, 1987. 2 v.: bibl. (Libros para el pueblo; 39)

Republication of 1952 study that leans toward description and celebration. In addition to biography, examines Montalvo's works, style, main ideas, and themes. Detailed bibliography, with few exceptions, has not been updated.

3444 Sarmiento, centenario de su muerte: recopilación de textos publicados por miembros de la institución. Prólogo de Enrique Anderson Imbert. Buenos Aires: Academia Argentina de Letras, 1988. 450 p.: bibl. (Biblioteca de la Academia Argentina de Letras: Serie Estudios académicos; 27)

Consists of 40 essays. Authors include Arrieta, Bataillon, Borges, Canal Feijóo, Carilla, Carrizo, Castagñino, A. Castro, Gálvez, Giusti, Henríquez Ureña, Mallea, Ocampo, Pagano, Pagés Larraya, Reyes, and Verdevoye.

3445 Schulman, Iván A. José Martí frente a la modernidad hispanoamericana: vacíos y reconstrucciones de la escritura modernista. (*Rev. Iberoam.*, 55:146/147, enero/junio 1989, p. 175–192)

Applies Angel Rama's observation that in Martí's early poetry and in *Ismael* a sense of precariousness and impending destruction prevails.

3446 Serrano Camargo, Rafael. Silva: imagen y estudio analítico del poeta. Bogotá: Ediciones Tercer Mundo, 1987. 290 p.: ill., ports.

Psychological study (40 p.) of the poet introduces a sentimentalized biography interspersed with Silva's poems.

3447 Sommer, Doris. Foundational fictions: when history was romance in Latin America. (*Salmagundi*, 82/83, Spring/Summer 1989, p. 111–141)

Through a discussion of Galván's *Enriquillo* (1882), Mármol's *Amalia* (1851), and Gallego's *Doña Bárbara* (1929), Sommer demonstrates "the almost inevitable coincidence between establishing modern nations and projecting their ideal histories through the novel." In these and other novels, romance and epic are the same in that they "marry national destiny to personal sentimentalism."

3448 Sommer, Doris. El mal de *María:* (con)fusión en un romance nacional. (*MLN*, 104:2, March 1989, p. 439–474)

Any new consideration of Jorge Isaacs' classic novel must begin with the well-documented views of this article. After exploring the literary, biographical, and historical influences affecting author's world vision, Sommer concludes that the protagonist's incurable sickness, which has no apparent textual motive, serves as a displaced analogy for Issacs's discomfort with his Jewish heritage.

3449 Sommer, Doris. Sab c'est moi. (*Hispamérica*, 16:48, 1987, p. 25–37)

Both the romantic female writer (Gertrudis Gómez de Avellaneda y Arteaga) and her protagonist Sab, a slave on the verge of revolt, find in literary enterprise an imperfect means for transgressing the symbolic order at the root of their respective oppression. In contrast to "populist" novels of the period, the sentiment here anticipates the emergence of an interracial Cuban identity that would appear in the post-independence period.

3450 *Todo es Historia.* Vol. 22, No. 255, sept. 1988– . Buenos Aires: Honegger. Issue devoted to centennial of Sarmiento's death includes essay by W. Katra, "Sarmiento en los Estados Unidos," interpreting last part of *Viajes* as a utopian projection of the traveler's disenchantment with Europe. Also includes essays on Sarmiento by J. Orione, A. Zigón, L. Vitale, H.R. Mancuso, and S. Berjman.

3451 Toledo, Arnaldo. Esteban Borrero y "El Ciervo Encantado." (*Islas*, 79, sept./dic. 1984, p. 51–70)

Study of the most appraised short story (1905?) of this poet and positivist philosopher (1849–1906). Story uses allegory to express Cuba's widespread disillusionment over the failed revolutionary attempt and North American intervention.

3452 Vedoya, Juan Carlos. Fierro y la expoliación del gaucho: ensayo. Buenos Aires: Univ. Nacional del Centro de la Provincia de Buenos Aires, 1986. 152 p.: ill.

Perceives José Hernández's poem *Martín Fierro* as emblematic of the *estancia rosista* perspective in aspects such as disdain for foreigners, absence of sheep and agriculture, emphasis on the world of cattle-raising, and focus on the *latifundista* lifestyle that prospered under Rosas.

3453 Verdevoye, Paul. Domingo Faustino Sarmiento, educar y escribir opinando (1839–1852). Buenos Aires: Editorial Plus Ultra, 1988. 480 p.: bibl. (Temas argentinos; 10)

Long-awaited translation of 1963 French study (see *HLAS 28:1162*).

3454 Villanueva Collado, Alfredo. José Asunción Silva y Karl-Joris Huysmans: estudio de una lectura. (*Rev. Iberoam.*, 55: 146/147, enero/junio 1989, p. 273–286)

Studies Silva's extensive notations written in the margins of a recently recovered copy of Huysmans's *A rebours* (1884).

3455 Vitier, Cintio. Martí en Marinello; Casal en Martí: la formación literaria de José Martí, según Juan Marinello. (*Anu. Centro Estud. Martianos*, 9, 1986, p. 213–230)

Celebrates Marinello's fertile encounter with Martí throughout several important essays. Points out how, in spite of the abyss separating Casal's decadent pessimism and Martí's revolutionary vision, the latter was able to understand how Casal shared his agony over their *patria desgarrada.*

MISCELLANEOUS (ESSAYS, MEMOIRS, CORRESPONDENCE, ETC.)

3456 Barrenechea, Ana María. Carta de Sarmiento a Rugendas. (*Nueva Rev. Filol. Hisp.*, 36:1, 1988, p. 407–416, appendix)

Includes text of and commentary on Sarmiento's 1849 letter to Rugendas, painter of South American scenes and types. Letter documents Sarmiento's self-promotion as writer and future statesman.

3457 Bello, Andrés. Obras completas de Andrés Bello. v. 25–26. Epistolario. 2a ed. facsimilar. Caracas: Fundación La Casa de Bello, 1981. 2 v.

Important prologue by O. Sambrano Urdaneta traces publishing history of Bello's correspondence. Volumes include letters to and from Bello (vol. 25, 1809–29; and vol. 26, to 1865). Publisher has included helpful alphabetical and onomastic indexes, as well as bio-bibliographical information about the correspondents.

3458 Cobo Borda, Juan Gustavo. José Asunción Silva, bogotano universal. Prólogo de Fernando Charry Lara. Bogotá: Villegas Editores, 1988. 382 p.: ill., ports. (Biblioteca de Bogotá)

Handsome volume, more celebratory than critical, combines introduction (80 p.), four *testimonios* of the poet by contemporaries, and 16 sketches about the "reception" of his work.

3459 Meo Zilio, Giovanni. Metodología y técnica de una traducción literaria: los juegos de palabras en *Martín Fierro*. (*Thesaurus*, 43:2/3, mayo/dic. 1988, p. 272–295)

Describes interesting process of translating word plays in the poem into familiar and colloquial Italian.

20th Century Prose Fiction
Mexico

FERNANDO GARCIA NUÑEZ, *Professor of Spanish, University of Texas at El Paso*

LA NARRATIVA DE ESTE BIENIO en México continúa su marcha acelerada con la participación indiscriminada de escritores con aureola casi mítica, primerizos y de las filas medias, cuyo conjunto exige al estudioso un ritmo de lectura intenso y sin descanso, visible en ejercicios críticos substanciales y en efemérides periodísticas día a día más numerosas.

En la narrativa quizás lo más destacado, a nivel colectivo, sea el afianzamiento cada vez mayor de los escritores pertenecientes a la todavía no bautizada generación de los que empiezan a publicar inmediatamente después de 1968: sus obras crecen en número y definición precursores de una próxima sorpresa magistral, no exenta al rastreo crítico profesional que ya la husmea en el quehacer de José Joaquín Blanco y su inmensa capacidad para captar el sentido del ahora en sus crónicas, (items **3468, 3466,** y **3467**), María Luisa Puga y su contar reflexivo e intimista (item **3498**), Federico Patán y la facilidad imaginativa (item **3493**), Rafael Ramírez Heredia y el contar conversacional (item **3501**) y Hugo Hiriart (item **3484**), Guillermo Samperio (item **3504**) y Hernán Lara Zavala (item **3486**) en la perfección del relato semifantástico, para no mencionar sino a los anotados en este bienio. La lista completa la proporcionan en sus estudios respectivos Francisco Vicente Torres y Reinhard Teichmann (items **3548** y **3547**), quienes, entre otros, incluyen además a Jesús Gardea, Ignacio Solares y Luis Arturo Ramos. A nivel individual sobresale el inagotable Carlos Fuentes con una novela de ritmo mágico y discursivo a la vez (item **3479**), rememoradora de su mejor trabajo, para desaliento de quienes lo creían en decadencia (item **3529**). También descuella Enrique Serna con relatos reveladores de sutileza en la escritura y de una imaginación con frecuencia potenciada al cuadrado (item **3505**) y Laura Esquivel con su primera novela, tan sabrosa en su lectura como las recetas que la constituyen (item **3477**).

Una ausencia cada vez más notable es la diminución de obras en las cuales la crisis mexicana de los 80 sea el tema fundamental, tal vez porque ella se ha integrado a la naturaleza del acontecer del país como sugieren José Joaquín Blanco (items **3468** y **3466**) y María Luisa Puga (item **3498**). Tampoco abundan los textos de recreación histórica, con excepción del ya mencionado de Fuentes y otro, de Jorge Aguilar Mora (item **3461**). En el bienio el gusto se dirige hacia la búsqueda de lo poético, inclusive en situaciones caóticas como las de las novelas dantescas de Carmen Boullosa (items **3469** y **3470**) y la ensoñadora de Alejandro Hernández (item **3483**). La poesía, en estados no tan extremos, surge avasallante en la "prosa de intensidades" de Alberto Ruy Sánchez (item **3503**), en las composiciones narrativas de Adolfo Castañón y Vicente Quirarte (items **3474** y **3499**), y se hace presente en la casi totalidad de las obras del bienio en mayor o menor grado.

En el terreno de la crítica resalta la publicación del primer volumen de un ambicioso proyecto antológico de Christopher Domínguez Michael (item **3511**), que anhela conjuntar lo mejor de la narrativa del país en un contexto crítico riguroso, mediante la selección de fragmentos tomados de unos 500 libros. Mucho de ello se patentiza ya en el volumen inicial, rubricado con el entusiasmo y la intuición del antologador, quien realiza su labor a sabiendas de que hasta el presente no existe una historia crítica de la literatura mexicana (ni de la narrativa), pero tampoco— y esto no lo menciona—un número respetable de ediciones críticas que sustentara con eficacia tanto una historia como una antología de esa naturaleza. Urge satisfacer estas necesidades de infraestructura para llevar a mejor efecto esa empresa, partiendo de la evidente disponibilidad de acervo crítico, como lo prueban, por ejemplo, dos distintivos acontecimientos de este período: las exhaustivas y magníficas recopilaciones de Merlin H. Forster y Julio Ortega (item **3516**) y de Julio Ortega y Alfredo Roggiano en el número especial de la *Revista Iberoamericana* (Vol. 55, Nos. 148/149), exclusivamente dedicado a la literatura mexicana, ambas bajo el auspicio del Instituto Internacional de Literatura Iberoamericana. En este mismo contexto destaca el interesantísimo estudio de John S. Brushwood (item **3512**), quien propone la teoría, previa aplicación al caso mexicano, de que las innovaciones narrativas vislumbran las transformaciones políticas y sociales.

La efervescencia de la narrativa mexicana se manifiesta también en la continuada práctica de los talleres literarios, auspiciados por el Instituto Nacional de Bellas Artes en todo el país, y los numerosos encuentros de escritores celebrados anualmente en diversas ciudades. A ello hay que aunar la gran actividad de difusión y crítica llevada a cabo en los suplementos literarios de los diarios y las secciones de las revistas y en las editoriales. En esta área es impresionante la labor de *La Jornada Semanal* y *Sábado,* de *Unomásuno;* decepcionante la decadencia del antes creativo *La Cultura en México,* de la revista *Siempre!;* y alentadora la incursión del equipo de *Vuelta* en el ámbito editorial.

PROSE FICTION

3460 Aguilar Melantzón, Ricardo. Aurelia. Ciudad Juárez, Mexico: Univ. Autónoma de Ciudad Juárez; México: Programa Cultural de las Fronteras, Consejo Nacional para la Cultura y las Artes, 1990. 119 p. (Col. Premio José Fuentes Mares; 3)

Colección de cuentos enmarcados principalmente en una frontera, geográfica (la del norte de México o la canadiense) o interior (la discernidora de diferencias más profundas), si bien en todos ellos se escucha el cadencioso ritmo del español de las ciudades fronterizas colindantes de Ciudad Juárez (Chihuahua) y El Paso (Texas), bellamente utilizado por un Aguilar cada vez más dueño de sus relatos. De éstos sobresalen "Puente Negro," por su maestría de contención al narrar una tragedia de indocumentados mexicanos, y "Sotavento," por la atmósfera casi fantástica que acompaña a un novio indocumentado.

3461 Aguilar Mora, Jorge. Una muerte sencilla, justa, eterna: cultura y guerra durante la Revolución Mexicana. México: Ediciones Era, 1990. 439 p., bibl.

Excelente libro que conjunta a la vez el género autobiográfico, el narrativo, el poético, el ensayístico y aún el crítico para incorporar a un discurso íntimamente personalizado la significación que la Revolución Mexicana (mito, literatura, historia, leyenda, etc.) tiene en la vida de un chihuahuense emigrado al Distrito Federal, quien al regresar a la ciudad de Chihuahua para realizar investigaciones históricas profesionales, de pronto se siente en la necesidad de reencontrarse a sí mismo en la tierra de sus ancestros.

3462 Agustín, José. Furor matutino. México: Editorial Diana, 1985. 192 p.

Selección antológica que el autor hace de su propia obra a los 20 años de la publicación de su primer libro. Los nueve textos escogidos (1964–84) son, según Agustín, los más representativos en su obra plural.

3463 Aura, Alejandro. Los baños de Celeste. México: Editorial Posada, 1989. 196 p.

Colección de cuentos cortos, los más de ellos con fuerte carga sensual y humorística, en los que Aura integra con acierto sus dotes de dramaturgo, poeta y actor. Esto resalta principalmente en "Los Baños de Celeste" y "Tratado de las Novias."

3464 Bermúdez, María Elvira. Cuentos herejes. México: Editorial Oasis, 1984. 39 p.: ill. (Los Libros del fakir; 53)

Colección de cuentos fantásticos en los cuales se conjugan las preocupaciones fundamentales de la humanidad (las relaciones de hombre y mujer, la simple comunicación, la muerte y Dios) en una representación casi alegórica. Ellas pueden surgir de circunstancias tan insignificantes como el caminar en sentido contrario a los demás ("Inusitadeidad").

3465 Betancourt, Ignacio. El muy mentado curso. México: Premiá, 1984. 101 p.

Composiciones narrativas desiguales en sus logros, cuya intención explícita es contraponer irónicamente la doctrina cristiana ortodoxa y timorata, a una concepción más heterodoxa y laxa. Para ello a cada una de las narraciones acompaña la debida censura eclesiástica que la aprueba o desaprueba. Este contrapunto en ocasiones hace surgir humor con un sabio distanciamiento irónico, pero en otras carece de originalidad. Esto lo acrecienta el innecesario y repetitivo "Anexo" de más de 15 páginas, que documenta lo ridículo de ciertas actitudes católicas ante el comunismo, sobre todo.

3466 Blanco, José Joaquín. Un chavo bien helado: crónicas de los años ochenta. México: Ediciones Era, 1990. 236 p.

Libro que narra en forma de crónica los malestares de la crisis mexicana de los años 80 con una prosa ágil, irónica y necesariamente salpicada de humor negro para conservar algo positivo en medio del desastre. Esta actitud permite la delineación prototípica de todo joven lúmpen mexicano: "Un Chavo Bien Helado," cuya actitud de total desesperanza de algún modo también comparte—aunque sin plena conciencia—la clase media, anestesiada con las canciones de los baladistas de moda ("Cuentos Rosas para una Ciudad Triste") y en eterna compulsión por compartir la falsa grandeza de la élite social mexicana ("The Mighty Mexicans: Próceres del Boom Petrolero").

3467 Blanco, José Joaquín. Cuando todas las chamacas se pusieron medias nylon, y otras crónicas. México: Joan Boldó i Clement, Editores, 1988. 207 p.

Obra indispensable en la perenne discusión sobre la idiosincracia de la cultura y de la identidad mexicanas en su camino a la modernidad. Lo substancial de él, más que en las crónicas urbanas de los años 1979–83, se encuentra en tres magistrales piezas sobre la filosofía de la cultura del país, donde Blanco combina la exposición ensayística con la concreción narrativa: "Identidad Nacional y Cultura Urbana," "La Ciudad de México: Aspectos de una Modernización" y "Boarding Pass."

3468 Blanco, José Joaquín. Los mexicanos se pintan solos: crónicas, paisajes, personajes de la Ciudad de México. Fotografías de Guillermo Castrejón *et al.* México: Pórtico de la Ciudad de México, 1990. 172 p.: ill.

La Ciudad de México de finales de los años 80 es la protagonista multifacética (en sus gentes, lugares y acontecimientos) de este libro de bocetos, retratos y estampas, más que de crónicas propiamente dichas, si se le compara con otros semejantes del autor. En él la prosa sutil e irónica de Blanco plasma un rostro monstruoso, pero atractivo, de la ciudad y sus gentes, sobre todo en el rastreo del desarrollo de sus barrios ("Coyoacán Tours" y "Zona Rosa") y costumbres ("Mañanitas a la Virgen" e Iztapalapa: Cristo y Fuego Nuevo").

3469 Boullosa, Carmen. Antes. México: Vuelta, 1989. 105 p. (La Imaginación) Novela rastreadora, a nivel poético y fantástico más que psicológico, del estadio pre-cedente a la conciencia y del darse de ésta última. Dicho estadio parece excluirse a la lógica de las consecusiones ordinarias para adentrarse en una sabia sinrazón muy cercana a la experimentada por los místicos, pero sin aura sagrada alguna. La narrativa de Boullosa, lo demuestra su segunda novela, sigue cánones no encontrados antes en ningún escritor mexicano.

3470 Boullosa, Carmen. Mejor desaparece. México: Océano, 1987. 107 p.: ill.

Novela de profundidades interiores indefinidas en torno a una presencia ubicua del mal ("eso") en el ámbito familiar, quizás propiciada por aberraciones paternas. Hay en ella un cierto tipo de caótico infierno no teológico sino humano, con uno que otro velado rasgo alegórico intransitivo con respecto a una realidad trascendente.

3471 Campbell, Federico. De cuerpo entero: Federico Campbell. México: Coordinación de Difusión Cultural, Dirección de Literatura, Univ. Nacional Autónoma de México: Ediciones Corunda, 1990. 59 p.

Supuesta autobiografía donde el autor opta por hablar de sí mismo en tanto ésto se manifiesta otorgándole la palabra a su familia para recordar de este modo a papá y a mamá: primero, por medio del diálogo con una de sus hermanas; después, introduciéndose al pensamiento rememorativo de otra hermana. Quizás con ello Campbell desee asentar lo ya establecido en sus obras de ficción: su materia favorita de fabulación es él mismo y sus padres, en sus respectivos espacios y tiempos.

3472 Campbell, Federico. Tijuanenses. México: Joaquín Mortiz, 1989. 175 p. (Serie del volador)

Libro que reúne una novela corta, ya publicada antes (*Todo los de las focas*) y cuatro cuentos que continúan a aquélla tan de cerca en su tono (la rememoración del pasado familiar) y temática (Tijuana) que parecen una sola obra. Si acaso hay cierto desplazamiento en la estancia autobiográfica en Hermosillo ("Anticipo de Incorporación"), pretexto para el reencuentro materno, y en la Ciudad de México ("Insurgentes Big Sur") que remite de nueva cuenta a Tijuana, el espacio primordial de "Los Brothers" y "Tijuanenses."

3473 Carballo, Marco Aurelio *et al.* El hombre equivocado: novela colectiva. México: Joaquín Mortiz, 1988. 162 p. (Nueva narrativa hispánica)

Novela experimental policíaca de un grupo de escritores de la misma generación que se propusieron, cada uno, continuar la novela en el capítulo escrito por el anterior, de acuerdo a previo sorteo. El resultado, pronosticado por ellos en la "Advertencia," es fallido. Tal vez lo más interesante de la novela pertenezca al futuro crítico: estudiar en ella los lazos aglutinantes de la generación de Marco Antonio Carballo, Joaquín Armando Chacón, Gerardo de la Torre, Hernán Lara Zavala, Vicente Leñero, David Martín del Campo, Silvia Molina, Aline Pettersson, Rafael Ramírez Heredia, Bernardo Ruiz y Guillermo Samperio, los autores.

3474 Castañón, Adolfo. El pabellón de la límpida soledad. México: Ediciones del Equilibrista, 1988. 85 p.

Ingeniosas composiciones narrativas—ninguna de ellas es un cuento—cuyo principal valor lo constituye el vago y sutil ambiente construído con abundante recurrencia de imágenes y cuidados conceptuales. Casi todas ellas aluden a los misterios de la lectura y la escritura en sus diversas etapas, incluída la fama ("Retrato de un Maestro Desconocido"), la venta de libros ("El Vendedor") y la función de los signos ortográficos ("Los Signos de Interrogación").

3475 Curiel, Fernando. Centinela de vista. México: Editorial Oasis, 1984. 38 p.: ill. (Los Libros del fakir; 61)

Colección de cuentos cortos y microrrelatos (máximas, proverbios y definiciones) irónicos, casi siempre apocalípticos y saturados de humor negro, dentro del ambiente económico, civil y cultural de tugurio de la Ciudad de México, extensivo también en algunos casos a los Estados Unidos de Norteamérica ("El Cerdo de Memphis"). En ellos el autor revela agudeza y maestría en la economía verbal.

3476 Espinosa, Alfredo. Infierno grande. Mexico: Plaza y Valdés Editores, 1990. 194 p. (Col. Platino)

Novela situada en Albores, un olvidado pueblo del norte de México, donde se conjuntan las ilusiones y los desengaños del país con motivo de la visita del Candidato.

Tal vez lo mejor de esta primera novela de Espinosa sea la atmósfera poética que circunda a Albores y a sus personajes, creada por el uso abundante de imágenes concatenadas.

3477 Esquivel, Laura. Como agua para chocolate: novela de entregas mensuales con recetas, amores y remedios caseros. México: Editorial Planeta Mexicana, 1989. 244 p. (Col. Fabula)

Novela en la que una sobrina narra la historia de su tía abuela, una mujer del norte de México, a principios del siglo, quien de alguna manera rompe con la tradición familiar ancestral de prohibir matrimonio a la primogénita para que se dedicara al cuidado exclusivo de su madre. En la narración se integran maravillosamente al discurso, a través de eficientes imágenes culinarias, los secretos de cocina y los amorosos, en un simulado contexto decimonónico de novela por entregas cuyos humorísticos capítulos se someten a la dirección titular del platillo y la concomitante receta del encabezado. Magnífica primicia la de Esquivel.

3478 Estrada, Josefina. Malagato. México: Plaza y Valdés Editores, 1990. 174 p.: ill. (Col. Platino)

Colección de cuentos reveladora de manejo certero de la escritura encaminada a detallar los resquicios de la pasión amorosa en contraste con otras fobias y pasiones, entre otras las religiosas (sobre todo la judía, caso inaudito en México). De éstas son un buen ejemplo "Satán en Tlatelolco," "El Judío de Jesús María," e "Italia."

3479 Fuentes, Carlos. La campaña. Madrid: Mondadori España, 1990. 241 p. (Narrativa Mondadori)

Magnífica novela en la cual un narrador protagónico relata la participación de uno de sus amigos en las luchas independentistas de Argentina, Chile, Perú, y México, intentando así el joven amigo abandonar las ilusiones de la Ilustración para asumir otras más combativas, las del Romanticismo. Bajo esa perspectiva la novela traza también la evolución ideológica en Hispanoamérica, pero adentrando asimismo al lector en un ritmo narrativo cercano al decimonónico, al principio, para después llevarlo por una mágica vorágine poética que culmina en el Alto Perú. La novela, lo apunta la página anterior a la titular, es la primera de una trilogía que incluirá también *La novia muerta* y *El baile del Centenario.*

3480 Galindo, Sergio. Terciopelo violeta. México: Grijalbo, 1985. 189 p. (Col. Narrativa)

Antología personal de 12 cuentos, escritos en orden de aparición tipográfica de 1985 a 1945, de entre la vastísima producción del autor. En todos ellos, pero principalmente en los más recientes ("El Tío Quintín") y ("Juego de Soledades"), permea un narrador en absoluto control de ambiente, conducta y habla de los personajes, los cuales son cada vez más fantásticos a pesar de encontrarse asidos a la realidad.

3481 Gardea, Jesús. Antología de cuentos: Recopilación de Mario Lugo. Ciudad Juárez, Mexico: Univ. Autónoma de Ciudad Juárez, 1989. 158 p. (Col. Premio José Fuentes Mares; 2)

La antología proporciona con la selección de 15 cuentos magistrales una muestra acertada de las diversas etapas en la cuentística de Gardea: cinco cuentos de *Los viernes de Lautaro,* cuatro de *Septiembre y los otros días,* tres de *Alba sombría* y otros tres de *Luces del mundo.*

3482 González de Alba, Luis. Jacob, el suplantador. México: J. Mortiz, 1988. 189 p. (Nueva narrativa hispánica)

Desigual novela de tónica homosexual cuyo espacio es el norte de México, la capital e Ixtapa-Zihuatanejo. El desarrollo de Esaú, el protagonista, a veces se interrumpe por amplias digresiones en torno a sus adláteres y se le fuerza en su inserción al ámbito homosexual.

3483 Hernández, Alejandro. Nos imputaron la muerte del perro de enfrente. México: Editorial Diana, 1988. 287 p.

Fascinante novela donde el investigador oficial de la muerte de un cacique cuenta sus pesquisas, pero sobre todo cómo poco a poco él mismo va inmiscuyéndose en el mundo aparentemente irracional y solipsista de los sospechosos primos, enfermos de soledad y tristeza. Los numerosos capítulos configuran un ambiente poético inasible, en el cual dicha enfermedad incurable es común a todos los habitantes del pueblo y transmisible a los que a él se acercan. La novela es original a pesar de su evidente afiliación a la narrativa de Juan Rulfo.

3484 Hiriart, Hugo. Ambar. México: Cal y Arena, 1990. 117 p.

En este libro, parecido a una novela en la cual se conserva mucho de las direcciones escénicas, Hiriart invita al lector a penetrar a un mundo sutilmente fantástico, tal vez semejante al de la primera infancia, lleno de aventuras maravillosas que nos remiten a su inolvidable *Cuadernos de Gofa.* Sólo que en el presente es tan visible la mano del dramaturgo que, de hecho (se dice al final) se le ha representado como obra de teatro.

3485 Ibargüengoitia, Jorge. Autopsias rápidas. Recopilációnde Guillermo Sheridan. México: Vuelta, 1988. 290 p. (La Reflexión)

Anécdotas, reflexiones, reseñas, cartas y memorias constituyen este primer volumen de la abundante prosa periodística de Ibargüengoitia, publicada desde 1969 en el periódico capitalino *Excélsior* y luego en la revista *Vuelta* hasta su muerte. La sabia selección de Sheridan incorpora los escritos relacionados con libros y escritura en una sección; y en otras respectivas a los correspondientes a reseñas cinematográficas y eventos autobiográficos. En todos ellos persiste el tono irónico y humorista del siempre cuidadoso escritor que fue Ibargüengoitia. A través de su mira puede contemplarse el desarrollo literario, social y político del México de los 70 que preludia la crisis de los 80 en "La Vida en México en 1977."

3486 Lara Zavala, Hernán. Antología personal. Xalapa, Mexico: Univ. Veracruzana, 1990. 213 p.

Selección de los cuentarios *De Zitilchén* (México: Joaquín Mortiz, 1981), *El mismo cielo* (México: Joaquín Mortiz, 1987), de otros cuentos y de ensayos críticos, precedida de una entrevista. La muestra traza con claridad los derroteros narrativos del autor: en el primer libro, la indagación personal en la ancestral península de Yucatán ejemplificada en "A la Caza de Iguanas"; y en el segundo, en el extranjero de "Correspondencia Secreta," entre otros.

3487 Lara Zavala, Hernán. Charras. México: J. Mortiz, 1990. 249 p.

Interesante novela creada a partir de un hecho histórico real: el asesinato, por mandato gubernamental, de un líder sindical de Yucatán en 1974. Desde un principio, el profético narrador omnisciente declara la consumación de ese hecho y se propone reconstruir con minucia cronológica de minutos, horas y días los posibles acontecimientos que determinaron la muerte del líder, así como las consecuencias que de ella se derivaron después. Un acierto del narrador es limitarse a contemplar la función que Charras tenía dentro del complicado y corrupto engranaje de poder, sin caer en la tentación populista de mitificarlo.

3488 León, Fabrizio. La banda, el consejo y otros Panchos. 2a ed. México: Grijalbo, 1984. 101 p., 12 leaves of plates: ill. (Col. Narrativa)

Trabajo de campo en el cual el investigador, en forma narrativa, pretende presentar la manera de pensar y vivir de los jóvenes pertenecientes a las incalculables bandas suburbanas que rodean al Distrito Federal, en especial las de Santa Fe. En la escritura del libro se utiliza un dialecto cercano al de la banda.

3489 Mansour, Mónica. Mala memoria. Presentación de Eraclio Zepeda. México: Editorial Oasis, 1984. 65 p. (Col. El Nido del Roc; 5)

Colección de cuentos derivados, de alguna manera, de rememoraciones y consecuencias de la masacre de Tlatelolco en 1968. Su mérito mayor está en el continuo estado de inseguridad y zozobra en que se envuelven todas las acciones. Esto cobra todavía mayor fuerza en los magníficos cuentos "Como si Nada" y "Acuartelado."

3490 Martínez, Herminio. La jaula del tordo. México: Editorial Oasis, 1985. 132 p. (Col. Letras del milenio; 19)

Cuentario acerca de las costumbres, leyendas, creencias y sabidurías campesinas del estado de Guanajuato, en las cuales campean por igual lo santo y lo profano. Entre todos los cuentos, destaca "Jesús María Coyote" por construirse tomando como base una letanía interminable de las numerosas yerbas curativas de la región.

3491 Mastretta, Angeles. Mujeres de ojos grandes. México: Cal y Arena, 1990. 180 p.

Conjunto de narraciones cortas (estampas, bocetos, cuentos) acerca de mujeres poblanas desde finales del siglo pasado hasta mediados del presente, según son recordadas por la historia oral recogida por una supuesta sobrina, la narradora, situada en la época contemporánea al lector. La mayoría de ellas asumen o fingen asumir el papel atribuído a la tradicional mujer mexicana, aunque su vida oculta rebase con mucho tal prototipo. La voz narrativa se desenvuelve, entre ellas, con ironía y humor.

3492 Pacheco, Cristina. Los dueños de la noche. México: Planeta, 1990. 360 p.: ill. (Espejo de México; 3)

Una treintena de entrevistas, editadas a la manera de relatos con trama y desenlace, constituyen este libro panorámico de los protagonistas de la cultura popular mexicana desde los años 40 hasta el presente (empresarios de espectáculos, deportistas afamados, rumberas, cantantes, compositores, etc.). En el libro se selecciona sólo parte de la actividad periodística de la autora durante 11 años, en el semanario capitalino *Siempre!*

3493 Patán, Federico. Puertas antiguas. México: Alianza Editorial Mexicana, 1989. 127 p. (Alianza literatura)

Novela cuyo narrador en primera persona elabora un universo profundo a través de inteligentes y lúdicas disquisiciones acerca de las cosas más rutinarias de la vida, pero desarrolladas en la interioridad de un yo imaginativo capaz de relacionar con soltura y naturalidad lo aparentemente disímil. En este sistema de escritura hacia adentro, poco o nada interesa la acción: el encuentro en la playa del narrador con su vecina del piso de arriba.

3494 Pettersson, Aline. Aline Pettersson: de cuerpo entero. Mexico: Univ. Nacional Autónoma de México; Ediciones Corunda, 1990. 64 p.

Interesante autobiografía ("cuento," dice la autora) en la que la novelista confiesa la dificultad para escribirla, a pesar de su profesión de letras. Recuerda niñez, adolescencia y edad adulta en tanto se manifiestan específicamente en sus diversas obras. Confiesa su afinidad personal y escritural a Josefina Vicens y proporciona su versión— a semejanza de José Agustín en *Ciudades desiertas*—de su estancia en el taller de escritores de Iowa.

3495 Poniatowska, Elena. Nada, nadie: las voces del temblor. México: Ediciones

Era, 1988. 311 p., 24 p. of plates: ill. (Biblioteca Era; 173/1)

Novela en la que Poniatowska, ayudada por 18 autores más (nombrados en la pág. 9), intenta recrear con rigor cronométrico el devastador temblor (19 sept. 1985) en la Ciudad de México y sus secuelas físicas, morales, sociales y políticas en la capital y el país entero; pero se pretende de alguna manera hacer que el lector escuche ahora la multiplicidad de voces que en esos trágicos momentos expresaron perspectivas diversas, a veces encontradas. Por ello el proyecto tiene algo de épico y anónimo.

3496 Prieto, Francisco. La inclinación. México: Plaza y Janés, 1986. 194 p.

Novela donde un narrador protagónico analiza con minucia y profundidad la problemática interior que orilló a su antiguo amigo de seminario a una conducta sexual demente y asesina, no alejada del todo de la potencial también en el narrador, quien vacila en su vocación sacerdotal.

3497 Prieto, Francisco. Si llegamos a diciembre. México: Premià, 1985. 90 p.: ill. (La Red de Jonás: Literatura mexicana; 28)

Novela saturada de acción, a veces ingenuamente manipulada, con el objeto de posibilitar un cambio psicológico en el protagonista, afectado por una indolencia profunda, según se reitera. Pero ésta es gratuita, pues nunca se elabora en el transcurso narrativo.

3498 Puga, María Luisa. La forma del silencio. México: Siglo Veintiuno Editores, 1987. 256 p. (La Creación literaria)

Novela cuya finalidad es precisamente mostrar la escritura de una novela, desde que se le concibe con espacios específicos (Acapulco, el Distrito Federal, el país), personajes determinados (papá, mamá, yo, los amigos y la crisis) y un tiempo delimitado (desde los años 50 del alemanismo hasta los críticos 80 del lópezportillismo); aunque en verdad el proyecto implica principalmente el ir trazando el desarrollo (desde la infancia hasta la edad adulta) del propio yo en palabras ya antes latentes, mas no del todo trazadas. El proceso narrativo se da con tan amigable intimidad y soltura que el lector no se siente un intruso en él.

3499 Quirarte, Vicente. Plenilunio de la muñeca. México: Editorial Oasis, 1984. 39 p.: ill. (Los Libros del fakir; 39)

Pequeña colección de cuentos poseedores, todos ellos, de una bella atmósfera poética circunscribidora tanto de su espacio como de sus personajes. Esto se nota más cabalmente en "Octubre de 1961," con la inolvidable figura de Lorca, el añorado primer amor; y en "Retrato de una Dama," la historia de una relación lesbiana en un trasfondo saturado del ambiente sublime del arte italiano. Quirarte se revela aquí con la misma excelencia que lo ha hecho en su poesía.

3500 Ramírez Heredia, Rafael. Rafael Ramírez Heredia: de cuerpo entero. México: Coordinación de Difusión Cultural, Dirección de Literatura, Univ. Nacional Autónoma de México, 1990. 64 p.

Lúdica autobiografía donde por todas partes transluce la soltura y el humor de los ya numerosos cuentarios y novelas del autor, quien se presenta a sí mismo en los diversos eventos de su vida, enraizados en la tierra mexicana a través de su gusto por las plantas de todas las regiones y sus variados nombres. Dicha variedad se replica en la pluralidad geográfica de sus familiares, amigos y preferencias musicales.

3501 Ramírez Heredia, Rafael. Los territorios de la tarde. México: J. Mortiz, 1988. 138 p. (Serie del volador)

Colección de cuentos aglutinados por el común tema del amor clandestino o legítimo y por la facilidad del autor para contar con sabrosura y humor, emparentados con el gusto popular de las canciones vernáculas ("Llegó Borracho el Borracho" y "Sombras Nada Más") o importadas ("Cuando Calienta el Sol") y con los rumores acerca de la vida íntima de los hombres en el poder. Esto acontece magistralmente en "Los Territorios de la Tarde," semblanza de los amoríos del ex-Presidente José López Portillo y una integrante de su gabinete, según puede deducir con claridad todo conocedor de ese período en la vida política mexicana.

3502 Roffiel, Rosamaría. Amora. México: Editorial Planeta Mexicana, 1989. 162 p.

Novela donde se relatan las peripecias por las que tienen que pasar las mujeres lesbianas en México para mantener sus relaciones en un ambiente machista, conservador y hostil. La utilización de ágiles diálogos es el recurso más socorrido y eficaz en ella (veáse la magnífica sección "No Cabe Duda:

el Gay-Set es el Gay-Set," por ejemplo); pero en ocasiones pierde naturalidad por la excesiva indoctrinación proselitista que lo acompaña.

3503 Ruy Sánchez, Alberto. La inaccesible. Tacámbaro, Mexico: Taller Martín Pescador, 1990. 12 p.

Mogador, la oriental ciudad de la narrativa de Ruy Sánchez, es descrita en esta hermosa composición de prosa poética ("prosa de intensidades," le llama el autor) con misteriosos y tentadores rasgos femeninos que la hacen simultáneamente deseable e inaccesible, a pesar del íntimo acercamiento amoroso de la voz narrativa.

3504 Samperio, Guillermo. Antología personal, 1971–1990: ellos habitaban un cuento. Xalapa, Mexico: Univ. Veracruzana, 1990. 234 p. (Ficción)

Selección de la variada narrativa de Samperio (cuentos, estampas, retratos, prosa poética, crónicas, etc.) publicada en 13 libros durante los últimos 20 años. El conjunto, aunado al "Diálogo con Guillermo Samperio," de Leo Eduardo Mendoza, ejemplifica su permanente inquisición en las formas de narrar que van de lo íntimamente filosófico a lo político y a lo social, pero conservando en todas las instancias hermoso dominio lúdico de cada una de sus palabras.

3505 Serna, Enrique. Amores de segunda mano. Xalapa, Mexico: Univ. Veracruzana, 1991. 163 p. (Ficción)

Colección de cuentos surgidos de la confrontación irónica, humorística e intensivamente seriada de acciones y actitudes enmarcadas en un acontecer real de amor, caridad y comunicación, con otras reflejas o "de segunda mano." En éstas últimas, aquéllas se manifiestan como distorsionadas, absurdas y carentes de sentido. La prosa acelerada y sagaz del joven autor logra crear cuentos dignos de antologarse, tales como "Hombre con Minotauro en el Pecho" y "Borges y el Ultraísmo."

3506 Su, Margo. Alta frivolidad. México: Cal y Arena, 1989. 200 p.

Recuento autobiográfico en cuyo curso el irónico yo narrativo se desenvuelve en sincronía a los fenómenos de cultura popular más importantes de la Ciudad de México de los últimos 40 años (el Waikikí, Tongolele, Los Panchos, María Victoria, Dámaso Pérez Prado, el Teatro Blanquita, etc.), los cuales a

su vez parecen ir conformando el rostro nocturno de la capital y el escondido del gobernante en turno. De esta forma el libro parece más un sabroso relato del acontecer mexicano de esa época que una autobiografía.

3507 Traven, B. Traven para jóvenes. Selección y prólogo de Ricardo Aguilar Melantzón y Rosa María Quevedo. Mexico: Consejo Nacional para la Cultura y las Artes, Instituto Nacional de Bellas Artes, 1990. 204 p. (Col. para jóvenes)

Bruno Traven, independientemente de su nacionalidad norteamericana, sueca o noruega, pertenece a la narrativa mexicana en concordancia a lo afirmado en el instructivo prólogo de esta amena antología. En ella se incluyen los populares cuentos "La Canasta," "San Antonio le Falló," "No hay Burro que se Regale" y "Macario;" así como fragmentos de las novelas *El tesoro de la Sierra Madre* y *El General*.

3508 Vallarino, Roberto. Las aventuras de Euforión. México: Edivisión Compañía Editorial; Editorial Diana, 1988. 144 p. (Novela)

Novela testimoniadora de la ilusión de cambio implícita en el alejamiento de la tierra patria (México) hacia San Sebastián (España) un poco antes del terremoto de 1985. Lo distinto del paisaje y de la gente en un principio deslumbra a Euforión, quien cree encontrar un paraíso en Europa, principalmente en el hermoso capítulo XIII ("La Tarde de Brujas"). La desilusión comienza al comprobar la problemática de la lucha separatista vasca, aunada a la represión policíaca tan semejante a la experimentada en México.

3509 Villoro, Juan. Albercas. México: J. Mortiz, 1985. 129 p. (Serie del volador)

Colección de cuentos caracterizados por iniciarse todos ellos dentro de un espacio real que insensible mas progresivamente se diluye en otro fantástico, como si a ambos los separara sólo un tenue velo cuyo descorrer realiza el narrador. No importa si esto acontece en la añoranza de la novia deseada durante la secundaria ("Espejo Retrovisor") o en los otoñales años de un hombre en su encuentro con una adolescente ("El Cielo Inferior").

3510 Zapata, Luis. Ese amor que hasta ayer nos quemaba. México: Editorial Posada, 1989. 213 p. (Letras de México)

Colección de ocho cuentos y una novela corta, de la cual se toma el título del
libro, de tema fundamentalmente homosexual. Aunque se publica hasta ahora, el
material pertenece a la obra primeriza de Zapata (1973–82); esta condición se revela en el
desarrollo narrativo, nunca tan logrado como
en obras posteriores del autor.

LITERARY CRITICISM
AND HISTORY

**3511 Antología de la narrativa mexicana del
siglo XX. v. 1.** Selección, introducciones y notas de Christopher Domínguez
Michael. México: Fondo de Cultura Económica, 1989. 1 v.: bibl., index. (Letras
mexicanas)

Gigantesco proyecto, a publicarse en
dos volúmenes, de presentar en forma selec-
tiva lo mejor de la exuberante narrativa mexicana del presente siglo en cinco libros a los
cuales precede una sólida e intuitiva introducción crítica, seguida de una somera ficha
biobibliográfica para cada uno de los autores,
pero sin establecer el contexto del fragmento
textual que se proporciona. Se asume un concepto narrativo que incluye, además del
cuento y la novela, la prosa poética, el afo-
rismo, la crónica y la prosa llana. La selección de este volumen comienza cronológicamente en 1912 con fragmentos de La ca-
mada, de Salvador Quevedo y Zubieta y La
llaga, de Federico Gamboa; y termina en
1969 con "Lolo Campa, el Venadito," de Ricardo Garibay y Complot mongol, de Rafael
Bernal. El criterio de selección, al menos en
el vol. 1, no parece muy definido en "Las Palabras Liminares," tal vez por la carencia—se
dice ahí—de una "historia crítica de la literatura mexicana;" los fundamentos de la cual
pretende trazar Domínguez Michael en el aparato crítico que acompaña a su obra. Sin desmerecer la evidente valía de este intento, es
obvio que en él no se incluyen una gran can-
tidad de materiales críticos que debieran haberse incorporado a una empresa de tal magnitud; la cual quizás podría llevarse más
cuidadosamente a cabo si se contara con un
equipo de investigadores que por varios años
y con los recursos bibliográficos a la mano la
elaborara. Hay algo de ingenuidad cuando el
recopilador antólogo sugiere que algunos aspectos de tal procedimiento son anacrónicos,

cuando dice: "Esta antología hubiera reque-
rido para su elaboración, apenas hace quince
años, una larga temporada en un cubículo de
Kansas o Austin." Pero es preciso reiterarlo, a
pesar de las deficiencias ordinarias en una
obra individual de tamaña envergadura, esta
antología implica un valioso comienzo para
realizar una valoración crítica global de esta
rica narrativa.

3512 Brushwood, John Stubbs. Narrative
innovation and political change in
Mexico. New York: P. Lang, 1989. 129 p.
(University of Texas studies in contemporary
Spanish-American fiction; 4)

Sólido estudio que propone una perspectiva revolucionaria en la aproximación
al análisis de la narrativa en general y de la
mexicana en particular. La nueva tesis considera que las innovaciones o cambios que ex-
perimenta la narrativa en un determinado
período pueden ser algunos de los indicadores
de reformas por venir en la vida pública; no
en el sentido de que aquéllas causen u oca-
sionen éstas, sino para significar que hay en
el ejercicio de la narrativa y de las demás
artes un cierto tipo de presciencia que detecta la transformación política y social del
futuro inmediato. La tesis de Brushwood no
intenta reivindicar el profetismo romántico
atribuido a poetas y artistas, sino hacer ver
tal presciencia en el caso concreto de México, a través de un complejo y riguroso análisis de las analogías del quehacer narrativo
y político en ese país. Brushwood concluye
que el relato revolucionario directo y verista,
de lectura más accesible que y el vanguardista, precede al populismo socialista de Cárdenas el inconformismo de la Generación de
la Onda, al activismo político de 1968.

3513 Campos, Marco Antonio. De viva voz:
entrevistas con escritores. Tlahuapan,
Mexico: Premià, 1986. 158 p.: bibl. (La Red
de Jonás. Estudios; 32)

Consiste de 20 entrevistas a poetas,
narradores y críticos hispanoamericanos,
sobre todo de México. Seis de ellas son de
narradores mexicanos (Rubén Salazar Mallén,
Josefina Vicens, Edmundo Valadés, Juan José
Arreola, Augusto Monterroso y Salvador Elizondo) y dos de críticos también de México
(José Luis Martínez y Emmanuel Carballo).
El entrevistador muestra conocimiento serio
de la obra del autor en turno, cuando en verdad se da la entrevista con su participación

en las preguntas; en otras ocasiones sólo se proporciona lo que parece ser la contestación por escrito a un cuestionario por él proporcionado al escritor.

3514 Carballo, Emmanuel *et al.* Revueltas en la mira. México: Univ. Autónoma Metropolitana, Dirección de Difusión Cultural, Depto. Editorial, 1984. 164 p.: bibl. (Molinos de viento; 18 [i.e. 23]: Serie Ensayo)

Selección de 10 estudios sobre la obra de Revueltas, tomada de la semana de ponencias en su honor llevadas a cabo a partir de abril 14, 1983 en la Univ. Autónoma Metropolitana. Destacan por sus aportaciones los artículos de Ignacio Trejo Fuentes ("Las Novelas de José Revueltas"), Adolfo Sánchez Vázquez ("La Estética Terrenal de Revueltas") y Miguel Espejo ("La Estética en José Revueltas").

3515 Coloquio Fronterizo, *1st, Tijuana, Mexico, 1987.* Mujer y literatura mexicana y chicana: culturas en contacto. Edición de Aralia López González, Amelia Malagamba Ansótegui y Elena Urrutia. México: Colegio de México, Programa Interdisciplinario de Estudios de la Mujer; Tijuana, México: Colegio de la Frontera Norte, 1988. 264 p.: bibl.

Una docena de ensayos exclusivamente sobre la mujer en la narrativa mexicana, sin uno sólo sobre la poesía. Dos generales sirven de introducción: "Caminos del Ser y de la Historia: la Narrativa Femenina en México," de Yvette Jiménez de Báez, y "La Sexualidad en la Narrativa Femenina Mexicana, 1970–1987: una Aproximación," de Peggy Job. Los estudios particulares abordan obras de Nellie Campobello, Elena Garro, Inés Arredondo, Amparo Dávila, Margo Glantz, Elena Poniatowska y María Luisa Puga.

3516 De la crónica a la nueva narrativa mexicana: coloquio sobre literatura mexicana. Edición de Merlin H. Forster y Julio Ortega. México: Editorial Oasis, 1986. 480 p.

Volumen dedicado a la literatura mexicana en general, producto de algunas de las presentaciones hechas durante el Vigésimo Congreso del Instituto Internacional de Literatura Iberoamericana ("Literatura Mexicana y Literatura Iberoamericana: Balance y Relación"), llevado a cabo en la Univ. de Texas

(Austin, 24–28 marzo, 1981). En el libro se incluyen más de 20 estudios sobre narrativa mexicana, principalmente de Juan Rulfo y de Carlos Fuentes, aunque también los hay sobre Alfonso Reyes, Martín Luis Guzmán, Rosario Castellanos, Elena Garro, Salvador Elizondo, José Emilio Pacheco, José Agustín y Gustavo Sainz, entre otros.

3517 A different reality: studies on the work of Elena Garro. Edited by Anita K. Stoll. Lewisburg: Bucknell Univ. Press; London: Associated Univ. Presses, 1990. 204 p.: bibl., index.

Esta es la obra crítica más completa sobre el teatro y la narrativa de Elena Garro hasta hoy. Además de los estudios sobre teatro, la constituyen una entrevista (indispensable para captar los frecuentes elementos autobiográficos en su obra), una recopilación biográfica y artículos acerca de *La casa junto al río, Testimonios sobre Mariana* y varios de sus cuentos.

3518 Domínguez Michael, Christopher. Martín Luis Guzmán: el teatro de la política. (*Vuelta*, 11:131, oct. 1987, p. 22–31, bibl., photos)

Incisivo ensayo donde se plantea la tesis de que el personaje omnipresente en las novelas de Guzmán es la política, presentada siempre en acción teatral: en *El águila y la serpiente* el problema a escenificar es el de la libertad y la acción moral o el de una dramática moral en la cual triunfa el actor político; en *La sombra del caudillo* los actores son los generales en pugna, quienes se disputan el poder; y en *Las memorias de Pancho Villa*, la voz del general se pierde sofocada por la de Guzmán, quien a través de la voz de Villa plantea sus opiniones sobre el pueblo.

3519 Domínguez Michael, Christopher. Notas sobre mitos nacionales y novela mexicana, 1955–1985. (*Rev. Iberoam.*, 55: 148/149, julio/dic. 1989, p. 915–924)

Ensayo taxonómico por su intención de trazar una clasificación de la novela mexicana (1955–85) tomando como ejes *Pedro Páramo, La región más transparente* y *El luto humano.* La novela de Juan Rulfo implicaría la muerte de la tragedia con el desmoronamiento del héroe trágico, el mito del poder; la de Fuentes, la novela de la burguesía que exalta el mito de la Nación; mientras que la de José Revueltas construye en el subsuelo de dichos mitos la utopía. Para el ensayista la época más sana fue el intermedio, acéfalo de mitos, de Salvador Elizondo, Fernando del Paso, José Emilio Pacheco y José Agustín, entre otros. Pero eso duró poco: los acontecimientos de 1968 obligaron a todos a volver al mito de la Nación y al submito de la Ciudad de México.

3520 Dorward, Frances R. The evolution of Mexican indigenista literature in the twentieth century. (*Rev. Interam. Bibliogr.*, 37:2, 1987, p. 145–159, bibl.)

Inteligente ensayo comprehensivo sobre la narrativa indigenista en México, en el cual se estudian los principales textos críticos de la materia (César Rodríguez Chiharro, Warren Lee Meinhardt, Joseph Sommers, Antonio A. Leal, Donald Lee Schmidt, Marta Portal y Judith L.W. Thompson), para concluir que en ellos se ha puesto más énfasis en el análisis temático que en el técnico y que se ha descuidado el estudio del cuento.

3521 Escalante, Evodio. Lectura ideológica de *Pedro Páramo*. (*in* De la crónica a la nueva narrativa mexicana. [see item **3516**] p. 295–303)

El ensayo rastrea el marco de *Pedro Páramo* en la tradición de la novela social mexicana, sobre todo en relación a *El resplandor*, de Mauricio Magdaleno, y *El luto humano*, de José Revueltas. La visión del mundo en todas estas novelas se focaliza en su concepción de la Revolución Mexicana: ésta, para Magdaleno, fue de un fracaso, aunque estableció la escuela rural, posible principio de una mejor vida; Revueltas comparte ese pesimismo, pero cree que en el fondo de la Revolución hay fuerzas que prometen un orden mejor de vida; mientras que para Rulfo la Revolución fue como si no hubiera sido, ante la decadencia total de Comala y el país.

3522 Foster, David William. Escrutando el texto de la revolución: *El águila y la serpiente* de Martín Luis Guzmán. (*Caravelle*, 53, 1989, p. 65–80)

Ensayo donde se estudia la novela de Guzmán en cuanto texto cultural a través del cual el autor transmite en forma retórica los hechos históricos de la Revolución.

3523 Gnutzmann, Rita. *Al filo del agua* de Agustín Yáñez y su modelo norte-

americano "Manhattan Transfer." (*Ibero-Am. Arch.*, 14:1, 1988, p. 1–20, bibl.)

Detallado estudio comparativo entre ambas novelas, fundamentado en la afirmación expresa de Yáñez de aplicar a su novela las técnicas de John Dos Passos. La autora muestra las coincidencias y las discrepancias entre ambas obras, así como la posibilidad de que las coincidencias pudieran provenir no directamente de la novela del norteamericano, sino de una tradición común también a Yáñez.

3524 Jara, René. Farabeuf: estrategias de la inscripción narrativa. Xalapa, México: Centro de Investigaciones Lingüístico-Literarias, Instituto de Investigaciones Humanísticas, Univ. Veracruzana, 1982. 93 p.: bibl., ill. (Cuadernos del centro; 15)

Interesantísimo estudio sobre la inagotable novela de Salvador Elizondo, vista bajo la perspectiva semiótica. Jara establece con claridad que la inasibilidad semántica de la novela proviene de su constante aurorreflexividad (verse a sí misma en tanto es escrita o leída) y de la esencia ambigua del hecho literario. De esta forma es posible narrar un instante que incluye en sí mismo vida, muerte, placer, dolor, comienzo y final interminables.

3525 Jiménez de Báez, Yvette. Escisión y unidad: *Pedro Páramo*, Susana San Juan y Lord Dunsany. (*Caravelle*, 53, 1989, p. 81–92)

La autora muestra la admiración de Rulfo por el escritor irlandés Lord Dunsany, cuyos libros, *Cuentos de un soñador* (1924) y *La montaña eterna* (1945), habrían tenido cierta influencia en la escritura de la novela del mexicano.

3526 Katra, William H. "No Oyes Ladrar los Perros": la excepcionalidad y el fracaso. (*Rev. Iberoam.*, 56:150, marzo 1990, p. 179–191)

Ensayo donde se propone una lectura filosófica del cuento: la cristiana y la existencialista, ambas justificadas en el desarrollo y la conclusión del relato. En la cristiana el padre simboliza a Cristo en lucha por salvar a Ignacio, su hijo; aunque las recriminaciones que le hace también lo asocian con el Dios veterotestamentario. En la existencialista, en versión sartreana, el padre, salve o no a su hijo (ser en-sí), con su actitud (ser para-sí) adquiere la condición de héroe.

3527 Klahn, Norma. Un nuevo verismo: apuntes sobre la última novela mexicana. (*Rev. Iberoam.*, 55:148/149, julio/dic. 1989, p. 925–935)

Ensayo sobre la novela escrita después del 68 y sus diferencias con la inmediatamente anterior. Mientras ésta última recurriría a un tiempo mítico cíclico en su búsqueda de identidad y orígenes, la primera utilizaría un tiempo lineal insertado en la realidad concreta de la vida cotidiana. Por ello estos novelistas simpatizan más con Carlos Monsiváis que con Octavio Paz y sus personajes, lejos de alcanzar el simbolismo de un Juan Preciado o un Artemio Cruz, surgen del espacio ubicable de la ciudad (burócratas, adolescentes, etc.) o el campo (mineros, campesinos, etc.). Sus numerosos miembros van desde José Agustín a Jesús Gardea y José Joaquín Blanco.

3528 Koch, Dolores M. El micro-relato en México: Torri, Arreola, Monterroso. (*in* De la crónica a la nueva narrativa mexicana. [see item **3516**] p. 161–177)

El ensayo muestra en forma detallada y clara, a través de la obra de Julio Torri, Juan José Arreola y Augusto Monterroso, las características temáticas y estilísticas del relato breve. Estas lo inscribirían dentro de un marco propio e independiente del género del cuento.

3529 Krauze, Enrique. La comedia mexicana de Carlos Fuentes. (*Vuelta*, 12:139, junio 1988, p. 15–27, photos)

Apasionado y personal ensayo donde Krauze cuestiona la honestidad intelectual de Fuentes en su interpretación ensayística de la realidad mexicana; además lo acusa de distorsionar la historia de México en sus obras de ficción y de no ser un verdadero mexicano. El escrito, de repercusiones periodísticas internacionales, rastrea el fundamento de sus imputaciones en casi cada una de las obras del novelista.

3530 Leal, Luis. Mariano Azuela: precursor de los nuevos novelistas. (*Rev. Iberoam.*, 55:148/149, julio/dic. 1989, p. 859–867)

Las novelas de Azuela, según Leal, se clasifican en naturalistas, de la Revolución, vanguardistas y políticas. De ellas las que más adelantan el camino de la nueva novela hispanoamericana, además de *Los de abajo*,

son las correspondientes a la etapa vanguardista (1923–32) y de entre ellas sobresale *La Malahora* (1923), en la cual ya se utilizan tiempos superpuestos, flashbacks, interrupción de escenas, desarrollo no cronológico, etc.

3531 Lorente-Murphy, Silvia. Juan Rulfo: realidad y mito de la Revolución Mexicana. Madrid: Pliegos, 1988. 134 p.: bibl. (Pliegos de ensayo; 33)

Estudio temático de la obra rulfiana la cual, según la autora, implicaría la devastación del mito de la Revolución Mexicana y un estilo sencillo oriundo del intento de Rulfo por ver el mundo con ojos populares y no intelectuales.

3532 Menton, Seymour. Las cuentistas mexicanas en la época feminista, 1970–1988. (*Hispania/Teachers*, 73:2, May 1990, p. 366–370, bibl.)

Recuento panorámico y crítico de la obra de las cuentistas mexicanas de esas dos décadas (Inés Arredondo, María Luisa Mendoza, Beatriz Espejo, Esther Seligson, Ethel Krauze), contrapuesto a la de las predecesoras (Elena Garro y Rosario Castellanos), para concluir que ha aumentado su número y publicaciones, pero sin haber logrado ninguna de ellas el superestrellato de algunos de los cuentistas hombres.

3533 Miller, Beth. Historia y ficción en *Oficio de tinieblas* de Castellanos: un enfoque gramsciano. (*in* De la crónica a la nueva narrativa mexicana. [see item **3516**] p. 407–421)

En el ensayo se utiliza el concepto marxista de Antonio Gramsci para hacer ver que en su novela Castellanos analiza la hegemonía y sus mitos concomitantes en la rebelión de los chamulas, así como su respectiva contrahegemonía y contramitología.

3534 Molloy, Sylvia. Desentendimiento y socarronería en *Anacleto Morones* de Juan Rulfo. (*in* De la crónica a la nueva narrativa mexicana. [see item **3516**] p. 319–328)

Incisivo estudio de los diversos tipos de voces encontrados en los escritos de Rulfo con énfasis en la voz chata o llana, la cual tiene un propósito también: esconder con palabras lo que no se quiere decir. Este juego, reiterado al máximo en el más "locuaz" de los cuentos de Rulfo (*Anacleto Morones*,) lleva a la socarronería de Morones y al desentendimiento de los propósitos de las mujeres que lo visitan.

3535 Moreno, Fernando. Carlos Fuentes: *La mort d'Artemio Cruz*, entre le mythe et l'histoire. Paris: Editions caribéennes, 1989. 152 p.: bibl., ill. (Col. Tropismes: Série 1, Une œuvre, un auteur)

Interesante estudio analítico de las oposiciones temáticas, estructurales, simbólicas y míticas en la novela de Fuentes, ocasionadas por el contexto histórico plural de la Revolución Mexicana, el verdadero protagonista, del cual Artemio Cruz es sólo un símbolo.

3536 Ortega, Julio. Carlos Fuentes: para recuperar la tradición De La Mancha; entrevista. (*Rev. Iberoam.*, 55 : 148/149, julio/dic. 1989, p. 637–654)

Informativa conversación donde Fuentes y Ortega dialogan sobre la importancia del lenguaje en *Cristóbal nonato*, novela en la cual surge de nueva cuenta uno de los personajes principales de Fuentes: la Ciudad de México. El también habla de su "estética de la novela," propuesta en la trilogía de *Aura, Cumpleaños* y *Una familia lejana*, entre muchas otras cosas.

3537 Paquete: cuento; la ficción en México. Edición, prólogo y notas de Alfredo Pavón. México: Univ. Autónoma de Tlaxcala, 1990. 213 p.

Recolección de 12 ponencias presentadas en el Primer Encuentro de Investigadores del Cuento Mexicano, (Tlaxcala, México, mayo 31-junio 1–2, 1989). Destacan los estudios de Emmanuel Carballo ("Del Romanticismo al Naturalismo"), Luis Leal ("La Revolución Mexicana y el Cuento"), Jaime Erasto Cortés ("Antologías de Cuento Mexicano") y Federico Patán ("La Narrativa de Edmundo Valadés").

3538 Patán, Federico. Contrapuntos. México: Univ. Nacional Autónoma de México, 1989. 127 p.

Patán es, los demuestran estos ensayos de narrativa mexicana contemporánea, riguroso analista de textos, además de sólido narrador. Dos de los estudios proporcionan una panorámica general ("La Capital en la Narrativa Mexicana Reciente" y "La Joven Narrativa"); los otros analizan por separado una o más obras individuales de Josefina Vicens (*Los años falsos* y *El libro vacío*), Sergio Ga-

lindo (*Nudo* y *Otilia Rauda*), Arturo Azuela (*Manifestación de silencios*), Sergio Pitol (*El desfile del amor*), Carlos Fuentes (*Gringo Viejo*) y Vicente Leñero (*Asesinato*).

3539 Paz, Octavio. Generaciones y semblanzas: escritores y letras de México. Edición de Octavio Paz y Luis Mario Schneider. México: Fondo de Cultura Económica, 1987. 693 p.: index. (México en la obra de Octavio Paz; 2. Letras mexicanas)

La sección titulada "Protagonistas y Agonistas: Narradores" (de aproximadamente 60 p.) se dedica a reproducir con variaciones leves, excepto en el caso de Josefina Vicens, ensayos ya publicados antes sobre narradores mexicanos: Vasconcelos, Agustín Yáñez, José Revueltas, Juan Rulfo, Jorge Ibarbüengoitia, Carlos Fuentes, Juan García Ponce y Salvador Elizondo. En todos, aunque principalmente en los dedicados a Revueltas y Fuentes, brilla la intuición crítica de Paz, quien con su palabra crítica parece definirlos en los fundamentos más importantes de su obra total.

3540 *Revista Iberoamericana*. Vol. 55., No. 148–149, julio/dic. 1989– . Número Especial Dedicado a Alfonso Reyes y a la Literatura Mexicana del Siglo XX. Edición de Julio Ortega y Alfredo Roggiano. Pittsburgh: Organo del Instituto Internacional de Literatura Iberoamericana, Univ. de Pittsburgh.

Copiosa y útil recopilación de estudios y entrevistas sobre la literatura mexicana de este siglo. En extensa selección sobre la narrativa (más de 200 p.) se encuentran estudios panorámicos sobre cuento, novela, poesía y narración, novela de la Revolución y nuevas promociones; además hay entrevistas y ensayos individuales sobre la obra de Alfonso Reyes, José Revueltas, Juan Rulfo, Elena Garro, Juan José Arreola, Arturo Azuela, Jorge Ibargüengoitia y Carlos Fuentes.

3541 Rubio de Lértora, Patricia. Funciones del nivel descriptivo en *Los recuerdos del porvenir*. (*Caravelle*, 49, 1987, p. 129–138)

Análisis de los índices del nivel de enunciación en la novela de Elena Garro para identificar el nivel descriptivo en cuanto uno de los elementos más decisivos en la ordenación del texto.

3542 Schärer, Maya. Del decir de los otros al otro decir en la obra de Juan Rulfo. (*in*

De la crónica a la nueva narrativa mexicana. [see item **3516**] p. 285–293)

En el artículo se analizan las "lagunas" o situaciones en las cuales no es posible comprobar si lo que se dice, casi siempre condenatorio, corresponde o no a la verdad en los cuentos de Rulfo. Luego se hace ver que lo mismo sucede en la laguna fundamental de *Pedro Páramo:* Juan Preciado va a Comala en busca de su padre impulsado por decires ajenos que poco a poco lo van envolviendo en "rumores" y "murmullos" incontables, los cuales hacen imposible el discernir la verdad.

3543 Siemens, William L. Encuentro con la Maga en *Terra Nostra.* (*in* De la crónica a la nueva narrativa mexicana. [see item **3516**] p. 343–352)

Rastreo de semejanzas entre la novela de Fuentes y la de Cortázar, sobre todo entre Polo-Celestina y Oliveira-La Maga; aunque también se extienden las analogías hacia *Cien años de soledad,* de Gabriel García Márquez.

3544 Soto, José. Tres aproximaciones a *José Trigo.* (*Rev. Chil. Lit.,* 30, nov. 1987, p. 125–154)

Extenso ensayo donde se establece que en la novela de Fernando del Paso hay un proceso de metaforización entre los conflictos sociales y políticos del movimiento ferrocarrilero de 1960 y los mitos de origen, muerte y resurrección. Por ello el tiempo lineal del movimiento se transforma en el cíclico del mito y, como en éste, el conflicto se resuelve cuando una de las fuerzas antagónicas es sacrificada.

3545 Stanton, Anthony. Estructuras antropológicas en *Pedro Páramo.* (*Nueva Rev. Filol. Hisp.,* 36:1, 1988, p. 567–606)

Extenso ensayo que analiza el modo en que la confusión o sustitución de estructuras antropológicas fundamentales, como el incesto y el parricidio, se convierten en la novela en mecanismos generadores de ambigüedad, semejante a la establecida en la estructura y el tema.

3546 Stevens, Kathryn L. Configuración de La Onda en un cuento de José Agustín. (*in* De la crónica a la nueva narrativa mexicano. [see item **3516**] p. 453–462)

Según Stevens el cuento "Cuál es la Onda," de José Agustín, sirve para caracterizar a la Generación de la Onda en su bús-

queda de un lenguaje propio y fresco, semejante al de la joven pareja de enamorados en el cuento, quienes para poder relacionarse precisan delimitar y definir su lenguaje.

3547 Teichmann, Reinhard. De la onda en adelante: conversaciones con 21 novelistas mexicanos. México: Editorial Posada, 1987. 551 p.: ports. (Letras de México)

Util conjunto de entrevistas, precedido de un sólido ensayo introductorio de 23 p. en el cual se proporciona el criterio de la selección, el esquema básico de las entrevistas, un bosquejo de cada autor individual y las características comunes a la narrativa mexicana, según se desprenden de las entrevistas. Teichmann menciona un segundo tomo de posterior aparición en el cual se incluirá a 35 o 40 autores más, pertenecientes también, según él, a la Generación de la Onda y a la posterior. Esta es la lista de los narradores incluidos en el presente tomo: José Agustín, René Avilés Fabila, Gerardo de la Torre, María Luisa Puga, Marco Antonio Campos, Federico Arana, Héctor Manjarrez, Agustín Ramos, David Martín del Campo, Arturo Azuela, Silvia Molina, Aline Pettersson, Ethel Krauze, Luis Zapata, Jorge Aguilar Mora, Humberto Guzmán, Daniel Leyva, Hugo Hiriart, Rafael Ramírez Heredia, Angeles Matretta y Eugenio Aguirre.

3548 Torres, Vicente Francisco. Narradores de fin de siglo. México: Univ. Autónoma Metropolitana, 1989. 131 p.

Colección de estudios individuales, acompañados de la respectiva entrevista, de narradores inmediatamente posteriores en publicación a la Generación de la Onda, que comienzan a escribir en 1970. A tales corresponderían, entre otros, Ignacio Solares (enlazador de una y otra generación), Jesús Gardea, Luis Arturo Ramos, Hernán Lara Zavala, Silvia Molina y Paco Ignacio Taibo II. Los estudios de Torres, aunque breves, son serios e informativos; además, conociendo tan a fondo la obra de sus entrevistados, las entrevistas ahondan en los puntos señalados en los estudios.

3549 Troiano, James J. Illusory worlds in three stories by Emilio Carballido. (*Hisp. J.,* 10:2, Spring 1989, p. 63–79, bibl.)

Análisis de los elementos que constituyen el mundo fantástico en tres cuentos del escritor mexicano, contenidos en *La caja vacía* (1962). El ensayista establece que Carballido es tan certero cuentista como dramaturgo, a pesar de no practicar tan frecuentemente el primer oficio.

3550 Volek, Emil. *Pedro Páramo* de Juan Rulfo: una obra aleatoria en busca de su texto y del género literario. (*Rev. Iberoam.*, 56:150, marzo 1990, p. 35–47)

Ingenioso y humorístico ensayo, aunque no por ello menos serio, acerca de los problemas que presentan las diversas versiones de la novela. Volek establece cronologías en apariencia precisas para diversos eventos importantes de la novela, pero hay otros que conservan fechas dudosas; algunas de éstas podrían ocasionar ciertos tropiezos en una lectura lógica de la novela. Pero, advierte Volek, las variantes y las dudas en el hacerse permanente del texto de *Pedro Páramo* caen muy bien dentro de la estructura abierta y plural de la obra.

Central America

RENE PRIETO, *Associate Professor of Spanish, Southern Methodist University*

THE MOST NOTICEABLE TREND in the prose fiction of Central America in the last two years is the overwhelming predominance of the short story. Such a turn is alarming for a number of reasons. To begin with, despite their many qualities, short stories have an inherent disadvantage: they are compact anecdotes rather than full-fledged fictional narratives. Under normal circumstances, this would not matter. All genres are welcomed and recognized for the place each occupies in the family of fiction. But what happens when other family members dwindle dramatically? In the past two years, hardly a novel, essay, or critical study has come out of Central America. Where have all the worthwhile writers gone? Where are the Augusto Monterrosos and the Monteforte Toledos who communicate through lavish plots and full-bodied character studies rather than through well-polished and sometimes facile anecdotes? What does this widespread tendency to write short stories to the almost total exclusion of other genres suggest about the state of Central American literature as we enter the 1990s?

Clues in answer to this question can be found when we examine the content of Central American writing. Much of it has political overtones, but what a far cry from the revolutionary zeal and zest for life of older authors writing only a short decade ago. Has the new generation run out of steam? Instead of the brillant, hopeful light that suffused Central American fiction, now all one detects through the iron grating of politics is a dim and disappointed glimmer. A militant literature that provided a revolutionary perspective of open fields and limitless horizons has shrivelled into a narrow fiction of exile and confinement exemplified by Horacio Castellanos Moya's "En Guinda," a story about two teenage brothers from El Salvador who must leave the country (item **3557**). The mood of Castellanos' original and trendy stories is depressed, and his characters are invariably trapped by conditions beyond their control, conditions that lead in turn to much defeatist introspection.

The theme of exile in the prose fiction coming out of Central America these days is not merely political, but moral and social as well. This is the case in V.A. Mora Rodríguez's title story in *Nora y otros cuentos* (item **3577**), a tale in which the heroine is pushed to her death by her own prejudiced and petty townsfolk. Regardless of the type of exile described by Central American authors, their characters are without exception estranged, set apart, and rejected by their own community, as in the case of Roberto Castillo's Premio Plural-winning story "La Laguna" (item **3558**). All of these tragic works emphasize a contemporary predicament, the diminishing capacity for communication among human beings today. Unlike fictional works of the previous generation, these stories are profoundly nihilistic.

The nihilism of these authors, however, is not the only reason for the estrangement of their characters. In Isis Tejeira's *Sin fecha fija* (item **3590**) and Irma Prego's *Mensajes al más allá* (item **3582**) the characters' difficulty in communicating is inherent to the condition of women as victims of repressive forces. Female characters in many works annotated below, such as those in Emilia Macaya Trejos' *La sombra en el espejo* (item **3574**) reject this state of victimization and embark in search of their true identity. This concern with feminism is not exclusive to fiction and is also evident in the field of Central American literary criticism. Examples are Luz Ivette Martínez's scholarly study of the four leading feminist writers of Costa Rica: Carmen Lyra, Yolanda Oreamuno, Julieta Pinto, and Carmen Naranjo (item **3598**). In recent years, the women of Central America have channeled their anger and frustration into works of literature, a tendency most noticeable in Costa Rica. Indeed, the fact that Costa Rica has become the most prolific center for aspiring authors of various tendencies, feminist or not (e.g., Emilia Macaya Trejos and Hugo Rivas) can be attributed to the nation's development of good publishing houses, the creation of intellectual support groups, and above all, the maintenance of a peaceful and tolerant climate in which to write.

With the exception of El Salvador, where militant literature is still being written (e.g., Juan Allwood Paredes' *María Elena y la liberación nacional*, item **3552**; and Oscar Benítez's *Las huellas de una lucha sin final*, item **3555**), there is a widespread tendency toward escapist writing in Central American countries: examples are Mauricio del Pinal's *Indianista* fantasy, *3-Caban* (item **3581**), and a timely reedition of Froylán Turcios' handsomely written gothic tale, *El vampiro* (item **3591**). Escapist literature, as well as a parallel and not unrelated tendency towards the depiction of despotic figures (e.g., Fernando Durán Ayanegui's *Tenés nombre de arcángel*, item **3565**), suggest that in Central America authors are relying on tropes, subterfuges, and fantasy in order to portray and condemn the overwhelming pandemonium of repression and violence that surrounds them.

As far as literary criticism and reeditions are concerned, several new publications deserve to be mentioned. *La novela del imperialismo en Centroamérica* by Esther María Osses (item **3599**) should be commended for its thoroughness and critical insight. Francisco Albizúrez Palma's article "El Contexto Social de Asturias" (item **3593**) also deserves mention because of its interesting exploration of the symbiotic relationship between society, author, and literary production. Of cultural interest to the general public and specialist alike, are two reeditions: 1) Pablo Antonio Cuadra's best selling ethnological study, *El nicaragüense* (item **3596**), an insightful and amusing look at the people of Nicaragua; and 2) Flavio Herrera's justly famous *Caos* (item **3570**), especially the poignant and beautifully written chapter on indigenismo entitled "El Muro."

PROSE FICTION

3551 Aguilar, Rosario. 7 relatos sobre el amor y la guerra. Ciudad Universitaria Rodrigo Facio, Costa Rica: Editorial Universitaria Centroamericana, 1986. 154 p. (Col. Séptimo día)

Written in a predominantly meta-phoric style, this new collection of short stories by Aguilar highlights the difficult living conditions in her native Nicaragua during and after the Revolution.

3552 Allwood Paredes, Juan. María Elena y la liberación nacional. El Salvador: Editorial EPACTA, 1987. 180 p.

Uninspired and badly disguised political harangue of little literary merit. The author of *Osicala* brings together a handful of characters from different social milieux who take part in the struggle to renew El Salvador.

3553 Antología del cuento hondureño. Edición de Jorge Luis Oviedo. Tegucigalpa: Editores Unidos, 1988. 167 p. (Col. Puerta de golpe)

Selection of short stories beginning with some written in the 1920s by the "Renovación" group (e.g., Arturo Martínez Galindo, Federico Peck Fernández, Arturo Mejía Nieto and Marcos Carías) and concluding with representative choices by contemporary authors such as Jorge Luis Oviedo.

3554 Argüello, Carlos Luis. El mundo de Juana Torres. San José: Editorial Costa Rica, 1985. 153 p.

Adolescent runaway's rite of passage in Costa Rica's banana plantations. Argüello's first person narrative borrows freely from Güiraldes' *Don Segundo Sombra* but remains original and highly entertaining.

3555 Benítez, Oscar René. Las huellas de una lucha sin final: novela. North Hollywood, Calif.: Evergreen Books, 1986. 189 p.

Highly unusual second novel by versatile young author of *Immortales* brings together sexuality, corruption, politics, and revenge in an apocalyptic manifesto. Highlights dramatic living conditions in present day El Salvador.

3556 Britton, Rosa María. La muerte tiene dos caras. San José: Editorial Costa Rica, 1987. 129 p.

String of fictionalized case studies on the theme of death written by a medical doctor turned writer. Recipient of Costa Rica's Fullbright Assn. 1985 Walt Whitman Award.

3557 Castellanos Moya, Horacio. Perfil de prófugo. México: Claves Latinoamericanas, 1987. 96 p.

Skillfully written short stories where *mal de vivre,* lust rather than sex, and revolutionary sympathies commingle. In their hopes, poses, and aspirations, characters are reminiscent of Horacio and "la Maga" in *Rayuela.*

3558 Castillo, Roberto. Figuras de agradable demencia. Tegucigalpa: Editorial Guaymuras, 1985. 141 p. (Col. Fragua)

One of the most original works to appear in print in Honduras in the last decade. Young author has a particular talent for character development. His story "El Loco Divino" offers quirky and disturbing portrayals of alienation, estrangement and madness.

3559 Certamen Permanente Centroamericano 15 de Septiembre, *Guatemala, 1985.* Certamen Permanente Centroamericano "15 de Septiembre" 1985: rama, literatura, subrama, cuento. Guatemala: Depto. de Actividades Literarias, Dirección General de Bellas Artes, Ministerio de Cultura y Deportes, 1986. 150 p.

These short stories by Luis de Lión, William Lemus and Manuel Corleto were awarded three first prizes in the Central American Literature Contest "15 de Septiembre." All three authors are markedly ironic, but no single tale stands out in terms of literary innovation except perhaps Lemus' saga in Santa Lucía Cotzumalguapa.

3560 Chong Ruiz, Eustorgio A. Diario de una noche de camino: cuentos. 2a ed. Panamá: E.A. Chong Ruiz, 1987. 76 p.: ill.

Short stories, written in colloquial language, in which children and rural themes play an important part. Chong has won several literary awards, among them one for children's literature.

3561 Chorres Guerrero, J. A. Remembranzas de una primavera. Panamá: [s.n.] 1987. 106 p.

Childhood memories provide a glimpse of a rapidly disappearing world: school vacations spent in the unpolluted countryside, miraculous Holy Weeks, dazzling story tellers, and venerable town elders.

3562 Cifuentes, Edwin. La nueva Esmeralda: la novela de París. México: J. Mortiz, 1987. 127 p. (Nueva narrativa hispánica)

Puerile transcription of *Notre Dame de Paris* in which Esmeralda is portrayed as a calculating female Robin Hood who strips the rich to help the poor and the gutters of Victor Hugo's original city are substituted by today's Metrorail system.

3563 Cruz, Luz María de la. Pequeños hombres; y, Relatos de fin de siglo. San José: Editorial Costa Rica, 1986. 107 p.

Two collections of short stories by Costa Rican author and twice winner of the Walt Whitman literary award.

3564 Curtis, Wilson. Variaciones sobre una conjetura. Managua: Editorial Nueva Nicaragua, 1987. 85 p.: ill.

Elegantly written stories among which a feline fantasy entitled "los Tatuadores" stands out. During its best moments, Curtis' prose can be likened to blank verse, such is his deft handling of language.

3565 Durán Ayanegui, Fernando. Tenés nombre de arcángel: novela. San José, Costa Rica: Ediciones Guayacán, 1988. 122 p.

Durán's original first novel introduces the figure of a boy named Gabriel as the conscience of a village mired in degradation. The pervasive lewdness and perversion tolerated and even protected by the townspeople serves as a metaphor of the passivity which allows despotism to prosper throughout the world.

3566 Escudos, Jacinta. Apuntes de una historia de amor que no fue. San Salvador: UCA Editores, 1987. 86 p. (Col. Gavidia; 27)

Political and military struggles that swept El Salvador during the 1970s (and paving the way for today's FMLN) provide the background for this love story.

3567 Gadea Mantilla, Fabio. Cartas de amor a Nicaragua. San José, Costa Rica: s.n., 1985. 206 p.: ill.

Collection of letters combine political messages and patriotic homilies by well-known Nicaraguan author and radio speaker. Gadea has written and often read these poignant messages in an attempt to rescue his country from what he views as "the claws of Soviet power." His discussion of trampled human rights, of political prisoners and *Miskito* massacres beg the attention of those wishing to understand the political and living conditions in revolutionary Nicaragua.

3568 González, Otto Raúl. El magnicida. Guatemala: Fundación Guatemalteca para las Letras, 1987. 162 p.

Second novel by Guatemalan diplomat and author who played an active role in the "Generation of 1940." González portrays a man on his deathbed who is haunted by reminiscences of younger days including a scheme to assassinate President Eisenhower.

3569 Herra, Rafael Angel. La guerra prodigiosa: novela. San José: Editorial Costa Rica, 1986 323 p.: ill.

Bizarre and imaginative work of fiction scrutinizes the nature of good and evil and the origins of Lucifer. Author is Univ. of Costa Rica professor and editor of the *Revista de Filogía*.

3570 Herrera, Flavio. Caos. Guatemala: Editorial Universitaria de Guatemala, 1982. 187 p.: port. (Col. Flavio Herrera; 2)

Timely reedition of author's last novel (first published in 1949). Turmoil, chaos and disorder rule over human beings and are often worse than the hurricanes and other natural phenomena that ravage the tropics. Herrera leaves behind his earlier *criollista* concerns to focus on the human condition. Particularly noteworthy is a poignant *Indigenista* chapter entitled "El Muro."

3571 Jaramillo Levi, Enrique. Ahora que soy él: cuentos. San José: Editorial Costa Rica, 1985. 92 p.

Collection of short stories with metaphysical themes reminiscent of Borges' by one of the better-known authors from Panama. Jaramillo Levi adroitly explores the nature of perception as well as the behavior of döppelgangers.

3572 Jiménez Veiga, Danilo. El paso del tiempo. San José: Ministerio de Cultura, Juventud y Deportes, 1985. 96 p.

Reminiscences of younger days, some are set in Costa Rica's banana plantations, others include sensitive meditations on unrequited love, religious crises, petit-bourgeois virtues, and the post-war years in Paris.

3573 Lyra, Carmen. Los otros cuentos de Carmen Lyra. San José: Editorial Costa Rica, 1985. 140 p.

Reedition of a crucial work by very important Costa Rican author (d. 1949). Lyra's greatest concerns—the importance of culture and education, the nexus between economic contradictions and social ones, the problem of the oppressed—are ubiquitous in these beautifully written and deeply moving stories.

3574 Macaya, Emilia. La sombra en el espejo. San José: Editorial Costa Rica, 1986. 99 p.: ill.

First collection of short stories by Costa Rican professor and specialist in methods of literary analysis. Woman rejects her secondary role in life and embarks in search of her own identity.

3575 Martínez, Yolanda C. Veinte cartas neuróticas desde Alabama. San Salvador: Clásicos Roxsil, 1987. 76 p. (Col. Novela)

Original as well as entertaining, this epistolary saga is as literal as its title suggests: 20 letters exchanged by a young couple are read and interpreted by a voyeuristic roommate.

3576 Monterroso, Augusto. La letra e: fragmentos de un diario. Mexico: Ediciones Era, 1987. 204 p. (Biblioteca Era)

Escritos periodísticos, a manera de diario, en los cuales el autor da a conocer en su siempre pulida prosa lecturas, amigos, viajes, actividades profesionales, etc. En conjunto los trozos proporcionan una idea general de la vida literaria en México y de la manera como planea y escribe Monterroso sus escuetos textos literarios. [F. García Núñez]

3577 Mora Rodríguez, V.A. Nora y otros cuentos. Ciudad Universitaria Rodrigo Facio, Costa Rica: Editorial Universitaria Centroamericana, 1986. 107 p. (Col. Séptimo día)

Three short stories by Costa Rican polymath now practicing psychiatry in New York City. "Nora," the title story, stands out for both the insights it provides into the psychological tensions of a small town as well as for its original writing style.

3578 El nuevo cuento hondureño. Selección e introducción de Jorge Luis Oviedo. Tegucigalpa: Dardo Editores, 1985. 129 p.

Consists of 13 short stories from Honduras in which the work of Julio Escoto and Marcos Carías stands out for its originality and craftsmanship.

3579 Oviedo, Jorge Luis. La gloria del muerto. Tegucigalpa: Editores Unidos, 1987. 75 p.

Portrait of a brutal *caudillo* representative of the many who pollute the Latin American landscape. Oviedo's Baroque writing style portrays a grotesque world with imagination and savagery.

3580 Pellecer, Carlos Manuel. El cantar de las tinieblas: novela. Guatemala: Librerías Artemis y Edinter, 1986. 232 p.

The story of two persecuted men (one of them a Catholic priest) who meet and become friends in an isolated village in the middle of the jungle. Reminiscent of Eustaquio Rivera's *La vorágine,* this rite-of-passage novel raises fundamental questions about human nature, idealism and the need to revolt.

3581 Pinal, Mauricio del. 3-Cabán: novela. Guatemala: CENALTEX, Ministerio de Educación, 1987. 255 p.: ill.

Indianista novel set in the city of Tikal during the Mayan classic period. Its romantic plot—the story of a young man living around 800 AD and of the three women in his life—is based on solid archaeological and ethnological information.

3582 Prego, Irma. Mensajes al más allá. Cuidad Universitaria Rodrigo Facio, Costa Rica: Editorial Universitaria Centroamericana, 1987. 181 p. (Col. Séptimo día)

Collection of short stories, many with a feminist theme. The banality of everyday life described by Prego is enlivened by her extraordinary handling of vocabulary and ironic perspective.

3583 Quesada, Roberto. El desertor. Honduras: G. Fiallos Paz, 1985. 108 p.

Written in colloquial style, this collection of short stories offers an ironic view of daily life in Honduras. Particularly noteworthy for its blend of literary themes and reality is the story entitled, "El Ultimo Habitante de Macondo."

3584 Quezada, Roberto. El filo de tu locura. 1a ed. del X aniversario de RIN-78. Guatemala: Grupo Literario Editorial RIN-78, 1988. 253 p. (Col. Literatura; 29)

Conventionally written second novel by award-winning author of *Ardillas enjauladas.* This dual love story of Hispanics in Los Angeles is, in fact, a profound reflection of more general concerns such as the validity of marriage and the equality between the sexes.

3585 Rivas, Hugo. Esa orilla sin nadie. San José: Ediciones Guayacán, 1988. 209 p.

The adventures of a handful of young men and women set in contemporary Costa Rica. Their political involvement and search for love blend together in Rivas' somewhat ponderous first novel.

3586 Robles Martínez, José. Más allá de la memoria. México: Plaza y Janés, 1987. 305 p.

Novel of political intrigue foretells

the destruction of a monstrous petrochemical empire in Veracruz. Skillfully written entertainment.

3587 Robleto, Octavio. Cuentos de verdad y de mentira. Managua: Editorial Nueva Nicaragua, 1986. 215 p. (Letras de Nicaragua; 22)

Consists of 32 short stories, fables and allegories by a twice winner of the "Rubén Darío" Award (1957–1958). Most fiction by this renowned Nicaraguan author has a surprise ending not unlike O. Henry's.

3588 Sagastume Gemmell, Marco Antonio. Recuento de cuentos y descuentos. Guatemala: Serviprensa Centroamericana, 1987. 84 p.: ill.

Consists of 16 anecdotes written with imagination and originality. Frequent puns and surprise endings are, no doubt, two of the reasons why Miguel Angel Asturias particularly enjoyed this collection.

3589 Salazar Herrera, Carlos M. Cuentos de angustias y paisajes. San José: Editorial El Bongo, 1988. 210 p.: ill.

Costumbrista short stories by the 1964 Magón Prize winner from Costa Rica. Uses straightforward prose to illustrate homespun moral lessons.

3590 Tejeira, Isis. Sin fecha fija. 2a ed. Panamá: s.n., 1986. 126 p.

Brilliant and original first-person narrative describes hardships of a woman ensnared by the repressive forces of society. Her unconditional surrender to the arbitrary dictates of a bigoted world force the reader to question and repudiate the ostensibly "respectable" family structure and convent education that promote such abject submission.

3591 Turcios, Froylán. El vampiro. 4a ed. Tegucigalpa: Baktún Editorial, 1986. 144 p.

Reprint of Turcios' handsomely written gothic tale, originally published in 1910 and set in Antigua, Guatemala. The heart of the novel is the passionate relationship of a teen-age couple whose romance ends up in tragedy.

3592 Vides, Méndez. Las catacumbas. Managua: Editorial Nueva Nicaragua, 1987. 99 p.

Three trapped tigers without the sense of humor. Winner of the 1986 literary prize

"Nueva Nicaragua," this short novel is an adroitly written and slow-moving account of nightlife in the tawdry bars of just about any Central American capital.

LITERARY CRITICISM AND HISTORY

3593 Albizúrez Palma, Francisco. El contexto social de Asturias. (*Let. Guatem.*, 4/5, 1985/1986, p. 37–54)

Examines the symbiotic relationship between society, author and literary production specifically regarding Miguel Angel Asturias' work. Provides useful overview of this author's evolution for the lay reader but is lacking in insights for the specialist.

3594 Albizúrez Palma, Francisco. Italia en la literatura guatemalteca. (*Let. Guatem.*, 4/5, 1985/1986, p. 15–35)

Article of general interest on a little-studied subject: the direct influence of Italy and of Italian literary sources on the work of Guatemalan authors beginning with Rafael Landívar (and his *Rusticatio Mexicana*) through Miguel Angel Asturias who completed his *Clarivigilia primaveral* in Italy.

3595 Araujo, Max. Hacia una nueva novela en Guatemala. (*Cult. Guatem.*, 6:3, sept./dic. 1985, p. 71–81, bibl.)

Interesting two-part article examines questions of morals and good taste in today's literature (e.g. a short story by Dante Liano entitled "Jorge Isaac Habla de María"). Author sees Joyce as the progenitor of modern experimental literature and identifies Rafael Arévalo Martínez, Flavio Herrera, Miguel Angel Asturias and Mario Monteforte Toledo as the first Guatemalan writers to break away from the mimetic tradition.

Bravo, Anne. *El Mercurio:* un discurso sobre la cultura, 1958–1980. See *HLAS 51:4875.*

3596 Cuadra, Pablo Antonio. El nicaragüense. San José: Libro Libre, 1987. 207 p. (Obras completas de Pablo Antonio Cuadra: Obra en prosa; 3. Serie literaria)

Best-selling ethnological essay in the tradition of Octavio Paz's *The Labyrinth of Solitude*. All-embracing reflection on the people of Nicaragua with chapters on humor and mockery as well as on the "Nica's" imagination, sobriety and split personality.

3597 **Fernández Cañizález, Víctor.** Análisis de la obra literaria de Tristán Solarte. Prólogo de Elsie Alvarado de Ricord. Panamá: Ediciones Librería Cultural Panameña, 1986. 383 p.: bibl., 1 port.

Erudite study of the great Panamanian poet and novelist, Tristán Solarte. Author's mostly biographical and psychological study includes chapters on Solarte's themes and influences, a comparison between his poetry and his prose, as well as exhaustive incursions into *Tres imágenes de la muerte en tres edades, El Guitarrista, El ahogado,* and *Confesiones de un magistrado.*

3598 **Martínez S., Luz Ivette.** Carmen Naranjo y la narrativa femenina en Costa Rica. Ciudad Universitaria Rodrigo Facio, Costa Rica: Editorial Universitaria Centroamericana, 1987. 463 p.: bibl. (Col. Signo)

Based on scholarly doctoral dissertation on the very important work of Costa Rican author Carmen Naranjo. Martínez places Naranjo within the mainstream of Costa Rican literature and, specifically, ot literature written by women (e.g., Carmen Lyra, Yolanda Oreamuno and Julieta Pinto). Martínez's approach is both panoramic and focused, especially in her monographic studies of these four leading women writers of Costa Rica.

3599 **Osses, Esther María.** La novela del imperialismo en Centroamérica: Literatura hispanoamericana general II. Maracaibo: Univ. del Zulia, Vicerrectorado Académico, 1986. 174 p.: bibl.

Collection of critical essays (on *Viento fuerte, Mamita Yunai, Prisión verde* and others) preceded by two introductory chapters on Spanish American fiction and on the novel of imperialism in Central America. Osses, a retired professor of literature and journalism, also reflects on the existence of an "authentic American language."

Hispanic Caribbean

CARLOS R. HORTAS, *Dean of Humanities and the Arts, Hunter College-City University of New York*
ENRIQUE SACERIO-GARI, *Associate Professor of Spanish, Bryn Mawr College*

THE WORKS REVIEWED DURING the past few years for this section reflect the socio-political confrontations that have faced the Caribbean for decades: individual freedoms, national sovereignty, Cuban diaspora, Puerto Rican identity. As no two Cuban jazzmen, or Caribbean bands, play the same tune in exactly the same way, writers and their critics interpret the region with different instruments. While Arturo Sandoval "flies to freedom" with his trumpet and enters the international market, Gonzalo Rubalcaba makes a guest appearance at the piano at the Montreux in Switzerland, but returns to a Cuba forever in crisis. Many of Cuba's best writers live abroad and would like their native land's long struggle for freedom to succeed by ending Communist intransigence. The best hope in and out of Cuba is not for free-market trumpeting nor for protectionist chords but for a true reconciliation that would lead to independence from all blocs. And the rest is literature or history. . . . And yet, now that a transition seems certain (inevitable) for Cuba's socialist regime, we could speculate about the things to come if not about a period gone by.

Many bibliographic sources now available for the study of Cuban prose writers can be found in Julio Martínez's *Fuentes bibliográficas para el estudio de la literatura cubana moderna* (item **3666**). One wonders about the value of "Relaciones Culturales Soviético-Cubanas: ¿Cómo Serán?" (item **3682**). If the latter reflects the traditional Cuban preference for *mutually* controlled exchange, the former points the way for scholars who wish to investigate the complex reality of Cuban literature, beyond ideological partisanship.

The listings which follow capture the transnational nature of the Hispanic Caribbean. For Reinaldo Arenas (item **3603**) this theme is represented by a doorman between worlds in Manhattan; for many Dominicans the tales revolve around the key year 1965, when US marines moved across their land.

With steady perseverance, specialists in Cuban literature have produced monographs on individual authors (items **3626, 3684, 3668, 3676, 3694** and **3645**) and movements (item **3674**), as well as the studies of the position and disposition of the wider Cuban text (item **3679**). For a discerning analysis of discourse and counter-discourse in antislavery narratives, see William Luis' *Literary bondage: slavery in Cuban narrative* (item **3664**). Pamela M. Smorkaloff's *Literatura y edición de libros: la cultura literaria y el proceso social en Cuba* (item **3691**) offers us an informative social history of book production in Cuba.

The literary and critical dreams of the Cuban Revolution produce testimonies and distressing affidavits. Miguel Barnet's "testimonial" contribution continues to receive critical attention and the high praise it deserves. Too often, Cuban controversy about critical discourse appears to be either ideological knee-jerking or consumed by a normative code of behavior (e.g., see Desiderio Navarro's "La Teoría y la Crítica Literarias: También una Cuestión Moral," item **3671,** and the assessment of the situation from abroad in items **3690, 3654, 3636, 3643** and **3635**). Severo Sarduy and Guillermo Cabrera Infante command universal critical attention *outside* Cuba. Lezama Lima and Carpentier now rule in all camps.

The modes of narration by Dominican writers and the manner in which the history of the Republic should be told are also subject to intense scrutiny in Neil Larson's "¿Cómo Narrar el Trujillato?" (item **3660**) and Efraín Barradas' "La Seducción de las Máscaras . . ." (item **3633**). Jenny Montero's *La cuentística dominicana* (item **3667**) and Bruno Rosario Candelier's *Tendencias de la novela dominicana* (item **3686**) are valuable essays on the Dominican short story and novel. The best work of fiction (item **3601**) and criticism (item **3627**) belong to the same person: José Alcántara Almánzar.

In the last few years Puerto Rican writers and critics have continued to publish critical editions of classic works of Puerto Rican literature. Socorro Girón's edition of Bonafoux's *Ultramarinos* (item **3637**) and Carmen I. Marxuach's edition of Zeno Gandías *La charca* (item **3625**) exemplify this trend. Never at a loss for essays which analyze and examine Puerto Rican life and mores, political and national identity, consumerism and the media, we have annotated below two particularly valuable collections of essays, *El tramo ancla* (item **3634**) and *Images and identities* (item **3657**). These essays are authored by writers of the moment who offer valuable insight and analysis of contemporary life and letters in Puerto Rico and of Puerto Rican life on the US mainland. We continue to see promising new writers each year who come forth with interesting contributions to the island's prose fiction. This year we particularly note the short stories of Luis López Nieves (item **3617**) and the recent novel of Edgardo Jusino Campos (item **3614**). Among the island's women writers, Rosario Ferré (item **3611**) has become a literary elder stateswoman of sorts, and continues to lead the way for others. *Reclaiming Medusa* (item **4930**), edited by Diana Vélez, is a good collection of short fiction by the island's best women writers.

PROSE FICTION

3600 Adán, Orestes. El Dorado. La Habana: Editorial Letras Cubanas, 1986. 138 p. (Col. Espiral)

Tale about a Cuban El Dorado, a small village that marks the road between Bayamo and the Sierra Maestra. In colonial days, the bayameses looked for gold in the mountains and later founded El Dorado near a golden stream. Good example of elementary revolutionary revisionism follows: all of Cuba's history from Carlos Manuel de Céspedes to the present prefigures Fidel Castro's policies, from capitalist gold to gold-plated development.

3601 Alcántara Almánzar, José. La carne estremecida. Santo Domingo: Fundación Cultural Dominicana, 1989. 154 p.

Excellent collection of short stories. "El Zurdo" (i.e. "The Left-Handed Man") speaks to his stepmother Rosario, who forced him to use his right hand as a child. At school he suffers the insults of "rightists" who favor right-handedness. As an adult writer, with Borges as blind guide, he listens to a performance of Ravel's piece for the left hand. Later, he plunges a right-handed knife into Rosario's womb. Throughout the story, the narrator speaks to Rosario's dead body. Other tales are as allegorical. They all question the superficial analysis of Dominican realities.

3602 Almánzar Rodríguez, Armando. Selva de agujeros negros para "Chichí la Salsa." Santo Domingo: Biblioteca Nacional, 1985. 147 p. (Col. Orfeo)

Good, wide-ranging collection of narrative exercises: letters, irony, violence. Good introduction places author in context as member of the 1960s generation. Many tales emphasize the struggle against Trujillo's tyranny. Pleads for the poor and the disadvantaged, the homeless and the unemployed trapped in a violent environment where guns are ready to fire against any suspicious person, including children.

3603 Arenas, Reinaldo. El portero. Miami: Ediciones Universal, 1990. 158 p. (Col. Caniquí)

Novel about a Cuban doorman in Manhattan, a good observer (watchman) of tenants and excellent talker with their ani-

mals! This work is a brilliant social fantasy and a piercing fable, with Arenas at the threshold of his deepest anguish.

3604 Cabrera, Raimundo Sombras que pasan. Prólogo, cronología, bibliografía y notas de Dolores Nieves. La Habana: Editorial Letras Cubanas, 1984. 366 p. (Biblioteca básica de literatura cubana)

Novel about early years of the struggle for Cuban independence from Spain. Covers political turmoil of 1870–73, during the "Guerra de los Diez Años." Author was jailed as teenager, during 1869–70, in Isla de Pinos.

3605 Cardoso, Onelio Jorge. La cabeza en la almohada. La Habana: Editorial Letras Cubanas, 1983. 57 p. (Ocuje)

Seven tales, two for children, with death or the threat of death as primary theme. Cardoso is at his best in "La Brasa," in which the dying protagonist recalls key incidents from his life. Once, after physically abusing his daughter because she carelessly (almost) stepped in front of a car, he swore to hold a burning coal in his hand if he hit her again. Recalling a neighbor who fatally burned herself, the protagonist wonders if he restrained himself from further abuse because of love for the child or because of fear of fire.

3606 Coll, Edna. Simplemente cuentos. San Juan, Puerto Rico: Esmaco Printers Corp., 1986. 126 p.

Pleasant anecdotes about daily life and customs with no real literary value. The writing is self-absorbed and very limited.

3607 Córdova Iturregui, Félix. El rabo de lagartija de aquel famoso señor rector y otros cuentos de orilla. Río Piedras, P.R.: Ediciones Huracán, 1986. 109 p.

Rather unimpressive short stories with weak story lines and a ruminative narrative style.

3608 El Cuento en Santo Domingo: selección antológica. Recopilación de Sócrates Nolasco. Santo Domingo: Biblioteca Nacional, 1986. 204 p.: bibl. (Col. Orfeo)

Collection of short stories by the most traditional names in Dominican letters. One curious piece is by Cuban independence hero Gen. Máximo Gómez, "El Sueño del Guerrero," a story which describes Columbus confessing his guilt to Gómez in 1889 at La Demajagua. Introduction is not helpful. Omission of key figures, for obvious political reasons, is regrettable.

3609 Delgado, Ana María. Habitación de por medio. Santurce, P.R.: Model Offset Print, 1987. 62 p.: ill.

Daughter's reflections on her relationship to her mother during the daughter's visit to her aged mother's sickbed. Narration consists mostly of daughter's thoughts, interspersed with snatches of conversation. Realistic dialogue, when it occurs, but narrative is tedious at times.

3610 Encarnación, Angel M. Las meninas de Avignon en Orgaz: novela. Santurce, P.R.: Jay-Ce Printing, 1986. 151 p.

Novel written in the linguistic spirit of *Tres tristes tigres*, full of puns, word games, and double entendres. Very funny at times, yet the narrative has no identifiable thread. Word associations and puns are at times forced and trite. Interesting but somewhat flawed experiment.

3611 Ferré, Rosario. Maldito amor. Río Piedras, P.R.: Ediciones Huracán, 1988. 186 p.

Important collection of excellent short stories by one of Puerto Rico's outstanding prose writers.

Ferré, Rosario. Sweet diamond dust. See item **4993.**

3612 Fonfrías, Ernesto Juan. El martirio de una familia humilde: novela. Río Piedras, P.R.: Impr. ESMACO, 1986. 144 p.: ill.

Anecdotal story about the tribulations of a family. Plodding, prosaic style which fails to sustain reader interest.

3613 González, José Luis. El oído de Dios. México: Ediciones Era, 1984. 58 p.: ill. (Biblioteca Era)

Not up to José Luis González's usual standards, this narrative never transcends the obvious. Denouement is flat and disappointing.

3614 Jusino Campos, Edgardo. Cita para la fiesta: novela. Río Piedras, P.R.: Editorial Cuarto Centenario, 1985. 249 p.

Excellent narrative by a writer who continues to grow. Well realized novel follows the lives of a group of men from adoles-

cence to adulthood and reveals their failures and successes, struggles and contradictions.

3615 Jusino Campos, Edgardo. Los reptiles incautos. P.R.: Editorial Edil, 1978. 107 p.

War in Vietnam as seen through Puerto Rican eyes, this narrative lacks the consistent tension that its subject demands. Uninterrupted narration with minimum of dialogue works well at times, but is not consistently engaging.

3616 Lezama Lima, José. Cuentos. La Habana: Editorial Letras Cubanas, 1987. 94 p. (Giraldilla)

Brief introduction presents five seldom studied "short stories"; "Fugados," "El Patio Morado," "Para un Final Presto," "Juego de las Decapitaciones," "Cangrejos, Golondrinas."

3617 López Nieves, Luis. Escribir para Rafa. Buenos Aires: Ediciones de la Flor, 1987. 220 p.

Wonderful collection of short stories, among which there is an epistolary narrative that is a real gem. Characterized by humor, irony and good insights into the human psyche, these stories are also imaginative and fresh. Excellent reading.

3618 Marqués, René. En una ciudad llamada San Juan: cuentos. 5a ed. Río Piedras, P.R.: Editorial Cultural, 1983. 233 p.

New edition of the by now classic collection of René Marqués' short stories dedicated to the city of San Juan. This edition includes 17 short stories, seven more than the first edition. Excellent stories, but no bibliographical or critical apparatus.

3619 Milanese, Otto Oscar. Tres gotas de misericordia. Santo Domingo: Taller, 1988. 102 p.

Collection of loose, uneven stories written in a style at times fluid, at others verbose. Includes some good pieces such as "Altares y Abismos" which satirizes the writing trade, others which explore the life of characters trapped in their houses, their past, their existential traces.

Reclaiming Medusa: short stories by contemporary Puerto Rican women. See item **4930.**

3620 Santiago de Figueroa, Evalina. Dulceamargo y otros cuentos: recuerdos de una década. Ponce, P.R.: Mairena, 1984. 77 p.: ill.

Traditional stories about the Puerto Rican countryside written in a realistic, anecdotal style. Although they lack a distinctive literary structure or development, they are interesting and revealing from the standpoint of human interest.

3621 Sarduy, Severo. Cocuyo. Barcelona: Tusquets, 1990. 209 p. (Col. Andanzas; 125)

Another dazzling fragmented novel by Sarduy without origin or outer limit. If *Colibrí* is "fixed motion" *Cocuyo* is (unpredictable) light quanta.

3622 Savariego, Berta. La "Mandolina" y otros cuentos: cuentos y cantos sefarditas. Miami: Ediciones Universal, 1988. 82 p. (Col. Caniquí)

Touching collection of short stories, poems, and recollecitons about Cuba's Sephardic community. Draws on a nostalgia for Israel and the pain of Sepharad to capture the deepest meaning of *diaspora*.

3623 Uribe, Pedro. Círculo de ceniza. Santo Domingo: Taller, 1986. 113 p. (Biblioteca Taller; 216)

Consists of 24 vignettes written in early 1980s. These so-called "micro-stories" are well-written. Many refer to the resistance to the Trujillo tyranny (e.g., Trujillo's daughter is the protagonist of one vignette). Some are stories of love in the darkest night. A more significant darkness concerns one narrator's blindness, which the prologue attributes to the author's poor eyesight. In "Condenados a la Sombra," the "blind" narrator seems courageous and powerful in his vision, as he looks into the darkness of the political landscape of the Trujillo era.

3624 Vivas Maldonado, José Luis. Mis cuentos. San Juan: Instituto de Cultura Puertorriqueña, 1986. 263 p.

Consists of 30 short stories selected from a number of the author's earlier publications. A few have been revised; five are published for the first time. Realistic narratives about Puerto Rican life are excellently written.

3625 Zeno Gandía, Manuel. La charca. Introducción y notas de Carmen Irene Marxuach. San Juan: Centro de Estudios

Avanzados de Puerto Rico y el Caribe, 1987. 294 p.: bibl.

Superbly annotated edition of Zeno Gandía's classic novel includes excellent critical introduction and appendices.

LITERARY CRITICISM AND HISTORY

3626 Aguirre, Mirta. Estudios literarios. La Habana: Editorial Letras Cubanas, 1981. 507 p. (Letras cubanas)

Good selection features three essays on Sor Juana Inés de la Cruz by Cuba's mainstream female poet-critic. Besides pieces on Guillén and Martí, she examines the "presence of México" in the works of Juan Marinello and the "Mexicanidad" of Ramón López Velarde's poetry. Includes essays on key figures from France and Italy (e.g. Machiavelli, Vico, Balzac).

3627 Alcántara Almánzar, José. Los escritores dominicanos y la cultura. Santo Domingo: Instituto Tecnológico de Santo Domingo, 1990. 226 p.: bibl., index. (Serie monografía; 21)

Essential book divided in three sections: "Three Poets;" "Writing and Society;" and "Writers and Culture." Study of the three poets (i.e., Manuel Rueda, Freddy Gatón Arce and Virgilio Díaz Ordóñez) may be the most appropriate introduction to the subsequent literary history, where author praises the major contribution of poets and hopes for more endurable talents in prose. Author is optimistic about the future, possibly because of a strong tradition of sociological analyses based on the works of Hostos and Henríquez Ureña. Tortuous events such as the Trujillo era and the April 1965 intervention still await their masterpieces. Author offers informative interpretation of Dominican history and letters.

3628 Almeida Bosque, Juan. Presidio. La Habana: Editorial de Ciencias Sociales, 1987. 88 p., 1 leaf of plates: ill. (Ediciones políticas)

Almeida's recollections of his imprisonment with Fidel Castro in the "presidio" at Isla de Pinos, after the assault on the Moncada barracks, are interwoven with his memoirs of the operation. Of interest to those who would like to study the library that was at the disposal of Castro and his companions during their incarceration.

3629 Alvarez-Borland, Isabel. The Pícaro's journey in the structure of *La Habana para un infante difunto.* (*Hispanófila*, 90, mayo 1987, p. 71–79, bibl.)

Explains the structure of Cabrera Infante's novel as five collective adventures ("the great fresco of Havana") interlaced with six individual episodes ("the psychological and sexual development of the protagonist") and the "Epílogo" (a synthesis of both series by means of an "outrageous parody of the womb").

3630 Anhalt, Nedda G. de. Eloísa Lezama Lima: una resistencia fogosa. (*Vuelta*, 12:143, oct. 1988, p. 24–31)

Interview with Lezama Lima's sister in the course of which Eloisa recounts her brother's views of literary life in revolutionary Cuba, various anecdotes from their childhood, and her assessment of his works. She regrets the publication in Cuba of her brother's adolescent poems or "la obra no pulida" (see also item **3631**).

3631 Armas, Emilio de. Inicio y escape de José Lezama Lima. (*Unión*, 3, julio/sept. 1987, p. 34–49)

Perceptive essay about Lezama Lima describes and comments on the manuscript of his first book of poems, *Inicio y escape*, whose date of composition appears to have been sometime between 1927–32. Poignant typographical mistake in the title *Inicio y escape de José Lez amaLima* discerns a Lezama who loves the (nail) file ("ama lima"), who loves to polish ("ama limar") his texts. Of course, Lezama is notorious for his own misspellings.

3632 Barnet, Miguel. Confesiones personales con palabras no escritas. (*Let. Cuba.*, enero/marzo 1987, p. 131–141, ill.)

Barnet talks about his early works of poetry (e.g., *La piedrafina y el pavorreal, La sagrada familia,*) his relation with other Cuban authors, and his research in New York for the novel *La vida real.*

3633 Barradas, Efraín. La seducción de las máscaras: José Alcántara Almánzar, Juan Bosch y la joven narrativa dominicana. (*Rev. Iberoam.*, 54:142, enero/marzo 1988, p. 11–25, bibl.)

Examines critical assessment of Juan Bosch by younger Dominican writers. Appraises differences between Bosch and others, especially José Alcántara Almánzar as representative of the younger group. Compares two short stories and their treatment of various literary or social issues: rural vs. urban setting, perspectives on sex, stylistic traits, degree of concern with literariness. Utilizes Harold Bloom's *Anxiety of influence* as a foundation for his reading "influences."

3634 Barsy, Kalman *et al.* El Tramo ancla: ensayos puertorriqueños de hoy. Edición de Ana Lydia Vega. Río Piedras: Editorial de la Univ. de Puerto Rico, 1989. 305 p. (Col. caribeña)

Collection of short essays on Puerto Rican life, literature and mores written by seven young Puerto Rican intellectuals. These informative, insightful and at times moving essays were previously published in *Claridad.*

3635 Benítez-Rojo, Antonio. Comments on Georgina Dopico Black's "The Limits of Expression: Intellectual Freedom in Postrevolutionary Cuba." (*Cuba. Stud.*, 20, 1990, p. 171–174)

Praises Black's article (see item **3636**) and states how literary works are also often rejected, confiscated or censored because of the authors' "improper conduct" rather than the "content or form" of the texts.

3636 Black, Georgina Dopico. The limits of expression: intellectual freedom in postrevolutionary Cuba. (*Cuba. Stud.*, 19, 1989, p. 107–142)

Detailed and analytical review of how, during different phases of Cuban cultural policy, socio political norms have been employed to "promote, prohibit or marginally tolerate" literary production. Excellent examination of censorship and self-censorship, illustrated by many examples of individual writers and literary genres.

3637 Bonafoux y Quintero, Luis. Ultramarinos. Edición de Socorro Girón. 2a ed. Ponce, P.R.: S. Girón, 1988. 305 p.: bibl.

New critical edition of Bonafoux's newspaper articles, first published in 1882. Fully annotated edition includes excellent bibliography.

3638 Bost, David H. History writing fiction: rediscovering America in *El mar de las* *lentejas.* (*SECOLAS Ann.*, 20, March 1989, p. 30–39, bibl.)

Uses Foucault and other Latin American historical novels in order to explore Benítez Rojo's novel, including aspects such as the process of historical identity in the course of which documentary materials are fictionally arranged to reconstitute a hi*story*.

3639 Bunke, Klaus. Testimonio-Literatur in Kuba: ein neues literarisches Genre zur Wirklichkeitsbeschreibung. Pfaffenweiler, Germany: Centaurus-Verlagsgesellschaft, 1988. 368 p.: bibl. (Reihe Sprach- und Literaturwissenschaft, 0177–2821; 12)

Overview of what the author considers a new genre—oral or written testimony as literature—uses examples from the Cuban Revolution and draws conclusions about Cuban society. A thorough examination of sources, including an index of testimonies. [G.M. Dorn]

3640 Cabrera, Francisco Manrique. Historia de la literatura puertorriqueña. Río Piedras, P.R.: Editorial Cultural, 1986. 384 p.: bibl., index. (Biblioteca de clásicos puertorriqueños)

Reprint of 1971 edition of useful history of Puerto Rican literature. Unfortunately, contents have not been updated since then.

3641 Carpentier, Alejo. Conferencias. Selección y edición de Virgilio López Lemus. La Habana: Editorial Letras Cubanas, 1987. 282 p. (Letras cubanas)

Selection of lectures (some are transciptions of "documentaries" filmed in 1973), prologues, political speeches and journalistic pieces from, among others: *Carteles; Bohemia; Gaceta de Cuba; Revolution y Cultura.*

3642 Carpentier, Alejo. Ensayos. La Habana: Editorial Letras Cubanas, 1984. 303 p.: bibl. (Letras cubanas)

Selection of essays drawn from *Tientos y diferencias, Razón de ser* and *La novela latinoamericana en vísperas de un nuevo siglo y otros ensayos.* Several were originally delivered as lectures. Also includes previously unpublished piece "Un Ascenso de Medio Siglo" (1977).

3643 Chaple, Sergio. A reply to Verity A. Smith's "Recent Trends in Cuban Criticism and Literature." (*Cuba. Stud.*, 20, 1990, p. 167–169)

Chaple regrets that Smith did not interview him during her 1987 trip to Cuba (see item **3690**). Points out several inaccuracies, especially concerning her characterization of Chaple's relationship with Desiderio Navarro. More to come from Smith, for sure.

3644 Chiampi, Irlemar. Sobre la teoría de la creación artística en *Los pasos perdidos*, de Alejo Carpentier. (*Cuad. Am.*, 14:2, marzo/abril 1989, p. 101–116)

Applies Vladimir Propp's functions to analyze pts. 19–32 of Chap. 5 of *Los pasos* in which the protagonist composes the threnody.

3645 Chiampi, Irlemar. Teoría de la imagen y teoría de la lectura en Lezama Lima. (*Casa Am.*, 30:177, nov./dic. 1989, p. 48–57)

"Lectura relacional (del texto como producto y de los textos que han influído en su productividad)" of the essay "Las Imágenes Posibles" (1948). Chiampi concludes that Lezama's essay should not be read as a poetics but as *poiesis* (creation and reception), that is as a production of the image by poet and reader. Lotman's model of the reader at work, as a text within a text producing meaning, comes to mind.

3646 Conferencia de Hispanistas, 6th, Saint Augustine, Trinidad and Tobago, 1983. La mujer en la literatura caribeña. St. Augustine, Trinidad: Univ. of the West Indies, 1983. 196 p.: bibl.

Proceedings of conference (Port-of-Spain, Trinidad and Tobago, April 1983) includes essays on Puerto Rican, Panamanian, Nicaraguan, Dominican, Cuban, and Colombian writers. Highlight is Ana Lydia Vega's essay on three Puerto Rican writers: Magali García Ramis, Carmen Lugo Filippi, and Carmen Valle.

3647 Criterios: Estudios de Teoría Literaria, Estética y Culturología Nos. 21–24, tercera época, enero 1987/dic. 1988– . La Habana: Casa de las Américas.

Special issue (made up of Nos. 21–24), consists of extraordinary collection of essays on variety of theoretical questions of literary analysis by renowned foreign critics. Four of 10 essays were read at "Primer Encuentro Internacional de Criterios" (La Habana,

Jan. 1987). Surprisingly, an essay, originally in Russian, has been translated not by Desiderio Navarro but by Rinaldo Acosta. *Criterios* is required reading for those interested in the politics of literary criticism in Cuba. Fredric Jameson and Jonathan Culler represented the US at the conference. Culler's essay "Post-Structuralist Criticism" is translated by Navarro.

3648 Dill, Hans-Otto. *El Siglo de las Luces* de Alejo Carpentier: la Revolución Francesa y el Caribe. (*Beitr. Roman. Philol.*, 28:2, 1989, p. 189–202)

Explores issues of revolutionary change as the creation of new dependencies in which Victor Hughes, *the merchant*, leads the way.

3649 Duchesne, Juan Ramón. Miguel Barnet y el testimonio como humanista. (*Rev. Crít. Lit. Latinoam.*, 13:26, 1987, p. 155–160)

Thoughtful essay on the ethnographic nature of testimonial narration. Exceptional for its semiotic considerations as it examines *Biografía de un cimarrón* in various contexts, from Plato to Bahktin, Lévi-Strauss to Gadamer, Martí to Fernando Ortiz and Barnet.

3650 Fama, Antonio. Cultura, historia e identidad en *Concierto barroco* de Alejo Carpentier. (*Rev. Crít. Lit. Latinoam.*, 14:27, 1988, p. 129–138)

Uses Lotman's *Semiótica de la cultura* to outline Carpentier's exploration of the "hybrid" nature of Latin American culture. Fama shows how European perceptions deprive the novel's characters of their Latin American authenticity, which is later recovered through transcodification of identity.

3651 Fernández Olmos, Margarita. La narrativa dominicana contemporánea: en busca de una salida. (*Rev. Iberoam.*, 54:142, enero/marzo 1988, p. 73–87)

Studies Pedro Vergés' *Sólo cenizas hallarás: bolero* (1980) and Efraím Castillo's *Curriculum: el síndrome de la visa* (1982). Using Jan Carew's and Angel Rama's discussions of the problems of economic and cultural marginalization, traces themes of exile and migration in both works.

Ferré, Rosario. Ofelia a la deriva en las aguas de la memoria. See item **5058.**

3652 Ferreras, Ramón Alberto. Negros. Santo Domingo: Editorial del Nordeste, 1983. 439 p. (Media isla; 4)

Book is dedicated to the *Negros jelofes* who carried out a slave insurrection during Christmas 1522. Chap. 4, "Hombres, Labores y Salarios" describes situation of black sugarcane cutters in a nutshell. Very informative work about Haitians in the Dominican Republic. Explains many of their rituals and adversities.

3653 González Echevarría, Roberto. Colón, Carpentier y los orígenes de la ficción latinoamericana. (*Torre*, 2:7, julio/sept. 1988, p. 439–452)

Examinando el uso que hace Carpentier de los textos de Colón en su última novela, *El arpa y la sombra* (1978), este trabajo explica por qué los novelistas latinoamericanos persisten en nutrir sus obras con "Crónicas de Indias." Varias características de éstas, que son la contrapartida de la novela moderna, explican esta persistencia: su calidad no literaria, de archivo que englobasaber y poder, su mezcla iconoclasta de discursos, su manipulación oficial de la información y su incapacidad de presentar la "verdad." En contacto con estos caracteres, el novelista moderno reconstruye el momento prístino de nombrar las cosas y hace de la historia latinoamericana un mito. Imprescindible para quien estudie las relaciones entre las letras del período colonial y la literatura contemporánea. [A.F. Bolaños]

3654 González Echevarría, Roberto. Cuban criticism and literature: a reply to Smith. (*Cuba. Stud.*, 19, 1989, p. 101–106)

González Echevarría responds to Smith (item **3690**) by defending his evaluation of the Cuban scene and pointing out that recent high-ranking appointments in the cultural bureaucracy suggest an increase of political control by lesser intellectual figures. Also refers to Castro's speeches and predicts that rectification will lead to "darker years."

3655 Graham-Jones, Jean and **Duleep Deosthale.** Interview with Guillermo Cabrera Infante. (*Mester*, 16:2, Fall 1987, p. 53–63)

Interview as stand-up comedy: Cabrera Infante talks about the movies and the theatre, his identity as an English subject who writes in Spanish, the words "word" "world" and "palabra," the title of a new book *Mea Cuba*.

3656 Hispanic immigrant writers and the identity question. v. 1–2. Edition and introduction by Silvio Torres-Saillant. Foreword by Pedro R. Monge. New York: Ollantay Press, 1989. 81 p. (Ollantay Press literature/conversation series; 1–2)

Vol. 1 is collection of papers and transcription of panelists' discussion with audience on topic of "Identity of Hispanic Writers in the New York Area," a symposium organized by the Ollantay Center for the Arts in Queens, N.Y. Also includes poems and short stories by panelists as well as good discussion of difficulty of designation "Hispanic" to refer to different nationalities. Vol. 2 ("Hispanic Immigrant Writers and the Family") includes readings by five Latin American creative writers of different cultural backgrounds who also present brief essays on the discussion topic. Includes photographs and transcription of "conversation" with the audience.

3657 Images and identities: the Puerto Rican in two world contexts. Edited by Asela Rodríguez de Laguna. New Brunswick, N.J: Transaction Books, 1987. 276 p.: bibl., index.

Excellent collection of essays which cover a gamut of topics, including Puerto Rican identity, ideology, literature and education. Very representative selections of important island and mainland authors.

3658 Irizarry, Estelle. La novelística de Enrique A. Laguerre: trayectoria histórica y literaria. Río Piedras, P.R.: Editorial Cultural, 1987. 213 p.: bibl., maps.

Comprehensive look at Laguerre's works, including how individual novels reflect the historical, political and social conditions in Puerto Rico. Includes stylistic analysis of the development of Laguerre's prose style and good bibliography and notes. Very useful work.

3659 Iznaga, Diana. La novela testimonio de Miguel Barnet: apuntes sobre una trilogía. (*Islas*, 83, enero/abril 1986, p. 123–141)

After stating that Barnet's *Biografía de un cimarrón*, *Canción de Rachel* and *Gallego* are out-of-print in Cuba, Iznaga Beira offers plot summaries and choice passages. In addition, she reviews Barnet's comments on these works and contrasts the lives and language of the novels' protagonists.

3660 Larson, Neil. ¿Como narrar el Trujillato? (*Rev. Iberoam.*, 54 : 142, enero/marzo 1988, p. 89–98)

According to author, the long Trujillo years (1930–61) have yet to be dealt with in Dominican fiction. Examines two works: 1) Juan Jimenes Grullón's *Una Gestapo en América* (1941), which is regarded as a superficial "historical portrait" of Trujillo and too 19th-century in its approach; and 2) Marcio Veloz Maggiolo's *De abril en adelante* (1975), which is much influenced by Cortázar and which attempts (and fails) to look at the Trujillo experience from a post-1965 perspective.

3661 Lezama Lima, José. Confluencias: selección de ensayos. Selección y prólogo de Abel E. Prieto. La Habana: Editorial Letras Cubanas, 1988. 429 p. (Letras cubanas)

Good selection of Lezama's essays, with an excellent prologue. Prieto successfully explains Lezama's poetic system. Less convincing is his presentation of Lezama's trail within the Revolution.

3662 Lezama Lima. Edición de Eugenio Suárez-Galbán. Madrid: Taurus, 1987. 398 p.: bibl. (Persiles; 182. Serie El Escritor y la crítica)

Assembles previously published articles on Lezama in the usual "El Escritor y la Crítica" mode. Selections are excellent.

3663 *Linden Lane Magazine*. Vol. 9, No. 4, oct./dic. 1990– . Princeton, N.J.: Linden Lane Magazine & Press.

Special double issue devoted to "Escritores y Artistas Cubanos en el Exilio." So many writers wished to participate that editors pledged to devote the next issue to the project.

3664 Luis, William. Literary bondage: slavery in Cuban narrative. Austin: Univ. of Texas Press, 1990. 1 v.: bibl. (Texas Pan American series)

Indispensable book for readers of the library of absences. Luis' commitment to texts outside the canon and his discerning analysis of discourse and counter-discourse of classic and contemporary anti-slavery narratives make him an essential critic today.

3665 Mac Adam, Alfred J. Seeing double: Cabrera Infante and Caín. (*World Lit. Today*, Autumn 1987, p. 543–548, bibl.)

Comprehensive review of Cabrera Infante's early literary activities in Cuba, especially his work as a film critic. Relates GCI's political activities before and after 1959 and includes many discerning comparisons to other literary figures (e.g., Eliot, Borges). Explores the relationship of biography and autobiography in the writings of GCI.

Márquez, Roberto. Nationalism, nation, and ideology: trends in the emergence of a Caribbean literature. See item **3277.**

3666 Martínez, Julio A. Fuentes bibliográficas para el estudio de la literatura cubana moderna. (*Rev. Interam. Bibliogr.*, 36:4, 1986, p. 473–485)

Essay achieves objective of its title as an informative piece on the bibliographical source (histories, bibliographies, dictionaries, anthologies, monographs) for the study of Cuban literature.

3667 Montero, Jenny. La cuentística dominicana. Santo Domingo: Biblioteca Nacional, 1986. 221 p.: bibl., ill., index. (Col. Orfeo)

Anthology of Dominican folktales and short stories preceded by Montero's introduction which sketches a basic concept of oral tales (i.e., "cuentos de camino") by using Propp. Montero also reviews short-story writing till 1965 emphasizing Juan Bosch and making an uneven appraisal of the ensuing historical processes and literary responses.

3668 Montero, Oscar. The name game: writing/fading writer in *De donde son los cantantes.* Chapel Hill: U.N.C. Dept. of Romance Languages: Univ. of North Carolina Press, 1988. 149 p.: bibl. (North Carolina studies in the Romance languages and literatures; 231)

Montero's work may be called "fair play with Sarduy." Sets down clearly the Lacanian rules of the analysis; works tenaciously at the edges of the reading table; and executes a winning hand with a well-worn French deck.

3669 Morales Carrión, Arturo. Mirada a ultramar. San Juan, P.R.: Biblioteca de Autores Puertorriqueños, 1985. 74 p. (Biblioteca de autores puertorriqueños)

Collection of short journalistic pieces which appeared in the Puerto Rican magazine *Avance* (1972–73). Most consist of political reflections on current events. Well-written and insightful, these essays are valuable to readers interested in political events of the early 1970s, especially as they relate to Puerto Rico.

3670 Moreiras, Alberto. Despatriación y política en la novela de Severo Sarduy. (*Rev. Crít. Lit. Latinoam.*, 14:27, 1988, p. 167–174, bibl.)

Departing from Enrico M. Santi's essay "Textual Politics: Severo Sarduy," Moreiras asserts that Heidegger's *Heimatlosigkeit* ("despatriación") and *Namenlosen* ("desnominación") can best describe Sarduy's work as journeying away from "patria" and "nombre."

3671 Navarro, Desiderio. La teoría y la crítica literarias: también una cuestión moral. (*Casa Am.*, 27:158, sept./oct. 1986, p. 134–161)

Here Navarro answers Guillermo Rodríguez Rivera's "Del Plagio, la Teoría y la Crítica," where GRR attempts to refute Navarro's charge that he had committed plagiarism in another article. All the dirty laundry under the Cuban sun.

3672 Navarro, Noel. Techo y sepultura. La Habana: Editorial Letras Cubanas, 1984. 428 p. (Ocuje)

According to Navarro, during a period he refers to as "epoca seudorrepublicana," it was easier to find one's grave than a roof over one's head. The work describes a ramshackle town in Cuba on the eve of the Revolution, a place in which political assassinations are routine, corpses float down rivers, ambulances go shrieking by.

3673 Nelson, Ardis L. *Holy smoke:* anatomy of a vice. (*World Lit. Today*, Autumn 1987, p. 590–597, photo)

Splendid essay on Cabrera Infante's first book in English. Analyzes its multilingual play as a Bakhtinesque Menippean version of the world of smoke from its "discovery" by Columbus to the Surgeon General labels.

3674 *Orígenes: revista de arte y literatura.* v. 1–7. Ed. facsimilar. México: El Equilibrista; Madrid: Ediciones Turner, 1989.

Facsimile edition of all issues of the literary magazine *Orígenes*, including two different printings of Nos. 35 and 36, after Lezama and Rodríguez Feo went their separate ways. Includes superb introduction, photographs, and comprehensive index.

3675 Palmer Bermúdez, Neyssa S. Las mujeres en los cuentos de René Marqués.

Río Piedras, P.R.: Editorial de la Univ. de Puerto Rico, 1988. 103 p.: bibl.

Very thorough look at the treatment of women in Puerto Rican short fiction and in the short stories of René Marqués. Provides sound psychological and stylistic analysis of female characters in Marqués' works. Contains good bibliography of primary and secondary sources.

3676 Pellón, Gustavo. José Lezama Lima's joyful vision: a study of *Paradiso* and other prose works. Austin: Univ. of Texas Press, 1989. 151 p.: bibl., ill., index. (The Texas Pan American series)

Stimulating introduction to Lezama Lima. After reviewing the different approaches to *Paradiso*, Pellón offers his reading of several important passages from Lezama's prose. Study is most illuminating for its comparative, intertextual, intersemiotic, strategies.

3677 Pellón, Gustavo. Portrait of the Cuban writer as French painter: Henri Rousseau, José Lezama Lima's alter ego. (*MLN*, 103:2, March 1988, p. 350–373)

Compares the relationship that Lezama and Rousseau each had with their respective cultural systems and explores Lezama's identification with Rousseau. Notes the similarities in the reception accorded to the works of both artists.

3678 Pensamiento y política cultural cubanos: antología. v. 2–4. Recopilación de Nuria Nuiry Sánchez y Graciela Fernández Mayo. La Habana: Editorial Pueblo y Educación, 1986–1987.

Selection of texts underpins cultural policies and political objectives of the Cuban Revolution: 1) its Afro-Cuban agenda (see selections in vol. 2 of Fernando Ortiz and Ernesto Che Guevara); 2) "El Quijote de La Habana" by Nicolás Guillén in vol. 3; and 3) Documents about (centralized) cultural initiatives (e.g., "Creación del ICAIC, 1959" and "Derecho de Autor, 1977" in vol. 4).

3679 Pérez Firmat, Gustavo. The Cuban condition: translation and identity in modern Cuban literature. Cambridge; New York: Cambridge Univ. Press, 1989. 185 p.: bibl., index. (Cambridge studies in Latin American and Iberian literature; 1)

Insightful essay examines particular modulations of the "Cuban voice" in several *criollista* texts. Its characteristics are seen as inextricably consolidated within a nationalist project and a transnational process. Concludes with a reading of Carpentier's *Los pasos perdidos:* a novel "written in a language that cannot be Spanish but refuses to be English."

3680 Pérez León, Roberto. Lezama, en la desmesura de la imagen: Premio Crítica 1985. La Habana: Depto. de Actividades Culturales Univ. de la Habana, 1987. 53 p.: bibl.

In the prologue Reynaldo González hopes that this essay will contribute to the "rescue" of Lezama from manipulative foreign critics. What follows is a simple list of Lezama quotations about three themes: Martí, food, and the city of Habana. We can imagine that "lo que (Pérez León) sabía de (Lezama) era infinitamente más de lo que nos dejó dicho."

3681 Ramos, Josean. Palabras de mujer. San Juan, P.R.: Editorial Univ. de América, 1988. 224 p.: ill., ports.

Wonderful, evocative "memoirs" from Felisa Rincón, former Mayor of San Juan and the woman who brought snow to the children of San Juan.

3682 Relaciones culturales soviético-cubanas: ¿cómo serán? (*Am. Lat./Moscú*, 2, 1990, p. 53–68, photos)

Transcription of round table discussion held in Moscow, at offices of the journal *América Latina* (June 25, 1989) the opening day of the "Primer Congreso de los Diputados del Pueblo de la URSS." One gathers from the interchange that, due to bureaucratic incompetence, the Cuban and Soviet peoples have been misinforming each other about their respective cultures since the signing of their first cultural agreement (1960). If Cuba is, as Carlos Martí Brenes remarks, the "puente natural entre los países socialistas y los de América Latina," few cultural products can be expected to cross that bridge under present Cuban conditions. Conspicuous by his absence at this meeting is Desiderio Navarro, who is mentioned and described by Luisa Campuzano as "un erudito en cultorología [sic] soviética."

3683 Rensoli Laliga, Lourdes. La cultura del poeta: la filosofía en el *Diario de José*

Lezama Lima. (*Rev. Bibl. Nac. José Martí,* 31:3, sept./dic. 1989, p. 73–99, bibl.)

Contends that Platonism is the central guide to Lezama's reflections in his diary (Oct. 18, 1939 to July 31, 1949). Concludes that for Lezama, the poet is a mystagogue who prepares others, by means of his orphic talents and the virtue of song, for an initiation into a deeper view of reality.

3684 Repilado, Ricardo. Cosecha de dos parcelas. La Habana: Editorial Letras Cubanas, 1985. 416 p. (Col. Crítica)

Excellent anthology of Repilado's essays. Vintage gathering from his native research grounds: readings of archival materials (e.g., correspondence of Céspedes) and of works by various contemporary writers (e.g., Fernández Retamar, Vitier, Soler Puig). Book opens with essays on Proust and Alfonso Reyes.

3685 Riccio, Alessandra. Lezama y la posibilidad infinita de Martí. (*Unión*, 3, julio/sept. 1987, p. 4–19)

Quoting extensively from Lezama on Martí (his image, his death), and drawing from Cintio Vitier's analysis of Lezama's poem "la casa del alibi," Riccio develops an informative comparative essay.

3686 Rosario Candelier, Bruno. Tendencias de la novela dominicana. Santiago, República Dominicana: PUCMM, 1988. 378 p.: ill. (Col. Estudios; 136)

After recounting main polemics of 1970 symposium on the novel in which discussion focused on the quality of the Dominican contribution to the genre, Rosario Candelier presents his "theory of the novel" and the historical factors that have conditioned its development in the Republic. Of great interest are three written responses to a questionnaire about the novel (Carlos Federico Pérez, Carlos Esteban Deive, Francisco Nolasco Cordero) and the transcription of three interviews (Aída Cartagena Portalatín, Manuel Mora Serrano, Marcio Veloz Maggiolo).

3687 Sarduy, Severo. Ensayos generales sobre el Barroco. México: Fondo de Cultura Económica, 1987. 323 p.: bibl., ill. (Col. Tierra firme)

This is Sarduy's "Summa Barroca" (or "General Theory of the Baroque"), with essays from *Escrito sobre un cuerpo* (1969), *Barroco* (1974), *La simulación* (1982) and

more recent material from *Nueva inestabilidad* (minus the illustrations). Here, Sarduy focuses on the manner scientists present new interpretations of natural phenomena. New visions require a convincing imagination, and a writer that can articulate transitions to new symbolic stages. Sarduy's view of the scientific world places him in the company of enthusiastically perplexed *Scientific American* "readers." Indispensable book for understanding his other fictions.

3688 Sarduy, Severo. Nueva inestabilidad. México: Vuelta, 1987. 71 p.: bibl., ill. (La Reflexión)

Retombée, achronic (coexistent) causality or discontinued (distant) similarity (creative writing and criticism as a double of cosmological speculation, against all hierarchy) takes Sarduy back to the first Baroque (origin?) and big-bangs to present (distant) reflections on scientific theories ever in the making. The last section "Fórmulas para Salir a la Luz," a knockout of a parody, cites fragments from ancient texts (and commentaries on them) and concludes with Sarduy's own simple verses accompanied by simple illustrations.

3689 Sklodowska, Elzbieta. Miguel Barnet: hacia la poética de la novela testimonial. (*Rev. Crít. Lit. Latinoam.*, 14:27, 1988, p. 139–149)

Useful and succinct account of the conflictive evolution of "the canonization of the peripheral and the marginalization of the canon" as shown in Barnet's tetralogy about the lives of Esteban Montejo (a runaway slave), "Rachel" (a chorus girl), Manuel Ruiz (a Galician immigrant in Cuba) and Julián Mesa (a Cuban emigrant in the United States). Sklodowska emphasizes the alternative offered by the ideological posture and poetics of the testimonial novel as contrasted with the "boom" esthetics.

3690 Smith, Verity A. Recent trends in Cuban criticism and literature. (*Cuba. Stud.*, 19, 1989, p. 81–99)

Smith's main purpose is to bring up to date González Echevarría's 1981 article "Criticism and Literature in Revolutionary Cuba" (see HLAS 44:5350). She reports on a 1987 trip to Cuba and maintains that the recent process of "rectification" of Cuban cultural policy makes González Echevarría's original assessments too categorical. She disagrees primarily on the degree of marginalization of Desiderio Navarro and Sergio Chaple (see also item **3643**).

3691 Smorkaloff, Pamela María. Literatura y edición de libros: la cultura literaria y el proceso social en Cuba. La Habana: Editorial Letras Cubanas, 1987. 372 p.: bibl. (Ensayo)

Social history of book production in Cuba. Following a review of the history of the publishing industry before 1959, the author presents an informative examination of the publishing policies for 1959–86.

3692 Tomos: Cincuentenario de la Biblioteca de Autores Puertorriqueños, 1935–1985. San Juan: Biblioteca de Autores Puertorriqueños, 1986. 341 p.: bibl., facsims. (Biblioteca de autores puertorriqueños)

Annotated catalog of publications of the Biblioteca de Autores Puertorriqueños (1935–present). Excerpts from major works and individual poems are also reproduced as part of the catalog.

3693 Valdés Carreras, Oscar. *El Habanero:* precursor; *Patria:* soldado. (*Univ. La Habana,* 233, sept./dic. 1988, p. 87–102)

Concise review of the history of the two publications. author compares Varela's "Mi América" with Martí's "Nuestra América" as well as their key passages about *patria* and *pueblo.* Article ends with reference to Varela's belief that Cuba's independence was inevitable.

3694 Valero, Roberto. El desamparado humor de Reinaldo Arenas. Miami, Fla.: Univ. of Miami, North-South Center, 1991. 412 p: bibl. (Col. Letras de Oro)

Cover shows photo of Roberto Valero and Reinaldo Arenas side by side, in Cuba(?). This is a hallucinatory book by an author too close (perhaps) to his subject. Nevertheless, a must reading for students of Arenas. After two long chapters devoted to a historical review of the impossibility of defining humor, Valera offers a unique critical analysis of all of Arenas' works. His reading, which refers to many Arenas scholars, critical theory, lost manuscripts and unpublished materials, is not limited to the themes of "humor y desolación." This study won the 1988–89 "Letras de Oro" Prize.

3695 Vásquez, Carmen. Acerca del *Retrato de un dictador* de Alejo Carpentier. (*Rev. Bibl. Nac. José Martí,* 30:3, sept./dic. 1988, p. 77–96)

Examination of Carpentier's literary and political activities in Europe before the fall of Machado serves as introduction to the text *Retrato de un dictador,* originally published in the magazine *Octubre* (Madrid, 1933). Vásquez makes a valuable contribution to the studies of the sources of Carpentier's dictator novel *El recurso del método.*

Andean Countries

JOSE MIGUEL OVIEDO, *Professor of Spanish, University of Pennsylvania*
RAYMOND LESLIE WILLIAMS, *Professor of Spanish, University of Colorado at Boulder*

DURANTE EL PERIODO CUBIERTO por este volumen, el predominio, cualitativo y cuantitativo, de la producción crítica sobre temas colombianos y peruanos sigue siendo dominante en el área; y, dentro de esa producción, los autores favoritos continúan siendo por cierto García Márquez y Vargas Llosa. Entre las obras dedicadas al primero, deben mencionarse las recopilaciones críticas realizadas por Harold Bloom (item **3700**) y por McGuirk y R. Cardwell (item **3699**). Otras recopilaciones son el fruto de reuniones académicas centradas en diversos temas de literatura contemporánea, algunos tan consabidos como el de literatura y violencia (item **3705**). En las recopilaciones de su producción crítica personal (items **3258** y **3696**), el colombiano Cobo Borda ofrece un poco de todo: ensayos, artículos, notas, entrevistas, que dan testimonio de su intensa actividad intelectual. Entre las recopilaciones dedicadas a la obra de un autor individual, las que se consagran a Alvaro Mutis (item **3703**) y a Fernando Charry Lara (item **4241**) merecen destacarse. Igualmente, se destaca una curiosa exhumación literaria: el hallazgo y publicación del *Diario secreto de Vargas Vila* (item **3704**).

Entre los trabajos críticos sobre Vargas Llosa, el aporte más valioso es el de Leopoldo Bernucci, que estudia su relación con Euclides da Cunha (item **3710**). Pero la mayor parte de estudios y recopilaciones dedicados a la literatura peruana tienen un marcado carácter de revisión y recuento de viejas o recientes tradiciones literarias. Esa es la intención principal en los trabajos aquí citados de Cornejo Polar (item **3711**) y Ortega (item **3717**), pero también en las selecciones de textos de autores como Vallejo (item **3719**), Ventura García Calderón (item **3713**) y Mariátegui (item **3715**). El volumen colectivo que revalúa el aporte creador y los contextos sociales de la "generación del 50" (item **4210**) inicia un proyecto crítico que puede resultar valioso.

Del Ecuador los trabajos de mayor interés son los dedicados a Pedro Jorge Vera (item **3707**) y Nelson Estupiñán (item **3708**), que representan inflexiones distintas de la novelística realista y comprometida del país; ambos libros tienen el mérito además de ser los primeros estudios de cierta extensión que se publican sobre esos autores. Y entre las contribuciones críticas sobre literatura venezolana cabe mencionar la edición de un volumen con dos novelas y un conjunto de relatos de Salvador Garmendia, más aparato crítico, dentro de la bien conocida Biblioteca Ayacucho (item **3722**). [JMO]

Major writers of the Andean region, such as Gabriel García Márquez and Mario Vargas Llosa, continued writing fiction, and publishers in the region were quite active. Caracas, Bogotá, Quito, Lima, and La Paz served as centers of a flourishing publishing industry, including such outlets as Editorial Planeta (which published national editions in Venezuela, Colombia and Ecuador), Tercer Mundo Editores, Editorial Oveja Negra (which distributed throughout the Andean region), and others. Colombia, which has been historically weak in publishing, became a leader in the Andean region.

Andean novelists, like many Latin American writers, have recently abandoned the grand schemes and "totalizing" works that had characterized much of their previous writing. García Márquez's *El general en su laberinto* (item **3737**) and Vargas Llosa's *El elogio de la madrastra* (item **3760**), for example, are far less ambitious and shorter than many of these writers' previous novels. Generally speaking, Andean writers published relatively brief and accessible works. Writers who published light and entertaining narrative fiction were the Ecuadorian Demetrio Aguilera Malta, the Peruvian Julio Ramón Ribeyro, and the Colombians Alvaro Mutis and Marco Tulio Aguilera Garramuño. Aguilera Malta's novel appeared posthumously (item **3745**), Ribeyro wrote a humorous and nostalgic volume of short fiction (item **3759**), and Mutis continued to novelize the life of a mythic character in the second volume of a series (item **3739**).

Several younger writers published very well written novels, including those by such recognized figures as the Peruvian Alfredo Bryce Echenique (item **3756**), the Venezuelan Denzil Romero (item **3763**), and the Peruvian Harry Belevan (item **3755**). Other young writers to appear on the scene were the Ecuadorian Eliécer Cárdenas Espinosa (item **3746**), and the Colombians Eduardo García Aguilar (item **3736**), Roberto Burgos Cantor (item **3732**), Evelio Rosero Diago (item **3741**), and Harold Kremer (item **3738**).

In accordance with a Latin American tradition, many Andean novelists assumed the role of social critics. Ecuador's Abdón Ubidia (item **3749**) and Jorge Velasco MacKenzie (item **3750**) published novels portraying the urban marginalized. Other social critics whose novels offered a contestatory voice were the Ecuadorian Alicia Yáñez Cossío (item **3752**), the Colombian Gustavo Alvarez Gardeazábal (item **3730**), the Ecuadorian Pedro Jorge Vera (items **3751, 3706,** and **3707**), and the Colombian Fernando Vallejo (items **3743** and **3744**). Each used a variety of techniques to denounce specific institutions in their respective countries.

Some novels produced in the late 1980s reflected a tendency toward reconsidering the political history of the 1960s. These revisionist works were typically written by authors involved in social and political movements in the university during the 1960s. Authors engaged in this type of revisionism were the Venezuelan Alicia Freilich (item **3764**), the Ecuadorian Raúl Pérez Torres (item **3747**), and the Peruvian Angel Avendaño (item **3753**).

The Andean region even witnessed the rare publication of erotic fiction with the appearance of the writing of the Venezuelan Rubén Monasterios (item **3762**) and the Colombian Marco Tulio Aguilera Garramuño (items **3728** and **3729**). [RLW]

LITERARY CRITICISM AND HISTORY
Colombia

3696 Cobo Borda, Juan Gustavo. La narrativa colombiana después de García Márquez y otros ensayos. Bogotá: Tercer Mundo Editores, 1989. 343 p.: (Crítica literaria)

Otra de las ya frecuentes recopilaciones de trabajos críticos del autor. Pese al título no sólo cubre narrativa colombiana, sino otros géneros y autores, como Borges, Rilke y Emir Rodríguez Monegal. [JMO]

3697 Congreso de Colombianistas, 5th, Cartagena, Colombia, 1988. De ficciones y realidades: perspectivas sobre literatura e historia colombianas; memorias. Recopilación de Alvaro Pineda Botero y Raymond L. Williams. Bogotá: Tercer Mundo Editores; Cartagena: Univ. de Cartagena, 1989. 397 p.: (Crítica literaria)

En estas actas del V Congreso de la Asociación de Colombianistas el lector encontrará un variado material crítico cuyos focos son las obras de Alvaro Cepeda Samudio, García Márquez, R.H. Moreno Durán, entre otros tópicos de literatura e historia colombiana. [JMO]

3698 Encuentro de la Asociación de Colombianistas, 1st, Antioquia, Colombia, 1984. Ensayos de literatura colombiana. Recopilación de Raymond L. Williams. Bogotá: Plaza & Janés, 1985. 283 p.: (Narrativa colombiana)

Fruto de una reunión de especialistas extranjeros, la mayoría de Estados Unidos, realizada en Antioquia en 1984, el presente volumen examina cuestiones literarias nacionales con un criterio regional (la literatura antioqueña, la literatura costeña) y dedica la última sección a nuevos autores y perspectivas, así como a temas de carácter político. [JMO]

3699 Gabriel García Márquez: new readings. Edited by Bernard McGuirk and Richard Andrew Cardwell. Cambridge; New York: Cambridge Univ. Press, 1987. 230 p.: (Cambridge Iberian and Latin American studies)

Este nuevo repertorio crítico sobre el autor fue concebido en 1983, después de que le otorgasen el Premio Nobel a García Márquez. A pesar del retraso con el que aparece, el volumen conserva interés pues ofrece aplicaciones de muy variados métodos críticos: formalista, antropológico, psicoanalítico, deconstructivo, etc. [JMO]

3700 Gabriel García Márquez. Edited and introduced by Harold Bloom. New York: Chelsea House, 1989. 306 p.: bibl., index. (Modern critical views)

Importante repertorio de trabajos críticos dedicados al novelista por autores norteamericanos e hispanoamericanos. Incluye aportes sustantivos, como los de Mario Vargas Llosa, Roberto González Echevarría y Michael Palencia-Roth. [JMO]

3701 García Ramos, Juan Manuel. *Cien años de soledad* de Gabriel García Márquez. Madrid: Alhambra, 1989. 107 p.: bibl., ill. (Guías de lectura; 3)

Esta es la guía de lectura más simple y breve que se pueda conseguir sobre la novela, a pesar de lo cual cubre suficientemente los aspectos principales del libro, incluyendo aspectos de enfoque narrativo, estructura, lenguaje, etc. [JMO]

3702 Pineda Botero, Alvaro. Del mito a la posmodernidad: la novela colombiana de finales del siglo XX. Bogotá: Tercer Mundo Editores, 1990. 212 p.: (Crítica literaria)

Es en el fondo un mero recuento o registro de novelas colombianas publicadas en la década del 80. La breve bibliografía del género que se ofrece al final del libro, quizá sea lo más valioso. [JMO]

3703 Tras las rutas de Maqroll el Gaviero: 1981–1988. Edición de Santiago Mutis Durán. Cali, Colombia: Proartes; Bogotá: Revista Literaria Gradiva, 1988. 418 p.: bibl., ill.

Fruto de un homenaje que se le rindió al autor en Cali en 1988, este valioso repertorio incluye tributos poéticos, numerosos trabajos críticos, algunas de páginas de creación de Alvaro Mutis, entrevistas y una extensa bibliografía. [JMO]

3704 Vargas Vila, José María. Diario secreto. Selección, introducción y notas de Consuelo Triviño. Bogotá: Arango Editores: Ancora Editores, 1989. 209 p.: ill.

Este es un verdadero hallazgo que se añade a la curiosa y escandalosa obra literaria del autor colombiano: Consuelo Treviño encontró y consultó las páginas de este diario, gracias a una información dada—según dice—por el propio Fidel Castro. La investigadora lo presenta con una introducción y una cronología. [JMO]

3705 Violencia y literatura en Colombia. Edición de Jonathan Tittler. Madrid: Orígenes, 1989. 223 p.: (Col. Tratados de crítica literaria)

El IV Congreso de la Asociación de Colombianistas no sólo se ocupó del soco-

rrido tema que las actas anuncian, sino de otros asuntos más generales de cultura y política nacionales, como el auge de las telenovelas y el proceso de pacificación. [JMO]

Ecuador

3706 Calderón Chico, Carlos. Pedro Jorge Vera se confiesa: política y literatura. Quito: Fondo Editorial de la UNP, 1985. 123 p., 1 leaf of plates: ill.

Contiene un largo diálogo con el narrador, en el que algunas preguntas del entrevistador son más extensas que las respuestas del entrevistado. La edición, modestísima, no incluye ni una bibliografía de Vera y ni siquiera un índice general. [JMO]

3707 Haritos, Mary J. Las novelas de Pedro Jorge Vera. Quito: Univ. Central del Ecuador, 1989. 133 p.:

En el que seguramente debe ser el primer libro crítico dedicado al novelista, la autora discute sobre todo las relaciones de su obra con las tesis del compromiso y la interpretación marxista que sostuvieron los hombres del Grupo de Guayaquil. Concluye que la obra de Vera contradice las fórmulas que él mismo ha defendido. [JMO]

3708 Richards, Henry J. La jornada novelística de Nelson Estupiñán Bass: búsqueda de la perfección. Quito: Editorial El Conejo, 1989. 149 p.: (Col. Ecuador/letras)

Primer trabajo crítico de cierta extensión que se le consagra al novelista. Analiza cada una de sus siete novelas y cubre aspectos esenciales de esa obra, como el componente ideológico, modo metaficcional, conciencia histórica, etc. Se trata de un aporte bastante valioso. [JMO]

Romero Arteta, Oswaldo. La literatura ecuatoriana en las tesis doctorales de las universidades norteamericanas desde 1943 a 1985. See item **48.**

3709 Sacoto, Antonio. Sobre el ensayo ecuatoriano contemporáneo. Quito: Centro de Investigación y Cultura, Banco Central del Ecuador, 1988. 160 p.: (Testimonio de la palabra; 3)

El estudio de este género en Ecuador es muy escaso. El autor brinda información interesante sobre su desarrollo a partir del medio siglo, pero habría sido más valioso que aparte de publicar sus entrevistas a seis ensayistas contemporáneos, hubiese hecho también un examen crítico de sus obras. [JMO]

Peru

3710 Bernucci, Leopoldo M. Historia de un malentendido: un estudio transtextual de *La guerra del fin del mundo* de Mario Vargas Llosa. New York: P. Lang, 1989. 242 p.: (Univ. of Texas studies in contemporary Spanish-American fiction, 0888–8787; 5)

Riguroso estudio de "intertextualidad" entre *Os sertões* de Euclydes da Cunha y *La guerra del fin del mundo* de Vargas Llosa, que muestra las deudas concretas que éste tiene con su modelo, así como sus variantes y divergencias creadoras. [JMO]

3711 Cornejo Polar, Antonio. La formación de la tradición literaria en el Perú. Lima: Centro de Estudios y Publicaciones, 1989. 199 p.: bibl., ill. (CEP; 97)

Haciendo un planteamiento polémico, el autor estudia la forma cómo aparecen en el Perú las tradiciones constitutivas de su literatura moderna y contemporánea: costumbrismo, nacionalismo, indianismo, indigenismo, etc. El propósito es mostrar la convivencia de formas literarias alternativas al lado de las hegemónicas. [JMO]

3712 Encuentro de Narradores Peruanos, 1st, Arequipa, Peru, 1965. Primer encuentro de narradores peruanos. 2a ed. Lima: Latinoamericana Editores, 1986. 269 p.

Se trata de una reedición del volumen del mismo título aparecido en 1965 y cuyo mayor interés hoy es de presentar testimonios personales de autores ya desaparecidos como José María Arguedas, Ciro Alegría y Sebastián Salazar Bondy. [JMO]

3713 García Calderón, Ventura. Obra literaria selecta. Selección y prólogo de Luis Alberto Sánchez. Caracas: Biblioteca Ayacucho, 1989. 317 p.: (Biblioteca Ayacucho; 139)

Con un breve pero suficiente prólogo de Luis Alberto Sánchez, ofrece una amplia selección de la obra en prosa y verso del escritor novecentista peruano, y hace accesibles (por primera vez en mucho tiempo) textos que necesitan relectura y revisión. [JMO]

3714 Manuel González Prada, profeta olvidado: seis entrevistas y un apunte. Edición de Willy F. Pinto Gamboa. Lima: Editorial Cibeles, 1985. 144 p.

El breve volumen reúne seis entrevistas, sólo algunas "olvidadas" como anuncia el título, realizadas al escritor por Mariátegui, Valdelomar, Vallejo y otros. Material útil para fijar la imagen que del autor tenían los hombres de su tiempo. [JMO]

3715 Mariátegui, José Carlos. Invitación a la vida heroica: antología. Selección y presentación de Alberto Flores Galindo y Ricardo Portocarrero Grados. Prólogo de Javier Mariátegui Chiappe. Lima: Instituto de Apoyo Agrario, 1989. 450 p.: (Serie Tiempo de historia; 5)

La novedad de esta antología es que recoge, en orden rigurosamente cronológico, más de un centenar de artículos, poemas y otros textos escritos por Mariátegui entre 1911–30. Su lectura permite observar el proceso de su vida intelectual y la variedad de intereses que la definieron. [JMO]

3716 Muñoz, Silverio. José María Arguedas y el mito de la salvación por la cultura. Lima: Editorial Horizonte, 1987. 174 p.: bibl. (Crítica literaria; 5)

El crítico chileno se concentra en dos libros iniciales de Arguedas (*Agua* y *Yawar fiesta*) para tratar de mostrar cómo evoluciona desde un "realismo" marcado por ciertos ideas de Maríategui, a una visión integradora de la cultura mestiza. [JMO]

O'Brien, Mac Gregor. Bibliografía de las revistas literarias peruanas. See item **45.**

3717 Ortega, Julio. Crítica de la identidad: la pregunta por el Perú en su literatura. México: Fondo de Cultura Económica, 1988. 223 p.: (Col. Tierra firme)

Una revisión muy personal de la forma cómo se va configurando la literatura peruana en ciertos momentos de su historia. Comienza con Guamán Poma y termina con Vargas Llosa, pero toma en consideración también a autores menos conocidos, como Juan de Arona y Luis Loayza. [JMO]

3718 Tenorio García, Víctor. Siete estudios del cuento peruano. Lima: CONCYTEC, 1988. 120 p.: bibl.

Usando el esquema estructuralista de análisis textual, el autor intenta una lectura detallada de narraciones breves de A. Valde-lomar, Ciro Alegría, J.M. Arguedas, J. Diez Canseco, J.R. Ribeyro, E. Congrains Martín y M. Vargas Llosa. Es una típica aplicación de la técnica general de explicación de textos en clase. [JMO]

Valcárcel Carnero, Rosina. Mitos: domina-ción y resistencia andina. See *HLAS* 51:1109.

3719 Vallejo, César. La cultura peruana: crónicas. Prólogo, recopilación, selec-ción, traducciones y notas de Enrique Ballón Aguirre. Lima: Mosca Azul Editores, 1987. 240 p.:

De su extensa obra periodística, la mayor parte escrita en Europa, se han entre-sacado estos 45 artículos cuyo tema es el Perú y su cultura. Algunos tienen interés para observar la evolución intelectual del au-tor. La exigencia del prologuista para que se haga la lectura "materialista" de estos textos, parace hoy más trasnochada que nunca. [JMO]

3720 Vargas Llosa, Mario. . . . Sobre la vida y la política: diálogo con Vargas Llosa [por] Ricardo A. Setti; Ensayos y conferencias [de] Mario Vargas Llosa. Buenos Aires: Edito-rial InterMundo, 1989. 271 p.: ill.

Hay en el volumen dos partes distin-tas: 1) un extenso diálogo con el autor; y 2) textos de algunas de sus conferencias y ensa-yos. Después de la aparición de los volú-menes de *Contra viento y marea*, la utilidad de esta sección es mucho menor. [JMO]

Venezuela

Discursos académicos. v. 1. See item **3121.**

3721 El ensayo literario en Venezuela: siglo XX; antología. v. 1. Edición de Gabriel Jiménez Emán. Caracas: Ediciones La Casa de Bello, 1987. 1 v.: (Col. Zona tórrida; 6: Antologías y selecciones)

Aunque se presenta como una antolo-gía, esta obra es más bien un catálogo: siendo sólo el vol. 1 de una recopilación mayor, pre-senta 22 ensayistas contemporáneos, el úl-timo de los cuales es un autor nacido en 1912. Más de 600 p. para cubrir ese período parece algo excesivo. [JMO]

3722 Garmendia, Salvador. *Los pequeños seres; Memorias de Altagracia* y otros

relatos. Edición de Oscar Rodríguez Ortiz. Caracas: Biblioteca Ayacucho, 1989. 321 p.: bibl. (Biblioteca Ayacucho; 143)

La primera novela (1950) y una mucho más reciente (1974) del narrador venezolano se reúnen aquí, junto con ocho cuentos, todo ello acompañado por un prólogo, cronología y bibliografía preparados por Oscar Rodríguez Ortiz. [JMO]

3723 Garrels, Elizabeth. Las grietas de la ternura: nueva lectura de Teresa de la Parra. Caracas: Monte Avila Editores, 1987. 150 p.: (Estudios)

Polémico trabajo que trata de demos-trar que, pese a lo generalmente afirmado, la novela *Las memorias de la Mamá Blanca* comparte el "espíritu feminista" de nuestro tiempo, lo que la haría una obra precursora. El análisis textual es minucioso, aunque a veces algo forzado para acomodar su tesis. [JMO]

Instituto de Investigaciones Literarias Gon-zalo Picón Febres. Diccionario general de la literatura venezolana. v. 1–2. See item **92.**

Ocampo López, Javier. Los orígenes ideológi-cos de Colombia contemporánea. See item **5373.**

3724 Uslar Pietri, Arturo. Arturo Uslar Pie-tri: semana de autor. Madrid: Instituto de Cooperación Iberoamericana, Ediciones Cultura Hispánica, 1988. 122 p.

Transcribe los diálogos sostenidos con el autor en la semana de homenaje que reci-bió en Madrid en 1986. Esos diálogos cubren los varios aspectos de su obra y persona: su actividad política, su labor periodística, sus ensayos y, sobre todo, la cuestión del "rea-lismo mágico," noción de la cual el autor es un pionero algo olvidado. [JMO]

PROSE FICTION
Bolivia

3725 Arguedas, Alcides. Raza de bronce: Wuata Wuara. Edición critica de Anto-nio Lorente Medina. Nanterre, France: ALLCA XX, 1988. 572 p.: bibl., ill. (Col. Ar-chivos; 11)

Originally published in 1919, *Raza de Bronce* now appears in a fine critical edition prepared by Antonio Lorente Medina. The Bolivian Arguedas (1879–1946) is widely recognized as the pioneer of the *indigenista* novel. This volume consists of an introduction and a note on philology by Lorente Medina, and an "advertencia" by Alcides Arguedas, followed by the text. The novel's text contains copious notes on the language and variances in the different editions. This excellent critical edition makes the novel accessible to a wide range of readers and scholars.

3726 Los mejores cuentos bolivianos del siglo XX. Recopilación de Ricardo Pastor Poppe. 2. ed., corr. y aum. La Paz: Editorial Los Amigos del Libro, 1989. 440 p.: bibl. (Enciclopedia boliviana)

Pastor Poppe has made a good selection of 23 important 20th-century Bolivian short stories. Provides brief note about each writer and commentary on the story. Authors appear in alphabetical order, but the anthology would have been more useful as an introductory text if some other organizational format had been used, placing each author in some literary or social context. This anthology is of limited use for the non-specialist in Bolivian literature.

3727 Rivas Alcocer, Luis. Kuntur Khawa: el gobernador de Inkallajta. La Paz: Editorial Los Amigos del Libro, 1987. 213 p. (Col. Premio Novela Erich Guttentag)

In some prefatory remarks, author explains his desire to write a novel with a "genuine Quechua taste." Plot deals with the epic Indian figure Kunturo Khawa, and author dedicates considerable space to creating this "Quechua taste" by description of local color. Characters occasionally sing and speak in Quechua, and these sections also appear in Spanish in the text. Also includes Quechua-Spanish dictionary at end. Although Rivas Alcocer was born in 1925, this book could have been written in the 19th century, and in many ways seems to have been.

Colombia

3728 Aguilera Garramuño, Marco Tulio. Mujeres amadas. Jalapa, México: Univ. Veracruzana, 1988. 190 p. (Ficción)

Entertaining novel relates development of a writer's love life. At the same time, it is a parody of numerous Western concepts of love, as well as an intertextual dialogue with love literature of different periods of literary history. Narrator's style and topics range from Sade to Proust. *Mujeres amadas* can be read as burlesque eroticism but, in any case, it signals yet another successful direction of this young Colombian's writing career.

3729 Aguilera Garramuño, Marco Tulio. Los placeres perdidos. Bogotá: Fundación Tierra de Promisión, 1989. 254 p. (Col. Narrativa)

Since bursting onto the literary scene in Colombia with his satiric and parodic novel *Breve historia de todas las cosas* (1975), Aguilera Garramuño has settled into teaching and writing in Mexico. He has established a well-earned reputation as one of Colombia's most imaginative and irreverent writers. *Los placeres perdidos* tells the story of Adolfo Montañovivas, a *bon vivant* from Cali, Colombia. Consummate lover, philosopher, and novelist, this protagonist belongs to a group of self-styled *frenápteros,* a neologism referring to their eccentric lives. Montañovivas lives a life of extremes, ranging from esoteric knowledge and wisdom to polymorphous perversity. Readers will recognize Cali in the 1970s, with its political and social disintegration which became more evident in the 1980s. Another well-written and entertaining book by one of Colombia's most talented young writers.

3730 Alvarez Gardeazábal, Gustavo. El último gamonal. Bogotá: Plaza & Janés, 1987. 177 p.

Alvarez Gardeazábal established a reputation in Colombia during the 1970s as one of the country's most talented young writers. He published several outstanding novels during that period. Unfortunately, his more recent work, including *El último gamonal,* has been less substantive. This novel recreates the history of a real-life *cacique* (or *gamonal* in Colombia) in provincial Colombia. In the 1980s, Alvarez Gardeazábal has been novelizing Colombia's power structure.

3731 Arciniegas, Triunfo. La lagartija y el sol. Bogotá: C. Valencia Editores, 1989. 78 p. (Col. Nueva narrativa; 6)

Arciniegas has published short fiction for children and adults, and now this young

(b. 1957) Colombian has written a short novel which postulates either a child or an adult as the reader. Arciniegas explores the possibilities of fable and allegory by using a lizard as main character. A protagonist indefatigably pursues his dream of reaching the sun in a simple story written in simple language.

3732 Burgos Cantor, Roberto. De gozos y desvelos. Bogotá: Planeta, 1987. 177 p. (Autores colombianos)

Burgos Cantor has begun to establish a noteworthy career writing fiction about Cartagena and the Caribbean coastal region of Colombia. His first two books of fiction, as well as these four stories, are intimately related to this area. These stories deal with its common folk: "Encarnación Mancera, mi Negra de Alma," for example, relates experiences of a working black woman.

3733 Duque López, Alberto. Alejandra. Bogotá: Planeta, 1988. 188 p. (Col. Autores colombianos)

Fourth novel by one of Colombia's most innovative writers who returns to the experimental language and structure of his first, *Mateo el flautista*. Title refers to two women named Alejandra with whom the protagonist maintains an ambiguous relationship. Novel is an intertextual labyrinth in which the reader finds a plethora of film and texts drawn from other fiction. It is also Duque López's best work since *Mateo el flautista*.

3734 Espinosa, Germán. Noticias de un convento frente al mar. Bogotá: Editorial Oveja Negra, 1988. 121 p.

Author of three excellent novels and various books of fiction and criticism, Espinosa offers an interesting departure from his historical fiction. These 14 brief stories, originally written in the 1970s-80s, range from satires of literary life in Bogotá to refined exercises in the fantastic. Cover story is a superbly written erotic anecdote of a young woman's lesbian affair in a convent. Espinosa remains one of the most talented secrets in Colombia.

3735 Espinosa, Germán. El signo del pez. Bogotá: Planeta, 1987. 231 p. (Autores colombianos)

One of Colombia's most accomplished stylists, Espinosa has gained a readership of discriminating Colombians over the past two decades. His fiction has been predominantly historical, and *El signo del pez* follows this pattern. Set in early Christian Rome, the novel consists of a revisionist interpretation of the origins of Christianity. Espinosa adds ironic and non-conventional twists to the traditional Christian story. Although not one of his best, it is well-written and accessible.

3736 García Aguilar, Eduardo. Bulevar de los héroes. México: Plaza y Valdés Editores, 1987. 238 p.

García Aguilar's second novel, set in Latin America and Paris, is a violent story of revolutionary guerrillas. Satirizes numerous Colombian political and literary institutions, particularly nation's adherence to Greek and Latin ideals until well into the 20th century. A violent yet humorous book written by one of Colombia's talented young writers (b. 1953).

3737 García Márquez, Gabriel. El general en su laberinto. Madrid: Mondadori, 1989. 286 p.: ill. (Narrativa Mondadori)

Nobel Laureate García Márquez has assumed the considerable challenge of novelizing the life of one of Latin America's most celebrated heroes, Simón Bolívar. García Márquez uses language and phraseology that the reader will recognize from his earlier fiction. In addition, his humanization of the hero figure is fascinating. Nevertheless, García Márquez seems excessively inhibited by the straitjacket of history. The result is the least successful novel that he has written to date.

3738 Kremer, Harold. Rumor de mar. Bogotá: Carlos Valencia Editores, 1989. 124 p. (Col. Nueva narrativa)

This volume consists of 26 short fictions that range in length from one paragraph to a few pages. Author alternates between very brief anecdotes (less than a page) to short stories a few pages in length. Kremer fictionalizes a bizarre and dreamlike world with overtones of Borges and Kafka. Many of these stories, particularly the very brief ones, question traditions and customs. With this volume, Kremer establishes his place as one of Colombia's more promising short fiction writers.

3739 Mutis, Alvaro. Ilona llega con la lluvia. Madrid: Mondadori, 1988. 140 p. (Narrativa Mondadori)

Since the 1950s Mutis has been writing about the mythic character Maqroll, whom he originally invented in his poetry. In his recent novel *La nieve del Almirante*, Mutis returns to Maqroll. Now Maqroll, one of the most mysterious characters of Latin American literature, appears once again. He is a traveler, sailor, philosopher and hedonist about whom Mutis writes with great intimacy. In this novel, Maqroll narrates as a wise person who lives new experiences in the Caribbean and Panama. Mutis' style is accessible and attractive. First published in Bogotá by Editoral Oveja Negra in 1987.

3740 Mutis, Alvaro. La última escala del *Tramp Steamer*. Bogotá: Arango Editores, 1989. 114 p. (Narrativa colombiana)

The *Tramp Steamer*, a small ship that travels mostly between the Caribbean and Europe, serves as the focal point for this light love story. The narrator is a small-time bureaucrat and writer who tells an attractive story of human relationships related to this boat. The personal tone and spiritual search relate this short novel to Mutis' recent fiction on the mysterious Maqroll figure, even though Maqroll is not a character in this book. Mutis continues to write an accessible fiction with a great sense of style and tone.

3741 Rosero Diago, Evelio. Juliana los mira. Barcelona: Anagrama, 1987. 200 p.

Rosero Diago's second book marks an astonishing improvement in this young Colombian novelist's writing career. It is an erotic story of a 10-year-old girl's sexual awakening. She engages in a relationship with another girl and observes the sexual activity of her parents, who are involved in a variety of affairs. The most remarkable innovation of this novel within a Colombian context is its empowering of the woman via the female gaze. Rosero Diago represents an interesting new narrative voice in Colombia.

3742 Sánchez, Héctor. El héroe de la familia. Bogotá: Tercer Mundo Editores, 1988. 188 p.

Author of nine books of fiction, Sánchez has established a reputation as one of Colombia's most productive satirists. Most of his work is about the common folk in small-town *tierra caliente* of Colombia (vaguely located in Sánchez's region of Tolima), and El héroe de la familia follows this tradition. Humorous work deals with popular myths that glorified Colombian soldiers that participated in the Korean War with the US. Protagonist returns to his town as a hero, even though he had never really gone to Korea.

3743 Vallejo, Fernando. Los caminos a Roma. Bogotá: Planeta, 1988. 123 p. (Autores colombianos. El río del tiempo; 3)

Third novel in his trilogy, *El río del tiempo*, Los caminos a Roma is a first-person analysis of Colombian society. Vallejo's condemnation is carried out from Rome and other European cities through which the Colombian protagonist carries out his odyssey. He inherits a series of Colombian societal and sexual myths, and questions a repressive Catholic tradition. Rare incursion into homosexuality in Colombia is another reason why Vallejo is one of the nation's most controversial young writers.

3744 Vallejo, Fernando. Los días azules. Bogotá: Planeta, 1987. 185 p. (Autores colombianos. El río del tiempo; 1)

First novel in author's trilogy, *El río del tiempo*, Los días azules is a first-person analysis of Colombian society. Written in an immediate present that frequently suggests the nostalgia typical of recent fiction from the region of Antioquia. Reader follows protagonist from primary school forward. Child becomes observer of Antioquian and Colombian social history of the 1950s and also experiences his *rite de passage*, seeing death. Vallejo's first condemnation of a degenerate and scandalous Colombian society brought him well-deserved renown and controversy in Colombia.

Ecuador

3745 Aguilera Malta, Demetrio. Una pelota, un sueño y diez centavos. Quito: Planeta-Letraviva; México: J. Mortiz, 1988. 170 p. (Nueva narrativa hispánica)

Aguilera Malta did not finish this novel before his death in 1981. Although one of Ecuador's greatest novelists of the century, this probably would not have been one of his better novels, even if he had completed it.

Simple in style and story, the novel focuses on two soccer players over a three hour period on an evening after a soccer game in which they play. The narration alternates between the players and characters who watch them on television, an interesting story told mostly in dialogue. The novel begins as a story of the dreams and myths associated with professional sport heroes, but ends as little more than an everyday love story. This denouement appears as a postscript written by Aguilera Malta's wife, who claims her husband told her the novel's ending before his death. Just as *La tía Julia y el escribidor* is one of Vargas Llosa's more entertaining but lesser works, this light novel will occupy a similar space in the total work of Aguilera Malta.

3746 Cárdenas Espinosa, Eliécer. Las humanas certezas. Quito: Planeta, 1985. 156 p. (Col. Narrativa ecuatoriana; 5)

Author's fourth book of fiction consists of an entertaining series of anecdotes focusing on life in the rural town of Chanquín. Each of the 14 chapters is narrated by a different animal or object in the town, such as a spider, a rat, a shirt, or a radio. Their narratives offer obviously different views of the town's reality, but they have in common their critique of Chanquín's modernization by outsiders. In each case, the changes ushered in by modernity, the Reforma Agraria, and the *cooperativa* lead to a breakdown of traditional lifestyles. Well-written book by one of Ecuador's best young writers.

3747 Pérez Torres, Raúl. Teoría del desencanto: novela. Quito: Planeta, 1985. 179 p. (Col. Narrativa ecuatoriana; 2)

Ecuadorian writer's first novel after publishing several volumes of short stories. Despite the title, this is not a work of theory or postmodern reflection on theory and fiction. Rather, it consists of the narrator-protagonist's nostalgic reflections on his life in Ecuador during the 1960s. An intellectual, the protagonist suffers from insomnia and self-doubt as he recalls life in the university, his numerous lovers, and his free life-style during the 1960s. Lack of plot, loose use of language, and ineffective narrative technique hamper this work.

3748 Rumazo, Lupe. Peste blanca, peste negra: novela. Prólogo de Leopoldo Zea. Caracas: Ediciones Edime, 1988. 318 p.

This Ecuadorian residing in Caracas has already published six books. Despite ambitious structure and references to a plethora of modern writers, this novel is actually rather traditional in its assumptions and difficult to read. Author uses traditional allegory as a consistent mode of communication. Story involves human relationships and individual crises.

3749 Ubidia, Abdón. Sueño de lobos. Quito: Editorial El Conejo, 1986. 233 p.

Novel about Ecuador's urban marginalized (*hampa*) deals with the daily lives and everyday anecdotes in an underworld of crime, drugs, pool halls, street vendors, and the like. The action, which leads to a bank robbery, takes place over a period of several months in 1980. The innovative structure consists of a rotating focus on the approximately half-dozen main characters. Interesting characterizations compensate for slow movement of the plot.

3750 Velasco Mackenzie, Jorge. El rincón de los justos. Quito: Editorial El Conejo, 1983. 176 p. (Grandes novelas ecuatorianas; 9)

Velasco Mackenzie's first novel is an experiment in portraying the marginalized underworld on the streets of Guayaquil, Ecuador. Different characters, such as Raymundo the cigarette seller, narrate their immediate experiences while an omniscient narrator provides perspective. All these narrators are very close to the experience recounted, providing insights into a very unique world for the foreign reader. This closeness, however, often makes the reading obscure and tedious. Valasco Mackenzie uses much colloquial language, demonstrating a control of different styles that is impressive for a first novel.

3751 Vera, Pedro Jorge. Por la plata baila el perro: novela. Quito: Planeta, 1987. 215 p. (Col. Narrativa ecuatoriana; 9)

The novel's cover shows a table topped with two glasses of cognac, a cigar, a pistol, stacks of money, and a woman's leg in dark stockings. The cheap and crude scene portrays well the fictional world Vera presents in the novel. This story of a corrupt family in Guayaquil portrays the city's decadence in all spheres of life, particularly in business and politics. From the novel's first chapter, the characters are capable of giving anything for money, including their bodies. Several sections of the novel, titled "La Ciudad," are narrated by the city of Guayaquil, providing an interesting juxtaposition of a family story with an urban story. Nevertheless, Vera's indictment of contemporary Ecuadorian society never gets beyond the obvious and the superficial.

3752 Yánez Cossío, Alicia. La casa del sano placer. Quito: Planeta, 1989. 238 p. (Col. Narrativa ecuatoriana; 13. Letraviva.)

One of Ecuador's established writers, Yánez Cossío uses a classic Latin American paradigm involving collaboration between the local government and the Church to carry out illegal schemes. In this particular case, a house of prostitution is the focus of the scheme. The *grand dame* who operates this institution soon has it competing with the town's other institutions. She is so successful that the provincial town changes in nature. Yánez Cossío demonstrates how the social construction of gender operates and she questions all traditional values whose legitimacy depends on the perversion of norms.

Peru

3753 Avendaño, Angel. Los cuervos de San Antonio. Lima: Ediciones Antawara, 1989. 203 p.

Avendaño has published some short fiction, and this first novel is one of those rare works set in the Peruvian city of Cusco. Uses Univ. San Antonio Abad as a microcosm for playing out national ideological conflicts of the 1960s–70s. Over 30 characters appear in rotating fashion, creating a kaleidoscope effect over a background of revolution, rebellion, *cheísmo*, and conflicts between students and police. Little story line but much on the experience of young Peruvian intellectuals during the period. Ending is more optimistic than most novels of this type.

3754 Balta Campbell, Aída. Sodoma, Santos y Gomorra. S.l.: Editorial El Quijote, 1986. 152 p.

Balta Campbell (b. Lima, 1957) has written extensively as a journalist and also been involved with theater and short fiction.

This first novel is set in the mythical and magical Latin American town of "Santos," and tells a 19th-century family story. Reminiscent of García Márquez, the novel includes prodigious events and people, gypsies, and a main character who is a jeweler and astrologer. In the end, the town of Santos disappears, rising to the sky like a silk kite. This young writer is still in search of her own voice.

3755 Beleván, Harry. Fuegos artificiales. Lima: Ediciones El Virrey, 1986. 151 p.

Beleván is known as the Peruvian author of fantastic fiction (novel and short stories). Volume includes 12 pieces more overtly political and theoretical than any of his previous fiction. First story, "Apuntes para Escribir la Historia de un Farsante," deals with a diplomat at the UN who gains an authentic social consciousness from his revolutionary son. Another story, "Turismo Típico," describes conflict between individuals and representatives of social institutions. Other stories deal with similar political themes and theory of literature.

3756 Bryce Echenique, Alfredo. El hombre que hablaba de Octavia de Cádiz: cuaderno de navegación en un sillón Voltaire. 2. ed. colombiana. Bogotá: Editorial Oveja Negra, 1988. 383 p. (Narrativa)

The Martín Romaña of Bryce Echenique's previous novel, *La vida exagerada de Martín Romaña*, is the protagonist and narrator of this work. As a continuation of the earlier novel, this one is also set in Paris. Martín is a professor in the Univ. of Nanterre; Octavia de Cádiz is the sister of one of his students. Bryce Echenique is as irreverent and humorous as in his previous work, making a game of his love affair a well as his novel. Narrator even addresses the issue of losing track of the plot. Highly entertaining book by one of Peru's most talented writers.

3757 Castillo Yzaguirre, Luis Juan. Granos de pólvora. Lima: Ediciones Identidad, 1987. 283 p.

Early part of this novel deals with class and political conflict; the implied narrator sympathizes with workers and the APRA. But as the novel reaches into the 19th-century historical past, it loses focus. Characters also digress with lengthy stories. Neither well-written nor well-organized.

3758 Iwasaki Cauti, Fernando. Tres noches de corbata y otras noches. Lima: Ediciones AVE, 1987. 93 p.

Fernando Iwaski Cauti is a young Peruvian writer (b. 1961) who has published several stories and essays. This first compilation of 12 stories was written between ages 20 and 25; it is brief fiction written in a traditional fashion. The story "La Sombra del Guerrero" deals with how past tradition affects the present, within the context of interaction between Latin American and Oriental cultures. Other stories represent an effort to explore ambiguous and non-empirical aspects of reality.

3759 Ribeyro, Julio Ramón. Sólo para fumadores. Lima: Editorial El Barranco, 1987. 146 p.

Writing under the shadow of Vargas Llosa has been Ribeyro's only literary problem. His work has invariably been as outstanding as the fiction found in this literary review volume of writings ranging from autobiographical anecdotes to formal short stories. Title story is a hilarious recounting of Ribeyro's intense and life-long relationship with cigarettes. Describes it as a sick relationship that leads to numerous physical ailments, avoiding all positive results derived from his anti-smoking treatments and therapy. The smoker remains as faithful to his addiction as do partners in sick relationships. Other pieces are nostalgic and humorous anecdotes from Ribeyro's youth in Peru.

3760 Vargas Llosa, Mario. Elogio de la madrastra. Barcelona: Tusquets, 1988. 198 p., 6 leaves of plates: ill. (La Sonrisa vertical; 58)

Vargas Llosa continues to surprise his readers by adding another dimension to his already broad range of writings. Author of such powerful historical and political novels as Conversación en la Catedral and La guerra del fin del mundo now turns to eroticism as the topic and painting as the inspiration for this brief novel. Playful possibilities of the erotic are played out in a triangle among husband, wife, and adolescent stepson. Paintings are six erotic works ranging from a 1648 work by Jordaens to a 1977 abstract painting by Fernando de Szyszlo. Cleverness and humor of novels

such as Pantaleón y las visitadoras and La tía Julia y el escribidor are also evident in this work.

Venezuela

3761 Chirinos, César. Mezclaje. Caracas: FUNDARTE, 1987. 190 p. (Cuadernos de difusión; 100)

Novel won Venezuela's Premio FUNDARTE de Narrativa (1985). Author of several books of fiction, Chirinos describes in Mezclaje the constant state of crisis in which the marginalized live. Narrator is a vagabond intellectual who frequently cites poets and is a friend of the poet Uyón Vivas, a major character who suffers rejection by a hostile society and from his own drunken boredom. All in all, Mezclaje is a plotless and rambling book that ends in a theory of fiction: a novel is the construction of a world around an idea.

3762 Monasterios, Rubén. El pájaro insaciable. Caracas: Alfadil Ediciones, 1989. 125 p. (Col. Ludens; 3)

Monasterios is a relatively unknown Venezuelan who writes excellent erotic fiction. Three stories in this volume are progressively more erotic, nearly crossing the boundary into pornography: 1) "In Amore Unicornis," relates an erotic seduction that ends with the protagonist functioning as voyeur to an erotic sex scene; 2) sexual obsessions and masochist tendencies of protagonist in "El Pájaro Insaciable" reach humorous dimensions; 3) "Una Noche de Abril," is perversely erotic and playful. These well-written and ironic tales are ultimately an attack on social and sexual conventions.

3763 Romero, Denzil. Entrego los demonios. Caracas: Alfadil Ediciones, 1986. 243 p. (Col. Orinoco; 10)

Romero's second novel is a humorous tour de force that relates the seven lives of the narrator-protagonist Ascelepius Calatrava Baca. Using conventions of the Spanish picaresque novel, author constructs the protagonist's story around 21 chapters, and begins each with a one-sentence plot resumé. Calatrava Baca is destined to granduer in his several lives as Pygmalian, king, prostitute, philosopher, etc. Hyperbolic language illustrates the protagonist's extraordinary erudition (e.g., constructs a Borgian "aleph" that enables him to observe all spaces and times in one point). Influenced by the fiction of Gabriel García Márquez and *Terra nostra* by Carlos Fuentes, this novel represents a successful effort by one of Venezuela's most talented younger writers.

3764 Segal, Alicia Freilich de. Cláper. Caracas: Editorial Planeta, 1987. 176 p.

First novel by Venezuelan journalist and essayist. Narrator-protagonist of *Cláper* relates her experiences in modern Venezuela and several European nations. Much is related to Venezuelan political and intellectual life (1950s–60s). Segal does not develop a consistent plot or other unifying element to connect disparate anecdotes of this novel. Essayistic asides are also distracting. Consequently, the self-indulgent narrator fails to engage the reader.

Chile

JOSE PROMIS, *Professor of Latin American Literature and Literary Criticism, University of Arizona*

ESTE BIENIO EXHIBE UN EXTRAORDINARIO aumento de la producción en prosa, la cual aparece fuertemente comprometida con la dinámica situación política en que vive el país. La generalidad de los textos prosísticos tiene como asunto, en unos casos más explícitamente que en otros, dicha circunstancia. Se publica un corto número de relatos que pretenden justificar el golpe militar de 1973 novelando los efectos que las condiciones históricas previas a ese año tuvieron sobre el comportamiento individual. Ejemplo de esta tendencia es la novela *Antonio Canario, sin voz para cantar,* de Eliana Cerda (item **3769**). Sin embargo, la tendencia dominante en la prosa del bienio es la desacralización del sistema político impuesto por el autoritarismo militar y—como consecuencia y proyección de lo anterior—de las notas aceptadas tradicionalmente como definidoras y características de la sociabilidad chilena.

Dentro de esta tendencia desacralizadora destacan por su número las novelas contestatarias, relatos cuya interpretación artística de la realidad es orientada para servir como instrumento de lucha contra el régimen militar imperante. Los narradores adscritos a esta tendencia asumen distintas perspectivas para representar la situación política chilena que los afecta. Claudio Jaque utiliza la ficción científica como metáfora de la opresión en *El ruido del tiempo* (item **3781**), mientras que Francisco Simón Rivas en *Todos los días un circo* (item **3790**) y Jorge Edwards en *El anfitrión* (item **3776**) desarrollan una visión fantástica del ambiente de la dictadura. La mayoría de las novelas, sin embargo, pretende entregar una imagen de la interioridad individual, buscando allí los efectos producidos por la política autoritarista: fractura o destrucción de la personalidad (items **3775, 3774** y **3771**), de las relaciones familiares (item **3785**), de los vínculos humanos fundamentales (item **3788**), etc. Entre las novelas que continúan desarrollando el tema del exilio sobresale por su extraordinaria riqueza narrativa *De cómo fue el destierro de Lázaro Carvajal,* de Walter Garib (item **3779**).

Los procesos de desacralización se extienden a ámbitos mayores en novelas como *La nueva provincia* de Andrés Gallardo (item **3778**), que desmitifica y satiriza las imágenes campesinas creadas por la prosa criollista, mientras que en *En el* *bosque, un ángel y un demonio* de Reinaldo Edmundo Marchant (item **3784**), esas mismas imágenes son transformadas en un mundo de alucinante irracionalidad. Por su parte, Patricio Manns en *Actas de Muerteputa* (item **3783**) continúa su proyecto narrativo de reemplazar la imagen de Chile entregada por la historia "oficial" reescribiéndola desde el punto de vista de los oprimidos y humillados sociales.

En la producción narrativa femenina destaca la publicación de *Eva Luna*, tercera novela de Isabel Allende (item **3766**). Aquí sólo cambia la ambientación; la figura de la mujer vuelve a ser representada como motor y sentido de la historia, y los motivos del relato son los característicos de sus dos primeras novelas. El influjo de Isabel Allende sobre las narradoras chilenas se comprueba con la publicación de *Doy por vivido todo lo soñado*, primera novela de Isidora Aguirre, la más famosa dramaturga chilena (item **3765**). La reedición de *La mampara* (item **3768**) es destacable porque comprueba la importancia que tuvo Marta Brunet en la renovación de la narrativa criollista todavía vigente en la década de 1940. Excelente imagen de las inquietudes actuales de las escritoras chilenas entregan los cuentos de *La mujer de yeso*, de Alejandra Basualto (item **3767**).

Respecto a la narración breve, la antología *Contando el cuento* (item **3801**) pretende dar a conocer a los narradores más jóvenes de Chile. Otro elemento digno de destacarse en este género es la reaparición de Carlos Olivárez, quien publica su segundo volumen de relatos: *Combustión interna* (item **3787**) después de 16 años de silencio.

Finalmente, en la narrativa testimonial de asunto literario destaca la nueva edición de la *Historia personal del "Boom"* escrita por José Donoso con la colaboración de su esposa, donde se agregan informaciones sobre lo ocurrido con los más prominentes novelistas hispanoamericanos después de 1972 (item **3801**). Y en la narrativa testimonial de asunto político, que tanta importancia ha adquirido durante los últimos años, sobresale *En el país prohibido*, de Volodia Teitelboim (item **3792**), prominente narrador social y una de las figuras políticas más perseguidas por el régimen militar.

En el terreno de la crítica, René Jara publica *El revés de la arpillera* (item **3805**), análisis del desarrollo de la literatura chilena escrito con el formato de los tradicionales "perfiles literarios." Dos contribuciones valiosas se suman a la bibliografía sobre la novela de la generación de 1938: Ted Lyon la considera un pequeño "boom" dentro de la literatura chilena (item **3808**) y Lon Pearson descubre la estructura estética que todos estos narradores parecieran haber utilizado (item **3810**). La obra de José Donoso, Isabel Allende y, secundariamente, de María Luisa Bombal sigue acaparando la atención predominante de los críticos. Sobre cada uno de estos autores se acumula una extensa información. Util es la bibliografía anotada de Isabel Picado sobre Donoso (item **3812**) y por su originalidad destacan los estudios de Carlos Cerda sobre *Casa de campo* (item **3798**) y de Fernando Burgos sobre *El jardín de al lado* (item **3797**). Marcelo Coddou publica el primer estudio de larga extensión dedicado a Isabel Allende, aunque se concentra principalmente en *La casa de los espíritus* (item **3799**). De entre los innumerables artículos dedicados a la novelista chilena, destacan los de Gloria Gálvez-Carlisle (item **3803**) y Sandra Boschetto (item **3796**), junto a la entrevista realizada por Verónica Cortínez (item **3800**). *María Luisa Bombal: apreciaciones críticas* (item **3794**) es el más útil e interesante volumen de ensayos críticos publicado sobre esta novelista durante el bienio, y la entrevista de Juan Armando Epple, *Nos reconoce el tiempo y silba su tonada* (item **3795**), es un documento indispensable para los interesados en estudiar la obra y el pensamiento de Fernando Alegría.

PROSE FICTION

3765 Aguirre, Isidora. Doy por vivido todo lo soñado. Barcelona: Plaza & Janés, 1987. 239 p. (Plaza & Janes/literaria)

Primera novela de la más famosa dramaturga chilena. Evocación de una historia familiar donde pasado y presente se sobreponen y se crea un mundo poético y fantasmagórico, en una línea similar a *La casa de los espíritus*, de Isabel Allende. Excelente manifestación de un nuevo modo narrativo en la novela chilena actual.

3766 Allende, Isabel. Eva Luna. Barcelona: Plaza y Janés Editores, 1987. 282 p.

Relato que se ambienta en Venezuela y asume la forma del género picaresco para presentar la historia de Eva Luna, prototipo de la individualidad femenina desarrollándose bajo regímenes autoritarios. Novela que confirma la maestría narrativa de la autora e insiste en los símbolos presentados en sus obras anteriores.

3767 Basualto, Alejandra. La mujer de yeso. Santiago: Ediciones Documentas, 1988. 80 p. (Documentas/literatura)

Relatos que intentan encontrar "lo femenino" oculto debajo de un lenguaje acuñado por los hombres. Excelente muestra de la literatura feminista chilena.

3768 Brunet, Marta. La mampara. Santiago: Editorial Universitaria, 1987. 87 p. (Col. Los Contemporáneos)

Reedición del excelente relato breve que en la fecha de su primera publicación (1946) contribuyó a reorientar la novela chilena desde su interés por lo telúrico hacia la indagación de los conflictos interiores del ser humano.

3769 Cerda, Eliana. Antonio Canario, sin voz para cantar. Santiago: Editorial Andrés Bello, 1987. 201 p.

Un narrador-niño relata sus vagabundeos por Santiago huyendo de la inestabilidad que se vive en su hogar. Su mirada descubre una imagen dramática de las condiciones sociales de Chile durante el régimen de la Unidad Popular. Se crea así una identidad entre las condiciones históricas del medio y las de los individuos que viven en él.

3770 Délano, Luis Enrique. La luz que falta. Santiago: Galinost-Andante, 1987. 224 p.

Novela póstuma que su autor terminó de redactar durante su exilio en Estocolmo.

3771 Délano, Poli. Como si no muriera nadie. Santiago: Planeta, 1987. 219 p. (Biblioteca del sur)

El título procede de un verso de Pablo Neruda y ampara a cuatro voces narrativas que rememoran momentos particulares de la historia chilena de los últimos 30 años, desde un tiempo inicial de inocencia y optimismo hasta culminar en el horror y la impotencia frente a la destrucción de la normalidad cotidiana.

3772 Díaz Eterovic, Ramón and Diego Muñoz Valenzuela. Contando el cuento: antología joven narrativa chilena. Santiago: Editorial Sinfronteras, 1987. 261 p.

Antología de relatos de los más jóvenes narradores chilenos (todos entre 17 y 35 años). Entrega también importante información sobre el desarrollo del cuento durante los últimos años y sobre cada narrador antologado en particular.

3773 Díaz Márquez, Luis. Cuentos coloraos [sic] para lectores verdes: un vino viejo en cueros nuevos. Río Piedras, P.R.: Ediciones Mairena, 1988. 113 p.: ill.

Entertaining short stories by Chilean author living in Puerto Rico are based on myths and legends from the island of Chiloé, on the southern tip of Chile. [C.R. Hortas]

3774 Domínguez Vial, Luis. Oh Capitán, mi Capitán. Santiago: Ediciones Melquíades, 1988. 167 p. (Ficción)

Presentación de la vida privada de oficiales que participaron en el pronunciamiento militar de 1973, estableciendo las contradicciones entre la responsabilidad que asumieron profesionalmente y su interioridad humana. Novela que representa muy bien las tendencias denunciativas del relato chileno actual. El título proviene de Walt Whitman y constituye un indicio para la comprensión del texto.

3775 Dorfman, Ariel. Máscaras. Buenos Aires: Editorial Sudamericana, 1988. 159 p.

Diferentes voces narrativas ponen en tela de juicio la confianza del lector en la solidez de la experiencia empírica. El lenguaje ilumina fuerzas opresivas que otorgan a la realidad un carácter pesadillesco. La novela es un nuevo paso del proyecto literario del autor para denunciar la situación chilena de los últimos años.

3776 Edwards, Jorge. El anfitrión. Santiago: Editorial Planeta del Sur, 1987. 201 p.

Novela que significa una variante importante en la producción del autor, quien abandona aquí el estilo realista para ensayar una interpretación fantástica de la realidad. Utilizando los motivos míticos del viaje a los infiernos y el pacto diabólico, el narrador presenta la imagen de un mundo alucinante, pero identificable con la realidad cotidiana chilena de los últimos años.

3777 Eltit, Diamela. El cuarto mundo. Santiago: Planeta, 1988. 129 p. (Biblioteca del sur)

Indagación del problema de la identidad a través de un experimento narrativo que destroza las relaciones familiares convencionales. Buen ejemplo de una tendencia desmitificadora presente en muchos novelistas jóvenes en Chile.

3778 Gallardo, Andrés. La nueva provincia. México: Fondo de Cultura Económica, 1987. 126 p.

Historia del espíritu separatista de un pueblo sureño que se autotransforma primero en provincia, después en república y finalmente en monarquía. El autor confirma un estilo narrativo iniciado en su novela *Cátedras paralelas* (ver *HLAS 50:3404*), donde la sátira, la ironía y la fantasía desmitifican estructuras y temas literarios tradicionales, y costumbres consideradas características de la sociedad chilena.

3779 Garib, Walter. De cómo fue el destierro de Lázaro Carvajal. Santiago: BAT, 1988. 307 p.

Premio Municipal de Literatura 1988 de Santiago. Una de las mejores novelas publicadas ese año. Con un lenguaje de extraordinaria riqueza y poderosa capacidad para crear imágenes se relata la historia de un pueblo a orillas del río Bío-Bío, al cual se convierte en espacio de fantasía donde transcurre el exilio de un participante de la revolución de 1891.

3780 González, Angel Custodio. Muerte del día en Capadocia. Santiago: Editorial Andrés Bello, 1988. 164 p.: map.

Premio María Luisa Bombal de Novela 1988.

3781 Jaque, Claudio. El ruido del tiempo. Santiago: Editorial Galinost, 1987. 366 p. (Narradores chilenos de hoy)

Relato de ficción científica de excelente factura. En un mundo futuro que posee identificables signos del presente, el narrador imagina la lucha de los oprimidos contra la tiranía, conflicto donde los límites entre dominación y libertad llegan también a confundirse.

3782 Lafourcade, Enrique. Las señales van hacia el Sur. Santiago: Editorial Planeta, 1988. 275 p. (Biblioteca del sur)

Nuevo planteamiento de un tema favorito del autor: la búsqueda por la propia identidad. Relato de los esfuerzos de un individuo para encontrar la compañera y un espacio en el mundo, imposibles ambos, en boca de un testigo que constituye la contrapartida del protagonista. El lenguaje exhibe la extraordinaria riqueza característica de todas las novelas del autor.

3783 Manns, Patricio. Actas de Muerteputa. Santiago: Editorial Emisión, 1987. 112 p.

Tercera novela del ciclo de las *Actas* iniciado con *Actas de Marusia* (versión cinematográfica de Miguel Littin) y *Actas del Alto Bío-Bío* (ver *HLAS 50:3412*), que continúa el proyecto desacralizador de los mitos creados en el discurso histórico tradicional sobre Chile y América con el objeto de presentar la imagen desconocida de la historia: la visión de las víctimas y de los oprimidos.

3784 Marchant, Reinaldo Edmundo. En el bosque, un ángel y demonio. . . . Santiago: Ediciones Mar del Plata, 1988. 149 p.

El nivel de la existencia cotidiana es reemplazado por el de un mundo de anormales fantasías donde el comportamiento racional es alterado o destruido. El lenguaje asume también una sintaxis extraña que produce imágenes insólitas, desconocidas en la narrativa chilena anterior. Novela representativa de la atracción hacia lo irreal que caracteriza a muchos novelistas jóvenes chilenos.

3785 Matta, Paulina. Album de fotografías. Santiago: Editorial A. Bello, 1987. 133 p.

Premio de Novela Andrés Bello 1986. Visión introspectiva de las experiencias de una mujer rodeada por las circunstancias históricas chilenas bajo el gobierno de Pinochet.

3786 Morand, Carlos. UltraOhtumba. Santiago: Ediciones Logos, 1988. 329 p.

Segunda parte de la historia del profesor Marcelo Belmar iniciada en *Ohtumba* (1979). El texto desmitifica con amarga ironía la vida académica chilena, así como en *Ohtumba* se desacralizaba la imagen de la vida universitaria en EE.UU.

3787 Olivárez, Carlos. Combustión interna. Santiago: Galinost, 1987. 134 p. (Narradores chilenos de hoy)

Segundo libro publicado por el autor 16 años después de su primer volumen de cuentos: *Concentración de bicicletas* (ver *HLAS 36:4439*). La angustia por sobreponerse a la soledad es el leitmotiv de la mayoría de este nuevo conjunto de relatos breves que confirman al autor como uno de los más eximios cultivadores del género en Chile.

One more stripe to the tiger: a selection of contemporary Chilean poetry and fiction. See item **4928.**

3788 Parra, Marco Antonio de la. El deseo de toda ciudadana. Santiago: Ediciones del Ornitorrinco, 1987. 215 p.

Primer Premio en el Concurso de Novela Ornitorrinco. Utilizando códigos del lenguaje cinematográfico y del relato policial, el autor desarrolla una historia originalmente diseñada como texto dramático que crea una atmósfera pesadillesca donde son perceptibles los motivos más característicos de la novela chilena actual: afanes de dominio, opresión, fractura de la personalidad, etc.

3789 Piña, Carlos. Crónicas de la otra ciudad. Santiago: Facultad Latinoamericana de Ciencias Sociales, 1987. 185 p.

Colección de cuentos que traen a la luz los espacios vitales subterráneos desapercibidos por la mirada inmediata que observa sólo el comportamiento superficial de los individuos.

3790 Rivas, Francisco Simón. Todos los días, un circo. Santiago: Planeta, 1988. 406 p. (Biblioteca del sur)

Primera novela publicada con el nombre completo del autor: Francisco Simón Rivas, quien omitía su apellido Rivas en sus novelas anteriores. El texto propone una visión fantástica de la historia chilena de los ultimos años y ensaya un desenlace sobrenatural para la dictadura establecida. Es, sin

duda, la novela más ambiciosa publicada por el autor hasta esta fecha, y una de las mejores del bienio 1987–88.

3791 Ruiz-Tagle, Carlos. El cementerio de Lonco. Santiago: Editorial Andrés Bello, 1987. 124 p.

Premio María Luis Bombal de Novela 1987. Las vidas mínimas de los habitantes de Lonco, un pueblito ubicado imaginariamente en el sur de Chile, crean un relato de fino humorismo y agradable lectura, en la tradición de la narrativa de José Santos González Vera y Carlos León.

3792 Teitelboim, Volodia. En el país prohibido. Concepción, Chile: LAR, 1988. 286 p.

El autor reúne recuerdos y experiencias que desde su punto de vista iluminan las condiciones reales de vida existentes en Chile durante los años del gobierno militar.

3793 Torres, Víctor. Laberinto sueco. Santiago: Ediciones Documentas, 1988. 185 p. (Literatura)

Relato de las amargas experiencias de los exiliados políticos chilenos en el extranjero. El texto se inscribe en la tendencia testimonial que predomina fuertemente en la producción novelesca chilena contemporánea.

LITERARY CRITICISM AND HISTORY

3794 Agosin, Marjorie; Elena Gascón-Vera; and Joy Renjilian-Burgy. María Luisa Bombal: apreciaciones críticas. Tempe, Arizona: Biligual Press/Editorial Bilingüe, 1987. 280 p.

Colección de 24 estudios sobre diferentes aspectos de la narrativa de Bombal, acompañada de una excelente bibliografía por Jorge Román-Lagunas.

3795 Alegría, Fernando; and Juan Armando Epple. Nos reconoce el tiempo y silba su tonada. Concepción, Chile: Ediciones LAR, 1987. 119 p. (Serie Memoria y Testimonio)

Una de las más extensas y completas entrevistas realizadas a Fernando Alegría, importantísima para conocer sus ideas sobre su obra y sus experiencias literarias durante medio siglo de actividad creadora.

3796 Boschetto, Sandra M. Dialéctica metatextual y sexual en *La casa de los espíritus* de Isabel Allende. (*Hispania/Teachers*, 72:3, Sept. 1989, p. 526–532, bibl.)

La casa de los espíritus interpretada como acto narrativo que trasciende las fronteras de sexo y de clase para culminar en un acto de perfecta reconciliación totalizadora, sentido final comunicado por la novela.

3797 Burgos, Fernando. Exilio y escritura: *El jardín de al lado.* (*Rev. Interam. Bibliogr.*, 37:1, 1987, p. 57–61)

El autor rechaza considerar la novela de Donoso como relato sobre el exilio, tal como lo ha hecho la mayoría de la crítica, para analizarla como expresión estética del sentimiento de la modernidad.

3798 Cerda, Carlos. José Donoso: originales y metáforas. Santiago: Editorial Planeta Chilena, 1988. 217 p.

Largo ensayo que trata de probar que *Casa de campo* da una imagen de la realidad social chilena a través de una visión metafórica totalizante. De este modo, la novela de Donoso se convierte en la gran novela social de Chile.

3799 Coddou, Marcelo. Para leer a Isabel Allende: introducción a *La casa de los espíritus.* Concepción, Chile: Ediciones LAR, 1988. 235 p.

Primer estudio de larga extensión publicado sobre la más famosa novelista chilena. Su autor establece la identidad literaria de Isabel Allende, el concepto de escritura a que responden sus relatos, su poética realista frente a la poética de lo real-maravilloso, la presencia de lo femenino en su interpretación de la realidad y sus técnicas narrativas más sobresalientes.

3800 Cortínez, Verónica. Polifonía: entrevista a Isabel Allende y Antonio Skármeta. (*Rev. Chil. Lit.*, 32, nov. 1988, p. 79–89)

Ambos entrevistados manifiestan sus puntos de vista sobre la naturaleza y la función de la novela hispanoamericana y sobre la situación y significado de su obra dentro del género.

3801 Donoso, José. Historia personal del "Boom:" nueva edición con apéndice del autor seguido de "El 'Boom' Doméstico" por María Pilar Donoso. Santiago: Editorial Andrés Bello, 1987. 178 p.

Al ensayo publicado en 1972, el autor agrega un apéndice sobre la suerte que después de esa fecha han corrido los narradores mencionados en la primera edición. Su esposa, María Pilar Donoso, complementa estos recuerdos desde su punto de vista personal.

3802 Fernández, Magali. El discurso narrativo en la obra de María Luisa Bombal. Madrid: Editorial Pliegos, 1988. 168 p.

Indagación de lo que la autora llama el "ser femenino" en el mundo narrativo de la Bombal, y de aquellos aspectos técnicos que la confirman como iniciadora de la novela contemporánea en Latinoamérica.

3803 Gálvez-Carlisle, Gloria. El sabor picaresco en *Eva Luna* de Isabel Allende. (*in* Mujer y sociedad en América. Edición de Juana Alcira Arancibia. Mexicali, México: Univ. Autónoma de Baja California; Westminster, Calif.: Instituto Literario y Cultural Hispánico, 1988, v. 1, p. 105–115)

Análisis de la manera como la tercera novela de Isabel Allende incorpora elementos de la tradición picaresca y, al mismo tiempo, altera dicho modelo de acuerdo a las circunstancias histórico-sociales de Latinoamérica.

3804 Guerra-Cunningham, Lucía. Texto e ideología en la narrativa chilena. Minneapolis: The Prisma Institute, 1987. 249 p.

Colección de ensayos sobre narrativa chilena, aparecidos previamente en diversas publicaciones, que entregan interesantes observaciones sobre cada uno de los temas tratados y, además, revelan la evolución intelectual de su autora.

3805 Jara, René. El revés de la arpillera: perfil literario de Chile. Madrid: Ediciones Hiperión, 1988. 275 p.

Desde un punto de vista subjetivo el autor revisa el desarrollo de la literatura chilena entregando sugerentes y útiles observaciones sobre aquellos temas, autores y períodos que establece en su texto.

3806 Jofré, Manuel Alcides. La novela chilena, 1965–1988. (Georgia series on hispanic thought)(*in* Los ensayistas: Chile, 1968–1988. Edición de José Luis Gómez-Martínez y Francisco Javier Pinedo. Athens, Georgia: Center for Latin American Studies, Univ. of Georgia, 1987/88, nos. 22–25, p. 191–206)

Apretada síntesis que pretende resaltar las características más sobresalientes del género y que culmina con la distinción entre una novela del interior y una novela del exterior después de 1973.

3807 López Morales, Berta. *Hijo de ladrón: novela de aprendizaje antiburguesa.* Santiago: Editorial La Noria, 1987. 179 p.

La novela más famosa de Manuel Rojas (1951, ver *HLAS 17:2416*) es interpretada como una experiencia de aprendizaje donde el protagonista debe vencer los obstáculos del capitalismo para ascender al nivel de una humanidad fraternal e igualitaria.

3808 Lyon, Ted. Presentación de la Generación Chilena del 38: una perspectiva de cincuenta años. (*Ibero-Am. Arch.*, 15:1, 1989, p. 19–32, bibl., facsims., tables)

Caracterización de la literatura producida por la Generación del 38 como un verdadero "Boom" interno que produjo una tradición literaria renovadora e inspiradora de los novelistas más jóvenes.

3809 Para una fundación imaginaria de Chile: la obra literaria de Fernando Alegría. Edición de Juan Armando Epple. Lima: Latinoamericana Editores, 1987. 229 p.

Volumen dedicado a un análisis exhaustivo de la obra del novelista chileno. Reúne ensayos de R. Brodsky, Alfonso Calderón, Hernán Lavín Cerda, Víctor Valenzuela, Fernando Aínsa y otros.

3810 Pearson, Lon. The Chilean Generation of 1938 and literary *estampa.* (*in*

Rocky Mountain Council on Latin American Studies, *36th, Fort Collins, Colo., 1988.* Proceedings. Las Cruces, N.M.: Center for Latin American Studies, New Mexico State Univ., p. 127–136)

Innovador artículo sobre la Generación del 38. El autor sugiere que la forma literaria de la *estampa* otorga a los miembros de dicha generación su perfil unitario al otorgarles un estilo artístico común. Pero además, la *estampa* afecta su visión de mundo y la forma en que la comunican a sus lectores.

3811 Petreman, David A. La obra narrativa de Francisco Coloane. Santiago: Editorial Universitaria, 1987. 174 p.: bibl. (Col. El Saber y la cultura)

Según el autor, las características esenciales de la chilenidad son comunicadas por Coloane en un lenguaje vital, sencillo y directo. Sin embargo, el verdadero interés del novelista es la indagación de los valores humanos universales que se manifiestan en tales características. Un merecido estudio sobre este poco conocido narrador chileno.

3812 Picado, Isabel. Bibliografía anotada seleccionada: la crítica de José Donoso. (*Hispania/Teachers*, 73:2, May 1990, p. 371–391)

Util y cuidadosa bibliografía que cubre hasta 1987 dividida en: 1) "Bibliografía General" que entrega información básica sobre el autor y sobre cada una de sus obras; y 2) "Bibliografía Anotada Seleccionada" que se organiza en orden alfabético de autores.

River Plate Countries

MARIA LUISA BASTOS, *Professor of Spanish, Lehman College and the Graduate School, City University of New York*
MAGDALENA GARCIA PINTO, *Associate Professor of Spanish, University of Missouri, Colombia*
MARIA CRISTINA GUIÑAZU, *Assistant Professor of Spanish, Lehman College, City University of New York*
SAUL SOSNOWSKI, *Professor and Chairman of the Department of Spanish and Portuguese, University of Maryland, College Park*

ARGENTINA

LA MAYORIA DE LOS TEXTOS reseñados en este capítulo del *Handbook* se publicaron entre 1985–88. Este informe fue redactado entre 1990–91. Una novela de Juan José Saer y una de Andrés Rivera se destacan entre lo mejor de la producción narrativa del período. Rivera centra *La revolución es un sueño eterno* (item **3861**) en la circunstancia patética de un personaje de la historia argentina, un gran orador privado del habla, cuyas reflexiones exponen el poder y la vulnerabilidad del autoanálisis. *La ocasión* de Saer (item **3865**), que ocurre en la llanura argentina en el siglo XIX, es una puesta en relato de lo ilusorio tanto de la pretensión de controlar la conducta ajena, como de suponer que es posible interpretar acertadamente actos, y sobre todo palabras, de otros. Saer dosifica el relato de manera que su sutileza irónica pasa casi inadvertida hasta el final, en que el dilema del personaje no se resuelve. Por caminos diversos, las dos novelas postulan la imposibilidad de poseer una supuesta verdad objetiva. En ambos libros, la historia—en los dos sentidos del término—se fragua mediante versiones autocorregidas con que sujetos extremadamente controladores tratan de reconstruir la "realidad:" su empresa está destinada a fracasar, ya que sólo disponen del recuerdo de sus percepciones, inevitablemente falaces por parciales. En otra tónica, *Tiempo de opresión* de Antonio Brailovsky (item **3816**) sugiere que la historia, a pesar de su naturaleza ficticia, puede iluminarnos, no tanto sobre el pasado sino sobre la falacia potencial de nuestras conjeturas sobre el presente.

Se han seguido publicando relatos referidos—en las formas más variadas—a la historia argentina reciente. Algunos, como los de Alicia Kozameh (item **3838**), parten de una inconfundible experiencia personal; su poder de convicción se debe a que lo anecdótico se ha depurado en beneficio de la tensión narrativa. Otros enjuiciamientos al terrorismo de Estado de la década de 1970 no se refieren en forma directa a circunstancias conocidas: son construcciones muy elaboradas, como *Partes de inteligencia* de Jorge Asís (item **3889**), *La vida entera* de Juan Carlos Martini (item **3846**) o los espléndidos relatos de Carlos Gardini (item **3831**).

En las *nouvelles* de *Pájaros de la cabeza* (item **3828**), Enrique Fogwill explora las posibilidades narrativas de distinto tipo de obsesiones. En general, sus relatos son como metáforas de una ubicua falta de integridad, provocada por una sociedad que transforma en necesidades muchas convenciones triviales.

La experiencia judía (items **3823** y **3827**) y los distintos aspectos del exilio son núcleo temático de antologías atractivas (item **3876**).

A la bastante copiosa producción de nuevos relatos y a la de textos aparecidos originariamente en el exilio, se agregan reediciones y antologías, a veces precedidas por prólogos en que el ditirambo vacío ocupa el lugar que debería reservarse para una evaluación orientadora. La falta de espacio no ha permitido anotar las reediciones, antologías, "selecciones personales" de Enrique Anderson Imbert, Antonio Di Benedetto, Sara Gallardo, Mempo Giardinelli, Eduardo Mallea, Ernesto Sábato, Bernardo Verbitsky, para dar unos pocos nombres. Se ha reeditado *Los oficios terrestres* de Rodolfo Walsh (item **3878**), suprimido como sus otros libros por el régimen militar que ocupó el poder entre 1976–83 y que en 1977 hizo desaparecer a su autor.

El 10 de julio de 1990, a los 57 años, murió Manuel Puig en Cuernavaca, México. Su última novela (item **3859**), cuya acción ocurre en Brasil, penúltimo exilio voluntario del autor, combina el tema de la nostalgia del lugar de origen con el de la nostalgia de la juventud. [MLB y MCG]

En cuanto a crítica literaria, como en años anteriores, el nombre de Borges encabeza la nómina de publicaciones recibidas. Algunos libros y numerosos artículos (juiciosamente excluidos de esta nómina) trajinan sus páginas y fatigan a sus obligados lectores; otros justifican ampliamente el interés constante en una obra fundacional. Por diversas razones corresponde destacar la original aproximación de

Grau (item **3936**); las propuestas teóricas de Block de Behar (item **3916**); el acceso a la esfera privada y memoriosa de Estela Canto (item **3922**); el desafío que anuncian las páginas de Balderston para un sector de la crítica (item **3911**). Decir "Borges, el mismo" alcanza, creo, para describir la insistente recuperación de conversaciones y recuerdos. La mera mención de una "marca" pareciera ser suficiente para la publicación de una cronología, de un Borges oral, de un diccionario del Borges público, mientras la justificada efemérides encuadra las páginas que celebran la entrega del Premio Cervantes. Son útiles para diferentes públicos las compilaciones de ensayos realizadas por H. Bloom (item **3938**), C. Cortínez (item **3927**), R. Cosse (item **3939**) y Gerard de Cortanze (item **3921**). El trabajo de Meneses constituye un aporte a la "arqueología" de Borges (item **3943**); la publicación de *Biblioteca personal: prólogos* (item **3918**), la recuperación de la lectura, uno de sus mayores hábitos y legados.

El cómputo de entradas favorece en segundo lugar a Sábato; siquiera en parte, ello quizá se deba a la publicidad generada por su igualmente meritorio Premio Cervantes—de ser así, cabe anticipar para el próximo bienio una respetable nómina de publicaciones en torno a Bioy Casares. Textos sobre Macedonio, Martínez Estrada, Arlt, Cortázar, Viñas, Puig y Piglia, reflejan una veta inagotable para la esfera académica cuyo lenguaje posiblemente no se reconocería en las construcciones propuestas por Nicolás Rosa (item **3952**). Entre los hallazgos de este período se destacan el estudio fundamental de John King sobre la revista *Sur* (item **3941**) y, en otro circuito, la nostálgica recuperación de las peñas de Buenos Aires de Antonio Requeni (item **3949**). Algunos estudios sobre la literatura escrita durante la dictadura militar, el libro-homenaje a Conti (item **3937**), y los diálogos con Sebreli (item **3957**) apuntan a zonas que merecen una atención mayor. Sigue siendo notoria—y lamentablemente casi una constante—la ausencia de estudios sobre autores cada vez menos jóvenes y poseedores (cada vez más) de una obra cuya importancia ya no requiere justificación alguna ante los guardianes de "los clásicos." [SS]

PARAGUAY

En el bienio que reseñamos destaca la publicación de una colección de cuentos sobre el Paraguay, en el contexto de la dictadura, de Manuel Argüello, *Las letras del diablo y otros cuentos* (item **3880**); la novela del prolífico cuentista destacado Mario Halley Mora, titulada *Los hombres de Celina* (item **3881**); y una colección de cuentos de Sara Karlik, *Demasiada historia* (item **3882**) muy emparentada con la narrativa de Horacio Quiroga, pero no imitación. Una muestra de la producción del relato corto en el Paraguay es la publicación de *Premio Cultura Hispánica 1984 de Cuentos* (item **3884**), entre los que se encuentra otro cuento de Sara Karlik.

Continúa en vigencia la publicación de textos escritos en la cárcel tales como *El contador de cuentos: resabios de prisión* (item **3891**), *Relatos de la cárcel: esta empecinada flor* (item **3897**), *Paloma de contrabando: textos escritos en las cárceles de Buenos Aires* (item **3914**) y *La otra orilla* (item **3903**).

En cuanto a crítica de la narrativa paraguaya, la figura de Augusto Roa Bastos domina lo publicado en este período por haber recibido el Premio Cervantes en 1989. La revista *Insula* dedica un tercio del vol. 521 al estudio de su obra (item **3970**). Hugo Rodríguez Alcalá publicó un volumen de textos críticos sobre *Poetas y prosistas paraguayos y otros breves ensayos* (item **3968**). [MGP]

URUGUAY

En el Uruguay se destaca la novela corta de Juan Carlos Onetti *Cuando entonces* (item **3899**); un nuevo volumen de Eduardo Galeano, *El libro de los abrazos* (item **3896**); y una nueva novela de Teresa Porzecanski, *Una novela erótica* (item **3901**).

Los estudios de crítica e historia literaria valiosos de este período son un artículo de Lucía Guerra Cunningham sobre la narrativa de Cristina Peri Rossi (item **3979**) y una bibliografía comentada de las revistas uruguayas publicadas entre 1885 y 1985 (item **3973**), que ofrece información sobre esta actividad tan importante en el quehacer literario intelectual de la América hispana. [MGP]

Sin desmerecer en modo alguno el esfuerzo por interrogar la producción de autores reconocidos como los uruguayos Horacio Quiroga (item **3981**), Felisberto (item **3982**), y Onetti (items **3980** y **3978**) y los paraguayos Roa Bastos (items **3961, 3970, 3962, 3963, 3965, 3966, 3971** y **3972**) y Bareiro Saguier (item **3964**), corresponde indagar sobre tantas otras obras que aguardan (¿pacientemente?) la atención de la crítica. Los caminos de esta práctica formal de la lectura nos aseguran que no cejarán los estudios sobre textos fundacionales; también que los claros y programáticos ensayos de Benedetti (items **3974** y **3975**) seguirán atrayendo a un núcleo fiel a toda su producción. Como en otras ocasiones, sin embargo, cabe reiterar la esperanza de ver una mayor amplitud en el marco atendido por la crítica académica. [SS]

PROSE FICTION
Argentina

3813 Aira, César. Canto castrato. Barcelona: J. Vergara Editor, 1984. 351 p. (Novela contemporánea)

La acción ocurre hacia 1783, en el submundo galante de la ópera y los admirados *castrati,* las intrigas del papado y de los nobles. *Tour de force* combina la aparente soltura contemporánea con el detallismo de la novela de intriga de la época barroca o de las reconstrucciones cinematográficas de los relatos galantes. [MLB]

3814 Albarracín, Raúl Alberto. Provincia II: relatos. Tucumán, Argentina: Biblioteca Alberdi, Instituto de Literatura Argentina, 1988. 163 p.

Selección de 15 relatos, algunos de los cuales fueron publicados anteriormente. La yuxtaposición de voces diversas y de tiempos históricos diferentes, así como el uso coloquial del lenguaje dan originalidad a la crítica social y política llevada a cabo en ambientes costumbristas provincianos. [MCG]

3815 Alvarenga, Martín. País alucinógeno: Travesura fantástica. Buenos Aires: Torres Agüero, 1988. 200 p.

Novela imaginativa que integra las experimentaciones de la vanguardia y del *nouveau roman* para crear un laberinto lingüístico, desde el cual el protagonista-escritor explora su conciencia, la función del lenguaje y el proceso creador. Analiza asimismo las fuerzas antagónicas que se combinan en el

tejido cultural del país. Premio Fondo Nacional de las Artes, 1987. [MCG]

3816 Brailovsky, Antonio Elio. El asalto al cielo. Buenos Aires: Sudamericana/ Planeta, 1985. 155 p.

La novela postula la parcialidad esencial de los registros de la historia. Pero también sugiere que, leídos con actitud crítica, esos registros incompletos del pasado pueden aclarar nuestra visión inevitablemente fragmentada del presente. [MLB]

3817 Briante, Miguel. Las hamacas voladoras y otros relatos. Estudio preliminar de María Rosa Lojo de Beuter. Buenos Aires: Puntosur Editores, 1987. 136 p. (Puntosur literaria)

Este narrador argentino pertenece a la Generación del 60 que se caracteriza por la producción de una narrativa poblada de exploraciones y replanteos culturales. Destacan "Capítulo Prímero," "El Héroe" y "Las Hamacas Voladoras." La primera edición de estos cuentos se hizo en 1964. Otras obras de este autor, no muy prolífico, pero sí ejemplo de las preocupaciones de su generación, son *Hombre en la Orilla* (1968) y *Ley del juego* (1983). Se cierra el volumen con un "Estudio Posliminar" de María Rosa Lojo. [MGP]

3818 Casas, Juan Carlos. Fraile Muerto. Buenos Aires: Editorial Atlántida, 1988. 386 p.: ill. (Col. Libro elegido: Novela Atlántida)

Novela. Narra las peripecias de unos ingleses que, atraídos por las riquezas del país se instalan en 1865 en la frontera cordobesa. De las luchas contra el suelo y contra el indio surgen las ilusiones, los recuerdos y el racismo de los extranjeros. Los epígrafes, provenientes de libros de viajeros y de autores locales (L.V. Mansilla, E. del Campo, J.B. Alberdi y otros), indican el tono entre histórico y costumbrista. [MCG]

3819 Castillo, Abelardo. El que tiene sed. Buenos Aires: Emecé Editores, 1985. 255 p.

En su delirio alcohólico, el protagonista procura rescatar su escritura y, junto con ella, su integridad. [MLB]

3820 Comte, Roberto. La otra vida: novela. Buenos Aires: Torres Agüero Editor, 1988. 120 p.

Novela fantástica que recuerda *Metamorfosis* o *Rayuela* aunque sin sus novedades narrativas. Un argentino de mediana edad transmigra al cuerpo y circunstancias de un industrial francés y desde su nueva situación intenta aclaraciones sobre la identidad de su yo verdadero. [MCG]

3821 Conteris, Hiber. El diez por ciento de vida: el test Chandler. Barcelona: Laia, 1986. 279 p. (Alfa 7)

"Homenaje a Raymond Chandler y Philip Marlowe," el relato—cuyo narrador es el famoso detective norteamericano—utiliza personajes, situaciones, lugares tomados de la ficción o de la vida del escritor norteamericano. [MLB]

3822 Cortázar, Julio. El examen. Madrid: Ediciones Alfaguara, 1987. 291 p.

Hacia el final de su vida, Cortázar decidió publicar este relato escrito en 1950 porque "me gusta su libre lenguaje, su fábula sin moraleja, su melancolía porteña, y también porque la pesadilla de donde nació sigue despierta y anda por las calles." [MLB]

3823 Cuentos judíos latinoamericanos. Selección y prólogo de Ricardo Feierstein. Buenos Aires: Milá Editor, 1989. 240 p. (Raíces; 43)

Consiste de 25 relatos de valor variado, con el común denominador del cuestionamiento e investigación de la identidad del judío latinoamericano. [MCG]

3824 Denevi, Marco et al. Enciclopedia secreta de una familia argentina. Buenos Aires: Editorial Sudamericana, 1986. 277 p.: index. (Narrativas argentinas)

En "artículos" que configuran una saga familiar paródica a partir de la llegada de un "adelantadito," Denevi se burla de las convenciones: de la historia; de la sociedad; de la literatura argentina e hispanoamericana desde los tiempos coloniales hasta la actualidad. [MLB]

3825 Di Benedetto, Antonio. Páginas de Antonio Di Benedetto. Seleccionadas por el autor. Estudio preliminar de Graciela Maturo. Buenos Aires: Editorial Celtia, 1987. 271 p. (Col. Escritores argentinos de hoy)

Cuentos seleccionados por el autor de *Zama* poco antes de su muerte en 1986. [MLB]

3826 Diaconú, Alina. Los ojos azules. Buenos Aires: Editorial Fraterna, 1986. 238 p.

La protagonista, abandonada por su marido, es sometida a un violento tratamiento psiquiátrico. Las fantasías desencadenadas por la droga constituyen el texto, que caricaturiza clichés de la literatura popular y de las series televisivas. [MLB]

3827 Feierstein, Ricardo. Mestizo. Estudio de Andrés Avellaneda. Buenos Aires: Milá, 1988. 331 p.: ill. (Col. imaginaria)

Replantea un tema tratado anteriormente por el autor: la integración de las familias judías de origen europeo a la sociedad latinoamericana—argentina, en este caso. La estructura policial resulta eficaz para relatar las peripecias de un personaje en busca de su identidad y de la solución a un crimen que ha presenciado. Con la técnica del *collage* se combinan sueños, fotografías y fragmentos de memorias. [MCG]

3828 Fogwill, Rodolfo Enrique. Pájaros de la cabeza. Buenos Aires: Catálogos Editora, 1985. 185 p.

Cada una de estas tres *nouvelles* ejemplifica y representa las dificultades, límites y posibilidades de una escritura que dé cuenta de obsesiones desencadenadas por motores diversos: la reflexión sobre los problemas de la narración; la frivolidad generada por el consumerismo estólido; las asociaciones incongruentes inducidas por las drogas. [MLB]

3829 Fontanarrosa, R. Nada del otro mundo, y otros cuentos. 2a ed. Buenos Aires: Ediciones de la Flor, 1988. 256 p.

Humor negro, parodia, secretas o explícitas alusiones literarias, reproducción de formas coloquiales, sirven para desmontar mitos populares o desacralizar los lugares comunes erigidos en entidades absolutas. [MLB]

3830 Gambaro, Griselda. Lo impenetrable. Buenos Aires: Torres Agüero Editor, 1984. 151 p.

Parodia de la "literatura erótica," escrita en Barcelona durante la dictadura argentina de la década del 70. [MLB]

3831 Gardini, Carlos. Sinfonía cero. Buenos Aires: Riesa, 1984. 228 p.

Seis cuentos y una novela breve que da título al libro de uno de los mejores escritores de su generación. [MLB]

3832 Guebel, Daniel. La perla del emperador. Buenos Aires: Emecé Editores, 1990. 269 p. (Escritores argentinos)

La novela se estructura en torno a la búsqueda de un objeto inaccesible, la perla del título, de valores metafísicos. Con gran maestría, la voz narrativa crea un ambiente de fantasía oriental en el que los relatos, a modo de muñecas rusas se contienen y espejean. Premio Emecé 1989–90. [MCG]

3833 Heker, Liliana. Zona de clivaje. Buenos Aires: Legasa, 1987. 284 p. (Nueva literatura)

Los equívocos y malentendidos de la protagonista no son del todo convincentes, pero Heker, que maneja con soltura el habla de los intelectuales jóvenes de las últimas décadas, transita con destreza por distintos puntos de vista narrativos. Primera novela de una narradora que se inició a principios de la década del 60 con un libro de cuentos que obtuvo la Mención Unica del Concurso Hispanoamericano de Literatura de Casa de las Américas. [MLB]

3834 Ibáñez, Oscar. El señor de los cuatro vientos. Buenos Aires: Plus Ultra, 1984. 287 p. (Nuestros novelistas)

Alegoría sobre la personalidad y la supuesta obra redentora de Perón. [MLB]

3835 Jurado, Alicia. Descubrimiento del mundo: memorias. v. 1. Argentina : Emecé Editores, 1989– . 1 v.

Autobiografía. Siguiendo las reglas tradicionales del género, Jurado narra el desarrollo de su carrera como escritora y explica la situación y la evolución de la mujer argentina en el siglo XX. [MCG]

3836 Korn, Francis. Más Amalias de las que se puede tolerar. Buenos Aires: Grupo Editor Latinoamericano; Emece Editores, 1989. 96 p. (Col. Escritura de hoy)

Ocho cuentos cuidadosamente narrados. Con mucha originalidad, combinan el incidente extraño, el mal comportamiento, los choques de sentimientos encontrados y las situaciones fantásticas. [MCG]

3837 Kovadloff, Santiago. Mundo menor. Buenos Aires: Torres Agüero Editor, 1986. 74 p. (Col. Primeras ediciones)

Dos *nouvelles* cuyas tramas, que se disimulan entre convenciones, minucias y prejuicios burgueses, denuncian la violencia que pervade todos los órdenes. [MLB]

3838 Kozameh, Alicia. Pasos bajo el agua. Buenos Aires: Editorial Contrapunto, 1987. 106 p.: ill. (Col. Nueva literatura argentina)

La autora ha trasmutado sus experiencias como prisionera política (1975–78) en ocho relatos bien construidos, sin escatimar detalles respecto de prácticas inadmisibles y sin caer en la truculencia. [MLB]

3839 Lojo de Beuter, María Rosa. Canción perdida en Buenos Aires al oeste. Buenos Aires: Torres Agüero Editor, 1987. 131 p.

Premio Fondo Nacional de las Artes 1986. Distintos miembros de una familia fundada por inmigrantes recuerdan e interpretan sus experiencias. La narración se ve entorpecida por exceso de lirismo, voluntarioso y convencional. [MLB]

3840 Lojo de Beuter, María Rosa. Marginales: cuentos, 1974–1980; Premio Fondo Nacional de las Artes, 1985, Unica Mención Concurso Emecé, 1980–1981. Buenos Aires: Epsilon Editora, 1986. 100 p. (Narrativa argentina contemporánea)

El vocabulario y la sintaxis de muchos de estos cuentos son como una "pátina de época" contraproducente, que desmerece y a veces encubre por completo su fuerza narrativa. [MLB]

3841 López, Fernando Eudoro. Arde aún sobre los años: novela. La Habana: Casa de las Américas, 1985. 264 p.

Premio Casa de las Américas 1985. Este *Bildungsroman* de un joven provinciano culmina con la Guerra de las Malvinas. La narración, ágil al principio, se hace reiterativa y acaba con una profesión de optimismo político, bien intencionada y harto ingenua. [MLB]

3842 Lugones, Leopoldo. Cuentos fantásticos. Edición, introducción y notas de Pedro Luis Barcia. Madrid: Castalia, 1987. 251 p. (Clásicos Castalia; 168)

Contiene 21 cuentos de Lugones, de distintas épocas, ordenados cronológicamente. [MLB]

3843 Luna, Félix. Soy Roca. Buenos Aires: Editorial Sudamericana, 1989. 495 p.: bibl., ill., plates.

Novela histórica en primera persona. Julio A. Roca narra su labor de comandante de la campaña del desierto y de presidente de Argentina en dos oportunidades (1880–86 y 1898–1904). La combinación de hechos históricos con anécdotas personales y el empleo del lenguaje coloquial confieren credibilidad e interés a la narración y explican que un texto muy documentado se haya convertido en "best seller." [MCG]

3844 Martelli, Juan Carlos. Debajo de la mesa. Buenos Aires: Legasa, 1987. 171 p. (Nueva literatura)

Novela de lectura laboriosa, en la que se yuxtaponen metonímicamente el tiempo, el espacio, los personajes, las alusiones políticas, la política como perversión sexual, la fantasía orgiástica como lucha por el poder, las teorías sobre la carga del significante. [MLB]

3845 Martini, Juan Carlos. El fantasma imperfecto. Buenos Aires: Editorial Legasa, 1986. 186 p. (Nueva literatura)

La novela mimetiza en su escritura muy detallista la sordidez del aeropuerto donde trascurre la acción. La economía y la atención al detalle están al servicio de un desenlace en que no se "explica" nada. [MLB]

3846 Martini, Juan Carlos. La vida entera. Introducción de Julio Cortázar. Buenos Aires: Editorial Legasa, 1987. 283 p. (Omnibus)

Enjuiciamiento del régimen militar instalado en 1976. El libro apareció por primera vez en España en 1981. En una escritura ponderada por Cortázar y Onetti, se fusiona la revelación críptica de los sueños (nombres alegóricos; espacio y tiempo indeterminados)

con la coherencia y el rigor de la vigilia razonadora. [MLB]

3847 Medina, Enrique. Buscando a Madonna. Buenos Aires: Editores Milton, 1987. 200 p.

La contratapa anuncia que "el hilo conductor" del relato es el "pensamiento femenino;" el texto, en cambio, es un mero repositorio de estereotipos sobre la mujer, un documento del sexismo masculino porteño de fines del siglo XX. El mimetismo fotográfico del lenguaje trasciende los límites de la caricatura, y lo hace inverosímil. [MLB]

3848 Mibashan, David. Vida y vuelta. Buenos Aires: Grupo Editor Latinoamericano; Emecé Editores, 1987. 127 p. (Col. Escritura de hoy)

Bajo epígrafe tomado de *Le mythe de Sisyphe*, Mibashan crea una novela psicológica de dos vertientes: el suicidio de un joven y su supervivencia en la persona su novia. El cuestionamiento de las relaciones íntimas queda en un plano superficial sin lograr un análisis exhaustivo. [MCG]

3849 Nicastro, Laura Diana. Oyó que los pasos. Buenos Aires: Corregidor, 1987. 158 p.

En muchos de estos 15 cuentos, las metáforas y símiles "poéticos" funcionan como distracciones innecesarias, ajenas al orden narrativo. En los mejores, se logra una tensión sostenida que se desanuda con eficacia. [MLB]

3850 Oliveri, Marta. El confinamiento. Buenos Aires: Editorial Legasa, 1989. 226 p. (Omnibus)

Novela en primera persona. La epístola y el fragmento del diario íntimo son las formas elegidas para la "confesión" de una vida. Con exceso de minuciosidad, el narrador sigue un intrincado hilo de Ariadna que indaga culpas y estados de ánimo y que plantea cuestiones filosóficas. Premio Fondo Nacional de las Artes 1988. [MCG]

3851 Orgambide, Pedro G. La convaleciente. Buenos Aires: Legasa, 1987. 160 p. (Nueva literatura)

La tesis de la novela es que volver del exilio exige tomar distancia con respecto al pasado y aceptar la nostalgia. La protagonista está movida a la vez por ese doble proceso y por un laborioso afán de reconciliación. [MLB]

3852 Orgambide, Pedro G. Historias imaginarias de la Argentina. Buenos Aires: Editorial Legasa, 1986. 206 p. (Nueva literatura)

Catorce relatos, una semblanza biográfica, opiniones críticas y bibliografía del autor. [MLB]

3853 Orgambide, Pedro G. La mulata y el guerrero. Buenos Aires: Ediciones del Sol, 1986. 178 p. (Los Nuestros; 3)

"Entretenimientos" relativamente breves, situados en "Los Orígenes," "Los Ayeres," "Como si Fuera Hoy." [MLB]

3854 Pampillo, Gloria. Estimado Lerner. Buenos Aires: Grupo Editor Latinoamericano, 1986. 137 p. (Col. Escritura de hoy)

Ocho cuentos fantásticos en que lo cotidiano adquiere cualidades extrañas. Con una admirable economía narrativa que combina lo grotesco, la ironía y el humor, el lenguaje familiar se transforma en juegos sutiles que descubren las complicadas relaciones humanas. Recuerda la narrativa de Silvina Ocampo. [MCG]

3855 Piglia, Ricardo. Prisión perpetua. Buenos Aires: Editorial Sudamericana, 1988. 209 p. (Col. Narrativas argentinas)

A los seis relatos publicados en *Nombre falso* (1975) se ha agregado una *nouvelle* que encabeza y da título a este volumen. [MLB]

3856 Posse, Abel. Los perros del Paraíso. Barcelona: Argos Vergara, 1983. 253 p. (Bibliotheca del fénice; 11)

Los "perros del paraíso" son los cancerberos que a lo largo de la historia de la conquista y colonización han sido instrumentos de los sucesivos oficialismos expoliadores. El texto es una sostenida parodia: de la grandilocuencia hispánica, el pretendido desenfado de los argentinos, la hipocresía y tapujos de los detentores del poder. [MLB]

3857 Posse, Abel. El viajero de Agartha. Buenos Aires: Emecé Editores, 1989. 252 p. (Escritores argentinos)

Novela de espionaje compuesta en torno a las notas de un agente nazi. Su misión: llegar a Agartha y ganar para la causa las fuerzas superiores del espíritu. Con ese marco, la novela indaga a nivel individual, la obsesión ideológica que culmina en el delirio. [MCG]

3858 Pozzi, Edna. El lento rostro de la inocencia. Buenos Aires: Emecé Editores, 1986. 206 p.

Premio Emecé 1985–86. La interferencia de lo subjetivo y lo político es el motor de este relato, organizado en secuencias narradas por los personajes o reconstruidas por una voz narrativa. [MLB]

3859 Puig, Manuel. Cae la noche tropical: novela. Barcelona: Seix Barral, 1988. 221 p. (Biblioteca breve)

En la que sería su última novela, Puig ensambla los temas del envejecimiento, el destierro, la pobreza extrema en un relato *sui generis,* a la vez irónico y nostálgico, que se lee con la avidez que suscitan los textos policiales. [MLB]

3860 Redondo, Víctor F.A. Las familias secretas. Buenos Aires: Catálogos Editora, 1986. 164 p.

El autor recibió el Premio de Poesía Jorge Guillén en 1980. Estos textos reiterativos—centrados en la obsesión por el sexo y las drogas—carecen casi por completo de una mínima tensión narrativa. [MLB]

3861 Rivera, Andrés. La revolución es un sueño eterno. Buenos Aires: Grupo Editor Latinoamericano; Emecé Editores, 1987. 170 p. (Col. Escritura de hoy)

El protagonista es Juan José Castelli, una de las figuras patéticas de la historia argentina. Su elocuencia, que en la vida real fue decisiva para el triunfo de la Revolución de 1810, se ha convertido en la crispada subjetividad del orador privado del habla por un cáncer de la lengua. Con lucidez extrema, el personaje consigue adueñarse de su destino al analizar por escrito, sin retaceos, tanto su pasado como la versión que su recuerdo le ofrece de los demás. [MLB]

3862 Rodrigué, Emilio. Ondina, supertramp. Buenos Aires: Editorial Sudamericana, 1987. 201 p. (Narrativas argentinas)

Relato de tono autobiográfico ("experimento en las ficciones de la veracidad," dice Rodrigué), en que se yuxtaponen escenas y consideraciones que rezuman una suerte de narcisismo intelectual entre exasperante e ingenuo. [MLB]

3863 Roffé, Reina. La rompiente. Xalapa, México: Univ. Veracruzana, 1987. 98 p.

Nouvelle premiada en el Concurso Internacional de Novela Breve, de San Francisco, Córdoba. Experiencias diversas de una protagonista tienen como aglutinante el sostenido sesgo introspectivo con que se las refiere. [MLB]

3864 Sáenz, Dalmiro and **Sergio Josevovshy.** El día que mataron a Cafiero. Montevideo: Puntosur Editores, 1987. 219 p.

Novela que critica los abusos del poder de las últimas décadas. Expone las luchas entre la guerrilla, la institución militar y los partidos políticos. [MCG]

3865 Saer, Juan José. La ocasión. Barcelona: Ediciones Destino, 1988. 249 p. (Col. Ancora y delfín; 614)

A mediados del siglo XIX, un ocultista que tiene que huir de Europa se establece en el campo, en la llanura argentina, donde un amigo criollo terrateniente lo protege. Irónicamente, la ciencia del protagonista no le sirve para resolver el problema que ocupa sus días: ¿su mujer lo engañó o no con su amigo criollo? Relato cargado de alusiones sutilmente anacrónicas, que sin entorpecer el ambiente "de época" remiten a nuestro tiempo, a la falacia de nuestra ilusión de control. Premio Nadal 1987. [MLB]

3866 Schmid, Silvia. Mabel salta la rayuela. Buenos Aires: Editorial Legasa, 1987. 113 p. (Omnibus)

Primer libro de narrativa de la autora de tres textos teatrales. Consiste de 15 cuentos de factura diversa, escritos con imaginación, ironía y sentido de la tensión narrativa. Premio Fondo Nacional de las Artes 1985–86. [MLB]

3867 Schopflocher, Roberto. Venus llega al pueblo. Buenos Aires: Grupo Editor Latinoamericano; Emecé Editores, 1986. 205 p. (Col. Escritura de hoy)

Catorce cuentos. Sobresalen los de leve tono moralizante que describen y critican la vida de los pueblos pequeños. [MCG]

3868 Sur, No. 358–359, enero-dic. 1986– . Buenos Aires: s.n.

Número dedicado a Manuel Mújica Láinez (1910–84) incluye textos de y sobre el escritor y una bibliografía. [MLB]

3869 Tizón, Héctor. Fuego en Casabindo. Estudio posliminar de Carmen Real.

Buenos Aires: Puntosur Editores, 1988. 122 p.: map. (Puntosur literaria)

Nueva versión de un relato fechado en 1968, parte del ciclo narrativo dedicado a rescatar la historia de la puna jujeña. [MLB]

3870 Torquelli, Américo Alfredo. En la selva por fin. Buenos Aires: El Cid Editor, 1980. 113 p.

Recopilación de relatos que obtuvo el Premio del Fondo Nacional de las Artes a la Produccíon Literaria Inédita de 1978. [MLB]

3871 Torre, Javier. Las noches de Maco. Buenos Aires: Editorial Legasa, 1986. 231 p. (Nueva literatura)

El texto, a veces excesivamente moroso, consigna desencuentros y antagonismos de una familia argentina que repiten o resultan de los conflictos ideológicos de las últimas décadas. [MLB]

3872 Torres Zavaleta, Jorge. El primer viaje. Buenos Aires: Emecé Editores, 1986. 190 p. (Escritores argentinos)

Viaje de iniciación de un joven que deberá afrontar fuerzas antagónicas y ambiguas en su primera experiencia amorosa. [MCG]

3873 Trías, Manuel. La miel amarga. Buenos Aires: Epsilon Editora, 1987. 152 p. (Narrativa argentina contemporánea)

Primera novela del autor. La narración en primera persona combina las memorias de unas vacaciones de la adolescencia con meditaciones sobre el proceso creador, la individualidad y la comunicación. Premio Fondo Nacional de las Artes, 1986. [MCG]

3874 Valenzuela, Luisa. Novela negra con argentinos. Barcelona: Plaza & Janés, 1990. 202 p. (Plaza & Janés literaria; 6)

Novela. Roberta Aguilar y Agustín Palant investigan los motivos que impulsaron a este último, al asesinato. Ambos protagonistas, escritores, emprenden un recorrido por una Nueva York sórdida y por momentos, grotesca. La narración sigue las tendencias experimentales de Bataille y Artaud y con gran dominio explora los límites y las relaciones entre realidad, delirio y ficción, cuerpo, teatro y escritura. Hay otras dos ediciones de la novela en español (Buenos Aires: Editorial Sudamericana, 1991 y Hanover, N.H.: Ediciones del Norte, 1990) y traducción al inglés de Tony Talbot (New York: Simon & Schuster, 1992). [MCG]

3875 Vanasco, Alberto. Al sur del Río Grande. Buenos Aires: Torres Agüero Editor, 1987. 124 p.

Historia de perseguidos políticos refugiados en São Paulo, Caracas, México, D.F. y Chile. [MLB]

3876 20 cuentos del exilio. Recopilación de Humberto Costatini. México: Editorial Tierra del Fuego, 1983. 177 p.

Costantini ha calificado de "provisoria" esta atractiva antología de relatos de 16 autores, muchos de ellos conocidos; inéditos o casi, los demás. [MLB]

3877 Verolin, Irma. Hay una nena que gira. Buenos Aires: T. Agüero, 1988. 174 p.

Estos cuentos son prácticamente una memoria de la infancia diseminada en situaciones variadas. La nostalgia, inevitable, está bien dosificada aunque a veces desestima lo narrativo en aras de lo poético. [MLB]

3878 Walsh, Rodolfo J. Los oficios terrestres. Buenos Aires: Ediciones de la Flor, 1986. 99 p.

Reedición de un volumen prohibido por el régimen militar, junto con el resto de las obras del autor. Textos ejemplares que amalgaman economía narrativa, escritura impecable, intuición de la inevitabilidad e insensatez de la violencia. [MLB]

3879 Wiede, Guillermo A. Jinetes de nombre muerto: romance de Entre Ríos, 1861–1871; novela. Ilustraciones de Sara Molas Quiroga. Buenos Aires: Grupo Editor Latinoamericano; EMECE Editores, 1988. 277 p.: ill. (Col. Escritura de hoy)

Primera novela del autor. Con la yuxtaposición de artículos periodísticos y de testimonios imaginarios recrea la crónica de la providencia de Entre Ríos en la segunda mitad del siglo XIX. [MCG]

Paraguay

3880 Argüello, Manuel E.B. Las letras del diablo y otros cuentos. Asunción: Editorial Meba, 1988. 139 p.

Interesante colección de cuentos sobre la vida en el Paraguay cuyo telón de fondo es la dictadura y el abuso de la autoridad, que llega en muchos casos al exceso. Esta colección contiene 15 cuentos de este autor que

también ha publicado poemas, además de ser actor y director de teatro. [MGP]

3881 Halley Mora, Mario. Cuentos, microcuentos y anticuentos. Asunción: El Lector, 1987. 140 p. (Col. literaria; 8)

Este escritor es dramaturgo (ver *HLAS 50:3808*), novelista y cuentista con obra prolífica. Recibió el Premio La República en 1981 por su novela *Los hombres de Celina* (Asunción: Ediciones NAPA, 1981, 168 p.). En esta colección se destacan los microcuentos. Este narrador se destaca en las letras paraguayas por su agilidad, la excelente tensión que logra en los cuentos, y el fino humor que maneja los relatos. En la última sección de esta colección se incluyen tres textos titulados "Anticuentos." [MGP]

3882 Karlik, Sara. Demasiada historia. Buenos Aires: Grupo Editor Latinoamericano, 1988. 140 p. (Col. Escritura de Hoy)

Escritora paraguaya residente en Chile desde 1962 ofrece en este conjunto de relatos una notable habilidad para el género que la relaciona con la cuentística de Horacio Quiroga en la fuerza de la tensión narrativa, en los temas, y en el ámbito geográfico en que los sitúa. El volumen está dividido en tres partes: 1) "En Escena;" 2) "Trabalengua;" y 3) "Demasiada Historia." [MGP]

3883 Karlik, Sara. Entre ánimas y sueños. Prólogo de Carlos Villagra Marsal. Asunción: Editorial Araverá, 1987. 129 p.: port. (Serie Narrativa; 5)

En 1987, el primer volumen de cuentos de esta autora paraguaya se tituló *La oscuridad de afuera* (Santiago: Ediciones Ergo Sum, 1986). *Entre ánimas y sueños* es su segundo libro que consta de 24 relatos cortos, construidos con muy poco material narrativo, que queda compensado con la intensidad de una no acción o stasis de sus personajes. Interesante colección para los interesados en la narrativa femenina hispanoamericana. [MGP]

3884 Premio Cultura Hispánica 1984 de Cuentos. Asunción: Instituto Paraguayo de Cultura Hispánica; Mediterráneo, 1984. 102 p.: ill. (Serie Antología premios)

En esta colección se reunen 18 cuentos de seis autores ganadores del Premio Cultura Hispánica 1984 patrocinado por el Instituto de Cultura Hispánica del Paraguay. Los cuentistas son: René Ferrer de Arrellaga, Moncho Azuaga, José de Jesús Aguirre, Neida de Mendonça, Sara Karlik de Arditi y Darío González. Estos textos ofrecen una diversidad que ilustra la actividad de la cuentística en el Paraguay. [MGP]

3885 Ramírez Santacruz, Gilberto. Esa hierba que nunca muere. Asunción: Ediciones Ñanduti Vive; Intercontinental Editora, 1989. 162 p.

Es la primera novela de este joven escritor cuyo tema central es la formación y derrota de los movimientos guerrilleros contra la dictadura del Gen. Stroessner en la década que corren entre los 50 y 60 aproximadamente. Es testimonio narrativo del desgarrado proceso histórico del Paraguay, asentado en relatos de revolucionarios que participaron en estos movimientos. [MGP]

3886 Roa Bastos, Augusto Antonio. Carta abierta a mi pueblo. Buenos Aires: Frente Paraguayo en Argentina, 1986. 69 p.

Un importante texto del novelista paraguayo en el que hace un llamamiento al pueblo del Paraguay con ocasión de conmemorarse los 50 años de la Guerra del Chaco. Invita a una reflexión sobre la historia y el espíritu nacional, para buscar el camino de la regeneración y conciliación nacional. [MGP]

3887 Saguier, Raquel. La niña que perdí en el circo. Prólogo de J.A. Rauskin. Asunción: RP Ediciones, 1987. 141 p.

Primera novela de esta autora paraguaya que ilustra una de las direcciones de la narrativa femenina actual en ese país. Se trata de una narración que va en busca de un encuentro entre la niña que quedó atrapada en la mujer adulta que la protagonista es y la mujer adulta que surge de esa niña. [MGP]

Uruguay

3888 Alfaro, Milita. Jaime Roos: el sonido de la calle. Montevideo: Ediciones Trilce, 1987. 87 p.: ill.

Entrevista con Jaime Roos, cultor de la música popular uruguaya, cuyo aporte ha tenido el apoyo masivo del público. A la entrevistadora le interesa en particular el tema de la identidad, que a lo largo de la conversación se desarrolla ampliamente. De interés para los interesados en la cultura urbana del Uruguay contemporáneo. [MGP]

3889 Asís, Jorge. Partes de inteligencia. v. 1. Montevideo: Puntosur Editores, 1987. 1 v.

Parodia del deterioro del significado de las palabras a que conduce, fatalmente, la actividad burocrática de los "Servicios" de inteligencia . El apego a la letra resulta en un discurso abstruso, generador de situaciones incoherentes y de prácticas inmorales equiparables a las del terrorismo institucionalizado. [MLB]

3890 Barros-Lémez, Alvaro. La larga marcha de lo verosímil: narrativa uruguaya del siglo XX. (*Casa Am.*, 39:170, sept./oct. 1988, p. 41–50)

Análisis de la narrativa uruguaya desde 1973—fecha de golpe de estado—hasta el presente. Ofrece una panorámica de las circunstancias sociales y políticas del Uruguay durante ese período que divide el autor en siete períodos. A partir de 1984 se inicia el proceso de apertura, aunque al comienzo está signado por movimiento lento que busca adaptarse a las nuevas circumtancias políticas. Barros-Lémez marca el estrecho lazo que vincula la narrativa y la producción poética con las circunstancias políticas en este país, que la lleva a los *Cielitos y diálogos patrióticos* del iniciador de la literatura "nacional," el gauchesco poeta Hidalgo. Traza luego las experiencias literarias a través de obras de tema rural y las obras de tema urbano. Siguiendo el pensamiento de Angel Rama, de quien es discípulo el autor de este artículo, se analizan los elementos que dan marco a la producción literaria uruguaya de fines del siglo anterior y del que estamos casi terminando. Importante artículo para los interesados en la narrativa uruguaya y en los procesos de transformación de la narrativa hispanoamericana. [MGP]

3891 Baumgartner, José Luis. El contador de cuentos: resabios de prisión. Montevideo?: Ediciones Atenea, 1986. 135 p.

Los narradores de estos 20 relatos fueron prisioneros políticos en alguna cárcel uruguaya, deducción que se hace por algunas escasas referencias a zonas urbanas de Montevideo. Estos cuentos cortos reconstruyen las variadas experiencias de las relaciones entre torturadores y torturados en el magro marco de las instituciones penitenciarias del Uruguay. Excelente muestra del género. [MGP]

3892 Benedetti, Mario. Despistes y franquezas. Montevideo; Arca: Nueva Imagen, 1989. 358 p.

Este libro de "entreveros literarios," resultado de cinco años de labor, reúne cuentos, viñetas humorísticas, enigmas policíacos, relatos fantásticos, fragmentos autobiográficos, poemas, parodias y graffiti, según descripción del autor. Estos textos están organizados en tres categorías: 1)"Despistes;" 2)"Franquezas;" y 3)"El Tiempo que no Llegó" que incluyen sólo dos de ellos. La categoría "libro-entrevero," confiesa Benedetti, ha sido una larga aspiración en su tarea literaria que se cumple aquí, y que queda justificada por considerarla "un signo de libertad creadora, y del derecho a seguir el derrotero de la imaginación y no siempre el de ciertas estructuras rigurosas y prefijadas." Deja fijada su genealogía en compañía de Oswald de Andrade, Macedonio Fernández y Augusto Monterroso. Recomendado para los interesados en explorar este género contemporáneo de alto linaje en las letras de América. [MGP]

3893 Burel, Hugo. Tampoco la pena dura: novela. Montevideo: Editorial Sudamericana, 1989. 334 p.

Este narrador es autor de *Esperando a la pianista*, (colección de cuentos, 1983,) *Matías no baja, novela* (1986) y *El Vendedor de sueños* (1986). Esta novela, enmarcada por una cita de "Las babas del diablo," tiene como protagonista un joven fotógrafo, pintor frustrado y buscador de una imagen que capte la eternidad. Está marcado por el desarraigo del que es víctima en el paisaje anticipador de nuevas realidades que es el año 1968 en el sur de América Latina. [MGP]

3894 Butazonni, Fernando *et al.* Cuentos de nunca acabar: antología erótica. Montevideo: Ediciones Trilce, 1988. 157 p.

Este volumen reúne 12 cuentos eróticos de 12 autores: Mario Benedetti, Fernando Butazzoni, Miguel Angel Campodónico, Juan Capagorry, Victor Cunha, Elvio Gandolfo, Juan Carlos Mondragón, Elbio Rodríguez Barulari, Alfredo Zitarrosa, y tres mujeres: Silvia Lago, Teresa Porzecanski y Elena Rojas. Colección de cuentos que interesará a los estudiosos del género, que viene precedida de un breve prólogo de los editores. [MGP]

3895 Cuentos bajo sospecha: antología. Dirigida por Mario Delgado Aparaín. Montevideo: Ediciones Trilce, 1989. 119 p.

Esta colección interesa porque reúne seis cuentos de Omar Prego, Juan Carlos Mondragón, Juan Flo, Mario Delgado Aparaín, Ariel Muñiz y Hugo Burel. Esta colección viene a llenar un poco el vacío editorial del género en el Uruguay. [MGP]

3896 Galeano, Eduardo H. El libro de los abrazos: imágenes y palabras. Montevideo: Ediciones del Chanchito," 1989. 265 p.: ill.

Un nuevo libro del escritor uraguayo cuya obra incluye hasta el presente volumen los siguientes títulos: *Las venas abiertas de América Latina; Vagamundo y otros relatos; La canción de nosotros; Días y noches de amor y de guerra; Memoria del fuego (v. 1, Los nacimientos, v. 2, Las caras y las máscaras, v. 3, El siglo del viento); Entrevistas y artículos;* y *El libro de los abrazos.* El epígrafe de este magnífico volumen señala desde donde se habla en estos textos: "Recordar: Del latín *re-cordis,* volver a pasar por el corazón." Además de la riqueza y extraordinaria amplitud de los temas que toca, esta colección va bellamente ilustrada por el autor, de allí que el subtítulo sea "imágenes y palabras." [MGP]

3897 Invernizzi, Claudio. Relatos de la cárcel: esta empecinada flor. Montevideo: Ediciones de Las Bases, 1986. 42 p.: ill.

El autor de este libro de escritos en la cárcel es periodista. Escribió para *Jaque* y *La Hora* y actualmente para *Las Bases.* Estuvo en la cárcel 1975–79. Estos textos son testimonio de la experiencia individual dentro de los infiernos de las cárceles de la dictadura uruguaya. [MGP]

3898 Levrero, Mario. Espacios libres. Estudio posliminar de Pablo Fuentes. Buenos Aires: Puntosur Editores, 1987. 318 p. (Puntosur literaria)

Excelente colección de cuentos de este narrador, autor asimismo de tres volúmenes adicionales: *La máquina de pensar en Gladys* (1970); *Todo el tiempo* (1982) y *Aguas salobras* (1983). Es autor de tres novelas: *La ciudad* (1970); *París* (1979) y *El lugar* (1981). Se considera parte del grupo de narradores que Angel Rama calificara de "Los Raros," cuyo precedente es Felisberto Hernández, cultor de literatura fantástica o imaginativa en la que predomina una lógica del relato que funciona en contra de las leyes de la causalidad, de elementos insólitos que pueden pertenecer a varios ámbitos, entre los cuales estarían lo onírico, crítica de la realidad y algunos elementos surrealistas. Estudio posliminar de Pablo Fuentes. [MGP]

3899 Onetti, Juan Carlos. Cuando entonces. Madrid: Mondadori, 1987. 99 p. (Narrativa Mondadori)

Excelente narración en cuatro partes del escritor uruguayo en donde se reflexiona sobre las percepciones de la realidad desde el exilio, incrustada en la historia de Magda: "Donde Magda es Nombrada;" "Donde Magda es Amada;" "Donde Magda es Apartada;" "Donde la Teletipo Escribe el Final." [MGP]

3900 Onetti, Juan Carlos. Cuentos secretos: Periquito el Aguador y otras máscaras. Introducción de Omar Prego. Montevideo: Biblioteca de Marcha, 1986. 262 p.: ill., plates. (Col. Letras)

Esta edición de *Cuentos secretos* se inicia con una introducción de Omar Prego sobre la cuentística del escritor uruguayo. Este volumen contiene tres partes: 1) "Reflexiones," ensayos breves aparecidos en *Marcha* (junio 1939–abril 1941); 2) "Los Cuentos en *El Semanario*," ocho cuentos, dos de ellos inéditos y reconocidos por el autor (i.e., "El Fin Trágico de Alfredo Plumet" y "Un Crimen Perfecto"); y 3) Anexo Documental," texto de un concurso de cuentos para autores uruguayos, ganado por Onetti bajo el sinónimo de H.C. Ramos y otros documentos relacionados con este concurso. El último documento del libro es una "receta" de como escribir un cuento que ningún crítico o lector onettiano debe desconocer. [MGP]

3901 Porzecanski, Teresa. Una novela erótica. Montevideo: Margén, 1986. 99 p. (Los Narradores; 2)

Novela de la destacable escritora uruguaya que juega con la seducción de título. Este texto es una reflexión sobre el escribir, sobre la intención de escribir una novela de amor, sobre la reflexión creadora que vive inserta en un medio de cotidianeidad. Este es su séptimo título de ficción. [MGP]

3902 Rodríguez Barilari, Elbio. Lugares comunes: novela. Montevideo: Ediciones de la Banda Oriental, 1987. 141 p. (Narradores uruguayos de hoy; 17)

Este autor uruguayo ha publicado antes una colección de cuentos. Esta novela recibió mención especial en el Primer Concurso Latinoamericano de Novela organizado por la Cámara Uruguaya del Libro en 1986. Plantea una reflexión sobre las condiciones humanas, precarias en que viven los personajes luego de una experiencia dura durante la dictadura. El personaje central se empeña en reconstruir su vida en medio de un contorno indiferente, cansado, mediante la experiencia solitaria en contraste con la vida de relación con antiguos y nuevos amigos. [MGP]

3903 Verzi, Horacio García. La otra orilla: novela. Montevideo: Proyección, 1987. 152 p. (Col. Letras; 5)

Este autor ha publicado *Las horas chicas* y *El mismo invisible pecho del cielo* (1983). La novela explora la problemática del desexilio, el abandono del país que lo recibió, la complejidad del reencuentro con el país y la sociedad que hubo que dejar, junto a otros aspectos de la vida humana en circunstancias coloreadas por el exilio y desexilio. [MGP]

LITERARY CRITICISM AND HISTORY
Argentina

3904 Acevedo, Hugo. Cuadros de una exposición. Buenos Aires: Nuevo Meridión, 1985. 165 p. (Col. Pensar América; 1)

Miscelánea de reflexiones sobre características nacionales (el uso del lenguaje, por ejemplo) y escritores (Borges, Neruda, Martínez Estrada, Alone, Sábato entre otros) precedidas por una carta de Antonio Di Benedetto. [MLB]

3905 Agheana, Ion Tudro. The meaning of experience in the prose of Jorge Luis Borges. New York: Peter Lang, 1988. 256 p.: bibl., index. (American university studies: Series II, Romance languages and literature; 71)

De las diversas "experiencias" que detecta en la prosa de Borges, y más que las conocidas filiaciones literarias (Cervantes, Shakespeare, Quevedo, Whitman, Shaw, Valéry y otros), llama la atención la sección dedicada a la "experiencia cromática" y el efecto final que se produce al deslizarse Borges hacia una ineludible preferencia por la penumbra—juego de luz y de sombra que, por otro lado, se anuncia desde sus primeros versos. [SS]

3906 Alifano, Roberto. Borges: biografía verbal. Barcelona: Plaza & Janés, 1988. 235 p.: bibl. (Biografías y memorias)

Poemas, recuerdos, datos, sueltos, entrañables lecturas, citas de conversaciones sostenidas a lo largo de muchos años, y las dos "autobiografías" de Borges (1972 y 1983) contribuyen a mantener un delicado equilibrio entre el ansia de acercarse al otro Borges y el escrupuloso respeto por sus letras. Alifano fue el "más cercano colaborador" de Borges durante 1978–85. [SS]

3907 Anarkos: literaturas libertarias de América del Sur, 1900; Argentina, Chile, Paraguay, Uruguay. Recopilación de Jean Andreu, Maurice Fraysse y Eva Montoya. Buenos Aires: Corregidor, 1990. 256 p.: bibl.

Una breve pero útil contextualización precede a esta antología única de poemas, proclamas y textos varios que se contraponen a esas otras apacibles manifestaciones estéticas que perduran como muestra de una época. [SS]

3908 Arlt, Mirta. Prólogos a la obra de mi padre. Buenos Aires: Torres Agüero, 1985. 202 p.: bibl. (Col. Primeras ediciones. Memoria del tiempo)

Si bien el dato biográfico es insoslayable—y si así se inscribe esta recopilación—las lecturas críticas de Mirta sobre la obra de Arlt revisten más que una mera curiosidad. El necesario distanciamiento es significativo en estas páginas que transitan tres décadas (1952–82). Son meritorios los apuntes sobre el teatro. [SS]

3909 Bacarisse, Pamela. The necessary dream: a study of the novels of Manuel Puig. Totowa, N.J.: Barnes & Noble Books, 1988. 285 p.: bibl., index.

Estudia siete novelas de Puig, desde *La traición de Rita Hayworth* (1968) hasta *Sangre de amor correspondido* (1982). Además de una cuidadosa interpretación de cada texto, se propone persuadir que "there has been no waning of Manuel Puig's powers with the last two or three novels, but that on the contrary, they constitute a rewarding literary experience if read with a mind not coloured by the assumptions created by the enjoyment of the first works, which in any case were also fundamentally serious and provocative." Merece consideración en la creciente bibliografía sobre Puig. [SS]

3910 Balderston, Daniel et al. Ficción y política: la narrativa argentina durante el proceso militar. Buenos Aires: Alianza; Minneapolis: Institute for the Study of Ideologies & Literature, Univ. of Minnesota, 1987. 121 p.: bibl. (Alianza estudio; 4)

Resultados de una reunión llevada a cabo en 1986 en la Univ. de Minnesota. Incluye los siguientes valiosos ensayos: Francine Masiello, "La Argentina Durante el Proceso: Las Múltiples Resistencias de la Cultura;" Beatriz Sarlo, "Política, Ideología y Figuración Literaria;" Marta Morello-Frosch, "Biografías Fictivas: Formas de Resistencia y Reflexión en la Narrativa Argentina Reciente;" Tulio Halperín Donghi, "El Presente Transforma el Pasado: El Impacto del Reciente Terror en la Imagen de la Historia Argentina;" David W. Foster, "Los Parámetros de la Narrativa Argentina durante el 'Proceso de Reorganización Nacional;'" y Daniel Balderston, "El Significado Latente en *Respiración artificial* de Ricardo Piglia y en *El corazón de junio* de Luis Gusmán." Buen complemento para el volumen *Represión y reconstrucción de una cultura: el caso argentino* (ver *HLAS 50: 3485*) que recoge los textos presentados en 1984 en la reunión de la Univ. de Maryland. [SS]

3911 Balderston, Daniel. Historical situations in Borges. (*MLN*, 105:2, March 1990, p. 331–349)

Mediante una serie de alusiones históricas y políticas que se hallan en los textos de Borges, rechaza la insistente concentración de la crítica en la "irrealidad." En una coda propone que "Borges' conception of history is not as close to that of Hayden White, for whom history is discourse, as to that of Fredric Jameson, for whom history is not narrative or textual, but an Other only partially recoverable to us in textual form." Estimulante anuncio de un libro en preparación. [SS]

3912 Barrenechea, Ana María. La maga en el proceso de escritura de *Rayuela*: pre-texto y texto. (*Explic. Textos Lit.*, 17:1/2, 1988/1989, p. 27–45)

Con el *Cuaderno de bitácora* de *Rayuela* en sus manos, se centra "específicamente en la Maga dentro del nivel de los personajes" para estudiar "*pre-texto* y *texto* con los supuestos de la nueva crítica genética," especialmente según Jean Bellemin-Noël. Rechaza que los borradores dependan de la obra publicada y adopta "La posición que reconoce la validez del pre-texto en sí (uno o varios) y les da categoría, junto con la novela conocida, de otras tantas propuestas en concurrencia." [SS]

3913 Bastos, María Luisa. Relecturas: estudios de textos hispanoamericanos. Buenos Aires: Hachette, 1989. 166 p.: bibl. (Col. Hachette universidad: Lengua-lingüística-comunicación)

Una colección mayor de ensayos producidos entre 1976–84, divididos en tres partes: 1) "La Nueva Palabra Española" (Alonso Carrió de la Vandera); 2) "Ingreso en la Modernidad" (Cambaceres, Rodó, Gómez Carrillo); y 3) Escrituras de la Ambigüedad" (M.L. Bombal, Rulfo, Borges, Bianco y Bioy Casares). Estos estudios responden legítimamente a las "repercusiones incalculables de lo verbal;" su rigor también les confiere un lugar privilegiado entre las innumerables (no infinitas) páginas que siguen suscitando algunos de estos autores. [SS]

3914 Bellessi, Diana. Paloma de contrabando: textos escritos en las cárceles de Buenos Aires. Buenos Aires: Torres Agüero Editor, 1988. 190 p.

Este texto se suma a la amplia colección de textos y narrativos y poemas escritos en las cárceles de los gobiernos militares sudamericanos. Esta colección reúne nueve textos escritos en las cárceles de Buenos Aires. Acompaña al volumen un "Léxico" que aclara el significado de los coloquialismos porteños para mejor comprensión del libro fuera del país. [MGP]

3915 Bioy Casares, Adolfo. Memoria sobre la pampa y los gauchos. Buenos Aires: Emecé Editores, 1986. 59 p.: ill.

Reedición de un atractivo texto de 1970 en que Bioy puntualiza matices con que la gente de su generación y clase social usaba y entendía las palabras del título. [MLB]

3916 Block de Behar, Lisa. Al margen de Borges. México: Siglo Veintiuno Editores, 1987. 219 p.: bibl. (Lingüística y teoría literaria)

Como para otros lúcidos teóricos de

las letras, Borges sigue siendo un hábito que pluraliza la reflexión sobre y desde sus propios textos, como lo verifican los textos y conferencias que recoge este importante volumen. "A Manera de Prólogo" es una guía eficaz para interpretar la sutil y compleja trama de estas lecturas. Incluye dos poemas ("El Don" y "1984") que Borges ofreciera para las publicaciones uruguayas *Maldoror* y *Jaque*. [SS]

3917 Block de Behar, Lisa. Dos medios entre dos medios: sobre la representación y sus dualidades. Buenos Aires?: Siglo Veintiuno Argentina Editores, 1990. 164 p.: bibl. (Lingüística y teoría literaria)

"Entre dos espacios, con procedimientos diferentes y propósitos semejantes, el autor, el lector, el traductor, el estudioso, detiene el discurso, combina textos, repite fragmentos que coinciden y hacen juego: con cada trazo descubre el sentido de una comunicación intersticial, procurando salvar en el espacio abierto entre palabras, los trozos dispersos, la inadecuación entre las cosas y las palabras que también son cosas. Por medio de su interpretación, cada uno intenta una crítica de *reparación:* cumpliendo con un gesto múltiple, *repara:* observa o compone, dispuesto a aclarar una voz por otra, un texto por otro, una lengua por otra, restituye, en cada caso, partes de un conocimiento anterior al que otra vez accede" (p. 12). Esta "confabulación" entre los intersticios de la palabra aflora en lecturas de Borges, de Jules Laforge, de Molière; en reflexiones sobre el cine, en pre-textos para teorizar, para significar. [SS]

3918 Borges, Jorge Luis. Biblioteca personal: prólogos. Madrid: Alianza Editorial, 1988. 132 p. (Alianza tres; 209)

"No sé si soy un buen escritor; creo ser un excelente lector o, en todo caso, un sensible y agradecido lector." Estos breves prólogos a una colección de libros heterogéneos editados en Argentina en 1985–86 constituyen un valioso catálogo de los gustos y las memorias de Borges en vísperas de su muerte. La galería de vastas preferencias incluyen entre sus 66 prólogos a Cortázar, Lugones, Groussac, Mujica Láinez, Martínez Estrada, Rulfo y Arreola. [SS]

3919 Borges, Jorge Luis. Textos cautivos: ensayos reseñas en *El Hogar* de Buenos

Aires. Edición de Enrique Sacerio-Garí y Emir Rodríguez Monegal. Ilustraciones extraídas de *El Hogar*. Barcelona: Tusquets, 1986. 338 p.: bibl., ill., facsims., ports. (Marginales; 92)

Reseñas y ensayos (1936–39) publicados en *El Hogar* de Buenos Aires. Recopilación valiosa para los lectores hedónicos y los profesionales. [MLB]

3920 Borges and his successors: the Borgesian impact on literature and the arts. Edited by Edna Aizenberg. Columbia: Univ. of Missouri Press, 1989. 1 v.: index.

Para ampliar los horizontes de la recepcíon de Borges "either by taking up totally unexplored 'succesions' or by considering better known ones in a new light," Aizenberg reunió trabajos de Ana María Barrenechea, Marta Morello-Frosch, Rafael Gutiérrez Girardot. Jaime Alazraki, Suzanne Jill Levine, Emir Rodríguez Monegal, Herman Rapaport, Malva Filer y otros. Una *mise au point* minuciosa del hebraísmo en la teoría literaria, de Aizenberg, y dos conferencias inéditas de Borges, "El Libro de Job" y "Spinoza" cierran un libro atractivo y útil. [MLB]

3921 Borges, l'autre: colloque de Cerisy. Dirigé par Gérard de Cortanze. Gourdon, France: D. Bedou; Antigramme, 1987. 172 p.: bibl.

La memorable presentación de Gérard de Cortanze (*"Tenebrae factae sun . . ."*) es seguida por una miscelánea de presentaciones de las que cabe destacar los aportes de G.M. Goloboff, M. Ezquerro, J. Ricardou, J.J. Saer, S. Yurkievich y A. Dujovne Ortiz. Variantes que van desde el rigor metodológico al culto de la simpatía. Se trata, como siempre en estos casos, de "Borges, él mismo." [SS]

3922 Canto, Estela. Borges a contraluz. Madrid: Espasa Calpe, 1989? 286 p.: ill. (Col. Austral; 93: Literatura)

Pocas mujeres frecuentaron tanto al Borges que se vislumbra de este lado del "contraluz." Recuerdos, cartas, y una larga amistad, agilizan la lectura de estas páginas que frecuentemente se descuelgan por la intimidad poco develada de Borges. Más vida que obra las animan, y no parece ser otro el propósito de algunos pasajes que ratifican misterios, o de otros que confirman lecturas largamente conocidas. [SS]

3923 Carter, E. Dale. Bibliografía de y sobre Julio Cortázar. (*Explic. Textos Lit.*, 17:1/2, 1988/1989, p. 251–327)

La más completa bibliografía hasta la fecha. Util material a pesar de un sorprendente "criterio" (¿error de armado? ¿incitación a los escasos juegos que toleran las bibliografías?) que separa partes de una misma sección anunciando "Más compilaciones," "Más artículos y reseñas" y, por partida doble, "Otros artículos y reseñas" . . . [SS]

3924 Catania, Carlos. Genio y figura de Ernesto Sábato. Buenos Aires: Editorial Universitaria de Buenos Aires, 1987. 186 p.: ill., plates, ports. (Genio y figura; 38)

Una explícita simpatía por Sábato y su mundo permiten la inmediata y fructífera sintonía con los ejes que urden su obra. Lúcida presentación en la que se destacan las "interpolaciones" dedicadas a *Sobre héroes y tumbas*. [SS]

3925 Chiáppori, Sergio. Trincheras de la vida. Buenos Aires: Plus Ultra, 1986. 139 p.

Textos periodísticos, convencionales y superficiales, sobre Ricardo Rojas, Enrique Finochietto, David Peña, Rafael Obligado, Ricardo Sáenz Hayes, Ganivet y Zweig, Rodolfo Alcorta, Martín Fierro y Luciano Santos, José Ingenieros, Florencio Sánchez, Jane Austen, Delmira Agustini, Pedro Figari, Eduardo Talero, Roberto Gache, Méndez Calzada, Cancela y Loncán, Eugenio Cambaceres. [MLB]

3926 Cortázar: iconografía. Investigación y selección de fotografías de Alba C. de Rojo. Selección de textos de Felipe Garrido. México: Fondo de Cultura Económica, 1986. 123 p.: bibl., ill., index. (Tezontle)

"Esta iconografía de Julio Cortázar es una suerte de artefacto del tiempo en nuestras manos, un artefacto que restituye la presencia de un hombre que ya no está pero que no se ha ido." Bello homenaje que merece el agradecimiento de todos sus (per)seguidores. [SS]

3927 Cortínez, Carlos et al. Con Borges: texto y persona. Buenos Aires: Torres Agüero Editor, 1988. 207 p.: bibl.

Selección del material publicado originalmente como *Simply a man of letters* (Orono: Univ. of Maine at Orono Press, 1982). Incluye una charla de Borges sobre el tema "simplemente un hombre de letras," sus comentarios a propósito de la traducción de cinco poemas al inglés, varias aproximaciones críticas y la transcripción de tres paneles que se ocuparon de "Borges y Chesterton," "Sobre la Traducción de Borges" y de "Borges: ¿Filósofo? ¿Poeta? ¿Revolucionario?." Esta edición incluye un poema de Enrique Molina ("Borges") aparecido en *La Nación* en 1986. [SS]

Cozarinsky, Edgardo. Borges in/and/on film. See item **5017.**

3928 Cuentistas y pintores argentinos. Selección y prólogos de Jorge Luis Borges. Buenos Aires: Ediciones de Arte Gaglianone; Círculo de Lectores, 1985. 277 p.: ill. (some col.), plates.

Las escuetas introducciones son variantes de las ideas de Borges sobre la literatura en general y sobre un aspecto—el fantástico—de la literatura argentina en particular. [MLB]

3929 Epica dadora de eternidad: Sábato en la crítica americana y europea. Selección y edición de A.M. Vázquez Bigi. Buenos Aires: Sudamericana/Planeta, 1985. 281 p.: bibl., ill.

La presentación del compilador anuncia el registro analítico de una llamativa colección de ensayos que se centra, como era de esperar, en las tres novelas de Sábato. Incluye estudios de Paul Verdevoye, Cesare Segre, Leo Pollmann, Salvador Bacarisse y Luis Wainerman, entre otros. [SS]

3930 Feinmann, José Pablo. La creación de lo posible. Buenos Aires: Editorial Legasa, 1986. 317 p. (Omnibus)

Recoge 32 ensayos publicados en su mayoría en la revista *Humor* (marzo 1984–enero 1986). Crónicas reflexivas, polémicas, incisivas, de un "filósofo peronista" para un período histórico en que el título de esta colección era aún promesa. [SS]

3931 Fernández, Macedonio. Obras completas. t. 7, Relato: cuentos, poemas y misceláneas. Edición de Adolfo de Obieta. Buenos Aires: Corregidor, 1987. 241 p. (Obras completas; t. 7)

Vol. 7 de las fundamentales *Obras completas*, ordenadas y anotadas por Adolfo de Obieta, incluye: el relato "Una Novela que Comienza" (Santiago, 1941); cuentos (entre ellos, los clásicos "Tantalia" y "El Za-

pallo que se hizo Cosmos"); Esquemas para Arte de Encargo;" "Géneros del Cuento;" "Poemas;" y "Miscelánea." Esta última y memorable sección incluye, entre otros, "Todoamor: *Innovación de una autobiografía* Hecha por Otro," (1922); "Evar Méndez" (publicado en 1925 en *Proa*); "La Conferencialidad y la Cachada" (*Destiempo*, 1937), y "Leopoldo Lugones: la Psique, Pistolera También" (1938). [SS]

3932 Fletcher, Lea. Una mujer llamada Herminia. Buenos Aires: Catálogos Editora, 1987. 116 p.: bibl.

Useful critical study of the life and work of Argentine author Herminia Brumana written from a feminist perspective. Includes bibliography and selections from her writings. [R. Prieto]

3933 Frugoni de Fritzsche, Teresita. Murena, un escritor argentino ante los problemas del país y de su literatura. Buenos Aires: El Imaginero, 1985. 132 p.: bibl. (El Imaginero; 12)

Breviario sobre la obra de Murena (1923–75) es útil como primera introducción a su mundo. [MLB]

3934 Gallo, Marta. In-trascendencia textual en *Respiración artificial* de Ricardo Piglia. (*Nueva Rev. Filol. Hisp.*, 35:2, 1987, p. 819–834, appendix, bibl.)

Postula que *Respiración artificial*, en una filiación que pasa por Borges, Cortázar y, singularmente, por *Cómico de la lengua* de Néstor Sánchez, "está hecho de transtextualidad: diferentes textos en yuxtaposición, superposición, transcripciones de citas, de cartas, de notas. La falta de articulación entre esos textos está subrayada hasta el punto que ese hiato, casi abismal, parece lo más importante en esta trascendencia textual." Por sobre todo, concluye, importa "la restauración de la experiencia de la lectura misma como ejercicio lúdico del arduo privilegio humano del lenguaje." [SS]

3935 Goloboff, Gerardo Mario. Genio y figura de Roberto Arlt. Buenos Aires: Editorial Universitaria de Buenos Aires, 1988. 149 p.: bibl. (Genio y figura; 39)

Excelente presentación de esta permanente y crecientemente admirada "máquina literaria." Según Goloboff, y a pesar de ciertas apariencias, Arlt asumió conscientemente una carrera literaria. "Ser escritor—dice—significa para Arlt decirlo todo, no ocultarse nada, perder 'el respeto de la literatura' en temas y en lenguaje, es decir, hacer entrar en ella no sólo las anécdotas y los personajes más insólitos sino también los pensamientos y las fantasías más descabelladas. Creado todo ello, naturalmente, por un léxico y por 'formas' igualmente desinhibidos, totalizadores." [SS]

3936 Grau, Cristina. Borges y la arquitectura. Madrid: Cátedra, 1989. 189 p.: bibl., ill. (Ensayos arte)

Reconoce desde el primer contacto de Borges con el espacio urbano una serie de nexos en varias instancias biográficas y aun en su temprana experiencia ultraísta. Analiza las relaciones literatura-arquitectura "en los recursos iconográficos, simbólicos y retóricos que Borges utiliza en la concreción del espacio; cómo afecta la propia estructura del texto al espacio percibido por el lector; si texto y arquitectura participan de una misma poética y a qué otras arquitecturas literarias o literaturas arquitectónicas remiten. En síntesis, se trata de tomar el espacio descrito por Borges y reconstruirlo en términos de arquitectura." Fascinante aproximación a mundos que evidentemente merecen nuevos tránsitos. [SS]

3937 Haroldo Conti, con vida. Recopilación de Néstor Restivo y Camilo Sánchez. Buenos Aires: Editorial Nueva Imagen, 1986. 211 p.: ill.

Libro-homenaje a uno de los mayores escritores de su generación desaparecido en 1976 durante la dictadura militar. Recoge testimonios de su familia, de padres salesianos, de maestros y alumnos, de sus colegas y de tantos otros que no se resignan a acatar la impunidad. Valioso documento sobre el autor de *En vida* (Barcelona: Barral Editores, 1971) y sobre años de infamia que no han silenciado ni a su obra ni a su memoria. [MLB]

3938 Jorge Luis Borges. Edited and with an introduction by Harold Bloom. New York: Chelsea House Publishers, 1986. 256 p.: bibl. (Modern critical views)

Mediante una generalmente acertada selección de artículos y capítulos de libros, la mayoría publicados originalmente en inglés, esta colección establece una crónica de la recepción que ha tenido la obra de Borges en algunos círculos académicos de EE.UU. a partir

de 1969, fecha de la breve introducción del compilador. Se destacan los ya conocidos aportes de Alazraki, Christ, Irby, Sturrock y Rodríguez Monegal, junto a las inteligentes observaciones de Shlomith Rimmon-Kenan (sobre "El Jardín de Senderos que se Bifurcan") y las propuestas críticas de Thomas R. Hart, Jr. ("Borges' Literary Criticism"), Paul de Man ("A Modern Master") y González Echevarría ("Borges and Derrida"). [SS]

3939 Jorge Luis Borges, el último laberinto: testimonios y estudios entre la memoria y el olvido. Coordinación de Rómulo Cosse. Montevideo: Librería Linardi y Risso, 1987. 364 p.: bibl., port.

Colección de ensayos ya publicados y de otros especialmente preparados para este volumen. Entre estos últimos cabe destacar "Borges y los Nuevos: Ruptura y Continuidad," de M. Morello—Frosch—particularmente por su lectura de la obra de Andrés Rivera—y las medulares reflexiones de "Paradoxa Ortodoxa" de L. Block de Behar. Las memorables declaraciones de Borges, esta vez aparecen en diferentes charlas a cargo de Milton Fornaro, Alfonso Lessa y Jorge Ruffinelli. Juan Fló elaboró para esta miscelánea "Una Reseña Crítica Tardía" a su polémico "Vindicación o Vindicta de Borges" (1978). No deja de ser valiosa la inflexión oriental de este volumen. [SS]

3940 Katra, William H. Contorno: literary engagement in post-Peronist Argentina. Rutherford: Fairleigh Dickinson Univ. Press; London: Associated Univ. Presses, 1988. 170 p.: bibl., index.

Ramón Alcalde, Tulio Halperín Donghi, Noé Jitrik, Oscar Masotta, Adolfo Prieto, León Rozitchner, Juan José Sebreli, David e Ismael Viñas, entre otros, estuvieron asociados con la revista *Contorno*, cuya breve vida (1953–59) marcó a una generación de intelectuales y cuya lectura sigue siendo imprescindible para comprender una de las décadas decisivas de la historia argentina. Aporte importante que también cuenta con una útil bibliografía de los autores de *Contorno*. [SS]

3941 King, John. *Sur:* a study of the Argentine literary journal and its role in the development of a culture, 1931–1970. New York: Cambridge Univ. Press, 1986. 232 p.: bibl., index. (Cambridge Iberian and Latin American studies)

Excelente estudio sobre una de las publicaciones fundacionales de América Latina. Además de ofrecer un sólido análisis de la revista y de los proyectos de Victoria Ocampo, de su entorno, y de lo que significa la ineludible *Sur* para una comprensión de estas décadas, este libro también constituye un aporte metodológico para comprender cómo se analiza una revista literaria. [SS]

3942 Lindstrom, Naomi. Jewish issues in Argentine literature: from Gerchunoff to Szichman. Columbia: Univ. of Missouri Press, 1989. 1 v.: bibl., index.

Importante panorama para el estudio de la veta cultural judía-argentina con una útil introducción al tema y un apresurado postfacio para citar autores que hubieran merecido una mayor atención. Analiza con seriedad obras de Gerchunoff, Tiempo, Verbitsky, Viñas, Rabinovich, Isaacson, Barnatán y Szichman. Valiosa guía bibliografíca. [SS]

3943 Meneses, Carlos. Cartas de juventud de J.L. Borges: 1921–1922. Madrid: Editorial Orígenes, 1987. 95 p.: bibl. (Tratados de testimonio)

"Dominado por la emotividad de la juventud"—al decir de Meneses—le dirige estas cartas al poeta mallorquín Jacobo Sureda (1901–31), poco antes de que con *Fervor de Buenos Aires* (1923) comenzara a ser Borges. Interesante presentación, seguida de documentos, textos breves y reproducciones facsimilares. [SS]

3944 Moreau de Justo, Alicia. Conversaciones con Alicia Moreau de Justo y Jorge Luis Borges. Entrevista de Blas Alberti. Buenos Aires: Ediciones del Mar Dulce, 1985. 148 p.: bibl., ports. (Ediciones del mar dulce; 5)

Testimonios de un conjunto de ocho entrevistas realizadas a "personajes de Buenos Aires" a lo largo de 1979–80. De este volumen, y para la reconstrucción de un sector argentino, importan más las declaraciones de quien fuera feminista, médica y la mujer del socialista Juan B. Justo. [SS]

3945 Muñoz, Elías Miguel. El discurso utópico de la sexualidad en Manuel Puig. Madrid: Pliegos, 1987? 151 p.: bibl. (Pliegos de ensayo; 21)

La liberación sexual como núcleo que atraviesa toda la obra de Puig, desde *La traición de Rita Hayworth* (1968) hasta sus últimas páginas. También examina el poder subversivo propio de otras estrategias discursivas de Puig al leer *Pubis angelical* (1979) y *Sangre de amor correspondido* (1982). [SS]

3946 Ndoye, El Hadji Amadou. Jazz, blues et littérature dans *Rayuela* de Julio Cortázar. (*Lang. Néo-Lat.*, 246, p. 35–78, bibl.)

Particularmente informativo para los que sólo tienen acceso a versiones francesas de la bibliografía cortazariana. Si bien el propósito inicial de Cortázar al unir armoniosamente jazz, blues y poesía, pudo haber sido la conquista de un campo ilimitado en que las artes estarían perpetuamente comunicadas, la indicación de Ndoye de que la música de los negros estadounidenses ha sido una manera de luchar contra la muerte y que "Cortázar a observé les paradox qui ont déchiré et fait vivre la musique d'un groupe éthnique opprimé," podría ser un asomo de la ideologización más explícita de algunos textos posteriores. [SS]

3947 Nudelstejer B., Sergio. Borges: acercamiento a su obra literaria. Presentación de Alfredo Cardona Peña. México: Costa-Amic Editores, 1987. 174 p.: bibl., ports.

Recorre algunos motivos centrales de la obra de Borges. Incluye fotos, cronología y una breve bibliografía. Estrictamente para no-iniciados.[MLB]

Paoli, Roberto. Borges y Schopenhauer. See item **5428.**

3948 Petrea, Mariana D. Ernesto Sábato: la Nada y la metafísica de la Esperanza. Madrid: Ediciones J. Porrúa Turanzas, 1986? 195 p.: bibl., indexes. (Ensayos)

Se propone demostrar que "La Nada y la Esperanza han sido el motivo esencial" de la vida y la obra de Sábato. Comienza con una semblanza del autor; luego de analizar el pensamiento de Sábato en su ensayística, revisa su expresión a través de los personajes y de la novela. Se limita a obras publicadas entre 1945–74. Sorprende que dada la tesis de la autora no haya pasado a la etapa crucial en que Sábato dirigió la CONADEP. [SS]

3949 Requeni, Antonio. Cronicón de las peñas de Buenos Aires. 3a ed. Buenos Aires: Corregidor, 1986. 174 p.: ill., plates, ports.

Más de 20 años de periodismo, recuerdos y testimonios de muchos de los participantes de la vida literaria porteña en las primeras décadas de este siglo ("tiempo en que aún había tiempo para despilfarrar ante la mesa de un café; época en la que era habitual ver conciliados verdad y pintoresquismo, pobreza y alegría, talento y desinterés") contribuyen al regocijo de este memorioso libro. [SS]

3950 Rivera, Juan Manuel. Estética y mitificación en la obra literaria de Ezequiel Martínez Estrada. Madrid: Pliegos, 1987. 202 p.: bibl. (Pliegos de ensayo; 20)

Tesis doctoral sobre la obra de Martínez Estrada (1895–1964) que se propone exponer "en forma dialéctica los encuentros y desencuentros que se dan en el pensamiento de este autor entre ideología y ciencia o—lo que es lo mismo—entre apariencia y estructura." Se centra en "la falsa osatura conceptual sobre la que el autor levantó su extraña y hermosa y anárquica metáfora." La bibliografía no es desdeñable. [SS]

3951 Rodríguez Monegal, Emir. Jorge Luis Borges: a literary biography. New York: Paragon House, 1988. 502 p.: bibl., ill., index, plates.

Reedición del volumen publicado por Dutton en 1978. [MLB]

3952 Rosa, Nicolás. Los fulgores del simulacro. Santa Fe, Argentina: Univ. Nacional del Litoral, Depto. de Extensión Universitaria, 1987. 396 p.: bibl. (Cuadernos de extensión universitaria; 15: Serie Ensayo)

"Estos textos, estos restos," titula Rosa a las páginas que presentan su recopilación de "ficción crítica" publicada entre 1970–86. Si tiene razón al decir que "Dicen más del decir que del dicho," se equivoca al pensar que sólo poseen una "incierta, improbable transcendencia." Incluye algunos trabajos inéditos junto a sus conocidas páginas sobre "Borges y la Crítica" (1972) y los lúcidos "'Tratados' sobre *Alambres* de N. Perlongher" (1987). [SS]

3953 Sábato, Ernesto R. Ernesto Sábato. Barcelona: Anthropos; Madrid: Ministerio de Cultura, Dirección General del Libro y Bibliotecas, Centro de las Letras Españolas, 1988. 124 p.: bibl., ports. (Ambitos literarios/Premios Cervantes; 10)

Obra de difusión a raíz del Premio Miguel de Cervantes que le fuera otorgado en 1984. Incluye tres ensayos (firmados por Dónoan, Marina Gálvez Acero y Trinidad Barrera), el discurso de Sábato en la entrega del premio, una conversación con Mónica Liberman, Luis García Martín y su devoto Arnoldo Liberman), una bibliografía y una cronología de su vida.

3954 Sábato, Ernesto R. Lo mejor de Ernesto Sábato. Selección, prólogo y comentarios del autor. Barcelona: Seix Barral, 1989. 237 p.

Ordenadas cronológicamente, esta mesurada selección incluye fragmentos de sus tres novelas, ensayos y reflexiones de *El escritor y sus fantasmas*, su memorable lecturarecordación de Pedro Henríquez Ureña, "El desconocido Da Vinci" y las breves palabras que pronunciara en el homenaje a Borges celebrado en la Bibliothèque Nationale de París. Apto cierre para señalar la continuidad del diálogo, del saber; una apuesta al futuro de la lucidez. [SS]

3955 Salvador, Nélida. Macedonio Fernández: precursor de la antinovela. Buenos Aires: Plus Ultra, 1986. 125 p. (Perfiles contemporáneos; 3)

Sólido y esclarecedor breviario sobre las propuestas de Macedonio, sus "doctrinas estéticas," la "teoría de la novela" que surge de sus textos y su larga repercusión. [SS]

3956 Schiminovich, Flora H. La obra de Macedonio Fernández: una lectura surrealista. Madrid: Editorial Pliegos, 1986? 229 p.: bibl. (Pliegos de ensayo; 18)

Se propone "indagar la posible relación de Macedonio Fernández con el surrealismo, teniendo en cuenta todas las dificultades que esa proposición supone, ya que no poseemos ninguna clave específica." Considera que la solución metafísica que Macedonio propone para conciliar antinomias fundamentales (v.g., vida/muerte, sueño/vigilia, . . .) lo relaciona con el "proyecto surrealista de llegar a un punto supremo de conciliación de los contrarios." Al confrontarlo con el surrealismo, las constantes de Macedonio ("la libertad, el metalenguaje, el amor y la eternidad") "adquieren su ímpetu y su sentido." [SS]

3957 Sebreli, Juan José. Las señales de la memoria: diálogos con Orfilia Polemann. Buenos Aires: Editorial Sudamericana, 1987. 254 p.

"Sebreli inventó un libro—dice su interlocutora—que es mezcla rara de diario confidencial, memoria, autobiografía, testimonio, reflexión en voz alta, ensayo y, ¿por qué no? algo de novela." Quizá no cabía otro modo de descubrir al autor de alguien que ha reflexionado medularmente sobre sus mundos, desde *Buenos Aires, vida cotidiana y alienación* hasta *Los deseos imaginarios del peronismo*. Una importante vertiente del pensar crítico, de una generación crítica. [SS]

3958 Stortini, Carlos Roberto. El diccionario de Borges: el Borges oral, el de las declaraciones y las polémicas. Buenos Aires: Editorial Sudamericana, 1986. 238 p.: bibl., index.

"Este trabajo está basado, fundamentalmente, en las expresiones públicas de Borges, a través de diálogos, declaraciones, entrevistas, reportajes y opiniones emitidas por el escritor, principalmente en diarios, periódicos y revistas." Una cuidadosa y, por lo general, feliz selección de citas del "Borges oral" (¿heredero, también en esta fase, del otro Macedonio?). Tal como lo deseara Stortini, este libro es "apto para todo público," especialmente para aquél que sabe que las frases ingeniosas no sustituyen al "Borges escrito." [SS]

3959 Valverde, Estela. David Viñas: en busca de una síntesis de la historia argentina. Buenos Aires: Editorial Plus Ultra, 1989. 298 p.: bibl.

Asumiendo el riesgo que implica una lectura que se sintoniza en la propia metodología que David Viñas utiliza en sus ensayos, Valverde elabora el trabajo más completo hasta la fecha sobre la polifacética obra del fundador de una particular vertiente de la crítica literaria argentina. Articula el análisis en torno a la línea literatura-política y a instancias medulares de la política argentina y su relación con la vida de Viñas. Excelente bibliografía. [SS]

3960 Villordo, Oscar Hermes. Genio y figura de Adolfo Bioy Casares. Buenos Aires: Editorial Universitaria de Buenos Aires, 1983. 207 p.: bibl., ill., plates. (Genio y figura; 35)

Minucioso acopio de datos sobre Bioy y su obra. Las opiniones, y aun las interpretaciones del propio Bioy, se registran con absoluto respeto. Texto útil aunque carente de distancia crítica. [MLB]

Paraguay

3961 Antúnez de Dendia, Rosalba. Augusto Roa Bastos: una interpretación de su primera etapa narrativa. (*Estud. Parag.*, 13:1/2, dic. 1985, p. 198–329)

Reconoce dos estapas literarias a partir de la publicación de *El trueno entre las hojas* (1953), siendo *Yo, El Supremo* el inicio de la segunda. La primera sería "de buceo en la realidad social, con características más bien regionales; todo ello a partir del tratamiento de los temas, el lenguaje, las motivaciones;" la segunda, que "trasciende los muros culturales paraguayos," poseería "claras aspiraciones universales y logros notables en ese sentido." A pesar de este criterio, ofrece datos útiles que están arraigados en la práctica y el goce del idioma guaraní. [SS]

3962 Augusto Roa Bastos y la producción cultural americana. Recopilación de Saúl Sosnowski. Buenos Aires: Ediciones de la Flor, México: Folios Ediciones, 1986. 262 p.: bibl., ill.

Excelentes textos sobre Roa Bastos y tres estudios sobre: la literatura de masas; Lezama Lima; la novela de la revolución mexicana. Ensayos de T. Halperín Donghi, D. Scott Palmer, W.R. Wright, A. Cornejo Polar, R.A. Borello, A. Roa Bastos, J. Ruffinelli, C. Pacheco, J. Franco, W.D. Mignolo, A. Prieto, E. Bejel, J. Aguilar Mora. [MLB]

3963 Bareiro Saguier, Rubén. Augusto Roa Bastos: caídas y resurrecciones de un pueblo. Montevideo: Ediciones Trilce; Paris: Editions caribéennes, 1989. 187 p.: bibl., ill., plates. (Coll. Tropismes. Série no 1, Une oeuvre—un auteur) (Col. Espejos)

Pocos conocen tan íntimamente a Roa Bastos y al Paraguay como el autor de este libro. Los fructíferos diálogos y los comentarios ocasionales de Bareiro Saguier constituyen una excelente presentación del autor de *Yo, El Supremo*. Predominan los planteos políticos, el impacto del exilio, el sentido de una literatura de ARB ve como "una huída del exilio hacia adelante." [SS]

3964 Bouzigues Lamoise, Dominique et al. Rubén Bareiro Saguier: valoraciones y comentarios acerca de su obra. Edición de Hugo Duarte Rodi y Carlos Villagra Marsal. Asunción: Arte Nuevo Editores: Editorial Araverá, 1986. 193 p.: bibl. (Serie Ensayos:

Arte Nuevo Editores; 9. Serie Ensayos: Editorial Araverá; 4)

Miscelánea de trabajos críticos, notas, apreciaciones y entrevistas. Volumen explícitamente destinado a profesores y estudiantes franceses(*Ojo por diente* fue seleccionado para el "Programa de l'agregation d'espagnol" en 1987), pero que por varias de las selecciones, trasciende ese puntual propósito. Incluye, entre otros, páginas de Roa Bastos, Jean Andreu, y Yurkievich. [SS]

3965 Campra, Rosalba. Lectura de un sistema textual: los cuentos de Augusto Roa Bastos. (*Nueva Rev. Filol. Hisp.*, 35:2, 1987, p. 789–817, appendix, bibl.)

Nota que la organización general de la narrativa de Roa Bastos contempla "por una parte, el retorno, en el interior de un mismo libro, de personajes y situaciones que remiten de un cuento a otro; por otra, la reproposición, en cada uno de sus libros, de cuentos ya publicados en los libros anteriores." Dejando de lado razones editoriales que tenderían a explicar este hecho, plantea a partir del concepto de macrotexto propuesto por María Corti, la "redefinición del sentido de un cuento según el sentido global del conjunto del que pasa a formar parte." Valiosa relectura dados los índices de *El trueno entre las hojas* (1953), *El baldío* (1966), *Los pies sobre el agua* (1967), *Madera quemada* (1967) y *Moriencia* (1969).

3966 Pacheco, Carlos. Muerte, binariedad y escritura en la cuentística de Augusto Roa Bastos. (*Hispamérica*, 18:52, 1989, p. 3–15)

Pacheco estudia algunos aspectos de la ficción corta de Roa Bastos para proponer un entendimiento más profundo de la concepción de la escritura y de la literatura del maestro paraguayo. Los cuentos que estudia aparecieron publicados en siete volúmenes, constituido por 43 relatos. Uno de los ejes temáticos que se explora es la muerte y el otro es la binariedad (vida-muerte) como modelo estético. [MGP]

3967 Rodríguez-Alcalá, Hugo. La incógnita del Paraguay y otros ensayos. Asunción: Arte Nuevo Editores, 1987. 196 p.: bibl. (Serie Ensayos; 11)

Colección de ensayos del crítico paraguayo que cubre un período de quince años es representivo de su labor crítica. Incluye temas como la labor crítica de Luis Alberto Sánchez y la literatura paraguaya; la obra de Fariña Núñez y Herib Campos Cervera; la narrativa paraguaya de la década que 1960–70; y Ferrater Mora, Francisco Romero, Henríquez Ureña y José Rulfo. [MGP]

3968 Rodríguez-Alcalá, Hugo. Poetas y prosistas paraguayos, y otros breves ensayos. Asunción: Mediterráneo; EDISA; Intercontinental Editora, 1988. 364 p.: bibl., ill.

El crítico paraguayo reúne en esta colección ensayos escritos después de su regreso al Paraguay, en 1983. Incluye estudios sobre poetas paraguayos: Alejandro Guanes, Julio Correa y Josefina Plá; sobre la generación poética de 1950; otra sección de cuatro textos sobre viajes en el tiempo y en el espacio, incluso uno sobre Elvio Romero; la sección titulada "Tres Poetas en sus Patrias Chicas;" otro conjunto de artículos sobre narradores; le sigue una sección sobre "Temas Literarios;" otra sobre "El Guaraní y el Castellano;" dos artículo sobre Alejandro Korn, uno sobre Borges en California. Concluye el volumen con un artículo sobre Dante y Rulfo. Valioso volumen sobre la literatura paraguaya. [MGP]

3969 Rodríguez-Alcalá, Hugo. Quince ensayos. Asunción: Criterio Ediciones, 1987. 216 p.: bibl., ill.

Esta miscelánea de ensayos, escritos a lo largo de su carrera académica, ofrece una clara semblanza de los alcances de este autor que se inicia en la literatura con dos poemarios que vierten sus experiencias durante la Guerra del Chaco. [MLB]

3970 Rubio, Fanny *et al.* Augusto Roa Bastos: una escritura, un pueblo. (*Insula*, 521, mayo 1990, p. 11–22, photos)

En este número de *Insula* se incluye una sección a la obra narrativa de Augusto Roa Bastos en ocasión de haber recibido el Premio Cervantes 1989. Los ensayos que aportan una nueva lectura de la novelística de Roa Bastos incluyen: Fanny Rubio "A.R.B.: Una Escritura Abierta;" Rosalba Campra "Los Cuentos de Augusto Roa Bastos o los Caminos de la Memoria;" Rafael Conde "En torno a *Hijo de Hombre*: la Primera Gran Novela de A.R.B;" Teresa Méndez-Faith "El Exilio en la Novelística de Roa Bastos;" Dante Liano "El Prisionero, Ténicas y Símbolos;" Dante Carignano "La Escritura o la

Suprema Representación del Ser;" Milagros Ezquerro "Estructura y sentido en *Yo, El Supremo;*" Edmundo Gómez Mango "Letra o Muerte: Aproximación Psicoanalítica a *Yo, El Supremo;*" Juan Calviño "Los Protocolos del Disparate Político: El Supremo como Dictacor/Dictador." Esta serie de ensayos está precedida por "Raíces, Ejes, Caminos de una Escritura" del compatriota de Roa Bastos y escritor Rubén Bareiro Saguier. [MGP]

3971 Tovar, Francisco. Las historias del dictador: *Yo, El Supremo,* de Augusto Roa Bastos. Barcelona: Edicions del Mall, 1987. 301 p.: bibl. (Llibres del mall. Sèrie ibèrica; 38)

Asentado en una razonable documentación histórica, articula las múltiples figuras del Dr. Francia hilvanando algunas de las complejidades de la novela de Roa Bastos y sugiriendo algunas claves para dilucidarlas. [SS]

3972 Las Voces del karaí: estudios sobre Augusto Roa Bastos. Edición de Fernando Burgos. Madrid: EDELSA EDI 6, 1988. 231 p.: bibl.

Este volumen recoge 18 ensayos presentados en 1985 en el primer coloquio organizado por la revista *Discurso Literario* en Oklahoma State Univ. Incluye estudios de D.W. Foster, F.E. Feito, A. Romero, V. Agüera, J.B. Kubayanda, y Carlos Pacheco. [SS]

Uruguay

3973 Barité, Mario and **María Gladys Ceretta.** Guía de revistas culturales uruguayas, 1885–1985. Prólogo de Jorge Ruffinelli. Montevideo: Ediciones El Galeón, 1989. 101 p.: ill., index. (Col. Ensayos; 1)

Excelente trabajo bibliográfico de las revistas publicadas en el Uruguay durante un siglo: desde 1885, con *Revista Nacional de Literatura y Ciencias Sociales,* hasta 1985, con *Grafo, Letras Femeninas del Uruguay.* El estudio registra el nombre de los editores y de los escritores y escritoras que participaron en cada una de las revistas reseñadas. Incluye unas 240 revistas, de las cuales el 60 por ciento apareció en la segunda mitad del siglo. Es la primera recopilación bibliográfica de este tipo para el Uruguay. Precede una in-

troducción de Jorge Rufinelli sobre el trabajo bibliográfico de Barité y Ceretta. [MGP]

3974 Benedetti, Mario. Crítica cómplice. Bogotá: Alianza Editorial Colombiana, 1988. 358 p.: bibl.

Importante recopilación que incorpora 37 trabajos críticos, algunos de ellos recientes, junto a una excelente selección de ensayos de seis libros anteriores—desde el temprano *Literatura uruguaya siglo XX* (1963) hasta *El ejercicio del criterio* (1981). Organizado en tres secciones, comienza con seis estudios de literatura uruguaya ("La comarca"), y luego se abre a una amplia sección americana y a lecturas de otros autores occidentales. Como lo adelanta su cortazariano título, todos ellos están guiados por la complicidad—"quizá una de las más importantes y productivas maniobras que el oficiante crítico realiza en su afán de entender, y también de comunicar"—y por la convicción que lo lleva a decir "¿Y qué es la crítica (ya que descifra, comprende, vincula, disfruta, revela, participa y se duele) sino un complejo y vital acto de amor?" Con ese tono sigular que lo hace accesible a un vasto público, Benedetti procura trascender el circuito cerrado y discriminatorio de las lecturas académicas estrictas y "excluyentes." [SS]

3975 Benedetti, Mario. Cultura entre dos fuegos. Montevideo: Univ. de la República, División Publicaciones y Ediciones, 1986. 143 p. (Col. Letras nacionales; 2a época, no. 2)

Conferencias, artículos, ponencias y ensayos breves escritos y publicados en su mayoría durante sus años de exilio (1979–86). Son particularmente reveladores de esos años "Los Temas del Escritor Latinoamericano en el Exilio," "Acción y Creación Literaria en América Latina" y "La Cultura, ese Blanco Móvil." [SS]

3976 Benedetti, Mario. Mario Benedetti: detrás de un vidrio claro. Entrevistado por Hugo R. Alfaro. Montevideo: Ediciones Trilce, 1986. 219 p.: bibl., plates, ports. (Col. Espejos)

Hugo Alfaro, redactor responsable de *Marcha* y fundador de *Brecha,* lleva a cabo la entrevista más dentenida con Benedetti. Importante contribución que, además de dar datos sobre la vida de MB, también recorre las instancias más cruciales de su obra literaria y de su actividad política. [MLB]

3977 Benedetti, Mario. Subdesarrollo y letras de osadía. Madrid: Alianza, 1987. 247 p.: bibl. (El Libro de bolsillo; 1263. Sección Literatura)

Recoge 16 ensayos breves, conferencias y artículos publicados entre 1963–86. Son particularmente importantes "El Escritor y la Crítica en el Contexto del Subdesarrollo" (1977), "La Cultura, ese Blanco Móvil" (1982) y el ensayo que le da título a esta colección (1968), publicado originalmente como "Temas y Problemas" en *América Latina en su literatura* (Mexico, Siglo XXI; UNESCO, 1972). Fundamental para los estudiosos de Benedetti y para una revisión del mapa crítico de estas décadas. [MLB]

3978 Concha, Jaime et al. Juan Carlos Onetti, papeles críticos: medio siglo de escritura. Coordinación de Rómulo Cosse. Montevideo: Librería Linardi y Risso, 1989. 294 p.: bibl.

Al igual que con su volumen sobre Borges, Cosse se propuso elaborar "un colectivo plural en los criterios y discutidor en la praxis, donde las distintas perspectivas y metodologías se disponen en dialécticas y complementarias oposiciones. Así el libro se cierra, efectivamente, en el acto de la lectura participativa y protagónica, capaz de integrar o seleccionar opciones críticas." Incluye ensayos de José Pedro Díaz, Juan Carlos Mondragón, Hilia Moreira, Noemí Ulla, Iber Verdugo, Jaime Concha, Ximena Moreno Aliste, Rómulo Cosse, Jorge Ruffinelli y Hugo Verani; un diálogo con Eduardo Galeano cuando le fuera otorgado a Onetti el Premio Cervantes, y una nota de Hugo Giovanetti. La cronología (útil) y la bibliografía (casi inexistente) estuvieron a cargo de Alvaro Barros-Lémez y Carlos Fagúndez. Valioso "reader." [SS]

3979 Guerra-Cunningham, Lucía. La referencialidad como negación del paraíso: exilio y excentrismo en *La nave de los locos* de Peri Rossi. (*in* Mujer y sociedad en América. Edición de Juana Alcira Arancibia. Mexicali, México: Univ. Autónoma de Baja California; Westminister, Calif.: Instituto Literario y Cultural Hispánico, 1988, v. 1, p. 45–56)

Guerra estudia las representaciones del exilio en esta obra principal de la narradora uruguaya en términos de sus connotaciones polisémicas. Está conformado en dos partes: "El Tapiz de la Creación: Centro y Sentido del Universo" y "Los Pliegues Alienantes de la Cultura Androcéntrica." El argumento central arriba a que en este texto Peri Rossi socaba el orden teleológico y destruye la perfección de la estructura representada en el tapiz medieval de la creación postulado como centro mítico. [MGP]

3980 Juan Carlos Onetti. Edición de Hugo J. Verani. Madrid: Taurus, 1987. 407 p.: bibl. (Persiles; 181: Serie El Escritor y la crítica)

Recopilación a cargo de uno de los mayores expertos de la obra de Onetti. La excelente "visión de conjunto" reúne aproximaciones de Rufinelli, Benedetti, Rama, J.P. Díaz, Aínsa, Claude Fell y Félix Grande. Entre estos estudios particulares son notables los de S. Molloy sobre *Los adioses*, de J. Ludmer sobre *Para una tumba sin nombre*, de J. Concha sobre *El pozo* y el del propio Verani sobre *La vida breve*. [SS]

3981 Speratti-Piñero, Emma Susana. Horacio Quiroga: precursor de la relación cine-literatura en la América Hispánica. (*Nueva Rev. Filol. Hisp.*, 36:2, 1988, p. 1239–1249)

Muestra "algunas respuestas a la atracción desafiante del séptimo arte y su universo" tal como se manifiestan en la producción de Horacio Quiroga (1878–1937). Además de lo elaborado en sus ensayos, el influjo del cine se registra en los cuentos "Miss Dorothy Phillips, mi Esposa" (1919), "El Espectro" (1921), "El Puritano" (1926) y "El Vampiro" (1927). También señala "aprovechamientos" en Bombal, Cortázar y Carpentier. [SS]

3982 Verani, Hugo J. Felisberto Hernández: la inquietante extrañeza de lo cotidiano. (*Cuad. Am.*, 14:2, marzo/abril 1989, p. 56–76)

La extrañeza que inicialmente distanciara a Felisberto de los lectores y de la crítica es precisamente la que, en última instancia, sirvió como clave de acceso para su posterior incorporación al mapa de los recuperados por los éxitos de los años 60. Excelente presentación de algunos de los rasgos que definen su singularidad y justifican la (tardía) atención que siguen mereciendo sus relatos. [SS]

Poetry

LUIS EYZAGUIRRE, *Professor of Spanish, University of Connecticut-Storrs*
MAGDALENA GARCIA PINTO, *Associate Professor of Spanish, University of Missouri, Columbia*
JAIME GIORDANO, *Professor of Spanish, the Ohio State University*
RUBEN GONZALEZ, *Associate Professor of Spanish, State University of New York at Old Westbury*
NORMA KLAHN, *Associate Professor of Spanish, University of California, Santa Cruz*
PEDRO LASTRA, *Professor of Spanish, State University of New York at Stony Brook*
OSCAR RIVERA-RODAS, *Professor of Spanish, University of Tennessee, Knoxville*
ARMANDO ROMERO, *Associate Professor of Spanish, University of Cincinnati*
GEORGE YUDICE, *Professor of Spanish, Hunter College-City University of New York*

LA PRODUCCION POETICA en este período ha sido muy apreciable, como podrá verse en los resúmenes regionales que siguen, y esto a pesar de las dificultades editoriales que padecen ciertas áreas, como Uruguay. Es por lo mismo particularmente meritoria la sostenida actividad de revistas dedicadas a difundir la creación poética y a registrar el trabajo crítico que ella genera: en este aspecto se destacan algunas publicaciones del Caribe y de Colombia.

Las relecturas y análisis de autores modernistas como R. Darío, L. Lugones y J. Herrera y Reissig (items **4213, 4216, 4220** y **4237**), y de poetas contemporáneos ya reconocidos como R. López Velarde (items **4233, 4258** y **4263**), G. Mistral (item **4231**), C. Vallejo (items **4235** y **4247**), P. Neruda (items **4240** y **4254**), J. Lezama Lima (items **4243** y **4245**) y O. Paz (items **4256, 4261, 4266,** y **4151**) concitaron el mayor interés de la crítica. Sobre esos autores hubo aportes analíticos significativos, que compensan felizmente la medianía que suele advertirse en este tipo de estudios.

El suceso más notable del período fue una distinción que honra a la poesía hispanoamericana en la persona y en la obra de Octavio Paz. [PL]

La poesía mexicana recibió su más alto homenaje con el Premio Nobel de Literatura otorgado a Octavio Paz en 1990. El premio no sólo reconoce la obra del poeta sino también la rica tradición literaria de su país. A raíz de este acontecimiento aparecieron numerosas entrevistas, artículos y ensayos en periódicos y revistas, junto a libros introductorios a la vida y obra de Paz, quien había recibido en 1988 el importante Premio Britannica.

La conmemoración del centenario del nacimiento de Ramón López Velarde (1988) suscitó varias reediciones y estudios. Entre éstos merecen mención especial los de Emmanuel Carballo (item **4233**), Allen Phillips (item **4258**) y Guillermo Sheridan (item **4263**). Con motivo de este centenario, el Congreso Estatal de Zacatecas le confirió a Allen W. Phillips la medalla "Ramón López Velarde."

La poesía de mujeres empieza a ser justamente reconocida no sólo en antologías generales (items **4001** y **3997**) sino en antologías especiales (items **3994** y **3987**) y con distinciones como el Premio de Poesía Aguascalientes entregados a Myriam Moscona en 1988 (item **4134**) y a Elsa Cross en 1989 (item **4053**).

A la producción de poetas ya establecidos internacionalmente como Homero Aridjis (item **4016**), Gerardo Deniz (item **4061**), Jaime García Terrés (item **4074**), Eduardo Lizalde (item **4119**) y José Emilio Pacheco (item **4144**), se suma el promisorio trabajo de una nueva generación, en la que se destacan las contribuciones de Efraín Bartolomé (items **4019** y **4020**), Alberto Blanco (item **4026**), Coral Bracho (item **4028**), Ricardo Castillo (item **4042**), Francisco Hernández (item **4095**), David Huerta (item **4096**), Silvia T. Rivera (item **4167**) y Verónica Volkow (item **4197**).

Junto a la actividad del Fondo de Cultura, Joaquín Mortiz y Premiá, aparecen ahora nuevas editoriales interesadas por la producción poética de los jóvenes, como Ediciones Toledo, Los Cuadernos de Malinalco, El Tucán de Virginia y la colección El Ala del Tigre, de la Univ. Nacional Autónoma de México. [NK]

En la medida en que aminoran en Centroamérica las poéticas de denuncia, las posturas antiimperialistas y la sencilla crónica de hechos desalentadores -todavía evidentes en Miguel Huezo Mixco, El Salvador (item **4098**), José Adán Castelar y Roberto Sosa, Honduras (items **4041, 4040** y **4185**) y en Ernesto Cardenal, Nicaragua, cuya inspiración creativa parece haberse agotado y desembocado en eternas crónicas (items **4032, 4033** y **4034**), vienen cobrando mayor fuerza aquellas tendencias que exploran las tensiones del lenguaje mismo: Laureano Albán, Costa Rica (item **4006**); los registros intimistas de las pequeñas luchas cotidianas: Italo López Vallecillos, El Salvador (item **4123**), Carmen Matute, Guatemala (item **4126**) y María Eugenia Ramos, Honduras (item **4163**); que sondean el erotismo: Enrique Jaramillo Levi, Panamá (items **4102** y **3993**) y Francisco de Asís Fernández, Nicaragua (item **4067**). El erotismo cobra mayor intensidad poética en el feminismo de las poetas: Julieta Dobles, Leonor Garnier, Lil Picado y Ana Istarú, Costa Rica (items **4065, 4075, 4159,** y **3984**), C. Matute y, especialmente, las antologías dispuestas por Luz Méndez de la Vega, Guatemala (items **3991** y **3998**) y Rosario Murillo, Nicaragua (item **4135**). La libertad de expresión personal ha llegado inclusive a la poetización del amor lesbiano por Nidia Barboza, de Costa Rica (item **4018**). Finalmente, el pastiche juguetón e irónico a la manera de Roque Dalton encuentra su continuación en Juan Chow, Nicaragua (item **4048**). [GY]

En el Caribe la crítica reafirma el valor de las figuras mayores de la poesía contemporánea de la zona: Nicolás Guillén (items **4090, 4214, 4228** y **4260**), José Lezama Lima (items **4110, 4243** y **4245**), Eliseo Diego (item **4063**), Pedro Mir (items **4128** y **4252**), Luis Lloréns Torres (item **4120**) y Luis Palés Matos (item **4242**). Los grupos de *Orígenes*, en Cuba, y "La Poesía Sorprendida," en la República Dominicana (items **4000** y **4224**), aún gozan de parcial atención.

Entre los poetas de promociones próximas es notoria no ya la disminución sino una casi total ausencia del elemento político, que hasta entrada la década de los 80 era estímulo y vivencia poética admirativa. Es claro que hay una diversificación de actitudes y direcciones, pero la poesía de más vuelo recala en el tema del arte y de la poesía misma, como se evidencia en las voces del puertorriqueño José Luis Vega (item **4194**) y del cubano José Pérez Olivares (items **4153** y **4154**). También merece mención aparte el interesante poemario del joven dominicano Juan Carlos Mieses (item **4127**), cuyas historias recuerdan la fortaleza de la poesía épica.

En julio de 1989, a los 87 años de edad, murió en La Habana el gran poeta cubano Nicolás Guillén. Su obra es como el modelo caracterizador de la tendencia negrista (década del 30) en el Caribe; se le reconoce también por su poesía social o de sostenido compromiso político. En octubre de 1990, a la edad de 42 años, murió en Puerto Rico Manuel Ramos Otero. Aparte de su obra narrativa deja publicado *El libro de la muerte* (1985, ver *HLAS 48:5862*), en cuyo centro gravita la experiencia homosexual.

Impresiona cómo las editoriales cubanas ayudan a divulgar la poesía, especialmente la de los jóvenes, aunque no siempre hay conciencia de calidad o del orden productivo. En Puerto Rico la *Revista del Instituto de Cultura Puertorriqueña* y *Mairena* merecen reconocimiento por su labor de difusión de la poesía, pero hasta

ahora no se advierten voces prometedoras. La revista *Cuadernos de Poética* acrecienta sus estrategias críticas y mantiene abiertas sus páginas a numerosos autores
jóvenes en la Republica Dominicana. [RG]

La actividad poética colombiana de estos años continúa su línea de intensidad, pero ya no sólo en lo referente a búsquedas y hallazgos poéticos sino en cuanto
a difusión: aunque no siempre privilegiada por los editores, la poesía ha encontrado
un apreciable apoyo en el auge editorial del país. Fernando Arbeláez, poeta de la
generación de *Mito*, publicó dos libros después de algunos años de silencio (items
4012 y **4011**). Se destaca también la reaparición de los poetas "nadaístas" Jaime Jaramillo Escobar (item **4101**) y Jotamario (item **4103**), junto a otros poetas de la década
del 60, Giovanni Quessep (item **4161**) y Jaime García Maffla (item **4072**). Entre los
autores más jóvenes sobresalen Juan Manuel Roca (item **4168**) y Santiago Mutis
(item **4137**). Los principales aportes de la poesía femenina fueron los de María Mercedes Carranza (item **4036**) y Orietta Lozano (item **4124**).

Debe mencionarse la sostenida labor de Mario Rivero en la dirección de la
revista *Golpe de Dados*, que en 1989 completó los 100 números; otras publicaciones importantes son *Gradiva* y *Casa Silva:* esta última registra las actividades
de la institución del mismo nombre, dedicada exclusivamente a promover la poesía
colombiana y latinoamericana. Una revista reciente que merece reseñarse junto a
las anteriores es *Verso Libre*.

Nota dolorosa en 1989 fue la muerte de los poetas Carlos Castro Saavedra y
Néstor Madrid Malo.

Los libros más importantes publicados en Venezuela durante este período pertenecen, casi en su totalidad, a poetas de las generaciones del 40 y 50–60. *Obra
poética* de Vicente Gerbasi procura una visión de conjunto del trabajo de una de las
personalidades mayores de la literatura venezolana de este siglo (item **4080**). Se destacan también dos libros de Juan Liscano (items **4118** y **4117**), y una nueva publicación de Juan Sánchez Peláez (item **4179**) que confirma el magisterio de su palabra
poética. De Ludovico Silva, recientemente fallecido, se publicó una obra que recoge
toda su producción de 1958–82 (item **4182**). Juan Calzadilla y Arnaldo Acosta
Bello, poetas representativos de los grupos "El Techo de la Ballena" y " Tabla Redonda," respectivamente, editaron libros significativos (items **4030** y **4003**).

En la poesía femenina, de amplia y apreciable trayectoria en Venezuela, los
aportes más interesantes fueron los de Margara Russotto (item **4176**) y Cecilia Ortiz
(item **4142**). [AR]

La producción poética de los últimos años en Bolivia ha demostrado cierto
equilibrio en tres áreas importantes: reedición de poetas ya consagrados; nuevos
libros de autores conocidos; y aparición de representantes de las generaciones jóvenes. Respecto a los primeros cabe destacar *Poesías* de Antonio José de Sainz (item
4177), obra que invita a revisar los conceptos propios de la transición modernista-
vanguardista, desde la perspectiva de la modernidad. La publicación en España de la
obra completa de Oscar Cerruto (item **4045**) confirma que se trata de un aporte valioso a la lírica hispánica contemporánea. Otros poetas ya conocidos—Alberto
Guerra (n. 1929), Jorge Suárez (n. 1932) y Jesús Urzagasti (n. 1941) publicaron nuevos volúmenes después de períodos de silencio impuestos por las dictaduras militares hasta hace 10 años (items **4089, 4186** y **4189**). Es notable la aparición masiva
de jóvenes valores, especialmente femeninos: Carmen Montero Ayala (item **4132**) y
Viviana Limpias (item **4114**). También sobresalen Alvaro Diez Astete (item **4064**),
Juan Ignacio Siles (item **4181**) y Jorge Campero (item **4031**).

En Ecuador se publicaron reediciones de autores conocidos y nuevas obras de poetas consagrados, como Euler Granda (item **4087**). En general, la poesía ecuatoriana muestra dos características más o menos comunes: por una parte, un esfuerzo por introducir formas y recursos expresivos novedosos en el lenguaje, y aunque no se podría señalar una obra que los logre plenamente, se deben destacar los libros de Raúl Arias (item **4015**) y Edgar A. García (item **4073**). Por otra parte, se advierte cierta uniformidad en la actitud emocional subyacente a la mayoría de los textos actuales: desencanto e incertidumbre, que a veces implica una visión desolada de la realidad.

El panorama de la poesía en el Perú se caracteriza fundamentalmente por la relectura y revaloración de poetas nacionales mayores, cuya figura dominante es César Vallejo. Son numerosas las reediciones de sus obras (item **4192, 4191** y **4193**) y los estudios críticos dedicados a su examen (items **4235, 4247** y **4282**). Otras revaloraciones de gran interés han sido las de Martín Adán (item **4248**) y Javier Heraud (items **4094** y **4244**). La atención que ha merecido Martín Adán permite reconsiderar el importante lugar de este poeta dentro del vanguardismo peruano, así como es también significativa la corriente de lectura que enfoca la obra de Heraud. Paralelamente deben destacarse un nuevo texto de Washington Delgado (item **4060**) y el volumen que reúne varios libros de Carlos Germán Belli, publicado en España (item **4022**). [ORR]

Importantes estudios, reediciones, antologías y biografías de los poetas chilenos consagrados aparecieron en este período: entre ellos, el excelente libro de Luis Arrigoitia sobre la prosa de Gabriela Mistral fue un preciso homenaje en el centenario del nacimiento de la escritora en 1989 (item **4231**). De Nicanor Parra se publicaron una cuidada reedición de *Poemas y antipoemas* (item **4150**) y una antología (item **4149**). Sobresalen también en este panorama dos selecciones poéticas de Pablo de Rokha, controvertido precursor de la vanguardia chilena (items **4171** y **4172**).

Una publicación muy destacable de estos años es la primera recolección de estudios sobre Neruda en inglés: el libro *Pablo Neruda* (item **4254**), editado por el conocido crítico Harold Bloom, es particularmente significativo para la literatura chilena en general. Debe señalarse también el evocador homenaje fotográfico de Luis Poirot (item **4277**), enriquecido con textos testimoniales de diversos escritores.

Publicaciones de y sobre Humberto Díaz Casanueva y Gonzalo Rojas demuestran el interés que suscita la poesía de ambos autores. Es consagratoria la *Obra poética* del primero, publicada por la Biblioteca Ayacucho, de Caracas (item **4062**). *Materia de testamento* (item **4170**) es volumen fundamental de Gonzalo Rojas, sobre quien apareció en Alemania un conjunto de estudios (item **4246**). De los poetas más próximos, el de mayor relevancia es Oscar Hahn, cuyo ejemplar libro de sonetos (item **4091**) apareció al mismo tiempo que se publicaba una recolección de estudios sobre su trabajo, dispuesta por Pedro Lastra y Enrique Lihn (item **4232**). Entre los poetas de promociones recientes merecen especial mención Pedro Vicuña (item **4195**) y Tomás Harris (item **4093**). Un lugar señero ocupa el rescate de la inquietante poesía de Rodrigo Lira, joven poeta muerto en 1981 y cuyo *Proyecto de obras completas* fue presentado por Enrique Lihn en 1984 (item **4115**).

La muerte de Enrique Lihn en 1988 empobrece en mucho el panorama cultural chileno, pero tres libros suyos editados en estos años invitan a meditar en la significación mayor de su obra: *Diario de muerte*, un sobrecogedor libro póstumo (item **4112**), *Album de toda especie de poemas* (item **4111**) y *Mester de juglaría* (item **4113**). [LE]

Durante este bienio se destaca en el Paraguay la figura de Elvio Romero, quien regresó al país después de casi 40 años de exilio. Dos de sus obras más importantes se reeditaron en el período (items **4173** y **4175**). En 1990 la Editorial Alcántara emprendió la publicación de sus *Poesías completas* en dos tomos (item **4174**): una manera fecunda de reivindicar al escritor tras su larga y obligada ausencia. El crítico Hugo Rodríguez Alcalá publicó en 1988 un volumen de ensayos sobre literatura paraguaya, en el que se incluyen informativos estudios sobre la obra poética de varios autores de distintas generaciones (item **3968**). Este libro será imprescindible para los interesados en el desarrollo de la poesía en Paraguay, un campo que ofrece posibilidades a los nuevos investigadores de poesía hispanoamericana contemporánea.

En Uruguay continuó la publicación de textos escritos en la cárcel o en el exilio, y que dan voz a las hasta ahora innombradas experiencias de la prisión política, de la tortura y de la muerte propia y ajena. De los autores ya establecidos, Mario Benedetti publicó dos volúmenes poéticos (items **4023** y **4024**), y Hugo Achugar una importante antología (item **4002**) que reúne sus libros anteriores desde 1977–89. Otro acontecimiento de gran interés fue la edición de la *Obra completa* de Bartolomé Hidalgo (item **3393**), que apareció precedida de un enjundioso prólogo-estudio de Antonio Pradeiro, responsable de la publicación. Es meritorio el esfuerzo de los poetas jóvenes, que editan en medio de serias dificultades económicas; pero el trabajo crítico en este género literario es escaso. [MGP]

En Argentina se ha visto un verdadero "retorno" poético; el más importante es probablemente el transitorio de Juan Gelman. Sus libros han sido reeditados, se empiezan a publicar sus obras completas y se divulga su producción en España durante el exilio (items **4076, 4077, 4078** y **4079**). La colección "Ultimo Reino" realiza una labor amplia, plural, y muchos de los nuevos y mejores poetas han aparecido allí. Se solidifica el prestigio de algunos poetas clásicos como Enrique Molina (item **4130**), Alberto Girri (items **4082, 4083, 4255, 4268** y **4273**) y Roberto Juarroz (items **4104** y **4105**), y empieza a reconocerse ampliamente a poetas como Néstor Perlongher (items **4156** y **4157**), probablemente uno de los más audaces entre los jóvenes. La abundancia de encuentros, congresos y recitales en todo el Cono Sur imprime un sello de vida a este renacer editorial que abarca toda el área. [JG]

ANTHOLOGIES

3983 Antología: *Ultimo Reino.* Buenos Aires: Ediciones Libros de Tierra Firme, 1987. 158 p. (Col. de poesía Todos bailan; 16)

Esta selección está constituida por 12 autores y puede ser de mucho interés para quienes deseen conocer a algunos de los poetas asociados a la revista *Ultimo Reino*, activa desde 1979. [JG]

3984 Antología de una generación dispersa. Edición de Carlos Ma. Jiménez, Jorge Bustamante, Isabel C. Gallardo. San José: Editorial Costa Rica, 1982. 198 p.: bibl.

A pesar del número de poetas incluidos, esta antología presenta una sensibilidad común que atestigua el destiempo, el desencuentro, el desequilibrio, el desgarramiento.

Una sensibilidad expresada a menudo en imágenes trilladas—"acariciar la soledad," "descender[] las llagas que [. . .] oprimen." Más que dispersa, parece una generación perdida en el aburrimiento, con algunas excepciones como Ana Istarú, quien enuncia una voz feminista que la salva del ripio enajenante. [GY]

3985 Brull, Mariano *et al.* Una antología de poesía cubana. Selección y presentación de Diego García Elío. México: Editorial Oasis, 1984. 239 p.: bibl. (Col. Percance; 6)

Reúne a un grupo significativo de poetas cubanos del siglo XX: Brull, Florit, Ballagas, Guillén y otros que se consagraron alrededor de la famosa revista *Orígenes* (ver item **3674**). Se echa de menos un estudio que sitúe y por lo menos describa las características más importantes de la obra de los escogidos. Es lamentable que tampoco se identifique el año ni el libro a que pertenecen los poemas seleccionados. [RG]

3986 50 años de poesía argentina contemporánea, 1930–1980. Compilación de Oscar Hermes Villordo. Buenos Aires: Revista Cultura, 1985. 180 p.: bibl. (Col. Unión Carbide)

Esta introducción a la poesía argentina (1930–80) es bastante completa en cuanto a los 62 nombres escogidos. Lamentablemente las últimas décadas están muy mal representadas, probablemente por limitaciones generacionales en el gusto estético. Pudo haber sido más estricta en las décadas iniciales. La calidad de los poemas escogidos no le suele hacer justicia a los poetas, pero considerando la vastedad del material, el esfuerzo en su conjunto es loable. [JG]

3987 The fertile rhythms: contemporary women poets of Mexico. Selected and edited by Thomas Hoeksema. Translated by Thomas Hoeksema and Romelia Enríquez. Pittsburgh: Latin American Literary Review Press, 1989. 126 p. (Discoveries)

A pesar del título complaciente de esta antología bilingüe, se reconoce su importancia al presentar nuevas poetas mexicanas en traducción. Las selecciones van precedidas de dos breves ensayos. En el primero Gabriel Zaid discute la constitución de su texto *Asamblea de poetas jóvenes de México* de 1980 dado que Hoeksema parte de ese texto para seleccionar a las poetas, nacidas entre 1950–62, que representan una nueva generación. El ensayo de Mary Crow, más interrogante que analítico, constata la dificultad de caracterizar una poesía en proceso. Entre las antologadas, con dos o tres poemas cada una, están Hilda Bautista, Sabina Berman, Coral Bracho, Kyra Galván, Pura López Colome, Blanca Luz Pulido, Perla Schwartz, Verónica Volkow. For comments on translation see item **4919**. [NK]

The image of black women in twentieth-century South American poetry: a bilingual anthology. See item **4921**.

3988 Nueva poesía argentina. Selección de Leopoldo Castilla. Madrid: Ediciones Hiperión, 1987. 103 p. (Poesía Hiperión; 116)

Util selección de poetas nacidos a partir de 1940, la mayor parte de ellos afectados por la conflictiva situación política de los

años 60 y 70, notablemente la dictadura militar desatada en 1976. Contiene 19 poetas, algunos de los cuales (por ej.: Guillerno Boido, Angel Leiva, Daniel Freidenberg, Rafael Felipe Oteriño, Diana Bellesi, Jorge Boccanera) son valores ya reconocidos. Los poemas seleccionados están escogidos con gusto. El efecto de conjunto es más uniforme de lo que es normal en una antología. [JG]

On the front line: guerrilla poems of El Salvador. See item **4927**.

One more stripe to the tiger: a selection of contemporary Chilean poetry and fiction. See item **4928**.

3989 Pájaro y volcán. Edición de Miguel Huezo Mixco. San Salvador: UCA Editores, 1989. 182 p. (Col. Gavidia; 30)

Indispensable muestra de poesía y testimonio centroamericano escrito por militantes y combatientes del FMLN en los frentes de guerra. Si bien predominan los temas vinculados a la lucha, también se sondea el amor, la existencia y, lo más sorprendente en este contexto, el ser mismo de la poesía. La mayoría de textos están insertos totalmente dentro de la tradición poética, contrastando marcadamente con los talleres populares en Nicaragua. [GY]

3990 Parvada: poetas jóvenes de Baja California, antología. Selección de Gabriel Trujillo Muñoz. Mexicali, Mexico: Univ. Autónoma de Baja California, .1985. 232 p.

Los talleres de las últimas dos décadas han impulsado "una explosión poética en Baja California" informa Gabriel Trujillo Muñoz en la esclarecedora introducción a esta antología que recoge la poesía escogida de 24 poetas nacidos entre 1940–65. Desde distintas tradiciones poéticas esta poesía registra realidades inéditas de la frontera. Entre los antologados se destacan: Jorge Ruiz Dueñas, Ernesto Trejo, Roberto Castillo Udiarte, Rosina Conde, Luis Cortés Bargallo, Daniel Sada, Gabriel Trujillo Muñoz, José Javier Villarreal. [NK]

3991 La poesía del Grupo RIN-78. Selección y comentarios de Luz Méndez de la Vega. Guatemala: Grupo Literario Editorial RIN-78, 1986. 229 p. (Col. Literatura; 28)

Valiosa antología, con extensos comentarios y bibliografía de los poetas del grupo RIN-78. Merecen mención Amable Sánchez

Torres y Hugo Cerezo Dardón por su poesía de tema existencial y denuncia social. Pero la verdadera novedad en la poesía guatemalteca, y que trasciende el escenario nacional, la constituye el enfrentamiento erótico y el feminismo de Ana María Rodas, Carmen Matute y la antóloga misma. [GY]

3992 Poesía en Aguascalientes: antología de poetas, siglos XIX y XX. Compilación de Alejandro Sandoval. México: Editorial Oasis, 1984. 251 p. (Col. Percance; 10)

Este volumen presenta a los poetas más importantes de los siglos XIX y XX de este estado. Más bien interesa por la introducción de Sandoval quien elabora sobre la importancia de los Juegos Florales que se llevan a cabo en el estado, y la influencia que tuvieron en el desarrollo de la literatura local. Esta tradición cumplió una función histórica y ha sido, de alguna manera, sustituída por el actual Premio Nacional de Poesía otorgado en Aguascalientes a poetas jóvenes cuyo manuscrito premiado publica Joaquín Mortiz. [NK]

3993 Poesía erótica de Panamá, 1929–1981. Selección y prólogo de Enrique Jaramillo Levi. México: Editorial Signos, 1982. 165 p.: bibl. (Col. Portobelo; 4. Serie Temas y conflictos)

Predomina el tema social y antiimperialista en la poesía panameña. No obstante, también hay un caudal de literatura erótica, que esta antología pretende recopilar. En un prólogo esclarecedor el recopilador ofrece el siguiente criterio de inclusión: "Toda manifestación de la vitalidad sexual humana, expresada . . . [como] el surgimiento de una profunda inquietud—necesidad (deseo) de expansión de los sentidos, cuyo referente suele ser la presencia (real o imaginaria) de otro cuerpo; y el instante en que la sexualidad en llamas alcanza su realización en otro." [GY]

3994 La poesía femenina contemporánea en México, 1941 a 1968. Introducción, selección y notas de Carlos González Salas. Ciudad Victoria, Mexico: Instituto Tamaulipeco de Cultura, 1989. 350 p.

Antología que busca recoger la poesía de las mujeres en México en un momento de productividad extraordinaria que va desde la generación de la *Revista Rueca* (1941) hasta la de poetas cuya obra surge durante 1959–71. Util prólogo, revisa antologías de la pro-

ducción femenina desde la Independencia. La edición, aunque a destiempo, registra una centena de poetas, cada una acompañadas de una introducción general y una bio-bibliografía, de interés para el estudioso. [NK]

3995 Poesía modernista hispanoamericana y española: antología. Estudio preliminar, edición y notas de Ivan A. Schulman y Evelyn Picon Garfield. Madrid: Taurus, 1986. 520 p.: bibl. (Temas de España; 154. Sección de clásicos)

Contra la divulgada escisión de "la expresión hispánica de la crisis universal decimonónica" en dos manifestaciones: "Modernismo" en Hispanoamérica y "98" en España, esta antología ilustra el período modernista como un fenómeno de conjunto. Considera a todos los poetas hispanoamericanos representativos, desde S. Díaz Mirón a D. Agustini. Más novedosa, a pesar de los desniveles de la muestra, es la parte dedicada a España, iniciada de manera polémica con Rosalía de Castro (1837–85), cuya presencia aquí parecerá discutible a más de un lector de la escritora gallega. Entre los autores peninsulares sobresalen notoriamente Unamuno, Valle Inclán, A. Machado y J. R. Jiménez. [PL]

3996 Poesía y gráfica contemporánea de Costa Rica. Prólogo de Jézer González. Selección de Alfonso Chase. San José: Editorial Costa Rica, 1986. 75 p.: ill.

Prólogo valioso en que se destacan las tradiciones poéticas costarricenses de este siglo: modernismo lugoniano y herriano más que dariano; renovación técnica a partir de la vanguardia en Eunice Odio, Mario Picado, Jorge Charpentier y Carlos Duverrán; la tríada de mayor importancia—Jorge Debravo, Laureano Albán y Alfonso Chase—en la segunda mitad del siglo XX; y la más destacada poesía femenina en América Latina: Julieta Dobles, Lil Picado, Mía Gallegos, Ana Istarú y Janina Fernández. [GY]

3997 Poetas de una generación, 1950–1959. Selección y prólogo de Evodio Escalante. México: Premiá: Coordinación de Difusión Cultural, Dirección de Literatura, UNAM, 1988. 177 p.: bibl. (Textos de humanidades)

Antología importante que junto a la de Jorge González de León (1981), cuya recopilación incluía la poesía de poetas nacidos entre 1940–49, se constituye como texto necesario para el estudioso de la poesía. Escalante mantiene en su prólogo que la poesía de esta generación, aunque en proceso, es una de las más ricas en la historia reciente de las letras mexicanas por "la profusión de registros, la gran variedad temática y el radicalismo experimental." Es, sin duda, una excelente introducción a poetas que anuncian una nueva voz para la poesía. Entre los poetas se encuentran Efraín Bartolomé, Alberto Blanco, Carmen Bullosa, Coral Bracho, Héctor Carreto, Ricardo Castillo, Sandro Cohen, Kyra Galván, Ricardo Hernández, Pura López Colomé, Fabio Morábito, Vicente Quirarte, Silvia Tomasa Rivera, Blanca Luz Varela y Verónica Volkow. [NK]

3998 Poetisas desmitificadoras guatemaltecas. Edición de Luz Méndez de la Vega. Guatemala: Tip. Nacional, 1984. 195 p.: bibl. (Col. Guatemala; 18: Serie José Batres Montúfar; 4)

Indispensable antología de composiciones innovadoras—desde la feminidad postmodernista a lo Storni hasta el feminismo actual—que rompen el tradicional acato de la poesía guatemalteca. El valioso prólogo analiza las circunstancias en que se produce esta desmitificación y a continuación se incluyen selecciones de diez poetas, incluyendo Alaíde Foppa, Isabel de los Angeles Ruano, Ana María Rodas y Carmen Matute. [GY]

3999 Sin otro profeta que su canto: antología de poesía escrita por dominicanas. Selección y prólogo de Daisy Cocco de Filippis. Santo Domingo: Taller, 1988. 231 p. (Biblioteca Taller; 263)

Con la antología se quiere delinear una tradición literaria femenina. La muestra comienza con poetas del 17 y llega hasta el presente. El prólogo analiza y desmitifica la imagen tradicional de la mujer en la poesía dominicana. Algunos nombres en la antología son cuestionables. Algunas poetas importantes son Salomé Ureña de Henríquez, Aída Cartagena Portalatín, Jeannette Miller y Sherezada (Chiqui) Vicioso. [RG]

4000 El Síndrome de Penélope en la poesía dominicana: antología básica. Santo Domingo: Biblioteca Nacional, 1986. 349 p.: ports. (Col. Orfeo)

La antología periodiza la poesía dominicana desde principios del siglo hasta la década del 80. En el prólogo se reconoce el período de la "Poesía Sorprendia" (1943) como el de mayor esplendor en su tradición. A pesar de su retórica preciosista, el prólogo llega a presentar una visión integral de la poesía de este siglo. Incluye los poetas dominicanos más importantes. Hay algunas inclusiones cuestionables; también hay exclusiones notorias, sobre todo en la generación a la que pertenecen los autores, por cierto, auto-incluídos. [RG]

4001 La sirena en el espejo: antología de poesía, 1972–1989. Selección de Manuel Ulacia, José María Espinasa y Víctor Manuel Mendiola. México: Ediciones El Tucán de Virginia: Fundación E. Gutman: Dirección de Difusión Cultural de la UNAM, 1990. 239 p. (Col. El texto colectivo. Serie Poesía)

Util antología cuyo prólogo revisa la poesía mexicana del siglo XX para situar a 23 poetas seleccionados que representan dos últimas generaciones en México. Separados por la experiencia del movimiento estudiantil del 68, la primera se define por su participación y lucha en la transformación radical de la sociedad. La segunda, más escéptica, se considera contestataria de ciertos discursos ideológicos. Ambas rechazan la poesía como instrumento explícitamente político o didáctico, aunque en sus poemas existan planteamientos ideológicos y éticos. Siguiendo la línea de José Emilio Pacheco piensan que la originalidad "consiste en hacer nuevo lo que ya existe en la tradición, o en todo caso, tal como lo entendió Eliot: volver a la palabra original." Entre los poetas se encuentran Efraín Bartolomé, Hilda Bautista, Alberto Blanco, Carmen Boullosa, Coral Bracho, Francisco Hernández, David Huerta, Fabio Morábito, Vicente Quirarte, Manuel Ulacia, Verónica Volkow. Una ficha bio-bibliográfica precede cada selección. [NK]

BOOKS OF VERSE

4002 Achugar, Hugo. Todo lo que es sólido se disuelve en el aire: 1977–1989. Montevideo: Arca, 1989. 132 p.

Este poemario cuyo título repite el epígrafe tomado del *Manifiesto Comunista* de K. Marx, lleva una portada que cita al Goya de "Los Sueños de la Razón . . . " Ambos "umbrales recortan la obra poética en un espacio en el que la existencia humana y la expresión poética de dicha experiencia se sostienen en los movimientos de la imaginación y en los juegos rituales que repiten el insistir del tiempo en su doble ritmo de stasis y transcurrir. Los poemas están organizados en tres secciones: 1) *Cuaderno verde, 1988–1989;* 2) *Todo lo que es sólido se disuelve en el aire: o ¿qué hay detrás de esa cortina?; Cuaderno de bitácora, 1984–1989;* y 3) *Las mariposas tropicales, 1977–1989.* La obra poética de Hugo Achugar es imprescindible para una apreciación cabal de la generación del 68 no sólo en el Uruguay sino también en Hispanoamérica [MGP]

4003 Acosta Bello, Arnaldo. Mar amargo. Caracas: Fundarte, 1988. 80 p. (Col. Delta; 21)

Arnaldo Acosta Bello (n. 1927) fue miembro fundador del grupo literario "Tabla Redonda," que junto con "Sardio" y "El Techo de la Ballena" recogen gran parte de la mejor producción poética venezolana de las décadas del 50 y 60. Poeta de honda reflexión existencial, Acosta Bello nos da en este libro una profunda muestra de su dirección poética. En ella, mediante un lenguaje denso y depurado, el poeta ahonda en lo desconocido, en el misterio que oculta el filo de las formas. [AR]

4004 Aguilar, Marco. Emboscada del tiempo. San José: Ediciones Zúñiga y Cabal, 1988. 70 p.: ill. (Col. Santamaría)

Desde los albores del "microbio solitario" hasta el contemporáneo envenenamiento y espanto nuclear, Aguilar *cuenta*—acaso demasiado narrativamente— la evolución de los seres humanos, movidos desde siempre por el proyecto de "quebrar[-] juntar . . . el cántaro del oído." Debe decirse que no es claro por qué se elige el género poético para contar (más que *cantar*) estas generalidades de condena y solidaridad humanas. [GY]

4005 Agustini, Delmira. Antología. Selección y prólogo de Esther de Cáceres. 2a ed. Montevideo: Ministerio de Educación y Cultura, 1986. 65 p. (Biblioteca Artigas: Col. de clásicos uruguayos; 69)

Esta selección de la poeta uruguaya realizada por Esther de Cáceres va precedida de un largo prólogo que revisa algunas de las lecturas de la obra de Agustini, pero no se indica de qué libro procede cada texto. Y hay una ausencia notable: falta "Visión" que no debería dejar de incluirse en una selección de la poesía de Agustini. [MGP]

4006 Albán, Laureano. Geografía invisible de América. San José: Editorial Costa Rica, 1983. 152 p.

En contraste con otras tentativas de contar/cantar el mundo precolombino, Albán recrea casi arqueólogicamente las cosmogonías nahua y maya en un lenguaje que— siguiendo las pautas de su "Manifiesto Trascendentalista" de 1977—busca el "continuo develamiento esencial de la realidad," aquí volcada hacia la "América trascendental, invisible, más allá de su historia y su geografía física." Procura, en otras palabras, recrear el fundamento poético acaso olvidado tras de tantas inmigraciones y fusiones culturales. [GY]

4007 Alegría, Claribel. Luisa en el país de la realidad. México: Joan Boldó i Climent, Editores: Univ. Autónoma de Zacatecas, 1987. 181 p.

Mosaico de poemas, anécdotas, recuerdos, deseos, este libro baraja retazos de una autobiografía ligeramente ficcionalizada, en la cual predominan, evocaciones personales pero a menudo intervenidas por referencias a la guerra civil. Es un acierto artístico la proyección de una sensibilidad poética que atraviesa formas expresivas tan diversas. [GY]

4008 Anguita, Eduardo. Definición y pérdida de la persona. Santiago: Editorial Universitaria, 1988. 20 p. (Col. Fuera de serie)

Poema que empieza situándose en un tiempo cuando "el mundo es una forma vacía." En un segundo tiempo, la luz de la creación "empieza a definir . . . los objetos." Se define luego la figura humana que, al final, se pierde, después de perder los goces de un "último amor." [LE]

4009 Arango, Gonzalo. Adangelios. Bogotá: Montaña Mágica, 1985. 141 p.: ill. (some col.)

El nadaísmo, como rebelión generacional, buscaba responder con violencia a la violencia colombiana, y logró su cometido de años de una lucha vital y poética desde casi todos los frentes de la cultura nacional. Gonzalo Arango (1932–76), líder máximo de este movimiento, representó por años al escritor comprometido profundamente con el cambio de todos los valores sociales. Sin embargo, y luego de innumerables altibajos en su trayectoria como pensador, al final de sus días había abrazado las fuerzas tradicionales del pensamiento cristiano, en un afán salvador. Este libro recoge una serie de poemas, de muy poca calidad literaria, que detallan este camino de redención. [AR]

4010 Arango, José Manuel. Poemas escogidos. Selección y prólogo de David Jiménez P. Medellín, Colombia: Editorial Univ. de Antioquia, 1988. 333 p. (Col. Premio nacional de poesía)

Arango (n. 1937) es uno de los poetas sobresalientes en la actualidad poética colombiana. Este libro es una selección de sus libros anteriores: *Este lugar de la noche* (1973); *Signos* (1978); *Cántiga* (1978). Se incluyen también algunos poemas dispersos y traducciones de poetas, especialmente norteamericanos. Transparencia, encantamiento, celebración, rito, son los vocablos que buscan atrapar lo que se desprende de estas páginas cargadas de una simple, y por qué no decirlo, extraña sabiduría verbal. [AR]

4011 Arbeláez, Fernando. Textos de exilio. Bogotá: Procultura, 1986. 79 p. (Nueva biblioteca colombiana de cultura. Serie breve. Literatura)

Divididos en tres partes: "Analectas y Signos," poemas de 1970 (ya publicados anteriormente); "Textos de Exilios;" y "El Pincel sobre la Seda," de más reciente factura. Este libro del poeta colombiano Arbeláez apunta en su conjunto a esa zona donde la oscuridad deviene claridad no sólo por sabia sencillez sino por afinación del instrumental poético. Arbeláez logra un encantamiento verbal no gracias a la abundancia sino a la depuración. [AR]

4012 Arbeláez, Fernando. El viejo de la ciudad = Ho geros tēs polēs The old man of the city. Traducción al griego de Rigas Kappatos. Traducción al inglés de Elizabeth Harrison. Bogotá: Banco Central Hipotecario, 1985. 105 p.

La presencia del poeta griego Constantino Cavafi en la poesía latinoamericana es relevante, así lo atestiguan poemas, citas, ensayos, traducciones, versiones, que se remontan hasta la década del 20. El presente libro del poeta colombiano Fernando Arbeláez (n.

1923) es una valiosa contribución a este culto reverencial y amistoso. La obra es un sólo poema extenso publicado en su original en español y traducido asimismo al griego por el poeta Rigas Kappatos y al inglés por Elizabeth Harrison. En un juego de interiores y exteriores que conducen nítidamente al mundo poético de Cavafi, Arbeláez contrapone la vida del poeta y la presencia fabulosa de su ciudad mítica: Alejandría. [AR]

4013 Arbeleche, Jorge. Antología. Montevideo: Ediciones Destabanda, 1987. 95 p.

Antología que celebra el 19 aniversario de la publicación del primer volumen de poesía de este autor. El volumen está precedido de un trabajo sobre la obra del poeta. La selección recoge poemas de *Sangre de la luz*, de *Los instantes*, *Las vísperas*, *Los ángeles oscuros*, *Alta noche*, *La casa de la piedra negra*, y *Poemas*, su última colección de 1987. Los temas recurrentes son la lucha de contrarios: luz-sombra, sed-agua, fuego-ceniza, amor-desamor, palabra-silencio, vida-muerte, día-noche, temas universales de la preocupación poética. [MGP]

4014 Arenas, Braulio. Discurso del gran poder. Santiago: Editorial La Noria, 1985. 33 p.

Reedición de un poema publicado por primera vez en 1952. Edición definitiva, y merecido homenaje a un buen poeta de larga trayectoria. Su obra se inició en 1940 con *El mundo y su doble*. [LE]

4015 Arias, Raúl. Trinofobias. Quito: Editorial El Conejo, 1988. 98 p. (Col. Metáfora)

Una intención evidente de renovación caracteriza a este poemario. Sus textos muestran un compromiso con la búsqueda de nuevas preocupaciones y expresiones poéticas, aunque todavía no logran concretar su búsqueda. De ahí que su sentido se reduce a la protesta y al rechazo de las concepciones poéticas tradicionales. [ORR]

4016 Aridjis, Homero. *Imágenes para el fin del milenio* y *Nueva expulsión del Paraíso*. México: Joaquín Mortiz, 1990. 137 p.

El más reciente y excelente poemario de esta figura notable de las letras mexicanas de las últimas generaciones. El texto reúne dos libros de poemas: el primero de 1986 y el segundo de 1990. Un hablante poético, heredero de distintas culturas, y desde variadas formas de versificación busca, en este fin de siglo, entender su pasado a través de la memoria colectiva; y su presente, a través de la reflexión y la mirada individual. Poemas que abarcan temas desde la conquista hasta el diario vivir en la Ciudad de México hoy. Su principio organizativo es el paso del tiempo. Contra la destrucción del tiempo se alza la palabra poética de Aridjis en varios destacados poemas sobre la muerte de los padres, reminiscentes de Jorge Manrique y Jaime Sabines: "Sentado junto a ti, veo más lejos tu cuerpo,/Acariciándote el brazo, siento más tu distancia,/Todo el tiempo te miro y no te alcanzo./Para llegar a ti hay que volar abismos./Inmóvil te veo partir, aquí me quedo. [NK]

4017 Barbarito, Carlos and **María Pugliese.** Páginas del poeta flaco [de] Carlos Barbarito. De uno y otro lado [de] María Pugliese. Buenos Aires: Filofalsía, 1988. 22 p.: ill.

Dos libros de poesía en uno, dependiendo de la manera como se lo sostiene en las manos. Barbarito tiene un innegable don de lenguaje como se demuestra en sus 11 poemas. Los textos de Pugliese son, a la vez, más tiernos y experimentales. [JG]

4018 Barboza, Nidia. Hasta me da miedo decirlo. Ciudad Universitaria Rodrigo Facio, Costa Rica: Editorial Universitaria Centroamericana, 1987. 90 p.: ill. (Col. Semilla)

Entre los diversos estados de ánimo de la mujer—amor, erotismo, miedo, ansiedad ante el envejecimiento o la incomunicación, predominan en este libro la descripción y exaltación gráficas del amor lesbiano: "Nuestros cuerpos se suspenden/en el espumaje del sudor," como si el verso consistiera en "los ritmos del arado entre las piernas." El último poema—"El Permiso"—reconoce las restricciones impuestas a este amor (socialmente) audaz: "Pero ella y yo/sólo podemos mirarnos/cuando él/no nos mira." [GY]

4019 Bartolomé, Efraín. Cuadernos contra el ángel. Querétaro, México: Univ. Autónoma de Querétaro, 1987. 75 p. (Col. Premios)

Entre los mejores poetas de la última generación, Bartolomé gana con este poemario el Premio Nacional de Poesía (1987) convocado por la Univ. Autónoma de Querétaro. Original uso de recursos poéticos tradicionales y vanguardistas en la lucha contra el án-

gel del mal y de la muerte. Elabora espacios de luz y sombra desde los cuales surge la voz que desafía la soledad, la muerte y la poesía misma. [NK]

4020 Bartolomé, Efraín. Ojo de jaguar. México: UNAM, 1990. 81 p.

Edición aumentada del poemario del mismo nombre que apareció en 1982. Poesía rica en imágenes sensoriales y cadencias rítmicas que cantan a la tierra natal del poeta, la selva chiapaneca. Versos que recrean una naturaleza exuberante desde donde se recrea la persona poética. [NK]

4021 Bellessi, Diana. Eroica. Buenos Aires: Ediciones Ultimo Reino, 1988. 126 p.

Nuevo poemario de Bellesi, con versos punzantes, llenos de sorpresa, seguros de su efectividad lírica. Los textos están distribuidos en tres secciones: 1) "Imagen del Texto Vivo;" 2) "Vaga Stella Dell'Orsa;" y 3) "Intempesta Nocte." [JG]

4022 Belli, Carlos Germán. Boda de la pluma y la letra. Madrid: Ediciones Cultura Hispánica, Instituto de Cooperación Iberoamericana, 1985. 182 p.: port.

Humor y agudeza crítica a través de un lenguaje poético conciso caracteriza a esta obra de uno de los poetas más originales de la actualidad en el Perú. Este volumen reúne ocho colecciones publicadas entre 1958–83, lo que implica casi la obra completa del autor, que después de este volumen publicó dos colecciones más. [ORR]

4023 Benedetti, Mario. Canciones del más acá. Madrid: Visor, 1989. 151 p.: ill. (Col. Visor de poesía; 243)

A instancias del editor, Benedetti reúne en este volumen 60 letras de canciones y poemas a los que se les puso música a partir de los años 60, realizados por 40 intérpretes individuales, dúos, coros y conjuntos vocales. La nómina de estos intérpretes figura en un apéndice al final del volumen. Entre ellos figuran Soledad Bravo, Alberto Favero, y Nacha Guevara, Pablo Milanés y Joan Manuel Serrat. [MGP]

4024 Benedetti, Mario. Yesterday y mañana. Madrid: Visor, 1988. 111 p. (Col. Visor de poesía; 222)

Colección de poemas estructurados en siete secciones: "Todo el tiempo;" "Entresueños;" "Yesterday y Mañana," "Sucede;"

"Ciudad Huella;" "Viñetas de mi Viñedo" y "Il Cuore." Podría decirse que la labor poética del uruguayo toma cuerpo en los siguientes versos: "mis versos grises son preguntas/ tiros al aire/ contraolvidos/ bordes de historia que son huesos . . . mis versos no son siempre grises/ los hay azules verdes rojos. Destacan los poemas "Corredores de Fondo," "John Lennon Dixit," "Yesterday," "La Vuelta de Mambrú" y "Límites." La intensificación de lo cotidiano en la vivencia universal, lo profundo y vital que se recoge de la cultura popular y el humor son algunos de sus rasgos importantes. [MGP]

4025 Berroa, Rei. Los otros. Santo Domingo: Imprenta Paz, 1983. 37 p.
El afán de entrega, de desprendimiento es la temática que las muestra las dotes líricas de este poeta. Ecos bien aprovechados de los multitudinarios Whitman y Mir se suman a estas composiciones de momentos felices. [RG]

4026 Blanco, Alberto. El libro de los pájaros. México: Ediciones Toledo, 1990. 50 p.
Establecido poeta de la generación de los 50 nos ofrece, en este su último poemario, y desde la mejor tradición de los bestiarios, versos que rinden homenaje a las aves y analógicamente expresan al hombre. Lirismo sensual y sensorial en cuya resonancia percibimos ecos del modernismo. [NK]

4027 Boullosa, Carmen. La salvaja. México: Fondo de Cultura Económica, 1989. 160 p. (Letras mexicanas)
Poeta, novelista y dramaturga, Boullosa reúne en este volumen una selección de sus poemarios anteriores y una sección inédita bajo el título de "La Infiel." De la más reciente generación de autores en México, la obra de Boullosa se destaca por su rebeldía contra formas poéticas anteriores. En estos versos la hablante se constituye desde la abstracción, en el espacio de la imaginación, la memoria, el deseo y los sueños para darle forma al mundo que la limita y a su propia liberación: "Cuando escribo esto es porque/ la rota bestia/la salvaja que soy/yo/por los aires/me he ido." [NK]

4028 Bracho, Coral. Bajo el destello líquido: poesía, 1977–1981. México: Fondo de Cultura Económica, 1988. 85 p.
Recoge los dos poemarios de esta joven poeta *Peces de piel fugaz* (1977) y *El ser qe va a morir* (1981). Imaginería vertiginosa y desbordante en un lenguaje expresivo y críptico que ubica al ser en un tiempo y espacio por descifrar. [NK]

4029 Calderón, Teresa. Causas perdidas. Santiago: Ediciones Artesanales, 1984. 73 p.: ill., plates
Sorprende este primer libro de esta joven poeta por la seguridad del lenguaje lírico con el que cuestiona el mundo y las cosas: la relación amorosa entre ellas. Poemas que ironizan el dolor de lo perdido o no conseguido, acogen la inevitabilidad de lo cotidiano, conjeturan sobre lo por venir. [LE]

4030 Calzadilla, Juan. Diario para una poesía mínima. Caracas: Editorial Mandorla, 1986. 67 p. (Col. Cármenes)
Perteneciente al grupo vanguardista venezolano de la década del 60, "El Techo de la Ballena," Juan Calzadilla (n. 1931) es en la actualidad uno de los poetas más destacados de su país. Su poesía, en un principio inmersa en la corriente estética surrealista, ha ido alejándose progresivamente del desborde oscuro y mágico de las imágenes en busca de un pensamiento poético que atiende más a la sabiduría que al esplendor verbal. Este libro, de tono epigramático y directo, está ya completamente inmerso en esta dirección de lucidez pre-socrática, si así podemos decir. [AR]

4031 Campero, Jorge. Sumarium común sobre vivos. La Paz: Tandem Editores, 1985. 68 p.: ill. (Col. Media Ave del Paraíso)
Es obra de un joven poeta boliviano. Una de sus características destacadas es el juego con la tradición y la crítica a la misma tradición en sus aspectos variados. La rebeldía que impulsa esa actitud se manifiesta mediante enunciados explícitos, la ironía o el sarcasmo. De cualquier modo, el efecto poético está siempre presente. [ORR]

4032 Cardenal, Ernesto. Cántico cósmico. Managua: Editorial Nueva Nicaragua, 1989. 581 p.
"Epopeya-científico-místico-revolucionaria" que a lo largo de casi 600 p. transcribe la fascinación de la ciencia. Como *Quetzalcóatl*, el libro representa un desplazamiento desde la poesía activista e inmediata a una visión del destino humano *sub specie aeternitas*. [GY]

4033 Cardenal, Ernesto. Quetzalcóatl. Madrid: Visor, 1988. 69 p. (Col. Visor de poesía; 228)

Recuento en verso de la leyenda de Quetzalcóatl y la historia de la fundación y derrota de la sociedad étnica tolteca. Parece una lección de historia para niños, con algunos comentarios apenas irónicos referentes a la actualidad: los turistas en Tenochtitlán dejan plásticos de picnic, el presidente llega al aeropuerto en su avión Quetzalcóatl, etc. Exenta de la función plegaria de antaño, la poesía de Cardenal deja de ser poética para incorporarse a la pedagogía, a la crónica, a la reinterpretación de la historia. [GY]

4034 Cardenal, Ernesto. Vuelos de victoria. León, Nicaragua: Editorial Universitaria, UNAN, 1987. 143 p. (Col. Poesía; 14)

Podría estarse de acuerdo con el decir de Roque Dalton de que la poesía no está hecha sólo de palabras, esperando que—como se presupone en estos poemas—la (ya no tan) "Nueva Nicaragua" rocíe de poesía a la mera crónica de hechos y nombres. Pero ello requiere que el contexto sea esperanzado. A partir de feb. 1990 la realidad nicaragüense ha dejado de infundir a la crónica de hechos con una carga poética. [GY]

4035 Cárdenas, Galel. Pasos de animal grande. 2a. ed. Tegucigalpa: Editores Unidos, 1986. 64 p. (Col. Vía Láctea)

La primera parte consiste en testimonios, en el estilo de los códices-crónicas maya y quiché de los crímenes contra el pueblo. La política penetra la atmósfera mítica asumida. En la segunda y tercera partes se lleva la existencia cotidiana a dimensiones metafísicas, con un imaginismo audaz, inspirado quizás en las vanguardias: "La carcajada es un reo extraño;" "El musgo de la reptilidad/va poblando esferoidalmente." [GY]

4036 Carranza, María Mercedes. Vainas: antología 1972–1983. Bogotá: Fundación Simón y Lola Guberek, 1987 146 p. (Col. literaria; 19)

El presente volumen recoge gran parte de la poesía escrita por María Mercedes Carranza (n. 1945) hasta el momento. Destacan en ella algunos rasgos propios a su grupo generacional post-nadaísta: aproximación directa al objeto poético, constante fricción de las palabras dentro del texto, escepticismo y rabia como respuesta lírica a una sociedad en crisis, búsqueda de diálogo, comunicación. [AR]

4037 Carriego, Evaristo. La canción del barrio y otros poemas. Introducción y se-

lección de Javier Adúriz. Buenos Aires: Editorial Biblos, 1985. 139 p. (Col. Poesía: Serie Menor; 5)

Otro de los varios mitos poéticos argentinos. Este volumen es utilísimo porque la selección es bastante comprensiva, incluye textos de sus seis libros, y permite hacerse una imagen relativamente completa del autor. Carriego (1883–1912) sale bastante bien de esta prueba como un versificador ingenioso y eficaz, y la relectura de sus textos resulta sorprendentemente atractiva. [JG]

4038 Casaus, Víctor. Amar sin papeles. La Habana: Editorial Letras Cubanas, 1988. 48 p. (Mínima; 32. Poesía)

El tema al centro de este libro es el amor. Un amor celebratorio, erótico, libre. Casaus es una especie de trovador urbano que, por el desenfado en su lenguaje, a veces recuerda al chileno Parra. [RG]

4039 Casazola Mendoza, Matilde. Amores de alas fugaces. La Paz: s.n., 1986. 53 p.

Discurso erótico femenino original—de esta autora boliviana—que reflexiona sobre una variedad de aspectos de la relación amorosa, desde una perspectiva cotidiana. Crítica, denuncia, demanda o requerimiento son formas por las que se manifiesta la intencionalidad de este discurso. Un delicado sentimiento de soledad y añoranza subyace a lo largo del volumen dividido en 35 textos numerados. [ORR]

4040 Castelar, José Adán. Sin olvidar la humillación, 1983–1984. Tegucigalpa: Talleres Tipolitográficos de López y Cía., 1987. 44 p.: ill.

Poemas que suscitan el dolor, la queja, el enojo frente a la intervención estadounidense en Centroamérica. De toda su poesía ésta es la más directamente denunciadora: "acuérdense de Vietnam, grandes cabrones!" [GY]

4041 Castelar, José Adán. Tiempo ganado al mundo. Presentación de Rigoberto Paredes. Tegucigalpa: Ediciones Librería Paradiso, 1989. 122 p.: ill. (Col. Poesía)

Gran talento que labra las palabras precisas si bien sencillas para transformar humildad, pobreza, fealdad, aburrimiento, humillación y enfado en verdaderos logros líricos, matizados por el humor, la ironía o la ternura: "No eres nadie, dice mi estatura [. . .]/ Pero algo nace en lo destruído [. . .]/sin pedir escaleras, sin desear/el trono de las direc-

ciones,/conforme con el trabajo que le doy a
la vida:/a esa débil que un día cambiaré por
algo/más hermoso." [GY]

4042 Castillo, Ricardo. Nicolás el camaleón,
antecedido por "Cienpiés tan Ciego."
México: Ediciones Toledo, 1989. 78 p.

Lenguaje que desde el reto y la agre-
sión busca nuevas formas para efectuar cambios en la realidad y en la poesía. Anti-poeta
inconforme e iconoclasta cuya experimenta-
ción formal y búsqueda de una voz original le
ha otorgado un sitio importante entre los
poetas jóvenes mexicanos. En este reciente
poemario elabora desde la tercera y segunda
personas la historia de "Nicolás, el Camaleón." Involucra al lector en un proceso de
autorrevelación impuesto por un hablante
acusativo. [NK]

4043 Castro Saavedra, Carlos. Oda a Colombia. Medellín, Colombia: Pluma, 1987.
207 leaves

La poesía de Carlos Castro Saavedra,
con fuerte influencia desde un principio de la
obra de Neruda, se ha distinguido por una dirección de exaltación de los valores regionales y autóctonos. Este libro, que toca diversos aspectos de la realidad y el paisaje
colombianos, no escapa a esta tradición telúrica. [AR]

4044 Cea, José Roberto. Los herederos de
Farabundo. 2a ed. San Salvador: Editorial Universitaria, Univ. de El Salvador, 1987.
146 p.

El poeta se vale de materiales testimoniales, documentales, míticos, experiencias populares y aún informes económicos en
la tentativa de crear un mosaico entre crónica y poema documental, hablado en diversos registros, ventrilocuando así las voces del
pueblo. [GY]

4045 Cerruto, Oscar. Poesía. Prólogo de
Juan Quirós. Notas, cronología y bibliografía de Pedro Shimose. Madrid: Ediciones Cultura Hispánica, Instituto de Cooperación Iberoamericana, 1985. 238 p.: port.

Contiene la obra completa de uno de
los poetas hispanoamericanos más importantes de la segunda mitad del siglo presente.
Sobriedad y riguroso manejo del lenguaje, así
como contenido profundo, caracterizan a esta
poesía, relativamente breve, publicada entre
1957-75. Con un prólogo de Juan Quirós,
la edición a cargo de Pedro Shimose incluye

notas, cronología y bibliografía. Cerruto (Bolivia, 1912-81) corresponde a la generación
de Octavio Paz, Lezama Lima, Nicanor Parra,
Enrique Molina, entre otros. [ORR]

4046 Charpentier, Jorge. Arrodillar la noche.
Heredia, Costa Rica: EUNA, 1988.
64 p. (Col. Barva. Serie Creación. Subserie
Poesía)

Algunos de estos poemas evocan la ilu-
sionada desesperanza vallejiana: "Bebo de la
vida [. . .]/a veces es muy ácido/el sabor."
Tentativa de transformar la desilusión y la
pérdida en nuevo potencial: "Debes convertir
el hambre/en verde espuma de los prados." Si
por una parte "ya la palabra no existe," por
otra "Te quiero a ti vida [. . .]/aunque la vida
duela tanto/tenerte en carne propia/amante
vida." [GY]

4047 Charpentier, Jorge. Diferente al
abismo y otros poemas. San José: Editorial Costa Rica, 1989. 203 p.: bibl.

Esta antología, que abarca 30 años de
producción, prologada por dos estudios, ofrece una muestra del lirismo parco y preciso,
casi transparente, de la voz de uno de los
poetas guatemaltecos más destacados de hoy
día. [GY]

4048 Chow, Juan. Oficios del caos. Managua: Unión de Escritores de Nicaragua,
Asociación Sandinista de Trabajadores de la
Cultura: Editorial Nueva Nicaragua, 1986.
163 p.: ill.

Ni metafísico ni político, Chow se
mueve en el hiperespacio posmoderno de la
citación: artistas de cine, boxeadores, la entera literatura mundial, toda Sagrada Escritura, el Jazz, y, claro, las referencias de riguer
si bien desrigormortizadas a revolucionarios
(Che, Rugama), todo esto inscripto en este
vasto museo poético de lo heteróclito. Y todo
muy en la onda y muy ubicuo, pues casi todos los poemas parecen haber sido escritos
siempre de paso, en hoteles, como se constata en la indicación de lugar al final de cada
composición. [GY]

4049 Cobo Borda, Juan Gustavo. Todos los
poetas son santos. México: Fondo de
Cultura Económica, 1987. 62 p. (Col. Tierra
firme)

Cada nuevo libro de Juan Gustavo
Cobo Borda (n. 1948) es la adición de unos
pocos poemas a poemas recogidos en sus libros anteriores. En él vuelven los temas desa-

cralizadores del discurso oficial colombiano, el amor, el sexo y el diálogo con otros poetas y escritores. Una nota diferente en este libro sería un ligero salir del coloquialismo predominante en su poesía para sumergirse en un tono más lírico. [AR]

4050 Córdova Iturregui, Félix. Militancia contra la soledad. Río Piedras: Ediciones Huracán, 1987. 77 p. (Col. La Flor del agua)

Lírica nostálgica del amor ausente. La emoción del amor—el amor rememorado—quiere ser instrumental para conocer ciertos aspectos de la condición humana, como los estados de tristeza, soledad o sufrimiento. El lenguaje, invocativo, a menudo se impone la búsqueda de la metáfora insólita. [RG]

4051 Cortés, Carlos. Los pasos cantados. Heredia, Costa Rica: Editorial de la Univ. Nacional, 1987. 127 p. (Col. Barva. Serie Creación. Subserie Poesía)

Predomina en este primer premio Certamen Una-Palabra 1986, una intervención verbal que frisa en la ironía y el humor aun tratando de los temas más serios, como si Roque Dalton o Ramón Gómez de la Serna escribieran las meditaciones vallejianas de *Trilce* (e.g., "Se va la luz:/¿no pagué el recibo/o es el fin del mundo?"). Cortés es el poeta más joven incluído en *Antología de una generación dispersa.* [GY]

4052 Costa du Rels, Adolfo. Poemas. Prólogo y versión de Eduardo Mitre. Ed. bilingüe. La Paz: Ediciones Altiplano, 1988. 71 p. (Col. Piedra libre)

Rico y refinado discurso poético que reelabora el mejor simbolismo de principios de siglo. Con un estudio previo de Eduardo Mitre, este volumen presenta una selección de *Amaretudine* (1949), libro publicado originalmente en francés. Costa du Rels (Bolivia, 1891–1979) ha sido un escritor bilingüe (narrador y dramaturgo) que vivió la mayor parte de su vida en París. En 1971 recibió el Premio Gulbenkian por su obra literaria. [ORR]

4053 Cross, Elsa. El diván de Antar. México: Joaquín Mortiz, 1990. 72 p.

Merecedora del Premio de Poesía Aguascalientes 1989. Cantos de amor desde un espacio idealizado y atemporal; una meditación reflexiva que busca a través de imágenes etéreas y sensuales captar los misterios del universo. [NK]

4054 Cuadra, Pablo Antonio. Esos rostros que asoman en la multitud: homenajes. San José: Libro Libre, 1985. 129 p. (Obra poética completa; 5. Serie literaria)

Las dos colecciones incluídas en este tomo consisten en retratos—en especial de "rostros anónimos." La primera tiene dos partes: 1) "Doña Andreíta y Otros Retratos," reúne composiciones de 1964–75; 2) En "Apocalipsis con Figuras: Managua-1972," el poeta rescata rostros de su pueblo de entre las ruinas del gran terremoto que destrozó la capital. Estos rostros consisten en hábiles manejos del lenguaje del retrato, compuesto no tanto de descripciones sino de registros y discursos que, en su particular encuentro, rezuman una manera de ser a la vez cotidiana y poética. [GY]

4055 Cuadra, Pablo Antonio. La ronda del año: poemas para un calendario. San José: Libro Libre, 1988. 127 p.: ill. (Obra poética completa; 7)

Estos 12 poemas fueron escritos en diversas épocas de casi medio siglo de fecunda actividad creadora. El poemario resulta así una singular muestra retrospectiva de la totalidad de la producción poética: el sentir religioso de los misterios cristianos; el fervor cívico de la preocupación por la redención de la historia; el enfrentamiento con el Poder. [GY]

4056 Cuadra, Pablo Antonio. Siete árboles contra el atardecer y otras poemas. Prólogo de Guillermo Yepes Boscán. San José: Libro Libre, 1987. 103 p.: ill. (Obra poética completa; 6)

Consiste en siete poemas escritos en los momentos más dramáticos y de transformación de Nicaragua, desde el terremoto (1972) hasta el triunfo de la revolución sandinista. En ellos se procura afirmar los límites y robustecer las defensas de lo personal frente a las amenazas de las catástrofes físicas y de la barbarie política. En *Otros poemas* Cuadra transita de la mitología botánica a la zoológica, sucumbiendo al "bello placer primitivo de cubrir los pensamientos humanos con las pieles zoológicas." El volumen está prologado por un excelente análisis de Guillermo Yepes Boscán, en el que se vinculan revolución política y renovación de la expresión del ser. [GY]

4057 Dalton, Roque. Un libro levemente odioso. Prólogo de Elena Poniatowska. San Salvador: UCA Editores, 1989. 137 p.: ill. (Col. Gavidia; 32)

Lejos de caer en la furia o desesperanza sociocrítica, este libro—recién editado por primera vez—es una de las pocas poesías que conduce a la risa constante ("Una erizante broma nada más/emboscada flagrante/puta poesía para Simular") y a la concomitante puesta en tela de juicio del status quo, inclusive el de su propia identidad comunista: ¿De qué puede servir un preservativo/en el asilo de ancianos?" (referente al partido comunista). [GY]

4058 Dalton, Roque. Un libro rojo para Lenin. Managua: Editorial Nueva Nicaragua, 1986. 239 p. (Col. Séptimo aniversario)

Verdadero acierto formal es esta política poética o poesía política, este collage (trozos de los textos de Lenin y del ensayo *Lenin* de 1924 de Lukács—clásico del llamado ultraizquierdismo—más materiales secundarios de Maiakovsky, Gramsci, Ho Chi Minh, Kim Il Sung, Fidel, Debray, Magdoff, testimonios salvadoreños, todo mezclado con los poemas de Dalton mismo) tiene como propósito la "vivifación poética" y flexibilización del leninismo como respuesta a la muerte del Che y la crisis de la estrategia guerrillera que implicaba su muerte. Dalton caracteriza el texto como "un poema inconcluso, en correspondencia con la revolución latinoamericana, como proceso de desarrollo . . . mientras viva el autor." [GY]

4059 Debravo, Jorge. Nostros los hombres. San José: Editoral Costa Rica: Ministerio de Cultura, Juventud y Deportes, 1988. 109 p.

Reedición de una obra capital de los 60, esta poesía expresa sencilla y llanamente la solidaridad o la protesta, llamando a compartir la emoción poética, las más de las veces, en su veta decepcionante y, las menos, en registros de esperanzada utopía. [GY]

4060 Delgado, Wáshington. Reunión elegida. Lima: Seglusa Editores: Editorial Colmillo Blanco, 1988. 155 p. (Col. Astrolabio)

Selección antológica realizada por el propio autor. Incluye poemas procedentes de ocho libros publicados entre 1955–70. Se trata de una colección de los textos preferidos por el propio poeta. Incluye además poe-mas no publicados antes. Es una poesía de aceptación de la realidad propia, pese a las deficiencias que su percepción denuncia. [ORR]

4061 Deniz, Gerardo. Grosso modo. México: Fondo de Cultura Económica, 1988. 124 p.: ill. (Letras mexicanas)

Con este último poemario Deniz confirma una ubicación original dentro de la poesía latinoamericana. Poemas que no permiten su inserción en ningún paradigma poético reconocible. Habla que se convierte en escritura y que envuelve al lector en un proceso de desciframiento en zonas verbales desconocidas. Los poemas atraen tanto por su novedad cuanto por el tono escéptico y la visión de un hablante que toma distancia emocional de su material. [NK]

4062 Díaz Casanueva, Humberto. Obra poética. Selección, prólogo, cronología y bibliografía de Ana María Del Re. Caracas: Biblioteca Ayacucho, 1988. 396 p.: bibl. (Biblioteca Ayacucho; 131)

Cuidada edición de mayor parte de la obra poética de Díaz Casanueva, excepto *El sol ciego* (1966); *El hierro y el hilo* (1980), del que se incluye sólo selección; *El niño de Robben Island* (1985); y *Vox tatuada* (1985). Buen prólogo, que revela aspectos claves de este valioso quehacer poético. Hay excelente cronología y bibliografía muy completa. [LE]

4063 Diego, Eliseo. Entre la dicha y la tiniebla: antología poética, 1949–1985. Selección y presentación de Diego García Elío. México: Fondo de Cultura Económica, 1986. 203 p.: ill. (Col. Tierra firme)

El mundo poético de Eliseo Diego lo constituyen, principalmente, las cosas que lo rodean: la familia, el paso de los días, su ambigua relación con un mundo originario: mundo que se nombra por primera vez o mundo recordado, "cercado de añoranzas." Pero su discurso no se regodea en lo anecdótico: sus símbolos emanan desde un tiempo interior. La primera sección de esta antología, *En la calzada de Jesús del Monte* (1949), muestra relaciones evidentes con la poesía de los 40 de Lezama Lima. Pero esas semejanzas se atenúan en la evolución de la poética de Diego, que se define en lo luminoso y preciso. [RG]

4064 Diez Astete, Alvaro. Abismo. La Paz: Ediciones Ojo Libertario, 1988. 59 p. Joven valor de la poesía boliviana. Su discurso está embargado por una visión existencial del ser humano desde una perspectiva de incertidumbre social y metafísica. Su lenguaje simbólico no puede prescindir de la ineludible presencia del ser en los límites extremos de la propia existencia, ni de un afán por conocer lo trascendente del ser, aunque éste es visto en la materialdad del cuerpo. Poesía reflexiva sobre la trascendencia de la vida y de la muerte. [ORR]

4065 Dobles, Julieta. Los delitos de Pandora. San José: Editorial Costa Rica, 1987. 87 p.

Poesía que procura trascender la negación de la palabra y la actividad de la mujer. Para ello se vale del mito, transformándolo más allá de sus limitaciones y traiciones en reconocimiento de "voces femeninas [que] lo inundan todo." La palabra, como el acto de la mujer, tiene doble sentido cotidiano y trascendente: "El mundo necesita ser barrido diariamente." La poesía es este acto de limpieza de la conciencia. [GY]

4066 España, Aristóteles. Dawson: poemas escritos en el Campo de Concentración de Isla Dawson, septiembre 1973-septiembre 1974. Santiago: Bruguera-Documentos, 1985–1987. 73 p.: ill., plates, ports.

Conmovedor poemario-testimonio de uno de los momentos más despiadados de la historia de Chile. A los 17 años, Aristóteles España los escribe en Campo de Concentración Isla Dawson (1973–74). Dice un poema: "Anoche al acostarme/ escuché ladridos/ en algún lugar del Campamento./ Y NO ERAN PERROS." Hay fotos y documentos de lugar y época. Lectura necesaria en lucha contra el olvido. [LE]

4067 Fernández, Francisco de Asís. Pasión de la memoria. Managua: Editorial Nueva Nicaragua, 1986. 137 p. (Letras de Nicaragua; 21)

El volumen recoge más de 20 años de trabajo poético, recorriendo un espectro de posibles registros poéticos en sus primeros versos, *A principio de cuentas* (1968), pasando por la poesía militante si bien siempre abierta al sentimiento, al paisaje y al goce, en *El cambio de estaciones* (1981), hasta la lograda plasticidad imaginativa e irónica, la exaltación erótica y la pasión de belleza, sin dejar por ello de denunciar la injusticia, en *Pasión de memoria* (1983–86). [GY]

4068 Fernández, Pablo Armando. El sueño, la razón (1948–1983). La Habana: Unión de Escritores y Artistas de Cuba, 1988. 433 p. (Bolsilibros Unión)

Este genuino poeta cubano junta aquí gran parte de la poesía que lo confirma como autor claro e inteligente. El amor, la amistad, la nostalgia (el paso del tiempo), la muerte, constantemente vuelven para encantar estas páginas de sencillez profunda. [RG]

The fertile rhythms: contemporary women poets of Mexico. See item **4919**.

4069 Florit, Eugenio. Castillo interior y otros versos. Miami, Fla.: Ultra Graphics Corp., 1987. 31 p.

Florit acostumbra una poesía contemplativa, limpia, ceñida, cerrada sobre sí misma. En este poemario hay dos aspectos notables: 1) la aspiración a un infinito armonioso y protector que puede ser Dios o la poesía misma y 2) el tiempo y la memoria, expresado de manera que recuerda a Cernuda y un tanto la concepción intelectual del tiempo en Borges. [RG]

4070 Freidemberg, Daniel. Diario en la crisis. Buenos Aires: Libros de Tierra Firme, 1986. 68 p. (Col. de poesía Todos bailan)

Uno de los mejores talentos de las últimas generaciones en Argentina: manejo de la sorpresa rítmica, sentido de la composición poemática, sensibilidad al borde de las palabras, don de intensidad y concentración líricas. Consta de tres partes homogéneas: 1) "Si Fuera Posible;" 2) "Diario en la Crisis;" y 3) "Arte Dificultosa." [JG]

4071 Galarza Zavala, Jaime. Poemas sin permiso. Quito: Ediciones Solitierra, 1986. 128 p.: ill.

Textos escritos entre 1967–84, productos de la represión política y el desencanto social. Comprometidos con una posición subversiva, conforman un discurso de queja y soledad, de protesta y subversión, propio de las situaciones políticas que han vivido casi todas las sociedades latinoamericanas bajo los regímenes militares dictatoriales en las últimas décadas. La protesta se extiende al sistema político de los EE.UU., señalado como propiciador de las dictaduras militares. [ORR]

4072 García Maffla, Jaime. En otoño debían caer todas las hojas de los libros. Bogotá: Fundación Fumio Ito, Pontificia Univ. Javeriana, 1987. 166 p. (Crítica y ensayo)

A la lucidez de una obra poética signada por el encantamiento verbal y la profundidad casi religiosa de los temas, el poeta colombiano Jaime García Maffla (n. 1944) añade estos ensayos cortos, viñetas de alcance más literario que periodístico. Valioso aporte que nos deja ver no sólo aspectos importantes de la obra de los poetas o narradores analizados sino que nos muestra al desnudo las direcciones de búsqueda del propio autor. [AR]

4073 García Rivadeneira, Edgar Allan. Sobre los ijares de Rocinante. Quito: TRAMA, 1990. 72 p.

Textos poéticos con efectos originales. Muy conscientes del valor y las posibilidades del lenguaje, manipulan las palabras con recursos variados de lexicalización, pero con una intención social definida y riqueza poética indudable. [ORR]

4074 García Terrés, Jaime. Las manchas del sol: poesía 1956–1987. Madrid: Alianza, 1988. 309 p.

Antología que reúne lo mejor de la producción de este poeta de la generación de Bonifaz Nuño, Castellanos y Sabines. Los poemas escogidos de *Las provincias del aire* (1956), *Los reinos combatientes* (1961), *Todo lo más por decir* (1971), *Corre la voz* (1980), y *Parte de mi vida* (1987) constatan la importancia de este poeta cuyo verso culto, clásico y razonado le ha merecido un lugar sólido en la poesía mexicana. [NK]

4075 Garnier Castro, Leonor. Agua de cactus. San José: Editorial Costa Rica, 1985. 61 p. (Libros de poesía)

La poeta se identifica—en derroche nerudiano—con los elementos naturales por los que el amante pasa eróticamente, quizás "para otras plenitudes," dejándola luego en estado de abandono que requiere que lo reinvente con su palabra. [GY]

4076 Gelman, Juan. Anunciaciones. Madrid: Visor, 1988. 74 p. (Col. Visor de poesía; 223)

Uno de los últimos libros de este clásico de nuestro tiempo y que probablemente sea uno de sus mejores. El hablante vuelve a su entorno personal después de sus extensos diálogos con poetas de otrora. Pero la aventura al pasado ha sido bien asimilada y el lenguaje resulta tan enriquecido que uno tiene

la impresión cierta de estar escuchando palabra fuerte e iluminada. La continuidad de los textos da al libro el carácter de un poema largo en el cual el lector pudiera quedarse horas, días, años. [JG]

4077 Gelman, Juan. Interrupciones I: *Relaciones, Hechos, Notas, Carta abierta, Si dulcemente, Comentarios, Citas.* Buenos Aires: Libros de Tierra Firme, Ediciones Ultimo Reino, 1988. 317 p. (Col. de poesía Todos bailan)

Excelente idea la de recolectar en un volumen una serie de libros de este gran poeta latinoamericano, casi todos ellos publicados fuera de Argentina durante sus años de exilio. Este primer volumen reúne: *Relaciones, Hechos, Notas, Carta Abierta, Si dulcemente, Comentarios, Citas.* Incluye un prólogo de Julio Cortázar: "Contra las telarañas de la costumbre." [JG]

4078 Gelman, Juan. Interrupciones II. Buenos Aires: Libros de Tierra Firme, 1986. 274 p.: ill. (Col. de poesía Todos bailan; 37)

Continúa la recolección de textos escritos por Gelman durante los 80, muchos de ellos inéditos al momento de publicarse este libro. Incluye: *Bajo la lluvia ajena: notas al pie de una derrota, Hacia el mar, Com-posiciones* y *Eso.* [JG]

4079 Gelman, Juan. Obras completas. v. 1, Violín y otras cuestiones; El juego en que andamos; Velorio del solo; Gotán. Buenos Aires: Libros de Tierra Firme, 1989. 155 p. (Col. de poesía Todos bailan; 85. Obras completas; 1)

Vol. 1 de lo que serán las *Obras completas* del autor. Una valiosa recapitulación hecha con calidad y fidelidad. [JG]

4080 Gerbasi, Vicente. Obra poética. Caracas: Biblioteca Ayacucho, 1986. 303 p. (Biblioteca Ayacucho; 122)

Importante libro que recoge en su totalidad la obra hasta el momento publicada de este gran poeta venezolano. Vicente Gerbasi (n. 1913) ha publicado numerosos libros de poesía entre los que destacan: *Mi padre el inmigrante* (1945) y *Los espacios cálidos* (1952), verdaderas contribuciones a la poesía latinoamericana. Atento a la presencia poética del paisaje y de su gente, Gerbasi toca con sus vigorosas y relampagueantes imágenes el espacio real de la poesía. [AR]

4081 Girondo, Oliverio. Antología. Selección y estudio preliminar de Aldo Pellegrini. Buenos Aires: Editorial Argonauta, 1986. 156 p.: bibl., port.

Un acierto esta segunda edición de una antología publicada en 1964 y que sigue siendo una eficaz manera de recorrer las diversas fases de la poesía de uno de los más significativos poetas del vanguardismo hispanoamericano, desde *Veinte poemas para ser leídos en el tranvía* (1922) hasta *En la masmédula* (1954). El prólogo de Aldo Pellegrini se resiente del paso del tiempo y del tono elogioso. [JG]

4082 Girri, Alberto. Cuestiones y razones. Prólogo de Jorge Cruz. Buenos Aires: Editorial Fraterna, 1987. 196 p.: bibl.

Volumen de entrevistas con un interlocutor que logra obtener respuestas de calidad por parte del poeta. La voz de Girri es convincente y no parece, en ningún momento, mediatizada por el entrevistador. Incluso llega a haber algunas declaraciones que permiten entender mejor algunos textos del autor. El prólogo, la cronología y la bibliografía que completan el libro son de utilidad. [JG]

4083 Girri, Alberto. Existenciales. Buenos Aires: Editorial Sudamericana, 1986. 117 p.

Hay varios excelentes poemas en este nuevo libro de Girri, una de las figuras claves de la lírica argentina contemporánea. Es poesía pulcramente trabajada, modalizada con inteligencia y segura de su maestría. La primera parte es la más original y novedosa, y es la que da título al poemario. Las otras dos, "Poema con Poemas" y "Versiones" son breves y sus juegos intertextuales parece añadidos sin mucha fe. [JG]

4084 Godoy Olivera, Miguel Angel. Los que no mueren en la cama: poética de la tortura. Montevideo: Centro Integración Cultural, 1988. 129 p.: ill. (Col. Escritos de la cárcel; 4)

Estos poemas fueron escritos en 1972 y los textos fueron recuperados en 1988. El material poético que encierra este volumen procede de los años de encarcelamiento de los autores. El volumen consta de 25 poemas electrizantes sobre las multifacéticas experiencias de la tortura recreada en este lenguaje poético. La introducción a la colección es valiosa para tener un panorama concreto del contorno de esta poesía y sus circunstancias de producción. [MGP]

4085 González Rojo, Enrique. Obra completa: verso y prosa, 1918–1939. Edición crítica de Guillermo Rousset Banda y Jaime Labastida. México: Instituto Nacional de Bellas Artes: Editorial Domés, 1987. 495 p.: photos, ports.

Este volumen recoge la prosa y poesía de González Rojo. El ensayo preliminar de Jaime Labastida lo ubica dentro del grupo de los "Contemporáneos" dándonos un trasfondo cultural de la época, mientras que el ensayo breve de Rousset Banda se concentra en el análisis de su poesía. [NK]

4086 González Tuñón, Raúl. Todos bailan: los poemas de Juancito Caminador. 2a ed. Buenos Aires: Libros de Tierra Firme, 1987. 84 p. (Col. de poesía Todos bailan; 10)

Una bella lectura del pasado que se lee con ánimos encontrados. Poesía llena del entusiasmo y dolor histórico de los años 30. Conmovedora reedición. [JG]

4087 Granda, Euler. Bla, bla, bla: poesía. Quito: Editorial Universitaria, 1986. 201 p.

Recopilación de poemas escritos en diferentes épocas (1957–84) por uno de los poetas contemporáneos más destacados del Ecuador. El volumen ofrece una perspectiva clara sobre la evolución de la obra poética de este autor, cuyo lenguaje se caracteriza por el vigor de la fuerza elocutiva y una rica y compleja heterogeneidad de imágenes. [ORR]

4088 Gravina, María. La leche de las piedras. Montevideo: DestaBanda, 1988. 64 p.

Esta poeta uruguaya, residente en Cuba por un tiempo, recibió el distinguido premio Casa de las Américas en 1979 por su libro *Lázaro vuela rojo*. *La leche de las piedras* es su segundo libro de 24 poemas de tono conversacional. Destacan en particular los que hacen uso del tono poético-epistolar y se marcan en el título con la palabra "Carta," "Carta de Setiembre de Setentaiocho," "Carta en Diciembre 80" y otros que ponen en movimiento la forma epistolar cuyo interlocutor es un amante imaginario. Esta forma del discurso poético ha encontrado en las mujeres un interesante desarrollo en la poesía femenina contemporánea. [MGP]

4089 Guerra Gutiérrez, Alberto. Hálito que se desgarra en pos de la belleza: la cotidianidad por renovar la vida. Oruro, Bolivia: Editora Lilial, 1989. 73 p.: ill. (Ediciones El Duende)

Otro poeta boliviano (n. 1929) ya conocido, pero ahora enfrentado a una visión desencantada e incierta de la realidad. Revela las preocupaciones de la poesía moderna respecto a la percepción sensible de la realidad y su aprehensión inteligible. Reflexión poética reiterada sobre aspectos del tiempo en el espacio inmediato del poeta: la geografía andina. [ORR]

4090 Guillén, Nicolás. El libro de los sonetos. Compilación y prólogo de Angel Augier. La Habana: Unión de Escritores y Artistas de Cuba, 1984. 178 p.

Esta compilación de sonetos permite apreciar la maestría absoluta de Guillén sobre esta forma clásica. Sus primeros sonetos muestran una clara influencia modernista; en éstos abundan los versos de amor. El libro sanciona otras fases de la poesía de Guillén: la negrista (e.g., "El abuelo") y la poesía comprometida. [RG]

4091 Hahn, Oscar. Estrellas fijas en un cielo blanco. Dibujos de Roser Bru. Santiago: Editorial Universitaria, 1988. 91 p.: ill. (Col. Los Contemporáneos)

Consiste de 21 sonetos bellamente editados. Prueba irrefutable de que Oscar Hahn es uno de los grandes poetas de Latinoamérica hoy. Diversas, prestigiosas tradiciones poéticas se combinan para decir una multifacética experiencia humana. Conviven textos que recrean la armonía de épocas clásicas con otros que sugieren la zarandeada condición actual. Textos como "De Cirios y de Lirios," "Gladiolos junto al Mar," "Agua Geométrica," son verdaderas joyas del arte del soneto. [LE]

4092 Hahn, Oscar. Poemas selectos. Prólogo de Fernando Kri M. Santiago: Ediciones Tertulias Medinensis, 1989. 31 p. (Breviarios. Serie Celeste; 2)

Volumen que recoge 28 poemas de diferentes libros de este "primer poeta de su generación," a juicio de Enrique Lihn. Selección muy rigurosa que revela la altura e intensidad poéticas de Hahn. Los poemas se ofrecen como nuevos y el libro como una novedad comprobatoria de los logros de esta poesía. [LE]

4093 Harris, Tomás. Diario de navegación. Concepción, Chile: Ediciones Cuadernos Sur, 1986. 47 p. (Cuadernos Sur de poesía)

Segundo libro de este joven poeta (n. 1956). Estructurado a partir del pre-texto del diario de navegación de Colón, los textos se mueven en el marco amplio de historia del continente. Dialogan entre sí y con momentos diversos del acontecer de América. Visión irónica y desencantada de la historia se expresa en las voces de los varios personajes desde los que habla el texto. [LE]

4094 Heraud, Javier. Poesía completa. Prólogo de Javier Sologuren. Lima: PEISA, 1989. 251 p.: ill. (Alma matinal)

Este volumen se presenta como "la recopilación más completa realizada hasta la fecha de importantes poemas inéditos." Abarca desde el primer poemario publicado en 1960 hasta los textos inéditos que dejó el autor. Un prólogo de Javier Sologuren informa sobre los antecedentes de la edición, así como ofrece una aproximación preliminar a la lectura del mismo. Por su calidad, es un volumen importante de un poeta muerto a sus 21 años mientras militaba en el Ejército de Liberación Nacional del Perú. [ORR]

4095 Hernández, Francisco. De cómo Robert Schumann fue vencido por los demonios. México: Ediciones del Equilibrista, 1988. 31 p.: music.

"Podría ser que la música y la poesía fueran una misma cosa, o tal vez dos cosas que se necesitan mutuamente como la boca y el oído," dice Novalis en el epígrafe que antecede este poema extenso que propone la relación íntima entre la música y la palabra. La partitura musical de "Nachtstucke" de Schumann acompaña los versos de inusual cadencia rítmica. El hablante poético dialoga con el compositor en una suerte de homenaje y recuento biográfico donde se recrea el mito del genio creativo. [NK]

4096 Huerta, David. Historia. Tlalpan, Mexico: Ediciones Toledo, 1990. 68 p.

Otro acierto de este joven poeta mexicano que desde un original y elevado lenguaje poético de verso libre y liberador nos cuenta la consabida historia de amor universal. Constitución de un hablante confesional y vulnerable con el que sufrimos la partida de la amada, la mutilación emocional del abandonado, la memoria que angustiosamente reconstituye la pasión erótica y el momento de máxima entrega, el adiós inevitable, el rencor abismal, y el terror de olvido que, sin misericordia, borra toda imagen anterior. [NK]

4097 Huerta, Efraín. Poesía completa. Edición a cargo de Martí Soler. Prólogo de David Huerta. México: Fondo de Cultura Económica, 1988. 621 p.: bibl., index. (Letras mexicanas)

Volumen que recoge la obra de este reconocido poeta de la generación de la revista *Taller* cuya poesía se define por su ubicación citadina, por su conciencia social y cívica, por su erotismo y pasión amorosa y por su humor irónico. Recoge su obra desde *Absoluto amor* (1935) hasta *Transa poética* (1979), e incluye *Dispersión total*, obra póstuma de 1986 y los poemas dispersos que aparecieron en periódicos y revistas. El prólogo de David Huerta y las fichas bibliográficas al final hacen de este un valioso texto para el estudioso de la poesía mexicana. [NK]

4098 Huezo Mixco, Miguel. El pozo del tirador. Ciudad Universitaria, San Salvador: Editorial Universitaria, Univ. de El Salvador, 1988. 106 p.

Poesía testimonial, en la guerra, ante el imperialismo, en el amor y la intimidad. En la primera parte "El Pozo del Tirador" procura "dejar el rastro" de la lucha; en la segunda, "La Canción del Burdelero" trata con sarcasmo la vida *degenerada*—simbolizada por la prostitución—que gozan los explotadores para así restregársela en su cara fastuosa e hipócrita. [GY]

4099 Ielpi, Rafael Oscar. Viajeros y desterrados. Santa Fe, Argentina: Univ. Nacional del Litoral, 1989. 71 p.

Poesía que mezcla historia, imaginación y experiencia personal. Hay un flujo casi narrativo-descriptivo que se lee con tranquilidad y gusto. Son versos casi sin pausas, sin ex-abruptos, y que comunican fácilmente su belleza. [JG]

4100 Jaramillo Agudelo, Darío. Poemas de amor. Bogotá: Fundación Simón y Lola Guberek, 1986. 90 p. (Col. literaria; 17)

Integrante de las últimas promociones de poetas colombianos, a la que se ha denominado "La generación sin nombre," Darío Jaramillo (n. 1947) ha publicado anteriormente dos libros de poemas: *Historias* (1974) y *Tra-*

tados de retórica (1978), con el cual obtuvo el Premio Nacional de Poesía. Este libro, dividido en cuatro partes, oscila entre un tono altamente lírico y sugerente donde predominan los temas del amor, la soledad, el abandono y la nostalgia, y una necesidad de correspondencias, vagamente coloquiales, con otros poetas y escritores. [AR]

4101 Jaramillo Escobar, Jaime. Poemas de tierra caliente. Medellín, Colombia: Univ. de Antioquia, 1985. 111 p. (Col. Premio nacional de poesía)

Poemas extensos, narrativos, éstos de Jaime Jaramillo Escobar (n. 1932), donde la imagen se logra por medio de conjunciones pictóricas y juegos verbales, y donde el discurso poético se adentra en la reflexión vital. Si en su primer libro de poemas, *Los poemas de la ofensa* (1966), un tono hermético contrastaba con cierta tendencia escatológica, producto tal vez de su inmersión en los temas de la violencia social, en este libro estos factores persisten aunque como nota distintiva se percibe una deliberada claridad en el poema. [AR]

4102 Jaramillo Levi, Enrique. Extravíos: poesía. Ciudad Universitaria Rodrigo Facio, Costa Rica: Editorial Universitaria Centroamericana, 1989. 82 p. (Col. Séptimo día)

Erotismo y fantasía comparten espacios descarnados en algunos poemas, mientras el clamor por la patria degradada presente o lejana, es desgarramiento en otros. La búsqueda existencial, personalísima, angustiosa es, sin embargo, el tema predominante, que poetizado, es modo de sobrevivencia: "Anticuerpo de amor/lo inmunizan [al poema]/ contra tanto desamparo/ . . . /Por eso sobrevive/la poesía;" "A fin de cuentas, *somos*;/y eso—como la poesía—/mientras dure es lo que importa." [GY]

4103 Jotamario. El profeta en su casa: paños menores. 2a ed. Bogotá: Fundación Simón y Lola Guberek, 1988. 135 p. (Col. literaria; 25)

Importante reedición del primer libro del poeta nadaista Jotamario (n. 1940), *El profeta en su casa* (1965), además de una colección de poemas dispersos escritos entre 1966–77 y hasta ahora no recogidos en libro. En la poesía de Jotamario se destacan la ironía, el humor, y una constante desacralización de los valores culturales y sociales instituidos, la cual fue una de las premisas de este movimiento vanguardista colombiano de los 60. [AR]

4104 Juarroz, Roberto. Novena poesía vertical, décima poesía vertical. Buenos Aires: Ediciones Carlos Lohlé, 1986. 142 p.

Continuación del sistemático trabajo poético de este gran poeta argentino bajo el título general de "poesía vertical." Con el tiempo, esta verticalidad se hace más profunda. Un libro imprescindible para visualizar el mundo lírico de Juarroz. [JG]

4105 Juarroz, Roberto. Poesía vertical: antología incompleta. Selección y prólogo de Louis Bourne. Madrid: Playor, 1987. 172 p.: bibl. (Nueva poesía)

Juarroz es uno de los grandes poetas hispanoamericanos actuales y ésta es una excelente antología modestamente llamada "incompleta." Louis Bourne ha trabajado con gusto y profundo conocimiento seleccionando un apreciable material de las diez colecciones de "poesía vertical" publicadas hasta la fecha. El libro tiene unidad y permite una lectura continua y coherente. [JG]

4106 Klein, Laura. A mano alzada. Buenos Aires: Libros de Tierra Firme, 1986. 59 p. (Col. de poesía Todos bailan; 14)

Las tres partes de este libro: 1) "Bajo Pena," 2) "En el Sillón de Inés," y 3) "Mano Alzada," exhiben la misma osadía de asociaciones lingüísticas que hacen a esta poesía sorpresiva e insinuante. [JG]

4107 Lamborghini, Leonidas C. El solicitante descolocada. Buenos Aires: Libros de Tierra Firme, 1989. 144 p. (Col. de poesía Todos bailan; 98)

Reúne tres conjuntos poéticos: 1) "Las Patas en las Fuentes," 2) "La Estatua de la Libertad," y 3) "Diez Escenas del Paciente." Ensalada lírica con un efecto de exuberante comicidad, desde la intertextualidad paródica o humorística hasta lo grotesco y delirante. Un gran sentido de lo insólito e irreverente que protege estos textos (casi siempre) de lo fácil y predecible. [JG]

4108 Landó, Cristina. Mitades vivas. Montevideo: Proyección, 1988. 64 p.: ill.

Conjunto de poemas en tiradas largas, agrupados en cuatro partes: 1) "Mitades Vivas," 2) "Sangreología," 3) "Siembra y Estiér-

col," y 4) "América." Poemas eróticos de excelente calidad, estructurados en un lenguaje de alta vibración, resonancia, casi con el ritmo herreriano (de Herrera y Reissig). [MGP]

4109 Larrea, Rafael. Bajo el sombrero del poeta. Quito: Editorial El Conejo, 1988. 108 p. (Col. Metáfora)

Miembro de la generación "tzántzica," se caracteriza por su observación alerta y crítica—aunque con mesura—de las diversas actividades de su realidad cotidiana. Se destaca la descripción y referencia a circunstancias sociales ecuatorianas, en las que descubre aspectos profundos e inadvertidos por la tradición y los hábitos. Demuestra así su afán de reforma y renovación. [ORR]

4110 Lezama Lima, José. Muerte de Narciso: antología poética. Selección y prólogo de David Huerta. México: Ediciones Era, 1988. 149 p. (Biblioteca Era; 172/1)

Más conocido como el autor de *Paradiso*, su obra poética, compleja e intrigante, ha tenido menos difusión. La introducción de David Huerta—poeta él mismo que, como Lezama, cultiva la vía de figuraciones (*Incurable*), busca interpretar el paradisíaco mundo verbal de un poeta que obsesivamente encubre el sentido de su escritura. [RG]

4111 Lihn, Enrique. Album de toda especie de poemas. Barcelona: Editorial Lumen, 1989. 154 p. (Poesía; 58)

Antología preparada por el autor poco antes de su muerte (1988). Incluye textos cuyo conjunto constituye un verdadero testamento poético. El libro se sitúa en un plano de autobiografía y poética reveladoras de la evolución humana y literaria de uno de los poetas más lúcidos de nuestro tiempo. Sin duda, la mejor antología de su poesía y la que muestra más plenamente todos sus registros poéticos. Indispensable para estudios sobre Lihn. [LE]

4112 Lihn, Enrique. Diario de muerte. Textos reunidos y transcritos por Pedro Lastra y Adriana Valdés. Santiago: Editorial Universitaria, 1989. 83 p. (Col. Fuera de serie)

Libro póstumo que revela el mundo ya desde los espacios de la muerte. Conjunción de palabra y circunstancia ofrecen testimonio poético lúcido y conmovedor. Indispensable grupo de poemas que reiteran la iluminadora coherencia de una de las obras mayores de la poesía chilena de todos los tiempos. [LE]

4113 Lihn, Enrique. Mester de juglaría. Madrid: Hiperión, 1987. 77 p.: port. (Poesía Hiperión; 108)

Selección en que el autor recoge siete de sus poemas mayores: "La Pieza Oscura" (1963), "Mester de Juglaría" (1966), "Beata Beatrix" (1975), "La Efímera Vulgata," "De lo Mismo," "Pena de Extrañamiento" y "Athinulis" (1986). Muestra facetas más definidoras de poesía de Lihn. Dice el poeta: "Estos poemas, tan distintos entre sí temporalmente, se me imaginan como las metamorfosis de una misma criatura descentrada." Así reunidos, estos poemas son corroboración irrefutable de los grandes méritos de esta poesía. [LE]

4114 Limpias Chávez, Viviana. Poemas bajo un sol ajeno. Santa Cruz, Bolivia: Cabildo, 1987. 78 p.: ill. (Col. de poesía La Bala perdida; 2)

Personalidad nueva en la poesía boliviana. Textos centrados en el tema del amor, constituyen un discurso erótico femenino renovador. Desde la perspectiva tradicional de la mujer en su rol social, pero sólo aparente, se enfrenta abiertamente a las manifestaciones típicas del tema y rechaza sus eufemismos en favor de una expresión directa pero con eficacia poética. [ORR]

4115 Lira, Rodrigo. Proyecto de obras completas. Santiago: Coedición Minga/Camaleón, 1984. 125 p.

Primera publicación que pertenece íntegramente a Lira. El prólogo de Enrique Lihn es un penetrante análisis del concepto de poesía, y reanuda un diálogo entre un poeta al comienzo de su trayectoria y otro en el punto más elevado de ella. Los poemas desestabilizan códigos de la comunicación poética para integrarse, dice Lihn, "en un contexto o . . . intertexto que les da resonancia y . . . coherencia." Libro que merece ser leído y meditado: desconcierta, obligando al lector a abandonar la comodidad de la norma. [LE]

4116 Liscano, Carlos. ¿Estará no más cargada de futuro? Montevideo: Vintén Editor, 1989. 60 p.

Poemas escritos en la cárcel y en el exilio que exploran el tiempo sin transcurrir, las posibilidades de la libertad, la poesía, la identidad del ser, entre los temas dominantes. El poemario contiene 52 poemas distribuidos en una serie variada de combinatorias estróficas configurados en un lenguaje de tendencia vanguardista junto a un marcado prosaísmo. Esta voz poética se diferencia de los poemas escritos en la cárcel de otros poetas en que combina en el mismo poemario dos movimientos: hacia la expresión del encierro y hacia la vida en el exilio. [MGP]

4117 Liscano, Juan. Vencimientos. Caracas: Galería Durban, 1986. 110 p.

Al paso de los años la obra del poeta venezolano Juan Liscano (n. 1915) ha tocado con gran profundidad muchos de los temas caros a la poesía latinoamericana: la reflexión sobre el paisaje americano, el erotismo, los mitos, la poesía misma, y los conflictos existenciales y vitales. Con un lenguaje casi directo, donde lo hermético presenta el rostro ilusorio de la sencillez, Liscano busca en este libro continuar un camino de develación y conocimiento que auna lo poético y lo religioso, en el sentido más-amplio de la palabra. El resultado es una hermosa suma de encantamiento y lucidez. [AR]

4118 Liscano, Juan. El viaje. Mérida, Venezuela: Univ. de Los Andes, Consejo de Publicaciones, between 1976 and 1987. 61 p. (Col. El Ciervo vulnerado. Serie Poesía)

Perdido el manuscrito durante varios años este libro fue recuperado gracias a la diligencia del profesor y crítico Jesús Serra. En él, Juan Liscano (n. 1915) nos narra poéticamente las aventuras espirituales del viaje interior. Conocimiento, mesura y lucidez se hermanan a versos de alta calidad lírica. [AR]

4119 Lizalde, Eduardo. Tabernarios y eróticos. México: Vuelta, 1988. 70 p. (La Imaginación)

Poemario desigual del iniciador del "Poetismo" en México. Lo más logrado son los poemas que construyen un hablante irónico e inconforme cuyas reflexiones impugnan la soledad, la vida diaria, el tiempo y la poesía. La última sección "Baja Traición" recoge una serie de traducciones de poetas célebres (Dante, Pessoa, Joyce, Blake, Rilke, etc.), sección que legitimiza Pacheco, que se encuentra en muchos poemarios recientes y que implícitamente define la traducción simultáneamente como traición y acto creativo. [NK]

4120 Lloréns Torres, Luis. Luis Lloréns Torres: antología: verso y prosa. Edición de Arcadio Díaz Quiñones. Río Piedras,

P.R.: Ediciones Huracán, 1986. 168 p.: ill.
(Col. Clásicos Huracán)

Esta cuidada edición se propone hacer accesible a un "clásico" de la literatura puertorriqueña. La antología muestra a un escritor complejo, no sólo porque se dispone del verso y la prosa, sino porque la variada selección de textos sanciona la proyección ideológica de quien, como ningún otro escritor puertorriqueño, quiso fundar una literatura *nacional*. La selección va acompañada de breves bibliografías de la obra de Lloréns, y de la crítica literaria sobre este autor. Abre el volumen un ejemplar estudio crítico de Arcadio Díaz sobre Lloréns Torres. [RG]

4121 Lojo de Beuter, María Rosa. Forma oculta del mundo. Buenos Aires: Ediciones Ultimo Reino, 1991. 75 p.

Con este libro la autora retoma ese lenguaje sin pausas artificiales que es el poema en prosa, y en el que ya había ofrecido textos maestros en *Visiones* (1984). El volumen está dividido en fases que ostentan nombres de insinuante pluralidad como "Magias," "Lunas," "Esperas," "Tránsitos," "Centros," "Transfiguraciones," y "Duelos." [JG]

4122 López-Adorno, Pedro. Las glorias de su ruina. Madrid: Playor, 1988. 60 p. (Nueva poesía)

En sus mejores momentos esta poesía recuerda a Lezama (pero sin Lezama), porque hay menos de elaboración del mito y la historia que de gozo en el regodeo de un lenguaje siempre oblicuo: la más cultivada evidencia. Sin embargo, hay algo de alucinante y de altura poética en estos versos que hace volver al lector a una de sus fuentes de inspiración, Sor Juana. [RG]

4123 López Vallecillos, Italo. Poesía completa. San José: Editorial Universitaria Centroamericana, 1987. 345 p.: facsims. (Col. Séptimo día)

Poeta intimista y comprometido (fundador de "La Generación Comprometida"), en busca de nuevos modos de acción para transformar la realidad, más bien en sentido surrealista y metafísico que material. Frente a su profunda tristeza radical procura asir "el lenguaje exacto del alma de las cosas," que parece encontrar en el discurso amoroso de su último libro inédito, *Del vulnerable amor*. En él amada y poema coinciden ("poema mío hecho carne") para rescatar "el oscuro perfil de la memoria." [GY]

4124 Lozano, Orietta. El vampiro esperado. Bogotá: Editorial Puesto de Combate, 1987. 101 p. (Col. La Flauta de pan)

Importante poeta colombiana de la más reciente promoción, Orietta Lozano (n. 1956) ha publicado anteriormente *Fuego secreto* (1983) y en 1987 obtuvo con este libro el Premio Nacional de Poesía. Su poesía, de frente a los grandes temas como el amor, la soledad, la existencia, se caracteriza por un uso fluido y atento de la imagen y la palabra poética. [AR]

4125 Masci, Luis. Los caballos de la lluvia. Caracas: Ediciones la Espada Rota, 1987. 101 p.

La obra poética de este autor incluye tres títulos: *Siglos secos* (1977), *Los pasos por volver y otros poemas* (1978–97) y *Los caballos de la lluvia*. Sus temas son el amor, la guerra y la circunstancia desgarradora de la transitoriedad del individuo. Las formas de los poemas descorden títulos, mayúsculas o signos de puntuación; los versos combinados en muy breves con muy largos precipitan el movimiento intenso del deseo, del acercamiento y la fuga, la inestabilidad del estar y del ser. La obra de este poeta deberá interesar a los estudiosos de la poesía lírica uruguaya y latinoamericana. [MGP]

4126 Matute, Carmen. Poeta sola. Guatemala: Grupo Literario Editorial RIN-78, 1986. 82 p. (Col. Literatura; 27)

Tentativa de conciliar el dilema existencial y el amor individual con la esperanza colectiva: "Por recorrer tu piel a pedacitos/ olvidó la piel agrietada/de la patria [. . .] sumergida en un orgasmo inacabable" que, no obstante deviene "enorme canasto de pan/ que se reparte para todos." [GY]

4127 Mieses, Juan Carlos. Flagellum Dei. Santo Domingo: Taller, 1987. 78 p.: ill. (Col. Poesía; 7)

El joven poeta dominicano se ubica en un ámbito que, de alguna manera, recuerda la épica. *Flagellum Dei*, El Azote de Dios, es un canto al bárbaro Atila, rey de los hunos. Su tránsito vencedor y su derrota son la historia que inspira esta lírica de gran imaginación. [RG]

4128 Mir, Pedro. Hay un país en el mundo. Ilustraciones de José Perdomo. Introducción de Marianne de Tolentino. Santo

Domingo: Taller, 1987. 33 p.: col. ill. (Biblioteca Taller; 247)

Reedición de uno de los tres grandes poemas de Mir. A Mir se le considera el poeta dominicano más importante del siglo XX. Es una edición artística, ilustrada por el pintor José Perdomo. Las pinturas se inspiran en el poema. La introducción de Marianne de Tolentino vincula las obras. [RG]

4129 Modern, Rodolfo E. Ascensión de lo grave. Buenos Aires: Torres Agüero Editor, 1987. 77 leaves

Modern es un poeta único en Hispanoamérica por su línea clásica, su precisión medular, su elaboración sobria. El título de uno de los 35 poemas que componen el libro expresa esta condición: "Juego Geométrico," donde su arte poética se resume en los versos finales: "pasarse en limpio: /exactamente." [JG]

4130 Molina, Enrique. Obras completas. t. 2, Obra poética. Buenos Aires: Corregidor, 1987. 477 p. (Obras completas; 2)

Necesaria recolección de la obra lírica de uno de los más grandes poetas de nuestro continente. Incluye desde *Las cosas y el delirio* (1941) hasta "Poemas Recientes." [JG]

4131 Moltedo, Ennio. Playa de invierno. Viña del Mar, Chile: Meridiana Editorial, 1985. 63 p.

Poesía que habla desde fuera esperando, o ya desesperando, poder entrar en "espectáculo" de una vida precaria: "Un lugar de luz a donde dirigir los pasos cuando el día cede a la noche." Lenguaje preciso y mesurado refuerza el sentido de resignación frente a la alienación de la voz poética. [LE]

4132 Montero Ayala, Carmen Rosa. Del otro lado de mis ojos. Santa Cruz, Bolivia: Editorial Cuimbae, 1990. 55 p.: ill., plate (Col. Poesía)

Una visión femenina refinada del sentimiento amoroso, que no abandona cierta actitud de nostalgia, caracteriza a esta poesía. El erotismo que cultiva es a un tiempo vigoroso y delicado. Se trata de un discurso poético nuevo en la poesía femenina boliviana. La configuración de sus imágenes, referidas a la manifestación del acto amoroso como pensamiento y como acto, se realiza espontánea y original. [ORR]

4133 Morales, Jorge A. Cabos sueltos Loose ends. San Juan, P.R.: Instituto de Cultura Puertorriqueña, 1989. 208 p.

Esta edición reúne cuatro poemarios: *Escribalazos* (1976), *Vine en busca de tu voz* (1981), *Baladas de Vellonera y otras consideraciones* (1981), y un libro nuevo, *Cabos sueltos/Loose ends*, donde, como en los primeros libros, se incluyen textos en inglés. Se aprovecha muy bien el discurso popular y el contexto cotidiano. El humor (que recuerda a Parra) se combina bien en estos versos. [RG]

4134 Moscona, Myriam. Las visitantes. México: Editorial Joaquín Mortiz, 1989. 74 p.

Segundo texto de esta joven poeta que mereció el Premio de Poesía Aguascalientes en 1988. Desfile de mujeres de ayer y de hoy recreadas desde la realidad, los mitos, las leyendas y la imaginación. Moscona, hija de extranjeros, torna el desarraigo en condición humana extremada en la experiencia femenina. La voz poética insiste en la mujer como visitante, como exiliada en búsqueda de un sitio constructivo y creativo para su naturaleza y sus proyectos. [NK]

4135 Murillo, Rosario. En las espléndidas ciudades. Managua: Editorial Nueva Nicaragua, 1985. 135 p. (Letras de Nicaragua; 13)

Se escribe para acomodar "un sitio para la esperanza," expresada ésta en amor— en la guerra junto al hombre, sobre la tierra, celebrando la vida. La sobrevivencia poética— aquí sobrevivencia de mujer—trasciende la realidad y lo biográfico: "Necesito amar el cielo con mis cantos/asaltar los recuerdos/y hacerlos lluvia renovando el zacate"; "Una mujer tiene que sobrevivir compartiendo/tiene que intentar lo imposible:/darle vuelta a la historia, sacudirla/en una sola mirada." [GY]

4136 Mutis, Alvaro. Sesenta cuerpos. Selección y notas de Jaime Jaramillo Escobar. Medellín, Colombia: Comité de Publicaciones, Univ. de Antioquia, 1985. 182 p. (Col. Premio Nacional de Poesía)

La crítica y los lectores han sido unánimes al considerar la obra de Mutis como una de las más importantes hoy en día en América Latina. El presente libro editado por el poeta nadaísta Jaime Jaramillo no sólo cumple con su tarea de difundir esta obra poética sino que permite observar el encuentro de dos generaciones. Al alterar el orden de publicación de los poemas y seguir una línea de estructuración del libro muy personal, Jaramillo nos da la lectura nadaísta de esta obra fundamental. [AR]

4137 Mutis Durán, Santiago. Soñadores de pájaros. Bogotá: Fundación Simón y Lola Guberek, 1987. 49 p. (Col. literaria; 20)

Silente y rigurosa la obra de este joven poeta colombiano ha encontrado por sí misma un lugar destacado dentro de la nueva poesía de este país. En ella se busca una imagen lírica que estalle con la fuerza de una imagen pictórica: plasticidad, color, sorpresa y una armonía surreal que colocan al hablante lírico en constante diálogo con pintores y artistas, entre ellos Remedios Varo, Leonora Carrington, Miró, Hooper, todos ellos "soñadores de pájaros." [AR]

4138 Neruda, Pablo. La insepulta de Paita. Caracas: Talleres Italgráfica, 1983. 66 p.: ill., plate, ports.

Edición contentiva del poema. Homenaje de la Sociedad Bolivariana de Venezuela a la memoria de Manuela Sáenz. Reproduce poema que es recuerdo y exaltación de la amante de Bolívar. Hay presentación de Oscar Rojas Jiménez y retrato de la "Libertadora del Libertador," como la llamara el propio Bolívar. [LE]

4139 Ochoa Romero, Quintín. Sobre un giro de espejos. Holguín, Cuba: Sección de Literatura, SPC de Holguín, 1988. 77 p.

El lirismo de este poeta sabe eslabonar situaciones cotidianas que les dan sabor a historias. Con sencillez y buen gusto vislumbra lo insólito en lo común. Mejores los poemas de temas amorosos. [RG]

4140 Oñate, Iván. Anatomía del vacío. Quito: Editorial El Conejo, 1988. 147 p. (Col. Metáfora)

Poesía de calidad, reflexiva sobre los objetos y situaciones de la cotidianidad. Su percepción, pese a las imágenes referenciales de las cosas concretas, no deja de ser desolada y con frecuencia remite a espacios del vacío y del absurdo, en una dimensión física y metafísica. El texto está dividido en seis partes: 1) Introducción; 2) La Guerra; 3) Abismos; 4) La Patria; 5) Baldíos; y 6) Cuerpos Prestados. [ORR]

4141 Orta Ruiz, Jesús. Entre, y perdone usted—. La Habana: Unión de Escritores y Artistas de Cuba, 1983. 203 p. (Bolsilibros Unión)

Comprehensive selection from the works of Cuban folk poet Jesús Orta Ruiz (n. 1922) known as "el Indio Naborí." Includes many of his earliest, scattered poems. [E. Sacerio-Garí]

4142 Ortiz, Cecilia. La pasión errante. Caracas: Monte Avila Editores, 1986. 43 p. (Col. Las Formas del fuego)

Las fuerzas del deseo, entremezclando pasión, eros, amor, desengaño, encuentros y desencuentros, invade la poesía de la poeta venezolana Cecilia Ortiz (n. 1951). La misma sigue la tradición de poetas que han hecho de la relación amorosa y de sus múltiples estallidos la carne de sus poemas. Bien escrita, síntesis de la imagen que toca como con agujas la realidad, ella prevalece gracias a la sinceridad desgarrante de su búsqueda. [AR]

4143 Osorio, Amílcar. Vana stanza: diván selecto, 1962–1984. Bogotá: Fundación Simón y Lola Guberek, 1989. 190 p. (Col. literaria; 32)

La trágica desaparición en 1985 del poeta nadaísta Amílcar Osorio (1940–85), dejó inconclusa una obra que desde la fundación del movimiento nadaísta venía perfilándose como novedosa, dadas su calidad y afán de aventura. El libro que aquí nos ocupa recoge poemas entre 1962–82 y es una buena muestra de una fase de la intención poética de Osorio. Dentro de un mundo encantado por las formas el hablante lírico se distancia para darnos en fragmentos, casi cubistas, el rostro de un ser atento a los reclamos del deseo y al imperio sensual de la realidad. [AR]

4144 Pacheco, José Emilio. Ciudad de la memoria: poemas 1986–1989. México: Ediciones Era, 1989. 64 p. (Biblioteca Era; 193/1)

Ultima y excelente entrega del reconocido poeta mexicano. Desde un sujeto impersonal habla desde la perspectiva del hombre contemporáneo quien, condenado al paso del tiempo, busca la permanencia a través de la memoria, "olvido que inventa." Aunque "ficción," se agudiza la memoria del poeta para darle forma al fin del milenio a "este siglo de muerte;" para recrear la ciudad desaparecida; para expresar los momentos fugaces. De manera original y provocativa, Pacheco vuelca, de nuevo, su mirada a la condición humana, singular y arbitraria. Rescata, otra vez, la poesía, como vía de conocimiento. [NK]

4145 Páez, José-Christian. Boceto por una joven muerte. Santiago: Editorial La Noria, 1986. 29 p.

Poemas de "amor" con un lenguaje audaz donde los diversos elementos que lo conforman se comunican en formas siempre cambiantes en camino a proponer sus sentidos. Perturbadoramente sugerentes de esa inquietante cercanía amor-muerte, Eros-Tánatos. Muestra logros poéticos interesantes. [LE]

4146 Pagés Lendián, Heriberto. Los nombres de la noche. La Habana: Editorial Letras Cubanas, 1987. 63 p. (Col. Espiral)

La experiencia decisiva en este poemario es la del tiempo. Hay un constante planteamiento del ineludible pero comprensible paso del tiempo. El tratamiento del tema recuerda a Machado y, con otras particularidades, a J.E. Pacheco. La soledad, el espacio vacío, la lluvia o la imagen del diluvio son otros motivos que guían estos poemas que, notablemente, se apartan de la poesía de ideología revolucionaria que acostumbraban publicar los jóvenes en las editoriales cubanas. [RG]

4147 Paoletti, Mario. Inventario. Talavera de la Reina, Spain: s.n., 1991. 1 v.

Paoletti continúa el modo de diálogo poético que iniciara en *Poemas con Arlt* (1983): recuerdos y recuentos, enumeraciones y restas, citas y tergiversaciones. Son versos inteligentes, escuetos, donde hay una virtud dominante: el ingenio, y como todo ingenio, a veces meramente ingenioso, otras amargo, trágico, pero nunca obvio. [JG]

4148 Parada Maluenda, José Manuel. Pido respeto. Ilustraciones de Nemesio Antúnez. Santiago: Editorial Emisión, 1986. 146 p.: ill. (some col.)

Se incluye por el valor que puede tener como testimonio de una época que no debiera clausurarse en Chile sin una reflexión seria sobre los destinos de países y seres humanos. La voluntad de poesía del autor de *Pido respeto*, si no el valor intrínseco de los poemas, debe validar esta inclusión. Ilustraciones de Nemesio Antúnez acompañan los textos poéticos. [LE]

4149 Parra, Nicanor. Chistes parra desorientar a la poesía. Prólogo y selección de María Nieves Alonso y Gilberto Triviños. Madrid: Visor, 1989. 216 p. (Col. Visor de poesía; 236)

Ultima antología de la poesía de Parra. Incluye textos desde *Poemas y antipoemas*

(1954) a *Hojas de Parra* (1985). Hay seis textos "inéditos" (1988). Buen prólogo y una buena selección. Buena selección que destaca el carácter desmitificador de esta poesía que no olvida la función social del vate. [LE]

4150 Parra, Nicanor. Poemas y antipoemas (1954). Edición de René de Costa. Madrid: Cátedra, 1988. 119 p.: bibl. (Letras hispánicas; 287)

Reedición importante que sigue fielmente la edición príncipe de Nascimento, Santiago de Chile, 1954. Informativa introducción de René de Costa relaciona las tres secciones del libro de Parra con tres movimientos de rechazo a modelos canónicos de la época: Mistral, Neruda, y él mismo (el "autor" contra el poeta). [LE]

4151 Paz, Octavio. Libertad bajo palabra: 1935–1957. Edición de Enrico Mario Santí. Madrid: Cátedra, 1988. 376 p.: bibl., index, port. (Letras hispánicas; 250)

Excelente y corregida edición de este libro singular que registra la formación poética de Paz (Premio Nobel 1990), y contiene varios poemas que están entre los más conocidos de la poesía hispanoamericana: "Himno entre Ruinas," "Piedra del Sol," y "El Cántaro Roto." La introducción de Santí narra las circunstancias bajo las cuales Paz elabora esta obra. Los comentarios informativos del editor y los varios análisis textuales hacen de éste un libro valioso para el estudio de Paz. [NK]

4152 Pellegrini, Aldo. Escrito para nadie: poemas inéditos, 1972/1973. Barcelona: Argonauta≤s Punxes, 1989. 106 p.: ill., plate. (Biblioteca de poesía; 1)

Aldo Pellegrini (1903–73) es conocido como poeta y crítico, y se le identifica con la fase vanguardista de la poesía hispanoamericana. Estos son los últimos poemas escritos por él. Están pulcramente editados por primera vez, y puede apreciarse el modo sencillo como el hablante lírico, apoyado en versos largos y desacentuados, penetra en las profundidades de la inteligencia surrealista. Se puede leer este libro como un verdadero réquiem. [JG]

4153 Pérez Olivares, José. A imagen y semejanza. La Habana: Depto. de Actividades Culturales, Univ. de La Habana, 1987. 45 p.

Poesía distinta a la que publica la mayoría de sus contemporáneos cubanos: desentreverada de los pactos ideológicos circunstanciales; no obstante, se potencia como abarcadoramente crítica. En la mayoría de los poemas prevalece la admiración por el arte (pintura y literatura) surrealista. [RG]

4154 Pérez Olivares, José. Caja de Pandora. La Habana: Editorial Letras Cubanas, 1987. 80 p.: ill.

En esta poesía fresca y atractiva se exalta la pintura, particularmente la francesa del siglo XIX y principios del XX. Aunque no desatiende el aspecto histórico—de hecho, hay frecuentes menciones históricas—, Pérez Olivares se regodea en el mundo del arte y la leyenda. [RG]

4155 Pérez Só, Reynaldo. Matadero. S.l.: Amazonia, 1986. 66 p.

Con la publicación de *Para morirnos de otro sueño* y *Tanmatra* a principios de la década del 70, Reynaldo Pérez-Só vino a presentarse como uno de los poetas jóvenes más interesantes de Venezuela. Sus poemas afirmaban un lenguaje preciso, sintético, altamente lírico, si bien herméticos en su busca de concisión. El peligro estaba en tropezar en la autocomplacencia, en el encandilamiento del ego acosado por decir la Palabra, con mayúsculas. Este libro, a pesar de algunos aciertos en la línea establecida antes, cae lastimosamente en estos escollos que señalamos. [AR]

4156 Perlongher, Néstor Osvaldo. Alambres. Buenos Aires: Ediciones Ultimo Reino, 1987. 63 p.

Néstor Perlongher (n. 1949, Buenos Aires) muestra en su segundo libro (el primero es *Austria-Hungría*, 1980) que es uno de los mejores poetas hispanoamericanos actuales. Verbalmente osado, combina palabras en composiciones que toman siempre de sorpresa, en un nivel de tragicomedia que hiere y fascina. Después de 23 poemas, hay una breve sección en prosa y un largo poema final: "Cadáveres." [JG]

4157 Perlongher, Néstor Osvaldo. Hule. Buenos Aires: Ediciones Ultimo Reino, 1989. 75 p.

Poeta de gran riqueza verbal, exuberancia imaginativa y constructiva. Este es su tercer libro: lo preceden *Austria-Hungría* (1980) y *Alambres* (ver item bi92–15245). Su estética "neobarrosa" se despliega grotesca y

osadamente en el "Preámbulo Barroso" con que se inicia la serie de 19 poemas, algunos de ellos extensos y minuciosos. [JG]

4158 Perrone, Alberto Mario. Derrota y despojo: poemas. Buenos Aires: Lugar Editorial, 1989. 64 p.: ill. (Col. de poesía El Divan Japonés)

Poemas de insólita belleza discursiva, versículos donde la reflexión histórica se hace lírica y se va adhiriendo a la sensibilidad del lector. El libro consta de seis poemas, cada uno de ellos basados en figuras de la historia latinoamericana, algunas conocidas como Colón, Sor Juana o Sarmiento, y otras que, aunque no lo sean tanto, resultan emotivas por su tragicidad. [JG]

4159 Picado, Lil. Vigilia de la hembra. San José: Editorial Costa Rica, 1985. 81 p.: ill.

Poemario amoroso escrito en un lenguaje en que se conjugan lo sensual y lo lírico, lo erótico y lo místico. Ante todo se canta desde y para el principio femenino del ser, arraigado en el cuerpo femenino: "Mi pecho ahora es campanario/gozándome por los senos." Si bien se insiste en el fundamento corpóreo y natural del ser femenino, las referencias al amante son abstractas, mucho más de lo que suele ser en la poesía mística. [GY]

4160 Pitty, Dimas Lidio. Rumor de multitud. Panamá: Editorial Mariano Arosemena, 1986. 63 p.

Visión testimonial de nuestra época y sus mitos, no tanto como denuncia sino como vivencia de la cotidianidad urbana. Se ironiza la cultura de masas y se buscan los rasgos deformados de la conciencia social a través de jergas, regionalismos, lenguas invasoras, mostrando así una imagen desarticulada del contexto nacional, sin dejar de lado una ternura expresada desde la perspectiva del hombre común. [GY]

4161 Quessep, Giovanni. Muerte de Merlín. Prólogo de Fernando Charry Lara. Bogotá: Instituto Caro y Cuervo, 1985. 116 p. (Serie La Granada entreabierta; 40)

Laboriosa, metódica, la obra de Giovanni Quessep (n. 1939) es consecuente con el dictamen que implica que el oficio del poeta es escribir. A este libro lo preceden seis libros de poesía, siendo el último de ellos *Poesía* (1985), que reúne los libros anteriores. La crítica ha sido unánime al señalar como características exteriores de la poesía de Quessep su revisión constante de la musicalidad en el poema, su arquitectura y, en fin, la precisión en el manejo de sus engranajes. Todos estos factores se manifiestan en este libro aunados a la convocatoria que hace el poeta al misterio, el exilio, el viaje sin destino o los lagos profundos de la desesperanza. [AR]

4162 Quirarte, Vicente. La luz no muere sola: poesía 1976–1984. México: Ediciones Gernika, 1987. 154 p. (El Nigromante. Serie Creación; 8)

Antología que reúne seis libros del autor publicados entre 1979–84. Se destacan los poemas de amor y los de la ciudad. En estos, el poeta desanda la Ciudad de México, recreando sus innumerables espacios y la gente que los habita. Define, y se define por, la ciudad en un lenguaje directo, de imágenes concretas y precisas que logran captar la vitalidad y la angustia que se vive diariamente en la capital. [NK]

4163 Ramos, María Eugenia. Porque ningún sol es el último. Presentación de Clementina Suárez. Tegucigalpa: Ediciones Librería Paradiso, 1989. 59 p.: ill. (Col. Poesía)

Este primer libro de Ramos (n. 1959) representa acaso la visión poética de una nueva generación que lleva la preocupación social a un plano más intimista, expresada en los registros del Vallejo más cotidiano. Se vislumbra en estos poemas una esperanza menos grandiosa o apocalíptica—la alborada del "nuevo hombre"—, que se aprecia en la humilde sobrevivencia, viéndola ya no como "el camino de ida" [al vacío], pues éste "puede ser en realidad el de regreso" a la reconstitución de la vida. [GY]

4164 Ramos Sucre, José Antonio. Las formas del fuego. Edición de Katyna Henríquez Consalvi. Prólogo de Salvador Garmendia. Madrid: Siruela, 1988. 541 p.: port. (El Ojo sin párpado; 12)

Valiosa edición de la obra del gran poeta venezolano José A. Ramos Sucre (1890–1930) a cargo de Katyna Henríquez Consalvi, y con un magnífico prólogo del escritor Salvador Garmendia. La obra de Ramos Sucre se caracteriza por una honda búsqueda que actualiza lo maravilloso. Por años el nombre de Ramos Sucre fue casi completamente desconocido para los lectores latinoamericanos; sin embargo, el empeño de algunos poetas venezolanos por sacar su obra del olvido ha permitido que el público lector pueda hoy reconocer en ella a una de las voces poéticas más importantes del continente. [AR]

4165 Renán, Raúl. Los urbanos. Fotografía de Arturo David Schmitter. México: Instituto Nacional de Bellas Artes; Guadalajara, Mexico: Gobierno del Estado de Jalisco, 1988. 85 p.: ill.

Fotografía de Arturo David Schmitter y grafía poética de Raúl Renán, se complementan en este bello libro que busca, a través de la imagen y la palabra, profundizar la experiencia urbana del Distrito Federal. El hablante poeta deambula por esta ciudad-monstruo, constituyente de espacios opresivos y liberadores. [NK]

4166 Restrepo, Elkin. Absorto escuchando el cercano canto de sirenas; Retrato de artistas. Medellín, Colombia: Ediciones Autores Antioqueños, 1985. 71 leaves: ill. (Col. Autores antioqueños; 12)

Cercano al nadaísmo en su última etapa. Elkin Restrepo (n. 1942) pronto se desafilió de esta línea de acción y emprendió solitario su camino en poesía. A una ya abundante obra poética donde se destacan *La sombra de otros lugares* (1973), *Memoria del mundo* (1974), *Lugar de invocaciones* (1977), *La palabra sin reino* (1982) y *Retrato de artistas* (1983), se añade este libro doble, ya que en él se reproducen *Retrato de artistas* y el que da pie al título. *Retrato de artistas* es tal vez uno de los libros más interesantes y hermosos de la nueva poesía colombiana. Un tono nostálgico, que atrapa en sus matices el aire viciado de los destellos de la fama, se mueve por este libro donde resucitan y mueren las estrellas de plástico del reino cinematográfico. [AR]

4167 Rivera, Silvia Tomasa. Duelo de espadas. México: Fondo de Cultura, 1987. 103 p.

Excelente volumen de una de las voces jóvenes y originales de la poesía mexicana. Recoge la poesía de *Duelo de espadas* (1984), *Poemas al desconocido, Poemas a la desconocida* (1984), y *Apuntes de abril* (1986). Anti-poeta, inspirada en Jaime Sabines, logra expresar realidades y vivencias inéditas, con un lenguaje directo, iconoclasta, y cargado de intencionalidad. [NK]

4168 Roca, Juan Manuel. País secreto, 1979–1987. Bogotá: Ediciones El Caballero Mateo, 1987. 87 p.

La poesía de Juan Manuel Roca (n. 1946) se inscribe en esa tierra de nadie que va de los extramuros del movimiento nadaísta a las fronteras del coloquialismo insurgente de los 70. Sin embargo, la imagen surreal, sorpresiva, lo uniría más con el nadaísmo. Imagen a su vez torturada por la violencia y el desamparo, cualidades propias del poeta que vive su país como un exilio, forzado a habitar en las lindes de la realidad. [AR]

4169 Rojas, Gonzalo. Antología personal. Prólogo de Eduardo Vázquez. México: Premiá: Coordinación de Difusión Cultural, Dirección de Literatura, UNAM, 1988. 95 p. (Textos de humanidades)

Importante recolección de textos que ofrece lo que el lector puede considerar lo más personal y propio del poeta. Son 51 poemas de entre los más notable de la obra de Gonzalo Rojas, uno de los mejores poetas contemporáneos en español. [LE]

4170 Rojas, Gonzalo. Materia de testamento. Madrid: Hiperión, 1988. 192 p.: port. (Poesía Hiperión; 130)

Recoge producción entre 1987–88, más otros poemas de volúmenes anteriores que aquí se incorporan como necesidad de este libro. Cada nuevo libro de Rojas ahonda en producción anterior y en la contradictoria condición del ser humano. En sus 70 años, Rojas ofrece los abundantes dones de su visión poética, de los que nosotros, afortunados lectores de *Materia de testamento*, nos apropiamos. [LE]

4171 Rokha, Pablo de. Epopeya de las comidas y las bebidas de Chile. Selección y prólogo de Carlos Droguett. La Habana: Casa de las Américas, 1986. 469 p. (Col. Literatura latinoamericana; 116)

Antología que vale la pena destacar porque muestra renovado interés por rescatar y difundir la obra de este cuestionado poeta (1894–1968). (Ver *Sinfronteras*, 1987, *Nueva antología de Pablo de Rokha*). Pese a violencia denostadora del lenguaje y desborde del sentimiento, sus muchos aciertos avalan la condición de precursor asignada a De Rokha. Incluye evocador vocabulario de términos chilenos y cuadro sinóptico de poeta y época. [LE]

4172 Rokha, Pablo de. Nueva antología de Pablo de Rokha. Edición de Naín Nó-

mez. Santiago: Sinfronteras, 1987. 189 p.

Promueve necesario conocimiento de obra de polémico poeta. Cuidadosamente editada por Naín Nómez, sugiere exuberancia de este exaltado precursor de la vanguardia en Chile. Selección es bastante completa e incluye textos de 1916 *Versos de infancia* hasta 1965 *Estilo de masas*. Hay, también, textos hasta ahora inéditos y dos textos póstumos. (ver item **4171**). [LE]

4173 Romero, Elvio. Despiertan las fogatas, 1950–1952. Con un poema de Nicolás Guillén. Ed. corr. y modificada. Asunción: Alcándara, 1986. 101 p. (Col. Poesía; 41)

Nueva edición de poemas del exilio, escritos entre 1950–52 que fuera corregida por el poeta paraguayo y entregadas desde esa circunstancia a la Editorial Alcándara, al celebrar esta respetable casa editorial cinco años de vida. Va precedida de un poema de Nicolás Guillén dedicado a Elvio Romero y José Asunción Flores. Es poesía social marcada por la nostalgia del pasado. Tiene dos partes: la primera consta de 29 poemas, la segunda de 11. [MGP]

4174 Romero, Elvio. Poesías completas. v. 1, Días roturados; Resoles áridos; Despiertan las fogatas; El sol bajo las raíces; De cara al corazón; Esta guitarra dura. v. 2, Un relámpago herido; Los innombrables; Destierro y atardecer; El viejo fuego; Los valles imaginarios; Libros de la migración; Inéditos. Asunción: Ediciones Alcándara, 1990. 2 v.: ill.

Importante la aparición de la obra poética completa en dos volúmenes de este gran poeta del Paraguay. Le preceden dos textos a manera de pórtico: una carta de Gabriela Mistral y un poema titulado "Elvio Romero/ Poeta Paraguayo" de Rafael Alberti. La poesía completa incluye los siguientes títulos: *Días roturados. Poemas de la Guerra Civil. Paraguay 1947: Resoles áridos* (1948–49): *De cara al corazón* (1955): *Esta guitarra dura* (1960) para el vol. 1. El vol. 2 se abre con una breve presentación de Miguel Angel Asturias, seguida de un poema titulado "Hacia el Paraguay Lejano" de Nicolás Guillén. Contiene este volumen los siguientes poemarios: *Un relámpago herido* (1963–66); *Los innombrables* (1959–73); *Destierro y atardecer* (1962–75); *El viejo fuego* (1977); *Los valles imaginarios* (1984); *Libro de la migración (Yby-Ñomimbyré)* (1958–64) y seis poemas inéditos. [MGP]

4175 Romero, Elvio. Resoles áridos, 1948–1949. Ed. corr., con um poema inédito. Asunción: Alcándara, 1987. 94 p.: 1 port. (Col. Poesía; 51)

Tercer poemario que apareció en el Paraguay por primera vez en los años 40 y que no tuvo reimpresión hasta la presente edición en 1987. Incluye correcciones y revisiones del autor, quien agrega además un texto inédito. Esta publicación celebra el regreso del poeta a su país después de casi 40 años de destierro. [MGP]

4176 Russotto, Margara. Viola d'amore: Caracas, 1981–1984. Caracas: Fundarte, 1986. 90 p. (Col. Cuadernos de difusión; 98)

Es tal vez Margara Russotto (n. 1946) una de las poetas venezolanas que ha sabido proyectar con mayor fuerza y firmeza su voz lírica. En sus libros anteriores, *Restos de viaje* (1979) y *Brasa* (1979), como en éste, hay un encuentro con lo vital que vigoriza el poema y le da a la palabra una resonancia de estallido, precisando en la metáfora, en la imagen, una visión de lucidez, de apertura. [AR]

4177 Sainz, Antonio José de. Poesías. Estudio sobre el autor y su obra de Eduardo Ocampo Moscoso. Cochabamba, Bolivia: Editorial Los Amigos del Libro, 1989. 263 p. (Col. Poesía; 850)

Poeta boliviano importante, aunque poco conocido, de la transición modernista-vanguardista. Su poesía se caracteriza por los rasgos de desencanto e incertidumbre que definen a la modernidad en la lírica hispánica. La relectura de este volumen, que reúne la obra completa del poeta (1894–1959), ofrece una información valiosa para estudiar no sólo el lenguaje poético de su autor sino también para volver al período vanguardista hispanoamericano desde la perspectiva de la modernidad. [ORR]

4178 Salazar Bondy, Sebastián. Todo esto es mi país. Con un recuerdo de Jaime García Terrés. México: Fondo de Cultura Económica, 1987. 221 p. (Col. Tierra firme)

Este volumen ofrece una visión contemporánea del Perú, particularmente de Lima, de uno de los poetas del siglo XX más importantes de ese país, aunque poco difundido internacionalmente. Reúne las ocho colecciones de poesía que ha publicado entre 1944–65, año en que falleció, más el volumen póstumo *Sombras como cosas sólidas*. [ORR]

4179 Sánchez Peláez, Juan. Aire sobre aire. Caracas: Tierra de Gracia Editores, 1989. 33 p. (Col. Rasgos comunes)

En la poesía latinoamericana la voz del poeta venezolano Juan Sánchez Peláez (n. 1922) se destaca por su singular maestría verbal y particular profundidad. Este libro, compuesto de 15 poemas, afirma categóricamente estas cualidades. En él las imágenes deslumbrantes que unen el sueño y la vigilia nos dan la realidad del poeta: habitante de un espacio donde la memoria desafía el tiempo y sus acechanzas. [AR]

4180 Sarduy, Severo. Un testigo fugaz y disfrazado: sonetos, décimas. Severo Sarduy. Barcelona: Edicions del Mall, 1985. 54 p. (Llibres del mall. Sèrie ibèrica; 16)

Colección de sonetos y décimas donde la metáfora enmarca el verdadero rostro de esta poesía: en Sarduy el deseo sexual inflamado—particularmente el que insinúa la relación homosexual—es el motivo de su aventura creadora. Mejores los sonetos que las décimas, donde se detecta a Quevedo y a otros escritores clásicos del eros. [RG]

Scarpa, Roque Esteban. Madurez de la luz. See item **390.**

4181 Siles, Juan Ignacio. Con las manos vacías de mariposas muertas. La Paz: Librería-Editorial Popular, 1987. 57 leaves: ill., plates.

Poesía de desencuentros, como resultado de una observación que descubre que la realidad se manifiesta con un orden ajeno a lo previsible. Su autor es un joven poeta boliviano (n. 1961), que apoya la producción de su discurso sobre la sorpresa, el desconcierto y el desencanto, y de algún modo rechaza lo tradicional. [ORR]

4182 Silva, Ludovico. Opera poética, 1958–1982. Caracas: Ediciones de la Presidencia de la República, 1988. 419 p.

Filósofo, crítico, poeta, el venezolano Ludovico Silva ha mantenido a lo largo de los años una incesante actividad intelectual. Su poesía, que recoge desde las formas cerradas del soneto clásico hasta la apertura del coloquialismo tremendista de las vanguardias de los 60, está impregnada de un continuo discurrir sobre la existencia y sus avatares. Este libro es una buena muestra de lo más relevante de ella. [AR]

4183 Silva Acevedo, Manuel. Desandar lo andado: poemas. Ottawa: Ediciones Cordillera, 1988. 120 p.: ill.

Volumen que ofrece lo mejor de uno de los buenos poetas chilenos de hoy. De 67 textos, 35 ya se incluían en *Palos de ciego* (1986). Aquí, esos textos muestran cambios en la organización estrófica, variantes tipográficas y un orden diferente. Así, se integran plenamente a esta colección. Libro revela varias e interesantes facetas de esta poesía. [LE]

4184 Silva Acevedo, Manuel. Palos de ciego. Concepción, Chile: Ediciones Literatura Americana Reunida, 1986. 61 p. (Serie del mirador. Portocaliú)

Poemas de amor cargados de un erotismo que estando siempre cerca de la muerte canta a los placeres de la carne y de la vida. Nuevo libro de un poeta muy valioso en contexto de poesía chilena. [LE]

4185 Sosa, Roberto. Secreto militar. Tegucigalpa: Editorial Guaymuras, 1985. 51 p. (Col. Salamandra)

Denuncia irónica y sarcástica de los responsables de la injusticia, en especial los dictadores legendarios de América Latina, desde Hernández Martínez hasta Ríos Montt. En "Secreto Militar" Sosa toma la célebre expresión de Rafael Heliodoro Valle ("La historia de Honduras se puede escribir en una lágrima") y la recrea: "La historia de Honduras se puede escribir en un fusil,/sobre un balazo, o mejor, dentro de una gota de sangre." [GY]

4186 Suárez, Jorge. Sinfonía del tiempo inmóvil, y otros poemas de amor. Santa Cruz, Bolivia: Editorial Casa de la Cultura, 1986. 60 p. (Serie Poesía)

Jorge Suárez (n. 1932) es un poeta de obra breve, pero de indiscutible calidad, como lo prueba este volumen de 24 textos. Trabajados con rigor, demuestran elaboración formal (métrica) y de contenido imaginativo inédito y personal. El aprecio de las formas clásicas se funde a la elaboración brillante de la imagen contemporánea, surgida de una percepción poética rica, varia y original. [ORR]

4187 Szinetar, Vasco. El libro del mal amado. Caracas: Editorial Mandorla, 1988. 41 p. (Col. Carmenes)

Con una voz casi susurrante, donde el silencio tiende a dejar su impronta en cada poema, la poesía de Vasco Szinetar (n. 1949) se destaca diferente dentro de su marco generacional venezolano. No hay en ella esos rasgos duros de escepticismo, rabia o ironía que prevalecieron junto al poema coloquial, directo. Más bien son poemas de alta emoción lírica donde el tema del amor y sus infortunios, tan difícil a veces, cae ligero, como golpe de plumas. Szinetar había publicado anteriormente *Esto que gira* (1980). [AR]

4188 Torres Santiago, José Manuel. Sobre casas de muertos va mi sombra. New York: J.M. Torres Santiago, 1988. 126 p. (Col. Ida y vuelta)

Quizás hasta este nuevo poemario la voz de Torres Santiago (n. 1940) se indentificó siempre con la poesía social y política que distingue la producción de los 60 en Puerto Rico. Aquí hay un evidente cambio de poética. Prevalece la nostalgia honda por el pasado, pero no por un pasado combativo; más bien el hablante es jalonado por recuerdos que devoran distancias y por la melancolía que emerge de la pérdida y la ausencia de lo que el tiempo va borrando -su antiguo barrio y la presencia de algunos seres queridos. Estos versos tienen ciertos ecos (Vallejo) y cierta iluminación que los hace perdurables. [RG]

4189 Urzagasti, Jesús. Yerubia. La Paz: Escuela de Artes Gráficas del Colegio Don Bosco, s.d. 20 p.

Volumen breve y de edición modesta, pero de excepcional calidad. Esta poesía muestra una elaboración ardua del lenguaje y de su distribución en versículos. Su visión, alerta y reflexiva de la realidad cotidiana y natural, descubre en lo ordinario percepciones inusitadas, sorprendentes y de alto valor poético. Su autor (n. 1941) se destaca en el panorama de la poesía boliviana e hispanoamericana. [ORR]

4190 Valera Mora, Víctor. Antología poética. Edición e introducción de Gabriel Jiménez Emán. Caracas: FUNDARTE, 1987. 119 p. (Col. Cuadernos de difusión; 102)

El poeta venezolano Víctor Valera Mora (1938–83) representa ese lado de la vanguardia poética de la década de los 60 en el que a una lucha existencial se agrega un enfrentamiento directo con la realidad social y política del país. Y esto se trasluce en su poesía "enguerrillada," como bien dice el escritor Gabriel Jiménez Emán en su acertada nota introductoria. [AR]

4191 Vallejo, César. Poemas en prosa; Poemas humanos; España, aparta de mí este cáliz. Edición e introducción de Julio Vélez. Madrid: Cátedra, 1988. 289 p.: bibl., ports. (Letras hispánicas; 278)

Aunque *Poemas en prosa* sigue la ordenación de las ediciones tradicionales, Vélez propone un nuevo orden para *Poemas humanos* de acuerdo a informaciones de la viuda del poeta y según relaciones temáticas. *España, aparta de mi este cáliz* sigue la edición de 1939 hecha en Barcelona. El volumen lleva como "Introducción" un ensayo interesante de Vélez sobre "La Dialéctica como Estrategia Poética." [ORR]

4192 Vallejo, César. Poemas humanos; España, aparta de mí este cáliz. Edición, introducción y notas de Francisco Martínez García. Madrid: Castalia, 1987. 269 p.: bibl., facsim., ill., index, plates, ports. (Clásicos Castalia; 159)

Esta edición se basa en los manuscritos reproducidos por Moncloa, de Lima, en la *Obra poética completa* de Vallejo. El estudio introductorio incluye un enfoque general de la obra del poeta en base a valoraciones individuales de cada uno de sus libros, aunque su interpretación final se apoya de un modo específico en *Trilce*. [ORR]

4193 Vallejo, César. Poesía completa. Edición crítica y estudio introductorio de Raúl Hernández Novás. La Habana: Editorial Arte y Literatura: Casa de las Américas, 1988. 404 p.: bibl., index. (Biblioteca de literatura universal)

Edición cuidadosa de lo que los editores consideran la poesía completa de Vallejo. La compilación ha sido producto de una labor crítica rigurosa realizada por el Centro de Investigaciones Literarias de la Casa de las Américas, Cuba. La edición está precedida por dos textos de Raúl Hernández Novás: un artículo preliminar que explica minuciosamente los fundamentos de la tarea realizada para la compilación y un ensayo extenso sobre la vida y la obra del poeta. [ORR]

4194 Vega, José Luis. Bajo los efectos de la poesía. Río Piedras, P.R.: Editorial de la Univ. de Puerto Rico/Editorial Cultural, 1989. 1 v.

Este poemario es celebración de la poesía. Una gran autoconciencia de su trabajo y una apasionante vocación por el arte son evidentes. Todo aquí encuentra un mayor mejor—sentido en la invención formal del poeta. Aun el tiempo y la historia se suspenden, desaparecen, se borran para siempre. Como una vez el amor, para este fino poeta puertorriqueño, el único recurso en la vida ahora es el arte. [RG]

4195 Vicuña, Pedro. Notas de viaje. Santiago: Ediciones Documentas, 1988. 33 p. (Documentas/literatura)

Uno de los poetas chilenos jóvenes más prometedores (n. 1956). Primer libro de Vicuña publicado en Chile. En poco más de una docena de poemas, sorprende por la capacidad transformadora de su lenguaje. Ofrece la realidad conocida envuelta en el misterio de lo imaginado. [LE]

4196 Villarreal, José Javier. Mar del norte. México: J. Mortiz, 1988. 80 p.

Texto ganador del Premio de Poesía Aguascalientes, 1987. Poesía solemne y prosaica que busca en los clásicos su ritmo y tono para decir los mares desérticos del norte. [NK]

4197 Volkow, Verónica. Los caminos. México: Ediciones Toledo, 1989. 53 p.

Diario de viaje, dedicado a la fotógrafa Graciela Iturbide que plasma el mundo a través de la imagen escrita. Dominio de la palabra en esta poesía depurada, directa, de ritmo hondo y cadencia sensual. Hablante reflexivo que se desplaza por los caminos laberínticos del espacio real y del yo interior para decirse, y decir el mundo. [NK]

4198 Westphalen, Emilio Adolfo. Belleza de una espada clavada en la lengua: poemas, 1930–1986. Lima: Ediciones Richkay, 1986. 1 v. (unpaged)

Este libro puede ser considerado como la obra completa de uno de los poetas más destacados del Perú contemporáneo (n. 1911). Incluye los textos publicados en seis colecciones, entre 1933–84, además de una inédita con los últimos poemas del autor, que en 1977 recibió el Premio Nacional de Cultura. [ORR]

4199 Wiethüchter, Blanca. En los negros labios encantados. Prólogo de Alba María Paz Soldán. Santa Cruz de la Sierra, Bolivia: Ediciones Altiplano, 1989. 55 p. (Col. Piedra libre)

Poesía íntima, sensual, de enunciados breves y de suspensos. El conjunto de los textos hacen un discurso que se elabora en la sugerencia y la interrupción. Se trata de una nueva voz femenina en la poesía boliviana. El volumen lleva un prólogo de Alba María Paz Soldán, que orienta certadamente sobre la lectura del volumen. [ORR]

4200 Zabaljáuregui, Horacio. Fondo blanco. Buenos Aires: Ediciones Ultimo Reino, 1989. 40 p.

Varios poemas de este conjunto resultan de alto nivel, con inspiración y dominio de la expresión lírica. Un poeta joven (n. 1955) que sobresale dentro de la promoción de "Ultimo Reino." [JG]

4201 Zamora, Daisy. En limpio se escribe la vida. Managua: Editorial Nueva Nicaragua, 1988. 125 p. (Letras de Nicaragua; 26)

Las primeras cuatro secciones consisten en diálogos, monólogos, retratos y testimonios de la mirada de mujeres con que se encuentra la poeta. Mujeres que sobreviven el ajetreo cotidiano o que están involucradas en la lucha. Destaca el lenguaje llano y conversacional que crea una atmósfera de intimidad. "Soltando estas Palabras" (sección V) consiste en un diálogo a voz única con los grandes poetas nicaragüenses. En la última sección se lanza una descarnada denuncia de Somoza y los EE.UU. y la celebración eufórica de la victoria sandinista. [GY]

4202 Zeller, Ludwig. Salvar la poesía, quemar las naves. Introducción de Alvaro Mutis. México: Fondo de Cultura Económica, 1988. 134 p.: ill. (Tierra firme)

Recoge textos de libros anteriores de este poeta, firme creyente en el surrealismo. Su surrealismo "no puede sino ser el de quien piensa que acaso seguimos viviendo en un desierto donde la vida es tan sólo la piel de un espejismo," apunta Alvaro Mutis en introducción. Otra prueba de la persistencia del ámbito surrealista en la poesía chilena. [LE]

GENERAL STUDIES

4203 Arancibia, Juana Alcira. Poesía telúrica del Noroeste argentino. Buenos Aires: Ayala Palacio Ediciones Universitarias, 1989. 206 p.: bibl.

Uno de los esfuerzos más completos por explicar lo telúrico y lo regional en literatura, especialmente en lírica. Después de un primer capítulo teórico bastante bien fundado en un amplio conocimiento de la tradición ensayística y narrativa argentina, se concentra en el estudio del grupo *La Carpa* y, por último, los tres poetas que la autora considera más representativos del Noroeste: Raúl Martín Galán, Manuel Castilla y Raúl Aráoz Anzoátegui. [JG]

4204 Arráiz Lucca, Rafael. Venezolanische poesie: un paseo para turistas. (*Insula*, 44:512/513, agosto/sept. 1989, p. 41–43)

Interesante y bien informado recuento de la actividad poética venezolana en lo que va de este siglo. Desde los poetas que heredaron y asimilaron la tradición modernista hasta los novísimos poetas de la década del 80, Arráiz, poeta él mismo, establece líneas, paralelismos, rupturas y tradiciones de una rica aunque no bien divulgada poesía. [AR]

4205 Beverly, John and Marc Zimmerman. Literature and politics in the Central American revolutions. Austin: Univ. of Texas Press, 1990. 1 v.

Sin lugar a dudas el estudio más ambicioso e importante de la literatura centroamericana desde los años 70 hasta el presente (con un repaso breve de la herencia dariana). Partiendo de una orientación más o menos postmoderna construida a partir de la postmarxificación—efectuada por los muy de moda Laclau y Mouffe—de la noción de lo "nacional-popular" gramsciana, los autores arguyen que la literatura—en especial la poesía y el testimonio—ha sido un agente importante en el proceso revolucionario en Nicaragua, El Salvador y Guatemala (¿implica esto que no se manifieste una voluntad revolucionaria poética en los otros países centroamericanos?), cuyos principales poetas de la hora son Ernesto Cardenal, Roque Dalton y Otto René Castillo. Casi en prensa cuando los sandinistas pierden en los comicios de feb. 1990, los autores son obligados por las circunstancias a mitigar su planteamiento, reconociendo que la literatura acaso ya no pueda considerarse el agente privilegiado del cambio social. [GY]

4206 Borgeson, Paul W., Jr. La Espiga Amotinada y la poesía mexicana. (*Rev. Iberoam.*, 55:148/149, julio/dic. 1989, p. 1177–1190)

Importante estudio de la trayectoria de este grupo (Bañuelos, Labastida, Oliva, Shelley, Zepeda), que con su libro de 1960, marcan una ruptura y un cambio en la historia de la poesía mexicana. Analiza la visión de conjunto y las biografías y poéticas individuales desde un enfoque dual—artístico y social—que, según el crítico, marca la obra de este grupo importante y poco estudiado hasta la fecha. [NK]

4207 Carrera Andrade, Jorge. Reflexiones sobre la poesía hispanoamericana. Quito: Casa de la Cultura Ecuatoriana Benjamín Carrión, 1987. 119 p.: bibl.

Incluye cinco ensayos sobre la poesía hispanoamericana, originalmente conferencias leídas en universidades del estado de New York en 1968. Constituyen una lectura e interpretación de esta poesía a partir de la perspectiva de uno de los principales poetas de la vanguardia hispánica. Los tres últimos ensayos se concentran en la poesía del siglo XX, particularmente en el vanguardismo. El volumen es un testimonio muy importante para el estudio de la poesía hispanoamericana contemporánea. [ORR]

4208 Dauster, Frank. Poetas mexicanos nacidos en las décadas de 1920, 1930 y 1940. (*Rev. Iberoam.*, 55:148/149, julio/dic. 1989, p. 1161–1175)

Orientador estudio general de los poetas mexicanos desde la generación de Bonifaz Nuño. La última sección esboza la producción de aquellos nacidos en los 40, promoción ya establecida y antologada, y todavía, como dice el crítico, difícil de caracterizar. [NK]

En breve: minimalism in Mexican poetry, 1900–1985. See item **4917.**

4209 Gatica, Héctor David. Mapa de la poesía riojana: y trayectoria cultural. Buenos Aires: Editorial Cisandina, 1989. 300 p.: bibl.

Lo excesivo del material que contiene este "mapa" queda compensado por el valor referencial que ello implica. Son 17 capítulos que dan cuenta de numerosas etapas históricas, grupos, escuelas, revistas que se han sucedido en la provincia argentina de La Rioja. [JG]

4210 La generación del 50 en la literatura peruana del siglo XX. v. 1, pt. 1. Lima:

Univ. Nacional de Educación Enrique Guzmán y Valle, Facultad de Humanidades y Artes, Depto. Académico de Literatura, 1989. 1 v.: bibl., ill. (some col.);

Vol. 1, dedicado a la poesía, de un proyecto de estudio y revisión de esta generación que renovó en su tiempo la literatura peruana. Contiene trabajos críticos de carácter general, testimonios orales de escritores, e iconografía. [J.M. Oviedo]

4211 González, Rubén. Crónica de tres décadas: poesía puertorriqueña actual, de los sesenta a los ochenta. Río Piedras, P.R.: Editorial de la Univ. de Puerto Rico, 1989. 230 p.: bibl.

El libro cumple con creces el sugestivo anuncio de su título. De especial importancia para el cabal conocimiento del proceso es el examen de los programas poético-ideológicos difundidos en diversas revistas de los 60 y el análisis del diálogo que los poetas del 70 entablan con su tradición. La excelente y cuidadosa antología de los 13 autores estudiados corrobora muy bien los puntos de vista sustentados en este volumen de consulta indispensable. [PL]

Higgins, James. Orígenes coloniales de la poesía peruana. See item **3321.**

4212 *Inti: Revista de Literatura Hispánica.* Nos. 26–27, otoño 1987-primavera 1988– . Providence, R.I.: Dept. of Modern Languages, Providence College.

Número dedicado por entero a la poesía, publica los diálogos de M.A. Zapata con 26 poetas hispanoamericanos. Cada caso incluye una muestra poética de la que también es responsable el editor. Los autores entrevistados son Carlos Germán Belli, Antonio Cisneros, J.G. Cobo Borda, Belkis Cuza Malé, Roberto Echavarren, Jorge Eduardo Eielson, Eduardo Espina, Rosario Ferré, Oscar Hahn, Rodolfo Hinostroza, Mercedes Ibáñez Rosazza, José Kozer, Pedro Lastra, Hernán Lavín Cerda, Juan Liscano, Liliana Lukin, Eduardo Milán, Alvaro Mutis, Heberto Padilla, Néstor Perlongher, Luis Rebaza Soraluz, Gonzalo Rojas, Armando Romero, Javier Sologuren, Ida Vitale y Saúl Yurkievich. [PL]

4213 Kirkpatrick, Gwen. The dissonant legacy of modernismo: Lugones, Herrera y Reissig, and the voices of modern Spanish American poetry. Berkeley: Univ. of California Press, 1989. 294 p.: bibl., index. (Latin American literature and culture)

Excelente y muy bien documentado estudio de dos personalidades poéticas del modernismo, cuyas obras se caracterizan por la subversión del canon. De especial interés son los apartados sobre la parodia y la ironía en el primer Lugones, y el entero capítulo dedicado a la dimensión transgresora de la poesía de Herrera y Reissig. La parte final de este importante libro puntualiza la significación del modernismo en la poesía del siglo XX y en particular en el trabajo de C. Vallejo, R. López Velarde y A. Storni. [PL]

4214 Kubayanda, Josaphat Bekunuru. The poet's Africa: Africanness in the poetry of Nicolás Guillén and Aimé Césaire. New York: Greenwood Press, 1990. 176 p.: (Contributions in Afro-American and African studies, 0069–9624; 138)

Detallado y rico trabajo sobre Guillén y Césaire, a quienes el crítico considera los dos poetas caribeños más importantes del siglo XX. Este estudio comparado afirma el concepto de negritud como un principio unificador de esta poesía. El trabajo tiende a ser algo emocional cuando, menos convincentemente, se considera la poesía de Palés Matos y otros poetas caribeños que han escrito poesía negrista o antillana. [RG]

4215 Lukin, B.V. Istoki narodnopoeticheskoi kul'tury Kuby:krest'ianskie improvizatory = Orígenes de la cultura poética popular en Cuba: repentistas guajiros. 273 p.: bibl., ill. music, plates.

Scholarly study of Cuban popular (and folk) poetry. Includes 152-item bibliography, several scores of ballads based on folk poems, and numerous illustrations of relevant individuals. [R.V. Allen]

4216 Marini Palmieri, Enrique. El modernismo literario hispanoamericano: caracteres esotéricos en las obras de Darío y Lugones. Prólogo de Graciela Maturo. Buenos Aires: F. García Cambeiro, 1989. 141 p.: bibl. (Col. Estudios latinomericanos; 34)

"Alquimia y hermetismo del verbo en su intencionalidad a la vez mágica, esotérica, ocultista y espiritual" forman parte inseparable del modernismo, dice Marini-Palmieri en el prefacio. La premisa no es nueva, pero sí lo es la eficacia de las verificaciones, realizadas con verdadera solvencia bibliográfica. [PL]

Las páginas que demuestran la erudición teosófica de Lugones y las que prueban la presencia de "Lycosthenes" en un cuento de Darío son ejemplos notables, entre otros, de las sorpresas que procura esta meritoria investigación. [PL]

4217 Müller-Bergh, Klaus. De Agú y anarquía a la Mandrágora: notas para la génesis, la evolución y el apogeo de la vanguardia en Chile. (*Rev. Chil. Lit.*, 31, abril 1988, p. 33–61, bibl.)

Estudio interesante que traza el desarrollo de la vanguardia chilena desde los balbuceos dadaístas de "Agú" (1920) hasta la fundación del núcleo surrealista Mandrágora (1938). Detalla revistas y documentos de la época y da cuenta del hervidero de tendencias vanguardistas. [LE]

Orígenes: revista de arte y literatura. v. 1–7. See item **3674.**

4218 Pailler, Claire. Mitos primordiales y poesía fundadora en América Central. Paris: Editions du Centre national de la recherche scientifique: Diffusion, Presses du CNRS, 1989. 183 p.: bibl., ill. (Amérique latine—pays ibériques)

Investigación de: 1) la poesía en su relación con la formación nacional y el uso del mito y la referencia al héroe (i.e., Sandino); 2) el elemento femenino en la poesía de los talleres populares; 3) el recurso a lo elemental en las poetas nicaragüenses de los 80; y 4) la multiplicidad de temas y recursos estilísticos en la poesía de Roque Dalton. Los comentarios—interesantes y valiosos—son, no obstante, más bien descriptivos que críticos, corroborando así la ideología poética de los poetas comentados. [GY]

4219 Perricone, Catherine R. A bibliographic approach to the study of Latin American women poets. (*Hispania/Teachers*, 71:2, May 1988, p. 262–287, bibl.)

Valiosa y muy completa bibliografía para el estudio de poetas latinoamericanas. Dividida en ocho secciones: 1) Obras de Referencia General; 2) Antologías; 3) Crítica Feminista; 4) Estudios Generales: Libros; 5) Estudios Generales: Artículos y Ensayos; 6) Antecedentes Históricos y Sociológicos; 7) Fuentes Primarias y Secundarias para 15 Poetas; y 8) Publicaciones Periódicas. [AR]

4220 Phillips, Allen W. Cuatro poetas hispanoamericanos entre el modernismo y la vanguardia. (*Rev. Iberoam.*, 55:146/147, enero/junio 1989, p. 427–449)

Excelente estudio de la poesía de Lugones, Herrera y Reissig, R. López Velarde y J.J. Tablada como manifestación de continuidad de las estéticas del modernismo y del vanguardismo, en aspectos esenciales de sus obras. Páginas de consulta indispensable, tan atractivas como informadas. [PL]

4221 La poesía chilena actual: 1960–1984, y la crítica. Edición de Ricardo Yamal. Concepción, Chile: Ediciones Literatura Americana Reunida, 1988. 343 p.: bibl. (Col. Estudios, tesis y monografías)

Recolección de ensayos que intenta proponer y definir un momento de la poesía chilena (1960–84). No logra su loable objetivo por la heterogeneidad de los ensayos y su dispar calidad. Hay buenos estudios aislados sobre Hahn, Zurita, Juan Luis Martínez, que desbordan la intención antológica del volumen. [LE]

4222 Poesía dominicana: desde sus inicios hasta la muerte del último tirano. Compilación de Abel Fernández Mejía. Santo Domingo: Editorial Tiempo, 1987. 115 p.

Sucinta introducción al estudio de la poesía dominicana. El crítico suele ilustrar sus hipótesis con ejemplos de la poesía. Además, se acomodan fichas de lectura (bibliográficas) de obras críticas y de teoría poética con algunos extractos de las mismas para reforzar sus razonamientos. [RG]

4223 Les poètes latino-américains et la guerre d'Espagne. Edition de Claude Fell. Paris: CRICCAL, Service des publications, Univ. de la Sorbonne nouvelle Paris III, 1986. 218 p.: bibl., ports.

Importante publicación de documentos y trabajos sobre el tema, dispuesta y prologada por Claude Fell. Entre los aciertos del editor debe anotarse la recopilación de textos que constituye la primera parte (p. 25–59): poemas inéditos de M.A. Asturias y algunos artículos de la época, infrecuentemente citados, de P. Neruda, C. Vallejo y otros escritores. En la segunda parte se recogen los siguientes ensayos críticos: A. Melon, "Guillén, Neruda, Vallejo: Trois Voix pour un Même Message?;" J. Lamore, "Cohérence Thématique de *España: poema en cuatro angustias y una esperanza*, de Nicolás Guillén;" N. Ly, "Engagement et Poétique: quel-

ques Remarques sur le Discours Poétique de Nicolás Guillén, Pablo Neruda et César Vallejo;" C. Cymerman, "L'Univers Antinomique d'*España en el corazón;*" M.C. Zimmermann, "Images et Mètres dans *España en el corazón;* C. Vásquez, "Voluntad de Canto: Pablo Neruda y Tres Poetas de la Resistencia Francesa;" S. Salaün, "César Vallejo: Poète Marxiste et Marxiste Poète;" S. Yurkievich, "*España, aparta de mí este cáliz:* la Palabra Partcipante;" A. Sicard, "Pensamiento y Poesía en *Poemas humanos* de César Vallejo: la Dialéctica como Método;" C. Esteban, "Quelques Remarques sur la Poétique de César Vallejo." [PL]

4224 Publicaciones y opiniones de *La Poesía Sorprendida.* San Pedro de Macorís, República Dominicana: Univ. Central del Este, 1988. 576 p.: ill. (Serie literaria; 15. Univ. Central del Este; 70)

Reimpresión facsímil de la revista *La Poesía Sorprendida* (1943–47); publicación que reunió a algunos escritores importantes que han pasado a la historia de la literatura latinoamericana como "los poetas sorprendidos." Este volumen recoge ensayos de cuatro de los integrantes del grupo que buscan explicar la constitución y estética de esta aventura poética dominicana. [RG]

4225 Rivera-Rodas, Oscar. El discurso modernista y la dialéctica del erotismo y la castidad. (*Rev. Iberoam.*, 55:146/147, enero/junio 1989, p. 43–62)

Describe la subversión del discurso erótico del romanticismo realizada por los modernistas. Una cuidadosa lectura semiótica del poema "Voz Extraña . . . " de Ricardo Jaimes Freyre comprueba eficazmente las observaciones iniciales. [PL]

Rodríguez-Alcalá, Hugo. Poetas y prosistas paraguayos, y otros breves ensayos. See item **3968.**

4226 Romero, Armando. El Nadaísmo colombiano o La búsqueda de una vanguardia perdida. Bogotá: Tercer Mundo Editores, 1988. 323 p.: bibl. (Crítica literaria)

Interesante y bien documentada historia de este movimiento poético, que se lee al mismo tiempo como testimonio de parte, pues el autor fue uno de los integrantes del polémico grupo de los años 60. A la descripción del origen y desarrollo del nadaísmo, hasta su receso en 1972 (p. 11–87) sigue una generosa antología de Gonzalo Arango, Jaime Jaramillo Escobar, Jotamario, Eduardo Escobar, Amílcar Osorio, Darío Lemos, Elmo Valencia, Alberto Escobar, Humberto Navarro, Jan Arb, Eduardo Zalamea y Armando Romero (p. 89–319). [PL]

4227 Rosario Candelier, Bruno. La creación mitopoética: símbolos y arquetipos en la lírica dominicana. Santiago, Dominican Republic: Pontificia Univ. Católica Madre y Maestra, 1989. 252 p.: bibl. (Col. Estudios; 130)

Imaginativo y documentado ensayo crítico sobre la recreación del mito en la poesía dominicana. Para el autor, la poesía que le da prioridad al mito es la más honda y la más expresiva. Se estudia el *uso vivencial* del mito en obras de Manuel del Cabral, Mieses Burgos y de algún integrante del grupo "La Poesía Sorprendida," como Manuel Rueda, entre otros poetas dominicanos. [RG]

4228 Sabourín, Jesús. Vanguardismo y poesía negrista en Cuba. (*Santiago*, 67, dic. 1987, p. 143–153)

Se propone explicar la poesía negrista como una conjunción de vanguardismo y otros rasgos específicos—y exclusivos, se implica—cubanos, como raza, tradiciones, humor, ritmo. El negrismo—propone el crítico—es más que una modalidad literaria; es una búsqueda de identidad del negro. La suma: Guillén. [RG]

4229 Schopf, Federico. Del vanguardismo a la antipoesía. Roma: Bulzoni, 1986. 284 p.: bibl. (Letterature iberiche e latino-americane)

Convincente estudio sobre vanguardismo en Chile e Hispanoamérica. Ofreciendo relecturas de textos poéticos inteligentemente seleccionados, y apoyado en textos teóricos de incuestionable pertinencia, Schopf desarrolla lúcido análisis de este transformador momento de la vida literaria. Destaca la sección "Antipoesía y Vanguardismo" que propone novedosas relaciones entre la antipoesía y sus probables fuentes literarias y culturales. Necesario para todo estudio sobre la vanguardia en Hispanoamérica. [LE]

SPECIAL STUDIES

4230 Agosin, Marjorie and **Inés Dölz-Blackburn.** Violeta Parra, santa de pura greda: un estudio de su obra poetica. Santiago: Editorial Planeta Chilena S.A., 1988. 190 p.: bibl., index.

Estudiar la obra de Violeta Parra como producción poética es lo que se proponen las autoras de este logrado trabajo crítico, nada hagiográfico, como podría sugerir su título. Por el contrario: se trata de una investigación rigurosa y de gran interés, que conjuga los valores de un oportuno despliegue informativo (tanto biográfico como histórico-cultural) con la claridad expositiva. El libro invita, de manera muy convincente, a leer a Violeta Parra como una personalidad de primer orden en la poesía chilena e hispanoamericana. [PL]

Alcántara Almánzar, José. Los escritores dominicanos y la cultura. See item **3627.**

Armas, Emilio de. Juan Marinello: crítico de la poesía martiana. See item **1868.**

4231 Arrigoitia, Luis de. Pensamiento y forma en la prosa de Gabriela Mistral. Río Piedras, P.R.: Editorial de la Univ. de Puerto Rico, 1989. 408 p.: bibl.

Libro excelente aparecido en centenario del nacimiento de Mistral. Revisión histórico-crítica de obra en prosa estructurada alrededor de: el poema en prosa (1914–24), el periodismo (1924–34), el "recado" (1935–54). Bibliografía muy completa y elaborada con esmero, de y sobre la Mistral. Indispensable a los estudios sobre el área. [LE]

4232 Asedios a Oscar Hahn. Edición de Pedro Lastra y Enrique Lihn. Santiago: Editorial Universitaria, 1989. 149 p.: bibl. (Col. El Saber y la cultura)

Bien meditada primera recolección de estudios sobre Hahn. Toma nota de material crítico a partir de *Arte de morir* (1977). Incluye algunos de los mejores estudios ya aparecidos y textos hasta ahora inéditos. Ya publicados, destacan artículos de Rosado, Hill, Waldo Rojas, O'Hara, Lihn. Publicados por primera vez, destacan los de Ina Cumpiano, Christine Legault, Adriana Valdés. "Notas" revelan amplitud y diversidad de obra de Hahn y diversidad de lecturas suscitadas. Son de Belli, O'Hara, Carmen Foxley, Beach-Viti, Legault, Jorge Guzmán, Lastra, Lihn. "Bibliografía de Oscar Hahn" es de Pedro Lastra. Fundamental para estudios sobre Hahn y sobre poesía chilena. [LE]

4233 Carballo, Emmanuel. Visiones y versiones: López Velarde y sus críticos, 1914–1987. México: INBA, 1989. 489 p.

Recopilación de ensayos sobre la obra del célebre poeta jerezano. Recoge desde la primera nota crítica que le dedica José Juan Tablada en 1914, hasta un ensayo por Marco Antonio Campos (1987). Casi todas las contribuciones han sido escritas por poetas o críticos mexicanos con la excepción de dos: Henríquez Ureña y Neruda. [NK]

4234 Chiles, Frances. Octavio Paz, the mythic dimension. New York: P. Lang, 1987. 224 p.: bibl. (American univ. studies. Series II, Romance languages and literature, 0740–9257; 6)

Estudio que examina la función del mito y su elaboración en la poesía y poética de Paz. [NK]

4235 Coloquio Internacional sobre César Vallejo, Grenoble, France, 1988. Caminando con César Vallejo: actas. Edición de Bruno Buendía Sialer. Lima: Editorial Perla-Perú, 1988. 306 p.: bibl., ill.

Actas del coloquio incluye 18 trabajos que en su mayoría se ocupan de la poesía de Vallejo. Entre los autores participantes figuran André Coyné, Washington Delgado, Américo Ferrari, James Higgins, Roberto Paoli y Alain Sicard. [ORR]

4236 Concha, Jaime. Gabriela Mistral. Madrid: Júcar, 1987. 237 p.: facsims., ill., ports. (Los Poetas; 68)

Selección antológica aparecida poco antes del centenario del nacimiento de Mistral (1889), primer Premio Nobel concedido a un escritor latinoamericano (1945). Precedida por introducción bibliográfica y estudios de *Desolación, Ternura, Tala, Lagar,* y *Poema de Chile* (póstumo, 1987). Destaca lo que se dice sobre *Tala* y *Poema de Chile.* [LE]

4237 Conil Paz, Alberto A. Leopoldo Lugones. Buenos Aires: Librería Huemul, 1985. 520 p.: bibl., ill., plates.

Conmovedor estudio de la vida intelectual, política y personal de Lugones. Especialmente logrados son los capítulos sobre la "transformación ideológica" en los años 20. Muy instructiva y convincente. [JG]

4238 Cristina Peri Rossi. Edición de Uberto Stabile. Valencia, Spain: Quervo, 1984. 71 p.: bibl., ill. (Quervo poesía; 7)

No. 7 de esta serie monográfica está dedicado a la obra de Cristina Peri Rossi. Contiene los siguientes trabajos: Uberto Sta-

bile, "La Esencia Ainvolucrada: Aproximación a Cristina Peri Rossi;" Ana Basualdo, "Clarividencia de Paisaje Gris," sobre tres libros de poemas y "Fragmentos de una Entrevista;" Helena Araujo, "'La Anunciación,' de Cristina Peri Rossi;" Luis Martul Tobío, "(In) conclusiones sobre la Obra de Cristina Peri Rossi;" y Hugo Verani, "La Rebelión del Cuerpo y del Lenguaje." Contiene también una selección de poemas de *Lingüística general, Diáspora, Correspondencia con Ana María Moix, Descripción de un naufragio* y de *Europa después de la lluvia.* [MGP]

4239 Edwards, Jorge. Retrato de un poeta. (*Vuelta,* 12:145, dic. 1988, p. 58–60, photo)

Evocadora semblanza de Lihn, cuya "poesía fue algo así como un diario de vida poético, poesía de paso por esta época y que pasaba por los extremos de la alegría, la reflexión, la exaltación lírica, la alabanza y la acusación, el fragmento, el discurso, el epigrama, el arte poética." Incluye poema de Pedro Lastra y otro de Lihn que remiten al asombroso ámbito de las correspondencias. [LE]

4240 Eipper, John E. Nuptial material: a model for translating Neruda's *Residence on earth.* (*Lat. Am. Lit. Rev.,* 17:34, July/Dec. 1989, p. 62–82, appendix)

Interesante estudio que, al proponer un "functional model for the English translation of the *Residence,*" revela aspectos importantes del sistema poético de Neruda. Adopta camino intermedio entre dos escuelas de traductores de Neruda: la "liberalist" de Ben Belitt, y la "literalist" de Donald Walsh. [LE]

4241 García Maffla, Jaime. Fernando Charry Lara. Bogotá: Procultura, 1989. 137 p.: bibl., ill. (Clásicos colombianos; 9)

Este volumen es un compendio esencial del poeta colombiano: aparte de la biografía y presentación crítica de su obra realizadas por el antólogo, incluye una antología, selección de textos sobre el autor, bibliografía activa y pasiva, y una cronología. Fuente de consulta muy útil para los interesados en Charry Lara. [J.M. Oviedo]

4242 González, Aníbal. La (sín)tesis de una poesía antillana: Palés y Spengler. (*Cuad. Hispanoam.,* 451/452, enero/feb. 1988, p. 59–72)

Inteligente artículo que discute cómo Palés Matos utiliza las teorías de Spengler sobre la cultura en su poemario *Tuntún* y en la glosa teórica sobre la cultura antillana (y el concepto de transculturación) que Palés elaborara. Es un trabajo completo y de interés. [RG]

4243 González, Reynaldo. Lezama Lima: el ingenuo culpable. La Habana: Editorial Letras Cubanas, 1988. 164 p.: ill., plates.

Libro atractivo que combina la crítica literaria y el documento testimonial en un intento de descifrar la prodigiosa inteligencia poética del escritor cubano. El texto incluye una entrevista de González a Lezama y un par de cartas—hasta entonces inéditas—del escritor a su amigo. [RG]

Gutiérrez Revuelta, Pedro. Lista de tesis doctorales presentadas en las universidades de los Estados Unidos en los últimos diez años, 1974/1984. See *HLAS 51:37*.

4244 Heraud Pérez, Cecilia. Vida y muerte de Javier Heraud: recuerdos, testimonios y documentos. Lima: Mosca Azul Editores, 1989. 237 p.: ill.

Es ciertamente el primer intento biográfico sobre el poeta guerrillero, escrito por su hermana y sobre documentación de primera mano. El relato biográfico se desarrolla tanto a través del dato documental como sobre las percepciones que la autora obtiene en su lectura de la obra literaria de su hermano. Volumen imprescindible para el estudio del poeta. [ORR]

4245 Hirshbein, Cesia Ziona. Las eras imaginarias de Lezama Lima. Caracas: Academia Nacional de la Historia, 1984. 157 p.: bibl., ill. (Biblioteca de la Academia Nacional de la Historia. Estudios, monografías y ensayos; 56)

Ensayo crítico que busca explicar las eras (espacios) imaginarias de Lezama Lima, considerando el mito y la historia (lo universal) como fuentes poéticas y filosóficas y su final resolución en una expresión americana. Es un estudio claro y abarcador que considera tanto al hombre como su poesía y narrativa. [RG]

4246 *Ibero-Amerikanisches Archiv.* Vol. 15, No. 1, 1989– . Taller Literario con Gonzalo Rojas. Berlin: Ibero-Amerikanisches Institut.

Vol. 15, No. 1 de la revista consiste de un excelente volumen que ofrece estudios importantes sobre la poesía de Gonzalo Rojas. Colaboran: Michael Nerlich, "Simetría del Agua: Encuentro con Gonzalo Rojas;" Gonzalo Rojas, "De donde Viene uno" (también prólogo a *Materia de testamento*); Ted Lyon, "Presentación de la Generación Chilena del 38: una Perspectiva de Cincuenta Años;" I. Howard Quackenbush, "La Autoconciencia Literaria en la Poesía de Gonzalo Rojas;" Estrella Bustos Ogden, "Del Espíritu de la Posmodernidad en la Poesía de Gonzalo Rojas;" Dieter Janik, "'Epitafio' y Epitafios en la Obra de Gonzalo Rojas;" Nelson Rojas, "Física y Metafísica en Gonzalo Rojas: 'La Viruta';" Juan Loveluck, "El Espacio como 'Abismo' en la Poesía de Gonzalo Rojas;" Marcelo Coddou, "Los Poemas Redivivos de Gonzalo Rojas y su Relacion con Paul Celan;" Russell M. Cluff, "Crónica de una Convivencia: Selección y Traducción de *Esquizotexto y otros poemas* de Gonzalo Rojas." Diversidad de perspectivas y lecturas revela riqueza de este universo poético. [LE]

4247 Jácome, Gustavo Alfredo. Estudios estilísticos en la poesía de César Vallejo. Quito: Editorial Casa de la Cultura Ecuatoriana, 1988. 193 p.: bibl.

Descripción de rasgos estilísticos del lenguaje poético de Vallejo. En una nota previa, el autor advierte que guiará su estudio por tres conceptos: la cotidianidad de la lengua, las rupturas del sistema y la disimilitud antitética. El libro concluye con capítulos biográficos sobre el poeta. [ORR]

4248 Kinsella, John. Lo trágico y su consuelo: estudio de la obra de Martín Adán. Lima: Mosca Azul Editores, 1989. 212 p.: ill.

Integrado por cuatro capítulos ("Introducción," "La Visión Trágica de la Vida," "La Búsqueda de la Trascendencia" y "La Evolución de la Obra de Adán"), este estudio abarca una obra poética de 50 años, mostrando su evolución y temas principales desde sus orígenes en las corrientes vanguardistas hasta las manifestaciones más contemporáneas del lenguaje poético de un destacado autor peruano. [ORR]

4249 Laforgue, Jules. Homenaje a Jules Laforgue. Montevideo: Ministerio de Educación y Cultura, 1987. 232 p.: bibl., ill. (some col.)

Elegante volumen dedicado al poeta franco-uruguayo con motivo de la visita del Presidente François Mitterrand al Uruguay. Contiene una biografía ilustrada con fotocopias de manuscritos del autor; un artículo de Lisa Block de Behar, "Jules Laforgue o las Metáforas del Desplazamiento;" el texto "Hamlet o las Consecuencias de la Piedad Filial;" una selección de poemas en francés y en español; selección de la correspondencia de Laforgue con Charles Ephrussi, Charles Henry y la Sra. de Mullezer; unas breves páginas sobre crítica del escritor. El volumen está ilustrado por artistas uruguayos. [MGP]

4250 Lastra, Pedro. Conversaciones con Enrique Lihn. 2a ed. Santiago: Atelier Ediciones, 1990. 194 p.: bibl., ill.

Reproduce—corregida—la edición aparecida en Xalapa (ver *HLAS 44:5494*). Agrega capítulo "Contrapunto de Sobrelibro" y actualiza bibliografía activa de Enrique Lihn. Indispensable para estudios sobre estos dos poetas (Lastra/Lihn) y para estudios sobre poesía chilena o hispanoamericana. [LE]

Lezama Lima, José. Confluencias: selección de ensayos. See item **3661.**

4251 Mansour, Mónica. Efraín Huerta: absoluto amor. Guanajuato, Mexico: Gobierno del Estado de Guanajuato, 1984. 228 p.: bibl., ill. (some col.)

Bello libro para el estudioso de Huerta que reproduce memorabilia de los archivos del poeta: originales, correspondencia, documentos, fotografías y otras obras gráficas que nos presenta la imagen del hombre público y del hombre privado. [NK]

4252 Matos Moquete, Manuel. Poética política en la poesía de Pedro Mir. (*Rev. Iberoam.*, 54:142, enero/marzo 1988, p. 199–211)

Pedro Mir, celebrado poeta dominicano, reconocido como poeta nacional, afinca sus temas en lo colectivo (social) y lo histórico. Su poesía, declara el crítico, además de frecuentar lo político, tiene valor de profecía. Apropiadas comparaciones con Whitman y Neruda. No es muy claro cuando, entre otras cosas, quiere ver la poesía de Mir como metapoesía. [RG]

4253 Minard, Evelyne. La poesía de Humberto Díaz-Casanueva. Prólogo de Saúl Yurkievich. Traducción de Alejandro Reyes.

Santiago: Editorial Universitaria, 1988. 216 p.: bibl., ill., plates. (Col. El Saber y la cultura)

Prolijo estudio basado en investigaciones estructuralistas y psicoanalíticas aplicadas a esta poesía. Pese a siete "tablas" que pretenden retener "sólo lo esencial" de los cinco capítulos del libro, la profusión de detalles oscurece el sentido de los ánalisis. Consciente del problema, la autora advierte sobre la dificultad del lector "para discernir en mis afirmaciones lo esencial de lo accesorio." [LE]

Ortega, Julio. Sobre el discurso político de Octavio Paz. See item **5340.**

4254 Pablo Neruda. Edited and with an introduction by Harold Bloom. New York: Chelsea House, 1989. 345 p.: bibl., ill., index. (Modern critical views)

Primera recolección de estudios sobre Neruda en inglés. Reconocido prestigio del editor, Harold Bloom, realza importancia del volumen. Sitúa la obra de Neruda en el contexto de la crítica universal en lengua otra que el español. Se inicia con presentación hecha por Federico García Lorca en Madrid (1935) y se cierra con estudio de Frank Menchaca, publicado aquí por primera vez. Otros estudios son de: Walter Holzinger; Frank Riess; Fernando Alegría; Amado Alonso; J. Coleman; Julio Cortázar; Rodríguez Monegal; Gordon Brotherston; J. Alazraki; B. Belitt; R. de Costa; Manuel Durán; J. Felstiner; Robin Warner; Enrico Mario Santí; Florence Yudin, A. Mac Adam. Herramienta indispensable para los estudios nerudianos. [LE]

4255 Pascoe, Muriel Slade. La poesía de Alberto Girri. Buenos Aires: Editorial Sudamericana, 1986. 290 p.

Muy completa y competente descripción de la poesía de Girri, tanto en sus aspectos formales como pragmáticos. Se estructura sobre tres fases: 1) "Denuncia y Testimonio (1946–55);" 2) "Soluciones (1956–63);" y 3) "Lucidez (1964–85)." [JG]

4256 Paz, Octavio and **Anthony Stanton.** Genealogía de un libro: *Libertad bajo palabra.* (*Vuelta*, 12:144, nov. 1988, p. 15–21)

Se discuten los antecedentes, los procesos de composición, y las lecturas influyentes; se aclaran datos importantes; se analizan poemas y poéticas en esta excelente y valiosa conversación en la que Paz traza detenidamente la historia de *Libertad bajo palabra.* [NK]

4257 Pedrazzoli, Julio C. Aproximaciones a la poesía de Juan L. Ortiz. Paraná, Argentina: Editorial de Entre Ríos, 1987. 111 p.: bibl., ill.

Este libro se autoconcibe como un homenaje y, a la vez, como introducción panorámica a la lectura de Juan Laurentino Ortiz (1895–1978), uno de los poetas más mitificados de la provincia argentina de Entre Ríos. El crítico consigue transmitir su pasión por la poesía y la persona del autor, y a través de abundante material y numerosas citas logra hacer comprensible la admiración que su personalidad lírica todavía ejerce sobre tantos lectores. [JG]

4258 Phillips, Allen W. Retorno a Ramón López Velarde. México: INBA y Univ. Autónoma de Zacatecas, 1989. 1 v.

Texto en conmemoración del centenario del iniciador de la poesía moderna en México. Phillips compila sus artículos aparecidos después de la publicación de su libro *Ramón López Velarde: el poeta y el prosista* en 1962 (ver *HLAS 26:1816*). Importante libro de este crítico, especialista de la obra del poeta zacatecano. [NK]

Rensoli Laliga, Lourdes. La cultura del poeta: la filosofía en el *Diario de José Lezama Lima.* See item **3683.**

4259 Romero, Roberto A. Emiliano R. Fernández: mito y realidad. Asunción: M. Kallsen, 1988. 129 p.: facsims., port.

Este libro reivindica la figura del poeta soldado Emiliano R. Fernández y su obra que fuera escrita durante la Guerra del Chaco. Esa guerra produjo una revaloración del guaraní como expresión de la nación paraguaya y estas composiciones son un reflejo de esa actitud. En este estudio se incluyen numerosos textos en guaraní con algunas traducciones al español. Un apéndice final contiene documentación sobre Ramírez. [MGP]

4260 Santana, Joaquín G. El joven Guillén. La Habana: Editora Abril, 1987. 93 p.: ill.

Amena y apologética biografía. No se ilumina ningún aspecto nuevo de la vida o de la obra de Guillén pero el trabajo podría incitar al menos informado. [RG]

4261 Santí, Enrico Mario. *Conversar es humano:* entrevista con Octavio Paz. (*Torre*, 3:9, enero/marzo 1989, p. 105–121)

Meritoria entrevista de este crítico cuyo conocimiento de la vida y obra de Paz sirvieron para estimular un diálogo animado y esclarecedor. Paz conversa sobre *El laberinto de la soledad, Posdata, El ogro filantrópico, El arco y la lira, El mono gramático,* la poesía moderna, la soledad, la cultura hispánica en EE.UU., etc. [NK]

4262 Scarano, Tommaso. Varianti a stampa nella poesia del primo Borges. Pisa, Italy: Giardini, 1987. 164 p.: bibl. (Collana di testi e studi ispanici. II, Saggi; 6)

Hay aquí abundante información y estudio potencialmente muy útil: el crítico estudia las variantes en textos poéticos fundamentales de Borges, y trata de extraer algunas conclusiones de ellas. La introducción ofrece una fundamentación minuciosa del trabajo, y va seguida de un reportorio de variantes en *Fervor de Buenos Aires, Luna de enfrente* y *Cuaderno San Martín.* Importante como libro de consulta. [JG]

4263 Sheridan, Guillermo. Un corazón adicto: la vida de Ramón López Velarde. Investigación iconográfica de Xavier Guzmán Urbiola. México: Fondo de Cultura Económica, 1989. 230 p.: bibl., ill., map (Tezontle)

Provocativa y más reciente biografía del reconocido poeta. Reconstrucción de una vida que parte de la investigación rigurosa para renovar el género. Alejándose del lenguaje académico entrega desde distintos registros, en un estilo claro, directo y literario una narración fluida y amena. Dice de su labor: "Reconstruí la cronología hasta donde me lo permitió la información asequible . . . después inevitablemente, conjeturé, concluí y adiviné hasta donde me lo permitió mi honestidad. Si preservé algunas ambigüedades, lo hice porque, impotente para resolverlas, supuse que el lector también tenía el derecho (y, quizá, la obligación de sopesarlas)." Las fotografías y reproducciones hacen de este un libro para coleccionistas. [NK]

4264 Szmulewicz, Efraín. Nicanor Parra: biografía emotiva. Santiago: Ediciones Rumbos, 1988. 209 p.: bibl., ports.

Biografía que recrea momentos importantes en la vida del poeta con miras a presentar una semblanza "desde el ángulo humano general." Intento por relacionar vida-obra se queda en lo más evidente. Interés radica en la evocación afectiva de detalles poco comentados de la biografía de Parra. [LE]

4265 Tanabe, Atsuko. Hokusaiwo aishita Mexico shijin [The Mexican poet who loved Hokusai: the Japanism of José Juan Tablada]. Tokyo: PMC Shuppan, 1990. 310 p.: bibl., ill.

Traces Mexican poet José Juan Tablada's contact with Japan in early 20th century and development of his genuine interest in Japanese arts and literature. [K. Horisaka]

4266 Ulacia, Manuel. Octavio Paz: poesía, pintura, música, etcetera; conversación con Octavio Paz. (*Rev. Iberoam.*, 55: 148/149, julio/dic. 1989, p. 615–636)

Diálogo informativo donde Paz discute su poesía, incluyendo su más reciente libro, *Arbol adentro*, y vuelve a temas como el muralismo, la *Revista Taller*, el arte moderno, la música, etc., con una visión y crítica renovada e iluminadora. [NK]

4267 Uno es el poeta: Jaime Sabines y sus críticos. Introduccíon y recopilación de Mónica Mansour. México: Secretaría de Educación Pública, 1988. 402 p.: bibl.

Recopilación de artículos, reseñas, correspondencia, testimonios y bibliografías sobre la obra del iniciador de la poesía coloquial en México, y ganador del Premio Nacional en 1983. Importante para el estudioso de Sabines, en razón del material proveniente de revistas, libros y periódicos publicados en México, aunque de difícil acceso en bibliotecas extranjeras. Completa este volúmen de excelente factura, la inclusión de varios discursos de Sabines al recibir premios regionales y nacionales. [NK]

4268 Vittor, Luis Alberto. Simbolismo e iniciación en la poesía de Alberto Girri. Buenos Aires: Editorial Fraterna, 1990. 270 p.: bibl.

Un intento interpretativo nada desdeñable: los textos de Girri se transforman en aventura de conocimiento, búsqueda de presencias que muy bien pudieran dar cuenta de una de las direcciones semánticas posibles de esta poesía. Pese a trabajar los poemas como jalones de un proceso de "iniciación mística," no hay demasiado exceso verbal en este sentido y, por la mayor parte, las aserciones del crítico parecen bastante convincentes, si no como la lectura correcta de Girri, como una posibilidad interpretativa. [JG]

4269 Zavala, Iris M. Rubén Darío bajo el signo del cisne. Río Piedras, P.R.: Editorial de la Univ. de Puerto Rico, 1989. 153 p.: bibl., ill.

Apoyándose en la teoría crítica de la ideología (con especial aporte de Voloshinov/ Bajtín y de la teoría de la recepción), se analiza cómo a partir de su posición de sujeto Darío produce en "los cisnes" "una puesta en escena y una proyección verídica 'imaginaria' de su situación histórica concreta," cuya naturaleza dialógica se inscribe en el inconsciente poético, estableciendo así un enigma que es a su vez como invitación al lector a construir un mundo imaginativo distinto a partir de los actos de lenguaje ilocutivos de los cisnes. [GY]

MISCELLANEOUS

4270 Arango, Gonzalo. Correspondencia violada. Recopilación de Eduardo Escobar. Bogotá: Instituto Colombiano de Cultura: Univ. de Antioquia: Gobernación del Depto. de Antioquia, 1980. 487 p. (Col. regionales; 2. Antioquia)

El poeta Eduardo Escobar nos presenta en este libro una selección bastante interesante de la correspondencia que Gonzalo Arango, fundador del movimiento nadaísta colombiano, sostuvo con algunos de los integrantes de este grupo vanguardista. Desafortunadamente las fechas de las cartas han sido suprimidas dificultando así la lectura crítica. [AR]

4271 Arlt, Roberto et al. Tango: prosa y poesía de Buenos Aires. Prólogo y selección de textos de Horacio Salas. Proyecto editorial y dirección de textos de Manrique Zago. Obras plásticas de Carlos Alonso et al. Fotografía de Jack Tucmanián et al. Buenos Aires: Manrique Zago Editorial, 1990. 152 p.: ill. (some col.)

Apasionante y rico mural bibliográfico sobre el tango, hecho con erudición, talento y buen gusto. Fotografías, dibujos, reproducciones de pinturas y afiches, etc., contribuyen al éxito del conjunto. Muy buena selección de ensayos donde se evita el simple homenaje. Se incluyen incluso textos de autores importantes que denigran el género. También, letras de tangos famosos. Y mucho más. [JG]

4272 Cuadra, Pablo Antonio. Aventura literaria del mestizaje y otros ensayos. Pablo Antonio Cuadra. San José: Libro Libre, 1988. 167 p. (Obras completas de Pablo Antonio Cuadra. Obras en prosa; 2)

Nueve ensayos en que se analizan los rasgos fundamentales del proceso dinámico que caracteriza la literatura nicaragüense desde los tiempos coloniales hasta el presente, plasmados en el encuentro y fusión de las herencias culturales autóctonas con la espiritualidad europea y cristiana. Emblema de esta fusión nacional es Darío. [GY]

4273 Ducmelic, Zdravko. Once rostros y un poema. Buenos Aires: Ediciones de Arte Gaglianone, 1988. 1 v. (unpaged): ill. (some col.)

Además del poema de Girri, "A la Expresión de una Dama en Quien Todo Va desde su Alma al Rostro," y de las versiones en inglés y francés de las que se acompaña, este libro vale por los excelentes dibujos de Zdravko Ducmelic. Una joya bibliográfica. [JG]

4274 Garmendia, Julio. La ventana encantada. Prólogo de Domingo Miliani. Caracas: Ediciones del Congreso de la República, 1986. 224 p.

La obra del escritor venezolano Julio Garmendia (1898–1977) junto con la del poeta José A. Ramos Sucre, verdaderos aportes a la literatura latinoamericana, ha encontrado por fin, al paso de los años, lectores cada vez más entusiastas. Así, esta edición de textos (poemas, cuentos, notas críticas) publicados en revistas y periódicos es una valiosa contribución al conocimiento de una obra que se distingue no sólo por la calidad y variedad de los temas sino por la actualidad de su escritura. El prólogo de Domingo Miliani es magnífico al ubicar críticamente al autor. [AR]

4275 Jornadas de Estudio del Consejo Episcopal Latinoamericano, Bogotá, 1988. Presencia de Dios en la poesía latinoamericana: Dios siempre vivo. Bogotá: Pontificia Univ. Javeriana, Sección de Pastoral de la Cultura: Secretariado para los No Creyentes, 1989. 332 p.: bibl. (Documentos CELAM; 111)

Interesantes trabajos distribuidos en tres secciones: 1) Propuestas que fijan marcos teológico-literarios de referencia; 2) Estudios sobre poetas hispanoamericanos: G. Mistral y P. Neruda (Hugo Montes); J.L. Borges (Oswaldo Pol); C. Vallejo (R. González Vigil y Yolanda Westphalen); V. Huidobro (Sarah de Mojica); E. Cardenal (M. Dolores Jaramillo); J. Carrera Andrade (Rafael Mirquez); J. de Lima (Armindo Trevisan), entre otros; y 3) tres ponencias dedicadas a la poesía colombiana. [PL]

4276 Kappatos, Rigas and Enrique Lihn. Los poemas de Athinulis. México: Premiá Editora S.A. (Libros del bicho), 1986. 1 v.

Curioso libro con poemas de Kappatos traducidos del griego e ilustraciones de Enrique Lihn. Hay dos textos de Lihn que reflexionan sobre el mundo del gato Athinulis y apuntan la faceta lúdico-afectiva del poeta muerto en 1988. [LE]

4277 Poirot, Luis. Neruda: retratar la ausencia. Madrid: Comunidad de Madrid, 1987. 231 p.: ill., ports.

Revelador homenaje gráfico. Hay fotografías de casas de Isla Negra y la Chascona, junto a textos poéticos de Neruda. Evoca vida y obra del poeta hasta el momento de publicación de este libro. Sección "testimonios" lleva fotografías y textos de escritores y amigos: Alberti, José Donoso, Nicanor Parra, Jorge Edwards, Cortázar, entre otros. Albertina Azócar, musa de *Veinte poemas,* trata de recordar el historiado "romance," y la voz de Delia del Carril apenas se oye a sus 103 años. Libro que todo amante de la poesía quisiera tener. [LE]

4278 Prosa hispánica de vanguardia. Edición de Fernando Burgos. Madrid: Orígenes, 1986. 270 p.: bibl., facsims., ill. (Tratados de crítica literaria. DiscursOrígenes)

Recoge 23 trabajos presentados en el simposio que sobre el tema tuvo lugar en Memphis State Univ. (abril 1985). Dos de estas contribuciones estudian interesantes aspectos de la producción poética del período considerado (1915–40): Klaus Müller-Bergh, "Indagación del Vanguardismo en las Antillas: Cuba, Puerto Rico, Santo Domingo, Haití;" y Paul W. Borgeson, "Los Versos 'Prosados' de César Vallejo." [PL]

4279 Romero, Armando. Gente de pluma: ensayos críticos sobre literatura latinoamericana. Madrid: Editorial Orígenes, 1989. 143 p.

La dosis de "arbitrariedad poética en el análisis" proclamada en el Prefacio es rasgo apreciable en estos ensayos, que buscan establecer un diálogo entre la literatura y la crítica como creación. Junto a sugerentes páginas dedicadas a narradores, sobresalen el comentario apreciativo de los últimos libros de V. Huidobro (*El ciudadano del olvido* y *Ver y palpar*); una perceptiva lectura de *La rosa profunda*, de J.L. Borges; agudas consideraciones sobre el sistema poético de Lezama Lima; una introducción a la obra de Aurelio Arturo (1906–74), y el examen, bien substanciado, de la querella entre academicismo y ruptura en la poesía colombiana. [PL]

4280 Salinas de Marichal, Solita. España en la poesía hispanoamericana, 1892–1975. Madrid: Fundación Juan March: Cátedra, 1987. 115 p. (Crítica literaria)

Cuatro conferencias dictadas en la Fundación Juan March (1987) sobre las relaciones con "lo español" de R. Darío, V. Huidobro, J.L. Borges, A. Reyes, C. Vallejo, P. Neruda, O. Paz. Señala la importancia que tuvo para ambos espacios culturales la intensidad de esas relaciones, renovadas en Hispanoamérica desde 1939 con la presencia de los poetas españoles exiliados. [PL]

4281 Urrutia, Matilde. Mi vida junto a Pablo Neruda. Barcelona: Seix Barral, 1986. 249 p.

Matilde rememora su vida junto al poeta. Detalla encuentros en Europa antes que la relación se hiciera pública. Reitera mucha información ya conocida. Contribución reside en la intimidad del tono y la recreación de la atmósfera de miedo en Chile en 1973. Comunica impacto que la muerte de Neruda causó en Chile, aparte del dolor personal de la autora. [LE]

4282 Vallejo, César. Desde Europa: crónicas y artículos, 1923–1938. Recopilación, prólogo, notas y documentación de Jorge Puccinelli. 2a ed. Lima: Ediciones Fuente de Cultura Peruana, 1987. 455 p.: facsims., ill., plates.

Importante recopilación de artículos publicados por el poeta en varios periódicos de Europa y América entre los años de 1923–38. Precede un prólogo con información de primera mano sobre la hemerografía de Vallejo. La recopilación ha sido realizada en 34 periódicos. [ORR]

Drama

GEORGE WOODYARD, *Professor of Spanish, University of Kansas*

THE NUMBER OF PLAYS published in this cycle is impressive and the quality is higher than before. There are new plays by known figures such as Carballido, Chocrón, Cossa, Dragún, Estorino, De la Parra, and Wolff. Also, the growing number of plays by women writers continues, an increase exemplified by authors such as Azcárate, Berman, Britton, Gambaro and Mosquera. Some plays still deal with purely sociopolitical issues, but the precentage is definitely decreasing in favor of more eclectic themes and approaches, including theater in exile (items **4284** and **4361**), historical (items **4342, 4354,** and **4359**), collective creations (items **4321** and **4327**), and myth (items **4364** and **4358**). Several excellent plays are written in a popular vein (items **4289** and **4336**). Plays from under-represented regions such as El Salvador and Yucatán appear here, as do the individual works of many of the younger Mexicans such as Castillo, Liera, Schmidhuber, Urtusástegui, and others. Finally a voice long silent returns in this cycle, Antón Arrufat (item **4293**).

Critical activity continues to pick up with many monographs and article-length studies. It is reassuring to note that Latin American theater criticism has become increasingly more objective as scholars apply tested critical methodologies instead of resorting to the all-too-frequent subjective commentary encountered in the past. Two excellent new books by Meléndez (item **4475**) and Taylor (item **4508**) approach the Latin American theater in a comprehensive way, utilizing appropriate critical tools in order to make enlightened comments. Burgess (item **4432**) employs the same methodologies in studying the Mexican theater of the younger generation. To complement these mainstream studies there are a number of new publications with a more specific focus on a particular author such as Iván García (items **4421**), Cabrujas (item **4424**), Griselda Gambaro (item **4512**), and Luis Rafael Sánchez (item **4476**). From a nationalist point of view, the Argentine theater is the most studied, with many new publications that document the Rosas period (item **4436**) and with special emphasis on the 1910s–20s (item **4465**). The attention to modernism as a theatrical phenomenon is a curious addition (items **4483** and **4504**). Colombia, Cuba and Chile also receive high marks for critical attention as does, surprisingly, the Dominican Republic. New histories of theater in Nicaragua (item **4423**) and Paraguay (item **4490**) are particulary welcome. An interesting item is Heidrun Adler's collection of essays by several authors designed as a handbook for a German audience, evidence of the growing appeal of Latin American theater in Europe (item **4420**). On the Iberian peninsula, the annual Cádiz festival of Latin American theater and the FITEI in Portugal constitute further proof of the Europeans' intense interest in Spanish American drama.

PLAYS

4283 Abreu Felipe, José. *Amar así.* Miami: Ediciones Universal, 1988. 46 p. (Col. Teatro)

Rare piece of Cuban underground theater, written in 1980, with a poetic flavor to its denunciation of political and social repression.

4284 Acosta, Iván. *Un cubiche en la luna:* tres obras teatrales. Houston: Arte Público Press, 1989. 128 p.

Three plays by a Cuban exiled in NY use techniques of *bufo* theater and the absurd to criticize Cuban politics, Latin American dictatorships in general, and in broad strokes, the incongruencies of life.

4285 Adellach, Alberto. *Por amor a Julia.* México: Editorial Tierra del Fuego, 1983. 139 p. (Series de Tierra del Fuego. Teatro)

Three short plays with Julia as the central figure. Each reflect Adellach's obsession with language and anti-fascist themes.

4286 Adolph, José B. Teatro. Peru: EFESCO, 1986. 120 p.

Four engaging plays from Peru: *Asedio y liberación del ciego y la parturienta, Trotsky debe morir, De buena familia y Amigos.* All have a social theme couched in natural, even jocose, language. In *De buena familia,*

for example, a revolutionary group fails at bank robbery and kidnaps a child which brings about their downfall, without violence.

4287 Aguirre, Isidora. *Retablo de Yumbel.* Concepción, Chile: Literatura Americana Reunida, 1987. 68 p.

Committed Chilean playwright analogizes the massacre of 19 people, victims of the 1973 coup whose remains were discovered in Yumbel in 1979, with the martyrdom of St. Stephen in Roman times.

4288 Aleandro, Norma. *Los chicos quieren entrar:* en un acto, con música y cuatro generaciones en escena. Buenos Aires: Torres Agüero Editor, 1989. 55 p.: ill. (Col. Cuarta pared; 5)

Lyrical little play, by one of Argentina's best known actresses, in praise of youth, music and life, focuses on tender relationships and unexplored meanings.

4289 *Allá en el Alto Piura: teatro popular.* Lima: Uctubri Qanchis, 1985. 42 p.

Popular (i.e., folkloric, picturesque) culture play portrays authentic experience of revolt against the *gamonal* on the high plains of Peru with consequences of actions.

4290 Alsina, Carlos María. *Limpieza:* obra de teatro en un acto. Buenos Aires: Torres Agüero Editor, 1988. 106 p.: ill., plates.

During Argentina's military atrocities

of the 1970s, Tucumán is "cleaned" of its undesirables. Alsina captures the inhumanity of this episode and this regime from the victims' point of view. Menacing helicopter provides a unifying linkage in this sobering play.

4291 Ardiles Gray, Julio. Personajes y situaciones: teatro. Buenos Aires: Torres Agüero Editor, 1989. 220 p. (Col. Primeras ediciones)

Four plays of varying length but invariably good quality: 1) *La noche del crimen perfecto* poses a curious interaction between a ventriloquist and his dummy; 2) *La muralla invisible* deals with discrimination, especially racial; 3) *Los cinco sentidos* dramatizes senses with surprise twists and endings; and 4) *Auto de fe en las Indias* reconstructs a modern-day auto-da-fé.

4292 Argüelles, Hugo. *Los cuervos están de luto; La ronda de la hechizada; El ritual de la salamandra.* México: Editores Mexicanos Unidos, 1985. 319 p.: plates, ports. (Teatro)

Three plays (1958–81) emphasize Argüelles' talent for destroying Mexican myths with magic and black humor, whether through rural family greed (*Los cuervos*), or indigenous spiritual conquests (*La ronda*), or in contemporary urban-bourgeois setting (*La salamandra*).

4293 Arrufat, Antón. *La tierra permanente.* La Habana: Editorial Letras Cubanas, 1987. 306 p. (Giraldilla)

Two-part (300 p.) play written in free verse for 12 men. Adapts the structure of an *auto sacramental* play in order to invoke the spirit of the land and the people. Telluric and magical, written between 1974–76.

4294 Avanzada: más teatro joven. Edición de Emilio Carballido. México: Editores Mexicano Unidos, 1985. 183 p. (Teatro)

Another in the series in which Carballido promotes the younger generation of Mexican playwrights. Consists of 10 good short plays, most by authors in previous volumes, with a variety of themes and techniques, all of them with good human interest and dramatic quality.

4295 Azcárate, Leonor. La pareja. Puebla, México: Univ. Autónoma de Puebla, 1986. 92 p. (Col. Difusión cultural. Serie teatro; 3)

Two separate plays by young Mexican women playwrights under a collective title reflect the common theme of difficulties and frustrations of male/female relationships, married or not. Azcárate's *Un día de dos* and Leñero's *Casa llena* present illuminating, if not pleasant, views on a familiar topic.

4296 Barbery Suárez, Oscar. *El portavoz.* Santa Cruz de la Sierra, Bolivia: Editorial Casa de la Cultura Raúl Otero Reiche, 1988. 85 p.: ill., plates. (Col. Autores cruceños. Serie Teatro)

When the son becomes addicted to cocaine, the entire family structure is threatened. Although stress on the family is evident, efforts to save the son are justified and successful.

4297 Basurto, Luis G. *El candidato de Dios.* México: Grijalbo, 1986. 83 p. (Col. Narrativa. Teatro)

When Pope John I died after only 33 days in office, the shortest term ever, certain mysteries surrounding his death were never explained. Basurto fictionalizes intrigue inside the Vatican walls in this fascinating play.

4298 Basurto, Luis G. Teatro de Luis G. Basurto: *Miércoles de ceniza y dos obras más.* México: Editores Mexicanos Unidos, 1986. 245 p.: ports. (Teatro)

Reprints three Basurto plays (1950s-60s) with religious themes: 1) *Miércoles de ceniza* is the encounter of a priest and a prostitute; 2) *Con la frente en el polvo* reveals the internal anguish of a doubting bishop; and 3) *Asesinato de una conciencia* is inspired by Camilo Torres and his life as a *guerrilla* presented within the framework of an *auto sacramental*. All suffer from the all-too-common Basurto hyperbole.

4299 Berman, Sabina. *Muerte súbita: obra de teatro original.* México: Editorial Katún, 1988. 67 p.: ill. (Teatro mexicano; 4)

Passion, betrayal and determination characterize this excellent three-character play in which a young novelist struggles with his best friend over his girl, his novel, his vision, and his life.

4300 Berman, Sabina. Teatro de Sabina Berman. México: Editores Mexicanos Unidos, 1985. 327 p.: ill. (Teatro. Serie Nueva Dramaturgia)

Collection of plays by one of Mexico's bright young women playwrights includes several short pieces in addition to three major plays: *Yankee* (formerly *Bill*), about an American veteran who interacts with a Mexican family; *Rompecabezas*, about Jacques Mornard, Trotsky's assassin in Mexico; and *Herejía*, about a 16th-century episode involving the Carvajal family and the Inquisition. Good technical control.

4301 Bonifaz Nuño, Alberto. *El derecho del señor.* 2a ed. México: Secretaría del Trabajo y Previsión Social, Unidad Coordinadora de Políticas, Estudios y Estadísticas del Trabajo, 1987. 160 p. (Cuadernos obreros; 18)

Lengthy (and only?) play by leading Mexican writer, first published in 1960 and reprinted here in honor of Mexico's struggle for social equality. Within a department-store setting, play's issues are sexual favoritism, workers' rights and responsibilities, and labor union policies. Reasonably good.

4302 Boullosa, Carmen. *Mi versión de los hechos.* Ilustraciones de José Luis Cuevas. México: Arte y Cultura Ediciones, 1987. 103 p.: ill. (Col. literaria. Serie Teatro; 1)

Peculiar and challenging conversation in non-traditional form, with resonances of the absurd, and of memories and feelings from the past.

4303 Brene, José R. *Pasado a la criolla y otras obras.* Prólogo de Rine Leal. La Habana: Editorial Letras Cubanas, 1984. 368 p. (Repertorio teatral cubano)

Four Cuban plays that reflect Brene's range of interest (Creole, colonial and contemporary) although none of these plays (*Pasado a la criolla, El ingenioso criollo Don Matías Pérez, Los demonios de Remedios, Fray Sabino*) achieves the spirit and success of his *Santa Camila de La Habana Vieja.*

4304 Britton, Rosa María. *Esa esquina del paraíso.* Panamá: Editorial M. Arosemena, 1986. 71 p. (Col. Ricardo Miró)

Concerns pain and trouble in the life of Panamanian women of different generations as they seek love, understanding and marriage in a bi-partite society with contrasting Latin and gringo values.

4305 Bruza, Rafael; Jorge Ricci; and **Mauricio Kartun.** *El clásico binomio* [de] Rafael Bruza y Jorge Ricci. *El partener* [de]

Mauricio Kartun. Santa Fe, Argentina: Univ. Nacional del Litoral, 1989. 112 p. (Serie Teatro argentino)

In the Bruza-Ricci play, two *tangueros* leave their homes and families full of promise about fame and fortune but the years pass by without success. In Kartun's *sainete tragicómico El partener,* the young modern-day gaucho goes in search of his vagabond father to share his misery and adventures.

4306 Buenaventura, Enrique. *La orgía.* Bogotá: Editorial La Oveja Negra, 1985. 53 p. (Biblioteca de literatura colombiana; 82)

Originally part of author's *Papeles del infierno,* this commentary on miserable socio political conditions from the perspective of a marginalized group of individuals is mordantly satirical.

4307 Buendía, Felipe. *Cuando el sol se apaga.* Notas a la edición de Pablo Macera, Fernando Fuenzalida y Max Hernández. Lima: Editorial e Impr. DESA, 1989. 70 p.

New version of classic Atahualpa story; this one differs in that Pizarro does not appear on stage which perhaps heightens the anguish of Atahualpa's final days and hours before his death.

4308 Cáceres Carenzo, Raúl. *Canek, caudillo maya: pieza épica y testimonial.* Mérida, México: Instituto de Cultura de Yucatán, Consejo Editorial, 1990. 93 p. (Col. Voces contemporáneas)

Yucatecan political theatre in support of revolutionary causes, exemplified here by Mayan leader Jacinto Canek in the 1761 uprising.

4309 Carballido, Emilio. *Ceremonia en el Templo del Tigre; Rosa de dos aromas; Un pequeño día de ira.* México: Editores Mexicanos Unidos, 1986. 172 p. (Teatro)

Three choice Carballido offerings: 1) *Ceremonia,* inspired by the US invasion of Grenada, combines *machismo* and ancient rites; 2) *Rosa* is an excercise in solidarity by two women against machismo; and 3) *Un pequeño día de ira* is a now classic protest play.

4310 Carballido, Emilio. *Silencio pollos pelones, ya les van a echar su maíz; Un pequeño día de ira; Acapulco, los lunes.* México: Editores Mexicanos Unidos, 1985. 237 p.: ill. (Teatro)

New edition of three well-known

farces by Carballido which unfortunately still ring as true now as when they opened years ago because of little change in Mexican (or world) social orders and conditions.

4311 Carballido, Emilio. Teatro 2. México: Fondo de Cultura Económica: CREA, 1988. 185 p. (Biblioteca joven; 55)

New edition of *Un vals sin fin por el planeta* (1970), *La danza que sueña la tortuga* (1956), and *Las estatuas de marfil* (1960), three well established plays in the Carballido repertory.

4312 Carballido, Reynaldo. *Tiempos revueltos.* Preámbulo de Emilio Carballido. México: Instituto Politécnico Nacional, 1987. 147 p.: ill. (Col. Textos literarios. Serie Teatro)

Six short plays, some more like dramatic sketches, attest to Reynaldo Carballido's talent for creative and natural dialogue. Mostly young people in real-life situations, dealing with sexual and social issues. Title play presents an interesting metatheatrical twist.

4313 Cárdenas Espinosa, Eliécer. *Morir en Vilcabamba:* teatro. Quito: Ediciones de la Pontificia Univ. Católica del Ecuador, 1988. 86 p.

When Richard Burton and Cantinflas meet in Vilcabamba, Ecuador, a site known as a paradise of longevity, they endure the pleasures and anguish of anonymity as they seek personal and professional immortality.

4314 Carreño, Virginia. *La misión de Roque: vida de San Roque González de Santa Cruz;* obra teatral. Buenos Aires: Ediciones Univ. del Salvador, 1988. 182 p.: ill.

Semi-documentary of the life and mission of Roque González de Santa Cruz, Jesuit missionary in Paraguay, killed by the Indians in 1628, and canonized in 1988. Episodic, not very dramatic.

4315 Carrillo, Hugo. *María:* versión dramática en dos actos de Hugo Carrillo de la novela homónima de Jorge Isaacs. Guatemala: Hugo Carrillo, 1983. 47 p.: photos

Tender interpretation of Jorge Isaacs' famous 19th-century novel, freely adapted for the stage.

4316 Carrillo, Hugo. *El Señor Presidente:* ritual bufo en dos jornadas. 2a ed., pri-

vada. Guatemala: Delgado Impresos, 1989. 85 p.: ill., plates.

In a remarkably efficient format Carrillo succeeds in capturing the myths and magic of Asturias' novel, translating the richness of Guatemalan folklore and politics to the stage through total theatre. Introduction by author plus photos.

4317 Castillo, Dante del. *Muñecas de magia y plata:* dos obras de teatro, *Las muñecas y Mulata con magia y plata* (comedia musical). Prólogo de Tomás Espinosa. México: Instituto Politécnico Nacional, 1987. 151 p. (Col. Textos literarios. Serie Teatro)

Two plays by one of Mexico's *jóvenes: Las muñecas* (1973) uses neighborhood bordello setting to examine middle-class tendencies to condemn others while ignoring one's own faults; *Mulata con magia y plata* is a musical comedy based on the history/legend of the famous "mulata de Córdoba" of the 16th century.

4318 Cerda, Carlos. *Lo que está en el aire.* Santiago: Sinfronteras, 1986. 62 p.

Mystery and suspense in the airport before flight time allow for different reactions to politically-motivated tensions and search for truth that leads to freedom. Excellent.

4319 Chocrón, Isaac E. *Clipper; Simón:* (teatro). Caracas: Alfadil Ediciones, 1987. 146 p. (Col. Orinoco; 2)

Two excellent plays by Chocrón: *Clípper* analyzes a Jewish household (autobiographical touches?) through the memories of a son on his first trip away from home. *Simón* focuses on Simón Bolívar and his relationships with his mentor Simón Rodríguez.

4320 Chocrón, Isaac E. *Mónica y el florentino; El quinto infierno; Amoroso.* 1a ed. conjunta en M.A. Caracas: Monte Avila Editores, 1987. 201 p. (Teatro; 3)

Reprints Chocrón's first three plays (1959–61) which set new standards at the time, breaking with realistic traditions of earlier era and launching the career of Venezuela's best known playwright. Includes brief introduction.

4321 5 obras, creación colectiva. Bogotá: Teatro La Candelaria, 1986. 414 p.

These five plays by La Candelaria, Bogotá's most celebrated theatre group, include their major successes from the 1970's: *Nosotros los comunes; La Ciudad Dorada; Guadalupe años sin cuenta; Los diez días que estremecieron al mundo;* and *Golpe de suerte.*

4322 50 años de teatro uruguayo: antología. v. 1–2. Selección y coordinación de Laura Escalante. Montevideo: Ministerio de Educación y Cultura, 1990. 2 v.: ill.

Anthology of 16 plays that span nearly 50 years (1933–81) and represent masterworks of Uruguayan theatre. Selections include Maggi's *La biblioteca,* Langsner's *Esperando la carroza,* and Rosencof's *Los caballos.* Each play is accompanied by brief biography, critical commentary, and reviews of productions.

4323 Concurso de Teatro, *2nd, Santo Domingo, 1987.* Concurso de Teatro, 1987. Santo Domingo: Taller, 1988. 177 p.: ill.

Five Dominican plays from a 1987 competition, of which the best is Juan Carlos Campos' *Hágase la mujer,* an entertaining piece in which God loses control and Man's request for a companion brings an unexpected response. The other plays are Germana Quintana's *No quiero ser fuerte,* Frank Disla's *Ultimo son,* William García's *La trama de San Miguel* and Angelo Valenzuela's *Un ladrón en mi casa.*

4324 Cossa, Roberto M. Teatro. v. 2. Buenos Aires: Ediciones de la Flor, 1990. 3 v.

In addition to the collectively-written *El avión negro,* this volume contains *La nona,* a metaphorical voracious octogenarian, and *No hay que llorar,* an exposé of sibling greed that hastens their mother's impending death.

4325 Cossa, Roberto M. *et al.* Teatro abierto 1982. Selección de Nora Mazziotti. Buenos Aires: Puntosur Editores, 1989. 145 p. (Teatro Puntosur. Col. Repertorio)

Of the 36 plays presented, seven are published here, presumably the best of the 82 season. All are pithy, committed. Selection includes: *El tío loco* (Roberto Cossa), *Príncipe azul* (Eugenio Griffero), *La casita de los viejos* (Mauricio Kartún), *De víctimas y victimarios* (Aarón Korz), *Prohibido no pisar el césped* (Rodolfo Paganini), *El Oficial Primero* (Carlos Somigliana), *Chorro de caño* (Gerardo Taratuto).

4326 Cossa, Roberto M. *Yepeto.* (*Conjunto,* 80, julio/sept. 1989, p. 77–97, photo)

One of Cossa's best, in which the implications of the Pinocchio story underlie the relations of a professor, his student and her friend.

4327 Cuatro obras del Teatro La Candelaria. Bogotá: Ediciones Teatro La Candelaria, 1987. 394 p.

Four of La Candelaria's major productions: 1) García's *El diálogo del rebusque* based on Quevedo's *Buscón;* 2) *Corre corre carigüeta* based on the tragedy of Atahualpa; 3) Fernando Peñuela's *La tras-escena* which sees a production of a Columbus play from behind the scenes; and 4) Patricia Ariza's *El viento y la ceniza* offers new view of mercenary conquest of the Americas. Good theatre and strong ideologies.

4328 Defilippis Novoa, Francisco. *He visto a Dios; Despertate, Cipriano.* Estudio preliminar y notas de Carlos A. Polemann Solá. Buenos Aires: Kapelusz, 1985. 149 p. (Grandes obras de la literatura universal; 161)

Excellent essay by Polemann Solá sets context for reprinting these last two plays by an exceptional playwright of the post-Sánchez period. Both plays belong to the vanguardist period (1929–30) of the Argentine grotesque.

4329 Denevi, Marco. Obras completas. v. 6. Buenos Aires: Ediciones Corregidor, 1989. 1 v.

Eight plays by Denevi (1957–75) reveal his critical eye, caustic humor and ironic touch. For example, in *El segundo círculo,* a man with a great reputation for womanizing is eternally beseiged by women, a new twist on Don Juan in Hell.

4330 Díaz Vargas, Henry. *Las puertas; Josef Antonio Galán; La encerrona del miedo.* Medellín, Colombia: Univ. de Antioquia, Depto. de Publicaciones, 1990. 183 p. (Col. Teatro)

Three plays by a promising young playwright from Medellín (b. 1948); *Las puertas* deals with local issues and local color. The other two relate to the late 18th-century uprising of Josef Antonio Galán (the *comuneros*).

4331 Dorr, Nicolás. Dramas de imaginación y urgencia. La Habana: Unión de Escritores y Artistas de Cuba, 1987. 340 p. (Contemporáneos)

Three *dramas de imaginación* and two *de urgencia* comprise this 1987 collection of Dorr's later plays. In spite of his good intentions to be more inventive, the plays still hew to the party line.

4332 Dragún, Osvaldo. *¡Arriba corazón!* Buenos Aires: Teatro Municipal General San Martín, 1987. 104 p.: ill., plates. (Teatro Municipal General San Martín; 20)

Dragún's autobiographical journey through time in three acts with Corazón Niño, Corazón Joven and Corazón Hombre in an Argentina shaken like an earthquake by political extremes.

4333 Estorino, Abelardo. Teatro. Prólogo de Salvador Arias. La Habana: Editorial Letras Cubanas, 1984. 394 p.: ill. (Repertorio teatral cubano)

Five plays by the best playwright to have remained in Cuba examine life and family values as they relate to the revolution. *El peine y el espejo* (1956) is a good forerunner of his classic *El robo del cochino* (1961). *La casa vieja* examines sexuality and ethics. The title of *La dolorosa historia del amor secreto* de Don José Jacinto Milanés is totally descriptive of the Cuban poet, and *Ni un sí ni un no* (1981) shows values in transition from traditional standards to the Revolutionary posture.

4334 Felipe, Carlos. Teatro. Edición a cargo de José A. Escarpanter y José A. Madrigal. Boulder, Colorado: Society of Spanish and Spanish-American Studies, 1988. 633 p.: bibl., ill. (Cuban literary studies)

Magnificent volume that embraces the complete works of Carlos Felipe, one of Cuba's most prominent playwrights of the century. Includes his 11 plays (1939–64) together with extensive analysis of the man and his oeuvre, as presented by José A. Escarpenter and José A. Madrigal.

4335 Fernández Tiscornia, Nelly. *Made in Lanús = Made in Buenos Aires.* Texto en edición bilingüe. Traducción al inglés de Raúl Moncada. Edición, prólogo y notas de Lilia Vietti. Buenos Aires: Editorial Legasa, 1990. 170 p.: bibl., ill.

Bilingual edition of play about exile and the anguish it creates both for those who go as well as for those who stay behind.

4336 Freidel, José Manuel. *Los infortunios de la Bella Otero y otras desdichas.* 1a ed. colombiana. Medellín, Colombia: Ediciones Otras Palabras, 1985. 88 p.

Exquisite little play with a complex popular culture background combined with commitment to socio political change.

4337 Gac Canales, Roberto. *Pactos con el diablo:* comedia en tres actos y seis cuadros. Rancagua, Chile: Centro Gráfico, 1984. 129 p.

Realistic play about exploitation, corruption and prostitution set in Yankee-owned mining company in Chile at turn of century.

4338 Gambaro, Griselda. Teatro. v. 3. Buenos Aires: Ediciones de la Flor, 1990. 1 v.

Consists of 12 short plays by Gambaro, ranging from *Viaje de invierno* to *Antígona furiosa*, that reveal her genius and her commitment to quality and originality in the Argentine theatre.

4339 García, Carlos Jesús. *Sueño y agonía de Toto de los espíritus.* Holguín, Cuba: Dirección Municipal de Cultura, 1987. 89 p.: ill.

Modern day Cuban morality story of greed and exploitation balanced by naive faith in humankind and the afterlife.

4340 García de la Mata, Helena. *El imbuche.* Buenos Aires: Torres Agüero Editor, 1989. 46 p.: ill. (Col. Cuarta pared; 6)

Man finds inner freedom within a jail, in spite of the Jailer and the Prostitute and through the symbol of the mythical bird, *the imbuche,* who appears before men of pure hearts.

4341 Garibay, Ricardo. *¡Lindas maestras!* México: J. Mortiz, 1987. 166 p. (Teatro del volador)

Four plays—*¡Lindas maestras!, ¿Cómo está tu ex-amante?, ¡Ay déjame que le quite su galán!,* and *Chippendale*—deal sympathetically with women's issues and perspectives ranging through divorce, infidelity, separation and even men's strip-tease.

4342 Goldenberg, Jorge and **Marisel Lloberas Chevalier.** *Cartas a Moreno. Acordate de la Francisca.* Buenos Aires : Teatro Municipal General San Martín, 1987.

102 p.: ill., plates. (Teatro Municipal General San Martín; 22)

Goldenberg play provides contemporary staging (with references to Sartre and Hitler) of letters written during the Argentine war of independence in order to give dramatic perspective to history (especially as metaphor) in the making; the second play is a humorous and satirical view of contemporary consumerism *a la americana.*

4343 González Delvalle, Alcibíades. *El grito del Luisón; Procesados del 70.* Asunción: El Lector, 1986. 99 p. (Col. Teatro; 2)

Two plays by Paraguay's leading playwright reveal his two tendencies: in *Procesados del '70,* the human interest aspect of the historic and bloody War of the Triple Alliance; and in *El grito del Luisón,* the mythic quality of personal interactions.

4344 González Delvalle, Alcibíades. *San Fernando:* drama histórico. Asunción: Editorial Nuestro Tiempo, 1989. 82 p.

Historical Paraguayan play about Gen. Solano López in the War of the Triple Alliance, considered to be sufficiently antipatriotic to be banned in Asunción even in the post-Stroessner period. Minimally satisfactory as theatre.

4345 El Grotesco criollo: Discépolo-Cossa: antología. Selección, introducción, notas y propuestas de trabajo de Irene Pérez. Buenos Aires: Ediciones Colihue, 1986. 172 p.: ill. (Col. literaria LYC (leer y crear); 074)

Designed as a textbook to interest students, this anthology focuses on the *grotesco criollo* and two of its major proponents. Includes good critical material, biobibliography and a play by each: *Stéfano* and *La nona.*

4346 Gudiño Kieffer, Eduardo. *Azazel.* Buenos Aires: Torres Agüero Editor, 1989. 87 p. (Col. Cuarta pared; 2)

Curious, poetic and anachronistic tale of witchcraft in the 16th century. Loosely based on historical account in which Gudiño Keiffer looks at narcissism, love and fidelity to one's self.

4347 Hinostroza, Rodolfo. *Apocalipsis de una noche de verano.* Lima: Instituto Nacional de Cultura, 1988. 159 p. (Col. Personae)

The overlay of Shakespeare's fairies

from the *Midsummer night's dream* provides a fascinating and erotic interchange with American soldiers fighting in Central America in Hinostroza's protest war and political/military involvement. Cumbersome but interesting.

4348 Hiriart, Hugo. Tres indagaciones teatrales: *La ginecomaquia, Simulacros, Intimidad.* México: J. Boldó i Climent, 1987. 141 p.

Hiriart's playful style is entertaining at times but of little transcendental value. Of the three plays included here—*La ginecomaquia, Simulacros* and *Intimidad*—the last is the most satisfying because of its technical experimentation with choral work and simultaneous dialogue.

4349 Inclán, Federico Schroeder. *Don Quijote murió del corazón.* Coyoacán, México: Univ. Autónoma Metropolitana-Xochimilco, 1985. 57 p. (Col. de teatro mexicano. Serie Dame el pie; 2)

From the confines of a mental hospital, a 20th-century Don Quijote and Sancho engage in some amusing revisionist history while retaining some of their original qualities.

4350 Kartun, Mauricio. *Chau Misterix.* Buenos Aires: Torres Agüero Editor, 1989. 72 p.: ill. (Col. Cuarta pared; 4)

Young boy's erotic fantasies intertwine with characters from a masquerade (Misterix, Doris Day, Marilyn Monroe, etc.) in intricate games of make-believe.

4351 Langsner, Jacobo. *Esperando la carroza.* Buenos Aires: Argentores, 1988. 83 p. (Argentores; 3)

Slow-moving modern-day "comedia de costumbres" which examines family structure, mores and behaviors around the episode of an old woman, disappeared and presumed dead.

4352 Leñero, Vicente. *La mudanza; La visita del ángel; Alicia, tal vez; La carpa:* teatro doméstico. México: Editores Mexicanos Unidos, 1985. 343 p.: ill. (Teatro)

Four of Leñero's more playful efforts (not documentary history) show his talent for manipulating tension, conflict (or lack of conflict) and human interest situations.

4353 Leñero, Vicente. *¡Pelearán! diez rounds.* México: Editores Mexicanos Unidos, 1986. 125 p.: ill. (Teatro)

Documentary play inspired by the story of Bobby Chacón mixes reality and fiction, boxing and theater, life and death.

4354 Leñero, Vicente. Teatro documental. México: Editores Mexicanos Unidos, 1985. 311 p.

Anthology of four of Leñero's documentary plays: 1) *Los traidores* (the *Excelsior* corruption); 2) *Pueblo rechazado* (psychoanalysis in the Cuernavaca monastery); 3) *Compañero* (Che Guevara); and 4) *El juicio* (the assassination of Alvaro Obregón). Includes introduction by Judith Bissett and interview by Kirsten Nigro.

4355 Leñero, Vicente. Tres de teatro. México: Cal y Arena, 1989. 279 p.

Three of Leñero's recent plays: 1) *Nadie sabe nada* is a thriller à la his own *La mudanza*; 2) *Jesucristo Gómez* is an adaptation of his novel *El evangelio según Lucas Gavilán*; and 3) *Martirio de Morelos* captures in his documentary style both the man and the hero.

4356 Licona, Alejandro. *Raptóla, violóla y matóla.* Nota previa de Tomás Espinosa. México: Instituto Politécnico Nacional, 1987. 139 p. (Col. Textos literarios. Serie Teatro)

Five short plays full of humor, often black, with twists and surprises at every turn. By one of Mexico's most promising young playwrights, these plays capture the imagination with a quick and witty idiom. Very playable.

4357 Liera, Oscar. Las dulces compañías. Culiacán, Mexico: Univ. Autónoma de Sinaloa, 1987. 75 p. (Teatro; 2)

Four pithy one-act plays that explore issues of sexuality and interpersonal relations through language and violent endings, written by one of Mexico's most talented young playwrights, prematurely deceased.

4358 *M.M. un mito:* y 4 obras ganadoras. México: Editores Unidos Mexicanos, 1984. 284 p.: ill, ports. (Teatro)

Prize winning plays in the Salvador Novo contest. Of the four one-acts, two deal with myth creation: Enrique Cisneros' *El campeón* details the formation of a young boxer, and Alberto Arteaga Olguín's *M.M. un mito* is a clever version of Marilyn Monroe. Urtusástegui's *¡Huele a gas!* is a mordant

satire on Mexico's nouveaux riches. Plus two others of comparable quality.

4359 Magaña, Sergio. *Moctezuma II; Cortés y la Malinche (los argonautas).* México: Editores Mexicanos Unidos, 1985. 236 p.: ill. (Teatro)

Reprint of two Magaña plays also includes author's interview. *Moctezuma II* (1953) captures the tragic splendor of the ill-fated emperor; *Cortés y la Malinche* (formerly *Los argonautas,* 1967) gives a comic-satiric view of the two main figures of the conquest.

4360 Maldonado, Premier. *Zaguaneando en el país de los encancaranublados* Premier Maldonado. Río Piedras, P.R.: Editorial Cultural, 1986. 59 p.: ill., plates.

Through the medium of farce, Maldonado projects a devastating analysis of the labyrinths of Puerto Rican identity, raising questions which transform themselves *ad infinitum* through self-denial. Very much like his *Escambronando* (see HLAS 50: 3812).

4361 Miranda, Jaime. *Regreso sin causa.* Santiago: Sinfronteras, 1986. 78 p.

Prize-winning play (1984) about exiled Chileans who make the difficult decision to return to their country, and the disillusion and antagonism they encounter on doing so. Both a Chilean and a universal experience of exile and return.

4362 Montalvo, Juan. *El libro de las pasiones.* Ed. sesquicentenario II Convención Nacional. Ambato, Ecuador: I. Municipio de Ambato, Consejo Editorial, 1987. 2 v. (Biblioteca Letras de Tungurahua; 24–25)

New edition of Montalvo's five plays which are amazingly agile in their political and religious themes and dialogues, considering Montalvo's lack of critical feedback. Excessively long critical study by Ricardo Descalzi introduces the volume.

4363 Mosquera, Beatriz. Teatro. Buenos Aires: Libros de Tierra Firme, 1987. 215 p. (Col. de teatro Babilonia; 1)

Five plays (written 1970–84) reveal Mosquera's clear talent for engaging dialogue. The two *Lunas* bracket two couples (neighbors and friends) undergoing personal anxieties caused by Argentina's socio political situation, circumstances which are exacerbated in the latter version.

4364 Novo, Salvador. *La dama culta* [de] Salvador Novo. *Hoy invita La Güera* [de] Federico S. Inclán. 1a ed. en Lecturas mexicanas. México: Secretaría de Educación Pública, Cultura, 1984. 142 p. (Lecturas mexicanas; 51)

Reprint of two Mexican plays: the Novo play (1951) satirizes the hypocrisy of the Mexican upper class; Inclán's play (1955) is an antihistorical version of the famous *güera* Rodríguez in an intentional time warp. Not the best of the 1950s.

4365 Novo, Salvador. *Yocasta o casi; La guerra de las gordas.* México: Editores Mexicanos Unidos, 1985. 224 p. (Teatro)

Reprint of two Novo plays of the early 1960s: 1) in *Yocasta o casi* a psychiatrist works on different levels of reality with an actress; and 2) *La guerra de las gordas (in Pipiltzintzin)* recounts sexual and other practices among 15th-century warring Mexicans.

4366 9 obras jóvenes. Recopilación de Emilio Carballido. México: Editores Mexicanos Unidos, 1985. 254 p. (Teatro)

No longer so young, the playwrights represented here embrace the best of the generation (i.e. Tomás Espinosa, Willebaldo López, Dante del Castillo, Miguel Angel Tenorio, Rascón Banda) plus others with fewer productions (Pilar Campesino, José López Arellano, José Ruiz Mercado, Silvia Marín). Plays cover interesting variety of themes ranging across politics, the Mexican bureaucracy, and youth, and including good portrayal of human relationships.

4367 Ocampo, Silvina and J.R. Wilcock. *Los traidores.* Buenos Aires: A. Korn Editora, 1988. 181 p.: ill.

Collaborative work written in verse in 1956 plays with palace intrigues and decadence of imperial Rome in the third century AD, clearly for metaphorical reasons.

4368 *Ollantay: cantos y narraciones quechuas.* Versiones de José María Arguedas, César Miró y Sebastián Salazar Bondy. Lima: Ediciones PEISA, 1986. 160 p. (Biblioteca peruana. Serie Narrativa)

Modernization in language, style and technique, by Cesar Miró and Sebastián Salazar Bondy, of cumbersome 18th-century original of this Incan classic.

4369 Ott, Gustavo. Teatro 5. Caracas: Textoteatro Ediciones, 1989. 265 p. (Teatro)

Five recent pieces by a young Venezuelan who specializes in denouncing social disorders in plays that are both trenchant and entertaining. Of the five, *Los peces crecen con la luna* may be the most substantive for its depiction of a power struggle in a country in deterioration.

4370 Parra, Marco Antonio de la. *La secreta obscenidad de cada día; Infieles; Obscenamente (in)fiel; o, una personal crónica de mi prehistoria dramatúrgica.* Santiago: Planeta, 1988. 201 p. (Biblioteca del sur)

Two plays by Chile's young star: 1) *La secreta obscenidad de cada día* puts two apparent exhibitionists (Freud and Marx) in front of a girls' school to cover their political intentions; and 2) *Infieles* entwines the loves and deceptions of two couples with Chile's political charades. Excellent theatre.

4371 Parrado, Gloria. Teatro. Gloria Parrado. La Habana: Editorial Letras Cubanas, 1984. 205 p.: ill. (Repertorio teatral cubano)

Ubiquitous theme of three Cuban plays is to praise the virtues of the revolution while attacking imperialism and capitalism.

4372 Parrado, Gloria. Tríptico. La Habana: Unión de Escritores y Artistas de Cuba, 1984. 188 p. (Manjuarí. Teatro)

Three plays from Cuba's republican period (1905) focus on women's perspectives and issues.

4373 Pavlovsky, Eduardo A. *Cámara lenta: historia de una cara.* 2. ed. Buenos Aires: Ediciones Búsqueda, 1987. 53 p. (Col. Literatura de hoy)

Ex-boxer faces ignominous end. Strong language and emotions, metaphorical of the deterioration of Argentina, portray the protagonist from hero to grave.

4374 Pavlovsky, Eduardo A. *El Señor Galíndez; y, Pablo.* Buenos Aires: Ediciones Búsqueda, 1986. 94 p. (Col. Literatura de hoy)

Reprinting of *El Señor Galíndez*, Pavlovsky's *tour de force* about dehumanized torture in Argentina, published here with *Pablo*, an enigmatic story of violence and disappearances.

4375 Pérez, Lupe and Leda Cavallina. *Ellas en la maquila.* San José: Editorial Costa Rica: Centro Nacional para el Desarrollo de la Mujer y la Familia, 1989. 92 p.

Based on a documentary, this amateur

play achieves its objectives by portraying the vicissitudes of life for women in a Costa Rican factory setting.

4376 Raad, Henry. *La nueva semilla.* Guayaquil, Ecuador: Poligráfica, 1986. 66 leaves: ill.

Written by a Lebanese in Guayaquil, the play speaks to issues and concerns of an ethnic community dealing with relocation and adaption. Transcendent values show through its local color.

4377 Radrigán, Juan. *La contienda humana.* Santiago: Ediciones Literatura Alternativa, 1989. 47 p.

Forceful two-character play tied to death and examination of conscience, values and human relationships during a time of national political strife (Chile during and after the coup). Radrigán is exceptionally effective in conveying the mores in popular idiom.

4378 Radrigán, Juan. *Pueblo del mal amor;* *Los borrachos de luna.* Chile: Editorial Ñuke Mapu, 1987. 94 p.

Pueblo del mal amor is an unusual Radrigán play, a poetic and allegorical account of rural exiles fleeing or deposed by the conflict between authority and individual rights; *Los borrachos de luna* also has Biblical overtones in portraying the oppressed couple José and María.

4379 Ramos-Perea, Roberto. *Módulo 104: revolución en el purgatorio.* Río Piedras, P.R.: Fundación René Marqués, 1986. 99 p.: plates, ports.

Strong indictment of the treatment of political prisoners in the Puerto Rican penitentiaries during the 1980–82 crisis.

4380 Ramos-Perea, Roberto. *Teatro de luna.* San Juan, P.R.: Ediciones Gallo Galante: Cía. de Teatro el Cemí, 1989. 121 p.: ill.

In *Llanto de luna* (1989) author laments Puerto Rican politics at end of last century in the context of Simón Bolívar's missing candelabra; *Obsesión* (1988) is equally violent, but modern with a surprising touch of extraterrestrials and UFO's.

4381 Rascón Banda, Víctor Hugo. Teatro del delito. México: Editores Mexicanos Unidos, 1985. 256 p.: ill. (Teatro)

Three plays by popular, if undisciplined, Mexican author: *Manos arriba* deals with corruption; *La fiera del Ajusco* concerns mother who kills her children out of despair; and *Máscara vs. cabellera* wrestling.

4382 Rascón Banda, Víctor Hugo. *Tina Modotti y otras obras de teatro.* México: SEP. 1986. 175 p. (Lecturas mexicanas; 2a ser., 63)

Title play documents Tina Modotti's life and involvement as a model in Mexico's leftist political movements; *Voces en el umbral* details, from the point of view of a miner's daughter, social conflicts in Chihuahua; *Playa azul* suggests intrigue in a coastal setting. Typical Rascón excesses.

4383 Reyes, Alfonso. Teatro completo. Monterrey, México: Instituto de la Cultura de Nuevo León, Dirección de Artes Escénicas, 1989. 131 p.: bibl.

First collection of Reyes' theatre provides ample evidence, in five short plays, of his astonishing abilities as a master poet and craftsman, even if dramatic values are lacking. *Ifigenia cruel* is best known; the *Cantata en la tumba de Federico García Lorca* is moving, as is the opereta *Landrú*.

4384 Río, Marcela del. *De camino al concierto:* monólogo. México: Univ. Autónoma Metropolitana, Unidad Xochimilco, 1986. 39 p. (Col. de teatro mexicano. Serie Dame el pie; 6)

Monologue by violinist on his death bed, inspired by author's own husband, Hermilio Novelo.

4385 Rivera, Virgilio A. *Aquel domingo en el club:* pieza en dos actos. México: Punto por Punto Editores, 1987. 71 p.

Middle-age male's marriage is threatened by vasectomy and suspected homosexual encounter. Interesting treatment of machismo in contemporary Mexican society.

4386 Rivera, Virgilio A. *El enemigo está en casa:* pieza en dos actos. México: Punto por Punto Editores, 1987. 70 p.

In mundane atmosphere of Cuernavaca, an examination of repressed hostilities and disintegration of family relations provide dramatic interest.

4387 Rivera Saavedra, Juan. *Los Ruperto.* Lima: Editora Latina, 1986. 69 p.

Vicissitudes of family life under poor economic conditions, especially in conflict with Church positions on contraception and abortion, recounted with black humor.

4388 Roa Bastos, Augusto Antonio. *Yo El Supremo:* pieza escénica en cuatro actos, prólogo y epílogo. (*Estud. Parag.*, 13:1/2, dic. 1985, p. 113–196)

Dramatization of *Yo El Supremo* by Roa Bastos himself produces text substantially different from the novel.

4389 Rodríguez, Abrahan. *Andoba, o, Mientras llegan los camiones.* La Habana: Editorial Letras Cubanas, 1985. 118 p. (Col. Espiral)

Oscar (Andoba) is the focal point in this Cuban play that shows (still) differing values and perspectives of a society in transition toward the "right" objectives.

4390 Rodríguez Muñoz, Alberto. *Zarabanda de los inocentes; El solitario viaje de regreso.* Buenos Aires: PROTEA, 1988. 124 p.

First play (1987) conjures up infinite reference to classical and historical figures (Castor and Pollux, Mohammed III, etc.) in a grand allegory of liberty; second (1976) anticipates the other with its word play, its strange humor and its metaphorical trip through life.

4391 Rodríguez Solís, Eduardo. *Las ondas de La Catrina.* México: Univ. Autónoma Metropolitana, Unidad Xochimilco, 1986. 59 p. (Col. de teatro mexicano. Serie Dame el pie; 5)

Entertaining series of encounters with "La Catrina," one of the many names of Death in Mexican culture.

4392 Rojas, Miguel. *El anillo del pavo real.* San José: Ediciones Guayacán, 1988. 47 p.

Lyrical and interesting short play derived from Costa Rican myths and legends about the sensual Zárate and her suitors.

4393 Rojas, Miguel. *Los nublados del día.* San José: Editorial Costa Rica, 1985. 128 p.: ill. (Libros de teatro)

Dramatized version of Gregorio Ramírez's heroic 19th-century life, who at age 27 died for Costa Rican independence. Realistic but sententious.

4394 Rojas Palacios, Jaime. *Autopsia de un joven triste:* drama en tres actos. México: Univ. Autónoma Metropolitana, Unidad Xochimilco, 1986. 99 p. (Col. de teatro mexicano. Serie Dame el pie; 11)

Somewhat forced effort to dramatize the life of a young boy, abandoned by his mother, who aspires to a theatrical career.

4395 Rosencof, Mauricio. *Los caballos; El combate en el establo; El saco de Antonio.* Montevideo: Librosur, 1985. 127 p. (Librosur literario; 2)

Consists of *Los caballos,* Rosencof's flawed play of 1976, and two one act strange and inconsequential plays. In *El combate en el establo,* José dialogues with the cow; *El saco de Antonio* deals with the repetitious rancor between two sisters over a man.

4396 Rovinski, Samuel. Tres obras de teatro. San José: Editorial Costa Rica, 1985. 292 p. (Libros de teatro)

Gobierno de alcoba reaffirms succession of malicious power systems; *La víspera del Sábado* reflects anxieties of expatriate Polish-Jewish family during World War II; *El laberinto* questions sanity of brilliant chemist with his toxic gas. Latter two are better, less rigidly realistic.

4397 Sabido, Miguel. *Pastorela regiomontana.* Monterrey, México: Secretaría de Educación y Cultura, Departamento Editorial, 1987. 84 p. (Serie Teatro; 1)

Playwright Sabido builds framework for Sabido, the researcher of the *pastorela,* to create an original work which he encourages others to adapt and perform in order to promote this Mexican form of popular culture.

4398 Sáenz, Dalmiro. *Las boludas.* Buenos Aires: Torres Agüero Editor, 1988. 76 p. (Col. Primeras ediciones)

Play (1988) is proof that torture in Argentina is still of dramatic concern, here imbedded in a context of sexuality and male/female role issues.

4399 Salazar Tamariz, Hugo. Teatro. Cuenca, Ecuador: Casa de la Cultura Ecuatoriana Benjamín Carrión, Núcleo del Azuay, 1986. 212 p. (Libros para el pueblo; 34)

Three realistic plays from Cuenca with elements of social protest but limited artistic merit: *La llaga, La falsa muerte de un ciclista, De por qué a la oportunidad la pintan calva.*

4400 Schmidhuber de la Mora, Guillermo. *Por las tierras de Colón:* drama latinoamericano en dos actos. Concepción, Chile: LAR, 1988. 81 p.

Winner of first Letras de Oro prize for theatre, this metatheatrical play about a Mexican actress performing a play and caught in the *bogotazo* of 1948 provides an excellent integration of theatre, life and political events.

4401 Shand, William. Teatro. Buenos Aires: Grupo Editor Latinoamericano, 1989. 328 p. (Col. Escritura de hoy)

Six plays by prolific Scot transplanted to Argentina concentrate on relationships in various settings, but they have a pedestrian quality in technical development coupled with some often bizarre premises that cloud their effectiveness.

4402 Somigliana, Carlos. *Amarillo; Amor de ciudad grande:* melodrama en dos actos. Buenos Aires: Municipalidad de la Ciudad de Buenos Aires, 1988. 154 p. (Teatro completo; 2)

Amarillo (1965) urges agrarian reform in the context of ancient Rome under Cayo Graco, a metaphor for social reform in Argentina. *Amor de ciudad grande* (1965) presents age-old story of love between soldier and prostitute, with comments about Argentina's social setting.

4403 Somigliana, Carlos. *De la navegación; Historia de una estatua.* Buenos Aires: Municipalidad de la Ciudad de Buenos Aires, 1988. 158 p. (Teatro completo; 3)

De la navegación (1969) uses Adriatic galley-ship of precolumbian times as metaphor of solidarity and freedom. *Historia de una estatua* (1983) brings to life illusions and disillusions of Lavalle (1820–40).

4404 Somigliana, Carlos. *El exalumno:* un acto de contrición, en dos actos; *La bolsa de agua caliente.* Buenos Aires: Municipalidad de la Ciudad de Buenos Aires, 1988. 120 p. (Teatro completo; 6)

Final volume in six-set series. *El exalumno* (1978) is a bizarre tale of former student returning after 20 years and finding himself trapped in strange circumstances. *La bolsa de agua caliente* (1966) provides ironic demonstration of justice in an unjust world. Somigliana's work is characterized in general by much interest in history, use of metaphor to address contemporary socio political situations, and an ear for good dialogue but with few concessions to humor or special techniques.

4405 Somigliana, Carlos. *Homenaje al pueblo de Buenoˌ Aires.* Buenos Aires: Municipalidad de la Ciudad de Buenos Aires, 1988. 59 p.: ill., plates. (Teatro completo; 1)

First of complete set of Somigliana's theater, published soon after his untimely death. *Homenaje* (1975) is a sardonic comment on power and lack of freedom.

4406 Somigliana, Carlos. *Oficial 10; La democracia en el tocador; El Nuevo Mundo; El avión negro.* Buenos Aires: Municipalidad de la Ciudad de Buenos Aires, 1988. 145 p. (Teatro completo; 5)

Three one-act plays and a collaborative work: *Oficial Primero* is a lecherous government official who eliminates his unwilling victims through control of habeas corpus; *El Nuevo Mundo* (1981) is a microcosm of venality and lechery in the style of the Marquis de Sade; *La democracia en el tocador* (1984) also deploys the Marquis de Sade with a libidinous and ironic touch. *El avión negro* (1970) marks a collaborative effort by Somigliana, Roberto Cossa, German Rozenmacher and Ricardo Talesnik and concerns Perón's return to Argentina in a mythic black airplane.

4407 Teatro colombiano, siglo XIX: de costumbres y comedias. Selección y notas de Carlos Nicolás Hernández. Bogotá: Tres Culturas Editores, 1989. 463 p.: ill.

Anthology of nine plays rescues some which were lost. Not great theatre but of historical value in documenting national customs and traditions.

4408 Teatro latinoamericano en un acto. Selección de Carlos Espinosa. La Habana: Casa de las Américas, 1986. 209 p. (Col. La Honda)

Seven of the best one-act plays in Latin America; the common denominator is a commitment to justice, equality and basic human rights.

4409 Tejeda de Tamez, Altaír. *Los mutantes y otras piezas.* México: Federación Mexicana de Escritores, 1985. 125 p.

Title play deals with moral decay ensuing from money and power; *Otoño muere en primavera* focuses on a provincial home peopled by prejudiced women; *Para pasar el día* concerns alcoholism.

4410 Tessier, Domingo. *Tablas, láminas, alambre de púas—y demases:* comedia en un aliento y un suspiro; *Prótesis:* teatro en una pieza. Chile: Editorial La Noria, 1985. 95 p. (Teatro)

Two plays of acceptable quality by leading figure of the Chilean stage. *Prótesis* is a strange one-act encounter between two older people in an hourly hotel; the other shows the impact of social disintegration during the Allende years on an upper-class family.

4411 Toscano, Carmen. *La llorona.* 2a ed. México: Fondo de Cultura Económica, 1985. 108 p.: ill., plates. (Col. popular; 306)

This 1958 play captures the legendary figure of *La llorona,* the supposed reincarnation of Cihuacóatl, in a mid-16th century Mexican setting.

4412 Urtusástegui, Tomás. *Vida, estamos en paz.* Mérida, México: Consejo Editorial de Yucatán, 1986. 135 p. (Libros yucatecos. Voces contemporáneas)

Four *ancianos* (three women, one man) live out their frustrations, their fond memories, their justifications and ultimately their fears of an unknown tomorrow, as they sort out their own relationships. Poignant and plausible.

4413 Varela, Carlos M.; Víctor M. Leites; and Alberto Paredes. Teatro uruguayo. Montevideo: ACTU/Signos, 1989. 193 p.

Three winners of Uruguay's annual Florencio Prize (1981–83) which share concern for family status, class consciousness, and issues of power and control.

4414 Velásquez, Gerardo. *Rubor helado.* Prólogo de Armando Partida Taizan. México: Instituto Politécnico Nacional, 1987. 131 p.: ill. (Col. Textos literarios. Serie Teatro)

Collection of five plays (*Vía libre, El cuarto más tranquilo, Hasta hacernos polvo juntos, Las viudas, Sobre las lunas*) with Velásquez's typical penchant for fragmentation, unusual relationships and experimental designs.

4415 Vilalta, Maruxa. Teatro II. México: Fondo de Cultura Económica, 1989. 497 p.: bibl., ill. (Colección popular; 399)

Five of Valalta's more recent plays: *Esta noche juntos amándonos tanto* (1970) captures an Ionesco-like ambiance of boredom and hostility; *Nada como el piso 16*

(1975) continues the hostilities with games of power and intrigue; *Historia de él* (1978) examines absurdities of power in Mexico's political system; *Una mujer, dos hombres y un balazo* (1981) contains four plays intertwined in 10 scenes; *Pequeña historia de horror (y de amor desenfrenado)* has ironic aspects of traditional English murder mystery. Vilalta has talent as a writer of the absurd dealing with concepts of love, power and the small ironies of life.

4416 Walsh, Rodolfo J. *La granada; La batalla.* Buenos Aires: Ediciones de la Flor, 1988. 139 p.: ill.

Two plays from mid-1960s illustrate with interesting scenic techniques atrocities of misguided military thinking and strategy and victims they produce, one of whom was the author himself, a "desaparecido" since 1976.

4417 Wolff, Egon. *Parejas de trapo; La balsa de la Medusa.* Prólogo de Agustín Letelier. Santiago: Editorial Universitaria, 1988. 186 p.: ports. (Col. Los Contemporáneos)

Two plays by Chile's premier playwright. *Parejas de trapo* (1960) is an early effort to deal with marital and economic issues; *La balsa de la Medusa* (1984) is a technical tour de force, based on Géricault's painting, of complex social and economic factors in conflict. Superb.

4418 Yuyachkani. *Encuentro de zorros: creación colectiva de Yuyachkani.* (*Conjunto,* 81, oct./dic. 1989, p. 29–50)

One of Yuyachkani's plays of strong social protest; contains long sections in Quechua with much music and dance.

4419 Zarlenga, Ethel Gladys. *Te presento un amigo.* Buenos Aires: Editorial Galerna, 1986. 85 p. (Col. Union Carbide)

Ingenuous but interesting family situation which nearly collapses when 50-year-old spinster announces plan to marry.

THEATER CRITICISM AND HISTORY

4420 Adler, Heidrun. Theater in Lateinamerika: ein handbuch. Berlin: Dietrich Reimer Verlag, 1991. 463 p.

Handsome collection of 15 essays, in German, by European and Latin American authors not only surveys recent activities in the field but demonstrates growing European interest in Latin American theater.

4421 Aguilú de Murphy, Raquel. Soledad e incomunicabilidad en la obra teatral de Iván García. (*Rev. Iberoam.*, 54:142, enero/marzo 1988, p. 259–269)

Study of three plays (1963–65) by Dominican Iván García traces aspects of the absurd.

4422 Altamirano, Ignacio Manuel. Obras completas. v. 10, Crónicas teatrales. México: Secretaría de Educación Pública, 1989. 1 v.

Nice compilation of theater reviews, mostly from 1868, with prologue by Héctor Azar, reveal Altamirano's interest in and deep understanding of the theater (e.g., production of Tamayo y Baus' *El drama nuevo* deserves its 20 p.).

4423 Arellano, Jorge Eduardo. Inventario teatral de Nicaragua. Managua: Biblioteca, Banco Central de Nicaragua, 1988. 227 p.: bibl., ill.

Only study to date of Nicaraguan theater from beginnings to present. For all its deficiencies (balance, typescript, style), it is enormously useful as a repository of information on Nicaragua.

Arlt, Mirta. Prólogos a la obra de mi padre. See item **3908.**

4424 Azparren Jiménez, Leonardo. Cabrujas en tres actos. Caracas: Ediciones El Nuevo Grupo, 1983. 105 p. (Teatro; 4)

Intense investigation of three plays by a leading Venezuelan playwright. 1) *Profundo* (the religious act); 2) *Acto cultural* (the cultural act); and 3) *El día que me quieras* (the political act). Makes internal comparisons of Cabrujas' valuable contributions to the stage.

4425 Azparren Jiménez, Leonardo. Teatro en crisis. Caracas: Fundarte, 1987. 104 p.: bibl. (Col. Antares; 5)

Compilation of selected articles, originally written for newspapers, that reflect author's views of major theater trends and developments in Venezuela (1978–86).

4426 Bixler, Jacqueline Eyring. Language in/ as action in Egon Wolff's *Háblame de Laura.* (*Lat. Am. Theatre Rev.*, 23:1, Fall 1989, p. 49–62)

Bixler uses speech-act theory to illu-

minate role of language as both content and form in this cryptic and complex play.

4427 Bixler, Jacqueline Eyring. Recasting the past: the dramatic debunking of Mexico's "official" story. (*Rev. Hisp. Mod.*, 42:2, dic. 1989, p. 163–72)

Clear and insightful analysis of three Mexican plays (Ibarguengoitia's *El atentado*, Willebaldo López's *Yo soy Juárez*, and Leñero's *Martirio de Morelos*) that demythifies and deconstructs three Mexican heroes.

4428 Bixler, Jacqueline Eyring. Vargas Llosa's *Kathie y el hipopótamo:* the theatre as self-conscious deception. (*Hispania/ Teachers*, 71:2, May 1988, p. 254–260, bibl.)

Perceptive study of ambiguities, illusion and perception in Vargas Llosa's second, less-studied play.

4429 Boiling, Becky. Crest or pepsodent: Jorge Díaz's *El cepillo de dientes.* (*Lat. Am. Theatre Rev.*, 24:1, Fall 1990, p. 93–104)

Boiling looks at this play within the context of Díaz's own critique of mass media and consumerism.

4430 Bonilla, María Rosa de and **Stoyan Vladich.** El teatro latinoamericano en busca de su identidad cultural. San José: Cultur Art, 1988. 327 p.: bibl

Title promises more than volume delivers. Study attempts to deal with performance aspects of theater by analyses of four plays by two groups—Colombia's TEC and Uruguay's El Galpón.

4431 Boyd, Jennifer. *Flores de papel* as criticism: the artist and the tradition. (*Lat. Am. Theatre Rev.*, 23:2, Spring 1990, p. 7–12)

Boyd points to Wolff's use of language as the controlling force in the artist's compulsion to assimilate, destroy and remake traditions.

4432 Burgess, Ronald D. Building a basic Spanish-American theatre bibliography. (*LARR*, 23:2, 1988, p. 226–233, bibl.)

Judicious commentary about strengths and weaknesses of bibliographical information in the field of Latin American theater.

4433 Burgess, Ronald D. The new dramatists of Mexico: 1967–1985. Lexington: Univ. Press of Kentucky, 1991. 166 p.

Impressive study of 215 plays by young generation of Mexican playwrights (b. 1938–54).

4434 Cajiao Salas, Teresa and **Margarita Vargas.** An overview of contemporary Latin American theater. (*in* Philosophy and literature in Latin America: a critical assessment of the current situation. Edited by Jorge J. E. Gracia and Mireya Camurati. Albany, N.Y.: State Univ. of New York Press, 1989, p. 132–139)

Brief but cohesive view of Latin American theater since the 1930s with original observations about the work of some groups (e.g. ICTUS) and role of political theater and theater of exile.

4435 Castagnino, Raúl Héctor. Circo, teatro gauchesco y tango. Buenos Aires: Instituto Nacional de Estudios de Teatro, 1981. 187 p.: bibl., ill.

With his usual attention to scholarly detail Castagnino organizes material, most of it published previously, into a helpful new format. Discusses influences of tango, the circus, and gaucho traditions on Argentine theater.

4436 Castagnino, Raúl Héctor. El teatro en Buenos Aires durante la época de Rosas. Buenos Aires: Academia Argentina de Letras, 1989. 2 v.: bibl., ill. (Biblioteca de la Academia Argentina de Letras. Serie Estudios académicos; 29)

Reprints long out-of-print 1944 ed. of massive work (781 p.) on the theater during Rosas' time (1830–52). Invaluable study of theaters, playwrights, plays and public itself during this challenging period of Argentine history.

Chambaud Magnus, Jaime. Directoras de escena novohispanas del siglo XVII. See item **3364.**

4437 50 años de teatro: Palacio de Bellas Artes. México: Instituto Nacional de Bellas Artes, Secretaría de Educación Pública, 1985. 147 p.: bibl., ill. (some col.)

Beautiful oversized history of the construction, inauguration and theater program in Mexico's Palacio de Bellas Artes for the 1934–84 period. Nicely documented and handsomely illustrated with photos and sketches.

4438 Cioppo, Atahualpa del *et al.* Diálogo en La Habana. (*Conjunto,* 80, julio/ sept. 1989, p. 35–53, photos)

Polemical discussion among several distinguished theater artists and critics about conditions of Latin American theater, with some especially contentious remarks about Cuba. Participants are Atahualpa del Cioppo, Miguel Rubio, Santiago García, Juan Carlos Gené, Nissim Sharim, Fernão Peixoto, José Solé, Enrique Dacal, Magaly Muguercia and Raquel Carrió.

4439 Couselo, Jorge Miguel. Pablo Podestá: entre la locura y el arte. (*Todo es Hist.,* 268, oct. 1989, p. 6–15, facsims., photos)

"Autobiography" of Podestá, one of Uruguay's leading theater figures, as related in first person by Couselo.

4440 Dauster, Frank. Bridging the quantum gap: considerations on the novelist as playwright. (*Lat. Am. Theatre Rev.,* 24:1, Fall 1990, p. 5–16)

Dauster suggests that five major novelists are successful in writing for the stage because they adapt easily to differing technical requirements.

4441 Dauster, Frank. *Los hijos del terremoto:* imágenes de un recuerdo. (*Lat. Am. Theatre Rev.,* 22:1, Fall 1988, p. 5–12)

Study of Dragún's autobiographical play, later called *Arriba corazón,* which incorporates intertextuality, irreal staging and flexible time.

4442 Diéguez Caballero, Ileana. Lo trágico en el teatro de René Marqués. La Habana: Depto. de Actividades Culturales, Univ. de La Habana, 1985. 80 p.: bibl.

On the basis of three plays author justifies Marqués' efforts to defend Puerto Rican identity in this fragmentary and poorly documented study.

A different reality: studies on the work of Elena Garro. See item **3517.**

Domínguez Michael, Christopher. Martín Luis Guzmán: el teatro de la política. See item **3518.**

4443 Dubatti, Jorge Adrián. Francisco F. Fernández y el teatro político de Entre Ríos. (*Rev. Estud. Teatro,* 6:15, 1987, p. 43–49, ill.)

Study of Fernández's *La Triple Alianza* (1870), long thought to be lost.

4444 Eidelberg, Nora. Teatro experimental hispanoamericano, 1960–1980: la realidad social como manipulación. Minneapo-

lis: Institute for the Study of Ideologies and Literature, 1985. 221 p. (Series towards a social history of hispanic and Luso-Brazilian literature)

Groups 19 thoughtful play analyses into three categories (ludic, didactic, popular) to produce excellent vision of the vanguard theater during an explosive period of development.

4445 Encuentro Internacional sobre Teatro Latinoamericano de Hoy, *1st, Paris, 1988.* Reflexiones sobre teatro latinoamericano del siglo veinte. Buenos Aires: Editorial Galerna, 1989. 240 p. (Serie Crítica de teatro latinoamericano; 1)

Compilation of selected papers presented at the first ITTCTL (Instituto Internacional de Teoría y Crítica de Teatro Latinoamericano) conference (Paris, 1988).

4446 Festival Internacional de Teatro, *8th, Caracas, 1990.* 8 Festival Internacional de Teatro. Caracas: Consejo Nacional de la Cultura/CONAC, Fundateneofestival, 1990. 82 p.: ill.

Good documentation with photos and commentaries on multi-national theater and dance festival of Caracas (1990).

4447 Festival Latinoamericano de Teatro, *2nd, Córdoba, Argentina, 1985.* II Festival Latinoamericano de Teatro. Córdoba, Argentina: Secretaría de Turismo, 1985. 140 p.: ill.

Second Córdoba festival is well documented with this collection of posters, reviews and photos of entries in theater and dance.

4448 Fischer, Virginia Fanny. Tres hombres de teatro. Santiago: Editorial Nascimento, 1985. 94 p.: ill., plates.

Vision of Chile's three giants of 1930s experimental theater movement: Pedro de la Barra, Agustín Siré and Pedro Orthous. Presented from personal, almost autobiographical perspective, rather than a critical viewpoint.

4449 Fontana, Roberto. Memoria en dos actos: mi testimonio sobre el Teatro Independiente de Montevideo. Montevideo: ARCA, 1988. 120 p.: ill., index.

First-person account of independent theater movement in Montevideo from 1942 on, but more objective and informative than most such memoirs.

4450 Foster, David William. José González Castillo's *Los invertidos* and the vampire theory of homosexuality. (*Lat. Am. Theatre Rev.*, 22:2, Spring 1989, p. 19–29)

Interesting study of early Argentine plays (1914) dealing with a taboo topic.

Fouchard, Jean. Le théâtre à Saint-Domingue. See item **4876.**

4451 Frugoni de Fritzsche, Teresita. El teatro de Eduardo Pavlovsky. (*Rev. Estud. Teatro*, 6:15, 1987, p. 50–57)

Brief review of Pavlovsky's plays, supposedly with psychoanalysis as the frame of reference.

4452 Gálvez Acero, Marina. El teatro hispanoamericano. Madrid: Taurus, 1988. 173 p.: bibl. (Historia crítica de la literatura hispánica; 34)

In attempting to cover entire spectrum of Spanish American theater from conquest to present, this slim book fails to present new ideas or new structures. Falls instead into pattern of listing plays and authors too numerous to discuss in merited detail.

4453 Gann, Myra S. Meaning and metaphor in *Flores de papel.* (*Lat. Am. Theatre Rev.*, 22:2, Spring 1989, p. 31–36)

Gann studies the canary as a complex metaphor in Wolff's play.

4454 García del Toro, Antonio. Mujer y patria en la dramaturgia puertorriqueña: proyecciones del sentimiento patrio en la figura de la mujer como protagonista de la dramaturgia puertorriqueña. Madrid: Playor, 1987. 267 p.: bibl., ports. (Biblioteca de autores de Puerto Rico)

Using three categories of women (earth-mother, marginal, and rebel), author discusses nine women as protagonists in Puerto Rican plays over 30-year period. Short on critical theory, book nevertheless makes interesting case for women (and not men) as the ultimate symbol of Puerto Rican patriotism.

4455 Gené, Juan Carlos. *Memorial del cordero asesinado.* (*Conjunto*, 78, 1989, p. 45–71)

Composite in memory of fallen heroes, "more or less assassinated" (e.g., Lorca, Neruda, Machado).

4456 Gerdes, Dick and **Tamara Holzapfel.** Melodrama and reality in the plays of

Mario Vargas Llosa. (*Lat. Am. Theatre Rev.*, 24:1, Fall 1990, p. 17–28)

Authors study Vargas Llosa's plays to show how melodramatic conventions can produce different effects in all three.

4457 Gnutzmann, Rita. *El beso de la mujer araña: de la novela al teatro.* (*Iberoromania*, 27/28, 1988, p. 220–234)

Serious and substantial study of the transformation of *El beso de la mujer araña* from narrative to theater.

4458 Golluscio de Montoya, Eva. Grotesco rioplatense y convención cocolichesca: *Stéfano* de Armando Discépolo. (*Lett. Am.*, 2:9/10, autunno 1981, p. 135–153)

Linguistic study of the *cocoliche pseudo sabir* which provides excellent systems for interpreting the Italian-based language of the grotesque.

4459 Gómez, Eduardo and **José Peréz.** Festival Iberoamericano de Teatro: aspectos del festival, Bogotá 88. (*Bol. Cult. Bibliogr.*, 25:16, 1988, p. 81–88, photos)

Insightful commentary on major performances of world theater festival (Bogotá, 1988).

4460 Guerra, Ramiro. Un teatro total popular en las parrandas remedianas. (*Islas*, 84, mayo/agosto 1987, p. 97–118, bibl.)

Substantial interpretive article about popular theater in Remedios, Cuba.

4461 Gutiérrez Nájera, Manuel. Espectáculos: teatro, conciertos, ópera, opereta y zarzuela, tandas y títeres, circo y acrobacia, deportes y toros, gente de teatro, el público, la prensa, organización y locales. Selección, introducción y notas de Elvira López Aparicio. Edición e índices de Ana Elena Díaz Alejo y Elvira López Aparicio. México: Univ. Nacional Autónoma de México, Impr. Universitaria, 1985. 287 p.: bibl., ill., index, plates, ports.

Only nine of 60 entries are theater reviews but 11 concern theater people. Lively entries reflect Gutiérrez Nájera's good taste as critic, his effervescent style and inevitable subjectivity.

Hiriart, Hugo. Ambar. See item 3484.

4462 Ita, Fernando de. La danza de la pirámide: historia, exaltación y crítica de las nuevas tendencias del teatro en México.

(*Lat. Am. Theatre Rev.*, 23:1, Fall 1989, p. 9–17)

Author regards radical staging and performance experiments by the Japanese director Seki Sano and by the 1950s group Poesía en Voz Alta as crucial for understanding recent developments in Mexican theater.

4463 Jornadas Nacionales de Investigación Teatral, 2nd, Buenos Aires, 1985. Segundas Jornadas Nacionales de Investigación Teatral. Buenos Aires: Asociación de Críticos e Investigadores Teatrales de la Argentina, 1986. 122 p.: bibl.,ill.

Compilation of abstracts of papers presented at conference (Buenos Aires, 1983), organized around principal theme of "Authors in Buenos Aires."

4464 Klein, Teodoro. Los conflictos teatrales de 1919 y 1921. (*Rev. Estud. Teatro*, 6:15, 1987, p. 36–42, facsim.)

Historical view of important period of reconsolidation in the Argentine theater.

4465 Klein, Teodoro. Una historia de luchas: la Asociación Argentina de Actores. Buenos Aires: Asociación Argentina de Actores, 1988. 64 p.: bibl., ill.

Study commissioned by Asociación Argentina de Actores to trace history and struggle to unionize the Argentine theater, complete with photos, graphs and documents.

4466 Larson, Catherine. Recollections of plays to come: time in the theatre of Elena Garro. (*Lat. Am. Theatre Rev.*, 22:2, Spring 1989, p. 5–17)

Studies synchronic and diachronic elements in eight of Garro's plays to show how perceptions of reality depend on this thematic and structural device.

4467 *Latin American Theatre Review.* Vol. 22, No. 1, Fall 1988 [through] Vol. 24, No. 2, Spring 1991– . Lawrence: Univ. of Kansas, Center of Latin American Studies.

In addition to articles annotated elsewhere in this section, these volumes contain reports on festivals in Argentina, Bogotá, Brazil, Cádiz, Manizales, Mexico, Miami, Peru and other locations; interviews with Pavlovsky, Dolores Prida, Antonio Corrales, Juan Antonio Hormigón, Carlos Morton and other theater luminaries; and other critical studies, book and performance reviews, and bibliography. Vol. 24, No. 2, Spring 1991 is a special issue dedicated to recent Argentine theater with Osvaldo Pellettieri as guest editor.

4468 Leal, Luis. Vida y muerte: el jardín como metáfora en *La hija de Rappaccini*. (*Ideas 92*, 1 : 1, Fall 1987, p. 71–75, bibl.)

Studies Octavio Paz's play in light of Nathaniel Hawthorne's story.

4469 Letras: cultura en Cuba. Prefacio y compilación de Ana Cairo Ballester. La Habana: Editorial Pueblo y Educación, 1987– . 3 v.: ill.

With a notable lack of cohesiveness, this four-part book has two parts on theater: 1) three plays by Virgilio Piñera (*Electra Garrigó*, *Jesús*, and *Aire frío*), with note of introduction; and 2) six essays by prominent Cuban theater scholars and commentators on diverse topics, ranging from José Antonio Ramos' work to theater of the Revolution.

4470 Magnarelli, Sharon. Dramatic irony and lyricism in historical theatre: *El pobre Franz* and *Falsa crónica de Juana La Loca*. (*Lat. Am. Theatre Rev.*, 22 : 2, Spring 1989, p. 47–57)

Magnarelli studies two plays, one Argentine, the other Mexican, to determine the role of dramatic irony and artistic license in historical theater.

4471 Marial, José. Teatro y país: desde 1810 a teatro abierto 1983. Buenos Aires: Ediciones AGON, 1984. 194 p.: bibl.

In this small volume Marial pretends to cover all of Argentine theater from the Revolution of 1810 to the Teatro Abierto of 1983, a feat which he accomplishes with inevitable superficiality.

4472 Martínez, Christine D. El valor de la libertad en el teatro de Guillermo Schmidhuber de la Mora. (*Lat. Am. Theatre Rev.*, 24 : 1, Fall 1990, p. 29–40)

On the basis of two Schmidhuber plays, author discusses the expression of freedom, not as a political force, but as the realization of one's potential.

4473 Martínez A., Gilberto Teatro, teoría y práctica. Prólogo de Alberto Aguirre. Medellín, Colombia: Ediciones Autores Antioqueños, 1986. 235 p.: bibl., ill. (Ediciones Autores antioqueños; v. 27)

Volume contains three plays by this Medellín actor/director/author (*Zarpazo*, *El horóscopo*, *Las vicisitudes del poder*) as well

as five of his essays on such topics as text, space and improvisation.

4474 Matas, Julio. Vuelta a *Electra Garrigó* de Virgilio Piñera. (*Lat. Am. Theatre Rev.*, 22 : 2, Spring 1989, p. 73–79)

Matas argues that the leading character in this play presents an existential kind of rebellion, contrary to the usual interpretation of the play as a satire of Cuban high middle-class mores.

4475 Meléndez, Priscilla. La dramaturgia hispanoamericana contemporánea: teatralidad y autoconciencia. Madrid: Pliegos, 1990. 189 p.

Important new critical study of six Latin American plays (by Usigli, Dragún, Luis Rafael Sánchez, Triana, Carballido and Vargas Llosa).

4476 Morales Faedo, Mayuli. Variaciones sobre la relación público-actor/personaje en el teatro de Luis Rafael Sánchez. (*Conjunto*, 80, julio/sept. 1989, p. 60–68, photos)

Valid and useful study of communication aspects of Sánchez's major plays.

4477 Morris, Robert J. The theatre of Gregor Díaz. (*Lat. Am. Theatre Rev.*, 23 : 1, Fall 1989, p. 79–87)

Morris studies Díaz's ten plays for their value as protest against social, religious and political abuse of the proletariat.

4478 Muguercia, Magaly. El teatro cubano en vísperas de la Revolución. La Habana: Editorial Letras Cubanas, 1988. 257 p.: bibl. (Giraldilla. Ensayo)

Detailed study of Cuban theater in three epochs before Castro: 1) renovation 1936–50; 2) transition, 1951–53; and 3) Batista years, 1954–58. Muguercia traces antecedents but always from a current Revolutionary perspective.

4479 Muguercia, Magaly. Teatro, en busca de una expresión socialista. La Habana: Editorial Letras Cubanas, 1981. 148 p. (Col. Espiral)

Compilation of essays (1972–78) which provide good documentation on the Cuban theater, especially around the pivot group (Teatro Político Bertolt Brecht) which Muguercia advised.

4480 Muñoz, Diego et al. Poética de la población marginal, teatro poblacional chileno, 1978–1985: antología crítica. Minneapolis: Prisma Institute, 1987. 439 p.: bibl., index. (Literature and human rights, 0893–9438; 3)

Three very substantial essays by Diego Muñoz, Carlos Ochsenius and José Luis Olivari establish antecedents and development of marginal theater (i.e., of the "poblaciones") in Chile during 1978–85 when the full economic and cultural effect of the Pinochet regime was felt. Also includes 20 examples of this marginalized theater. Excellent and useful volume.

4481 Neghme Echeverría, Lidia. La resistencia cultural en *El toro por las astas* de Radrigán. (*Lat. Am. Theatre Rev.*, 22:1, Fall 1988, p. 23–28)

One of Radrigán's best plays dealing with resistance to the Chilean dictatorship among marginal classes.

4482 Neglia, Erminio Giuseppe. El hecho teatral en Hispanoamérica. Roma: Bulzoni, 1985. 216 p.: ill. (Letterature iberiche e latino-americane)

Collection of 12 essays (including several reprints) on different themes (language, torture, etc.) and playwrights (Huidobro, Triana etc.) confirms the richness of the theater material and the commonality of themes and techniques throughout the hemisphere.

4483 Neglia, Erminio Giuseppe. El teatro modernista en Hispanoamérica. (*in* Louisiana Conference on Hispanic Languages and Literatures, *6th, New Orleans, 1985.* Selected proceedings. Edited by Gilbert Paolini. New Orleans: Tulane Univ., 1985, p. 267–274)

Lugones' two short plays owe a debt to Jose Martí; Enrique Larreta's six plays have characteristics of modernism, even if not fully developed.

4484 Nigro, Kirsten F. Pop culture and image-making in two Latin American plays. (*Lat. Am. Lit. Rev.*, 17:33, Jan./June 1989, p. 42–49, bibl.)

Penetrating study of Cabrujas' *El día que me quieras* and Fuentes' *Orquídeas a la luz de la luna* that points up the intertextual relations with Gardel and Dolores del Río/María Félix.

4485 Ordaz, Luis. Las máscaras dramáticas de Roberto Arlt. (*Rev. Estud. Teatro,* 6:15, 1987, p. 3–14, bibl., photo)

Valuable study of Arlt's theater, even though the referents of the "mask" remain unclear.

4486 Padilla Galvez, Norma. Lo grotesco en el teatro de Hugo Carrillo. Guatemala: Univ. de San Carlos, Facultad de Humanidades, 1983. 124 p.: bibl., facsims., photos, tables.

Written as thesis, this study examines the grotesque in Carrillo's theater as literary style and historical component.

Pasquariello, Anthony M. Theatre in colonial Spanish America: religious and cultural impact. See item 3343.

4487 Pellettieri, Osvaldo. El sistema de la gauchesca teatral alrededor de 1983: *Juan Soldao* de Orosman Moratorio, entre Juan Moreyra y Calandria. (*Rev. Estud. Teatro,* 6:15, 1987, p. 28–35)

Further analysis of the evolution of the gauchesque theater in the late 19th century.

4488 Pereira, Joseph R. The black presence in Cuban theatre. (*Afro-Hisp. Rev.,* 2:1, Jan. 1983, p. 13–18)

Unique and invaluable study of the black author and black influence in the Cuban theater from colonial times to present.

4489 Pianca, Marina. El teatro cubano en la década del ochenta: nuevas propuestas, nuevas promociones. (*Lat. Am. Theatre Rev.*, 24:1, Fall 1990, p. 121–34)

Study of recent Cuban theater in light of reforms and self-criticism launched around 1985.

4490 Plá, Josefina. Cuatro siglos de teatro en el Paraguay: el teatro paraguayo desde sus orígenes hasta hoy, 1544–1988. v. 1. Asunción: Univ. Católica Nuestra Señora de la Asunción, Depto. de Teatro, 1990– . 1 v.: bibl., ill.

Vol. 1 of projected set on Paraguayan theater history contains useful information for years 1544–1870.

4491 Pujol, Sergio A. El teatro argentino y la industria cultural, 1910–1930. (*Todo es Hist.*, 248, feb. 1988, p. 52–69, bibl., photos)

Examines development of the River Plate theater after Sánchez's death looking for influences, forces and conflicts.

4492 Quackenbush, L. Howard. Borges' tragedy. (*Hispanófila*, 92, enero 1988, p. 77–86, bibl., ill.)

Fascinating study of Borges's story "El Milagro Secreto" which author examines for its dramatic qualities.

4493 Ramos-Perea, Roberto. Perspectiva de la nueva dramaturgia puertorriqueña: ensayos sobre el nuevo teatro nacional. San Juan: Ateneo Puertorriqueño, 1989. 93 p. (Cuadernos del Ateneo. Serie de teatro; 1)

Collection of Ramos-Perea's talks and previous publications focuses on development of political-action theater in Puerto Rico since 1986, especially as it relates to questions of Puerto Rican identity.

4494 Rela, Walter. Diccionario de autores teatrales uruguayos; &, Breve historia del teatro uruguayo. Montevideo: Proyección, 1988. 138 p.

Contains bio-bibliographical information on 19th and 20th-century Uruguayan playwrights. Preceded by brief historical overview of Uruguay's theater from beginning to present.

4495 *Revista del Instituto Nacional de Estudios de Teatro.* Vol. 5, No. 13, 1986– . Buenos Aires: Instituto Nacional de Estudios de Teatro.

The origins and development of *Juan Moreira*, a dramatic phenomenon in the River Plate for more than 100 years, are examined in 10 informative articles.

4496 Reynolds, Bonnie H. Violence and the sacred in a den of thieves. (*Lat. Am. Theatre Rev.*, 23:1, Fall 1989, p. 19–26)

Reynolds studies Puerto Rican Roberto Ramos-Perea's play *Cueva de ladrones* to distinguish between positive and negative forms of violence and their impact on society.

4497 Rizk, Beatriz J. El nuevo teatro latinoamericano: una lectura histórica. Minneapolis: Prisma Institute, 1987. 143 p.: bibl. (I & L)

Valuable analysis of the so-called "New Theater" in Latin America (i.e., anti-bourgeois theatre commited to social and political issues and action). Rizk studies themes and techniques, focusing on the *creación colectiva* with particular emphasis on Colombia.

4498 Rodríguez, Franklin. Del teatro precolombino hacia la nueva poética teatral latinoamericana. (*Cultura/Quito*, 9:26, sept./dic. 1986, p. 219–241)

Fascinating and thoughtful piece with extensive commentary on precolumbian theater as precedent for later Spanish American plays as conceptualized by José Martí and later Artaud.

4499 Rojas, Mario A. *Gulliver dormido* de Samuel Rovinski: una parodia del discurso del poder. (*Lat. Am. Theatre Rev.*, 24:1, Fall 1990, p. 51–64)

Rojas uses a semantic, syntactic and pragmatic discourse analysis to uncover Rovinski's linguistic devices to parody the ruling class.

4500 Rosso, Ignacio. Anatomía de un genio: Florencio Sánchez. Montevideo: Ediciones de la Casa del Estudiante, 1988. 157 p.: bibl., ill.

Testimonial to Sánchez's life and works which provides abundant information, sometimes in telegraphic style, without pretension of critical value.

4501 Las rutas del teatro: ensayos y diccionario teatral. Edición de Giorgio Antei. Traducciones de Giorgio Antei, Fernando Arenas y Amparo Torres. Bogotá: Centro Editorial, Univ. Nacional de Colombia, 1989. 265 p.: bibl., ill.

Sandwiched between a theater dictionary and six general essays by the likes of Appia, Artaud and Clive Barker are five useful entries on Colombian and Latin American theater by Antei, Buenaventura and others.

4502 Salazar del Alcázar, Hugo. Teatro y violencia: una aproximación al teatro peruano de los 80. Lima: Centro de Documentación y Video Teatral: Jaime Campodónico, 1990. 52 p.: bibl., ill.

Brief and informative if poorly organized commentary on the political activism of such groups as Cuatrotablas and Yuyachkani, together with the role played by Sendero Luminoso in Peru's theater.

4503 Santana González, Gilda. Apuntes para el estudio de la crítica teatral de José Martí. La Habana: Depto. de Acitividades Culturales, Univ. de La Habana, 1985. 115 p.: bibl.

Ephemeral appearance of this publication belies rich value of its contents as a substantial contribution to Martí's involvement in and support of theater.

4504 Schmidhuber de la Mora, Guillermo. El Modernismo hispanoamericano y el teatro: una reflexión. (*Rev. Iberoam.*, 55: 146/147, enero/junio 1989, p. 161–171)

Valuable incursion into an area little studied: relationship of modernism to Latin American theater. Examines two texts of José Martí with brief commentaries on other plays.

4505 Shen, Virginia. El nuevo teatro de Colombia: posturas estéticas e ideológicas en *Soldados* de Carlos José Reyes. (*in* Rocky Mountain Council on Latin American Studies, *36th, Fort Collins, Colo., 1988*. Proceedings. Las Cruces, N.M.: Center for Latin American Studies, New Mexico State Univ., p. 137–144)

Examination of *Soldados* which relates the characterization in the play, inspired by Alvaro Cepeda Samudio's novel, with figures of the historical event.

4506 Suárez Durán, Esther. De la investigación sociológica al hecho teatral. La Habana: Editorial de Ciencias Sociales, 1988. 81 p.: bibl. (Sociología)

Abstract and theoretical application, without any working examples, of Stanislavski's and Brecht's ideas to the work of Teatro Escambray in Cuba.

Surtz, Ronald E. Pastores judíos y Reyes Magos gentiles: teatro franciscano y milenarismo en Nueva España. See item **3354**.

4507 Taylor, Diana. Framing the revolution: Triana's *La noche de los asesinos* and *Ceremonial de guerra*. (*Lat. Am. Theatre Rev.*, 24:1, Fall 1990, p. 81–92)

Posits interesting questions about the revolutionary aspects and function of Triana's two major plays.

4508 Taylor, Diana. Theatre of crisis: drama and politics in Latin America. Lexington: Univ. Press of Kentucky, 1991. 277 p.

Most exciting study of the Latin American theater in some time. Taylor chooses five major playwrights (Triana, Gambaro, Carballido, Buenaventura and Wolff) and plays written 1965–70 to make original and complex observations.

4509 Thomas, Eduardo. Ficción y creación en cuatro dramas chilenos contemporáneos. (*Rev. Chil. Lit.*, 33, abril 1989, p. 61–70)

Solid metatheatrical interpretation of four Chilean plays: Díaz's *El cepillo de dientes* and *El locutorio*; Heireman's *El tony chico*; and de la Parra's *La secreta obscenidad de cada día*.

4510 Toro, Fernando de *et al*. Teatro argentino de los 60: polémica, continuidad y ruptura. Recopilación de Osvaldo Pellettieri. Buenos Aires: Corregidor, 1989. 241 p.: bibl. (Col. Imagen del drama)

Excellent and varied collection of essays on Argentine theater of the 1960s, introduced by Osvaldo Pellettieri, and written by Argentines and North Americans. Provides an overview of the movement and also focuses on particular authors: Dragún, Gambaro, Rozenmacher, Somigliana, Talesnik, Pavlovsky and others.

4511 Trejo, Pacheco, Novión, Vacarezza. Recopilación de Edmundo Guibourg. Buenos Aires: A-Z Editora, 1987. 93 p. (Escritores argentinos por autores argentinos; 2)

Introductory essay by the venerable Guibourg outlines the antecedents of the Argentine sainete and provides background, both critical and personal, on four authors represented in this volume by brief selections illustrative of their style and technique.

4512 Ure, A. *et al*. Poder, deseo y marginación: aproximaciones a la obra de Griselda Gambaro. Recopilación de Nora Mazziotti. Buenos Aires: Puntosur Editores, 1989. 150 p.: bibl. (Teatro Puntosur. Col. Bambalinas)

Nine mostly excellent articles by eight different authors attempt to explain the Gambaro phenomenon through close analysis of her themes, language, ability to capture human reality in the theater (with some attention to her narrative). Extremely useful collection.

4513 Urquiza, Juan José de. El Cervantes en la historia del teatro argentino. Buenos Aires: Teatro Nacional Cervantes, 1985. 90 p.: ill.

As the title indicates, a history of the Teatro Cervantes, an indomitable force in the Argentine theater since 1921.

4514 Vanrell Delgado, Juan María. La historia de la Comedia Nacional. Montevideo: Intendencia Municipal de Montevideo,
1987. 249 p.: ill., plates.
Chronology of the National Theatre
of Montevideo from its inception in 1947
through 1986 with skeletal references to all
productions and a few photos.

4515 Velasco, María Mercedes de. El nuevo
teatro colombiano y la colonización
cultural. Bogotá: Editorial Memoria, 1987.
207 p.: bibl.
Thoughtful analysis of Colombian theater establishes antecedents before examining contribution of the "nuevo teatro" in
which La Candelaria (Santiago García), the
TEC (Enrique Buenaventura), Carlos José
Reyes and Jairo Aníbal Niño brought new
theoretical conceptions to the stage, challenging earlier traditional and colonizing
forms.

4516 Vélez, Joseph F. Dramaturgos mexicanos según ellos mismos. México: Compañía Editorial Impresora, 1990. 119 p.
Interesting self-commentaries by 16
leading Mexican playwrights.

BRAZIL
Novels

REGINA IGEL, *Associate Professor, Department of Spanish and Portuguese, University of Maryland, College Park*

THE SUFFERING INFLICTED ON Brazil by the dictatorship of 1964 as well as the social chaos that has engulfed the nation since are leading subjects in many recent novels. Nevertheless, traditional genres and themes such as the historical and psychological novel, the plight of the Brazilian poor in urban and rural areas, the saga of the nation's immigrants and Indians, and science fiction continue to attract Brazilian writers. Another interesting development is the reissue of important out-of-print Brazilian novels, some published more than 50 years ago.

After Brazil's return to democracy, the end of censorship led to a boom in fiction, particularly in works dealing with the dictatorship. These novels provided a catharsis for Brazilians who had lived through one of the most dramatic and repressive chapters in their history. Indeed, the methodology of oppression and repression are detailed in innumerable personal accounts reported in the form of novels, diaries, chronicles, or documentaries. Above all, the fictional works emphasize the impact and consequences of the military dictatorship on individuals, families, and on the country as a whole. The overriding feelings conveyed by this "testimonial literature" or reportorial narrative are astonishment, rebellion, impotence, and despair, as well as the need to forewarn Brazilians against historical amnesia. Many of these novels are notable for their innovative narrative strategies, imaginative expression, original development, and other features characteristic of a postmodernist sensibility. These works stand in contrast to the few conventional novels annotated below which adhere to more traditional writing patterns.

Two important works on the subject of the abuse and suffering endured by Brazilians under the military regime are Cardoso's *Meu pai, acabaram com ele* (item **4531**) and *Diário de Berê* (item **4530**), novels that make innovative use of the narrative voice. Horrifying accounts of people victimized by military oppressors are included in Faria's *Autópsia* (item **4540**) and Glauco's *Os cogumelos vermelhos do* *outono* (item **4545**). Not even adolescents were spared the upheavals of the 1960s. Powerful portrayals of young people growing into love and maturity under these appalling circumstances appear in the following novels: Diniz Netto's *Armadilha do destino* (item **4537**), Andrade's *Perdido no meio da rua* (item **4518**), Bahia's *Ensiname a ler: conspirando contra o amor* (item **4520**), and Batista's *O camaleão no abismo* (item **4523**). That the old and the middle aged were as persecuted as the young is the subject of a novel by Amaral, *Luísa: quase uma história de amor* (item **4517**). Practically every geographic region of Brazil has generated fiction on the repressive policies of the dictatorship and their impact on Brazilians. In Rio Grande do Sul, Cristaldo's *Ponche verde* (item **4535**) follows a group of individuals through their exile in Europe. In Pernambuco, Berto's *Nunca houve guerrilha em Palmares* (item **4525**) focuses on early struggles at the outset of the military takeover. There is even an ironic narrative of conflicting ideologies, past and future, in Leitão's *O hóspede do tempo* (item **4551**), in which a formerly right-wing father requests help from a liberal friend in order to hide his leftist son from military persecutors.

Additional social and political issues are explored in novels such as Carrero's *Viagem no ventre da baleia* (item **4532**), Lacerda's *Manual de tapeçaria* (item **4550**), and in Escobar's "punky" *Speedball* (item **4538**), a satire on Brazil written in a language filled with foreign words. Coincidentally, the need to preserve and protect the Portuguese language of Brazil against foreign influences is the subject of Bernardes' novel *Memorias do vento* (item **4524**).

The prevalence of satire, irony and parody in Brazilian fiction today is exemplified by novels such as Marcos Rey's allegorical *Memórias de um gigolô* (item **4563**) and *A sensação de setembro: ópera tropical* (item **4564**), a sort of opera buffa. The text of Maranhão's *Rio de raivas* (item **4553**) confirms its author's gloomy perspective whereas Fonseca's *Bufo & Spallanzani* (item **4543**), already translated into English, is a best-seller in Brazil.

A more traditional approach to fiction is apparent in works such as Bulhões' *As quatro estações* (item **4527**), and Bandeira's *Espere um pouco, Solano* (item **4521**), a novel that uses a political pamphleteering style. Oswaldo França Jr.'s *No fundo das águas* (item **4544**) and Portes' *Maruim* (item **4561**) deal with the fate of the doomed populations of two different towns. Rónai's *O terceiro tigre* (item **4565**) concerns an author's tribulations as a novelist. Other personal quandaries are explored by Campos in *A boa guerra* (item **4529**), a narrative about how Brazil's financial problems affect the mental health of a businessman and by Daniel in *Alegres e irresponsáveis abacaxis americanos* (item **4536**), a novel about the predicament of homosexuals. Other personal predicaments are adroitly examined in Celina's *Afonso Contínuo, santo de altar* (item **4534**), a well-crafted literary tribute to a humble man which is also a *roman à clef*. The nature of love and infatuation between man and woman are treated in two separate novels: Luzilá Ferreira's *Muito além do corpo* (item **4542**), a work of singular spirituality, wisdom, and poetry, and in Luiz Vilela's *Graça* (item **4570**), a witty exploration of a protagonist's macho attitudes towards the novel's female character. A feminist sensibility governs Marilene Felinto's *O lago encantado de Grongonzo* (item **4541**), a novel in which everything a woman values is destroyed.

Novels about the various immigrant experiences in Brazil are well represented in this *HLAS* volume: the Japanese are featured in Ana Suzuki's *Flor de vidro* (item **4568**) and in Cecília Murayama's *Sayonara, e já que assim deve ser . . .* (item **4557**); the Italians in Lacava's *Vinho amargo* (item **4549**), which takes place in Rio Grande do Sul; the Germans in Boos Jr.'s *Quadrilátero: livro um; Matheus* (item **4526**); and the Lebanese (or "Syrian-Lebanese" as these immigrants were known at the turn of the century) in Emil Farhat's *Dinheiro na Estrada* (item **4539**) a narrative which unfolds in several geographic areas.

The perennial struggle over the use and ownership of Brazilian land, a leitmotif in the nation's history and literature, is once again the dominant theme of many works of fiction. The abuse and misuse of land by unscrupulous men is portrayed in a new edition of Barroso's *Os posseiros* (item **4522**). Although first published 31 years ago, the novel's depiction of an ancient and widespread problem is as timely today as it was then. Land is also the subject of Carvalho's *Carro doce* (item **4533**), an ironic and bitter portrayal of life among the Northeast's sugarcane planters. Jacob's *A gaiola tirante rumo do rio da borracha* (item **4547**) deals with confrontations between rubber plantation owners and the humble peasants of the Amazon basin. Set in the same region, Tocantins' *As ruínas de Suruanã* (item **4569**) evokes life on the island of Marajó, a region rarely portrayed in Brazilian literature.

A theme inseparable from the Brazilian struggle over land is the subjugation of the nation's indigenous population. Two recent novels depict confrontations between the white man and the first Brazilian natives: Marques' *Extermínio* (item **4554**) centers on colonial policies designed to either convert the Indians to a European notion of discipline, better described as slave labor, or to annihilate them. The other novel, Kuperman's *O pai de todos* (item **4548**) encompasses the entire world but focuses on several Indian villages in Brazil, denouncing iniquities perpetrated against their inhabitants.

Another Brazilian minority group victimized by unfair treatment throughout the nation's history is blacks. Historical novels about African slaves and their descendants still in chains—actually, if not visibly—include Pinaud's *Malvados mortos* (item **4560**), a story of the hatred and injustice that permeated the institution of slavery, and also Oscar's *Curukango Rei* (item **4559**) about a black leader nicknamed "King" who led a doomed slave rebellion. The terror experienced by blacks in colonial times also affected whites who happened to hold different religious beliefs from those of the Portuguese colonizers. Neves' prize winning *As chamas na missa* (item **4558**) conveys the persecutions suffered by non-Christians (i.e. "New Christians" and Jews) during the time of the Inquisition. The Church and religion are also the subject of a novel that portrays the little-known, charismatic heroine Santa Dica in Moura's *Sete léguas de paraíso* (item **4556**). Finally, in another historical novel, narrated at many levels, author Maria José de Queiroz tells the story of *Joaquina, filha de Tiradentes* (item **4562**), the natural daughter of "the Martyr of Independence," and the frustrations which eroded her life.

Among other eclectic and recent novels are *Horizonte de eventos* (item **4528**), a "sci-fi" version of the future; Márcio Souza's *O brasileiro voador: um romance mais-leve-que-o-ar* (item **4567**), a satirical interpretation of Santos Dumont's contribution to aviation. Reeditions included *A família Agulha* (item **4546**), a humoristic work about Brazilian society in the 1800s published nearly a century ago by Guimarães Jr.; the renowned *Macunaíma* (item **4519**); and three massive volumes of Josué Montello's works reissued on the occasion of his 70th birthday (item **4555**).

To conclude, one can state that the Brazilian novel is enjoying a renaissance. Departures from traditional styles and the success of original and experimental approaches to narrative confirm the vitality of the genre. These new novels attest to the rebirth of creativity in a society formerly frozen by the repression of a police state and still undergoing great socioeconomic turmoil.

4517 Amaral, Maria Adelaide Santos do. Luísa: quase uma história de amor. Rio de Janeiro: Editora Nova Fronteira, 1986. 275 p.

Describes life among cultivated, upper-middle-class, middle-aged Brazilians in São Paulo during the military rule of the 1960s. Luisa, the protagonist, exemplifies the anxieties of intellectuals who had nowhere to go during the persecutions of the 1970s, and whose values and ideals were shattered by the times. One of the few novels about the dictatorship which understates the theme of physical torture, while pointing out the significance and impact of psychological torments that resulted in wounds possibly as deep and lasting as those inflicted by the tortures.

4518 Andrade, João Batista de. Perdido no meio da rua: romance. São Paulo: Global Editora; Secretaria de Estado da Cultura, 1989. 108 p.

While young and idealistic students and workers envision a just future for their country, military forces conspire against them. Novel portrays last hours of freedom and first experiences of dictatorship of members of a progressive party in São Paulo. Plot reveals how betrayal evolves into guilt and apprehension into terror.

4519 Andrade, Mário de. Macunaíma: o herói sem nenhum caráter. Ilustrações de Rita Loureiro. 2a. ed. Belo Horizonte, Brazil: Editora Itatiaia, 1985. 154 p., 44 p. of plates: bibl., col. ill.

Richly illustrated edition of classic by one of the founders of the Week of Modern Art in Brazil (1922). Telê P.A. Lopes' commentary "Rapsódia e Resistência" is informative, scholarly, and insightful.

4520 Bahia, Juarez. Ensina-me a ler: conspirando contra o amor. Petrópolis, Brazil: Vozes, 1989. 125 p. (Col. Romances Vozes)

Concerns male and female lovers and their commitment to and plans for social revolution in Brazil in the 1960s. He is a revisionist Communist, and she, a progressive Catholic activist. Narrative combines social science theories with political strife and romantic interludes. Provides overview of Brazil's struggle for democracy in the 20th century.

4521 Bandeira, Elisa. Espere um pouco, Solano. São Paulo: EDICON, 1987. 319 p.: ill.

Novel uses dialogue among students, farmers, peasants, and factory workers to expose vulnerability of Brazil's working classes and corruption of its ruling elite. Other themes addressed are emergence of feminism in opposition to male chauvinism, growing awareness of injustice, and rise of socio-political consciousness among Brazilians in the face of persistent oppression over the last 30 years.

4522 Barroso, Maria Alice. Os posseiros. Rio de Janeiro: Editora Record, 1986. 300 p.

Concerns perennial Brazilian struggle over land between *posseiros* (peasants who work abandoned fields) and *grileiros* (who claim to own the fields). In 1955, when novel was first published, rights of the former were barely acknowledged by a few journalists and politicians, while the government favored the latter. Despite some improvement, problem persists today. Told from the *posseiro's* viewpoint, the novel's reissue confirms persistence and severity of the problem. Author presents a large social canvas of life in the Brazilian backlands, enriched by psychological insights. See also *HLAS 48:6030.*

4523 Batista, Ramiro. O camaleão no abismo. Belo Horizonte, Brazil: Editora Itatiaia, 1986. 200 p. (Col. Buriti; 43)

Love story traces the predicament of a man and woman trying to survive physically and spiritually during the Brazilian dictatorship of the 1960s. Author uses irony and parody to develop his roman-à-clef characters; the female protagonist is based on the celebrated poet Adélia Prado. Narrative is interlaced with excerpts and quotations from authors such as Balzac, Nabokov, and Chico Buarque de Holanda.

4524 Bernardes, Carmo. Memórias do vento. Rio de Janeiro: Editora Marco Zero, 1986. 201 p. (Col. Histórias do pau-brasil)

Journalist/protagonist is committed to the linguistic decolonization of his country. Regards foreign imports as grave threats to Brazilian national culture. Stresses his *caipira* (provincial) heritage, which he discusses in articles in his Goiás newspaper. Posits that Brazilian writers have a vast array of expressions they should preserve in their writings. Uses picaresque style to expose urban life in slums, inhabitants of which exemplify the vitality of Brazilian speech in proverbs, spontaneous rhymes, sayings.

4525 Berto, Luiz. Nunca houve guerrilha em Palmares. Porto Alegre, Brazil: Mercado Aberto, 1987. 315 p. (Série Novo romance; 12)

Passionate narrative concerning tragic outcome of sociopolitical events in Pernambuco in mid-1960s focuses on how democratically-elected Governor Miguel Arraes was deposed by an alliance formed among local oligarchs, traditional Catholic Church representatives, and the Americans (in the person of an arms dealer). This "anticommunist league" declared war on destitute sugarcane peasants (cassacos) and their political leaders, all of whom were even further victimized by another union between the coronéis and the sugar producers (usineiros). Author refers to Pernambuco of the 1960s as a social "laboratory."

4526 Boos Júnior, Adolfo. Quadrilátero: livro um—Matheus; romance. São Paulo: Melhoramentos, 1986. 450 p.

Dense novel concerns tribulations endured by German immigrants to Brazil towards the end of the 19th century. Narrative's structure applies pattern inspired by four elements—Earth, Wind, Fire, and Water—to lives of four characters: Matheus, Natalia, Paula, and Rudolf. Covers their struggle to settle in the backlands and their rejection by earlier German immigrants. Narrative combines collective and personal memories. A difficult, somewhat puzzling work.

4527 Bulhões, Antônio. As quatro estações. Rio de Janeiro: Editora Guanabara, 1986. 324 p.

Novel concerns men and women suffering from tuberculosis and confined to a sanatorium-residence at the time of World War II. One patient writes about the development of mankind, while others experience love and lust. Conversations range from self-analysis to religion to order and chaos in the world beyond the sanatorium. Somewhat reminiscent of Thomas Mann's The magic mountain.

4528 Calife, Jorge Luiz. Horizonte de eventos: romance. Rio de Janeiro: Editora

Nova Fronteira, 1986. 327 p. (Padrões de contato; 2)

A sequel to Padrões de contato (see HLAS 48:6127), this novel rotates beyond planet Earth. Angela Duncan, heroine of the previous novel, appears 38 years later but still age 25 in the year 3040. By then she leads "Eden Seis," a floating colony whose mixed population is a cross between earthlings and inhabitants from other planets and galaxies. Interesting science fiction writer is very popular in Brazil.

4529 Campos, Arnaldo. A boa guerra. Porto Alegre, Brazil: Mercado Aberto, 1986. 90 p. (Série Novelas; 27)

Unusual narrative concerns businessman destroyed by Brazil's economic crisis who is facing bankruptcy. Novel incorporates a failed love affair, a listless marriage, and a frantic search for financial solutions. Radio's medical bulletins on dying President-Elect Tancredo Neves symbolize the nation's and the protagonist's decline and hopelessness.

4530 Cardoso, Luiz Pereira. Diário de Berê. São Paulo: Estação Liberdade, 1988. 159 p.

Somewhat of a continuation of Meu pai, acabaram com ele (see item **4531.** Concerns political fate of Tulio Sr., his incarceration after the military coup of 1964, and the effect of this incarceration on his household (i.e., wife, two daughters, son, maid, chauffeur, dog). Novel shifts between wife's memoirs read by one daughter and the children's interpretations of their father's absence. Narrative is designed as a sort of documentary on the capricious and arbitrary acts of the military police against vulnerable citizens devoid of legal protection. After seven years of mourning and suspense, and lacking any knowledge of Tulio Sr.'s ultimate fate, his family, led by his wife, must reinvent and redirect life without father/husband/friend to lead the way.

4531 Cardoso, Luiz Pereira. Meu pai, acabaram com ele. Rio de Janeiro: Editora Guanabara, 1986. 122 p.

Concerns torture and death of a father/husband by the police during President Emilio Médici's rule. Narrated from three viewpoints: 1) a daughter, who is also jailed along with father and mother; 2) a maid who distances herself from a conflict she perceives as an "upper class" problem; and

3) the youngest child, a seven-year-old boy whose account takes precedence over the others. The father's eventual death reveals the family's hidden strengths and weaknesses. Unusually sympathetic narrative about the nation's middle class, generally scorned in most Brazilian novels about this heinous period. See also item **4530.**

4532 Carrero, Raimundo. Viagem no ventre da baleia. Recife, Brazil: Tempo Brasileiro; Fundação do Patrimônio Histórico e Artístico de Pernambuco, Secretaria de Turismo, Cultura e Esportes do Governo de Pernambuco, 1986. 190 p.

Dense, complex novel of ideas about Brazil's perennial socio-political problems. Dialogues, anecdotes, and fragmented narratives encompass many subjects ranging from education to religion to idealism of anti-establishment young militants. Also deals with role of Catholic Church in struggles between peasants and landowners.

4533 Carvalho, Romeu de. Carro doce. Rio de Janeiro: Anima, 1986. 147 p.: ill.

Regional novel about life in the backlands of Brazil's Northeast. Describes man's relationship to the land in the work of planting, harvesting, and care of the soil. Author's depiction of the Northeast landscape is reminiscent of the old-fashioned and romantic style of José de Alencar. On the other hand, Carvalho's commitment to social change places him on a par with other contemporary novelists. His novel is basically an account of the persecutions and injustices endured by the Northeast peasants who formed the "Ligas Camponesas" or peasant leagues that were crushed by the military in the 1960s.

4534 Celina, Lindanor. Afonso Contínuo, santo de altar. Rio de Janeiro: Editora Nova Fronteira, 1986. 213 p.

Author, the recipient of numerous awards for fiction, here describes the relationships among judges and lawyers as well as the janitorial staff in a Belém courthouse, a sort of fantastic pantheon known as the "Palácio da Justiça." Author stresses the corruption that permeates the local society and, ironically, the disdain for human justice characteristic of legal experts. Narrator is Antônio, a humble janitor who stands in sharp contrast to the judges and lawyers. His kindness and other qualities make him,

in the author's words, a "santo de altar" (saint in a niche). This satirical and humorous *roman-à-clef* novel caused quite a stir in Belém's society at the time of book's publication.

4535 Cristaldo, Janer. Ponche verde. Rio de Janeiro: Nórdica, 1986. 279 p.

Concerns young Rio Grande do Sul Brazilians who went into exile in Europe in the 1970s to escape the military dictatorship. Novel relates their personal soul-searching and reevaluation of Brazil from a foreign perspective. Their decision to return is stimulated by their desire to reform the country from within. Writing is clear; use of literary devices is balanced; and author's perceptive portrayal of individuals away from their country of origin is convincing.

4536 Daniel, Herbert. Alegres e irresponsáveis abacaxis americanos: romance. Rio de Janeiro: Espaço e Tempo, 1987. 333 p. (Col. Ficções deste espaço e tempo; 4)

Complex narrative concerns lives of a large group of homosexuals traced through 12 episodes or "sequences." Each deals with gay men in 1980s who lived between rejection and acceptance by society, relating their individual struggles that ranged from hesitation regarding sexual tendencies to fear of being infected with AIDS. Some episodes describe tragic decisions about life-and-death situations, while others reflect the more enjoyable aspects of sexual relations. Uses long dialogues in the style of an hermeneutic essay to convey the ancient Greeks' worship of sex, pursuit of physical health, and search for a balanced life.

4537 Diniz, Tailor Netto. Armadilha do destino. Porto Alegre, Brazil: Mercado Aberto, 1988. 71 p. (Série Novelas; 44)

Two adolescents discover love during the "euphoric" 1970s decade in Brazil. Their encounter with frustration and disillusion parallels the nation's own trajectory from euphoria to repression and decline. Narrative stresses middle-class support of the military and indifference to the suffering of the poor.

4538 Escobar, Pepe. Speedball. Porto Alegre, Brazil: L&PM Editores, 1987. 175 p. (Col. Olho da rua)

Kinetic and experimental novel about the chaotic circumstances of today's world. Perspective shifts from specific individuals to the universe as a whole, and ranges from Brazil to Australia. Portuguese is the dominant language, followed by English and including a variety of other languages. Lucid, intelligent critique of modern politics as a grotesque development of Western civilization. A literary equivalent of films by Fellini and Coppola, the narrative is hyperbolic, radical, charismatic, and magnetic.

4539 Farhat, Emil. Dinheiro na estrada: uma saga de imigrantes. São Paulo: T.A. Queiroz Editor, 1987. 359 p., 1 leaf of plates: port.

Novel about Lebanese immigrants (i.e., "Syrian-Lebanese," called *turcos* by Brazilians) is based on letters written by immigrant brothers to their mother in Lebanon. Letters describe geographic regions where jobs are offered, providing large social canvas of Brazil at the time of railroad-building (e.g., Madeira-Mamoré). Mother's replies are filled with self-deprecating humor. Epistolar novel reveals how immigrants dealt with the values of a new society.

4540 Faria, Alvaro Alves de. Autópsia: romance. São Paulo: Traço Editora, 1986. 83 p.

Novel reissued almost 20 years after its initial publication provides graphic depiction of civil rights violations perpetrated by the military during Emilio Garrastazu Médici's dictatorship. Men and women confined to the police torture chambers would leave mutilated both physically and spiritually, if not dead. Narrative describes this infernal scenario, noting the helplessness, confusion, and ignorance of these victims, whether naive leftists, intellectuals, or politicized factory workers, in their confrontations with the police.

4541 Felinto, Marilene. O lago encantado de Grongonzo. Rio de Janeiro: Editora Guanabara, 1987. 151 p.

Intensely introspective novel consists of a monologue. Protagonist is a married woman and mother who returns to a mythical town where she may have spent a bitter childhood. While recalling her past, she attempts to justify her mistrust of women by noting her betrayal and mistreatment by mother, grandmother, girlfriends, and female teachers. Novel explores the nature of friendship among women.

4542 Ferreira, Luzilá Gonçalves. Muito além do corpo: romance. São Paulo: Editora Scipione; Fundação Nestlé de Cultura, 1988. 79 p.

Author uses man's body as the text of a narrative that will retrieve passages of the narrator's childhood while formulating an ideology of love. Author establishes a blueprint for feminine but apolitical writing. Novel with a spiritual dimension and a strong intellectual focus. Recipient of Third Prize in the 1988 *Premio Bienal Nestlé de Literatura Brasileira.*

4543 Fonseca, Rubem. Bufo & Spallanzani. 2a. ed. Rio de Janeiro: F. Alves, 1985. 337 p.

Acclaimed by Brazilian critics as one of the author's best, this ironic and witty novel is about the craft of writing fiction. Concerns idiosyncrasies of a fastidious detective and narrator's involvement in bizarre, unsolved crimes. Uses postmodern plurality of plots in which one novel is written within another along concurrent narrative voices. Portrays multitude of Brazilian lifestyles, ranging from bourgeois conservatives to transvestites, lesbians, and hippies. As if anticipating a deconstructionist approach, author has fashioned a series of narrative building blocks held together by the curiosity of a detective on the trail of several murders.

4544 França Júnior, Oswaldo. No fundo das águas. Rio de Janeiro: Editora Nova Fronteira, 1987. 169 p.

Projected dam will result in the conversion of a region into a lake. The fate of hundreds of characters is linked by prospect of waters flooding and covering all that mattered in their life. Process involves events ranging from litigation to robberies and assassinations among competing interests. Rural Brazil is portrayed as a sort of laboratory in which all sorts of new experiments in living are tried, adopted, and discarded. A sense of doom pervades the novel.

4545 Glauco, Luiz. Os cogumelos vermelhos do outono. Rio de Janeiro: Livraria Editora Cátedra, 1989. 215 p.

Stresses torture and other abuses of the military police against defenseless young political activists imprisoned during the dictatorship. Told from viewpoint of such a victim of the regime, describes life of the marginalized and destitute and contrasts it with that of the rich. Innovative narrative incorporates newspapers' "social columns" about such lifestyles and also plays with Portuguese language to create various effects.

4546 Guimarães Júnior, Luís. A Família Agulha: romance humorístico. 2a. ed. Rio de Janeiro: Presença, 1987. 244 p. (Col. Resgate; 9)

Welcome reissue for laymen and scholars of a forgotten 19th-century novel, a genre little known in today's Brazil. Ironic and witty narrative about the lifestyle of the Brazilian urban middle class in the 1900s. Critic Flora Susskind's foreword notes the author's humor in exposing the pretensions and nonsense that pervade that world.

4547 Jacob, Paulo. A gaiola tirante rumo do rio da borracha: romance. Rio de Janeiro: Editora Cátedra, 1987. 188 p.

Paulo Jacob does for the Amazon Basin what Guimarães Rosa did for the *sertão*. Powerful narrative portrays feverish world of killings, robberies, greed, and distrust among rich farmers, and hopes for a better life among the region's poor. Provides fascinating, panoramic view of a society on the brink of financial and social bankruptcy following arrival of an international business network intent on exploiting and destroying the Amazon region.

4548 Kuperman, Mário. O pai de todos: romance. Rio de Janeiro: Philobiblion, 1985. 251 p. (Col. Prosa brasileira; 9)

Plot traces activities of a group of idealistic young people concerned with contemporary issues of vital importance for the survival of mankind. They struggle to promote issues related to ecology, birth control, equality, and feminism. The young idealists operate in an atmosphere of danger and repression in several Third World impoverished regions that range from Asia to Africa to an Indian enclave in Brazil. Somewhat didactic novel that includes dialogues and discussions that will interest ecologists and sociologists.

4549 Lacava, Eloy. Vinho amargo. Caxias do Sul, Brazil: EDUCS; Porto Alegre, Brazil: EST, 1987. 186 p. (Col. Imigração italiana; 85)

Historical novel deals with repercussions of World War I in Santa Teresa, an isolated Italian colony in Rio Grande do Sul.

Narrative describes political and social circumstances among Italian expatriates who settled in the Brazilian pampas. Covers a period of 30 years and events such as the Spanish flu, Anarchists, and political conflicts that preceded the "Estado Novo," as well as the semi-fascist Vargas regime.

4550 Lacerda, Nilma Gonçalves. Manual de tapeçaria: romance. Rio de Janeiro: Philobiblion; Fundação Rio, 1986. 231 p. (Col. Prosa brasileira; 13)

First Prize for Literature (Rio de Janeiro, 1985). Narrative about young female teacher who sees herself as surrogate mother of her pupils and counselor to their parents. Postmodernist, complex structure underlies deceptively simple plot. Narrative strongly critical of lack of civic responsibility in Brazil for marginalized citizens, especially children. Among accomplishments of this exceptional novel are a sophisticated and original use of language and complex narrative techniques.

4551 Leitão, José Maria. O hóspede do tempo. Porto Alegre, Brazil: Mercado Aberto, 1987. 136 p. (Série Novelas; 32)

Memoirs of former guerrilla who escaped the brutal persecution that began after the Brazilian military coup of 1964. Advised by his father to seek refuge in a friend's house, the narrator learns about his father's past as a right-wing advocate who supported policies that caused many problems to the friend who is now the young man's protector. An awareness of cycles of history repeating themselves permeates the narrative, providing an ironic, if sometimes confusing, perspective.

4552 Luft, Lya Fett. Exílio: romance. Rio de Janeiro: Editora Guanabara, 1987. 201 p.

Outcast and isolated woman examines her failed life as wife, mother, lover, daughter, sister, and medical doctor, roles not necessary of her own choice. She searches for reasons that would explain the ruptures in her life. Mostly she attempts to understand the influence and memory of her mother. Doubts and questions are posed to a weird dwarf, a sort of super-ego who follows her everywhere but provides no answers.

4553 Maranhão, Haroldo. Rio de raivas. Rio de Janeiro: F. Alves, 1987. 278 p.

Outpouring of scatology and profanity overwhelms an otherwise insightful and panoramic view of life in Belém do Pará, the author's hometown. Exposes corrupt activities of political leaders, some local clergy, landowners, and journalists. In contrast to author's previous works, noted for their subtle satire and manifestation of literary skills, here the writer concentrates his attack on the most sordid aspects of life in Belém as if determined to wreak vengeance upon his hometown. (See also *HLAS 46:6057*.)

4554 Marques, Aracyldo. Extermínio: romance. Rio de Janeiro: Livraria Editora Cátedra, 1986. 204 p.

Epic novel follows the efforts of native Indians in Brazil who struggle to preserve their lifestyle and, ultimately, their life, as they face persecution and death at the hands of Portuguese settlers during first years of colonization. Narrative describes the cruel clash between European and native cultures. Lyrical passages provide insight into the Indians' innocence. Tupi vocabulary is used to describe their social habits, religion, and food.

4555 Montello, Josué. Romances e novelas. Rio de Janeiro: Editora Nova Aguilar, 1986. 3 v.: bibl., ill. (Biblioteca luso-brasileira; 32: Série brasileira)

Three volumes published on 70th birthday of major Brazilian writer include 16 novels and four short stories, and critics' introductions. Preceded by "Confissões de um Romancista," wherein author highlights his literary career. Enhanced by pictures, chronology, updated bibliography, and a "map" of the city of São Luís as portrayed in his fiction.

4556 Moura, Antônio José de. Sete léguas de paraíso. São Paulo: Global Editora, 1989. 282 p.: ill. (Singular & plural)

Historical novel based on real incident concerns so-called "Republic of Angels" founded by young charismatic woman and followers in the Goiás backlands in mid-1920s. After witnessing an apparition of the Virgin Mary, *Santa Dica* began to perform miracles, to preach salvation before the end of the world, and to attract a mass following. The Catholic Church and the State declared war on her. Novel describes the misfortunes of this "female version of Antônio Conselheiro."

4557 Murayama, Cecília. Sayonará: e já que assim deve ser. Campinas, Brazil: ICEA Gráfica e Editora, 1988. 282 p.

Another novel, possibly autobiographical, about Japanese immigration to Brazil. This is a Shakespearean love story in which Japanese expatriates prevent the marriage of a son to a Brazilian Caucasian woman. Author explores New World's impact on a thousand-year-old tradition.

4558 Neves, Luiz Guilherme Santos. As chamas na missa: romance. Rio de Janeiro: Philobiblion; Fundação Rio, 1986. 105 p. (Col. Prosa brasileira; 15)

Ironic narrative describes climate of terror created by the Inquisition in colonial Brazil. Gives as examples Father Vieira's Baroque speeches, accusations against New Christians and Crypto-Jews found in Holy Office Archives, and hypocritical litanies chanted by Dominicans and other religious orders. Author's extensive historical and linguistic research are evident in the novel. Awarded Third Prize in the 1985 Fundação Rio's *Premio Rio de Literatura*.

4559 Oscar, João. Curunkango rei. Prefácio de Barbosa Lima Sobrinho. Niterói, Brazil: Cromos Editora, 1988. 213 p.

Semi-historical novel about Brazilian slavery. Protagonist is slave who leads a rebellion against his masters, and loses. Survivors manage to preserve their spiritual dignity and sense of inner freedom despite abuses. Author's narrative and dialogue make excellent use of the rich and diverse lexicon of slave languages and speech in colonial Brazil.

4560 Pinaud, João Luiz Duboc. Malvados mortos: Paty do Alferes, 1838. Rio de Janeiro: Expressão e Cultura, 1988. 170 p.: ill.

Novel about the heroic struggles of slaves who fled sugarcane plantations (*engenhos*) to seek refuge in *quilombos*, remote colonies made up of fugitive slaves. Protagonist is Manoel Congo, most recalcitrant of *quilombo* chiefs, who was captured and condemned in Rio de Janeiro (1838–39). Subject is Congo's trial, which generated much publicity at the time, due to defendant's great intelligence and courage. Author combines fictional narrative with factual excerpts (e.g., legislation). Includes glossary of relevant terms and interesting illustrations.

4561 Portes, Max de Figueiredo. Maruim: romance. São Paulo: Melhoramentos, 1986. 93 p.

In the style of a Guimarães Rosa, author uses folk songs and folk wisdom to tell a love story in an environment populated by local chieftans who control the town's destiny. Narrator's personal view of world changes, and he overcomes his own prejudices. Awarded First Prize in the 1986 Premio Bienal Nestlé de Literatura Brasileira.

4562 Queiroz, Maria José de. Joaquina, filha do Tiradentes: romance. São Paulo: Marco Zero, 1987. 297 p. (Histórias do pau-brasil)

Historical novel about the ideals of Joaquina, the illegitimate daughter of Joaquim José da Silva Xavier, Brazil's independence hero (1746–92) who was nicknamed "O Tiradentes." After death of "O Tiradentes" by hanging, mother and daughter fled from Portuguese Crown's authorities through vast areas of Brazil. Intensely personal psychological account of Joaquina's life also focuses on the impact of poverty, low self-esteem, and fear on two abandoned women during adverse political times.

4563 Rey, Marcos. Memórias de um gigolô: romance. 12a. ed. São Paulo: Editora Atica, 1986. 224 p. (Col. de autores brasileiros; 96)

Postmodernist novel concerns individual who serves as metaphor for alienated urban man. A parasite, the *gigolô* reveals his adventures with women, their lovers and husbands, São Paulo's secret night life, etc. A Brazilian film and TV soap were based on this novel which has been translated into English (see *HLAS 50:4317*).

4564 Rey, Marcos. A sensação de setembro: opereta tropical. São Paulo: Editora Atica, 1989. 167 p.

Written as if it were a combination novel/opera buffa, this work is a satire of the upper and middle classes of urban Brazil. Families are strangers under one roof bent on the pursuit of money and pleasure. Those who deviate are viewed as bizarre and eventually are punished by the family.

4565 Rónai, Cora. O terceiro tigre. Rio de Janeiro: Editora Nova Fronteira, 1986. 154 p.

Postmodernist novel develops interca-lated set of double voices: a female's narrative ponders her bourgeois upbringing, boring lifestyle, and agonies of creating fiction; the male's discourse is focused on the actual writing of a novel. In addition to a self-reflective pattern, these texts have in common the incorporation of established authors' ideas and concepts such as Borges' "third tiger" of the title, a narrative *leitmotif*. Novel also draws on Jungian interpretation of dreams.

4566 Sá, Irene Tavares de. Fazenda da Estrela: romance. Prefácio de Rachel de Queiroz. Rio de Janeiro: Livraria Agir Editora, 1988. 226 p.

Ultra-romantic novel about a lonely and bored man who fathers the son of his ignorant and poor maid. After she dies, he raises the boy. Despite the somewhat trite plot, the novel makes interesting use of narrative voices that alternate among a subjective, autobiographical speaker, an aloof story teller, and a third narrator. Also includes convincing atmosphere of mystery and good descriptions of forests and other wild landscapes.

4567 Souza, Márcio. O brasileiro voador: um romance mais-leve-que-o-ar. Rio de Janeiro: Editora Marco Zero, 1986. 263 p. (Col. Histórias do pau brasil)

Renowned author of *The emperor of the Amazon* (see *HLAS 44:6334*) returns to the successful style of that novel. Using the "feuilleton" method, Souza retraces life of Alberto Santos-Dumont (1873–1932), Brazilian pioneer aviator/inventor and national hero. Santos-Dumont's great achievements notwithstanding, author mocks his looks, friends, romantic adventures, and bourgeois lifestyle.

4568 Suzuki, Ana. Flor de vidro. Rio de Janeiro: Editora Record, 1987. 152 p.

Brazilian descendants of Japanese immigrants are contrasted with their traditional predecessors. Novel's young characters prefer to attend the *karaokes* (singing nightclubs popular in São Paulo) rather than places favored by their parents. A Japanese-Brazilian youth returns to Brazil from Tokyo after hearing a Brazilian love song over a long-distance call. Like the *ikebana* sessions taught by old Japanese masters, the Brazilian song is also a ritual, a recall from Brazil.

Those born in Brazil are rooted in that country rather than in an ancestral homeland.

4569 Tocantins, Sylvia Helena. As ruínas de Suruanã: romance marajoara. Belém, Brazil: Gráfica Falangola, 1987. 249 p., 7 leaves of plates: ill.

Concerns life in the island of Marajó at the mouth of the Amazon River, a region rarely the subject of fiction in Brazil. Plot focuses on activities of rich landowners and rulers of an area populated by an impoverished and humiliated population living in subhuman conditions. Narrative makes effective use of dialect, folktales, and the island's extraordinary history. Includes glossary and illustrations.

4570 Vilela, Luiz. Graça: romance. São Paulo: Estação Liberdade, 1989. 226 p.

Novel makes witty use of contemporary Portuguese language through author's play of words and concepts. When not engaged in sex, male character pontificates on a variety of subjects while his female, a carnal creature almost devoid of brains, listens. The *machista* tendencies of Brazilian men are portrayed in the picture of the male as thinker and speaker and the female strictly as sex object.

Short Stories

MARIA ANGELICA GUIMARÃES LOPES, *Associate Professor, Department of Spanish, Italian, and Portuguese, University of South Carolina, Columbia*

BECAUSE MOST OF THE BOOKS REVIEWED for *HLAS 52* were published between 1982–88 (and the great majority in 1986–87), the present assessment of the genre in Brazil is not that much different from the one in *HLAS 50* which covers 1982–87 (with one-third of them published in 1984–86). The economic instability which limited if not the writing at least the publication of short-story collections remains as it was five years ago. In other words, publishing houses have been forced to reduce the publication of stories and settle for more lucrative fare such as best-seller translations, self-help manuals, educational texts, and works of famous authors which always guarantee sales. Also profitable are reprints of classics and successful recent story collections.

Still, from the economic and name-recognition viewpoint, there are incentives for story writers, both established and new. Literary associations, governmental and other entities, and universities work together to award prizes for good story writing. Some of the most lucrative of these are issued by corporations such as Nestlé, with its prestigious "Bienal de Literatura" awarded to various literary genres. The Brazilian public pays attention to literary events and sometimes writers do attain celebrity status. Although authors are often advised to write novels because "stories don't sell," the genre is nevertheless popular in Brazil. Indeed, the story long ago replaced poetry as the first contact of most readers with Brazilian literature.

The deaths of several literary figures in the last years is a cause for regret. The dean of "crônicas," Rubem Braga, and José Cândido de Carvalho, a writer of fantastic tales, lived to ripe old ages, but Oswaldo França Júnior's death in a car accident at a relatively young age cut short an impressive literary career.

Among the many themes of the recent Brazilian story, the most notable one is black liberation (items **4581, 4588, 4589, 4602,** and **4619**). Most authors of these works are "committed" in the Sartrean sense of *engagé* and belong to the Quilombhoje Group (i.e., "Heroic Slave Rebellion Today"). This black movement is of necessity different from the one in the US where miscegenation is not as pervasive as in Brazil. It is also different from movements such as *négritude* in countries with predominantly black populations such as those in the Caribbean. After Gilberto Freyre (1900–87) published his classic studies of the biological and spiritual miscegenation of Brazil, it has been regarded as one of the major elements of the nation's identity and culture. Brazil is perceived as a fusion of aboriginal, European (mainly Portuguese), and African elements: for generations, schoolchildren have recited that Brazil is "the flower of three sad races" (Bilac). For the intellectuals and artists who are members of Quilombhoje, helping fellow blacks out of economic difficulties is as important as telling them and other Brazilians about significant African traditions.

Feminism, a dominant theme in previous years, is not as pervasive in stories canvassed for this *Handbook*. It is true that Schmaltz (item **4623**) deals with these issues in a splendid manner, and that Ferreira (item **4591**) and Freitas (item **4592**) are also very good. The intelligent irony in Tavares' stories (item **4630**) is also notable. Still, one misses the variety and wealth of women authors who in the 1970s-80s wrote from a female perspective (see *HLAS 46*, p. 516).

Overall, most collections examined for *HLAS 52* show a balanced concern for style as well as a vital awareness of current Brazilian reality. Among established writers who continue to produce are Pólvora, Ramos, and Dourado, with the latter two expanding their fictional territory and honing their craft. Dourado's marvelous tales have made his mythical Duas Pontes a very real *locus* in Brazilian fiction (item **4590**). Younger writers Abreu, José, and Martins have "arrived" after producing a sizable corpus of consistently good fiction (items **4571, 4572, 4597,** and **4606**).

The reissue of out-of-print works by writers such as Athanázio (item **4576**), and Porto Alegre (item **4617**) not only honor these deserving authors, but also serve to introduce young Brazilians to their cultural and literary history. Young and contemporary writers, on the other hand, continue to submit their stories to literary contests that serve to promote new talent.

Overall, a pessimistic mood permeates most of the fiction annotated below, with two exceptions: the inventiveness and good humor of Mariotti's and Krahl's tales brought frequent smiles to this reviewer's lips (items **4605,** and **4599**).

To conclude, one could say that there are no major departures from the last biennium. The subjects range widely from concern for the dispossessed, to anguish and fear of life's dangers, to the enchantment and magic of childhood. Stylistically, these stories vary from matter-of-fact journalistic style to ultra-literary tales of Baroque convolution and word play. There is no doubt that despite the economic crisis and other problems the genre continues to thrive in Brazil.

4571 Abreu, Caio Fernando. Morangos mofados. São Paulo: Brasiliense, 1982. 145 p.: ill. (Cantadas literárias; 5)

Themes are isolation (Leibniz's monads), mystery of the self, multiple personalities, male homosexual feelings and encounters, madness, and death. Narrative portrays an oneiric, often menacing world in which electric light mingles with starlight. Describes physical and mental suffering of prisoners. Uses "molded strawberries" and figs as metaphor for people. Extremely well-written by recognized author with major prizes and many readers (see also *HLAS 40:6111* and item **4572**).

4572 Abreu, Caio Fernando. O ovo apunhalado. 3a. ed. Rio de Janeiro: Salamandra Editora, 1984. 172 p.

Third, revised edition of well-received work in which author deals with the diversity of love, solitude, and other feelings, as well as fate. Its everyday world includes angels, robots, and murderous objects. Lucid and magical stories often present child's viewpoint. Author is novelist, playwright, and cinema critic (see also *HLAS 42:6111* and item **4571**).

4573 Almeida, Paulo Kruel de. Olho de
    ronda: contos. Porto Alegre, Brazil:
Movimento, 1986. 89 p. (Col. Rio Grande; 81)
    Conveys the sense of despondency and impotence that permeates the life of the poor in a manner that is both realistic and surrealistic. The atmosphere is one of doom and hopelessness. Almeida's protagonists are often plural—crowds as collective characters living out their fate in dramatic, suspenseful stories. Clearly this is a writer that should be watched and especially read.

4574 Angelo, Ivan. A face horrível: contos.
    Rio de Janeiro: Editora Nova Fronteira,
1986. 223 p.
    Revised stories reveal interesting differences between the generations and the political situation of Brazil during two distinct periods (1960s and 1980s). Author is adept at showing the "element of surprise that one finds under the dust of everyday." Includes previously published stories which made their author famous at the time (1958–62). Distinguished collection by famous writer that makes excellent reading (see also *HLAS 44:6010*).

4575 Aragão, Adrino. As três faces da es-
    finge: contos. Natal, Brazil: Clima
Artes Gráficas, 1985. 95 p.
    Fine stories by Northeastern writer portray the region and its inhabitants for the interested reader.

4576 Athanázio, Enéas. Tapete verde. São
    Paulo: Editora do Escritor, 1983. 79 p.:
appendix. (Col. do escritor; 67)
    Regional stories by Santa Catarina author bring characters and situations to the fore with dramatic force. Includes essays on Athanázio and on Monteiro Lobato's and Godofredo Rangel's fiction.

4577 Báril, Fischel. A cabeça no lugar: con-
    tos. Porto Alegre, Brazil: Movimento,
1985. 78 p. (Col. Rio Grande; 74)
    Author's second collection presents several family members in difficult situations (disarray, sickness, infatuation, passion,

and death). Written with economy and perception, these are intense, moving stories. Both collections are not only very readable, but literary works of art as well. Worthy of further exposure (see also *HLAS 46:6079*).

4578 Barreto, Antônio *et al.* Um prazer
    imenso: contos eróticos masculinos.
Seleção de Jeferson de Andrade. Rio de Janeiro: Editora Record, 1986. 115 p.
    This collection of erotic tales by male authors is uneven and ranges from very fine to mediocre. Collection is also a response to two hugely successful compilations of stories by women writers: *Muito prazer* (see *HLAS 46:6122*) and *O prazer é todo meu* (Rio: Editoria Record, 1984).

4579 Boos Júnior, Adolfo. A companheira
    noturna: contos. São Paulo: Melhora-
mentos, 1986. 107 p.
    Mysterious tales written in an earthy style can be read either as parables or as simple narratives. Ironic, incisive, and polished, they depict dramatic and even extreme situations such as a nuclear explosion, a shipwreck, or revenge. The prize-winning tales have a dreamlike atmosphere. Also, "The Nocturnal Companion" of the title is a spider.

4580 Borges, Fernando. A companheira:
    contos. Porto Alegre, Brazil: Movi-
mento, 1987. 71 p. (Col. Rio Grande; 85)
    Important collection by Rio Grande do Sul author consists of stories set in the border town of Figueiras. Some deal with city-dwellers, others with country-folk. Characters and incidents in both are vivid (see also *HLAS 48:6166*).

4581 *Cadernos Negros: Contos.* Vol. 10,
    1987→. São Paulo: Editora e Gráfica
Xavier Ltda. 147 p.: bibl.
    Entire volume of *Cadernos Negros* is devoted to stories by members of *Quilombhoje* (the name of a black artistic and social movement in São Paulo), which examine different aspects in the lives of Brazilian blacks. Also emphasizes century-old African lore passed from grandfather to young man, who in turn will pass it on to his own grandchildren. Earnest, well-written book combines different approaches and perspectives that range from the matter-of-fact documentary to styles that are allegorical and surrealistic.

4582 Carvalho, André. Toda mulher é culpada: contos. Rio de Janeiro: Editora Record, 1989. 108 p.

Well-written stories with fine dialogue are not as simplistic or misogynistic as title implies. They deal with female characters drawn from several socioeconomic strata. Author was awarded prestigious Casa de las Américas Prize for previous work.

4583 Cavalcante, Joyce M.F. O discurso da mulher absurda. São Paulo: Global Editora, 1985. 96 p.

Lively and competently written collection that is in many ways a book with a thesis. Topic is sexual woman and her like in the 1970s-80s. In several of these action-cum-meditation pieces, the protagonists (author's alter ego?) resemble one another like sisters.

4584 Ceres, Heliônia. Rosália das visões: contos. São Paulo: Canopus, 1984. 93 p.

Well-crafted stories in which the inner life of characters is conveyed with a delicate touch.

4585 Contos da repressão. Rio de Janeiro: Editora Record, 1987. 150 p.

Important anthology of stories by distinguished writers, selected and prefaced by Fábio Lucas. These "repression stories" provide a painful account of the 1964–84 period, Brazil's "Never Again" (i.e., *Nunca Más*, which was the title given by Argentine writer Ernesto Sábato to a famous report on repression in his own country).

4586 Coralina, Cora. Estórias da casa velha da ponte. São Paulo: Global Editora, 1985. 95 p.

Moving, quaint, and often perceptive stories by Brazilian who became famous literary personality in her old age.

4587 Costa, Eduardo Alves da. A sala do jogo. São Paulo: Estação Liberdade, 1989? 240 p.

Anthology of six novelettes that range from science fiction to black magic to an ingenious version of Scheherazade's story. These whimsical tales, each written in its own lexicon, make entertaining reading. [R. Igel]

4588 Cunha Júnior, H. Negros na noite. São Paulo: EDICON, 1987. 79 p.: ill.

Very well written fiction conveys ideology of black liberation, for both men and women, among São Paulo intellectuals. A lucid, moving, and intelligent book. The story "Os Alfinetes" ("Pins") is a witty reworking of Machado de Assis' famous "Apólogo." Includes fine illustrations by Marizilda Menezes.

4589 Delazari, Benedita. Filhos da miséria e outras histórias: contos. 2a. ed. São Paulo: Editora Pannartz, 1988. 95 p.: ill.

The "children of misery" of the title are the poor in the big city. With simplicity and dignity, Delazari tells about the homeless, factory workers, and latchkey children in a tough world which is even tougher for those who are poor and black. In one story, however, characters enjoy power and success as young artists and intellectuals. Writer's clear narrative line and ethical concerns make for convincing stories.

4590 Dourado, Autran. Violetas e caracóis. Rio de Janeiro: Editora Guanabara, 1987. 197 p.

More parables about the mythical setting of Duas Pontes, Minas Gerais, where inhabitants eventually are expected to "declare" their madness, and where Quixotes and Sanchos abound. Many are characters from previous Dourado works (see *HLAS 46:6091* and *HLAS 48:6174*). Major themes are universal: illusion and reality, madness and sanity, good and evil. Dourado treats them in the manner of Machado and Guimarães Rosa. One doctor prescribes "violets" as a remedy to a beautiful, melancholic girl; another prescribes "snails." Brilliant, moving collection by major Brazilian writer.

4591 Ferreira, Sonia Nolasco. Você jurou que eu ia ser feliz. São Paulo: Global Editora, 1986. 207 p. (Col. múltipla)

Five novellas focus on upper-middle class women in Brazil and abroad. Unlike their mothers, these are career women who face new conflicts and different problems. These very well-written stories are psychological studies with traditional plots that include some innovative devices such as interior monologue and time shift.

4592 Freitas, Ana Maria. Um tango, por favor: contos e novelas. Rio de Janeiro: Nórdica, 1987. 166 p.

Notion of "tango" is decoded as lust,

passion, betrayal, and possibly death. Told from a female viewpoint, these stories focus on middle-class housewives as well as career women. Although author is from the Northeast, stories have a *carioca* flavor, being both exuberant and ironic. Well worth reading.

4593 Genauer, Beyla. Levantar vôo: contos. Rio de Janeiro: Philobiblion, 1986. 97 p. (Col. Prosa brasileira; 18)

Strong, incisive stories by Jewish-Brazilian writer about her milieu. They deal with repressed anger, misunderstandings, and aimless lives.

4594 Giffoni, Luís. A jaula inquieta: conto. São Paulo: Editora Scipione, 1988. 77 p.

Hard to believe that these are author's first stories. Excellent compilation noted for its stylistic economy, elegance, imaginative plots, and firm characterization. Serendipitous book in which allegories and moral tales resound with ironic echoes of Poe and Machado de Assis.

4595 Hilst, Hilda. Com os meus olhos de cão e outras novelas. São Paulo: Editora Brasiliense, 1986. 309 p.

Powerful stories tell of narrator's lifelong introspection and resulting actions. Rather than plot, the tales reveal "landscapes of the soul" through which the reader follows the narrator's dense, contorted consciousness. Hilst is a well-known poet whose stories are impressive but far from easy reading.

4596 Hoffmann, Ricardo L. A casa da matéria. Capa e ilustrações de Odil Campos. Florianópolis, Brazil: Fundação Catarinense de Cultura; São Paulo: M. Ohno, 1987. 60 p.: ill. (some col.).

According to author, these are "elegies in prose for the house of matter." Are they poetic meditations? Stories? Actually, they are cosmogonic, metaphysical, oneiric, static, beautiful pieces. Their convoluted syntax demands patient reading.

4597 José, Elias. O grito dos torturados: contos. Rio de Janeiro: Editora Nova Fronteira, 1986. 159 p.

Fine stories about dreams and mysterious events. Title story (English translation: "Scream of the Victims of Torture") is an impressive examination of the corruption gen-

erated by injustice. In "O Reencontro," two former revolutionaries who were lovers meet again. "Idolatria" portrays a nun/psychoanalyst and her patient (see also *HLAS 42:3137*).

4598 Jovens contos eróticos. Prefácio de Principelho Mon Petit. São Paulo: Editora Brasiliense, 1987. 180 p.: ill.

Out of 2,000 erotic tales submitted for a contest, the 20 collected here are the winners. Quite a few are well done. Irreverent, farcical, and literary, they portray sex from diverse perspectives.

4599 Krahl, Neori Rafael. Folhas avulsas penduradas num cabide. Florianópolis, Brazil: FCC Edições, 1987. 62 p.

Wonderful stories by young lawyer usually told by first-person narrator. They focus on a small boy's village, a world which the child perceives as exotic. Other characters are a collection of warm, likable eccentrics. Humor and perspective are reminiscent of Guimarães Rosa's tales. Collection was awarded State of Santa Catarina Virgílio Várzea Prize for 1986.

4600 Lessa, Ivan. Garotos da fuzarca. Seleção de Diogo Mainardi. São Paulo: Cia das Letras, 1986.] 143 p.: ill.

Some of the "party girls" of the title are irreverent, occasionally delirious pieces. Author's style is a surrealistic cocktail consisting of clichés, history, jokes. Although not exactly stories in the accepted sense, these pieces make for exciting if difficult reading. According to Rubem Fonseca, Lessa is a "great writer . . . one of the damned."

4601 Lima Barreto. Os melhores contos. Seleção de Francisco de Assis Barbosa. São Paulo: Global Editora, 1986. 172 p.: bibl.

Compilation by famous, tragic author acclaimed by some as Machado de Assis' successor. Wonderful, bitter stories tell what it meant to be poor and mulatto in Rio during the 20th century's first quarter. Characters comprise politicians, orphans, servants, millionaire merchants, and kept women during Brazil's *belle époque*. Includes introduction and bibliography by F.A. Barbosa, a noted Barreto scholar.

4602 Lopes, Nei. Casos crioulos. Rio de Janeiro: CCM Editores, 1987. 67 p.: ill. (Col. Voz do Brasil)

Lively *Stories of black people* deal

with narrator's adventures in Rio. The milieu is bohemian, with musicians (samba composers, dancers) whose lives center around Carnival. Collection was deservedly complimented by another Rio native, the lexicographer and grammarian Antônio Houaiss. Paean to Rio by popular music composer and author who has written on the black experience in Brazil.

4603 Maia, Vasconcelos. Cação de areia: uma estória de sexo e violência nos mares da Bahia. São Paulo: Edições GRD, 1986. 70 p.

Consists of one long and two short stories by well-known Bahian writer whose leading characters are fishermen. Describes modern daily life represented by 1970s hippies against the timeless background of the fishermen's lives in Bahia de Todos os Santos. Passion, brutality, irony, and suspense are sustained throughout. Rarely has a reader felt, seen, and almost smelled the ocean as in these remarkable tales.

4604 Mansur, Gilberto. A fome do mundo: contos. São Paulo: Melhoramentos, 1986. 61 p.

Winner of Third Prize in the 1986 Premio Bienal Nestlé de Literatura Brasileira. Tales deal with unusual topics in a sophisticated, literate, and clever style. Some read like visions, such as the one about donkeys working in an underground mine, or another about the man who tries to change the course of a river. A fine collection.

4605 Mariotti, Humberto. Um circo só de mágicos. São Paulo: Global Editora, 1987. 110 p. (Col. múltipla)

Almost all these stories are nocturnal as well as imaginative, playful, and good-humored. Rather than sinister, night is seen as the accomplice of play and games. The surrealistic atmosphere and plots of author's first book (see HLAS 42:6145) are also present in these narratives. An entertaining book of high comedy.

4606 Martins, Julio Cesar Monteiro. Muamba. Rio de Janeiro: Editora Anima, 1985. 112 p.

Book's title, Muamba, is defined by the dictionary as "purse contents; exchangeable merchandise." Stories are infused with author's keen powers of observation and irony. They range from realistic to fantastic,

and the settings from the Amazon to the Andes to the cities. Martins' cinematic ability is evident in his fluid presentation of fantastic images and skillful editing techniques. Well worth reading, as are author's previous collections: *Torpalium* (see HLAS 42:6148); *Sabe quem dançou esta noite?* (see HLAS 42:6147); and *O oeste de nada* (see HLAS 46:6115).

4607 Mattos, Cyro de. Duas narrativas rústicas. Rio de Janeiro: Livraria Editora Cátedra; Itabuna, Brazil: Fundação Henrique Alves dos Reis, 1985. 48 p.

Prize-winning stories in which Bahia author depicts the region's rural areas. "Inocentes e Selvagens," for example, tells of the drought and, as Mattos' other stories, lovingly portrays the interactions between human beings and other animals.

4608 Moreira, Virgílio Moretzsohn. Jogos do instante. Rio de Janeiro: Editora Nova Fronteira, 1986. 220 p.

Book's narratives are subdivided into stories and *crônicas.* Witty stories about a varied cast of characters suggest the mysteries of their inner life. Fine collection (including the *crônicas*).

4609 Moutinho, Irene. As irmãs de Caim. Rio de Janeiro: Philobiblion, 1987. 114 p. (Col. Prosa brasileira; 21)

Three richly suggestive stories (*Mandarins de Amanda, Aurélio no castelo,* and *Prólogo?*) about jealous siblings recall the legend of Cain and Abel. In *Mandarins,* a sister is haunted by guilt for her mistreatment of a dead twin. In *Aurélia,* told like a medieval legend, an adolescent orphan has been wronged by a domineering male. In *Prólogo?,* two sisters confront the death of a child in a tropical forest, one sister abandoning the other in order "to meet Cain." [R. Igel]

4610 Nepomuceno, Eric. 40 dólares e outras histórias. Rio de Janeiro: Editora Guanabara, 1987. 171 p. ;

Beautifully crafted tales animated by mysterious characters in settings that are "tense and intense." A more accomplished set of stories than the author's previous and notable collection (see HLAS 50:3974).

4611 Oliveira, Ariosto Augusto de. A noite do galo doido: contos. São Paulo: Brasiliense, 1986. 70 p. (Cantadas literárias; 43)

Subtitled *Tales of perversion, wickedness, and desire,* these well-crafted stories are bitter and wry. They use lively language to provide psychological insights into the mind and imagination of white-collar criminals. Some stories are excellent monologues. Oliveira belongs to Rubem Fonseca's school and is a talent worthy of attention.

4612 Osório, Laci. Ibirapuytã. Porto Alegre, Brasil: Tchê!, 1987. 70 p. (Continente)

Competent stories by ex-political prisoner whose literary works were banned in 1964. In them, Osório tried to raise his readers' political consciousness.

4613 Pellegrini Júnior, Domingos. Os meninos crescem. Rio de Janeiro: Editora Nova Fronteira, 1986. 245 p.

Includes some revised stories taken from *Os meninos* (see *HLAS 42:6154*) as well as new ones. Earthy, moving, and humorous tales that focus on a pubescent boy growing up in a large family in southern Brazil (see also *HLAS 40:7446*).

4614 Peres, Arino. Contos & pontos. Brasília: Instituto Nacional do Livro; Belo Horizonte, Brazil: Editora Itatiaia, 1988. 99 p. (Col. Buriti; 44)

Includes several notable pieces by author who is also a physics professor, poet, and journalist of which the best is "Tia Dão" ("Aunt Dão"). A tour-de-force "biography" of a senile woman who dies alone, this is a dramatic account entirely free of bathos or clichés.

4615 Pires, Cornélio. Conversas ao pé do fogo. Ed. fac-similar. São Paulo: Impr. Oficial do Estado, 1987. 252 p.

Another reprint of 1921 collection consisting chiefly of pleasant tales about rural folk (i.e., the *caipira* personality). Based on considerable research, these stories are important because of their documentary value.

4616 Pólvora, Hélio. Mar de Azov: contos. São Paulo: Melhoramentos, 1986. 111 p.

Four long stories told in flashback that deal with childhood and extended family in Bahia. Incisive, sometimes even brutal, these tales cover the same territory as author's 1983 collection, *O grito da perdiz* (see *HLAS 48:6196*). Although a fine collection, it lacks

Perdiz's sustained narrative and lyrical voice (see also *HLAS 38:7394*). Winner of first prize in the 1986 Prêmio Bienal Nestlé de Literatura Brasileira.

4617 Porto Alegre, Apolinário. Paisagens: contos. Estudo crítico de Regina Zilberman. Estudo biobibliográfico e fixação de texto de Maria Eunice Moreira. Porto Alegre, Brazil: Movimento; Brasília: MinC/Pró-Memória, Instituto Nacional do Livro, 1987. 131 p.: bibl. (Col. Resgate; 2. Col. Rio Grande; 82)

These well-wrought, dramatic, sometimes ghostly stories set in a historical Rio Grande do Sul are Brazilian classics by a famous writer. Collection includes important introductory essay by Regina Zilberman, and bibliography.

4618 Ramos, Ricardo. Os amantes iluminados. Rio de Janeiro: Rocco, 1988. 116 p.

Deeply felt but unsentimental stories which constitute another achievement in Ramos' distinguished career. Like his previous collections, these tales also deal with life in the big city of São Paulo (see also *HLAS 38:7398, HLAS 42:6157,* and *HLAS 46: 6125*). Several narratives relate the theme of dying or dead friends. Highly recommended collection.

4619 Ribeiro, Esmeralda Malungos e milongas: conto. São Paulo : Autoria Quilombhoje, 1988. 61 p.

African words of title convey essence of collection: *malungos* (i.e., comrades) and *milongas* (i.e., stories, news, dances). Emphasizes solidarity of the adult children of a black family making a living in São Paulo. Ribeiro is a member of black group *Quilombhoje.* (*Quilombo* was the name of a historical slave rebellion; *hoje* means "today.") Her book celebrates 11th anniversary of *Quilombhoje.* Stories are clear and pleasant to read, as well as didactic.

4620 Sabino, Fernando Tavares. Os melhores contos. Rio de Janeiro: Editora Record, 1986. 200 p.

Most of these stories were initially published as *crônicas* (a special Brazilian genre published as newspaper columns). Their fluid narrative conveys the acute sensibility, powers of observation, and humor of their famous author. Sabino makes writing seem so easy! A definite *carioca* flavor is conveyed to the reader by the young, the old, sassy children, and even pets.

4621 Saboya, Natércia Campos de. Iluminuras: conto. São Paulo: Editora Scipione, 1988. 100 p.

Placing second in the short story category in the 1988 Prêmio Bienal Nestlé de Literatura Brasileira, collection consists of clear narratives that emphasize magical settings, while characters intermingle with the commonplace. Dedicated to Luis da Câmara Cascudo, the foremost scholar of Brazilian folklore, this collection of "illuminations" with their conjurings of wind, benevolent sorceresses, fishermen, and mermaids deserves to become a classic.

4622 Sarney, José. Norte das águas. Presentación de Jaime Lusinchi. Prólogos de Josué Montello, Léo Gilson Ribeiro, y Luci Teixeira. Traducción de Elvira Beroes. Ilustraciones de Antonio Almeida. Ed. bilingüe, 1. ed. en español. Caracas: Presidencia de la República; Monte Avila Editores, 1989. 456 p.: bibl., ill.

Bilingual Portuguese-Spanish edition of stories by former President of Brazil José Sarney. Includes prefaces by three Brazilian critics, and illustrations (see also *HLAS 50:3983* and *HLAS 44:6119*).

4623 Schmaltz, Iêda. Atalanta: contos. Rio de Janeiro: J. Olympio Editora; Instituto Nacional do Livro, Fundação Nacional Pró-Memória, 1987. 127 p.

Stories by prize-winning poet and fiction writer are influenced by Jung's ideas and accordingly divided into the four elements of being: Shadow, Animus, Anima, and Self. As imaginative, dense, and rich as Schmaltz's previous *Miserere* (see *HLAS 44:6038*), these stories trace the difficulties in the lives of female and male characters. The poet Schmaltz has a keen ear for popular diction and is also admirable for her reweaving of classical lore and myth. Important collection by major feminist author.

4624 Scliar, Moacyr. A orelha de Van Gogh: contos. São Paulo: Companhia das Letras; Editora Schwarcz, 1989. 163 p.

Elliptic, imaginative, and amusing fables written in a fluid, pleasant style by noted story writer/physician whose work has been translated into 12 languages. Author

dissects society's evils in recreations of biblical accounts and fairy tales.

4625 Silveira, Joel. O dia em que o leão morreu: contos. Rio de Janeiro: Editora Record, 1986. 155 p.

Classic stories by distinguished reporter who covered military actions of Brazilian troops in Italy during World War II. Tales imbued with nostalgia for a more innocent world. Some are written for children; others, dealing with the war, show compassion for both allied and enemy soldiers (see also item **4626 and 4638**).

4626 Silveira, Joel. O Generalíssimo e outros incidentes. Rio de Janeiro: Espaço e Tempo, 1987. 236 p. (Col. Ficções deste espaço e tempo; 4)

Extremely well-written pieces that are more memoirs than stories. Author is illustrious journalist who is particularly interested in certain political and historical events (e.g., the OAS Conference of 1960 when Cuba was expelled from the organization; the awarding of the Nobel Prize to Vicente Aleixandre), and in specific Brazilian figures such as Afonso Arinos and Cardinal Arns, both of whom figure in his narratives as fine characterizations (see also item **4625**).

4627 Simões, João Manuel. O túnel circular: contos. Rio de Janeiro: Philobiblion, 1986. 126 p. (Col. Prosa brasileira; 16)

Stories by poet and literary critic are philosophical fables and conundrums, carefully constructed by skilled craftsman. Influenced by modern literary currents such as myth, surrealism, and magical realism.

4628 Steen, Edla van. Até sempre. São Paulo: Global Editora, 1985. 183 p. (Col. múltipla)

Paradoxical title (English translation: *Until always*) introduces stories by southern Brazilian writer about the conflicted and tortuous world of German immigrants in the region. Not only are family relationships depicted as difficult, painful, and inextricable, but characters actually perish from lack of love. Includes good portrayals of the grotesque elements in this world.

4629 Strelzuk, Paulo. Os amarrados. Porto Alegre, Brazil: Tchê!, 1985. 90 p.

Outstanding first collection by new author who has the ability to focus on isolated incidents and specific characters in families to reveal sordid, frightening, and humorous aspects of characters' lives. Taut, intense stories accomplished with great literary skill.

4630 Tavares, Zulmira Ribeiro. O mandril. Posfácio de Vilma Arêas. São Paulo: Editora Brasilense, 1988. 136 p.

A superior collection of finely wrought hybrid pieces that consist of stories-cum-*crônicas*, prose-poems, actual poems, etc. Most of them express wry comments about nature (the *mandril* of the title is a monkey) as well as humans. Author is poet, essayist, and winner of major prose prize for her novel *O nome do bispo* (see *HLAS 50:3950*). For author's previous collection of stories, see *HLAS 46:6138*.

4631 Várzea, Virgílio. A canção das gaivotas. Organização de Lauro Junkes. Florianópolis, Brazil: Editora Lunardelli, 1985? 235 p.

Scholarly reedition of Brazilian classic. Várzea is Santa Catarina's foremost fiction writer. His beautiful stories deal mostly with the ocean.

4632 Vilaça, Adilson. A possível fuga de Ana dos Arcos. Vitória, Brazil: Fundação Ceciliano Abel de Almeida, Univ. Federal do Espírito Santo, 1984. 137 p. (Col. Letras capixabas; 12)

Elliptical stories of great power and impact about a violent and ruthless world. Most of Vilaça's characters are outlaws: thieves, prostitutes, drug addicts, as well as victims of police brutality. Despite the pervasive violence, the stories are moving and poetic. Collection won State of Espírito Santo Prize in 1983. Includes very favorable introduction by João Antônio, a writer who deals with similar characters.

Crônicas

RICHARD A. PRETO-RODAS, *Professor, Division of Modern Languages and Linguistics, University of South Florida*

MANY OF THE SELECTIONS chosen for this section underline the *crônica's* paradoxical nature as a genre dependent on ephemeral topics which nonetheless assumes permanent literary significance in the hands of a talented writer. Decades after appearing in newspapers, magazines, and anthologies, many long unavailable pieces by some of Brazil's most popular authors are once again readily accessible. Accordingly, fans of such masters as João do Rio, Carlos Drummond de Andrade, Rubem Braga, Raquel Queiroz, and Fernando Sabino can now renew their acquaintance, and young readers can savor the best *crônicas* from the first half of this century. With respect to Carlos Drummond de Andrade, a recent publication of his final columns from the *Jornal do Brasil* (item **4635**) provides a fitting conclusion to an astonishingly long and fruitful cultivation of a genre that few would still regard as "minor."

Besides the reissues of anthologies long out of print, there are fine examples of collections by younger writers who build on past successes in other areas, such as the novelist João Ubaldo Ribeiro (item **4658**), the poet and essayist Affonso Romano de Sant'Anna (items **4661** and **4662**), and the memorialist Eliezer Levin (item **4651**). Moreover, the trend towards the *crônica* as a national genre no longer confined to Rio de Janeiro continues in these collections by writers for newspapers from north to south. Little Santa Catarina, for example, is home and setting for no fewer than five of the works annotated below: Sousa (item **4665**) Cardozo (item **4640**), Hamms (item **4648**), Costa Ramos (item **4657**), and Souza (item **4666**), while

Brasília serves as the focal point for the journalist Márcio Cotrim (item **4645**). There is also something of a first in the work of Nei Costa whose *Ciranda da cidade* (item **4643**) began not on the written page at all but rather as commentary over the radio for a São Paulo station.

Since the *crônica* is sparked quite literally by anything of interest, its thematic content defies classification. One can, however, detect certain preferences that reflect the times. As noted in 1986 and 1988, the turbulent state of Brazilian society in an era of little censorship accounts for the interest in topics pertaining to inflation, crime, social disintegration, and ecological disasters. There is also increasing awareness of the need for a feminist perspective as evidenced in works by Affonso Romano de Sant'Anna (items **4661** and **4662**) and Lindolfo Paoliello (item **4653**). They also, along with others, express growing concern over AIDS in Brazilian society. Not surprisingly, the general tone has grown more reflective and a bit pessimistic in comparison to older writers or, indeed, in comparison to earlier works by veteran practitioners of the genre who now express a darker view of reality. To be sure, one can also find many comic moments including a peculiarly Brazilian penchant for malice and risqué situations as demonstrated by Hamms (item **4648**) and Drummond (items **4634, 4635, 4646,** and **4633**).

An especially noteworthy development concerns a self-conscious use of language and genre as point of departure. Thus, there are moments when Portuguese itself is the topic. The subtlety of grammar, for instance, is a topic in Sabino's *As melhores crônicas* (item **4659**), while Paoliello (item **4653**), Sant'Anna (items **4661** and **4662**), and Ramos (item **4657**), lament the proliferation of technical and bureaucratic jargon at the expense of a more direct use of language. A curious inversion of the traditional linguistic standard is suggested by Ubaldo Ribeiro's humorous reflections on the impact of Brazilian soap operas on the speech patterns of television viewers in Portugal (item **4658**). The *crônica* itself, whether as a genre or a journalistic event, provides thematic material for Hamms (item **4648**), Bergman (item **4637**) and Cardozo (item **4640**), while all of Carlos Drummond de Andrade's *De notícias e não-notícias* (item **4634**) is an exercise in adapting the genre to the style and tone of a newspaper's sundry departments.

The selections below represent only one reader's choice of the best from dozens of collections, and even these can be further ranked with respect to literary significance. As a genre, however, the *crônica* certainly provides the most graphic portrayal of contemporary Brazilian society in all its colorful diversity and exuberance.

4633 Andrade, Carlos Drummond de. Crônicas, 1930–1934. Belo Horizonte, Brazil: Governo do Estado de Minas Gerais, Secretaria de Estado da Cultura, 1987. 228 p.: ill.

This collection provides a sampling of the very earliest pieces of the late master's work written in Belo Horizonte under the pen names of "Antônio Crispim" and "Barba Azul." Each column was intended to be read in "Just One Minute" (the subtitle of this anthology), and bears the mark of naughty flappers and a certain flashy inconsequentiality. Not surprisingly, pretty women, love's pangs, new hats, and Charlie Chaplin and Greta Garbo are invoked in these short pieces, each of which faces cartoons, ads, and other graphics from the period. Even a heavy topic, like yet another orthographic convention, elicits a light touch.

4634 Andrade, Carlos Drummond de. De notícias e não-notícias faz-se a crônica. Rio de Janeiro: Editora Record, 1987. 200 p.

This tour de force collection demonstrates a theory of the *crônica* in its very execution. As "news" and "non-news," the genre can reflect all the possible categories of a major newspaper, in this case *Jornal do Brasil.* Author brings his genius to bear on all his paper's departments, from international happenings and the editorial page to the children's corner, classifieds, and the horoscope. The selections, some of which have been anthologized before, reflect the style and tone appropriate to each department.

4635 Andrade, Carlos Drummond de. Moça deitada na grama. Rio de Janeiro: Editora Record, 1987. 218 p.

While several of these selections have already appeared in book form, others represent the writer's columns for *Jornal do Brasil* during final months of his life collected here for the first time. His dry wit and irony, leavened with generous doses of compassion, remain undiminished as he reflects on issues and events large and small, from politics and inflation to the semiotics of t-shirts and to helping a child write an essay "On The Mouth." There is an undercurrent of revolt against restrictions of simple pleasures (like the title's girl lying on the grass in the park) in a society indifferent to widespread corruption and rampant street crime.

4636 Barreto, Paulo. A alma encantadora das ruas. Rio de Janeiro: Prefeitura da Cidade do Rio de Janeiro, Secretaria Municipal de Cultura, Departamento Geral de Documentação e Informação Cultural, 1987. 206 p.: bibl. (Biblioteca carioca; 4)

New edition of pieces by João Paulo Baretto, early 20th-century *carioca* writer whose very penname (João do Rio) proclaims his main inspiration, his beloved Rio de Janeiro. Assuming stroller's perspective, he sketches a varied cityscape with a preference for the downtrodden and marginal such as gypsies, prisoners, Portuguese laborers, dock tattoo artists, and street vendors whose wares include produce, books, and prayers guaranteed to work.

4637 Bergman, João. Cacareco: o mais votado. 2a. ed. Porto Alegre, Brazil: Tchê!, 1985. 119 p.: ill.

A *gaúcho* voice from the past is heard in these provocative samples by "Jotabé," who wrote for the *Folha da Tarde* in the 1950s until his death at 38. Famous in his time for his densely-written columns characterized by an absence of dialogue and by rambling sentences (the subject of one of these pieces), JB is unfailingly sophisticated and witty as he gently mocks politicians, beauty queens, high society, and soccer. His Porto Alegre is plagued by mosquitos and other airborne visitors in the first reports of flying saucers. In several selections this gifted author writes about experiences in various European countries.

4638 Braga, Rubem. Crônicas da guerra na Itália. Rio de Janeiro: Editora Record, 1985. 323 p.

Third edition of *crônicas* written by author while a correspondent for *Diário Carioca* accompanying Brazilian troops during their World War II campaign in Italy. Footnotes have been added to supplement what wartime censorship once forbade. In addition there are several *crônicas* written in subsequent years, most notably one relating a visit to old battlefields a quarter of a century later. One still reads with real pleasure these moving accounts of young Brazilians as they valiantly toiled up the Italian peninsula during the fall of 1944 and winter of 1944–45. Author stresses the Brazilians' multiracial composition in their war against the Nazi belief in Aryan superiority (see also item **4625**).

4639 Braga, Rubem. O verão e as mulheres. 4a. ed. Rio de Janeiro: Editora Record, 1986. 119 p.

Fourth edition of author's popular *A cidade e a roça* accordingly provides the best of Braga's work from 1953–55. One is struck by how gentle and whimsical life seemed 35 years ago as compared to contemporary *crônicas* by this author and others. The effect of summer's languors on women (which provides the new title), the winter solstice, Mothers' Day, and a humble rural worker offer some of the more notable highlights from this popular anthology.

4640 Cardozo, Flávio José. Beco da lamparina: crónicas. Florianópolis, Brazil: Diário Catarinense; Editora Lunardelli, 1986. 157 p.

All selected from Cardozo's regular contributions to *O Diário Catarinense*, these *crônicas* are especially striking in their graphic portrayals of conflict and confusion, from surfers at odds with fishermen to hospital mixups to the hilarious consequences of dialing sex-by-phone instead of the fire department. The genre becomes its own inspiration when author writes of other authors of *crônicas* in the news, or when one of his columns sparks reader response deserving of a follow-up. Elections and the art of eating watermelon invite author's comments, as do the dangers of a water bed in a tryst involving an errant husband subject to seasickness.

4641 Colasanti, Marina. Aqui entre nós. Rio de Janeiro: Rocco, 1988. 187 p.

Most of this collection consists of advice and essays from the women's magazine *Nova*. There are however some notable *crônicas* illustrating the long road that still lies ahead for Brazilian women as they move towards social equality.

4642 Congílio, Mariazinha. E por falar nisso—: crônicas. São Paulo: Editora Soma, 1985. 119 p.

Certainly one of Brazil's most prolific writers of *crônicas* with no fewer than a dozen collections in print, author has assembled yet another volume of her reflections on gossip, anecdotes, and conversations overheard on the bus. Her tone is often confessional, and her style is sometimes breezy and always quintessentially colloquial.

4643 Costa, Nei. Ciranda da cidade: crônicas em prosa e verso. São Paulo: Ahimsa, 1986. 94 p.

This entry represents a departure from the usual in that these pieces were delivered orally in one-minute spots on the radio. Author, a talkshow host for a São Paulo station, captures all the "here and now" with his comments on each day's major public interest story, from prison inmate riots and the effects of the budget crunch on social services to chicanery and adulterous affairs among the bourgeoisie.

4644 Costa Júnior, Paulo José da. Delito e delinqüente: novas crônicas. São Paulo: Editora Revista dos Tribunais; Secretaria de Estado da Cultura, 1982. 135 p.

Collection of incidents culled from author's years as a trial lawyer in São Paulo, these *crônicas* reflect a simpler time when call girls could cause turmoil in the court room by identifying *all* the parties to a suit in a country where "important people don't stay in jail." There are many revealing instances of women's subaltern place in Brazilian society and examples of the notorious leniency shown to wife-killers.

4645 Cotrim, Márcio. O outro lado do concreto amado: crônicas. Brasília: Thesaurus, 1987. 200 p.

Title's pun provides the dominant tone of these bittersweet pieces about the development of Brasília. The city's chamber-of-commerce enthusiasm for clean air, sunny skies, low crime rates, and a truly national population, all characteristics of Brazil's capital, is tempered by the ever more chaotic traffic, urban sprawl, vandalism, and the occasional frost, drought, and deafening hordes of cicadas. On balance, though, Brazil's melting-pot city is still a diplomat's dream assignment.

4646 Drummond, Olavo. O amor deu uma festa. Rio de Janeiro: Editora Nova Fronteira, 1987. 289 p. (Crônicas)

Drawing from his base in Belo Horizonte, this writer conveys the pace of city life. His view hones in on the off-center (and, often, the off-color) as he focuses on the ironies of contemporary values. Love, lust, and jealousy are no match for the ravages of time, while ego needs often lead to religious obsession, sexual adventures, and outright criminal behavior. Author is equally effective as he reflects on foreign experiences such as a visit to New York's Delancey Street for a Sunday shopping spree or a poetic moment amid the opulence of central Tokyo.

4647 Espínola, Waldir Reis. Lembranças e andanças: crônicas. Natal, Brazil: Clima; Fundação José Augusto, 1986. 166 p.

Mixed bag of tourist's impressions (positive about Spain, very negative about the US) and occurrences in author's native Natal. Espínola is a self-confessed cynic who attributes all motivation to sex and greed. His writing, though, is lively and holds our interest as he delves into the psyche of middle-class Brazil as the century nears its end.

4648 Hamms, Jair Francisco. A cabra azul. Florianópolis, Brazil: Editora Lunardelli, 1985. 164 p.: ill.

Only the title piece has never previously appeared in print in this collection of generally light-hearted views of Florianópolis, with a tendency towards the off-color account and bizarre dreams involving Pedro Alvares Cabral in happy camaraderie with the samba king, Noel Rosa. Boisterous poets and satire abound, with more than a little sexism in evidence.

4649 Hypolito, Adriano. Imagens de povo sofrido. Petrópolis, Brazil: Vozes, 1982. 118 p.

Reprints of a Catholic cleric's ministry among the downtrodden of Rio's suburbs. We read of lively and, in the main, likable individuals imperiled by a system that finds them at best embarrassing and at worst superfluous.

4650 Leite, Ronildo Maia. O destino das ruas: crônicas. Recife, Brazil: Rede Globo Nordeste, 1985. 250 p.: ill.

Originally read on television programs, these selections constitute a "poetic tour of the city" of Recife and are profusely illustrated to show warts and all. View of flooded streets, grime, and street urchins amounts to poetic revenge against venal urban planners and municipal authorities in general. Occasional column on carnival and nostalgia hardly offsets a bleak glimpse of urban decay and violence.

4651 Levin, Eliezer. Crônicas de meu bairro. São Paulo: Editora Perspectiva, 1987. 152 p.

São Paulo's Jewish neighborhood of Bom Retiro (the title of author's memoirs published some years ago) is the focus of these evocative glimpses of a world in transition, as new arrivals from Japan and Korea gradually replace earlier immigrants from the shtetls of Eastern Europe. Paradox abounds in the author's tragic-comic, bitter-sweet perspective in presenting such issues as the generation gap, the debatable propriety of sardines as a substitute for herring after a prayer meeting, and the dubious relevance of a Yiddish press to a young public raised and educated in Portuguese.

4652 Martins, Dileta Silveira. A crônica modernista de João Bergman. (Veritas, 31:122, junho 1986, p. 223–252)

Chapter from a doctoral thesis on The history and types of crônicas in Rio Grande do Sul where author is Coordinator of Literature and Art at the Catholic Univ. Work is perceptive study of craft and art of João Bergman, whose Cacareco: o mais votado is reviewed here (item 4637). Self-parody, irony, and word play are all considered as "an intel-

ligent response to the mediocrity and insipid nature of daily life."

Moreira, Virgílio Moretzsohn. Jogos do instante. See item 4608.

4653 Paoliello, Lindolfo. O país das gambiarras. Rio de Janeiro: Editora Record, 1986. 197 p.

Collection of author's columns from Estado de Minas for 1983–86. Title piece sets the tone as he pokes fun at his countrymen's tendency towards finding quick-fix temporary solutions (gambiarras) at the expense of reason and permanent remedies. We read of the threat of AIDS in the context of public ignorance and prejudice, the scourge of professional jargon, the gradual corrosion of Aleijadinho's famous sculptures by acid rain, and the central place of soccer in the national consciousness. Coping in our time requires a ready smile (the topic of one selection) and insight (a basic ingredient for the crônica). Indeed, the genre serves as a theme for several of these selections.

4654 Pellegrino, Hélio. A burrice do demônio. 2a. ed. Rio de Janeiro: Rocco, 1988. 220 p.

Recently deceased psychiatrist and social critic reflected a leftist-Catholic perspective in his columns for Jornal do Brasil and O Estado de São Paulo. Much to consider in his views of Ronald Reagan's infatuation with the contras, Jânio Quadros as an agent of Thanatos, the death penalty, and Glasnost. His most memorable pieces are probably those inspired by the funeral of Carlos Drummond de Andrade and an evocation of Clarice Lispector.

4655 Peralva, Osvaldo. O espião de Colônia: crônicas. Rio de Janeiro: Paz e Terra, 1985. 138 p. (Col. Literatura e teoria literária; 55)

Foreign correspondent for A Folha de São Paulo, author has assembled 47 columns from past assignments, mostly in Eastern Europe and Asia. The "spy" of the title turns out to be a Brazilian adventurer with no sinister designs. Angered by oppression whether from the left or right, author provides original view of places and events made famous in recent years including Saigon on the eve of its collapse.

4656 Queiroz, Rachel de. A donzela e a moura torta. Rio de Janeiro: Academia

Brasileira de Letras, 1987. 294 p., 8 p. of plates: ill., ports. (Col. Academia Brasileira; 3)

Collection of *crônicas* by the "first lady of Brazilian literature" includes columns written for magazines and newspapers dating as far back as 1940. Readers of *O Cruzeiro* and *Última Hora* will recall author's sharp insights concerning popular superstitions and politics. Also, her views of such matters as the American presence in wartime Recife and the role of "married" priests in the hinterland continue to hold our attention a half-century later. Nostalgia is also inevitable as she recalls the Rio suburb of Governador before the bridge linked the island to the mainland.

4657 Ramos, Sérgio da Costa. A emulsão de Ulysses. São Paulo: Global; Florianópolis, Brazil: Editora Lunardelli, 1988. 193 p.

Wide range of themes, all treated with subtle irony and a perceptive eye. Author underlines social and historical relevance of topics such as moustaches and beards as fads, positive aspects of a lazy day, Christmas creches, and lynching the Judas effigy at Easter. Other topics covered—the tyranny of tests (including those we dread to pass such as military induction), inflation, urban sprawl, scandalous Carnival celebrations—all seem to call for the magic elixir of the title. Author also despairs of the garbled "Spanish" that Brazilian politicians like to affect when conferring with Hemispheric counterparts.

4658 Ribeiro, João Ubaldo. Sempre aos domingos. Rio de Janeiro: Editora Nova Fronteira, 1988. 274 p.

Respected novelist with film credits and translations abroad considers life in Rio and sojourns in the US and Portugal to provide sometimes zany, often critical, and always perceptive views on such matters as quitting smoking cold turkey or abjuring liquor at social gatherings. He is on the mark in discussing inflation or reporting a conversation between dishwashers on the sexual ambiguities of Carnival in the time of AIDS. Language buffs find much to ponder in pieces dealing with the impact of Brazilian soap operas on middle-class Portuguese and the invasion of ill-digested American English in Brazil's "smart set."

Sabino, Fernando Tavares. Os melhores contos. See item **4620.**

4659 Sabino, Fernando Tavares. As melhores crônicas. Rio de Janeiro: Editora Record, 1986. 208 p.

Delightful collection which certainly deserves a better binding. Reader is swept along as Sabino parries with auto mechanics and a hypochondriac friend. Other themes are subtleties of Portuguese grammar, literary significance of Cervantes, and origins of famous quotes. Contemplative notes are sounded as he considers old age, perils of jogging, the Brazilian character, and the rise of technical jargon. Not coincidentally there are evocations of other literary masters such as Rubem Braga, Carlos Drummond de Andrade, and Manuel Bandeira.

4660 Sabino, Fernando Tavares. As melhores histórias. Rio de Janeiro: Editora Record, 1986. 217 p.

Some of these have appeared in other collections (e.g., *Festa de aniversário*) as *crônicas*, a fact which simply underlines the uncertain borders between short stories, stories, and *crônicas*. All show the author's skill in recreating a memorable moment, one which usually begins as a simple event that quickly escalates into an imbroglio, such as an interview at a noisy airport that ends with the author jammed into a phone booth with an elephantine reporter just as his plane is about to leave. Author is always well served by his wit and expressive style.

4661 Sant'Anna, Affonso Romano de. O homem que conheceu o amor. Rio de Janeiro: Rocco, 1988. 224 p.

As in other collections by this author, one finds a penchant for lyrical reflection and a sense of social responsibility. Pieces on AIDS include real pathos and not a little anger directed at bureaucrats and politicians. Elegiac tone extends to Andean Indians, deaf-mutes in Brazil, a growing awareness of old age and death, and several elegies for such figures as the ill-fated Pixote and Carlos Drummond de Andrade.

4662 Sant'Anna, Affonso Romano de. A mulher madura. Rio de Janeiro: Rocco, 1986. 173 p.

All of the author's work is eminently readable and quite often gripping. A fusion of the topical and literary, the pieces range from the light ("Kisses") and gossipy ("Orson Welles in Brazil") to the darker side of contemporary Brazilian life. Especially critical of machismo, urban alienation, rock music, and the plight of Indians. A frequent theme deals with converting catastrophe into new possibilities whether in earthquake-devasted Mexico City or in the life of an abused wife.

4663 Santos, Herbert de Jesus. Um dedo de prosa. São Luís, Brazil: Concurso Literário do SIOGE, Prêmio Maranhão Sobrinho, 1985. 130 p.: ill., ports.

Like Recife's Ronildo Leite, this *cronista* from São Luis do Maranhão strains the cordial tone of the genre as he hones his pen on examples of bureaucratic neglect and political chicanery. Perhaps half of the selections are more properly short stories and memoirs. His love for São Luis is apparent throughout.

4664 Scisinio, Alaôr Eduardo. Crônica que te quero conto. Rio de Janeiro: Achiamé, 1986. 133 p.

Fusing the two genres as is suggested in the title does not diminish the topical and "ephemeral" sources of inspiration in Rio's poorer neighborhoods. The Lebanese tailor, the laundress, the school chum who now does odd jobs all share the urban stage with samba schools and bisexual mistresses. These and other residents of a largely Afro-Brazilian demi-monde represent a departure from the genre's usual middle-class setting and bourgeois mores.

4665 Sousa, Abelardo. Um líder na rota do cronista. Florianópolis, Brazil: Editora Lunardelli, 1986. 104 p.

It must be noted that some of these columns approach political boosterism on behalf of a popular public figure in Florianópolis; however, they are also well written vignettes about one of Brazil's most charming cities. Urbanization and ecology are clearly dominant concerns of the newspaper in which these pieces originally appeared.

4666 Souza, Silveira de. Canário de assobio. Ilustrações de Hassis. Florianópolis, Brazil: Editora Lunardelli, 1986. 108 p.: ill.

Tone is rather ponderous and even grim for *crônicas*, but there is unmistakable reportorial zeal and literary talent in these

selections. One piece about a vigilante death squad's "work" is especially chilling, and a move to a new apartment block is memorable for its sense of anonymity and alienation. A recent widower's reaction to his late wife's favorite silk dress reinforces a somber note only occasionally lightened by moments involving family portraits and the title piece.

4667 Tatagiba, Fernando. Rua. Vitória, Brazil: Fundação Ceciliano Abel de Almeida/UFES, 1986. 118 p. (Col. Letras capixabas; 23)

While short stories and commentaries comprise most of this book, there are six true *crônicas* dealing with the contemporary scene in the writer's city of Vitória. The tone is decidedly bohemian in reflections on transvestites and on the disappearance of a gay bar, and in lyrical evocations of a Vitória vanishing under the onslaught of gentrification. Especially poignant is the relation of an impoverished father who cannot afford to buy a Christmas toy for his son from an equally poor child vendor.

4668 Veríssimo, Erico. Galeria fosca. Pesquisa e organização de Cristina Penz. Rio de Janeiro: Editora Globo, 1987. 136 p.

While the novels of this late writer remain for the most part readily available, some of his short stories and *crônicas* are here accessible for the first time in many years. His fans will immediately feel at home in these moments from the 1930s-40s with their sentimental *gaúcho* strongmen who cry at the movies, a time when rumbles of European fascism sent occasional ripples across this placid provincial milieu. Eulogy receives new meaning in his light-hearted tribute to the recently-deceased Monteiro Lobato.

4669 Veríssimo, Luís Fernando. A mesa voadora: crônicas de viagem e comida. 2a. ed. Rio de Janeiro: Editora Globo, 1982. 141 p.: ill. (Col. Sagitário)

Revised and expanded version of first edition (1978) by enormously popular humorist provides memorable moments drawn from travels to farflung places in search of adventure and good food. His love-hate view of the US is tempered by a lively sense of humor, which also accounts for his affection for Rio despite its "rapid loss of importance as the cultural center" of Brazil.

Poetry

RALPH E. DIMMICK, *General Secretariat, Organization of American States*

AS USUAL, VERSIFICATION CONTINUES to constitute a favorite pastime for Brazilians at all social and intellectual levels, from the working classes to José Sarney, President of the Republic (1985–90), and a vast amount of this output finds its way into print. Not unsurprisingly, it is difficult to detect any single overriding trend in such a flood of activity. Retarded Parnassians and Symbolists flourish alongside neomodernists, practitioners of *poesia concreta*, and individuals such as Sebastião Nunes (item **4717**) who resort to every conceivable shock device so that they may be considered the farthest of the far-out.

In general, the most rewarding reading is provided by figures of established reputation: Walmir Ayala (item **4678**), Astrid Cabral (items **4681** and **4682**), Mário Chamie (item **4687**), Ferreira Gullar (items **4695** and **4696**), Hilda Hilst (item **4697**), Lêdo Ivo (item **4698**), Lara de Lemos (item **4701**), Thiago de Mello (item **4708**), João Cabral de Melo Neto (items **4709, 4710, 4711,** and **4712**), and Olga Savary (items **4733** and **4734**), for example. Stella Leonardos seems to have turned from works of personal inspiration to pastiches based on delvings into history and folklore (items **4702, 4703,** and **4704**). A figure who looms ever larger on the literary scene is Gilberto Mendonça Teles. A new volume of his collected lyric works (item **4740**) attests to both his enduring dedication to poetic composition and the skill he exhibits in handling the art. Public appreciation of his effort is evidenced by a huge volume devoted to literary criticism of his work (item **4821**) and a perceptive study by Darcy França Denófrio (item **4822**).

Scholarly endeavor has produced several works of note. The variorum edition of *Martim Cererê* (item **4730**) clarifies with fascinating detail that few authors have ever effected such frequent and substantial changes in a text as did Cassiano Ricardo in the case of his most celebrated opus. While Mário de Andrade tinkered rather less with his compositions, Diléa Zanotto Manfio's attempt to arrive at a definitive text (item **4674**) should prove of valuable assistance to all researchers into the poetic oeuvre of the "pope" of modernism. Those investigating the transition to that movement may wish to look at the newly collected works of Theodemiro Tostes (item **4741**) and the volume devoted to the previously unrecorded Parnassian beginnings of Ascenso Ferreira (item **4691**). Scholars concerned with lessfamiliar earlier aspects of Brazilian literature may be interested by new editions of works by Bernardo Taveira Júnior (item **4738**) and Fontoura Xavier (item **4745**).

The understanding of *poesia concreta* has been furthered by the issuance of the collected compositions of its leading exponent, Augusto de Campos (item **4683**), and new light has been shed on the personality of Bandeira Tribuzi by the publication of his social protest verse (item **4744**).

The centennial of Manuel Bandeira's birth provided the occasion for a critical edition of *Carnaval* (item **4679**), a collective tribute sponsored by the Univ. Federal do Rio de Janeiro (item **4827**), and an unusually perceptive presentation of selections from his work by Ivan Junqueira (item **4680**).

A few names of promise are annotated by the *Handbook* for the first time: Sérgio Antunes (item **4676**), Luiz Coronel (item **4688**), Lya Luft (item **4705**), and Heloisa Severiano Ribeiro (item **4729**). In an apparently new publishing development, successful writers of popular songs have taken to issuing their collected lyrics in book form. The most ambitious effort of this sort is represented by the volume pùt out by Antônio Carlos Jobim (item **4699**).

Regionalism has its stronghold in Rio Grande do Sul. A good sampling of *gaúcho* poetry is provided by the *Antologia da estância da poesia crioula* (item **4675**), and an extended analysis of its characteristics and development has been furnished by Donaldo Schüler (item **4830**).

Black writers are sufficiently numerous and active that a journal devoted to their efforts, *Cadernos Negros* (item **4819**), has published at least 11 issues. The sincerity of the protest which most of this output embodies cannot be questioned, but its literary value is less evident. That black literature is a relatively recent phenomenon is made clear by the anthology organized by Oswaldo de Camargo (item **4728**).

An analogous effort was undertaken by Bernardo Kocher and Eulalia Maria Lahmeyer Lobo in compiling an anthology of poems of protest written by, or addressed to, workers of the turn of the century and shortly thereafter (item **4720**); once again the compositions in question are of more interest to the social historian than to the literary scholar.

4670 Affonso, Ruy. Cancioneiro de um jogral de São Paulo. São Paulo: M. Ohno Editor, 1985. 334 p.: ill. (Col. Toda a poesia; 1)

Skilled versifier in techniques ranging from conventional to concretist, Ruy Affonso shows to better advantage in the light of verse of later years (e.g., "Contraponto Paulistano") than in the "serious" compositions of his beginnings.

4671 Aires, Aidenor. Via viator: poesia. São Paulo: Melhoramentos, 1986. 125 p.

Gilberto Mendonça Teles aptly observes: "*Via viator* constitui . . . uma viasacra poética em que a paisagem goiana e a mitologia pessoal do poeta se fundem" in a *mestiçagem* characteristic of present-day Goiás.

4672 Alvim, Francisco. Poesias reunidas, 1968–1988. Desenho de Pedro de A. Alvim. São Paulo: Livraria Duas Cidades, 1988. 336 p.: ill. (Claro enigma)

"Autoridade" ("Onde a lei não cria obstáculos / coloco labirintos") well exemplifies the best of Alvim's compositions, vacillating between epigram and *poema-piada*.

4673 Andrade, Carlos Drummond de. Poesia errante: derrames líricos (e outros nem tanto, ou nada). Rio de Janeiro: Editora Record, 1988. 159 p.

Evidence of a great poet's originality of concept and imaginative way with words can be found even in these occasional verses and

other minor compositions, here published posthumously, mainly for the first time.

4674 Andrade, Mário de. Poesias completas. Edição crítica de Diléa Zanotto Manfio. Belo Horizonte, Brazil: Editora Itatiaia; São Paulo: Editora da Univ. de São Paulo, 1987. 535 p.: bibl., ill. (some col.). (Obras completas de Mário de Andrade; 2)

Editor attempts to establish definitive text of all but the "immature" verse of "the Pope of modernism." Provides variants, commentaries, descriptions of first editions, and explanatory notes.

4675 Antologia da Estância da Poesia Crioula. Porto Alegre, Brazil: Editora SULINA, 1987. 395 p.: bibl., ill., index.

Includes works of 183 writers, some as distinguished as Augusto Meyer, versifying for the most part in the folk vein. They attest to the enthusiasm of *gaúchos* for Rio Grande do Sul.

4676 Antunes, Sérgio. Primeira vez. Pinturas de Yvan Theys. São Paulo: M. Ohno Editor, 1986. 77 p., 1 leaf of plates: ill., ports.

Antunes' ironic humor and lyric imagination are exemplified by this reflection on elections: "O sorriso do velho senador/ vai desmanchando no poste,/ lentamente,/ erodido pela chuva/ e pela memória."

4677 Archanjo, Neide. Poesia, 1964 a 1984: antologia. Seleção e estudo crítico de

Pedro Lyra. Rio de Janeiro: Editora Guanabara, 1987. 244 p.: bibl.

From elegiac and metaphysical beginnings, Archanjo moved to concerns with events of the day and eventually to a search for self in relation to the Luso-Brazilian world. Critical bibliography and comments.

4678 Ayala, Walmir. Os reinos e as vestes. Rio de Janeiro: Editora Nova Fronteira, 1986. 68 p. (Poesia brasileira)

Poet's consciousness of being but one element of nature in a universe where "as formas perenemente fluídas/ ou vagas/ sonham o eterno equilíbrio" is expressed with poignancy and felicitous simplicity.

4679 Bandeira, Manuel. Carnaval. Redação de Júlio Castañon Guimarães e Rachel Teixeira Valença. Rio de Janeiro: Editora Nova Fronteira; Fundação Casa de Rui Barbosa, 1986. 96 p.: 1 port. (Poesia brasileira)

Still largely conventional, Bandeira's second published book included works (e.g., "Os Sapos") foreshadowing modernism. Present variorum text reveals relatively few changes made by author in lifetime; includes a few of his handwritten notes.

4680 Bandeira, Manuel. Testamento de Pasárgada: antologia poética. Seleção, organização e estudos críticos de Ivan Junqueira. Rio de Janeiro: Editora Nova Fronteira, 1981. 288 p.: bibl. (Col. Poiesis)

Junqueira's organization of selections by aspect and perceptive introductions to each division provide new insight into, and appreciation of, a major 20th-century poet.

4681 Cabral, Astrid. Lição de Alice: poemas, 1980–1983. Rio de Janeiro: Philobiblion, 1986. 111 p. (Col. Poesia sempre; 7)

"Colho os frutos do mundo/ mas já contaminados/ do mofo das lembranças/ sujos de mim, imundos" writes Cabral, conscious of the conflict between illusion and reality in this life, of the certainty of its end, and of the uncertainty that lies beyond. The poet at her best.

4682 Cabral, Astrid. Visgo da terra. Manaus, Brazil: Edições Puxirum, 1986. 104 p.

Whitmanesque rhapsodies recalling the Manaus of the poet's girlhood days.

4683 Campos, Augusto de. Viva vaia: poesia, 1949–1979. São Paulo: Brasiliense, 1986. 255 p.: ill., port.

Collected compositions of the leading exponent of *poesia concreta*. Sectional titles such as "Equivocábulos" and "Enigmagens" suggest emphasis on visual associations, eventually carried to the point that words and letters become mere elements of design.

4684 Campos, Geir. Cantos do Rio: roteiro lírico do Rio de Janeiro. Rio de Janeiro: Civilização Brasileira; Instituto Municipal de Arte e Cultura, 1982. 113 p. (Col. Poesia hoje; 60)

Poet's charming capsule—like reflections (lyric, comic, nostalgic, ironic) on sites and sights in Rio de Janeiro.

4685 Carvalho, Mariajosé de. Romance de Lampião. Ilustrações de Aldemir Martins. São Paulo: R. Kempf Editores, 1986. 52 p.: ill.

In "Romance de Lampião" Carvalho makes effective sophisticated use of folk material; in "Mar do Sul" she resorts to concretist *palavra-puxa-palavra* while maintaining a connected line of thought.

4686 Castro, Nei Leandro de. Musa de verão: 50 poemas mais ou menos livres. Natal, Brazil: Edições Clima, 1984. 111 p.: ill.

Witty erotic verse, evidencing both a clever intellect and true poetic feeling.

4687 Chamie, Mário. A quinta parede. Rio de Janeiro: Editora Nova Fronteira, 1986. 154 p. (Poesia brasileira)

Fear of, and desire for, freedom are voiced by a soldier, a worker, a priest, and a psychiatrist in a cycle reflective of mixed national feeling in the period of Brazil's return to democracy.

4688 Coronel, Luiz. Agonias migratórias: os retirantes do sul. Porto Alegre, Brazil?: Delphos Serviços Técnicos, 1983? 67 p.: ill.

Reminiscent of *Vida e morte severina*, this tragedy of the rural worker who seeks employment in the city raises *gaúcho* speech to an exceptional poetic level.

4689 Cruz, Geraldo Dias da. Rio dos signos. Rio de Janeiro: J. Olympio Editora; Brasília: Instituto Nacional do Livro, Fundação Nacional Pró-Memória, 1986. 58 p.

Poet's consciousness of the transitory nature of the world is heightened by "a descoberta absurda/ Da inexistência antes de morrer."

4690 **Cuti.** Flash crioulo sobre o sangue e o sonho. Belo Horizonte, Brazil: Mazza Edições, 1987. 57 p.

Lyric explosion of protest against racial discrimination, poverty, and other social evils, marked by power of conviction and rhythmic sweep.

4691 **Ferreira, Ascenso.** Eu voltarei ao sol da primavera. Organização de Jessiva Sabino de Oliveira. Palmares, Brazil: Fundação Casa da Cultura Hermilo Borba Filho; Recife, Brazil: Secretaria da Educação do Estado de Pernambuco,Depto. de Cultura, 1985. 146 p.

Hitherto unknown Parnassian beginnings of the famous "provincialist" modernist, published in Pernambucan newspapers, 1913–19.

4692 **Fontela, Orides.** Rosácea. São Paulo: R. Kempf Editores, 1986. 70 p.

Fontela excels in mini-poems capturing the essence of a moment or object (e.g, the pyramid in "Ei-la/ dor de milhares força/ de humanidade/ anônima/ do faraó/ nem cinzas").

4693 **Freitas, Lenilde.** Desvios. São Paulo: J. Scortecci Editor, 1987. 89 p.: ill.

Poe-like air of nightmare pervades these enigmatic but fascinating compositions.

4694 **Garcia, Pedro.** Indice de percurso. São Paulo: M. Ohno Editor; Florianópolis, Brazil: Fundação Catarinense de Cultura, 1986. 83 p.: ports. (Col. Jubileu; 2)

"Palavra metálica/ liga misteriosa/ habitante soturna/ do reino do medo" typifies the suggestions a single word (here, "cádmio") evokes for the poet.

4695 **Gullar, Ferreira.** Barulhos, 1980–1987. Rio de Janeiro: J. Olympio Editora, 1987. 93 p.

Sober, concise, reiterating Gullar's solidarity with the poor and oppressed, charged with melancholy for departed friends, these compositions show the poet at his mature best.

4696 **Gullar, Ferreira.** Crime na flora, ou, ordem e progresso. Rio de Janeiro: J. Olympio Editora, 1986. 71 p.

Written 30 years before publication, this melange of prose and poetry is best described as a surrealist dream in pentecostal language.

4697 **Hilst, Hilda.** Sobre a tua grande face. Grafismos de Kazuo Wakabayashi. São Paulo: M. Ohno Editor, 1986. 24 leaves: ill.

Love, not as corporal union but as spiritual fusion, inspires these intensely passionate lyrics. Hilst at her best.

4698 **Ivo, Lêdo.** Mar oceano: poesia. Rio de Janeiro: Editora Record, 1987. 102 p.

Recollections of youth, thoughts of death, and reflections on eternity alternate with erotic motifs in this autumnal volume.

4699 **Jobim, Antonio Carlos.** Ensaio poético: Tom e Ana Jobim. Rio de Janeiro: Passaredo, 1987. 139 p.: ill. (some col.).

Photographs, lyrics to some of Jobim's successes, and delightfully amusing reminiscences of one of the stars of Brazilian popular music.

4700 **Leal, César.** Constelação: poesia. Estudos críticos de Sebastién Joachim e Cassiano Ricardo. Rio de Janeiro: F. Alves; Recife, Brazil: Prefeitura da Cidade do Recife, Conselho Municipal de Cultura, 1986. 270 p.

Leal's collected verse runs from the relatively conventional to visual experimentation, from tributes to the heroes of Recife's past to compositions aping the formulas of physics.

4701 **Lemos, Lara de.** Palavravara. Rio de Janeiro: Philobiblion, 1986. 104 p. (Col. Poesia sempre; 10)

Restraint in both language and revealed feeling heightens the lyric and emotional impact of Lemos' compositions, each of which represents an "Árduo intento/ de reter por milênios/ o pássaro em seu último/ vôo."

4702 **Leonardos, Stella.** Estado de poesia. Rio de Janeiro: Philobiblion; Fundação Rio, 1987. 147 p. (Col. Poesia sempre; 15)

Celebration of Rio de Janeiro state in compositions in the folk manner, on themes drawn from history, legend, popular beliefs, and customs of the area.

4703 **Leonardos, Stella.** Mural pernambucano. Rio de Janeiro: J. Olympio Editora; Recife, Brazil: FUNDARPE, 1986. 72 p.

Wedding erudition with popular tradition, Leonardos celebrates the history, folklore, artisans, and writers of Recife.

4704 **Leonardos, Stella.** Romanceiro da Abolição: poesia. São Paulo: Melhoramentos, 1986. 159 p.

Based on research into Afro-Brazilian folklore, incorporates fragments of work songs, extensive African-language vocabulary, and elements of history and legend into a tribute to the black contribution to Brazil.

4705 Luft, Lya Fett. O lado fatal. Rio de Janeiro: Rocco, 1988. 97 p.

In verse of touching simplicity and sincerity, Luft recalls Hélio Pellegrini, her husband of little more than two years.

4706 Matos, Gregório de. Gregório de Matos. Seleção e notas de Higino Barros. Porto Alegre, Brazil: L&PM Editores, 1986. 183 p. (Rebeldes & malditos; 9)

This well-annotated selection makes abundantly clear why the stinging (and foul-mouthed) 17th-century satirist was known as "Boca do Inferno."

4707 Mattos, Cyro de. Lavrador inventivo: poesia. Rio de Janeiro: Livraria Editora Cátedra; Brasília: Instituto Nacional do Livro, Fundação Nacional Pró-Memória, 1984. 92 p.

Mattos is seen at his concise, imaginative best in this description of the crab: "Perdeu o pescoço/ de tanto buscar o depois/ anda para trás/ procurando a manhã do tempo."

4708 Mello, Thiago de. Num campo de margaridas. Rio de Janeiro: Philobiblion, 1986. 123 p. (Col. Poesia sempre; 11)

Abandoning political concerns, Mello turns to the great lyric themes of God, love, and nature, treating them in a simple, highly personal manner, admirable in effect.

4709 Melo Neto, João Cabral de. Agrestes: poesia, 1981–1985. Rio de Janeiro: Editora Nova Fronteira, 1985. 160 p. (Poesia brasileira)

While these recollections of Recife, Seville, Senegal, and Ecuador, and readings of foreign authors are tinged with the disabused melancholy of advancing age, the poet declares: "Escrever é sempre o inocente/ escrever do primeiro livro."

4710 Melo Neto, João Cabral de. Crime na Calle Relator: poesia. Rio de Janeiro: Editora Nova Fronteira, 1987. 82 p. (Poesia brasileira)

Anecdotic in subject matter, largely Pernambucan or Andalusian in motif, conversational in style, these poems are pervaded by a curious air of surrealism.

4711 Melo Neto, João Cabral de. Museu de tudo e depois, 1967–1987. Rio de Janeiro: Nova Fronteira, 1988. 339 p. (Col. Poesia brasileira)

Gathering together a major poet's production of the past two decades, this volume complements his *Poesias completas* of 1968 (see *HLAS 32:4833*).

4712 Melo Neto, João Cabral de. Poesia completa, 1940–1980. Prefácio de Oscar Lopes. Lisbon: Imprensa Nacional-Casa da Moeda, 1986. 452 p. (Escritores dos países de língua portuguesa; 5)

Portuguese edition of Melo Neto's complete verse attests to the broad appeal of its largely regional inspiration.

4713 Monteiro, Benedicto. O cancioneiro do Dalcídio. Rio de Janeiro: PLG Comunicação; Belém, Brazil: Falangola Editora, 1985. 133 p.

Surprisingly successful elaborations on poetic phrases extracted from four novels by Dalcídio Jurandir.

4714 Mota, Eduardo. Horas de agora. Recife, Brazil: Edição FUNDARPE, 1984. 86 p., 1 leaf of plates: port. (Col. Capibaribe; 6)

The significance of the simplest of objects and acts (e.g., the silencing of words when the paper on which they are written is thrown in the trash) provides motifs for Mota's brief, haunting compositions.

4715 Mund Júnior, Hugo. Flauta de espuma. Apresentação de Silveira de Souza. Brasília: Lavras Editora, 1986. 76 p.

Gracefully musical six-line poems capture fleeting aspects and moods of sea and shore.

4716 Mund Júnior, Hugo. Véspera do coração. São Paulo: M. Ohno Editor; Florianópolis, Brazil: Fundação Catarinense de Cultura, 1986. 82 p. (Col. Cultura catarinense: Série Literatura)

Atmospheric poems are evocative of mood rather than event, strongly sensuous in appeal.

4717 Nunes, Sebastião G. Antologia mamaluca e poesia inédita. v. 1. Sabará, Brazil: Edições Dubolso, 1988. 1 v.: ill.

Attempt to *épater le bourgeois* by an

assemblage of words and graphic images which the author characterizes as "pornô nouveau."

4718 Oliveira, Marilda Vasconcelos de. A mão e o fuso: poesias. Prefácio de Bartyra Soares. Ilustrações de Gil Vicente. Rio de Janeiro: José Olympio Editora, 1988. 91 p.: ill.

Emotionally, the poet sees herself as a function of others: "Refaço-me/ desfaço-me/ a cada instante/ . . . sou tua presença em mim."

4719 Oliveira, Silvio Roberto de. Terrabalada. Rio de Janeiro: F. Alves, 1987. 139 p.

"Só tu—Recife—escolheste/ as pontes como legado/ as águas como vestidos/ o mangue por principado" writes Oliveira, whose Northeast is not the droughtland interior but the engulfing, annihilating swampland of the coast.

4720 Ouve meu grito: antologia de poesia operária, 1894–1923. Redação de Bernardo Kocher e Eulalia Maria Lahmeyer Lobo. São Paulo: Editora Marco Zero; Rio de Janeiro: UFRJ-PROED, 1987. 151 p.: bibl. (História em cadernos; 2)

Exaltation of the labor movement, international solidarity, social criticism, anticlericalism, and incitement to direct action are a few of the themes inspiring verse addressed to workers, generally by their fellows, in the first quarter of the century. Helpful introductory essays by editors.

4721 Paes, José Paulo. A poesia está morta mas juro que não fui eu. Desenho de Rubens Matuck. São Paulo: Livraria Duas Cidades, 1988. 72 p.: ill. (Claro enigma)

Author of these clever, epigrammatic compositions defines his poetics thus: "conciso? com siso/ prolixo? pro lixo."

4722 Paes, José Paulo. Um por todos: poesia reunida. Introdução de Alfredo Bosi. São Paulo: Brasiliense, 1986. 219 p.: ill.

After conventional beginnings, Paes satirized Brazilian history in mock-archaic form and currently uses concretist devices for wry, humorous commentary on present-day society.

4723 Pena Filho, Carlos. Livro geral. Ilustrações de Hélio Feijó. Recife, Brazil: Editora Raiz, 1983? 142 p.: ill.

One regrets the untimely death of this poet of Recife and cultivator of the Portuguese lyric tradition, whose work, marked by elegance and freshness of touch, continues to attract readers.

4724 Percia, Vicente de. Voamar: não quero trabalhar neste verão. Rio de Janeiro: Dois Pontos, 1986. 106 p.: ill. (some col.).

"Qual atitude diante dum encontro/ de constante adeus?" asks Percia, evoking nostalgically and in lyrically suggestive imagery the "conjunto de apegos" representing home.

4725 Pinto, Romildo Gouveia. Holinda: inventário poético da herança flamenga em Pernambuco. São Paulo: J. Scortecci Editor, 1987. 43 p.

Pinto's mysterious evocations of Olinda's Dutch past are heightened by contrast with acid flashes of present-day reality.

4726 Pires, Cornélio. Musa caipira: as estrambóticas aventuras do Joaquim Bentinho (o Queima-Campo). Tietê, Brazil: Prefeitura Municipal de Tietê, 1985. 170 p.: ill.

Reissue of verse and Münchhausen-like tales in the *caipira* manner, very popular in the first decades of the century, plus a glossary of dialectal terms.

4727 Quintana, Mário. Preparativos de viagem. Rio de Janeiro: Editora Globo, 1987. 133 p.: facsims.

Personal favorites of a sentimental, superficial, prolific (and extraordinarily popular) poet, drawn from his half-century of composition. Printed text accompanied by autograph facsimiles.

4728 A razão da chama: antologia de poetas negros brasileiros. Coordenação e seleção de Oswaldo de Camargo. Colaboração de Paulo Colina e Abelardo Rodrigues. São Paulo: Edições GRD, 1986. 122 p.

With the classic exceptions of Luis da Gama, Gonçalves Crespo, and Cruz e Sousa, black consciousness appears to be a relatively recent phenomenon in Brazil: two-thirds of authors represented here were born after 1950.

4729 Ribeiro, Heloisa Severiano. Digamos assim. Rio de Janeiro: Editora Nova Fronteira, 1987. 92 p.

"Livre, sem a ilusão da verdade,/ passeio no além do que sou e penso" declares Ribeiro in verse admirable for precision and conciseness of language and restrained but deeply felt emotion.

4730 Ricardo, Cassiano. Martim Cererê: o Brasil dos meninos, dos poetas e dos heróis. Edição crítica de Marlene Gomes Mendes, Deila Conceição Peres, e Jayro José Xavier. Rio de Janeiro: Edições Antares; Brasília: Instituto Nacional do Livro, Fundação Nacional Pró-Memória, 1987. 409 p.: bibl., facsims. (Antares universitária)

Modernist classic *Martim Cererê* was continuously, often radically, revised by its author in 12 editions published in his lifetime. Providing a definitive text plus all variants, present volume is a monument to scholarly effort, fascinating to all interested in accompanying a poet's creative process.

4731 Ripoll, Lila. Ilha difícil: antología poética. Seleção e apresentação de Maria da Glória Bordini. Porto Alegre, Brazil: Editora da Univ. Federal do Rio Grande do Sul, 1987. 135 p.

Ripoll's graceful, unpretentious, intimist verse, centering on love, death, and childhood memories, is greatly superior to her militant outcries against social injustice.

4732 Rocha, Wilson. A forma do silêncio: poesia reunida. Rio de Janeiro: J. Olympio Editora; Fundação Cultural do Estado da Bahia, 1986. 141 p.: ill.

Spirit of ancient Greece and Rome relives in Rocha's graceful, lapidary compositions.

4733 Savary, Olga. Hai kais. São Paulo: R. Kempf Editores, 1986. 127 p.: port.

Outstripping the Japanese model in length of line and breadth of subject matter (here generally erotic), these three- or four-line compositions (about half previously unpublished) nonetheless preserve *haiku* virtues of concision and power of suggestion.

4734 Savary, Olga. Linha-d'água. Prefácio de Felipe Fortuna. Desenhos de Kazuo Wakabayashi. São Paulo: M. Ohno-Hipocampo Editores, 1987. 44 p.: ill. (Col. Toda a poesia; 2)

Water-inspired erotic compositions ("pátria é o que eu chamo poesia/ e todas as sensualidades: vida./ Amor é o que eu chamo mar,/ é o que eu chamo água.")

4735 Schmidt, Augusto Frederico. Canto da noite. Ilustrações de Santa Rosa. 3a. ed. Rio de Janeiro: Editora Nova Fronteira, 1986. 83 p., 8 leaves of plates: ill. (Poesia brasileira)

At the height of modernism, the lushly romantic verse of a hard-headed businessman enjoyed great success. These 1934 rhapsodies on love, nature, and eternity reflect Schmidt's "mocidade, com as suas crises, os seus deslumbramentos e as suas lágrimas."

4736 Simões, João Manuel. Sonetos escolhidos. Seleção e apresentação de Ênio Silveira. Estudo crítico final de Jesus Bello Galvão. Rio de Janeiro: Philobiblion, 1986. 85 p. (Col. Poesia sempre; 5)

Classic sonnets, Parnassian in vocabulary but modern in spirit and thoroughly personal in expression ("se, criador ou artesão, modelo/ com o barro do verbo estas figuras,/ é porque as trago em mim: são o meu selo.")

4737 Sousa, Afonso Félix de. Qüinquagésima hora & horas anteriores: poesia. Rio de Janeiro: Philobiblion, 1987. 107 p. (Col. Cavalo azul; 1)

Crepuscular verse (1976–84) of an aging poet meditating on dead friends, the meaning of life, and the prospect of extinction, plus unpublished compositions from earlier years.

4738 Taveira, Bernardo. Provincianas. Fixação de texto, estudos crítico e biobibliográfico de Carlos Alexandre Baumgarten e Maria Eunice Moreira. Coordenação de Regina Zilberman. Porto Alegre, Brazil: Movimento, 1986. 103 p. (Poesiasul; 58. Col. Resgate; 4)

First published in 1886; significant as a "texto pioneiro na tematização da vida campeira rio-grandense."

4739 Távola, Artur da. Calentura. Rio de Janeiro: Editora Nova Fronteira, 1986. 82 p. (Poesia brasileira)

Sometimes by plays on words, sometimes by plays on ideas, poet presents a cubistic view of life, viewed simultaneously from a variety of angles.

4740 Teles, Gilberto Mendonça. Hora aberta: poemas reunidos. Rio de Janeiro: J. Olympio Editora; Brasília: Instituto Nacional do Livro, Fundação Nacional Pro-Memória, 1986. 589 p.: bibl., ill.

Of two substantial additions to Teles' *oeuvre*, preferable to the clever but contrived exercises of "& Cone de Sombras" are the more personal, less formal compositions of "Plural de Nuvens," in which he lays bare "a sofreguidão de um brasileiro na sensualidade do idioma."

4741 Tostes, Theodemiro. Obra poética de Theodemiro Tostes. Porto Alegre, Brazil: Fundação Paulo do Couto e Silva, 1988. 175 p.

Collected poems, some previously unpublished (and indicative of a transition to modernism) of an unduly neglected *gaúcho*, literarily active in the 1920s, whose blend of late symbolism and the popular tradition possesses great musical charm.

4742 Trevisan, Armindo. Antologia poética. Porto Alegre, Brazil: Mercado Aberto, 1986. 182 p.

As Trevisan's concerns have advanced from the purely personal to the social and spiritual areas, his style has achieved increasing simplicity and conciseness.

4743 Trevisan, Armindo. O moinho de Deus. Caxias do Sul, Brazil: EDUCS, 1985. 81 p.

Sincerity, simplicity, and grace mark these poem-prayers. If the religious approach is traditional, the concerns expressed and the figures of speech employed are fully contemporary.

4744 Tribuzi, Bandeira. Tropicália consumo&dor. Prefácio de Oswaldino Marques. São Luís, Brazil: Edições SIOGE, 1985. 78 p.: port. .

Apparently first edition of better than usual verse of social protest ("a nossa ração é o nosso canto,/ um canto feito de contida raiva,/ duras palavras, carne insatisfeita, amor asperamente conquistado/ e recusada vida!").

4745 Xavier, Fontoura. Opalas. 5a. ed. Porto Alegre, Brazil: Centro de Pesquisas Literárias, Pró-Reitoria de Pesquisa e Pós-Graduação, Pontifícia Univ. Católica do Rio Grande do Sul, 1984. 130 p.

Extensive critical material enriches this reprint of an 1884 work, representative of the transition period between Romanticism and Parnassianism, when poets "se batiam pela *Nova Idéia*, pelo realismo, pela ciência, pela poesia social."

Drama

JUDITH ISHMAEL BISSETT, *Associate Professor of Spanish and Portuguese, Miami University, Oxford, Ohio*

POLITICAL PROTEST AND THE ILLUSTRATION of contemporary social and political problems through the dramatization of historical events are still evident in Brazilian drama. Yet, as the theater confronts changes in society and the institutions which controlled and repressed theatrical production for two decades, playwrights are reaching beyond politics in their search for a coherent dramatic voice. According to Yan Michalski in a speech on Brazilian theater (item **4774**), many writers find expression in a return to memories of childhood or adolescence. In "From *Abertura* to *Nova Repúbilca:* Politics and the Brazilian Theater of the Late Seventies and Eighties" (item **4759**), Severino João Albuquerque notes the same trend, but adds another—dramatic adaptations of other literary genres.

Alarme geral by Zaza Sampaio (item **4755**) is an example of the continuing presence of committed drama on the Brazilian stage. This play, banned during 1979–82, portrays the relationship between jailer and prisoner as the two characters discuss the meaning of freedom. Like playwrights Augusto Boal and Chico Buarque de Holanda, Luis Alberto de Abreu employs history to examine the problem of the economic and political invasion of Brazil by foreign powers in *Xica da Silva* (item **4746**). Here, after Xica's Portuguese lover leaves, she must deal with the consequences of her actions. In an effort to gain power and social acceptance through her association with Fernandes, Xica cruelly represses her own people.

Although Mário Prata's *Besame mucho* (item **4753**) does not deal precisely with childhood memories, it does represent a journey back in time. The characters explore relationships which began in the 1960s and continued through the 1980s. In *A volta do marido pródigo* (item **4754**), Paulo Hecker Filho, in collaboration with the author, dramatizes a short story by Guimarães Rosa. Like the " Grupo Macunaíma" and others mentioned by Severino Albuquerque, Hecker Filho sought dramatic expression through the adaptation of another literary form.

Recent critical studies examine Brazilian playwrights and theater groups as both artists and significant elements in the development of national theatrical history. The two works on José de Alencar (items **4768** and **4761**) come to similar conclusions, but the latter takes a more theoretical approach. Sábato Magaldi's study of Nelson Rodrigues (item **4772**) provides the reader with an excellent analysis of the playwrights's work as well as an evaluation of his contributions to the theater. Teatro Arena is the focus of Margo Milleret's "Acting into Action: Teatro Arena's *Zumbi*"(item **4775**) and Claudia de Arruda Campos' *Zumbi/Tiradentes e outras histórias contadas pelo Teatro de Arena de São Paulo* (item **4764**). While Milleret concentrates on *Zumbi*, Arruda Campos does a more extensive study of the theater. Both examine Teatro Arena's significance as an innovator as well as its relationship with Brazilian society and the audience.

Brecht no Brasil: experiências e influências (item **4777**) also looks at Brazilian theater from an historical point of view. The majority of these papers by important critics and playwrights were read at a symposium held in Brazil during Aug. 1986.

Brazilian theater, now in a period of transition and, in many cases, self-evaluation, continues to seek new forms of expression. As Severino Albuquerque affirms, both young and old playwrights will transform the structure of theater in Brazil.

ORIGINAL PLAYS

4746 Abreu, Luís Alberto de. *Xica da Silva.* São Paulo: Martins Fontes, 1988. 90 p.

Well-written version of the story of Xica da Silva and João Fernandes. Xica struggles to rise above her station by using Fernandes' money and power. When Fernandes, unsuccessful in manipulating the diamond trade, is sent back to Portugal, Xica is left to face the effects of her past cruelty to others.

4747 Alencar, Hunald de. *Os maguinus; Uma vez, o amor—; Quem matou o público?.* Aracaju, Brazil: s.n., 1987. 126 p.: ill.

Os maguinus depicts life and oppression of workers in Northeast. *Uma vez, o amor* consists of a conversation between a man and a prostitute concerning an opportunity missed. *Quem matou o público?* concerns actors and author discussing the relationship between theater and life.

4748 Comparato, Doc. *Nostradamus, o príncipe das profecias*: peça para teatro em dois atos. São Paulo: Editora Clube do Livro, 1988. 175 p.: bibl., ill.

Tells the story of the life and prophecies of Nostradamus from 1525 until his death in 1566. Follows his persecution by the Inquisition, his pardon, and difficulties dealing with his gift. Author includes a description of how each scene was constructed. Bibliography of historical references. Produced in 1986.

4749 Desligue o projetor e espie pelo olho mágico: comédia de Hilton Have em 3 atos. (*Rev. Teatro*, 463, julho/agôsto/set. 1987, p. 34–64)

Two homosexuals are forced to masquerade as heterosexuals due to an invasion by members of their families. Series of comic misunderstandings follow, but do not result in any change in the pair's original relationship.

4750 Gomes, Laércio. *Os longos dias da vingança.* Belém, Brazil: SEMEC, 1984. 64 p.: ill. (Cadernos de cultura: Teatro; 3)

Regional theater. Author has written plays, musicals, and music for Carnaval since 1934. This play is a loosely-connected story concerning evil aristocrat who persecutes the family of one of his servants. Scenes of Indians, Candomblé, and magic are interspersed throughout the central structure of the work.

4751 Oliveira, Marco Antônio de. *A ameaça.* Belém, Brazil: Edições SEMEC, 1985. 67 p. (Teatro)

Takes place in Amazon region during the first regency, 1836. Government soldiers confront a mother and her pregnant daughter, accusing them of hiding a revolutionary. Violent struggle ensues in which two soldiers and the daughter are killed, resulting in the elimination of evil but at great sacrifice.

4752 Pimentel, José. Heróis pernambucanos no teatro ao ar livre: *Frei Caneca; Batalha dos Guararapes.* Prefácio de Leonardo Dantas Silva. Recife, Brazil: Governo de Pernambuco, Secretaria de Turismo, Cultura e Esportes, Fundação do Patrimônio Histórico e Artístico de Pernambuco, Diretoria de Assuntos Culturais, 1987. 169 p., 16 p. of plates: ill. (some col.). (Col. pernambucana; 2a. fase, 35)

Introduction gives historical background for two plays in volume. Both written for outdoor presentation. Each deals with the Dutch invasion and the area's heroic efforts to gain freedom. Once this was achieved, inhabitants were betrayed by Brazilian government. Brechtian structures emphasize theme of treason and personal choice.

4753 Prata, Mário. *Bésame mucho.* Porto Alegre, Brazil: L&PM Editores, 1987. 176 p.

Written in 1982, play has been made into a film. Consists of a series of scenes beginning in 1982 and going back in time. Friends who are also writers interact with each other and their spouses. Most scenes have sex as a focal point. Theme: friendship, love, and marriage.

4754 Rosa, João Guimarães and **Paulo Hecker Filho.** *A volta do marido pródigo.* Porto Alegre, Brazil: Tchê!, 1987. 108 p. (Teatro brasileiro)

Adapted from "Sagarana," a short story by Guimarães Rosa. Concerns a worker in Minas Gerais who leaves his wife to see what women in Rio are like. When he returns, she is living with his former benefactor. Eventually, he convinces her to return. Off-stage voice and toads comment on action.

4755 Sampaio, Zaza. *Alarme geral* & outros textos. Fortaleza, Brazil: Secretaria de Cultura e Desporto, 1984. 264 p. (Col. Balaio de teatro; 8)

Title play was banned in 1979 but released in 1982. Deals with conversation between a woman and her jailer about freedom. Other plays are discussions, primarily between two characters, concerning life, loneliness, and freedom.

4756 Tourinho, Nazareno and **Valter Freitas.** *A greve do amor* [de] Nazareno Tourinho; *Fiau babau* [de] Valter Freitas. Belém, Brazil: Edições SEMEC, 1986. 109 p. (Teatro)

A greve do amor opens with Brechtian narrator who tells origin of the play. Written in dialect, it tells story of a municipality rumored to have placed a tax on pregnant women. *Fiau babau* is a children's play which discusses political oppression and the suppression of culture in terms they can understand.

4757 Tourinho, Nazareno. *Lei é lei e está acabado.* Belém, Brazil: Grafisa Offset, 1984. 79 p.: ill.

Author's note explains that censors allowed production of the play but not publication of the text. A lengthy one act tells story of a dying beggar, the prostitute who tries to save him, and a policeman who is reluctant to help. In the end, the beggar explains his life and dies.

4758 Trachta, João. *Nossa Senhora Aparecida:* drama sacro em cinco atos. São Paulo: Edições Loyola, 1988. 77 p.

Adaptation of historical novel published in 1944 and produced on radio in Tupí in 1955. Edited and prepared for further production in 1986. Concerns a family during time of the *bandeirantes*. A husband leaves and is thought dead. An evil second husband is stopped by miracles from stealing family's property.

HISTORY AND CRITICISM

4759 Albuquerque, Severino João. From *Abertura* to *Nova República:* politics and the Brazilian theater of the late seventies and eighties. (*Hispanófila*, 96, mayo 1989, p. 87–95, bibl.)

Excellent treatment of censorship during and after military regime. Provides historical overview to 1979 and examines censorship occurring today. Reviews playwrights of 1980s. States that most have turned away from political commitment to 1) examination of individual experience through a return to childhood; and 2) adaptation of texts from other genres.

4760 Albuquerque, Severino João. Representando o irrepresentável: encenações de tortura no teatro brasileiro da ditadura militar. (*Lat. Am. Theatre Rev.*, 21:1, Fall 1987, p. 5–18, bibl.)

Discusses theater's political position (1964–68) and its difficulties with military regime (1969–74). In one instance the play *Papa Highirte* was honored by Ministry of Education and immediately seized by Federal Police. Examines five plays written during the dictatorship, focusing on verbal and nonverbal language in torture scenes.

4761 Appel, Myrna Bier. Idéias encenadas: o teatro de Alencar. Porto Alegre, Brazil: Movimento, 1986. 157 p.: bibl. (Col. Ensaios; 24)

Study arranged thematically. Outlines Alencar's dramatic theory and uses it as basis of analysis of works. Includes detailed critical quotations. Finds that although playwright identified with French realists, romantic elements were constantly present in his plays. However, he brought to stage many previously-ignored social questions and used Brazilian language.

4762 Arêas, Vilma Sant'Anna. Na tapera de Santa Cruz: uma leitura de Martins Pena. São Paulo: Martins Fontes, 1987. 282 p.: bibl. (Col. Leituras)

Best study on the subject. [W. Martins]

4763 Autran, Paulo. Paulo Autran. Rio de Janeiro: Ministério da Cultura, Instituto Nacional de Artes Cênicas, Biblioteca Edmundo Moniz, CENACEN, 1987. 38 p.: ill., ports. (Ciclo de palestras sobre o teatro brasileiro; 6)

Autran speaks about Teatro Brasileiro de Comédia (TBC). Recalls TBC's formation and dissolution. Counters criticism that TBC did not present Brazilian plays or use Brazilian directors by indicating Antunes Filho's work with the Teatro and pointing out that Teatro paved way for Arena. Includes questions from audience.

4764 Campos, Cláudia de Arruda. *Zumbi, Tiradentes* e outras histórias contadas pelo Teatro de Arena de São Paulo. São Paulo: Editora Perspectiva; Editora da Univ. de São Paulo, 1988. 170 p.: ill. (Col. Estudos; 104: Teatro)

Beginning with 1958, author chronicles transformation of theater from national to international, aesthetic to political. Discusses social history at time Arena appeared, plays presented, and social and political effect of theater. Concludes that *Zumbi* and *Tiradentes* were flawed (thematically repetitive) but did introduce new forms. Studies newspaper reviews of productions.

4765 Carvalheira, Luiz Maurício Britto. Por um teatro do povo e da terra: Hermilo Borba Filho e o Teatro do Estudante de Pernambuco. Prefácio de Maximiano Campos. Recife, Brazil: Governo de Pernambuco, Secretaria de Turismo, Cultura e Esportes, Fundação do Patrimônio Histórico e Artístico de Pernambuco, Diretoria de Assuntos Culturais, 1986. 248 p., 30 p. of plates: bibl., ill., ports. (Col. pernambucana; 2a. fase, 27)

Studies theatre in Recife during 1940s-50s with emphasis on Teatro do Estudante de Pernambuco. Mentions influence of *autos* and foreign drama. Concentrates on Hermilo Borba Filho's importance in development of national as well as regional theatre. Includes historical background and interviews with Borba's students and colleagues.

4766 Castillo, Rubén and Aderbal Júnior.
Conversaciones con un director de teatro. Montevideo: Ediciones de la Banda Oriental, 1986. 99 p.

Prize-winning director interviewed in Uruguay discusses various aspects of theater and public (i.e., what is popular theater?). Provides detailed description of work with actors and the text. Other subjects include: role of critics, Brazilian playwrights, theater groups, history of theater in Brazil. Characterizes theater in 1980s.

4767 Costa, Marta Morais da et al. Teatro no Paraná. Rio de Janeiro: Ministério de Cultura, INACEN, 1986. 55 p.: bibl. (Col. Exposições; 1)

Four essays cover history of theater production in Paraná up to 1980. Provides valuable information on authors and on theater groups in Curitiba and other cities. Bibliography after each chapter.

4768 Faria, João Roberto. José de Alencar e o teatro. Prefácio de Décio de Almeida Prado. São Paulo: Editora Perspectiva; Editora da Univ. de São Paulo, 1987. 176 p., 1 p. of plates: bibl., ill., ports. (Col. Estudos; 100: Teatro)

Semi-biographical study gives detailed description of each play, including censorship and political problems. Discusses playwright's efforts to nationalize theater and romantic character of his work. Format: 1) social, literary, and biographical background; 2) summary; and 3) analysis. Includes excerpts from reviews and comments of censors.

4769 Gama, Oscar. História do teatro capixaba: 395 anos. Vitória, Brazil: Fundação Cultural do Espírito Santo; Fundação Ceciliano Abel de Almeida, 1981. 233 p.: bibl., ill., ports. (Col. Estudos capixabas; 3)

Begins with discussion of "dehumanization" of theater, the effect of mass media. Outlines history of region from colonial period to 1980. Describes plays written in area, starting with Anchieta. Excellent overview of role of autos in conversion of Indians. Lists playwrights, theater groups, festivals, and plays in chronological order.

4770 Kühner, Maria Helena. A comunicação teatral: de 1980 a 1983. Rio de Janeiro: Associação Carioca de Empresários Teatrais, 1983. 112 p., 16 p. of plates: ill.

Outlines work in theater (1980–83) with some reference to earlier years beginning in 1974. Includes information on spectators, production, advertising, tendencies, and innovations. Gives statistics on plays, such as prices charged and number of productions. Lists theaters in Rio with addresses and telephone numbers.

4771 Kühner, Maria Helena. Maria Helena Kühner. Rio de Janeiro: Ministério da Cultura, Instituto Nacional de Artes Cênicas, Biblioteca Edmundo Moniz, CENACEN; Pedidos para a Livraria Ver e Ler, 1985? 48 p.: ill. (Ciclo de palestras sobre o teatro brasileiro; 3)

Lecture by Kühner. Main points include: transformation of man and society, collective experience, recovery of history, use of language and significance of the study of its history. Also treats effect of mass media on theater. Concludes that today theater must not be a prisoner to external forces, nor a game.

4772 Magaldi, Sábato. Nelson Rodrigues: dramaturgia e encenações. São Paulo: Editora Perspectiva; Editora da Univ. de São Paulo, 1987. 200 p.: bibl., ill. (Estudos; 98: Teatro)

Detailed study of playwright's work begins with Brazilian theater history and indicates Rodrigues' innovations. Chronicles production and reception of his plays. Includes sections on characters, themes, dramatic structure, and productions, with illustrations. Concludes that Rodrigues excels due to his view of reality beneath social veneer. Includes bibliography.

4773 Meiches, Mauro and Sílvia Fernandes. Sobre o trabalho do ator. São Paulo: Editora Perspectiva; Editora da Univ. de São Paulo, 1988. 177 p.: bibl., ill. (Col. Estudos; 103: Teatro)

Author proposes to establish specific approach to an actor's work as it relates to production. Each chapter examines construction of characters in specific plays. Actors and groups studied include: Rubens Correa, Marília Pera, Antonio Fagundes, Paulo Autran, Asdrúbal Touxe o Trombone, and Carlos Moreno. Includes bibliography and illustrations.

4774 Michalski, Yan. Yan Michalski. Rio de Janeiro: Ministério da Cultura, Instituto Nacional de Artes Cênicas, Biblioteca Edmundo Moniz, CENACEN, 1986. 40 p.: ill. (Ciclo de palestras sobre o teatro brasileiro; 2)

Author's lecture reviews his books and recounts Brazilian theater history after 1964. Points out that the theater, active during years of persecution, entered a period of crisis in a less repressive atmosphere. Writers like Naum Alves de Souza now utilize childhood memories as a dramatic focus.

4775 Milleret, Margo. Acting into action: Teatro Arena's *Zumbi. (Lat. Am. Theatre Rev.,* 21 : 1, Fall 1987, p. 19–27, bibl.)

Traces history of Teatro Arena from its beginning in 1953. Study emphasizes the play *Zumbi,* considered by Boal to represent a turning point: the moment when the group attempted to change rather than reflect reality. Describes the play in production, and points out elements which made it answer audience's political and intellectual needs.

4776 Neves, João das. João das Neves. Rio de Janeiro: MinC-INACEN, 1987. 56 p.: ill. (Ciclo de palestras sobre o teatro brasileiro; 5)

One of the founders of Grupo Opinião and an award-winning author of children's books reviews his relationship with the theater. States that Aníbal Machado and his daughter had most influence on his work with language. Outlines his experience with Centro Popular de Cultura and describes the production of *Último carro.*

4777 Peixoto, Fernando *et al.* Brecht no Brasil: experiências e influências. Organização e introdução de Wolfgang Bader. Rio de Janeiro: Paz e Terra, 1987. 284 p.: bibl., ill.

Consists primarily of papers read at Brecht Symposium in Brazil (Aug. 1986). Introduction provides comments on participants. Peixoto examines Brechtian theory. Other papers by, for example, Boal, Michalski, Magaldi, deal with Brecht's writings, his work in movies and theatre, and transformations and influence of Brecht in Brazil. Lists criticism and Brazilian performances of playwright.

4778 Vasconcellos, Luiz Paulo. Dicionário de teatro. Porto Alegre, Brazil: L&PM Editores, 1987. 231 p.: bibl.

Presented by Yan Michalski, volume contains more than 600 terms both universal and pertaining to Brazil. Includes, for example, *agitprop* and *tropicalismo.* Short definitions are based on reference works such as *Oxford companion to the theatre.* Useful to scholars and students working with drama in Portuguese.

4779 Vásina, Elena. El teatro: documento de la historia. (*Am. Lat./Moscú,* 6 : 114, junio 1987, p. 87–94, photos)

Treats political and social drama by Plínio Marcos, João Ribeiro Chaves Netto, Oduvaldo Viana Filho, Millor Fernandes, and Leilah Assunção. Focuses on change in committed theater, and states that Brazilian theater in the 1980s portrays not the great figures of the 1960s but ordinary people caught up in terrible events.

Literary Criticism and History

WILSON MARTINS, *Professor Emeritus of Portuguese, New York University*

THE ONLY MAJOR WORK of literary criticism and history published during this biennium was the three-volume *História crítica do romance brasileiro* (item **4784**). Otherwise, the decline in theory and the concomitant rise in literary history in all its manifestations continues (see *HLAS 48,* p. 565). Note the increase in the number of biographies (items **4799, 4801, 4802, 4805, 4806, 4807, 4809, 4810, 4812,** and

4816), or specific studies about particular authors (items **4797, 4798, 4800, 4820, 4825, 4813, 4814, 4832, 4815, 4818,** and **4833**).

Criticism of poetry has been more catholic, ranging from the well-known João Cabral (item **4833**), Augusto dos Anjos (item **4814**), Castro Alves (item **4824**), Mário de Andrade (item **4823**), and Cecília Meireles (item **4825**), to minor poets such as Quintana (item **4832**), and Mário Faustino (item **4820**).

Critical studies of fiction are also noted by their wide-ranging interests and special emphases on female authors such as Clarice Lispector (items **4809** and **4816**), Patrícia Galvão (item **4801**), or Lygia Fagundes Telles (item **4814**). Note also the first comprehensive (very sympathetic) biography of Lúcio Cardoso (item **4802**).

Of course, that perennial subject, the great Machado de Assis, is gaining even more stature as recent criticism defines him as a post-modern of high caliber (item **4806;** see also *HLAS 46:6373* and *HLAS 48:6398*).

GENERAL

4780 Arrigucci Júnior, Davi. Enigma e co-
mentário: ensaios sobre literatura e ex-
periência. São Paulo: Companhia das Letras,
1987. 238 p.: bibl.
 Sundry essays on Manuel Bandeira,
Rubem Braga, Antônio Callado, Fernando
Gabeira, and Murilo Rubião; and also Juan
Rulfo, Julio Cortázar, and Jorge Luís Borges.

**4781 Bibliografia comentada de obras capi-
xabas.** Vitória, Brazil: Univ. Federal do
Espírito Santo, Biblioteca Central, 1987. 159
p.: 1 port.
 Invaluable reference (see also *HLAS
46:6322*).

**4782 Curso A Semana de Arte Moderna de
22, Sessenta Anos Depois,** *São Paulo,
1982.* Anais. São Paulo: Secretaria de Estado
da Cultura, 1984. 257 p.: bibl., index.
 Valuable compilation of convenient
information that includes an excellent bibliography about the 1922 *Semana de Arte
Moderna.* See also item **4794.**

4783 Leonel, Maria Célia de Moraes. *Estética*—revista trimensal, e modernismo. São Paulo: Editora HUCITEC; Brasília: Instituto Nacional do Livro, Fundação
Nacional Pró-Memória, 1984. 219 p.: bibl.
(Linguagem e cultura)
 History of important modernist journal (see also *HLAS 42:6391, HLAS 42:6418,
HLAS 42:6435,* and *HLAS 42:6444*).

4784 Linhares, Temístocles. História crítica
do romance brasileiro, 1728–1981. v.
1–3. Belo Horizonte, Brazil: Editora Itatiaia;
São Paulo: Editora da Univ. de São Paulo,
1987. 3 v.: bibl., indexes. (Col. Reconquista
do Brasil; 2a. sér., 116–118)
 As of now the best and most comprehensive study of the Brazilian novel (see also
item **4791**).

4785 A literatura no Brasil. v. 1–6. Direção
de Afrânio Coutinho e Eduardo de
Faria Coutinho. 3a. ed., rev. e atualizada. Rio
de Janeiro: J. Olympio Editora; Niterói, Brazil: Univ. Federal Fluminense, 1986. 6 v.:
bibl., index.
 See *HLAS 38:7605* and item **4791.**

4786 Machado, Janete Gaspar. A literatura
em Santa Catarina. Porto Alegre, Brazil: Mercado Aberto, 1986. 111 p.: bibl. (Série
Revisão; 23)
 See item **4793.**

4787 Marotti, Giorgio. Black characters in
the Brazilian novel. Translated by Maria O. Marotti and Harry Lawton. Los Angeles: Center for Afro-American Studies, Univ.
of California, 1987. 448 p., 18 p. of plates:
(Afro-American culture and society, 0882–
5297; 6)
 Competent and scholarly work, but
adds little to the well-known works by Raymond Sayers and Gregory Rabassa (see *HLAS
48:6352*).

4788 Míccolis, Leila. Do poder ao poder.
Porto Alegre, Brazil: Tchê!, 1987. 133
p.: bibl., ill. (some col.). (Universidade crítica; 3)
 Although partisan and clearly vindica-
tory, this work is invaluable for the wealth of
information provided on "marginal literature" of the 1960s–70s.

4789 Montello, Josué. Diário da tarde: 1957–1967. Rio de Janeiro: Editora Nova Fronteira, 1988. 772 p.

Follow-up of author's memoirs (see *HLAS 48:6432*).

4790 Muricy, José Cândido de Andrade. Panorama do movimento simbolista brasileiro. v. 1. 3a. ed., rev. e ampliada. São Paulo: Editora Perspectiva, 1987. 1 v.: bibl., ill. (Col. Textos; 6)

See *HLAS 40:7749* and *HLAS 48:6409*.

4791 Pereira, Lúcia Miguel. História da literatura brasileira: prosa de ficção, de 1870 a 1920. Belo Horizonte, Brazil: Editora Itatiaia; São Paulo: Editora da Univ. de São Paulo, 1988. 330 p.: bibl., index, port. (Col. Reconquista do Brasil; 2a. série, 131)

Useful contribution that was part of an unsuccessful attempt to produce a collective literary history (see also items **4785** and **4784**).

4792 O perfeito cozinheiro das almas deste mundo: diário coletivo da garçonnière de Oswald de Andrade, São Paulo, 1918. Textos de Mário da Silva Brito e Haroldo de Campos. Transcrição tipográfica de Jorge Schwartz. Ed. fac-similar. São Paulo: Editora Ex Libris, 1987. 256 p.: facsims.

Interesting literary oddity consists of collective journal about and by friends and associates of Oswald de Andrade.

4793 Sachet, Celestino. A literatura catarinense. Florianópolis, Brazil: Editora Lunardelli, 1985. 350 p.

Another in a series of regional literary histories (see also item **4786** and *HLAS 48:6354*, with cross-references.

4794 Saraiva, Arnaldo. O modernismo brasileiro e o modernismo português: subsídios para o seu estudo e para a história das suas relações. v. 1. Porto, Portugal: s.n., 1986. 1 v.: bibl.

Includes wealth of new research and corrects many persistent mistakes, while clarifying important details of literary history (see also item **4782**).

4795 Senna, Homero. História de uma confraria literária: o Sabadoyle. Rio de Janeiro: Xerox do Brasil, 1985. 127 p.: ill., index, ports. (Biblioteca reprográfica Xerox; 24)

Important contribution to the history of Brazilian literary life in the 20th century.

4796 Süssekind, Flora. Cinematógrafo de letras: literatura, técnica e modernização no Brasil. Brazil: Companhia das Letras; São Paulo: Editora Schwarcz, 1987. 170 p., 14 p. of plates: bibl., ill., ports.

Interesting research that examines how the rapid process of modernization with its technological innovations has affected Brazilian literature.

PROSE FICTION

4797 Alcoforado, María Letícia Guedes. *Bom-crioulo* de Adolfo Caminha e a França. (*Rev. Let./São Paulo*, 28, 1988, p. 85–93, bibl.)

Under a somewhat misleading title, this essay calls attention to two neglected naturalists, namely Adolfo Caminha and Abel Botelho, and their possible relationship.

4798 Almeida, Nelly Alves de. Estudos sobre quatro regionalistas: Bernardo Elis, Carmo Bernardes, Hugo de Carvalho Ramos, Mário Palmério. 2a. ed. Goiânia, Brazil: Editora da Univ. Federal de Goiás, 1985. 502 p.: bibl. (Col. Documentos goianos; 15. Publicação; 104)

Textbook, first published in 1968, is of interest because of the information included.

4799 Andrade, Ana Luiza Britto Cezar de. Osman Lins, crítica e criação. São Paulo: Editora Hucitec, 1987. 239 p.: bibl., ill. (Linguagem e cultura)

Sympathetic reading that presents Osman Lins as one of the major contemporary Brazilian writers (see also item **4804** and *HLAS 48:6394*).

4800 Antelo, Raúl. Na Ilha de Marapatá: Mário de Andrade lê os hispano-americanos. Prefácio de Alfredo Bosi. São Paulo: Editora HUCITEC, 1986. 360 p., 6 p. of plates: bibl., ill., ports. (Linguagem e cultura)

Mário de Andrade read widely, including Spanish-American writers. Antelo's excellent research is a valuable contribution to an aspect of Andrade's career that is beginning to be explored (see also *HLAS 42:6344, HLAS 42:6428, HLAS 46:5005, HLAS 48:5648*, and *HLAS 48:6379*).

4801 Bloch, Jayne H. Patrícia Galvão: the struggle against conformity. (*Lat. Am. Lit. Rev.*, 14:27, Jan./June 1986, p. 188–201)

Recently rediscovered as a satellite of Oswald de Andrade, the political activist Patrícia Galvão is attracting the interest of "born-again oswaldians." Here is the whole story in a nutshell.

4802 Carelli, Mario. Corcel de fogo: vida e obra de Lúcio Cardoso, 1912–1968. Tradução de Júlio Castañon Guimarães. Rio de Janeiro: Editora Guanabara, 1988. 250 p., 9 p. of plates: bibl., ill.

First comprehensive biography of Cardoso is also sensitive, well-informed, and discreet.

4803 Costa, Edison José da. Quarup, tronco e narrativa. Curitiba, Brazil: Scientia et Labor, 1988. 197 p.: bibl.

Careful reading of Callado's work (see also *HLAS 48:6397*).

4804 Daniel, Mary L. Critique of the critics: Osman Lins' essay-novel *A Rainha dos Cárceres da Grécia*. (*Lat. Am. Lit. Rev.*, 14:27, Jan./June 1986, p.145–158, bibl.)

Excellent reading of an Osman Lins novel shows once more that he was a cerebral novelist who wrote as if fiction were a mathematical theorem (see also items **4799** and **4808**).

4805 De Oliveira, Celso Lemos. Understanding Graciliano Ramos. Columbia, S.C.: Univ. of South Carolina Press, 1988. 188 p.: bibl., index. (Understanding contemporary European and Latin American literature)

Useful guide for students and lay readers designed "to provide a brief introduction to the life and writings of prominent authors" (see also item **4807**).

4806 Fitz, Earl E. Machado de Assis. Boston: Twayne Publishers, 1989. 165 p.: bibl., index, port. (Twayne's world authors series; TWAS 809: Latin American literature)

Excellent survey in the well-established tradition of Twayne's monographic series.

4807 Garbuglio, José Carlos; Alfredo Bosi; and Valentim Facioli. Graciliano Ramos. São Paulo: Editora Atica, 1987. 480 p.: bibl., ill., ports. (Col. Escritores brasileiros: Antologia & estudos; 2)

Roughly, 36 percent of the volume is devoted to texts about Graciliano Ramos (or GR); 28 percent to an anthology of his writings; 17 percent to his biography (very detailed and proficient); six percent to a roundtable discussion; and five percent to a bibliography (also very good). Practical, useful, and convenient, this work is probably not unique but overall an excellent working tool for students of GR (see also item **4805**).

4808 Igel, Regina. Osman Lins: uma biografia literária. São Paulo: T.A. Queiroz Editor, 1988. 174 p.: bibl., ill., ports. (Biblioteca de letras e ciências humanas: série 1a., Estudos brasileiros; 4)

Valuable account of the late, great novelist in which Igel uses Lins' life to illuminate his work. Carefully researched and written study which includes numerous documents and interviews with Lins. Second part is a fine and solid study of the writer's non-fiction works as well as of his masterpiece *Avalovara*.[M.A. Guimarães Lopes]

4809 Novello, Nicolino. O ato criador de Clarice Lispector. Rio de Janeiro: Presença, 1987. 142 p.: bibl.

Another addition to the growing literature on Lispector (see also item **4816** and *HLAS 48:6392*).

4810 Pereira, Joacil de Britto. José Américo de Almeida: a saga de uma vida. João Pessoa, Brazil: Instituto Nacional do Livro, 1987. 631 p.: bibl., ports.

Although somewhat sycophantic and at times digressive, this work is possibly the most complete and comprehensive of all the biographies of José Américo de Almeida. Provides useful data on the political life of Brazil since the 1920s.

4811 Picchio, Luciana Stegagno. Brazilian anthropophagy: myth and literature. (*Diogenes/Philosophy*, 144, Winter 1988, p. 116–139)

Scholarly coverage of a theme related to the work of Oswald de Andrade.

4812 Ribeiro, José Antônio Pereira. O universo romântico de Joaquim Manoel de Macedo. São Paulo: Roswitha Kempf, 1987. 137 p.: bibl., facsims.

Somewhat amateurish and intellectually naive study of a writer that has been unfairly underestimated.

4813 Sena, Jorge de. Machado de Assis and his "carioca" quintet. Translated by Isabel de Sena. (*Lat. Am. Lit. Rev.*, 14:27, Jan./June 1986, p. 9–18)

Author proposes that the last five of Machado's novels should be regarded as an esthetic whole structured around the central axis of *Dom Casmurro*. Technically the *carioca* quintet is a work in the modern vein rather than a novel in the romantic or realistic tradition (see also item **4806**).

4814 Silva, Vera Maria Tietzmann. A metamorfose nos contos de Lygia Fagundes Telles. Rio de Janeiro: Presença Edições, 1985. 210 p. (Col. Atualidade crítica; 7)

"Metamorphosis" is the term given by some to "corrections" or textual variants. Add this book to the ever-increasing studies on Lygia Fagundes Telles.

4815 Valente, Luis Fernando. Parody and carnivalization in the novels of Márcio Souza. (*Hispania/Teachers*, 70:4, Dec. 1987, p. 787–793, bibl.)

Self-explanatory title.

4816 Varin, Claire. Clarice Lispector: rencontres brésiliennes. Laval, Canada: Trois, 1987. 241 p.: photos. (Col. Vedute)

Interesting and valuable compilation of Lispector's interviews and confessions, the editor's somewhat whimsical policies notwithstanding. Includes excellent photos. Note the correction of Lispector's birth date, which is 1920 rather than 1925 as believed until now (see also item **4809**).

4817 Vieira, Nelson H. Testimonial fiction and historical allegory: racial and political repression in Jorge Amado's Brazil. (*Lat. Am. Lit. Rev.*, 17:34, July/Dec. 1989, p. 6–23)

Reading of Jorge Amado exposes common misreadings that plague studies of his work.

4818 Ward, Teresinha Souto. O discurso oral em *Grande sertão—veredas*. São Paulo: Livraria Duas Cidades, 1984. 149 p.: bibl.

The rhetorical oral style of *Grande sertão: veredas* is a common criticism of this work. This study provides comprehensive coverage of such criticism throughout the years.

POETRY

4819 *Cadernos Negros*. Vol. 9, 1986– . São Paulo: Gráfica Scortecci.

Serial publication devoted to poetry of *négritude* evidences growing interest in the topic. [R.E. Dimmick]

4820 Chaves, Albeniza de Carvalho e. Tradição e modernidade em Mário Faustino. Belém, Brazil: Univ. Federal do Pará, Gráfica e Editora Universitária, 1986. 344 p.: bibl., port.

Minute, apologetic reading of Mário Faustino, a poet who became a cult figure after his tragic death at a young age.

4821 Crítica e poesia: antologia de textos críticos sobre a poesia de Gilberto Mendonça Teles. Organização, introdução e notas de Dulce Maria Viana. Goiânia, Brazil: Secretaria de Estado da Cultura, 1988. 700 p.: bibl., index, port.

Impressive evidence of the interest Teles' poems have evoked among contemporaries at home and abroad. [R.E. Dimmick]

4822 Denófrio, Darcy França. Poesia contemporânea: G.M.T., o regresso às origens. Porto Alegre, Brazil: Livraria Editora Acadêmica, 1987. 90 p.: bibl., ill., index.

Analyses of *Hora aberta* and *Plural de nuvens*, treating Gilberto Mendonça Teles' handling of the relationship between the physical and metaphysical worlds and his transubstantiation of the commonplace into the poetic. [R.E. Dimmick]

4823 Haberly, David T. The depths of the river: Mário de Andrade's "Meditação sôbre o Tietê." (*Hispania/Teachers*, 72:2, May 1989, p. 278–282, bibl.)

Good reading of Andrade's poem.

4824 Hill, Telenia. Castro Alves e o poema lírico. 2a ed. rev. e aum. Rio de Janeiro: Tempo Brasileiro, 1986. 181 p.: bibl., ill. (Biblioteca Tempo universitário; 54)

Another reading of Castro Alves (67 p.), followed by a "small anthology" (25 p.).

4825 Kovadloff, Santiago. Cecília Meireles: entre lo secular y lo sagrado. (*Cuad. Hispanoam.*, 463, enero 1989, p. 45,60)

Interesting analysis of a solitary figure of contemporary Brazilian poetry. See also *HLAS 48:6413*.

4826 Manuel Bandeira: um novo itinerário: exposição comemorativa do centenário do seu nascimento. Rio de Janeiro: Fundação Casa de Rui Barbosa, 1986. 43 p.: bibl., facsims., ports. (Memória literária; 10)
Useful and informative.

4827 Manuel Bandeira, 1886-1986. Coordenação de Elódia F. Xavier. Rio de Janeiro: Univ. Federal do Rio de Janeiro, PROED, 1986. 142 p.: bibl., ill.
Of this collection of reminiscences and critical essays honoring the centennial of the poet's birth, Gilberto Mendonça Teles' "A Experimentação Poética de Bandeira" merits particular attention. [R.E. Dimmick]

4828 Rosa, Sérgio Ribeiro. Cantares do Maranhão: exegese da obra poética de José Sarney. Rio de Janeiro: Arte Contemporânea, 1985. 76 p.: ports. (Leituras de poesia; 1)
Rather than a systematic study of President Sarney's verse, Rosa has written a running commentary on a single composition, "Os Marimbondos de Fogo." [R.E. Dimmick]

4829 Santiago, Socorro. Uma poética das águas: a imagem do rio na poesia amazonense contemporânea. Manaus, Brazil: Edições Puxirum, 1986. 140 p.
Influence of the river on Amazonian poets as reflected in the images they use, the social life they depict, and the regional beliefs and universal myths on which they draw. [R.E. Dimmick]

4830 Schüler, Donaldo. A poesia no Rio Grande do Sul. Porto Alegre, Brazil: Mercado Aberto; IEL, 1987. 347 p.: bibl. (Série Documenta; 22)
Extended analysis of the idiosyncratic development of poetry in Rio Grande do Sul, emphasizes conflict between the *texto monárquico*, which exalts the individual and tends toward the grandiloquent, and the *texto arcaico*, which gives expression to the collectivity in everyday terms. [R.E. Dimmick]

4831 Silva, De Castro e. Augusto dos Anjos: o poeta e o homem. 2a. ed. Campinas, Brazil: Editora LISA, 1984. 229 p., 13 leaves of plates: ill.
For the first edition of this work (1961), Silva rewrote his pioneering *Augusto dos Anjos: poeta da morte e da melancolia*

(1944). Thus he could claim that "everything is new here" (see *HLAS 42: 6420*).

4832 Távora, Araken. Encontro marcado com Mário Quintana. Porto Alegre, Brazil: L&PM Editores, 1986. 31 p.: ports.
Interesting autobiographical information about a minor poet.

4833 Zenith, Richard. João Cabral de Melo Neto: an engineer of poetry. (*Lat. Am. Lit. Rev.*, 15:30, July/Dec. 1987, p. 26–42)
Finally, an excellent reading of Cabral's poetry that is more than the usual paraphrasing.

MISCELLANEOUS (ESSAYS, MEMOIRS, CORRESPONDENCE, ETC.)

4834 Brant, Vera. Ensolarando sombras. Rio de Janeiro: F. Alves, 1986. 175 p.: facsims., ports.
Eminently readable thanks to author's lively sense of humor and uninhibited mode of expression, these memoirs provide vivid pictures of early life in Brasília and of such figures as "Helena Morley" and Juscelino Kubitschek. [R.E. Dimmick]

4835 Leite, Ascendino. Os dias memoráveis. Rio de Janeiro: EdA Edit., 1987. 292 p.: index. (Jornal literário; 12)
In addition to numerous reflections on Euclydes da Cunha, interesting pictures of Marques Rebêlo and Luiz da Câmara Cascudo distinguish this latest addition to the journal of a self-confessed "renitente e apagado moralista literário." [R.E. Dimmick]

4836 Neves, Tancredo. Tancredo: máximas e citações. Compilação e comentário de Carlos Laranjeira. Apresentação de Adhemar de Barros Filho. São Paulo: A.T. Color, 1985. 126 p.: index.
Quotes on public figures and issues from a president-elect who never took office; of interest primarily to historians. [R.E. Dimmick]

4837 Nunes, Raimundo. Pedro Nava: memória. São Paulo: Editora Ateniense, 1987. 445 p.: bibl.
Neither a biography of Nava nor a systematic commentary on his work, but rather notes and reflections relative thereto. [R.E. Dimmick]

FRENCH AND ENGLISH WEST INDIES AND THE GUIANAS

ETHEL O. DAVIE, *Assistant Vice President for Academic Affairs, West Virginia State College*
NAOMI M. GARRETT, *Professor Emeritus, West Virginia State College*

THERE HAS BEEN A CONSIDERABLE EXPANSION of literature from the French and English West Indies and The Guianas during this biennium, with the bulk of this increase being produced in French-speaking areas.

Prose fiction, particularly novels, led all genres in Haiti and Martinique. These novels treat mainly historical events, current social and political problems, and the writers' cultural backgrounds. While several established authors such as Edouard Glissant (item **4847**), Jean Métellus (items **4855** and **4867**), René Depestre (item **4846**), and prolific popular writer Tony Delsham (items **4843, 4844,** and **4845**) are represented, there are also a number of talented novices annotated below. It is worthy of note that the prestigious Prix Renaudot was awarded in 1988 to Depestre for his novel, *Hadriana dans tous mes rêves* (item **4846**). Prose production in English areas consists principally of short stories and one drama.

Collections of verse by major poets allow access to their important works. French poets are principally from the two islands previously cited, while English poetry in this *HLAS* represents a continuum from the Bahamas to Trinidad and Guyana. Small Anglophone islands add their contributions, some for the first time.

Heightened interest in Caribbean literature is indicated by the number of critical studies from several parts of the world. In recent years the region's writers have served as a fertile source for topics of study not only in the West Indies but in Europe and the US. Diverse critical studies are multilingual in expression and content: scholars deal simultaneously with writings from several different language areas and critics often write in languages other than their own. In this connection, special mention should be made of the report from the pluridisciplinary colloquium, *La période révolutionnaire aux Antilles* (item **4874**), which shows the reciprocal influence of the Haitian and French revolutions on literature and philosophical ideas on both sides of the Atlantic.

Much important research has been conducted on the theater (items **4882** and **4876**), the Francophone novel, and major Caribbean authors. Whether writers should use European or indigenous languages remains a principal concern. Derek Walcott (item **4902**) was awarded the Nobel Prize for literature in 1992.

FRENCH WEST INDIES AND FRENCH GUIANA
Prose Fiction

4838 Beaulieu, Raymond. La canne debout: roman. Port-au-Prince: Impr. des Antilles, 1988. 399 p.

In a financial agreement between the two governments on Hispaniola, Haitian peasants are conscripted to work in Dominican cane fields. Influenced by tales of the 1937 massacre of Haitians under similar circumstances, one young man escapes to the hills and becomes an inspiration to the impoverished community. Brutal treatment of workers and the murder of many returning to Haiti lead to a violent uprising against local officials. Author, not always skillful in handling subplots, shows an interesting style. Portrays the downtrodden sympathetically but is pessimistic about their future. Includes helpful glossary of Creole terms.

4839 Blandin-Pauvert, Arlette. Au temps des Mabos: les blancs créoles de la Guadeloupe au début du siècle. Fort-de-France: Désormeaux, 1986. 190 p. (Col. Les Grands romans des Antilles-Guyane)

Author reminisces about the 19th-century golden age for white youth of favored French colonial origin. Praises early planters' constructive activities, while protesting the hostile contemporary public's unjust neglect and reprobration of their accomplishments. Planters' deeds are remembered in the oral tradition of prestigious older families on Guadeloupe.

4840 Burnet, Mireille. La chienne du quimboiseur. Paris: Editions Caribéennes, 1986. 126 p. (Série Tropicalia)

Popular fiction about sorcery in Martinique. Mysterious disappearance of a magician's wife is followed by arrival of a devoted and jealous female dog causing fear and suspicion. Not until another woman appears to share the magician's life is the matter resolved. Melodramatic supernatural ending.

4841 Cabort-Masson, Guy. La mangrove mulâtre. Saint-Joseph, Martinique: La Voix du Peuple, 1986. 282 p. (Roman historique martiniquais)

In 1842 a young lawyer is sent from Paris to his native Martinique to investigate the misfortunes of a formerly successful French merchant there. Investigation uncovers much about relationships among slaves, free mulattoes, and French masters, the *békés*, as well as the machinations of each group in the era just prior to abolition.

4842 Cabort-Masson, Guy. Pourrir, ou, martyr un peu. Illustrations de René Corail. Martinique: La Voix du peuple, 1987. 252 p.

Memoir concerning formation of an intelligent island youngster who is able to succeed in the competitive, socially restricted educational system but nevertheless revolts. Admitted through family influence to noted French Ecole Normale, he is unable to conform to its regulations. After reaching cadet rank at St. Cyr, he is sent to Algeria where he becomes involved in that conflict. Interesting insights into the education of a Martinican rebel (1943–60).

4843 Delsham, Tony. L'ababa. . Fort-de-France: Editions M.G.G., 1987? 258 p.

Young Martinican discovers that his only child, a girl, is so severely handicapped that she will never be able to speak or function normally. His wife, unable to accept her daughter's condition, leaves the family and flees to France. The successful businessman father devotes his life to the daughter who becomes insanely jealous of her father's female friends. Solution gives an unusual twist to the story. Interesting psychological study.

4844 Delsham, Tony. L'impuissant. Fort-de-France: Editions M.G.G., 1986. 204 p.

After several years of a nearly perfect marriage a successful young Martinican businessman discovers that he is impotent. Medicine, psychiatry, naturopathy, sorcery—all prove futile as the protagonist learns that his problem is hereditary. Unexpected event prevents tragic ending.

4845 Delsham, Tony. Panique aux Antilles. Fort-de-France: Editions M.G.G., 1985. 188 p.

Talented popular writer has turned out an interesting tale of murder and political wrong-doing. Principal character is detective especially attractive to women, but his affairs do not prevent solving a difficult case. Seven gruesome murders turn out to be the work of one improbable suspect.

4846 Dépestre, René. Hadriana dans tous mes rêves: roman. Paris: Gallimard, 1988. 195 p.

Fanciful story by well-known Haitian poet René Dépestre. Beautiful young daughter of wealthy French family living in Jacmel becomes thirsty as she leaves home for her wedding. She drinks a refreshing lemonade and falls dead as she pronounces her marriage vows. After her burial the young bride miraculously escapes the zombification that had been carefully planned for her. Author uses amusing tale to mock life and social customs in his native city.

4847 Glissant, Edouard. La case du commandeur: roman. Paris: Editions du Seuil, 1981. 253 p.: appendix, ill.

Story of fictionalized Martinican woman born in late 1920s provides opportunity for tracing family ancestry back to African forebears. Events in the heroine's life as well as her ancestors and descendants form the body of this family saga. Appendix provides sketch of main family lines. Magic realism and author's characteristic style make this an intriguing novel.

4848 Godart, Jacques G. Pourquoi les campêches saignent-ils? Port-au-Prince: Impr. H. Deschamps, 1987. 199 p.

Dramatic novel of adultery, vengeance among mean-spirited Haitian peasantry. Prix Deschamps, 1987.

4849 Hermary-Vieille, Catherine. L'épiphanie des dieux: roman. Paris: Gallimard, 1983. 190 p.

Young Frenchwoman decides to remain in Haiti after the death of her diplomat husband. Falling in love with the Haitian Minister of the Interior, she becomes involved with local politics and religion when her maid's lover assassinates an important American. Author sees similarity between the main characters and Haitian voodoo gods.

4850 Hermine, Micheline. Les iguanes du temps. Paris: Editions Caribéennes, 1988. 175 p.

Stranger—evidently French—leaves the plane as it makes a stop in Cayenne, French Guiana. Young man at airport directs him to distant area where he will not be detected or questioned. Fleeing a life sentence, the stranger lives in a secluded community protected by the sea, failing to divulge his name or identity even to those who befriend him. Exile's descriptions of natural surroundings and of his relationships form the basis of this unusual novel.

4851 Lamarre, Joseph M. Tragi-comédie à Quisqueya: roman. Port-au-Prince: Impr. Le Natal, 1987. 104 p.

Novel about president of fictitious Caribbean nation who maneuvers his people as a dramatist does his characters. Several heroes emerge—the most important being a group of rebellious university students who, though the revolution fails, do not relinquish hope. They are determined to prepare a better rebellion. In epilogue, the dictator's son becomes president after the father's death. Vein of humor runs throughout.

4852 Mattioni, Mario D. Emamori: les premières années de la colonisation en Martinique. Fort-de-France: Désormeaux, 1986. 156 p. (Col. Les Grands romans des Antilles-Guyane)

Romanticized historical novel of early French colonial period on Martinique idealizes the noble savage. Real and fictional events and people are combined in interesting story. Insights into customs and mores of the Calinas, known to settlers as Caraibes. Conversations are distorted by simultaneous renderings in French and Indian, plus inserted translations.

4853 Mattioni, Mario D. Ma Nou l'esclave: sous l'administration de Du Parquet. Fort-de-France: Désormeaux, 1986. 157 p. (Col. Les Grands romans des Antilles-Guyane)

Historical fiction continues story of colonization of Martinique and includes characters from author's earlier *Emamori* (1986). Severin, a young Frenchman adopted by the Calina tribe, meets African Ma Nou and together they join to fight French oppression. In an era when conquest was accepted normal procedure, an otherwise enlightened, sympathetic French official abets destruction of subjugated races.

4854 Maximin, Daniel. L'Isolé soleil roman. Paris: Éditions du Seuil, 1981. 313 p.

First work of fiction by young Guadeloupean poet. Supposedly written by young female compatriot, novel consists of family correspondence, diaries and journals through several generations. Covers events from arrival of the Spaniards to the 1940s Vichy regime. Political attitudes, natural phenomena, and relations with other islands are brought into play. Author uses symbolism, allusions and paraphrase to good advantage.

4855 Métellus, Jean. Les cacos: roman. Paris: Editions Gallimard, 1989. 303 p.

Novel depicts life and actions during early years of US occupation of Haiti. Based on factual events, story fictionalizes leading characters involved in that historic era. Important roles of religion, politics, patriotism, collaboration, attitudes of the occupiers, and heroism are presented realistically. Aid to understanding present-day Haiti.

4856 Novastar, Charles. Le macho et la fille du macoute: roman. Port-au-Prince: Choucoune, 1987. 181 p. (Série Récit/roman; 3)

Exceptional novel by talented author

about a modern Don Juan. Narrator combines psychological observations on sexuality with adept narrative techniques. Insights into modern behavior patterns. Preface on Creole language is of interest to linguists.

4857 Papillon, Margaret. La marginale: roman. Port-au-Prince: H. Deschamps, 1987. 263 p.

Story of young woman of Haitian upper-middle class during Duvalier regime. Raped by unknown assailant during Carnival, she gives birth to son to whom she devotes her life. Young woman has other unfortunate experiences before finally finding happiness where least expected. Intriguing story despite traces of melodrama.

4858 Tareau, Marc. Le procès d'identité: roman. Chenove, France: Editions Bayardère, 1987. 157 p.

Group of young Martinicans are embittered by their lack of opportunities at home and privileges accorded to French continentals. Additionally, their subjection to racial prejudice in France leads them to revolt. They plan to lead rebellion against conditions and to fight for their island's independence. Revolution fails but leader's trial provides occasion to express opinions on Martinican identity. Interesting story despite persistent polemical tone.

Poetry

4859 Charles, Pradel. Aube aux éclats: poèmes. Port-au-Prince: Impr. Xpress, 1986. 32 p.

First verse of young poet concerned with questions of love. Includes preface by Margareth Lizaire.

4860 Fethière, Sténio. Clartés: poèmes. Les Cayes, Haïti: S. Fethière, 1987? 27 leaves

Patriotic poems written while author was political prisoner. They sing of Haiti and laud the martyrs and all who have fought bravely for the country throughout her history. Published posthumously.

4861 Glissant, Edouard. Pays rêvé, pays réel: poème. Paris: Seuil, 1985. 103 p.

Collection of short, intellectually engaging poems is one long song of praise and

love for Martinique and ancestral Africa. The majority find their inspiration in the natural phenomena, history and people of the poet's native island.

4862 Laraque, Paul. Sòlda mawon. Pòtoprens, Haiti: Edisyon Sanba; Flushing, N.Y.: Haitian Book Centre, 1987. 91 p.

Well expressed poems in Creole and French saluting heroes in Haitian history from the first arrival of Europeans on the island up to the present. Jean F. Brierre, one of Haiti's greatest poets, does the French translation.

4863 Lizaire, Margareth. Ondes vides. Port-au-Prince: Impr. La Diffusion, 1987. 47 p.

In her second volume of verse (see *HLAS 46:6412*), the young poet still attacks injustice and pleads for the underprivileged in Haiti, but in softer, more sonorous tones.

4864 Rosarion, Ulrick. Voix des saisons. Port-au-Prince: Impr. des Antilles, 1983. 155 p.

Volume of rhythmic poetry uses mainly the classic alexandrine reminiscent of earlier Haitian verse. The poet, who is also judge of the Civil Court, sings of lost loves and hopes and the passage of time, with an occasional, faint expression of joy.

4865 Sachy. Floraison d'or; Raisins amers; Raison de croire. Port-au-Prince: Impr. II, 1987. 160 p.

Lyrical verse of seasoned writer presented under a pseudonym gives delicate pictures of Haiti, her past and people. The poet also sings of his own experiences, dreams, and hopes for the future. He meditates upon life, love, and the common fate of man. The refreshing collection is introduced by two outstanding Haitian writers.

4866 Tavernier, Janine. Naïma, fille des dieux: poèmes. Préface de Jean F. Brierre et Roger Dorsinville. Sherbrooke, Canada: Editions Naaman, 1982. 75 p. (Col. Création; 113)

Latest volume by Janine Tavernier (see also *HLAS 26:2139* and *HLAS 34:4340*) takes its name from the first group of poems. Exiled from her beloved Haiti, the poet expresses her suffering and nostalgia in majestic yet anguished tones.

Drama

4867 Métellus, Jean. Anacaona: théâtre. Paris: Hatier, 1986. 160 p.: map. (Col. Monde noir poche; 38)

Dramatic presentation concerns history of Haiti's earliest known inhabitants. Gentle, trusting natives welcome the arrival of Columbus, believing in the Spaniards' offers of friendship and peace. However, the Europeans' greed, desire for power, and determination to convert the Indians led to the death of the gentle queen and the virtual extermination of the natives. Well-known poet and novelist displays noteworthy musicality in his dramatic verse.

4868 Namphy, Elizabeth Abbott. Tropical obsession: a universal tragedy in four acts set in Haiti. Port-au-Prince: Editions Henri Deschamps, 1986. 100 p.: ill.

Young Haitian peasant leaves his unhappy home because of his mother's death. Abandoned by his father, he goes to Port-au-Prince where he is educated by Catholic priest and becomes very successful. But his very ill father has taken steps that will destroy the son and his family. Young man returns to his village to seek aid from the voodoo gods and discovers the reasons for his father's actions. Drama of love, hatred, broken promises, and reconciliation reveals many peasant customs and beliefs.

Special Studies

4869 Almeida, Lilian Pestre de. Oralité et création dans la production caraîbéenne: Guillén, Césaire et quelques autres. (*Conjonction*, 180, 1988, p. 37–77)

Analyzes traditional oral forms, emphasizing riddles and their functions, *comptines*, and story-telling as represented in the works of Guillén, Césaire and other area writers in French, Spanish and Portuguese. Concludes that use of oral forms is often regarded as surrealism by the uninformed, particularly in Césaire's works.

4870 Antoine, Régis. Le souci humaniste dans les littératures des Antilles francophones. (*Philol. Prag.*, 32 : 3, 1989, p. 140–152, bibl.)

Resumé of the literature of Haiti, Martinique and Guadeloupe traces the islands' geophysical, historic, and linguistic similarities relative to their literary history. Evolutionary pattern is similar for all three, but differences are reflected in writings. Penetrating observations of works of major authors.

4871 Arnold, Albert James Modernism and negritude: the poetry and poetics of Aimé Césaire. Cambridge, Mass.: Harvard Univ. Press, 1981. 318 p.: bibl., index.

Critical analysis of the writings and ideas of Martinican poet and dramatist Aimé Césaire. Creator of the term *negritude*, he is portrayed as thoroughly steeped in his African background and highly influenced by French surrealists. Using a dense association of images and metaphors from African traditions and racial memory, Césaire expresses the pent-up emotions of blacks in their struggle for freedom and equality. With a choice selection of words, syntax and metaphors, he speaks for his people, wishing to develop a truly Martinican personality while guiding blacks everywhere to their rightful place in world society.

4872 Aubin, Danielle. Approche du roman historique antillais. (*Présence Afr.*, 148, 1988, p. 30–43, bibl.)

Reviews five novels from Haiti, Martinique and Guadeloupe. Based on historic incidents during revolutionary periods and real personnages, the novels are concerned with slavery, *marronage*, and open rebellion, showing African slaves in a different perspective than that ordinarily presented by white Creole writers.

4873 Catálogo de la Exposición Bibliográfica Haitiana. Santo Domingo: Biblioteca Nacional, 1988. 39 p.

Selected bibliography of Haitian works available in the Biblioteca Nacional, Santo Domingo. Collection of writings in French, Spanish, and English deals with politics, history, science, literature, etc. Valuable for early periods but lists few current writers.

4874 Colloque international pluridisciplinaire sur la période révolutionnaire aux Antilles, *Fort-a-France et Pointe-à-Pitre, 1986.* Proceedings: la période révolutionnaire aux Antilles: images et résonances; littérature, philosophie, histoire sociale, histoire des idées. Coordination de Roger Toumson et Charles Porset. Schœlcher, Martinique: Groupe de Recherche et d'Étude des Littératures et Civilisations de la Caraïbe et des Amériques Noires, Univ. des Antilles et de la Guyane; Paris: Centre d'Etude de la Littérature Française des XVIIe et XVIIIe Siècles du C.N.R.S., Univ. de Paris-Sorbonne, 1987? 615 p.: bibl.

Volume of multi-disciplinary scholarly papers deserves important place in Haitian research. Contains varied collection of comparative studies on social history, literature, and civilization during French revolutionary period as revealed in both Caribbean and French literatures. Analysis maintains that the contradiction of slavery's persistence throughout the century of Enlightenment haunted the conscience of civilized peoples and was present in major works of the period.

4875 Dominique, Max. Castera: critique et poésie. (*Conjonction*, 180, 1988, p. 81–109)

Assessment of Castera's poetry and criticism concludes that his writing reflects a serious consideration of the art and contains a close correspondence to proletarian positions. Article notes influence of Roumain and Alexis on Castera, and his concern for major question of language of expression.

4876 Fouchard, Jean. Le théâtre à Saint-Domingue. Port-au-Prince: H. Deschamps, 1988. 294 p.: bibl. (Regards sur le temps passé; 5)

Interesting and well-documented study of theater in Saint Domingue from the organization of the first dramatic group in 1740 until the declaration of Haitian independence. According to author, theaters were established in all major and minor cities, the most elaborate at Port-au-Prince. Actors and actresses from Paris and domestic troupes gave outstanding performances in operatic and strictly dramatic works. Descriptions of the theater as show place and social center of colonial life, comments on audiences, synopses of less well-known presentations, and critical views are all authenticated by citations from reviews and periodicals of the time.

4877 González, José Emilio. La antilla reencontrada de Jean-Claude Bajeux. (*Rev. Inst. Cult. Puertorriq.*, 92/93, abril/sept. 1986, p. 81–89)

Thoughtful, meticulous critique (in Spanish) of Haitian Jean-Claude Bajeux's published dissertation (in French) on three major Caribbean poets from different language areas. Thoughtful and complimentary analysis of works of Claude McKay, Luis Palés Matos, and Aimé Césaire, sustains thesis that *négritude* is a global attribute of the Caribbean area.

4878 Hoffmann, León-François. Bibliographie des oeuvres de Jean Price-Mars. (*Conjonction*, 172, 1987, p. 116–131, appendix)

Definitive bibliography of the prolific writer Jean Price-Mars' substantial body of work. Includes materials from previously published bibliographies plus texts from parliamentary discourse. Hoffman's meticulous research will form important resource for further studies.

4879 Hoffmann, León-François. Esclavitud y tensiones raciales en Haití a través de la literatura. (*Anu. Estud. Am.*, 43, 1986, p. 353–364, bibl.)

Traces psychological and social effects of slavery and revolt on the Haitian population as expressed in the literature. In Haiti, the only New World country where freedom was achieved by force of armed slave rebellion, the people never have been ashamed of their origins. On the contrary, they have gloried in the exploits of their brave ancestors. At that period in history, mulattoes occupied a privileged status and were landed proprietors owning one-fourth of all slaves. Because of their advantages of education and wealth, mulattoes quickly filled the power vacuum left by white expulsion. Unfortunately, as the literature testifies, racial discord between a light-skinned upper class, a powerful black professional group, and a disenfranchised poor black agrarian class still persists.

4880 Hoffmann, Léon-François. Le roman haïtien: idéologie et structure. Sherbrooke, Canada: Editions Naaman, 1982. 329 p.: bibl., index. (Col. Etudes; 36)

Scholarly monograph discusses 156 Haitian novels (1859–1980). Author authoritatively examines their origins and national characteristics, and explores their themes, stylistics, and linguistic aspects. Last chapter on originality of the Haitian novel draws some interesting conclusions, opening avenues for further research. Includes comprehensive bibliography.

4881 Lahens, Yanick Jean-Pierre. Autour de deux jeunes poètes haïtiens. (*Conjonction*, 172, 1987, p. 92–106, bibl.)

Study of the power of words to transform the world as evidenced in the works of Robert Manuel and Robert Berrouët-Oriol. Explores intertextually *rythmicité*, treatments of syntax, levels of language, and registers. Examines Marie Chauvet's *Amour, colère, folie*, concluding that literature should no longer serve as faithful report of the established order.

4882 Regards sur le théâtre. Bourg-Abymes, France: Centre Antillais de Recherches et d'Etudes, 1980. 176 p.: bibl., ill., maps. (CARE, 0336–7487; 6)

Collection of articles devoted chiefly to discussion of theater development in Francophone and Anglophone Caribbean. First presentations were European and generally for the colonists. In the British islands a domestic theater began in the early 1900s. Subjects mirrored concerns of the people: economic, social, political, racial, and gender problems. Caribbean theater has become more sophisticated through major writers such as Derek Walcott and Aimé Césaire.

4883 Turian Cardozo, Jacqueline. On ne guérit pas de son enfance. Port-au-Prince: Editions H. Descamps, 1987. 220 p., 2 p. of plates: ports.

Charming memoirs of a happy childhood in a mid-20th century gifted Haitian household. Mentions renowned literary, political, and administrative friends and relatives. Of general and scholarly interest.

4884 Victor, Gary. Albert Buron, ou, profil d'une "élite." Port-au-Prince: Imprimeur II, 1988. 230 p.

Brilliant political and social satire of contemporary local society by Haitian journalist. Albert Buron, the central figure and epitome of corruption, symbolizes decadent politicians whose likeness can be recognized easily by their compatriots.

ENGLISH WEST INDIES AND GUYANA
Prose Fiction

4885 Catalyn, James J. Reading roasts and other writings. Nassau: Nassau Guardian, 1986. 86 p.

Collection of political satire, social commentary, and roasts featuring outstanding Bahamian citizens. Skits and songs portray island society. Folk speech intermingled with standard English highlights aspects of the culture.

4886 Charles, Faustin. The black magic man of Brixton. London: Karnak House; Zed Books, 1985. 91 p.

Collection of interesting tales set in Britain by Trinidadian writer. Old man uses magic to teach ancient island values to immigrants corrupted by hard life in urban London ghetto. Attacks modern racism, hypocrisy, crime and immorality.

Dabydeen, David and **Nana Wilson-Tagoe.** Selected theses in West Indian literature: an annotated bibliography. See item **36.**

4887 Lazare, Alick. Native laughter. Roseau, Dominica: Tropical Printers, 1985. 167 p.

Interesting collection of short stories and poetry built around author's native island, Dominica. Nine stories present humourous but sympathetic view of small island life and people. Poems depicting native culture show a more serious attitude.

4888 Lockhart, Anthony. Man in the hills. Roseau, Dominica: Tropical Printers, 1987? 56 p.

Four stories portray middle-class life on Dominica. Title drawn from first tale about young student who leaves home and college in rebellion against actions of his tyrannical father and practices of a corrupt government.

4889 Senior, Olive. Summer lightning and other stories. Essex, England: Longman Group Ltd., 1986. 134 p. (Longman Caribbean writers)

Well-known writer's collection of short stories set in rural Jamaica depicts events from ordinary lives in realistic detail. Characters' speech is rendered in natural patois.

Poetry

4890 Bissundyal, Churaumanie. Cleavage: a poem on East Indian immigration to British Guyana. East Demerara, Guyana: C. Bissundyal, 1986. 64 p.

Long poem concerning indentured East Indians leaving their homeland for British Guiana. Describes indignities of the voyage and hardships suffered in their new life but offers promise of brighter future for their descendants.

4891 Brathwaite, Edward Kamau. Jah music. Mona, Jamaica: Savacou Cooperative, 1986. 60 p.

Collected examples from scattered sources of major poet's early genius. Noteworthy poems dedicated to jazz musicians displays Brathwaite's virtuosity in synchronizing language with music.

4892 Carter, Martin. Selected poems. Foreword by Ian McDonald. Georgetown, Guyana: Demerara Publishers Ltd., 1989. 198 p.: bibl.

Collection spans production of one of Guyana's major poets (1952–84). Poems of rebellion, defeat and disillusion highlight the work covering a turbulent period in Guyanese history from independence to uneasy early 1980s. Contains brief bibliography of Carter's poetry and political and critical writings during his long successful career.

4893 Clarke, Clayton. Selected poems. S.l.: s.n., 1987? 21 p.

Consists of 15 excellent poems mainly about the poet's Caribbean island.

4894 Collie, S. Sidney. Island breezes: a collection of poems and short stories. Nassau: s.n., 1985. 41 p.: ill.

Collection of poems and stories inspired by life and scenes on the Bahamas' smaller islands. Traditions and local color pervade selections in this first well-presented volume. Illustrations.

4895 Dream rock. Edited by Edward Kamau Brathwaite. Introduction by Winnie Risden-Hunter. Kingston: Jamaica Information Service, 1987. 34 p.

Consists of 31 poems by eight talented young Jamaicans. Selected and edited by poet Edward Kamau Brathwaite and dedicated to the memory of his wife.

4896 Escoffery, Gloria. Loggerhead. Kingston: Sandberry Press, 1988. 48 p. (Caribbean poetry series; 1)

Though this is her first published volume, the talented poet has had verse included in Caribbean collections and reviews.

Primarily a painter, she presents realistic pictures of scenes, places, and actions.

4897 Khalideen, Rosetta. Portrait in poetry: a collection of poems. Georgetown, Guyana: R. Khalideen, 1989. 30 p.

Small collection of interesting verse pays tribute to the poet's East Indian heritage, to her family, and to Guyana, her native land. Several poems had appeared earlier in literary reviews.

Kubayanda, Josaphat Bekunuru. The poet's Africa: Africanness in the poetry of Nicolás Guillén and Aimé Césaire. See item **4214.**

4898 Robinson, Nelcia. Pictures remain: a collection of 13 poems. Kingstown, St. Vincent and the Grenadines?: Alternatives Ltd., 1987. 16 p.

Personal experiences, thoughts, and concerns of her compatriots provide the subject of this second volume by promising young poet.

4899 Robinson, Nelcia. Poetry is feeling. Kingstown, St. Vincent and the Grenadines?: Alternatives Limited, 1987. 32 p.

First efforts in verse reveal the poet's widespread interest in her island, its life, its people and their concerns. Several poems show talent and sensitivity of expression and observation.

4900 Seetahal, Bhadase. Arrivals and departures. Introduction by Bhoendradatt Tewarie. St. Augustine, Trinidad and Tobago: B. Seetahal, 1986. 52 p.

Much of the verse in this collection, some of which appeared earlier in literary magazines, deals with loss, isolation, stifled dreams, frustrated ambitions and a general concern for society. Despite a vein of pessimism, the talented young poet expresses hope for a brighter future.

4901 Seymour, Arthur J. Selected poems. Georgetown, Guyana: Labour Advocate Job Print, 1983. 52 p.

Collection of poems selected from the best of Seymour's earlier published verse. Volume designed for use in Guyanese schools shows the poet's art in expressing love of country, its history, and its legends.

4902 Walcott, Derek. Collected poems, 1948–1984. New York: Farrar, Straus & Giroux, 1986. 515 p.: bibl., index.

Excellent selections from the best of Walcott's published verse. All phases of his work are represented, showing the excellence of the poet's art whether he is writing of his deepest thoughts, acquaintances, or travels, or reminiscing over his childhood and native island.

Drama

4903 Edgecombe, David. *Coming home to roost:* a play in two acts. Plymouth, Montserrat: Summit Communications, 1988. 63 p.

Two-act drama portrays effects of envy and jealousy between two brothers on the island of Montserrat. Older brother labors hard seeking security, while the younger, more ambitious, leaves his young family to study in England. Rivalry causes great pain and nearly destroys the young brother's family.

Special Studies

4904 Cooper, Carolyn. "That Cunny Jamma Oman": the female sensibility in the poetry of Louise Bennett. (*Jam. J.*, 18:4, Nov. 1985/Jan. 1986, p. 2–9, bibl., ill., photos)

Author analyzes Bennett's rendering of female psychology in the context of domestic relations and work situations. Women tolerate masculine condescension but not subservience, depending on *Anansi*-like guile for successful manipulation of dominating males. *Anansi* is incorrectly identified as "Akan Creator God."

4905 Dabydeen, David and **Nana Wilson-Tagoe.** Selected themes in West Indian literature: an annotated bibliography. (*Third World Q.*, 9:3, July 1987, p. 921–960)

Significant discussion of Anglophone West Indian literature shows that common elements in the islands' background, history, and experiences have resulted in the region's writers sharing interests and concerns. Anti-imperialism, nationalism, race, island family life, migration, politics, are major themes addressed in both prose and poetry. Annotated bibliography of selections supports authors' theories.

4906 Davidas, Lionel. Vision de l'Inde et de la diaspora indienne à travers l'oeuvre de l'émigré trinidadien V.S. Naipaul. (*Rev. CERC*, 3, 1986, p. 97–106)

Eminent Trinidadian writer V.S. Naipaul has made several attempts to explore his Indian heritage as seen in *An area of darkness* and *India: a wounded civilization.* His vision remains negative in both works, as does his portrayal of India's uncertainty, being a continent poised between tradition and modernity.

4907 Focus on West Indian literature: booklist. Kingston: Jamaica Library Service, 1985. 45 p.

Catalog of miscellaneous West Indian book exhibit reflects a wide range of subjects for public consumption. Includes pamphlets and periodicals.

4908 O'Connor, Teresa F. Jean Rhys: the West Indian novels. New York: New York Univ. Press, 1986. 247 p.: bibl., index.

Critical study distinguished by special empathy for the works of Jean Rhys. Concludes that preoccupation with social, cultural, and personal elements characterizes her writings. Carefully reviews her publications, unpublished manuscripts, and reference materials. Interviews with Rhys and her intimates confirm critic's conclusion that her writings are intensely autobiographical and reveal a lonely, unhappy childhood. Alienation resulting from the colonial experience, disruptive family relationships, and an episode of sexual abuse affected both her life and works.

4909 Taylor, Patrick. The narrative of liberation: perspectives on Afro-Caribbean literature, popular culture, and politics. Ithaca, N.Y.: Cornell Univ. Press, 1989. 251 p.: bibl., index.

Thorough study of the development of a liberating consciousness among peoples of the Caribbean with intent to create national cultures. Using history, religion, folklore, from their African and colonial past, Afro-Caribbean writers interpret present conditions with a view to creating societies based on recognition of human freedom and cultural dignity. Writers' goal is to lead their people from an attitude of colonialism to a liberated culture. Chief among writers studied are psychiatrist and political activist Frantz Fanon, poet and dramatist Derek Walcott, and novelist George Lamming. Provides selected bibliography.

TRANSLATIONS INTO ENGLISH FROM THE SPANISH AND PORTUGUESE

CAROL MAIER, *Professor of Spanish, Kent State University, Ohio*
DAPHNE PATAI, *Professor of Portuguese, University of Massachusetts at Amherst*

TRANSLATIONS FROM THE SPANISH

TO THE EXTENT THAT NUMBERS can provide reason for encouragement, the quantity of translations from the Spanish during the current biennium is cause for celebration. With the exception of theater (an area in which the only recent titles fall in the next volume of the *Handbook*), there has been a notable increase of work in all categories. In addition, this increase includes both significantly more translations of work by women and many translations of works by writers little known or unknown in English. To be sure, there is more than one new book each by Carpentier, Fuentes, García Márquez, Neruda, Paz, and Vargas Llosa. There are also, however, enough titles linked with less familiar names to suggest an alteration in the tendency noted by Michael Scott Doyle (item **5050**) and others to publish primarily "a handful of superstars in translation." There have also been several significant reissues which have brought back into print such important titles as Fernando Alegría's *Changing centuries* (Pittsburgh: Latin American Literary Review Press, 1988), Miguel Angel Asturias' *Men of maize* (London: Verso, 1988), Adolfo Bioy Casares' *Plan for escape* (St. Paul, Minn.: Graywolf Press, 1988), José Lezama Lima's *Paradiso* (Austin: Univ. of Texas Press, 1988), Augusto Roa Bastos' *Son of man* (New York: Monthly Review Press, 1988), and Luisa Valenzuela's *He who searches* (Elmwood Park, Ill.: Dalkey Archive Press, 1987).

Nor is it necessary to speak only of the greater number of books published. On the contrary, among those publications one finds highly accomplished work by translators whose names North American readers have seen often (such as Edith Grossman, Suzanne Jill Levine, Margaret Sayers Peden, and Eliot Weinberger) and others whose names they may not recognize (Daniel Balderston, Thomas Christensen, Evelyn Picon Garfield, and Katherine Silver, to name only a few who could be listed here). Many of the anthologies also contain excellent translations, and these collections often introduce translators new to the profession as well as writers hitherto unavailable in English.

Fortunately, it is also possible to report an increase in the quantity and quality of the attention paid to both Hispanic literature in translation and to the activity of translation itself. No doubt this reflects, at least to some extent, the frequent mention of translation in critical discussions within and across diverse disciplines. This trend is exemplified by publications such as Andrew Benjamin's *Translation and the nature of philosophy* (New York: Routledge, 1989), Vicente L. Rafael's *Contracting colonialism: translation and Christian conversion in Tagalog society under early Spanish rule* (Ithaca: Cornell Univ. Press, 1988), and James Boyd White's *Justice as translation* (Chicago: Univ. of Chicago Press, 1990). Works more specific to Hispanic studies are Daphne Patai's introduction to *Brazilian women speak: contemporary life stories* (item **2982**) and Gustavo Pérez Firmat's *The Cuban condition: translation and identity in modern Cuban literature* (item **3679**). Although such discussion frequently explores the negative aspects of translation as "conquest," it also proposes that translation can be what Homi K.

Babha noted in "The Commitment to Theory" (in *New Formations*, 5, Summer 1980) as "a place of hybridity," in which, to use translator's terms, neither source nor target text (or culture) predominates.

With respect to Hispanic literature, a growing interest in this "place of hybridity" has occasioned events like the Latin American Book Fair now held annually in New York City and "Translating Latin America," a conference that took place at SUNY-Binghamton (April, 1990). These conferences, like the annual meeting of the American Literary Translators Association (ALTA) and special sessions held at other conferences, highlight the activity of translation through commentaries and readings. In addition, several translators of Spanish literature have received recent national recognition: in 1988, for example, Gregory Rabassa was awarded the Wheatland Prize for his contribution to international literary exchange and Cedric Belfrage received a Special Citation from the PEN Translation Committee for his translations of work by Eduardo Galeano (item **5019**); Suzanne Jill Levine received the Elinor D. Randall Translation Award in 1990 for her translation of an Adolfo Bioy Casares novel (item **4984**); and Eliot Weinberger was featured in press coverage about Octavio Paz in the fall of 1990 when Paz won the Nobel Prize for Literature.

Although reviewers of Spanish literature in translation have been notoriously slow to acknowledge this recognition by according translation serious consideration, it is possible to cite several publications in which, with some regularity, the translator's work receives more than a cursory adjective. Thus it is no longer only in *Review* and *World Literature Today* that one looks for thoughtful response to work in translation but also to *American Book Review*, for example, or *The Women's Review of Books, The Voice Literary Supplement*, or *The Nation*. Moreover, numerous literary journals and magazines advertise a commitment to publishing original work in translation. *American Poetry Review* comes to mind most immediately, but many others could be named as well.

A further indication of increased visibility on the part of translation can be noted in the apparently increased frequency with which translators are reflecting in writing on their practice. The sizeable list of entries annotated below under "Bibliography, Theory, and Practice," makes this clear. It is also corroborated by the extensive translator's remarks that accompany some of the books under review here (e.g., Maureen Ahern, item **4913,** and Julian Palley, item **4942,** writing about their respective translations of Rosario Castellanos; Diana Vélez about *Reclaiming Medusa*, item **4930;** and Robert Mezey's comments about translating *Tungsten*, item **5010**). As might be expected, not all translators, readers, and reviewers agree about the appropriateness of granting translation a space so prominent and so "academic." Their very disagreement, however, especially when presented publicly, serves to problematize the practice of translation and to encourage consideration of the mediation it inevitably involves. See, for example, Dan Bellm's remarks on *A Rosario Castellanos reader* in "A Woman who Knew Latin" (*The Nation*, June 26, 1989, p. 135–139) or the comments in *Publishers Weekly* (July 8, 1989, p. 49) about *Reclaiming Medusa.*

Lest it seem that all the recent attention to translation makes it unnecessary to reiterate the concerns about accessibility expressed in the last volume of the *Handbook* (see *HLAS 50*, p. 590–591), it is important to comment as well on what can only be considered continuing resistance to work in translation. Although manifest in many ways, this resistance is perhaps articulated best in reviewers' appraisals of translation and their responses to translators' comments. Not only is a long translator's preface apt to annoy some readers because of its intrusiveness, a translation bearing lengthy baroque sentences is likely to be judged harshly by a reviewer not familiar with the stylistics of the original. Or conversely, and this is more often the case, the translations described as "fluent," "readable," and "idiomatic" are those in which the sentence structure and syntax most resemble those of English.

This preference for "readability," as Lawrence Venuti has argued (item **5064**), is integrally related to other factors that continue to predominate in the publication and distribution of Latin American literature in North America. Those factors include translation's marginal place in the publishing industry (summarized succinctly by James Marcus in "Foreign Exchange: How Books Break the Language Barrier," *The Voice Literary Supplement*, Feb. 1990), the relative lack of information about Latin America and its literatures on the part of editors and reviewers, and an intense but market-dependent demand for translated material from the "Third World." Thus, the short publication runs for translations noted previously are still prevalent, and it is often not the large publishing firms, but the small presses— with budgets frequently linked to funding which is harder and harder to obtain— that take the risks involved in introducing the work of unfamiliar or controversial writers. What is more, there is still no definitive source of information regarding which titles have been translated and by whom. In his *A to Z*, Jason Wilson offers a praiseworthy attempt to correct this situation single-handedly (item **5066**); he also comments on recent trends in the publication of Latin American fiction in English in "Some Here, Some There" (*The Times Literary Supplement*, 14–20 July 1989). The fact that literary translators continue to be poorly compensated also has a negative effect on accessibility, occasioning hasty work or work that drags on indefinitely because it must be done "on the side."

In short, then, despite the number of books translated from the Spanish, work in translation from Spanish America has not yet been truly "received" in Anglo America, much less received in a context that even approximates its own. Johnny Payne remarks on this with respect to practice (item **5062**); it is also expressed cogently in the editor's afterword to *Latin Americans in New York City* (item **4929**) and the comment that ". . . authors can only sit back and watch while their work, often intended to foment social and political change in their country, is packaged here as aesthetic commodities and read only as universal allegories or exotic travel guides." A further example would be the use by a major university press of "Emergent Literatures" to title a collection that includes work by José Revueltas and Clarice Lispector.

All of the factors discussed above have borne directly on the writing of the reviews in this section, and I hope they will be kept in mind as those reviews are consulted. In particular, I hope that my attention to the practice of translation will be seen as an effort to make translation more visible and more nuanced by encouraging the reading of works in translation as "versions" that are themselves readings. In doing so, I have attempted to be more descriptive than evaluative, although I have not hesitated to indicate work that appears careless or inconsistencies between a translator's stated approach and his or her practice. The *Handbook* is one of the few publications offering serious consideration to translation itself. For this reason I believe that annotations printed in the "Translation" chapter of the *Handbook* must serve as short reviews that provide not only bio-bibliographical information but also raise and explore theoretical issues associated with the activity of translation.

In the same spirit, I have quoted from other reviewers with some frequency, often with the purpose of presenting contrasting opinions. If I seem to have made or reported fewer evaluations with respect to anthologies, it has been because I wanted to summarize their contents as fully as possible within the limited space available. My preference, however, is for anthologies that include a clear editorial statement about the criterion or criteria for selection and that provide sufficient bio-bibliographical information for further reading and research. These aspects of an anthology are as much elements of translation as the transferal of words from one language to another.

The reviews in this volume of the *Handbook* include books published between April 1988 and Aug. 1990. Books received after Sept. 1, 1990 will be reviewed in *HLAS 54*. Except in a very few cases, I have been able to consult both Spanish and English versions of every title reviewed; exceptions are noted. Finally, although I have referred to several reissues, the large volume of new works in translation makes it impossible for reissues to be annotated here.

Readers will note that the Portuguese section of "Translation into English from Spanish and Portuguese" has been considerably expanded. Not only are there more reviews, there is also a separate essay about Brazilian literature in English translation. These additions should make it possible to provide more thorough coverage of work in both languages, and I am grateful to Daphne Patai for her willingness to join me as a collaborator. She is responsible for the annotations of work translated from the Portuguese and for the essay about Brazilian literature. I have prepared the annotations about translations from the Spanish and the section on "Bibliography, Theory, and Practice."

It is with regret that I conclude this introduction by noting the deaths of two highly esteemed translators of Spanish American literature, Cedric Belfrage and Gregory Kolovakos. Both left numerous outstanding translations and made important contributions to the practice, and praxis, of translation. [CM]

TRANSLATIONS FROM THE PORTUGUESE

The past few years have seen a small but steady production of translations from Brazilian literature, published by both trade houses and university presses. Although the diversity of outlets, lack of centralization of translation efforts, and inadequate databases make it difficult to become aware of all translations, especially those that are not reviewed in the major newspapers and journals, it seems safe to conclude that there are two main paths by which translations from Brazilian literature originate. One is through trade publishers (with Thomas Colchie acting as agent for many Brazilian writers), the other through university presses responding to individual initiatives by translators (often teachers of Portuguese). The types of books accepted by these two processes naturally differ, since university presses are able to publish small editions of works for which a trade publisher might not see a sufficient market. In both cases, however, a major problem with translations from Brazilian literature—perhaps shared by others literatures perceived as "minor"—is that these translations may have little visibility and short lifespans. A survey of existing translations of Brazilian literature reveals that a great many works have appeared over the years, only to disappear again quickly. Nor do bookshops normally stock even such Brazilian "classics" as Machado de Assis, as they might stock comparable Russian or French writers.

While several series exist (e.g., the Texas Pan American Series, which has kept alive translations of Graciliano Ramos and Rachel de Queiroz, for example; or the Univ. of Minnesota Press' new series on Emergent Literatures), no series specifically devoted to the publication of translations of Brazilian literature has been undertaken by a university press. Such a series—which would make available not only current Brazilian writers but also "classics" like José de Alencar, Lima Barreto, and Júlia Lopes de Almeida—would do much to make the field more visible and, by mutual reinforcement, to keep translations in print.

In the absence of such publishing programs, the small scale and hit-and-miss nature of the current practice of translation in this field mean that the cultural image of Brazil propagated abroad is likely to be distorted, serving North American fads and commercial priorities on the one hand, or the idiosyncratic tastes and contacts of individual translators on the other, rather than adequately representing Brazil's diversity and cultural production. Furthermore, books cannot usually be adopted for classroom use if they are unavailable in reasonably priced paperbacks, which consigns Brazilian literature to continuing neglect even in this period of emphasis on curricular reform and cultural diversity. In such a situation, visibility may depend upon name association. Thus, Susan Sontag's introduction to the Farrar, Straus reprint of Machado's *Epitaph of a small winner* may bring that "neglected" ("by whom?" one may well ask) masterpiece some much deserved attention, and Grace Paley's brief introduction to Clarice Lispector's *Soulstorm* (item **5029**) is surely intended to serve the same function.

The present crop of books reveals that two writers, in particular, are currently enjoying significant visibility through translation of their works: Moacyr Scliar and Clarice Lispector. The imaginative and captivating Scliar is being brought out primarily by Ballantine Books, which has published many of Scliar's works in the past half dozen years. Lispector's fiction, more difficult and hermetic, is finding diverse outlets in English with both university and trade presses. But it is Jorge Amado who continues to be the Brazilian writer with the highest name-recognition in the US, Bantam Books having paid $250,000 for the English-language rights to *Tocaia Grande* (item **5033**; see also *HLAS 50:3920*). In conjunction with the publicity attendant upon such an advance, Avon reissued, through its Bard Series, many of its existing Amado translations and undertook, as well, to publish a hitherto untranslated early novel, *Capitães da Areia* (item **5032**).

Several New York publishers have recently brought out other Brazilian works in an on-going effort to hit upon a "big book" that would capture the public eye and wallet. Nélida Piñon, João Ubaldo Ribeiro, and Moacyr Scliar were the lucky authors selected. But Brazilian literature, even when it appears in translation, is seldom widely reviewed or regularly stocked. Thus, victim of a pernicious and hard-to-break cycle, it continues to be little known.

In the brief reviews that follow, I have focused on these works *as translations.* Because some of my judgments may seem harsh, let me add that almost all the translations are perfectly readable and enjoyable. It is one thing, however, to read a work only in English; it is quite another to compare it with the original. I have done the latter, and this has afforded me a general sense of some of the common failings of these translations. Most damaging, in my judgment, is, in the case of prose, a surprising inattentiveness to details of style. Thus, for example, repetitions crafted into the original are too often ignored by translators, while elsewhere repetitions not found in the original are introduced; lapses occur in euphony and register, where such lapses do not characterize, or serve any function in, the original; and translators, inadvertently or not, take on the role of editors. In some instances, the same translator will do much better with short works than with long ones by the same author, as if the sheer bulk of a novel has led to more hurried work or to a sense that each phrase mattered less. In making these criticisms, I am fully aware of the enormous labors involved in literary translation. But we need not only more translations from Brazilian literature but also better ones, so that we, as translators, at least offer no pretext for its continued marginalization. [DP]

ANTHOLOGIES

4910 And we sold the rain: contemporary fiction from Central America. Edited by Rosario Santos. New York: Four Walls Eight Windows, 1988. 239 p.: bibl.

Twenty stories, each by a different contemporary author. Thirteen translators. Editor defines her purpose as an effort to "counterbalance the dehumanizing effect of media reporting" with stories that present Central American people, history and culture. Introduction by Jo Anne Engelbert traces the history of the Central American story as both popular tale and written narrative. Substantial biographical paragraph for each writer.

4911 The book of fantasy. Edited by Jorge Luis Borges, Silvina Ocampo, and Adolfo Bioy Casares. Introduction by Ursula K. Le Guin. New York: Viking, 1988. 384 p.

Numerous selections in this revised version of the *Antología de la literatura fantástica* include the work of many translators. Le Guin's introduction is less informative than Borges's "Prólogo" and "Postdata," which it replaces, and Le Guin focuses on Borges as "fantasist" par excellence, to the exclusion of the other editors. She does, however, recount the conceptualization of the original anthology (1940) and offer a pleasing preface to this rich collection.

4912 Borge, Tomás. Have you seen a red curtain in my weary chamber?: poems, stories, and essays. Introduction, translation, and notes by Russell Bartley, Kent Johnson, and Sylvia Yoneda. Willimantic, Conn.: Curbstone Press; New York: Talman Co., 1989. 160 p. : ill. ;

Consists of poetry, short stories, and essays written between 1955–87, including an interview with Sandinista leader and author Borge (1987) and "Critical Comments" by poet Carlos Martínez Rivas. Somewhat laudatory introduction provides general information about Borge's life and writing. Although translators' effort to create "faithful reflections" leads at time to overly literal versions or awkward phrasing, their work conveys both Borge's political commitment and his tenderness. Title is from "Ya no" (poem, 1977). Poems *en face.*

4913 Castellanos, Rosario. A Rosario Castellanos reader: an anthology of her poetry, short fiction, essays, and drama. Edited and with a critical introduction by Maureen Ahern. Translated by Maureen Ahern and others. Austin: Univ. of Texas Press, 1988. 378 p.: bibl., index. (The Texas Pan American series)

Volume of generous selections, including "The Eternal Feminine," a farce translated by Diane E. Marting and Betty Tyree Osiek. Ahern's extensive preliminary material offers biographical and bibliographical information about Castellanos and a critical study, based on feminist scholarship in translation theory and literary criticism, about Castellanos' work and its translation. This analysis has benefited some of the translations more than others; the strongest pieces in English are essays and drama.

4914 Celeste goes dancing, and other stories: an Argentine collection. Edited by Norman Thomas di Giovanni. Translated by Norman Thomas di Giovanni and Susan Ashe. San Francisco: North Point Press, 1990. 184 p.

A frankly "personal affair," di Giovanni's collection includes 14 stories by an equal number of authors he believes should be known, or better known, in English. With one exception, the stories were written in the 1980s; all of them are by living writers. Di Giovanni is an accomplished North American translator now living in England, as the English in these translations with Susan Ashe indicates. Provides an informative biography for each writer as well as an engaging introduction.

4915 Clamor of innocence: Central American short stories. Edited by Barbara Paschke and David Volpendesta. San Fran-

cisco: City Lights Books; Eugene, Or.: Sub-
terranean Co., 1988. 174 p. ;

Wide selection of 31 stories by different authors. Several of the writers are already
familiar to readers in English (Miguel Angel
Asturias, Ernesto Cardenal, Manlio Argueta,
Carmen Naranjo, Sergio Ramírez), but many
others are translated here for the first time.
Work by 13 translators. Very brief "Notes"
on writers and translators open volume and
provide only introductory commentary.

**4916 Conductors of the pit: major works by
Rimbaud, Vallejo, Césaire, Artaud and
Holan.** Translated, edited, and introduced by
Clayton Eshleman, with co-translations by
Annette J. Smith and František William
Galan. New York: Paragon House, 1988. 230
p.: bibl., ports.

Includes translations of Vallejo's *Sermones de la barbarie* based on Eshleman's
work with José Rubia Barcia in *César Vallejo: the complete posthumous poetry* (see
HLAS 42:6648). Changes may seem minor
(isolated words here and there), but many of
them make dramatic differences that would
repay comparative study with the earlier version (the removal of "eh," e.g., in "Goes Running, Walking, Fleeing").

**4917 En breve: minimalism in Mexican po-
etry, 1900–1985.** Translated by Enrique R. Lamadrid and E.A. Mares. Edited by
Enrique R. Lamadrid. Santa Fe, N.M.: Tooth
of Time Books, 1988. 79 p.

Intriguing examples of the short form
by 28 writers from José Juan Tablada to Ernesto Trejo. Prologue traces history and significance of minimalist verse in Mexico,
identifying Tablada, Octavio Paz, and Efraín
Huerta at the center of a meeting between
the "epigrammatic tradition of the West" and
the "contemplative imagist tradition of the
East." Some renditions are apropriately agile
and striking, others less dynamic. *En face.*

**4918 The Faber book of contemporary Latin
American short stories.** Edited by
Nick Caistor. Pbk. ed. London; Boston: Faber
and Faber, 1990. 187 p.

"Determinedly oppositional," according to Gerald Martin (in the "London Times
Literary Supplement"), "Caistor has balanced
left-oriented stories . . . by including perhaps
the most provocatively anti-revolutionary
story by a Cuban writer since 1959." There

are only four women here in 20 stories, but
12 countries including both Brazil and the
US (represented by Chicano writer Rolando
Hinojosa). Short, insightful introduction.
Good translations by various translators,
with authors Hinojosa and João Ubaldo Ribeiro translating their own work.

**4919 The fertile rhythms: contemporary
women poets of Mexico.** Selected and
edited by Thomas Hoeksema. Translated by
Thomas Hoeksema and Romelia Enríquez.
Pittsburgh, Pa.: Latin American Literary Review Press, 1989. 126 p. (Discoveries)

From Gabriel Zaid's *Asamblea de poetas jóvenes de México* (1980), Hoeksema selected 22 women born between 1951–60; of
them, Coral Bracho is no doubt the strongest
and the most challenging for her translators.
Gabriel Zaid's comments about the "intellectually unisex" nature of the generation to
which these poets belong are likely to anger
some. Mary Crow has responded by posing
several leading questions and stressing the
"love of language" in the work of the women
anthologized. For literary critic's comment
see item **3987.**

4920 Formations. Vol. 5, No. 1, Fall 1988– .
Madison, Wis.: Univ. of Wisconsin
Press.

Issue entitled "The disturbing, the
bizarre: contemporary Argentine short
stories." Editor Luisa Valenzuela names 12
stories as her "favorites." Stories are also
unified, she explains, by the prevalence of
the "bizarre," which is manifested in each
through the "custom-made dream." Selections begin with Macedonio Fernández. Argentine authors best known in English have
been omitted in favor of others not as familiar. Translators are Toby Talbot, Magdalena
García Pinto, and Maurita Ugarte.

**4921 The image of black women in twenti-
eth-century South American poetry:
a bilingual anthology.** Edited and translated
by Ann Venture Young. Washington: Three
Continents Press, 1987. 1 v.

Poems by 15 writers from Colombia,
Ecuador, Peru, Uruguay, and Venezuela "in
which the black female is the central figure."
Translations are restrained, even flat at
times, but Young does highlight a figure
whose importance has been virtually overlooked by critics writing in both English and

Spanish. Introduction briefly surveys Peninsular and Spanish American literatures with respect to *negras, morenas,* and *mulatas,* three terms that would have benefited from a more nuanced explanation.

4922 Juana Inés de la Cruz, Sor. A Sor Juana anthology. Translated by Alan S. Trueblood. Foreword by Octavio Paz. Cambridge, Mass.: Harvard Univ. Press, 1988. 248 p.: index.

Selections comprise a representative sampling of poetry including "First Dream" in its entirety, "The Reply to Sor Philothea," and excerpts from "The Divine Narcissus." Trueblood's extensive introduction surveys Sor Juana's life and work; his preface focuses on the translations, especially the difficult question of rhyme. Translations are careful and accurate, although readers will no doubt find some of them ("The *Villancicos*" for example) more satisfying than others. Poems *en face,* except for "First Dream."

4923 Landscapes of a new land: fiction by Latin American women. Edited by Marjorie Agosin. Buffalo, N.Y.: White Pine Press, 1989. 194 p.

In her introduction, Agosin explains a dual purpose: to make known in English "distinguished authors in their own countries . . . little recognized abroad;" "to show the wide range of themes, images, and use of language encountered in . . . Latin American narrative written by women." Includes 22 stories rendered by 18 translators and drawn from 10 countries (including Brazil), arranged thematically. Also provides biographical notes for authors and translators. Information about publication of the individual stories in Spanish would have made the volume even more useful.

4924 *Literary Review.* Vol. 32, No. 4, Summer 1989. Madison, N.J.: Fairleigh Dickinson Univ.

Special issue on "Argentine Writing in the Eighties." Guest editor Wiliam H. Katra has selected work from seven poets, two dramatists, and 13 fiction writers to present what he terms a "pivotal" decade in Argentine literature. His introductory essay outlines recent Argentine history and describes the writing included. Katra's implicit intent was a "representative overview," but actual criteria are not stated. Collaboration of 22

translators. Generous introductory information about each author.

4925 Lives on the line: the testimony of contemporary Latin American authors. Edited and with an introduction by Doris Meyer. Berkeley: Univ. of California Press, 1988. 314 p.: bibl.

Wide selection of essays written 1960–86 by 30 authors from 12 countries, each of whom is presented individually with biographical and bibliographical information. All pieces share a concern with what Meyer refers to as "testimony" (a term it would have been well to qualify, given the current interest in the *testimonio*). Brief introductory overview, but too sketchy for adequately examining the writer's role in Latin American society.

4926 Nicaraguan peasant poetry from Solentiname. Translated with an introduction by David Gullette. Albuquerque, N.M.: West End Press, 1988. 209 p.: bibl.

Translation of *Poesía campesina de Solentiname* (1980, see *HLAS 46:5646*), this volume represents "the fruits of the first of Nicaragua's poetry workshops." Translator's introduction outlines a biography of Ernesto Cardenal, Mayra Jiménez's role in developing the workshops, and the radicalization of the Solentiname community. Brief information about each poet; short bibliography; glossary of words and names specific to Nicaragua, which translator has wisely allowed to remain in Spanish. *En face.*

4927 On the front line: guerrilla poems of El Salvador. Edited and translated by Claribel Alegría and Darwin J. Flakoll. Willimantic, Conn.: Curbstone Press, 1989. 89 p.

Some of these poets may be known to readers in English; others are anonymous or identified only by a first name. (Roque Dalton, whose work has been translated previously, has not been included.) What all of the poets share is the experience of fighting "on the front line" of the FMLN. Some of the translations seem inappropriately "literary," but most convey well the commitment and immediacy of the poems. *En face.*

4928 One more stripe to the tiger: a selection of contemporary Chilean poetry and fiction. Edited and translated by Sandra Reyes. Fayetteville: Univ. of Arkansas Press, 1989. 311 p.: index.

Selections from 21 poets and stories by 10 fiction writers intended as a "cross-section" of Chilean writing "since the late sixties." This has been achieved, although better-known poets receive a disproportionate number of poems, and the anthology includes little work by women. In most instances, Reyes works well with a wide variety of writers, and she has an impressive command of idiomatic English. Short introduction and very brief information about writers. Poems *en face.*

4929 The Portable Lower East Side. Vol. 5, Nos. 1–2, 1988– . New York: PLES.

Special issue entitled "Latin Americans in NYC." An anthology of work (nonfiction, fiction, poetry, and photographs) by 28 artists from Central and South America and the Caribbean. Several of the authors are well known in the US (e.g., Luisa Valenzuela, Eduardo Galeano), but many undoubtedly appear here in English for the first time. Various translators. Editorial "Afterword" contains unusually direct observations about the politics of publishing and promoting Latin American literature in English translation.

4930 Reclaiming Medusa: short stories by contemporary Puerto Rican women. Edited and translated by Diana Lourdes Vélez. San Francisco: Spinsters/Aunt Lute, 1988. 161 p.: ill.

Consists of 12 well-translated selections from work by Rosario Ferré, Carmen Lugo Filippi, Mayra Montero, Carmen Valle, and Ana Lydia Vega. In her introduction, Vélez explains the stories' "commonality of spirit" as the questioning of "women's place" in both Puerto Rico and Latin America. Preface discusses translation strategies for dealing with culturally specific words and expressions, and examines other issues related to the translator's "allegiance." Spanish originals included for two selections. Brief biographical information about each writer.

4931 Salmagundi. Nos. 82–83, Spring/ Summer 1989– . Saratoga Springs, N.Y.: Skidmore College.

Special issue entitled "The Writer in Latin America" is devoted mainly to writing and criticism. Fiction by Ariel Dorfman, Guillermo Cabrera Infante, José Donoso, Luisa Valenzuela, and Rosario Ferré. Poems by Gonzalo Rojas and Herberto Padilla.

Memoir by Ernesto Sábato. Various translators.

4932 Short stories by Latin American women: the magic and the real. Compiled and edited by Celia Correas de Zapata. Houston, Tex.: Arte Publico Press, 1990. 224 p.

Highly eclectic selection of 31 authors rendered by 25 translators. Zapata provides short introduction to (the absence of) "women's literature, stictly speaking, in Latin America." Her purpose: to show "flesh-and-blood individuals endowed with free will," created by what she terms a "new sensibility." Brief foreword by Isabel Allende. Both Allende and editor, somewhat patronizingly, contend that women who write give voice to other, silent women, "in the more backward areas of the continent" (Zapata). Biographical paragraphs for both authors and translators.

4933 Untold sisters: Hispanic nuns in their own works. Edited by Electa Arenal and Stacey Schlau. Translated by Amanda Powell. Albuquerque: Univ. of New Mexico Press, 1989. 450 p.: bibl., ill., index.

Although this volume is not a literary anthology per se, it includes some important colonial texts published in both modern Spanish and Powell's well-crafted "modern American idiom" (her definition). Chap. 5 contains some selections from the *apóstolas* of Peru, and Chap. 6 offers writings by "aristocratic, bourgeois, and Indian nuns of Mexico." For literary critic's comment see item **3371.**

4934 Woman who has sprouted wings: poems by contemporary Latin American women poets. Edited by Mary Crow. 2nd. ed. Pittsburgh, Pa.: Latin American Literary Review Press, 1987. 205 p. (Discoveries)

To her first edition (see *HLAS 48: 6525*), editor has added work by Olga Orozco, Adélia Prado, and Ana María Rodas. Biographies of poets (now 17) have been updated and errata corrected.

4935 Women's fiction from Latin America: selections from twelve contemporary authors. Edited with translations by Evelyn Picon Garfield. Detroit: Wayne State Univ. Press, 1988. 355 p.: bibl., ports. (Latin American literature and culture)

Authors selected are from seven countries, one of which is Brazil. Selections, intended as a "representative sample," include

19 short stories, a one-act play, and four excerpts from novels. Brief introduction explains choices; a substantial biographical sketch precedes the work of each writer; and individual bibliographies provide listings of authors' principal work in English translation as well as pertinent secondary sources. Picon Garfield has done most of the translations, and in general her work is excellent.

4936 You can't drown the fire: Latin American women writing in exile. Edited by Alicia Partnoy. Pittsburgh, Pa.: Cleis, 1988. 258 p.: bibl.

Poetry and prose from 35 authors, most whom have left their countries since 1970, in versions by 25 translators. Explicit, three-fold purpose: "to build cultural bridges; to destroy stereotypes about Latin American women; and to denounce political repression." Partnoy acknowledges regretfully the impossibility of including all countries. Even so, Cuba is a conspicious absence, given the book's title. Very brief biographical information for each writer; selected bibliography. For literary critic's comment see item **3289**.

TRANSLATIONS FROM THE SPANISH
Poetry

4937 Agosin, Marjorie. Women of smoke. Translated by Naomi Lindstrom. Edited by Yvette E. Miller. Pittsburgh, Pa.: Latin American Literary Review Press, 1988. 115 p.: ports. (Discoveries)

Although results are mixed, Lindstrom is to be credited with having taken some definite risks in these translations. At times her willingness to draw out Agosin's suggestions leads to striking lines or images. In other instances, overtranslation subtracts rather than adds subtlety and the register in English seems far too colloquial. Brief preface by Carmen Naranjo. *En face.*

4938 Agosin, Marjorie. Zones of pain. Translated by Cola Franzen. Introduction by Robert Pring-Mill. Buffalo, N.Y.: White Pine Press, 1988. 72 p.

Marjorie Agosin's title alludes to the bond she feels with Chile's "buried women" and "searching mothers." Franzen has translated her poetry extensively, and Pring-Mill does well to praise these versions in his short

introduction, where he points to Franzen's use of "the stark intensity of English monosyllables" to convey the "more sonorous verbal music" of the Spanish. *En face.*

4939 Alegría, Claribel. Woman of the river. Translated by Darwin J. Flakoll. Pittsburgh, Pa.: Univ. of Pittsburgh Press, 1989. 95 p. (Pitt poetry series)

Although it would certainly be foolish to suggest that the quality of a translation might be judged by the response to the original it occasions, it does seem safe to credit Flakoll's fine traslations of these poems with some of the enthusiastic and thoughtful reviews they have received, in *The Village Voice*, for instance, or in *The Women's Review of Books.*

4940 Belli, Gioconda. From Eve's rib. Translated by Steven F. White. Introduction by Margaret Randall. Willimantic, Conn.: Curbstone Press; New York: Talman Co., 1989. 121 p.

Representative selection of both early and recent work. In her brief introduction, Randall points to the "strong parallel" in the poems between "the intimacy of the couple" and the struggles of the Nicaraguan revolution. White conveys this simultaneity; he works more skillfully, however, with the narrative strain in Belli's work than with her lyricism and eroticism, whether in entire poems or in individual images. *En face.*

4941 Cardenal, Ernesto. Nicaraguan new time. Translated by Dinah Livingston. London: Journeyman Press, 1988. 96 p.

Of 30 poems included here, eight were written before the revolution and 22 after. As poems, Livingston's translations are uneven. The directness of many of her images, however, offers an interesting contrast, and one worth further study, to versions by Jonathan Cohen (see *HLAS 50:4239*) and Marc Zimmerman (see *HLAS 50:4238*), especially with respect to images dealing with women.

4942 Castellanos, Rosario. Meditation on the threshold: a bilingual anthology of poetry. Translation and introduction by Julian Palley. Tempe, Ariz.: Bilingual Press/ Editorial Bilingüe, 1988. 176 p.: bibl.

Selection of 43 poems, most of which date from 1950 ("Al Pie de la Letra") and after. (Translator clearly prefers these later poems to earlier ones which he finds "feminine.") Introductory material includes essay on Castellanos' feminism by Gabriella de Beer, and a translator's preface and extensive introduction written in what Julian Palley defines as a "Lacanian context." Tone of translations tends to be elevated, and Palley's choice of words somewhat formal and latinate. *En face.*

4943 Castellanos, Rosario. The selected poems of Rosario Castellanos. Translated by Magda Bogin. Edited by Cecilia Vicuña and Magda Bogin. St. Paul, Minn.: Graywolf Press, 1988. 105 p. (A Palabra sur book)

This collection, which according to editors "makes no pretense of being representative," includes some of Castellanos' less anthologized poems. Bogin has been justly praised as "a poet with a love of language to match Castellanos' own" (*The Nation*). She has retained the "gently elevated . . . feel of Castellanos' diction," but her versions are supple and moving. Introductory essay by Chilean poet Cecilia Vicuña. *En face.*

4944 Dorfman, Ariel. Last waltz in Santiago and other poems of exile and disappearance. Translated by Edith Grossman with the author. New York: Penguin Books, 1988. 78 p. (Penguin poets)

Translation of *Pastel de choclo* (1986). Readers in English, like the reviewers who have written about this collection, may have mixed reactions to Dorfman's poems and his use of various personae to give voice to the suffering of others. Any question of his poetics, however, need not include speculation about the quality of these translations; they are excellent.

4945 Guillén, Nicolás. The daily daily. Translated and with an introduction by Vera M. Kutzinski. Berkeley: Univ. of California Press, 1989. 139 p.

Highly (and appropriately) inventive "reading" of *Diario que a diario* (1972). Kutzunski provides an exemplary translator's introduction in which she discusses this unusual and little studied poem and places it with respect to Guillén's work. She also comments on specific challenges involved in translating into English a subversive "gathering" of widely diverse texts in which English is itself subverted. *En face.*

4946 Hahn, Oscar. The art of dying. Translated by James Hoggard. Pittsburgh,

Pa.: Latin American Literary Review Press, 1987. 95 p. (Discoveries)

In his preface James Hoggard offers valuable comments about translating *Arte de morir* (1977) and portry written in the romance languages. In particular, he explains his own decision not to "recreate" in English Hahn's sound patterns. Despite this deliberate cultivation of difference, the results "often represent questionable choices on the part of the translator" (*Small Press*). *En face.*

4947 Huidobro, Vicente. Altazor, or, A voyage in a parachute, 1919: a poem in VII cantos. Translated by Eliot Weinberger. St. Paul, Minn.: Graywolf Press, 1988. 167 p. (Palabra sur)

Using no footnotes or critical explanations other than a brief introduction, Eliot Weinberger has attempted, as he explains, "to translate everything" according to Huidobro's "vision of poetry: as a divine game of language." He has succeeded admirably: " . . . as its discourse becomes more disarticulated, the 'translation,' while less literal, is laudably more inventive" (*Review*).

4948 Juana Inés de la Cruz, *Sor.* Selected sonnets. Translated by Sandra Sider. Saskatoon, Canada: Peregrina Publishing Co., 1987. 1 v.

"Representative selection" of 35 sonnets in awkward translations studded with forced, frequently ludicrous rhymes. Of interest only to translation students or scholars who wish to examine multiple versions in English.

4949 Juarroz, Roberto. Vertical poetry. Translated from the Spanish by William Stanley Merwin. San Francisco: North Point Press, 1988. 161 p.

Bilingual selection from nine volumes of *Poesía vertical*, plus one recent poem. In addition to these fine translations, Merwin includes foreword that both places Juarroz among his contemporaries and explains the nature of his poetry, which is "extremely formal " although "neither metrical nor rhymed." Also provides (auto)biographical information about Juarroz and comments by Julio Cortázar written after a reading of *Second vertical poetry*. *En face.*

Meo Zilio, Giovanni. Metodología y técnica de una traducción literaria: los juegos de palabras en *Martín Fierro*. See item **3459.**

4950 Neruda, Pablo. The house in the sand: prose poems. Translated by Dennis Maloney and Clark M. Zlotchew. Foreword by Marjorie Agosin. Afterword by Ariel Dorfman. Minneapolis, Minn.: Milkweed Editions, 1990. 122 p.: ill.

Strong effort that nevertheless exemplifies some of the difficulties faced by Neruda's translators: how to best render the rich mix of scientific and sonorous language found in poems like "La Arena" and "Premio Nobel en Isla Negra?". Translators have opted here for longer structures that stay close to the Spanish, and for frequent cognates. Thus, they have greater success with the shorter pieces and with the more narrative sections of the longer poems. Collection includes much of the work (unfortunately without Milton Roguin's photographs) published previously in *The house at Isla Negra*, a chapbook (White Pine Press: 1988). *En face.*

4951 Neruda, Pablo. Late and posthumous poems, 1968–1974. Introduction by Manuel Duran. Edited and translated by Ben Belitt. New York: Grove Press, 1988. 239 p.: bibl.

Ben Belitt defines as "personal" both the selection of these poems (from nine volumes) and his goal: to make available in English "a single protean identity" in Neruda's work, and to nudge readers beyond the poet's best-known books. These are dynamic but controversial translations, and some readers will disagree with Manuel Durán's praise for the extent to which Belitt's own poetry "is intertwined with his translation." *En face.*

4952 Neruda, Pablo. The sea and the bells. Translated by William O'Daly. Port Townsend, Wash.: Copper Canyon Press, 1988. 125 p.

Ben Belitt has referred to O'Daly's translations of Neruda's posthumous poems as "scrupulous," and the extreme care suggested by that word is evident in this, his fourth volume. Perhaps it is inevitable that such close attention to the text will result in unrestrained poems that feel at times *overly* cautious. In her thoughtful review of O'Daly's work (in *Review*, 41), Edith Grossman has discussed these strengths and weaknesses at length. *En face.*

4953 Neruda, Pablo. The yellow heart. Translated by William O' Daly. Port

Townsend, Wash.: Copper Canyon Press, 1990. 109 p.

Although O'Daly does not refer specifically to the practice of translation, he alludes to what may be the greatest challenge for a translator of Neruda when he explains that the work is unified by a "restlessness" and "multiplicity" that any other single individual is not likely to comprehend fully. At least implicity, then, O'Daly acknowledges that his versions will undoubtedly both please and disappoint, at times within the same poem. Long descriptive introduction places the poems with respect to Neruda's later work. *En face.*

4954 Paz, Octavio. A tree within. Translated by Eliot Weinberger. New York: New Directions Pub. Corp., 1988. 164 p.: index. (A New Directions paperback; 661)

Volume reprints both Spanish originals and English versions published in *The collected poems of Octavio Paz* (see HLAS 50:4259). Here, however, all of the translations are by Weinberger. As Paz's "official translator," Weinberger is one of the two North Americans who know him best (*The New York Times*), and Weinberger's work is truly outstanding, whether in a long poem like the final "Letter of Testimony" or some of the shorter poems at the beginning of the collection.

4955 Rojas, Gonzalo. Schizotext and other poems. Translated by Russell M. Cluff and L. Howard Quackenbush. New York: P. Lang, 1988. 135 p.

In their brief introduction, translators explain the five categories into which they have divided their selections. Their work is careful but flat, despite an evident familiarity with Rojas' poetry (item in Theory section: "Crónica de una convivencia"). Although the two languages are split across facing pages, the English versions in themselves do not convey the plays, tensions, and intensity that characterize the Spanish. *En face.*

4956 Storni, Alfonsina. Selected poems. Edited by Marion Freeman. Translated by Marion Freeman, Mary Crow, Jim Normington, and Kay Short. Buffalo, N.Y.: White Pine Press, 1987. 65 p.

Despite the wide recognition accorded Storni in South America, her work as a whole has yet to be well translated into English. This volume contains a brief biographical introduction and a representative selection. Translations, however, are uneven, and some of them are quite awkward. Collaboration between Mary Crow and Marion Freeman has yielded the most felicitous results.

4957 Vallejo, César. The black heralds. Translated by Richard Schaaf and Kathleen Ross. Pittsburgh, Pa.: Latin American Literary Review Press, 1990. 174 p. (Discoveries)

Close, lexically accurate reading that permits flashes of Vallejo's lyricism. How well these versions could stand "on their own" as English poems is questionable, however. Includes brief chronology of Vallejo's life and work. *En face.*

4958 Vallejo, César. César Vallejo: a selection of his poetry. Translations, introduction, and notes by James Higgins. Wolfeboro, N.H.: F. Cairns, 1988. 1 v. (Hispanic bilingual texts; 1)

As defined by Higgins, these versions are intended "as a text for students and to introduce Vallejo's prose to general readers." Although the extensive introduction describes Vallejo's life and work, one questions whether translations with "no pretension to do justice to the poetic richness of Vallejo's originals" will convey what Higgins refers to as their "sense," much less their "spirit." *En face.*

4959 Zeller, Ludwig. "The Marble Head" and other poems. Translated by A.F. Moritz and Beatriz Zeller. Introduction by José Miguel Oviedo. Oakville, N.Y.: Mosaic Press, 1986. 1 v.

Even without access to the Spanish, it is evident that these are listless, disappointing translations, especially since Zeller's work on the cover testifies to an energy not conveyed in English. Oviedo's introductory essay makes the reader wish that more writing on this Chilean poet (b. 1927) now living in Canada were available in English.

Brief Fiction and Theater

4960 Benítez-Rojo, Antonio. "The Magic Dog" and other stories. Selection, edition, and introduction by Frank Janney. Hanover, N.H.: Ediciones del Norte, 1990. 261 p.: bibl.

Drawn mainly from three collections by Antonio Benítez-Rojo, many of these stories were also published in *Estatuas sepultadas y otros relatos* (Ediciones del Norte, 1984). Good to excellent translations by various translators, several of whom have rendered Cuban Spanish inventively. Brief but informative introduction by Frank Janney (but his parenthetical definition of *choteo* as "jive humor" suggests a misleading correspondence).

4961 Carrington, Leonora. "The seventh horse" and other tales. Translations by Kathrine Talbot and Anthony Kerrigan. New York: E.P. Dutton, 1988. 197 p.: ill.

Most of the stories by this English-born surrealist writer and painter have been translated from the French. A few, however, were written in English, and three—two stories and "The Invention of Mole," a brief play—were originally written in Spanish and set in Mexico, where Carrington lived for over 40 years. Translations from the Spanish are by Anthony Kerrigan.

4962 Dorfman, Ariel. My house is on fire. Translated from the Spanish by George Shivers with the author. New York: Viking, 1990. 167 p.

Reviewers have found Dorfman's fiction to be uneven here. The translations of these eleven stories from *Cría ojos* (1970) are good, however. The use of Americanisms may strike a reader as inappropriate (*The New York Times Book Review*), but it also reflects the dislocation of Dorfman's characters and contributes an immediacy, even an eeriness, to his stories.

4963 Fuentes, Carlos. Constancia: and other stories for virgins. Translated by Thomas Christensen. New York: Farrar, Straus, Giroux, 1990. 340 p.

Perhaps the best evaluation of (and praise for) this translation can be found in the appreciation of Fuentes' "bumpy luminousness" and "unexpected intersection of myths" that the translation makes possible (*The Christian Science Monitor*). To cite one fine example of the translator's agility: the play with the title and with the translation itself, in "La Desdichada."

4964 García Ponce, Juan. Encounters. Translated by Helen Lane. Introduction by Octavio Paz. Hygiene, Colo.: Eridanos Press, 1989. 116 p. (The Eridanos library; 13)

"The Cat," "The Square," "Anticipation," and "The Seagull" (almost a novella) are the four pieces included here. Gene H. Bell-Villada (*The New York Times*) found the translation "about as perfect as a translation can be." Although some passages suggest that this praise is excessive, Helen Lane's work does convey well the mystery and innocence that Octavio Paz discusses as characteristics of García Ponce's narrative.

4965 Martínez Estrada, Ezequiel. "Holy Saturday" and other stories. Translated by Leland H. Chambers. Pittsburgh, Pa.: Latin American Literary Review Press, 1988. 159 p. (Discoveries)

In addition to the title story, this volume contains "Marta Riquelme," "Examination Without Honor," and "The Deluge." Informative, succinct introduction discusses Martínez Estrada's fiction and relates it to the essays for which he is better known. An accurate translation, but one that would be more satisfying if the translator had relied less consistently on Spanish syntax and cognates.

4966 Muñiz-Huberman, Angelina. Enclosed garden. Translated by Lois Parkinson Zamora. Pittsburgh, Pa.: Latin American Literary Review Press, 1988. 103 p. (Discoveries)

In her introduction Zamora cites the "complex cultural and historical context" of *Huerto cerrado, huerto sellado* as her greatest challenge. It is one she has met well. The use of footnotes could be debated, but here they are neither numerous nor intrusive. Zamora has apparently misjudged, however, the difficulties presented by Angelina Muñiz Huberman's poetic prose. Although accurate, the English often lacks resonance and depends on the Spanish to an extent that is stifling.

4967 Naranjo, Carmen. There never was a once upon a time. Translated by Linda Britt. Pittsburgh, Pa.: Latin American Literary Review Press, 1989. 94 p.: ill. (Discoveries)

In her description of the "seemingly disorganized discourse" that characterizes these stories from *Nunca hubo alguna vez,* Linda Britt has identified the greatest transla-

tion difficulty presented by this volume. In some instances, it is a challenge Britt has met well, even inventively. In others, what she terms a child's "unpredictable syntax" is rendered clumsily and the words used by the narrator are not those likely to be chosen by children.

4968 Ocampo, Silvina. Leopoldina's dream. Translated by Daniel Balderston. New York: Penguin Books, 1988. 205 p. (Penguin short fiction)

". . . [W]hat we write: that is what we are . . . ," Silvina Ocampo states in her brief introduction; and Daniel Balderston has rendered that "being" well in his translations of this highly poetic prose. The selection of 32 stories has been made from four of Ocampo's books; a longer introduction to her work would have been welcome.

4969 Onetti, Juan Carlos. Goodbyes and stories. Translated by Daniel Balderston. Austin: Univ. of Texas Press, 1990. 174 p. (The Texas Pan American series)

In addition to *Los adioses,* Daniel Balderston has included nine stories from *Cuentos completos.* His work stays close to the Spanish, too close perhaps at times, but his readings convey the peculiar distanced emotion he has identified as a distinguishing characteristic of Onetti's fiction. The introduction is excellent. The translation of *Goodbyes* was co-winner of the Eugene M. Kayden National Translation Award for 1987.

4970 Palma, Clemente. Malignant tales. Translated from the Spanish by Guillermo I. Castillo-Feliú. Lanham, Md.: Univ. Press of America, 1988. 65 p.: bibl.

Translation of the four *Historietas malignas* (Lima, 1925). Brief but informative introduction to Clemente Palma and his controversial work, which is far less known than that of his famous father. The translator has managed to convey the stories' "highly erudite language" and the *fin-de-siècle* ambience, but at times the English is merely awkward. Numerous footnotes are intrusive and unnecessary.

4971 Piñera, Virgilio. Cold tales. Translation by Mark Schafer. Revised by Thomas Christensen. Introduction by Guillermo Cabrera-Infante. Hygiene, Colo.: Eridanos Press; New York: Rizzoli International, 1988. 282 p.: port. (The Eridanos library; 8)

Translator Mark Schafer has done a good job with the tension between the intense "heat" in these stories and their coldness which—according to Piñera—is "deceptive." The volume includes 43 stories of varying length, a brief foreword by the author, and "The Death of Virgilio," Guillermo Cabrera-Infante's biographical introduction.

4972 Rey Rosa, Rodrigo. The beggar's knife. Translated by Paul Bowles. San Francisco: City Lights Books, 1985. 95 p.

An instance of English translation preceding publication in Spanish, this volume is based on *El cuchillo del mendigo* (Guatemala, 1986), which was not available for review. Rey Rosa left his native Guatemala in 1980; in Tangier he met Paul Bowles, who has published two other collections of his work in English translation: *The path doubles back* (1982) and *Dust on her tongue* (1989).

4973 Ribeyro, Julio Ramón. Silvio in the rose garden and other stories. Translated by María Rosa Fort and Frank Graziano. Gettysburg, Pa.: Logbridge-Rhodes, 1989. 101 p.

What one reviewer (Wolfgang A. Luchting, *World Literature Today*) has referred to as a "safe" selection of "four splendid stories." The translations, however, are disappointing, suggesting haste or lack of care. Close adhesion to Spanish syntax and cognates has led the translators to write frequently ungrammatical and inconsistent English.

4974 Ricci, Julio. Falling through the cracks. Translated by Clark M. Zlotchew. Pittsburgh, Pa.: Latin American Literary Review Press, 1989. 81 p.

A collection of seven stories drawn from five books. Zlotchew provides an engaging introduction that evidences his own ease with Julio Ricci's work as well as presenting the Uruguayan writer. These are good translations, even if one might wish that in a story like "Mr. Szomogy's Best Friend"— where Szomogy's speech is heavily accented— the translator shared Ricci's linguistic inventiveness.

4975 Sorrentino, Fernando. "Sanitary Centennial" and selected short stories. Translated by Thomas C. Meehan. Austin:

Univ. of Texas Press, 1988. 186 p. (The Texas Pan American series)

Reviewers of Fernando Sorrentino's brief novel and six stories in English have agreed that, in general, the translations are quite good. Meehan's work with Sorrentino's wordplays and culture-specific references raises questions, however, about how a translator of fiction might best approach humor and parody. The solutions here are, for some readers, overly academic: Meehan's introduction runs to 20 p., and there are 30 footnotes for the title novel alone.

4976 Valenzuela, Luisa. Open door: stories. Translated by Hortense Carpentier *et al.* San Francisco: North Point Press, 1988. 201 p.

There are some excellent translations in this volume, which includes work by Hortense Carpentier, J. Jorge Castello, Helen Lane, Christopher Leland, Margaret Sayers Peden, and David Unger. The selection was made by Luisa Valenzuela herself. It comprises stories from three collections: *Clara, Strange Things Happen Here*—both previously published in English—and *Up among the eagles* (*Donde viven las águilas*), which has not appeared in English before.

Novels

4977 Adán, Martín. The cardboard house. Translated and with an introduction by Katherine Silver. St. Paul, Minn.: Graywolf Press, 1990. 103 p. (A Palabra sur book)

According to Silver, this translation was made "image by image," a method that proved to be very appropriate for the poetic prose of *La casa de cartón*. Silver is also to be praised for her introduction, in which her own eloquent text has been interspersed with phrases of Martín Adán.

4978 Alegría, Claribel and **Darwin J. Flakoll.** Ashes of Izalco: a novel. Translated by Darwin J. Flakoll. Willimantic, Conn.: Curbstone Press; New York: Talman Co., 1989. 173 p.

"Workmanlike" translation, according to one reviewer (Fran Handman, *The New York Times Book Review*) whose single adjective, something of a left-handed compliment, is surprisingly accurate. Given the continual alternation of voices in this novel, one would expect more variation in tone and style. On the other hand, the uniformity does not prevent a reader from following the voices or from being moved by them.

4979 Alegría, Claribel. Luisa in realityland. Translated from Spanish by Darwin J. Flakoll. Willimantic, Conn.: Curbstone Press; New York: Talman Co., 1987. 152 p.

The challenge in this novel of fragments is the continual alternation of prose and poetry selections. Although Claribel Alegría's (English) language has been praised for its "presence as words" (*American Book Review*), the mix of lyric and narrative is not always successful, as Electa Arenal indicates in a review that is unusually attentive to Alegría's craft as a writer (*New Directions for Women*, Jan./Feb. 1989).

4980 Allende, Isabel. Eva Luna. Translated from the Spanish by Margaret Sayers Peden. New York: Knopf, 1988. 271 p.

Although Isabel Allende's third novel has drawn mixed response in English, praise for its translator has been virtually unanimous. One could quibble about an infelicitous choice of words here or there, or about occasional instances of careless punctuation or syntax, but as Dan Bellm observed, Margaret Sayers Peden seems to have gotten Allende's "elegant, mischievous tone just right."

4981 Arenas, Reinaldo. Old Rosa: a novel in two stories. Translated from the Spanish by Ann Tashi Slater and Andrew Hurley. New York: Grove Press, 1989. 106 p.

Although published here as a single novel, these two stories were written several years apart and have been published separately in Spanish (*Vieja Rosa*, 1966 and *Arturo, la estrella más brillante*, 1971). Excellent translations of Arenas' highly lyric prose.

4982 Arias, Arturo. After the bombs. Translated by Asa Zatz. Willimantic, Conn.: Curbstone Press, 1990. 1 v.

Highly successful translation of this novel is indicated by a reviewer's ability to describe, quite accurately and with no apparent knowledge of Spanish, Arias' style, even the construction of his sentences (Alan West, *Voice Literary Supplement*). The one element absent from that style in English would be Arias' play with language itself—his dis-

tinctly Guatemalan Spanish and the frequent abrasion of English within it.

4983 Benítez-Rojo, Antonio. Sea of lentils. Translated by James Maraniss. Introduction by Sydney Lea. Amherst: Univ. of Massachusetts Press, 1990. 201 p.: 1 map.

According to one reviewer (Frederick Luciani, *The New York Times Book Review*), thanks to Antonio Benítez-Rojo and the "obstinate power of the literary imagination," this de-centered novel "remains convincing and compelling." Certainly such gratitude should also extend to the translator who has worked skillfully with multiple narratives and rendered in English, with only a slip or two in syntax, a section as challeging as chap. 19. Sydney Lea's introduction offers information about the author and comments about North American unfamiliarity with Caribbean narrative.

4984 Bioy Casares, Adolfo. The adventures of a photographer in La Plata. Translated by Suzanne Jill Levine. New York: E.P. Dutton, 1989. 169 p.

This most recent of Levine's translations of Adolfo Bioy Casares has won high praise. Iván Stavans, for instance, drew attention to Levine's ability to retain the "flavor of the Argentine colloquialisms." Also, for her work with this novel, Levine was named the recipient of the Elinor D. Randall Translation Award, the first PEN/West prize given in the category of translation.

4985 Bioy Casares, Adolfo. The dream of heroes. Translated from the Spanish by Diana Thorold. New York: Dutton, 1988. 212 p.

There are a few unnecessary footnotes towards the beginning of the novel and Thorold's English seems somewhat clipped, but generally this version of *El sueño de los héroes* reads well. "It's only 33 years late in English translation," according to the *London Observer*—a remark that is clearly more praise than complaint.

4986 Campobello, Nellie. Cartucho; and, My mother's hands. Translated by Doris Meyer and Irene Matthews. Introduction by Elena Poniatowska. Austin: Univ. of Texas Press, 1988. 129 p. (A Texas Pan American paperback)

In general, good translations by both translators. In *Cartucho*, Meyer has met well the challenge of rendering a child's voice, although at times her word choice makes the register too elevated. (The occasional footnotes and explanations of untranslated terms also seem inappropriately adult.) Matthews also has worked successfully with the different, poetic prose in *Las manos de mamá*. Campobello's long prologue to her work (1960) would have been welcome, but there is helpful introductory material: the translators each have provided a "note," and Poniatowska's introduction places Campobello with respect to her contemporaries.

4987 Carpentier, Alejo. The chase. Translated by Alfred J. Mac Adam. New York: Farrar, Straus, Giroux, 1989. 121 p.

For this "sensitive and idiomatic" version of *El acoso*, Mac Adam has been praised deservedly (Gustavo Pérez Firmat, *Review*). His translation is not the first, however, as *Manhunt*, a translation by Harriet de Onís, was published in 1959.

4988 Carpentier, Alejo. Concierto barroco. Translated by Asa Zatz. Tulsa, Okla.: Council Oak Books/Hecate with Univ. of Tulsa; Chicago: Independent Publishers Group, 1988. 135 p.: bibl. (Fiction&)

A difficult task, the translation of *Concierto barroco*, because of the "unnatural demands" Carpentier's prose places on English. Translator Zatz has qualified success here. On the one hand, his work makes clear the "overflowing, baroque" nature of the Spanish sentences (*Publishers Weekly*). On the other, the English sentences are far less graceful; many seem forced, because of inelegant, or even incorrect, grammar.

4989 Carpentier, Alejo. The harp and the shadow: a novel. Translated by Thomas Christensen and Carol Christensen. San Francisco: Mercury House; St. Paul, Minn.: Consortium Book Sales & Distribution, 1990. 159 p.

Excellent translation. There are occasional discordances (Columbus' "Okay, okay, no problem"), but the translators have worked marvelously with Carpentier's prose. Their long sentences are fluent and graceful, thanks to skillful transformations that evoke Spanish patterns while honoring rules of English syntax. Brief translators' preface is interesting for the contrast noted between North and Latin American responses to the conquest.

4990 Conteris, Hiber. Ten percent of life. New York: Simon & Schuster, 1987. 220 p.

Several small but important changes indicate that author collaborated in English version of his novel. As Patricia Hart has explained ("Revisiting Chandler and Recreating Marlowe in Híber Conteris's *El diez por ciento de la vida*" in *The Journal of the Midwest Modern Language Association* (23:2, Fall 1990, p. 9–10), the translation of Raymond Chandler's Philip Marlowe "back" into English presents a particular challenge. Although the English reads well and the work is not inaccurate, Hart finds the language awkward and "unsatisfying." Unfortunately, the translator (Deborah Bergman?) is not clearly identified.

4991 Di Masso, Gerardo. The shadow by the door. Translated from the Spanish by Richard Jacques. London: Zed Books; Totowa, N.J.: Biblio Distribution Center, 1985. 96 p.

Jacques does well to call attention to *La penumbra*'s original title and his reasons for altering it. His apology for the "loss" should not mislead a reader, however, because this is a fine translation that skillfully conveys Di Masso's "simple lyrical style" (Lisa Valenzuela, *The New York Times Book Review*) and the horrors recounted in his novel. Translator's brief introduction effectively places the work, which occurs in an unnamed country.

4992 Donoso, José. Curfew: a novel. Translated from the Spanish by Alfred J. Mac Adam. New York: Weidenfeld & Nicolson, 1988. 310 p.

Competent, yet not completely satisfactory version of *La desesperanza*. Thinking, no doubt, of an English reader's possible impatience with Donoso's long, complex sentences, Mac Adam has done considerable recasting. His own sentences are not always graceful, though, and this weakens the descriptive passages of the novel. Faster-moving sections of dialogue represent Donoso more accurately.

4993 Ferré, Rosario. Sweet diamond dust. Translated from the Spanish by the author. New York: Available Press; Ballantine Books, 1988. 197 p.

Although a North American may find

Rosario Ferré's prose "elaborate" (e.g., David Cohen, in *American Book Review*, points to a 43-line sentence), Ferré herself has referred to a "pruning" of the Spanish sentences in *Maldito amor* so as to achieve in English a more practically-oriented language. The result is a noticeably different work, but one in which the specifically Puerto Rican elements of the narrative have been retained, even accentuated. (See Ferré's comments in item **5058.**)

4994 Fuentes, Carlos. Christopher unborn. Translated from the Spanish by Alfred J. Mac Adam and the author. New York: Farrar Straus Giroux, 1989. 531 p.

Given the role of language in this novel, it is no wonder that the translation has received far more than the customary nod from reviewers. Iván Staváns has even recounted its "story" in *American Book Review* (Sept./Oct. 1990). As the translator tells it, at one point in his work he spent a week "isolated from the world" with the author and their publisher, turning *Cristóbal nonato* into a book written in English. Some readers may find the relentless wordplay in that book exasperating; others no doubt will savor its hybridity and admire the translation.

4995 García Márquez, Gabriel. The general in his labyrinth. Translated from the Spanish by Edith Grossman. New York: A.A. Knopf; Random House, 1990. 285 p.: map

Edith Grossman's achievement in the translation of this novel will be clear to her readers. It was also made evident in an unusual way, however, to the participants of the Translating Latin America Conference (April 1990), when her reading of the book's opening section demonstrated the sensitivity and skill with which she had worked.

4996 García Márquez, Gabriel. Love in the time of cholera. Translated from the Spanish by Edith Grossman. New York: Alfred A. Knopf, 1988. 348 p.

No doubt some readers worried when they learned that, with this novel, Gabriel García Márquez had a "new" translator. Fortunately, any such apprehension was unfounded, because Edith Grossman's work is outstanding, as Thomas Pynchon remarked in an unusually long reviewer's comment about the quality of her translation (*The New York Times Book Review*).

4997 Martínez, Tomás Eloy. The Perón novel. Translated by Asa Zatz. New York: Pantheon Books, 1988. 357 p.

As several reviewers have pointed out, even in Zatz's "fluent" translation (Jay Cantor, *The New York Times Book Review*), North American readers unfamiliar with recent Argentine history may be unable to appreciate fully the imaginative "truth" of this novel. Or, perhaps, the translator "is not always successful in picking up the nuances of Martínez's parody" (Jean Franco, *The Nation*). A further possibility: the contextualizing or explanation that make parody comprehensible to an outsider is incompatible with "ease of reading."

4998 Martínez Moreno, Carlos. El infierno. Translated by Ann Wright. Introduction by John King. London: Readers International, 1988. 266 p.

Good, confident, and idiomatic translation of *El color que el infierno me escondiera*, Martínez Moreno's latest novel (1981) and his first to be translated into English. King's concise introduction provides information on the Tupamaros and the Uruguayan social and literary context.

4999 Molloy, Sylvia. Certificate of absence. Translated by Daniel Balderston with the author. Austin: Univ. of Texas Press, 1989. 125 p. (Texas Pan American series)

In a gesture that encourages a rethinking of the novel in both languages, the translators of *En breve cárcel* have replaced the Spanish title, and the stanza by Quevedo from which it was taken, with a poem and a title from Emily Dickinson. Otherwise, their version follows the Spanish closely and conveys fully, if with a bit less immediacy, a woman's persistent writing "so as to be able to reread herself and continue to live."

5000 Moyano, Daniel. The devil's trill. Translated by Giovanni Pontiero. London: Serpent's Tail, 1988. 119 p.

Excellent translation of *El trino del diablo* based on the original edition (1974). Pontiero has worked well with the "dazzling nonsympathy . . . of dissonant music" (described in a glowing review in *The Village Voice*), and with the challenge of a disturbing melody at once lyrical and sinister.

5001 Peri Rossi, Cristina. Ship of fools. Translated by Psiche Hughes. New York: Readers International, 1989. 1 v.

"Wonderfully translated novel" or one in which "the bad news is the translation?" The difference between Mary G. Berg's praise (*Belles Lettres*) and Dan Bellm's annoyance (*Voice Literary Supplement*) is instructive. Berg believes that Hughes has "managed to preserve the [book's] extraordinary tone of verbal harmony and gentleness," whereas Bellm points out that the price of fluent English involves inaccuracies, small omissions, and the breaking of "long, rhythmic sentences into little bits as if to condense and improve the style."

5002 Piñera, Virgilio. Rene's flesh. Translated by Mark Schafer. Boston: Eridanos Press, 1990. 256 p.

In order to achieve what the novel's jacket advertises as a "translation of great liveliness," Schafer has taken several decisive steps. First, alerting the English-language reader to "the volatile ambivalence of the word *carne* unquestionably works well. Others, such as the omission of substantial passages of description and the streamlining of Piñera's prose, raise questions about reworking and updating a text so as to highlight its "story" and make for more "readable" English.

5003 Posse, Abel. The dogs of paradise. Translated from the Spanish by Margaret Sayers Peden. New York: Atheneum, 1989. 301 p.

"Translators inevitably call upon countless resources . . . for information and terminology beyond their personal knowledge," Margaret Sayers Peden writes in her Translator's Note. On reading it and this outstanding translation, one cannot fail to remark on the truly diverse and extensive research demanded by Abel Posse's "secularized vision" of 1992 and his "portentous language" (*The New York Times Book Review*).

5004 Revueltas, José. Human mourning. Translated by Roberto Crespi. Minneapolis: Univ. of Minnesota Press, 1989. 208 p. (Emergent literatures)

Fortunately, the (unintended?) rhymes that detract from the opening of this translation are misleading. In fact, Crespi's new version of *El luto humano* is a good one, with a tone appropriate to the bitterness and pain in Revueltas' novel. (*The stone knife*, a previous translation by H.R. Hayes, was published in

1947.) Octavio Paz's introduction includes his largely negative review of the edition published in 1943, and a rectification dated 1979 in which he discusses Revueltas' "Christian Marxism."

5005 Rivabella, Omar. Requiem for a woman's soul. Translated by Paul Riviera and Omar Rivabella. New York: Random House, 1986. 116 p.

Although the translation cannot be annotated because it was not possible to consult the Spanish original, the English version of this novel has received high praise. Rivabella is an Argentine journalist who now lives in New York City. The focus of his book, as presented through the eyes of a young woman, is "torture itself . . . sometimes so horrible that death comes as a relief to its victims" (*The New York Times Book Review*).

5006 Sábato, Ernesto R. The tunnel. Translated by Margaret Sayers Peden. New York: Available Press; Ballantine, 1988. 138 p.

In what more than one reviewer has referred to as a "fine new translation," Margaret Sayers Peden has restored the metaphor that titles *El túnel*. (Harriet de Onís' version of 1950 was known as *The outsider*). This is not to suggest, however, that Peden's work is more literal. On the contrary, she offers a highly colloquial reading in which the narrator addresses his reader(s) directly.

5007 Soriano, Osvaldo. Winter quarters: a novel of Argentina. Translated by Nick Caistor. Columbia, La.: Readers International, 1989. 192 p.

Caistor, according to Alberto Manguel, has found a "wry English voice" for his translation of *Cuarteles de invierno* (*Times Literary Supplement*). For Manguel, that voice is "full of felicities," especially with respect to "the Argentine swear words." Richard Eder also points to Caistor's translation of what he terms the "tone of cordial abusiveness" specific to Argentina (*Los Angeles Times Book Review*) which, in his view, Caistor translates "rough and awkward."

5008 Taibo, Paco Ignacio. An easy thing. Translated by William I. Neuman. New York: Penguin Books, 1990. 230 p. (Penguin crime fiction)

Writing early in 1990, Charles Champlin welcomed *An easy thing* as "an outstanding discovery" (*Los Angeles Times Book Review*). He also praised the translation as "lively and colloquial." This is an accurate description, although the most interesting aspect of Neuman's work is its intriguing mix of highly idiomatic English and the constant, very specific presence of both Mexico City and Mexican Spanish.

5009 Valdivieso, Mercedes. Breakthrough. Translated by Graciela Daichman. Introductions by Margo Glantz and Fernando Alegría. Pittsburgh, Pa.: Latin American Literary Review Press, 1987. 96 p. (Discoveries)

Translation of *La brecha* sufficiently adequate that a reader can describe the narrator's "smooth, captivating voice" (Barbara Benham, *Belles Lettres*). Same reader also remarks, however, that the novel "might seem quaint" were the story not still timely. That this comment is possible owes to a stiltedness in the translation which, as Mary G. Berg points out (*Chasqui*), ". . . adds yet another layer of awkwardness . . . each sentence bashing angrily against a reader's sensibilities." Brief introductions by Margo Glantz and Fernando Alegría.

5010 Vallejo, César. Tungsten: a novel. Translated by Robert Mezey. Foreword by Kevin J. O'Connor. Syracuse, N.Y.: Syracuse Univ. Press, 1988. 133 p.

No matter what readers in English decide about the place of this novel with respect to Vallejo's work, or about the assessments of that work and of Vallejo's Marxism made by O'Connor and Mezey, the translation need not be questioned. Mezey's version reflects both his own skill as a poet and a respect for Vallejo that, when necessary, allows him to interpret with both confidence and caution. Foreword and translator's preface are thoughtful, informative, and candid.

5011 Vargas Llosa, Mario. In praise of the stepmother. Translated by Helen Lane. New York: Farrar, Straus, Giroux, 1990. 149 p.: ill.

Whether this novel is truly "hot" or merely rather warm is a topic of some disagreement among critics. Translation is a good one, though, and occasional questions about word choice or register do not prevent the English from conveying the shifts and play in *El elogio de la madrastra*. On the

other hand, the effect of the color plates is lessened by their altered placement in the text.

5012 Vargas Llosa, Mario. The storyteller. Translated by Helen Lane. New York: Farrar, Straus, Giroux, 1989. 245 p.

Widely reviewed, Helen Lane's translation of *El hablador* was recognized for the high-quality work that English-language readers have come to expect from this prolific translator. The only point of disagreement occured, as one might anticipate, with respect to the sections narrated in the words of the "storyteller." Dan Bellm (*Voice Literary Supplement*) found that the translation "captures perfectly the strangeness" of those words. According to John Butt, however, the storyteller's sections are too "familiar;" also, "the passage between the Western and Amerindian chapters is a shade too easy, and inflicts less culture shock than it should" (*Times Literary Supplement*).

5013 Vicens, Josefina. The false years. Translated and with an introduction by Peter G. Earle. Pittsburgh, Pa.: Latin American Literary Review Press, 1989. 94 p. (Discoveries)

Excellent translation of *Los años falsos* (1982) that conveys well the intensity of the monologue addressed by a 19-year-old boy to his dead father. Introduction, originally a book review of the novel in Spanish, offers unnecessary summary, but also provides information about Josefina Vicens and the place of her work in Mexican narrative.

5014 Zapata Olivella, Manuel. Chambacu, black slum. Translated by Jonathan Tittler. Pittsburgh, Pa.: Latin American Literary Review Press, 1989. 128 p. (Discoveries)

Competent translation that conveys Manuel Zapata Olivella's "staccato style" and the presence of different registers in *Chambacú: corral de negros*. Tittler's English is somewhat stiff in the most lyrical passages, however, especially when it comes to dialogue. This leads one to ask if there might not have been a more appropriate vehicle in English for translating Afro-Colombian Spanish.

Essays, Interviews, and Reportage

5015 Agosin, Marjorie. Women of smoke: Latin American women in literature.

Translated by Janice Molloy. Trenton, N.J.: Red Sea Press, 1989. 1 v.

This book has been given the same title as a volume of Agosin's poetry (see item **5015**), but is a collection of essays. Their topic: women of Latin America, who (as writers, for example, or activists, or mothers of the Plaza de Mayo) have been trapped, like Agosin's native Chile, "behind a veil of smoke." In general, translator seems to have read and worked with care; Spanish originals not available.

5016 Cortázar, Julio. Nicaraguan sketches. Translated by Kathleen Weaver. New York: Norton, 1989. 142 p.

As David Volpendesta has explained (*In These Times*), Weaver's intention here was to create an English-language version of *Nicaragua tan violentamente dulce*, but also to "expand the common North American perception of Cortázar as a highly European-ized writer . . . " This double purpose is reflected both in the translator's introductory essay, which stresses Cortázar's consistent concern for Latin American issues, and in the "fluency" of the translations. Those translations are good, although in them Cortázar's characteristically long sentences have become almost journalistic and they have not always been recast in the most felicitous way.

5017 Cozarinsky, Edgardo. Borges in/and/on film. Translated by Gloria Waldman and Ronald Christ. New York: Lumen Books, 1988. 117 p.: bibl.

This translation and updating of *Borges en/y/sobre cine* includes numerous film reviews by Borges and two essays by Edgardo Cozarinsky about Borges' influence on the cinema and the films that have been based on his work. Also: a substantial introduction by Cozarinsky, brief notes by Ronald Christ and Adolfo Bioy Casares, and translators' footnotes and filmographies. Translations, which are excellent, offer good examples of working with long, complex Spanish sentences.

5018 Fernández Retamar, Roberto. "Caliban" and other essays. Translated by Edward Baker. Foreword by Fredric Jameson. Minneapolis: Univ. of Minnesota Press, 1989. 139 p.: bibl., index.

The "other essays" are "Caliban Re-

visited," "Against the Black Legend" (in a new translation), "Some Theoretical Problems of Spanish-American Literature," "Prologue to Ernesto Cardenal," and a preface for North American readers by Fernández Retamar. Except for the title essay (done by Lynn Garafola, David Arthur McMurray, and Roberto Márquez), Baker is responsible for the translations, which are accurate if not always elegant. Information about the original publication of individual pieces would have been helpful.

5019 Galeano, Eduardo H. Memory of fire. v. 1, Genesis. v. 3, Century of the wind. Translated by Cedric Belfrage. New York: Pantheon Books, 1985. 2 v.: bibl.

In Spanish, the final passage of Galeano's trilogy is a letter to his publisher. In the English edition, that letter is addressed to his translator, a conclusion that seems highly fitting given what Galeano has termed the long, intimate "brothership between the two. (See Galeano's comments about their relationship in Sam Stagg's "Eduardo Galeano," *Publishers Weekly*, June 3, 1988.) Critical responses to Galeano's poetic "unofficial" history vary according to reviewer's aesthetic and ideological persuasions; Belfrage, however, "is present throughout the book as a sympathetic intelligence, a parallel sensibility" (George Black, *Mother Jones*).

5020 Padilla, Heberto. Self-portrait of the other. Translated by Alexander Coleman. New York: Farrar, Straus, Giroux, 1990. 247 p.

On the one hand, this translation manifests the "gentle ironic detachment" that Roberto González Echevarría has noted in Padilla's *La mala memoria* as something "unique in Latin American literature" (*The New York Times Book Review*). On the other, the English version is rendered less than satisfactory by imprecisions in word choice and phrasing and by frequent omissions, at times of only a clause, at times of a paragraph or more. The poem's epigraph is a poem by Belkis Cuza Malé, translated by Alastair Reid.

5021 Partnoy, Alicia. The little school: tales of disappearance & survival in Argentina. Translated by Alicia Partnoy with Lois Athey and Sandra Braunstein. Illustrated by Raquel Partnoy. Pittsburgh, Pa.: Cleis Press, 1986. 136 p.: ill.

English translation of *La escuelita* is noted here in spite of the fact that the Spanish version, due to be published in Chile, was not available. Partnoy's book has been read and discussed widely and highly praised, in particular with respect to the *testimonio*.

5022 Paz, Octavio. Sor Juana, or, the traps of faith. Translated by Margaret Sayers Peden. Cambridge, Mass.: Harvard Univ. Press, 1988. 547 p.: appendix, bibl., index.

It is unfortunate and unfair that in the numerous reviews of this biography there are so few mentions of Peden's superb work as its translator. Or that the praise she has received should thank her for "adroitly excising the original's verbosity" (*Library Journal*). In fact, not only does the English follow Octavio Paz's structures and style quite closely, but Paz refers in his prologue to changes and omisions in the English-language edition for which he himself was responsible. The appendix includes a translation of the "Carta de la Madre Juana Inés de la Cruz escrita al R.P.M. Antonio Núñez de la Compañía de Jesus." Glossary of Spanish terms.

5023 Rodó, José Enrique. Ariel. Translation, reader's reference, and annotated bibliography by Margaret Sayers Peden. Foreword by James W. Symington. Prologue by Carlos Fuentes. Austin: Univ. of Texas Press, 1988. 156 p.: bibl., index.

Praised repeatedly for allowing José Enrique Rodó's classic text to become not merely accessible but even "exciting" (*Choice*), Peden's practice has been best described by Carlos Fuentes in his introduction. Peden, Fuentes explains, "while being perfectly faithful . . . eliminates long sentences and subordinate clauses in favor of shorter phrases that say exactly the same things written by Rodó . . . " Translator has included an exhaustive "Reader Reference" list and an extensive annotated bibliography of *Ariel*.

5024 Sarduy, Severo. Written on a body. Translated by Carol Maier. New York: Lumen Books, 1989. 131 p.

Translation of *Escrito sobre un cuerpo* and the first third of *La simulación.*

5025 Timerman, Jacobo. Chile: death in the south. Translated from the Spanish by Robert Cox. New York: Knopf: Random House, 1987. 133 p.

In his translation of *Chile: el galope muerto*, Cox offers a highly readable version in English, and at the same time closely follows both Timerman's "mixture of reportage, political analysis and philosophical reflecting" (J.M. Coetzee) and the immediacy of the testimonies included in the interchapters.

5026 Timerman, Jacobo. Cuba: a journey. Translated from the Spanish by Toby Talbot. New York: A.A. Knopf, 1990. 125 p.

Translation by Tony Talbot from an unpublished Spanish manuscript.

TRANSLATIONS FROM THE PORTUGUESE
Poetry

5027 Bandeira, Manuel. This earth, that sky: poems. Translated with notes and introduction by Candace Slater. Berkeley: Univ. of California Press, 1989. 247 p.: index. (Latin American literature and culture; 1)

Bilingual edition of over 100 poems selected primarily from post-1930s books of this outstanding poet, with excellent introduction situating Bandeira's work in constant oscillation between nontranscendence and transcendence—earth and sky. Unable to convey the original's formal qualities, the translations nonetheless suggest Bandeira's simplicity, thematic range, and enormous appeal.

5028 Prado, Adélia. The alphabet in the park: selected poems of Adélia Prado. Translated and with an introduction by Ellen Watson. Middletown, Conn.: Wesleyan Univ. Press, 1990. 63 p.

Delightful and informative introduction demonstrates why Watson is precisely the right translator for Prado's work. Excellent, resonant translations of Prado's richly evocative verse (selected from her first three books). Prado's poems, at times transcendent but always rooted in everyday life, constantly "change their many minds," in Watson's apt phrase.

Brief Fiction and Theater

5029 Lispector, Clarice. Soulstorm: stories. Translated with an afterword by Alexis Levitin. Introduction by Grace Paley.

New York: New Directions Pub., 1989. 175 p.

Volume unites two collections of short texts—stories, meditations, sketches—from the 1974 books *A via crucis do corpo* and *Onde estivestes de noite*. Paley's three-page introduction is advertising, unlike Levitin's valuable and brief afterword. Translations are convincing: attentive and yet creative in finding solutions to the problems of Lispector's characteristic tones and rhythms.

5030 Marcos, Plínio; Leilah Assunção; and Consuelo de Castro. 3 contemporary Brazilian plays in bilingual edition. Edited by Elzbieta Szoka and Joe W. Bratcher. Austin, Tex.: Host Publications, 1988. 527 p.: bibl., ill.

Brief introduction to Brazilian theater by Margo Milleret and biographical and critical commentaries present three contemporary playwrights to a foreign readership. Elzbieta Szoka translates Marcos' *Dois perdidos numa noite suja* (a two-man existential struggle); Lydia Gouveia Marques translates Assunção's *Boca molhada de paixão calada* (about games married people play); and Celina Pinto translates Castro's *Aviso prévio* (a Beckett-like two-actor play). All three translations are poor, and the design of the volume—with each complete English version followed by the Portuguese—is a mistake.

5031 Scliar, Moacyr. The enigmatic eye. Translated by Eloah F. Giacomelli. New York: Ballantine Books, 1989. 100 p.

Consists of 26 very short stories, some previously published as long ago as 1962, from Scliar's 1986 volume. These are off-beat tales of the fantastic and the mundane, the mysterious, ludicrous, and profound, narrated in Scliar's characteristic deadpan tone. Excellently translated with great care, fluency, and tact, the volume displays Scliar's considerable talents.

Novels

5032 Amado, Jorge. Captains of the sands. Translated from Portuguese by Gregory Rabassa. New York: Avon, 1988. 248 p.

Sixth of Amado's early series, "The Bahian Novels." Originally published in 1937, this story of abandoned children in Sal-

vador owes its belated appearance in English to Bantam's 1988 publicity effort on behalf of *Showdown*. Translation displays Rabassa's usual skill and fluency, but also the carelessness that at times mars his work.

5033 Amado, Jorge. Show down. Translated by Gregory Rabassa. Toronto, Canada; New York: Bantam Books, 1988. 422 p.

Although very readable, this translation of Amado's 1984 novel (derivative of his own earlier works, especially *Gabriela*) is uneven and at times careless. Most startling, however, is the discovery that this is, unannounced, an edited and abriged version, with perhaps 20 percent (i.e., phrases, sentences, paragraphs) of the original omitted, as if Amado's prolix style were excessive for an American audience.

5034 Anjos, Cyro dos. Diary of a civil servant. Translated by Arthur Brakel. Rutherford, N.J.: Fairleigh Dickinson Univ. Press; London: Associated University Presses, 1988. 179 p.: bibl.

Elegantly written philosophical novel, originally published in 1937, is finally available in English thanks to Brakel, whose translation is eloquent, faithful and fluent, capturing the tone and diction of the original. Brakel's solid introduction sets the novel in its historical and literary context. With translator's notes.

5035 Azevedo, Aluísio. Mulatto. Translated by Murray Graeme MacNicoll. Edited by Daphne Patai. Introduction by Daphne Patai and Murray Graeme MacNicoll. Rutherford, N.J.: Fairleigh Dickinson Univ. Press; London: Associated University Presses, 1990. 298 p.: bibl.

Azevedo's controversial 1881 exposé of his native São Luis do Maranhão in the years before the abolition of slavery. Considered by many to be the first naturalist novel produced in Brazil, it is an intense expression of the abolitionism, anticlericalism, and republicanism sweeping through Brazil in the 1870s. With translator's notes.

5036 Cunha, Helena Parente. Woman between mirrors. Translated by Fred P. Ellison and Naomi Lindstrom. Austin: Univ. of Texas Press, 1989. 132 p. (The Texas Pan American series)

Claiming the introspective, consciousness-exploring Lispectorian mantle, Cunha contributes to the growing body of women's fiction with this challenging and complex novel (her first, originally published in 1983) of alienation and self-discovery. The translation, preceded by a good introduction, is competent but uneven, at times lapsing into an inappropriate register.

5037 Dourado, Autran. The bells of agony. Translated from the Portuguese by John M. Parker. London: P. Owen; Chester Springs, Pa.: Dufour Editions, 1988. 236 p.

First published in 1974, this historical novel of Vila Rica in the 18th century is structured like a classical tragedy but also has contemporary political relevance, as the translator explains in a short and helpful introduction. Faithful and fluent translation effectively captures the heavy, even oppressive quality of the original.

5038 Fonseca, Rubem. Bufo & Spallanzani. Translated by Clifford E. Landers. New York: Dutton, 1990. 249 p.

Fonseca's complex and delightful 1985 novel: love story, mystery, black comedy, and metafiction in one. Superbly translated, it reads like an original work of fiction that is witty, full of verve, intriguing, all the while being rigorously accurate and faithful to the details, phrasing, style, and tone of the original.

5039 França Júnior, Oswaldo. Beneath the waters. Translated by Margaret A. Neves. New York: Ballantine Books, 1990. 165 p.

Another minimalist fiction (originally published in 1987) by this author who died in 1989; it is an unbroken series of vignettes on the human costs of modernization, written in a stripped-down, bare-bones style. Translation is at times too literal, other times too free, in effect editing the original. In particular, errors that make no sense in English should have been caught.

5040 Lispector, Clarice. Near to the wild heart. Translated with an afterword by Giovanni Pontiero. New York: New Directions, 1990. 192 p.

Lispector's first novel (published in 1944) has finally appeared in English, with an engaging brief afterword by the translator. Lispector's lyrical and introspective language is effectively recreated here, although compared to the Portuguese, the translation is at times careless, especially in introducing traces of a masculine perspective absent from the original.

5041 Lispector, Clarice. The passion according to G.H. Translation by Ronald W. Sousa. Minneapolis: Univ. of Minnesota Press, 1988. 173 p. (Emergent literatures)

In a brief introductory note, Sousa explains why his version of Lispector's famous 1964 novel about a woman's self-imposed initiation rite is "more conventional than the original," thereby losing some of original's ambiguity and idiosyncracy. Translation is fluent, readable, and in large part faithful in its awkwardness and groping.

5042 Lispector, Clarice. The stream of life. Translated by Elizabeth Lowe and Earl E. Fitz. Foreword by Hélène Cixous. Minneapolis: Univ. of Minnesota Press, 1989. 114 p. (Emergent literatures)

With a foreword one-third the length of the work, Cixous threatens to bury this fluent and readable translation of Lispector's 1973 meditation (some of which also appears, in slightly altered form, in her later *Soulstorm*). This is Lispector as a virtual caricature of herself, and will please only dedicated fans.

5043 Piñon, Nélida. The republic of dreams: a novel. Translated from the Portuguese by Helen Lane. New York: Knopf, 1989. 663 p.

Intriguing family saga about Spain and Brazil, and the writing of fiction and history, originally published in 1984. The translation is generally faithful and reads extremely well, but some inexplicable decisions have been made by the translator and there is occasional carelessness with euphony, register, and repetitions.

5044 Ribeiro, João Ubaldo. An invincible memory. Translated by the author. New York: Harper & Row, 1989. 504 p.

This revisionist historical novel of Bahia, originally published in 1984, is reminiscent of (and much praised by) Jorge Amado. Its English publication provides an excellent occasion for a study of translation itself, so rare is it for an author to act as his own translator, let alone do it with such a superb sense of English, at once exceedingly faithful to his original and yet innovative.

5045 Scliar, Moacyr. Max and the cats: a novel. Translated by Eloah F. Giacomelli. New York: Ballantine Books, 1990. 99 p.

Scliar's 1981 parable of Max on land and sea, in Germany and in Brazil, his adventures with felines marking the stages of his passage. The characteristic Scliar style—a detached tone, and straightforward narrative intermingling memories and dreams and fantastic and everyday events—is very successfully recreated.

5046 Scliar, Moacyr. The strange nation of Rafael Mendes. Translated by Eloah F. Giacomelli. New York: Harmony Books, 1987. 309 p.

Panoramic family saga of New Christians past and present, set during one catastrophic day in the life of a Brazilian businessman. The translation is very readable, though on occasion it takes excessive liberties in its recourse to idiomatic expressions not in the Portuguese.

5047 Scliar, Moacyr. The volunteers. Translated by Eloah F. Giacomelli. New York: Available Press, 1988. 151 p.

Scliar's lyrical 1979 tale of Christians, Jews, and Arabs, and of the events leading to an ill-fated voyage from Porto Alegre to Haifa in search of the lost Jerusalem. Reads well but with occasional awkwardness and repetition in the English, and, more mysteriously, omits most but not all chapters' epigraphs from Camões.

5048 Torres, Antônio. Blues for a lost childhood: a novel of Brazil. Translated with an introduction by John M. Parker. Columbia, La.: Readers International, 1989. 202 p.

Originally published in 1986, this novel, at once lyrical and political, moves between the materially impoverished Northeast and the morally impoverished urban South. Text reads well in English, but is rather loosely translated from the Portuguese. Translator has added "color," as if he considered the Portuguese too monotonous, and has utilized a register at times too formal, other times too colloquial.

BIBLIOGRAPHY, THEORY, AND PRACTICE

5049 Annual Conference of the American Translators Association, 28th, Albu- querque, N.M., 1987. Across the language gap: proceedings. Edited by Karl Krummer. Medford, N.J.: Learned Information, Inc., 1987. 1 v.

Of particular interest to Latin Americanists are: Jo Anne Englebert, "But Is It English?: English Poetic Idiom and the Translation of Neruda" (p. 205–208); "This Side of Meaning: The Importance of Consultation in Literary Translation" (p. 209–214); and Clifford E. Landers, "Using Tone in Literary Translation" (p. 215–219).

5050 Annual Conference of the American Translators Association, 29th, Seattle, Wash., 1988. Learning at the crossroads: proceedings. Edited by Deanna Lindberg Hammond. Medford, N.J.: Learned Information, Inc., 1988. 1 v.

See especially: Michael Scott Doyle, "Hispanic Fiction in Translation: Some Considerations Regarding Recent Literary Theory" (p. 213–221); and Jean R. Longland, "Translating Brazilian and Portuguese Poetry" (p. 479–482).

5051 Annual Conference of the American Translators Association, 30th, Washington, 1989. Coming of age: proceedings. Edited by Deanna Lindberg Hammond. Medford, N.J.: Learned Information, Inc., 1989. 1 v.

Of particular interest is: Clifford E. Landers, "A (Highly Compressed but All-Too-Typical) Day in the Life of a Literary Translator," an article concerning the translation of Rubem Fonseca's *Bufo & Spallanzani* (p. 329–334).

5052 The art of translation: voices from the field. Edited by Rosanna Warren. Boston: Northeastern Univ. Press, 1989. 290 p.: bibl., ill., index.

Collection of "witness by practitioners" that spans many aspects of literary translation. Of particular interest to Latin Americanists are: Suzanne Jill Levine's article about translating Manuel Puig's *Boquitas pintadas*; J. Jorge Klor de Alva's on colonial discourse and classical Nahuatl; Dennis Tedlock's one-act play about translating the *Popul Vuh*.

5053 Barrenechea, Ana María. El texto poético como parodia del discurso crítico: los últimos poemas de Susana Thénon. (*Dispositio*, 11:30/32, 1987, p. 255–272)

Discussion of numerous ways in

which, in the work of Argentine poet Susan Thénon, translation is manifest as both theory and practice, particularly in poems written since *Distancias*. Detailed analysis of one poem: "Poema con Traducción Simultánea."

5054 Chamberlain, Lori. Gender and the metaphorics of translation. (*Signs*, 13:3, Spring 1988, p. 454–472)

Chamberlain's concern with gender and the "*representation* of translation" leads to an incisive historical survey of the metaphors traditionally used in Western culture to discuss translation as a "struggle for authority." She also comments on the usual failure to accord authority to translators; and she calls for a feminist theory and practice of translation that would rely on "the double-edged razor of translation as collaboration," a theory she finds suggested in the writing of a Latin American poet and two women translators of Latin American literature.

5055 Cluff, Russell M. Crónica de una convivencia: selección y traducción de *Esquizotexto y otros poemas* de Gonzalo Rojas. (*Ibero-Am. Arch.*, 15:1, 1989, p. 117–131, bibl., facsims.)

Discussion of author's joint translation with L. Howard Quackenbush (see item **4955**). Interesting for the description of a collaborative translation and for reproduction of successive versions of one poem.

5056 The craft of translation. Edited by John Biguenet and Rainer Schulte. Chicago: Univ. of Chicago Press, 1989. 153 p.: bibl. (Chicago guides to writing, editing, and publishing)

Essays collected here focus on translation practice as charted by translators who have retraced and examined their steps in the preparation of specific texts. Languages and perspectives vary, but, as the editors note, there is a remarkable recurrence of practical considerations. Among the contributors are two of the foremost translators of Latin American literature: Margaret Sayers Peden ("Building a Translation, the Reconstruction Business: Poem 145 of Sor Juana Inés de la Cruz") and Gregory Rabassa ("No Two Snowflakes are Alike: Translation as Metaphor").

5057 Encuentro Nacional de Traductores, 1st, Lima, 1986. Actas. Edición de Mariana Mould de Pease *et al.* Lima: Univ.

Ricardo Palma; Univ. Femenina Sagrado Corazón, 1988. 2 v.: bibl., ill.

Preceedings, almost entirely in Spanish, include papers read at the conference as well as transcriptions of workshops and roundtable sessions. Some presentations are literary; others deal with the translation of highly technical and scientific texts, legal documents, or materials from the humanities and social sciences. All of the presentations are concerned with translation into Spanish (from English, French, German, and Japanese), but many offer commentary that will interest translators who work from the Spanish. The pieces vary: some are quite anecdotal; others employ a theoretical approach (i.e., stylistic, linguistic, semiotic).

5058 Ferré, Rosario. Ofelia a la deriva en las aguas de la memoria. (*in* El coloquio de las perras. San Juan, P.R.: Editorial Cultural, 1990, p. 67–82.)

Translator of her own work, Rosario Ferré explores what she defines as the impossibility of transcribing cultural identity. Her example is the conversion of *Maldito amor* into *Sweet diamond dust* (item **4993**), but her comments extend to numerous other works and to a reflection on cultural and linguistic differences between Spanish and English. This is an intriguing meditation on both writing and translation.

5059 Harrison, Regina. Signs, songs, and memory in the Andes: translating Quechua language and culture. Austin: Univ. of Texas Press, 1989. 233 p.: bibl., ill., index.

As defined by its author, this book is one of "translations of culture." Harrison's extensive reflections on her own assumptions and inevitable "intrusions" as a translator, however, and her comments about the ethics of translating material in circumstances of considerable or even extreme imbalance, provide numerous analogues with the translation of literary texts. Readers may question some of her observations, but in so doing they will be addressing issues seldom discussed fully with respect to literature in translation.

5060 Merwin, William Stanley. Translating Juarroz and Noren: working papers. (*in* Translating poetry: the double labyrinth. Edited by Daniel Weissbort. Iowa City: Univ. of Iowa Press, 1989, p. 138–143)

Brief comments by Merwin about translation in general and about his particular translations of poems by Roberto Juarroz (from the Spanish, a language he knows) and Lars Noren (from the Swedish, a language with which Merwin is not familiar). Includes draft and final version of Juarroz's "Fifth Vertical Poetry, #27 (see item **4949**).

5061 Meta. Vol. 34, No. 1, 1989– ; Vol. 35, No. 3., 1990– . Montréal: Univ. de Montréal.

Most articles in *Meta* are written in French, but many issues contain articles pertinent to Latin America. In Vol. 34, No. 1, see: Celestino Fernández: "Humor and Satire in Mexican Immigration *Corridos:* A Study of Languages and Cultures in Contact" (p. 91–101). Vol. 35, No. 3, is a special issue entitled "Translation in the Spanish and Portuguese World." Articles on literary translation include: Luis Enrique Jara, "Le Traducteur: Instance d'Enonciation dans *Chronique d'une morte annoncé (Crónica de una muerte anunciada);*" Eva Wysk Koch, "A German Connection?: Context-Description of Literary Translation Efforts in Southern Brazil;" Suzanne Jill Levine, "The Subversive Scribe: Translating Manuel Puig;" and H. Guttenkunst Prade, "Brazilian Literature in Translation."

5062 Payne, Johnny. Translating the fiction of fascism. (*Hisp. J.,* 11:1, Spring 1990, p. 107–119)

On the basis of Nelson Marra's *El Guardaespaldas*, Payne discusses strategies for translating language that speaks of "the culture of fear" only to those familiar with "the linguistic and literary codes and their referents that develop under intensive state terror." Despite the highly specific nature of Payne's example, his suggestions for alerting an uninformed reader about how a text is to be read are pertinent to many Latin American works.

5063 Translation Review. No. 27, 1988 [through] Nos. 30/31, 1989– . Richardson, Tex.: Univ. of Texas at Dallas.

Journal devoted exclusively to issues of translation. Includes essays and reviews of interest to *Handbook* users. With respect to translation of literature from Latin America, see: Irene del Corral, "Humor: When Do We Lose It?" (about the translation of Jorge Ibar-

güengoitia's *Los relámpagos de agosto*) in No. 27, 1988, p. 25–27; Gustavo Godoy, "'What's in a Name?:—A Fish Called Pig,' or, How *Bahía de cochinos* Became 'Bay of Pigs'" in No. 28, 1988, p. 33–34; and Clifford E. Landers, "Back to the Violent Land: Reassessing the Putnam Translation of *Terras Do Sem Fim*" in Nos. 30/31, 1989, p. 38–40.

5064 Venuti, Lawrence. The translator's invisibility. (*Criticism,* 28:2, Spring 1986, p. 179–212)

In his discussion of Ben Belitt's translation of Pablo Neruda's verse play *Splendor and death of Joaquín Murieta*, Venuti examines Belitt's use of dialect as an example of translation made "visible." His thesis: that through resistance a reader can be engaged with a text far more directly than through "readability." This is an article with important implications for Latin American literature in translation, as both practice and product.

5065 Weinberger, Eliot. Nineteen ways of looking at Wang Wei: how a Chinese poem is translated. Exhibit and commentary by Eliot Weinberger. Further comments by Octavio Paz. Mount Kisco, N.Y.: Moyer Bell, 1987. 53 p.: bibl.

Deceptively small book that engages many—if not all—of the principal issues of literary translation. Weinberger presents 19 "incarnations" of a four-line poem by Wang Wei (ca. 700–761). He accompanies each with an incisive although often prescriptive commentary, which, for this reason, seems to be at odds with his purpose. Octavio Paz's discussion addresses his own version of the poem and the changes it has undergone.

5066 Wilson, Jason. An A to Z of modern Latin American literature in English translation. London: Institute of Latin American Studies, 1989. 95 p.: bibl.

Alphabetical entries, by author, include translated and original titles, genre, publication information, and translator. Also, a section of anthologies, a brief general "Bibliography on Translations," and a short introduction. With the exception of Sor Juana, Wilson lists authors who published from the period of Latin American Independence to July 1, 1989. North Americans will find this a valuable resource, despite some inevitable omissions and errors. In addition to being quite complete, it cites work published in England which has been neither reviewed nor distributed in the US.

JOURNAL ABBREVIATIONS

Afro-Hisp. Rev. Afro-Hispanic Review. Washington.

Am. Lat./Moscú. América Latina. Academia de Ciencias de la Unión de Repúblicas Soviéticas Socialistas. Moscú.

An. Acad. Geogr. Hist. Guatem. Anales de la Academia de Geografía e Historia de Guatemala. Guatemala.

An. Inst. Invest. Estét. Anales del Instituto de Investigaciones Estéticas. Univ. Nacional Autónoma de México. México.

Anu. Centro Estud. Martianos. Anuario del Centro de Estudios Martianos. Centro de Estudios Martianos. La Habana.

Anu. Estud. Am. Anuario de Estudios Americanos. Consejo Superior de Investigaciones Científicas; Univ. de Sevilla, Escuela de Estudios Hispano-Americanos. Sevilla, Spain.

Anu. Let. Anuario de Letras. Revista de la Facultad de Filosofía y Letras, Univ. Nacional Autónoma de México. México.

Beitr. Roman. Philol. Beiträge zur Romanischen Philologie. Rütten & Loening. Berlin.

Bol. Cult. Bibliogr. Boletín Cultural y Bibliográfico. Banco de la República; Biblioteca Luis-Angel Arango. Bogotá.

Cad. Negros. Cadernos Negros. São Paulo.

Caravelle. Caravelle. Cahiers du monde hispanique et luso-brésilien. Univ. de Toulouse, Institute d'études hispaniques, hispano-americaines et luso-brésiliennes. Toulouse, France.

Casa Am. Casa de las Américas. La Habana.

Conjonction. Conjonction. Bulletin de l'Institut français d'Haïti. Port-au-Prince.

Conjunto. Conjunto. Revista de Teatro Latinoamericano. Comité Permanente de Festivales; Casa de las Américas. La Habana.

Criterios/La Habana. Criterios: Revista de Teoría Literaria, Estética y Culturología. Casa de las Americas. La Habana.

Criticism. Criticism. Wayne State University Press. Detroit.

Cuad. Am. Cuadernos Americanos. Editorial Cultura. México.

Cuad. Hispanoam. Cuadernos Hispanoamericanos. Instituto de Cultura Hispánica. Madrid.

Cuba. Stud. Cuban Studies. Univ. of Pittsburgh, Center for Latin American Studies. Pittsburgh, Penn.

Cult. Guatem. Cultura de Guatemala. Univ. Rafael Landívar. Guatemala.

Cultura/Quito. Cultura. Banco Central del Ecuador. Quito.

Diogenes/Philosophy. Diogenes. International Council for Philosophy and Humanistic Studies (Paris); Berg Publishers. Oxford, England.

Dispositio. Dispositio. Dept. of Romance Languages, Univ. of Michigan. Ann Arbor.

Estud. Parag. Estudios Paraguayos. Univ. Católica Nuestra Señora de la Asunción. Asunción.

Explic. Textos Lit. Explicación de Textos Literarios. Dept. of Spanish and Portuguese, California State Univ. Sacramento.

Formations. Formations. Univ. of Wisconsin Press. Madison, WI.

Hisp. J. Hispanic Journal. Indiana Univ. of Pennsylvania, Dept. of Foreign Languages. Indiana, Penn.

Hisp. Rev. Hispanic Review. Univ. of Pennsylvania, Dept. of Romance Languages. Philadelphia, Penn.

Hispamérica. Hispamérica. Takoma Park, Md.

Hispania/Teachers. Hispania. American Assn. of Teachers of Spanish and Portuguese; Univ. of Southern California. Los Angeles.

Hispanófila. Hispanófila. Univ. of North Carolina. Chapel Hill, N.C.

Histórica/Lima. Histórica. Pontificia Univ. Católica del Perú, Depto. de Humanidades. Lima.

Historiogr. Bibliogr. Am. Historiografía y Bibliografía Americanista. Escuela de Estudios Hispano-Americanos de Sevilla. Sevilla, Spain.

Ibero-Am. Arch. Ibero-Amerikanisches Archiv. Ibero-Amerikanisches Institut. Berlin.

Iberoromania. Iberoromania. Max Niemeyer Verlag. Tübingen, Germany.

Ideas 92. Ideas '92. North-South Center and the Latin American Studies Program, Univ. of Miami. Coral Gables, Fla.

Insula. Insula. Madrid.

Integr. Latinoam. Integración Latinoamericana. Instituto para la Integración de América Latina. Buenos Aires.

Inti. Inti: Revista de Literatura Hispánica. Providence College, R.I.

Islas. Islas. Univ. Central de Las Villas. Santa Clara, Cuba.

Jam. J. Jamaica Journal. Institute of Jamaica. Kingston.

Lang. néo-lat. Les Langues néo-latines. Société des langues néo-latines.

LARR. Latin American Research Review. Latin American Research Review Board. Univ. of New Mexico, Albuquerque, N.M.

Lat. Am. Lit. Rev. Latin American Literary Review. Carnegie-Mellon Univ., Dept. of Modern Languages. Pittsburgh, Penn.

Lat. Am. Perspect. Latin American Perspectives. Univ. of California. Newbury Park, Calif.

Lat. Am. Theatre Rev. Latin American Theatre Review. Univ. of Kansas, Center of Latin American Studies. Lawrence, Kan.

Let. Cuba. Letras Cubanas. La Habana.

Let. Guatem. Letras de Guatemala. Univ. de San Carlos de Guatemala, Facultad de Humanidades, Instituto de Estudios de la Literatura Nacional.

Lett. Am. Letterature d'America. Bulzoni Editore. Roma.

Lexis. Lexis. Pontificia Univ. Católica del Perú. Lima.

Linden Lane Mag. Linden Lane Magazine. Princeton, N.J.

Lit. Rev. Literary Review. Fairleigh Dickinson Univ., Madison, N.J.

Mester. Mester. Univ. of California, Dept. of Spanish and Portuguese. Los Angeles, Calif.

Meta. Meta: Journal des traducteurs/ Translators Journal. Univ. de Montréal. Canada.

MLN. MLN. Modern Language Notes. Johns Hopkins Univ. Press. Baltimore, Md.

Neophilologus. Neophilologus. H.O. Tjeenk Willenk, etc. Groningen, The Netherlands.

Nueva Rev. Filol. Hisp. Nueva Revista de Filología Hispánica. El Colegio de México. México.

Philol. Prag. Philologica Pragensia. Academia Scientiarum Bohemoslovenica. Prague.

Portable Lower East Side. The Portable Lower East Side. New York.

Présence Afr. Présence Africaine. Paris.

Rev. Andin. Revista Andina. Centro Bartolomé de las Casas. Cusco, Perú.

Rev. Bibl. Nac. José Martí. Revista de la Biblioteca Nacional José Martí. La Habana.

Rev. CERC. Revue du CERC. Centre d'études et de recherches caraïbéennes, Univ. des Antilles-Guyane, Guadeloupe. Point-à-Pitre.

Rev. Chil. Lit. Revista Chilena de Literatura. Univ. de Chile, Depto. de Literatura. Santiago.

Rev. Crít. Lit. Latinoam. Revista de Crítica Literaria Latinoamericana. Latinoamericana Editores. Lima.

Rev. Estud. Colomb. Revista de Estudios Colombianos. Asociación de Colombianistas Norteamericanos; Plaza &ampersand; Janés. Bogotá.

Rev. Estud. Hisp. Revista de Estudios Hispánicos. Univ. of Alabama, Dept. of Romance Languages, Office of International Studies and Programs. Univ., Alabama.

Rev. Estud. Teatro. Revista de Estudios de Teatro. Instituto Nacional de Estudios de Teatro. Buenos Aires.

Rev. Hisp. Mod.   Revista Hispánica Moderna. Hispanic Institute, Columbia Univ. New York.

Rev. Iberoam.   Revista Iberoamericana. Instituto Internacional de Literatura Iberoamericana; Univ. de Pittsburgh. Pittsburgh, Penn.

Rev. Indias.   Revista de Indias. Consejo Superior de Investigaciones Científicas, Instituto Gonzalo Fernández de Oviedo. Madrid.

Rev. Inst. Cult. Puertorriq.   Revista del Instituto de Cultura Puertorriqueña. San Juan, P.R.

Rev. Inst. Nac. Estud. Teatro.   Revista del Instituto Nacional de Estudios de Teatro. Buenos Aires.

Rev. Interam. Bibliogr.   Revista Interamericana de Bibliografía. Organization of American States. Washington.

Rev. Let./São Paulo.   Revista de Letras. Univ. Estadual Paulista. São Paulo.

Rev. Lit. Cuba.   Revista de Literatura Cubana. Unión de Escritores y Artistas de Cuba. La Habana.

Rev. Teatro.   Revista de Teatro. Sociedade Brasileira de Autores Teatrais. Rio de Janeiro.

Salmagundi.   Salmagundi. Skidmore College. Saratoga Springs, New York.

Santiago.   Santiago. Univ. de Oriente. Santiago, Cuba.

SECOLAS Ann.   SECOLAS Annals. Southeastern Conference on Latin

American Studies; West Georgia College. Carrollton, Ga.

Signs.   Signs. The Univ. of Chicago Press. Chicago.

Sur.   Sur. Buenos Aires.

Texte.   Texte: revue de critique et de théorie littéraire. Trinity College. Toronto, Canada.

Thesaurus.   Thesaurus. Instituto Caro y Cuervo. Bogotá.

Third World Q.   Third World Quarterly. Third World Foundation; New Zealand House. London.

Todo es Hist.   Todo es Historia. Buenos Aires.

Torre.   La Torre. Univ. de Puerto Rico. Río Piedras, P.R.

Transl. Rev.   Translation Review. Univ. of Texas at Dallas. Richardson.

Unión.   Unión. Unión de Escritores y Artistas de Cuba. La Habana.

Univ. La Habana.   Universidad de La Habana. Habana.

Univ. San Carlos Guatem.   Universidad de San Carlos de Guatemala. Univ. de San Carlos. Guatemala.

Veritas.   Veritas. Pontificia Univ. Católica do Rio Grande do Sul. Pôrto Alegre, Brazil.

Vuelta.   Vuelta. México.

World Lit. Today.   World Literature Today. Univ. of Oklahoma. Norman, Okla.

MUSIC

ROBERT STEVENSON, *Professor of Music, University of California, Los Angeles*

UNDER THE HEADINGS "MUSIC, "Music and Literature," "Music and Society," and "Musicians," the 1988 *Hispanic American Periodicals Index (HAPI)* (Univ. of California, Los Angeles, p. 336–338), listed 107 articles published in 1987–88 in 31 different periodicals. However, only one of the 31 is a music magazine published in Latin America. None of the following seminal magazines was indexed: *Art: Revista da Escola de Música e Artes Cênicas da Universidade Federal da Bahia; Correspondência Musicológica* (São Paulo: Sociedade Brasileira de Musicologia); *Heterofonía* (México, D.F.); *Pauta* (México: Univ. Autónoma Metropolitana); *Revista del Instituto de Investigación Musicológica Carlos Vega* (Buenos Aires); *Revista de Musicología* (Sociedad Española de Musicología); *Revista Musical de Venezuela* (Caracas: Instituto Latinoamericano de Investigaciones y Estudios Musicales Vicente Emilio Sojo); *Temas de Etnomusicología* (Buenos Aires: Instituto Nacional de Musicología Carlos Vega). Two years later, only *Revista Musical de Venezuela* among the above had joined HAPI's lust of indexed periodicals.

As for other indexes: in January 1989, *The Music Index: a Subject-Author Guide to Music Periodical Literature* (Warren, Mich.: Harmonie Park Press) did index *Art*, *Heterofonía*, and *Pauta*. Nonetheless, it again was of but limited use to anyone specializing in Latin American music, because it indexed none of the other periodicals listed in the previous paragraph. These absences from the most complete indexes now being published, *HAPI* and *The Music Index*, explain the present perilous state of Latin America music studies—both in and outside Latin America. Only with utmost difficulty can librarians even discover what specialized music magazines are being published, much less find a dealer who will supply them.

So far as reviews of books and music appearing in these magazines go, they should alert librarians to desirable purchases. But a spot check in late 1990 of the music and music literature purchases that have been made by 12 leading university libraries in five Western states confirms the absence of not only all but one or two music periodicals published in Latin America, but also of all such book and music items listed in *HLAS 48:7047, HLAS 48:7050-7056, HLAS 48:7074, HLAS 48: 7076, HLAS 48:7123, HLAS 48:7127, HLAS 48:7128, HLAS 48:7149*, and *HLAS 48:7160*.

The decade of the 1990s must therefore take for its first goal not publication, but circulation. Some ways must be found to make Latin American music and music book purchases as easy for public and university librarians of good will as are purchases of the vastly more expensive music and books emanating from Germany, France, and Italy. At one of the Study Sessions of the International Musicological Society programmed for the week of April 3–10, 1992 in Spain (hosted by the Real Conservatorio Superior de Música, in Madrid) the participants focused on "The

Dissemination of Music and Music Literature published in the Iberian World." Whether any panaceas for the most pressing problem that now confronts Latin American music specialists were then found, is doubtful. But at least during the Quincentennial the problem was looked at in all its magnitude and urgency.

GENERAL

5067 Alposta, Luis. El tango en Japón. Buenos Aires: Corregidor, 1987. 171 p.: ill.

Covers history of tango in Japan to 1980, the centenary of its introduction to that country. In 1929 the cellist Matsubara gathered a Montparnasse tango band that played in Tokyo clubs; in 1931 the Paris Moulin Rouge Tango Ensemble led by *bandoneón* player Maurice Dufour debuted in Florida Dance Hall (Tokyo). Their success was so great that they continued performing in Japan to 1936. At the close of 1933, the Japanese pianist Kaoru Ban formed a new tango ensemble; however, much greater success awaited the Teito Tango Band, directed by Akira Yoshiro (Kiyoshi Sakurai, second violin), that began in 1934 with a mixture of Argentine and French tangos.

5068 Cancionero rioplatense, 1880–1925. Edición, prólogo, y selección de Carla Rey de Guido y Walter Guido. Caracas: Biblioteca Ayacucho, 1989. 583 p.: appendices, bibl., ill. (Biblioteca Ayacucho; 137)

Availing themselves of the microfilms of 643 octavo pamphlets and books totaling more than 23,000 p., not counting newspaper clippings gathered by the German polymath Robert Lehmann-Nitsche during his residence in the River Plate region and deposited at the Ibero-Amerikanisches Institut of Berlin, the editors organized the poetry under four headings, with subdivisions within the first and second headings. For musicians, the "Datos Biobibliográficos de Autores y Compositores" (p. 539–554) will be extremely welcome, as will many of the footnotes to the poems and especially the editors' paragraph on the *cifra, estilo, vidalita, canción criolla, vals, polca, habanera, mazurca, milonga,* and tango (p. i-lix).

5069 Cetrangolo, Annibale. Musica italiana nell'America coloniale: premesse, cantate del veneto Giacomo Facco. Padova, Italy: Liviana Editrice, 1989. 155 p.: bibl., ill., music. (Saggi; 21. Quaderni dell'IMLA)

Contains transcriptions of seven cantatas for solo voice by Giacomo Facco (1676–1753), with continuo parts by Emanuela Marcante (p. 71–137). Facco, the subject of Uberto Zanolli's 270-p. panegyric *Giacomo Facco Maestro de Reyes: introducción a la vida y la obra del gran músico veneto de 1700* (México: Don Bosco, 1965), never visited the Western Hemisphere, but like the nearly 65 other Italians listed in Cetrangolo's *catalogo provvisorio* (p. 53–57), his printed and manuscript works were circulated in the New World. This beautifully printed book was reviewed in *Revista Musical Chilena* (44:173, enero/junio 1990, p. 126).

Collazo, Bobby. La última noche que pasé contigo: 40 años de farándula cubana. See *HLAS 51:4680.*

5070 Dictionnaire de la musique. Direction de Marc Vignal. Paris: Larousse, 1987. 882 p., 160 p. of plates: col. ill.

In this idiosyncratic one-volume lexicon Cuba and Mexico gain articles, but not Argentina, Chile or Peru. Statements included in the unsigned Latin American articles are frequently questionable or wrong and are always out of date. Without any attempt at bibliography or work-lists, this Larousse does at least boast pretty pictures, mostly in color. Pictureless Alberto Ginastera (1916–83) entry gets 22 lines; his "pupil" Kagel, also born in Buenos Aires (1931), gets 72.

5071 Duckles, Vincent Harris and **Michael A. Keller.** Music reference and research materials: an annotated bibliography. 4th ed., rev. New York: Schirmer Books; Toronto: Collier Macmillan Canada; New York: Maxwell Macmillan International, 1992. 714 p.: index.

Latin American coverage in this manual is so defective as to border on the ludicrous. Spain and Portugal fare only slightly better.

5072 Etnomusicólogo norteamericano Dr. Steve Loza dictó cursos en la Facultad de Artes de la Universidad de Chile. (*Rev.*

Music. Chil., 43:172, julio/dic. 1989, p. 114–115)

During a residency in Chile (Aug.-Dec. 1989), Loza gave highly successful courses, lectures, and programs at Santiago, Valparaíso, and Valdivia, introducing Chileans to regional and popular musics of Mexico and the Caribbean.

5073 Hosiasson, José. El jazz e Hispano-América: interesante caso de retroalimentación. (*Rev. Music. Chil.*, 42:169, enero/junio 1988, p. 37–42, facsims.)

"Chilean Aces of Jazz" recorded *Rosetta* and *Copenhagen* at Santiago in 1944 (Vic-Ch 90–0341), and *Jazz Me Blues* and *Darktown Strutters Ball* in 1945 (Vic-Ch 90–0466). The members in 1944 were Lucho Aranguiz (tpt), Ángel Valdés (tbn), Woody Wolf (clt), Mario Escobán (ten), Hérnan Prado (p), Raúl Salinas (g), Iván Cazaban (bs), and Víctor Tapia (d). Author lists honor roll of 28 latins who distinguished themselves as jazz performers in the US or in Europe.

5074 Illari, Bernardo. A propósito del tardío siglo XVIII latinoamericano: tres compositores galantes de América del Sud. (*in* Conferencia Anual de la Asociación Argentina de Musicología, *1st, Buenos Aires, 1987.* Actas. Buenos Aires: Asociación Argentina de Musicología, 1988, p. 3–21, bibl., music)

Combating the prevalent view that Latin American music declined in artistic value 1750–1800, Illari offers excellent reviews of Salve Regina settings by Bartolomé Massa Mazza (1721–99), Juan Manuel Olivares (1769–97), and José Emérico Lobo de Mesquita (d. 1805). Transcriptions of Massa's fourth of five movements, Et Jesum (p. 10–12), of a portion of the opening verse of Olivares' Salve (p. 17), and of Lobo de Mesquita's entire three-movement Salve (p. 18–20) admirably reinforce Illari's verbal analyses. This article offers a model of what work needs to be done by future Latin American musicologists.

5075 Instrumentos musicales de América Latina y el Caribe. Caracas: Editorial Binev, C.A., 1988 135 p.: bibl., plates.

Preceded by an anonymous introduction summarizing the history of indigenous American instruments and an explanation of the Hornbostel-Sachs system of classifying instruments, the main body of this manual consists of succinct descriptions and catalog data on idiophones (p. 19–38), membranophones (p. 39–55), chordophones (p. 57–69), and aerophones (p. 71–96), gathered for deposit in a future Venezuelan museum. Valuable indexes of instruments by categories (p. 125–129) and by countries (p. 131–135) conclude this handsome volume.

5076 Kuss, Malena. Bernal Jiménez, Miguel; Boero, Felipe; Castro, Juan José; García Caturla, Alejandro; Ginastera, Alberto; Gutiérrez y Espinosa, Felipe; López Buchardo, Carlos. (*in* Pipers Enzyklopädie des Musiktheaters. München: Piper Verlag, 1986, 1987, 1989, v. 1, p. 317–318, 377–378, 503–505; v. 2, p. 325–327, 380–386, 623–624; v. 3, p. 549–550)

These seven invaluable encyclopedia articles include in-depth discussion of at least one opera by the cited composer and conclude with an up-to-date bibliography.

5077 Kuss, Malena. Toward a comprehensive approach to Latin American music bibliography: theoretical foundations for reference sources and research materials. (*in* Latin American masses and minorities: their images and realities. Madison, Wis.: Seminar on the Acquisition of Latin American Library Materials; Memorial Library, Univ. of Wisconsin, 1987, v. 2, p. 615–678)

No one is better equipped than the author of "Current State of Bibliographic Research in Latin American Music" (Fontes Artis Musicae, 34:4, Oct./Dec. 1984, p. 20–39) to confront the miasma through which Latin American music bibliographers must walk.

5078 Langevin, André. Música andina: breve introducción bibliográfica. (*Rev. Andin.*, 7:2, dic. 1989, p. 575–579)

Although this is an attentive survey of literature going back as far as R. and M. D'Harcourt's classic 1925 text, the oldest item in the discography is dated 1966 (Mountain Music of Peru, Folkways FE 4339). The author delays to the end listing items that he considers primarily of interest to specialists. He makes no claim to exhaustiveness.

5079 Milanca Guzmán, Mario. Claudio Arrau y Teresa Carreño. (*Araucaria Chile*, 42, 1988, p. 115–125)

In contrast with Horowitz, who became tense after only a few octaves, Carreño played Liszt's 6th Hungarian Rhapsody without ever tiring. Arrau recalls that she once played the last three concertos of Beethoven with Nikisch, never showing fatigue.

5080 Montaño Army, Mary. *Zarzuelas:* Spanish operetta in the New World. (*Palacio*, 91:2, Fall 1985, p. 19–25, facsims., photos)

Manuel Areu's collection of 116 19th-century zarzuelas, mostly in piano-vocal scores (often incomplete), was transferred to the Univ. of New Mexico Fine Arts Library in 1972. Sixty-two are one-act zarzuelas, 40 are two- or three-act, and 14 are of undetermined length. Born at Madrid in 1845, Areu arrived at Havana in 1868, thence departing on a long tour of Cuba and of Mexico. At Mexico City he married a voice pupil, Pilar Pautret, who died in 1900, leaving him with six children. After years of zarzuela performances throughout Mexico, the family escaped during the Pancho Villa epoch, locating during the Depression in Los Angeles. Manuel returned to Mexico City in 1934 and died there at age 97 in 1942. His archive of performed zarzuelas is unsurpassed in US university libraries. The facsimiled playbills document performances at such theatres as the Arbeu (1897) in Mexico City, the Juárez (1911) in Ciudad Juárez, and the Cananea (1916) in the state of Sonora.

5081 Morgan, Robert P. Twentieth-century music: a history of musical style in modern Europe and America. New York; London: W.W. Norton & Co., 1991. 554 p.

Chapter on Latin America (p. 315–322) is the most superficial and uninformed in this trendy book.

5082 The Norton/Grove concise encyclopedia of music. Edited by Stanley Sadie. New York: W.W. Norton, 1988. 850 p.: ill.

In all respects, including Latin American and Iberian coverage, this is a much better one-volume lexicon than the 1987 one-volume Larousse. Dates of birth and death are exact; many more Latin American composers are profiled; stylistic summaries are better informed; and the nonpareil editorship of Sadie and his assistant Alison Latham is in evidence throughout.

5083 Pérez Perazzo, Alberto. Ritmo afrohispano antillano, 1865–1965. Caracas: Publicaciones Almacenadoras Caracas, 1988. 240 p., 34 p. of plates: bibl., ill., index.

Beginning in 1922, radio in Cuba, Puerto Rico, and Mexico began popularizing *los discos de moda.* Chaps. 6–25 contain a variety of valuable data concerning popular urban music through 1965.

5084 Rico Salazar, Jaime. Cien años de boleros: su historia, sus compositores, sus intérpretes y 500 boleros inolvidables. Bogotá: Centro de Estudios Musicales; Academia de Guitarra Latinoamericana, 1987. 454 p.: ill., indexes, music, ports.

After an introductory chapter on the Spanish bolero, the compiler devotes a chapter each to Cuba, Mexico, Puerto Rico, Argentina, Chile, Central America, and Colombia, listing each nation's foremost bolero composers and giving thumbnail biographies and portraits of most. The *cancionero* (p. 175–442) contains the "500 boleros" advertised in the title, each with superimposed chord names above the texts (no melodies), and each credited to its author. Alphabetical indexes of the boleros by title and of the composers and interpreters follow (p. 446–454). The "Curiosidades en la Historia de Bolero" (p. 172–173) contains the true names of nine artists who used pseudonyms and reveals many other interesting tidbits.

5085 Roldán, Waldemar Axel. Antología de música colonial americana. Buenos Aires: El Ateneo, 1986. 259 p.

Transcriptions of 16 religious pieces by Juan de Araujo, Fabián García Pacheco, Antonio Durán de la Mota, Manuel Gaytán y Arteaga, Ignacio Quispe, José de Orejón y Aparicio, Sebastián Durón, Manuel Mesa y Carrizo, and Roque Ceruti (plus *Hanacpachap Cussicuinin,* 1631, probably by Juan Pérez Bocanegra). García Pacheco, Gaytán y Arteaga, and Durón never visited the Western Hemisphere.

5086 Roldán, Waldemar Axel. Catálogo de manuscritos de música colonial de la Biblioteca Nacional de Bolivia. Lima: Proyecto Regional del Patrimonio Cultural y Desarrollo, PNUD, UNESCO; La Paz: Instituto Boliviano de Cultura, 1986. 1 v.

After transfer from the Sucre cathedral music archive and augmented by the Julia Fortún collection formerly at La Paz, the Bolivian National Library collection now houses the works cataloged under "La Paz" and "Sucre" headings in Robert Stevenson's

Renaissance and Baroque Musical Sources in the Americas (see *HLAS 36:4516*). Other works from the cathedral archive surfacing after 1970 bring the total to 1,238 pieces, 760 of which are anonymous. Villancicos in Spanish composed after 1680 dominate the collection. The reviewer in *Revista de Musicología* (Madrid: 12:1, 1989, p. 316–317) alphabetically listed the 82 named composers. (Sample errors: Arguimbau should be Arquimbau; George Saint should be Saint-Georges.)

5087 Seeger, Anthony. Correndo entre gabinete e campo: o papel da transcrição musical em etnomusicologia. (*Rev. Mus. Paul.*, 33, 1988, p. 173–191)

Renewed consideration of the knotty problems of transcription and analysis of indigenous songs uses case study of the Suya *agache ngere* songs uttered in unison by seated adult males in rainy season. Ambience, ritual, and text are frequently superior to pitch and rhythm in defining song character. European notation too often falsifies the inner nature of indigenous music.

5088 Torres, Rodrigo. Creacíon musical e identidad cultural en América Latina: Foro de Compositores Cono Sur. (*Rev. Music. Chil.*, 42:169, enero/junio 1988, p. 58–85, ill.)

The Chilean Agrupación Musical Anacrusa sponsored Encuentro de Música Contemporánea at the Goethe Institut (2nd, Santiago, 1987). Participants included Juan Orrego-Salas, Gerardo Gandini, Alicia Terzián, Luis Szarán, Corúin Aharomian, Cirilo Vila, Oscar Bazán, and Antonio Guarello. Moderator Rodrigo Torres summarizes the discussion. Although the problem of "identity" was bruited, the chief problem—propagating the musicians' works beyond narrow boundaries—remained nearly insoluble.

5089 Turnbull, Robert. The opera gazetteer. New York: Rizzoli, 1988. 240 p.: ill., index.

The shocking inaccuracies of this manual include making Toscanini a director for the "whole Teatro Colón" in 1913; spelling Mozart's Munich opera *Idomineo;* and claiming that the first performance of *Idomeneo* at the Colón was in the 1970s instead of 1963. Richard Strauss' *Elektra*, first heard at the Colón in 1923, was not preceded by

"prologues in the form of two bad one-act Italian operas." Heitor (not "Hector") Villa-Lobos wrote no opera called *Jesus;* the Teatro Amazonas at Manaus does not have a "capacity of only 800." At Santiago the early seasons were not dominated by a composer named "Mercandante." "Paiagua" was not the composer of *Catalina de Guisa* (Paniagua was). The "first Venezuelan opera (*Virginia*)" did not have its world premiere in 1973 and was not sponsored by "President Guzmán Blanco." Plácido Domingo had triumphed at Mexico City long before 1975 (in 1961, in *Amelia Goes to the Ball* and *Fedora*, and also in Paris).

ARGENTINA

5090 Alberto Ginastera: a complete catalogue of his published works. Introduction by Aurora Natola-Ginastera and Malena Kuss. New York: Boosey & Hawkes, 1986. 1 v.

Revised and updated edition of *Alberto Ginastera: a catalogue of his published works* (London: New York: Boosey & Hawkes, 1976, 20 p.)

Arlt, Roberto et al. Tango: prosa y poesía de Buenos Aires. See item **4271.**

5091 Caamaño, Roberto and Carmen García Muñoz. Treinta años de la Facultad de Artes y Ciencias Musicales. (*Rev. Inst. Invest. Musicol. Carlos Vega*, 10:10, 1989, p. 7–32)

Caamaño's preface rightly signals the uniqueness of the music faculty in the Univ. Católica Argentina, there being nothing comparable in Buenos Aires or anywhere else in Argentina. After a documented year-by-year history of the faculty, García Muñoz lists the 27 members of the faculty in 1989 and the 73 who taught previously, and concludes with a year-by-year list of all the graduates with the degrees of either *licenciatura* or *profesor superior de música* (grouped under the specialties of composition, musicology and criticism, music education, choral and orchestral directing, and, for the *licenciatura*, sacred music). Amalia (Pola) Suárez Urtubey, who in 1964/65 was among the licenciates in musicology, obtained her doctorate from UCA in 1972; García Muñoz (*licenciatura* in musicology in 1966/67) obtained her doctorate—only the third granted by UCA—in 1989.

5092 Collier, Simon. The life, music & times of Carlos Gardel. Pittsburgh, Pa.: Univ. of Pittsburgh Press, 1986. 340 p., 8 p. of plates: bibl., ill., index. (Pitt Latin American series)

This best biography of Latin America's "first (and in many ways greatest) superstar of light entertainment"—who is remembered for 1,443 recorded songs (most of them tangos), triumphal tours of Europe, and French and US films—provides a model of how biographies of popular entertainers should be written. Only thing lacking is musical analysis. See also Carlos Gardini's translation *Carlos Gardel: su vida, su música, su época* (Buenos Aires: Editorial Sudamericana, 1988).

5093 Deschner, Ana María and **Olga Inés Zaffore.** El jazz y sus antecedentes en nuestro país. (*in* Conferencia Anual de la Asociación Argentina de Musicología, *1st, Buenos Aires, 1987.* Actas. Buenos Aires: Asociación Argentina de Musicología, 1988, p. 24–32, bibl.)

Around 1900 Harold Philips, cakewalk artist from the US of African descent, became known as a "brillante pianista." In 1924 Jazz America arrived: comprising eight to ten instrumentalists led by Gordon Stretton, the group played Abdullah Club. In 1927 came Sam Wooding, an African-American with this jazz band, playing at the Teatro Maipo and Gran Cine Florida. Ken Hamilton and his Band Boys, four of whom imitated the sounds of instruments, debuted in 1933 at the Buenos Aires Centro de Arquitectura.

5094 Franze, Juan Pedro. William Davis: un maestro de danzas. (*Rev. Inst. Invest. Musicol. Carlos Vega*, 9:9, 1988, p. 35–63, bibl.)

On July 18, 1829 *The British Packet* announced the opening of a dancing school to be run by William Davis, an arrival from North America. On March 3, 1833, he called himself "a resident of the State of Rhode Island now residing in Buenos Ayres" and identified himself as a man of "colour," ready to "prove himself to the generous public by dancing the Minuet de la Cour and the Gavotte, likewise the Jacky Tar's hornpipe on the 4th of March." On Dec. 13, 1834, he an-

nounced that dressed as a Turk he would dance the French quadrille "with four beautiful young ladies of his own colour, taught by him . . . next the Sailor's Hornpipe, 25 steps, French Gavot and Minuet de la Cour, Mrs. Cooper's Hornpipe, 25 steps, Jack's the Lad with 25 steps." On July 4, 1835, one *British Packet* correspondent "witnessed an African dance, in a small mansion in a bye-street of San Nicolas" where "three black young ladies, attired in the highest style of fashion, and three young gentlemen of the same complexion, were dancing minuets à la mode d'Angola, to the music of the tom-tom." After an absence that took him to England, France, and Boston during which he collected new dances "more attractive than those which have been presented here," Davis reappeared on July 24, 1841, with an advertisement in *The British Packet*. Again, in the *Packet* of May 8, 1848, he "respectfully informs his public and his friends that he has returned to this city" to resume his dancing classes.

5095 García Muñoz, Carmen. Cartas de Juan Carlos Paz. (*Rev. Inst. Invest. Musicol. Carlos Vega*, 10:10, 1989, p. 313–320)

Paz's 11 letters dating from Aug. 1936-May 1941 include one to Václav Smetácek at Prague written June 12, 1937, in which he attributes his secession from Grupo Renovación to the group's conservative musical stance. In a long, undated letter to compatriot Luis Gianneo he bewailed the "impaciencia y desorden en el artista americano: quiere llegar pronto." Paz's approving correspondents included Paul Pisk and Henry Cowell.

5096 García Muñoz, Carmen. Materiales para una historia de la música argentina: la actividad de la Sociedad Nacional de Música entre 1915 y 1930. (*Rev. Inst. Invest. Musicol. Carlos Vega*, 9:9, 1988, p. 149–194)

José André, Felipe Boero, Ricardo Rodríguez, and Josué Teófilo Wilkes founded the Sociedad Nacional de Música on Oct. 18, 1915, along with associate founders Carlos López Buchardo, Floro Ugarte, Constantino Gaito, Celestino Piaggio, Pascual De Rogatis, José Gil, Cesar Stiatessi, and Carlos Pedrell. By government decree of 1940 the name was changed to Asociación Argentina de Compositores. Between Nov. 5, 1915, and Dec. 16,

1930, the Sociedad sponsored 100 programs given at the Museo Nacional de Bellas Artes, the Salón La Argentina, the Sálon "Amigos del Arte," and intermittently at various locales in Buenos Aires, La Plata, Rosario, Córdoba, and Bahía Blanca. In addition to works (mostly of the chamber or solo variety) by the composers named above, the Sociedad sponsored performances of numerous compositions by Ernesto Drangosch, Raúl H. Espoile, Alejandro Inzaurraga, and Alberto Williams. Performers included the composers themselves, pianists Juan Carlos Paz, Eduardo Risler, and Ricardo Viñes, and singers, string players, and flute, clarinet, and harp players of excellent quality. This admirable author meticulosly lists the works performed, the interpreters, dates and places of performances.

5097 García Muñoz, Carmen. Materiales para una historia de la música argentina: las revistas musicales: *Bibelot*. (*Rev. Inst. Invest. Musicol. Carlos Vega*, 9:9, 1988, p. 131–136)

The 72 issues of *Bibelot: Revista Musical* published at Buenos Aires (1903–05) came out weekly through issue 11 and thenceforth fortnightly. Adolfo Cipriota directed it through issue 52. Among the 51 musical selections published in *Bibelot*, all but three were by Argentines, either native-born or long domiciled in the country. Issue 31 included five musical selections; 15 issues lacked any music. The most eligible composers were Julián Aguirre, Celestino Piaggio, and Jaime Bustamante. Most of the selections were piano pieces or songs with lyrics in French, Italian, or Spanish. Although not intended as a literary periodical, the "Notas Ligeras, Delicadamente Breves" promised in the first issue often turned bitter, sarcastic, and even vituperative.

5098 García Muñoz, Carmen. Materiales para una historia de la música argentina: las colecciones musicales en la primera mitad del siglo XIX. (*Rev. Inst. Invest. Musicol. Carlos Vega*, 10:10, 1989, p. 351–364)

Among printed sources listed are *La Moda* (23 numbers, 1837–38) and *Boletín Musical* (16 issues, Aug.-Dec. 1837); among manuscripts are the so-called Julianita López notebook and the seven Ruibal notebooks, containing mostly unattributed salon pieces, but others credited to Argentine J.B.A. (Juan

Bautista Alberdi), Juan Pedro Esnaola, F.M. Cordero, and to Europeans Bassini, Cramer, "Henrique Bolman," and "Berdi" (Verdi). With her usual scrupulous scholarship, author lists the contents and whereabouts of each collection.

Grebe Vicuña, María Ester. El *tayil* mapuche, como categoría conceptual y medio de comunicación trascendente. See item **5186.**

5099 Kuss, Malena. Alberto Ginastera: musikmanuskripte. Winterthur, Switzerland: Amadeus Verlag, 1990. 40 p.

In 1986 the Paul Sacher Stiftung in Basel, Switzerland, became the depository of the manuscripts brought from Buenos Aires to Geneva in 1971 by Alberto Ginastera (1916–83) as well as of his later compositions. Besides his 54 works with opus number, the Stiftung holds manuscripts of works withdrawn by Ginastera from his catalog, his film and stage music, and 23 p. of unidentified material.

5100 Kuss, Malena. Felipe Boero: *El matrero*, 12 Juli 1929, Teatro Colón, Buenos Aires. (*in* Pipers Enzyklopädie des Musiktheaters. v. 1. München, Germany: Piper Verlag, 1986, p. 377–378, ill.)

Encyclopedia article. Kuss also authored articles on *Proserpina e lo straniero* (1952) by Juan José Castro, *Bomarzo* (1967) and *Don Rodrigo* (1964) by Alberto Ginastera, *Il sogno di Alma* (1914) by Carlos López Buchardo, *Huemac* (1916) by Pascual De Rogatis, and *Marianita limeña* (1957) by Valdo Sciammarella for this encyclopedia, entered under composers' names. For a list of her other articles published in this encyclopedia, see item **5076.**

5101 Mansilla, Silvina Luz. Alfredo Pinto, 1891–1968. (*Rev. Inst. Invest. Musicol. Carlos Vega*, 9:9, 1988, p. 119–129)

At age 22, after completing studies at Naples Conservatorio di Musica, Alfredo Angel Pinto emigrated to Buenos Aires, first establishing himself as a pianist. From 1920 he composed extensively. Among his four one-act operas, *Gualicho*, with libretto by Rosario Beltrán Núñez, was mounted at the Colón in 1940. His Inca legend ballet *El Pillán* was danced at the Colón in 1949. Alfredo Casella conducted the premiere of his symphonic poem *Eros* in 1930 at the Teatro Politeuma.

5102 Móndolo, Ana María. Alfredo L.
Schiuma, 1885–1963. (*Rev. Inst. Invest. Musicol. Carlos Vega*, 10 : 10, 1989,
p. 321–346.)

Born at Spinazzola, Italy, Alfredo Luis
Schiuma (1885–1963) reached Buenos Aires
in 1888 with his family. Following in the
footsteps of his musician father Raphael
Schiuma (1844–1940), he became a distinguished violinist, composer, and choral and
orchestra director. Among his six operas,
four were produced at Buenos Aires: *Amy
Robsart* (1917); *La Sirocchia* (1920), later retitled as *Litigio de Amor* (1932); *Tabaré*
(1923); *Las Vírgenes del Sol* (1938). Despite a
resolution presented in 1963 to the H. Consejo Deliberante de la Ciudad de Buenos
Aires to publish piano-vocal scores of *Tabaré*
and *Las Vírgenes del Sol*, they remain unpublished, as does the rest of his extensive
oeuvre (which is now guarded by the author
of this excellent article).

5103 Móndolo, Ana María. Catálogo clasificado de la obra de Celestino Piaggio.
(*Rev. Inst. Invest. Musicol. Carlos Vega*, 9 : 9,
1988, p. 79–94)

Born at Concordia, Entre Ríos prov.,
Celestino Piaggio (1886–1931) died at Buenos
Aires. His compositions (songs, piano pieces,
a C minor overture for full orchestra written
1913–14) are youthful works antedating
1920. After a European sojourn during which
he made headway in Romania as a conductor,
in 1921 he returned to Buenos Aires and
served Argentine music by promoting and
conducting the works of his compatriots.
From 1924 to his death he was subdirector
of the Conservatorio de Música de Buenos
Aires, an Alberto Williams entity.

5104 Móndolo, Ana María and **Néstor Ramón Cenal.** Roberto García Morillo.
(*Rev. Inst. Invest. Musicol. Carlos Vega*,
10 : 10, 1989, p. 33–71)

Chronological table of the composer's
works (p. 35–64)—grouped under such
genres as stage music, orchestral, orchestra
with soloists and with soloists and chorus,
chamber works, piano solos, voice with
piano, and juvenilia—reveals the enormous
fecundity of this composer born at Buenos
Aires in 1911. For forty years a newspaper
critic (*La Nación* 1938–79), author of six
books, and frequent transcriber of other Argentine composers' works, García Morillo
also received a host of prizes and other distinctions, and was rector of the Conservatorio Nacional de Música (1972–79).

5105 Moreno Cha, Ercilia. El Instituto Nacional de Musicología Carlos Vega.
(*Rev. Inst. Invest. Musicol. Carlos Vega*, 9 : 9,
1988, p. 95–103)

By Argentine government decree, in
1971 the former Instituo de Musicología Nativa (under the Secretaría de Cultura since
1961) became the Instituto Nacional de Musicología, with a staff of 15. By Dr. Arturo
López Peña's resolution in 1973, the name
"Carlos Vega" was added, to honor the paladin of Argentinian musicology who in 1931
had founded the Gabinete de Musicología
Indígena, ancestor of the present Instituto
Nacional.

5106 Roldán, Waldemar Axel. Música colonial en la Argentina: la enseñanza musical. Buenos Aires: El Ateneo, 1988. 133 p.:
appendices, bibl., facsims.

Data concerns 18th-century teaching
methods, performances, and (in appendices)
documents relating to colonial music in the
Argentine Archivo General de la Nación; reviewed in *Latin American Music Review*
(10 : 1, 1989, p. 186–187).

5107 Rosselli, John. The opera business and
the Italian immigrant community in
Latin America, 1820–1930: the example of
Buenos Aires. (*Past Present*, 127, May 1990,
p. 155–182)

The purpose of this documented article is threefold: "to study Italian singers in
Latin America from about 1820 as part of the
great stream of Italian migration; to set out
the growth of opera into an important business, particularly in Buenos Aires, between
1870 and 1930; and to ask how this illustrates the relationship between the large Italian community and the immense, almost
empty country that was its host."

5108 Stevenson, Robert Murrell. Zipoli's
transit through dictionaries: a tercentenary remembrance. (*Inter-Am. Music Rev.*,
9 : 2, Spring/Summer 1988, p. 21–89, bibl.,
facsims., ill.)

This compendium of all information
available in 1988 on Domenico Zipoli (1688–
1726) brings up to date the material on him

published in The New Grove (1980, v. 20, p. 696–697), and is fleshed out with a transcription of his Mass copied at Potosí in 1784, formerly housed in the Sucre Cathedral music archive where it was discovered by Stevenson in 1959.

5109 Suárez Urtubey, Pola. Juan Bautista Alberdi: teoría y praxis de la música. (*Rev. Inst. Invest. Musicol. Carlos Vega,* 10:10, 1989, p. 157–199, bibl.)

Contrary to the opinions of the rank and file of Alberdi's biographers, music played as significant a role in his formative years as it did in the lives of Giuseppe Mazzini, Nietzsche, and Schopenhauer. With great acuity the author analyzes Alberdi's *Ensayo sobre un método nuevo para aprender a tocar el piano* and *El espíritu de la música a la capacidad de todo el mundo* (both dated 1832), and identifies his sources. Next, she evaluates the repercussions of Alberdi's *Ensayo.* She concludes with "Obras Escritas de Alberdi sobre Música."

5110 Terzián, Alicia. Impulsadora del americanismo en la música. (*Rev. Music. Chil.,* 43:171, enero/junio 1989, p. 112–113)

Terzián (b. Córdoba, 1936) is profiled biographically in both Aaron I. Cohen's *International encyclopedia of women composers,* 2d ed. (New York: Books and Music, 1987, vol. 2, p. 693), and in *Dizionario enciclopedico universale della musica e dei musiciti; le biografie* (Torino, Italy: Unione Tipografico-Editrice Torinese, 1988, vol. 8, p. 7).

5111 Veniard, Juan María. Arturo Berutti: un argentino en el mundo de la ópera. Buenos Aires: Instituto Nacional de Musicología Carlos Vega, Dirección Nacional de Música, Secretaría de Cultura, Ministerio de Educación y Justicia, 1988. 365 p., 8 p. of plates: bibl., ill.

Among 19th-century Latins, Arturo Berutti (1858–1938) had more operas produced than any other except Carlos Gomes. The eight produced were *Vendetta* (1890), *Evangelina* (1892–3), *Tarass Bulba* (1893–4), *Pampa* (1896), *Yupanki* (1897–9), *Khrysé* (1900–1), *Horrida nox* (1904), and *Glieroi* (1906–9). Berutti's truncated archive, presented in 1979 to the Instituto Nacional de Musicología Carlos Vega by J.M. Insaurralde,

provided Veniard the data contained in this valuable book.

5112 Zipoli, Domenico. Missa in F. (*Inter-Am. Music Rev.,* 9:2, Spring/Summer 1988, p. 35–89)

Robert Stevenson's transcription and realization of Zipoli's Mass copied in 1784 at Potosí, which was discovered by Stevenson in the Sucre, Bolivia, cathedral archive in 1959 (see *The music of Peru: aboriginal and viceroyal epochs,* Washington: Organization of American States, 1960, p. 178–179).

BOLIVIA

5113 Auza León, Atiliano. Simbiosis cultural de la música boliviana. La Paz: Producciones CIMA, 1989. 151 p.: ill.

Valiant attempt to bring under control inaccessible biographical data. Born at Sucre (1928), Auza León graduated from the Escuela Normal Integra José Antonio de Sucre and the Conservatorio Nacional at La Paz before studying violin and composition at the Centro Latinoamericano de Altos Estudios Musicales del Instituto Torcuato Di Tella at Buenos Aires in 1966. Upon returning to Bolivia, he occupied numerous posts which are listed here along with his compositions and literary products (p. 72). Book profiles such important comtemporaries as: Rogers Becerra Cassanovas (b. Trinidad, 1924), Ernesto Cavour (b. La Paz, 1940), Emilio Gutiérrez Illanas (b. Depto. de Cochabamba, 1925), Humberto Iporre Salinas (b. Potosí, 1915), Ernesto Lafaye (1915–1988), Pastor Acha Martínez (b. Villa Abecia, 1928), Jaime Mendoza Nava (b. La Paz, 1925), Gustavo Navarre Viscarra I (b. La Paz, 1931), Néstor Olmos Molina (b. La Paz, 1926), Gilberto Rojas E. (b. Cochabamba, 1938), and Milo Soruco Arancibia (b. Tarija, 1927). Author also profiles or lists interpreters and conductors (p. 121–145).

5114 Boletín. No. 1, enero/feb. 1988–; No. 2, marzo/abril 1988–; No. 3, mayo/junio 1988–; No. 4, julio/agosto 1988–; No. 8, nov. 1988–; No. 9, dic. 1988–. Bibliografía sobre Música Tradicional. Cochabamba, Bolivia: Centro de Documentación de Música Boliviana; Centro Pedagógico y Cultural Portales.

Prepared by Walter Sánchez, each *Boletín* contains 100 bibliographic references ordered alphabetically. Nos. 3 and 8 list articles in newspapers published at La Paz, Cochabamba, Santa Cruz, Sucre, and Potosí. These newspaper articles are all the more important because Bolivia lacks periodicals specifically devoted to music.

5115 Boletín. No. 6, oct. 1988– . Música Autóctona del Norte de Potosí. Cochabamba, Bolivia: Centro Pedagógico y Cultural Portales; Centro de Documentación de Música Boliviana.

In conjution with the 8th Festival Nacional Luz Milá Patiño, organized by the Centro de Documentación de Música Boliviana and coordinated in 1988 by Luz María Calvo, the centro sponsored a *boletín* dedicated to the autochthonous music in the region north of Potosí. In this issue Walter Sánchez offers two maps of the region; describes the chief instruments and their use; and correlates musical happenings with the all-important agricultural calendar.

5116 Boletín. No. 10, enero/feb. 1989– .
Apuntes sobre la Música Aymara en el Período Prehispánico. Cochabamba, Bolivia: Centro de Documentación de Música Boliviana; Centro Pedagógico y Cultural Portales.

Relying extensively on Ludovico Bertonio's *Arte breve dela lengua aymara* (Rome, 1603), expanded into *Vocabulario dela lengua aymara* (Lima [Juli], 1612), Walter Sánchez explains such terms as *haylli, kochu, quicutha, maketa, haccutha, quechuya, sokhatha, huallatha, huayno,* and identifies names for instruments—among them *sicu, ayarichi, pincullo, quepa,* and *saccapa.*

5117 Cavour Aramayo, Ernesto. El charango: su vida, costumbres y desventuras. La Paz: Producciones CIMA, 1988. 310 p.: bibl., ill., ports.

The author (b. La Paz, 1940) founded the *charango* trio *Los Jairas* that in 1965 won first prize in the Primer Festival Latinoamericano de Folklore at Salta, Argentina, and in 1979 toured Japan (p. 232). The present omnigatherum of 55 chapters follows an unpredictable sequence: origins of the *charango,* areas where it is played, variant reentrant tunings of its five double-string courses (p. 70–76), *charango* constructions, its place

in Bolivian education, lives of famous players, and its diffusion throughout the world. Much of the information is now dated; publication of the book had been planned originally for 1980. Properly edited and indexed, it could have been a prime document.

5118 Terceros Rojas, Armando and **Alex Parada Serrano.** Libro de oro de los intérpretes de la música cruceña. Santa Cruz de la Sierra, Bolivia: AP Indústrias Gráficas, 1989. 249 p.: ill.

Contains biographies (with exact birthdates) of 107 performers and 6 band directors and histories of: different duos, trios, and larger groups, six Santa Cruz radio stations, the Cine "Palace Theatre," and three Sombrero E Sao festivals. The chief instrument of three-fourths of the interpreters is guitar; Lyra company in La Paz issued one-fourth of the 78 rpms and LPs; La Pascana *confiteria* in Sierra de la Cruz was the locale favored by 29.2% of the performers; Pena de Bloming (La Bamba) by 12.5%; only 31.7% of the artists were either music professionals or teachers of music. The most recorded composer is Godofredo Núñez Chávez, born in 1924 at Montero, Santa Cruz dept.; next is Nicolás Menacho Tarabillo (Jiguerillo), born at Santa Cruz in 1925. Both studied at the Colegio Nacional Florida, from which 25.5% of the personalities in this book emerged. This excellent compilation, financed by Cerveceria Santa Cruz S. A., is not likely to be bettered any time soon.

BRAZIL

5119 Andrade, Mário de. Dicionário musical brasileiro. Coordenação de Oneyda Alvarenga e Flávia Camargo Toni. Brasília: Ministério da Cultura; São Paulo: Instituto de Estudos Brasileiros da Univ. de São Paulo; Editora da Univ. de São Paulo; Belo Horizonte, Brazil: Editora Itatiaia, 1989. 701 p.: bibl., ill. (Col. Reconquista do Brasil; 2a sér.,162)

Andrade (1893–1945) began the present dictionary in 1929, but did not complete it before his death; he bequeathed what he had done on it (3,754 terms) to his disciple Alvarenga. In reality the present subject dictionary is hers. In 1982, she gathered about her a group of assisting researchers and guided the work's elaboration until her death. Terms such as *bossa nova* and *tropicália* do not appear. The data concerning dances and instruments not indigenous to Brazil are frequently misleading, out-of-date, and even wrong. Perhaps these deficiencies are due to the absence of any recent foreign dictionaries from the bibliography (the most recent English-language dictionary was the third edition of Grove).

5120 Appleby, David P. Heitor Villa-Lobos: a bio-bibliography. New York: Greenwood Press, 1988. 358 p.: bibl., index, 1 port. (Bio-bibliographies in music, 0742–6968; 9)

Representing years of devoted effort to bring the sprawling and enormous Villa-Lobos bibliography under control, this valiant attempt omits books as important as Erico Veríssimo's *A volta do Gato Preto* (Rio, 1956), and easily available articles such as "Heitor Villa-Lobos's Los Angeles Connection" and "Brazilian Report of Villa-Lobos's First Los Angeles Visit," both in *Inter-American Music Review* (9:1, Fall/Winter 1987). Berkeley, California is misspelled, as is also the name of the conductor whose orchestra Villa-Lobos conducted in Los Angeles. The compendious listing of Lisa Peppercorn's writings on Villa-Lobos is extremely welcome. Arminda's death before publication of this book enabled Appleby to reveal that she misrepresented her age by five years. In a future reprinting, the very important literature that appeared in the 1987 centennial year of the composer's birth should be assessed, and the "Works" section amplified with bibliographic references to articles having to do with the listed compositions.

5121 Baptista Filho, Zito. A ópera. Rio de Janeiro: Editora Nova Fronteira, 1987. 705 p.: index.

Of the 222 operas analyzed in this volume, 16 are by Brazilians. Extremely valuable are the plot summaries, names of librettists, tables of singers, and histories of productions. Alphabetically by composer, the Brazilians are: Oswaldo Passos Cabral (b. 1905), *Siloé*; Antônio Carlos Gomes (1836–1896), *Lo schiavo, Fosca, Il Guarany, Maria Tudor, A noite do Castelo, Salvator Rosa*; Mozart Camargo Guarnreri (b. 1907), *Pedro Malazarte*; Francisco Mignone (1897–1986), *O Chalaça, O Contratador de Diamantes, O Inocente, O sargento de milicias*; José de

Lima Siqueira (b. 1907), *A compadecida*; Heitor Villa-Lobos (1887–1959), *Izaht, A Menina das nuvens, Yerma.*

5122 Barros, Ermelinda Azevedo Paz de Souza. Heitor Villa-Lobos: o educador. (*in* Prêmio grandes educadores brasileiros: monografias premiadas, 1988. Brasília: Ministério da Educação, Instituto Nacional de Estudos e Pesquisas Educacionais, 1989, p. 59–183, bibl., facsims., music, tables)

According to the author, Villa-Lobos' greatest service to his country was as an educator. In 1980 Jeanne Venzo Clement completed a 2-vol. doctoral thesis at the Sorbonne entitled *Villa-Lobos educateur*. Maria Célia Machado's *Heitor Villa-Lobos* (Rio: Francisco Alves; Univ. Federal de Rio de Janeiro, 1987); and Villa-Lobos' own publications, especially his *O ensino popular da música no Brasil* (Rio: Depto. de Educação do Distrito Federal, 1937), *Programa do ensino de música* (Rio: Depto. Educação do Distrito Federal, Série C, Programas e Guias de Ensino, 6, Secretaria Geral de Educação e Cultura, 1937), and "Educação Musical" in *Boletín Latino Americano de Música* (6:495–588, abril 1946), provide insight into his monumental efforts at making singing instruction and choral festivals mandatory throughout the nation—or at least in the Federal District during Getúlio Vargas' presidency. The author enriches her monograph with transcriptions of interviews (Dec. 1986-Sept. 1987) with 11 musical leaders who knew Villa-Lobos personally. She also gives facsimiles of three items in Villa-Lobos' *Collecção Escolar* (*As creançãs*, canção a 4; *O Gaturamo*, coro a 3; and *Meu Brasil*, an instrumentally accompanied samba).

5123 Béhague, Gerard. Mignone famiglia di musicisti brasiliani di origine italiana. (*in* Dizionario enciclopedico universale della musica e dei musicisti: le biografie, v. 5. Torino, Italy: Unione Tipografico-Editrice Torinese, 1988, p. 91–92, bibl.)

Profiles four Mignone family members, including Francisco Mignone (1897–1986) who was born the year after his father Alferio (1875–1960) emigrated from Italy to accept a position as flutist with São Paulo Teatro municipal orchestra.

5124 Bispo, Antonio Alexandre. Fundamentos gnosticistas do pensamento sincretístico no Brasil: a necessidade absoluta de uma revisão da literatura a respeito dos cultos afro-brasileiros. (*Corresp. Musicol.*, 2, 1989, p. 18)

During a colloquium (Bonn, 1989) the editor of this bulletin countered the prevalent notion that Brazilian slaves were the first to link African deities, such as Oxumaré, Oxum, Yemanjá, Xango, Omulu, Exu, Ogum, Yansa, and Ossaim with Catholic saints. Linking of such instruments as *atabaques* with religious concepts was already prevalent in the Iberian peninsula long before 1500.

5125 Bispo, Antonio Alexandre. Semiologia gregoriana no contexto histórico-musicológico do mundo de língua portuguesa. (*Corresp. Musicol.*, 3 : 1, 1990, p. 1–8)

In one of his most questionable *ipse dixits*, Mário de Andrade claimed that plainchant is incapable of inspiring expressive art music; rather, only popular song can do so (*Obras completas*, vol. 7, São Paulo, 1963, p. 38). Among Gregorian specialists now active in Brazil, Ir. Maria do Redentor, C.S.A. (Eleanor Florence Dewey) ranks among the highest. Her brilliant trajectory is covered in this valuable article.

5126 Brasilien: Einführung in Musiktraditionen Brasiliens. Herausgegeben von Tiago de Oliveira Pinto. Mainz, Germany; New York: Schott, 1986. 227 p.: bibl., ill. (some col.), index. (Welt Musik)

Preceded by the editor's overview, this introduction to Brazilian musical traditions contains 12 articles. Articles by Menezes Bastos and Travassos explore ethongraphic events in High Xingu locales; António Alexandre Bispo emphasizes Portuguese inherence in the music heard during Brazilian Catholic festivities; Julieta de Andrade's article on *cururu* deals with song duels in São Paulo state. The editor and José Maria Tenório Rocha cooperatively discuss "Bandas de Pífanos, die Instrumental-Ensembles des Nordoestens." Afro-Brazilian music finds its exponents in the editor who writes on *candomblé* music and on "Capoeira, das Kampfspiel aus Bahia." Kazadi wa Makuna analyzes the "Bamba-meu-Boi" in Maranhão. Essays on *chôro* ensembles and Rio's samba schools lightly touch on popular currents. In her review (*Ethnomusicology*, 34 : 1, Winter 1990, p. 16–167), Maria Elizabeth Lucas disparaged

the emphasis on the music of northeastern Brazil, the neglect of popular music traditions, and the "passé" view of Brazilian music as consisting of three separable strands.

5127 Calado, Carlos. Jazz ao vivo. São Paulo: Editora Perspectiva, 1989. 206 p.: ill. (Debates; 227: Música)

Wielding a wide lens camera, the author gives newspaper-worthy profiles of Courtney Pine (b. London, 1964), Herbie Hancock (b. Chicago, 1940), Bobby McFerrin (b. New York, 1950), Sarah Vaughan (b. Newark, 1924), Egberto Gismonti (b. Carmo, Brazil, 1947), André Geraissati, and more than 50 others who have toured Brazil or become fetishes by reason of their recordings.

5128 Carvalho, Hermínio Bello de. O canto do pajé: Villa-Lobos e a música popular brasileira. Rio de Janeiro: Espaço e Tempo, 1988. 186, 11 p. of plates: bibl., ill., ports. (Col. Pensando o Brasil; 8)

Fifteen miscellaneous studies of unequal value following this order: 1) "Arquivos;" 2) "Nem Pensar;" 3) "Milagre Villa-Lobos;" 4) "Donga, Memórias de um Gravador;" 5) "Oscar Cáceres, uma Fieira de Histórias;" 6) "Villa-Lobos e a Música Popular;" 7) "Mimita e Villa-Lobos;" 8) "Mindinha de Villa-Lobos;" 9) "Herivelto Martins: Ele era um Chato;" 10) "Villa e o Modinheiro Paulo Tapajós;" 11) "Villa: um Caleidoscópio;" 12) "Sodade do Cordão;" 13) "Mario e Villa-Lobos;" 14) "Villa-Lobos e o Violão;" and 15) "Olga Praguer: Uma Grande Paixão."

5129 Carvalho, Piedade. Villa-Lobos: do crepúsculo à alvorada. Rio de Janeiro: Tempo Brasileiro, 1987. 151 p.: bibl., music.

Prefacing her book with an original poem, author declares at the outset that chronology—when a work was written, how it reflected its ambience—takes no priority with her. Instead, she prefers to examine Villa-Lobos' psyche. After quoting his statement, "My works are emotional letters that I wrote to posterity without hope of response," she offers this book as the response to "his letters to posterity."

5130 Coelho, Vera Penteado. Informações sobre um instrumento musical dos índios waurá. (*Rev. Mus. Paul.*, 33, 1988, p. 193–224, bibl., ill.)

The *kauka atain* is a slim recorder with four finger holes. Some two feet in length, it measures only an inch in diameter at the blow hole. The mouth end is covered with forest birds' wax. The Waura, who play it standing, sitting, or dancing, live in an Alto Xingo locality. The transcriptions (p. 213–219) of four lengthy solo gracenoted wide-skipping melodies recorded by the author in 1980 contain numerous partials of the fundamentals (d f f# b; B d f). The player, Yawalá, identified as the son and heir apparent of chief Malakuyawá, plays the *kauka atain* in curing rituals as does his father.

5131 Concerto com obras de autores brasileiros na véspera do dia da independência em Bonn. (*Coresp. Musicol.*, 2, 1989, p. 18–19)

A 1989 colloquim on traditional Brazilian musical usages closed at Bonn with a concert including the following works: Henrique Oswald (1852–1931), *Sonata, op. 21*; Luis Levy (1897–1986), *Tres valsas para fagote*; José Siqueira, *Tres estudos para trompa e piano* (1964); Osvaldo Lacerda, *Tres peças para trompa e piano* (1983); Gilberto Mendes, *Rancheira para fagote e piano* (1987); Breno Blauth, *Sonatina T 48 para trompa e piano* (1974).

5132 Consulate General of Brazil, Los Angeles. Ricardo Tacuchian in the USA, 1987–1990. Preface by Celso Diniz. Foreword by Aurelio de la Vega. Los Angeles: Consulate General of Brazil, s.d. 21 p.

Includes information on concerts, reviews, lectures, and honors received by the Armenian-descended Brazilian composer (b. Rio de Janeiro, 1939) during his three years in the US.

5133 Dias, Marie Thérèse Odette Ernest. Sarau da República. (*Humanidades/ Brasília*, 7 : 1, 1990, p. 5–9, bibl., ill.)

In 1889, the day that the republic was proclaimed, there was sung in the streets of Rio de Janeiro not the hymn with music by Francisco Manuel da Silva, but the *Marseillaise*, with new "positivist" Brazilian text by Montenegro Cordeiro. Bushmann e Guimarães published 1,000 copies, each selling for 1,000 réis. French influences dominated the music of the year—in the variety shows (*A República: Revista dos acontecimentos de 1889* with music by Aluísio Azevedo, and *Frotzmac* with music by Leocádio Rayol); and in the quadrilles (*O Príncipe Imperial*,

Os lanceiros da república, and Ernesto Nazareth's quadrille *Chile-Brasil* danced on Nov. 9, 1889, at the last court ball of Pedro II's reign).

5134 Eisenhood, Elizabeth D.; Joseph C. Hickerson; and Therese Langer. Brazil recordings in the Archive of Folk Culture. Washington: American Folklife Center, Library of Congress; 1990. 4 p.

Cataloged holdings of Afro-Bahian, tribal, and regional musics. Many are copies from other collections.

5135 Fonseca, Maria da Conceição Rezende. A música na história de Minas colonial. Belo Horizonte, Brazil: Editora Itatiaia; Brasília: Instituto Nacional do Livro, 1989. 765 p.: bibl.

Dedicated to her husband Aurélio, and prefaced by *homenagem* to the Minister of culture José Aparecido de Oliveira, this omnigatherum of clippings and citations testifies to the devotion of the author to the art of music. Waldemar de Almeida Barbosa sent the author a testimonial dated May 17, 1990 stating: "Sua pesquisa foi profunda. Trata-se de obra de fôlego em que pormenorizou a formação histórica e musical de Minas." An example of the author's unindexed, unfootnoted prose is the following. "J.S. Bach tinha uma mensagem a transmitir à humanidade através da música: mostrar a glória de Deus através de sua Biblia e sua relação com os homens." (p. 448). The praiseworthy intentions of this compendium are seriously compromised by its scrapbook format, haphazard and inadequate footnoting, purple prose when the author is not quoting others, absence of musical examples, and its lack of even so basic a necessity as a paged table of contents.

5136 Hino Constitucional do D. Pedro I divulgado na Alemanha do século XIX. (*Coresp. Musicol.*, 3 : 1, 1990, p. 13–17, facsims., ill., music)

The Rio Biblioteca Nacional has a copy of the Portuguese edition of Pedro I's hymn, composed March 31, 1821, and first sung in the Real Teatro São João at Rio on May 13, at Praia Grande (now Niterói) on July 20, in the provinces soon thereafter, and in Lisbon at the Teatro São Carlos on August 24. The city of Munich has both the Portuguese edition and a more carefully printed Munich edition of Pedro I's "Hino," with German text translated by W. Gerhard.

5137 Horta, Luís Paulo. Villa-Lobos: uma introdução. Rio de Janeiro: J. Zahar Editor, 1987. 165 p., 16 p. of plates: bibl., ill., ports.

Prepared by the (since 1970) music critic for *Jornal do Brasil*, this introduction contains a chronology, thumbnail analysis of works, and a catalog organized by Arminda Villa-Lobos that was published in 1965 (revised version, 1972) by the Museu Villa-Lobos. Another popularization published to mark the composer's centenary, this work deifies him.

5138 Instrumentos musicais brasileiros. Coordenação de Ricardo Ohtake. Texto de João Gabriel de Lima. Fotos de Romulo Fialdini. São Paulo?: Rhodia, 1988. 212 p.: bibl., ill. (chiefly col.).

This lavish coffee-table book contains superb photos, mostly in color, of instruments housed in collections at São Paulo, Recife, Belo Horizonte, Bahia, and Rio de Janeiro. The four sections, "Sounds of the Forest," "Instruments Played by Hands," "Urban Instruments," and "Magic Craft of Inventors," follow no scientifically recognized classification scheme, nor are there any indexes.

5139 Lange, Francisco Curt. La actividad musical en la Capitanía General de Minas Gerais, Brasil, siglo XVIII. (*Rev. Music. Venez.*, 9:26, sept./dic. 1988, p. 45–65)

Lange's first Brazilian researches centered at Rio and São Paulo in 1934. Ten years later he began investigating the previously unknown musical history of Minas Gerais. He bought the inherited archive of Justino da Conceição, and then that of Orozimbo Parreiras containing an *antifona* of José Joaquim Emérico Lobo de Mesquita dated 1787. Subsequently, Lange was able to identify and save approximately 50 works by this important Minas Gerais mulatto composer (d. Rio, 1805). The stitching together of the dispersed and abandoned fabric of Minas Gerais musical life in the late 18th century entitles Lange to a primordial place among musicologists specializing in Latin America.

5140 Marlos Nobre en Londres. (*Rev. Music. Chil.*, 42:169, enero/junio 1988, p. 95–96)

On April 28, 1988, sponsored by the Latin American and Caribbean Society (LACCS) and the Brazilian Embassy, Nobre (b. Recife, 1939) conducted the St. John's orchestra playing his *Ukrinmakinkrin*, 1964 (soprano, flute, oboe, trumpet, piano); cantata *O Canto Multiplicado*, 1972 (soprano and string orchestra); *Desafio VII*, 1968 (short concerto for viola and strings); *Variações Ritmicas*, 1963 (piano and percussion); and *Primer Cuarteto*, 1967 (strings).

5141 Mesquita, José Joaquim Emérico Lobo de. Tercio: para solista, coro e orquestra de cordas, 1783. Texto [i.e. prefácio] de Maria da Conceição Rezende Fonseca. Rio de Janeiro: FUNARTE, Instituto Nacional de Música, Projeto Memória Musical Brasileira, 1985. 1 score (66 p.).

Lobo de Mesquita (1746–1805), a free mulatto, was born at Vila do Principe do Serro Frio. After 20 years at Arraial do Tejuco (Diamantina), where he performed numerous musical functions, he transferred in 1798 to Vila Rica (Ouro Preto) and in 1800 to Rio where he was organist of the Venerável Ordem Terceira do Carmo until his death. The *tercio* shown in facsimile (p. 37–66), his sole extant work in autograph score (strings, continuo, SAB), today survives at the Museu da Música da Arquidiocese de Mariana. Rezende's thematica catalog (p. 14–33) of 78 works—62 with incipits—by Mesquita, or attributed to him, was saluted by F.C. Lange in a certificate dated at Belo Horizonte Aug. 21, 1989.

Mott, Luiz Roberto de Barros. Acotundá: raízes setecentistas do sincretismo religioso afro-brasileiro. See item **657.**

5142 Muricy, José Cândido de Andrade et al. Carlos Gomes: uma obra em foco. Rio de Janeiro: FUNARTE, Instituto Nacional de Música/Projeto Memória Musical Brasileira, 1987. 215 p.: bibl., facsims., music, ports.

Chapters by Vicente Salles, "Carlos Gomes: Passagem e Influência em Várias Regiões Brasileiras;" Bruno Kiefer, "A Obra Pianística de Antônio Carlos Gomes;" Léa Vincour Freitag, "Carlos Gomes: As Canções de Câmara;" and Luis Heitor Corrêa de Azevedo, "Projeção no exterior" were commissioned by the Instituto Nacional de Música/Funarte in the sesquicentennial year of Gomes' birth. The succeeding chapters, devoted to individual operas dated 1861–91, and to the choral symphonic poem (*Colombo*, 1892), were published in the centennial Gomes number of *Revista Brasileira de Música* (3:2, p. 201–316). Convenient as it is to have the 1936 essays on *A noite do Castelo, Joana de Flandres, Il Guarany, Fosca, Salvator Rosa, Maria Tudor, Lo schiavo*, and *Condor* back in print, each is extremely dated in its approach; each obviously takes no account of intervening scholarship; and each is less desirable because footnotes that were on the page in 1936 are now placed at ends of chapters. If funds to commission new studies of the operas were unavailable, it would have been much better to have published a facsimile edition of the 1936 (478 p.) Gomes number integrally.

5143 Peppercorn, Lisa M. Heitor Villa-Lobos: profilo del compositore brasiliano. (*Nuova Riv. Music. Ital.*, 19:2, 1985, p. 254–267)

The vertiginous catapulting of Villa-Lobos to universal fame at age 57 resulted in no small part from F.D. Roosevelt's Good Neighbor Policy. Peppercorn, whose Villa-Lobos bibliography is huge, made a career writing articles about him, but without ever winning the affection of Brazilianists.

5144 Pequeno, Mercedes Reis. Brazilian music publishers. (*Inter-Am. Music Rev.*, 9:2, Spring/Summer 1988, p. 91–104, facsims., ill., music)

Editor's translation and revision of Reis Pequeno's article "Impressão Musical no Brazil" in *Enciclopédia da música brasileira: erudita, folclórica, popular* (São Paulo: Art Editora, 1977, v. 1, p. 353–363). Prior to 1900, no country in Latin America boasted a greater number of music publishers and publications than Brazil. This article is the most detailed and authoritative ever issued on music publication in a Latin American country.

5145 Perrone, Charles A. Masters of contemporary Brazilian song: MPB [Música Popular Brasileira], 1965–1985. Austin: Univ. of Texas Press, 1989. 253 p., 5 p. of plates: bibl., index, ports.

The author, who was assistant professor of Portuguese and Luso-Brazilian culture and literature at the Univ. of Florida when this book was published, devotes chaps. 1–5 to lyrics sung by Chico Buarque de Hollanda, Caetano Veloso, Gilberto Gil, Milton Nasci-

mento and the pair João Bosco and Aldir Blanc. Although attractively presented so far as analysis of texts goes, the musical comments run in this vein: "Bosco's vocal attack—curt, repetitive, hardly melodious at the outset—acoustically shapes a bellicose mood." Minus musical notations, the book also diminishes copyright problems (see "Permissions," p. 251–253) by offering only English translations for the overwhelming majority of the lyrics discussed. His Univ. of Texas PhD dissertation (University Microfilms 85–27632, 1985), from which "an appreciable portion of this book was adapted and which is titled *Lyric and lyrics: the poetry of song in Brazil*," did include Portuguese texts and is therefore much more useful to the student of the songs as such.

5146 Personalidades: Pe. Jaime Cavalcanti Diniz. (*Corresp. Musicol.*, 1, 1989, p. 15–20)

Diniz died on May 27, 1989. The preeminent musicologist of northern Brazil, this necrology is the fullest account of his life and career accessible in a journal circulating outside Brazil, but it does not tell where he died (presumably Recife).

5147 Personalidades: Ernst Widmer. (*Corresp. Musicol.*, 3:1, 1990, p. 21–23)

Ernst Widmer (1927–90), a resident since 1956 in Bahia where Hans Joachim Koellreutter hired him to teach in the Univ. Federal da Bahia, died in his natal city—Aarau, Switzerland. Widmer's pupils included Lindemberg Cardoso, Fernando Cerqueira, January Oliveira, and at least six other members of the Grupo de Compositores da Bahia founded by him in 1966. This useful necrology lists Widmer's chief work through opus 127 (1981).

5148 Rossi, Franco. Villa-Lobos, Heitor. (*in* Dizionario enciclopedico universale della musica e dei musicisti: le biografie, v. 8. Torino, Italy: Unione Tipografico-Editrice Torinese, 1988, p. 243–246, bibl.)

Longest and most detailed of any Latin American's biography in this encyclopedia, article goes beyond material in other music lexicons.

5149 Silva, Marília Trindade Barboza da. Negro em roda de samba: herança africana na música popular brasileira. (*Tempo Bras.*, 92/93, jan./junho 1988, p. 105–118)

The so-called samba *Pelo Telefone*, recorded in 1902 by Ernesto dos Santos (Donga), was in reality a *maxixe* or Brazilian tango. In 1892 Ernesto Nazareth published the polca-tango *Rayon D'Or*, and in 1893, *Brejeiro*.

5150 Stevenson, Robert Murrell. Brazilian report of Villa-Lobos's first Los Angeles visit. (*Inter-Am. Music Rev.*, 9:1, Fall/Winter 1987, p. 9–10)

Erico Veríssimo (1905–1975), Villa-Lobos's interpreter during his 1944 visit, rated him "um homem distraído, desligante e egocéntrico" (*A volta do gato preto*, Rio, 1956, p. 331).

5151 Stevenson, Robert Murrell. First Portuguese New World encounter. (*Inter-Am. Music Rev.*, 8:2, Spring/Summer 1987, p. 99)

Pedro Álvares Cabral's fleet that departed from Lisbon March 8, 1500 and reached Brazil at Corôa Vermelha, Baía Cabrália April 22, 1500 carried numerous musical instruments, including *trombetas, atabaques, sistros, tambores, frautas, pandeiros*, and *gaitas*. At sung Mass celebrated April 26, 70 Indians heard music by several Franciscans—among whom were organist Frei Maffei and singer Frei Pedro Neto. After Mass a bagpipe player from the fleet provided music which the Tupinquin Indians danced. On Thursday, April 30, they danced to the sound of a *tamboril*.

5152 Stevenson, Robert Murrell. Heitor Villa-Lobos's Los Angeles connection: a centennial tribute. (*Inter-Am. Music Rev.*, 9:1, Fall/Winter 1987, p. 1–8, ill.)

On Nov. 26, 1944 at Los Angeles's Philharmonic Auditorium—Villa Lobos conducted his first concert in the US. However, Werner Janssen had introduced two excerpts from Villa-Lobos' *Bachianas Brasileiras No. 2* to Los Angeles audiences on Oct. 30, 1941. *Magdalena* awaited July 26, 1948, for its world premiere at Los Angeles; it then traveled to San Francisco (Aug. 16) and to Billy Rose's Ziegfeld Theater in New York City (Sept. 20) where it remained for 88 performances.

5153 Toni, Flávia Camargo. Mário de Andrade e Villa-Lobos: pesquisa e texto. São Paulo: Centro Cultural São Paulo, 1987. 120 p.: bibl., ports.

This collection of Andrade's published comments is preceded by his unpublished criticisms. While fully aware that Villa-Lobos' national as well as international successes stemmed from the approbation that he had won at Paris from critics such as Henry Prunières (1886–1942) and artists such as Artur Rubinstein, Andrade resented their reasons for embracing Villa-Lobos. In Prunières's judgment, what the Americas had to offer Paris was solely sensuality, exoticism, and savagery, but he was so ignorant of Brazil that he named Buenos Aires as its capital. Andrade was among the first to utterly discount Villa-Lobos' "dating" of his own works, and he also pioneered in demonstrating how deceptive Villa-Lobos was when he fattened his catalog with self-proclaimed new works that were in reality mere arrangements and compendia of earlier compositions given different names. No composer exceeded Villa-Lobos in self-puffery and deceit, and none so lacked any ability to evaluate his own works. As Jorge Coli remarks in his synthesis that prefaces this present book, Andrade detested Villa-Lobos' tasteless appetite for the colossal that urged him onward during Getúlio Vargas' presidency.

5154 Valença, José Rolim. Modinha: raízes da música do povo. São Paulo: Dow, 1985. 120 p.: bibl., ill. (chiefly col.).

Collection of color plates—showing instruments, title pages, music scores, performers' and composers' likenesses—serves as a visual history to 1900. The text surrounding the illustrations moves from the *corno e buzina* played by the Indians whom Vaz da Caminha heard in 1500, through the gamut of colonial theater, dance, and church sounds, to the upsurge of art music during the imperial period. The last three photographs show the cylinder and gramophone tentatives at sound reproduction popular in Brazil at the end of the last century.

5155 Vasconcelos, Ary. Carinhoso, etc.: história e inventário do choro. v. 1. Rio de Janeiro: Gráfica Editora do Livro, 1984 271 p.

Lengthy discography (p. 55–264), through titles beginning with the word *dois*, of the *polcas, tangos brasileiros, valsas, mazurcas, maxixes, xotes*, and (in some cases) *sambas* and *marchas* recorded by urban instrumental groups from 1902. In total, Vasconcelos anticipates a discography of 10,000 records. He began compiling it in 1978, listening once or twice to each recording. Also contains a historical survey of popular urban instrumental ensemble music from 1870–1983 (p. 17–51). Topping the list of *choro* classics, each with 27 recordings, come *Tico-Tico no Fuba* (Zequinha de Abreu) and *Brejeiro* (tango or *maxixe brasileiro* composed in 1893 by the carioca Ernesto Nazareth (1863–1934) who with 215 compositions ranks as the all-time greatest contributor to *choro* repertory). This very useful fact-filled volume concludes with author's detailed curriculum vitae (p. 265–271).

5156 Vendramini, Maria do. São Paulo: o carrilhão da Sé volta a tocar. (*Corresp. Musicol.*, 3 : 1, 1990, p. 17)

In Sept. 1989 Gerard de Waardt played the inaugural concert on the 61-bell carrillon installed in 1959 by Petit & Fritsen, but not played for 23 years. He also gave a course completed by 14 would-be carrilloneurs.

5157 *Yara de Prantl: ópera teuto-brasileira.* (*Corresp. Musicol.*, 1, 1989, p. 11–12)

Josef Prantl (1896–1951) succeeded in having his opera *Yara* (libretto by Otto Adolf Nohel, d. 1932) premiered at Joinville on Jan. 17, 1936, with local performers, and mounted later that year at Curitiba. His career as well as that of other local musicians is told in Elly Herkenhoff's *Era uma vez um simples caminho . . .* (Joinville, Brazil: Fundação Cultural, Arquivo Histórico, 1987, 225 p. bibl.).

THE CARIBBEAN (EXCEPT CUBA)

5158 Allen, Rosemarie. Una panorámica del calypso en Curazao. (*Montalbán*, 20, 1988, p. 205–228)

Anthropological study of the role of calypso among English-speaking inhabitants of Curaçao provides a brief historical overview of the period prior to the arrival of these immigrants, and then describes their social and economic situation as well as the development and influence of the calypso. [R. Hoefte]

5159 Averill, Gage. Haitian dance bands, 1915–1970: class, race, and authenticity. (*Lat. Am. Music Rev.*, 10 : 2, Fall/Winter 1989, p. 203–235, bibl.)

Extracted in part from the author's Univ. of Washington dissertation *Haitian dance band music: the political economy of exuberance,* this article explores race and class in Latin American and Caribbean popular music. In the summer of 1955 Nemours Jean-Baptiste, leader of the Ensemble Aux Calebasses, initiated *konpa dirèk* as a Haitian adaptation of the Dominican *merengue.* Previously, Haitian *mereng* was harmonized I-IV-V7, but in much Dominican and Cuban music V7-I sufficed. Up to now, *konpa* musicians have favored the two-chord vamp in the main section (the so-called mother *konpa*).

Bilby, Kenneth M. War, peace, and music: The Guianas. See *HLAS 51 : 4670.*

5160 La canción de arte en Puerto Rico. Prólogo de Leonardo Egurbida. Río Piedras, P.R.: Asociación Nacional de Compositores de Puerto Rico, 1986. 123 p.: music.

Contains 29 art songs with piano or guitar accompaniment by Luis M. Álvarez, Rafael Aponte Ledée, Carlos Cabrer, Ernesto Cordero, Jack Delano, Narciso Figueroa, José Daniel Martínez, Carlos O. Morales, Luis Antonio Ramírez, José Rodríguez Alvira, Raymond Torres Santos, Carlos Vázquez, and Amaury Veray. Composed 1963–85, songs in this anthology are intended for performance, not as paper music inviting serial analysis. The problem with the anthology is its limited distribution outside the island.

5161 Cidoncha, Ileana. Plenitud profesional y personal. (*Nuevo Día*, Suplemento {Retrato{, 14 oct. 1990, p. 70–71)

Details career of Annie Figuroa Laugier, the leading Caribbean area music librarian and wife of Donald Thompson.

5162 Dauphin, Claude. Musique du vaudou: fonctions, structures et styles. Sherbrooke, Canada: Editions Naaman, 1986. 182 p.: bibl., ill. (some col.), music. (Col. Civilisations; 18)

In her review in *Latin American Music Review* (10 : 2, Fall/Winter 1989, p. 298–302), Lois E. Wilcken admits this Haitian author's competence in describing *vodoun* music in European terms, but questions his allying three song genres "derived from Chapter Five's corpus" to the rites Yanvalou-Mayo, Pétro, and Gedé, and the *manjé yanm.* She also contends that he goes astray in leaving "the mistaken impression in Chapter Two that the four families of drum patterns given are definitive for all of Haiti." Dauphin also errs in classifying the rhythmic pattern called *kasé* as the master drummer's "attempt to foil a malevolent spirit, to confuse it and thus send it away."

5163 Deglans, Kerlinda and Luis E. Pabón Roca. Cátalogo de música clásica contemporánea de Puerto Rico. Río Piedras, P.R.: Pro-Arte Contemporáneo, 1989. 197 p.

Catalogs works by 25 composers, including those by: Carlos Vázquez (b. Mayagüez, 1952), first president of the Puerto Rican Asociación Nacional de Compositores; Carlos Cabrer (b. San Juan, 1950) who succeded Vázquez as president; well-established composers Rafael Aponte Ledée (b. Guayma, 1938) and Héctor Campos Parsi (b. Ponce, 1922); José Enrique Pedreira (1904–59) and José Ignacio Quintón (1881–1925); foreign-born composers Jack Delano (b. Kiev, Russia, 1914), Ignacio Morales Nieva (b. Spain), José Rodríguez Alvira (b. Havana, 1954), Francis Schwartz (b. Rosenberg, Texas, 1940); and female composers Esther Alejandro (b. New York, 1947) and Awilda Villarini. Works of each composer are listed alphabetically by title, followed by subtitle, instrumentation, year written, duration, publisher, and recordings.

5164 Díaz Díaz, Edgardo. Crónica sobre una gira artística de Anita Otero Hernández, 1886–1887. (*Rev. Inst. Cult. Puertorriq.*, 92/93, abril/sept. 1986, p. 42–50, photos)

In order to raise funds for her piano studies at Paris, Anita Otero (b. Humacao, 1861) began a Puerto Rican tour with a concert in her home town Sunday night, Feb. 14, 1886, during which she played Weber's *Concertstück*, Op. 79. She was assisted by local artists not only at Humacao but also at the other locales. A table (p. 47–50) gives names and functions of assisting artists at 12 of the events and adds brief newspaper comments published after 10 of the 13 concerts. Otero's Puerto Rican repertory included Juan Morel Campos' *Vals de concierto* and *No me toques* (*danza*); Ramón Sarriera's *Mazurca brillante* dedicated to her; and Manuel G. Tavárez's *Potpourrit de aires del país*. In 1892, when she left New York City for a brief visit home, Rubén Darío apostrophized her in his poem *El País del Sol* and on another occasion called her the "Artista de América."

5165 Holguín Veras, Miguel A. Elila Mena: el drama de su vida. Santo Domingo: Editora Corripio, 1983. 235 p.: bibl., ill., index.

Elila Luisa del Carmen Mena Costa (1918–70) was the daughter of the notable Dominican composer and conductor Luis Emilio Mena (1895–1964). March 30, 1955, she played Rachmaninoff's Concerto, Op. 18, with the Dominican Orquesta Sinfónica Nacional in the Salón de Actos de la Gobernación Provincial de Santiago and weeks later at the capital. On June 13, 1956, one month after the inauguration of the Palacio de Bellas Artes, she played it again a third time. After her death the Escuela Elemental de Música at Santo Domingo, which she had directed for many years, took her name. In *The New York Times* (17 : 5, July 8, 1972), Allen Hughes favorably reviewed the New York début recital of her pianist son, Oscar Luis Valdez Mena (b. Santo Domingo, 1942).

5166 La Croes, Eric M. *Tumba di Karnaval de Curazao.* (*Montalbán*, 20, 1988, p. 229–245, bibl.)

Anthropological examination of the *tumba di karnaval*, the basic rhythm of Curaçao. La Croes defines and gives examples of the different musical rhythms of the *tumba* and compares this music to the calypso of Trinidad. [R. Hoefte]

5167 Lizardo, Fradique. Instrumentos musicales folklóricos dominicanos. v. 1, Idiófonos y membranófonos. Santo Domingo: UNESCO, 1988. 457 p.: bibl., ill.

Lizardo (b. Santo Domingo, 1930) studied in Sweden(1964–67) and Denmark (1969–73). In 1957 he began profuse publication, extending to 32 items listed in his bibliography here. In this book he gathers all hitherto available information concerning idiophones and membranophones now or formerly known in the island. This omnigatherum was published "con el apoyo del Fondo Internacional para la Promoción de la Cultura," a UNESCO entity.

5168 Mondoza de Arce, Daniel. Panorama of the music in the Cathedral of San Juan, Puerto Rico. (*Lat. Am. Music Rev.*, 10 : 1, Spring/Summer 1989, p. 53–68)

A Puerto Rican bishop complained to Charles IV in a letter dated Oct. 1792 about the low quality of plainchant singing. Thirteen succentors held the post between 1738–

1810; on Jan. 1, 1811 the San Juan chapter hired on an interim basis Juan Vicens y Llibert as succentor. Domingo de Andino died in 1820, whereupon Vicens was promoted to first organist. After Vicens' death in 1830, Isidro Martí followed him as first succentor. The death of Martí's successor Ramón de Seguer on April 8, 1857 brought to a close the succession of Spanish-born succentors. This article includes a list of first and second succentors and organists in San Juan Cathedral 1756–1857.

5169 Price, Richard and Sally Price. Two evenings in Saramaka. Musical transcriptions by Kenneth M. Bilby. Chicago: Univ. of Chicago Press, 1991. 417 p.: bibl. ill., map.

Authors joined the Saramaka Maroons for two tale-telling wakes to hear Saramaka folktales. Narrative, song, dance, and social interaction merge in these two evenings. The volume is set in the more general context of African-American tale-telling. Includes more than 50 songs in musical notations. [R. Hoefte]

Quintero Rivera, Angel G. La música puertorriqueña y la contra-cultura domocrática: espontaneidad libertaria de la herencia cimarrona. See item **1585.**

5170 Rosemain, Jacqueline. La musique dans la société antillaise: 1635–1902, Martinique, Guadeloupe. Paris: L'Harmattan, 1986. 183 p.: bibl., ill., music. (Col. Recherches et documents monde antillais)

Chaps. 1–2 treat 1635–1714 and 1714–89 in the colonies of Guadeloupe and Martinique; Chap. 3 covers the years of the first abolition of slavery (1789–1802); Chap. 4 deals with period of slavery's return; Chaps. 5–6 cover events up to the eruption of Mont Pelée that destroyed Saint-Pierre, cultural capital of the two islands. When buttressed by documents, the treatment is indisputable, but the speculations on the origins of the *beguine, calenda,* and *chica* can be questioned. Reviewed favorably by Jocelyne Guilbault in *Latin American Music Review* (9:2, Fall/Winter 1988, p. 272–274).

Seminar on the Calypso, St. Augustine, Trinidad and Tobago, 1986. Papers. See *HLAS* 51:4737.

5171 Thompson, Donald. El ambiente musical en Puerto Rico en la década de 1880. (*Cupey*, 6:1/2, enero/dic. 1989, p. 122–139)

Brilliant exposition of all phases of musical life in the island during the 1880s, documented from notices in *El Boletín Mercantil, El Buscapié, Puerto Rico Ilustrado, Boletín Eclesiástico,* and six other periodicals, of which La Ópera, issued March-June 1887, was especially valuable. The *Catálogo General de la existencia del almacén de música de Olimpio Otero* (Humacao: 1883) documents 112 composers (many with 30 or 40 works), and sales of metronomes, pianos, and other instruments. Opera companies crisscrossed the island with repertories of the old and new. Zarzuelas crowded the boards; some, such as *Don Mamerto* (libretto by Sotero Figueroa; music by Morel Campos; premiered at Ponce in La Perla Theater November 27, 1881), were by native-born composers.

5172 Thompson, Donald. Music in Puerto Rican public ceremony: *fiestas reales, fiestas patronales, ferias,* and *exposiciones.* (*Inter-Am. Music Rev.,* 10:2, Spring/Summer 1989, p. 135–141)

Thompson's list provides a guide to the mainly unknown body of information concerning music in Puerto Rican public life found in official and semi-offical reports and similar documents.

5173 Thompson, Donald. Notes on the inauguration of the San Juan, Puerto Rico, Municipal Theater. (*Lat. Am. Music Rev.,* 11:1, Spring/Summer 1990, p. 84–91)

Entries in the journal of Ralph Waldo Emerson's brother, Edward Bliss, permit citing the February 26, 1832, concert in the Coliseo (now the Teatro Tapia—on which construction had begun in Sept. 1824), as the inaugural musical event. The singers were the English tenor William Pearman, born at Manchester in 1792, and soprano Ann Pearman, his wife.

5174 Thompson, Donald. The Puerto Rican *danza:* nostalgia in motion. (*Qué pasa,* 42:1, Jan. 1990, p. 8–11, ill.)

Between 1850–1930 the *danza* all but monopolized piano publications by such renowned composers as Manuel Gregorio Tavárez (1843–83, 45 salon *danzas*); Juan Morel Campos (1857–96, 300 *danzas*); and Braulio Dueño Colón (1854–1934). After obsolescence, it began to be revived in the 1960s.

5175 Witmer, Robert. Kingston's popular music culture: neo-colonialism to nationalism. (*Jam. J.*, 22:1, Feb./April 1989, p. 11–18, bibl.)

Edited version of "'Local' and 'Foreign:' The Popular Music Culture of Kingston, Jamaica, before Ska, Rock Steady and Reggae," (*Latin American Music Review*, Summer 1987), which in turn was based on a chapter in Witmer's Univ. of Illinois dissertation *The popular music culture of Kingston, Jamaica: background and recent change*. European transplants are labelled "colonial" and therefore denigrated. Author blesses American jazz and blues that filtered through to Kingston urban masses, but warns against prideful recollection of jazz bands that played in hotels accessible only to the wealthy. Although radio broascasting began November 17, 1939, ZQI broadcast only four hours daily as late as 1947. By 1955 Radio Jamaica and Radiffusion (RJR) was broadcasting 118 hours weekly, but even then "relied almost exclusively on British and American record and subscription services."

CENTRAL AMERICA

5176 Acevedo Vargas, Jorge Luis. La música en las reservas indígenas de Costa Rica. San José: Editorial de la Univ. de Costa Rica, 1987. 197 p.: bibl., ill., music.

Author of *La muscia en Guanacaste* (1980, see *HLAS 46:1043*), Acevedo returns with an opulent book containing chapters on: 1) the "cultural roots" of Costa Rica's indigenous communities; 2) precolumbian musical instruments; 3) music on Costa Rican Indian reservations (Guatuzo malekus, Guaymi, Brunkas y Térrabas, Cabecares y Bribris); and 4) Costa Rican indigenous melodies. After 9 *anexos* (p. 159–183), the author adds five easy piano pieces composed by himself (p. 159–195). All the music (including pitches sounded by precolumbian ocarinas) is written on five-line staff in uninflected tempered scale-notes (no diactritics). Lacks analytic index.

Healy, Paul F. Music of the Maya. See *HLAS 51:302*.

5177 Lehnhoff, Dieter. Espada y pentagrama: la música polifónica en la Gua-

temala del siglo XVI. Guatemala: Centro de Reproducciones, Univ. Rafael Landívar, 1986. 154 p., 6 leaves of plates: bibl., ill., index.

Born at Guatemala City in 1955, the author studied there and at the Mozarteum in Salzburg before obtaining his PhD in 1990 at Catholic Univ. in Washington. In 1984 he initiated as a continuing project the rescue of historic Guatemalan music. The present excellent review of 16th-century music in Guatemalan culminates in Chap. 5 with an authoritative discussion of the works of Hernando Franco, Pedro Bermúdez, and Gaspar Fernández, the three outstanding composers of European birth active in the cathedral at Antigua. The most prolific of these was Bermúdez, a native of Granada who served as *maestro de capilla* at Antequera before emigrating to Cusco, transferring thence to Guatemala in 1597, where during the next five years he composed and/or had copied 18 of his compositions, the largest of which is a *Missa de Bomba, a 4*, in Cathedral Choirbook I, 152–169, parodying Mateo Flecha's ensalada *La Bomba*.

5178 La música de Guatemala en el siglo XVIII Music from eighteenth-century Guatemala. Recopilación e introducción de Alfred E. Lemmon. Antigua, Guatemala: Centro de Investigaciones Regionales de Mesoamérica; South Woodstock, Vt.: Plumsock Mesoamerican Studies, 1986. 1 score (174 p.): bibl.

Prefaced by a catalog of 38 works by Manuel José de Quiroz, *maestro de capilla* of Guatemala 1738–65, and of 149 by his nephew Rafael Antonio Castellanos, *maestro* 1765–91, this edition of four works by Quiroz and nine by Castellanos (12 *villancicos* and one psalm) is supplemented with transcription by Joseph Coll's *Levanten Pendones* sung in Guatemala Cathedral in honor of Charles III's coronation. Lester D. Brothers authoritatively reviewed this publication in *Notes of the Music Library Association* (46:1, Sept. 1989, p. 226–228), as did Rui Vieira Nery in *Latin American Music Review* (9:1, Spring/Summer 1988, p. 109–112).

5179 Yurchenco, Henrietta. El baile de las canastas y otras sobrevivencias del teatro prehispánico maya-quiché. (*An. Acad. Geogr. Hist. Guatem.*, 62:60, enero/dic. 1986, p. 75–87, music)

In 1945 Yurchenco visited Guatemala for the first time, witnessing a dance drama in the Icxil village of Chajul (Quiché dept.). Accompanied by trumpet, tun (teponaztli), and tortoise carapace, the *Baile de las Canastas* lasted nine scenes and told the story of shaman Matagtanic who with others went hunting for the quetzal, the national bird. Having pity, the hunters let the bird live, but on taking the bird home, it turned into a lover of the shaman's daughter Mariquita, and from her gained maize seed. The translator of this article signals various errors. The trumpet part transcribed by Jennifer Sooke is mostly descending pentaphonic melody; the textless voice part includes many repeated notes grouped in 16th-note and 8th-note patterns.

CHILE

5180 Bustos, Raquel. La musicología en Chile: la presente década. (*Rev. Music. Chil.*, 42 : 169, enero/junio 1988, p. 27–36, bibl.)

The Chilean musical investigators most published during the 1980s were Samuel Claro-Valdés, Manuel Dannemann, Ernesto González G., Juan Pablo González R., María Ester Grebe, Margot Loyola, María Isabel Mena, Luis Merino Montero, and Carmen Peña; the most concentrated teaching occured between 1974–82.

5181 Cifuentes, Luis. Fragmentos de un sueño: Inti-Illimani y la generación de los 60. Santiago: Ediciones Logos, 1989. 310 p.

Inti-Illimani began as a student group at the Univ. Técnica del Estado in 1967; began recording in August 1967; toured Argentina with five members in 1968; turned into a professional touring group in July 1971; toured Cuba and six other Latin American countries in 1972 and Europe in 1973; recorded *La Nueva Canción Chilena* at Milan in March 1974; gave 134 presentations in 12 countries in 1975, 108 in 11 countries in 1977, and 122 in ten in 1979; made its first digital and first compact disc in 1984 in Germany; appeared with John Williams at Edinburgh in 1986; signed a contract with CBS (Columbia Broadcasting Company) in 1987; and disembarked at Pudahuel on Sept. 18, 1988, after 15 years of exile abroad. In Oct. 1988 the seven-member group appeared

in Argentina with Bruce Springsteen, Sting, and Peter Gabriel during the World Tour of Amnesty. Mostly written as a series of interviews with members of the group, the book contains nine chapters; Chap. 8 (p. 236–261) deals with music, and Chap. 9 gives prognostications of future political developments.

5182 Claro, Samuel. Domingo Santa Cruz Wilson. (*Inter-Am. Music Rev.*, 9 : 1, Fall/Winter 1987, p. 115–116)

A titan among South Americans, Santa Cruz is here remembered for his unique grandeurs.

5183 Claro, Samuel. Herencia musical de las tres Españas en América. (*Rev. Music. Chil.*, 43 : 171, enero/junio 1989, p. 7–41, bibl.)

A synthesis of this extended account of the *cueca's* lineage, stretching back to Muslim Spain, was read at the Smithsonian Institution's symposium, "Musical Repercussions of 1492" (Washington, D.C., 1988). Immigrants to the Americas included a large proportion of Andalusians of Arab descent, who brought with them an oral culture that preserved Iberian poetic and musical forms handed down from Ziryab (789–857) and his successors.

5184 Claro, Samuel *et al.* Iconografía musical chilena. v. 1–2. Santiago: Ediciones Univ. Católica de Chile, 1989. 2 v.: ill. (Investigaciones)

This monumental work, first of its kind in Latin America, occupied the investigators for almost a decade (beginning in 1979). The catalogs of visual images are divided under these headings in vol. 1: 1) organología; 2) músicos; 3) arquitectura y entorno; 4) artes plásticas y de representación; and in vol. 2: 5) impresos; 6) manuscritos; 7) numismática, heráldica y genealogía; 8) sociedad, congresos, grupos musicales, círculos, centros, facultades, institutos, etc.; and 9) personas afines. The six annexes index: 1) nombres de personas; 2) títulos de obras musicales; 3) lugares; 4) editores e casas editoras de música; 5) especies musicales; and 6) teatros. Small b/w photographs scattered one or two to a page throughout the catalog vivify many of the entries. Ramón Carnicer appeared on a 1947 Chilean commemorative stamp (v. 2, p. 845), the only stamp cataloged. The compilers of this catalog deserve a commemorative stamp.

5185 Estreno de *Ritual de la Tierra, del Viento y del Fuego*, por el Ballet Nacional Chileno. (*Rev. Music. Chil.*, 42:169, enero/junio 1988, p. 98–99)

At the Teatro Baquedano in Santiago on May 27, 1988, the Ballet Nacional Chileno successfully premiered the mentioned work, with choreography by Sergio Zapata and music by Guillermo Rifo, who mixed taped sounds with those of a large orchestra directed by Lothar Kooenigs. The storyline, a rare puberty ceremony of the Onas who inhabit the largest island in Tierra del Fuego, was developed in 14 scenes and suggested by Hain.

5186 Grebe Vicuña, María Ester. El *tayil* mapuche, como categoría conceptual y medio de comunicación trascendente. (*Inter-Am. Music Rev.*, 10:2, Spring/Summer 1989, p. 69–75)

Tayil is a powerful type of ritual song, released by the gods only to a few privileged humans whom they specifically choose. These elect few can by *tayil's* power provoke the descent of the gods to reenact on earth their supernatural doings. Categories of *tayil* are determined by the sex of the *tayilutufe* (interpreter of *tayil*), by the age of a given *tayil*, and by the beneficence of the spirits evoked by a given *tayil*. In Chile, *tayil* is the legacy of shamans—especially women shamans. Grebe concludes with a table in which she juxtaposes the characteristics of *tayil* as reported by observers of Argentine Mapuches, with what she has observed among Chilean Mapuches.

5187 Jara, Joan. Víctor Jara: un canto no truncado. Concepción, Chile: Literatura Americana Reunida, 1988. 268 p., 16 p. of plates: ill. (Col. Memoria y testimonio)

Memories of the English dancer Joan Alison Turner Roberts, who left Chile Oct. 15, 1973, with her two daughters after the Sept. death of Víctor Jara, the famous singer-poet laureate of the Allende regime and her companion since Oct. 1961. The epilogue (p. 253–261) contains the texts of eight of his songs copyrighted 1966–71.

5188 Lemmon, Alfred E. Jesuit chroniclers and historians of colonial Spanish America: sources for the ethnomusicologist. (*Inter-Am. Music Rev.*, 10:2, Spring/Summer 1989, p. 119–129, music)

Bernard Havestadt's 76 songs published in 1777 in his *Chilidúgú pars sexta, notae musicae ad canedum in clavichordio, cantiones partis tertiae a n. 650 usque ad n. 676* are but one example of the very numerous Jesuit writings that document the musical practices of New World Indians to whom Jesuits ministered before the order's expulsion.

5189 Mansilla, Luis Alberto. Claudio Arrau: la magia y el genio. (*Araucaria Chile*, 42, 1988, p. 97–114)

The only pianist of the younger generation completely approved by Arrau is Daniel Barenboim. On the other hand Mauricio Pollini and Ivo Pegorlic salute him as "um monumento." However, they do criticize him for neglecting contemporary music, relying almost exclusively on masterpieces that he learned in his youth while studying with Martin Krause at Berlin. He remained a Chilean citizen until 1979 and "solo los impuestos le hicieron aceptar la nacionalidad norteamericana."

5190 Merino, Luis. Acario Cotapos: centenario del nacimiento de un pionero solitario. (*Rev. Music. Chil.*, 43:171, enero/junio 1989, p. 107–111, ill.)

Cotapos (1889–1969) received the Chilean National Arts prize in 1960. Despite a reduced works lists, he served as a bridge between Santiago and the other world capitals where he spent many years, among them: New York (1916–1925); Paris; Madrid (1934–1938); and Buenos Aires (1945–1947).

5191 Merino, Luis. Bienvenida a Gustavo Becerra. (*Rev. Music. Chil.*, 42:170, julio/dic. 1988, p. 87–89)

Transcript of welcome words pronounced in the Sala Isidora Zegers of the Facultad de Artes, Aug. 23, 1988, initiating the "Encuentro con el Compositor Gustavo Becerra." After a biennium as Chilean Cultural Attaché in Bonn (1971–73), Becerra elected to remain in East Germany teaching in the Univ. of Oldenburg (lower Saxony), founded in 1973. In issue 161 of *Revista Musical Chilena* (enero/junio 1984), Becerra publ4ished "La Música en la Universidad de Oldenburgo."

5192 Merino, Luis. Cinco efemerides en la creación musical chilena. (*Rev. Music. Chil.*, 41:167, enero/junio 1987, p. 44–47)

1985 marked the centennial of the death of José Zapiola and Federico Guzmán, and of the birth of Pedro Humberto Allende Sarón (1885–1959). Alberto García Guerrero (1886–1959) left Chile in 1914; worked the next five years chiefly in New York; and in 1919 settled in Toronto where his pupils included John Beckwith, Ray Dudley, Glenn Gould, R. Murray Schafer, and 20 leading Canadian-born musicians. Carlos Isamitt (1887–1974) won the Premio Nacional de Arte in 1965.

5193 Merino, Luis. Discurso pronunciado en el acto de entrega de estudios en honor de Domingo Santa Cruz. (*Rev. Music. Chil.*, 42:169, enero/junio 1988, p. 40–57)

With his accustomed magisterial powers, the author supervised the *Festschrift* of 17 articles that *Anales de la Universidad de Chile* (quinta serie, no. 11, agosto 1986) consecrated to the memory of an unsurpassed giant in the history of Latin American art music.

Merino, Luis. Repercusiones nacionales e internacionales de la visita a Chile de José White. See item **5212.**

Morris, Nancy E. Canto porque es necesario cantar: the new song movement in Chile, 1973–1983. See *HLAS 51:4912.*

Ochoa Campos, Moisés. La chilena guerrerense. See item **5234.**

Pérez de Arce A., José. Flautas arqueológicas del extremo sur andino. See *HLAS 51:521.*

5194 Ruiz, Martín. Flores musicales del exilio chileno: Inti-Illimani cumple veinte años. (*Araucaria Chile*, 42, 1988, p. 83–94)

Members of the group affirmed their solidarity with Unidad Popular during interviews. Group was in Rome at the time of the *golpe*, having left Chile June 29, 1973, to take part in the Festival Mundial de la Juventud in East Berlin.

5195 Sergio Ortega: compositor de tres óperas para el bicentenario de la Revolución Francesa. (*Rev. Music. Chil.*, 43:172, julio/dic. 1989, p. 87–88)

Responding to the bicentenary, Ortega composed three pageant operas. *Messidor* premiered in Oct. 1988 at Argenteuil; *Le Louis perdu* premiered at Pantin in Feb. 1989; and *Les contes de la Révolution à Aubervilliers* premiered at Aubervilliers in June 1989. Michel Swiercheski was the mu-

sical director; Gerald Destal the scenic director; and Francis Combes wrote the librettos.

5196 Stevenson, Robert Murrell. Nino Marcelli: fundador de la Orquesta Sinfónica de San Diego. (*Rev. Music. Chil.*, 41:167, enero/junio 1987, p. 26–43)

Nino Marcelli (b. Rome, 1890; d. San Diego, Calif., 1967) grew up in Santiago, where he had a distinguished career before emigrating to the US in 1916. His orchestral *Suite Araucana* won first prize in the 1923 New York Stadium competition and was premiered at the City College Stadium Aug. 9, 1923. Settling in San Diego, California, in 1920, he founded the San Diego Symphony Orchestra, which he conducted through the summer of 1937.

5197 Stevenson, Robert Murrell. Nino Marcelli: founder of the San Diego Symphony Orchestra. (*Inter-Am. Music Rev.*, 10:1, Fall/Winter 1988, p. 113–123)

Nino Marcelli entered the Santiago national conservatory in 1900. Enrique Soro instigated Nino's appointment on April 1, 1910, to teach *solfège*, and on June 7, 1910, to teach horn on the Chilean national conservatory. Between April 9 and May 30, 1913 Nino conducted all 9 Beethoven symphonies in the Teatro Unión Central at Santiago; he was the first to do so in Chile.

5198 Torres Alvarado, Rodrigo. Gabriela Mistral y la creación musical en Chile. (*Rev. Music. Chil.*, 43:171, enero/junio 1989, p. 42–106, facsims., ill., music)

The present exemplary article—worthy of highest praise—is a revised version of p. 1–158 of the author's 420-page tesis de musicología supervised by Luis Merino: *Presencia de Gabriela Mistral y Pablo Neruda en la música chilena* (Santiago: Facultad de Artes de la Univ. de Chile, 1983). The purpose of the article is to identify and give a global vision of the musical works based on Mistral's poetry. The 40 composers whose Mistral-based works are listed in the catalog (p. 67–102) include nearly all the stellar names in Chilean 20th-century composition.

5199 Towner, Margaret. Violeta Parra: una artista popular chilena. (*Rev. Univ./ Tabasco*, 10/11, dic. 1985/marzo 1986, p. 20–30, bibl.)

Hagiographic account of the life of Violeta Parra (1917–67), whose achievements as singer, guitarist, collector of folksongs, poet, painter, weaver of tapestries, pottery maker, and political reformist were testimony to her own individual genius; and whose misfortunes were the fault of others. The men at fault included: the railroad worker Luis Cereda with whom she spent a miserable decade and by whom she bore children in 1938 and 1941; Luis Arce, her second husband, whom she left to make her way in Europe with Communist Party funding; and Gilbert Fabré, the Swiss who accompanied her back to Chile in late 1964 after her second European sojourn, only to break her heart by abandoning her. The chronology in this article is shaky: she cannot have sailed for Europe in 1934 leaving her latest baby with her second husband, and have married her first husband in 1936.

5200 Urrutia-Blondel, Jorge. (*in* Dizionario enciclopedico universale della musica e dei musicisti: le biografie, v. 8. Torino, Italy: Unione Tipografico-Editrice Torinese, 1988, p. 135–136)

Despite the composer's death in 1981, this ineffective entry has him still alive in 1988. His birthdate is also wrong: Urrutia-Blondel was born at La Serena, Sept. 17, 1903 (not 1905), and died at Santiago, Chile, July 5, 1981.

5201 Vicuña Lyon, Magdalena. In memoriam: Pedro Núñez Navarrette, 1906–1989. (*Rev. Music. Chil.*, 43:171, enero/junio 1989, p. 141)

Born at Constitución Aug. 3, 1906, composer and educationist Núñes Navarrete died at Santiago Jan. 5, 1989.

5202 Villagra, Nelson. Víctor Jara: un adiós imposible. (*Araucaria Chile*, 42, 1988, p. 29–38)

Homage to Jara on what would have been his 50th birthday. An actor in the Chilean films *El chacal de Nahueltoro* and *Tres tristes tigres*, the author emigrated to Cuba after the *golpe* and was living in Canada in 1988.

COLOMBIA

5203 Antología de música religiosa, siglos xvi-xviii: Archivo Capitular, Catedral de Bogotá. Estudio y transcripción de Egberto Bermúdez. Bogotá: Presidencia de la Repú-

blica de Colombia, 1988. 1 score (91 p., 11 p. of plates).

In addition to the Epiphany villancico a 4, *Monarcas generosos* by Juan Hidalgo, a *madrileño* who died in 1685 without ever having visited the Western Hemisphere, this sumptuous volume offers transcribed works by four Bogotá Cathedral *maestros de capilla:* Gutierre Fernández Hidalgo (odd-verse *Magnificat Secundi toni*); José Casacante; Juan de Herrera; and Salvador Romero (*Lamentatio, Lectio 3: Feria VI in Parasceve*, solo voice with unfigured bass). The elegantly reproduced facsimiles of scattered music manuscript pages in Bogotá Cathedral archive preceding the transcriptions add value to this lavish publication.

5204 Escobar, Luis Antonio. La música en Santafé de Bogotá. Bogotá: Impresión Sandri, 1987. 169 p.: bibl., ill. (some col.).

This beautiful volume, illustrated with full-color plates, was financed by the Lotería de Cundinamarca, Corporación Financiera de Cundinamarca, and Empresa de Licores de Cundinamarca. After preliminaries on aboriginal manifestations comes a section on "Instrumentos de la Colonia" (p. 121–147), followed by "Primeros Músicos."

5205 Pinaud B., Moisés. Ficha biográfica del Maestro Guillermo Espinosa Grau. (*Universal Dominical*, 9 dic. 1990)

Born at Cartagena on Jan. 9, 1905 to parents Mateo Espinosa and Pura Grau de Espinosa, Guillermo Espinosa died at Washington, D.C. on July 5, 1990. He completed primary and secondary studies at San Pedro Claver Colegio in Cartagena, and pursued music at the Escuela de Música (now Instituto Musical de Cartagena) before enrolling at the Royal Conservatory at Milan. After directing the Music Division of the Organization of American States (1953–75) he remained in Washington. Other informative articles concerning him were published in *El Universal* of Cartagena on Nov. 20, Nov. 27, and Dec. 8, 1990.

CUBA

5206 Acosta, Leonardo. From the drum to the synthesizer: study of a process. (*Lat. Am. Perspect.*, 16:2, Spring 1989, p. 29–46, bibl.)

In this incantatory essay, African influences are apostrophized, European contexts reviled. In their generation García Caturla and Roldán best exemplified affirmative response to African beat. Ranging widely over such diverse territory as jazz in and out of Cuba, the rejection of African-American vocal styles in Cuba, guitars versus electric guitars and synthesizers, this essayist is prolific of *ipse dixits* but chary of dates and other specifics.

5207 Carreira, Xoan M. "Chane": un músico para Curros Enríquez. (*Nosa Terra*, 9, 1987, p. 39–41, music)

Born at Santiago de Compostela in 1856, José Castro González ("Chane") emigrated to Havana in 1893, there distinguishing himself as choral director and composer. To honor the Galician poet Carlos Enríquez, who had preceded him to Cuba, he set four of his poems.

5208 Fernández, Nohema. La contradanza cubana y Manuel Saumell. (*Lat. Am. Music Rev.*, 10:1, Spring/Summer 1989, p. 116–134, bibl., music)

Each of the two parts of a *contradanza* consists of a repeated eight-measure section, making a total of 32 bars. The majority of the 58 *contradanzas* by Havana-born Saumell (1817–70) bear titles relating them to local events or persons. Their rhythmic delights give him the kind of unique stature that Scott Joplin enjoys in the domain of rag.

5209 Giro, Radamés. Leo Brouwer y la guitarra en Cuba. La Habana: Editorial Letras Cubanas, 1986. 226 p.: bibl., music. (Giraldilla)

Publishers say that "Giro, after exploring archives, periodicals, concert programs, specialized texts and other relevant publications, is able to give us a coherent vision of the numerous schools and methods of guitar playing that flowed into popular and concert currents in Cuba." Having done all this in Chaps. 1–2, Giro next analyzes Brouwer as the culminating exponent of the Cuban guitar in "La Guitarra Alcanza su Espiral Eterna." In Chap. 5 (the last) he pays tribute to other contemporary Cubans who have contributed to the literature and propagation of the guitar. The music examples (p. 135–207) are so poorly reproduced that most are illegible and therefore useless. The book suffers drastically from lack of an index.

5210 González, Jorge Antonio. La composición operística en Cuba. La Habana: Editorial Letras Cubanas, 1986. 591 p.: ill., music, ports. (Música)

Lacking a bibliography and any analytic index, this survey contains footnoted references to Alejo Carpentier's *La música en Cuba* (La Habana: Editorial Letras Cubanas, 1979), but most of the footnotes express the author's opinion. No reference is made to author's previous cooperative endeavor with Edwin T. Tolón—their 472-page *Operas cubanas y sus autores* (See *HLAS 9:4775*), of which the present book is essentially an expanded, politically correct version. The summaries of opera plots remain very welcome but numerous mistakes need correction. For instance, on the first page the author errs on calling February 16, 1738, the date that opera first "made its formal entry in Spain." Also, Antonio Rosales, not Manual V. García, set Ramón de la Cruz's *El licenciado Farfulla*.

5211 Hernández Balaguer, Pablo. Los villancicos, cantadas y pastorelas de Esteban Salas. La Habana: Editorial Letras Cubanas, 1986. 193 p.: bibl., music. .

This posthumous publication includes the incipits of 45 Christmas pieces by Cuba's chief colonial composer (p. 138–160). The editors also print the texts (p. 161–190) of *villancicos* sung to music by Joseph Puig, Joseph Durán, Esteban Salas himself, Fray Manuel Lazo de la Vega, and Juan París, the maestro in Santiago de Cuba Cathedral who succeeded Salas. The bibliography itemizes seven of Hernández Balaguer's publications dated 1960–64. Most welcome now will be republications of the music of Esteban Salas first issued in 1961–62 (p. 192). The 36 documents consulted by Hernández Belaguer (see p. 192–193) testify to his unique diligence and perspicacity.

5212 Merino, Luis. Repercusiones nacionales e internacionales de la visita a Chile de José White. (*Rev. Music. Chil.*, 44:173, enero/junio 1990, p. 65–113, bibl., music)

In this nonpareil account of the visit to Chile (Jan. 1878–May 1879) of the internationally celebrated Cuban mulatto concert violinist, Merino touches all bases. He meticulously lists all White's concerts and other musical activities, and concludes with a lengthy disquisition on the *zamacueca* arranged for concert by White which was subsequently popularized and imitated in Brazil and in France. Merino's ancillary data concerning persons and places is of supreme value.

5213 Milanca Guzmán, Mario. José White en Venezuela. (*Rev. Music. Chil.*, 44 : 173, enero/junio 1990, p. 25–64, bibl., ill.)

In this meticulous account, the author expands on Cuban violinist White's visit by offering extremely welcome data on the three Caracas concerts given in 1876 by another Cuban violinist, Claudio Brindis de Salas. (See *HLAS 40: 9097* for related article concerning these two violinists' visits to Caracas.) Ramón de la Plaza was not only author but also composer of a *barcarola* sung at White's second Caracas concert April 2, 1877.

5214 Rodríguez, Victoria Eli. Apuntes sobre la creación musical actual en Cuba. (*Lat. Am. Music Rev.*, 10:2, Fall/Winter, 1989, p. 287–297)

Prominent among dance bands in 1989 were Juan Fornell y la Orquestra Los Van Van, Adalberto Álvarez y Su Grupo, Chuco Valdés e Irakeré, Orquesta de Pachito Alonso, and Wilfredo Naranjo y la Original de Manzanillo. Concert composers active in the island ranged from Leo Brouwer, Juan Blanco, and Carlos Fariñas to José Ángel Pérez Puentes "y otros más, que harían muy extenso el listado."

5215 Toledo, Armando. White en Cuba. (*Rev. Music. Chil.*, 44: 173, enero/junio 1990, p. 5–24, bibl., ill.)

Born at Matanzas on New Year's eve night 1835, José Silvestre White was the son of a free African, María Escolástica, and a merchant who acknowledged him legally as his son in 1855, but who had begun teaching him violin in 1840. In 1843 he studied with José Miguel Román and later with Pedro Haserf. At 19 years of age he played 16 instruments, according to his father, who also credited him with having composed 13 types of dances, many of them scored for small orchestra. On March 21, 1854, he joined with L.M. Gottschalk in a concert at Mantanzas, during which he played his own *Melodías sobre aires cubanos, Variaciones sobre el Carnaval de Venecia*, and *Fantasía sobre*

[Rossini's] *Guillermo Tell*. Gottschalk helped raise funds for his departure for Paris May 27, 1855 aboard the French frigate La Clementina. On Dec. 8, 1854, his *Missa a 4* and on May 27, 1855, his Palm Sunday Passion were performed in San Carlos Parish, Matanzas. In Paris both he and Sarasate began lessons with Jean Delphine Alard (1815–1888) the same day, June 14, 1856. White returned home to be present at his father's death in Feb. 1859, thereafter touring the island until his farewell at Matanzas Oct. 4, 1860, which concert closed with his patriotic *Pot-pourri sobre aires cubanos*. He made his last visit to Cuba at the end of 1874, concertizing at Matanzas in Jan. 1875, at Santiago Feb. 20, and March 7, at the Tacón in Havana April 10, 19, and 22, 1875. Next month José Martí welcomed him to Mexico City where White gave sensationally successful concerts May 25 and June 11 (see *HLAS 48: 7124*).

5216 Wistuba Alvarez, Vladimir. La música de Leo Brouwer. (*Araucaria Chile*, 42, 1988, p. 129–134)

Extracted from a book to be published with the title *Lo cubano en las obras tempranas para guitarra de Leo Brouwer*, this article by a musicologist residing at Helsinki stresses his close affinity with the visual arts and his early desire to become a painter.

ECUADOR

5217 Godoy Aguirre, Mario. Florilegio de la música ecuatoriana. Guayaquil, Ecuador: Editorial del Pacífico, 1988? 606 p.: bibl., ill., music.

According to the bibliography (p. 605–606) the author published *Educación Musical* (Editorial Del Pacífico) and *La Navidad y los Reyes en Riobamba* (Riobamba: Editorial Pedagógica Freire), both in 1983. Volume includes author's summary of Ecuadorian music history, crafted chiefly from out-of-date secondary sources, but containing such facts as these: the Salesians opened their Escuela de Artes y Oficios at Riobamba Nov. 7, 1891; it was closed by the liberal regime in 1895, but reopened in 1897; the Asociación Musical Santa Cecilia was founded at Guayaquil in 1891; Claudio Rosa directed the Sociedad Filantrópica at Guayaquil. Pt. 2 contains song texts and music. Mostly handcopied, the music is variously given subtitles such as *pasillo, pasacalle, tonada, valse, albazo, habanera, fox incaico, bambuco, sanjuanito, yaraví,* and *capishca.* Although not rigidly adhered to, the order is alphabetical by first word in the main title. Nearly all *letras* and music are credited to named individuals, but without any attempt to identify them. Collection lacks an index of the composers' and lyricists' names, and for this and other reasons volume is unwieldly.

5218 Hickman, Ellen. Lithophones from Ecuador. (*Archaeol. Music.,* 1, 1988, p. 52–55)

Reports on prehistoric stone sounding slabs from the Ecuadorian coast in three languages, English, German, French.

Idrovo Urigüen, Jaime. Instrumentos musicales prehispánicos del Ecuador: estudio de la exposición "Música milenaria." See *HLAS 51:562.*

MEXICO

5219 Alcaraz, José Antonio. —en una música estelar: de Ricardo Castro a Federico Alvarez del Toro. México: CENIDIM, 1987. 141 p. (Col. Ensayos; 5)

Collection of brevities previously published in unnamed locales contains worthwhile comments on Carrillo's *Symphony in D* (1901) revived for the composer's centenary in 1975, on Castro's piano concerto written between 1885–87 but premiered in Antwerp in Dec. 1904, and on works by 14 20th-century Mexicans.

5220 Barce, Ramón. Manuel Enríquez. (*Ritmo,* 586, marzo 1988, p. 112–113, ill.)

Article contains composer's photo and an excerpt from his *Ambivalencia* for violin and cello.

5221 Barce, Ramón. Rodolfo Halffter. (*Ritmo,* 585, feb. 1988, p. 96–97)

Profile of a composer claimed equally by Spain and Mexico.

5222 Brothers, Lester D. Francisco López Capillas, first great native New-World composer: reflections on the discovery of his will. (*Inter-Am. Music Rev.,* 10:2, Spring/Summer 1989, p. 101–118, facsims., music)

López Capillas, whose Masses and Magnificats form MS M. 2428 at the Madrid National Library, died at Mexico City Jan. 18, 1674 (not 1673, as reported by Antonio de Robles in his *Diario de Sucesos Notables, 1665–1703*). His will, discovered by Robert Stevenson in the Archivo General de Notarías, Distrito Federal, Francisco de Quiñones, Libro 547Q (olim 325), 1674, folios 8–11, certifies his birth at Mexico City and gives abundant details concerning his family and possessions.

5223 Carmona, Fernando. Homenaje a Silvestre Revueltas. (*Plural,* 19–9:225, junio 1990, p. 77–87)

Panegyric, timed to coincide with the 50th anniversary of the composer's death. His sympathetic contact with street people is stressed, rather than his formative years in Chicago where he studied with the best teachers then available.

5224 Carredano, Consuelo. Servir a la música: entrevista a Miguel García Mora. (*Pauta,* 8:29, enero/marzo 1989, p. 28–39, ill.)

At age 77, the Mexico City native García Mora recalls having recorded in 1968 the piano concerto by his harmony and composition teacher, José Rolón (1883–1945), with the Orquesta Sinfónica Nacional conducted by Luis Herrera de la Fuente (RCA-MKL/S-1815, side 2). His nine longplays recorded 1955–1987 begin with *Valses mexicanos de 1900* (Musart, MCD-3001) and continue with albums of Mexican concert piano music (chiefly dances) to 1959, when his *Ritmos de América* (Masart MCD-3020) included Lecuona on side 1 and Villa-Lobos, Migone, and Lorenzo Fernández on side 2. García Mora gave the first Mexican performance of Maurice Ravel's *Gaspard de la nuit* at Sala Wagner June 26, 1930.

5225 Castrillón, María Teresa. Amgélica Morales: máxima pianista mexicana. (*Pauta,* 9:33, enero/marzo 1990, p. 56–58, photo)

Born Jan. 22, 1911, at Mexico City, Morales studied in Europe with Egon Petri, Isidor Philipp, and Emil Sauer (whom she married). She played her début New York recital at age 18 (*The New York Times,* Feb. 21, 1929, 32:5). Despite many years of teaching at the Universities of Kansas and Oklahoma

she never exchanged her Mexican citizenship for that of the US.

5226 50 años de música [en el] Palacio de Bellas Artes. [Recopilación de] Manuel Enríquez *et al.* Mexico: Instituto Nacional de Bellas Artes, Secretaría de Educación Pública, 1986. 539 p.: bibl., facsims., ill., music, ports. (some col.).

This luxuriously-published oblong contains a photographic record of season-by-season highlights of the first 50 years of the Palace of Fine Arts. The *cuadro sinóptico* (p. 219–539) provides a detailed listing of every event from the day of opening (Sept. 29, 1934) through Dec. 16, 1984. Under each date, the compilers of this extremely valuable itemization give: 1) type of concert; 2) interpreters; 3) director; 4) soloist(s); 5) chief works performed; and 6) composer of each chief work. The 797 illustrations (p. 13–213), accompanied by running commentary on the 50 seasons, include some musical scores and program facsimiles, but consist mostly of b/w photographs of performers, conductors, and composers. The Imprenta Madero, responsible for this magnificent bound volume, printed 1,000 copies (see also item **5227.**)

5227 50 años de ópera [en el] Palacio de Bellas Artes. [Recopilación de] Carlos Días Du-Pond *et al.* Mexico: Instituto Nacional de Bellas Artes, Secretaría de Educación Pública, 1986. 252 p.: bibl., ill., ports. (some col.).

Like *50 años de música,* its companion hardbound volume (see item **5226**), this lustrous oblong opens with the same one-page repeated "presentations" by Miguel González Avelar, Secretary of Public Education, and Javier Barros Valero, Director General of the National Institute of Fine Arts. The plan of both volumes is the same: first, season-by-season highlights (in this book, 1935–84), illustrated with photographs (many more in color in this volume); and second, a "synoptic table" (p. 177–252) in which are itemized all the operas and *zarzuelas* produced at the Palace of Fine Arts from March 22, 1935, through Nov. 4, 1984, recording names of the chief singers, the orchestra, scenic and choral directors of each work, and names of dancers and ballet groups. The 605 illustrations (p. 18–167) are accompanied by season-by-season running commentary.

5228 Cortez M., Luis Jaime. Silvestre Revueltas: 3; la primera orfandad. (*Pauta,* 8:29, enero/marzo 1989, p. 17–22, ill.)

In his first surviving letter, dated Jan. 5, 1916, at Mexico City, where he lived with a friend of his father while studying music, Silvestre (b. Dec. 31, 1899, at Santiago Papasquiaro, Durango state) tells his mother (Romana Sánchez Árias de Revueltas) that he has promised his teacher Rafael J. Tello (1872–1946) to learn counterpoint in five months. Nonetheless he complains of idle days and of his separation from others of his own age. In his letter to his parents dated April 17, 1917, he assures them that he is not traipsing about but instead that his studies are going well, despite his longing for home. His well-to-do businessman father paid for his study and living at Mexico City.

5229 Crouch, Marjorie K.; Joseph C. Hickerson; and Therese Langer. Mexico recordings in the Archive of Folk Culture. Washington: American Folklife Center, Library of Congress, 1990. 5 p. (Library of Congress Folk Archive Finding Aids; 7)

Cataloged holdings of tribal music (discs and tapes) and of some regional mestizo groups. Most are copies from other collections.

5230 Enríquez, Manuel. 50 años de música en el Palacio de Bellas Artes. (*Plural,* 18:206, nov. 1988, p. 49–56, ill.)

Carlos Chávez directed the inaugural concert in the Mexico City Palace of Fine Arts Sept. 29, 1934. The Orquesta Sinfónica de México founded by him in 1928 with support of the Sindicato de Filarmónicos del Distrito Federal gave the majority of concerts in the Palace during the first decade after its opening. Other conductors included Ansermet, Stokowski, Kleiber, Beecham, and Monteux, during the first epoch. Most of Revueltas' works were premiered in the Palace. This valuable article contains a global review of activities up to 1988.

5231 Lavalle, Josefina. El jarabe—: el jarabe ranchero o jarabe de Jalisco: Versión recopilada por Francisco Sánchez Flores. México: Centro Nacional de Investigación, Documentación e Información de la Danza José Limón, INBA, 1988. 219 p.: bibl., ill., music.

Taking issue with Gabriel Saldívar, whose *El jarabe* (1937) remains a standard

authority, the author dates the music to which Anna Pavlova danced the *jarabe* March 18, 1919 in the Teatro Arbeu as having been compiled by Mexico City native Manuel Castro Padilla (1897–1940) in 1919, not in 1905 when he was only eight years old. Despite the printing of musical examples upside down (p. 84, 88, 91) the music of the *Jarabe jalisciense* (Chap. 6), its choreography (Chap. 5), and pictures of the appropriate dance costumes (Chap. 7) go beyond Saldívar, making this a valuable addition to the *jarabe* literature.

5232 Medina, Angel. Un nuevo manuscrito del tratado de guitarra de Vargas y Guzmán, Cádiz, 1773. (*Inter-Am. Music Rev.*, 10:2, Spring/Summer 1989, p. 61–67, ill.)

Before emigrating to Mexico, Vargas y Guzmán resided at Cádiz, where in 1773 he prepared a preliminary draft of his *Explicación para tocar la guitarra* (Veracruz, 1776; copies of the 1776 version, with differences, exist at the Archivo General de la Nación, Mexico City, and at the Newberry Library, Chicago). The music at the end of the 1773 manuscript treatise comprises nine minuets, a passepied, and three other short pieces.

Navarrete Hernández, Mario. Cuatro instrumentos musicales prehispánicos. See *HLAS* 51:340.

5233 Negrete, Diana. Jorge Negrete. México: Editorial Diana, 1988. 391 p.: ill.

In this authorized biography of the *charro cantor* who starred in 41 Mexican films 1937–55, the daughter of Jorge Alberto Negrete Moreno (1911–53) portrays him as a knight in shining armor, *sans peur et sans reproche*.

5234 Ochoa Campos, Moisés. La chilena guerrerense. Chilpancingo de los Bravos, Mexico: Gobierno del Estado de Guerrero, 1987. 140 p.: bibl., ill. (Serie Fuentes; 2)

The Chilean ships commanded by Admiral Cochrane that arrived at Acapulco port Jan. 25, 1822, carried sailors who remained in the region until the squadron's departure two months later. They introduced the *cueca* that in Guerrero became the *chilena*. The origins of the *cueca* are African according to Benjamín Vicuña Mackenna (1831–86), but Peruvian in the opinion of Antonio Acevedo Hernández. Carlos Vega claimed that "el ori-gen de todos los bailes y canciones populares sudamericanos era limeño." The author of the present posthumous monograph (1927–85) studied at Rome and Santiago de Chile. He was for many years director of the Seminario de Ciencia Política at the Univ. Nacional Autónoma de México.

5235 Parker, Robert L. Diego Rivera, Frida Kahlo y Carlos Chávez: colaboración, desilusión y retribución. (*Heterofonía*, enero/feb./marzo 1987, p. 6–29, ill.)

When Chávez authorized a catalog of his works in 1971, the data concerning *H.P. Caballos de vapor*, premiered at Philadelphia March 31, 1952, excluded any mention of his chief collaborator, Diego Rivera. On Feb. 26, 1952, Chávez informed Rivera that a mural commissioned by the Instituto Nacional de Bellas Artes could not be shown in a forthcoming May 1952 Exposición de Arte Mejicano Antiguo y Moderno at Paris. Rivera countered by publicly accusing Chávez of being a dictator interested solely in bureaucratic power, an enemy of all the Mexican composers, and a tool of imperialism. This important article also contains a wealth of information concerning Rivera's twice-married painter wife Frida Kahlo, and her relations with Chávez.

5236 Premio "Robert Stevenson" fue ganado por musicólogos mexicanos. (*Rev. Music. Chil.*, 43:172, julio/dic. 1989, p. 118)

Juan José Escorza and José Antonio Robles Cahero won the $5,000 first prize awarded by the Organization of American States in 1988 for their edition of Juan Antonio de Vargas Guzmán's *Explicacíon para tocar la guitarra* (Veracruz, 1776).

5237 Pulido Silva, Esperanza. Robert Stevenson, mexicanista. (*Inter-Am. Music Rev.*, 10:2, Spring/Summer 1989, p. 93–99)

Excerpts from correspondence with the *directora* of Heterofonía dated Feb. 19, 1974–Jan. 31, 1986.

5238 Querol Gavaldá, Miguel. Notas biobibliográficas sobre compositores de los que existe música en la catedral de Puebla. (*Inter-Am. Music Rev.*, 10:2, Spring/Summer 1989, p. 49–60, facsims., music)

Biobibliographical information on 15 17th-century and 14 18th-century composers in Puebla Cathedral music manuscripts, correcting and amplifying Alice Ray [Catalyne]'s defective article "Music of the Sixteenth to Eighteenth Centuries in the Cathedral of Puebla, Mexico" *Yearbook of the Inter-American Institute for Musical Research* (Tulane Univ., 2, 1966). Typical of her gross mistakes, Ray confused Fabián [García] Pacheco with Francisco Javier García Fajer.

5239 Revueltas, Silvestre. Escritos de Revueltas. (*Pauta*, 9:33, enero/marzo 1990, p. 50–55, ill.)

Succinct program notes for Orquestra Sinfónica Nacional performances Oct. 15 and Dec. 1, 1933, of his own *Cuanáhuac* and *Esquinas*, and of such other works as *Don Juan* by Richard Strauss, *Classic Symphony* by Prokofiev, and *La Valse* by Ravel, given in fall 1933 and 1935 seasons.

5240 Ruiz Tarazona, Andrés. En el centenario de Salazar. (*Scherzo*, 5:47, sept. 1990, p. 94–97, ill.)

Born at Madrid, Adolfo Salazar (1890–1958) emigrated in 1939 to Mexico City where he continued publishing books, articles, and reviews that were "ansiosamente buscados por la juventud estudiosa española durante la dictadura."

5241 Saavedra, Leonora. 50 años de música de concierto en México. (*Plural*, 17:200, mayo 1988, p. 45–51, bibl., ill.)

Before 1950, guest conductors of pick-up orchestras in the expensive Palacio de Bellas Artes included Rocabruna (1936), Iturbi (1939), Limantour (1942), Erich Kleiber (1942–43), Horenstein (1944–45), and Roemer (1948). After 1950, only orchestras and instrumental ensembles subsidized by the government gave concerts. Concert life never found support of the proletarian masses.

5242 Saavedra, Leonora. Los escritos periodísticos de Carlos Chávez: una fuente para la historia de la música en México. (*Inter-Am. Music Rev.*, 10:2, Spring/Summer 1989, p. 77–91)

Chávez's ca. 225 journalistic contributions—the bulk of them newspaper articles for *El Universal* beginning in 1924 when he was 25 years old and continuing with interruptions to 1960—form a neat packet at the Archivo General de la Nación, Mexico City. Saavedra judiciously analyzes, quotes, and summarizes. Chávez's egoism prevented him from endorsing any currents in Mexican music that did not flow through him. As a po-

lemicist, he was never gracious or yielding. On the other hand, he supremely valued the approval that US musical powers bestowed, and did everything possible to cultivate and continue it.

5243 Stevenson, Robert Murrell. Aztec organography. (*Inter-Am. Music Rev.*, 9:2, Spring/Summer 1988, p. 1–19, bibl., ill.)

Treats musical instruments current among the precontact Aztecs.

5244 Stevenson, Robert Murrell. Catalogue of Newberry Library Mexican choirbooks (Case MS VM 2147 C36). (*Inter-Am. Music Rev.*, 9:1, Fall/Winter 1987, p. 65–73, facsims.)

The Newberry choirbooks contain a rich store of works by Renaissance and Baroque composers ranging from Hernando Franco and Francisco Guerrero to Juan de Lienas, Thomas Luis de Victoria, and Fabián Ximeno—here exhaustively itemized.

5245 Stevenson, Robert Murrell. Ferrer, Manuel Ygnacio. (*Inter-Am. Music Rev.*, 8:1, Fall/Winter 1986, p. 41, 80–88, 120–125, music)

Born at San Antonio, Baja California, in May 1832, Ferrer emigrated in 1850 to San Francisco, where, after ranking as the leading concert guitarist in the area and publishing prolifically, he died June 1, 1904. His *Compositions and arrangements for the guitar* (San Francisco: Mathias Gray, 1882) contain the Mexican national anthem, a Mexican Waltz, his own *Los lindos ojos* (*danza habanera*), and his Mexican compatriot Miguel S. Arévalo's *La súplica* (*danza habanera*).

5246 Stevenson, Robert Murrell. Mexican baroque polyphony in foreign libraries. (*Inter-Am. Music Rev.*, 9:1, Fall/Winter 1987, p. 55–64)

Updated and augmented version of Stevenson's "Mexican Colonial Music Manuscripts Abroad" (*Notes of the Music Library Association* 29:2, Jan. 1972, p. 203–214).

5247 Stevenson, Robert Murrell. Mexico City cathedral music, 1600–1675. (*Inter-Am. Music Rev.*, 9:1, Fall/Winter 1987, p. 75–114, music)

Excerpts from Antonio Rodríguez Mata and Luis Coronado's passions, a *gallego* by Fabián Ximeno, and a Magnificat by Francisco López Capillas illustrate the varied styles embraced by successive cathedral chapelmasters.

PARAGUAY

5248 Sequera, Guillermo. Cosmofonía de los indígenas mbya del Paraguay. (*Caravelle*, 49, 1987, p. 65–75, bibl.)

Among instruments of European derivation, the Mbya revere as sacred the bowed *rave* (a descendant of the rabel rebeck, the *rave* is tuned in fifths) and the plucked *kuminjare* (a five-course, doubled-string). The wood for both is from the revered *yary* (cedar) tree; the strings are of nylon. Women more frequently than men play the cane syrinx of six or seven tubes (*mimby pu*). Men play the vertical flute (*mimby puku*), made of cane and open at both ends.

PERU

5249 Chaumeil, Jean-Pierre. Las fiestas: abandono y supervivencia. (*Shupihui*, 13:45/46, enero 1988, p. 37–46, ill., music)

Extracted from his book *Los Yaguas del Nor-Oriente Peruano* (Lima: Centro de Investigación Antropológica de la Amazonia Peruana, 1987, p. 161–168), this article includes 16 rhythmic and melodic incises transcribed from Yagua dances recorded in Dec. 1971 (San Antonio de Arambaza) and Sept. 1973 (in Maposa). The Yaguas no longer celebrate festivals handed down from pre-contact times. The instruments pictured in this article include syrinx, *quena, cascabeles,* and snare drum, but not the pair of *trompas de corteza* used to evoke the *runda* spirit.

5250 Chirif, Alberto; Stefano Varese; and Josafat Roel P. Voces e instruments de la selva. (*Shupihui*, 13:45/46, enero 1988, p. 123–136, music)

Originally published as liner notes for an album of the same title issued in 1969 by the Casa de la Cultura Peruana, the six Aguaruna songs here notated were recorded between April and June of that year in the Aguaruna reserves of Nazareth and Facunda bordering the Chiriyaca river. The Aguaruna rate as the best singers, according to the annotations. The Campa occupy a vast zone between the Apurimac river and the Upper Ucayalí. Their three songs and three instrumental pieces here transcribed were recorded during February 1967 in the area between Oventeni mission, the Upper Shitani river, and the lake Tzirompiani region where a *curandero* named Poshano lived. The Campa instrumental pieces include one for mouth bow called *piompirintzi*, and another pair (pieces 10 and 17) for a flute called *jonkamentotzi* which married woman should not play in social gatherings, because of their seductive associations. Both men and women may properly play it to amuse and beguile themselves when traversing forest trails.

5251 Kike Pinto, Arturo. Afinaciones de la guitarra en Ayacucho. (*Bol. Lima*, 9:49, enero 1987, p. 83–87, bibl., ill., music)

After consultation with Ayacucho guitarists Raúl García Zárate and Manuel Prado, the author itemizes possible tunings of the Andean six-course guitar, with each tuning befitting a certain key. Because the tunings with the top course e¹ and the next-to-bottom B/ contain a tritone, these are popularly known as "devil" tunings (*diabolus in musica*).

5252 Paniagua L., Félix. Los creadores de la música puneña. (*Bol. Lima*, 9:51, mayo 1987, p. 61–89)

Extremely welcome biographies of 16 composers born in or near Puno, many of them provided with exact dates of birth and lists of works. In alphabetical order, they are: Mariano Béjar Pacheco, Víctor Echave Cabrera, Rosendo Huirse Nuños (1880–1971), Augusto Masías Hinojosa (b. 1932), Victor Masías Rodriguez (1900–73), Néstor Molina Galindo, Virgilio Palacios Ortega, Julián Palacios Ríos (1887–1974), Augusto Portugal Vidangos, J. Eladio Quiroga Rosado (1908–57), Alberto Rivarola Miranda (1892–1958), Carlos Conrado Robins Burgos (1895–1959), Edgar Valcárcel Arze (b. 1932), Theodoro Valcárcel Caballero (1900–42), Castor Vera Solano (1913–76), and Juan Visa Choquemamani.

5253 Pinilla, Enrique. La música de la selva peruana. (*Shupihui*, 13:45/46, enero 1988, p. 9–35, music)

According to Pinilla, nine-tenths of *selva* music consists of songs, many times unaccompanied—despite the cataloging of over 500 forest area instruments. The sounds of the Amazonian fauna find frequent echo in forest songs. Among the more than ten hours of taped forest music heard by Pinilla in 1963, the Culima Aribal songs were notable for the complexity of the scales that sometimes bordered on the microtonal character of Nazca antara emissions. The Shipibo songs contained melodic cells that were at times expanded into motives or "themes," and their songs occasionally "modulated" from one "minor" mode to another (A minor to E minor, as example on p. 35). An Aguaruna tribal melody could modulate from major to its tonic minor (G major to G minor). Pinilla comments unsympathetically on forest music studies by Fritz Bose (Berlin, 1934), Patsy Adams (*Folklore Americano*, 10:10, 1962), Lila Wistrand (*Ethnomusicology*, 13:3, 1969), and Rodolfo Holzmann (*Panorama de la música tradicional del Perú*, Lima, 1966). On the other hand, he approves of Alberto Chirif and Stefano Varese's liner notes for "Voces e instrumentos de la Selva: Aguaruna-Campas," an LP issued in 1969 under auspices of the Casa de la Cultura Peruana and the Instituto Raúl Porras Barrenechea.

5254 La sangre de los cerros: antología de la poesía quechua cantada. Transcripción de Raúl R. Romero y Rosalina [i.e. Rosa Elena] Vásquez. Recopilación de Rodrigo Montoya *et al.* Lima: CEPES, 1987. 107 p. of music. (Serie Cultura peruana; 2)

Collection of 170 tunes transcribed by ethnomusicologists Romero and Vásquez complements some half of the 333 Quechua song texts published by Rodrigo Montoya and Luis Montoya with the cooperation of Edwin Montoya in their book *Urqukunapa Yawarnin: la sangre de los cerros; antología de la poesía quechua cantada* (Lima: Cepes; Mosca Azul Editores; Univ. Nacional Mayor San Marcos, 1987). In the introduction (p. 7–10), Romero explains that, as a rule, only one strophe is fitted to each tune, the other strophes published in the 1987 anthology being fitted at the singer's discretion. The 1987 anthology is also a necessary complement because each song is there typed, assigned to its place of origin, given an author, and translated into Spanish. As for the music: deviations from the European tempered scale (indicated by diacritics) and glissandos are salient features of the vocal style. Over half the 170 tunes are pentatonic. Another large number are either triadic or four-note melodies. The meter shifts at will, even

though the basic quarter-note pulse (indicated by metronome marks) remains steady. As witnessed to by the transcribers, high pitch ("screaming") and "harsh" timbre continue characterizing Andean vocal style. Seven tune transcriptions derive from previous Andean song anthologies; the rest of the tunes were transcribed from commercial disks, taped versions made *in situ*, or sung by commissioned informants.

5255 Turino, Thomas. Structure, context, and strategy in musical ethnology. (*Ethnomusicology*, 34:3, Fall 1990, p. 399–412, bibl., ill.)

Introducing his discussion of the Fiesta de la Cruz which he visited and participated in at the rural Aymara district of Conima in southern Peru May 3, 1986, the author, who was then in Peru, writes: "In recent years it had been customary for the community of Huata, located within the district to perform *imillani* (a 'coming out' dance for young girls) accompanied by panpipes, and for various ensembles from the communities of Checasaya to dance *achachk'umu* with *pitus* (side-blown flutes). Formerly, the community of Japisi had performed the *chokelas* (vertical end-notched flutes) for the fiesta, but this tradition has effectively passed out of existence. In 1986, only a single, costumed *achachk'umu* ensemble of Checasaya danced." Turino ventures that the reasons for the fiesta's decline was the "badness" of the music in 1986 and the "cover-up" of the "badness."

5256 Vásquez Rodríguez, Chalena and **Abilio Vergara Figueroa.** ¡Chayraq!: carnaval ayacuchano. Lima: Centro de Desarrollo Agropecuario; Asociación de Publicaciones Educativas, 1988. 395 p.: bibl., ill., index.

All 75 songs and instrumental pieces transcribed in this sumptuous volume were recorded during the 1987 carnival at Ayacucho. In contrast with the transcriptions in *La sangre de los cerros*, every song transcribed herein is accompanied by its complete text (all strophes) and by its translation into Spanish. The songs are all transcribed in C major, G major, or A minor. The meter is almost invariably 6/8, and the songs never deviate from gapped scales. For those who do not read five-line music notation, graphs of the melodies frequently underlie the staves. The styles of the individual composers to whom the songs are ascribed—Alberto Morales, Rufino Pizarro, Elancio Pillaca, Jorge Gamboa, Juan Rojas, Jesús Pillaca, Julia and Bertha Godoy, Roberto Arce, Ranulfo Fuentes, and many others (p. 152–364)—never differ from the style of the numerous songs attributed to "creación colectiva." The educational ends that the volume is intended to serve are reinforced by "how-to-play" diagrams of the *quena* (p. 221–222), the guitar (p. 228), and diagrams of the choreography for dances and *comparsas* (p. 62, 72, 269, 275).

URUGUAY

Alfaro, Milita. Jaime Roos: el sonido de la calle. See item **3888**.

5257 Paraskevaidis, Graciela. *Mburucuyá* de Eduardo Fabini: una aproximación analítica. (*in* Conferencia Anual de la Asociación Argentina de Musicología, *1st, Buenos Aires, 1987.* Actas. Buenos Aires: Asociación Argentina de Musicología, 1988, p. 155–170, music)

With the aid of 20 short music excerpts, the author examines the structure of *Mburucuyá*, a symphonic work by Eduardo Fabini (1882–1950). The fourth of his five orchestral works composed between 1899 and 1937, *Mburuyá* (Guarani word for a brightly colored flower) was composed 1932–33 as a score for a ballet in one act of three scenes, the argument deriving from poem by the Uruguayan Fernán Silva Valdés (1887–1975). Lamberto Baldi conducted the première given by the Orquesta Sinfónica del SODRE April 15, 1933, and repeated it in the Buenos Aires Teatro Colón in 1936. Erich Kleiber conducted OSSODRE in a 1941 performance. The première of *Mburucuyá* as a ballet in the Estudio Auditorio of SODRE awaited 1954.

VENEZUELA

5258 Calcaño, José Antonio. La ciudad y su música: crónica musical de Caracas. Prólogo de Rházes Hernández López. Cronología de Walter Guido. 2a ed., aum. Caracas: Fundarte, 1980. 518 p.: bibl., ill., index. (Col. Rescate. Col. Caracas; 1)

Published in 1958 and in facsimile in 1980, Calcaño's magnum opus received short shrift in *HLAS 22 : 5723* from a reviewer unfamiliar with the terrain. Caracas-born Calcaño (1900–80) left a history that still remains the best in its class. The present edition closes with a conscientious list of the literature cited or used by him and an index of names. Until a better general history is written, some self-abnegating Venezuelan would do musicology a favor by footnoting, correcting and updating Calcaño.

5259 Castillo Didier, Miguel. Cayetano Carreño, 1774–1836: en torno a su cuna y su obra. (*Lat. Am. Music Rev.*, 11 : 1, Spring/Summer 1990, p. 36–62, bibl.)

During the lifetime of his father, Alejandro Carreño (d. 1791), the composer signed himself "Joseph Cayetano del Carmen," only adding Carreño as his surname when applying in 1792 for the chair of music in the Univ. de Caracas. This richly documented article elucidates the heretofore murkier aspects of Cayetano's biography and gives an autoritative listing of 49 attributed works—of which 20 survive. Six of these the author minutely analyzes, recommending them for recording.

5260 López Chirico, Hugo. La "cantata criolla" de Antonio Estévez: un análisis de la obra y de su inserción en el nacionalismo musical latinoamericano y venezolano. Caracas: Consejo Nacional de la Cultura, Instituto Latinoamericano de Investigaciones Musicales Vicente Emilio Sojo, 1987. 349 p., 1 folded leaf of plates: bibl., ill., music. (Serie de investigaciones; 6)

Exhaustive analysis of a work first conceived in 1948 and premiered in 1954 by the Orquesta Sinfónica Venezuela, a work now considered the chief masterpiece of Venezuelan nationalism. Gerard Béhague enthusiastically reviewed this book in *Latin American Music Review* (11 : 1, Spring/Summer 1990, p. 102–106), calling it an "obra magistral cuya seriedad y perspicacia sirven de modelo para cualquier estudio analítico de esta índole."

Milanca Guzmán, Mario. José White en Venezuela. See item **5213**.

5261 Milanca Guzmán, Mario. Reynaldo Hahn, caraqueño: contribución a la biografía caraqueña de Reynaldo Hahn Echenagucia. Caracas: Academia Nacional de la Historia, 1989. 264 p., 42 p. of plates: bibl., ill. (Biblioteca de la Academia Nacional de la Historia: Estudios, monografías y ensayos; 121)

With his accustomed acuity the author has identified the composer's father Carl as Jewish; born in 1822 at Hamburg (son of Rubin and Caroline [Levy] Hahn), he was baptized Apr. 20, 1853, before marrying on May 22, 1853, a native of Curaçao residing at La Guaira, María Elena Echenagucia Ellis (b. 1831). Not only as a minutely detailed account of the infancy of the composer (who had 12 brothers and sisters) but also of all aspects of the business, social, and governmental life of the extended Hahn family (Carl had three siblings at Caracas), this volume is extremely valuable. Reynaldo was born in Altagracia parish Aug. 9, 1874; baptized tardily Mar. 9, 1876; and taken with this family in a vessel departing from Venezuela for France April 20, 1878, never thereafter to return to Caracas.

5262 Milanca Guzmán, Mario. Teresa Carreño: gira caraqueña y evocación, 1885–1887. Caracas: Depto. de Relaciones Públicas de Lagoven, 1987. 138 p.: bibl., ill. (Cuadernos Lagoven)

After a 23-year absence, Carreño returned to her native land in 1885 for a concert tour that lasted until Sept. 1886. From March 15 to April 24, 1887, she managed and conducted an opera season. After the first six chapters entitled "Gira Caraqueña," the author draws parallels between her career and Arrau's. According to Arrau, "She was a goddess with incredible projection and energy. I believe that I never heard another pianist fill the old Philharmonic Hall in Berlin with her quantity of sound. Her octaves were fantastic, her velocity incredible." He heard her play the last three Beethoven concertos in one evening, with Nikisch conducting.

5263 Milanca Guzmán, Mario. Teresa Carreño: cronología y manuscritos. (*Rev. Music. Chil.*, 42:170, julio/dic. 1988, p. 90–133, bibl., ill., facsims.)

In this definitive study of Carreño's first decade, buttressed by 24 facsimiled documents, author recovers data for a detailed chronology (p. 98–106) that is a model of exactness and prodigality. Nothing can be more minute and meticulous than this author's work on 19th-century Venezuelan musical figures, insofar as their careers can be documented from contemporary newspapers, government, and ecclesiastical documents.

5264 Noguera Messuti, Luis. 30 años de historia gráfica de la ópera en Caracas. Caracas: Seguros La Seguridad Compañía Anónima, 1985. ca. 350 p.: chiefly ill., ports.

The compiler gathered in this coffee-table volume his b/w photographs of participants in operas given at Caracas 1955–85. Lacks index, table of contents, or other finding aids.

5265 Peñín, José. Realidad de la musicología en Venezuela. (*Rev. Music. Venez.*, 10:27, enero/abril 1989, p. 45–61)

In *La cuidad y su música* José Antonio Calcaño hid his vast learning: his amiable and ductile prose entranced the reader. But retracing his steps now can be extremely difficult, since his fundamental book lacks bibliographic footnotes. The first dated Venezuelan composition is Caro de Boesi's 1779 Mass. This work, along with the rest of Venezuela's colonial musical heritage, came to light quite by chance when in 1929 Ascanio Negreti stumbled on a cache of manuscripts behind a staircase in the building now housing the Escuela de Música José Ángel Lamas.

5266 Sangiorgi Dupret, Felipe. El maestro Vicente Emilio Sojo: vida y obra. (*Rev. Music. Venez.*, 10:27, enero/abril 1989, p. 77–102)

Apart from an evaluation of Sojo's fundamental place in Venezuelan music history, this article contains an extremely useful year-by-year chronological summary of the events in his life (p. 90–96) followed by a listing of his works by category.

JOURNAL ABBREVIATIONS

An. Acad. Geogr. Hist. Guatem. Anales de la Academia de Geografía e Historia de Guatemala. Guatemala.

Araucaria Chile. Araucaria de Chile. I. Peralta Ediciones. Pamplona, Spain.

Archaeol. Music. Archaeología Musicalis. Moeck Verlag und Musikinstrumentenwerk. Celle, Germany.

Bol. Lima. Boletín de Lima. Revista Cultural Científica. Lima.

Boletín/Cochabamba. Boletín. Centro de Documentación de Música Boliviana.

Caravelle. Caravelle. Cahiers du monde hispanique et luso-brésilien. Univ. de Toulouse, Institute d'études hispaniques, hispano-americaines et luso-brésiliennes. Toulouse, France.

Corresp. Musicol. Correspondência Musicológica. Sociedade Brasileira de Musicologia. S&tildea&o Paulo.

Cupey. Cupey. Colegio Universitaria Metropolitano. Río Piedras, Puerto Rico.

Ethnomusicology. Ethnomusicology. Society for Ethnomusicology. Ann Arbor, Mich.

Heterofonía. Heterofonía. México.

Humanidades/Brasília. Humanidades. Editora Univ. de Brasília. .

Inter-Am. Music Rev. Inter-American Music Review. Robert Stevenson. Los Angeles, Calif.

Jam. J. Jamaica Journal. Institute of Jamaica. Kingston.

Lat. Am. Music Rev. Latin American Music Review. Univ. of Texas. Austin.

Lat. Am. Perspect. Latin American Perspectives. Univ. of California. Newbury Park, Calif.

Montalbán. Montalbán. Univ. Católica Andrés Bello, Facultad de Humanidades y Educación, Institutos Humanísticos de Investigación. Caracas.

Nosa Terra. A Nosa Terra, a Nosa Cultura. Vigo, Spain.

Nuevo Dia. El Nuevo Día. El Día, Inc. San Juan, Puerto Rico.

Nuova Riv. Music. Ital. Nuova Rivista Musicale Italiana. Edizioni RAI, Radiotelevisione Italiana. Torino, Italy.

Palacio. El Palacio. School of American Research; Museum of New Mexico;

Archaeological Society of New Mexico. Santa Fe, New Mexico.

Past Present. Past and Present. London.

Pauta. Pauta. Univ. Autónoma Metropolitana. México.

Plural. Plural. Excelsior Compañía Editorial. México.

Que Pasa. Que Pasa. Tourism Co. San Juan, Puerto Rico.

Rev. Andin. Revista Andina. Centro Bartolomé de las Casas. Cusco, Perú.

Rev. Inst. Cult. Puertorriq. Revista del Instituto de Cultura Puertorriqueña. San Juan, P.R.

Rev. Inst. Invest. Musicol. Carlos Vega. Revista del Instituto de Investigación Musicológica Carlos Vega. Univ. Católica. Buenos Aires.

Rev. Mus. Paul. Revista do Museu Paulista. São Paulo.

Rev. Music. Chil. Revista Musical Chilena. Univ. de Chile, Facultad de Ciencias y Artes Musicales y de la Representación. Santiago.

Rev. Music. Venez. Revista Musical de Venezuela. Instituto Latinoamericano de Investigaciones y Estudios Musicales Vicente Emilio Sojo, Consejo Nacional de la Cultura (CONAC). Caracas.

Rev. Univ./Tabasco. Revista de la Universidad. Univ. Juárez Autónoma de Tabasco. Villahermosa, Mexico.

Ritmo. Ritmo. Publilat. México.

Scherzo. Scherzo: Revista de Música. Scherzo Editorial. Madrid.

Shupihui. Shupihui. Centro de Estudios Teológicos de la Amazonia. Iquitos, Peru.

Tempo Bras. Tempo Brasileiro. Rio de Janeiro.

Universal Dominical. El Universal Dominical. Cartagena, Colombia.

PHILOSOPHY: LATIN AMERICAN THOUGHT

JUAN CARLOS TORCHIA ESTRADA, *General Secretariat, Organization of American States*

EL CONTENIDO DE ESTA SECCION sigue determinado por la inclusión de los siguientes materiales: 1) los trabajos críticos sobre filósofos, obras y corrientes filosóficas propios de (o desarrollados en) América Latina (por ejemplo, sobre Leopoldo Zea o Francisco Romero, o sobre el existencialismo en Latinoamérica); 2) el pensamiento, los escritos y la influencia de autores que, sin ser filósofos profesionales o académicos, han utilizado ideas filosóficas y han influido sobre la marcha de las ideas generales o la orientación práctica de la sociedad (el ejemplo paradigmático es el de los "pensadores" del siglo XIX); 3) las expresiones ideológicas (en el sentido de bases conceptuales y programas de acción de corrientes y grupos políticos) que son propias de América Latina, tanto por creación como por adaptación, y que son o han sido, en mayor o menor grado, operantes, sea en el mundo de las ideas, sea en la realidad misma (el marxismo, por ejemplo); 4) las interpretaciones generales sobre América Latina, sobre su cultura y su identidad, el sentido de su historia, de su presente y de su futuro, cuando todo eso es percibido desde un punto de vista filosófico o el de una ideología de acción; 5) el problema de la filosofía latinoamericana, largamente debatido entre algunos filósofos de la región; 6) la historia política, social, económica, religiosa, institucional, literaria, etc., de América Latina o sus componentes, cuando es vista desde el ángulo de la historia de la filosofía, de las ideas o de las ideologías; 7) los trabajos que examinan las relaciones entre las ideas y la realidad histórica. Esta descripción puede no ser exhaustiva, a la vez que ignora de propósito la tangencia o sobreposición con respecto a otras secciones del *Handbook*; pero es una aproximación razonable. Sintéticamente, diríamos que la sección abarca: la crítica filosófica; el vasto campo que se conoce con el nombre no muy preciso pero por ahora imprescindible de 'historia de las ideas'; y las ideologías en que se manifiesta el pensamiento político, tomado este último en un sentido muy amplio.

Por decisión de política editorial no se incluyen, desde el *HLAS 46*, reseñas de la producción filosófica latinoamericana "original," es decir, aquella que quiere ser contribución a las diferentes disciplinas filosóficas (teoría del conocimiento, metafísica, filosofía de la historia, etc.), ni obras o artículos de crítica sobre filosofía europea (o cualquier otra no latinoamericana). Por extensión de esa misma política también se omiten, a partir de este número, las noticias sobre obras filosóficas latinoamericanas recientemente publicadas, que desde el mencionado *HLAS 46* se incluian en la introducción. No hay en estas forzosas limitaciones ningún juicio de valor.

A la misma vez que para no afectar la economía del volumen es necesario ser selectivo, el criterio de inclusión es amplio en cuanto a fechas de publicación. Si un escrito tiene verdadero valor para los propósitos de la sección y el investigador puede beneficiarse con su conocimiento, se incluye, aunque su fecha de publicación se remonte a algunos años atrás. La idea es constituir un *corpus*, si no exhaustivo, por lo menos tan representativo como sea posible, además de informar sobre las publicaciones recientes. Es más, la bibliografía acumulada clama por un análisis historiográfico, por un examen crítico retrospectivo, para decantar el valor de referencia o de uso de materiales que se han reunido a lo largo de más de 50 años.

A continuación se señalan los aspectos más salientes del contenido de la presente sección, según las subdivisiones habituales.

GENERAL

Obras generales destacables por su valor filosófico o por su utilidad se encuentran varias. Ante todo, debe señalarse *Discurso desde la marginación y la barbarie,* de Leopoldo Zea (item **5324**), que quizás pueda considerarse la culminación del pensamiento del gran maestro mexicano como filósofo de la historia de América, después de libros como *América en la historia* (1957, ver *HLAS 21:4775*) y *Filosofía de la historia americana* (1976). Lo característico de su última obra es la extensión de las tesis que ya había avanzado en su producción anterior, a ciertos sectores del propio mundo europeo.

Son dignas de mención también dos expresiones españolas que muestran el interés peninsular por el pensamiento latinoamericano: *Filosofía de Hispanoamérica: aproximaciones al panorama actual* (item **5284**); y *El pensamiento español contemporáneo y la idea de América* (item **5304**). Esta última representa la visión de españoles contemporáneos que vivieron tanto en España como en el exilio hispanoamericano. (Vale la pena recordar aquí el libro de José Luis Abellán, *La idea de América,* ver *HLAS 46:7501*).

La preocupación por la identidad latinoamericana, vista desde este lado del Atlántico, junto con el tema del sentido de la filosofía en América Latina, es el asunto de la antología de Jorge Gracia e Iván Jaksic, *Filosofía e identidad cultural en América Latina* (item **5291**). Jorge Gracia es también compilador, junto con Mireya Camurati, de una obra que se ocupa de la filosofía y la literatura latinoamericanas contemporáneas: *Philosophy and literature in Latin America: a critical assessment of the current situation* (item **5308**). Aunque esta última tiene la misma intención que la incluida en el item **5284,** los capítulos de la parte filosófica presentan un panorama mucho más rico. Una de las conclusiones parecería ser la existencia de un saludable pluralismo filosófico en la región. (Gracia es también el compilador de *Latin American philosophy in the twentieth century,* ver *HLAS 50:4566*). Por último,—en el sentido de *last but not least*—en este panorama sobresale también el libro de Richard Morse, *New World soundings* (item **5297**), muy digno de ser meditado.

Entre los trabajos monográficos debe mencionarse, por su calidad, el de John Lynch, *Hispanoamérica, 1750–1850* (item **5295**). Muy orientador sobre una amplia gama crítica es también *Imagología del bueno y del mal salvaje,* de Juan Antonio Ortega y Medina (item **5303**).

Dos temas se reiteran en esta subsección: el del indigenismo y el de la teología de la liberación. Sobre el primero de ellos pueden verse los artículos de Albizu Labbe (item **5267**); Barabas (item **5270**); Goncharova (item **5289**); y *L'Utopia selvaggia* (item **5319**) , título no muy feliz según las cosas se ven hoy en día. La característica común a los tres últimos es la atención que prestan a los movimientos actuales promovidos por los propios indígenas—lo que se ha dado en llamar "indianismo," para distinguirlo del "indigenismo" tradicional. (Obras anteriores sobre el asunto son: *Pensamiento indigenista del Ecuador,* ver *HLAS 50:4644* y *El pensamiento indigenista,* ver *HLAS 46:7608.*) En cuanto a la teología de la liberación, nos hemos referido a ella en la introducción del *HLAS 50.* Aquí se recogen seis trabajos: uno panorámico (item **5285**); dos de fuerte tono combativo (items **5269** y **5317**); uno de naturaleza analítico-crítica (item **5293**); y dos de un autor que se ha ocupado de ella reiteradamente desde el campo de la filosofía: Enrique Dussel (items **5282** y **5283**). Huelga decir que hemos sido altamente selectivos. En cuanto a Dussel, encontramos tres artículos que hacen referencia a su obra (uno de ellos proveniente del campo soviético): (items **5306, 5307** y **5328**).

MEXICO

Lo más saliente de la producción sobre México está representado por: un libro colectivo sobre Clavigero (item **5331**); un artículo sobre el krausismo en México, de Charles Hale (item **5333**), con la calidad que se espera de este autor; un ensayo de Enrique Krauze sobre Vasconcelos (item **5335**), con el que se ve reiterada la impresión de que Krauze se cuenta entre los mejores ensayistas hispanoamericanos actuales; un buen libro de Tzvi Medin sobre Leopoldo Zea (item **5338**); y una investigación de especial interés y buena factura de Rosaura Ruiz Gutiérrez sobre el darwinismo en México, que se asocia de inmediato a *La polémica del darwinismo en México,* de Roberto Moreno (ver *HLAS 50:4602*).

A lo dicho anteriormente sobre el indigenismo deben agregarse otros dos trabajos sobre el mismo tema pero referidos al caso particular de México. Ellos son: el libro de Bonfil Batalla, *México profundo* (item **5330**), combativo pero que no podría ignorarse, y un artículo de Gunther Marihold (item **5337**), que es una buena visión de conjunto.

AMERICA CENTRAL

En América Central (donde incluimos Panamá) se destacan: la reedición de la obra clásica de Constantino Láscaris sobre las ideas filosóficas en Costa Rica (item **5344**) y una antología—posiblemente única—de las ideas políticas en Panamá, a cargo de un buen conocedor del asunto, Ricaurte Soler (item **5346**).

CARIBE INSULAR

Un artículo sobre el movimiento obrero en Puerto Rico (item **5348**) y otro sobre los orígenes del socialismo en el mismo país (item **5347**) tratan asuntos poco explorados. (Estos artículos deben ponerse en relación con otros que se ocupan del marxismo y el socialismo en diferentes países: Costa Rica, (item **5345**); República Dominicana, (item **5356**); Venezuela, (item **5360**); Chile, (item **5402**); América Latina en general, (item **5286**). Siempre dentro de Puerto Rico, Maldonado-Denis continúa su labor de difusión e interpretación de Hostos, con una antología del clásico antillano (item **5352**) y otra de ensayos sobre él (item **5359**). En lo que respecta a Cuba, Martí sigue siendo un tema permanente. Señalamos un iluminador y sensato ensayo de Carlos Ripoll (item **5357**), y el libro de Maldonado-Denis sobre Martí y Hostos (item **5355**). Otros trabajos sobre el pensamiento cubano producidos en Cuba (items **5350, 5351, 5354** y **5315**), continúan en la tónica interpretativa del marxismo-leninismo tradicional.

VENEZUELA

Como es frecuente, Bolívar es un tema que se reitera. Lo mismo ocurre con Andrés Bello (items **5361** y **5368**). Por otra parte, en esta entrega hay varias expresiones del interés por el positivismo venezolano. Susana Strozzi brinda una buena contribución sobre Julio C. Salas (item **5369**); lo mismo puede decirse del libro de Luisa Poleo Pérez sobre Rafael Villavicencio (item **5366**); Francisco Gotera se refiere al propio Villavicencio y otros tres autores positivistas en un ensayo sobre los orígenes del positivismo en Maracaibo (item **5362**); y Harwich Vallenilla (item **5364**) insinúa la existencia de una tendencia revisionista en el país para tratar esa corriente. (Sobre literatura referente al positivismo venezolano ver *HLAS* 50, p. 646).

COLOMBIA

Lo más saliente es la obra colectiva *La filosofía en Colombia: historia de las ideas* (item **5372**), de evidente valor dentro de la bibliografía sobre el pensamiento colombiano. Se une a dos oportunas empresas que señalamos en el volumen anterior: una bibliografía y una antología, ambas del siglo veinte (ver *HLAS 50:4631-4632*). Sobre filosofía en Colombia ver también, en esta edición, item **5296**.

ECUADOR

Hay que señalar una vez más la labor que viene cumpliendo el Banco Central del Ecuador con su serie Biblioteca Básica del Pensamiento Ecuatoriano. Hemos recogido aquí tres nuevos volúmenes: sobre el "arielismo" (item **5379**); sobre el pensamiento estético (item **5381**); y sobre la utopía en el Ecuador, a cargo de Arturo A. Roig (item **5382**), quien ha contribuido mucho a que en pocos años Ecuador descubriera sus fuentes de historia de las ideas. Sobre Ecuador ver también items **5277** y **5276** en la subsección de obras generales.

PERU

Trabajos críticos sobre Mariátegui y Haya de la Torre constituyen lo más numeroso de lo recogido sobre Perú. De ello, lo más importante es la publicación del primer volumen de una edición de los *Escritos juveniles* de Mariátegui (item **5390**) y, sobre Haya, un artículo que afirma la estrecha relación entre los orígenes del APRA y el anarquismo (item **5393**). Reediciones de González Prada (item **5387**) y de Víctor Andrés Belaúnde (item **5384**) completan el cuadro de lo más saliente.

BOLIVIA

Interesa sobre todo una reunión de escritos sobre Gabriel René Moreno (item **5394**).

CHILE

En la producción sobre Chile descuella, con mucho, el libro de Iván Jaksic, *Academic rebels in Chile: the role of philosophy in higher education and politics* (item **5399**). Obra de largo aliento, repasa la actividad y el pensamiento filosóficos desde 1810 hasta la década de los años 70 de nuestro siglo; pero a la vez que sigue ese desarrollo muestra las relaciones entre la filosofía y la secularización de la sociedad chilena en el siglo XIX, y la tensión entre la filosofía como empresa teórica y las exigencias de la praxis política en el siglo XX, en especial durante el movimiento de reforma universitaria a partir de 1960. Es una excelente contribución.

BRASIL

A pesar de ser Brasil uno de los países en que más se produce historia nacional de las ideas, lo reunido para esta edición no tiene la riqueza de otras veces. Esto no quiere decir que no haya trabajos útiles, como una bibliografía de la literatura marxista en Brasil (item **5407**) y un conjunto de testimonios y ensayos sobre el anarquismo (item **5408**); pero lo más saliente es el libro organizado por Antonio Paim sobre el Apostolado Positivista (item **5403**), y la obra de Riolando Azzi, *A cristandade colonial* (item **5406**). De interés también es la *História das idéias no Brasil*, de José Antonio Tobias (item **5412**).

URUGUAY Y PARAGUAY

Muy escaso es lo que se ha recogido sobre estos países en esta ocasión. Paraguay es evidentemente un país que requiere búsquedas documentales sobre historia de las ideas, que posiblemente se encuentren en publicaciones periódicas y en la prensa de los siglos XIX y XX, a pesar de que el clima político durante largos lapsos no ha sido proclive al pluralismo de opiniones. Con respecto a Uruguay, ver también item **5286.**

ARGENTINA

Aunque diferentes, como puede verse en las entradas individuales, sobresalen varias obras de conjunto: *Filosofía americana e identidad: el conflictivo caso argentino*, de Hugo Biagini (item **5417**); *Filosofía y nación*, de José Pablo Feinman (item **5420**); *Ensayos argentinos*, de Adelmo Montenegro (item **5426**); *Orígenes de la democracia argentina: el trasfondo krausista* (item **5427**); y *En busca de la ideología argentina*, de Oscar Terán (item **5438**). Todas están estructuradas como reunión de artículos. Tanto el libro de Biagini como el de Terán, así como *Orígenes de la democracia argentina*, sobrepasan la temática nacional.

Alberdi y Sarmiento son también objeto de atención reiterada. En cuanto al primero, hay una nueva edición del *Fragmento preliminar al estudio del derecho* (item **5416**); una selección de sus *Escritos póstumos*, al cuidado de Oscar Terán (item **5436**); y un trabajo descriptivo de conjunto (item **5444**). Sobre Sarmiento se destacan los aportes de Félix Weinberg (items **5443** y **5442**). Oscar Terán, además de las contribuciones mencionadas más arriba, ha elaborado dos antologías: una sobre Aníbal Ponce (item **5437**) y otra sobre José Ingenieros (item **5439**).

GENERAL

5267 Albizu Labbe, Francisco. Trajectoire(s) de l'indigenisme latino-américain. (*Etud. ibér. ibéro-am.*, 26, 1983, p. 105–120)

Visión panorámica del indigenismo desde la colonia hasta el siglo XX (o desde Las Casas hasta Mariátegui). Esquemático, pero de utilidad. Deja para otro artículo la fase más actual, en la cual el pensamiento y la acción provienen de los propios indios.

5268 Altman, Werner *et al*. El Populismo en América Latina. México: Univ. Nacional Autónoma de México, Coordinación de Humanidades, Centro Coordinador y Difusor de Estudios Latinoamericanos, 1983. 135 p.: bibl. (Nuestra América; 7)

Contiene cuatro trabajos: Lucía Sala de Tourón, "Algunas Reflexiones sobre el Populismo en América Latina" (busca precisar el sentido del término "populismo" y trata principalmente de dos autores: Octavio Ianni y Ernesto Laclau); Marcos Winocur, "El Populismo en América Latina" (también tiende a una clarificación, pero con casos concretos de gobiernos latinoamericanos, y luego examinando en particular el peronismo); Werner Altman, "Cárdenas, Vargas y Perón: una Confluencia Populista" (examina las propuestas y las correspondientes realidades de los tres casos, especialmente destacando la función del Estado); y Mario Miranda Pacheco, "El Populismo en Bolivia" (estudia el caso particular de este país). Orientados los autores por simpatías de izquierda política, una afirmación que se reitera en estos artículos es que los populismos no intentaron cambiar las estructuras económico-sociales.

5269 Arduini, Juvenal. Horizonte de esperança: teologia da libertação. São Paulo: Edições Paulinas, 1986. 195 p.: bibl. (Col. Fermento na massa)

Intensa defensa de la teología de la liberación. Habla de una "conspiración" contra ella.

5270 Barabas, Alicia M. Movimientos étnicos religiosos y seculares en América Latina: una aproximación a la construcción de la utopía india. (*Am. Indíg.*, 46:3, julio/sept. 1986, p. 495–529, bibl.)

Caracterización y búsqueda del significado de los movimientos indios de América Latina, tanto religiosos y milenaristas (más abundantes en el pasado) como seculares (más frecuentes en el siglo XX). La autora tiende a poner énfasis en el carácter político y descolonizador de esos movimientos, aun en el caso de los religiosos. Utiliza abundantes ejemplos para mostrar esta tesis.

5271 Borja y Borja, Ramiro. Raíces filosóficas del pensamiento político hispanoamericano. (*Rev. Hist. Am.*, 99, enero/junio 1985, p. 77–146)

Precede al tema hispanoamericano un largo ensayo de naturaleza teórica sobre sociedad, orden, derecho, etc., en el cual se percibe la influencia del tomismo. La parte dedicada a Hispanoamérica se relaciona con aquella estructura teórica previa, y trata de lo político-social en la colonia y en la emancipación, con frecuente referencia a la España medieval. El enfoque es más bien de historia del derecho y de las instituciones.

5272 Bravo Lira, Bernardino. Feijóo y la Ilustración católica y nacional en el mundo de habla castellana y portuguesa. (*Jahrb. Gesch.*, 22, 1985, p. 99–122)

Caracterización de Feijóo como representante de la "Ilustración católica" en España, es decir, de un espíritu ilustrado que se mantiene dentro de los límites de la fe. Para el autor, la de Feijóo fue a la vez una Ilustración "católica y nacional."

5273 Brunner, José Joaquín. Los debates sobre la modernidad y el futuro de América Latina. Montevideo: CLAEH, 1987. 75 p.: bibl. (Materiales para el debate contemporáneo; 14)

Obra importante como búsqueda de claridad sobre un tema conceptualmente poco definido. Se concreta mediante tres subtemas: modernidad, modernismo, modernización. No pretende grandes conclusiones sino abrir el camino a una difícil reflexión. En este sentido, el esfuerzo queda logrado.

5274 Casal, Juan Manuel. Sobre los fundamentos de una filosofía latinoamericana. (*Am. Merid.*, 5, 1985, p. 23–34)

Discute la posición de José Pablo Feinman y de Silvio Juan Maresca respecto de una "filosofía nacional latinoamericana." Intenta contribuir a la fundamentación de dicha filosofía con su propia meditación. Lo característico del trabajo es que acepta la necesidad de una filosofía latinoamericana expresiva de la liberación, pero critica lo que en ese orden se ha logrado hasta el momento.

5275 Casas, Bartolomé de las. The only way. Edited by Helen Rand Parish; translated by Francis Patrick Sullivan. New York: Paulist Press, 1992. 281 p.: bibl., index. (Sources of American spirituality)

Primera versión inglesa de *De unico vocationis modo omnium gentium ad veram religionem* (*Del único modo de atraer a los pueblos a la verdadera religión*). El texto que se ha conservado de esta obra de Las Casas es el llamado *Manuscrito de Oaxaca*, que han reproducido las versiones castellanas de Millares Carlo y Hanke (México: 1942) y de Castañeda Delgado y García del Moral (Madrid: 1990). En cambio, el que se adopta en la presente edición sería una "restauración" o vuelta a un texto anterior, más breve y desprovisto de materiales académicos que, aunque también de manos de Las Casas, recargan inútilmente, según la autora, al originario instrumento de evangelización. En un apéndice (p. 237–243) se señalan las diferencias con el *Manuscrito de Oaxaca*. Además del texto, la obra contiene una extensa introducción biográfica sobre Las Casas (con adelanto de noticias que se contendrán en el libro de Parish de próxima aparición: *Las Casas: the untold story*), apéndices biográficos y textuales, y bibliografía.

5276 Cerutti Guldberg, Horacio. De varia utópica. Bogotá: Publicaciones Univ. Central; Instituto Colombiano de Estudios Latinoamericanos y del Caribe, 1989. 237 p.: bibl., ill. (Pensamiento latinoamericano; 7. Ensayos de utopía; 3)

El tema de la utopía en América Latina está presente en todos los trabajos. En "La Utopía de 'Nuestra América' en el Pensamiento Cuencano" rescata dos autores "utópicos" ecuatorianos: Benigno Malo ("El Nuevo Mapa de América," 1866) y José Peralta ("La Esclavitud de la América Latina," 1927). En cuanto a la expresión, la nota dominante es el tono de compromiso político del autor.

5277 Cerutti Guldberg, Horacio. Hacia una metodología de la historia de las ideas (filosóficas) en América Latina. Guadalajara, México: Univ. de Guadalajara, 1986. 174 p.: bibl. (Col. Ensayos latinoamericanos; 1)

De los varios artículos reunidos en este libro destacamos: 1) referentes al Ecuador: "Aproximación a la Historiografía del Pensamiento Ecuatoriano" y "Situación de los Estudios Filosóficos y Sociales en el Ecuador en la Actualidad" (ver *HLAS 48:7602*); 2) sobre la historiografía del pensamiento latinoamericano: "Filosofía Latinoamericana e Historia de la Filosofía" (tal vez lo más importante del volumen); y 3) sobre el problema de la filosofía latinoamericana: "Problemas de Método en el Estudio de la Función de la Filosofía en la Realidad Americana." Buena parte de los trabajos son de naturaleza programática. Uno de los principales propósitos es crear una historia "materialista" de las ideas latinoamericanas.

5278 Cerutti Guldberg, Horacio. Sugerencias para el tratamiento del tema utópico en el siglo XIX. (*Rev. Hist. Am.,* 99, enero/junio 1985, p. 73–76)

Lo utópico se entiende no según la concepción habitual que lo hace sinónimo de lo irrealizable, sino como prefiguración del cambio o mejoramiento deseables. En el pensamiento latinoamericano del siglo XIX señala tres momentos utópicos: la Ilustración, el liberalismo y el movimiento obrero (ver número 5276).

5279 Codo, Wanderly et al. Psicología política latinoamericana. Coordinación de Maritza Montero. Caracas: Editorial Panapo; Texto-Volúmen, 1987. 407 p.: bibl., index.

Libro pionero en un campo poco desarrollado. La idea es rastrear lo que exista de psicología política en América Latina y darle a la disciplina un carácter propio, respondiendo a la realidad de las sociedades de la re-gión. El volumen se introduce con una revisión bibliográfica de la psicología política en América Latina entre 1956–86. También hay contribuciones metodológicas; estudios agrupados bajo el título general de "Identidad, Alienación y Conciencia;" y otros ensayos de naturaleza más específica dentro de la disciplina que se propone fundamentar.

5280 Congreso Interamericano de Filosofía, 11th, Guadalajara, Mexico, 1985. El perfil de la ciencia en América: actas. Recopilación de Juan José Saldaña. México: Sociedad Latinoamericana de Historia de las Ciencias y la Tecnología, 1986. 140 p.: bibl. (Cuadernos de Quipu; 1)

La mayoría de los trabajos expresan preocupación por la peculiaridad que debiera corresponder a la historiografía de la ciencia latinoamericana, y aun por lo que debe ser la ciencia y la investigación en la región. Así: Hebe Vessuri, "Los Papeles Culturales de la Ciencia en los Países Subdesarrollados;" José Sala Catalá, "La Ciencia Iberoamericana entre su Historia y su Filosofía;" Antonio Lafuente, "La Ciencia Periférica y su Especialidad Historiográfica;" Xavier Polanco, "La Ciencia como Ficción: Historia y Contexto;" Juan José Saldaña, "Marcos Conceptuales de la Historia de las Ciencias en Latinoamérica: Positivismo y Economicismo." Otros son de naturaleza monográfica: Celina A. Lértora Mendoza, "Contribuciones Argentinas a las Ciencias Humanas y Sociales;" Luis Carlos Arboleda, "Mutis entre el Rigor Wolffiano y la Intuición Cartesiana."

Congreso Internacional sobre Andrés Bello y el Derecho Latinoamericano, *Roma, 1981.* Andrés Bello y el derecho latinoamericano. See item **5361.**

5281 Cullen, Carlos A. Reflexiones desde América. v. 1, Ser y estar: el problema de la cultura. v. 2, Ciencia y sabiduría: el problema de la filosofía en Latinoamérica. Rosario, Argentina: Editorial Fundación Ross, 1986. 2 v.: bibl.

Estos dos volúmenes contienen trabajos filosóficos (entre otros, sobre la cultura y la hermenéutica) y ensayos relativos a la filosofía latinoamericana. Destacamos entre estos últimos: "El Ethos Barroco: Ensayo de Definición de la Cultura Latinoamericana a través de un Concepto Sapiencial;" "Sabiduría Popular y Cultura en América;" "Sentido y Función de la Filosofía en la Argentina de Hoy;" y "La Filosofía Necesaria en América Latina." Se puede situar al autor, de modo general, dentro de la filosofía de la liberación. En particular parece cercano al pensador argentino Rodolfo Kusch.

5282 Dussel, Enrique D. Hipótesis para una historia de la teología en América Latina. Bogotá: Indo-American Press Service, 1986. 98 p.: bibl. (Col. Iglesia nueva; 71)

La teología de la liberación sirve aquí como criterio de organización y periodización de la historia de la teología en América Latina en general. Así, de las seis etapas que el autor distingue en esa historia, tres serían formas de "teología de la liberación:" la que se preocupó por la situación del indio, simbolizada en el Padre Las Casas; la que acompañó al movimiento de Independencia; y la teología de la liberación propiamente dicha, de nuestros días. Las otras tres, de signo diferente, quedan de todas maneras caracterizadas—por contraste—con la teología de la liberación.

5283 Dussel, Enrique D. Racismo, América Latina negra e teologia da libertação: situação do problema. (*in* Escravidão negra e história da Igreja na América Latina e no Caribe. Edição da Comissão de Estudos de História da Igreja na América Latina (CEHILA). Petrópolis, Brazil: Editora Vozes Ltda., 1987, p. 217–237, tables)

El fenómeno del racismo encontraría adecuada explicación en el nivel de la ideología, específicamente como ideología de dominación. Luego pone en relación este fenómeno con la teología de la liberación, afirmando que el racismo es un desafío para esa orientación teológica.

Ecodesarrollo: el pensamiento del decenio. See *HLAS 51:2771.*

Fals-Borda, Orlando. Reflexiones sobre democracia y participación. See *HLAS 51:4528.*

5284 Filosofía de Hispanoamérica: aproximaciones al panorama actual: curso para profesores de Univ. del Instituto de Ciencias de la Educación de la Univ. de Barcelona; Barcelona, 15, 16 y 18 de junio de 1987. Coordinación del curso y de la edición de Eudaldo Forment Giralt. Barcelona, Spain: Instituto de Ciencias de la Educación, Univ. de Barcelona; Promociones Publicaciones Universitarias, 1987. 203 p.: bibl.

Recoge conferencias dictadas en el Instituto de Educación de la Univ. de Barcelona. Es indicativo, por lo tanto, del interés por el asunto en España. Los temas tratados son los siguientes: "Importancia y Actualidad de la Filosofía Hispanoamericana," panorama general a cargo de Alain Guy; "Espacio, Tiempo y Lenguaje de la Filosofía Hispánica," por Antonio Heredia, trabajo que se sitúa en el ámbito más amplio de lo "hispánico," que comprende también a España; "El Pensamiento Filosófico en la Obra de Carlos Vaz Ferreira," por José María Romero; "Aspectos de la Influencia de Ortega y Gasset en Hispanoamérica," por Francisco López Frías; "La Filosofía de la Liberación," por Raúl Fornet-Betancourt; y "La Metafísica de la 'Habencia' de Basave Fernández del Valle," por Eudaldo Forment Giralt.

5285 Foroohar, Manzar. Liberation Theology: the response of Latin American Catholics to socioeconomic problems. (*Lat. Am. Perspect.,* 13:3, Summer 1986, p. 37–57, bibl.)

Panorama de la historia, las bases y las principales afirmaciones de la teología de la liberación en América Latina. Se ocupa más de los aspectos políticos y sociales que de los propiamente teológicos. El movimiento es visto con simpatía.

5286 Frugoni, Emilio. Génesis, esencia y fundamentos del socialismo. v. 1–2. 2. ed. Montevideo: Ediciones de la Banda Oriental, 1989. 2 v.: bibl. (Obras de Emilio Frugoni; 5–6)

Reproduce—lamentablemente sin advertencia, introducción ni aparato crítico alguno—el libro de Frugoni sobre el socialismo, que es en realidad una historia de ese movimiento en sus diversas variantes. Casi la mitad del vol. 2 está dedicado al socialismo en América, interesando a esta Sección lo correspondiente a México, el Aprismo, Argentina, Uruguay, Chile y Venezuela. Frugoni fue el principal—y clásico—representante del socialismo en el Uruguay.

5287 Gissi B., Jorge. Identidad latinoamericana: psicología y sociedad. Santiago: Impresión Gráfica Andes, 1987. 211 p.: bibl., ill.

Conjunto de trabajos sobre temas psicológicos, pero algunos cercanos a la antropología social o cultural. El que interesa directamente a esta Sección es: "Identidad, Carácter Social y Cultura Latinoamericana," el cual básicamente retoma la reiterada denuncia sobre el colonialismo, el trato hacia los indios, el eurocentrismo, etc.

5288 Glaubert, Earl. J.G. Herder and Spanish cultural nationalism. (*in* Culture and Nationalism in Latin America. Edited by Victor Dahl. San Diego, Calif.: San Diego State Univ. Press, 1986, p. 1–11)

Breve pero útil trabajo sobre Julián Sanz del Río (1814–69), propagador del krausismo in España. El autor considera que el krausismo "can be thought of as a Spanish derivation of Germanic cultural nationalistic thought." El tema interesa por la repercusión del krausismo en América Latina.

5289 Goncharova, Tatiana. El indioamericanismo moderno: filosofía de la historia. (*Am. Lat./Moscú*, 2, 1985, p. 25–38)

El artículo es interesante y útil en cuanto expone y resume el pensamiento de algunos autores indígenas (Fausto Reinaga, por ejemplo), y muestra la diferencia de ese pensamiento con la filosofía y la cosmovisión occidentales. Parte del interés del artículo proviene, por lo tanto, del tema, es decir, de que el indigenismo que trata es una forma nueva y la más reciente dentro de la tradición indigenista.

5290 González Casanova, Pablo. Recuerdo y recreación del clásico: Marxismo y liberación en América Latina. Morelia, Mexico: Univ. Michoacana de San Nicolás de Hidalgo; Centro de Estudios Latinoamericanos Salvador Allende, 1985. 47 p., 8 p. of plates: bibl., facsim., ports. (Col. Historia de los trabajadores de América Latina; 1)

Interesa la segunda parte del libro: "Difusión del Marxismo en América Latina." Destaca a dos promotores: Germán Avé Lallemant (1835–1910), quien actuó en Argentina hacia fines del siglo XIX; y Carlos Baliño (1848–1926), marxista cubano. En este recuento también se incluye a Martí, pero según el autor no por marxista sino por revolucionario. (Sobre Baliño véase también item **5350.**)

González Stephan, Beatriz. La historiografía literaria hispanoamericana: agenda para problemas de la literatura nacional. See item **3378.**

5291 Gracia, Jorge J.E. and **Ivan Jaksic.** Filosofía e identidad cultural en América

Latina. Caracas: Monte Avila Editores, 1988. 446 p.: bibl. (Col. pensamiento filosófico)

Respondiendo a su título, esta antología entrelaza dos temas: 1) el de la identidad de América Latina (expresado en textos de Vasconcelos, Nicol, Schwartzmann, Mayz Vallenilla, entre otros); y 2) el del sentido y naturaleza de la filosofía latinoamericana (textos de Alberdi, Gaos, Zea, Frondizi, Salazar Bondy, Roig, Salmerón, Miró Quesada). La introducción ataca el problema de la filosofía latinoamericana desde dos ángulos: un provechoso examen crítico de los supuestos del problema, ponderando aciertos y desaciertos de las posiciones que se han adoptado frente a él; y un comprensivo panorama de su desarrollo histórico, trabajado principalmente en base a los autores representados en la antología. Se completa con una útil bibliografía.

Guerra Córdoba, Alexis and **Luis Ignacio Suárez Mesa.** Simón Bolívar y la Universidad latinoamericana. See item **5363.**

5292 Gutiérrez Girardot, Rafael. La concepción de Hispanoamérica de Alfonso Reyes, 1889–1959. (*Rev. Occident.*, 106, marzo 1990, p. 100–114)

Alta apreciación de Alfonso Reyes, por su labor literaria, desde luego, pero también por su aporte a la interpretación de Hispanoamérica y su cultura. Aunque no sin algún tono de manifiesto, es el tipo de escrito que merece lectura detenida y consideración atenta de sus afirmaciones.

5293 Hundley, Raymond C. Radical liberation theology: an evangelical response. Wilmore, Ky.: Bristol Books, 1987. 141 p.: bibl., ill.

Lo substantivo del libro es una crítica—más bien de tono sereno y comprensivo—a la teología de la liberación, tanto católica como protestante, desde el punto de vista de la posición evangélica. La base de la disidencia es la concepción y el uso de la Escritura. Son interesantes los datos que da sobre el movimiento teológico protestante "Iglesia y Sociedad en América Latina" (ISAL), fundado en 1959, al cual el autor considera antecedente inmediato de la teología católica de la liberación.

5294 López Portillo, Felicitas. Algunas consideraciones sobre el pensamiento conservador del siglo XIX. (*Rev. Hist. Am.*, 99, enero/junio 1985, p. 55–61)

Llama la atención sobre el hecho de que el pensamiento conservador latinoamericano ha sido poco estudiado, y señala algunos aspectos de él, basándose en el libro antológico de José Luis Romero, *Pensamiento conservador, 1815–1898* (Caracas: Biblioteca Ayacucho, 1978).

Luzbetak, Louis J. If Junípero Serra were alive: missiological-anthropological theory today. See *HLAS 51:712.*

5295 Lynch, John. Hispanoamérica, 1750–1850: ensayos sobre la sociedad y el Estado. Bogotá: Centro Editorial, Univ. Nacional de Colombia, 1987. 128 p.: bibl.

El libro está de hecho dividido en dos partes: 1) dos nutridos y bien informados ensayos de conjunto sobre la época anterior a la Independencia, el primero sobre las condiciones económicas y sociales y el segundo sobre la influencia de las ideas; y 2) dos estudios sobre los caudillos hispanoamericanos de la Independencia. Son de particular interés los capítulos "El Pensamiento Político de la Ilustración y su Influencia en la Independencia Hispanoamericana" y "Las Reformas Borbónicas y la Reacción Hispanoamericana, 1765–1810." Además de la seria información, caracteriza al autor su equilibrio crítico y su respeto por la complejidad de los fenómenos históricos que trata.

5296 Marquínez Argote, Germán. Sobre filosofía española y latinoamericana. Bogotá: Univ. Santo Tomás, Facultad de Filosofía, Centro de Investigaciones, 1987. 306 p.: bibl. (Biblioteca colombiana de filosofía; 8)

Corresponden al tema de esta Sección los siguientes artículos: "Horizontes Históricos de la Metafísica: Hacia una Metafísica en Latinoamérica;" "Zubiri Visto desde Latinoamérica;" "Benthamismo y Antibenthamismo en Colombia" (véase también **5371** y **5372**); "Fernándo González Ochoa, ¿Filósofo Colombiano?;" "El Problema de la Filosofía Latinoamericana y su Recepción en Colombia." En este último se alude a la discusión sobre la filosofía latinoamericana y en especial se muestra el caso de Colombia con datos muy útiles. (El artículo se publicó anteriormente en *Franciscanum*, 28:83, 1986.)

Merrim, Stephanie. The apprehension of the new in nature and culture. See item **3331.**

5297 Morse, Richard M. New World soundings: culture and ideology in the Americas. Baltimore, Md.: Johns Hopkins Univ. Press, 1989. 298 p.: bibl. (Johns Hopkins studies in Atlantic history and culture)

Por el estilo y la presentación de su contenido, es un libro más flexible que la clásica obra académica con su tesis central y su aparato de pruebas. Pero esto no debe llevar a confusión sobre la extensión del conocimiento del autor, la amplitud de sus fuentes, y su razonamiento. Es un libro rico en vistas no convencionales y en sugerencias para pensar. La temática va desde incursiones en la lingüística hasta Puerto Rico como cruce de culturas, pasando por la relación entre cultura y política en América Latina y el estado de los estudios latinoamericanos en los Estados Unidos. Aunque la obra desafía la fácil descripción, es de lectura imprescindible, especialmente por parte de los estudiosos latinoamericanos, que encontrarán en ella la visión desde otra cultura, pero con gran conocimiento y aguda percepción del modo latinoamericano de pensar.

5298 Muguerza, Javier. José Ferrater Mora: *De la materia a la razón* pasando por la ética. (*Rev. Latinoam. Filos.*, 15:2, julio 1989, p. 219–238)

Extenso, inteligente y por momentos informal comentario a la obra de Ferrater Mora, *De la materia a la razón* (1980), última parte de la valiosa creación filosófica de dicho autor.

5299 Münnich Busch, Susana. Nietzsche, Latinoamérica y la afirmación de lo propio. (*Estud. Públicos*, 20, primavera 1985, p. 349–363)

Se apoya en afirmaciones de Nietzsche para mostrar la necesidad de que todo pensamiento filosófico tenga por objeto la realidad propia. Una de sus afirmaciones es: en Latinoamérica "no existe una cultura filosófica propiamente latinoamericana."

Myth and the imaginary in the New World. See *HLAS 51:147.*

5300 *Nuestra América.* Año 4, No. 11, mayo/agosto 1984– . México: Univ. Nacional Autónoma de México, Centro Coordinator y Difusor de Estudios Latinoamericanos.

Este número está dedicado a la filosofía de la liberación, pero hay artículos que exceden esa temática. Horacio Cerutti Guldberg, en la Presentación, cree que se debe hablar de "filosofías *para* la liberación latinoamericana," lo cual implicaría, por un lado, que el movimiento no sería homogéneo, y por otro, que sería una especie de pensamiento instrumental, al servicio de la praxis liberadora. Los artículos son los siguientes: Enrique Dussel, "La 'Cuestión Popular' " (en polémica con Cerutti, defiende una interpretación del concepto de "pueblo" que lo distingue del de "clase" y lo deslinda del "populismo"); Edgard Montiel, "¿Conformismo o Subversión Creadora?: Un Dilema de la Filosofía Latinoamericana" (sostiene que toda doctrina filosófica debe ser revisada críticamente desde la realidad latinoamericana); María Luisa Rivara de Tuesta, "Augusto Salazar Bondy: Filosofía e Ideología en Latinoamérica y en el Perú" (señala que Salazar Bondy vendría a ser la combinación de las dos modalidades del pensamiento latinoamericano: la filosofía académica y el pensamiento ideológico o inclinado a la praxis; artículo útil también para la historia del tema de la filosofía latinoamericana y para los orígenes de la filosofía de la liberación); Arturo A. Roig, "Cuatro Tomas de Posición a Esta Altura de los Tiempos" (valioso testimonio, de parte de una figura de gran importancia dentro del pensamiento americanista, que se refiere aquí a los orígenes y desarrollos de la filosofía de la liberación y a su posición actual frente a ese movimiento); Ofelia Schutte, "Crisis de Identidad Occidental y Reconstrucción Latinoamericana" (considera que Leopoldo Zea y Arturo A. Roig, por un lado, y Enrique Dussel, por otro, representan dos modos por medio de los cuales la filosofía latinoamericana está forjando su propia identidad cultural); Gregor Saverwald, "Civilización y Barbarie" (con difícil lenguaje trata varios autores, pero especialmente a Juan Luis Segundo en su libro *Espesor de nuestra realidad*); Manuel Velázquez, "Consciencia Histórica: Posibilidad para una Filosofía de la Historia desde América Latina" (artículo de compleja presentación sobre la obra de Leopoldo Zea); Abelardo Villegas, "América Latina, Revolución y Lucha de Clases: un Ensayo Categorial" (en parte es reflexión sobre los temas de su libro *Reformismo y revolución en América Latina*, pero también examina las experiencias socialistas en Chile y Cuba).

5301 Ocampo López, Javier. Historia de la cultura hispanoamericana, siglo XX. Bogotá: Plaza & Janés, 1987. 297 p.: bibl., ill. (Selección Cultura colombiana; 57. Literatura)

Con las características de un panorama general, incluye manifestaciones filosóficas de ideas generales, literarias, historiográficas y educativas, de artes plásticas, y de cultura popular.

5302 Ortega y Medina, Juan Antonio. El ensayo cubano de Alejandro de Humboldt desde la perspectiva historiográfica mexicana. (*Jahrb. Gesch.*, 25, 1988, p. 673–693)

El grueso del artículo se dedica a la exposición del *Ensayo político sobre la isla de Cuba*, de Alejandro de Humboldt. En la "Conclusión," sin desmerecer los grandes méritos del sabio alemán y su incuestionable lugar en la historia científica del Nuevo Mundo, afirma que "fue un inconsciente instrumento de la penetración burguesa en la América hispana." Humboldt habría contribuido al conocimiento necesario para la penetración capitalista y proporcionado valiosa información a los gobernantes de Estados Unidos.

5303 Ortega y Medina, Juan Antonio. Imagología del bueno y del mal salvaje. México: Univ. Nacional Autónoma de México, 1987. 149 p., 16 p. of plates: bibl., ill. (Serie Historia general/Instituto de Investigaciones Históricas; 15)

Este libro, que resulta ser una guía útil para navegar en una extensa bibliografía, es de hecho un comentario a los siguientes escritos: "Sobre la Naturaleza Bestial del Indio Americano;" de Edmundo O'Gorman; "¿Hombres o Bestias?," de Lino Gómez Canedo; *Los grandes momentos del indigenismo en México*, de Luis Villoro; *La imagen del indio en el español del siglo XVI*, de Josefina Zoraida Vázquez; *L'exotisme américain dans la littérature française au XVIe. siècle*, de Gilbert Chinard; *América en el espíritu francés del siglo XVIII*, de Silvio Zavala; *La disputa del Nuevo Mundo*, de Antonello Gerbi; *Die "Wilden" und die "Zivilisierten"* (*Los salvajes y los civilizados*), de Urs Bitterli; y *The savages of America*, de Roy Harvey Pearce. También trata el tema de Ariel y Calibán en varios autores.

Parellada, Juan Ramón. Simón Bolívar, Libertador: una interpretación española. See item 5365.

5304 El Pensamiento español contemporáneo y la idea de América. v. 1, El pensamiento en España desde 1939. v. 2, El pensamiento en el exilio. Coordinación de José Luis Abellán y Antonio Monclús. 1. ed. Barcelona, Spain: Anthropos, 1989. 2 v. (Pensamiento crítico/Pensamiento utópico; 42–43)

Aunque trata del pensamiento español, lo que otorga a esta obra particular interés para Hispanoamérica es que tanto el pensamiento en España como el pensamiento español en el exilio son examinados en función del tema común de "la idea de América." La época tratada abarca desde la Guerra Civil española hasta la actualidad. Vol. 1 se divide en tres grandes partes: 1) El Pensamiento Conservador; 2) La Evolución desde el Oficialismo; 3) El Pensamiento Independiente (destacándose aquí el capítulo de Abellán sobre Laín Entralgo). Vol. 2 cubre diferentes zonas de Hispanoamérica. México, como era de esperar, ocupa una gran extensión; pero también se presta atención a Colombia, Venezuela, Argentina y Chile. Algunos de los autores tratados en esta parte son: José Gaos, José Prat, Justino de Azcárate, Manuel García-Pelayo, Francisco Ayala, Claudio Sánchez Albornoz y Leopoldo Castedo. Por su amplitud, por los textos que reproduce antológicamente, por sus indicaciones bibliográficas y por su tema central, se trata de una obra de verdadera importancia.

5305 El pensamiento latinoamericano en el siglo XIX. México: Instituto Panamericano de Geografía e Historia, 1986. 208 p.: bibl. (Pub.; 419)

Conjunto de trabajos cuyos temas se extienden, en el tiempo, entre finales del siglo XVIII y comienzos del XX. Los que tienen una directa vinculación con la historia de las ideas son los siguientes: Carlos Paladines, "La Herencia Ilustrada;" Rodolfo M. Agoglia, "La Fundamentación Jurídica de la Sociedad y el Estado;" Ricuarte Soler y Rubén Darío Rodríguez Patiño, "Proyectos de Unificación Hispanoamericana durante el Siglo XIX;" Horacio Cerutti Guldberg, "Aproximación a Dos Exponentes del Género Utópico Gestados en el Seno de la Ideología Liberal;" Arturo A. Roig, "El Siglo XIX Latinoamericano y las Nuevas Formas Discursi-

vas;" Carlos Stoetzer, "Positivismo, Realismo y Naturalismo: Ciencia;" Arturo Ardao, "Idealismo Latinoamericano del 900;" Leopoldo Zea, "Latinoamérica entre la Dependencia y la Emancipación;" y María Helena Rodríguez Ozán, "Inmigración, Surgimiento del Movimiento Obrero y Emergencia de las Clases Medias."

5306 Pérez Alvarez, Lorenzo. Un vacío en la historia de las ideas en América Latina: la mujer. (*Rev. Filos./Maracaibo*, 6, 1986, p. 135–147)

Destaca la labor filosófica de Enrique Dussel sobre la liberación de la mujer, y estima que las mujeres deben repensar toda la historia del pensamiento y elaborar su propia filosofía de la liberación femenina.

5307 Petiáksheva, Natalia. "Ética de la liberación" de Enrique Dussel. (*Am. Lat./Moscú*, 8:104, agosto 1986, p. 32–39, ill.)

La lectura es atenta y la crítica respetuosa, pero finalmente se reduce a señalar los vacíos que la doctrina examinada tendría para cumplir con los requisitos de una posición marxista. Señala en las teorías de Dussel (y de otros de orientación semejante) "la falta de atención a las premisas socioeconómicas de la liberación real," y afirma que "crean una simple apariencia de enfoque radical," permaneciendo, de todas maneras, "dentro del margen de la ideología burguesa."

5308 Philosophy and literature in Latin America: a critical assessment of the current situation. Edited by Jorge J.E. Gracia and Mireya Camurati. Albany: State Univ. of New York Press, 1989. 279 p.: bibl., index. (SUNY series in Latin American and Iberian thought and culture)

Los trabajos referidos a filosofía latinoamericana son: "Contemporary Argentinian Philosophy" (Hugo E. Biagini); "On the Diversity of Brazilian Philosophical Expression" (Onésimo Teotonio Almeida); "Philosophy in Brazil Today" (Fred Gillete Sturm); "Mexican Philosophy in the 1980s: Possibilities and Limits" (Oscar R. Martí); y "Philosophy in Other Countries in Latin America" (Jorge J.E. Gracia). En el caso de Argentina se destacan dos tendencias: la filosofía de la liberación y la filosofía analítica, aunque se indica que varias otras están también representadas. En lo que respecta a México y Brasil, los autores dan a entender que existe un intenso pluralismo filosófico, sin mayores conflictos ni grandes predominios. En estos países, el tema de la posibilidad de una filosofía latinoamericana quedaría en segundo plano, reemplazado por la práctica misma de la filosofía, sin cuestionamientos previos. Hay bibliografías sobre Argentina y México, además de una bibliografía general. La obra, útil de por sí, lo es más aún para el público de habla inglesa.

Popescu, Oreste. Estudios en la historia del pensamiento económico latinoamericano. See *HLAS 51:1618.*

Ramos, Julio. Saber decir: literatura y modernización en Andrés Bello. See item **3439.**

5309 Reperterio de filósofos Latinoamericanos Directory of Latin American philosophers. Compilación y edición de Jorge J.E. Gracia. Buffalo: Council on International Studies and Programs, State Univ. of New York at Buffalo, 1988. 122 p. (Special studies/ Council on International Studies and Programs; 156)

Contiene aproximadamente 350 entradas con nombres de personas que se dedican a la filosofía en América Latina, con los datos básicos, entre otros, de fecha de nacimiento, educación y obra publicada. El compilador antepone interesantes comentarios estadísticos, entre los cuales se destacan los referentes a las áreas de especialización de los filósofos incluidos. Es el único instrumento informativo en su género en lo que se refiere a América Latina.

5310 Rey de Guido, Clara. Contribución al estudio del ensayo en Hispanoamérica. Caracas: Academia Nacional de la Historia, 1985. 143 p.: bibl., index. (Biblioteca de la Academia Nacional de la Historia. Estudios, monografías y ensayos; 58)

Se trata de una bibliografía sobre el ensayo hispanoamericano, precedida de un extenso estudio preliminar. Obra de real utilidad.

5311 Roig, Arturo Andrés. Acotaciones para una simbólica latinoamericana. (*Cultura/Quito,* 9:26, sept./dic. 1986, p. 203–214)

Publicado anteriormente en *Reflexão* (9:30, 1984, ver *HLAS 50:4575*).

Rojas, Alejandro. La política como celebración de la vida y como construcción de espacios de esperanza. See *HLAS 51:4929.*

Sala Catalá, José. Crónica de Indias e ideología misional. See item **846.**

5312 Sánchez Agesta, Luis. La democracia en Hispanoamérica: un balance histórico. Madrid: Ediciones Rialp, 1987. 305 p.: bibl. (Libros de historia; 21)

Obra de síntesis, enfocada desde la historia constitucional. De utilidad para la historia de las ideas.

5313 Sánchez-Blanco, Francisco. Descubrimiento de la variedad humana y formación del espíritu moderno en la España del siglo XVI: el impacto del Nuevo Mundo. (*Rev. Indias,* 45:175, enero/junio 1985, p. 181–199)

Quiere mostrar cómo el concepto de "diversidad" a cuyo reconocimiento contribuyó la nueva realidad americana, chocaba, en el siglo XVI, contra conceptos tradicionales. Aunque la rigidez religiosa no permitió aprovecharlo debidamente, la novedad del Nuevo Mundo facilitó el sentido para la variedad antropológica y cultural. Artículo de interés.

5314 Sánchez Vázquez, Adolfo. El marxismo en la América Latina. (*Casa Am.,* 30:178, enero/feb. 1990, p. 3–14)

El autor es un filósofo hispano-mexicano de orientación marxista, que se ha ocupado especialmente de cuestiones de estética y de filosofía de la praxis. Este artículo es un panorama sobre el tema del título, elaborado con criterio personal e independiente. Se detiene con mayor extensión en Mariáteagui y en la Revolución Cubana. Señala también la relación entre el marxismo y la teología de la liberación. (Sobre el autor, ver *HLAS 50* p. 648).

5315 Seminario Científico Internacional,*Buenos Aires, 1988.* El Pensamiento revolucionario del comandante "Che" Guevara : intervenciones y debate. Buenos Aires: Dialéctica, 1989. 263 p. (Col. Política y sociedad)

Se reproducen las declaraciones y la participación en los debates de los asistentes al seminario. Aproximadamente unos 50 de ellos fueron latinoamericanos, miembros, de una forma o de otra, de la izquierda política de la región.

5316 Seminário de Estudos Latino-Americanos, *5th, Porto Alegre, Brazil, 1984.*

Os intelectuais nos processos políticos da América Latina. Coordenação de Maria Susana Arrosa Soares. Porto Alegre, Brazil: Univ. Federal do Rio Grande do Sul; Brasília: Conselho Nacional de Desenvolvimento Científico e Tecnológico, 1985. 251 p.: bibl.

La función del intelectual es vista, por los distintos autores, según diferentes temas: los partidos políticos, la educación, el Estado, la cultura, la democracia, etc. Algunos trabajos ilustran sobre la situación en determinados países latinoamericanos.

5317 Silva Gotay, Samuel. La transformación de la función política en el pensamiento teológico caribeño y latinoamericano. (*Rev. Mex. Sociol.*, 48:3, julio/sept. 1986, p. 129–161)

El autor es uno de los representantes más radicalizados de la teología de la liberación, y este artículo así lo muestra, por el alto grado de secularización que tiene su propuesta, el lenguaje utilizado, y la estrecha relación con el marxismo.

5318 Soler, Ricaurte. José Gaos y la historiografía de las ideas en América. (*Casa Am.*, 30;178, enero/feb. 1990, p. 107–111, photos)

Apreciación muy positiva de Gaos como historiador de las ideas latinoamericanas.

5319 L'Utopia selvaggia: teoria e prassi della liberazione indigena in America Latina. Emanuele Amodio, curatore. Ragusa, Italy: La Fiaccola, 1984. 215 p.: bibl., ill. (Edizioni La Fiaccola; 16)

El subtítulo es explicativo de la intención del libro. Contiene textos y pronunciamientos de ideólogos y agrupaciones indígenas de los siguientes países: Chile, Argentina, Paraguay, Bolivia, Perú, Ecuador, Colombia, Venezuela y Brasil. El interés reside en que los textos, de no muy amplia difusión en América Latina, aparezcan en un idioma europeo distinto del español.

5320 Villegas, Abelardo. Esquema para el estudio de la filosofía latinoamericana en el siglo XIX. (*Rev. Hist. Am.*, 99, enero/junio 1985, p. 147–156)

Valiosas indicaciones sobre los temas y corrientes filosófico-ideológicas que podrían componer un libro sobre el pensamiento latinoamericano en el siglo XIX.

5321 Wojcieszak, Janusz. Dylemat uniwersalizmu i partykularyzmu w hispanoamerykańskiej filozofii kultury lat 1900–1960 [The dilemma of Universalism and Particularism in the Spanish-American philosophy of culture in 1900–1960]. Warszawa: Centro de Estudios Latinoamericanos, Univ. de Varsovia, 1989. 272 p. bibl. (Studia i Materiały, 0867–3543; 1)

Analysis of the development of the notions of Spanish-American identity and culture is presented through the universalist concepts of Rodó and members of Mexico's Ateneo de la Juventud, and through other ideas such as Bolivian "mysticism of the earth," *Argentinidad, Peruanidad,* and *Lo Mexicano.* [M. Nalewajko]

5322 Yáñez, Eugenio. La Doctrina Social de la Iglesia y la política en América Latina. (*Opciones*, 14, mayo/agosto 1989, p. 177–194, ill.)

Descripción y defensa de la Doctrina Social de la Iglesia, que ha sido revitalizada, según el autor, por Juan Pablo II con su última encíclica, *Sollicitudo Rei Socialis.* Reconoce que dicha doctrina ha sido criticada por movimientos radicalizados, pero entiende que los cristianos no requieren de otro instrumento para cumplir con sus inquietudes sociales.

5323 Zavala, Silvio Arturo. Las Casas en el mundo actual. (*Caravelle*, 45, 1985, p. 5–20.)

Mirada de conjunto sobre la obra polémica de Las Casas, por una autoridad en el tema. Destaca el valor permanente de las doctrinas lascasianas. De particular interés son las ideas sobre la esclavitud.

5324 Zea, Leopoldo. Discurso desde la marginación y la barbarie. Barcelona: Anthropos, Editorial del Hombre, 1988. 284 p.: bibl. (Pensamiento crítico/pensamiento utópico; 29)

Ensayo de filosofía de la historia que complementa y da culminación a las tesis que Zea expresó en sus obras anteriores más personales, como *América en la historia* (1957) y *Filosofía de la historia americana* (1976). El tema de la (injustificada) marginalidad de ciertos pueblos o sociedades (ejemplificado en libros anteriores con el caso de América Latina) se extiende ahora a la historia de España, Portugal, Rusia y "Britania."

Fundamental para el conocimiento de la filosofía de Zea, cuya significación para el pensamiento americanista actual es innecesario destacar.

5325 Zea, Leopoldo. Filosofía de lo americano. Prólogo de Hernando Restrepo Toro. México: Centro de Estudios Económicos y Sociales del Tercer Mundo; Editorial Nueva Imagen, 1984. 420 p.: bibl. (Col. Cuadernos americanos; 6)

Recoge artículos publicados por Leopoldo Zea in la revista *Cuadernos Americanos* (México, 1942–81).

5326 Zea, Leopoldo. Hispano-América siglo XIX: ruptura y reencuentro. (*Cuad. Am.*, 19:1, enero/feb. 1990, p. 97–107)

La expresión "Hispano-América" se refiere al conjunto de España y la América Española. Originan la meditación del autor textos de José Gaos que ven el movimiento de Independencia de Hispanoamérica como correlativo de un intento similar de España para sacudirse la mentalidad imperial.

5327 Zemskov, Valeri. Conquista, polémica del siglo XVI sobre el Nuevo Mundo y orígenes de la tradición humanística latinoamericana: pts. 1–2. (*Am. Lat./Moscú*, 3, 1985, p. 26–41 and 4, 1985, p. 38–54)

Ensayo de síntesis. La segunda parte está dedicada casi enteramente a Las Casas. Vincula a éste (y al humanismo español del siglo XVI) con los orígenes de una cultura propiamente latinoamericana. Orientación más amplia de lo que haría prever la fuente en que aparece. Para comentario de un historiador, vease *HLAS 50:950*. Para comentario de un especialista de literatura, vease *HLAS 50:3017*.

5328 Zimmermann, Roque. América Latina, o não-ser: uma abordagem filosófica a partir de Enrique Dussel, 1962–1976. Petrópolis, Brazil: Vozes, 1987. 264 p.: appendices, bibl., ill.

Expone, con franca simpatía hacia la filosofía de la liberación, la obra de Enrique Dussel producida hasta 1976. En apéndices se incluyen dos trabajos de Dussel (ambos de 1985) y una bibliografía de este autor.

MEXICO

5329 Aguilar Monteverde, Alonso *et al.* Pensamiento político de México. v. 1,

La independencia. México: Editorial Nuestro Tiempo, 1986. 1 v.: bibl. (Col. Pensamiento político de México)

La obra tiene propósitos de divulgación. Una parte considerable se dedica a seguir los resultados de la labor historiográfica sobre el tema. En el prólogo se menciona el objetivo de mostrar la formación del capitalismo en el país y sus consecuencias.

5330 Bonfil Batalla, Guillermo. México profundo: una civilización negada. México: Secretaría de Educación Pública; CIESAS, 1987. 250 p.: bibl. (Foro 2000)

Resumidamente, el propósito de la obra es: 1) utilizar el conjunto de conocimientos establecidos sobre las culturas indígenas (el "México profundo") para destacar la negación que se hizo de ellas por parte de los sectores representativos de la cultura occidental (el "México imaginario"); 2) señalar la función clave que en ese proceso le correspondió a la dominación colonial; y 3) proponer un proyecto nacional que reconozca ambas realidades pero que de al "México profundo" un lugar que supere su negación actual. Aunque el autor se sitúa, en general, en una posición extrema, se trata de una obra digna de atención.

5331 Francisco Xavier Clavigero en la Ilustración mexicana, 1731–1787. Compilación de Alfonso Martínez Rosales. Prólogo de Antonio Gómez Robledo. México: Colegio de México, Centro de Estudios Históricos, 1988. 91 p.: bibl., index.

Recoge cinco conferencias organizadas por el Colegio de México con motivo del segundo centenario de la muerte de Clavigero, importante figura de la Ilustración mexicana. Contiene: "Clavigero: Defensor de los Idiomas Indígenas frente al Desprecio Europeo," por Dorothy Tanck de Estrada; "Francisco Xavier Clavigero, S.J., 1731–1787," por Xavier Cacho, S.J.; "Clavigero, Historiador de la Ilustración Mexicana," por Elías Trabulse; "La Cultura Italo-Mexicana de los Jesuitas Expulsos," por Alfonso Martínez Rosales; y "Un Mexicano en Europa" (que es una síntesis de la vida y de los valores representados por Clavigero). Antonio Gómez Robledo comenta estos trabajos en el Prólogo.

5332 González Rojo, Enrique. Ensayo sobre las ideas políticas de José Revueltas. México: Editorial Domés, 1987. 181 p.: bibl. (Obra filosófico-política; 4)

José Revueltas (1914–76) fue un novelista y militante de izquierda mexicano. Este libro da idea de su evolución ideológica. Estudia con detalle su obra *Ensayo sobre un proletariado sin cabeza* (1962), y dedica el capítulo final a la última etapa de su pensamiento político. Expresa variadas críticas a Revueltas, pero desde una posición relativamente cercana y no sin cierta simpatía.

5333 Hale, Charles A. El gran debate de libros de texto en 1880 y el krausismo en México. (*Hist. Mex.*, 35 : 2, oct./dic. 1985, p. 275–298, bibl.)

Trabajo interesante y que aporta útiles datos sobre un momento de la Escuela Nacional Preparatoria de México. Relaciona la cuestión pedagógica con la historia local y las influencias intelectuales europeas. Una de las principales tesis es el peso menor del krausismo en México frente al positivismo y al espiritualismo. Otra tesis es la mayor influencia de las corrientes filosóficas francesas frente a las españolas. Imprescindible para el estudio de la cultura filosófica mexicana.

5334 Knight, Alan. El liberalismo mexicano desde la Reforma hasta la Revolución: una interpretación. (*Hist. Mex.*, 35 : 1, julio/sept. 1985, p. 59–61, bibl.)

El liberalismo es enfocado aquí como sustrato y bandera de diversos movimientos políticos, los cuales a su vez determinaron en la práctica la evolución del liberalismo. Abarca la historia sociopolítica de México desde 1854 hasta 1910.

5335 Krauze, Enrique. José Vasconcelos en 1921: arquitecto del espíritu. (*in* Cultura urbana latinoamericana. Recopilación de Richard Morse y Jorge Enrique Hardoy. Buenos Aires: Consejo Latinoamericano de Ciencias Sociales, 1985, p. 95–102)

Fino e inteligente ensayo en el cual la obra educativa de Vasconcelos se ve como una manifestación de su modalidad filosófica más personal y de su identificación con el pensamiento de Plotino (ver también *HLAS 46:7547*).

León Portilla, Miguel. Time and reality in the thought of the Maya. See item **534.**

5336 Lida, Clara E. La Casa de España en México. México: Colegio de México, 1988. 201 p.: bibl., index. (Jornadas; 113)

Describe los orígenes y el desarrollo de la Casa de España en México, creada por el Presidente Cárdenas para absorber a la intelectualidad española exiliada con motivo de la Guerra Civil. La Casa se convirtió posteriormente en El Colegio de México. Crónica muy útil de una institución y un grupo de profesionales e intelectuales que son ya parte de la historia de la cultura en México.

López Austin, Alfredo. The human body and ideology: concepts of the ancient Nahuas. See item **538.**

5337 Marihold, Günther. Kontinuität und Wandel des indigenistischen Denkens in Mexiko. (*Ibero-Am. Arch.*, 12 : 1, 1986, p. 49–71, bibl.)

Ajustada visión de conjunto del desarrollo del pensamiento indigenista en México. Buena bibliografía. Incluye resumen en español.

5338 Medin, Tzvi. Leopoldo Zea: ideología, historia y filosofía de América Latina. México: Univ. Nacional Autónoma de México, Coordinación de Humanidades, 1983. 157 p.: bibl.

Posiblemente sea uno de los estudios que mejor permiten comprender el pensamiento de Zea, en sí y en su desarrollo. En el último capítulo se examinan las críticas que se han dirigido a la obra de Zea por parte, entre otros, de William Raat, A.F. Shulgovski, Zdenek Kourim y los filósofos mexicanos de la escuela analítica, como Luis Villoro.

Millares Carlo, Agustín. Cuatro estudios biobibliográficos mexicanos: Francisco Cervantes de Salazar, Fray Agustín Dávila Padilla, Juan José de Eguiara y Eguren, José-Mariano Beristáin de Souza. See item **972.**

5339 Nodar Manso, Francisco. Antonio Caso: el mito de su liberal mentalidad político-social. (*Can. J. Lat. Am. Caribb. Stud.*, 9 : 18, 1984, p. 31–55)

Duro ataque contra Antonio Caso y su pensamiento. Se concentra en los aspectos políticos e ideológicos: su relación con el porfirismo, el socialismo, la religión y el feminismo, entre otros.

5340 Ortega, Julio. Sobre el discurso político de Octavio Paz. (*Social. Particip.*, 33, marzo 1986, p. 89–95)

Crítica respetuosa a las posiciones políticas de Octavio Paz desde el ángulo de visión de una izquierda supuestamente distinta de la criticada por el escritor mexicano. No hay mucha precisión sobre esta forma de izquierda, pero uno de sus rasgos parecería ser su poca confianza en la democracia formal.

5341 Ruiz Gutiérrez, Rosaura. Positivismo y evolución: introducción del darwinismo en México. México: Coordinación General de Estudios de Posgrado [y] Facultad de Ciencias, Univ. Nacional Autónoma de México, 1987. 263 p.: bibl. (Col. Posgrado; 2)

Una de las principales tesis de la obra es que la aceptación del darwinismo en México se produjo antes en círculos de pensamiento filosófico y social que en el campo propio de la biología, por no estar esta última suficientemente desarrollada. Estudia: 1) la situación de las ciencias naturales en México en la segunda mitad del siglo XIX y comienzos del XX; 2) las discusiones sobre el darwinismo en la Sociedad Metodófila Gabino Barreda; 3) la obra de Alfonso Luis Herrera (1868–1942); y 4) las manifestaciones del darwinismo social. La obra es imprescindible para el tema (ver también *HLAS 50:4602*).

West, Delno C. Medieval ideas of apocalyptic mission and the early Franciscans in Mexico. See item **1098**.

5342 Zermeño P., Guillermo and **Rubén Aguilar.** Hacia una reinterpretación del sinarquismo actual: notas y materiales para su estudio. México: Univ. Iberoamericana, Depto. de Historia, 1988. 205 p.: bibl.

El tema de este libro es el pensamiento y la acción de la Iglesia Católica en México durante el siglo XX, tal como se manifestaron a través de instituciones como Acción Católica, Unión Nacional Sinarquista y otras. Consta de una introducción, breve pero clara; de un examen de la bibliografía sobre el tema; y de una sección documental.

AMERICA CENTRAL

5343 Arellano, Jorge Eduardo. Bosquejo ideológico de Augusto Sandino. (*Cuad. Hispanoam.*, 424, oct. 1985, p. 5–28, bibl.)

Presenta de manera clara y ordenada, con gran simpatía hacia el personaje, el ideario de Sandino. Si bien es exagerada la afirmación del autor en el sentido de que el luchador nicaragüense hizo una contribución significativa a la historia de las ideas en América Latina, son de interés otros aspectos destacados por el artículo, a saber: 1) las manifestaciones de Sandino sobre la unidad hispanoamericana; 2) el hecho de que la "redención de los oprimidos" pueda haber sido un motivo central de su tarea, junto con el combate contra la ocupación de su país; 3) la aparente absorción de ideas sindicalistas durante su estadía en México.

Blanco, Gustavo and **Orlando Navarro.** El solidarismo: pensamiento y dinámica social de un movimiento obrero patronal. See *HLAS 51:4628*.

Chandler, David Lee. Juan José de Aycinena: idealista conservador de la Guatemala del siglo XIX. See item **1429**.

Cuadra, Pablo Antonio. Aventura literaria del mestizaje y otros ensayos. See item **4272**.

5344 Láscaris Comneno, Constantino. Desarrollo de las ideas filosóficas en Costa Rica. 3a ed. San José: Univ. Autónoma de Centro América; Editorial Studium, 1983. 514 p. (Clásicos costarricenses)

Se trata de la 3a. edición de esta obra clásica y hasta el momento única sobre el tema. La primera se publicó en 1965 (ver *HLAS 30:5043*). La segunda, con algunos agregados, tiene fechado su prólogo en 1975. Esta tercera es póstuma y aparentemente reproduce sin cambios la segunda. Va antecedida de una nota de Guillermo Malavassi sobre Láscaris.

5345 Mora, Arnoldo. Los orígenes del pensamiento socialista en Costa Rica. San José: Depto. Ecuménico de Investigaciones, 1988. 47 p. (Col. universitaria)

Además de útiles indicaciones sobre la vida política costarricense del siglo XIX, estudia la figura de Félix Arcadio Montero, fundador del Partido Independiente Democrático.

Palmer, Steven. Carlos Fonseca and the construction of Sandinismo in Nicaragua. See item **1478**.

5346 El pensamiento político en Panamá en los siglos XIX y XX. Compilación de Ricaurte Soler. Panamá: Univ. de Panamá, 1988. 593 p.: bibl. (Biblioteca de la cultura panameña; 6)

Antología de textos políticos, que se

extiende entre 1821 y fechas recientes. De hecho viene a constituir una historia política del Istmo. Cada capítulo va precedido de una nota introductoria del recopilador. La mayor parte del volumen está dedicada al siglo XX. El autor no oculta sus propias preferencias, pero ello no afecta al carácter único del libro en la literatura sobre el tema, ni a su valor documental.

Sandino, Augusto César. Sandino without frontiers: selected writings of Augusto César Sandino on internationalism, Pan-Americanism, and social questions. See item **1495.**

CARIBE INSULAR

Amigó Jansen, Gustavo. La posición filosófica del Padre Félix Varela. See item **1718.**

5347 Dávila Santiago, Rubén. El derribo de las murallas: orígenes intelectuales del socialismo en Puerto Rico. Río Piedras, P.R.: Editorial Cultural, 1988. 223 p.: bibl.

Con simpatía para los procesos que describe, los temas del libro son: las organizaciones obreras, sus centros de estudio y sus publicaciones. La época analizada corresponde al final del siglo XIX y los comienzos del XX. Se trata principalmente del anarquismo, o "socialismo libertario," el cual, según el autor, constituye en Puerto Rico "la primera expresión ideológica del socialismo." En lo que se refiere a los centros de estudio fundados por las organizaciones obreras, el libro hace una contribución pionera para el caso de Puerto Rico.

5348 Dávila Santiago, Rubén. El pensamiento social obrero a comienzos del siglo XX en Puerto Rico. (*Rev. Hist./San Juan*, 1:2, julio/dic. 1985, p. 146–167, bibl.)

Texto de una conferencia. Visión panorámica del movimiento obrero en Puerto Rico a fines del siglo XIX y comienzos del XX. Se concede especial atención al aspecto de ideas y sus manifestaciones en publicaciones periódicas. En lo que respecta al "socialismo libertario," se mencionan expresiones coetáneas y semejantes en otros países de América Latina.

5349 Ette, Ottmar. Apuntes para una Orestíada americana: José Martí y el diálogo intercultural entre Europa y América Latina. (*Rev. Crít. Lit. Latinoam.*, 11:24, feb. 1986, p. 137–146, bibl.)

Lo más importante de este artículo para esta sección es la comparación entre Martí y Sarmiento en relación con los indios y con la dicotomía "civilización-barbarie."

5350 Gómez García, Carmen. Acerca de la periodización del pensamiento social de Carlos Baliño, el primer marxista cubano. (*Islas*, 82, sept./dic. 1985, p. 32–47)

Sobre Carlos Baliño (1848–1926), compañero de Martí y uno de los fundadores del Partido Comunista Cubano en 1925. Baliño es considerado "el primero en difundir el pensamiento marxista en Cuba." Se sigue el desarrollo de sus ideas y actividades a lo largo de su vida (ver item **5290**).

5351 Guadarrama González, Pablo. Valoraciones sobre el pensamiento filosófico cubano y latinoamericano. La Habana: Editora Política, 1986. 198 p.: bibl.

El método de interpretación consiste en apreciar cuánto los autores estudiados se acercan o se alejan del marxismo-leninismo. Aun dentro de esta postura, no es desaprovechable el artículo panorámico: "Algunas Particularidades del Positivismo en Cuba." Destacamos dos posiciones que sirven para situar al autor en el contexto de preocupaciones muy generalizadas de la filosofía latinoamericana actual: 1) Bastaría con abrazar "la filosofía del proletariado" para dar por resuelto el reiterado problema de la autenticidad del pensamiento latinoamericano; y 2) La búsqueda de una filosofía latinoamericana se ha producido "para evadir la creciente propagación de la filosofía marxista-leninista en este Continente."

Hernández, Pablo María. Historia del pensamiento pedagógico en la República Dominicana. See *HLAS 51:2618.*

5352 Hostos, Eugenio María de. América, la lucha por la libertad. Estudio preliminar por Manuel Maldonado-Denis. Edición especial del sesquicentenario de Eugenio María de Hostos. San Juan, P.R.: Ediciones Compromiso, 1988. 336 p.: bibl.

Antología de escritos de Hostos, compuesta principalmente por cartas y artículos, con énfasis, según el compilador, en "Hostos como sociólogo, educador y revolucionario." El estudio preliminar de Maldonado-Denis— autor de otras dos ediciones de Hostos—

abarca la biografía del pensador puertorriqueño, su obra de sociólogo y maestro, y su
"acción como revolucionario antillano." Libro de evidente utilidad, porque los escritos
seleccionados no son siempre de fácil acceso.
Una edición anterior había sido publicada en
México por la editorial Siglo XXI, en 1981
(ver item **5359**).

5353 Jimenes Grullón, Juan Isidro. La filosofía de José Martí. Santo Domingo:
Biblioteca Nacional, 1986. 217 p.: bibl.,
ports.

Los aspectos filosóficos de los escritos
de Martí son indagados afanosamente por el
autor, que profesa al personaje intensa simpatía. Este esfuerzo, sin embargo, excede lo
que los textos de Martí pueden tener de filosofía propiamente dicha. El prólogo indica
que el libro fue escrito "hace más de dos décadas," pero hay indicios que podrían poner
su elaboración hacia fines de la década del
40. (Aparentemente se habría publicado anteriormente en Cuba.)

**5354 Jornada Científica Internacional, *La
Habana, 1983.*** 30 aniversario del
asalto al Cuartel Moncada. La Habana: Instituto de Filosofía, Academia de Ciencias de
Cuba; Editorial de Ciencias Sociales, 1986.
851 p.: bibl. (Filosofía)

Este extenso volumen, que contiene
ponencias que fueron presentadas en 1983,
puede contribuir al conocimiento del pensamiento "oficial" cubano, por la abundancia
de material escrito desde una perspectiva
previsiblemente partidaria. Seis ponencias se
refieren al pensamiento en Cuba. Sus temas
y autores respectivos, en ese orden, son:
Carlos Baliño (Carmen Gómez García—ver
también item **5350**); el positivismo (Pablo
Guadarrama González); los movimientos
anarquistas (María M. Hernández Pacheco);
Felipe Poey (Gabino La Rosa Corzo); el pensamiento político en el siglo XIX (Olivia Miranda); y la relación de Diego Vicente Tejera
con Martí (Carlos del Toro González).

5355 Maldonado-Denis, Manuel. Ensayos
sobre José Martí. Río Piedras, P.R.:
Editorial Antillana, 1987. 92 p.: bibl.

Contiene cinco ensayos: "Martí ante
Bolívar;" "Martí y Hostos" (posiblemente el
más logrado como estudio); "Martí y su Concepto de Revolución;" "Martí y Albizu Campos;" y "Martí y Fanon." Por momentos la

prosa es exaltada, y atraviesa todo el libro el
tema del colonialismo y la independencia de
Cuba y Puerto Rico.

Miranda Francisco, Olivia. El pensamiento
de Félix Varela: coherencia y sistematicidad
en sus ideas filosóficas, políticas y sociales.
See item **1790**.

5356 Paulino Ramos, Alejandro. Las ideas
marxistas en la República Dominicana. Santo Domingo: Editora Universitaria,
USAD, 1985. 103 p.: appendix, bibl., ill. (Publicaciones de la Universidad Autónoma de
Santo Domingo; 453)

Breve crónica de la introducción de
ideas marxistas en la República Dominicana durante el siglo XX, con un apéndice
documental.

5357 Ripoll, Carlos. Martí: democracy and
anti-imperialism. Coral Gables, Fla.:
Institute of Interamerican Studies, Graduate
School of International Studies, Univ. of Miami, 1985? 15 p. (Occasional paper; 1985–2)

Las ideas sobre democracia y antiimperialismo son vistas y comprendidas en
la experiencia histórica y personal de Martí.
Aunque muy breve, es un ensayo clarificador
frente a la apropiación que tanto el pensamiento de derecha como el de izquierda han
hecho de ciertas afirmaciones de Martí.

5358 Ruano, Argimiro. Los orígenes de la
moral liberal en Puerto Rico. pts. 1/2.
(*Rev. Rev. Interam.*, 13:1/4, Winter/Spring
1983, p. 49–84; 14:1/4, Winter/Spring 1984,
p. 110–121)

Util solamente en cuanto algunos datos (y cierta literatura sobre el tema) son
poco conocidos, especialmente en el resto de
América Latina.

Valdés Carreras, Oscar. El Habanero: precursor; Patria: soldado. See item **3693**.

Vila Vilar, Enriqueta. Intelectuales españoles
ante el problema esclavista. See item **1855**.

5359 Visiones sobre Hostos. Selección, prólogo y notas de Manuel Maldonado-
Denis. Caracas: Biblioteca Ayacucho, 1988,
567 p.: bibl. (Col. Paralelos)

Se compone de ensayos y testimonios
sobre Eugenio María de Hostos. Algunos son
clásicos, otros más recientes. Entre los autores se cuentan: Miguel Angel Asturias, Rufino Blanco Fombona, Juan Bosch, Antonio

Caso, José Ferrer Canales, José A. Franquiz, Pedro Henríquez Ureña, Mauricio Magdaleno, Víctor Massuh, José L. Méndez Muñiz, Gabriela Mistral, Emilio Rodríguez Demorizi y Carlos Arturo Torres. "La Vocación Caribeña y Latinoamericana de Eugenio María de Hostos" es el título de la presentación del volumen, a cargo del compilador, buen conocedor del clásico puertorriqueño. Publicación oportuna (ver item **5352**).

VENEZUELA

5360 Antología del pensamiento revolucionario venezolano. Recopilación de Alexander Moreno. Prólogo de J.R. Núñez Tenorio. Caracas: Ediciones Centauro, 1983. 484 p.: ill., indexes.

Se reunen textos de la izquierda venezolana de las últimas décadas.

5361 Congreso Internacional sobre Andrés Bello y el Derecho Latinoamericano, Roma, 1981. Andrés Bello y el derecho latinoamericano. Caracas: La Casa de Bello, 1987. 530 p.: bibl.

Contiene 29 ponencias (algunas de gran extensión) de autores latinoamericanos y europeos (predominando entre estos últimos los italianos). La obra está subdividida en tres partes: 1) Andrés Bello y el derecho internacional en América Latina; 2) universidad y derecho romano en la formación del jurista, según Andrés Bello; y 3) el Código Civil de Andrés Bello: unidad y especificidad del sistema jurídico latinoamericano. La de mayor interés para esta sección es la primera.

5362 Gotera Alarce, Francisco. Maracaibo en los orígenes del positivismo. Maracaibo, Venezuela: Univ. del Zulia, Facultad Experimental de Ciencias, 1987. 151 p.: bibl.

Lo principal del libro es la exposición de cuatro autores: Rafael Villavicencio (1838–1920) (ver item **5366**); Francisco Eugenio Bustamante (1839–1921), evolucionista y a su modo teísta; Luis López Méndez (n. 1861), escritor de ideas positivistas; y Luis Razetti (1862–1932), quien llamó a Haeckel "mi maestro predilecto."

5363 Guerra Córdoba, Alexis and Luis Ignacio Suárez Mesa. Simón Bolívar y la Universidad latinoamericana. (*Bol. Acad. Nac. Hist./Caracas*, 69:274, abril/junio 1986, p. 413–435, bibl.)

El tema del artículo es el pensamiento de Bolívar sobre la Universidad, según se expresa en "medidas legislativas que adopta el Libertador en materia de creación y reorganización de la Universidad en seis países sudamericanos . . . " Sostiene el autor que estas ideas bolivarianas se adelantan a la Reforma Universitaria originada en Córdoba (Argentina) en 1918 (ver también *HLAS 40:9523*).

5364 Harwich Vallenilla, Nikita. Venezuelan positivism and modernity. (*HAHR*, 70:2, May 1990, p. 127–144)

Se desprende del artículo que habría una corriente revisionista en la apreciación de los positivistas venezolanos. Tal sería el caso de Arturo Sosa Abascal (ver *HLAS 50:4626*) y el del propio autor. Esta nueva apreciación pondría menos énfasis que la tradicional en la crítica al positivismo venezolano por su apoyo a la dictadura de Juan Vicente Gómez.

5365 Parellada, Juan Ramón. Simón Bolívar, Libertador: una interpretación española. S.l.: Ediciones de la Presidencia de la República, 1986. 48 p., 12 p. of plates: ports.

La virtud de este ensayo reside en ver el pensamiento político de Bolívar desde el ángulo de las ideas políticas en España durante la época de la Emancipación ("querella" entre conservadores y liberales, Constitución de Cádiz, etc.).

5366 Poleo Pérez, Luisa Margarita. Rafael Villavicencio, del positivismo al espiritualismo. Caracas: Academia Nacional de la Historia, 1986. 219 p.: bibl., facsims., index, port. (Biblioteca de la Academia Nacional de la Historia. Estudios, monografías y ensayos; 72)

Trabajo monográfico y a la vez antológico sobre Rafael Villavicencio (1838–1920), positivista venezolano seguidor de Comte, adherente también al transformismo darwiniano, y no carente a la vez de rasgos espiritualistas y teístas. La primera parte del libro es un análisis de las ideas de Villavicencio en relación con Comte. La segunda (después de establecer conclusiones y una cronología) contiene tres discursos académicos de Villavicencio, de 1889, 1900 y 1911, respectivamente. Buena bibliografía. (Ver también item **5362**).

5367 Romero, Aníbal. La idea de la política en el pensamiento de Simón Bolívar.

Caracas: Editorial Ateneo de Caracas, 1985. 145 p.: bibl. (Col. Historia)

Bolívar habría cumplido con las dos grandes y complementarias exigencias de la política: la de ser realista y sujetar los principios a los hechos, y la de tratar de cambiar la realidad de los hechos en virtud de principios y objetivos ideales.

5368 Sasso, Javier. Andrés Bello como filósofo. (*Rev. Latinoam. Filos.*, 15:2, julio 1989, p. 239–251)

Discute dos aspectos de la interpretación de Arturo Ardao en *Andrés Bello, filósofo* (ver *HLAS 50:4620*), sobre la relación entre Bello y Berkeley en lo que se refiere a la abstracción y al inmaterialismo. (Sobre Sasso y el pensamiento de Bello, ver también *HLAS 48:7592-7593.*)

5369 Strozzi, Susana. Julio C. Salas: biografía y política en el positivismo venezolano. Caracas: Fondo Editorial Lola de Fuenmayor, Centro de Investigaciones Históricas, Univ. Santa María, 1986. 141 p.: appendices, bibl. (Col. breve; 1)

Julio César Salas (1870–1933) pertenece al grupo de los positivistas venezolanos, aunque dentro de él es una figura menor. Es autor, entre otros escritos, de *Lecciones de sociología aplicada a la América* (1914) y, sobre todo, de *Civilización y barbarie* (1919), obra en la cual trata de hallar las razones del retraso de las naciones hispanoamericanas. Esta breve monografía sobre Salas sitúa al personaje en su medio histórico (especialmente el económico-social), traza su biografía y examina *Civilización y barbarie*. Contiene una cronología, apéndices documentales y bibliografía. Buena contribución al conocimiento de un autor no muy difundido.

5370 Uribe Celis, Carlos. Bolívar y Marx: dos enfoques polémicos. Bogotá: Ediciones Tercer Mundo, 1986. 190 p.: bibl.

Contiene un análisis del famoso escrito de Marx sobre Bolívar. Ese texto es analizado en sus fallas historiográficas y luego comentado.

COLOMBIA

5371 Benthamismo y antibenthamismo en Colombia. Selección e introducción por Germán Marquínez Argote. Bogotá: Editorial El Buho, 1983. 223 p.: bibl., ports. (Col. Pensamiento colombiano)

Esta antología recoge textos publicados en Colombia (1822–73) relacionados con el pensamiento de Bentham. Son manifestaciones de una polémica y van desde ordenanzas sobre la enseñanza hasta piezas académicas, pasando por material periodístico. Una breve introducción de Germán Marquínez Argote traza las líneas generales de la polémica aludida. La reunión y publicación de estos textos es una feliz contribución a la historia de las ideas en Colombia. (Sobre el mismo autor y el mismo tema, ver item **5372.**)

Henderson, James D. Conservative thought in twentieth century Latin America: the ideas of Laureano Gómez. See item **2351.**

5372 Marquínez Argote, Germán et al. La filosofía en Colombia: historia de las ideas. Bogotá: Editorial el Búho, 1988. 444 p.: bibl., ill. (Col. Universitas)

Esta obra colectiva es la primera que abarca la totalidad del proceso histórico de la filosofía en Colombia. El subtítulo, "Historia de las ideas," indica la intención de atender a formas de pensamiento que van más allá de la filosofía académica y que se enlazan con otros hechos históricos, especialmente los sociales. Los capítulos y sus autores son: Roberto Salazar Ramos, "Los Procesos Ideológicos de la Conquista," "Los Procesos Ideológicos de la Pacificación," y "Romanticismo y Positivismo;" Joaquín Sabalza Iriarte, "La Filosofía Colonial;" Germán Marquínez Argote, "Filosofía de la Ilustración," "Los Procesos Ideológicos de la Emancipación," y "Benthamismo y Antibenthamismo;" Leonardo Tovar González, "Tradicionalismo y Neo-Escolástica;" German Marquínez Argote y Eudoro Rodríguez Albarracín, "Sociedad y Cultura: hacia la Secularización de la Filosofía;" Daniel Herrera Restrepo, "La Filosofía en la Colombia Contemporánea;" Eudoro Rodríguez Albarracín, "El Socialismo: Praxis y Teorías." La obra se inicia con una introducción del último de los autores nombrados: "Problemática sobre la Historia de las Ideas Filosóficas," que es una contribución al concepto de "historia de las ideas." También el último capítulo es de naturaleza general: Marquínez Argote trata el problema de la filosofía latinoamericana y su recepción en

Colombia. Algunos de los capítulos de la obra reproducen las presentaciones que aparecieron en la serie antológica *Pensamiento Colombiano*, de la Editorial El Buho. Obra muy oportuna.

Marquínez Argote, Germán. Sobre filosofía española y latinoamericana. See item **5296.**

5373 Ocampo López, Javier. Los orígenes ideológicos de Colombia contemporánea. México: Instituto Panamericano de Geografía e Historia, 1986. 122 p.: bibl. (Instituto Panamericano de Geografía e Historia; 417)

Este útil panorama presenta las corrientes de pensamiento en Colombia desde mediados del siglo XIX hasta fechas recientes. Establece relaciones con la vida política del país y con su literatura. Un capítulo especial ("Optimismo y Pesimismo ante la Realidad de Nuestra América") se dedica a lo escrito en Colombia sobre la interpretación de la realidad hispanoamericana. Contiene buena bibliografía.

5374 Los radicales del siglo XIX: escritos políticos. Selección, prólogo y notas de Gonzalo España. Bogotá: Ancora Editores, 1984. 176 p.

Se refiere a los políticos liberales colombianos del siglo XIX. El carácter progresista de éstos, según el prologuista, contrasta con los representantes liberales del siglo XX. Los textos seleccionados—acompañados de breves anotaciones—son, entre otros, de Miguel Samper, Tomás Cipriano de Mosquera, Salvador Camacho Roldán, Aníbal Galindo y Manuel Murillo Toro.

5375 Shulgovski, Anatoli. La comuna de Bogotá y el socialismo utópico. pts. 1–2. (*Am. Lat./Moscú*, 8, agosto 1985, p. 45–56 and 9, sept. 1985, p. 47–56)

Narración de los hechos ocurridos con motivo del acceso al poder del general José María Melo en 1854, que dio lugar a lo que se ha denominado la "Comuna de Bogotá" o la "República de los Artesanos." Señala brevemente movimientos similares en Chile, Venezuela y México. Independientemente de ciertas obvias simpatías políticas del autor, se trata de un artículo interesante sobre un fenómeno poco conocido dentro de la historia de las ideas en América Latina.

5376 Torres, Camilo. Camilo Torres, sacerdote y guerrillero: revolución popular;

imperativo de cristianos y marxistas. Selección y prólogo de Héctor Gally. Buenos Aires: Ediciones Unidad, 1986. 164 p.: bibl.

Conjunto de escritos y cartas del sacerdote revolucionario colombiano Camilo Torres (1929–1966). Hay indicación de fechas de los escritos pero no de sus fuentes. La intención es primordialmente de difusión política.

5377 Valderrama Andrade, Carlos. Del lenguaje a la filosofía: itinerario de Miguel Antonio Caro. (*Bol. Acad. Colomb.*, 39:166, 1989, p. 219–239)

Se estudian, de Miguel Antonio Caro (1843–1909), sus ideas sobre la gramática en relación con Destutt de Tracy y su concepción de las ideas innatas. Los textos considerados son: "Informe sobre los *Elementos de ideología* de Tracy" (1870) y "Ligera Excursión Ideológica" (1872).

5378 Velásquez A., Francisco Mario; Carlos H. Uribe Celis; and Eduardo Santa. Vida y obra del profesor Luis López de Mesa. Medellín, Colombia: Univ. de Antioquia, Editorial U. de A., 1985. 393 p.: bibl.

Luis López de Mesa (1884–1967), médico psiquiatra, escritor y hombre público colombiano, es autor, entre otras obras, de *Escrutinio sociológico de la historia colombiana* (1955) y *De cómo se ha formado la nación colombiana* (1934). Aplicó el darwinismo social al estudio de la historia. Esta obra se compone de tres trabajos sobre López de Mesa.

ECUADOR

5379 El Arielismo en el Ecuador. Estudio introductorio y selección de Nancy Ochoa Antich. Quito: Banco Central del Ecuador; Corporación Editora Nacional, 1986. 355 p.: bibl. (Biblioteca básica del pensamiento ecuatoriano; 29)

Antología que presenta escritos ecuatorianos sobre José Enrique Rodó y lo que se ha dado en llamar el "arielismo." Los autores representados son: Gonzalo Zaldumbide (1885–1965); Alfredo Espinoza Tamayo (m. en 1918), de quien se ha publicado, en la misma colección, *Psicología y sociología del pueblo ecuatoriano* (1918, póstumo); Julio César Endara (1899–1969); Alejandro Andrade Coello (en esta parte se reproducen cartas de Rodó); y José María Velasco Ibarra, varias veces presidente de Ecuador. El "Estudio Introductorio" es más una expresión de las ideas personales de su autora frente a problemas actuales que un intento de comprender históricamente a los autores seleccionados.

Cerutti Guldberg, Horacio. De varia utópica. See item **5276.**

5380 Lara, Jorge Salvador. Notas acerca del pensamiento de los próceros quiteños de 1809. (*Rev. Hist. Am.*, 99, enero/junio 1985, p. 41–53)

Examina el "Alegato" de Manuel Rodríguez de Quiroga, participante en el frustrado movimiento de independencia producido en Quito en 1809. Esta pieza jurídica es considerada por el autor como "la primera justificación escrita de las luchas americanas por la emancipación." Se estudian también "las raíces ideológicas" del mencionado movimiento, en las cuales el autor encuentra tanto la línea tradicional española como el pensamiento de la Ilustración. Este último aspecto del trabajo es de particular interés.

5381 Pensamiento estético ecuatoriano. Estudio introductorio y selección de Daniel Prieto Castillo. Quito: Banco Central del Ecuador; Corporación Editora Nacional, 1986. 368 p.: bibl. (Biblioteca básica del pensamiento ecuatoriano; 24)

Obra antológica. Recoge escritos explícitamente dedicados a temas estéticos, excluyendo materiales incidentalmente referidos al asunto en obras de otra índole. El "Estudio Introductorio" destaca los principales temas que se reiteran en la literatura seleccionada (paisaje, arte y filosofía, la imitación, entre otros). Los autores representados son: Jesús Quijada, César Alfonso Pastor, Federico González Suárez, Angel Modesto Paredes, Ricardo Larraín y Bravo, Atanasio Viteri, Aurelio Espinoza Pólit y José María Vargas. Los textos son, en general, de la primera mitad del siglo XX, y algunos posteriores. Útil bibliografía y, en conjunto, una buena guía para el investigador.

Roig, Arturo Andrés. Rasgos biográficos de Rodolfo Mario Agoglia. See item **5432.**

Sacoto, Antonio. Juan Montalvo, el escritor y el estilista. v. 1–2. See item **3443.**

5382 La utopía en el Ecuador. Estudio introductorio y selección de Arturo

Andrés Roig. Quito: Banco Central del Ecuador; Corporación Editora Nacional, 1987. 468 p. (Biblioteca básica del pensamiento ecuatoriano; 26)

Obra antológica de temática muy amplia, porque no se basa en el concepto corriente de "utopía," sino en lo que el autor denomina "función utópica." Hay textos de Juan Velasco, Fray Antonio de Zúñiga, León Pinelo, Eugenio de Santa Cruz y Espejo, Benigno Malo, Fray Vicente Solano y Rafael Villamar, entre otros. El "Estudio Introductorio" es de hecho parte de la obra filosófica personal de Auturo Andrés Roig.

PERU

5383 Angotti, Thomas. The contributions of José Carlos Mariátegui to revolutionary theory. (*Lat. Am. Perspect.*, 13:2, Spring 1986, p. 33–57, bibl.)

Visión general de Mariátegui—altamente elogiosa—y de las varias y encontradas interpretaciones a que ha dado lugar el autor peruano. De esas interpretaciones, según el autor, la de los comunistas ha sido la más acertada. Afirma que el desencuentro de Mariátegui con la Komintern no justifica concluir que aquél dejó de ser comunista.

5384 Belaúnde, Víctor Andrés. La vida universitaria. Nota preliminar de Domingo García Belaúnde. 2a ed. Lima: Okura Editores, 1987. 76 p.

Oportuna reedición de escritos de la primera época del pensador peruano Víctor Andrés Belaúnde (1883–1966), sobre el tema de la universidad (en general y en el caso de Perú). Belaúnde giró más tarde hacia una posición católica militante. Los ensayos recogidos fueron escritos entre 1908–17. Interesa para la historia de las ideas en Perú y para el movimiento de Reforma Universitaria en América Latina.

5385 Chang-Rodríguez, Eugenio. Poética e ideología en José Carlos Mariátegui. 2a ed. Trujillo, Perú: Editorial Normas Legales, 1986. 243 p., 1 leaf of plates: bibl., index, port.

La edición de este libro realizada en España (1983) fue reseñada en *HLAS 50:4650.*

5386 Delgado, Carlos. Haya de la Torre: los escritos de 1923. (*Social. Particip.*, 31, sept. 1985, p. 25–34)

Examina con detalle el primer libro de Haya de la Torre, *Por la emancipación de América Latina,* aparecido en 1927 pero compuesto por artículos y mensajes de 1923. Considera que en estos escritos se encuentra "mucho del sello personalista y mesiánico" que tendría luego el movimiento aprista, y que están basados en "una clara inspiración marxista."

5387 González Prada, Manuel. Obras. v. 2., pt. 4. Prólogo y notas de Luis Alberto Sánchez. Lima: Ediciones Copé, Depto. de Relaciones Públicas de PETROPERU, 1985. 1 v.

Este volumen reproduce dos libros póstumos de González Prada, tal como fueron publicados por la Editorial Imán, de Buenos Aires: *Propaganda y ataque* (1939) y *Prosa menuda* (1941). Esas ediciones estuvieron a cargo de Alfredo González Prada, hijo del escritor peruano. Aquí se mantienen las numeras notas aclaratorias que este último preparó para las mencionadas ediciones de Buenos Aires. Antecede al volumen una breve nota de Luis Alberto Sánchez.

5388 Hurtado Oviedo, Víctor. Hayismo, leninismo. Lima: Bahía Ediciones, 1987. 107 p.: bibl.

Conjunto de trabajos periodísticos que ensalzan las virtudes del joven Haya de la Torre en la época de su libro *El antiimperialismo y el APRA.*

5389 Luna Vegas, Ricardo. Sobre las ideas políticas de Mariátegui: refutando a sus tergiversadores. Lima: Ediciones Unidad, 1984. 48 p.

Consta de cuatro artículos, entendidos como sendas "refutaciones" a interpretaciones de Mariátegui por parte de José Aricó, Alberto Flores Galindo, Patricio Ricketts y Luis Alberto Sánchez. El punto de vista del autor es el de un miembro del Partido Comunista Peruano.

5390 Mariátegui, José Carlos. Escritos juveniles: la edad de piedra. v. 1. Estudio preliminar, compilación y notas de Alberto Tauro. Lima: Biblioteca Amauta, 1987. 1 v.: bibl., ports. (Obras completas de José Carlos Mariátegui. Biblioteca Amauta)

La publicación de los *Escritos juveniles* de Mariátegui está planeada en varios

volúmenes, que harán parte a su vez de las *Obras completas* a cargo de la Biblioteca Amauta. Este primero se dedica a poesía, cuento y teatro. (El subtítulo: "La Edad de Piedra," responde a una expresión del propio Mariátegui, quien renegó de esa parte juvenil de su producción.) La línea divisoria entre el "primer" Mariátegui y el autor maduro suele ponerse en 1919, año en que comenzó una estadía en Europa, estimada como decisiva para su formación y sus ideas. Alberto Tauro— quien, en el "Estudio Preliminar," pacientemente y con gran conocimiento de detalle extrae todo lo que es posible de las primerizas contribuciones de Mariátegui—deja entrever que podría no haber tan tajante separación entre una época y otra del autor de los *Siete ensayos.*

Mariátegui, José Carlos. Invitación a la vida heroica: antología. See item **3715.**

5391 Martínez Riaza, Ascención. Función de la prensa en los orígenes del liberalismo peruano: la opinión pública ante la independencia. (*Rev. Indias*, 45 : 175, enero/junio 1985, p. 87–110)

Estudia la función y el contenido de la prensa doctrinal peruana en el primer cuarto del siglo XIX. Contiene también consideraciones sobre la prensa en los orígenes del liberalismo español. Trabajo aprovechable. De la misma autora: *La prensa doctrinal en la independencia del Perú: 1811–1824* (Madrid, 1985).

5392 Szlajfer, Henryk. Sobre el pensamiento y praxis política de José Carlos Mariátegui, de manera polémica. (*Estud. Latinoam.*, 10, 1985/1986, p. 187–204)

Analiza la etapa final de Mariátegui (1927–30), sus esfuerzos por fundar y mantener el Partido Socialista Peruano, y sus desacuerdos con la Komintern. Establece sus tesis en contraposición al libro de Flores Galindo, *La agonía de Mariátegui* (1980). Frente a la imagen de un Mariátegui víctima, señala aquellas características de la acción política de Mariátegui que explicarían su fracaso ante la Komintern e, internamente, ante el avance del aprismo. Para el autor, la gloria de Mariátegui seguirá inalterada como autor de los *Siete ensayos.*

5393 Tejada, Luis. La influencia anarquista en el APRA. (*Social. Particip.*, 29, marzo 1985, p. 97–110)

Muestra los inicios del anarquismo y

el anarco-sindicalismo en Perú a comienzos del siglo, y la relación de Haya de la Torre con ese movimiento, revelada en su primer libro *Por la emancipación de América Latina*. Afirma que, en los orígenes del APRA, "su base social militante" habría sido, "en medida considerable, libertaria." Concluye: "Nuestra hipótesis es que el aprismo es la expresión orgánica del proceso de politización que sufre el anarco-sindicalismo en la década del 20." Trabajo muy aprovechable.

BOLIVIA

5394 Estudios sobre Gabriel René Moreno: homenaje al sesquicentenario del nacimiento de Gabriel René Moreno, 1986. Santa Cruz, Bolivia: Casa de la Cultura Raúl Otero Reiche, 1986. 240 p.: bibl. (Serie Ensayo)

Seis trabajos sobre el historiador y bibliógrafo boliviano Gabriel René Moreno (1836–1908). Se trata de artículos anteriormente publicados, siendo el más antiguo de 1910 y los más recientes de 1961. Son los siguientes: Hernando Sanabria Fernández, "Gabriel René Moreno;" Emilio Finot, "Gabriel René Moreno en el Primer Centenario de su Nacimiento;" Emilio Finot, "Gabriel René Moreno y sus Obras;" Gunnar Mendoza, "Gabriel René Moreno, Bibliógrafo Boliviano;" Enrique Kempff Mercado, "En Torno a Gabriel René Moreno;" y Humberto Vázquez Machicado, "La Sociología de Gabriel René Moreno." Este último se refiere a las ideas de Gabriel René Moreno sobre el tema de las razas.

5395 Ferrufino Llach, Clara. Tamayo y el hombre boliviano. La Paz: Editorial Gisbert, 1987. 203 p.: bibl.

Expone de manera más bien elemental el pensamiento de Franz Tamayo (1879–1956), especialmente sus ideas sobre el carácter nacional. Ese pensamiento se pone también en relación con el de autores como Felipe Segundo Guzmán, Alcides Arguedas y Jaime Mendoza.

5396 Sacoto, Antonio. Alcides Arguedas y el positivismo hispanoamericano. (*Cultura/Quito*, 8:23, sept./dic. 1985, p. 281–290)

Se trata en realidad de una breve pero dura crítica a los conceptos de Alcides Arguedas (pensador boliviano, 1879–1946) sobre el indio y el mestizo, en su obra *Pueblo enfermo* (1910).

CHILE

5397 Bio-bibliografía de la filosofía en Chile desde 1980 hasta 1984. Dirección de Fernando Astorquiza Pizarro. Santiago: Univ. de Chile, Facultad de Filosofía, Humanidades y Educación; Instituto Profesional de Santiago, Escuela de Bibliotecología y Documentación, 1985. 118 p.: ill., indexes.

Esta bibliografía continúa una anterior (ver *HLAS48:7621*) del mismo título pero que abarcó desde el siglo XVI hasta 1980. Contiene más de 400 entradas de libros y artículos, además de datos biográficos básicos de algunos autores y varios índices.

Bravo, Anne. *El Mercurio:* un discurso sobre la cultura, 1958–1980. See *HLAS 51:4875*.

Cánepa, Gina. Folletines históricos del Chile independiente y su articulación con la novela naturalista. See item **3407.**

5398 Guzmán Brito, Alejandro. Portales y el derecho. Santiago: Editorial Universitaria, Univ. Metropolitana de Ciencias de la Educación, 1988. 134 p.: bibl. (Col. Fuera de serie)

Contiene cuatro trabajos sobre Diego Portales, figura conservadora que dominó la vida política chilena entre 1829 y 1837. Las investigaciones se refieren a su formación en materia de derecho, a su posible lectura de Montesquieu y a su acción para promover el *corpus* legislativo de su país.

Ibáñez Santa Maria, Adolfo. Estatismo y tradicionalismo en Mario Góngora. See item **2578.**

5399 Jaksic, Ivan. Academic rebels in Chile: the role of philosophy in higher education and politics. Albany: State Univ. of New York Press, 1989. 259 p.: (SUNY series in Latin American and Iberian thought and culture)

Sigue el curso del pensamiento filosófico chileno desde la Independencia hasta años recientes, pero no tratándolo aisladamente, sino en su vinculación con los acontecimientos políticos y, muy especialmente, con la concepción y la marcha de la educación superior. Por ello, con ser hasta el momento la mejor historia de las ideas filosóficas en Chile, el libro trasciende ese objetivo y es un modelo de interpretación de esas ideas en su contexto histórico. Obra de la mayor importancia en la reciente producción historiográfica sobre el pensamiento latinoamericano.

5400 Jocelyn-Holt, Alfredo. El desarrollo de una conciencia pública en Lastarria y Sarmiento. (*Estud. Públicos*, 17, verano 1985, p. 213–233)

Se desea lograr un análisis del liberalismo (en particular, el chileno), "partiendo . . . de los textos . . . y de las categorías y términos usados, hasta llegar a comprender el lenguaje o discurso político liberal . . ." Se toman como ejemplos las categorías de "lo público" y "lo privado" en José Victorino Lastarria y Domingo F. Sarmiento.

Millar Carvacho, René. El obispo Alday y el Probabilismo. See item **2222.**

5401 Ortega y Gasset en Chile. Compilación de José Moure Rodríguez. Santiago: Ediciones Logos, 1988. 235 p.: ill.

Recoge los ecos periodísticos de la visita de Ortega a Chile en 1928. Además, reúne 16 artículos y ensayos sobre el filósofo español, publicados, presumiblemente, en Chile. De los artículos periodísticos se indica fuente y fecha; de los ensayos, no. Recopilación oportuna, porque llena un vacío en la documentación sobre la resonancia de Ortega en Hispanoamérica, y complementa lo que con frecuencia se ha escrito para el caso de Ortega y la Argentina.

5402 El pensamiento socialista en Chile: antología, 1893–1933. Compilación de Eduardo Devés V. y Carlos Díaz. Santiago: América Latina Libros, 1987. 234 p., 16 leaves of plates: ill., ports.

Antología de indudable valor documental para el estudio de las ideas socialistas en Chile desde fines del siglo XIX hasta 1930, aproximadamente. El contenido está dividido en los siguientes temas: 1) Victor José Arellano y el Primer Socialismo; 2) El Socialismo Ácrata; 3) El Socialismo "Científico;" 4) Luis Emilio Recabarren; 5) El Pensamiento Socialista hasta 1910; 6) El Socialismo de los Discípulos de Recabarren; 7) El Pensamiento de las Agrupaciones Socialistas hacia 1930; 8)

Los Postulados Socialistas de la República del 4 de junio de 1932; 9) Los Postulados de los Fundadores del Partido Socialista de Chile. Cada capítulo documental va precedido de una breve presentación.

BRASIL

5403 O Apostolado positivista e a República. Seleção e introdução de Antônio Paim. Brasília: Câmara dos Deputados; Editora Univ. de Brasília, 1981. 108 p.: bibl. (Biblioteca do pensamento político republicano; 2)

Miguel Lemos (1854–1917) funda en 1881 la Iglesia Positivista Brasileña (o Apostolado Positivista), que llegó a ser una de las grandes expresiones del positivismo en Brasil. La presente obra es de carácter documental y contiene manifestaciones del Apostolado referentes al advenimiento de la República y a la política del período republicano. En la breve pero iluminadora introducción de Antônio Paim, este autor concluye que el Apostolado no influyó directamente en la creación de la República. Obra de obvia utilidad.

5404 Araújo, José Carlos Sousa. Igreja Católica no Brasil: um estudo de mentalidade ideológica. São Paulo: Edições Paulinas, 1986. 114 p.: bibl. (Col. Estudos e debates latino-americanos; 18)

Tiene por tema específico el comportamiento de la Iglesia en Brasil entre 1890 y 1922, es decir, durante casi todo el período de la "República Velha" o Primera República (1890–1930). Estudia tres cartas pastorales de ese lapso, examinándolas como discurso religioso y como modalidad de comunicación. Las encuentra expresivas del enfrentamiento con la mentalidad liberal republicana.

5405 Athayde, Hélio. Atualidade de Euclides: vida e obra. Rio de Janeiro: Presença, 1987. 218 p.: bibl. (Col. Atualidade crítica; 11)

Con abundantes citas de otros críticos, narra la vida de Euclides da Cunha (1866–1909) y la elaboración de *Os sertões* (1902). Examina esta obra capital y otras publicaciones posteriores del autor brasileño. Un capítulo se destina a la relación entre *Os sertões* y *Facundo*, de Domingo Faustino Sarmiento.

5406 Azzi, Riolando. A cristandade colonial: um projeto autoritário. São Paulo: Edições Paulinas, 1987. 233 p.: bibl. (História do pensamento católico no Brasil; 1)

Estudia la función de las ideas (específicamente, el pensamiento católico) en el proyecto de colonización lusitano y en la sociedad resultante. Por la preocupación de vincular los aspectos de pensamiento con realidades históricas más amplias, y por los resultados concretos que logra, es una obra de historia de las ideas muy atendible.

5407 Carone, Edgard. O marxismo no Brasil: das origens a 1964. Rio de Janeiro: Dois Pontos Editora, 1986. 264 p.: bibl.

Extensa bibliografía de la literatura marxista (y sobre el marxismo) en Brasil. Incluye no sólo obras teóricas, sino también de historia, testimoniales y lo que el autor denomina "literatura proletaria." La introducción es de gran riqueza informativa y en parte compensa el hecho de que la bibliografía no es anotada.

Centro de Documentação do Pensamento Brasileiro. Catálogo do acervo. See item 72.

Fernandes, Florestan. Florestan Fernandes. See *HLAS 51:5042.*

5408 Libertários no Brasil: memória, lutas, cultura. Organização de Antonio Arnoni Prado. São Paulo: Brasiliense, 1986. 308 p.: bibl.

Conjunto de testimonios y ensayos sobre el anarquismo en Brasil. Una parte está dedicada a las manifestaciones de esa tendencia que se dieron en el campo de la cultura.

5409 Oberacker, Carlos H. Os intelectuais brasileiros e a cultura alemã, 1800–1930. (*Jahrb. Gesch.*, 25, 1988, p. 591–606)

Útil para conocer la asimilación de la cultura alemana por parte de un grupo de autores durante el período señalado en el título. La característica común a todos es que debieron enfrentarse a la cultura francesa predominante, a la cual criticaron. Tienen especial relieve, por supuesto, Tobias Barreto y la Escuela de Recife, pero también otros juristas e historiadores. El artículo es resumen de un libro de próxima aparición: *Amigos da cultura alemã no Brasil.*

Osiel, Mark J. Going to the people: popular culture and the intellectuals in Brazil. See *HLAS 51:5077.*

5410 Pessoa, Lilian de Abreu. Aspectos do pensamento alemão na obra de Tobias Barreto. São Paulo: Univ. de São Paulo, Faculdade de Filosofia, Letras e Ciências Humanas, 1985. 135 p.: bibl., facsims. (Boletim; 46. Departamento de Letras Modernas; 17. Curso de Língua e Literatura Alemã; 05)

Basándose en un estudio de la biblioteca de autores alemanes que perteneció a Tobias Barreto (1839–1889), ilustra sobre la influencia de esos autores y sobre cómo el pensador sergipano los siguió o interpretó. Se concentra en tres temas: la literatura, las ideas filosóficas y las ideas religiosas. (En filosofía se destaca el monismo de Haeckel y Noiré.) El trabajo quiere también contribuir al examen del germanismo en Brasil (ver item **5409**).

5411 Scantimburgo, João de. O Brasil e a Revolução Francesa. São Paulo: Livraria Pioneira Editora, 1989. 337 p.: bibl. (Col. Novos Umbrais)

Expone la influencia de la Revolución Francesa (y de las ideas iluministas) en Portugal, y luego en Brasil.

5412 Tobias, José Antônio. História das idéias no Brasil. São Paulo: Editora Pedagógica e Universitária, 1987. 188 p.: bibl.

La obra se propone ser una historia de las ideas, pero no solamente filosóficas, sino también de otras que, aunque no sistemáticas, han sido determinantes en la historia de Brasil. De hecho viene a resultar también una interpretación de esa historia.

PARAGUAY

5413 Irala Burgos, Adriano. La ideología política del doctor Francia. 2a ed. Asunción?: C. Schauman Editor, 1988. 98 p.

Aunque maneja algún material documental, se trata principalmente de un ensayo. Tal vez lo más significativo sea el análisis de la nota de Francia del 20 de julio de 1811 dirigida a las autoridades de Buenos Aires, expresando la decisión de mantener al Paraguay independiente de esas autoridades.

URUGUAY

5414 Ciclo de conferencias: las ideas filosóficas que influyeron en la formación

del Uruguay contemporáneo. Montevideo: Fundación Prudencio Vázquez y Vega; Distribuye, Blanes, 1988. 88 p. (Serie Cuadernos)

Conjunto de conferencias de interés para el conocimiento de la influencia del espiritualismo y el krausismo en la vida política del Uruguay. Figuras relacionadas con esa influencia son José Battle y Ordóñez y Prudencio Vázquez y Vega, este último mucho menos conocido que el primero, y que murió muy joven.

ARGENTINA

5415 Alad'in, Valerii Gerasimovich. Problema cheloveka i obshchestva v filosofii Argentiny. Moskva: Izd-vo Universiteta druzhby narodov, 1986. 162 p.: bibl.

Interpretation (pre-glasnost) by Soviet philosopher of the history of Argentine thought. [R.V. Allen]

5416 Alberdi, Juan Bautista. Fragmento preliminar al estudio del derecho. Introducción y notas de Ricardo Grinberg. Buenos Aires: Editorial Biblos, 1984. 319 p.: bibl.

Reproduce la edición de 1837 de esta obra clásica de Alberdi. La introducción comenta el *Fragmento*, especialmente en relación con la política de la época. Se añaden al texto numerosas notas aclaratorias. Se agrega también una breve pero útil bibliografía sobre Alberdi.

5417 Biagini, Hugo Edgardo. Filosofía americana e identidad: el conflictivo caso argentino. Buenos Aires: Editorial Universitaria de Buenos Aires, 1989. 342 p.: bibl. (Temas)

El alto número de trabajos recogidos en este volumen (publicados anteriormente algunos, inéditos otros) hace difícil referirse por extenso al contenido. El libro toca una variedad de temas: la identidad argentina y latinoamericana; relaciones intelectuales con Estados Unidos; historiografía sobre el pensamiento argentino e historia reciente de ese pensamiento; krausismo y democracia; positivismo y nacionalidad. Lo mismo ocurre con autores: son objeto de consideración Sarmiento, Alberdi, Macedonio Fernández, Juan B. Justo, Ortega y Gasset, Eduardo Mallea y Vicente Fatone, entre otros. Mejor afirmado en lo monográfico que en lo ensayístico, el autor explora también temas más restringi-

dos y menos transitados: la revista *La Filosofía Positiva* o el pensamiento de Homero Guglielmini, para citar sólo dos ejemplos. Aunque había publicado otros libros, este volumen "establece" a Biagini en el conjunto de los autores con mayor obra realizada sobre pensamiento argentino y, por extensión, latinoamericano. Las manifestaciones expresas del propio autor lo vinculan a la figura de Arturo A. Roig. For literature specialist's comment see item **3406.**

5418 Buchrucker, Cristian. La "tentación fascista" en la Argentina. (*Criterio/Buenos Aires*, 58:1951, 12 sept. 1985, p. 481–487)

Repasa manifestaciones de intelectuales argentinos adherentes al fascismo, antes y después de 1945 (año que puede considerarse el comienzo de la etapa peronista), con útiles citas. Considera que una de las causas que favorecieron esa adhesión fue la falta de un pluralismo político fuerte. Del mismo autor: *Nacionalismo, fascismo y peronismo* (tesis doctoral, Berlín, 1982).

5419 Corbière, Emilio J. El marxismo de Enrique del Valle Iberlucea. Buenos Aires: Centro Editor de América Latina, 1987. 137 p. (Biblioteca Política Argentina; 198)

Enrique del Valle Iberlucea (1877–1910) fue senador nacional argentino, periodista, escritor y militante de orientación marxista. Este libro, de indudable valor por ser el personaje estudiado poco conocido, contiene un breve pero muy útil estudio preliminar de Emilio J. Corbière, textos de del Valle Iberlucea y documentación inédita.

Cullen, Carlos A. Reflexiones desde América. v. 1, Ser y estar: el problema de la cultura. v. 2, Ciencia y sabiduría: el problema de la filosofía en Latinoamérica. See item **5281.**

5420 Feinmann, José Pablo. Filosofía y nación: estudios sobre el pensamiento argentino. 3rd ed. Buenos Aires: Editorial Legasa, 1986. 191 p. (Ensayo crítico)

Contiene ensayos sobre: Mariano Moreno y la Revolución de Mayo; Juan Bautista Alberdi; el *Facundo* de Sarmiento; José Hernández y el *Martín Fierro*; y la posición del interior de Argentina frente a Buenos Aires en la segunda mitad del siglo XIX, simbolizada en la figura del caudillo Felipe Varela. (El valor que se atribuye a éste en la historia

del pensamiento es obviamente exagerado.)
En cuanto a caracterización general de la posición del autor, no coincide con la corriente
historiográfica "liberal;" pero tampoco es
"revisionista" (en el sentido que se da al término en la historiografía argentina) ni neo-
marxista. Abundante en juicios rotundos,
pero no prescindible.

Foster, David William. The Argentine generation of 1880: ideology and cultural texts.
See item **3417.**

5421 Galasso, Norberto. Ramón Doll: socialismo o fascismo. Buenos Aires: Centro Editor de América Latina, 1989. 141 p.:
bibl. (Biblioteca Política argentina; 275)

Crítico literario y social de tono agu-
damente iconoclasta, Ramón Doll (m. en
1970) fue originariamente adherente al Partido Socialista de Juan B. Justo, aunque sin
ser marxista. Defendió luego un nacionalismo popular, y concluyó en la vertiente nacionalista de tipo fascista, antipopular y anti-
semita. El autor de este libro, que ve a su
personaje con simpatía aunque no comparte
todas sus posiciones, lo enfoca desde la óp-
tica de lo que en Argentina se donomina "izquierda nacional," de la cual—dice—Doll
podría considerarse precursor por algunas de
sus facetas.

5422 Graziano, Frank. Divine violence:
spectacle, psychosexuality and radical
Christianity in the Argentine "Dirty War."
Boulder, Colo.: Westview Press, 1992. 328 p.:
bibl., index.

Los componentes de la represión militar durante la llamada "Guerra Sucia" en la
Argentina, sobre todo la extendida práctica
de la tortura y las manifestaciones ideológicas de la Junta gobernante, reciben una compleja interpretación que va más allá de la visión política habitual. Los elementos de esa
interpretación son psicoanalíticos (Lacan),
foucaultianos (en especial el Foucault de
Surveiller et punir), semióticos, religiosos,
mitológicos y etnológicos (rituales de sacrifi-
cios humanos). Es posible que para algunos
lectores quede como cuestión abierta el alcance explicativo de esa hermenéutica con
respecto al fenómeno de la "guerra sucia" en
su totalidad, con independencia de la opinión
que merezcan las interpretaciones de hechos
y motivaciones particulares.

5423 Isaacson, José *et al.* Pensar la Argentina. Buenos Aires: Plus Ultra, 1986.
166 p. (Col. Temas contemporáneos; 7)

Dos artículos interesan específicamente a esta Sección: Gregorio Weinberg,
"Ideas y Modelos;" y Norberto Rodríguez
Bustamante, "Hacia la Modernización de la
Argentina." El primero, sugestivo y aprovechable en muchos aspectos a pesar de su
brevedad, destaca la función de las ideas (o de
la "Inteligencia Crítica") en la adopción de
"modelos" o grandes orientaciones para la
marcha de la Argentina en momentos clave
de su historia. El segundo, desde una perspectiva metodológica que combina la historia
con la sociología, examina el siglo
1880–1980 teniendo como eje la teoría sociológica de la modernización.

5424 Lacay, Celina. Sarmiento y la formación de la ideología de la clase dominante. Buenos Aires: Editorial Contrapunto,
1986. 157 p.: bibl. (Col. La Historia revisada)

El tema principal de esta monografía
es el *Facundo*, de Sarmiento. La tesis final
sería la siguiente: Sarmiento legitimó una
ideología por medio de una interpretación
(una "imagen") de la realidad argentina de la
época que no fue objetiva, sino que sirvió a
los propósitos de un programa. El programa
tuvo sus beneficiarios: la "clase dominante."

5425 Lértora Mendoza, Celina A. La actividad filosófica femenina en Argentina
actual. (*Reflexão*, 33, set. 1985, p. 65–79,
bibl.)

El artículo es de utilidad e interés
desde el punto de vista de la sociología de la
profesión filosófica. También resulta informativo sobre la actividad filosófica en Argentina en las últimas décadas.

5426 Montenegro, Adelmo. Ensayos argentinos. Córdoba, Argentina: Univ. Nacional de Córdoba, Dirección General de
Publicaciones, 1984. 212 p.: bibl., port.

Contiene ensayos sobre la cultura y la
identidad argentinas, la generación del 80,
Sarmiento, Rivadavia, Ricardo Rojas, Lugones, Victoria Ocampo, Francisco Romero y
Ortega en la Argentina. Todos escritos en el
estilo ensayístico que busca más la apreciación de conjunto que la visión de detalle.

**5427 Orígenes de la democracia argentina:
el trasfondo krausista.** Compilación de

Hugo Edgardo Biagini. Buenos Aires: Secretaría de Cultura de la Nación, Fundación Friedrich Ebert; Editorial Legasa, 1989. 238 p. (Ensayo crítico)

Este excelente volumen contiene las exposiciones hechas en un simposio sobre el tema que da título al libro. La mayoría de los trabajos se ocupan del krausismo (y el krauso-positivismo) español, en tanto otros tratan de las resonancias de esas corrientes en Argentina. Al krausismo en la Argentina se refieren: 1) Hugo Biagini en la presentación del volumen, trazando un útil inventario de las manifestaciones krausistas en el pensamiento de dicho país; 2) Arturo A. Roig, en "La Cuestión de la 'Eticidad Nacional' y la Ideología Krausista," centrado en la ideología del presidente Irigoyen (Roig es autor de *Los krausistas argentinos*, único libro sobre el asunto, que ahora ve desde una perspectiva más radicalizada, con mayor acento en los conflictos de clase y la influencia de éstos en la superestructura de pensamiento.); 3) Osvaldo Alvarez Guerrero, "Krausismo y Radicalismo" (se refiere al partido político argentino llamado Radical), que es un artículo breve pero con propuestas muy sensatas. En lo que se refiere al krausismo peninsular, son sumamente iluminadores los artículos: "Institucionistas y Socialistas," de Elías Díaz; y "El Krauso-Positivismo en la Crisis de Fin de Siglo," de José Luis Abellán; pero hay otros también de gran interés y buena realización. Sobre el krausismo en Uruguay ver item **5414**).

5428 Paoli, Roberto. Borges y Schopenhauer. (*Rev. Crít. Lit. Latinoam.*, 11:24, feb. 1986, p. 173–208)

Presenta, de manera acuciosa, los motivos del pensamiento de Schopenhauer que fueron asimilados por Borges, que pasaron a ser parte de su *Weltanschauung* y que se manifestaron en su creación literaria. De esto último se ofrecen abundantes ejemplos para cada tema.

Prieto, Adolfo. El discurso criollista en la formación de la Argentina moderna. See item **3438**.

5429 Quijada, Mónica. Manuel Gálvez: 60 años de pensamiento nacionalista. Buenos Aires: Centro Editor de América Latina, 1985. 139 p.: bibl. (Biblioteca Política argentina; 102)

Exposición de las ideas políticas del ensayista y novelista argentino Manuel Gálvez (1882–1962), con abundantes referencias al contexto—especialmente político—de la época. Interesa para el tema del nacionalismo y el fascismo en la Argentina. Obra muy aprovechable.

5430 Quijada, Mónica. Utopía y realidad en el pensamiento nacionalista argentino: Manuel Gálvez. (*Rev. Indias*, 45:176, julio/dic. 1985, p. 523–556)

Es en parte resumen y en parte reproducción parcial de la obra de la misma autora, *Manuel Gálvez: sesenta años de pensamiento nacionalista* (ver item **5429**).

5431 Rocca, Carlos J. Juan B. Justo y Alejandro Korn en el socialismo argentino. La Plata, Argentina: Editorial Alas, 1988. 65 p.: bibl.

No es obra de investigación, sino más bien de recordación y homenaje. Destaca la función del pensamiento de Korn en el ideario del socialismo democrático argentino.

5432 Roig, Arturo Andrés. Rasgos biográficos de Rodolfo Mario Agoglia. (*Cultura/Quito*, 9:25, mayo/agosto 1986, p. 221–228, bibl.)

Breve pero emotiva semblanza de Rodolfo Mario Agoglia (1920–85), profesor y pensador argentino que enseñó en su país y en Ecuador. Muy oportuna la inclusión, al final, de la lista de escritos filosóficos de Agoglia. Además de temas de filosofía antigua y de filosofía de la historia, se ocupó de filosofía latinoamericana, especialmente del pensamiento en el Ecuador.

5433 Solano Villamil, Germán. El filosofar en Latinoamérica: el contexto argentino. (*Franciscanum*, 28:83, mayo/agosto 1986, p. 141–189)

Este trabajo es, de hecho, preámbulo al del mismo autor sobre Francisco Romero (ver item **5434**). Está realizado principalmente sobre fuentes secundarias.

5434 Solano Villamil, Germán. El filosofar en Latinoamerica: pt. 2, El pensamiento de Francisco Romero. (*Franciscanum*, 28:84, sept./dic. 1986, p. 351–406, bibl.)

Trabajo de naturaleza expositiva y general, escrito desde un punto de vista espiritualista cristiano, que expresa alto aprecio por el filósofo argentino.

5435 Stoetzer, O. Carlos. Raíces intelectuales de la Constitución argentina de 1853. (*Jahrb. Gesch.*, 22, 1985, p. 295–339)

Trabajo de síntesis sobre los antecedentes—incluidos los españoles –, las influencias extranjeras y las bases filosóficas de la Constitución argentina de 1853. Trata especialmente el problema religioso en dicha Constitución.

5436 Terán, Oscar. Alberdi póstumo. Buenos Aires: Punto Sur Editores, 1988. 283 p.: bibl., index.

Los escritos póstumos de Juan Bautista Alberdi (1810–84) ocupan 16 volúmenes, no críticamente organizados. El presente libro es una selección de esos escritos, comentados por Terán en un ensayo que precede a la parte antológica. Contiene también un índice sumario de los citados 16 volúmenes, una cronología biográfica de Alberdi y una bibliografia.

5437 Terán, Oscar. Aníbal Ponce—el marxismo sin nación? México: Ediciones Pasado y Presente; Siglo XXI Editores, 1983. 251 p.: bibl. (Cuadernos de pasado y presente; 98)

Antología del ensayista y pensador argentino Aníbal Ponce (1898–1938). Los textos recogidos son en general breves y poco conocidos, excepto una larga transcripción de *Humanismo burgués y humanismo proletario.* En la introducción, Terán traza la evolución del pensamiento de Ponce, desde su inicial liberalismo hasta su adhesión al marxismo. El marxismo de Ponce—examinado en el contexto de las ideas de la época y oportunamente comparado con el de Mariátegui—es considerado por Terán como proclive a una visión internacional y poco atenido a las peculiaridades latinoamericanas, y en particular al problema nacional argentino. Poco conocidas son dos notas de Ponce sobre Alejandro Korn y una sobre Vasconcelos que aparecen en el volumen.

5438 Terán, Oscar. En busca de la ideología argentina. Buenos Aires: Catálogos Editora, 1986. 253 p.: bibl., ill. (Col. Armas de la crítica)

Reúne varios trabajos, cuyo "hilo conductor," según el propio autor, "es la reflexión que ellos contuvieron acerca del problema de la nación." Los trabajos son los siguientes: "Positivismo y Nación en América Latina;" "Poderes de la Nación: Educar y Encerrar, Incursiones en el Positivismo Mexicano;" "José Ingenieros o la Voluntad de Saber;" "El Primer Antimperialismo Latinoamericano;" "Mariátegui: la Nación y la Razón;" "Aníbal Ponce o el Marxismo sin Nación;" "La Libertad Tolerante de Alejandro Korn;" y "Rasgos de la Cultura Argentina en la Década de 1950." Como puede observarse, el contenido va más allá del título del libro. Más que estudios monográficos se trata de ensayos interesados en relacionar los contenidos de ideas con las ideologías político-sociales y con la realidad histórica a que éstas últimas responden.

5439 Terán, Oscar. José Ingenieros: pensar la nación. Madrid; Buenos Aires: Alizana Editorial, 1986. 295 p. (Alianza Bolsillo; 13)

Se trata de una selección de textos del psiquiatra y pensador argentino. El "Estudio Preliminar" es un extenso ensayo que sigue la línea trazada por el pensamiento de Ingenieros a partir de sus escritos juveniles, con énfasis especial en las ideas político-sociales y su aplicación a la sociedad argentina (pensamiento de "la nación"). La selección de textos también está guiada por esta perspectiva.

5440 Torchia Estrada, Juan Carlos. Alejandro Korn: profesión y vocación. México: Univ. Nacional Autónoma de México, Centro Coordinador y Difusor de Estudios Latinoamericanos, 1986. 241 p.: appendix.

Contiene estudios sobre la actividad psiquiátrica de Korn (especialmente su tesis de grado, de 1883) y sobre su pensamiento filosófico (metafísica y religión, historia de la filosofía, socialismo ético). Uno de los artículos tiene carácter de ensayo bibliográfico. En apéndice se reproducen cartas de Alejandro Korn a Francisco Romero, de los años 1924–27.

5441 Vargas, Otto. El marxismo y la revolución argentina. v. 1. Buenos Aires: Editorial Agora, 1987. 1 v.: bibl.

Ensayo interpretativo sobre la organización de la clase obrera argentina desde la segunda mitad del siglo XIX hasta la fundación del Partido Comunista en 1918. El punto de vista que domina los juicios de valor es el de un militante de ese Partido. Esto explica las apreciaciones negativas sobre otras formas de socialismo en la Argentina, y especialmente sobre la figura de Juan B. Justo, fundador del Partido Socialista argentino.

Waisman, Carlos H. La ideología del nacionalismo de derecha en Cabildo, 1973–1983. See *HLAS 51:5003.*

5442 Weinberg, Félix. La antítesis sarmientina: "civilización-barbarie" y su percepción coetánea en el Río de la Plata. *(Cuad. Am.*, 13:1, enero/feb. 1989, p. 97–118)

Excelente contribución a la comprensión del *Facundo.* Expone antecedentes de la oposición "civilización-barbarie" en la literatura de la época que muestran que la expresión no fue exclusiva de Sarmiento. Luego analiza comentarios al *Facundo*, aparecidas en Buenos Aires y Montevideo y contemporáneas a la publicación del libro.

5443 Weinberg, Félix. Las ideas sociales de Sarmiento. Buenos Aires: Editorial Universitaria de Buenos Aires, 1988. 201 p.: appendices, bibl. (Temas)

Valioso conjunto de estudios que muestran buen conocimiento de los escritos de Sarmiento, y no sólo de los más divulgados. Se analiza el pensamiento social del autor argentino y sus ideas sobre la inmigración, la industrialización y la educación. También se enfoca a Sarmiento en el contexto de la vida política argentina durante la década de 1880 y como autor de *Argirópolis.* Contiene apéndices documentales.

5444 Zuccherino, Ricardo Miguel. Juan Bautista Alberdi, ideólogo del siglo XXI: análisis integral de su obra. Prólogo de Enrique de Gandía. Buenos Aires: Ediciones Depalma, 1987. 280 p.: bibl.

La mayor parte de la obra está destinada a describir la producción de Alberdi— libros tanto como breves escritos—agrupando los materiales por épocas.

JOURNAL ABBREVIATIONS

Am. Indíg. América Indígena. Instituto Indigenista Interamericano. México.

Am. Lat./Moscú. América Latina. Academia de Ciencias de la Unión de Repúblicas Soviéticas Socialistas. Moscú.

Am. Merid. América Meridional. Sociedad Regional de Ciencias Humanas. Montevideo.

Bol. Acad. Colomb. Boletín de la Academia Colombiana. Bogotá.

Bol. Acad. Nac. Hist./Caracas. Boletín de la Academia Nacional de la Historia. Caracas.

Can. J. Lat. Am. Caribb. Stud. Canadian Journal of Latin American and Caribbean Studies. Univ. of Ottawa. Ontario, Canada.

Caravelle. Caravelle. Cahiers du monde hispanique et luso-brésilien. Univ. de Toulouse, Institute d'études hispaniques, hispano-americaines et luso-brésiliennes. Toulouse, France.

Casa Am. Casa de las Américas. La Habana.

Criterio/Buenos Aires. Criterio. Editorial Criterio. Buenos Aires.

Cuad. Am. Cuadernos Americanos. Editorial Cultura. México.

Cuad. Hispanoam. Cuadernos Hispanoamericanos. Instituto de Cultura Hispánica. Madrid.

Cultura/Quito. Cultura. Banco Central del Ecuador. Quito.

Estud. Latinoam. Estudios Latinoamericanos. Polska Akademia Nauk, Instytut Historii. Varsovia.

Estud. Públicos. Estudios Públicos. Centro de Estudios Públicos. Santiago.

Etud. ibér. ibéro-am. Etudes ibériques et ibéro-americaines. Annales de la Faculté des lettres et sciences humaines de Nice. Nice, France.

Franciscanum. Franciscanum. Revista de las ciencias del espíritu. Univ. de San Buenaventura. Bogotá.

HAHR. Hispanic American Historical Review. Conference on Latin American History of the American Historical Assn.; Duke Univ. Press. Durham, N.C.

Hist. Mex. Historia Mexicana. Colegio de México. México.

Ibero-Am. Arch. Ibero-Amerikanisches Archiv. Ibero-Amerikanisches Institut. Berlin.

Islas. Islas. Univ. Central de Las Villas. Santa Clara, Cuba.

Jahrb. Gesch. Jahrbuch für Geschichte von Staat, Wirtschaft und Gesellschaft Lateinamerikas. Köln, Germany.

Lat. Am. Perspect. Latin American Perspectives. Univ. of California. Newbury Park, Calif.

Nuestra Am. Nuestra América. Centro Coordinador y Difusor de Estudios Latinoamericanos, Univ. Autónoma de México. México.

Opciones. Opciones. Centro de Estudios de la Realidad Contemporánea, Academia del Humanismo Cristiano. Santiago.

Reflexão. Reflexão. Pontificia Univ. Católica de Campinas. São Paulo.

Rev. Crít. Lit. Latinoam. Revista de Crítica Literaria Latinoamericana. Latinoamericana Editores. Lima.

Rev. Filos./Maracaibo. Revista de Filosofía. Univ. de Zulia. Maracaibo, Venezuela.

Rev. Hist. Am. Revista de Historia de América. Instituto Panamericano de Geografía e Historia, Comisión de Historia. México.

Rev. Hist./San Juan. Revista de Historia. Asociación Histórica Puertorriqueña. San Juan.

Rev. Indias. Revista de Indias. Consejo Superior de Investigaciones Científicas, Instituto Gonzalo Fernández de Oviedo. Madrid.

Rev. Latinoam. Filos. Revista Latinoamericana de Filosofía. Centro de Investigaciones Filosóficas. Buenos Aires.

Rev. Mex. Sociol. Revista Mexicana de Sociología. Instituto de Investigaciones Sociales, Univ. Autónoma de México. México.

Rev. Occident. Revista de Occidente. Publicación mensual. Madrid.

Rev. Rev. Interam. Revista/Review Interamericana. Univ. Interamericana. San Germán, P.R.

Social. Particip. Socialismo y Participación. Ediciones Socialismo y Participación. Lima.

INDEXES

ABBREVIATIONS AND ACRONYMS

Except for journal abbreviations which are listed: 1) at the end of each major
disciplinary section (e.g., Art, History, Language, etc.); 2) after each journal title in
the *Title List of Journals Indexed* (p. 797); and 3) in the *Abbreviated List of Journals
Indexed* (p. 807).

a.	annual
ABC	Argentina, Brazil, Chile
A.C.	antes de Cristo
ACAR	Associação de Crédito e Assistência Rural, Brazil
AD	Anno Domini
A.D.	Acción Democrática, Venezuela
ADESG	Associação dos Diplomados de Escola Superior de Guerra, Brazil
AGI	Archivo General de Indias, Sevilla
AGN	Archivo General de la Nación
AID	Agency for International Development
a.k.a.	also known as
Ala.	Alabama
ALALC	Asociación Latinoamericana de Libre Comercio
ALEC	*Atlas lingüístico etnográfico de Colombia*
ANAPO	Alianza Nacional Popular, Colombia
ANCARSE	Associação Nordestina de Crédito e Assistência Rural de Sergipe, Brazil
ANCOM	Andean Common Market
ANDI	Asociación Nacional de Industriales, Colombia
ANPOCS	Associação Nacional de Pós-Graduação e Pesquisa em Ciências Sociais, São Paulo
ANUC	Asociación Nacional de Usuarios Campesinos, Colombia
ANUIES	Asociación Nacional de Universidades e Institutos de Enseñanza Superior, Mexico
AP	Acción Popular
APRA	Alianza Popular Revolucionaria Americana, Peru
ARENA	Aliança Renovadora Nacional, Brazil
Ariz.	Arizona
Ark.	Arkansas
ASA	Association of Social Anthropologists of the Commonwealth, London
ASSEPLAN	Assessoria de Planejamento e Acompanhamento, Recife
Assn.	Association
Aufl.	Auflage (edition, edición)
AUFS	American Universities Field Staff Reports, Hanover, N.H.
Aug.	August, Augustan
aum.	aumentada
b.	born (nació)
B.A.R.	British Archaeological Reports
BBE	Bibliografia Brasileira de Educação
b.c.	indicates dates obtained by radiocarbon methods
BC	Before Christ

bibl(s).	bibliography(ies)
BID	Banco Interamericano de Desarrollo
BNDE	Banco Nacional de Desenvolvimento Econômico, Brazil
BNH	Banco Nacional de Habitação, Brazil
BP	before present
b/w	black and white
C14	Carbon 14
ca.	*circa* (about)
CACM	Central American Common Market
CADE	Conferencia Anual de Ejecutivos de Empresas, Peru
CAEM	Centro de Altos Estudios Militares, Peru
Calif.	California
Cap.	Capítulo
CARC	Centro de Arte y Comunicación, Buenos Aires
CARICOM	Caribbean Common Market
CARIFTA	Caribbean Free Trade Association
CBD	central business district
CBI	Caribbean Basin Initiative
CD	Christian Democrats, Chile
CDI	Conselho de Desenvolvimento Industrial, Brasília
CEBRAP	Centro Brasileiro de Análise e Planejamento, São Paulo
CECORA	Centro de Cooperativas de la Reforma Agraria, Colombia
CEDAL	Centro de Estudios Democráticos de América Latina, Costa Rica
CEDE	Centro de Estudios sobre Desarrollo Económico, Univ. de los Andes, Bogotá
CEDEPLAR	Centro de Desenvolvimento e Planejamento Regional, Belo Horizonte
CEDES	Centro de Estudios de Estado y Sociedad, Buenos Aires; Centro de Estudos de Educação e Sociedade, São Paulo
CEDI	Centro Ecumênico de Documentos e Informação, São Paulo
CEDLA	Centro de Estudios y Documentación Latinoamericanos, Amsterdam
CEESTEM	Centro de Estudios Económicos y Sociales del Tercer Mundo, México
CELADE	Centro Latinoamericano de Demografía
CELADEC	Comisión Evangélica Latinoamericana de Educación Cristiana
CELAM	Consejo Episcopal Latinoamericano
CEMLA	Centro de Estudios Monetarios Latinoamericanos, Mexico
CENDES	Centro de Estudios del Desarrollo, Venezuela
CENIDIM	Centro Nacional de Información, Documentación e Investigación Musicales, Mexico
CENIET	Centro Nacional de Información y Estadísticas del Trabajo, Mexico
CEPADE	Centro Paraguayo de Estudios de Desarrollo Económico y Social
CEPA-SE	Comissão Estadual de Planejamento Agrícola, Sergipe
CEPAL	Comisión Económica para América Latina y el Caribe
CEPLAES	Centro de Planificación y Estudios Sociales, Quito
CERES	Centro de Estudios de la Realidad Económica y Social, Bolivia
CES	constant elasticity of substitution
cf.	compare
CFI	Consejo Federal de Inversiones, Buenos Aires
CGE	Confederación General Económica, Argentina
CGTP	Confederación General de Trabajadores del Perú
chap(s).	chapter(s)
CHEAR	Council on Higher Education in the American Republics
Cía.	Compañía
CIA	Central Intelligence Agency
CIDA	Comité Interamericano de Desarrollo Agrícola
CIDE	Centro de Investigación y Desarrollo de la Educación, Chile; Centro de Investigación y Docencias Económicas, Mexico

CIE	Centro de Investigaciones Económicas, Buenos Aires
CIEDLA	Centro Interdisciplinario de Estudios sobre el Desarrollo Latinoamericano, Buenos Aires
CIEDUR	Centro Interdisciplinario de Estudios sobre el Desarrollo Uruguay, Montevideo
CIEPLAN	Corporación de Investigaciones Económicas para América Latina, Santiago
CIESE	Centro de Investigaciones y Estudios Socioeconómicos, Quito
CIMI	Conselho Indigenista Missionário, Brazil
CINTERFOR	Centro Interamericano de Investigación y Documentación sobre Formación Profesional
CINVE	Centro de Investigaciones Económicas, Montevideo
CIP	Conselho Interministerial de Preços, Brazil
CIPCA	Centro de Investigación y Promoción del Campesinado, Bolivia
CIPEC	Consejo Intergubernamental de Países Exportadores de Cobre, Santiago
CLACSO	Consejo Latinoamericano de Ciencias Sociales, Secretaría Ejecutiva, Buenos Aires
CLASC	Confederación Latinoamericana Sindical Cristiana
CLE	Comunidad Latinoamericana de Escritores, Mexico
cm	centimeter
CNI	Confederação Nacional da Indústria, Brazil
CNPq	Conselho Nacional de Pesquisas, Brazil
Co.	Company
COB	Central Obrera Boliviana
COBAL	Companhia Brasileira de Alimentos
Col.	Collection, Colección, Coleção
col.	colored, coloured
Colo.	Colorado
COMCORDE	Comisión Coordinadora para el Desarrollo Económico, Uruguay
comp(s).	compiler(s), compilador(es)
CONCLAT	Congresso Nacional das Classes Trabalhadoras, Brazil
CONDESE	Conselho de Desenvolvimento Econômico de Sergipe
Conn.	Connecticut
COPEI	Comité Organizador Pro-Elecciones Independientes, Venezuela
CORFO	Corporación de Fomento de la Producción, Chile
CORP	Corporación para el Fomento de Investigaciones Económicas, Colombia
Corp.	Corporation, Corporación
corr.	corrected, corregida
CP	Communist Party
CPDOC	Centro de Pesquisa e Documentação, Brazil
CRIC	Consejo Regional Indígena del Cauca, Colombia
CSUTCB	Confederación Sindical Unica de Trabajadores Campesinos de Bolivia
CTM	Confederación de Trabajadores de México
CUNY	City University of New York
CVG	Corporación Venezolana de Guayana
d.	died (murió)
DANE	Departamento Nacional de Estadística, Colombia
DC	developed country; Demócratas Cristianos, Chile
d.C.	después de Cristo
Dec./déc.	December, décembre
Del.	Delaware
dept.	department
depto.	departamento
DESCO	Centro de Estudios y Promoción del Desarrollo, Lima
Dez./dez.	Dezember, dezembro
dic.	diciembre, dicembre

disc.	discography
DNOCS	Departamento Nacional de Obras Contra as Secas, Brazil
doc.	document, documento
Dr.	Doctor
Dra.	Doctora
DRAE	*Diccionario de la Real Academia Española*
ECLAC	UN Economic Commision for Latin America and the Caribbean, New York and Santiago
ECOSOC	UN Economic and Social Council
ed./éd.(s)	edition(s), édition(s), edición(es), editor(s), redactor(es), director(es)
EDEME	Editora Emprendimentos Educacionais, Florianópolis
Edo.	Estado
EEC	European Economic Community
EE.UU.	Estados Unidos de América
EFTA	European Free Trade Association
e.g.	*exempio gratia* (for example, por ejemplo)
ELN	Ejército de Liberación Nacional, Colombia
ENDEF	Estudo Nacional da Despesa Familiar, Brazil
ESG	Escola Superior de Guerra, Brazil
estr.	estrenado
et al.	*et alia* (and others)
ETENE	Escritório Técnico de Estudos Econômicos do Nordeste, Brazil
ETEPE	Escritório Técnico de Planejamento, Brazil
EUDEBA	Editorial Universitaria de Buenos Aires
EWG	Europaische Wirtschaftsgemeinschaft. *See* EEC.
facsim(s).	facsimile(s)
FAO	Food and Agriculture Organization of the United Nations
FDR	Frente Democrático Revolucionario, El Salvador
FEB	Força Expedicionária Brasileira
Feb./feb.	February, Februar, febrero, febbraio
FEDECAFE	Federación Nacional de Cafeteros, Colombia
fev./fév.	fevereiro, février
ff.	following
FGTS	Fundo de Garantia do Tempo de Serviço, Brazil
FGV	Fundação Getúlio Vargas
FIEL	Fundación de Investigaciones Económicas Latinoamericanas, Argentina
film.	filmography
fl.	flourished
Fla.	Florida
FLACSO	Facultad Latinoamericana de Ciencias Sociales
FMI	Fondo Monetario Internacional
FMLN	Frente Farabundo Martí de Liberación Nacional, El Salvador
fold.	folded
fol(s).	folio(s)
FRG	Federal Republic of Germany
FSLN	Frente Sandinista de Liberación Nacional, Nicaragua
ft.	foot, feet
FUAR	Frente Unido de Acción Revolucionaria, Colombia
FUNAI	Fundação Nacional do Indio, Brazil
FUNARTE	Fundação Nacional de Arte, Brazil
FURN	Fundação Universidade Regional do Nordeste
Ga.	Georgia
GAO	General Accounting Office, Wahington
GATT	General Agreement on Tariffs and Trade
GDP	gross domestic product

GDR	German Democratic Republic
GEIDA	Grupo Executivo de Irrigação para o Desenvolvimento Agrícola, Brazil
gen.	gennaio
Gen.	General
GMT	Greenwich Mean Time
GPA	grade point average
GPO	Government Printing Office, Washington
h.	hijo
ha.	hectares, hectáreas
HLAS	*Handbook of Latin American Studies*
HMAI	*Handbook of Middle American Indians*
Hnos.	hermanos
HRAF	Human Relations Area Files, Human Relations Area Files, Inc., New Haven, Conn.
IBBD	Instituto Brasileiro de Bibliografia e Documentação
IBGE	Instituto Brasileiro de Geografia e Estatística, Rio de Janeiro
IBRD	International Bank for Reconstruction and Development (World Bank)
ICA	Instituto Colombiano Agropecuario
ICAIC	Instituto Cubano de Arte e Industria Cinematográfica
ICCE	Instituto Colombiano de Construcción Escolar
ICE	International Cultural Exchange
ICSS	Instituto Colombiano de Seguridad Social
ICT	Instituto de Crédito Territorial, Colombia
id.	*idem* (the same as previously mentioned or given)
IDB	Inter-American Development Bank
i.e.	*id est* (that is, o sea)
IEL	Instituto Euvaldo Lodi, Brazil
IEP	Instituto de Estudios Peruanos
IERAC	Instituto Ecuatoriano de Reforma Agraria y Colonización
IFAD	International Fund for Agricultural Development
IICA	Instituto Interamericano de Ciencias Agrícolas, San José
III	Instituto Indigenista Interamericana, Mexico
IIN	Instituto Indigenista Nacional, Guatemala
ILDIS	Instituto Latinoamericano de Investigaciones Sociales, Quito
ill.	illustration(s)
Ill.	Illinois
ILO	International Labour Organization, Geneva
IMES	Instituto Mexicano de Estudios Sociales
IMF	International Monetary Fund
Impr.	Imprenta, Imprimérie
in.	inches
INAH	Instituto Nacional de Antropología e Historia, Mexico
INBA	Instituto Nacional de Bellas Artes, Mexico
Inc.	Incorporated
INCORA	Instituto Colombiano de Reforma Agraria
Ind.	Indiana
INEP	Instituto Nacional de Estudios Pedagógicos, Brazil
INI	Instituto Nacional Indigenista, Mexico
INIT	Instituto Nacional de Industria Turística, Cuba
INPES/IPEA	Instituto de Planejamento Econômico e Social, Brazil
INTAL	Instituto para la Integración de América Latina
IPA	Instituto de Pastoral Andina, Univ. de San Antonio de Abad, Seminario de Antropología, Cusco, Peru
IPEA	Instituto de Pesquisa Econômica Aplicada, Brazil
IPES/GB	Instituto de Pesquisas e Estudos Sociais, Guanabara, Brazil

IPHAN	Instituto de Patrimônio Histórico e Artístico Nacional, Brazil
ir.	irregular
IS	Internacional Socialista
ITT	International Telephone and Telegraph
Jan./jan.	January, Januar, janeiro, janvier
JLP	Jamaican Labour Party
Jr.	Junior, Júnior
JUC	Juventude Universitária Católica, Brazil
JUCEPLAN	Junta Central de Planificación, Cuba
Kan.	Kansas
km	kilometers, kilómetros
Ky.	Kentucky
La.	Louisiana
LASA	Latin American Studies Association
LDC	less developed country(ies)
LP	long-playing record
Ltd(a).	Limited, Limitada
m	meters, metros
m.	murió (died)
M	mille, mil, thousand
M.A.	Master of Arts
MACLAS	Middle Atlantic Council of Latin American Studies
MAPU	Movimiento de Acción Popular Unitario, Chile
MARI	Middle American Research Institute, Tulane University, New Orleans
MAS	Movimiento al Socialismo, Venezuela
Mass.	Massachusetts
MCC	Mercado Común Centro-Americano
Md.	Maryland
MDB	Movimiento Democrático Brasileiro
MDC	more developed countries
Me.	Maine
MEC	Ministério de Educação e Cultura, Brazil
Mich.	Michigan
mimeo	mimeographed, mimeografiado
min.	minutes, minutos
Minn.	Minnesota
MIR	Movimiento de Izquierda Revolucionaria, Chile and Venezuela
Miss.	Mississippi
MIT	Massachusetts Institute of Technology
ml	milliliter
MLN	Movimiento de Liberación Nacional
mm.	millimeter
MNC	multinational corporation
MNR	Movimiento Nacionalista Revolucionario, Bolivia
Mo.	Missouri
MOBRAL	Movimento Brasileiro de Alfabetização
MOIR	Movimiento Obrero Independiente y Revolucionario, Colombia
Mont.	Montana
MRL	Movimiento Revolucionario Liberal, Colombia
ms.	manuscript
M.S.	Master of Science
msl	mean sea level
n.	nació (born)
NBER	National Bureau of Economic Research, Cambridge, Massachusetts
N.C.	North Carolina

N.D.	North Dakota
NE	Northeast
Neb.	Nebraska
neubearb.	neubearbeitet (revised, corregida)
Nev.	Nevada
n.f.	neue Folge (new series)
N.H.	New Hampshire
NIEO	New International Economic Order
NIH	National Institutes of Health, Washington
N.J.	New Jersey
NJM	New Jewel Movement, Grenada
N.M.	New Mexico
no(s).	number(s), número(s)
NOEI	Nuevo Orden Económico Internacional
NOSALF	Scandinavian Committee for Research in Latin America
Nov./nov.	November, noviembre, novembre, novembro
NSF	National Science Foundation
NW	Northwest
N.Y.	New York
OAB	Ordem dos Advogados do Brasil
OAS	Organization of American States
Oct./oct.	October, octubre, octobre
ODEPLAN	Oficina de Planificación Nacional, Chile
OEA	Organización de los Estados Americanos
OIT	Organización Internacional del Trabajo
Okla.	Oklahoma
Okt.	Oktober
op.	opus
OPANAL	Organismo para la Proscripción de las Armas Nucleares en América Latina
OPEC	Organization of Petroleum Exporting Countries
OPEP	Organización de Países Exportadores de Petróleo
OPIC	Overseas Private Investment Corporation, Washington
Or.	Oregon
OREALC	Oficina Regional de Educación para América Latina y el Caribe
ORIT	Organización Regional Interamericana del Trabajo
ott.	ottobre
out.	outubro
p.	page(s)
Pa.	Pennsylvania
PAN	Partido Acción Nacional, Mexico
PC	Partido Comunista
PCCLAS	Pacific Coast Council on Latin American Studies
PCN	Partido de Conciliación Nacional, El Salvador
PCP	Partido Comunista del Perú
PCR	Partido Comunista Revolucionario, Chile and Argentina
PCV	Partido Comunista de Venezuela
PD	Partido Democrático
PDC	Partido Demócrata Cristiano, Chile
PDS	Partido Democrático Social, Brazil
PDT	Partido Democrático Trabalhista, Brazil
PEMEX	Petróleos Mexicanos
PETROBRAS	Petróleo Brasileiro
PIMES	Programa Integrado de Mestrado em Economia e Sociologia, Brazil
PIP	Partido Independiente de Puerto Rico
PLN	Partido Liberación Nacional, Costa Rica

PMDB	Partido do Movimento Democrático Brasileiro
PNAD	Pesquisa Nacional por Amostra Domiciliar, Brazil
PNC	People's National Congress, Guyana
PNM	People's National Movement, Trinidad and Tobago
PNP	People's National Party, Jamaica
pop.	population
port(s).	portrait(s)
PPP	purchasing power parities; People's Progressive Party of Guyana
PRD	Partido Revolucionario Dominicano
PREALC	Programa Regional del Empleo para América Latina y el Caribe, Organización Internacional del Trabajo, Santiago
PRI	Partido Revolucionario Institucional, Mexico
Prof.	Professor, Profesor(a)
PRONAPA	Programa Nacional de Pesquisas Arqueológicas, Brazil
prov.	province, provincia
PS	Partido Socialista, Chile
PSD	Partido Social Democrático, Brazil
pseud.	pseudonym, pseudónimo
PT	Partido dos Trabalhadores, Brazil
pt(s).	part(s), parte(s)
PTB	Partido Trabalhista Brasileiro
pub.	published, publisher
PUC	Pontifícia Universidade Católica
PURSC	Partido Unido de la Revolución Socialista de Cuba
q.	quarterly
rev.	revisada, revista, revised
R.I.	Rhode Island
s.a.	semiannual
SALALM	Seminar on the Acquisition of Latin American Library Materials
SATB	soprano, alto, tenor, bass
sd.	sound
s.d.	*sine datum* (no date, sin fecha)
S.D.	South Dakota
SDR	special drawing rights
SE	Southeast
SELA	Sistema Económico Latinoamericano
SENAC	Serviço Nacional de Aprendizagem Comercial, Rio de Janeiro
SENAI	Serviço Nacional de Aprendizagem Industrial, São Paulo
SEP	Secretaría de Educación Pública, Mexico
SEPLA	Seminario Permanente sobre Latinoamérica, Mexico
Sept./sept.	September, septiembre, septembre
SES	socioeconomic status
SESI	Serviço Social da Indústria, Brazil
set.	setembro, settembre
SI	Socialist International
SIECA	Secretaría Permanente del Tratado General de Integración Económica Centroamericana
SIL	Summer Institute of Linguistics (Instituto Lingüístico de Verano)
SINAMOS	Sistema Nacional de Apoyo a la Movilización Social, Peru
S.J.	Society of Jesus
s.l.	*sine loco* (place of publication unknown)
s.n.	*sine nomine* (publisher unknown)
SNA	Sociedad Nacional de Agricultura, Chile
SPP	Secretaría de Programación y Presupuesto, Mexico
SPVEA	Superintendência do Plano de Valorização Econômica da Amazônia, Brazil

sq.	square
SSRC	Social Sciences Research Council, New York
SUDAM	Superintendência de Desenvolvimento da Amazônia, Brazil
SUDENE	Superintendência de Desenvolvimento do Nordeste, Brazil
SUFRAME	Superintendência da Zona Franca de Manaus, Brazil
SUNY	State University of New York
SW	Southwest
t.	tomo(s), tome(s)
TAT	Thematic Apperception Test
TB	tuberculosis
Tenn.	Tennessee
Tex.	Texas
TG	transformational generative
TL	Thermoluminescent
TNE	Transnational enterprise
TNP	Tratado de No Proliferación
trans.	translator
UABC	Universidad Autónoma de Baja California
UCA	Universidad Centroamericana José Simeón Cañas, San Salvador
UCLA	University of California, Los Angeles
UDN	União Democrática Nacional, Brazil
UFG	Universidade Federal de Goiás
UFPb	Universidade Federal de Paraíba
UFSC	Universidade Federal de Santa Catarina
UK	United Kingdom
UN	United Nations
UNAM	Universidad Nacional Autónoma de México
UNCTAD	United Nations Conference on Trade and Development
UNDP	United Nations Development Programme
UNEAC	Unión de Escritores y Artistas de Cuba
UNESCO	United Nations Educational, Scientific and Cultural Organization
UNI/UNIND	União das Nações Indígenas
UNICEF	United Nations International Children's Emergency Fund
Univ(s).	university(ies), universidad(es), universidade(s), université(s), universität(s), universitá(s)
uniw.	uniwersytet (university)
Unltd.	Unlimited
UP	Unidad Popular, Chile
URD	Unidad Revolucionaria Democrática
URSS	Unión de Repúblicas Soviéticas Socialistas
US	United States
USAID	*See* AID.
USIA	United States Information Agency
USSR	Union of Soviet Socialist Republics
UTM	Universal Transverse Mercator
UWI	Univ. of the West Indies
v.	volume(s), volumen (volúmenes)
Va.	Virginia
V.I.	Virgin Islands
viz.	*videlicet* (that is, namely)
vol(s).	volume(s), volumen (volúmenes)
vs.	versus
Vt.	Vermont
W.Va.	West Virginia
Wash.	Washington

Wis.	Wisconsin
WPA	Working People's Alliance, Guyana
Wyo.	Wyoming
yr(s).	year(s)

TITLE LIST OF JOURNALS INDEXED

For journal titles listed by abbreviation, see *Abbreviation List of Journals Indexed* (p. 807).

The Accounting Historians Journal.
Academy of Accounting Historians. University, Alabama. (Account. Hist. J.)

Afro-Hispanic Review. Washington. (Afro-Hisp. Rev.)

Agricultural History. Agricultural History Society. Univ. of Calif. Press. Berkeley. (Agric. Hist.)

Alfa. Univ. de São Paulo, Faculdade de Filosofia, Ciências e Letras. Marília, São Paulo. (Alfa)

Allpanchis. Instituto de Pastoral Andina. Cusco, Peru. (Allpanchis)

Amazonía Peruana. Centro Amazónico de Antropología y Aplicación Práctica, Depto. de Documentación y Publicaciones. Lima. (Amazonía Peru.)

América Indígena. Instituto Indigenista Interamericano. México. (Am. Indíg.)

América Latina. Academia de Ciencias de la Unión de Repúblicas Soviéticas Socialistas. Moscú. (Am. Lat./Moscú)

América Meridional. Sociedad Regional de Ciencias Humanas. Montevideo. (Am. Merid.)

American Ethnologist. American Ethnological Society. Washington. (Am. Ethnol.)

American Historical Review. American Historical Assn., Washington. (Am. Hist. Rev.)

American Indian Quarterly. Southwestern American Indian Society; Fort Worth Museum of Science and History. Hurst, Tex. (Am. Indian Q.)

American Speech. Columbia Univ. Press. New York. (Am. Speech)

The Americas. Academy of American Franciscan History. Washington. (Americas/Francisc.)

Anais do Museu Paulista. São Paulo. (An. Mus. Paul.)

Anales de la Academia de Geografía e Historia de Guatemala. Guatemala. (An. Acad. Geogr. Hist. Guatem.)

Anales de la Universidad de Chile. Santiago. (An. Univ. Chile)

Anales del Instituto de Investigaciones Estéticas. Univ. Nacional Autónoma de México. México. (An. Inst. Invest. Estét.)

Annales du Midi. Edouard Privat Editeur. Toulouse, France. (Ann. Midi)

Annales: économies, sociétés, civilisations. Centre national de la recherche scientifique de la VIe Section de l'École pratique des hautes etudes. Paris. (Ann. écon. soc. civilis.)

Antropología e Historia de Guatemala. Instituto de Antropología e Historia de Guatemala. Guatemala. (Antropol. Hist. Guatem.)

Antropológica. Fundación La Salle de Ciencias Naturales; Instituto Caribe de Antropología y Sociología. Caracas. (Antropológica)

Anuario. Univ. Nacional de Rosario, Escuela de Historia. Argentina. (Anuario/Rosario)

Anuario. Instituto de Investigaciones Históricas Dr. José Gaspar Rodríguez de Francia. Asunción. (Anu. Inst. Invest. Hist./Asunción)

Anuário Antropológico. Tempo Brasileiro. Rio de Janeiro. (Anu. Antropol.)

Anuario de Estudios Americanos. Consejo Superior de Investigaciones Científicas; Univ. de Sevilla, Escuela de Estudios Hispano-Americanos. Sevilla, Spain. (Anu. Estud. Am.)

Anuario de Estudios Centroamericanos. Univ. de Costa Rica. San José. (Anu. Estud. Centroam.)

Anuario de Letras. Revista de la Facultad de Filosofía y Letras, Univ. Nacional Autónoma de México. México. (Anu. Let.)

Anuario del Centro de Estudios Martianos. Centro de Estudios Martianos. La Habana. (Anu. Centro Estud. Martianos)

Anuario IEHS. Univ. Nacional del Centro de

la Provincia de Buenos Aires, Instituto de Estudios Histórico-Sociales, Argentina. (Anu. IEHS)

Anuario Mariateguiano. Empresa Editora Amauta. Lima. (Anu. Mariateg.)

Apuntes. Univ. del Pacífico, Centro de Investigación. Lima. (Apuntes/Lima)

Araucaria de Chile. I. Peralta Ediciones. Pamplona, Spain. (Araucaria Chile)

Arbor. Consejo Superior de Investigaciones Científicas. Madrid. (Arbor)

Archaeología Musicalis. Moeck Verlag und Musikinstrumentenwerk. Celle, Germany. (Archaeol. Music.)

Archaeology. Archaeology Institute of America. Cambridge, Mass. (Archaeology)

Archivo Ibero-Americano. Revista de Estudios Históricos. Los Padres Franciscanos. Madrid. (Arch. Ibero-Am.)

Archivum Historicum Societatis Iesu. Roma. (Arch. Hist. Soc. Iesu)

Asclepio. Consejo Superior de Investigaciones Científicas, Instituto Arnau de Vilanova de Historia de la Medicina, Archivo Iberoamericano de Historia de la Medicina y Antropología Médica. Madrid. (Asclepio)

Atenea. Univ. de Concepción. Chile. (Atenea/Concepción)

Behavioral and Social Sciences Librarian. The Haworth Press, New York. (Behav. Soc. Sci. Libr.)

Beiträge zur Romanischen Philologie. Rütten &ampersand; Loening. Berlin. (Beitr. Roman. Philol.)

Bermuda Journal of Archaeological and Maritime History. Bermuda Maritime Museum. (Bermud. J. Archaeol. Marit. Hist.)

Boletim do Museu Paraense Emílio Goeldi. Nova série: antropologia. Conselho Nacional de Desenvolvimento Científico e Tecnológico, Instituto Nacional de Pesquisas da Amazônia. Belém, Brazil. (Bol. Mus. Para. Goeldi)

Boletim Informativo e Bibliográfico de Ciências Sociais: BIB. Associação Nacional de Pós-Graduação e Pesquisa em Ciências Sociais. Rio de Janeiro. (ANPOCS BIB)

Boletín. Centro de Documentación de Música Boliviana. (Boletín/Cochabamba)

Boletín Americanista. Univ. de Barcelona, Facultad de Geografía e Historia, Depto. de Historia de América. Barcelona. (Bol. Am.)

Boletín Bibliográfico. Agencia Mexicana del ISBN, Dirección General del Derecho del Autor. Mexico . (Bol. Bibliogr./México)

Boletín Cultural y Bibliográfico. Banco de la República; Biblioteca Luis-Angel Arango. Bogotá. (Bol. Cult. Bibliogr.)

Boletín de Antropología Americana. Instituto Panamericano de Geografía e Historia. México. (Bol. Antropol. Am.)

Boletín de Estudios Latinoamericanos y del Caribe. Centro de Estudios y Documentación Latinoamericanos. Amsterdam. (Bol. Estud. Latinoam.)

Boletín de la Academia Colombiana. Bogotá. (Bol. Acad. Colomb.)

Boletín de la Academia Hondureña de la Lengua. Tegucigalpa. (Bol. Acad. Hondur. Leng.)

Boletín de la Academia Nacional de la Historia. Caracas. (Bol. Acad. Nac. Hist./Caracas)

Boletín de la Academia Nacional de la Historia. Buenos Aires. (Bol. Acad. Nac. Hist./B. Aires)

Boletín de Lima. Revista Cultural Científica. Lima. (Bol. Lima)

Boletín del Archivo Histórico Arquidiocesano Francisco de Paula García Paláez. Guatemala. (Bol. Arch. Hist. Arq.)

Boletín del Archivo Histórico de Miraflores. Presidencia de la República, Secretaría General. Caracas. (Bol. Arch. Hist. Miraflores)

Boletín del Centro de Investigaciones Históricas. Facultad de Humanidades, Univ. de Puerto Rico. Río Piedras. (Bol. Centro Invest. Hist.)

Boletín del Instituto Americano de Estudios Vascos. Instituto Americano de Estudios Vascos. Buenos Aires. (Bol. Inst. Am. Estud. Vascos)

Boletín del Instituto de Historia Argentina y Americana Dr. Emilio Ravignani. Facultad de Filosofía y Letras, Univ. de Buenos Aires. Buenos Aires. (Bol. Inst. Hist. Ravignani)

Boletín del Museo del Hombre Dominicano. Santo Domingo. (Bol. Mus. Hombre Domin.)

Boletín Histórico del Ejército. Montevideo. (Bol. Hist. Ejérc.)

Boletín Nicaragüense de Bibliografía y Documentación. Biblioteca, Banco Central de Nicaragua. Managua. (Bol. Nicar. Bibliogr. Doc.)

Bulletin. Association France-Haïti. Paris. (Bulletin/Paris)

Bulletin de la Société d'histoire de la Guadeloupe. Archives départementales avec le concours du Conseil général de la Guadeloupe. Basse-Terre, W.I. (Bull. Soc. hist. Guadeloupe)

Bulletin de l'Institut français d'études andines. Lima. (Bull. Inst. fr. étud. andin.)

Bulletin du Bureau national d'ethnologie. Bureau national d'ethnologie. Port-au-Prince, Haiti. (Bull. Bur. natl. ethnol.)

Bulletin du Centre d'histoire des espaces atlantiques. Talence-Cedex, France. (Bull. Cent. hist. atl.)

Bulletin hispanique. Univ. de Bordeaux; Centre national de la recherche scientifique. Bordeaux, France. (Bull. hisp.)

Bulletin of Latin American Research. Society for Latin American Studies. Glasgow, Great Britain. (Bull. Lat. Am. Res.)

Business History Review. Harvard Univ. Graduate School of Business Administration. Boston, Mass. (Bus. Hist. Rev.)

Cadernos Negros. São Paulo. (Cad. Negros)

California History. California Historical Society. San Francisco. (Calif. Hist.)

Canadian Journal of Latin American and Caribbean Studies. Univ. of Ottawa. Ontario, Canada. (Can. J. Lat. Am. Caribb. Stud.)

Caravelle. Cahiers du monde hispanique et luso-brésilien. Univ. de Toulouse, Institute d'études hispaniques, hispano-americaines et luso-brésiliennes. Toulouse, France. (Caravelle)

CARE. Centre Antillais de Recherches et d'Etudes. Editions Caribéennes, Paris. (CARE)

Caribbean Quarterly. Univ. of the West Indies. Mona, Jamaica. (Caribb. Q.)

Caribbean Studies. Univ. of Puerto Rico, Institute of Caribbean Studies. Río Piedras, Puerto Rico. (Caribb. Stud.)

Casa de las Américas. La Habana. (Casa Am.)

Catholic Historical Review. American Catholic Historical Assn.; The Catholic Univ. of America Press. Washington. (Cathol. Hist. Rev.)

Centro de Estudios Puertorriqueños Bulletin. Hunter College, City University of New York. New York. (Cent. Estud. Puertorriq. Bull.)

Church History. American Society of Church History, Univ. of Chicago. Ill. (Church Hist.)

Comparative Studies in Society and History. Society for the Comparative Study of Society and History; Cambridge Univ. Press. London. (Comp. Stud. Soc. Hist.)

Conjonction. Bulletin de l'Institut français d'Haïti. Port-au-Prince. (Conjonction)

Conjunto. Revista de Teatro Latinoamericano. Comité Permanente de Festivales;

Casa de las Américas. La Habana. (Conjunto)

Correspondência Musicológica. Sociedade Brasileira de Musicologia. São Paulo. (Corresp. Musicol.)

Cristianismo y Sociedad. Junta Latinoamericana de Iglesia y Sociedad. Montevideo. (Cristianismo Soc.)

Criterio. Editorial Criterio. Buenos Aires. (Criterio/Buenos Aires)

Criterios: Revista de Teoría Literaria, Estética y Culturología. Casa de las Americas. La Habana. (Criterios/La Habana)

Criticism. Wayne State University Press. Detroit. (Criticism)

Cuadernos Americanos. Editorial Cultura. México. (Cuad. Am.)

Cuadernos de Historia. Univ. de Chile, Facultad de Humanidades y Educación, Depto. de Ciencias Históricas. Santiago. (Cuad. Hist.)

Cuadernos del CLAEH. Centro Latinoamericano de Economía Humana. Montevideo. (Cuad. CLAEH)

Cuadernos Hispanoamericanos. Instituto de Cultura Hispánica. Madrid. (Cuad. Hispanoam.)

Cuadernos Hispanoamericanos: Los Complementarios. Instituto de Cooperación Iberoamericana. Madrid. (Cuad. Hispanoam. Complement.)

Cuban Studies. Univ. of Pittsburgh, Center for Latin American Studies. Pittsburgh, Penn. (Cuba. Stud.)

Cultura. Banco Central del Ecuador. Quito. (Cultura/Quito)

Cultura de Guatemala. Univ. Rafael Landívar. Guatemala. (Cult. Guatem.)

Cupey. Colegio Universitaria Metropolitano. Río Piedras, Puerto Rico. (Cupey)

Dados. Instituto Universitário de Pesquisas. Rio de Janeiro. (Dados)

De Gids. Meulenhoff. Amsterdam. (Gids)

Dédalo. Univ. de São Paulo, Museu de Arqueologia e Etnologia. São Paulo. (Dédalo)

Desarrollo Económico. Instituto de Desarrollo Económico y Social. Buenos Aires. (Desarro. Econ.)

Diogenes. International Council for Philosophy and Humanistic Studies (Paris); Berg Publishers. Oxford, England. (Diogenes/Philosophy)

Dispositio. Dept. of Romance Languages, Univ. of Michigan. Ann Arbor. (Dispositio)

Documentos de Arquitectura y Urbanismo:

DAU. Instituto de Investigación de Arquitectura y Urbanismo. Lima. (Doc. Arquit. Urban.)

Les Dossiers de l'Outre-Mer. Centre National de Documentation des Departments d'Outre-Mer (CENADDOM). Talence, France. (Doss. Outre-mer)

Economía. Pontificia Univ. Católica del Perú, Depto. de Economía. Lima. (Economía/Lima)

Estudios de Cultura Maya. Centro de Estudios Mayas, Univ. Autónoma de México. México. (Estud. Cult. Maya)

Estudios de Historia Moderna y Contemporánea de México. Univ. Nacional Autónoma de México. México. (Estud. Hist. Mod. Contemp. Méx.)

Estudios de Historia Novohispana. Univ. Nacional Autónoma de México, México. (Estud. Hist. Novohisp.)

Estudios Latinoamericanos. Polska Akademia Nauk, Instytut Historii. Varsovia. (Estud. Latinoam.)

Estudios Paraguayos. Univ. Católica Nuestra Señora de la Asunción. Asunción. (Estud. Parag.)

Estudios Públicos. Centro de Estudios Públicos. Santiago. (Estud. Públicos)

Estudios Sociales. Centro de Investigación y Acción Social de la Compañia de Jesús. Santo Domingo. (Estud. Soc./Santo Domingo)

Estudos Econômicos. Univ. de São Paulo, Instituto de Pesquisas Econômicas. São Paulo. (Estud. Econ./São Paulo)

Estudos Históricos. Associação de Pesquisa e Documentação Histórica. Rio de Janeiro. (Estud. Hist./Rio de Janeiro)

Ethnographisch-Archäologische Zeitschrift. Deutscher Verlag Wissenschaften. Berlin. (Ethnogr.-Archäol. Z.)

Ethnohistory. American Society for Ethnohistory. Duke Univ., Durham, N.C. (Ethnohistory)

Ethnologia Polona. Polish Academy of Sciences, Institute for the History of Material Culture. Wrocław, Poland. (Ethnol. Pol.)

Ethnomusicology. Society for Ethnomusicology. Ann Arbor, Mich. (Ethnomusicology)

Ethnos. Statens Etnografiska Museum. Stockholm. (Ethnos)

Etnía. Museo Etnográfico Municipal Dámaso Arce. Municipalidad de Olavarría, Provincia de Buenos Aires. Olavarría, Argentina. (Etnía)

Etudes créoles. Comité international des études créoles. Montréal. (Etud. créoles)

Etudes ibériques et ibéro-americaines. Annales de la Faculté des lettres et sciences humaines de Nice. Nice, France. (Etud. ibér. ibéro-am.)

Explicación de Textos Literarios. Dept. of Spanish and Portuguese, California State Univ. Sacramento. (Explic. Textos Lit.)

The Florida Historical Quarterly. The Florida Historical Society. Jacksonville, Fla. (Fla. Hist. Q.)

Folklore Americano. Instituto Panamericano de Geografía e Historia, Comisión de Historia, Comité de Folklore. México. (Folk. Am.)

Formations. Univ. of Wisconsin Press. Madison, WI. (Formations)

Franciscanum. Revista de las ciencias del espíritu. Univ. de San Buenaventura. Bogotá. (Franciscanum)

Heterofonía. México. (Heterofonía)

HISLA. Lima. (HISLA)

Hispamérica. Takoma Park, Md. (Hispamérica)

Hispania. American Assn. of Teachers of Spanish and Portuguese; Univ. of Southern California. Los Angeles. (Hispania/Teachers)

Hispania. Instituto Jerónimo Zurita, Consejo Superior de Investigaciones Científicas. Madrid. (Hispania/Madrid)

Hispanic American Historical Review. Conference on Latin American History of the American Historical Assn.; Duke Univ. Press. Durham, N.C. (HAHR)

Hispanic Journal. Indiana Univ. of Pennsylvania, Dept. of Foreign Languages. Indiana, Penn. (Hisp. J.)

Hispanic Review. Univ. of Pennsylvania, Dept. of Romance Languages. Philadelphia, Penn. (Hisp. Rev.)

Hispanófila. Univ. of North Carolina. Chapel Hill, N.C. (Hispanófila)

Histoire, économie et sociéte. Editions C.D.U. et S.E.D.E.S., Paris. (Hist. écon. soc.)

Historia. Univ. Católica de Chile. Instituto de Historia. Santiago. (Historia/Santiago)

Historia Boliviana. Cochabamba. (Hist. Boliv.)

Historia Mexicana. Colegio de México. México. (Hist. Mex.)

Historia Paraguaya. Anuario de la Academia

Paraguaya de la Historia. Asunción. (Hist. Parag.)

Historia, Urbanismo, Arquitectura, Construcción, Arte: HUACA. Facultad de Arquitectura, Urbanismo y Artes de la Univ. Nacional de Ingeniería. Lima. (HUACA)

Historia y Sociedad. Depto. de Historia, Univ. de Puerto Rico. Río Piedras, Puerto Rico. (Hist. Soc./Río Piedras)

Histórica. Pontificia Univ. Católica del Perú, Depto. de Humanidades. Lima. (Histórica/Lima)

Historiografía y Bibliografía Americanista. Escuela de Estudios Hispano-Americanos de Sevilla. Sevilla, Spain. (Historiogr. Bibliogr. Am.)

History of Religions. Univ. of Chicago. Chicago, Ill. (Hist. Relig.)

History Workshop. Ruskin College, Oxford Univ., England. (Hist. Workshop)

Hómines. Univ. Interamericana de Puerto Rico. San Juan. (Hómines)

Humanidades. Editora Univ. de Brasília. (Humanidades/Brasília)

Ibérica. Cahiers ibériques et ibéro-américains de l'Univ. de Paris-Sorbonne. Paris. (Ibérica)

Ibero-Americana. Scandinavian Assn. for Research on Latin America (NOSALF). Stockholm. (Ibero-Am.)

Ibero-Amerikanisches Archiv. Ibero-Amerikanisches Institut. Berlin. (Ibero-Am. Arch.)

Iberoromania. Max Niemeyer Verlag. Tübingen, Germany. (Iberoromania)

Ideas '92. North-South Center and the Latin American Studies Program, Univ. of Miami. Coral Gables, Fla. (Ideas 92)

Información Bibliográfica. Libros de Edición Argentina; Cámara Argentina del Libro. Buenos Aires. (Inf. Bibliogr.)

Insula. Madrid. (Insula)

Integración Latinoamericana. Instituto para la Integración de América Latina. Buenos Aires. (Integr. Latinoam.)

Inter-American Music Review. Robert Stevenson. Los Angeles, Calif. (Inter-Am. Music Rev.)

International Labor and Working Class History. Study Group on International Labor and Working Class History. New Haven, Conn. (Int. Labor Work. Class Hist.)

Inti: Revista de Literatura Hispánica. Providence College, R.I. (Inti)

Investigaciones y Ensayos. Academia Nacional de la Historia. Buenos Aires. (Invest. Ens.)

Islas. Univ. Central de Las Villas. Santa Clara, Cuba. (Islas)

Jahrbuch für Geschichte von Staat, Wirtschaft und Gesellschaft Lateinamerikas. Köln, Germany. (Jahrb. Gesch.)

Jahresbibliographie Bibliothek für Zeitgeschichte. Bernard & Graefe Verlag. Koblenz, Germany. (Jahresbibliogr. Bibl. Zeitgesch.)

Jamaica Journal. Institute of Jamaica. Kingston. (Jam. J.)

Journal of Anthropological Research. Univ. of New Mexico. Albuquerque, N.M. (J. Anthropol. Res.)

Journal of Caribbean History. Caribbean Universities Press. St. Lawrence, Barbados. (J. Caribb. Hist.)

Journal of Church and State. J.M. Dawson Studies in Church and State, Baylor Univ., Waco, Tex. (J. Church State)

The Journal of Conflict Resolution. Univ. of Michigan, Dept. of Journalism. Ann Arbor, Mich. (J. Confl. Resolut.)

The Journal of Developing Areas. Western Illinois Univ. Press. Macomb, Ill. (J. Dev. Areas)

The Journal of European Economic History. Banco di Roma. Rome. (J. Eur. Econ. Hist.)

Journal of Historical Geography. Academic Press. London; New York. (J. Hist. Geogr.)

Journal of Interamerican Studies and World Affairs. Institute of Interamerican Studies, Univ. of Miami. Coral Gables, Fla. (J. Interam. Stud. World Aff.)

Journal of Latin American Lore. Univ. of California, Latin American Center. Los Angeles, Calif. (J. Lat. Am. Lore)

Journal of Latin American Studies. Centers or Institutes of Latin American Studies at the Universities of Cambridge, Glasgow, Liverpool, London, and Oxford. Cambridge Univ. Press. London. (J. Lat. Am. Stud.)

Journal of Social History. Carnegie Mellon Univ., Pittsburgh, Pa. (J. Soc. Hist.)

Journal of the Southwest. Southwest Center, Univ. of Arizona. Tucson. (J. Southwest)

Journal of the West. Manhattan, Kan. (J. West)

Journal of Women's History. Indiana Univ. Press. Bloomington, Ind. (J. Women's Hist.)

Les Langues néo-latines. Société des langues néo-latines. (Lang. néo-lat.)

Lateinamerika Studien. Univ. Erlangen-Nürnberg, Sektion Lateinamerika. Nürnberg, Germany. (Lat.am. Stud.)

Latin American Literary Review. Carnegie-Mellon Univ., Dept. of Modern Languages. Pittsburgh, Penn. (Lat. Am. Lit. Rev.)

Latin American Music Review. Univ. of Texas. Austin. (Lat. Am. Music Rev.)

Latin American Perspectives. Univ. of California. Newbury Park, Calif. (Lat. Am. Perspect.)

Latin American Research Review. Latin American Research Review Board. Univ. of New Mexico, Albuquerque, N.M. (LARR)

Latin American Theatre Review. Univ. of Kansas, Center of Latin American Studies. Lawrence, Kan. (Lat. Am. Theatre Rev.)

Letras Cubanas. La Habana. (Let. Cuba.)

Letras de Guatemala. Univ. de San Carlos de Guatemala, Facultad de Humanidades, Instituto de Estudios de la Literatura Nacional. (Let. Guatem.)

Letras de Hoje. Pontifícia Univ. Católica do Rio Grande do Sul. Pôrto Alegre, Brazil. (Let. Hoje)

Letterature d'America. Bulzoni Editore. Roma. (Lett. Am.)

Lexis. Pontificia Univ. Católica del Perú. Lima. (Lexis)

Linden Lane Magazine. Princeton, N.J. (Linden Lane Mag.)

Linguistic Inquiry. MIT Press. Cambridge, Mass. (Linguist. Inq.)

Literary Review. Fairleigh Dickinson Univ., Madison, N.J. (Lit. Rev.)

Lotería. Lotería Nacional de Beneficencia. Panamá. (Lotería)

Luso-Brazilian Review. Univ. of Wisconsin Press. Madison, Wis. (Luso-Braz. Rev.)

Mesoamérica. Centro de Investigaciones Regionales de Mesoamérica. Antigua, Guatemala. (Mesoamérica/Antigua)

Mester. Univ. of California, Dept. of Spanish and Portuguese. Los Angeles, Calif. (Mester)

Meta: Journal des traducteurs/Translators Journal. Univ. de Montréal. Canada. (Meta)

Mexican Studies/Estudios Mexicanos. Univ. of California, Berkeley. (Mex. Stud.)

Military Affairs. American Military Institute. Washington. (Mil. Aff.)

Miscelánea Histórica Ecuatoriana: Revista de Investigaciones Históricas de los Museos del Banco Central del Ecuador. Museos del Banco Central del Ecuador. Quito. (Misc. Hist. Ecuat.)

MLN. Modern Language Notes. Johns Hopkins Univ. Press. Baltimore, Md. (MLN)

Montalbán. Univ. Católica Andrés Bello, Facultad de Humanidades y Educación, Institutos Humanísticos de Investigación. Caracas. (Montalbán)

Neophilologus. H.O. Tjeenk Willenk, etc. Groningen, The Netherlands. (Neophilologus)

New Mexico Historical Review. Historical Society of New Mexico; Univ. of New Mexico. Albuquerque, N.M. (N.M. Hist. Rev.)

New World: A Journal of Latin American Studies. New World Inc., New Orleans, La. (New World)

Nieuwe West-Indische Gids. Martinus Nijhoff. The Hague. (Nieuwe West-Indische Gids)

A Nosa Terra, a Nosa Cultura. Vigo, Spain. (Nosa Terra)

Novos Estudos CEBRAP. Centro Brasileiro de Análise e Planejamento. São Paulo. (Novos Estud. CEBRAP)

NS/NorthSouth/NordSud/NorteSur/NorteSul. Canadian Assn. of Latin American Studies. Univ. of Ottawa. (NS)

Nuestra América. Centro Coordinador y Difusor de Estudios Latinoamericanos, Univ. Autónoma de México. México. (Nuestra Am.)

Nueva Revista de Filología Hispánica. El Colegio de México. México. (Nueva Rev. Filol. Hisp.)

El Nuevo Día. El Día, Inc. San Juan, Puerto Rico. (Nuevo Dia)

Nuevo Texto Crítico. Dept. of Spanish and Portuguese. Stanford Univ., Calif. (Nuevo Texto Crít.)

Numen. International Assn. for the History of Religions. Leiden, The Netherlands. (Numen)

Nuova Rivista Musicale Italiana. Edizioni RAI, Radiotelevisione Italiana. Torino, Italy. (Nuova Riv. Music. Ital.)

Opciones. Centro de Estudios de la Realidad Contemporánea, Academia del Humanismo Cristiano. Santiago. (Opciones)

Orbis. Centre international de dialectologie générale. Louvain, Belgium. (Orbis/ Louvain)

Pacific Historical Review. Univ. of California Press. Los Angeles and Berkeley, Calif. (Pac. Hist. Rev.)

El Palacio. School of American Research; Museum of New Mexico; Archaeological Society of New Mexico. Santa Fe, New Mexico. (Palacio)

Past and Present. London. (Past Present)

Pauta. Univ. Autónoma Metropolitana. México. (Pauta)

Philologica Pragensia. Academia Scientiarum Bohemoslovenica. Prague. (Philol. Prag.)

Plural. Excelsior Compañía Editorial. México. (Plural)

Política y Sociedad. Univ. de San Carlos de Guatemala, Instituto de Investigaciones Políticas y Sociales. Guatemala. (Polít. Soc./Guatemala)

Population. Institut national de'Etudes démographiques. Paris. (Population)

The Portable Lower East Side. New York. (Portable Lower East Side)

Présence Africaine. Paris. (Présence Afr.)

Punto y Coma. Univ. del Sagrado Corazón. Santurce, Puerto Rico. (Punto Coma)

Quaderni Storici. Facoltà di Economia e Commercio, Instítuto de Storia e Sociologia. Ancona, Italy. (Quad. Stor.)

Que Pasa. Tourism Co. San Juan, Puerto Rico. (Que Pasa)

Reflexão. Pontificia Univ. Católica de Campinas. São Paulo. (Reflexão)

Relaciones. El Colegio de Michoacán. Zamora, Mexico. (Relaciones/Zamora)

Repertorio Histórico de la Academia Antioqueña de Historia. Medellín, Colombia. (Repert. Hist. Acad. Antioq. Hist.)

Res Gesta. Instituto de Historia, Facultad de Derecho y Ciencias Sociales, Univ. Católica Argentina. Rosario, Argentina. (Res Gesta)

Revista Andina. Centro Bartolomé de las Casas. Cusco, Perú. (Rev. Andin.)

Revista Antioqueña de Economía y Desarrollo. Fundación para la Investigación y la Cultura. Medellín, Colombia. (Rev. Antioq. Econ. Desarro.)

Revista Brasileira de Historia. ANPUH. São Paulo. (Rev. Bras. Hist.)

Revista Chilena de Historia y Geografía. Sociedad Chilena de Historia y Geografía. Santiago. (Rev. Chil. Hist. Geogr.)

Revista Chilena de Literatura. Univ. de Chile, Depto. de Literatura. Santiago. (Rev. Chil. Lit.)

Revista de Africa y Medio Oriente. Centro de Estudios de Africa y Medio Oriente. La Habana. (Rev. Afr. Medio Oriente)

Revista de Antropologia. Univ. de São Paulo, Faculdade de Filosofia, Letras e Ciências Humanas; Associação Brasileira de Antropologia. São Paulo. (Rev. Antropol./São Paulo)

Revista de Ciencias Sociales. Univ. de Puerto Rico, Colegio de Ciencias Sociales. Río Piedras, P.R. (Rev. Cienc. Soc./Río Piedras)

Revista de Crítica Literaria Latinoamericana. Latinoamericana Editores. Lima. (Rev. Crít. Lit. Latinoam.)

Revista de Estudios Colombianos. Asociación de Colombianistas Norteamericanos; Plaza & Janés. Bogotá. (Rev. Estud. Colomb.)

Revista de Estudios de Teatro. Instituto Nacional de Estudios de Teatro. Buenos Aires. (Rev. Estud. Teatro)

Revista de Estudios Extremeños. Diputación de Badajoz, Institución de Servicios Culturales. Badajoz, Spain. (Rev. Estud. Extremeños)

Revista de Estudios Hispánicos. Univ. of Alabama, Dept. of Romance Languages, Office of International Studies and Programs. Univ., Alabama. (Rev. Estud. Hisp.)

Revista de Estudios Políticos. Instituto de Estudios Políticos. Madrid. (Rev. Estud. Polít.)

Revista de Filosofía. Univ. de Zulia. Maracaibo, Venezuela. (Rev. Filos./Maracaibo)

Revista de Historia. Univ. Nacional de Costa Rica, Escuela de Historia. Heredia, Costa Rica. (Rev. Hist./Heredia)

Revista de Historia. Univ. Federal de Rio Grande do Sul. Porto Alegre, Brazil. (Rev. Hist./Porto Alegre)

Revista de História. Univ. de São Paulo, Faculdade de Filosofia, Letras e Ciências Humanas, Depto. de História. São Paulo. (Rev. Hist./São Paulo)

Revista de Historia. Asociación Histórica Puertorriqueña. San Juan. (Rev. Hist./San Juan)

Revista de Historia de América. Instituto Panamericano de Geografía e Historia,

Comisión de Historia. México. (Rev. Hist. Am.)

Revista de Indias. Consejo Superior de Investigaciones Científicas, Instituto Gonzalo Fernández de Oviedo. Madrid. (Rev. Indias)

Revista de la Academia Guatemalteca de Estudios Genealógicos, Heráldicos, e Históricos. Guatemala. (Rev. Acad. Guat. Estud. Geneal.)

Revista de la Biblioteca Nacional José Martí. La Habana. (Rev. Bibl. Nac. José Martí)

Revista de la Junta de Estudios Históricos de Mendoza. Mendoza, Argentina. (Rev. Junta Estud. Hist. Mendoza)

Revista de la Universidad. Univ. Juárez Autónoma de Tabasco. Villahermosa, Mexico. (Rev. Univ./Tabasco)

Revista de Letras. Univ. Estadual Paulista. São Paulo. (Rev. Let./São Paulo)

Revista de Literatura Cubana. Unión de Escritores y Artistas de Cuba. La Habana. (Rev. Lit. Cuba.)

Revista de Occidente. Publicación mensual. Madrid. (Rev. Occident.)

Revista de Oriente. Colegio Universitario de Humacao, Univ. de Puerto Rico. Humacao, Puerto Rico. (Rev. Oriente)

Revista de Teatro. Sociedade Brasileira de Autores Teatrais. Rio de Janeiro. (Rev. Teatro)

Revista del Archivo Nacional. San José, Costa Rica. (Rev. Arch. Nac.)

Revista del Archivo Nacional de Historia, Sección del Azuay. Casa de la Cultura Ecuatoriana, Núcleo del Azuay. Cuenca, Ecuador. (Rev. Arch. Nac. Hist. Azuay)

La Revista del Centro de Estudios Avanzados de Puerto Rico y el Caribe. Centro de Estudios Avanzados de Puerto Rico y el Caribe. San Juan. (Rev. Cent. Estud. Av.)

Revista del Instituto de Cultura Puertorriqueña. San Juan, P.R. (Rev. Inst. Cult. Puertorriq.)

Revista del Instituto de Investigación Musicológica Carlos Vega. Univ. Católica. Buenos Aires. (Rev. Inst. Invest. Musicol. Carlos Vega)

Revista del Instituto Nacional de Estudios de Teatro. Buenos Aires. (Rev. Inst. Nac. Estud. Teatro)

Revista do Instituto de Estudos Brasileiros. Univ. de São Paulo, Instituto de Estudos Brasileiros. São Paulo. (Rev. Inst. Estud. Bras.)

Revista do Museu Paulista. São Paulo. (Rev. Mus. Paul.)

Revista Europea de Estudios Latinoamericanos y del Caribe = European Review of Latin American and Caribbean Studies. Center for Latin American Research and Documentation; Royal Institute of Linguistics and Antropology. Amsterdam. (Rev. Eur.)

Revista Geográfica. Instituto Geográfico Militar del Ecuador, Depto. Geográfico. Quito. (Rev. Geogr./Quito)

Revista Hispánica Moderna. Hispanic Institute, Columbia Univ. New York. (Rev. Hisp. Mod.)

Revista Iberoamericana. Instituto Internacional de Literatura Iberoamericana; Univ. de Pittsburgh. Pittsburgh, Penn. (Rev. Iberoam.)

Revista Interamericana de Bibliografía. Organization of American States. Washington. (Rev. Interam. Bibliogr.)

Revista Interamericana de Bibliotecología. Univ. de Antioquía, Escuela Interamericana de Bibliotecología. Medellin, Colombia. (Rev. Interam. Bibl.)

Revista Latinoamericana de Filosofía. Centro de Investigaciones Filosóficas. Buenos Aires. (Rev. Latinoam. Filos.)

Revista Mexicana de Sociología. Instituto de Investigaciones Sociales, Univ. Autónoma de México. México. (Rev. Mex. Sociol.)

Revista Musical Chilena. Univ. de Chile, Facultad de Ciencias y Artes Musicales y de la Representación. Santiago. (Rev. Music. Chil.)

Revista Musical de Venezuela. Instituto Latinoamericano de Investigaciones y Estudios Musicales Vicente Emilio Sojo, Consejo Nacional de la Cultura (CONAC). Caracas. (Rev. Music. Venez.)

Revista Novos Rumos. São Paulo, Brazil. (Rev. Novos Rumos)

Revista Paraguaya de Sociología. Centro Paraguayo de Estudios Sociológicos. Asunción. (Rev. Parag. Sociol.)

Revista/Review Interamericana. Univ. Interamericana. San Germán, P.R. (Rev. Rev. Interam.)

Revue de la Société haïtienne d'histoire et géographie. Port-au-Prince. (Rev. Soc. haïti.)

Revue du CERC. Centre d'études et de recherches caraïbéennes, Univ. des Antilles-Guyane, Guadeloupe. Point-à-Pitre. (Rev. CERC)

Revue française d'histoire d'Outre-mer. Société de l'histoire des colonies françaises. Paris. (Rev. fr. hist. Outre-mer)

Revue historique. Presses Universitaires de France. Paris. (Rev. hist./Paris)

Ritmo. Publilat. México. (Ritmo)

Salmagundi. Skidmore College. Saratoga Springs, New York. (Salmagundi)

Santiago. Univ. de Oriente. Santiago, Cuba. (Santiago)

Scherzo: Revista de Música. Scherzo Editorial. Madrid. (Scherzo)

SECOLAS Annals. Southeastern Conference on Latin American Studies; West Georgia College. Carrollton, Ga. (SECOLAS Ann.)

Shih chieh li shih [World History]. Chungkuo she hui k'o hsüeh ch'u pan she [Institute of World History Studies]. Pei-ching. (Shih chieh li shih)

Shupihui. Centro de Estudios Teológicos de la Amazonia. Iquitos, Peru. (Shupihui)

Signs. The Univ. of Chicago Press. Chicago. (Signs)

The Sixteenth Century Journal. Sixteenth Century Journal Publishers. Kirksville, Mo. (Sixt. Century J.)

Slavery and Abolition. Frank Cass & Co., Ltd., London. (Slavery Abolit.)

Social and Economic Studies. Univ. of the West Indies, Institute of Social and Economic Research. Mona, Jamaica. (Soc. Econ. Stud.)

Socialismo y Participación. Ediciones Socialismo y Participación. Lima. (Social. Particip.)

Sociologus. Berlin. (Sociologus)

Studi Emigrazione. Centro Studi Emigrazione. Roma. (Stud. Emigr.)

Suplemento Antropológico. Univ. Católica de Nuestra Señora de la Asunción, Centro de Estudios Antropológicos. Asunción. (Supl. Antropol.)

Sur. Buenos Aires. (Sur)

Techniques & Culture. Maison des Sciences de l'Homme. Paris. (Tech. Cult.)

Temas Americanistas. Univ. de Sevilla, Escuela de Estudios Hispanoamericanos, Seminario de Historia de América. Spain. (Temas Am.)

Tempo Brasileiro. Rio de Janeiro. (Tempo Bras.)

Texte: revue de critique et de théorie littéraire. Trinity College. Toronto, Canada. (Texte)

Thesaurus. Instituto Caro y Cuervo. Bogotá. (Thesaurus)

Third World Quarterly. Third World Foundation; New Zealand House. London. (Third World Q.)

Tlalocan. Instituto de Investigaciones Antropológicas, Instituto de Investigaciones Históricas, Univ. Autónoma de México. México. (Tlalocan)

Todo es Historia. Buenos Aires. (Todo es Hist.)

La Torre. Univ. de Puerto Rico. Río Piedras, P.R. (Torre)

Translation Review. Univ. of Texas at Dallas. Richardson. (Transl. Rev.)

Ultramarines: bulletin des amis del archives d'Outre-mer. Institut d'histoire du pays d'outre-mer. Aix-en-Provence, France. (Ultramarines)

Unión. Unión de Escritores y Artistas de Cuba. La Habana. (Unión)

El Universal Dominical. Cartagena, Colombia. (Universal Dominical)

Universidad de La Habana. Habana. (Univ. La Habana)

Universidad de San Carlos de Guatemala. Univ. de San Carlos. Guatemala. (Univ. San Carlos Guatem.)

Universitas Humanística. Pontificia Univ. Javeriana, Facultad de Filosofia y Letras. Bogotá. (Univ. Humaníst.)

Veritas. Pontificia Univ. Católica do Rio Grande do Sul. Pôrto Alegre, Brazil. (Veritas)

Vozes. Editôra Vozes. Petrópolis, Brazil. (Vozes)

Vuelta. México. (Vuelta)

The Western Historical Quarterly. Western History Assn.; Utah State Univ., Logan, Utah. (West. Hist. Q.)

World Literature Today. Univ. of Oklahoma. Norman, Okla. (World Lit. Today)

Zeitschrift für Kulturaustausch. Institut für Auslandsbeziehungen. Stuttgart, Germany. (Z. Kult.austausch.)

Bol. Inst. Hist. Ravignani. Boletín del Instituto de Historia Argentina y Americana Dr. Emilio Ravignani. Facultad de Filosofía y Letras, Univ. de Buenos Aires. Buenos Aires.

Bol. Lima. Boletín de Lima. Revista Cultural Científica. Lima.

Bol. Mus. Hombre Domin. Boletín del Museo del Hombre Dominicano. Santo Domingo.

Bol. Mus. Para. Goeldi. Boletim do Museu Paraense Emílio Goeldi. Nova série: antropologia. Conselho Nacional de Desenvolvimento Científico e Tecnológico, Instituto Nacional de Pesquisas da Amazônia. Belém, Brazil.

Bol. Nicar. Bibliogr. Doc. Boletín Nicaragüense de Bibliografía y Documentación. Biblioteca, Banco Central de Nicaragua. Managua.

Boletín/Cochabamba. Boletín. Centro de Documentación de Música Boliviana.

Bull. Bur. natl. ethnol. Bulletin du Bureau national d'ethnologie. Bureau national d'ethnologie. Port-au-Prince, Haiti.

Bull. Cent. hist. atl. Bulletin du Centre d'histoire des espaces atlantiques. Talence-Cedex, France.

Bull. hisp. Bulletin hispanique. Univ. de Bordeaux; Centre national de la recherche scientifique. Bordeaux, France.

Bull. Inst. fr. étud. andin. Bulletin de l'Institut français d'études andines. Lima.

Bull. Lat. Am. Res. Bulletin of Latin American Research. Society for Latin American Studies. Glasgow, Great Britain.

Bull. Soc. hist. Guadeloupe. Bulletin de la Société d'histoire de la Guadeloupe. Archives départementales avec le concours du Conseil général de la Guadeloupe. Basse-Terre, W.I.

Bulletin/Paris. Bulletin. Association France-Haïti. Paris.

Bus. Hist. Rev. Business History Review. Harvard Univ. Graduate School of Business Administration. Boston, Mass.

Cad. Negros. Cadernos Negros. São Paulo.

Calif. Hist. California History. California Historical Society. San Francisco.

Can. J. Lat. Am. Caribb. Stud. Canadian Journal of Latin American and Caribbean Studies. Univ. of Ottawa. Ontario, Canada.

Caravelle. Caravelle. Cahiers du monde hispanique et luso-brésilien. Univ. de Toulouse, Institute d'études hispaniques, hispano-americaines et luso-brésiliennes. Toulouse, France.

CARE. CARE. Centre Antillais de Recherches et d'Etudes. Editions Caribéennes, Paris.

Caribb. Q. Caribbean Quarterly. Univ. of the West Indies. Mona, Jamaica.

Caribb. Stud. Caribbean Studies. Univ. of Puerto Rico, Institute of Caribbean Studies. Río Piedras, Puerto Rico.

Casa Am. Casa de las Américas. La Habana.

Cathol. Hist. Rev. Catholic Historical Review. American Catholic Historical Assn.; The Catholic Univ. of America Press. Washington.

Cent. Estud. Puertorriq. Bull. Centro de Estudios Puertorriqueños Bulletin. Hunter College, City University of New York. New York.

Church Hist. Church History. American Society of Church History, Univ. of Chicago. Ill.

Comp. Stud. Soc. Hist. Comparative Studies in Society and History. Society for the Comparative Study of Society and History; Cambridge Univ. Press. London.

Conjonction. Conjonction. Bulletin de l'Institut français d'Haïti. Port-au-Prince.

Conjunto. Conjunto. Revista de Teatro Latinoamericano. Comité Permanente de Festivales; Casa de las Américas. La Habana.

Corresp. Musicol. Correspondência Musicológica. Sociedade Brasileira de Musicologia. S&tildea&o Paulo.

Cristianismo Soc. Cristianismo y Sociedad. Junta Latinoamericana de Iglesia y Sociedad. Montevideo.

Criterio/Buenos Aires. Criterio. Editorial Criterio. Buenos Aires.

Criterios/La Habana. Criterios: Revista de Teoría Literaria, Estética y Culturología. Casa de las Americas. La Habana.

Criticism. Criticism. Wayne State University Press. Detroit.

Cuad. Am. Cuadernos Americanos. Editorial Cultura. México.

Cuad. CLAEH. Cuadernos del CLAEH. Centro Latinoamericano de Economía Humana. Montevideo.

Cuad. Hispanoam. Cuadernos Hispanoamericanos. Instituto de Cultura Hispánica. Madrid.

Cuad. Hispanoam. Complement. Cuadernos Hispanoamericanos: Los Complementarios. Instituto de Cooperación Iberoamericana. Madrid.

Cuad. Hist. Cuadernos de Historia. Univ. de Chile, Facultad de Humanidades y Educación, Depto. de Ciencias Históricas. Santiago.

Cuba. Stud. Cuban Studies. Univ. of Pittsburgh, Center for Latin American Studies. Pittsburgh, Penn.

Cult. Guatem. Cultura de Guatemala. Univ. Rafael Landívar. Guatemala.

Cultura/Quito. Cultura. Banco Central del Ecuador. Quito.

Cupey. Cupey. Colegio Universitaria Metropolitano. Río Piedras, Puerto Rico.

Dados. Dados. Instituto Universitário de Pesquisas. Rio de Janeiro.

Dédalo. Dédalo. Univ. de São Paulo, Museu de Arqueologia e Etnologia. São Paulo.

Desarro. Econ. Desarrollo Económico. Instituto de Desarrollo Económico y Social. Buenos Aires.

Diogenes/Philosophy. Diogenes. International Council for Philosophy and Humanistic Studies (Paris); Berg Publishers. Oxford, England.

Dispositio. Dispositio. Dept. of Romance Languages, Univ. of Michigan. Ann Arbor.

Doc. Arquit. Urban. Documentos de Arquitectura y Urbanismo: DAU. Instituto de Investigación de Arquitectura y Urbanismo. Lima.

Doss. Outre-mer. Les Dossiers de l'Outre-Mer. Centre National de Documentation des Departments d'Outre-Mer (CENADDOM). Talence, France.

Economía/Lima. Economía. Pontificia Univ. Católica del Perú, Depto. de Economía. Lima.

Estud. Cult. Maya. Estudios de Cultura Maya. Centro de Estudios Mayas, Univ. Autónoma de México. México.

Estud. Econ./São Paulo. Estudos Econômicos. Univ. de São Paulo, Instituto de Pesquisas Econômicas. São Paulo.

Estud. Hist. Mod. Contemp. Méx. Estudios de Historia Moderna y Contemporánea de México. Univ. Nacional Autónoma de México. México.

Estud. Hist. Novohisp. Estudios de Historia Novohispana. Univ. Nacional Autónoma de México, México.

Estud. Hist./Rio de Janeiro. Estudos Históricos. Associação de Pesquisa e Documentação Histórica. Rio de Janeiro.

Estud. Latinoam. Estudios Latinoamericanos. Polska Akademia Nauk, Instytut Historii. Varsovia.

Estud. Parag. Estudios Paraguayos. Univ. Católica Nuestra Señora de la Asunción. Asunción.

Estud. Públicos. Estudios Públicos. Centro de Estudios Públicos. Santiago.

Estud. Soc./Santo Domingo. Estudios Sociales. Centro de Investigación y Acción Social de la Compañia de Jesús. Santo Domingo.

Ethnogr.-Archäol. Z. Ethnographisch-Archäologische Zeitschrift. Deutscher Verlag Wissenschaften. Berlin.

Ethnohistory. Ethnohistory. American Society for Ethnohistory. Duke Univ., Durham, N.C.

Ethnol. Pol. Ethnologia Polona. Polish Academy of Sciences, Institute for the History of Material Culture. Wrocław, Poland.

Ethnomusicology. Ethnomusicology. Society for Ethnomusicology. Ann Arbor, Mich.

Ethnos. Ethnos. Statens Etnografiska Museum. Stockholm.

Etnía. Etnía. Museo Etnográfico Municipal Dámaso Arce. Municipalidad de Olavarría, Provincia de Buenos Aires. Olavarría, Argentina.

Etud. créoles. Etudes créoles. Comité international des études créoles. Montréal.

Etud. ibér. ibéro-am. Etudes ibériques et ibéro-americaines. Annales de la Faculté des lettres et sciences humaines de Nice. Nice, France.

Explic. Textos Lit. Explicación de Textos Literarios. Dept. of Spanish and Portuguese, California State Univ. Sacramento.

Fla. Hist. Q. The Florida Historical Quarterly. The Florida Historical Society. Jacksonville, Fla.

Folk. Am. Folklore Americano. Instituto Panamericano de Geografía e Historia, Comisión de Historia, Comité de Folklore. México.

Formations. Formations. Univ. of Wisconsin Press. Madison, WI.

Franciscanum. Franciscanum. Revista de las ciencias del espíritu. Univ. de San Buenaventura. Bogotá.

Gids. De Gids. Meulenhoff. Amsterdam.

HAHR. Hispanic American Historical Review. Conference on Latin American History of the American Historical Assn.; Duke Univ. Press. Durham, N.C.

Heterofonía. Heterofonía. México.

HISLA. HISLA. Lima.

Hisp. J. Hispanic Journal. Indiana Univ. of Pennsylvania, Dept. of Foreign Languages. Indiana, Penn.

Hisp. Rev. Hispanic Review. Univ. of Pennsylvania, Dept. of Romance Languages. Philadelphia, Penn.

Hispamérica. Hispamérica. Takoma Park, Md.

Hispania/Madrid. Hispania. Instituto Jerónimo Zurita, Consejo Superior de Investigaciones Científicas. Madrid.

Hispania/Teachers. Hispania. American Assn. of Teachers of Spanish and Portuguese; Univ. of Southern California. Los Angeles.

Hispanófila. Hispanófila. Univ. of North Carolina. Chapel Hill, N.C.

Hist. Boliv. Historia Boliviana. Cochabamba.

Hist. écon. soc. Histoire, économie et sociéte. Editions C.D.U. et S.E.D.E.S., Paris.

Hist. Mex. Historia Mexicana. Colegio de México. México.

Hist. Parag. Historia Paraguaya. Anuario de la Academia Paraguaya de la Historia. Asunción.

Hist. Relig. History of Religions. Univ. of Chicago. Chicago, Ill.

Hist. Soc./Río Piedras. Historia y Sociedad. Depto. de Historia, Univ. de Puerto Rico. Río Piedras, Puerto Rico.

Hist. Workshop. History Workshop. Ruskin College, Oxford Univ., England.

Historia/Santiago. Historia. Univ. Católica de Chile. Instituto de Historia. Santiago.

Histórica/Lima. Histórica. Pontificia Univ. Católica del Perú, Depto. de Humanidades. Lima.

Historiogr. Bibliogr. Am. Historiografía y Bibliografía Americanista. Escuela de Estudios Hispano-Americanos de Sevilla. Sevilla, Spain.

Hómines. Hómines. Univ. Interamericana de Puerto Rico. San Juan.

HUACA. Historia, Urbanismo, Arquitectura, Construcción, Arte: HUACA. Facultad de Arquitectura, Urbanismo y Artes de la Univ. Nacional de Ingeniería. Lima.

Humanidades/Brasília. Humanidades. Editora Univ. de Brasília.

Ibérica. Ibérica. Cahiers ibériques et ibéro-américains de l'Univ. de Paris-Sorbonne. Paris.

Ibero-Am. Ibero-Americana. Scandinavian Assn. for Research on Latin America (NOSALF). Stockholm.

Ibero-Am. Arch. Ibero-Amerikanisches Archiv. Ibero-Amerikanisches Institut. Berlin.

Iberoromania. Iberoromania. Max Niemeyer Verlag. Tübingen, Germany.

Ideas 92. Ideas '92. North-South Center and the Latin American Studies Program, Univ. of Miami. Coral Gables, Fla.

Inf. Bibliogr. Información Bibliográfica. Libros de Edición Argentina; Cámara Argentina del Libro. Buenos Aires.

Insula. Insula. Madrid.

Int. Labor Work. Class Hist. International Labor and Working Class History. Study Group on International Labor and Working Class History. New Haven, Conn.

Integr. Latinoam. Integración Latinoamericana. Instituto para la Integración de América Latina. Buenos Aires.

Inter-Am. Music Rev. Inter-American Music Review. Robert Stevenson. Los Angeles, Calif.

Inti. Inti: Revista de Literatura Hispánica. Providence College, R.I.

Invest. Ens. Investigaciones y Ensayos. Academia Nacional de la Historia. Buenos Aires.

Islas. Islas. Univ. Central de Las Villas. Santa Clara, Cuba.

J. Anthropol. Res. Journal of Anthropological Research. Univ. of New Mexico. Albuquerque, N.M.

J. Caribb. Hist. Journal of Caribbean History. Caribbean Universities Press. St. Lawrence, Barbados.

J. Church State. Journal of Church and State. J.M. Dawson Studies in Church and State, Baylor Univ., Waco, Tex.

J. Confl. Resolut. The Journal of Conflict Resolution. Univ. of Michigan, Dept. of Journalism. Ann Arbor, Mich.

J. Dev. Areas. The Journal of Developing Areas. Western Illinois Univ. Press. Macomb, Ill.

J. Eur. Econ. Hist. The Journal of European Economic History. Banco di Roma. Rome.

J. Hist. Geogr. Journal of Historical Geography. Academic Press. London; New York.

J. Interam. Stud. World Aff. Journal of Interamerican Studies and World Affairs.

Institute of Interamerican Studies, Univ. of Miami. Coral Gables, Fla.

J. Lat. Am. Lore. Journal of Latin American Lore. Univ. of California, Latin American Center. Los Angeles, Calif.

J. Lat. Am. Stud. Journal of Latin American Studies. Centers or Institutes of Latin American Studies at the Universities of Cambridge, Glasgow, Liverpool, London, and Oxford. Cambridge Univ. Press. London.

J. Soc. Hist. Journal of Social History. Carnegie Mellon Univ., Pittsburgh, Pa.

J. Southwest. Journal of the Southwest. Southwest Center, Univ. of Arizona. Tucson.

J. West. Journal of the West. Manhattan, Kan.

J. Women's Hist. Journal of Women's History. Indiana Univ. Press. Bloomington, Ind.

Jahrb. Gesch. Jahrbuch für Geschichte von Staat, Wirtschaft und Gesellschaft Lateinamerikas. Köln, Germany.

Jahresbibliogr. Bibl. Zeitgesch. Jahresbibliographie Bibliothek für Zeitgeschichte. Bernard &ampersand; Graefe Verlag. Koblenz, Germany.

Jam. J. Jamaica Journal. Institute of Jamaica. Kingston.

Lang. néo-lat. Les Langues néo-latines. Société des langues néo-latines.

LARR. Latin American Research Review. Latin American Research Review Board. Univ. of New Mexico, Albuquerque, N.M.

Lat. Am. Lit. Rev. Latin American Literary Review. Carnegie-Mellon Univ., Dept. of Modern Languages. Pittsburgh, Penn.

Lat. Am. Music Rev. Latin American Music Review. Univ. of Texas. Austin.

Lat. Am. Perspect. Latin American Perspectives. Univ. of California. Newbury Park, Calif.

Lat.am. Stud. Lateinamerika Studien. Univ. Erlangen-Nürnberg, Sektion Lateinamerika. Nürnberg, Germany.

Lat. Am. Theatre Rev. Latin American Theatre Review. Univ. of Kansas, Center of Latin American Studies. Lawrence, Kan.

Let. Cuba. Letras Cubanas. La Habana.

Let. Guatem. Letras de Guatemala. Univ. de San Carlos de Guatemala, Facultad de Humanidades, Instituto de Estudios de la Literatura Nacional.

Let. Hoje. Letras de Hoje. Pontifícia Univ. Católica do Rio Grande do Sul. Pôrto Alegre, Brazil.

Lett. Am. Letterature d'America. Bulzoni Editore. Roma.

Lexis. Lexis. Pontificia Univ. Católica del Perú. Lima.

Linden Lane Mag. Linden Lane Magazine. Princeton, N.J.

Linguist. Inq. Linguistic Inquiry. MIT Press. Cambridge, Mass.

Lit. Rev. Literary Review. Fairleigh Dickinson Univ., Madison, N.J.

Lotería. Lotería. Lotería Nacional de Beneficencia. Panamá.

Luso-Braz. Rev. Luso-Brazilian Review. Univ. of Wisconsin Press. Madison, Wis.

Mesoamérica/Antigua. Mesoamérica. Centro de Investigaciones Regionales de Mesoamérica. Antigua, Guatemala.

Mester. Mester. Univ. of California, Dept. of Spanish and Portuguese. Los Angeles, Calif.

Meta. Meta: Journal des traducteurs/ Translators Journal. Univ. de Montréal. Canada.

Mex. Stud. Mexican Studies/Estudios Mexicanos. Univ. of California, Berkeley.

Mil. Aff. Military Affairs. American Military Institute. Washington.

Misc. Hist. Ecuat. Miscelánea Histórica Ecuatoriana: Revista de Investigaciones Históricas de los Museos del Banco Central del Ecuador. Museos del Banco Central del Ecuador. Quito.

MLN. MLN. Modern Language Notes. Johns Hopkins Univ. Press. Baltimore, Md.

Montalbán. Montalbán. Univ. Católica Andrés Bello, Facultad de Humanidades y Educación, Institutos Humanísticos de Investigación. Caracas.

N.M. Hist. Rev. New Mexico Historical Review. Historical Society of New Mexico; Univ. of New Mexico. Albuquerque, N.M.

Neophilologus. Neophilologus. H.O. Tjeenk Willenk, etc. Groningen, The Netherlands.

New World. New World: A Journal of Latin American Studies. New World Inc., New Orleans, La.

Nieuwe West-Indische Gids. Nieuwe West-Indische Gids. Martinus Nijhoff. The Hague.

Nosa Terra. A Nosa Terra, a Nosa Cultura. Vigo, Spain.

Novos Estud. CEBRAP. Novos Estudos CEBRAP. Centro Brasileiro de Análise e Planejamento. São Paulo.

NS. NS/NorthSouth/NordSud/NorteSur/ NorteSul. Canadian Assn. of Latin American Studies. Univ. of Ottawa.

Nuestra Am. Nuestra América. Centro Coordinador y Difusor de Estudios Latinoamericanos, Univ. Autónoma de México. México.

Nueva Rev. Filol. Hisp. Nueva Revista de Filología Hispánica. El Colegio de México. México.

Nuevo Dia. El Nuevo Día. El Día, Inc. San Juan, Puerto Rico.

Nuevo Texto Crít. Nuevo Texto Crítico. Dept. of Spanish and Portuguese. Stanford Univ., Calif.

Numen. Numen. International Assn. for the History of Religions. Leiden, The Netherlands.

Nuova Riv. Music. Ital. Nuova Rivista Musicale Italiana. Edizioni RAI, Radiotelevisione Italiana. Torino, Italy.

Opciones. Opciones. Centro de Estudios de la Realidad Contemporánea, Academia del Humanismo Cristiano. Santiago.

Orbis/Louvain. Orbis. Centre international de dialectologie générale. Louvain, Belgium.

Pac. Hist. Rev. Pacific Historical Review. Univ. of California Press. Los Angeles and Berkeley, Calif.

Palacio. El Palacio. School of American Research; Museum of New Mexico;

Archaeological Society of New Mexico. Santa Fe, New Mexico.

Past Present. Past and Present. London.

Pauta. Pauta. Univ. Autónoma Metropolitana. México.

Philol. Prag. Philologica Pragensia. Academia Scientiarum Bohemoslovenica. Prague.

Plural. Plural. Excelsior Compañía Editorial. México.

Polít. Soc./Guatemala. Política y Sociedad. Univ. de San Carlos de Guatemala, Instituto de Investigaciones Políticas y Sociales. Guatemala.

Population. Population. Institut national de'Etudes démographiques. Paris.

Portable Lower East Side. The Portable Lower East Side. New York.

Présence Afr. Présence Africaine. Paris.

Punto Coma. Punto y Coma. Univ. del Sagrado Corazón. Santurce, Puerto Rico.

Quad. Stor. Quaderni Storici. Facoltà di Economia e Commercio, Instítuto de Storia e Sociologia. Ancona, Italy.

Que Pasa. Que Pasa. Tourism Co. San Juan, Puerto Rico.

Reflexão. Reflexão. Pontificia Univ. Católica de Campinas. São Paulo.

Relaciones/Zamora. Relaciones. El Colegio de Michoacán. Zamora, Mexico.

Repert. Hist. Acad. Antioq. Hist. Repertorio Histórico de la Academia Antioqueña de Historia. Medellín, Colombia.

Res Gesta. Res Gesta. Instituto de Historia, Facultad de Derecho y Ciencias Sociales, Univ. Católica Argentina. Rosario, Argentina.

Rev. Acad. Guat. Estud. Geneal. Revista de la Academia Guatemalteca de Estudios Genealógicos, Heráldicos, e Históricos. Guatemala.

Rev. Afr. Medio Oriente. Revista de Africa y Medio Oriente. Centro de Estudios de Africa y Medio Oriente. La Habana.

Rev. Andin. Revista Andina. Centro Bartolomé de las Casas. Cusco, Perú.

Rev. Antioq. Econ. Desarro. Revista Antioqueña de Economía y Desarrollo. Fundación para la Investigación y la Cultura. Medellín, Colombia.

Rev. Antropol./São Paulo. Revista de Antropologia. Univ. de São Paulo, Faculdade de Filosofia, Letras e Ciências Humanas; Associação Brasileira de Antropologia. São Paulo.

Rev. Arch. Nac. Revista del Archivo Nacional. San José, Costa Rica.

Rev. Arch. Nac. Hist. Azuay. Revista del Archivo Nacional de Historia, Sección del Azuay. Casa de la Cultura Ecuatoriana, Núcleo del Azuay. Cuenca, Ecuador.

Rev. Bibl. Nac. José Martí. Revista de la Biblioteca Nacional José Martí. La Habana.

Rev. Bras. Hist. Revista Brasileira de Historia. ANPUH. São Paulo.

Rev. Cent. Estud. Av. La Revista del Centro de Estudios Avanzados de Puerto Rico y el Caribe. Centro de Estudios Avanzados de Puerto Rico y el Caribe. San Juan.

Rev. CERC. Revue du CERC. Centre d'études et de recherches caraïbéennes, Univ. des Antilles-Guyane, Guadeloupe. Point-à-Pitre.

Rev. Chil. Hist. Geogr. Revista Chilena de Historia y Geografía. Sociedad Chilena de Historia y Geografía. Santiago.

Rev. Chil. Lit. Revista Chilena de Literatura. Univ. de Chile, Depto. de Literatura. Santiago.

Rev. Cienc. Soc./Río Piedras. Revista de Ciencias Sociales. Univ. de Puerto Rico, Colegio de Ciencias Sociales. Río Piedras, P.R.

Rev. Crít. Lit. Latinoam. Revista de Crítica Literaria Latinoamericana. Latinoamericana Editores. Lima.

Rev. Estud. Colomb. Revista de Estudios Colombianos. Asociación de Colombianistas Norteamericanos; Plaza &ampersand; Janés. Bogotá.

Rev. Estud. Extremeños. Revista de Estudios Extremeños. Diputación de Badajoz, Institución de Servicios Culturales. Badajoz, Spain.

Rev. Estud. Hisp. Revista de Estudios Hispánicos. Univ. of Alabama, Dept. of Romance Languages, Office of International Studies and Programs. Univ., Alabama.

Rev. Estud. Polít. Revista de Estudios Políticos. Instituto de Estudios Políticos. Madrid.

Rev. Estud. Teatro. Revista de Estudios de Teatro. Instituto Nacional de Estudios de Teatro. Buenos Aires.

Rev. Eur. Revista Europea de Estudios Latinoamericanos y del Caribe European Review of Latin American and Caribbean Studies. Center for Latin American Research and Documentation; Royal Institute of Linguistics and Antropology. Amsterdam.

Rev. Filos./Maracaibo. Revista de Filosofía. Univ. de Zulia. Maracaibo, Venezuela.

Rev. fr. hist. Outre-mer. Revue française d'histoire d'Outre-mer. Société de l'histoire des colonies françaises. Paris.

Rev. Geogr./Quito. Revista Geográfica. Instituto Geográfico Militar del Ecuador, Depto. Geográfico. Quito.

Rev. Hisp. Mod. Revista Hispánica Moderna. Hispanic Institute, Columbia Univ. New York.

Rev. Hist. Am. Revista de Historia de América. Instituto Panamericano de Geografía e Historia, Comisión de Historia. México.

Rev. Hist./Heredia. Revista de Historia. Univ. Nacional de Costa Rica, Escuela de Historia. Heredia, Costa Rica.

Rev. hist./Paris. Revue historique. Presses Universitaires de France. Paris.

Rev. Hist./Porto Alegre. Revista de Historia. Univ. Federal de Rio Grande do Sul. Porto Alegre, Brazil.

Rev. Hist./San Juan. Revista de Historia. Asociación Histórica Puertorriqueña. San Juan.

Rev. Hist./São Paulo. Revista de História. Univ. de São Paulo, Faculdade de Filosofia, Letras e Ciências Humanas, Depto. de História. São Paulo.

Rev. Iberoam. Revista Iberoamericana. Instituto Internacional de Literatura Iberoamericana; Univ. de Pittsburgh. Pittsburgh, Penn.

Rev. Indias. Revista de Indias. Consejo Superior de Investigaciones Científicas, Instituto Gonzalo Fernández de Oviedo. Madrid.

Rev. Inst. Cult. Puertorriq. Revista del Instituto de Cultura Puertorriqueña. San Juan, P.R.

Rev. Inst. Estud. Bras. Revista do Instituto de Estudos Brasileiros. Univ. de São Paulo, Instituto de Estudos Brasileiros. São Paulo.

Rev. Inst. Invest. Musicol. Carlos Vega. Revista del Instituto de Investigación Musicológica Carlos Vega. Univ. Católica. Buenos Aires.

Rev. Inst. Nac. Estud. Teatro. Revista del Instituto Nacional de Estudios de Teatro. Buenos Aires.

Rev. Interam. Bibl. Revista Interamericana de Bibliotecología. Univ. de Antioquía, Escuela Interamericana de Bibliotecología. Medellin, Colombia.

Rev. Interam. Bibliogr. Revista Interamericana de Bibliografía. Organization of American States. Washington.

Rev. Junta Estud. Hist. Mendoza. Revista de la Junta de Estudios Históricos de Mendoza. Mendoza, Argentina.

Rev. Latinoam. Filos. Revista Latinoamericana de Filosofía. Centro de Investigaciones Filosóficas. Buenos Aires.

Rev. Let./São Paulo. Revista de Letras. Univ. Estadual Paulista. São Paulo.

Rev. Lit. Cuba. Revista de Literatura Cubana. Unión de Escritores y Artistas de Cuba. La Habana.

Rev. Mex. Sociol. Revista Mexicana de Sociología. Instituto de Investigaciones Sociales, Univ. Autónoma de México. México.

Rev. Mus. Paul. Revista do Museu Paulista. São Paulo.

Rev. Music. Chil. Revista Musical Chilena. Univ. de Chile, Facultad de Ciencias y Artes Musicales y de la Representación. Santiago.

Rev. Music. Venez. Revista Musical de Venezuela. Instituto Latinoamericano de

Investigaciones y Estudios Musicales Vicente Emilio Sojo, Consejo Nacional de la Cultura (CONAC). Caracas.

Rev. Novos Rumos.   Revista Novos Rumos. São Paulo, Brazil.

Rev. Occident.   Revista de Occidente. Publicación mensual. Madrid.

Rev. Oriente.   Revista de Oriente. Colegio Universitario de Humacao, Univ. de Puerto Rico. Humacao, Puerto Rico.

Rev. Parag. Sociol.   Revista Paraguaya de Sociología. Centro Paraguayo de Estudios Sociológicos. Asunción.

Rev. Rev. Interam.   Revista/Review Interamericana. Univ. Interamericana. San Germán, P.R.

Rev. Soc. haïti.   Revue de la Société haïtienne d'histoire et géographie. Port-au-Prince.

Rev. Teatro.   Revista de Teatro. Sociedade Brasileira de Autores Teatrais. Rio de Janeiro.

Rev. Univ./Tabasco.   Revista de la Universidad. Univ. Juárez Autónoma de Tabasco. Villahermosa, Mexico.

Ritmo.   Ritmo. Publilat. México.

Salmagundi.   Salmagundi. Skidmore College. Saratoga Springs, New York.

Santiago.   Santiago. Univ. de Oriente. Santiago, Cuba.

Scherzo.   Scherzo: Revista de Música. Scherzo Editorial. Madrid.

SECOLAS Ann.   SECOLAS Annals. Southeastern Conference on Latin American Studies; West Georgia College. Carrollton, Ga.

Shih chieh li shih.   Shih chieh li shih [World History]. Chung-kuo she hui k'o hsüeh ch'u pan she [Institute of World History Studies]. Pei-ching.

Shupihui.   Shupihui. Centro de Estudios Teológicos de la Amazonia. Iquitos, Peru.

Signs.   Signs. The Univ. of Chicago Press. Chicago.

Sixt. Century J.   The Sixteenth Century Journal. Sixteenth Century Journal Publishers. Kirksville, Mo.

Slavery Abolit.   Slavery and Abolition. Frank Cass & Co., Ltd., London.

Soc. Econ. Stud.   Social and Economic Studies. Univ. of the West Indies, Institute of Social and Economic Research. Mona, Jamaica.

Social. Particip.   Socialismo y Participación. Ediciones Socialismo y Participación. Lima.

Sociologus.   Sociologus. Berlin.

Stud. Emigr.   Studi Emigrazione. Centro Studi Emigrazione. Roma.

Supl. Antropol.   Suplemento Antropológico. Univ. Católica de Nuestra Señora de la Asunción, Centro de Estudios Antropológicos. Asunción.

Sur.   Sur. Buenos Aires.

Tech. Cult.   Techniques & Culture. Maison des Sciences de l'Homme. Paris.

Temas Am.   Temas Americanistas. Univ. de Sevilla, Escuela de Estudios Hispanoamericanos, Seminario de Historia de América. Spain.

Tempo Bras.   Tempo Brasileiro. Rio de Janeiro.

Texte.   Texte: revue de critique et de théorie littéraire. Trinity College. Toronto, Canada.

Thesaurus.   Thesaurus. Instituto Caro y Cuervo. Bogotá.

Third World Q.   Third World Quarterly. Third World Foundation; New Zealand House. London.

Tlalocan.   Tlalocan. Instituto de Investigaciones Antropológicas, Instituto de Investigaciones Históricas, Univ. Autónoma de México. México.

Todo es Hist.   Todo es Historia. Buenos Aires.

Torre.   La Torre. Univ. de Puerto Rico. Río Piedras, P.R.

Transl. Rev.   Translation Review. Univ. of Texas at Dallas. Richardson.

Ultramarines.   Ultramarines: bulletin des amis del archives d'Outre-mer. Institut d'histoire del pays d'outre-mer. Aix-en-Provence, France.

Unión.   Unión. Unión de Escritores y Artistas de Cuba. La Habana.

Univ. Humaníst.   Universitas Humanística. Pontificia Univ. Javeriana, Facultad de Filosofia y Letras. Bogotá.

Univ. La Habana.   Universidad de La Habana. Habana.

Univ. San Carlos Guatem.   Universidad de San Carlos de Guatemala. Univ. de San Carlos. Guatemala.

Universal Dominical.   El Universal Dominical. Cartagena, Colombia.

Veritas.   Veritas. Pontificia Univ. Católica do Rio Grande do Sul. Pôrto Alegre, Brazil.

Vozes.   Vozes. Editôra Vozes. Petrópolis, Brazil.

Vuelta.   Vuelta. México.

West. Hist. Q.   The Western Historical Quarterly. Western History Assn.; Utah State Univ., Logan, Utah.

World Lit. Today.   World Literature Today. Univ. of Oklahoma. Norman, Okla.

Z. Kult.austausch.   Zeitschrift für Kulturaustausch. Institut für Auslandsbeziehungen. Stuttgart, Germany.

SUBJECT INDEX

Abbeville, Claude d', 607.
Abela, Eduardo, 364.
El Abolicionista, 1808.
Abolition (slavery), 738. Antigua, 1756. Barbados, 1744. Brazil, 2885, 2894, 2896, 2990, 3020, 3064, 3093, 3111. British Caribbean, 1735. Caribbean Area, 1710. Cuba, 1528, 1719–1721, 1743, 1776, 1779, 1808, 1833, 1853. French Caribbean, 1730. Grenada, 1734. Guadeloupe, 1627–1628, 1631, 1729, 1749, 1781, 1831. Guyana, 1592. Martinique, 1733, 1831. Peru, 2445, 2484. Saint Kitts, 1734. Suriname, 1635.
Abortion. Brazil, 3105.
Abstract Art, 293. Brazil, 455.
Academia Nacional de San Carlos, 313.
Academia Venezolana Correspondiente de la Española, 3121.
Acadians. French Guiana, 1647.
Acción Democrática (Venezuela), 1444, 2325, 2338.
Acculturation, 152, 832. Argentina, 2290, 2677. Borderlands, 1700. Brazil, 611. Central America, 1392. Chile, 590. Ecuador, 2113. Guatemala, 1387, 1406. Mayas, 501, 521. Mexico, 497, 518, 530–531, 537, 954, 991, 994, 1102. Paraguay, 2294. Peru, 586, 2445. Spaniards, 1609. Uruguay, 2860.
Aché. *See* Guayaqui.
Acosta, José de, 754.
Acosta de Samper, Soledad, 3382.
Acre, Brazil (state). History, 2983.
Adán, Martín, 4248, 4977.
Advertising. Brazil, 478. Cuba, 1797.
Aeronautics. *See* Aviation.
Aesthetics. Brazil, 437. Mexico, 327. Precolumbian Art, 120.
African Influences. Art, 363. Brazil, 485, 657, 3238, 4704. Caribbean Area, 363, 720, 3277, 4909. Catholicism, 5124. Cuba, 4228, 4488, 5206. Dance, 5094. Music, 5083, 5206. Poetry, 4214. Puerto Rico, 1585. Religion, 857, 5124.
Africans. Brazil, 485. Caribbean Area, 1588. Cuba, 1528, 1788. Peru, 2513.

Afro-Americans. *See* Blacks.
Agoglia, Rodolfo Mario, 5432.
Agrarian Reform. Argentina, 2721, 2783. Bibliography, 40. Bolivia, 2533, 2541. Central America, 40. Colombia, 2072. Costa Rica, 1490. Guatemala, 1440, 1452–1454. Mexico, 934, 952, 1134, 1166, 1248, 1251, 1275, 1280, 1300, 1310, 1328. Peru, 2443, 2463.
Agribusiness. Brazil, 2910. Guatemala, 1466. Venezuela, 2315.
Agricultural Colonization, 739. Argentina, 2720, 2770. Brazil, 3045. French Guiana, 1647. Uruguay, 2866.
Agricultural Credit. Argentina, 2652. Peru, 2512. Puerto Rico, 1801.
Agricultural Development. Argentina, 2733–2734. Bolivia, 2542. Brazil, 3041. Colombia, 2361. Costa Rica, 1448, 1487. Guatemala, 1373, 1390. Mexico, 511. Peru, 2458. Suriname, 1572.
Agricultural Geography. Costa Rica, 1494.
Agricultural Industries. *See* Agroindustry.
Agricultural Labor. Argentina, 2276. Bolivia, 2542–2543. Brazil, 2949, 2994–2995, 4533. Chile, 2577. Guatemala, 1411. Peru, 2476, 2506, 2519. Rio de la Plata, 2257.
Agricultural Policy. Argentina, 2688, 2721, 2730, 2783. Bolivia, 2533. Brazil, 3054. Colombia, 2369. Costa Rica, 1457. Guatemala, 1439. Mexico, 1134, 1170, 1248, 1273, 1275, 1307, 1328. Peru, 2488. Puerto Rico, 1737.
Agricultural Productivity. Argentina, 2262. Brazil, 2998. Mexico, 1216.
Agricultural Systems, 717, 814. Bolivia, 2541, 2543. Caribbean Area, 1587. Chile, 2577. Colombia, 2071. Paraguay, 2237, 2256. Peru, 2443.
Agricultural Technology. Brazil, 2887. Guadeloupe, 1522. Guatemala, 1373. Martinique, 1522.
Agriculture, 761. Argentina, 640, 2262, 2730. Bolivia, 2196, 2540. Brazil, 2932, 2994, 3115. Colombia, 2072. Costa Rica, 1413. Cuba, 1711, 1722. Ecuador, 673. Guade-

Church History, 971. Colonial Administration, 971. Colonial History, 81. Dominicans (religious order), 990, 1401. Insurrections, 539. Land Tenure, 990. Population Studies, 560.

Chibás, Eduardo, 1935.

Chicama River Valley (Peru). Trade Unions, 2487.

Chicanos. *See* Mexican Americans; Mexicans.

Chichimecs (indigenous group). History, 547.

Chilam Balam, 508.

Childbirth. Brazil, 2952.

Children. Brazil, 3072.

Children's Literature, 3560. Bibliography, 46. Puerto Rico, 46.

Chilean Aces of Jazz, 5073.

Chilean Influences. Mexico, 5234. Music, 5234.

Chileans. US, 5196.

Chillán, Chile (city). Urbanization, 2584.

Chillón Valley (Peru). Social Structure, 601.

Chimalpahin Cuauhtlehuanitzin, Domingo Francisco de San Antón Muñón, 504, 551.

Chimborazo, Ecuador (prov.). Caciquismo, 656.

Chimu (indigenous group), 117.

Chinese, 729–731. Peru, 2476, 2495, 2506, 2513.

Chinese Influences, 731.

Chiquinquirá, Colombia (town). Religious Art, 256.

Chiriguano (indigenous group). Bolivia, 2200.

Chocano, José Santos, 3390.

Chocó, Colombia (dept.), 2392. Dialectology, 3191. Race and Race Relations, 2366.

Chocó (indigenous group, Brazil). *See* Shocó.

Choquehuanca, José Domingo, 2439.

Christianity, 1998. Bibliography, 43. Literature, 3276. Mexico, 496–498. Syncretism, 857. Yucatán Peninsula, 501.

Christiano Junior, 3025, 3050.

Chronology. Cuba, 1895. Literature, 3252.

Chunay, Dionsio, 1379.

Chuquisaca, Bolivia (city). History, 2198.

Church Architecture. Chile, 2212. Colombia, 258. Cuba, 246. Guatemala, 230, 235. Honduras, 244. Mexico, 170, 172, 174, 180, 185, 195, 198, 200, 202, 205, 207–209, 220, 223, 226. Nicaragua, 229. Peru, 267, 269, 273–274, 276. Viceroyalty of New Spain (1540–1821), 190. Viceroyalty of Peru (1542–1822), 266.

Church History, 751, 777, 782, 809, 818, 822, 858, 887, 1998, 5275. Argentina, 2232, 2681, 2723–2725, 2769, 2798. Barbados, 1757. Bibliography, 978. Bolivia, 264. Borderlands, 1701. Brazil, 2890, 2908, 2928, 2972, 3075. Caribbean Area, 1622. Chile, 2211–2212, 2224, 2558, 2564, 2579, 2595. Colombia, 2054, 2339, 2380. Cuba, 1787. Ecuador, 2080, 2089, 2095, 2112, 2120, 2423. El Salvador, 1383. Guatemala, 1349, 1383, 1401, 1406. Mexico, 206–207, 497, 549, 551, 932–933, 948, 953, 962, 971, 978, 982, 988–989, 995, 1002, 1009, 1029–1030, 1045, 1063, 1067, 1069, 1072–1073, 1087, 1091, 1126, 1156, 1164, 1214, 1230, 1304, 1315, 1401. Paraguay, 2246–2247, 2305, 2822, 2825. Peru, 562, 2105, 2131, 2134, 2160, 2164, 2474. Puerto Rico, 1581, 1784. Rio de la Plata (region), 2241. Saint-Barthélemy, 1558. Spanish Caribbean, 1617. Trinidad and Tobago, 1557. Uruguay, 2798. Venezuela, 2026. Viceroyalty of Peru (1542–1822), 2184. War of the Pacific (1879–1884), 2579. Yucatán Peninsula, 527, 1042.

Church Records. Guatemala, 1349.

Church-State Relations, 858. Argentina, 2646, 2681, 2723, 5435. Brazil, 5404. Chile, 2564, 2602. Colombia, 2350, 2380. Cuba, 1563, 1894, 1913, 1961. Dominican Republic, 1579. Guatemala, 1424. Mexico, 193, 1156, 1166, 1212, 1230, 1234–1235, 1245–1246, 1304, 1315. Paraguay, 2238, 2264, 2822. Peru, 2450, 2474–2475, 2489, 2526. Venezuela, 2026.

Churches. Chile, 251. Colonial Architecture, 805. Colonial Art, 805. El Salvador, 233. Guatemala, 236. Honduras, 239. Mexico, 173, 191, 200, 206, 211.

Churriguera, José, 227.

CIA. *See* Central Intelligence Agency.

Cien años de soledad, 3701.

Cienfuegos, Cuba (prov.). Slaves and Slavery, 1760. Sugar Industry and Trade, 1760.

El Ciervo Encantado, 3451.

CIPEC. *See* Consejo Intergubernamental de Países Exportadores de Cobre y la Minería.

Círculo Israelita (Bolivia), 2546.

Cities and Towns, 734, 852. Argentina, 250, 2270, 2635, 2726, 2776. Aztecs, 218. Bolivia, 2198. Brazil, 2954, 3071, 4646, 4650, 4665, 4667. Caribbean Area, 1580. Chile, 2206, 2216, 2575, 2584, 2591, 2609. Colombia, 261, 2060, 2344. Costa Rica, 1370. Cuba, 1568, 1619. Culture, 735. Ecuador, 2091, 2098, 2421. French Caribbean, 1646. Guadeloupe, 1565, 1580, 1678. Guatemala,

Elizondo, Salvador, 3524.
Emigration and Immigration. *See* Migration.
En la sangre, 3402.
ENAMI. *See* Empresa Nacional de Minería.
Encomiendas. Argentina, 2245. Colombia, 2058. Guatemala, 1380. Peru, 578, 2175. Viceroyalty of Peru (1542–1822), 2176.
Encyclopedias. Argentina, 5100. Dominican Republic, 87. Mexico, 96. Music, 5082.
Engineering. Brazil, 3040. Cuba, 355. Dictionaries, 3166.
Engineers. Argentina, 2641.
Enlightenment, 752–753, 827, 5272, 5278. Argentina, 2272. Brazil, 5411. Colombia, 2055. Congresses, 5331. Ecuador, 5380. Mexico, 5331. Peru, 2183. Rio de la Plata (region), 2241. Slaves and Slavery, 4874. Viceroyalty of New Granada (1718–1810), 2055, 2057. Viceroyalty of Rio de la Plata (1776–1810), 2274.
Enríquez, Carlos, 5207.
Enríquez, Manuel, 5220.
Enríquez, Martín, 1032, 2153.
Enríquez, Miguel, 1616.
Enriquillo, 3430.
Ensayo político sobre la isla de Cuba, 5302.
Entralgo Vallina, Elías, 56.
Entre Ríos, Argentina (prov.). History, 2672. Newspapers, 2790.
Entrepreneurs. Borderlands, 1130. Brazil, 2996. Colombia, 2384. Costa Rica, 1487. Jamaica, 1560. Mexico, 1011, 1020. Spanish Conquest, 998.
Entreprenuers. Puerto Rico, 1816.
Environmental Protection. Caribbean Area, 1604.
Epigraphy. *See* Inscriptions.
Ercilla y Zúñiga, Alonso de, 3303.
Errázuriz Valdés, Maximiano, 2572.
Escobar, Patricio, 2820.
Escobar Rodas, Cecilio, 2812.
Escola Guignard (Belo Horizonte, Brazil), 471.
Escorza, Juan José, 5236.
Esmeraldas, Ecuador (prov.). Caudillos, 2430. Politicians, 2418.
Espejo, Eugenio, 3324.
Espinar, José Domingo, 1442, 2396.
Espiñeira, Pedro Angel de, 2224.
Espinosa Grau, Guillermo, 5205.
Espinosa Medrano, Juan de, 2138, 3366.
Espionage, US. Chile, 2581.
Espíritu Santo, Brazil (state). Theater, 4769.
Esquiú, Mamerto, 2646.
Esquizotexto, 5055.

Essays, 3288. Bibliography, 5310.
Essequibo, Guyana (region). Boundary Disputes, 2033.
Estado do Mato Grosso (newspaper), 3045.
Estética, 4783.
Estévez Aponte, Antonio, 5260.
Estupiñán Bass, Nelson, 3708.
Ethics. Brazil, 2890, 2965. Chile, 2222. Puerto Rico, 5358.
Ethnic Groups and Ethnicity, 898, 900. Argentina, 2292, 2633, 2666, 2673, 2682, 2707, 2717, 2737, 2770, 2782. Bolivia, 685. Brazil, 2889, 2946, 3048. British Caribbean, 1596. Chile, 2568, 2620. Chinese, 731. Colombia, 2366. Cuba, 1788. Ecuador, 570–571, 588, 2113, 2425. Guatemala, 1454. Haiti, 1777. Jamaica, 1560, 1597. Literature, 3269. Mexico, 927, 957, 977, 1078, 1102, 1122, 1147, 1185, 1321. Nicaragua, 1475. Paraguay, 612, 2306. Peru, 610, 676, 2513, 2522. Puerto Rico, 1582. Suriname, 1544, 1648, 1766. Trinidad and Tobago, 1874. Uruguay, 2860, 2864, 2875.
Ethnographers. Mexico, 557.
Ethnography. Argentina, 2278. Venezuela, 2321.
Ethnohistorians. Ecuador, 622.
Ethnohistory. Bolivia, 2200. Borderlands, 1702. Chile, 603. Congresses, 603. Ecuador, 604, 2087, 2123, 2125. Guatemala, 1369, 1374. Historiography, 636. Incas, 682. Mexico, 1004. Nicaragua, 1475.
Ethnology. Chile, 2601.
Ethnomusicology, 5087. Brazil, 5126. Chile, 5188. Jesuits, 5188. Peru, 5249–5250, 5253–5256.
Etymology. Argentina, 3167. Geographical Names, 3186. Mestizos and Mestizaje, 3158. Mexico, 3135. Spanish Language, 3167, 3169, 3174.
European Influences. Argentina, 2668, 2707. Caribbean Area, 3277. Chile, 384. Cuba, 2707. Mexico, 5333. Peru, 608.
Europeans. Argentina, 2710. Peru, 2453, 2513.
Eva Luna, 3803.
Evangelicalism, 5293.
Excavations. Florida, 1699. Jamaica, 1513. Mexico, 194.
Executive Power. Ecuador, 2427.
Exhibitions. Architecture, 314. Argentina, 370–371, 373. Bolivia, 379. Brazil, 444, 446, 457–458, 467. Caribbean Area, 363. Chile, 389, 391. Colombia, 392, 400. Costume and Adornment, 143. Dominican Re-

public, 347, 366–367. France, 465. Jamaica, 234, 351. Martinique, 356. Masks, 142. Mayas, 125. Mestizos and Mestizaje, 149. Mexico, 127, 178, 186, 196, 303, 305, 310–311, 316, 320, 322–323, 325–326, 329. Modern Art, 286–287. Painting, 417. Precolumbian Art, 131. Sculpture, 186. Silverwork, 160. Spain, 196. Uruguay, 417. Venezuela, 419, 421–422, 429.

Exiles. Argentina, 2766, 3876. Authors, 3260, 4936. Bibliography, 42. Biography, 3260. Chile, 2619, 3770, 3793, 3797, 5181, 5194. Colombia, 2407. Cuba, 359, 1747, 1767, 1814. Feminism, 3289. Jews, 3255. Literature, 3260. Puerto Rico, 1724, 1726. Spain, 5304, 5336. Women, 3289.

Expedición Malaspina (1789–1794), 2008.

Expeditions, 736, 747, 750, 756, 762, 785, 790, 793–794, 799, 803–804, 820, 835, 853, 862, 2003, 2008, 2015–2016, 2019. Borderlands, 1115, 1699, 1703. Caribbean Area, 1638, 1842. Central America, 1393. Easter Island, 2221. Mexico, 1027–1028. Nicaragua, 1375. Peru, 2491, 2529. Puerto Rico, 1686. Russia, 2491. Spain, 884. Viceroyalty of New Grenada (1718–1810), 2074.

Explicación para tocar la guitarra, 5232.

Explorers. Argentina, 2304. Brazil, 2929. Chile, 2159, 2223. Peru, 2141, 2159.

Export Promotion. Guatemala, 1506.

External Debt, 874, 1294. Argentina, 2659. Colombia, 2362, 2409. Dominican Republic, 1991. Ecuador, 2362. Mexico, 1294, 1316. Peru, 2468. Venezuela, 2362.

Eyzaguirre, Jaime, 2594.

Fabini, Eduardo, 5257.

Facundo, 5424, 5442.

Fagoaga Family, 179.

Falcão, Armando, 3007.

Falcão, João, 3008.

Falkland Islands, 2280. History, 2679.

Falkland/Malvinas War, 2732.

Family and Family Relations. Argentina, 2302, 2781. Brazil, 2900–2901, 2924, 2927, 2937, 2943–2944, 2976, 3071. Chile, 2210. Ecuador, 2083, 2419. Guatemala, 1366. Mexico, 980, 1001, 1011, 1024, 1039, 1080, 1123. Nicaragua, 1425.

Fantastic Art. Brazil, 458.

Fantastic Literature, 3254, 3262, 4911. Chile, 3799.

Farabeuf, 3524.

Farrapos Revolution (Brazil, 1835–1845), 2969, 3082.

Fascism. Argentina, 2649, 2713, 2741, 5418, 5421, 5429–5430. Brazil, 3096. Dominican Republic, 1990. Mexico, 1244. Peru, 2462. Puerto Rico, 1863.

Faustino, Mário, 4820.

Fausto, 3386, 3428.

Feather-Work. Brazil, 484.

FEDECAMARAS. *See* Federación Venezolana de Cámaras y Asociaciones.

Federación de Trabajadores de Campeche, 924.

Federación Nacional de Cafeteros de Colombia, 2346.

Federación Obrera Regional Argentina, 2727.

Federal-State Relations. Argentina, 2785. Colombia, 2373, 2391. Mexico, 1202, 1230, 1329.

Federalism. *See* Federal-State Relations.

Feijóo y Montenegro, Benito Jerónimo, 5272.

Felguérez, Manuel, 310.

Feminism, 912. Argentina, 2632, 2643, 2651, 2763, 3932. Brazil, 3013, 3019. Chile, 2574, 3766–3767, 3799, 3802. Costa Rica, 3598. Cuba, 1916. Exiles, 3289. Literature, 3253, 3261, 3286. Mexico, 1274, 3364. Peru, 2501. Philosophy, 5306. Puerto Rico, 1514–1515. Uruguay, 2872.

Fernández, Emiliano R., 4259.

Fernández, Francisco F., 4443.

Fernández, Macedonio, 3955–3956.

Fernández de Córdoba, Francisco, 2162.

Fernández de Córdoba Family, 2161.

Fernández de Oviedo y Valdés, Gonzalo, 3301, 3331, 3338.

Ferrater Mora, José, 5298.

Ferré, Rosario, 5058.

Ferreira, Alexandre Rodrigues, 2923.

Ferreira Aldunate, Wilson, 2857.

Ferrer, Manuel, 5245.

Fertility. *See* Human Fertility.

Festivals. Guatemala, 235. Incas, 707.

Figari, Pedro, 415.

Fignolé, Daniel, 1900.

Figueres Ferrer, José, 1449.

Figueroa, Baltasar de, 259.

Figueroa, Baltasar Vargas de, 259.

Figueroa, Gaspar de, 259.

Figueroa Laugier, Annie, 5161.

Filipinos, 1026.

Film Criticism, 5017.

Finance, 833. Andean Region, 904. Dictionaries, 3159, 3213, 3224. Ecuador, 2424. Historiography, 806. Military History, 800.

Financial Institutions. *See* Banking and Financial Institutions.

1830. Suriname, 1766. Trinidad and Tobago, 1810, 1874. Uruguay, 2298, 2870, 2876. Venezuela, 2310. Women, 913, 1208, 1530, 1980.

Labor Market. Brazil, 3020. Mexico, 1036. Peru, 2476. Venezuela, 2315.

Labor Policy, 107. Brazil, 3041. Chile, 2608.

Labor Supply, 814. Argentina, 2245, 2262, 2276, 2296, 2771. Bolivia, 2191. Borderlands, 1108. Brazil, 2915, 2940, 3063, 3078. Chile, 646, 2215, 2610. Colombia, 2070. Guyana, 1592. Panama, 1499. Peru, 2129, 2506. Rio de la Plata (region), 2261, 2297. Trinidad and Tobago, 1667. Venezuela, 2309.

Labra, Rafael María de, 1808.

Lacerda, Carlos, 3037.

Lacret Morlot, José, 1715.

Ladinos. Guatemala, 1454, 1466.

Laforgue, Jules, 4249.

Lágrimas del corazón, 3413.

Laguerre, Enrique A., 3658.

Lam, Wifredo, 349.

Land Owners. Bolivia, 2542. Brazil, 2887, 3076. Costa Rica, 1457. French Caribbean, 1730. Mexico, 931, 990, 1146, 1301–1302.

Land Reform. *See* Agrarian Reform.

Land Settlement. Argentina, 2289. Borderlands, 1119. Brazil, 3045. Chile, 2209, 2227. Colombia, 2066. Ecuador, 2086. French Guiana, 1647. Guatemala, 1404. Mexico, 1112.

Land Tenure. Argentina, 2678. Belize, 1422. Bolivia, 2540–2541. Borderlands, 1107– 1108. Brazil, 2887, 4522. Chile, 2205, 2577. Colombia, 2070–2072. Costa Rica, 1416, 1448, 1491. Cuba, 1577. Ecuador, 655. Guatemala, 1426. Law and Legislation, 506. Mayas, 525. Mexico, 506, 952, 969, 1113, 1134, 1178, 1216, 1218, 1321, 1328, 1344. Peru, 2512, 2519. Social Conflict, 4522. Venezuela, 2043.

Land Use, 717. Bolivia, 2533. Caribbean Area, 1604. Colombia, 2071, 2361, 2370. Costa Rica, 1494. Guatemala, 1426, 1439, 1466. Panama, 1378.

Landa, Diego de, 1042.

Landowners. Ecuador, 2419.

Landscape Painting. Cuba, 1521. Haiti, 1521. Hydroelectric Power, 420. Venezuela, 420.

Language and Languages. Congresses, 3125, 3190. Uruguay, 3139. Venezuela, 3199.

El Lápiz (Mérida, Venezuela), 2324.

Lara, Venezuela (state). Bibliography, 18.

Larrea, Carlos Manuel, 2097.

Larrea Family, 2097.

Láscaris Comneno, Constantino, 5344.

Laso de la Vega, Francisco, 2228.

Latacunga, Ecuador (city). Religious Art, 277.

Latifundios. Mexico, 1056.

Latin American Area Studies. Germany, 110. US, 62.

Latin American Influences. Japan, 3279, 5067.

Latin Americanists. Directories, 23. France, 1589. Germany, 23. The Netherlands, 740. US, 890, 925, 2978. USSR, 99.

Latin Americans. US, 4.

Latorre, Lorenzo, 2869.

Law and Legislation, 760, 847, 863, 5361. Argentina, 2628, 2754, 2762, 5416, 5435. Artisans, 784. Audiencia of Guatemala, 1376. Borderlands, 1125. Brazil, 2916, 3020. Chile, 2217, 2604, 5398. Colombia, 5371. Costa Rica, 1491. Cuba, 1731, 1853. Cultural Property, 215. Dictionaries, 3220– 3221. History, 5271. Mexico, 215, 506, 1005. Panama, 1396. Paraguay, 2815, 2840. Public Opinion, 841. Uruguay, 2762, 2851. Women, 1125.

Lawyers, 5361. Argentina, 2762. Costa Rica, 1483. Public Opinion, 841. Uruguay, 2762.

Lazo Pérez, Mario, 1929.

Leal, Luis, 59.

Lebanese. Brazil, 4539. Uruguay, 2875.

Legends. Borderlands, 1703. Mexico, 1143. Peru, 606, 2148. Suriname, 5169.

Legislators. Brazil, 84. Directories, 84. Uruguay, 2857.

Lehmann-Nitsche, Robert, 5068.

Leite, Ascendino, 4835.

Lempira (cacique), 1395.

Leñero, Vicente, 4427.

León, Luis L., 1300.

León, Nicaragua (city), 1372.

León Pinelo, Antonio de, 823, 847.

Lexicology. Authors, 3171. Brazil, 3212. Colombia, 3173. Creole Languages, 3248. Cuba, 3157. History, 3168. Mestizos and Mestizaje, 3158. Mexico, 3172. Portuguese Language, 3229, 3237. Puerto Rico, 3162, 3197. Spanish Language, 3163, 3171, 3174. Venezuela, 3136, 3163.

Lexicons. *See* Dictionaries.

Lezama Lima, José, 3630–3631, 3645, 3661–3662, 3676–3677, 3680, 3683, 3685, 4245.

Liberalism, 867, 873, 5278. Argentina, 2656, 2780. Bolivia, 2549. Brazil, 2941, 3046. Chile, 2618, 5400. Colombia, 2342, 2351,

Magnin, Juan, 2117.
Maids. *See* Domestics.
Maize. *See* Corn.
Makuna. *See* Macuna.
Malaspina, Alessandro, 736, 790, 803, 862, 1027, 2008, 3317.
Maldonado, Estuardo, 404.
Maldonado, Juan, 2042.
Maldonado, Pedro de, 2004.
Maldonado, Pedro Vicente, 687.
Malnutrition. *See* Nutrition.
Malvinas, Islas. *See* Falkland Islands.
Managua, Nicaragua (city). Insurrections, 1476.
Manaure, Mateo, 434.
Manaus, Brazil (city). Poetry, 4682.
Manfort, Díaz, 1169.
Manifiesto de Montecristi, 3424.
Manley, Michael, 1931.
Manuel, Robert, 4881.
Manuscripts, 755, 778, 787, 847. Argentina, 2670. Brazil, 2958. Easter Island, 2221. Ecuador, 2112. Guatemala, 1371. Honduras, 1395. Huarochirí, 626, 678. Mexico, 948, 988–989, 1006, 1031, 1079, 1086. Peronism, 2709. Peru, 564. Wars of Independence, 2068.
Maps and Cartography. Archives, 80. Colombia, 2055. Guiana Region, 2033. Mexico, 522, 959. Peru, 2529. Venezuela, 2030, 2046.
Mapuche (indigenous group), 565, 3303. Acculturation, 590. Chile, 2226. History, 635. Shamanism, 5186. Silverwork, 150. Songs, 5186.
Maqroll, el Gaviero (fictitious character), 3703.
Maqueo Castellanos, Esteban, 1210.
El mar de las lentejas, 3638.
Maracaibo, Venezuela (city). City Planning, 436. Commerce, 2073. Philosophers, 5362. Transportation, 2073.
Marajó Island (Brazil), 4569.
Maranhão, Brazil (state). Architecture, 480. Insurrections, 3061. Photography, 473.
Marcelli, Nino, 5196–5197.
María, 3437, 3448, 4315.
Mariátegui, José Carlos, 2516, 3715, 5314, 5383, 5385, 5389–5390, 5392.
Marillac, Jules, 356.
Marinello, Juan, 1868, 3455.
Maritime History, 2000, 2003. Argentina, 2242. Caribbean Area, 1618, 1620. Cuba, 1764. Peru, 2438, 2507, 2523. Viceroyalty of Peru (1542–1822), 2001, 2018.

Markets. Antigua, 1756. Guatemala, 1390. Mexico, 1018–1019.
Markham, Clement R., 2494.
Marmontel, Jean François, 2491.
Máro, Antonio, 405.
Maroons. Brazil, 2906, 2918, 2960. Colombia, 2076. Cuba, 1623. Dominican Republic, 1541. French Guiana, 1532. Guadeloupe, 3249. Haiti, 1548. Jamaica, 1641. Legends, 5169. Mexico, 957. Music, 5169. Panama, 1407, 2076. Peru, 2182, 2445. Rites and Ceremonies, 5169. Suriname, 1584, 1665, 1685, 1691, 5169. Venezuela, 2037.
Marqués, René, 3675, 4442.
Marriage, 767, 808. Argentina, 2244, 2302. Borderlands, 1109. Brazil, 2944, 2962, 3091. Ecuador, 584. Martinique, 1733. Mexico, 980, 1039, 1077. Venezuela, 2039.
Marroquín, Agustín, 1227.
Marryshow, Theophilus Albert, 1979.
Martí, José, 1708, 1720, 1748, 1751, 1759, 1769, 1774, 1783, 1812, 1824, 1843–1845, 1851, 1868, 3396, 3400–3401, 3418, 3424, 3426, 3429, 3445, 3455, 3685, 4503–4504, 5349, 5353, 5355, 5357.
Martim Cecerê, 4730.
Martín Fierro, 3452, 3459.
Martín Rivas, 3415.
Martínez de Rozas, Ramón, 2217.
Martínez Estrada, Ezequiel, 3950, 4965.
Martínez Gracida, Manuel, 147.
Martínez Holguín Family, 2419.
Martius, Karl Friedrich Phillip von, 2903.
Marulanda Vélez, Manuel, 2340.
Marx, Karl, 5370.
Marxism, 1981, 5290, 5307, 5314, 5317, 5351. Argentina, 5419, 5437, 5441. Bibliography, 5407. Brazil, 5407. Colombia, 5376. Cuba, 1936, 1946, 5350. Dominican Republic, 5356. Literature, 3283. Peru, 5383, 5386, 5388–5389, 5392.
Masks. Exhibitions, 142. Guatemala, 238. Mesoamerica, 146. Mexico, 142.
Masonry. *See* Freemasonry.
Masons. *See* Freemasonry.
Mass Media. Argentina, 2272, 3438. Brazil, 3081, 3099. Chile, 2569. Mexico, 1311, 1334. Peru, 5391. Political Ideology, 5391. Venezuela, 2332.
Massa, Bartolomé, 5074.
Massacres. Dominican Republic, 1917, 1992. El Salvador, 1438. Peru, 2470.
Mastai Ferretti, Juan María. *See* Pius IX, *Pope.*

AUTHOR INDEX

Cardoza y Aragón, Luis, 300–301
Cardozo, Flávio José, 4640
Cardozo Galué, Germán, 10
Cardwell, Richard Andrew, 3699
Carelli, Mario, 488, 4802
Carli, Gianrinaldo, 771
Carlson, John B., 130
Carmagnani, Marcello, 1155, 2205
Carmona, Fernando, 5223
Carneiro, Maria Luiza Tucci, 2985
Caro, Miguel Antonio, 3387
Caron, Aimery, 1605
Carone, Edgard, 2986–2988, 5407
Carpentier, Alejo, 3641–3642, 4987–4989
Carpentier, Hortense, 4976
Carpio, Manuel, 3388
Carranza, María Mercedes, 4036
Carrasco, Adrián, 2090
Carrasco, Eduardo, 388
Carrasco, Pedro, 500
Carrascosa-Miguel, Pablo, 3408
Carredano, Consuelo, 5224
Carreira, António, 2910
Carreira, Xoan M., 5207
Carreño, Antonio, 3302
Carreño, Virginia, 155, 4314
Carrera Andrade, Jorge, 4207
Carrera Verdugo, José Miguel, 2566
Carrero, Raimundo, 4532
Carriego, Evaristo, 4037
Carril, Bonifacio del, 369
Carrillo, Hugo, 4315–4316
Carrington, Leonora, 4961
Carrington, Selwyn H.H., 1642
Carrió de la Bandera, Alonso. See
    Concolorcorvo
Carrión, Benjamín, 2411
Carrizosa de López, María, 2342
Carroll, Patrick James, 957
Cartas de cabildos hispanoamericanos: Audiencia de México, 958
Cartas de los obispos de Cartagena de Indias durante el período hispánico, 1534–1820, 2054
Cartay Angulo, Rafael, 1527
Carter, E. Dale, 55, 3923
Carter, Martin, 4892
Cartografía histórica de la Nueva Galicia, 959
Carvalheira, Luiz Maurício Britto, 4765
Carvalho, André, 4582
Carvalho, Hermínio Bello de, 5128
Carvalho, José Murilo de, 2989–2990
Carvalho, Marcus J.M. de, 2881
Carvalho, Mariajosé de, 4685

Carvalho, Piedade, 5129
Carvalho, Romeu de, 4533
Carvallo, Gastón, 2315
Carybé, 460
Casa de la Cultura Franz Tamayo, 379
A Casa do Pinhal, 2991
Casado Arboniés, Francisco Javier, 772
Casal, Juan Manuel, 5274
Casalecchi, José Enio, 2992
Casals Marcén, Manuel, 3161
Casanova Guarda, Holdenis, 590
Casas, Bartolomé de las, 773–775, 786, 5275
Casas, Juan Carlos, 3818
Casasola, Agustín Víctor, 1256
Casaus, Víctor, 1987, 4038
Casazola Mendoza, Matilde, 4039
Cassá, Roberto, 1880
Castagneto, Giovanni Battista, 451
Castagnino, Raúl Héctor, 4435–4436
Castañeda Delgado, Paulino, 776
Castañeda García, Carmen, 927, 1003
Castañón, Adolfo, 3474
Castelar, José Adán, 4040–4041
Castellanos, Alfredo Raúl, 249, 2851
Castellanos, Isabel, 1528
Castellanos, Jorge, 1528
Castellanos, Rafael Antonio, 5178
Castellanos, Rosario, 4913, 4942–4943
Castellanos Cambranes, Julio, 1350, 1426
Castellanos Moya, Horacio, 3557
Castello Branco: testemunhos de uma época, 2993
Castera, Pedro, 3389
Castilla, Leopoldo, 3988
Castillero Calvo, Alfredo, 1377–1378, 1427
Castillo, Abelardo, 3819
Castillo, Dante del, 4317
Castillo, Edward D., 1105
Castillo, Efraim, 347
Castillo, Hugo F., 2652
Castillo, José R. del, 1257
Castillo, Ricardo, 4042
Castillo, Roberto, 3558
Castillo, Rubén, 4766
Castillo Didier, Miguel, 5259
Castillo-Feliú, Guillermo I., 4970
Castillo Lara, Lucas Guillermo, 2029
Castillo Mathieu, Nicolás del, 2003
Castillo Meléndez, Francisco, 1606–1607
Castillo Yzaguirre, Luis Juan, 3757
Castor, Suzy, 1881
Castrillón, María Teresa, 5225
Castrillón Arboleda, Diego, 255
Castro, Consuelo de, 5030
Castro, Eduardo Batalha Viveiros de, 597